W9-CPV-735

COST ACCOUNTING

TRADITIONS AND INNOVATIONS

ALSO FROM THESE AUTHORS:

Managerial Accounting, Second Edition

800 pages   Full-Color   Hardcover or Looseleaf
0-314-07014-1 (Annotated Instructor's Edition)
0-314-07591-7 (Student's Edition)

A BUSINESS DECISION-MAKING APPROACH

Managerial Accounting emphasizes the practical rather than the theoretical, showing students how real companies use accounting concepts and techniques to make effective business decisions. Students will learn when accounting information is needed, the techniques available to provide that information, the details needed to perform the techniques, and the benefits and limitations of the information provided in response to a manager's needs.

ACCOUNTING ACROSS DISCIPLINES

Raiborn, Barfield and Kinney promote accounting as a cross-functional discipline that provides information useful to all types of business people and for all types of organizations such as manufacturers, service companies, and not-for-profits – both domestic and international. *Cross-Functional Application Strategies* appear at the end of each chapter to show how all the major disciplines (management, finance, economics, and accounting) relate to the chapter material.

CURRENT AND INNOVATIVE COVERAGE

➤ **Quality** is discussed in-depth in *Chapter 2: Management Accounting in a Quality Environment* and included in nineteen *News Notes*. Quality discussion questions at the end of each chapter challenge students to make difficult quality-related decisions and to discuss and consider the consequences.

➤ **International coverage** begins in Chapter 1 and is continued throughout the text. This includes the use of three international company *On-Sites* and twenty *News Notes*.

➤ **Ethics discussions** at the end of each chapter, challenge students to debate legal and ethical behavior in business.

FOLLOWING REAL COMPANIES, REAL PEOPLE

On-Sites open each chapter to show students how chapter topics affect businesses on a daily basis. All of the *On-Sites* are new to this edition. A *Site Analysis* section at the end of each chapter indicates how the company reacted to or resolved the *On Site* situation.

ACCOUNTING IN THE NEWS

News Notes are boxed clips (3 to 8 per chapter) from recent periodicals. The excerpts are keyed with a logo as one of the following: ethical, quality, general business, or international. More than 90% of the *News Notes* are new to this edition.

AN EXCELLENT SUPPLEMENT PACKAGE

When you adopt *Managerial Accounting, Second Edition* you not only get a great book, you get a great supplement package. From acetates to software to videos – we have it all. Be sure to ask your local representative about the extensive supplement package that accompanies this text.

REQUEST YOUR REVIEW COPY TODAY

If you're interested in a text that lets your students spend less time preparing information and more time using it, ask your local ITP representative to send you an examination copy of *Managerial Accounting, Second Edition* by Raiborn, Barfield and Kinney.

THIRD EDITION

COST ACCOUNTING

TRADITIONS AND INNOVATIONS

JESSE T. BARFIELD
LOYOLA UNIVERSITY, NEW ORLEANS

CECILY A. RAIBORN
LOYOLA UNIVERSITY, NEW ORLEANS

MICHAEL R. KINNEY
TEXAS A&M UNIVERSITY

SOUTH-
WESTERN
COLLEGE
PUBLISHING

COPYEDITING   Kathy Pruno
COMPOSITION   Parkwood Composition Services, Inc.
TEXT DESIGN   Metier, Inc.
PAGE LAYOUT   Maureen McCutcheon
COVER PHOTO   © David McGlynn/FPG International

WEST'S COMMITMENT TO THE ENVIRONMENT

In 1906, West Publishing Company began recycling materials left over from the production of books. This began a tradition of efficient and responsible use of resources. Today, 100% of our legal bound volumes are printed on acid-free, recycled paper consisting of 50% new fibers. West recycles nearly 27,700,000 pounds of scrap paper annually—the equivalent of 229,300 trees. Since the 1960s, West has devised ways to capture and recycle waste inks, solvents, oils, and vapors created in the printing process. We also recycle plastics of all kinds, wood, glass, corrugated cardboard, and batteries, and have eliminated the use of polystyrene book packaging. We at West are proud of the longevity and the scope of our commitment to the environment.

West pocket parts and advance sheets are printed on recyclable paper and can be collected and recycled with newspapers. Staples do not have to be removed. Bound volumes can be recycled after removing the cover.

Production, Prepress, Printing and Binding by West Publishing Company.

Copyright © 1991, 1994 By WEST PUBLISHING COMPANY
Copyright © 1998   By SOUTH-WESTERN COLLEGE PUBLISHING
    5101 Madison Road
    Cincinnati, OH 45227

04 03 02 01 00 99 98 97   8 7 6 5 4 3 2

Library of Congress Cataloging-in-Publication Data

Barfield, Jesse T.
    Cost accounting : traditions and innovations / Jesse T. Barfield,
Cecily A. Raiborn, Michael R. Kinney.—3rd ed.
      p. cm.
    Includes index.
    ISBN student edition 0-538-88047-3
        annotated edition 0-538-88137-2
        looseleaf edition 0-538-88138-0
    1. Cost accounting. I. Raiborn, Cecily A. II. Kinney, Michael
R. III. Title.
HF5686.C8B2758   1997
657'.42—dc20

                        96-32426
                        ∞ CIP

Brief Contents

Contents

2 Organizational Strategy and Accounting   38

3 Considering Quality in an Organization   74

PART II   SELECTING, ANALYZING, AND TRACKING COSTS   113

4   Cost Terminology and Cost Flows   114

5 Allocating Indirect Costs   160

6 Activity-Based Cost Systems for Management   220

PART III PRODUCT COSTING METHODS   279

7 Job Order Costing   280

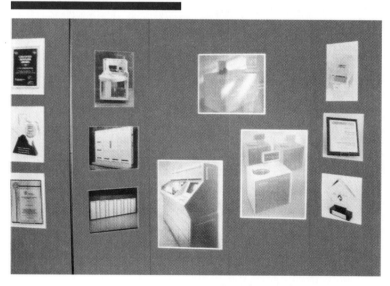

8   Process Costing   324

9   Special Production Issues: Lost Units and Accretion   366

10 Cost Allocation for Joint Products and By-Products 410

11 Standard Costing   448

PART IV COST PLANNING   511

---

12 Variable Costing and Cost-Volume-Profit Analysis   512

13 Relevant Costing   566

14 The Master Budget   618

PART V COST CONTROL   673

15 Introduction to Cost Management Systems   674

16 Cost Control for Noninventory Costs   708

17 Control of Inventory and Production   754

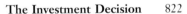

PART VI DECISION MAKING   805

18 Capital Budgeting   806

19 Responsibility Accounting and Transfer Pricing in Decentralized Organizations   870

PART VII PERFORMANCE EVALUATION   923

---

20 Measuring Short-Run Organizational Performance   924

21 Measuring Long-Run Organizational Performance   964

22 Rewarding Performance 994

APPENDIX A PRESENT VALUE TABLES   1028

Using the Ethics Discussion
APPENDIX B Questions   1034

Preface

Contemporary business expects an accounting graduate to possess solid knowledge of the interrelated areas of cost and management accounting. Both are concerned with producing, reporting, and interpreting internal information for managers. Cost accounting determines the cost of manufacturing products and/or providing services in organizations involved in a conversion process. Conversion can include transforming a raw material into a finished good or an idea into a set of architectural plans. Product and service costs are needed both for internal management decisions and for cost of goods sold and inventory valuation on external financial statements. The broader area of management accounting, of which cost accounting is a part, involves the provision of accounting information for the managerial functions of planning, controlling, evaluating performance, and making decisions. Thus, management accounting is applicable in all organizations regardless of whether they engage in a conversion process.

The distinction between these two accounting areas is becoming increasingly blurred because of overlapping job functions, growth in information technology, and institution of new production methods that require the availability of more nontraditional information. Therefore, this text addresses both cost and management accounting issues by including coverage of traditional product costing methods as well as innovative topics such as accounting and organizational strategy, activity-based costing and management, quality costs, cost management systems, accounting effects of a just-in-time philosophy, use of nonfinancial and long-term performance measures, and performance rewards.

AUDIENCE

This book is written for students aspiring to become professional accountants and pursuing professional credentials such as Certified Management Accountant (CMA), Certified in Financial Management (CFM), Certified Public Accountant (CPA), and/or Certified Internal Auditor (CIA). The text presents the essential issues of cost and management accounting thoroughly but concisely for use in a one- or two-semester course in a college accounting program. Before taking cost accounting, students will ordinarily have taken a principles of accounting or financial accounting course.

STRUCTURE

The text's chapter sequence reflects both curriculum characteristics and the authors' pedagogical preferences. Because many universities stress product cost computations in the first (or only) cost accounting course, we have placed the various product costing techniques (job order, process, joint, standard, and absorption/variable) at the beginning of the text in Chapters 7 to 12. In addition, topics such as standard costing and variance analysis are generally covered simultaneously in a cost accounting course even though standard costing is truly a product costing or planning topic whereas variance analysis is a management control and performance evaluation topic.

Part 1 (Chapters 1 through 3) provides a foundation in both the current business environment (including strategic and quality considerations) and management accounting. Part 2 (Chapters 4 through 6) presents a variety of issues related to cost terminology, cost flows, and the allocation of overhead costs. This section considers the roles of activity-based costing and activity-based management in modern world-class businesses. Part 3 (Chapters 7 through 11) demonstrates the systems and methods of product costing, accounting for product shrinkage and expansion, and treatment of joint process costs. These chapters constitute the traditional cost accounting viewpoint in that the focus is on determining cost for use in valuation on financial statements. Parts 4 through 7 (Chapters 12 through 22) concentrate on managerial information needs and processes. These chapters are divided into the areas of planning (Chapters 12 to 14), controlling (Chapters 15 to 17), decision making (Chapters 18 and 19), and performance evaluation (Chapters 20 to 22).

The text's chapter sequence is only one way that the topics may be covered; other potential sequences are provided in the preface to the Instructor's Manual. Each chapter is written in a fairly stand-alone fashion, assuming that the basic definitions have been covered. Because the end-of-chapter exercises and problems predominantly relate directly to the material within the chapter, an instructor wishing to vary the sequence of chapters should find few difficulties in assigning end-of-chapter material. If a problem in one chapter includes a significant use of another chapter's material, it is so designated in the heading to the problem. (For example, a standard costing problem may also be designated as a process costing problem.)

The following changes to the third edition of *Cost Accounting Traditions and Innovations* increase the text's teachability and real-world focus and enhance the student's comprehension and intellectual skills.

CHANGES IN THE THIRD EDITION

Because of its innovative topics, student orientation, readability, and inclusion of real-world applications and ethics, the previous editions of this text were very well received. The third edition continues these positive features from earlier editions; improves upon them by increasing their coverage as well as that of quality issues, multinational businesses, and modern business techniques such as Internet usage; and incorporates suggestions from users and reviewers for organizational and pedagogical changes.

The Accounting Education Change Commission (in its "Position Statement Number One: Objectives of Education for Accountants") has been instrumental in providing guidance on improving and expanding the text's pedagogical features. The AECC has indicated that it is essential for accounting graduates to possess strong communication, intellectual, and interpersonal skills as well as to understand professional ethics and make value-based judgments. Thus, to encourage students to improve their communication and intellectual skills, we have expanded the quantity of essay and "logic" problems in end-of-chapter materials, student study guide, and test bank. The end-of-chapter essay and logic problems directed at developing these skills are presented under the heading Communication Activities. To promote interpersonal skills, the Instructor's Manual provides ideas for group projects that may be assigned for oral or written presentation. And, to improve the process of analyzing and making ethical decisions, we have included more real-world ethics discussion questions in the end-of-chapter materials and a short end-of-text appendix about using these questions.

Pedagogy

Each chapter contains an "Introducing" and "Revisiting" segment about a real organization. Through these chapter openers and closures, students are shown how the topics included in the chapter affect businesses on a daily basis. The opening vignettes have been selected to illustrate all types of organizations (domestic/international, profit/not-for-profit, large/small, and manufacturing/service). Some featured organizations are Ford Motor Co., ITT Sheraton, The Procter & Gamble Company, Binney & Smith Inc., Boeing Co., Genentech, Inc., Entergy Corporation, and Dell Computer Corp. Although a real organization's data cannot be used in chapter numerical computations (for competitive reasons), comparable data for an illustrative company in the same type of business are used throughout the chapter.

To reinforce the real-world perspective and maintain student interest, the chapters continue to contain boxed "News Note" examples from the current business press featuring up-to-date applications of text concepts in real-world situations. These "Notes" are keyed with graphic icons as being primarily related to one of the following areas of interest: general business, international, and quality. There are approximately three to five notes per chapter featuring such companies as Delta Wire, The HON Company, Hewlett-Packard, Intel, McDonnell Douglas Corp., and Toshiba.

The international and service dimensions of business have been heavily integrated in the chapters, illustrative examples, and end-of-chapter materials. Such inclusions reflect the ever-increasing global expansion of business enterprises and the diminished quantity of manufacturing in the United States.

Approximately 25 percent of the end-of-chapter material is new; some of these items reflect real-world situations. An attempt has been made to provide at least two exercises for each key concept in the chapter. Many of the new end-of-chapter materials are unstructured thought problems that require students to use their analytical skills to excerpt and organize relevant information from a set of facts. Such end-of-chapter materials are designed to enhance the students' intellectual skills rather than provide a mechanism for rote recalculation of text examples.

In addition to the end-of-text glossary, page references for chapter definitions are included for each key term in each chapter.

Topics are provided in parentheses for all exercises and problems to indicate the nature of the material included in the end-of-chapter item. These lead-ins make it easier for faculty to select end-of-chapter materials that reinforce chapter objectives or for students to select additional materials to supplement assigned homework.

Organization

Chapter 1 begins with a section on changes in the American business environment. This section discusses differences between the traditional short-run perspective and the emerging strategic perspective as well as differences between techniques used by smaller businesses versus those of advanced manufacturing firms. Inclusion of this section helps students to understand the business environment of which they will be a part.

Chapter 2 is a new chapter that discusses organizational strategy as the underlying linkage for all business activities and how such strategy relates to and is supported by accounting information.

The topics of conversion and stages of production are covered in Chapter 4 along with the discussions of direct material, direct labor, and overhead.

Chapter 5 combines coverage of use of predetermined overhead rates and allocation of factory and service department costs. Chapter 6 presents activity-based management and activity-based costing concepts.

The absorption and variable costing discussion has been shortened and integrated into the cost-volume-profit information in Chapter 12. This change makes the student aware of the need for variable costing figures in determination of breakeven level and in computation of volume levels necessary to generate specific profit amounts.

Chapter 15, "Designing a Cost Management System," is new and discusses the development, implementation, and maintenance of a continuous feedback system for communicating and using internal accounting information for all managerial functions.

The prior editions' two chapters on capital budgeting have been combined into one in deference to the primacy of this topic in finance courses.

Organizational performance has been separated into two chapters: one related to short-run (and more traditional) performance measurements; the other to long-run (and typically more innovative) performance measurements.

STYLE

This text is extremely student-oriented and integrates procedural methods with the conceptual and behavioral aspects of information that help students solve real-world problems. The authors have endeavored to make the text highly readable and to provide numerous examples, models, and illustrations of real-world applicability. The coverage is up-to-date and presents the effects on accounting of phenomena such as just-in-time inventory management, flexible manufacturing systems, and expanded global markets.

Features in the text (such as learning objectives, opening and closing vignettes, news notes, chapter summaries, demonstration problems, and a full range of end-of-chapter materials) have been designed to promote the learning process, provide a high student interest level, and make the text a valuable student resource. The inclusion of quality concepts, international business considerations, discussions of diverse types of organizations, and end-of-chapter materials focusing on actual quality and ethical issues reinforces the applied nature of the text and assists faculty to make the course information more relevant to the students.

INSTRUCTOR SUPPORT MATERIALS

The instructor support package is an innovative response to the growing demand for creative and effective teaching methodologies. The supplements are designed to provide a comprehensive resource package for all faculty adopting this text; the materials used will depend on the faculty member's interest areas, class size, equipment availability, and teaching experience. All supplements not prepared by the authors have been reviewed by the authors for consistency and accuracy with the textual materials.

Annotated Instructor's Edition   This special edition of the text was prepared by the authors and contains a variety of margin notes to improve and enhance teaching effectiveness and efficiency. The margin notes include:

- *Teaching Notes* that provide additional clarification of points or examples that might be used in class
- *Points to Emphasize* that indicate logical "checkpoints" of student clarity on subject matter
- *Points to Consider* that indicate questions to generate student responses which indicate understanding of text material
- *Teaching Transparency* notations that indicate points at which selected transparencies can be used (the transparency masters are included in the Instructor's Manual)
- *Video Icons* that identify points at which videos supplied by West Publishing could be used to enhance or reinforce text material
- *Check Figures* that provide solutions to numerical end-of-chapter materials

Instructor's Manual   This manual (developed by Gregory K. Lowry of Mercer University) provides a listing of terminology, a lecture outline summary, an assignment classification table (indicating the topical breakdown and level of difficulty of end-of-chapter items, some CMA exam multiple-choice questions for use as additional test materials or for quizzes, and a selected bibliography of current readings for each chapter. Masters for over 40 teaching transparencies referenced in the Annotated Instructor's Edition are also included at the end of this volume. These masters are *not* duplicates of textual exhibits, but rather provide additional perspectives on text materials.

Solutions Manual   This volume, prepared by the authors and independently reviewed and checked for accuracy, contains complete solutions to each question, exercise, problem, and case in the text. Some suggested discussion points or (if from professional exams) complete answers are provided for the ethics and quality questions, but no distinct right-or-wrong answers are given. This volume also contains a copy of the Student Check Figures.

Solution Transparency Acetates   Approximately 250 acetates are provided from the solutions manual for all numerical end-of-chapter materials.

PowerPoint Presentation/Transparency Masters   This package (prepared by Donna S. Dietz of Concordia College) is a state-of-the-art presentation graphics program for Microsoft Windows™. All transparency material is preloaded onto the program, which gives instructors the opportunity to customize (by editing, adding, or deleting material) transparencies so they are specific to classroom needs. Illustrations include additional problems with solutions, definitions, charts, graphs, figures, and other visual support not found in the text. PowerPoint Presentation's animation allows for scalable type, type manipulation, shape and color blends, and variable zoom. Transparency masters are black and white printouts of each slide in the presentation.

Test Bank   The Test Bank has been prepared by Chandra Schorg of Texas Woman's University and contains over one thousand multiple-choice, short exercise, and short discussion questions with related solutions. It has been updated from the second edition to include approximately 30 percent new materials. Two to three additional computational problems have been added for each numerically based chapter.

WesTest™   This supplement is a computerized version of the hard-copy test bank. WesTest includes edit and word processing features that allow test customization through the addition, deletion, or scrambling of test selections. WesTest is available in DOS, Windows, and Macintosh formats.

Videos   Because the video packages accompanying the previous editions were so highly praised, additional new videos are available. There are an average of three to four video segments of various lengths per chapter. All of the previously available videos from the Association for Manufacturing Excellence—"On the Road to Manufacturing Excellence," "We're Getting Closer," and "Managing the Supply Chain" are available to adopters. Multiple years of the video library titled "Strengthening America's Competitiveness: Resource Management Insights for Small Business Success" are also available. These videos were developed by the Blue Chip Enterprise Initiative, sponsored by Connecticut Mutual Life Insurance Company, the U.S. Chamber of Commerce, and *Nation's Business* magazine. This initiative seeks out and recognizes businesses that have demonstrated exceptional management of key resources to meet challenges and emerge stronger. Almost every chapter in the text has one or more videos to accompany it; points of reference for classroom use are fully integrated in the Annotated Instructor's Edition. These tapes are provided free to qualified adopters.

Video Guide   A video guide has been developed to accompany the video package and provide information on length, alternative points of usage within the text, highlights to address, and some discussion questions to stimulate classroom discussion.

STUDENT SUPPORT MATERIALS

Student supplements are essential to the provision of a quality supplement package and are important in helping students to learn on their own—a factor stressed by the Accounting Education Change Commission. The following items are available for students.

Student Study Guide   This study guide is a chapter-by-chapter manual that allows students, through independent review and self-examination, to gain additional exposure and reinforce the materials detailed in the text. The study guide contains chapter learning objectives, overviews, detailed chapter notes, and self-test questions. The study guide has been updated to include approximately 40 percent new materials, and two to three additional computational problems have been added for each numerically based chapter. In addition, several projects are included for each chapter that allow students to exercise their written and oral communication and logic skills and, at the same time, develop their interpersonal skills through interaction with other students.

Student Check Figures   For instructors who wish to provide students with answers to end-of-chapter materials, this list has been prepared by the authors from the solutions contained in the solutions manual. The check figures provide a reference point answer for all numerical end-of-chapter materials, except those for which the provision of a check figure would be inappropriate. Check figures are available free of charge, when ordered to be shrink-wrapped with the textbook.

Spreadsheet Templates (developed by Greg Lowry of Mercer University) allows students to solve selected end-of-chapter exercises and problems using Excel®. This package, which includes student and instructor disks, requires students to identify the issues of the problem, program the necessary formulas, and input the data from the exercise or problem.

Practice Sets Two practice sets are available to supplement students' understanding of specific text materials.

Weston Manufacturing: An Activity-Based Costing Case, prepared by Bob Needham of Bucknell University, illustrates activity-based costing using a manufacturing company that produces agricultural irrigation systems and customized commercial irrigation systems. This practice set concentrates on determination of cost drivers and their use in assigning overhead costs to products. It can be used when teaching Chapter 6 or in conjunction with several chapters from the text to show the student the impact of activity-based costing on decision making. A solutions manual is available for instructors.

Laser Logos, Inc. is a computerized practice set that was written by Dana Forgione of The University of Baltimore and L. Murphy Smith of Texas A&M University. It provides students with the opportunity to develop a complete master budget and to use the budgeted information to make managerial decisions. A solutions manual indicates how the practice set can be used in conjunction with Chapter 14 or as a continuing problem for the entire term. The student workbook is available in IBM-compatible format with a disk.

Student Notetaking Guide This unique supplement includes copies of the transparencies provided to instructors. They are printed at fifty percent normal size on full sheets, with space for students to take lecture notes. Detailed outlines are also provided.

Insights: Readings in Cost Accounting, a readings book, is available for those faculty who wish to supplement text assignments with articles from the current business press. This softcover book contains approximately 20 selections from *FORTUNE*, *Management Accounting*, *Journal of Accountancy*, and *Journal of Cost Management* that discuss contemporary issues in cost and management accounting.

English as a Second Language Supplement is available for students for whom English is a second language. This supplement, prepared by Luis Guillén, contains a Spanish glossary of all key terms found in the text.

Acknowledgments

We would like to thank all the people who have helped us during the revision of this text. The constructive comments and suggestions made by the following reviewers were instrumental in developing, rewriting, and improving the quality, readability, and student orientation of *Cost Accounting: Traditions and Innovations* 3rd edition.

C. Richard Aldridge	Western Kentucky University
Tarek Amer	Northern Arizona University
C. Douglas Cloud	Pepperdine University—Malibu
Henry H. Davis	Eastern Illinois University
Nena Hankins	Kent State University
Judith Harris	Bryant College
Phil Jones	University of Richmond
Robert C. Kee	University of Alabama
David E. Keys	Northern Illinois University
Greg Lowry	Mercer University
Donald Madden	University of Kentucky

Annie McGowan   Texas A&M University
Robert Putnam   University of Tennessee at Martin
Joe Weintrop   Baruch College

Special mention must be given to Margie Boldt at the University of Oklahoma, Annie McGowan at Texas A&M University, and Cynthia Kreisner at Austin Community College for their hard work as problem checkers and to Joel Ridenour for his arduous task of obtaining all the necessary permissions. In addition, use of materials from the Institute of Management Accountants and American Institute of CPAs, the various periodical publishers, and the featured organizations have contributed significantly to making this text a truly useful learning tool for the students. Lastly, the authors thank all the people at West Publishing (Rick Leyh, Alex von Rosenberg, Cathy Story, Holly Henjum, Elsa Peterson, Kathy Pruno, and Erin Ryan Titcomb) who have helped us on this project, and our families and friends for their support and encouragement during this process.

Jesse Barfield
Cecily Raiborn
Mike Kinney

OVERVIEW

CHAPTER

1

The Contemporary Environment of Cost and Management Accounting

LEARNING OBJECTIVES

After completing this chapter, you should be able to answer these questions:

1. What significant changes are taking place in the business environment?

2. How do financial and management accounting relate to each other?

3. How are management and cost accounting related?

4. What is the scope of management accounting?

5. What important indications exist that management accounting is a profession?

6. (Appendix) How are organizations structured?

Ford Motor Company

January 1, 1995, welcomed in a new era for Ford Motor Company. Ford's U.S. and European operations were formally merged into one "superorganization"; the Asian and Latin American operations are being integrated into the global organization more slowly.

Ford's restructuring plan focuses on ways to eliminate $2 billion to $3 billion from purchasing, product development, and other operating costs by the end of the 1990s. At the base of this plan is the idea that the company needs to create and use the same systems and processes to design, build, and sell only slightly differentiated products in worldwide locations. Prior to the implementation of the Ford 2000 plan, the company had significant overlapping products and duplicated engineering efforts, with the various North American and European sectors operating as "self-contained units" with unique product mixes of vehicles, engines, and components. In making the decision to restructure, Ford executives did a significant amount of benchmarking on "how not to do things" so as to avoid mistakes such as those made by General Motors in its 1984 massive reorganization.

Assembly plants at Ford Motor Company are viewed as being almost as efficient as the best Japanese factories, but the company's high product development spending hurts financial results. One of the new tasks will be to better use computers to perform simulations to test vehicle designs rather than to hand-build expensive prototypes. Also, interdisciplinary engineering teams will be used to reduce the time-to-market of new vehicles. And, to shrink the approximately $37 billion per year in purchasing costs, Ford will begin standardizing parts over vehicle lines which, in turn, will allow the company to buy in larger quantities; the company will seek to make these purchases from a limited number of suppliers around the world who are willing to forego some profit margins in exchange for the increase in business.

SOURCE: Adapted from Neal Templin, "Ford's Trotman Gambles on Global Restructuring Plan," *Wall Street Journal* (April 22, 1994), p. B3. Reprinted by permission of *The Wall Street Journal*, © 1994 Dow Jones & Company, Inc. All Rights Reserved Worldwide.

In making the decision to restructure Ford Motor Company, top management needed to consider numerous issues that would affect the financial health of the company for years to come. The costs, including those for vehicle redesign for commonality of parts, review of suppliers, and reorganization of the management team, had to be weighed against the potential benefits to be gained. To make such a determination, Ford's leaders needed monetary and nonmonetary information that would help them to analyze and solve problems by reducing uncertainty. Accounting, often referred to as the language of business, provides much of that necessary information. Accounting language has two primary "variations": financial accounting and management accounting. Cost accounting is a subset of both financial and management accounting.

Financial accounting focuses on the needs of external users (stockholders, creditors, and regulatory agencies) and is dedicated to processing information about historical, monetary transactions. The basic output of the financial accounting process is a set of financial statements that have been prepared using generally accepted accounting principles. Alternatively, **management accounting** focuses on the information needs of an organization's internal managers—needs that are related to the

financial accounting

management accounting

EXHIBIT 1-1

Levels of Intelligence
Gathering

Broadest scope, including environmental
scanning, market research and analysis,
and competitive intelligence

Business Intelligence

Broad scope, assimilating all of the
competitor intelligence; provides an
early warning of opportunities and
threats, such as new acquisitions or
or alliances and future competitive
products and services

Competitive
Intelligence

Competitor
Analysis

Narrow focus on an individual competitor profile

SOURCE: Stan Whiteley, "The Management Accountant as Intelligence Agent," *CMA Magazine*
(February 1996), p. 3. Reprinted from an article appearing in *CMA Magazine* by Stan Whiteley,
February 1996 issue, with permission of The Society of Management Accountants of Canada.

planning, controlling, and decision-making functions of those managers. Some management needs are satisfied by historical, monetary information based on generally accepted accounting principles. Other needs require forecasted, qualitative, and frequently nonfinancial information that has been developed and computed for specific decision purposes.

business intelligence system

The environment in which an organization operates affects the information needs of its managers. Companies need to be certain that they have a proper **business intelligence** (BI) **system** or "formal process for gathering and analyzing information and producing intelligence to meet decision making needs."[1] In addition to the need for information about internal processes, a BI system requires knowledge of markets, technologies, and competitors. As shown in Exhibit 1–1, subsets of the BI system are competitive intelligence and competitor analysis.[2]

To help in understanding the underlying elements of a BI system, this chapter first presents an overview of the contemporary business environment. The chapter then explains the information generated by financial, management, and cost accounting. To further clarify the management/cost accounting function, the chapter discusses the professional management accounting certification, management/cost accounting standards, and the ethics code for U.S. management accountants.

CHANGES IN THE BUSINESS ENVIRONMENT

Because the accounting function reflects its surrounding environment, the first essential is to understand how business has changed in the past 50 years. Some of these changes are listed in Exhibit 1–2.

[1] "U.S. Companies Slow to Develop Business Intelligence," *Deloitte & Touche Review* (October 16, 1995), p. 1.
[2] Stan Whiteley, "The Management Accountant as Intelligence Agent," *CMA Magazine* (February 1996), p. 3. For more information, see the Society of Management Accountants of Canada's Management Accounting Guideline 39: Developing Comprehensive Competitor Intelligence.

	"THE OLD DAYS"	→	"THE NEW AGE"
Major type of business—U.S.*	Manufacturing		Service
Wage rates	Low		High**
Major workforce	Human		Machine
View of market	Domestic		International
Performance measurement focus	Production		Consumer
Product variety	Limited		Virtually unlimited
Size of production lots	Large		Limited
Legal environment	Regulated		Deregulated
Social consciousness	Obligatory		Responsive

*Other countries were often primarily involved in service activities or limited manufacturing, choosing to import many of their "hard" goods. Many of these countries have now shifted to manufacturing and exporting activities.
**In industrialized nations.

EXHIBIT 1–2

Changes in the Business Environment

Type of Business and Workforce

Traditionally, the American economy was heavily manufacturing based. Since the end of World War II, however, the economy has shifted toward more service businesses in the United States and more manufacturing in other countries. Currently in the United States, jobs in the service sector compose approximately 70 percent of the workforce, and this percentage is predicted to continue to rise. High wage rates and fringe benefit costs have contributed to the movement of manufacturing to other countries. As indicated in Exhibit 1–3, average hourly wage rates in industrialized nations are fairly high, which helps to explain why many manufacturing jobs have been lost to less industrialized locations.

As the cost of labor has increased, some U.S. companies have chosen to establish **maquiladoras** (or *maquilas*) in Mexico. As of 1994, there were approximately 2,100 maquilas, employing about 579,000 workers.[3] Operations such as these in Mexico or in other countries with comparatively lower wage rates provide lower costs and, therefore, potentially higher profits for the American companies. Ford, for example, is considering new plants in China, India, and Southeast Asia.[4] But, some manufacturers are acting in direct contradiction to such alternatives: according to a survey by the international accounting firm of Ernst & Young, "less than one-third of the 659 major investments abroad by U.S. manufacturers in 1991 went to countries with low labor rates."[5] Companies are often first looking for a customer base, technology, financial incentives, and low corporate tax rates.

maquiladoras

Germany	$27.37	France	$17.10	Korea	$6.33
Japan	21.38	Canada	15.73	Taiwan	5.47
Sweden	18.81	Britain	13.68	Hong Kong	4.79
United States	17.10	Spain	11.46	Mexico	2.57

SOURCE: U.S. Department of Labor, *International Comparisons of Hourly Compensation Costs for Production Workers* (Bureau of Labor Statistics, 1994). Reprinted from November 20, 1995 issue of *Business Week*, by special permission, copyright © 1995 by McGraw-Hill, Inc.

EXHIBIT 1–3

Average Per-Hour Labor Rates for Manufacturing Workers, 1994 (in U.S. dollars)

[3] Hayes Ferguson, "Tijuana Assembly Factories Booming," *(New Orleans) Times-Picayune* (April 26, 1995), p. A1.
[4] Jerry Flint, "One World, One Ford," *Forbes* (June 20, 1994), p. 41.
[5] Lucinda Harper, "U.S. Manufacturers in 1991 Invested Largely in Industrialized Countries," *Wall Street Journal* (October 20, 1992), p. A2.

CAD systems have helped General Motors and other auto makers design cars more effectively and efficiently than was possible in the past.

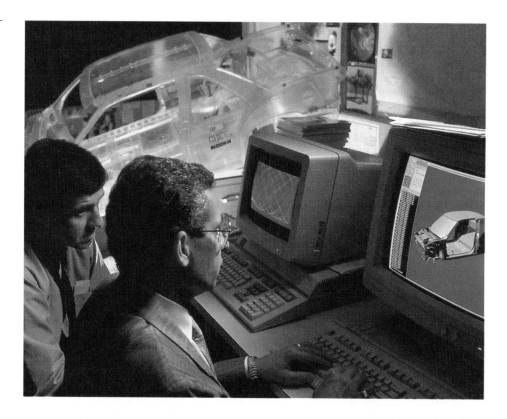

Increased Technology

Many companies are not looking to invest abroad, but simply to lower costs at home. One simple way to reduce costs is to increase quality. Many times cost reductions and quality improvements point directly to automation, which reflects the change from labor-intensive businesses to machine-intensive businesses. This operational evolution has occurred both in the work area and in the information technology area. The availability of data and the ability to process information efficiently have increased dramatically. Technology has affected all areas of an organization through the use of the low-cost, high-processing capabilities of personal computers (PCs). In engineering, **computer-aided design** (CAD) systems have made it easier to visualize and quickly generate prospective product designs. CAD systems contribute to quality processes by allowing companies to issue fewer and fewer **engineering change orders** (ECOs) after production is in process. An ECO affects the way in which a product is manufactured by modifying the design, parts, process, or even quality of the product. The current attitude is that planning is critical to a production process: "let's get it right *before* production begins."

computer-aided design

engineering change orders

computer-aided manufacturing

CAD systems are often integrated with **computer-aided manufacturing** (CAM) techniques. CAM refers to using computers to control production processes through the use of numerically controlled (NC) machines, robots, and automated assembly systems. These systems reduce the amount and cost of labor, produce a high quantity of consistently high-quality goods, and afford management the ability to respond quickly to changes in market needs and demands. Additionally, CAM systems may be used in place of human labor to perform dangerous or boring jobs.

Company managers have also decided, in many instances, to make a wide variety of products—offering hundreds of choices in product selection. To accomplish this, manufacturers need to be able to change rapidly from one production run to another

It Might Take Time to Recoup, But It's Worth It

[Kohler Company, the bathroom fixture giant, is 120+ years old and still family-owned. Thus, the company is able to view its spending] as "generational investments," where the concept of a five- or ten-year depreciation is not necessary. By the early 1970s most competitors had come to the conclusion that cast-iron tubs and sinks were passé. [Companies like American Standard and Crane] began replacing their cast-iron products with lighter-weight, cheaper-to-make acrylic fixtures. Starting in 1972, [when Herb Kohler took over as chairman, he] invested tens of millions of dollars to overhaul Kohler Co.'s ancient coal-fired cast-iron foundry. First, he replaced it with a more efficient process called electric melt. In the mid-1980s he invested in robots to automate the operation that puts enamel on cast-iron tubs. American Standard and Crane bet wrong. Today Kohler continues to sell huge volumes of cast-iron tubs quite profitably. "The cast-iron bathtub remains the best, most durable product that one can buy," says Kohler. "[We] are able to process the material inexpensively . . . because we invested over a long period of time in process technology . . . ." Some Kohler stock recently changed hands at $102,500 a share, a twelve-fold increase since 1979.

SOURCE: Gary Samuels, "Generational Investor," *Forbes 400* (October 16, 1995), pp. 71–72. Reprinted by permission of *Forbes* magazine. © Forbes Inc., 1995.

and to produce limited quantities of numerous items. Many companies are installing **flexible manufacturing systems** (FMSs) in which a single factory turns out multiple variations of products through the use of computer-controlled robots. Nissan, a firm believer in flexible manufacturing, "describes its strategy as 'five anys': to make anything in any volume anywhere at any time by anybody."[6] This type of production requires a high level of investment in equipment as well as in research and development. Increases in product variety cause many additional costs for ordering and stocking components in a manufacturing company. Ford, however, is trying to increase product variety while reducing costs. To do so, the company is committed to a limited number of basic car platforms, each of which will "have the same engine, transmission, and other major components around the world, but have styling tailored to local tastes."[7]

flexible manufacturing systems

The increased use of computers has also affected accounting by providing less costly and more flexible data analyses. Data can now be easily formatted in a variety of ways to suit managerial, financial, tax, and regulatory needs. The traditional accounting notion of using different costs for different purposes has become even more easily achievable.

Technology cost in automated companies is becoming quite high, and many managers in such firms are now taking a long-run, rather than the traditional short-run, perspective in making decisions. This changed perspective helps entities achieve a competitive edge by using innovative approaches to production, measuring production costs over a product's entire life, and focusing on product quality and customer service. The above News Note on Kohler Company illustrates the benefits of a long-run perspective.

Concepts involving the long-run perspective and its nontraditional information needs are presented in subsequent chapters. Because all companies have not developed to the same state-of-the-art stage, the more traditional cost accounting techniques and information continue to be used in less technologically intense firms.

---

[6] Thomas A. Stewart, "Brace for Japan's Hot New Strategy," *Fortune* (September 22, 1992), p. 72.
[7] Flint, "One World."

globalization

VIDEO VIGNETTE

Whirlpool (in AME—Going Global)

global economy

European Union

North American Free Trade Agreement

General Agreement on Tariffs and Trade

dumping

International Perspective

As technology has improved, the world has essentially become smaller. The **globalization** of markets involves a changeover in local markets from competition among national or local suppliers to competition among international suppliers. Companies and consumers now realize that choices for the sale and purchase of products and services are international rather than domestic and, thus, operations take place in a global economy.

The **global economy** includes the international trade of goods and services, international movement of labor, and international flows of capital and information.[8] In addition to technology, trade agreements that reduce the fiscal barriers to the movement of goods and services between countries also contribute to a global economy. Remarkable progress in this area has been achieved, as evidenced by the European Union, the North American Free Trade Zone, and the renegotiations of the General Agreement on Tariffs and Trade.

The **European Union** (EU) (sometimes referred to as the Single Market) began in 1957 as the European Economic Community. The EU comprises twelve member nations: Belgium, Denmark, France, Germany, Greece, Ireland, Italy, Luxembourg, the Netherlands, Portugal, Spain, and the United Kingdom.[9] Through trade initiatives, the EU has eliminated virtually all barriers to the flow of capital, labor, goods, and services among member nations and created the world's largest single market prior to the establishment of the North American Free Trade Zone.

Following Europe's lead, Canada, Mexico, and the United States formed the North American Free Trade Zone market alliance through the 1994 enactment of the **North American Free Trade Agreement** (NAFTA). Although not as comprehensive as the EU agreement, NAFTA nevertheless establishes a new level of market integration in the three bordering countries. NAFTA essentially provides for the duty-free transfer of goods if the following conditions are met: (1) the goods are 100 percent grown, mined, and/or produced in a NAFTA country, or (2) components made in a NAFTA country comprise at least 60 percent of the product's retail price or 50 percent of its manufacturing cost. Some duties will, however, be retained for up to 15 years to protect certain industries that are extremely sensitive to import competition (such as shoes and glassware). When implemented in its entirety, this trade zone will encompass approximately 370 million people having a combined economic output of over $6.5 trillion.[10]

A significant worldwide trade agreement is the **General Agreement on Tariffs and Trade** (GATT). The GATT's objective is to provide a "level playing field" for trade among the 100+ signatory nations. When the GATT was originally signed in 1947, the average tariff was almost 40 percent; after seven revisions, the average tariff has been reduced to approximately 3 percent.[11] In addition to reducing and standardizing the tariffs on goods traded among the signatories, the most recent GATT discussions (the Uruguay Round) also instituted provisions related to intellectual property, technical standards, import licenses, customs regulations, exchanges of services, and product dumping. (**Dumping** refers to selling products abroad at prices lower than the ones charged in the home country or in other national markets.)

The exchange-of-service provision may become especially important to accountants. First, the GATT establishes the groundwork for eliminating many barriers currently existing to professionals who wish to open offices abroad or to the types

[8] Paul Krugman, *Peddling Prosperity*, quoted by Alan Farnham in "Global—or Just Globaloney," *Fortune* (June 27, 1994), p. 98.
[9] Turkey and Austria are also considering membership in the EU.
[10] Charles P. Heeter, Jr., "NAFTA Opens New Markets for CPAs," *Journal of Accountancy* (March 1994), p. 70.
[11] "A Guide to GATT," *The Economist* (December 4, 1993), p. 25.

N E W S
N O T E

Another Potential Bribery Scandal?

Lockheed Martin Corp. faces three separate federal grand jury investigations into suspected improper payments to foreign officials and middlemen, including one prompted by a sweeping South Korean payoff scandal.

The recent flurry of inquiries centers on transactions including multibillion dollar sales of F-16 Falcon fighter jets and P-3 antisubmarine planes to Korea during the early 1990s, according to U.S. law officials. Also under investigation are the activities of a consultant in Taiwan who already has been implicated in an alleged bribery scheme involving other U.S. defense firms.

[G]rand juries sitting in Los Angeles and Fort Worth are looking into, among other things, commissions and consulting fees paid to sell F-16s in 1991 to South Korea, which purchased a total of nearly $20 billion of U.S.-built military equipment between 1990 and 1993. U.S. prosecutors are following leads developed by their South Korean counterparts as part of a 1993 bribery and influence-peddling scandal that resulted in the arrest or dismissal of dozens of generals, senior civilian procurement officials and prominent politicians in that country.

Lockheed Martin officials have acknowledged they are especially sensitive about overseas-payment investigations because the company had to pay $24.8 million to the government [in early 1995] as part of an agreement under which it pleaded guilty to conspiring to violate U.S. antibribery laws involving sales of Lockheed C-130 aircraft to Egypt.

SOURCE: Andy Pasztor and Jeff Cole, "Lockheed Martin Faces 3 Federal Probes into Possible Payments for Foreign Sales," *Wall Street Journal* (September 5, 1995), p. A6. Reprinted by permission of *The Wall Street Journal,* © 1995 Dow Jones & Company, Inc. All Rights Reserved Worldwide.

expect company managers to adopt an anticipatory or proactive role in social responsibility. Health, safety, and environmental issues, as well as corporate ethics, are high-priority concerns of all corporate stakeholders, both external and internal, and many companies have introduced a code of ethics as an integral part of the corporate culture.

V I D E O
VIGNETTE

Quaker Oats Code of Conduct and/or U.S. Sprint

If ethical business practices are not adhered to voluntarily, laws and regulations will be adopted to mandate such practices. One example of the U.S. government's stand on ethics is the **Foreign Corrupt Practices Act** (FCPA). This law was enacted to prevent bribes from being offered or given (directly or indirectly) to foreign officials to influence those individuals (or to cause them to use their influence) to obtain or retain business. Additionally, the FCPA mandates that a company maintain accurate accounting records and a reasonable system of **internal control.**[13] The intentions of this provision are that internal control systems would prevent or detect foreign bribes and would ensure that all transactions entered into by the firm were properly accounted for and legal. Unfortunately, even the best system of internal control may not prevent or detect circumstances that arise from employee or management collusion or circumvention of the system. For example, as indicated in the above News Note, bribery may simply be viewed as "the way to do business" in certain places. But attitudes such as this are changing and moves are being made to encourage less corrupt business practices.

Foreign Corrupt Practices Act

internal control

Businesses must operate under the established laws of the country in which those businesses are incorporated and of the countries in which business is practiced. Although laws can institute "roadblocks" to unethical activity, such activity can only be effectively prevented by a code of ethical conduct that has been internalized by company employees. Accountants hold a variety of roles in organizations, and "there is no guarantee that [those accountants] can avoid some of the pitfalls and problems

---

[13] An internal control is any measure used by management to protect assets, promote the accuracy of records, ensure adherence to company policies, or promote operational efficiency.

EXHIBIT 1–4

Most Desired Types of
Business Intelligence

AREA	% OF COMPANIES SURVEYED CURRENTLY RECEIVING INTELLIGENCE	% OF COMPANIES SURVEYED NEEDING BETTER INTELLIGENCE
Competitor activities	87	76
Changing market structure	82	67
Customer/supplier activities	81	55
Emerging technology initiatives	73	63
Regulatory climate	73	36
Political climate	68	32
Global economic conditions	52	32

SOURCE: The Futures Group, *Ostriches and Eagles: Competitive Intelligence Capabilities in U.S. Companies* (Glastonbury, CN); cited in "U.S. Companies Slow to Develop Business Intelligence," *Deloitte & Touche Review* (October 16, 1995), p. 1.

that engulf our society today, but, clearly, the most important first step is the pursuit of and dedication to high ethical standards."[14]

Each of the aforementioned changes in the contemporary business environment has affected the production process (or the provision of service) and managers' information needs. Exhibit 1–4 indicates the types of information that are most desired by company managers to improve the business information system. Note that the survey indicates "that relatively few [U.S.] companies track or feel compelled to track global economic conditions, which does not augur well for U.S. competitiveness in an increasingly global economy."[15]

But, by necessity, the costs of changing processes, expanding markets, and gathering information are reflected in a business's operations. To remain in business, a company must make a profit on its operating activities. To do so, it must determine which of its products and services are the most attractive to consumers and at what price. At the same time, the company has to be able to produce the product or perform the service at a cost that provides a reasonable profit margin. The selling prices of many goods are set by the marketplace rather than the individual producer. Thus, to generate reasonable profit margins, companies must contain costs and/or enhance products rather than raise selling prices. Information about the cost of producing a product or providing a service is determined from, and accounted for, in the company's accounting system.

RELATIONSHIP OF FINANCIAL AND MANAGEMENT ACCOUNTING

Accounting information is supposed to address three different functions: (1) provide information to external parties (stockholders, creditors, and various regulatory bodies) for investment and credit decisions; (2) estimate the cost of products produced and services provided by the organization; and (3) provide information useful for making decisions and controlling operations. Financial accounting is designed to meet external information needs and to comply with generally accepted accounting principles. Management accounting attempts to satisfy internal information needs and to provide product costing information for external financial statements. The primary differences between these two accounting disciplines are given in Exhibit 1–5.

Financial accounting must comply with the generally accepted accounting principles (currently established by the Financial Accounting Standards Board [FASB], a private-sector body). The information used in financial accounting is typically historical, quantifiable, monetary, and verifiable. These characteristics are essential to the uniformity and consistency needed for external financial statements. Financial

---

[14] Howard L. Siers, "Are We Really a Corporate Conscience?" *Management Accounting* (August 1991), p. 20.
[15] "U.S. Companies."

	FINANCIAL	MANAGEMENT
Primary users	External	Internal
Primary organizational focus	Whole (aggregated)	Parts (segmented)
Information characteristics	Must be	May be
	Historical	Current or forecasted
	Quantitative	Quantitative or qualitative
	Monetary	Monetary or nonmonetary
	Verifiable	Timely and, at a minimum, a reasonable estimate
Overriding criteria	Generally accepted accounting principles	Situational relevance (usefulness)
	Consistency	Benefits in excess of cost
	Verifiability	Flexibility
Recordkeeping	Formal	Combination of formal and informal

EXHIBIT 1–5

Financial and Management Accounting Differences

accounting information is usually quite aggregated and related to the organization as a whole. In some cases, a regulatory agency such as the Securities and Exchange Commission (SEC) or an industry commission (such as banking or insurance) may mandate financial accounting practices. In other cases, financial accounting information is required for obtaining loans, preparing tax returns, and understanding how well or poorly the business is performing.

By comparison, management accounting provides information for internal users. Managers are often concerned with individual parts or segments of the business rather than the whole organization, so management accounting information commonly addresses such individualized concerns rather than the "big picture" of financial accounting. For example, in addition to determining overall corporate profitability, Ford management needs information about the profitability of each of its product lines and each of its geographically diverse divisions.

Management accounting is not required to adhere to generally accepted accounting principles in providing information for managers' internal purposes. It is, however, expected to be flexible in serving management's needs and be useful to managers' functions. A related criterion is that **cost-benefit analysis** should justify the provision of information; that is, information should be developed and provided only if the cost of producing that information is less than the benefit of having it. These two criteria, though, must be combined with the financial accounting information criteria of verifiability, uniformity, and consistency, because all accounting documents and information (whether internal or external) must be grounded in reality rather than whim.

Nonetheless, from a management accounting perspective, managerial needs are more important than financial accounting requirements; thus, as indicated in the following News Note, flexibility is the hallmark of modern management accounting. For example, managers are often constrained by time when making decisions. They often need to accept less precise, but more timely, information for internal decision-making purposes rather than to delay a decision until the precise information required for external reporting can be obtained.

The objectives and nature of financial and management accounting differ, but all accounting information tends to rely on the same basic accounting system and set of accounts. The accounting system provides management with a means by which costs

cost-benefit analysis

Multiple Costs Are Often Necessary

[T]he truth of a cost is . . . closely linked to the ability of the manager to identify opportunities and to place values on these opportunities. . . . [A useful] definition of true cost focuses on the relation of the cost value to the decision faced by a manager. That is, the accuracy of a cost is a function of the correspondence between the decision a manager has to make and the relevance of the cost for that decision. In this scheme, the more closely a cost value matches that needed by a manager for a particular decision, the more accurate the cost.

Under this approach, managers are interested in different costs for different decisions. The manager will want more than a single value for cost—he or she wants a flexible system that provides a variety of cost analyses on demand.

SOURCE: Germain Boër, "Five Modern Management Accounting Myths," *Management Accounting* (January 1994), pp. 24–25. Reprinted from *Management Accounting*. Copyright by Institute of Management Accountants, Montvale, NJ.

are accumulated from input of materials through the production process until completion and, ultimately, to cost of goods sold. Although technology has improved to the point that a company can have different accounting systems designed for different purposes, most companies still rely on a single system to supply the basic accounting information. The single system typically focuses on providing information for financial accounting purposes, but its informational output can be adapted to meet most internal management requirements.

Account balances in the accounting system are summarizations of many individual details. External financial statements are prepared from account balances and represent past transactions. In reviewing external financial statements, managers may find some useful information, but often the information is either outdated or lacking in sufficient detail. The information needs of management typically involve day-to-day operational questions; answers to these questions sometimes require details not available in aggregated account balances. Managers may also need information involving estimates of *future* quantities or costs of resources that are not recorded in account balances.

Accounting records provide detail beyond the balances that appear on external financial statements. These records include data that can be formatted and manipulated in numerous ways in response to management's changing needs. Management accountants are often asked to gather and analyze data and make estimates regarding some problem management wishes to solve. For example, management may need information on the estimated cost of producing a new product and whether plant capacity is sufficient for the additional production. Management accountants obtain and study the information necessary to make those estimates and present the estimates to management. The basis for the estimates may begin with the historical data recorded in accounting records, but virtually it never ends there.

RELATIONSHIP OF MANAGEMENT AND COST ACCOUNTING

Institute of Management Accountants

Management accounting has been defined by the **Institute of Management Accountants** (IMA)[16] as including almost all manipulations of financial information for use by managers in performing their specified organizational functions and, additionally, in ensuring the proper use and handling of an entity's resources. The objectives of management accounting (shown in Exhibit 1–6) reflect the comprehensive

[16] The IMA's definition of management accounting is "the process of identification, measurement, accumulation, analysis, preparation, interpretation, and communication of financial information used by management to plan, evaluate, and control within an organization and to assure appropriate use of and accountability for its resources." [Institute of Management Accountants (formerly National Association of Accountants), *Statements on Management Accounting Number 2: Management Accounting Terminology* (Montvale, N.J.: NAA, June 1, 1983), p. 65.]

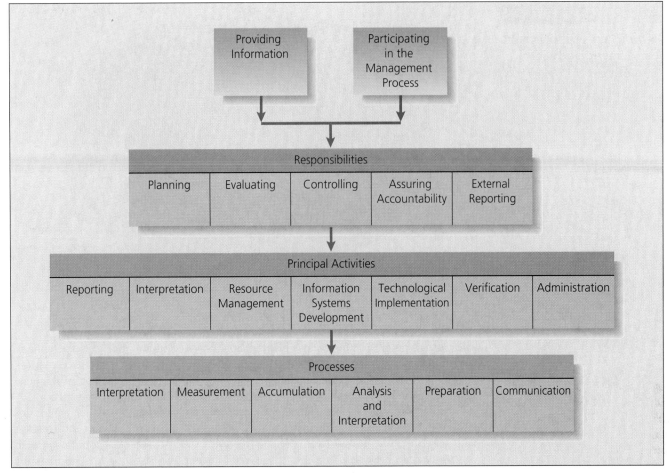

SOURCE: Institute of Management Accountants (formerly National Association of Accountants), *Statement on Management Accounting Number 1B: Objectives of Management Accounting* (Montvale, NJ; NAA, June 17, 1982), pp. 8–9. Copyright by Institute of Management Accountants (formerly National Association of Accountants), Montvale, NJ.

EXHIBIT 1–6

Objectives of Management Accounting

nature of this accounting area. The functions of cost accounting are focused primarily at the "processes" level in that exhibit. Thus, cost accounting is an integral part of the broader field of management accounting.

Cost accounting is defined as "a technique or method for determining the cost of a project, process, or thing. . . . This cost is determined by direct measurement, arbitrary assignment, or systematic and rational allocation."[17] The appropriate method of determining cost depends on the circumstances that generate the need for information. Various costing methods are illustrated throughout the text.

cost accounting

Although cost information was originally designed for internal managerial use, this purpose was diminished at the time of the 1929 stock market crash when the emphasis shifted to product costing, inventory valuation, and fair and proper financial statement presentation. The financial statement applications of cost information are still important, but the current trend is to refocus cost information for managerial use in planning, controlling, performance evaluating, and decision making.

Central to a cost accounting system is the process for tracing various input costs to an organization's outputs (products or services). This process uses the traditional accounting form of recordkeeping—general and subsidiary ledger accounts. Accounts containing cost and management accounting information include those dealing with

[17] Institute of Management Accountants (formerly National Association of Accountants), *Statements on Management Accounting Number 2: Management Accounting Terminology* (Montvale, N.J.: NAA, June 1, 1983), p. 25.

EXHIBIT 1–7

Relationship of Financial, Management, and Cost Accounting

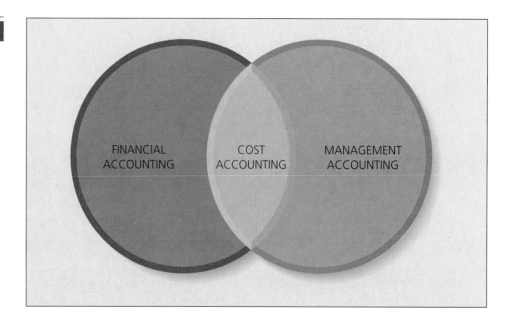

sales, procurement (materials and plant assets), production and inventory, personnel, payroll, delivery, financing, and funds management.[18] However, not all cost information is reproduced on the financial statements. Correspondingly, not all financial accounting information is useful to managers in performing their daily functions.

Although differences exist between the information provided for management decisions and financial accounting statements, both use a subset of the same information and share the same physical accounts and records. A well-designed accounting system can be flexible enough to meet management's needs and also provide the basis for preparation of external financial statements. Because two recordkeeping systems might be cumbersome and potentially redundant, cost information is generally kept in the same accounts as financial accounting information and much of the product cost information developed by cost accounting techniques is used in external financial statement accounts. However, some professionals have suggested that the use of different accounting systems for different purposes might be justified.

Cost accounting creates an overlap between financial accounting and management accounting. Cost accounting integrates with financial accounting by providing product costing information for financial statements and with management accounting by providing some of the quantitative, cost-based information managers need to perform their tasks. Exhibit 1–7 depicts the relationship of cost accounting to the larger systems of financial and management accounting. None of the three areas should be viewed as a separate and exclusive "type" of accounting. The boundaries of each are not clearly and definitively drawn and, because of changing technology and information needs, are becoming increasingly blurred.

The cost accounting overlap causes the financial and management accounting systems to articulate or be joined together to form an informational network. Because these two systems articulate, accountants must understand how cost accounting provides costs for financial statements and supports management information needs. Organizations that do not manufacture products may not require elaborate *cost* accounting systems. However, even service companies need to understand how much their services cost to provide so that those companies can determine whether it is cost-effective to be engaged in particular business activities. Regardless of the need to develop cost information, most organizations need to budget for future periods,

---

[18] With reference to accounts, this text will focus primarily on the set of accounts that depicts the internal flow of costs.

make decisions about operational performance, and analyze alternative courses of action. All of these functions require the use of *management accounting* concepts and techniques.

SCOPE OF MANAGEMENT ACCOUNTING

Management accountants should strive to recognize what information management needs, why it is needed, and how to provide it in the most understandable and timely manner so that the information is useful in decision making. Managers often want or need information about activities that technically fall outside the production process, but that are related to production. For example, managers need information for making decisions about (1) acquiring and financing production capacity; (2) determining which products to market; (3) pricing jobs, products, or services; (4) determining the best method of delivering finished goods to warehouses; (5) locating the best property for production facilities; and (6) financing the costs of production. To help make such decisions, managers frequently use management accounting information.

Data and information are distinctly different. **Data** are bits of knowledge or facts that have not been summarized and categorized in a manner useful to a decision maker; **information** has been carefully chosen from a body of data and arranged in a meaningful way. Data are not useful in managerial functions. Managers must combine information with experience and judgment to create knowledge that is used in solving problems and making decisions.

data

information

Management accountants can help managers in the decision-making process by providing both quantitative and qualitative information. (Some information, such as the number of production defects during a period, contains both quantitative and qualitative elements.) Quantitative information permits managers to view the numerical impact of alternative choices. Examples of quantitative information include monetary amounts, number of units of product expected to be sold in the next period, and time

There is such a thing as information overload! Reports should summarize data in an organized manner and should be sent only to those persons who actually need the information being provided.

needed for a robot to perform a specific production task. Alternatively, qualitative information provides facts that help to eliminate some of the inherent uncertainty related to choices. Qualitative information relates to the nature of an item; for instance, the management accountant might provide information on the raw material quality of different suppliers. The purchasing agent can then combine quantitative (price) and qualitative (quality) information to determine from which supplier to buy raw materials. The supplier offering the lowest materials cost may not provide goods of sufficiently reliable quality to justify purchasing materials from it.

Any single type of information about "cost" may not be useful in performing all management functions. For example, the replacement cost of machinery is useful information for planning because it indicates the amount of insurance to purchase. Alternatively, machinery replacement cost is not useful in controlling operations because current depreciation charges are based on historical cost.

goals

In focusing on the future, managers set goals and objectives. **Goals** are desired results or conditions contemplated in qualitative terms; these are often included in the organization's mission statement. To implement a mission statement and/or goals, the organization must determine targeted **objectives** that can be expressed in quantitative terms. These objectives should be written so as to be achievable within a preestablished period.

objectives

Role in Planning

planning

Translating the goals and objectives for a business and developing a strategy for achieving them in a systematic manner is called **planning.** Organizations should develop short-term, intermediate-term, and long-term plans (strategy). Short-term plans, which are prepared in more detail than long-term plans, are used by managers as a basis for the control and performance evaluation functions.

VIDEO
VIGNETTE

Starlight Publishing, Inc. (Blue Chip Enterprises)

The planning functions in large and small organizations tend to differ. Large organizations typically have a more established planning process that encompasses all planning horizons, recognizes the organization's place in the competitive structure, and communicates the plans throughout the organization for a "shared-values" perspective. Small organizations' managers, on the other hand, often plan only for the short run, simply trying to fit into the marketplace, and are either unable or unwilling to communicate, or do not recognize the value of communicating, plans to subordinates. But, regardless of how much planning is performed, the need for accounting information is critical to success.

In conducting the planning function, managers depend heavily on the management accountant. Long-term plans typically address issues such as market share, which is based on projections of costs, prices, volume, quality, and service. Short-term plans may be in the form of budgets for resources such as cash, inventory, and personnel. Budgets are based, in part, on the management accountant's knowledge of operational and financial activities and relationships. The budgeting process results in projected financial statements that allow managers to evaluate the prospective results of their plans before such plans are implemented.

Role in Controlling and Performance Evaluation

Planning is the basis for the management control and performance evaluation functions. **Controlling** is the exertion of managerial influence on operations so that they will conform to plans. Essentially, the control process first involves setting performance **standards** or norms against which actual results are measured. The management accountant helps in determining standards for various quantities, times, and costs in all operating areas. Performance is then measured and compared to the standards on a scheduled basis; the management accountant's role is to provide managers with timely, appropriate, and accurate reports.

controlling

standards

Using the analyses provided by the management accountant, managers can conduct a **performance evaluation** to determine whether operations are proceeding according to plan or whether actual results differ significantly from those that were expected. In the latter case, adjustments to operating activities may be needed. After performance is measured during the control process, managers must then evaluate the effectiveness and efficiency of that performance.

The successful accomplishment of a task reflects **effectiveness,** whereas performing tasks to produce the stated yield at the lowest cost from the resources used is **efficiency.** For example, it is effective for the production supervisor to lubricate production machinery, but it is more efficient to use a lower-paid maintenance worker to perform that task. Efficiency is greatest when the ratio of quality outputs to the related inputs is greatest. The best performance achieves effectiveness and maximizes efficiency.

performance evaluation

effectiveness

efficiency

Role in Decision Making

A manager's ability to manage depends on good **decision making**—choosing the most efficient course of action to achieve a specified objective. To make appropriate choices, managers need information related to alternative solutions. Managers, then, are information users and accountants are information providers. Accountants must recognize that the information they produce influences behavior and that clear communications must exist between the providers and users of accounting information. The following News Note discusses vocabulary as a prime difficulty in the communication process.

decision making

For information to be used as a sound basis for making decisions, accountants must understand why managers want the information and ascertain that information is being used appropriately. The quantity of information desired is based, in part, on

You Said It, But I Didn't Understand It

NEWS NOTE

Communication occurs when an exchange of messages results in shared meaning. Whether or not effective communication has resulted depends upon the way in which thoughts are translated by the sender into words and how the receiver translates these words back into thoughts. This "translation stage" is where problems begin in the communication process.

Differences in vocabulary seem to lie at the very root of any communication breakdown between accountants and non-accountants. The non-accountant receiver must feel somewhat like the doctor's patient when the physician discusses the diagnosis of an ailment using medical vocabulary. [Accounting professionals use what seem to them to be "basic" terms to communicate messages to individuals with little or no understanding of the meaning of those terms—thus, losing the message in the transmission.] In another scenario, the receiver may "read" an entirely different meaning into the message that the sender had not intended.

Therefore, accountants must think about who their prospective listeners are and choose the level of language accordingly.

Frequently receivers do not know that they do not understand what has been communicated. For example, an accountant may use the term cost when referring to the historical cost of an asset. Unfortunately, the term cost has many different meanings and can be easily misinterpreted (even by many accountants).

[Four possible ways to help overcome communication problems include using more descriptive (less technical) words when possible, using visual aids, watching for nonverbal clues of misunderstanding, and providing a mechanism for feedback.]

SOURCE: Benny Sachry and Betty A. Kleen, "Effective Communication with Non-Accountants," © 1995, excerpted with permission, *New Accountant*, November/December 1995.

VIDEO
VIGNETTE

Luster Construction Management
(Blue Chip Enterprises)

the expected consequences of the decision. The more important the decision, the more relevant information it is desirable to have.

Thus, the purpose of management accounting is twofold. First, it must provide the basis for appropriately estimating cost valuations needed for external financial statement presentations (balance sheet inventory values and income statement cost of goods/services sold). Second, it must provide sufficient, useful information to help managers adequately perform their functions of planning, controlling, evaluating performance, and making decisions. These two purposes are separate and distinct. Accomplishing the first does not necessarily or automatically satisfy the second, nor does accomplishing the second automatically accomplish the first. Each management function requires the use of some particular set of cost or management accounting information.

THE MANAGEMENT ACCOUNTING PROFESSION

common body of knowledge

Because of their many functions, management accountants are expected to be versed in a wide variety of topics. The IMA specified the **common body of knowledge** (CBK) presented in Exhibit 1–8 as the minimum knowledge needed by a person to function effectively as a management accountant. A review of the various areas covered by the CBK indicates that management accountants need to be versed in theories and techniques from economics, management, finance, marketing, and statistics in addition to accounting. For example, economics provides a sound base from which to analyze the organization's operating environment and to perform various financial planning functions. The depth of knowledge in any subject area depends on the individual's career level and functional responsibility area.

The common body of knowledge specified for management accountants should not be viewed as being permanently fixed. As changes occur in the business world, the knowledge needed by management accountants will also evolve. Changes most likely will be reflected as expansions, not contractions, in the CBK. Examples of recent changes causing innovations in the CBK for management accountants include the emergence of robotics and other computerized automation, management strategies developed in post–World War II Japan, and vastly improved information technology. The knowledge needed for a career in management accounting must be gained from *both* the classroom and work experience—each enhances the other and neither can stand alone.

Beginning in 1972, prior to the issuance of the CBK statement, the IMA (then the National Association of Accountants) offered a comprehensive examination designed to test an individual's knowledge of technical accounting skills as well as other

EXHIBIT 1–8

Common Body of Knowledge for Management Accountants

Core Knowledge Areas		
INFORMATION AND DECISION PROCESSES	ACCOUNTING PRINCIPLES AND FUNCTIONS	ENTITY OPERATIONS
■ Management decision processes ■ Internal reporting ■ Financial planning and performance evaluation	■ Organizational structure and management ■ Accounting concepts and principles	■ Principal entity operations ■ Operating environment ■ Taxation ■ External reporting ■ Information systems

SOURCE: Institute of Management Accountants (formerly National Association of Accountants), *Statements of Management Accounting Number 1D: The Common Body of Knowledge for Management Accountants* (Montvale, NJ: NAA, June 3, 1986), p. 2. Copyright by Institute of Management Accountants (formerly National Association of Accountants), Montvale, NJ.

related business fields. The comprehensive examination related to management accounting is currently administered by the Institute of Certified Management Accountants (ICMA), an IMA affiliate organization. The **Certified Management Accountant** (CMA) designation provides evidence that its holders have professional status, and it affords a means for management accountants to demonstrate educational attainment and competency in specific areas of knowledge. In addition to passing the examination, CMAs must qualify through work experience and maintain certain continuing education requirements that are reviewed and evaluated by the ICMA staff.

The CMA exam lasts two days and covers topics in all areas important to an upper-level management accountant. The exam has four sections: (1) Economics, Finance, and Management; (2) Financial Accounting and Reporting; (3) Management Reporting, Analysis, and Behavioral Issues; and (4) Decision Analysis and Information Systems. Each section of the exam is considered by practicing professionals to be "job pertinent." CMA candidates who have passed the Certified Public Accountant (CPA) examination are given credit for Part 2.

Although the CMA is a relatively recent designation, thousands of individuals have obtained certificates, many of whom are also CPAs. In fact, a significant proportion of the members of the American Institute of Certified Public Accountants actually work as management accountants rather than as public accountants. A knowledge of management accounting is useful to CPAs because it helps them to understand client organizations and accounting functions.

A CPA is granted, by individual states, the right to offer auditing services to the public. Thus, the CPA certificate is both a professional designation *and a basis for licensing* by which the states monitor and regulate public accounting. In contrast, the CMA is not a license because CMAs are employed by organizations that do not need to be "protected" by the government. The CMA and CPA do not compete with, but rather complement, each other.

The CMA program continues to grow and gain recognition from the business community. Rewards for attainment include salary differentials (see Exhibit 1–9) and promotions. In the future, the CMA may be considered a basic credential in the business world for high-level management accounting positions.

The Canadian organization that corresponds to the IMA is the **Society of Management Accountants of Canada.** The organization is composed of 29,000 members, of whom 26,000 are CMAs and 3,000 are professional program students. The Canadian CMA program differs from the American one in that there are two exams (an entrance and a comprehensive final). Between taking these two examinations, the aspiring CMA must obtain practical experience while participating in a demanding professional program that concentrates on management theory and practice, professionalism, ethics, and emerging management accounting issues. The accompanying

Certified Management Accountant

Society of Management Accountants of Canada

EXHIBIT 1–9

Average Salary Differentials between No Certification and CMA and/or CPA

AGE RANGE	NO CERTIFICATION	CMA CERTIFICATION	CPA CERTIFICATION	CMA & CPA CERTIFICATION
19–29	$32,457	$42,566	$38,662	$ 40,258
30–39	50,280	59,431	57,848	65,562
40–49	56,568	70,687	72,777	72,773
50–59	67,599	71,695	79,128	123,666
60 and over	69,009	*	85,331	*

*Data not reported because the number of respondents is insufficient to ensure individual confidentiality. Data based on IMA membership survey.

SOURCE: Karl E. Reichart and David L. Schroeder, "Salaries 1995," *Management Accounting* (June 1996), p. 22. Reprinted from *Management Accounting.* Copyright by Institute of Management Accountants, Montvale, NJ.

NEWS NOTE

The Importance of a Professional Designation

A professional designation is a highly valued personal asset. Once acquired, a member has a choice—live off the principal value, probably for a short period of time or increase the equity value of the designation.

Being a professional in today's markets is competitive. There is no certainty of employment and standing still in career development is an invitation to redundancy.

Individually and collectively, we have a lot to gain in ensuring that equity growth underpins our professional designation. That equity growth is our competitive advantage. Like any other asset with value, it means we must ensure our reputation, our uniqueness, our investment, and our legal standing.

We believe that CMA designation is the starting point of a successful career, not the destination. Once the designation is earned, the skill base and knowledge surrounding it should be constantly updated and improved. In the same way that total quality is a process of continuous improvement in an organization, professionalism should be seen as a life-long process of continuous improvement. . . .

SOURCE: Doug Dodds, "A Professional Designation: The CMA's Competitive Edge," *CMA Magazine* (February 1995), p. 2. Reprinted from an article appearing in *CMA Magazine* by Doug Dodds, February 1995 issue, with permission of The Society of Management Accountants of Canada.

News Note discusses the importance of the CMA designation, but the benefits are equally applicable to *any* professional designation, including the CPA (Certified Public Accountant), CA (Chartered Accountant), JD (Juris Doctorate), CFP (Certified Financial Planner), and CLU (Certified Life Underwriter).

Management and Cost Accounting Standards

Management accountants can use different costs and different information for different purposes, because their discipline does not have to adhere to generally accepted accounting principles when providing information for managers' internal use. In the United States, financial accounting standards are established by the Financial Accounting Standards Board (FASB), a private-sector body. No similar board exists to define universal management accounting standards. However, a public-sector board called the **Cost Accounting Standards Board** (CASB) was established in 1970 by the U.S. Congress to promulgate uniform cost accounting standards for defense contractors and federal agencies.

Cost Accounting Standards Board

The CASB produced 20 cost accounting standards (of which one has been withdrawn) from its inception until it was terminated in 1980 (see Exhibit 1–10). The CASB was re-created in 1988 as an independent board of the Office of Federal Procurement Policy. The board's objectives are to

- Increase the degree of uniformity in cost accounting practices among government contractors in like circumstances;
- Establish consistency in cost accounting practices in like circumstances by each individual contractor over periods of time; and
- Require contractors to disclose their cost accounting practices in writing.[19]

Although CASB standards do not constitute a comprehensive set of rules, compliance is *required* for companies bidding on or pricing cost-related contracts for the federal government.

In contrast to the CASB, the IMA cannot promulgate legally binding cost accounting standards, but it does produce nonbinding guidelines in the areas of cost

[19] Robert B. Hubbard, "Return of the Cost Accounting Standards Board," *Management Accounting* (October 1990), p. 56.

NUMBER	TOPIC
401	Consistency in estimating, accumulating, and reporting costs
402	Consistency in allocating costs incurred for the same purpose
403	Allocation of home office expenses to segments
404	Capitalization of tangible assets
405	Accounting for unallowable costs
406	Cost accounting period
407	Use of standard costs for direct material and direct labor
408	Accounting for costs of compensated personal absence
409	Depreciation of tangible capital assets
410	Allocation of business unit general and administrative expenses
411	Accounting for acquisition costs of material
412	Composition and measurement of pension cost
413	Adjustment and allocation of pension cost
414	Cost of money as an element of the cost of facilities capital
415	Accounting for the cost of deferred compensation
416	Accounting for insurance costs
417	Cost of money as an element of the cost of capital assets
418	Allocation of direct and indirect costs
419	Not published
420	Accounting for independent research and development costs and bid and proposal costs

SOURCE: Darrel A. Sourwine, "Putting the Pieces Together," *Management Accounting* (July 1991), p. 45. Reprinted from *Management Accounting.* Copyright by Institute of Management Accountants, Montvale, NJ.

EXHIBIT 1–10

CASB Standards

and management accounting called **Statements on Management Accounting** (SMAs). These pronouncements are developed by the Management Accounting Practices (MAP) Committee of the IMA after a rigorous developmental and exposure process to ensure their wide support.

Statements on Management Accounting

The first SMAs concentrated on the development of a framework for management accounting and included objectives and terminology. SMA topics such as objectives and the common body of knowledge were introduced earlier in this chapter. Later SMAs addressed management accounting practices and techniques such as determining direct labor cost, computing the cost of capital, and measuring entity performance.

As of early 1995, the Society of Management Accountants of Canada had issued 30 **Management Accounting Guidelines** (MAGs) that advocate appropriate practices for specific management accounting situations. These MAGs cover issues such as postinvestment audits of capital projects, cash and accounts receivable management, implementing JIT production systems and target costing, becoming ISO 9000 registered, and product life cycle management. Like the SMAs, MAGs are not requirements for organizational accounting, but merely suggestions.

Management Accounting Guidelines

Although the Institute of Management Accountants, Cost Accounting Standards Board, and Society of Management Accountants of Canada have been instrumental in standards development, much of the body of knowledge and practice in management accounting has been provided by industry practice and economic and finance theory. Thus, no "official" agency publishes generic management accounting standards for all companies, but there is wide acceptance of (and, therefore, authority for) the methods presented in the text. The development of cost and management accounting standards and practices indicates that management accountants are interested and involved in professional recognition. Another indication of this movement is the adoption of ethics codes by both the Institute of Management Accountants and the various provincial societies in Canada.

Ethics for Management Accountant Professionals

Because of the pervasive nature of management accounting and the organizational level at which many management accountants work, the IMA believed that some guidelines were necessary to help its members with ethical dilemmas. Thus, Statement of Management Accounting 1C, *Standards of Ethical Conduct for Management Accountants*, was adopted in June 1983. These standards are in the areas of competence, confidentiality, integrity, and objectivity. The IMA Code of Ethics is reproduced in Exhibit 1–11.

EXHIBIT 1–11

Standards of Ethical Conduct for Management Accountants

COMPETENCE
Management accountants have a responsibility to:
Maintain an appropriate level of professional competence by ongoing development of their knowledge and skills.
Perform their professional duties in accordance with relevant laws, regulations, and technical standards.
Prepare complete and clear reports and recommendations after appropriate analyses of relevant and reliable information.

CONFIDENTIALITY
Management accountants have a responsibility to:
Refrain from disclosing confidential information acquired in the course of their work except when authorized, unless legally obligated to do so.
Inform subordinates as appropriate regarding the confidentiality of information acquired in the course of their work and monitor their activities to assure the maintenance of that confidentiality.
Refrain from using or appearing to use confidential information acquired in the course of their work for unethical or illegal advantage either personally or through third parties.

INTEGRITY
Management accountants have a responsibility to:
Avoid actual or apparent conflicts of interest and advise all appropriate parties of any potential conflict.
Refrain from engaging in any activity that would prejudice their ability to carry out their duties ethically.
Refuse any gift, favor, or hospitality that would influence or would appear to influence their actions.
Refrain from either actively or passively subverting the attainment of the organization's legitimate and ethical objectives.
Recognize and communicate professional limitations or other constraints that would preclude responsible judgment or successful performance of an activity.
Communicate unfavorable as well as favorable information and professional judgments or opinions.
Refrain from engaging in or supporting any activity that would discredit the profession.

OBJECTIVITY
Management accountants have a responsibility to:
Communicate information fairly and objectively.
Disclose fully all relevant information that could reasonably be expected to influence an intended user's understanding of the reports, comments, and recommendations presented.

SOURCE: Institute of Management Accountants (formerly National Association of Accountants), *Statements on Management Accounting Number 1C: Standards of Ethical Conduct for Management Accountants* (Montvale, NJ: NAA, June 1, 1983). Copyright by Institute of Management Accountants (formerly National Association of Accountants), Montvale, NJ.

EXHIBIT 1–12

Resolution of Ethical Conflict

When faced with significant ethical issues, management accountants should follow the established policies of the organization bearing on the resolution of such conflict. If these policies do not resolve the ethical conflict, management accountants should consider the following courses of action:

- Discuss such problems with the immediate superior except when it appears that the superior is involved, in which case the problem should be presented initially to the next higher managerial level. If satisfactory resolution cannot be achieved when the problem is initially presented, submit the issues to the next higher managerial level. If the immediate superior is the chief executive officer, or equivalent, the acceptable reviewing authority may be a group such as the audit committee, executive committee, board of directors, board of trustees, or owners. Contact with levels above the immediate superior should be initiated only with the superior's knowledge, assuming the superior is not involved.
- Clarify relevant concepts by confidential discussion with an objective advisor to obtain an understanding of possible courses of action.
- If the ethical conflict still exists after exhausting all levels of internal review, the management accountant may have no other recourse on significant matters than to resign from the organization and to submit an informative memorandum to an appropriate representative of the organization.

Except where legally proscribed, communication of such problems to authorities or individuals not employed or engaged by the organization is not considered appropriate.

SOURCE: Institute of Management Accountants (formerly National Association of Accountants), *Statements on Management Accounting Number 1B: Objectives of Management Accounting* (Montvale, NJ: NAA, June 1, 1983). Copyright by Institute of Management Accountants (formerly National Association of Accountants), Montvale, NJ.

Accountants have always been regarded as individuals of conviction, trust, and integrity. The most important of all the standards listed are those designated under integrity. These are statements about honesty of character and embody the essence and intent of U.S. laws and moral codes. Standards of integrity should be foremost in business dealings on an individual, group, and corporate level.

Many items expressed in the code appear to be ideas that would be apparent to any reasonable and moral individual. Reading the standards closely, however, causes one to wonder how departures will be determined. For example, the confidentiality standards refer to being "legally obligated" to disclose information. Does this refer only to information specifically covered in statutory law or could it also refer to requests for information in a civil lawsuit?[20] Additionally, what if one were morally obligated to disclose information, but not legally obligated to do so? Would disclosure then be a violation of the code of ethics? To provide some increased guidance, the IMA offers the steps listed in Exhibit 1–12 as a course of action for resolution of problems.

In Canada, ethics is one of the themes in the Society's two-year professional program. Codes of professional ethics for CMAs vary in Canada because those codes must comply with provincial legislation and the bylaws of the provincial societies.

As with all codes of ethics, the IMA and Canadian Society codes should be viewed as goals for professional behavior. Such codes cannot address every potential situation. Moreover, each individual operates under his or her own personal code of ethics; thus, those persons lacking high standards will not be deterred from unethical behavior by either a mandated or a voluntary code. However, the IMA and Canadian Society codes do provide benchmarks by which management accountants can judge their conduct.

[20] Statutory law is composed of those laws that have been enacted by a legislative body. A civil lawsuit involves one citizen suing another, possibly for breach of contract.

REVISITING

Ford Motor Company

Ford Chairman Alex Trotman says going global will mean easier adoption of the best methods wherever Ford finds them. The company envisions huge cost savings from engineering a product only once. The savings, in turn, could help Ford finance the billions of dollars needed in the near future for new products and new plants. Says [retired Ford chairman Philip Caldwell of the Chinese and Indian markets]: "Fifty percent to 60% of the world's population is not being served by the Ford Motor Co. If we go about as we have in the past, the economics won't leave much left over for pursuit of these new market opportunities."

It's not surprising that Ford should push a global strategy further and faster than its rivals. After all, Henry Ford was one of the first U.S. industrialists to push overseas, and the company has always pursued a fair degree of cross-border integration.

One danger in the new strategy is that the cost in time and money of pulling together so many resources will swamp potential savings. "We are dealing with different cultures, different manufacturing processes, different government regulations, five hours difference in time," opines another Detroit veteran who knows Ford inside out. "How do you run operations from that philosophical and physical distance?"

"It's a risk, sure," says former Ford chairman Philip Caldwell. "But doing nothing is a risk, too. I think [Ford 2000] is a risk worth taking." [And it is well-assured that Ford management undertakes this risk with the best business intelligence system, including accounting information, available to it.]

SOURCE: Jerry Flint, "One World, One Ford," *Forbes* (June 20, 1994), p. 41. Reprinted by permission of *Forbes* magazine. © Forbes Inc., 1994.

CHAPTER SUMMARY

The accounting language has two primary variations: financial accounting and management accounting. Cost accounting is a mutually shared subset of both financial and management accounting. Cost accounting's role in financial accounting focuses on accumulating production costs to determine valuations for external financial statement presentations. Its role in management accounting is to provide information for managers' planning, controlling, performance evaluation, and decision-making needs.

With the numerous recent changes in the business environment (including ethical considerations), management's information needs have significantly expanded in scope and variety. The objectives and common body of knowledge for the management accounting discipline indicate the pervasive nature of the subject matter. Management accountants must be flexible in meeting management's information requirements; this flexibility is thought to be the hallmark of modern management accounting. Management and financial accounting overlap in their uses of the same underlying data and system of accounts, although the focus of each differs (internal and external, respectively). Cost and financial accounting information is primarily monetary in nature, whereas management accounting information often includes qualitative and quantitative nonmonetary information. Management accounting is viewed as encompassing the broader purposes of providing information to assist managers in planning, controlling, evaluating performance, and making decisions. In any case, the primary value of the information is its ability to reduce managers' uncertainty in carrying out their functions effectively and efficiently.

Official, binding cost and management accounting standards do not exist except for pricing cost-related contracts to the federal government. There are, however, numerous guidelines on procedures and practices related to cost and management accounting; most of these have been developed through the efforts of the Institute of Management Accountants and the Society of Management Accountants of Canada. These organizations have instituted certification programs for management accountants and have formulated codes of ethics for the individuals in this profession, indicating the degree of professionalism management accounting has attained.

APPENDIX

Organizational Structure

An organization is a system composed of humans, nonhuman resources, and commitments configured to achieve certain explicit and implicit goals and objectives. This appendix provides some general information regarding organizational structure. Entity structure normally evolves from its nature, policies, and goals because certain designs are more conducive to specific types of operations. For example, a manufacturer will have an organizational segment known as the production center; a wholesaler will not.

An **organization chart** illustrates an entity's functions, divisions, and positions and how these are related. An important aspect of reviewing an organization chart is the determination of line and staff employees. A **line employee** is directly responsible for achieving an organization's goals and objectives; a **staff employee** is responsible for providing advice, guidance, and service to line personnel. Accountants may be viewed as line or staff personnel depending on their job titles, functions, and the firm's size and structure. Most accountants are considered staff employees and are, therefore, responsible for providing line managers with timely, complete, and relevant information to improve decision making and reduce uncertainty.

organization chart

line employee
staff employee

However, this traditional line and staff classification scheme may be fading. More responsibility for financial controls and information is being given to line management, and financial personnel are taking on more responsibility for nonfinancial objectives such as quality. Data are being captured on-line with less need for processing and more need for analysis. Thus, the management group is beginning to operate more as a team and less as actors and advisors.

The organization chart also indicates the lines of authority and responsibility. The right (usually by virtue of position or rank) to use resources to accomplish a task or achieve an objective is called **authority.** This concept differs from **responsibility,** which is the obligation to accomplish a task or achieve an objective. Authority can be delegated or assigned to others; ultimate responsibility cannot be delegated.

authority
responsibility

Although organization charts permit visualization of a company's structure, they do not present all factors necessary to understand how an organization functions. Informal relationships and informal channels of communication (the **grapevine**) that exist in the organization are not shown on an organization chart. The grapevine is an extremely important factor that influences the way in which things are accomplished in an organization. In addition, at any given level of the organization, it is impossible to discern from the organization chart who wields more power or has more status, authority, and responsibility. Nonetheless, an organization chart does provide a basic diagram of certain official chains of command and channels of communication.

grapevine

Exhibit 1–13 presents an organization chart for the Lakisha Corporation, which manufactures a variety of equipment. This chart indicates two positions under the vice president of finance: treasurer and controller. The duties of these two individuals are often confused. The **treasurer** of a corporation generally handles the actual resources and does not have access to the accounting records. Specific duties of the treasurer normally include directing the following: handling cash receipts, disbursements, and balances; managing credit and collections; maintaining bank relations and

treasurer

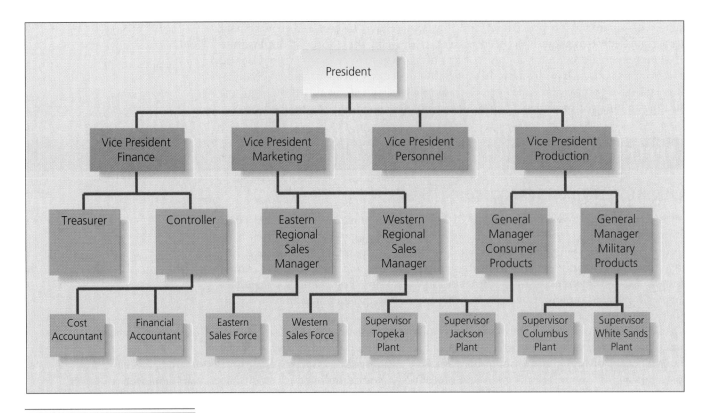

EXHIBIT 1–13

Organization Chart for
Lakisha Corporation

controller

arranging financing; managing investments; and insuring company assets. These functions are in contrast to those of the **controller** who supervises operations of the accounting system, but does not handle or negotiate changes in actual resources.

In many organizations, the controller is the chief accountant and is responsible for maintaining and reporting on both the cost and financial sets of accounts. The controller should see that the accounting system provides the amount of detail needed for internal and external purposes, while having a minimum amount of redundancy within the accounts. The controller is responsible for designing and maintaining the company's internal control system as well as helping management interpret accounting information. Interpreting accounting information allows the controller to exercise his or her technical abilities by assisting managers in determining the relevance of certain information to a decision, the need for additional accounting data, and the financial consequences of potential actions.

Other internal accounting staff positions may include the cost/management and financial accountants and their workers. The cost/management accountant is primarily concerned with internal information relating to the development of product or service cost; the financial accountant is primarily concerned with transactional information necessary to develop external reports. Companies may also have accountants in internal audit and tax departments.

matrix structures

In addition to the traditional hierarchical line-staff organization structure just discussed, some companies have adopted **matrix structures.** In this type of organization, functional departments and project teams exist simultaneously. Thus, an individual reports to two managers (one in the functional area and one in the project team), which provides a dual authority system. This structure is often used in organizations such as R&D companies and consulting firms that require significant coordination of personnel and that must respond to a rapidly changing environment.

authority (p. 27)

business intelligence (BI) system
   (p. 4)

Certified Management Accountant
   (CMA) (p. 21)

common body of knowledge (CBK)
   (p. 20)

computer-aided design (CAD) (p. 6)

computer-aided manufacturing
   (CAM) (p. 6)

controller (p. 28)

controlling (p. 18)

cost accounting (p. 15)

Cost Accounting Standards Board
   (CASB) (p. 22)

cost-benefit analysis (p. 13)

data (p. 17)

decision making (p. 19)

dumping (p. 8)

effectiveness (p. 19)

efficiency (p. 19)

engineering change order (ECO)
   (p. 6)

European Union (EU) (p. 8)

financial accounting (p. 3)

flexible manufacturing system (FMS)
   (p. 7)

Foreign Corrupt Practices Act
   (FCPA) (p. 11)

General Agreement on Tariffs and
   Trade (GATT) (p. 8)

global economy (p. 8)

globalization (p. 8)

goal (p. 18)

grapevine (p. 27)

information (p. 17)

Institute of Management
   Accountants (IMA) (p. 14)

internal control (p. 11)

line employee (p. 27)

management accounting (p. 3)

Management Accounting Guidelines
   (MAGs) (p. 23)

maquiladora (p. 5)

matrix structure (p. 28)

North American Free Trade
   Agreement (NAFTA) (p. 8)

objective (p. 18)

organization chart (p. 27)

performance evaluation (p. 19)

planning (p. 18)

responsibility (p. 27)

Society of Management Accountants
   of Canada (p. 21)

staff employee (p. 27)

standard (p. 18)

Statements on Management
   Accounting (SMAs) (p. 23)

treasurer (p. 27)

World Trade Organization (WTO)
   (p. 9)

1. Differentiate between the focuses and outputs of financial and management accounting. Explain the similarities between the two disciplines.

2. Wage rates are higher in industrialized than nonindustrialized nations. What reasons can you give for such a situation?

3. What changes are occurring in the perspectives and information needs of managers as the ability of technology to provide information increases and the cost of technology in highly automated companies decreases?

4. Ford Motor Company is attempting to increase product variety and reduce costs simultaneously. How would the following types of organizations implement the same strategy?
   a. Fast-food restaurant
   b. Teddy bear manufacturer
   c. Insurance company

5. What are some of the additional information needs of managers as firms advance from domestic to international markets? Why would such information be valuable?

6. What factors might hinder the implementation of a single market in Europe? What factors might hinder the implementation of NAFTA? Which hindrances do you believe would be most difficult to overcome and why?

7. How would you define ethics? What constitutes ethical behavior?

8. What are the benefits and drawbacks of having ethics mandated as a function of law versus as a function of voluntary compliance (such as the implementation of an internal code of ethics)?

9. Discuss why the following chapter statement is true: "The selling prices of many goods are set by the marketplace rather than the individual producer."

10. In general, the practice of management accounting is less regulated than financial accounting.
    a. Discuss the roles of the FASB, IMA, and the CASB (or, in Canada, the Canadian Institute of Chartered Accountants and the Society of Management Accountants) on the practice of cost and accounting.
    b. Which of these bodies has binding authority over firms' accounting practices? Why or how?

11. Flexibility is said to be the hallmark of modern management accounting, whereas standardization and consistency describe financial accounting. Explain the reason(s) why there is a difference in the focus of these two accounting systems.

12. Is cost accounting a subset of management accounting or is management accounting a subset of cost accounting? Why?

13. Assume that you are in the process of preparing a research paper for a class in microeconomics. Discuss some differences of which you might be aware between data and information.

14. What are the basic management functions and how might management accounting information help in each of these?

15. Define efficiency and effectiveness. What is the relationship of each to performance?

16. Why is it important to have a written common body of knowledge for management accountants? Why might that CBK change over a period of time?

17. Can an individual be both a CMA and a CPA (or, in Canada, a Chartered Accountant)? If so, why is there no conflict between these two professional designations?

18. Do generally accepted cost and management accounting standards exist? If so, indicate how they are or were established.

19. List the topical areas that comprise the IMA's (or, in Canada, the Society of Management Accountants') Code of Ethics. Why do you believe each of these areas was chosen?

20. Why does the IMA have a standardized code of ethics for the entire United States, but Canada's Society of Management Accountants' code is independently determined by province?

21. *(Appendix)* Explain the benefits and limitations of using an organization chart to explain the workings of a company or the interactions between individuals.

22. *(Appendix)* Colonial Realty Company is just starting operations, and members of its board of directors are discussing the organizational structure. The firm will engage in commercial sales, residential sales, and property management and also maintain leasing services for businesses and individuals. At this time Colonial Realty will have two branch locations. Using this information and your other knowledge of business operations, prepare a high-level organization chart for Colonial Realty Company.

23. (*Terminology*) Match the following lettered terms on the left with the appropriate numbered description on the right.

5   **a.** Business intelligence system
10   **b.** GATT
7   **c.** Goal
6   **d.** Financial accounting
1   **e.** Objective
3   **f.** NAFTA
8   **g.** Effectiveness
2   **h.** WTO
4   **i.** Globalization
9   **j.** Efficiency

1. A target expressed in quantitative terms
2. An international trade dispute arbitrator
3. A trade agreement among Canada, Mexico, and the United States
4. A change in market focus from domestic to international
5. The process of gathering and analyzing information to meet decision-making needs
6. An information system designed to meet the needs of external users
7. A desired result, expressed qualitatively
8. A measure of success of an endeavor
9. A measure of output achieved relative to resources consumed
10. The international trade agreement that created the largest world market

24. (*Difference between financial and management accounting*) The words and phrases below describe or are associated with either financial (F) or management (M) accounting. Indicate for each item with which system it is most closely associated.
   a. FASB
M **b.** Relevant
M **c.** CASB
   d. Verifiable
M **e.** Focus on parts of organization rather than whole organization
   f. Emphasis on consistency of information between periods
   g. Historical
M **h.** Internal focus
   i. SEC
M **j.** Future oriented
M **k.** Emphasis on timeliness
   l. External focus
M **m.** Cost-benefit analysis
M **n.** Flexible in meeting user needs

25. (*Business intelligence system; possible team project*) You are the management accountant for a nationwide chain of music/video stores. Your boss is interested in opening a store in London, England. He wants you to prepare a short presentation on such a market opportunity.
   a. If you were allowed to have three other people to work with you on this presentation, what types of internal organizational positions would you want them to have and why?
   b. Prepare a written presentation about the business intelligence system that might be needed to support or contradict this store opening.

26. *(Change in business activity; possible team project)* You have been asked to address a group of junior high school students on the changes in business activity in your country over the last 50 years. Do library or Internet research and prepare your oral presentation (with appropriate notes and source citations) for this group.

This activity can also be conducted as a team project by having the second and third members of the team prepare similar presentations on Japan and Germany.

27. *(Technology in business; possible team project)* Find a local business that is highly automated and interview several members of that organization about the following:
- The additional costs of the automation
- The additional benefits of the automation
- Any difficulties related to the automation (including personnel adjustments)

Prepare a written or video analysis of your interviews.

28. *(Cost-benefit analysis)* Prepare a short oral presentation using cost-benefit analysis to prove that your college education is worthwhile.

29. *(Cost-benefit analysis)* In April 1995, "the Senate Judiciary Committee cleared a bill to require federal agencies to conduct extensive cost-benefit analyses before issuing many regulations." [Timothy Noah, "Bill Requiring U.S. Agencies to Conduct Cost-Benefit Analyses Gains in Senate," *Wall Street Journal* (April 28, 1995), p. B2.]
- **a.** Investigate the status of the proposed cost-benefit rules.
- **b.** How would one determine the cost of regulations?
- **c.** Why would the use of cost-benefit analysis be difficult for the U.S. (or any other) government?
- **d.** Why would such a bill have a built-in exclusion for certain regulations (ones that cost the economy less than $50 million or $100 million per year, using either the Dole or Roth bill, respectively)?

30. *(Globalization)* The current trend has been to reduce the barriers to flows of capital, resources, technology, and labor across national borders. This trend has accelerated with the European Union, the North American Free Trade Agreement, and the signing of the Uruguay Round of the GATT. Use the library as a resource to help you prepare a paper to do the following.
- **a.** Discuss how the trend of decreasing national fiscal and physical barriers has created more of a global marketplace.
- **b.** Determine how this trend of globalization has affected management practices in your country.

31. *(Regs.)* Within the last two decades, U.S. businesses moved from an era of minimal regulation to the current environment that includes compliance with numerous social regulations. Businesses no longer have the freedom to design and produce products without regard to social considerations, nor do they have complete control over marketing practices and pricing policies. Social regulations have had an enormous impact on businesses, causing economic and continuity concerns. Despite the fact that overregulation by the government has been criticized, polls indicate that the majority of Americans continue to support most forms of social regulation.

Listed below are five agencies that have been created for the implementation and administration of social regulations:

Food and Drug Administration (FDA)
Consumer Product Safety Commission (CPSC)
Environmental Protection Agency (EPA)
Occupational Safety and Health Administration (OSHA)
Equal Employment Opportunity Commission (EEOC)

  a. Discuss the general reasons for the dramatic increase in the social regulation of business during the last two decades.

  b. Describe the social concerns that gave rise to each of the five areas of social regulation administered by the agencies listed above.

  c. Discuss how each area of social regulation has affected the business community.

  (CMA)

32. *(Pro/con FCPA)* The FCPA prohibits U.S. firms from giving bribes in foreign countries, although giving bribes is customary in some countries, and non-U.S. companies operating in foreign countries may not be similarly restricted. Thus, adherence to the FCPA could make competing with non-U.S. firms more difficult in foreign countries. Do you think that bribery should be considered so ethically repugnant to Americans that companies are asked to forgo a foreign custom and, thus, the profits that could be obtained through observance of the custom? Prepare both a pro and a con position for your answer, assuming you will be asked to debate one position or the other.

33. *(Environmental protection)* You have just been elected president of the United States. One of your most popular positions was that you would reduce the costs of doing business in the United States. When asked how you intended to accomplish this, you replied, "By seeking to repeal all laws that create unnecessary costs. Repealing these laws will be good not only for business but also for the consumer, because product prices will be reduced." Congress heard the message and has decided to repeal all environmental protection laws. Discuss the short-term and long-term implications of such a policy.

34. *(Globalization)* The United States provides an ethnically, racially, and culturally diverse workplace. Some people have argued that this plurality may be a competitive handicap for U.S. businesses. For example, communicating may be difficult because some workers do not speak English, motivating workers may be complicated because workers have diverse work ethics, and work scheduling may be difficult because of differing religions and ethnic holidays. Conversely, others have argued that Japan has a competitive advantage because its population is much more homogeneous.

  a. What are the advantages of a pluralistic society in the global marketplace?

  b. On balance, does America's plurality give it a competitive advantage or place it at a competitive disadvantage? Discuss.

35. *(Appendix)* An organization chart illustrates the functions, divisions, and positions in a company and how these are related.

  a. In viewing an organization chart, is it possible to determine the type of business conducted by the firm? Explain.

  b. Can one identify all the lines of communication in the firm from an organization chart? Explain.

36. *(Appendix)* Contact an alumnus of your school or a business person whom you know and ask his or her help in preparing an organization chart for the business for which that individual works.

---

37. *(Appendix)* Rockelle Inc. is a holding company with three major divisions as depicted on the accompanying organizational chart. The three division presidents report directly to Martin Willis, the vice president of corporate operations. In general, Rockelle has preferred a decentralized relationship with these three divisions; however, the managers of planning for each division have an indirect reporting relationship to Anne Kleine, the vice president of corporate finance, who is responsible for coordinating the corporate planning process.

CASES

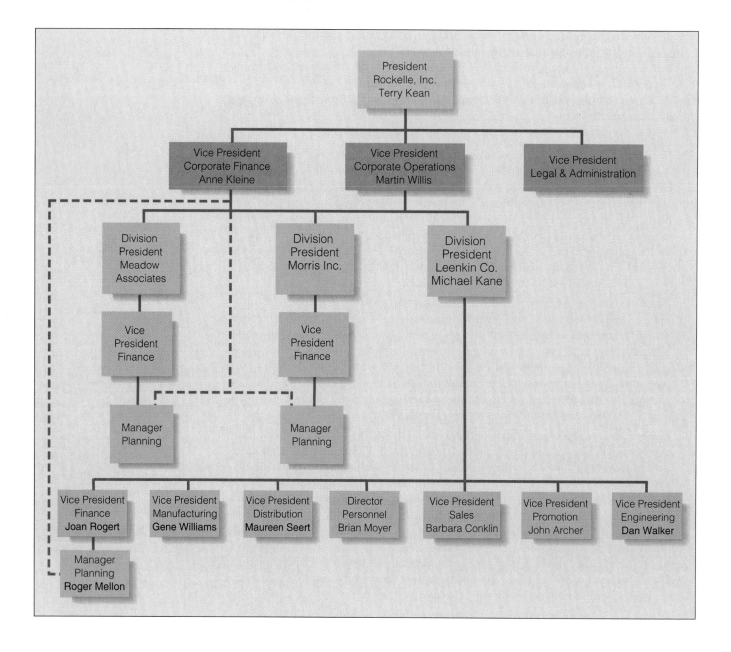

The organizational chart also displays the internal reporting relationships within Leenkin Company. A description of each vice president's area follows.

- Joan Rogert's responsibilities as vice president of finance include financial planning, general accounting, and cost accounting. Roger Mellon reports to Rogert and manages the planning function for the division.
- Gene Williams, vice president of manufacturing, oversees the production of Leenkin's main product, office furniture.
- Maureen Seert, vice president of distribution, handles the packaging and distribution of the office furniture through a network of wholesalers.
- As director of personnel, Brian Moyer is responsible for the sales relationships with retail outlets.
- John Archer, vice president of promotion, produces all advertising material, including a bimonthly catalog of Leenkin's products.
- Dan Walker, vice president of engineering, is responsible for product development and design, machine implementation, time study analysis, and quality control.

   a. Define line and staff functions in an organization.

   b. Describe any potential conflicts that may occur between line and staff employees in this organization based only on your understanding of the organizational chart and descriptions of job responsibilities.

   c. Discuss the benefits and disadvantages of the indirect reporting relationship of Roger Mellon.

   d. Identify the job function of each of the following individuals at Leenkin Company as a line or a staff function, and explain why.

      1. Gene Williams

      2. Joan Rogert

      3. Maureen Seert

      4. Dan Walker

(CMA adapted)

38. You are the owner and manager of a small auto repair shop that does routine maintenance, major repairs, and body work. Business is good and your monthly financial statements show that your shop is consistently profitable. Cash flow is becoming a small problem, however, and you may need to take out a loan from the bank. You have also been hearing customer complaints about time delays and price increases.

   a. What piece or pieces of accounting information do you think is/are most important to take with you to discuss a possible loan with your banker?

   b. What piece or pieces of accounting information do you think is/are most important in ascertaining the business activities of your repair shop in regard to addressing time delays and price increases? What about non-accounting information?

   c. Can the various information in parts a and b be gathered from the accounting records directly? Indirectly? If not at all, where would you need to look for such information?

39. Some U.S. businesses have opted to take advantage of the low wage rates, sometimes lax environmental laws, and peso devaluation in Mexico by establishing maquiladoras. Maquilas have surpassed tourism and oil as the prime generator of dollars in Mexico.

ETHICS AND QUALITY DISCUSSION

But there's a downside to the good news, which has come at the expense of the very people who make the factories run.

The plant workers, many of whom lived in deplorable conditions by U.S. standards even before the [peso] devaluation, are worse off. Their wages have increased only slightly or not at all, while the price of everything from milk to rent has risen sharply.

Tijuana's narrow, pothole riddled steets are congested, its sewer system inefficient. Conditions are especially decrepit in the shantytowns where the maquiladora workers live. Raw sewage runs down the dirt paths that lead to houses many live in, often one- or two-room shacks made of plywood or concrete block. Some lack running water or electricity.

Maquiladora managers say they're torn between employee raises and increased profits, complicated by a need to satisfy the Mexican government, which wants to keep wages down to curb inflation.

[SOURCE: Hayes Ferguson, "Tijuana Assembly Factories Booming," *(New Orleans) Times-Picayune* (April 26, 1995), p. A1. © The Times-Picayune Publishing Corporation.]

   a. Discuss the ethics of operating maquiladoras from the perspective of a U.S. business.

   b. Discuss the ethics of operating maquiladoras from the perspective of a Mexican worker.

   c. As the manager of a U.S. business, discuss some methods of enhancing the positive impacts of maquiladoras and minimizing the negative impacts. How might (has) the North American Free Trade pact affect(ed) maquiladoras?

40. Withers Computers manufactures computers and their components. The purchasing agent informed the owner, Bill Withers, that another company has offered to supply keyboards for Wither's computers at prices below those at which Withers can make them. Incredulous, Mr. Withers hired an industrial consultant to explain how this situation could exist. It seems that the supplier is suspected by the consultant of using many illegal aliens to work in the company plant at substandard wages. The purchasing agent and the plant manager believe that Withers Computers should buy the keyboards from the supplier as "no one can blame us for his hiring practices and will not even be able to show that we knew of those practices."

    a. What are the short-run advantages, including ethical issues, of buying from the external supplier?

    b. What are the long-run advantages, including ethical issues, of buying from the external supplier?

    c. What do you think Mr. Withers should do and why?

41. Ethics can be viewed in both a moral and a legal sense. Discuss the following:

    a. The similarities and differences that can exist between what is moral and what is legal

    b. The positive and negative aspects of a corporate code of ethical conduct emphasizing the legal sense of ethics rather than the moral

42. Middle managers and employees often feel pressure to conform to the ethical standards set by upper management, even if this means compromising personal principles. Discuss the following:

    a. Why such compromises would occur

    b. The advantages and disadvantages of such compromises

    c. Ways to avoid making such compromises

43. The term *whistleblower* is used to describe a person who informs on the wrongdoings of others, especially in a business or government organization. Discuss the following:

    a. Why people often do not "blow the whistle" on wrongdoing

    b. The positive and negative considerations that must be given to the information provided by whistleblowers

    c. How to encourage whistleblowing

44. In May 1995, a trade dispute arose with Japanese auto companies about potential discrimination as to purchasing American-made parts. President Clinton threatened trade sanctions against these firms relative to the Japanese luxury cars that were being imported into the United States. This dispute was presented to the World Trade Organization for resolution.

    a. Use library or Internet resources to determine the substantive issues of this dispute, including that of parts quality.

    b. Do you think such trade sanctions are in violation of a free market economy? Why or why not?

    c. If you had had the U.S. vote on the resolution of this matter, how would you have voted and why? The Japanese vote? The German vote?

45. *Starbucks Coffee Co. has adopted broad guidelines aimed at improving working conditions at its foreign coffee suppliers. The guidelines are believed to be the first ever by a big U.S. importer involving an agricultural community.*

    Starbucks's guidelines call for the Seattle company's overseas suppliers to pay wages and benefits that at least "address the basic needs of workers and their families." For example, the company wants suppliers to only allow child labor when it doesn't "interfere with mandated education." It also wants suppliers to help workers gain "access to safe housing, clean water and health facilities and services." In addition, the guidelines endorse the rights of workers to free association and to "work because they want or need to, but not because they are forced to do so."

Global human-rights activists applauded the guidelines. "This is going to be a benchmark for a lot of importers of agricultural commodities," says Robert Dunn, president of Business for Social Responsibility, a trade group.

Starbucks, however, doesn't plan to punish any suppliers that violate the code.

[SOURCE: G. Pascal Zachary, "Starbucks Asks Foreign Suppliers to Improve Working Conditions," *Wall Street Journal* (October 23, 1995), p. B4. Reprinted by permission of *The Wall Street Journal*, © 1995 Dow Jones & Company, Inc. All Rights Reserved Worldwide.]

    a. Assuming the suppliers abide by Starbucks's code, what short-run and long-run effects might be created relative to Starbucks's products? (Consider both positive and negative effects.)

    b. If you were managing a supplier operation for Starbucks in a low-wage country (for example, Guatemala), would you be inclined to abide by the policy? Why or why not?

    c. Levi Strauss, Reebok, and Nike have recently endorsed codes that threaten to stop doing business with suppliers that allow substandard working conditions. As a customer of these companies, would you necessarily be in favor of such a policy? Why or why not?

46. In any profession, there is usually some type of designation of achievement. Accounting has numerous professional designations, two of which are the CMA and CPA.

    a. Do you believe that the quality of a person's work can be determined based solely on whether he or she has obtained one or more professional certifications? Why or why not?

    b. Do you believe that the attainment of a professional certification is an indicator of the quality of work a person will perform? Why or why not?

    c. Discuss possible reasons for the salary differentials shown in Exhibit 1–9 for certified versus noncertified accountants.

INTERNET ACTIVITIES

47. Journalists, like accountants, are in the business of generating information. The Society of Professional Journalists, Sigma Delta Chi, has a code of ethics that has existed (with updates) since 1926. The code of ethics can be found at http://.town.hall.org/places/spi/ethics.html. Read the code of ethics for journalists and compare it with the code of ethics provided in the chapter from the Institute of Management Accountants. What do the differences between the codes suggest are major differences between the professions of accounting and journalism? What do the similarities between the codes suggest are major similarities between the two professions?

48. Visit the web site of the Institute of Management Accountants (http://www.rutgers.edu/accounting/raw/ima/). Review materials relating to the CMA designation including the required examination. Write an E-mail message to your instructor briefly describing the benefits that you would expect to derive from earning the CMA designation.

49. The opening and closing vignettes to this chapter feature Ford Motor Co. The official Ford Motor Co. home page (http://www.ford.com) contains discussions of important milestones in the history of the company. Read the "Model A Story" which describes the production and production environment of one of Ford's early cars. Use the opening vignette and the Model A Story as the basis to write a brief report in which you identify the five most significant changes that have occurred at Ford from the era of the Model A to today. Also, describe how you think the accounting system has changed from the early days of Ford Motor Co. to today.

CHAPTER

Organizational Strategy and Accounting

LEARNING OBJECTIVES

After completing this chapter, you should be able to answer these questions:

1. What primary factors help determine an organization's strategies?

2. What is meant by the three generic mission structures of build, hold, and harvest?

3. What is a core competency and how does it relate to outsourcing?

4. What constitutes a firm's intellectual capital and why is it important?

5. Why should a firm's strategies change over time?

6. How does accounting relate to organizational strategies?

7. What is strategic resource management?

8. What is the "value chain" and why is it important to management?

9. How does a firm compute its cost of capital and why is this cost important to managers?

Matsushita Electrical Industrial Company

Matsushita, a Japan-based company, is the largest consumer electronics maker in the world. Its consolidated sales in 1994 amounted to 6,948 billion yen, or roughly $69 billion. Worldwide, the company employs more than 265,000 people. Consumers are familiar with many of the popular brand names of the company's products including Panasonic, National, and Technics. Identifying new ways to maintain company growth is a major concern for Matsushita's top management.

In early 1991, Matsushita purchased MCA Inc., the U.S. film and entertainment conglomerate, for approximately $5.6 billion or about 15 times MCA's annual earnings. The purchase was designed to link Matsushita's hardware and software production capabilities with MCA's ability to deliver entertainment products and services. Of particular interest to Matsushita was the potential to develop multimedia computer products.

In making the investment in MCA, Matsushita executives recognized that much of MCA's value was tied to the expertise of its executives, including chairman, Lew Wasserman, and president, Sidney Sheinberg. Both individuals were highly respected in the U.S. entertainment industry and had been principal players in MCA's past successes. It was widely believed that MCA would not function as effectively under alternative management. Accordingly, Matsushita management recognized the need to keep Wasserman and Sheinberg at the helm of MCA rather than replace them.

Unfortunately, conflict soon developed between MCA's two top managers and Matsushita executives. The conflict revolved around the extent to which MCA would be independent of Matsushita in making new investments and defining the entertainment company's future direction. Wasserman and Sheinberg wanted relative autonomy in making these decisions for MCA. Matsushita top management wanted to be certain that MCA's growth was consistent with the original logic of synergism for making the investment in MCA.

As the rift between the two management groups grew, Wasserman and Sheinberg threatened to leave MCA and affiliate with competitors or form new entertainment ventures. In October 1994, top executives from Matsushita met with Wasserman and Sheinberg for five hours in an attempt to resolve differences. The outcome was a stalemate. Upon leaving the meeting, Matsushita executives must have been wondering why they ever would have spent $5.6 billion to purchase MCA.

SOURCES: Adapted from Thomas R. King and John Lippman, "Sale of MCA Being Discussed by Matsushita; Japanese Parent Weighing Several Options; Parties Include Bronfman, TCI," *Wall Street Journal* (March 31, 1995), p. A3; Richard Turner, "MCA's Talk with Parent Inconclusive, Matsushita Seems Open to Selling Unit," *Wall Street Journal* (October 20, 1994), p. A4. Reprinted by permission of *The Wall Street Journal,* © 1994, 1995 Dow Jones & Company, Inc. All Rights Reserved Worldwide.

In making the MCA investment, Matsushita executives were defining a new strategy for both companies: to link the complementary capabilities of two firms to create new technology and products. In the broadest sense, a strategy is a long-term plan that is formulated to fulfill an organization's goals and objectives. Such a plan must express the actions and resource allocations needed to achieve the desired outcomes.

This chapter explains the role of strategy in directing an organization's operations and conceptually links strategy creation and implementation with the accounting system. Strategy spans three organizational functions in which accountants interact with managers: planning, controlling, and decision making. Although the majority of the chapter's discussion of strategy reflects the perspective of a profit-seeking business, many of the concepts also apply to governmental and not-for-profit entities.

Does Your Organization
Have a Good Strategy?

1. Who are your five most important competitors?
2. Is your firm more or less profitable than these firms?
3. Do you generally have higher or lower prices than these firms, for equivalent product/service offerings? Is this difference due mainly to the mix of customers, to different costs, or to different requirements for profit?
4. Do you have higher or lower relative costs than your main competitors? Where in the cost structure (for example, cost of raw materials, cost of production, cost of selling, cost of distributing, cost of advertising and marketing) are the differences most pronounced?
5. [What are] the different business segments which account for 80% of your profits? [You will probably find that you are in many more segments than you thought, and that their profit variability is much greater.] If you cannot define the segments that constitute 80% of your total profits, you need to conduct a detailed product line profitability review.
6. In each of the business segments defined above, how large are you relative to the largest of your competitors? Are you gaining or losing relative market share?
7. In each of your important business segments, what are your customers' and potential customers' most important purchase criteria?
8. How do you and your main competitors in each segment rate on these market purchase criteria?
9. What are the main strengths of the company as a whole, based on aggregating customers' views of your firm in the segments that comprise most of your profits? What other competencies do you believe the firm has, and why do they seem to be not appreciated by the market?
10. Which are your priority segments, where is it most important to the firm as a whole that you gain market share? How confident are you that you will achieve this, given that other firms may have targeted the same segments for share gain? What is your competitive advantage in these segments and how sure are you that this advantage is real rather than imagined? (If you are not gaining relative market share, the advantage is probably illusory.)

SOURCE: Richard Koch, *The Financial Times Guide to Management and Finance* (London: Financial Times/Pitman Publishing, 1994), p. 359.

DETERMINING ORGANIZATIONAL STRATEGY

strategy

Each organization has a fundamental purpose or mission for which that organization was brought into existence. In addition, each organization has implicit and/or explicit goals that must be satisfied for the organization to satisfy its mission. **Strategy** is the link between an organization's goals and objectives and the activities actually conducted by the organization. "The strategy an organization implements is an attempt to match the skills and resources of the organization to the opportunities found in the external environment."[1] Hence, strategy often determines the extent to which an organization is successful in satisfying its goals. Most organizations have individual strategies for each business unit as well as an overall corporate strategy that integrates the separate business unit strategies to ensure synergy across the units, allocates resources to the units, develops an overriding corporate culture, and provides an organizational direction and momentum. Exhibit 2–1 provides a checklist of questions that need to be answered if an organization is to have a comprehensive strategy.

Because each organization has a unique set of opportunities and constraints, even organizations in the same industries will have unique sets of strategies that are feasible and likely to be successful. Exhibit 2–2 provides a model of the major factors that managers must consider in determining an organization's strategy. Because strategy is formulated as the basis of achieving the firm's goals and objectives, strategy gives direction to an organization's operations so that the organization will succeed. In

[1] Thomas S. Bateman and Scott A. Snell, *Management: Building Competitive Advantage* (Chicago: Irwin, 1996), p. 117.

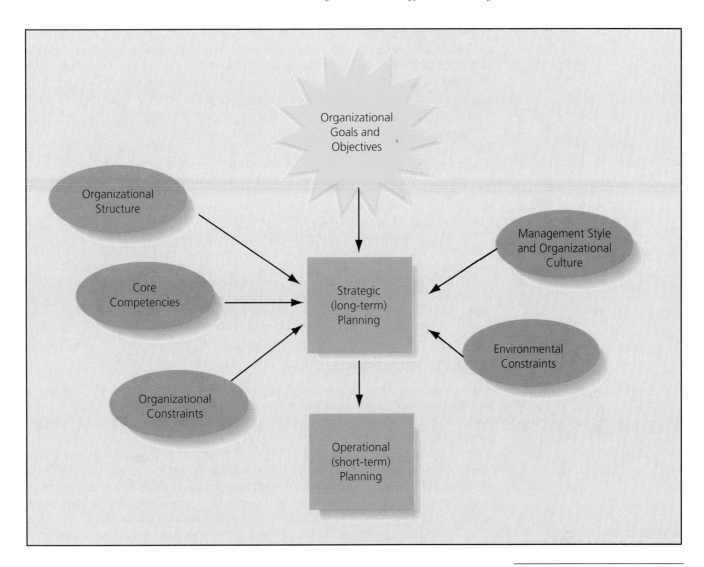

Organizational Goals and Objectives

Organizational Structure

Core Competencies

Organizational Constraints

Management Style and Organizational Culture

Environmental Constraints

Strategic (long-term) Planning

Operational (short-term) Planning

profit-oriented firms, one typical goal is to maximize shareholder wealth. To illustrate, consider the following excerpts from BellSouth's 1995 Summary Annual Report:

> BellSouth is focused on three key strategies that combine our dedication to customer service with our commitment to growing the value of your investment:
> 1. Strengthen our leadership position as the Southeast's premier communications company. (What are we doing in our region to stay on top? Plenty. Marketing aggressively. Selling new products and services. Keeping our prices competitive. Building on a strong, unified brand name.)
> 2. Continue to profitably grow our domestic wireless business. (As customer demand for mobile telecommunications continues to explode in the U.S., BellSouth will maintain its profitable growth by pricing and packaging services that set us apart from the competition.)
> 3. Grow our international businesses and expand into new markets. (Our international strategy is focused on the geographic regions that provide the best investment opportunities, and on creating new revenue streams by offering customers a wider array of services.)[2]

Goals likely will be formulated for the other major stakeholders such as customers, employees, and suppliers.

[2] BellSouth, *1995 Summary Annual Report*, pp. 5ff.

EXHIBIT 2–2

Model of Factors in Determining Organizational Strategy

V I D E O
VIGNETTE

New England Construction Co., Inc. (Blue Chip Enterprises)

To have predetermined "roadmaps" for their activities, even governmental and not-for-profit entities specify their goals relative to their unique missions. For example, the following mission, vision, and value statements of the Utah State Tax Commission incorporate that organization's goals and objectives:

[M]ission
Our mission is to collect revenue for the state and local governments and to equitably administer tax and assigned motor vehicle laws.
Vision
We are enthusiastically committed to a standard of excellence that exceeds customer expectations. We continuously focus on courtesy, accuracy, efficiency, consistency, and professionalism.
Values
We must uphold our public trust.
We value quality, which is the balance of efficiency and effectiveness.
We value job expertise and knowledge with consistent and dependable application of laws, rules, practices, and procedures.
We value integrity, including honesty, trust, and respect for self and others.
We value clear, meaningful, and concise communication with customers.
We value self-motivated employees and environments that encourage initiative.
We value empowered employees with their attendant accountability.[3]

Organizational Structure

Top managers of large organizations arrange their businesses into logical segments to implement strategy. Such segments (usually called divisions) are typically created based on product lines. Management seeks to define segments so that the arrangement facilitates organizational control.

Grouping similar products into a single segment offers several benefits. First, it allows for learning and accumulation of knowledge by product and market. Second, it allows realization of synergies in production. Third, it facilitates management of resources with respect to long-term/short-term trade-offs. Last, it allows a rational method of strategic management that is focused on the segment level.

A key to defining segments, managing resources, and implementing strategies is to organize segments relative to their missions. There are three generic missions for organizational segments: **build mission, hold mission,** and **harvest mission.** These missions are defined in Exhibit 2–3.

build mission

hold mission

harvest mission

EXHIBIT 2–3

Generic Strategic Missions

- **Build** This mission implies a goal of increased market share, even at the expense of short-term earnings and cash flow. A business unit that follows this mission is expected to be a net user of cash; that is, the cash flow from its current operations would usually be insufficient to meet its capital investment needs. Business units with "low market share" in "high growth industries" typically pursue a "build" mission.
- **Hold** This strategic mission is geared to the protection of the business unit's market share and competitive position. The cash outflows for a business unit that follows this mission generally equal the cash inflows. Businesses with "high market share" in "high growth industries" typically pursue a "hold" mission.
- **Harvest** The harvest mission implies a goal of maximizing short-term earnings and cash flow, even at the expense of market share. A business unit that follows the harvest mission is a net supplier of cash. Businesses with "high market share" in "low growth industries" typically pursue a "harvest" mission.

SOURCE: Vijay Govindarajan and John K. Shank, "Strategic Cost Management: Tailoring Controls to Strategies." Reprinted with permission from *The Journal of Cost Management for the Manufacturing Industry* (Fall 1992), © 1992, Warren Gorham & Lamont, 31 St. James Avenue, Boston, MA 02116. All rights reserved.

[3] Taken from the Internet; E-mail address: taxmaster@email.state.ut.us.

Obviously, the organizational segments with a build mission are the objects of most strategic planning, because these units are expected to be operated for the long run. Segments with a harvest mission require little strategic planning; their role is to generate cash and at some point they will probably be sold or spun off as other segments start to mature.

Segment mission is highly related to the product life cycle. The **product life cycle** refers to the sequential stages that a product passes through from the time the idea is conceived until production of the product is discontinued. This concept is presented in detail in Chapter 6. The build mission is appropriate for products that are in the early stages of the product life cycle, and the harvest mission is appropriate for products in the final stages of the life cycle.

When top managers create organizational segments, one challenge is to identify ways to make each segment's manager operate according to that segment's mission. For example, if a segment has a harvest mission, that segment is expected to generate cash that will, in part, be used by segments pursuing build missions. Top management does not want "harvest" segments to be consumers of resources. Consequently, methods need to be identified to ensure that the managers of such segments have an incentive to generate cash rather than consume it.

The way in which authority (and responsibility) for making decisions is distributed in the organization reflects the organizational structure. As discussed in the appendix to Chapter 1, an organizational chart may be used to communicate the authority structure in an organization.

There is a continuum of feasible structures, with one extreme having all authority for making decisions being retained by top management or **centralization.** At the other end of the continuum is **decentralization,** in which the authority for decision making is distributed to many people in the organization, including lower-level managers. Making decentralization an effective organizational structure requires employee **empowerment**—giving people the authority and responsibility to make decisions about their work. Pete Coors, CEO of Coors Brewing, explains empowerment as follows: "We're moving from an environment where the supervisor says, 'This is the way it is going to be done and if you don't like it go someplace else,' to an environment where the supervisor can grow with the changes, get his troops

product life cycle

centralization

decentralization

empowerment

Empowering workers automatically necessitates training and sharing information with them. Knowledge of how their jobs affect where the organization is headed helps keep workers moving toward appropriate goals and objectives.

together and say, 'Look, you guys are operating the equipment, what do you think we ought to do?' "[4]

Although strategy creation is most often the domain of only top management, a highly centralized organization creates a short-term constraint on organizational strategy. The decisions to be made in creating and implementing a successful strategy are heavily influenced by the expertise of the individuals involved. Centralized firms would have difficulty following a diversification strategy (as in a conglomerate), because top management might lack the necessary and critical industry-specific knowledge. For example, one problem in the Matsushita/MCA merger was the conflict involved between the decision to acquire MCA (Matsushita's strategy) and decisions made by MCA's top executives (strategy implementation).

kaizen

In most organizations, it is lower-level managers who are responsible for strategy implementation. If higher-level management insists on maintaining all authority, the people who deal directly with the issues (whether problems or opportunities), who have the most relevant information, and who can best foresee the consequences of decisions are not making the decisions. For example, Cummins Engine Company's Jamestown Plant in Lakewood, New York, began a JDIT-kaizen training program in which employees are empowered to "just do it" (JDIT). (**Kaizen** is a Japanese philosophy of continuous improvement.) This program has resulted "in 61 documented process improvements. Tangible results include higher quality, lower cost, reduced cycle times, improved safety, less inventory, and more efficient use of personnel."[5] In today's fast-changing and competitive operating environment, implementation of a decentralized organizational structure is almost imperative and typically cost-beneficial.

Core Competencies

core competency

A second factor that highly affects feasible organizational strategies is that organization's core competencies. A **core competency** is a higher proficiency relative to competitors in a critical function or activity. Core competencies are the roots of competitiveness and competitive advantage. Technological innovation, engineering, product development, or after-sale service are some examples of core competencies. Core competencies may be industry-specific or firm-specific. For instance, the Japanese electronics industry is viewed as having a core competency in miniaturization of electronics; Sony Corporation has a core competency of utilizing such miniaturizations in product development.[6] Nike views one of its core competencies as research and development for product design and marketing rather than production. Except for the technical components of the "Nike Air" systems, Nike does not produce shoes: manufacturing is performed by Asian collaborators with core competencies in shoe production.[7] One of Motorola's core competencies is development of wireless communication.

V I D E O
VIGNETTE

Lanzar Sound Corp. (Blue Chip Enterprises)

outsourcing

Knowledge of an organization's core competencies is useful in strategy development. When an organization does something better or less expensively than its competitors, it has a foundation for market success. Managers attempt to develop strategies that will exploit the organization's core competencies. In doing so, firms have begun outsourcing activities that are not viewed as core competencies. **Outsourcing** means contracting with outside vendors for necessary goods or services rather than producing the goods or performing the services in-house.

---

[4] Alan Wolf, "Golden Opportunities," *Beverage World* (February 1991).
[5] David L. Taylor and Ruth K. Ramsey, "Empowering Employees to 'Just Do It'," *Training & Development* (May 1993).
[6] Roger Tunks, *Fast Track to Quality* (New York: McGraw-Hill, 1992), p. 240.
[7] William G. Zikmund and Michael d'Amico, *Marketing* (Minneapolis/St. Paul: West Publishing, 1996), p. 110.

1. Improve company focus
2. Gain access to world-class capabilities
3. Accelerate the benefits of reengineering
4. Share risks
5. Free non-capital resources
6. Make capital funds available
7. Reduce operating costs
8. Obtain cash infusion
9. Obtain resources not available internally
10. Eliminate a function that is difficult to manage

SOURCE: Composite of the Outsourcing Institute survey of 1,200 companies, member experiences, and published research; reported in "Outsourcing: Redefining the Corporation of the Future," *FORTUNE* (December 12, 1994), p. 58. © 1994 Time Inc. All rights reserved.

EXHIBIT 2–4

Top Ten Reasons
to Outsource

In making outsourcing decisions, a company should first define its primary outsourcing objectives. This definition indicates which of the reasons given in Exhibit 2–4 will be satisfied by outsourcing. An understanding of these underlying issues is essential before selecting a **contract manufacturer** (or **contract vendor**) to provide the outsourced work.

contract manufacturer

contract vendor

A contract manufacturer or vendor cannot be chosen unless the contracting organization first defines the specific requirements, including performance considerations, for the outsourced work. The following News Note discusses a network organization that "brokers" the outsourced work for other companies and also indicates the importance of requirements specification. (A **network organization** is a flexible organization structure that establishes a working relationship among multiple entities, usually to pursue a single function.)

network organization

Inexpensive and Correct, But Time and Subject Are Issues

NEWS NOTE

In 1991, Edward Leonard founded the Electronic Scriptorium, a Leesburg, Va., company that farms out dozens of data-entry projects to hard-working monks in monasteries across the country. Contracting out data-entry projects is not new . . . and, at first blush, the idea of using monks for the tedious task may seem like a gimmick. But consider the economics. Many companies farm out their data-entry work to offshore companies, where labor is cheap. According to Leonard, such data-entry clerks are available for around $30 per hour in places like Ireland and India. Leonard's hourly rate: less than $20. Support costs are minimal because there are no direct supervisors. No computer equipment is provided. No technical assistance. No office space rental. No health care costs.

It's not only the reasonable prices that attract new customers. Law firms like Tucker, Flyer & Lewis in Washington, D.C., trust the monks to enter sensitive case information with discretion.

[Unfortunately,] working with a monastery places certain constraints on Leonard's capitalist sensibilities. Brother Thomas Baxter at the Monastery of the Holy Cross in Chicago and his fellow monks avoid jobs with high-pressure deadlines. Those constrictions recently kept Leonard from pursuing a transcription project worth possibly $100,000 from Johns Hopkins University because the deadline was far too tight. "The data-entry work can't dominate our day," says Brother Thomas.

The Scriptorium also hesitates to work with certain companies, such as Lockheed Martin [because of its weapons production activities] on moral grounds. Leonard says that he would probably not accept work from publications that some consider indecent—*Playboy*, for instance.

SOURCE: James Daly, "A Match Made in Heaven," *Forbes ASAP* (June 5, 1995), pp. 27ff. Reprinted by permission of *FORBES* magazine. © Forbes Inc., 1995.

By outsourcing non-core-competency activities, a company is adopting a strategy of concentrating on the development of its core competencies and devoting additional resources to those sets of skills or expertise that represent potential sources of competitive advantage. A company may develop partnerships, engage in joint ventures, form strategic alliances, or merge with another company with the intention of linking the core competencies of the two organizations. Such endeavors may create a market opportunity that neither firm could successfully exploit alone. For example, Matsushita's expertise in developing specific types of consumer hardware and software is viewed as a core competency. MCA possesses special competencies in developing and marketing certain types of entertainment products. Thus, the purchase of MCA by Matsushita was a strategy developed to exploit core competencies of both firms.

Target firms in mergers are not necessarily receptive to the merger offer. Managers of target firms may be fearful of a merger motivated by strategic considerations because it often requires strategic changes in the target firm. Consider the fact that, in the 1980s, raiders in corporate America attacked conglomerate corporations that could be broken up and sold in parts. Raiders were able to make profits by either selling the parts for a collective price that exceeded the bid price for the corporate shares or by selling the equity back to the target at an inflated price (called "green mail"). In the 1990s, the raiders are major corporations such as General Electric Company, International Business Machines, Inc., and Johnson & Johnson. These companies are engaging in "strategic mergers" rather than seeking quick market gains. "Since early 1994, about 85% of the hostile bidders were 'strategic' buyers, compared with about half in the 1980s."[8]

Organizational Constraints

Managers must acknowledge and deal with a variety of organizational constraints in making strategic decisions for their firms. In almost all cases, these constraints are of a short-term nature because opportunities exist to overcome the constraints. The decision to pursue one or more of these opportunities reflects, in part, the organizational strategy.

Implementation of most strategies requires some capital investment, and one of the primary constraints faced by all organizations is the level of capital availability. This constraint is much more important in some organizations than in others. Companies almost always have some ways of acquiring new capital such as additional borrowings or sales of equity. Before attempting to eliminate a capital constraint, however, management must answer two questions: (1) can the capital be obtained at a reasonable cost, and (2) would reallocation of current capital be more effective and efficient? The News Note on the next page addresses this second issue.

intellectual capital

Another significant constraint on organizational strategy is the level of the firm's **intellectual capital** or "the intangible assets of skill, knowledge, and information."[9] Intellectual capital encompasses human capital and structural capital. Human capital is reflected in the knowledge and creativity of an organization's personnel.

> Human capital matters because it is the source of innovation and renewal, whether from brainstorms in a lab or new leads in a sales rep's little black book. But growth in human capital—through hiring, training, and education—is pointless if it cannot be exploited. That requires structural intellectual assets, such as information systems, knowledge of market channels and customer relationships, and management focus, which turn individual know-how into the property of a group.

---

[8] Steven Lipin, "Big Corporations Making Knockout Bids Take the Fight Out of Friendly Rescuers," *Wall Street Journal* (November 8, 1995), pp. C1, C11.

[9] Thomas A. Stewart, "Your Company's Most Valuable Asset: Intellectual Capital," *FORTUNE* (October 3, 1994), p. 68. © 1994 Time Inc. All rights reserved.

Money May Have Nothing to Do with It

"If only we had more resources, we could be more strategic." Every experienced manager will recognize that lament. Yet it is clear that copious resources cannot guarantee continued industry leadership. Tens of billions of dollars later, no one can accuse GM of not being "strategic" in its pursuit of factory automation. If anything, GM was *too* strategic. The company's ability to invest outpaced its ability to absorb new technology, retrain workers, reengineer work flows, rejuvenate supplier relationships, and discard managerial orthodoxies.

Conversely, if modest resources were an insurmountable deterrent to future leadership, GM, Philips, and IBM would not have found themselves on the defensive with Honda, Sony, and Compaq. NEC succeeded in gaining market share against AT&T, Texas Instruments, and IBM despite an R&D budget that for most of its history was more modest in both absolute and relative terms than those of its rivals. Toyota developed a new luxury car for a fraction of the resources required by Detroit. IBM challenged Xerox in the copier business and failed, while Canon, a company only 10% the size of Xerox in the mid-1970s, eventually displaced Xerox as the world's most prolific copier manufacturer. CNN in its adolescence managed to provide 24 hours of news a day with a budget estimated at one-fifth that required by CBS to turn out 1 hour of evening news. Performance like this isn't just lean manufacturing; it's lean everything.

SOURCE: Reprinted by permission of *Harvard Business Review*. An excerpt from "Strategy as Stretch and Leverage," Gary Hamel and C. K. Prahalad (March–April 1993), p. 78. Copyright © 1993 by the President and Fellows of Harvard College; all rights reserved.

For managers and shareholders, structural capital counts most: It doesn't go home at night or quit and hire on with a rival; it puts new ideas to work; and it can be used again and again to create value, just as a die can stamp out part after part.[10]

If a company has limited intellectual capital, shifts in strategy will be difficult to pursue.

People must perceive opportunities for improvement and translate them into strategic innovations. The innovations may reflect technological advancements that, at least until the innovations are adopted by others, could provide the company a core competency. For example, Dallas-based Amtech Corporation used a previously patented radio-beam system to develop electronic tracking devices. Company management took a strategic focus on transportation functions because the devices were able to provide extremely speedy data readings. The State of Oklahoma is one of Amtech's many customers, having installed transceivers for windshield toll tags at toll plazas throughout Oklahoma, almost eliminating toll collectors and "lowering the state's annual toll collection costs from $180,000 a lane to $16,000 a lane—a $4 million annual savings. The system cost the state $12 million to install."[11]

Other examples of the use of intellectual capital to promote core competencies and affect strategy include the creation of new health care products from biotechnology developments, the use of the Internet to offer a variety of products and services electronically, and the use of automatic teller machine technology to produce machines that disburse tickets to sporting events.

A third constraint faced by companies is technology availability, which explains why many current strategic decisions involve technology acquisition. When one company develops certain technology, its competitors seek to obtain, use, and possibly increase the value of that technology to minimize the long-run competitive advantage of the developer. "One of the most consistent patterns in business is the failure of leading companies to stay at the top of their industries when technologies or markets

[10] Ibid., pp. 71–72.
[11] R. Lee Sullivan, "Fast Lane," *Forbes* (June 4, 1994), p. 112.

The way in which managers interact with their peers and subordinates is a key indicator of organizational culture.

change."[12] Acquiring new technology is one way to create new strategic opportunities, allowing a company to do things better or faster—assuming that the company has trained its human resources in the use of that technology.

Management Style and Organizational Culture

management style

Management style and organizational culture are two important and related variables in determining organizational strategy. An organization's **management style** reflects the preferences of managers in how they interact with other stakeholders in the organization. Management style greatly influences the way the firm engages in transactions or "contracts" and is manifested in managerial decisions, interpersonal and interorganizational relationships, and resource allocations. Managerial style is inherent in decisions about labor practices, labor/capital mix, financing mix, supplier relationships, pricing practices, and production technology.

Researchers have documented differences between typical Western and Japanese managers in managerial styles relating to organizational strategies. These differences have been found in worker/manager relations, product pricing, managerial performance evaluation, technology acquisition, and organizational financing. The relative success of many Japanese businesses has caused managers of many non-Japanese firms to attempt to adopt or replicate features of Japanese management. The style of management is important to the accounting function because it affects the role of accounting information in planning, controlling, and decision making.

organizational culture

Organizational culture is the set of basic assumptions about the organization and its goals and ways of doing business. "It is a system of shared values about what is important and beliefs about how the world works. A company's culture provides a framework that organizes and directs people's behavior on the job."[13] Thus, organizational culture describes an organization's norms in internal and external, as well as formal and informal, transactions.

Management style and organizational culture are influenced heavily by the national culture of the organization, the extent of diversity in the workforce, and the personal

VIDEO
VIGNETTE

Marc Fruchter Aviation (Blue Chip Enterprises)

[12] Joseph L. Bower and Clayton M. Christensen, "Disruptive Technologies: Catching the Wave," *Harvard Business Review* (January–February 1995), p. 43.
[13] Bateman and Snell, *Management*, p. 268.

Southwest's Corporate Culture Is Grounded in Simple Gestures

NEWS NOTE

Time after time, academics and competitors have analyzed the employee-motivation techniques of Southwest Airlines. But many didn't fully understand the secret behind its productive work force. Maybe they didn't look carefully enough at Colleen C. Barrett.

Ms. Barrett, the No. 2 executive at Southwest and the highest-ranking woman in the airline industry, is keeper of the airline's corporate culture. Though the airline has doubled in size [between 1991 and 1995], now topping 20,000 employees, Ms. Barrett has devised ways to preserve Southwest's underdog standing and can-do spirit. Her trademark: simple gestures.

It's one thing to make employees feel valued and coax them to do what's right for customers. Institutionalizing that across a coast-to-coast airline is another thing altogether.

Long before "empowerment" became a management buzz word, Ms. Barrett was giving employees freedom from centralized policies. She constantly reinforces the company's message that employees should be treated like customers and continually celebrates workers who go above and beyond the call of duty. And when she sensed the carrier was outgrowing its personality-kid-among-the-impersonal-giants image, she created a "culture committee" of employees charged with preserving Southwest's spirit.

When Southwest was having problems with workers at its Los Angeles International Airport station recently, Ms. Barrett swung the culture committee into action, dispatching employees to fill in for local supervisors so the supervisors could address morale and efficiency problems. Now the station is considered one of the most efficient. . . .

To Ms. Barrett, building loyalty breeds better performance. Southwest employees are well-paid compared with counterparts at other airlines. Celebrations are an important part of work, from spontaneous "fun sessions" to Christmas parties beginning in September to a lavish annual awards banquet, where the individual's contribution to the whole is glorified.

SOURCE: Scott McCartney, "Airline Industry's Top-Ranked Woman Keeps Southwest's Small-Fry Spirit Alive," *Wall Street Journal* (November 30, 1995), pp. B1, B2. Reprinted by permission of *The Wall Street Journal*, © 1995 Dow Jones & Company, Inc. All Rights Reserved Worldwide.

experiences and philosophies of the top management team. These variables have a significant role in determining whether the communication system tends to be formal or informal, whether authority is likely to be centralized or decentralized, whether relations with employees tend to be antagonistic or cooperative, and how control systems are designed and used. Like many of the other influences on organizational strategy, management style and organizational culture can be changed over time. In most cases, however, these variables are more frequently changed because of management turnover rather than because existing management changed its philosophy and business practices. The above News Note demonstrates how management style and organizational culture can influence strategy and organizational performance.

Environmental Constraints

A final factor affecting organizational strategy is the environment, which is composed of numerous constraints. An **environmental constraint** is any limitation on strategy options caused by external cultural, fiscal (such as taxation structures), legal/regulatory, or political situations. Because environmental constraints are not under the direct control of an organization's management, these factors tend to be longer run than the ones previously mentioned. This is not to say that the environment cannot be changed, only that such changes typically require time.

environmental constraint

EXHIBIT 2–5

Interactions of
Environmental Constraints
on the Organization

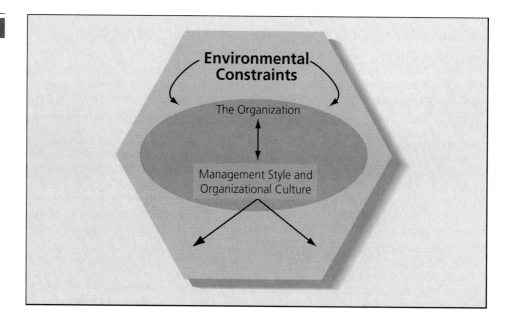

Many companies involved in global competition have recognized that culture may affect strategy because products and services that sell well in one part of the world may be ignored in markets in other parts of the world. The food industry provides an excellent example of the influence of culture on strategic initiatives. In 1988, Campbell Soup Company purchased a Puerto Rican canned bean brand called Casera. The objective was to acquire a product that would be marketable to Hispanics, particularly in the New York and Miami markets. Campbell management, however, discovered that many Hispanics in the United States would not buy the beans. In investigating the reasons for the poor market performance, Campbell found that Miami Hispanics are largely from Cuba; Cubans prefer black beans and the Casera brand were pinto beans. Campbell eventually sold the brand to an Hispanic company.[14]

To illustrate a fiscal constraint, prior to the adoption of the North American Free Trade Agreement (NAFTA), strategic investment in North America was frequently affected by the fact that firms in Canada, Mexico, and the United States were subject to large import duties and taxes on many classes of manufactured goods produced in one country and sold in another. NAFTA was enacted to reduce the level of such taxes and duties. As a result, firms are more free to locate investment (such as new production facilities) in the geographical North American area that will provide the greatest return on investment.

As discussed in the final segment of this chapter, Matsushita eventually resolved the conflict with MCA management by selling a majority of its stake in the firm to Seagram Company. In deciding to purchase the stake in MCA, Seagram had to divest itself of other stock holdings to avoid violating U.S. antitrust laws. Thus, these laws constrained the set of choices available in the strategic investment decision made by Seagram.

The operating environment of an organization does not operate in isolation from the other factors affecting corporate strategy. Exhibit 2–5 provides a model of the interactions of the environment on an organization and its managers. The environmental constraints significantly affect the organization and help define usable management styles. Management through its actions and the organizational culture influence the organization and may work to affect the operating environment through numerous activities (including attempts to change laws).

[14] Yumiko Ono, "Kraft Hopes Hispanic Market Says Cheese," *Wall Street Journal* (December 13, 1995), p. B7.

In developing operational strategies, businesses must consider the impacts those strategies will have on organizational stakeholders. Strategy formulation is the foundation level of organizational planning. If done successfully, it should meet one of the primary goals of all businesses: generation of profits. This goal is necessary so that shareholders can obtain wealth maximization, employees can retain their jobs, and creditors can be paid. Customers are the sources of business revenues, and revenues are generated only if a firm's products and services are seen as value-adding in the eyes of its customers. Thus, profitability is generally accomplished by providing customers with desired products that are delivered on time and at a reasonable cost.

Measurement of profitability is a function of the accounting information system. As indicated in Exhibit 2–6, organizational management, in determining what strategies to pursue, must consider the financial implications of its actions. If management does not believe the results are acceptable, revisions will be made to either the objectives or the strategies selected to achieve those objectives.

To best assess financial implications, organizational strategy needs to be expressed in short-term **operational plans,** which reflect the details of implementing and maintaining an organization's strategic plans. Operating plans are normally formalized in a **master budget** or pro forma set of financial statements. The master budget serves as an important managerial tool in directing business activities to conform with the firm's goals and objectives. This outcome is ensured by making the strategic plan the foundation of the operating plans as was shown in Exhibit 2–2.

Budgets are typically prepared using generally accepted accounting principles. However, as important as the financial accounting system may be in assessing current or projected profitability, it does not provide all the information needed by management to make decisions. "Exclusive focus on financial results and budgets does not

ROLE OF ACCOUNTING IN ORGANIZATIONAL STRATEGY

operational plans

master budget

EXHIBIT 2–6

The Planning Process

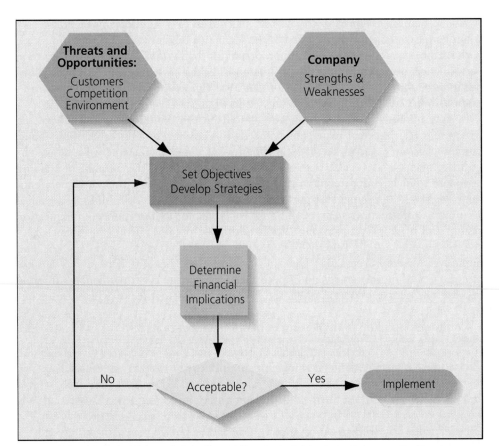

SOURCE: Roland T. Rust, Anthony J. Zahorik, and Timothy L. Keiningham, *Return on Quality* (Chicago: Probus Publishing Company, 1994), p. 116.

encourage managers to invest and build for longer-term competitive advantage."[15] Also, according to noted management author Peter Drucker:

> The standard concepts and tools of [traditional financial reporting] are inadequate to control operations because all they provide is a view of the skeleton of a business. What's needed is a way to examine the soft tissue.
>
> Financial accounting, balance sheets, profit-and-loss statements, allocation of costs, etc., are an X-ray of the enterprise's skeleton. But much as the diseases we most commonly die from—heart disease, cancer, Parkinson's—do not show in a skeletal X-ray, a loss of market standing or failure to innovate do not register in the accountant's figures until the damage is done.[16]

Fortunately, organizations now have the technological capabilities to easily expand their data collection activities to satisfy both external and internal information requirements. Professor Germain Boër (Vanderbilt University) has referred to this as having a core set of data that satisfies FASB, SEC, and other regulatory requirements as well as tax information. This core data set will be surrounded by "rings of data" that allow individual managers to start and stop capturing certain information that is relevant for their activities.[17] Following are some types of nonfinancial information that relate to the factors managers must consider in making strategic decisions.

Control and Decision Making

Accounting information plays a vital role in linking the objectives of top managers to the incentives of segment managers. In general, accounting information is the basis for measuring or evaluating the efficiency and effectiveness of segment managers. The incentive of segment managers to be attentive to the accounting performance measures arises from the fact that both their performance evaluation and their performance rewards are tied to the accounting measurements.

For accounting to provide the correct incentives to a segment manager, the accounting measurements must be tied to the segment's mission. Accordingly, long-term performance measures are more appropriate for build missions, and shorter-term performance measures are more appropriate for harvest missions. The use of accounting information to evaluate the performance of segment managers is referred to as **responsibility accounting** and is discussed in detail in Chapters 19 through 22.

responsibility accounting

In determining whether a company should have a centralized or decentralized structure, organizational management needs to consider, among other things, how rapidly decisions need to be made, willingness of upper management to allow subordinate managers to make potentially poor decisions, and the amount of training necessary to make empowered workers understand and evaluate the consequences of their decisions. Assessment of these factors requires the use of traditional financial accounting information such as the costs of a viable organization communication system and of employee training. What cannot be obtained from the financial accounting system are the benefits of better communication, more rapid decisions, and high levels of employee skills. Determination of these benefits necessitates the use of estimates of future returns and **opportunity costs** (the potential benefits forgone because one course of action is chosen over another)—neither of which are recognized under GAAP.

opportunity costs

Companies deciding to implement empowerment concepts also typically introduce teams to the organization structure. Exhibit 2–7 differentiates between the traditional

---

[15] Michael Goold and John Quinn, *Strategic Control: Milestones for Long-Term Performance* (London: The Economist Books Ltd/Hutchison, 1990); cited in Tony Barnes, *Kaizen Strategies for Successful Leadership* (London: Pitman Publishing, 1996), p. 135.

[16] "Drucker on Soft Tissue Metrics," *Datamation* (September 1, 1994), p. 64.

[17] Germain Boër, "Management Accounting Beyond the Year 2000," *Journal of Cost Management* (Winter 1996), pp. 46–47.

WORK GROUP	TEAM
■ Strong, clearly focused leader ■ Individual accountability ■ Group's purpose is same as the broader organizational mission ■ Individual work-products ■ Runs efficient meetings ■ Measures its effectiveness indirectly by its influence on others (e.g., financial performance of the business) ■ Discusses, decides, and delegates	■ Shared leadership roles ■ Individual and mutual accountability ■ Specific team purpose that the team itself delivers ■ Collective work-products ■ Encourages open-ended discussion and active problem-solving meetings ■ Measures performance directly by assessing collective work-products ■ Discusses, decides, and does real work together

SOURCE: Reprinted by permission of *Harvard Business Review.* An excerpt from "The Discipline of Teams" by Jon R. Katzenbach and Douglas K. Smith, March-April 1993. Copyright © 1993 by the President and Fellows of Harvard College; all rights reserved.

EXHIBIT 2–7

Differentiating between Groups and Teams

view of "groups of workers" with the current view of "teams." Introduction of teams requires new measurement systems to assess group (rather than only individual) performance and, if appropriate, to integrate those new measurements with any organizational pay-for-performance plans. These types of measurements and information often reflect the nonmonetary production quantities that are important management accounting data rather than the dollar figures commonly found in the financial accounting system.

Costs and Organizational Management

A company can evaluate its core competencies only by analyzing its activities and comparing them to internal or external benchmark measurements. Some comparison metrics will relate to costs: how much does it cost an organization to make a product or perform a service compared to the amount for which that product or service could be acquired externally? To make fair comparisons, a company must be reasonably certain of the validity of its costs. Unfortunately, a recent survey of over 200 financial and operating executives in North America by Lawson Software and Price Waterhouse LLP showed that less than half of the respondents "had confidence in the accuracy of the cost data available to them. . . . Operating executives in particular consistently asked for more accurate, timely, and detailed information from their systems."[18]

To help overcome these defects in the information system, some companies are now reporting additional information under an **activity-based management** (ABM) system. ABM refers to a set of analytical tools that relate organizational processes and activities to customer value. The object of ABM is to eliminate those activities (and thereby, the costs) that do not add value from the perspective of a customer. As part of an ABM system, a company may adopt **activity-based costing** (ABC) to determine costs based on the activities incurred to make a product or perform a service. As discussed in Chapter 6, significant differences between traditional costs and ABC costs are generally found in companies that manufacture numerous complex products (or perform numerous types of services) in differing volumes. In the previously mentioned survey, "executives whose organizations used ABC as part of a continuous cost analysis system rated the quality of their cost data much higher than those who used ABC only sporadically, and higher than nonusers of ABC."[19]

activity-based management

activity-based costing

[18] Mary Lee Geishecker, "New Technologies Support ABC," *Management Accounting* (March 1996), p. 44.
[19] Ibid.

Key Four Inc. (Blue Chip
Enterprises)

A company using valid costs may find that a product can be produced (or a service activity can be performed) externally less expensively than internally. This information, however, is not sufficient to mandate outsourcing. Although outsourcing is an excellent way to obtain the best knowledge, experience, and methodology available in a process activity, companies need to recognize that when an activity is outsourced, some degree of control is given up. Thus, company management should carefully evaluate the viability of activities to be outsourced using, for example, the risk pyramid shown in Exhibit 2–8. Such a procedure allows a company to maintain some balance with regard to outsourcing.

Company management may make a decision not to outsource, even though costs would be less, because of nonmonetary considerations. The function may be considered too critical to the organization's long-term viability (such as product research and development); the company may be pursuing a core competency relative to this function; or issues such as product/service quality, time of delivery, flexibility of use, or reliability of supply cannot be resolved to the company's satisfaction. In such instances, company management may want to reevaluate its activities relative to this function to attempt to perform the function at the lower cost quoted by the external firm.

If outsourcing is chosen, the company should prepare a comprehensive list of criteria to use for contract manufacturer or vendor selection and communicate these criteria to the potential suppliers. Although monetary considerations may be important, corporate management generally recognizes that some nonmonetary needs (such as those mentioned above) are even more critical.

After a contract manufacturer or vendor has been selected, the company must perform regular monitoring and evaluating. Again, financial accounting information may be important and is easily assessed: the invoices received from the contract manufacturer must be for the amount originally quoted per unit of product or service. But other performance criteria must be evaluated also, such as whether the vendor shipped defective parts or whether goods were delivered late.

EXHIBIT 2–8

Outsourcing Risk Pyramid

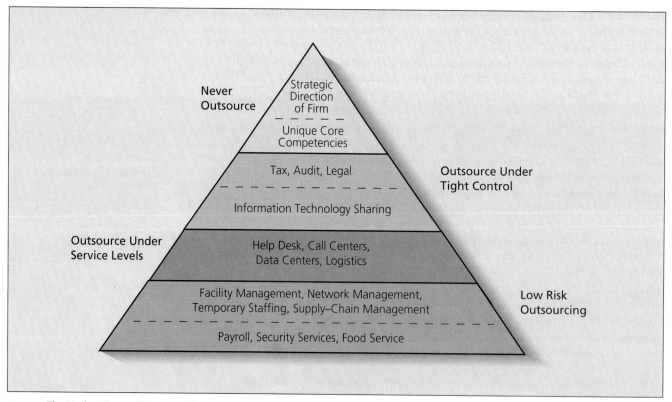

SOURCE: The Yankee Group, "Innovators in Outsourcing," *Forbes* (October 23, 1995), p. 266.

Consider the following example. In 1994, Southern Pacific Rail Corporation hired IBM to handle its computing activities for the subsequent 10 years. Unfortunately, due to IBM's inexperience in dealing with railroads, "computer breakdowns delayed accounting reports, and when connections failed at a major California rail-car-switching yard, a technician was left to direct 1,200 cars a day by hand. On other occasions, Southern Pacific's maintenance director had to wait for weeks for help from IBM's distant workers."[20]

This illustration serves to emphasize that the prices charged for the services rendered is not the only necessary or appropriate measurement of vendor performance. Only by integrating certain nonmonetary measurements (number of defective units or number of days late) with monetary measurements (the cost of customer returns of defective products or the cost of canceled orders because of an inability to deliver on time) can management determine the efficiency and effectiveness of its outsourcing plan and whether that plan is a good business strategy.

Historically, many firms did not consider the accounting function to be a core competency and, thus, many accounting activities were outsourced. However, firms are now discovering that the knowledge of accountants can be a source of strategic advantage and have sought to identify and exploit linkages between strategy and the accounting function. Many firms are now acknowledging the importance of having an internal capability in management accounting.

Capital Markets, Organizational Growth, and Competition

New strategic initiatives, including development of new products and services, are possible only if capital (both monetary and intellectual) is available for new investment. Corporate managers depend on public capital markets to acquire the funds necessary to pursue new investment. To attract capital, managers must have a proven record of developing products and services that add value to customers who, in turn, provide firms with revenues that generate profits for the shareholders.

Because capital is a primary organizational constraint, companies are concerned about the cost of the capital (COC) that they can acquire. Most firms have a variety of sources for capital, and each type of financing device is issued for different reasons and requires a different method to compute its cost. O'Brien Company is used to illustrate the various cost-of-capital computations.

DEBT   Debt primarily includes long-term notes and bonds. Because debt creates a tax deductible interest cost, the cost of debt is the after-tax cost of interest. The following formula indicates the computations for the cost of a new debt issuance:

$$k_d = YR(1 - TR)$$

where k_d = cost of debt
YR = yield (effective) rate[21]
TR = tax rate

O'Brien Company is planning a $10,000,000 bond issue. The stated rate on the debt is 7 percent, but the bonds are expected to sell at a price that will yield a rate of 8 percent. The company is in a 40 percent tax bracket. The cost of O'Brien's contemplated debt issuance is

$$k_d = .08 \ (1 - .40)$$
$$= .08 \ (.60)$$
$$= 4.8\%$$

[20] Louise Lee, "Hiring Outside Firms to Run Computers Isn't Always a Bargain," *Wall Street Journal* (May 18, 1995), p. A1.
[21] The current yield rate is computed as the periodic interest payment divided by the market value of the debt.

Each $1 of interest expense reduces O'Brien's taxable income by $1, which causes a $.40 reduction in tax expense. Therefore, the net effective cost of interest expense to O'Brien is 60 percent of the yield rate, or 4.8 percent.

PREFERRED STOCK EQUITY   Preferred stock has characteristics of both bonds (debt) and common stock (equity). Generally, preferred dividend payments have a fixed schedule and amount, as do debt interest payments. However, because preferred dividends are not tax deductible and are paid from after-tax earnings, no tax adjustment is made when the cost of capital is computed for preferred stock. The calculation for the cost of preferred stock is

$$k_p = D \div MP$$

where k_p = cost of preferred stock equity

D = annual dividend amount

MP = market price per share

In addition to the debt issue mentioned above, O'Brien Company is considering issuing 5,000 shares of $100 par value, 9 percent preferred stock. The preferred stock is expected to sell for $115 per share. The cost of O'Brien's proposed preferred stock issuance is

$$k_p = \$9 \div \$115$$
$$= 7.8\%$$

O'Brien will receive $115 for each share of preferred stock, but will pay only the 9 percent dividend on the $100 par value. Thus, the company has an approximate 7.8 percent effective dividend rate on each share.

COMMON STOCK EQUITY   The largest source of capital in most corporations is common stock equity, which refers to the common stock, paid-in capital, and retained earnings of a firm. One difficulty in determining the cost of common stock equity is that no specified interest or dividend payments are required for common stock. This lack of contractual payments creates difficulty in measuring the cost of common equity capital.

One method that can be used to compute common stock equity COC is based on the rate of return that stockholders expect to earn in future dividends on a company's common stock. Dividends paid on common stock are not tax deductible and are not affected by the tax rate. The cost of common stock equity can be computed as follows:

$$k_c = (D \div MP) + g$$

where k_c = cost of common stock equity

D = expected annual dividend amount

MP = market price per share

g = expected average annual growth rate

The expected average **growth rate** is an estimate of the increase expected in dividends or in market value per share of stock. The growth rate is a function of a company's predicted earnings, dividend policy, and market price appreciation per share.

growth rate

Assume that O'Brien Company expects to pay a $5 per-share dividend on common stock this year. Current market price of the common stock is $60 per share, and the company's average annual growth rate of 4 percent is expected to continue indefinitely. The cost of O'Brien's common stock equity is computed as

$$k_c = (\$5 \div \$60) + .04$$

$$= .08333 + .04$$

$$= 12.33\%$$

The **weighted average cost of capital** is a measure of the overall cost of capital from all sources. As a measure of the average cost of capital, the computation involves weighting the cost of each capital component by the percentage of total capital obtained from that source. The weighted average cost of capital is computed as follows:

weighted average cost of capital

$$K_T = (k_d \times \text{Debt\%}) + (k_p \times \text{Preferred Equity\%}) + (k_c \times \text{Common Equity\%})$$

To illustrate, assume O'Brien aims for a capital mix of 30 percent debt, 30 percent preferred equity, and 40 percent common equity. O'Brien's weighted average cost of capital would be:

$$K_T = (k_d \times \text{Debt\%}) + (k_p \times \text{Preferred Equity\%}) + (k_c \times \text{Common Equity\%})$$

$$= (4.8 \times .30) + (7.8 \times .30) + (12.33 \times .40)$$

$$= 8.71\%$$

The key tool managers use to allocate capital, and thereby determine which strategic initiatives will be pursued, is the capital budget. The **capital budget** is management's plan for capital investment. This budget (covered in detail in Chapter 18) is a major communication device for interaction between managers and managerial accountants in all kinds of organizations. Although the capital budget has traditionally focused on estimates of the quantitative benefits to be provided by new investments, many companies are now also incorporating estimates of qualitative benefits, especially in technology investments.

capital budget

The acquisition and use of new technologies often allow firms to be the first to bring a product to market. Rapid time-to-market for new products has become a critical performance dimension and is a primary requirement for success in the global market, especially relative to innovative products and services. Many advantages are associated with being the first to introduce a new product. For example, in introducing an innovative product, a firm can command a much higher price because the product will have no direct competitors, and competitors will be forced to lower prices on their less innovative products. Another advantage is gaining economies of scale over competitors due to higher volume production; the highest volume producer can eventually sell at lower prices than competitors by having a lower cost per unit.

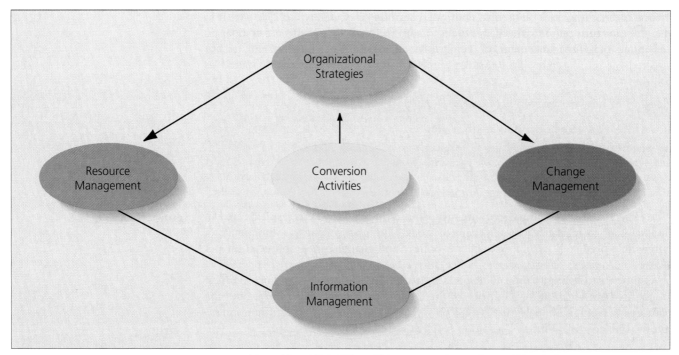

SOURCE: Adapted from W. P. Birkett, "Management Accounting and Knowledge Management," *Management Accounting* (November 1995), pp. 44–48. Reprinted from *Management Accounting*. Copyright by Institute of Management Accountants, Montvale, NJ.

EXHIBIT 2–9

Variables in Strategic Resource Management

target costing

strategic resource management

A new accounting tool that relates directly to strategic planning and product development is target costing. **Target costing** (discussed more fully in Chapter 6) is a process of determining an allowable cost for a product that is inferred from projecting a market price for the product and subtracting a required profit margin. It is a powerful planning tool because it causes collaboration across functional specialties in determining ways to reduce costs in the product design stage so that a more profitable product can eventually be launched. This discussion is continued in Chapter 18.

Unfortunately, the acquisition of cutting-edge technology—including that for new product development—frequently creates a mismatch in the timing of costs and benefits as measured by traditional GAAP-based rules. Thus, costs are recorded and recognized in the early years of the investment, whereas the benefits created by the new technology are recorded and recognized in later years. Additionally, financial accounting does not recognize benefits such as faster delivery time, customer satisfaction, or more rapid time-to-market of new products. Consequently, management accountants must rely on other measurement methods to better capture the costs and benefits of high-tech investments and help managers better evaluate the strategic implications of those investments.

Strategic resource management (SRM) involves the organizational planning for deployment of resources to create value for customers and shareholders. Key variables in the success of SRM are the management of information and the management of change in responding to threats and opportunities. Exhibit 2–9 depicts these important relationships.

SRM is concerned with the following issues:[22]

- how to deploy resources to support strategies;
- how resources are used in, or recovered from, change processes;
- how customer value and shareholder value will serve as guides to the effective use of resources; and
- how resources are to be deployed and redeployed over time.

[22] Adapted from W.P. Birkett, "Management Accounting and Knowledge Management," *Management Accounting* (November 1995), pp. 44–48.

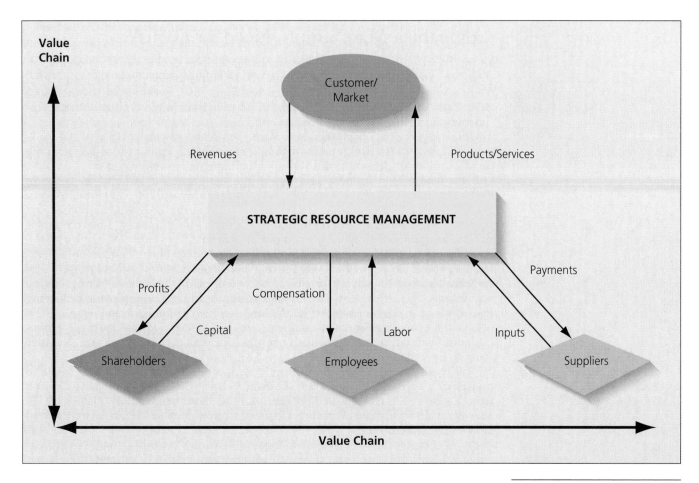

These areas of concern cannot be measured by financial accounting because they are often concerned with nonmonetary information and measurements. Thus, managerial accounting provides the necessary estimates designed to help management address these issues and focus on strategic objectives.

Exhibit 2–10 indicates that information is a key linkage between managing resources and managing change in directing the internal processes of a business. This relationship reflects the concept of a business intelligence system as discussed in Chapter 1. Managers, as the agents of change, must have information on internal processes, markets (customers), technologies, and competitors to direct proactive changes to new market opportunities and responsive changes to actions of competitors. The management accounting function is responsible for providing much of the information that is required by managers. Thus, for management accounting to make a valuable contribution to strategic management, it must find ways to provide managers with useful information to manage resources relative to value and time.

The foundation of SRM is the **value chain** or the set of processes that convert inputs into products and services for the firm's customers. As shown in Exhibit 2–10, the value chain includes the processes of suppliers as well as internal processes. By focusing on the value chain, managers are able to determine which activities in the firm create value for customers. This value is reflected in the prices charged for products and services and, thus, in revenues earned by the firm. By accentuating the activities that are value-adding in customers' eyes and by reducing or eliminating the non-value-adding activities, managers are able to operate their firms more efficiently and effectively.

For their contributions to the value chain, employees earn compensation and suppliers earn revenues. One requirement of successful competition is to gain cooperation of everyone in the value chain and communicate a perception to them that today's business competition is between value chains more so than between individual businesses. Once this concept is accepted, members of the value chain become aware

EXHIBIT 2–10

The Value Chain and Strategic Resource Management

value chain

NEWS
NOTE

Companies May Simply Need to Focus!

In the 1960s, conglomerates—corporations made up of dozens or even hundreds of disparate companies—were all the rage. James Ling gained fame building Ling-Temco-Vought (LTV) after starting out by selling stock from a booth at the Texas State Fair. In a mix of fear and mockery, Charles Bluhdorn's Gulf & Western Industries was satirized as Engulf & Devour.

Ultimately, the old conglomerates became hopelessly unwieldy. LTV's 1986 bankruptcy was the nadir. And now few flamboyant acquirers, similar to LTV's Mr. Ling or ITT's Harold Geneen in the 1960s are building new conglomerates.

But a funny thing happened on the way to the graveyard: A new generation of management realized that the problem wasn't necessarily with the conglomerate concept—the idea that companies could grow by acquiring disparate businesses and thereby achieve some protection from the cycles of a single industry. They concluded that the concept had simply careened out of control.

Today, these conglomerate chief executives, including James Hardymon at Textron, Lawrence A. Bossidy at Allied Signal and Richard Smith at Harcourt General Inc., are focusing on a relatively few, rather than many, businesses. While slowing acquisitions, they are working harder on the nitty-gritty job of improving productivity. Hands-on-management, cost cutting and selective pruning are in vogue.

Like their forebears, the new conglomerate chiefs are promising that their various businesses will create synergies, with one-plus-one making more than two. And they seem to be finding some.

"We're all focusing a little bit more and, I believe, becoming a little easier to understand," says Mr. Hardymon, Textron's chairman. Since coming to Textron from Emerson Electric Co. in 1990, he has done more than sell off businesses. He also has made acquisitions, but they are fewer than in the past and are geared toward enhancing existing lines.

But in addition, Mr. Hardymon is pressing Textron's remaining units, from helicopters to golf carts, to better manage cash flow and control inventories. Moreover, he brings together twice a year Textron's division heads, who used to see little of each other. He also has started training programs that draw in others from various groups. "We've had most of our manufacturing groups visit two auto-parts divisions to learn how they turn inventories 70 times a year," he says. "That helps trying to get throughput. Instead of taking 24 months to build a helicopter, it's now 14, and we're pushing for 12." Despite buying Acustar last year, Textron cut inventories by $100 million and freed up cash.

SOURCE: William M. Bulkeley, "A New Mix: Conglomerates Make a Surprising Comeback; Many Focus on Fewer Lines of Business, Emphasize Efforts to Reduce Costs; Predicting an Urge to Merge," *Wall Street Journal* (March 1, 1994), p. A1. Reprinted by permission of *The Wall Street Journal*, © 1994 Dow Jones & Company, Inc. All Rights Reserved Worldwide.

that information must be shared among all entities in the value chain. For example, "some customers with purchasing clout are already demanding cost justifications for proposed price increases by their suppliers."[23]

Strategic resource management in a conglomerate may be extraordinarily challenging. The conglomerate form of organization exists when there is a common owner of a set of diversified businesses. This type of entity makes financial sense only if synergies can be achieved across the individual business units. Otherwise, the units would be just as successful operating as individual entities. Value must be created laterally across business units as well as within vertical value chains involving individual business units. Although synergies or economies in operation may be somewhat obvious in the vertical value chain, they may be much more difficult to identify in conglomerates. However, as the above News Note indicates, the diversity in the operations and core competencies of the subunits can be a source of synergy.

[23] George Foster, "Management Accounting in 2000," *Journal of Cost Management* (Winter 1996), p. 36.

Who Should Get the Money?

**NEWS
NOTE**

Many executives who run America's large corporations are at a crossroads. With profits high, they must decide what to do with all the cash now flowing in. Plow it into the business? Or please many shareholders, perhaps by buying back stock? As earnings momentum slows, more and more executives will be wrestling with that seemingly enviable question—and finding a decision difficult. At General Signal Corp., they already are.

"We have a full plate of what to do with our money, including paying down debt from acquisitions," says Nino Fernandez, head of investor relations at the electronics maker. But the stock of the Stamford, Conn., company took a dive recently, to about $29 a share from $35, after management said second-half profit growth wouldn't be as robust as analysts had predicted.

Lately, several big shareholders have begun urging General Signal to divert cash from paying down debt, as management prefers, to propping up the stock. A popular, though expensive, way to bolster the price is to repurchase shares on the open market—thus reducing the supply and, by spreading profits over fewer shares, enabling per-share earnings to increase faster than total net income.

A lot is riding on such decisions. If many companies carry out big buybacks, the reduction in shares outstanding could buoy stock prices in the short run. But it could prove costly in the long run if, as some companies say, they thereby lose their painfully acquired competitive edge in world markets.

Indeed, some Wall Street analysts applaud the major long-term investments made by many U.S. companies and regard any retreat as a strategic mistake.

SOURCE: Fred R. Bleakley, "Reinvest High Profits or Please Institutions?" *Wall Street Journal* (October 16, 1995), pp. A1, A8. Reprinted by permission of *The Wall Street Journal*, © 1995 Dow Jones & Company, Inc. All Rights Reserved Worldwide.

One of the most significant challenges of efficiently and effectively managing an organization is balancing the short-run and long-run demands for resources. A rational application of resources must prioritize strategic resource needs and balance short-term and long-term value considerations. Although the term *resources* includes all organizational assets, including people, frequently cash is the resource that is the focus of managerial attention. As the above News Note indicates, managers and shareholders often differ on whether cash should be used to pay dividends or repurchase stock, or be reinvested in strategic growth opportunities.

In addition to balancing the application of resources to short- and long-term value creation, managers must also take care to structure strategic initiatives such that they allow flexibility in operational management. Stated another way, in making long-term commitments of resources, managers must consider how they affect short-term management of resources.

For example, General Motors was forced to hire temporary workers at a time when it was paying full wages and benefits to 8,300 workers who were doing nothing.[24] This situation was caused by booming sales of some models and sluggish sales of others. Because different models are produced in different plants, layoffs were occurring in some areas while overtime was being paid in others. Under terms of a GM agreement with the United Auto Workers Union, workers cannot be forced to work at any plant that is more than 50 miles from their home plant.

**MANAGING
RESOURCES ACROSS
TIME**

[24] Neal Templin and Joseph B. White, "Corporate Focus: GM Goes to Great Lengths to Match Workers and Work; Idled Employees Resist Transfers to Bustling Plants, Temporary Hires Step Up," *Wall Street Journal* (April 21, 1994), p. B4.

REVISITING

Matsushita Electrical Industrial Company

Rather than lose the executives in MCA who were keys to its successful operation, Matsushita elected to sell the majority of its stake in the company. Seagram Company purchased 80 percent of Matsushita's holdings in MCA in April 1995. Matsushita realized about $5.6 billion from the sale. During the term of the investment in MCA, the dollar had depreciated dramatically relative to the yen. Hence, Matsushita needed to realize about $10 billion to avoid a large loss on the sale. Booking the loss on the sale caused Matsushita's overall operations to post its first pre-tax loss in the company's history. At about the same time, Sony Corporation, another giant Japanese electronics firm, booked a $2.7 billion loss on its investment in Columbia/Tristar, a competitor of MCA.

With $5.6 billion of cash, Matsushita is again facing an important strategic decision: where and in what to invest the money. At least some of the cash may be converted to yen and reinvested in Japan, but most likely some of the cash will be invested in new factories in various parts of the world to produce product components. In terms of strategic resource management, the sale of MCA represents a decision by Matsushita to redeploy its financial resources in hopes of achieving a greater return. With over 70 research and development facilities operating globally, Matsushita has ample opportunities for new investment.

SOURCES: Matsushita's Internet Home Page; Thomas R. King and John Lippman, "Sale of MCA Being Discussed By Matsushita; Japanese Parent Weighing Several Options; Parties Include Bronfman, TCI," *Wall Street Journal* (March 31, 1995), p. A3; David P. Hamilton, "Business Brief: Matsushita Reports Pretax Loss of $1.32 Billion for Its First Period," *Wall Street Journal* (August 25, 1995), p. B4. Reprinted by permission of *The Wall Street Journal*, © 1995 Dow Jones & Company, Inc. All Rights Reserved Worldwide.

CHAPTER SUMMARY

Strategic planning is perhaps the most important contribution that high-level managers make to their organizations. Strategic planning provides long-term direction for organizations and is a necessary link between the organization's goals and objectives and its routine functions. Without strategic planning there would be no foundation for operational planning or organizational budgeting.

The creation of organizational strategy is affected by several factors. Organizational structure determines the distribution of authority and responsibility in the organization. By segmenting the totality of business operations into logical segments, different strategies can be implemented for different segments. Frequently segments are organized along product lines. In turn, product line strategies and missions are influenced by product life cycle considerations.

Core competencies determine which strategies would be feasible relative to the knowledge and internal capabilities of the organization. Core competencies should be exploited by an organization's strategies. Technological innovation, product and process engineering, product development, and after-sale service are examples of core competencies.

Strategy is also constrained by internal factors, such as availability of human, structural, and financial capital, and by technology. Internal constraints tend to be short term and usually can be overcome in the longer run.

Management style affects strategy by influencing the normal business practices and protocol for interactions among crucial parties such as employees, customers, and suppliers. Related to managerial style is the constraint of organizational culture. Organizational culture is the set of values shared by organizational participants.

Last, factors external to the firm such as government regulations, laws, and fiscal structures limit strategic options. Typical constraints of this type include external culture, fiscal barriers, legal/regulatory structures, and political considerations. These constraints are often long term and more difficult for managers to influence or control.

Today, the accounting function can contribute not only to the operational management of organizations but also to the strategic management and implementation of strategies. Budgets are frequently used as tools to link operational and strategic plans. One of the most important control budgets is the capital budget. This budget involves an understanding of the costs associated with alternative long-term sources of organizational financing. Collectively, the costs of debt and preferred and common equity compose the cost of capital of a firm.

Strategic resource management is a tool that provides a conceptual link between organizational strategy and resource deployment and provides for involvement of the accounting function. The key focus in strategic resource management is the value chain, or the string of activities that convert organizational inputs into outputs. This effort has provided a renewed emphasis on the importance of management accounting.

KEY TERMS

activity-based management (p. 53)
activity-based costing (p. 53)
build mission (p. 42)
capital budget (p. 57)
centralization (p. 43)
contract manufacturer (p. 45)
contract vendor (p. 45)
core competency (p. 44)
decentralization (p. 43)
empowerment (p. 43)
environmental constraint (p. 49)
growth rate (p. 57)
harvest mission (p. 42)
hold mission (p. 42)
intellectual capital (p. 46)
kaizen (p. 44)

management style (p. 48)
master budget (p. 51)
network organization (p. 45)
operational plan (p. 51)
opportunity cost (p. 52)
organizational culture (p. 48)
outsourcing (p. 44)
product life cycle (p. 43)
responsibility accounting (p. 52)
strategic resource management
  (p. 58)
strategy (p. 40)
target costing (p. 58)
value chain (p. 59)
weighted average cost of capital
  (p. 57)

SOLUTION STRATEGIES

Cost of Capital Computations:

$$\text{Cost of debt: } k_d = YR(1 - TR)$$

where k_d = cost of debt

YR = yield (effective) rate

TR = tax rate

$$\text{Cost of preferred stock: } k_p = D \div MP$$

where k_p = cost of preferred stock equity

D = annual dividend amount

MP = market price per share

$$\text{Cost of common stock equity: } k_c = (D \div MP) + g$$

where k_c = cost of common stock equity

D = expected annual dividend amount

MP = market price per share

g = expected average annual growth rate

Weighted Average Cost of Capital:

$$K_T = (k_d \times \text{Debt\%}) + (k_p \times \text{Preferred Equity\%}) +$$
$$(k_c \times \text{Common Equity\%})$$

DEMONSTRATION PROBLEM

Whitman Chemical is in the process of preparing its capital budget for 1998. The capital budget is an important tool of Whitman's management in executing strategic plans. To fully implement its growth initiatives, the company needs to raise $50,000,000 of new capital in 1998. In compiling the capital budget, the cost of capital components must be determined. Whitman finances its operations using a mix of common and preferred stock and long-term debt. Its desired capital mix is 40 percent debt, 10 percent preferred equity, and 50 percent common equity. The following information provides details regarding each source of capital.

- For Whitman's level of risk, new bonds can be issued to yield 9 percent before taxes.
- Whitman's combined federal and state income tax rate is 40 percent.
- Whitman can issue its 6 percent, $100 par value preferred stock for $90 per share.
- The current market price of Whitman's common stock is $50; the current expected annual dividend price is $4, and the dividend has been growing at a rate of 4 percent annually.

Required:

a. Compute the expected cost of debt for the 1998 capital budget.
b. Compute the expected cost of preferred equity for the 1998 capital budget.
c. Compute the expected cost of common equity for the 1998 capital budget.
d. At the given capital mix, compute the weighted average cost of capital for 1998.

Solution to Demonstration Problem

a. Cost of debt: $k_d = YR(1 - TR)$

$$= .09(1 - .40)$$
$$= .09(.60)$$
$$= 5.4\%$$

b. Cost of preferred stock: $k_p = D \div MP$

$$= (\$100 \times .06) \div \$90$$
$$= 6.67\%$$

c. Cost of common stock equity: $k_c = (D \div MP) + g$

$$= (\$4 \div \$50) + .04$$
$$= 12\%$$

d. Weighted average cost of capital: $K_T = (k_d \times \text{Debt \%}) + (k_p \times \text{Preferred Equity \%}) +$
$$(k_c \times \text{Common Equity \%})$$

$$K_T = (k_d \times .4) + (k_p \times .10) + (k_c \times .5)$$
$$= (5.4 \times .4) + (6.67 \times .10) + (12 \times .5)$$
$$= 8.83\%$$

1. What is organizational strategy? Why would each organization have a unique set of strategies?

2. How can the division of a business into smaller segments facilitate strategy formulation and execution?

3. What are the three generic missions of subunits? How do the objectives of organizational segments differ across the three missions?

4. How is the concept of subunit mission related to the concept of product life cycle?

5. What are the two ends of the continuum of organizational authority? Provide one organizational example that would "fit" each end of the continuum, and explain why that authority structure would be appropriate for that organization or type of organization.

6. How do core competencies constrain the feasible set of alternative organizational strategies?

7. Does the acquisition of new technology automatically overcome quality or speed problems? Why or why not?

8. Why are many companies relying more on suppliers and less on internal capacities for some conversion processes and organizational inputs?

9. How do firms use mergers to execute organizational strategies?

10. "If an organization can borrow money or sell stock, it does not have a capital constraint." Is this statement true or false? Discuss the rationale for your answer.

11. How does workforce diversity affect organizational culture?

12. How can a change in governmental laws or regulations create a strategic opportunity for a firm? Give an example.

13. Differentiate between operational planning and strategic planning. Is one more important than the other? Why or why not?

14. What roles does the accounting system play in the formulation or execution of strategies?

15. Why are companies concerned about their costs of capital? How is the cost of capital determined?

16. "Most companies determine product or service price by adding a reasonable profit margin to costs incurred." Discuss the validity of this statement.

17. How does the value chain interface with strategic resource management?

18. In the value chain view of an organization, which stakeholder is the focus of attention in determining whether a process is value-added or non-value-added? Explain.

19. Why is time such an important consideration in the management of organizational resources?

20. Compare and contrast the following concepts:
    a. Decentralization and empowerment
    b. Groups and teams
    c. Conversion activities and value chains
    d. Strategic planning and operational planning
    e. Activity-based management and activity-based costing
    f. Environmental constraints and organizational constraints
    g. Management style and organizational culture

EXERCISES

21. *(Terminology)* Match the following lettered terms on the left with the appropriate numbered description on the right. If a description has no match, assign it to letter k.

   a. Build mission
   b. Harvest mission
   c. Hold mission
   d. Kaizen
   e. Target costing
   f. Value chain
   g. Strategic resource management
   h. Core competency
   i. Decentralization
   j. Product life cycle
   k. None of the above

   1. Distributing decision-making authority throughout the firm
   2. Sequential stages, from idea conception to discontinuance, through which a product passes
   3. Protecting competitive position
   4. Determining amount resulting from subtracting a required profit margin from a projected market price
   5. Maintaining most decision-making authority by top management
   6. Maximizing short-term earnings and net cash generated, even at the expense of market share
   7. Having a higher proficiency relative to competitors in a critical function or activity
   8. Philosophy of continuous improvement
   9. Benefit forgone by accepting an alternative
   10. Increasing market share, even at the expense of short-term profits and cash inflow
   11. Planning for deployment of resources to create value for customers and shareholders
   12. Set of processes of company and its suppliers to convert inputs into products and services

22. *(Terminology)* Match the following lettered terms on the left with the appropriate description on the right. If a description has no match, assign it to letter k.

   a. Strategy
   b. Intellectual capital
   c. Activity-based management
   d. Network organization
   e. Responsibility accounting
   f. Empowerment
   g. Management style
   h. Environmental constraint
   i. Operational plans
   j. Outsourcing
   k. None of the above

   1. Giving people authority and responsibility to make decisions about their work
   2. Contracting with outside suppliers to produce goods or services in preference to producing them internally
   3. A long-range plan formulated to fulfill a firm's goals and objectives
   4. A firm's intangible assets of skill, knowledge, and information
   5. Continuous improvement

6. Reflect(s) the details of implementing and maintaining firm's strategic plans
7. A set of analytical tools relating company processes to customer value, especially for eliminating activities that create little or no customer value
8. Expected annual increase in dividends or per-share stock market value
9. Preferences of managers in how they interact with other stakeholders in the organization
10. Limitation on strategy options caused by an external influence
11. Using accounting information to evaluate managers
12. A firm that is part of a group adding value to a common product or service

23. *(Cost of capital)* Helen's Custom Fashions Inc. has the following composition of its capital structure:

Long-term debt (bonds)	30%
Preferred stock	15%
Common stock equity	55%
Total	100%

The before-tax interest on the bonds is 9 percent. The company's tax rate is 34 percent. The per-share dividend amount on the preferred stock is $6, and the stock is currently selling for $90 per share. Common stock is currently selling at $80, and its expected per-share dividend is $5. The company's expected annual growth rate is 2 percent. Calculate the following:
a. After-tax cost of the bonds
b. Cost of the preferred stock equity
c. Cost of common stock equity
d. Weighted average cost of capital

24. *(Weighted average cost of capital)* Westover Industrial has the following current capital structure:

COMPONENT	MARKET VALUE	AFTER-TAX COST OF CAPITAL
Bonds	$1,000,000	5.5%
Preferred stock equity	500,000	9.0%
Common stock equity	5,000,000	12.0%

The company is planning to expand by $2,000,000. Funds for this expansion are to be raised 40 percent from debt and 60 percent from common stock. The after-tax cost of the capital components are expected to remain the same.
a. Determine the firm's weighted average cost of capital before and after expansion.
b. Why would the firm's weighted average cost of capital decline in the two calculations made in part a?

25. *(Weighted average cost of capital)* Cleveland Distillery has the following components in its corporate structure:

Bonds payable (12% stated rate)	$10,000,000
Premium on bonds payable	397,980
9%, $100 par preferred stock	2,000,000
Paid-in capital on preferred	100,000
$20 par common stock	8,500,000
Retained earnings	6,700,000

The bonds were originally issued 10 years ago at \$10,795,960 with a 20-year life. Interest on the bonds is paid and amortized on an annual basis. The company uses straight-line amortization of bond discounts or premiums. The market yield of the bonds has not changed since the date of issue. The preferred stock was issued at \$105 per share, and it is currently selling for \$120. Common stockholders will receive a dividend of \$3 next period. The most recent trading price of a common share is \$45. Cleveland Distillery's management has promised a dividend growth rate of 5 percent per year, and the tax rate for the company is 40 percent.

a. Determine the cost of capital for the bonds.

b. Determine the cost of capital for the preferred stock.

c. Determine the cost of capital for the common stock.

d. Determine the weighted average cost of capital using the following capital mix: bonds, 40 percent; preferred stock, 15 percent; and common stock, 45 percent.

COMMUNICATION ACTIVITIES

26. *(Coping with regulatory change)* Most Americans probably don't see a huge difference between \$4.78 and \$5.15. Then again, most Americans don't work at Popeye's Chicken & Biscuits fast-food restaurants.

The \$4.78 is the average hourly wage earned by the 20 or so employees at the Popeye's store here on City Line Avenue. These are the fry cooks and biscuit makers, the floor sweepers and the cash-register jockeys doing some of the jobs at the bottom of the economic pyramid. The \$5.15 is what the Clinton administration proposes as the new minimum hourly wage. For workers here, it would mean a raise.

For store manager Mohammed Isah, however, the extra 37 cents an hour is a big deal. "Where is the extra productivity going to come from?" asks Mr. Isah. He is mapping contingency plans to cut some jobs if the higher wage is imposed.

[SOURCE: Bernard Wysocki, Jr., "A Hot Potato: A Popeye's Chain Frets Over How to Handle a Minimum-Pay Rise," *Wall Street Journal* (April 24, 1996), pp. A1, A6. Reprinted by permission of *The Wall Street Journal*, © 1996 Dow Jones & Company, Inc. All Rights Reserved Worldwide.]

As a hired consultant of Mr. Isah, prepare a written report that provides suggestions of changes Mr. Isah should consider in developing his contingency plan to respond to an increase in the statutory minimum wage.

27. *(Mergers and Spin Offs)* Two activities that are common in the global marketplace are mergers and spin-offs. A merger occurs when one company absorbs another. A spin-off involves the division of a single company into two or more independent firms. Mergers and spin-offs are strategic-level actions.

Go to your university library and conduct a search of business journals for articles about mergers and spin-offs. Use the articles you find as a basis for preparing an oral report. The oral report should be informative regarding the primary reasons that corporate managers merge and spin off businesses.

28. *(Core competencies)* As a team, make a list of the core competencies of your college or university and explain why you believe these items to be core competencies. Make appointments with your dean, one vice president, and if possible, the president of your college or university and, without sharing your list, ask these individuals what they believe the core competencies to be and why. Prepare a video presentation that summarizes, compares, and contrasts all the lists. Send copies of the tapes to each of the individuals you interviewed.

29. *(Subunit mission)* In 1995 and 1996, AT&T split up (spun off) its businesses into three independent corporations. One of the businesses is Lucent Technologies. Following are some of the significant items from the company's first-quarter earnings report for 1996:

1996 RELATIVE TO 1995

Network equipment revenue	up 17%
Domestic sales	up 12%
Microchip revenue	up 26%
R&D spending	up 2%
S, G, & A expenses	up 6.9%

For the quarter, the company reported a net loss of $103 million.

[SOURCE: John J. Keller, "Lucent Reports a Narrow Loss, Strong Revenue," *Wall Street Journal* (April 25, 1996), p. B12. Reprinted by permission of *The Wall Street Journal*, © 1996 Dow Jones & Company, Inc. All Rights Reserved Worldwide.]

Write a brief report describing how you would interpret the above financial information under the following circumstances:
a. Lucent's strategy is oriented toward growth.
b. Lucent's strategy is oriented toward harvesting profits from mature businesses.

30. *(Outsourcing)* In an unusually sweeping "outsourcing" arrangement, Dell Computer Corp. [has decided to] hand over responsibility for all its shipping to a single management company. The contract with Roadway Logistics Systems is designed to improve distribution of Dell's products as well as transportation of inbound materials, and should help the mail-order personal computer vendor control shipping costs. Currently, 40% of the cost of a Dell product can be attributed to logistics. "We expect multimillion-dollar savings annually." As the company projected its growth, Dell would have been required to hire 1,000 to 2,000 additional workers for its distribution management. Instead, it turned to outsourcing.

[SOURCE: Scott McCartney, "Unit of Roadway to Do All Shipping for Dell Computer," *Wall Street Journal* (February 15, 1995), p. B8. Reprinted by permission of *The Wall Street Journal*, © 1995 Dow Jones & Company, Inc. All Rights Reserved Worldwide.]

Prepare an oral report to the board of Dell Computer Corp. discussing the major risks and benefits of outsourcing compared to the alternative of having in-house distribution capacity.

31. *(Organizational mission)* Few companies have blended vision, mission, and performance more articulately than Levi Strauss. Its core curriculum training program is designed to synthesize output with values collectively constructed around trust and teamwork. Its statement reads, in part: "The mission of Levi Strauss & Co. is to sustain profitable and responsible commercial success by marketing jeans and selected casual apparel under the Levi's brand. . . . We all want a company that our people are proud of and committed to, where all employees have an opportunity to contribute, learn, grow, and advance based on merit . . . and to have fun in our endeavors."

[SOURCE: Michael H. Mescon and Timothy S. Mescon, "Management with a Mission," *Sky Magazine* (June 1995), p. 28.]

Prepare a brief written report relating the preceding materials from Levi Strauss to the major concepts discussed in this chapter.

CASES

32. *(Strategy execution)* Gulf Pharmaceutical manufactures prescription drugs for humans and animals. The company was formed in 1940, and over the next 55-plus years grew to become one of the largest pharmaceutical companies in the United States. In 1996, the company's sales were $4.5 billion and its net income was $350 million. Although the company has some foreign operations, domestic production and sales account for over 90 percent of current sales and profits. In the United States, the company's operations are divided into two operating divisions, Human Products and Animal Products.

The president of Gulf, Maxine Green, has been increasingly concerned about the growth rate of the firm and the inability of the firm to develop marketable products using emerging biotechnology. Ms. Green has expressed doubts about whether the firm has adequately invested in research and development for biotech products and whether her division managers are too short-term in their planning and decision priorities. As she has been in the process of analyzing this problem, she has gathered the following facts that she feels could be related to the problem.

- Decision making at Gulf Pharmaceutical is decentralized. Division managers have the authority to make most major decisions involving operations and investment. There is some review of capital expenditures at the corporate level, but only rarely are decisions of division managers questioned.

- Division managers are paid a base salary plus a bonus based on the amount of annual profit generated. For the most recent year, 1997, each division manager earned a bonus roughly equal to 1 percent of net divisional profits. There is no incentive pay that is linked to market share of products, sales revenue, or stock price.

- Both divisional managers are about 55 years old and will probably retire before age 65.

- Competitive success in the drug industry relies principally on R&D efforts and the ability to bring products to market before competitors.

- The company reported record profits in 1990. Since that time its profits have been stagnant.

    a. From the preceding discussion, what is the apparent mission (build, hold, or harvest) of the two divisions of Gulf Pharmaceutical as implied by Ms. Green's findings? Explain.

    b. Do the two division managers hold a different view of their divisional missions than that held by the company's president? Explain.

    c. Using concepts discussed in this chapter, identify the causes for the failure of the company's two divisions to invest in biotechnology product development.

    d. What recommendations would you make to Ms. Green to address the problems that you identified in part c?

33. *(Acquisition of new technology)* Balton Industrial Solutions Company supplies various manufacturing firms with production technology including conveyor systems. One of the company's most popular products is a conveyor system that is used in bottling operations for various bottled food products. One of the key components of the conveyor system is a mechanical sensor that controls the loading of empty bottles onto the conveyor belt. In the event the sensor is operating outside of normal tolerances, bottles will be unevenly spaced (causing problems in the fill operation such as spilling and partially filled bottles) or bottles will be too tightly packed on the conveyor system causing them to break. Broken glass on the conveyor line is a potentially serious problem in the event the glass shards fall into undamaged bottles and are shipped to customers. Broken glass can also cause damage to the conveyor system.

Product managers at Balton believe that the next generation of conveyor systems must be equipped with a computer-controlled sensor rather than a mechanical sensor. The defect rate of products produced on conveyor systems using a mechanical sensor is too high relative to customer expectations. The mechanical sensor is also difficult to adjust when production switches between products that utilize different sized bottles. The company's production capabilities do not presently extend to production of computerized equipment.

To produce computerized sensors, Balton would be required to invest in new production technology and build facilities to house the production equipment. Additional costs would be incurred for employee training, research, and product design and development. A secondary cost consideration is the effect of the required investment on the firm's cost of capital. The capital markets would perceive this type of investment to be more risky than other assets held by the firm, because of the magnitude of the required investment and the firm's lack of experience in dealing with computer technology. Management has estimated that the cost of capital of the firm would rise by 2.5 percent over its existing level if investment in the computer sensor production equipment is made.

a. Describe for the management of Balton options that they might consider to purchase of the production equipment and technology required to produce computerized sensors.

b. For options that you identified in part a, describe the major benefits and risks of each option.

c. Of the options identified in part a, as well as the option of purchasing the required equipment, which would you recommend? Why?

---

34. The October 16, 1995, issue of *Fortune* discusses the outsourcing relationship between Saks Fifth Avenue and Deloitte & Touche LLP: Deloitte & Touche provides the internal audit function for Saks. Such relationships are no longer unusual. Use library resources or personal interviews to help answer the following questions.

a. Other than cost savings, what benefits can be gained by outsourcing the internal audit function to an external public accounting firm?

b. What, if any, ethical issues could arise if the CPA firm that performed the organizational audit also performed the internal audit work?

35. In 1993, the U.S. Congress passed the Family and Medical Leave Act. This act requires employers to allow workers to take up to 12 weeks per year of unpaid, job-protected leave. Leave can be taken only for specified reasons such as to care for a newborn child or ailing spouse, or for personal health reasons.

Employees are eligible for leave if they've worked for an employer for at least one year, and for 1,250 hours over the previous 12 months, and if there are at least 50 employees working for their employer within a 75-mile radius of the work site.

Libby Sartain, a Southwest Airlines vice president and a member of the Society for Human Resource Management, said some employees have used the law's provisions to avoid working overtime. Others apply for pregnancy leave under the act and take off time for morning sickness.

"Often, it seems we are running a (Family Medical Leave Act) processing business instead of an airline," Sartain said.

But because the major reason for family leave is childbirth, people like Christie Sens, who has had two babies in the past three years, think the law is a blessing.

Her latest baby arrived a month early last February, and she developed a blood clot in her leg. Family leave allowed her to recuperate in the hospital without worrying about losing her school-teaching job.

[SOURCE: Knight-Ridder Newspapers, "Family Leave's Cost," *Akron Beacon Journal* (May 2, 1996), pp. A1, A4. Reprinted by permission: Tribune Media Services.]

a. With regard to controlling the quality of organizational output, what would be the greatest concerns you would have as a manager in dealing with the Family Medical Leave Act?

b. How could compliance with terms of this act positively affect the quality of work in an organization?

c. What are the ethical obligations of employees in requesting leave under the authority of this act?

36. One of the most prominent trends in business today is to outsource noncore functions. It requires little analysis to determine that outsourcing equates to loss of jobs for workers who formerly executed activities associated with the outsourced function. With this fact in mind, it is not difficult to understand that outsourcing is often an issue of contention between managers and workers.

In no American business is outsourcing likely to be more hotly debated than at General Motors. Compared to its North American rivals, Ford and Chrysler, General Motors currently outsources a far smaller percentage of its required components. To illustrate, General Motors presently outsources about 30 percent of its required parts. This compares to 50 percent for Ford and 70 percent for Chrysler.

Ford and Chrysler were never as vertically integrated as GM, and they moved more quickly in the 1980s to spin off or abandon parts businesses that

ETHICS AND QUALITY DISCUSSION

couldn't compete on the basis of cost with outside suppliers. GM now finds itself in a very difficult dilemma. On the one hand, the company needs to discontinue many noncore functions to become more cost competitive. On the other hand, its unionized labor force is poised to resist these efforts to protect its jobs. GM will soon begin negotiations with United Auto Workers to structure its future labor contracts.

[SOURCE: Adapted from Rebecca Blumenstein, Nichole M. Christian, and Gabriella Stern, "GM to Break With Peers in UAW Talks (Auto Maker Ready to Risk Another Strike on Cost Issue)," *Wall Street Journal* (April 26, 1996), pp. A2, A4. Reprinted by permission of *The Wall Street Journal*, © 1996 Dow Jones & Company, Inc. All Rights Reserved Worldwide.]

a. As a GM executive negotiating with the UAW, how would you seek to structure the labor contract with the UAW?

b. In your opinion, is greater reliance on outsourcing by GM in the long-term best interests of UAW members working for GM?

c. What ethical responsibility do firms such as GM bear to the employees who are displaced by outsourcing?

37. One resource that all firms need to survive and grow is capital. As discussed in the chapter, entities can obtain a capital mix consisting of debt, equity, and hybrids of debt and equity. Each organization tries to obtain capital at the lowest possible cost.

Various analysts follow public debt and equity issues in order to provide information to the investing public about expected future returns and risk considerations. Such analysts serve an important role in capital markets because they make information about securities available to investors at relatively low cost. These analysts can have a large impact on security prices.

One of the biggest players in the business of investment analysis is Moody's Investors Service Inc. One service Moody's provides is to assign a rating to pending and existing bond issues (debt financing). The impact of these ratings is significant: a higher rating translates into a lower interest rate (and a lower rating translates into a higher interest rate) for the issuing company.

Moody's has recently caught the attention of government regulators because of its practice of providing unsolicited ratings for pending bond issues. Some bond issuers have suggested that Moody's bullies them into buying a Moody's bond rating.

Sometimes, Moody's aggressive tactics seem to induce issuers to include them in their transactions. In 1994, Lehman Brothers Holdings Inc. was preparing to underwrite about $1 billion of bonds for GPA Group, an Irish aircraft-leasing company. Unlike the skimpy fees earned on insured municipals [bonds] deals, these so-called asset-backed transactions could generate as much as $400,000 in fees for ratings companies. Issuers such as GPA rely on their investment advisers to select which firms will rate the securities. And Lehman officials decided to hire S&P and Fitch.

Moody's response: Too bad. Moody's says it had an obligation to bondholders to rate the bonds, especially because GPA was under severe financial distress.

In the end, Lehman decided to include Moody's. Moody's says it persuaded the investment bankers of the value of its ratings. But the bankers say they feared that without all the available information, Moody's would issue a low unsolicited rating and drive up borrowing costs.

[SOURCE: Charles Gasparino, "Triple-A-Dispute: Unsolicited Ratings From Moody's Upset Some Bond Issuers," *Wall Street Journal* (May 2, 1996), pp. A1, A6. Reprinted by permission of *The Wall Street Journal*, © 1996 Dow Jones & Company, Inc. All Rights Reserved Worldwide.]

As an individual who relies on Moody's bond ratings to make investment decisions, evaluate Moody's practice of providing unsolicited bond ratings from the following:

a. An ethical perspective

b. A risk-management perspective

38. On the Internet, find the mission, vision and values statements for several companies. Compare and contrast the statements. What do the statements reveal about the strategies of the companies? What do the statements reveal about what managers feel are the key elements to organizational success?

39. Using Internet sources, find the corporate organizational chart for a company and a discussion of the company's competitive strategy. Include a copy of the organizational chart in a report in which you address whether the organizational structure (displayed in the organizational chart) is consistent with the firm's strategy. Also, by examining the organizational chart, what is revealed about the company's core competencies and values?

40. To raise capital from public issues of debt or equity securities in the U.S., companies must comply with laws and regulations enforced by the Securities and Exchange Commission. Many of these rules relate to disclosure requirements that companies must meet before issuing securities. Searching Internet sources, find information on Rule 504, Regulation D, of the Securities Act of 1933. Considering information you find, discuss changes in disclosure requirements initiated by Rule 504 and how these changes would affect the cost of capital of a small publicly traded corporation.

INTERNET ACTIVITIES

CHAPTER

3

Considering Quality in an Organization

LEARNING OBJECTIVES

After completing this chapter, you should be able to answer these questions:

1. What forces are currently creating a greater worldwide demand for higher quality?

2. How is quality defined and from whose viewpoint should it be evaluated?

3. What basic characteristics comprise product quality and service quality?

4. Why do companies engage in benchmarking?

5. Why is total quality management significant and what is necessary to make it work?

6. What types of quality costs will a company have and how are those costs related?

7. Why has the Malcolm Baldrige National Quality Award become so widely sought?

8. Why should a firm be concerned with international quality standards?

9. How can managers instill quality as part of the organizational culture?

ITT Sheraton Corporation

ITT Sheraton Corporation is a worldwide hospitality network focused on quality. It owns, leases, manages, or franchises nearly 450 hotel and related properties in 64 countries. ITT Sheraton's revenues in 1994 were nearly $4 billion. Its mission statement is as follows:

> At ITT Sheraton, we are committed to becoming the number one hospitality company in the world by attracting and retaining the best employees, and by providing total customer satisfaction in order to increase long-term profits and value for our owners and ITT.

Sheraton's origin dates back to 1937, when the company's founders, Ernest Henderson and Robert Moore, acquired their first hotel—the Stonehaven—in Springfield, Massachusetts. Within 2 years, they purchased three hotels in Boston and before long expanded their holdings to include properties from Maine to Florida. At the end of its first decade, Sheraton was the first hotel chain to be listed on the New York Stock Exchange.

Innovation and expansion have been the keys to Sheraton's progress. The company began expanding internationally in 1949 with the purchase of two Canadian hotel chains. "Reservatron," launched in 1958, became the industry's first automated reservations system, making Sheraton the first chain to centralize and automate the reservations function. Sheraton was also the first to develop a toll-free 800-number system for direct consumer access.

The Sheraton Guest Satisfaction System—a comprehensive program of staff orientation and training, launched in 1987—has become an important industry contribution. Concentrating on guest service and staff service attitudes, the Sheraton Guest Satisfaction System is unique in its concept and in its measurable service delivery aspects. Industry studies, such as the D. K. Schifflet Travel Lodging Index, which rate consumer preferences and attitudes toward chains and their service satisfaction, reflect the positive impact of the system for Sheraton with travelers.

SOURCE: ITT Sheraton, North American Division Headquarters, 60 State Street, Boston, Massachusetts 02109, 1995.

ITT Sheraton has long demonstrated a commitment to a high level of customer satisfaction and to continuous improvement. This commitment is an integral part of the firm's formula for success. Managers at ITT Sheraton and numerous other entities have come to recognize that high quality is a fundamental organizational strategy for competing in a global economy.

Businesses, both domestic and foreign, are scrambling to attract customers and are able to offer more choices than in the past. Consumers are more aware of the greater variety of product choices that are available to satisfy their wants and needs. Additionally, consumers recognize the extent of their options for quality, price, service, and lead time. Nondomestic products are often selected by customers because of the perceived value of those products. These considerations have motivated producers to improve product quality and customer service. This cycle of successive stimulus-response actions among consumers and producers has caused many firms to adopt a dynamic approach about continuously improving the quality of their processes and products or services to satisfy consumer demand.

This chapter discusses quality issues such as total quality management, quality costs, quality standards, and quality culture. Because quality affects costs, accountants must understand the trade-offs involved between having higher and lower product/

VIDEO
VIGNETTE

Video Lottery Consultants (Blue
Chip Enterprises)

service quality. The management of many organizations has come to understand that current expenditures on quality improvement may be more than recouped by future cost reductions and sales volume increases. Because current quality improvements normally benefit the firm into future periods, costs of making such improvements should be viewed by management as recoverable investments with the potential for profit generation and not as expenses or losses. As expressed by the vice president of Video Lottery Consultants (Bozeman, Montana) after a quality program cut product failures by two-thirds: "We have been paid back many times for the effort and the price that we're willing to pay upfront for our quality."[1]

WHAT IS QUALITY?

To improve its product or service quality, an organization must agree on a definition of the term. Originally, after the Industrial Revolution helped manufacturers to increase output and decrease cost, quality was defined as conformity to designated specifications, and making certain that conformity existed was left to inspectors. Dr. W. Edwards Deming, one of the most famous of the experts on quality control, defines quality as "the pride of workmanship."[2] On a less individualized basis, Philip Crosby (another noted quality expert) defines quality as "conformance to requirements."[3] This definition was also adopted by the American Society for Quality Control, which defines requirements as follows: "Requirements may be documented as specifications, product descriptions, procedures, policies, job descriptions, instructions, purchase/service orders, etc., or they may be verbal. Requirements must be measurable or they are not valid."[4] The following News Note stresses conformity to requirements, but explains that conformity must be judged by customers.

quality

Thus, a fairly all-inclusive definition of **quality** is the sum total of all the characteristics of a product or service that influence its ability to meet the stated or implied needs of the person acquiring it. Quality must be viewed from the perspective of the

NEWS
NOTE

Who Defines Quality?

Quality is not what the planning and producing individuals may think or wish it to be. It is exactly what exists in the mind of the customer when he or she receives and personally appraises the product or service. This includes the internal customer, recipient of internal support service or work in process, as well as the external customer. In short, the meaning of quality is directly related to *customer satisfaction*; it is still best defined as "conformance to customer requirements." Any other definition for quality leaves too much room for interpretation and bias, making it impossible to work with. . . .

The "customer first" conceptual approach to the definition of quality suggests that a company bases all its quality standards, or performance standards, on the customers' requirements. This starts with the end customer and works back up the direct and support work-process paths through all internal customers. It also suggests that these standards be established in each and every company operation as an essential ingredient for consistency in the satisfaction of all customers. Lest you be misled by not viewing this task in its proper perspective, setting quality standards means being committed to paying careful attention to details because that is what the customer notices; and it is always wrong to assume or guess what the customer really needs or expects.

SOURCE: Jack Hagan, *Management of Quality* (Milwaukee, WI: ASQC, 1994), p. 18. © 1994 American Society for Quality Control. Reprinted with permission.

[1] "Video Lottery Consultants" (Blue Chip Enterprises, 1992), video.
[2] Rafael Aguayo, *Dr. Deming* (New York: Simon & Schuster, 1990), p. xi.
[3] Philip B. Crosby, *Quality Is Free* (New York: New American Library, 1979), p. 15.
[4] American Society for Quality Control, *Finance, Accounting and Quality* (Milwaukee, WI: ASQC, 1990), p. 3.

user rather than the provider and relates to both performance and value. This perspective on quality arose because of more competition, heightened public interest in product safety, and an increase in litigation relative to products and product safety. The responsibility for quality has become not simply a production issue, but a company profitability and longevity issue. All entity processes (production, procurement, distribution, finances, and promotion) are involved in quality improvement efforts. Therefore, the two related perspectives of quality reflect (1) the totality of internal processes that generate a product or service and (2) the customer's satisfaction with that product or service.

Production View of Quality

Productivity is measured by the quantity of units of good output generated from a specific amount of input during a time period. Any factor that either slows down or stops a production process or that causes unnecessary work (redundancy) is an impediment to productivity. **Activity analysis** can be used to highlight such factors. The various repetitive actions performed in making a product or providing a service are detailed and classified in value-added (VA) and non-value-added (NVA) categories. **Value-added activities** increase the worth of the product or service to the customer; **non-value-added activities** consume time and costs but add no value for the consumer. Minimizing or eliminating the non-value-added activities increases productivity and reduces costs.

activity analysis

value-added activities

non-value-added activities

Some important internal NVA activities include storing products for which there is little immediate demand, moving materials unnecessarily, and having unscheduled production interruptions. Another non-value-added activity is caused by supplier quality problems: having to inspect incoming components. To minimize or eliminate this particular NVA activity some companies require their suppliers to provide only zero-defect components. The accompanying News Note about Softub, a $15-million

---

Reduce Defect Costs by Carefully Screening Vendors

NEWS NOTE

Two-thirds of Softub's product cost is in materials purchased from about 200 vendors, which range from large producers of sheet metal to mom-and-pop makers of nuts and bolts. Softub strives to keep its inventory low, so if a vendor's goods are faulty, part of the spa maker's line is quickly shut down and workers are sent home. Two years ago, after several incidents involving substandard parts, Softub decided to do things differently.

The big change: an audit team, led by purchasing agent Gary Anderson, goes out to grill vendor candidates. Ten of Softub's 130 employees participate; an engineer may check on technical specifications, for example. The team members receive information about the vendor, as well as trade-journal articles with tips on evaluating suppliers. They spend anywhere from two hours to two days with each prospect, getting to know everyone from the president to the factory workers while noting things such as oil slicks around the machinery.

To ensure that the audits would be effective, Anderson designed a vendor survey form, which acts primarily as a checklist. "It isn't a cure-all; it's only part of the analysis. But it forces the team to focus on specific areas so we don't forget anything when we're on a visit," he says. The form also generates discussion about crucial issues, such as timeliness of delivery. Back at Softub, copies of the completed form go to purchasing, quality control, operations, and the finance department for their input. Anderson also verifies a supplier's claims with at least three of its other customers. When all the information is in—and after all necessary product testing has been completed—management meets and selects one vendor.

SOURCE: Stephanie Gruner, "The Smart Vendor-Audit Checklist," *Inc.* (April 1995), p. 93. Reprinted with permission, *Inc.* Magazine, April 1995. Copyright 1995 by Goldhirsh Group, Inc., 38 Commercial Wharf, Boston, MA 02110.

Even in St. Gallen, Switzerland, Levi Strauss is known for the high quality of its products.

quality control

statistical process control

control charts

builder of hot tubs in Chatsworth, California, indicates that the company does quality audits on its 200 vendors to ensure the quality of purchased materials.

Factors causing production redundancy include the need to reprocess, rework, replace, and repair those items that did not conform to specifications. The quality of the production process largely determines the product's failure rate, longevity, and breakage tendencies. Further, the amount of waste, rework, and scrap generated by production efforts is related to production process quality. Production technology, worker skill and training, and management programs can, in large part, control the quality of the production process. If the impediments to good production are reduced or eliminated, increases in productivity and higher quality products can be expected. Some techniques that increase productivity and enhance quality include having suppliers preinspect materials for quality, having employees monitor and be responsible for their own output, and fitting machinery for mistake-proof operations.

All attempts to reduce variability and defects in products reflect the implementation of **quality control** (QC). QC places the primary responsibility for the quality of a product or service at the source—the maker or provider. Many companies use **statistical process control** (SPC) techniques to analyze where fluctuations occur in the process. SPC is based on the theory that a process has natural variations over time, but that "errors," which can result in defective goods or poor service, are typically produced at points of uncommon variations. Often these variations are eliminated after the installation of computer-integrated manufacturing systems, which have internal controls to evaluate deviations and sense production problems.

To analyze the process variations, a variety of **control charts** are developed by recording the occurrences of some specified measure(s) of performance at preselected points in a process. Charts, such as the one shown in Exhibit 3–1, graph actual process results and indicate upper and lower control limits. For example, a process is considered to be in or out of control depending on how well results remain within established limits. The charts must be prepared consistently and accurately for an intelligent analysis to be made about the out-of-control items. Although the development and use of such charts is outside the scope of this text, the management accountant is directly involved in selecting appropriate performance measures and helping to interpret the charts. Often the measures selected to prepare control charts are nonfinancial, such as number of defective parts, amount of waste created, and time taken to complete a task. Selection of performance measures to investigate

VIDEO
VIGNETTE

Oregon Cutting Systems
(in AME—We're Getting Closer)

EXHIBIT 3–1

Control Chart

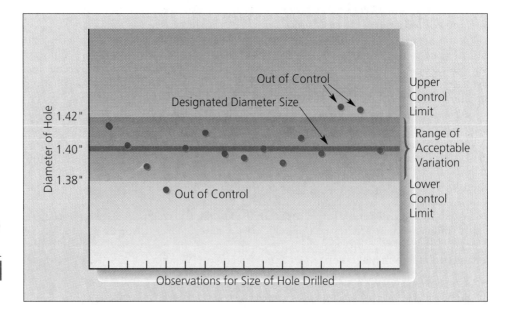

quality is further discussed in Chapters 20 and 21. In effect, using SPC causes a process to "talk" about what is occurring. If observers "listen," they can sometimes prevent potential out-of-control occurrences from happening.

Consumer View of Quality

Every customer who acquires a product or service receives a set of characteristics consisting of considerations such as range of features, convenience, promptness in delivery, warranty, credit availability, and packaging. The consumer's view of quality encompasses much more than whether the product or service delivers as it was intended, its rate of failure, or the probability of purchasing a defective unit. The customer perceives quality as the ability of a product or service to meet and satisfy all specified needs. Businesses entering markets dominated by quality producers must understand both their customers' quality expectations and their competition's quality standards. For example, when Cambex Corporation (Waltham, Massachusetts) began selling computers, it focused on the reliability and service effectiveness provided by IBM, Cambex's acknowledged lead competitor.

Exhibit 3–2 provides eight basic characteristics that would commonly be included in any customer's definition of product quality. An obvious difference exists between the first six and the last two quality characteristics: level of objectivity. The first six product quality characteristics can be reasonably evaluated through objective methods, whereas the last two are strictly subjective. Thus, the first six are significantly more susceptible to control by the organization providing the product than the final two.

High-quality service also has some commonly acknowledged characteristics. These important dimensions of service quality, presented in Exhibit 3–3, are key elements in ITT Sheraton's quality plan.

VIDEO VIGNETTE

Cambex Corporation (Blue Chip Enterprises) and/or Nypro (in AME—Going Global)

EXHIBIT 3–2

Characteristics of Product Quality

1. Performance—relates to a product's primary operating characteristics
2. Features—describes the secondary characteristics that supplement a product's basic function
3. Reliability—addresses the probability of a product's likelihood of performing within a specified period of time
4. Conformance—relates to the degree to which preestablished standards are matched by the product's performance and features
5. Durability—measures a product's economic and technical life
6. Serviceability—measures the ease with which the product is repaired
7. Aesthetics—relates to a product's appeal to the senses
8. Perceived quality—relates to image, brand names, and other indirect measures of quality

SOURCE: Reprinted from "What Does 'Product Quality' Really Mean?" by David Garvin, *Sloan Management Review* (Fall 1984), pp. 25–43 by permission of publisher. Copyright 1984 by the Sloan Management Review Association. All rights reserved.

EXHIBIT 3–3

Characteristics of Service Quality

- Reliability—the ability to provide what was promised, dependably and accurately
- Assurance—the knowledge and courtesy of employees, and their ability to convey trust and confidence
- Tangibles—the physical facilities and equipment, and the appearance of personnel
- Empathy—the degree of caring and individual attention provided to customers
- Responsiveness—the willingness to help customers and provide prompt service

SOURCE: A. Parasuraman, Leonard L. Berry, and Valarie Zeithaml, "Perceived Service Quality as a Customer-Based Performance Measure: An Empirical Examination of Organizational Barriers Using an Extended Service Quality Model," *Human Resource Management* 30(3) (Fall 1991), pp. 335–364.

grade

All customers cannot afford the same grade of product or service. **Grade** refers to the addition or removal of product or service characteristics to satisfy additional needs, especially price. Customers hope to maximize their satisfaction within the context of their willingness and ability to pay. They view a product or service as a

value

value when it meets the highest number of their needs at the lowest possible cost (cost includes purchase price plus the costs of operating, maintaining, and ultimate disposal of an item). Thus, although customers may have a collective vision of what constitutes "high quality," some of them may choose to accept a lower grade of product or service because it satisfies their functional needs at a lower cost.

To illustrate the difference between quality and grade, assume Mark Hennen is in the market for a new car. He needs the car to travel to and from work, run errands, and go on vacation and has determined that reliability, gas mileage, safety, and comfort are features that are most important to him. He may believe the Rolls Royce to be the highest grade of car available, but his additional needs are that the car be within his price range and that repair parts and maintenance be readily available and within his budget. Thus, he will search for the highest quality product of the grade that maximizes the set of remaining dimensions.

Customers often make quality determinations by comparing a product or service to an ideal level of a characteristic rather than to another product or service of the same type or in the same industry. For example, Sara Payne frequently stays at ITT Sheraton hotels on business trips. On a recent trip, she called a car rental agency to arrange for a car. Sara may compare the quality of service she received from the car rental agency with the high-quality service she typically receives from Sheraton rather than how well she was served in the past by another car rental company. Sara is unconcerned that car rental agency employees may not have had the same customer satisfaction training as Sheraton employees or that the Sheraton corporate culture is dedicated to high quality, whereas the car rental agency may not have yet made such a commitment. This type of comparison, when formalized in organizations, is called competitive benchmarking.

BENCHMARKING

benchmarking

Benchmarking means investigating, comparing, and evaluating a company's products, processes, and/or services against those of companies believed to be the "best in class." Such comparisons allow a company to understand another's production and performance methods, so that the first company can identify its strengths and weaknesses. Because each company has its own unique philosophy, products, and people, "copying" is neither appropriate nor feasible. Therefore, a company should attempt to imitate those ideas that are readily transferable, but, more importantly, to upgrade its own effectiveness and efficiency by improving on methods in use by others. Ethical considerations of benchmarking are presented in the following News Note.

Although benchmarking against direct competitors is necessary, it also creates the risk of becoming stagnant. To illustrate, General Motors, Chrysler, and Ford historically competitively benchmarked among themselves and, over time, their processes became similar. But then import competition came, which had totally different—and better—processes. It was like three club tennis players who all had similar levels of skill and who knew each other's games inside and out—and then Pete Sampras walked on the court.[5]

For this reason, additional comparisons should be made against companies that are the best in a specific characteristic rather than necessarily the best in a specific industry. Some examples of U.S. companies that are recognized as world-class leaders in certain disciplines are Allen-Bradley (flexible manufacturing), American Express (billing and collection), Disney (equipment maintenance), Federal Express (worker training), Levi Strauss (supplier management), and L. L. Bean (distribution and logistics).[6] It is against companies such as these as well as their international counter-

[5] Beth Enslow, "The Benchmarking Bonanza," *Across the Board* (April 1992), p. 20.
[6] "America's World-Class Champs," *Business Week* (November 30, 1992), pp. 74–75.

Benchmarking and Ethics

Since the responsible exchange of closely held information is an important part of what makes benchmarking a viable process, ethical and legal questions are paramount.

The process itself, however, can be self-policing, says Don Swire, director of research and development at the Strategic Planning Institute. Swire notes that if you go into a sophisticated company to benchmark, and you don't play by the rules, "then you don't know what benchmarking is all about." In the end, you look stupid as well as shady. Eric Thor, a benchmarking specialist at the International Benchmarking Clearinghouse, concurs: "If you want to do anything with these companies again, you'd better do it right."

The Council on Benchmarking, the Clearinghouse and other organizations have devised protocols and codes of conduct, which participants are expected to follow voluntarily. They center on issues of equal exchange, restricted use of learned data, and avoidance of anti-trust issues (no discussions on cost and price, and no illegalities such as bid rigging, bribery or price fixing). They also outline such courtesies as on-site visit and meeting preparation, adherence to agendas and third-party contact (obtaining permission before you give out a request for a contact's name).

Benchmarkers are concerned about how to value intellectual property—patented processes, specifically. Thor has put together two legal symposia for members thus far. "Knowing what to share and what not to share, how much something is worth to you, and how much to reveal and when to reveal it, is a main topic," he says.

Those traditionally sensitive "red zones" of discussion might be challenged by organizations as more of them become competent benchmarkers, says Michael J. Spendolini, a consultant and author of *The Benchmarking Book*. He contends that organizations "will become more aggressive in defining the range of acceptability" in selecting benchmarking topics.

SOURCE: Barbara Ettorre, "Ethics, Anti-Trust and Benchmarking," *Management Review* (June 1993), p. 13. Reprinted, by permission of publisher, from *Management Review* (June 1993) © 1993. American Management Association, New York. All rights reserved.

N E W S
N O T E

parts that others should benchmark. Exhibit 3–4 suggests some questions that need to be answered to provide the proper focus for benchmarking.

There are two types of benchmarking: results and process. In **results benchmarking,** the end product or service is examined and the focus is on product/service specifications and on performance results using a process called "reverse engineering." Results benchmarking helps companies determine which other companies are

results benchmarking

- Have you designed your benchmarking activities to improve competitiveness in the marketplace, customer-perceived quality versus competitors, market share, and business results? Or are you just fixing mistakes and errors?
- Do you focus on generating revenue, or on reducing costs—or on both? Don't answer "both" unless you can really track the impact of benchmarking and reengineering-derived ideas back to the actual revenues generated or costs reduced.
- Who should carry out this market-driven benchmarking? It should be the people who are going to have to implement the changes—the business general manager and an interfunctional team. They should go through a quality profiling process and list:
  a. What they think the key purchase criteria are—and will be.
  b. How important each quality attribute is (expressed as a percentage of 100).
  c. How they think customers perceive their business' performance and that of competitors on a scale of 1 to 10.

SOURCE: Bradley T. Gale, "Quality Profiling: The First Step in Reengineering and Benchmarking." This excerpt is reprinted from *Strategy & Leadership* (formerly *Planning Review*) May/June 1995 with permission from the Strategic Leadership Forum, The International Society for Strategic Management.

EXHIBIT 3–4

Some Questions about Benchmarking Activities

1. Determine the specific area in which improvements are desired and/or needed.

2. Select the characteristic that will be used to measure quality performance.

3. Identify the best-in-class companies based on quality characteristics. Remember that these companies do not have to be industry, product, or service specific.

4. Ask for cooperation from the best-in-class companies. This may be handled directly or through a consulting firm. Be prepared to share information and respect requests for confidentiality.

5. Have the people who are associated with the specific area being analyzed collect the needed information.

6. Analyze the "negative gap" between the company's product, process, or service and that of the best-in-class firm.

7. Act on the negative gap analysis and make improvements.

8. Do not become complacent. Strive for continuous improvement.

EXHIBIT 3–5

Steps in Benchmarking

VIDEO VIGNETTE

Xerox
(in AME—On the Road to Manufacturing Excellence)

process benchmarking

the "best in class." Chrysler uses two teardown facilities located at its product development centers to focus on competitors and to provide better interaction among engineering, design, and manufacturing. By studying design differences between its own and its competitors products, the firm seeks vital information to be researched for quality improvements.[7]

Focusing on the practices and the ways the best-in-class companies achieved their results is called **process benchmarking.** It is in this arena that noncompetitor benchmarking is extremely valuable. For example, after Xerox saw its market being eroded by the Japanese, the company found that one of its problem points was its warehousing and shipping functions. Recognizing that L. L. Bean, a catalog company, performed these functions extremely well, Xerox benchmarked against L. L. Bean and used that information to help redesign Xerox warehouses.[8]

The process of implementing benchmarking is detailed in Exhibit 3–5. Some companies have more steps and others have fewer, but all have a structured approach. Once the negative gap analysis is made, everyone in the firm is expected to work both toward closing that gap and toward becoming a best-in-class organization.

Through benchmarking, companies are working to improve their ability to deliver high-quality products from the perspectives of both how the products are made and how they are perceived by the customer. Integrating these two perspectives requires involvement of all organizational members in the implementation of a total quality management (TQM) system.

VIDEO VIGNETTE

Spectra-Physics (in AME—Lean Machines)

[7] Paul A. Stergar and James H. Cypher, "Teardown Keeps Chrysler Focused on the Competition," *Cost Management Insider's Report* (June 1995), pp. 12–13.
[8] Jeremy Main, "How to Steal the Best Ideas Around," *Fortune* (October 19, 1992), pp. 102–104.

All employees must be involved in a total quality management system. Involvement means empowering people to do their jobs and giving those individuals the appropriate tools and information to make empowerment viable.

Total quality management is a "management approach of an organization, centered on quality, based on the participation of all its members and aiming at long-term success through customer satisfaction, and benefits to all members of the organization and to society."[9] Thus, there are three important tenets of TQM:

1. It necessitates an internal managerial system of planning, controlling, and decision making.
2. It requires participation by everyone in the organization.
3. It focuses on improving goods and services from the customer's point of view.

The Quality System

The total quality movement requires the implementation of a system that provides information about the quality of processes so that managers can plan, control, evaluate performance, and make decisions. Consideration of quality has not historically been part of the planning process. More often it involved an after-the-fact measurement of errors because a certain level of defects was simply tolerated as part of the "natural" business process. Action was not triggered until a predetermined error threshold was exceeded.

In contrast, a total quality system should be designed to promote a reorientation of thinking from an emphasis on inspection to an emphasis on prevention, continuous improvement, and building quality into every process and product. This reorientation should indicate any existing quality problems so that managers can set goals and

TOTAL QUALITY MANAGEMENT

total quality management

[9] ISO 8402, *Total Quality Management* (1994), definition 3.7.

VIDEO
VIGNETTE

Rheaco Inc. (Blue Chip
Enterprises)

identify methods for quality improvements. The system should also be capable (possibly through the use of statistical methods) of measuring quality and providing feedback on quality improvements. Last, the system should encourage teamwork in the quality improvement process. In other words, the system should move an organization away from product inspection (finding and correcting problems at the end of the process) to proactive quality assurance (building quality into the process so that problems do not occur).

Employee Involvement

TQM recognizes that all organizational levels share the responsibility for product/service quality, and interactions among employee levels are changing the way managers do their jobs. Upper-level management must be involved in the quality process, develop an atmosphere that is conducive to quality improvements, set an example of commitment to TQM, and provide positive feedback when improvements are made. Workers should be made to feel as though they are part of the process of success, not the creators of problems. Encouraging employee suggestions and training workers to handle multiple job functions help improve efficiency and quality. At ITT Sheraton, for example, multifunctional work teams are commonly used to facilitate effective problem solving. Consider also the formation of teams at Boston's Published Image Inc., as discussed in the following News Note.

VIDEO
VIGNETTE

Devine Lighting, Inc. and/or
A.C. Peterson Farms, Inc. and/or
Russell's Service Ctr., Inc. (Blue
Chip Enterprises)

Product/Service Improvement

Total quality management focuses management attention on the relationship between the internal production/service process and the external customer. This approach has designated consumer expectations as the ultimate arbiter of satisfaction.

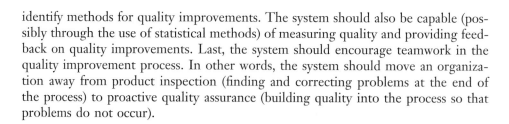

NEWS NOTE

It's Not a Game!

Published Image Inc. doesn't use the "game." Fine. But Published Image does have teams (with captains), coaches (instead of managers), and scoreboards (by which team members monitor their progress), all of which may indicate that the essence of game-playing lies not in the word but in the concept. For Published Image, at any rate, it's a whole new way of doing business.

[In 1993], says founder Eric Gershman, the company was in danger of growing itself to death. Newsletters-in-process moved laboriously from edit to art to production, hitting bottlenecks along the way. "People were working till one or two in the morning—but they were often sitting around waiting for other departments to do their jobs." The CEO decided drastic measures were in order.

In September [1993], Gershman told his employees to say goodbye to the old company. Henceforth, they would be working in teams—"little Published Images," as the boss put it. They would be responsible for their own clients' newsletters, start to finish.

Today teams with names like Quality Matters essentially run their businesses. A team salesperson lines up clients. Team operations people produce the product. Scoreboards in each team's area track numbers such as quarterly sales. A recently installed bonus system, pegged partly to sales and partly to quality scores, offers employees a "win" of up to 40% of salary. When a team reaches a certain level of output, it splits—and junior people on the old team can move into more senior positions on the new.

Since the changeover, says Gershman, earnings are up 35%, and the company's own customer-satisfaction measures are up 78%. But don't call it a game—even though the Quality Matters team will soon be installing a new, larger scoreboard.

SOURCE: John Case, "Games Companies Play," *Inc.* (October 1994), p. 52. Reprinted with permission, *Inc.* Magazine, October 1994. Copyright 1994 by Goldhirsh Group, Inc., 38 Commercial Wharf, Boston, MA 02110.

Therefore, TQM requires that companies first know who their customers are. ITT Sheration understands this basic premise and has virtually eliminated check-in and check-out time for guests who are ITT Sheraton Club International members by storing guest information in a reservation system.

In analyzing their customers, some companies may want to stop serving some groups of customers in line with cost-benefit analysis. Some customers simply cost more than they add in revenues and/or other benefits to the organization. The concept that shedding one or more sets of customers would be good for business is difficult to believe at first, but most organizations have some clients who drain, rather than improve, their ability to provide quality products and service.

Smart businesses pick customers—and learn from them. Although some customers consistently add value along several dimensions, other customers are value-subtractors: What they cost in time, money, and morale outstrips the prices they pay. Having the courage to identify, and then "fire" low-value customers is a healthy first step. It helps ensure that valued customers receive the best possible service and that potential customers recognize that the company cares about quality.[10]

After determining who its value-adding customers are, a company must then understand what those customers want. The primary characteristics currently desired by customers appear to be quality, value, and "good" service. Good service is an intangible; it means different things to different people. But most customers would agree that it is reflective of the interaction between themselves and organizational employees. "In the broadest sense, customer service is a group of processes that helps [an organization] handle inquiries, orders, complaints, and problems while enhancing the logistical, administrative, and distribution functions of [the] organization."[11] Frequently, only service quality separates one product from its competition.

Poor service can be disastrous. Data indicate that "70 percent of customers stop doing business with companies because of perceived rude or indifferent behavior by an employee—over three times the total for price or product quality (20 percent)."[12] Although instituting "customer service" programs can improve a company's image, such programs should not be taken to the extreme. As noted above, some customers are not cost-beneficial—often those demanding exorbitant service and not willing to pay the related price.

A company can increase its product and service quality by investing in **prevention costs,** which are intended to improve quality by preventing product defects resulting from dysfunctional processing. Amounts spent on improved production equipment, training, and engineering and modeling are considered prevention costs. Complementary to prevention costs are **appraisal costs,** which represent quality control costs incurred for monitoring; these costs compensate for mistakes not eliminated through prevention activities. Both of these costs can be expected to cause a reduction in another group of costs known as failure costs. **Failure costs** represent internal losses, such as scrap or rework, and external losses, such as warranty costs, handling customer complaints, litigation, or recalling defective products. The results of TQM indicate that the ultimate net effect of these cost trade-offs is an overall decline in costs. Also, by eliminating non-value-added activities and installing technologically advanced equipment, productivity will increase.

Lower costs mean that the company can contain (or reduce) selling prices; and customers, pleased with the higher quality at the same (or lower) price, perceive they have received value and will buy more. These factors create larger profits for the company. These profits can be reinvested in research and development activities to generate new high-quality products or services. Or the profits can be used to train

prevention cost

appraisal cost

failure cost

[10] Michael Schrage, "Fire Your Customers!" *Wall Street Journal* (March 16, 1992), p. A12.

[11] Jeffrey M. Margolies, "When Good Service Isn't Good Enough," *(Price Waterhouse) Review* (No. 3, 1988), pp. 25–26.

[12] Scott J. Simmerman, "Improving Customer Loyalty," *B & E (Business & Economic) Review* (April–June 1992), p. 4.

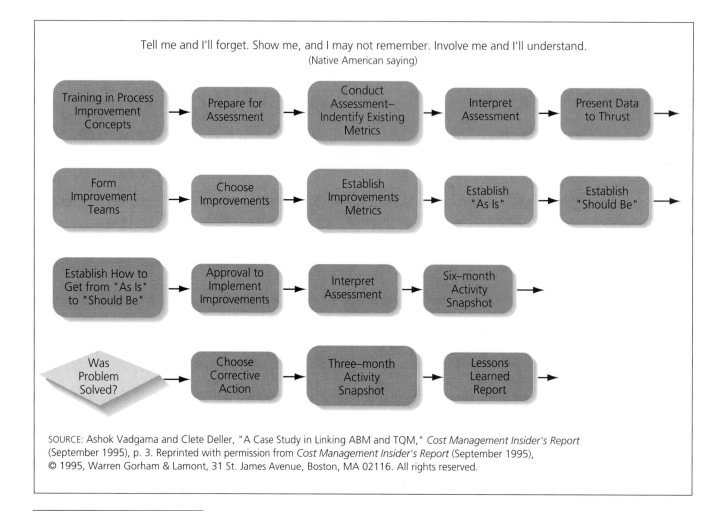

Tell me and I'll forget. Show me, and I may not remember. Involve me and I'll understand.
(Native American saying)

EXHIBIT 3–6

Generic Process
Improvement Methodology

workers to provide even higher quality products and services than are currently available. This cycle of benefit will continue in a company that is profitable and secure in its market share—two primary goals of an organization. Exhibit 3–6 presents a generic process improvement methodology used in training workers and conducting quality improvement projects.

QUALITY COSTS

VIDEO
VIGNETTE

Glacken Industries, Inc. (Blue
Chip Enterprises)

As mentioned in the previous section, the TQM philosophy indicates that total costs will decline, rather than increase, as quality improvements are made in an organization. *Zero defects* means that there is nothing to correct and customers are happy. Thus, total quality management also includes the idea that it is the *lack* of high quality that is expensive. Understanding the types and causes of quality costs can help managers prioritize improvement projects and provide feedback that supports and justifies improvement efforts.

Two types of costs comprise the total quality cost of a firm: (1) cost of quality compliance or assurance and (2) cost of noncompliance or quality failure. The cost of compliance equals the sum of prevention and appraisal costs. Compliance cost expenditures are incurred to eliminate the present costs of failure and maintain that

COSTS OF COMPLIANCE		COSTS OF NONCOMPLIANCE	
Prevention Costs	Appraisal Costs	Internal Failure	External Failure

Employees:

- Hiring for quality
- Providing training and awareness
- Establishing participation programs

Customers:

- Surveying needs
- Researching needs
- Conducting field trials

Machinery:

- Designing to detect defects
- Arranging for efficient flow
- Arranging for monitoring
- Incurring preventive maintenance
- Testing and adjusting equipment
- Fitting machinery for mistake-proof operations

Suppliers:

- Arranging for quality
- Educating suppliers
- Involving suppliers

Product Design:

- Developing specifications
- Engineering and modeling
- Testing and adjusting for conformity, effective and efficient performance, durability, ease of use, safety, comfort, appeal, and cost

Before Production:

- Receiving inspection

Production Process:

- Monitoring and inspecting
- Keeping the process consistent, stable, and reliable
- Using procedure verification
- Automating

During and After Production:

- Conducting quality audits

Information Process:

- Recording and reporting defects
- Measuring performance

Organization:

- Administering quality control department

Product:

- Reworking
- Having waste
- Storing and disposing
- Reinspecting rework

Production Process:

- Reprocessing
- Having unscheduled interruptions
- Experiencing unplanned downtime

Organization:

- Staffing complaint departments
- Staffing warranty claims departments

Customer:

- Losing future sales
- Losing reputation
- Losing goodwill

Product:

- Repairing
- Replacing
- Reimbursing
- Recalling
- Handling litigation

Service:

- Providing unplanned service
- Expediting
- Serving after purchase

EXHIBIT 3–7

Types of Quality Costs

zero level in the future; thus, they are proactive on management's part. Furthermore, effective use of prevention costs can even minimize the costs of appraisal. Alternatively, the cost of noncompliance results from production imperfections and is equal to internal and external failure costs. Exhibit 3–7 presents specific examples of each type of quality cost.

Information about production *quality* or lack thereof is contained in inspection reports, SPC control charts, and customer returns or complaints. Information about quality *costs*, on the other hand, is partially contained in the accounting records and supporting documentation. However, because the accounting records are commonly kept with an eye toward financial accounting, the behavior of quality costs relative to changes in activity as well as the appropriate drivers for these costs must be developed or estimated for quality management purposes. The need to estimate quality costs makes it essential for the management accountant to be involved in all activities—from system design to cost accumulation of quality costs.

Historically, quality costs have not been given separate recognition in the accounting system. In most instances, the cost of quality is "buried" in a variety of general ledger accounts, including Work in Process Inventory and Finished Goods Inventory (for rework, scrap, preventive maintenance, and other overhead costs), marketing/advertising expense (for product recall, image improvement after poor products were sold, or surveys to obtain customer information), personnel costs (for training), and engineering department costs (for engineering design change orders and redesign).

In determining the cost of quality, actual or estimated costs are identified for each item listed in Exhibit 3–7. If these costs were plotted on a graph, they would appear similar to the cost curves shown in Exhibit 3–8. If the firm spends larger amounts on prevention and appraisal costs, the number of defects is lower and the costs of failure are smaller. If less is spent on prevention and appraisal, the number of defects is greater and failure costs are larger. The external failure costs curve begins moving toward vertical when a certain number of defects are encountered by customers. The ultimate external failure cost is reached when customers will no longer buy a given product or any other products made by a specific firm because of the perception of poor quality work.

By developing a system in which quality costs are readily available or determinable, the management accountant is able to provide useful information to managers trying to make spending decisions by pinpointing the areas that would provide the highest cost-benefit relationships. Additionally, quality cost information will indicate how a shift in one or more curves will affect the others.

Exhibit 3–9 shows the location in the production-sales cycle where the types of quality costs are usually incurred. An information feedback loop (indicated by the bold line in this exhibit) should be in effect to link the types and causes of failure

EXHIBIT 3–8

Relationships among Quality Costs

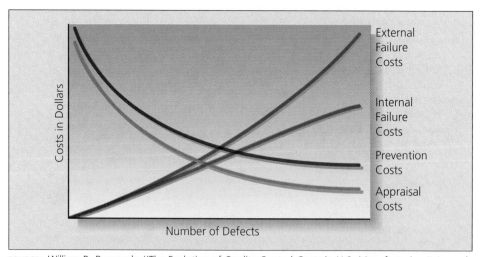

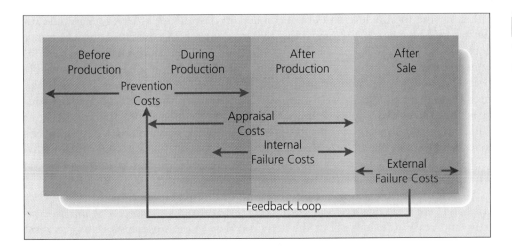

EXHIBIT 3–9

Time-Phased Model for
Quality Costs

costs to prevention costs to be subsequently incurred. Alert managers and employees continuously monitor the nature of failures to discover their causes and adjust prevention activities to close the gaps that allowed the failures to occur. These continuous rounds of action, reaction, and action are essential to continuous improvement initiatives.

Theoretically, if prevention and appraisal costs were prudently incurred, failure costs would become zero. However, prevention and appraisal costs would still be incurred to achieve zero failure costs. Thus, total quality costs can never be zero. This is not to disregard the knowledge that the benefits of increased sales and greater efficiency should exceed all remaining high quality costs. In this sense, the cost of high quality is free. Management needs to analyze the quality cost relationships and spend money for quality in ways that will provide the greatest benefit. Such an analysis requires that the cost of quality be measured to the extent possible and practical and the benefits of quality costs be estimated.

MEASURING THE COST OF QUALITY

Pareto analysis is one way management can decide where to concentrate its quality prevention cost dollars. This technique classifies the causes of process problems according to impact on an objective. For example, a company that makes refrigerators might subclassify its warranty claim costs for the past year according to the type of product failure as follows:

Pareto analysis

Cost of Type of Failure

MODEL	ELECTRICAL	MOTOR	STRUCTURAL	MECHANICAL	TOTAL DOLLARS
ZT 100	$14,000	$16,000	$13,000	$ 3,000	$ 46,000
MX 2000	11,000	14,000	7,000	3,000	35,000
All other	6,000	10,000	3,000	4,000	23,000
Total	$31,000	$40,000	$23,000	$10,000	$104,000

MODEL	DOLLARS	% OF TOTAL	CUMULATIVE % TOTAL
ZT 100	$ 46,000	44	44
MX 2000	35,000	34	78
All other	23,000	22	100
Total	$104,000	100	

Listing the total failure costs of all models in descending order of magnitude indicates that models ZT 100 and MX 2000 account for 78 percent of total warranty cost claims. Also, the largest single source of warranty claims cost is caused by problems with refrigerator motors. Therefore, management should focus efforts on further analysis on what causes models ZT 100 and MX 2000, and the motors on all models, to generate the greatest warranty claims costs. This knowledge permits management to devote the appropriate portion of its prevention efforts to minimizing or eliminating these specific problems. This kind of analysis should be conducted sufficiently often for trends to be detected quickly and adjustments to be made rapidly. ITT Sheraton uses Pareto analysis to prioritize service problems and, thus, focus on where to devote the majority of its problem-solving efforts.

A company desiring to engage in TQM and continuous improvement should record and report its quality costs separately so that managers can plan, control, evaluate, and make decisions about the activities that cause those costs. However, just having quality cost information available does not enhance quality. Managers and workers must consistently and aggressively use the information as a basis for creatively and intelligently advancing quality.

A firm's chart of accounts can be expanded to accommodate either separate tracing or allocating quality costs to new accounts. Exhibit 3–10 lists some suggested accounts that will help management focus on quality costs. Opportunity costs, including forgone future sales and a measure of the firm's loss of reputation, are also associated with poor quality. Although opportunity costs are real and may be estimated, they are not recorded in the accounting system because they do not result from specific transactions.

If the firm has a data-based management system, the information resulting from an expanded chart of accounts can alternatively be generated by coding transactions representing quality costs. Coding will permit these transaction types and amounts to be reformatted so that reports detailing the costs of quality can be provided as shown (using assumed numbers) in Exhibit 3–11. This report makes two important assumptions: stable production and a monthly reporting system. If wide fluctuations in production or service levels occur, period-to-period comparisons of absolute amounts may not be appropriate. Amounts may need to be converted to percentages to have any valid meaning. Additionally, in some settings (such as a just-in-time environment), a weekly reporting system would be more appropriate because of the need for continuous monitoring.

EXHIBIT 3–10

New Quality Accounts

PREVENTION COSTS	APPRAISAL COSTS
Quality Training	Quality Inspections
Quality Participation	Procedure Verifications
Quality Market Research	Measurement Equipment
Quality Technology	Test Equipment
Quality Product Design	

INTERNAL FAILURE COSTS	EXTERNAL FAILURE COSTS
Reworking Products	Complaints Handling
Scrap and Waste	Warranty Handling
Storing and Disposing Waste	Repairing and Replacing Returns
Reprocessing	Customer Reimbursements
Rescheduling and Setup	Expediting

	COST OF CURRENT PERIOD	COST OF PRIOR PERIOD	% CHANGE FROM PRIOR PERIOD	CURRENT PERIOD BUDGET	% CHANGE FROM BUDGET
PREVENTION COSTS					
Quality Training	$ 4,700	$ 4,500	+ 4	$ 5,000	− 6
Quality Participation	8,200	8,400	− 2	8,000	+ 3
Quality Market Research	11,000	8,800	+25	12,000	− 8
Quality Technology	9,600	10,800	− 11	15,000	− 36
Quality Product Design	16,600	12,200	+36	16,500	+ 1
Total	$ 50,100	$ 44,700	+12	$56,500	− 11
APPRAISAL COSTS					
Quality Inspections	$ 3,300	$ 3,500	− 6	$ 3,000	+ 10
Procedure Verifications	1,200	1,400	− 14	1,500	− 20
Measurement Equipment	2,700	3,000	− 10	3,200	− 16
Test Equipment	1,500	1,200	+25	1,500	0
Total	$ 8,700	$ 9,100	− 4	$ 9,200	− 5
INTERNAL FAILURE COSTS					
Reworking Products	$ 8,500	$ 8,300	+ 2	N/A*	
Scrap and Waste	2,200	2,400	− 8	N/A	
Storing and Disposing Waste	4,400	5,700	−23	N/A	
Reprocessing	1,800	1,600	+13	N/A	
Rescheduling and Setup	900	1,200	−25	N/A	
Total	$ 17,800	$ 19,200	− 7		
EXTERNAL FAILURE COSTS					
Complaints Handling	$ 5,800	$ 6,200	− 6	N/A	
Warranty Handling	10,700	9,300	+15	N/A	
Repairing and Replacing Returns	27,000	29,200	− 8	N/A	
Customer Reimbursements	12,000	10,700	+12	N/A	
Expediting	1,100	1,300	− 15		
Total	$ 56,600	$ 56,700	+ 0		
Total Quality Costs	$133,200	$129,700	+ 3	$65,700	+103

*TQM advocates planning for zero defects; therefore, zero failure costs would be included in the budget.

EXHIBIT 3–11

Cost of Quality Report

Exhibit 3–12 provides formulas for calculating an organization's total cost of quality, using prevention, appraisal, and failure categories. Some amounts used in these computations are, by necessity, estimates; however, it is a well-accepted approach in business to use reliable estimates rather than choosing not to perform the calculations because of the lack of verifiable or precise amounts. This situation reflects the idea discussed in Chapter 1 that management accountants are more apt to use estimated figures than financial accountants because of management's need for timely, rather than totally precise, information.

Consider the following July 1997 operating information for the Lee Company:

Defective units (D)	1,200	Units reworked (Y)	600
Profit for good unit (P_1)	$25	Profit for defective unit (P_2)	$15
Cost to rework defective unit (r)	$5	Defective units returned (D_r)	200
Cost of return (w)	$8	Prevention cost (K)	$30,000
Appraisal cost (A)	$6,200		

EXHIBIT 3–12

Formulas for Calculating
Total Quality Cost

CALCULATING LOST PROFITS

Profit Lost by Selling Units as Defects = (Total Defective Units − Number of Units
Reworked) × (Profit for Good Unit − Profit for Defective Unit)

$$Z = (D - Y)(P_1 - P_2)$$

CALCULATING TOTAL INTERNAL COSTS OF FAILURE

Rework Cost = Number of Units Reworked × Cost to Rework Defective Unit

$$R = (Y)(r)$$

Cost of Processing Customer Returns = Number of Defective Units Returned × Cost
of a Return

$$W = (D_r)(w)$$

Total Failure Cost = Profit Lost by Selling Units as Defects + Rework Cost + Cost of
Processing Customer Returns

$$F = Z + R + W$$

CALCULATING THE TOTAL QUALITY COST

Total Quality Cost = Defect Control Cost + Total Failure Cost

$$T = (\text{Prevention Cost} + \text{Appraisal Cost}) + \text{Total Failure Cost}$$
$$T = K + A + F$$

Prevention and appraisal costs are total estimated amounts; no formulas are
appropriate. As the cost of prevention rises, the number of defective units should
decline. Additionally, as the cost of prevention rises, the cost of appraisal should
decline; however, appraisal cost should never become zero.

SOURCE: James T. Godfrey and William R. Pasewark, "Controlling Quality Costs," *Management Accounting* (March 1988), p. 50. Reprinted from *Management Accounting.* Copyright by Institute of Management Accountants, Montvale, NJ.

Substituting these values into the formulas provided in Exhibit 3–12 provides the following results:

$$Z = (D - Y)(P_1 - P_2) = (1{,}200 - 600)(\$25 - \$15) = \$6{,}000$$

$$R = (Y)(r) = (600)(\$5) = \$3{,}000$$

$$W = (D_r)(w) = (200)(\$8) = \$1{,}600$$

$$F = Z + R + W = \$6{,}000 + \$3{,}000 + \$1{,}600 = \$10{,}600 \text{ total failure cost}$$

$$T = K + A + F = \$30{,}000 + \$6{,}200 + \$10{,}600 = \$46{,}800 \text{ total quality cost}$$

Of the total quality cost of $46,800, Lee Company managers will seek to identify the causes of the $10,600 failure costs and work to eliminate them. The results may also affect the planned amounts of prevention and appraisal costs for future periods.

High quality allows a company to improve current profits, either through lower costs or, if the market will bear, higher prices. But management is often more interested in business objectives other than short-run profits. An example of an alternative, competing objective is that of increasing the company's market share. Indeed, if increasing market share were an objective, management could combine the strategies of increasing quality while lowering prices to attract a larger market share.

When quality is increased by giving greater attention to prevention and appraisal activities, overall costs decline and productivity increases. Lower costs and greater productivity support lower prices that, in turn, often stimulate demand. The result is greater market share, higher long-run profits, and, perhaps, even greater immediate profits.

Any quality program should seek to meet the following three objectives:

- The organization should achieve and sustain the quality of the product or service produced so as to continuously meet the purchaser's stated or implied needs.
- The organization should give its own management confidence that the intended quality level is being achieved and sustained.
- The organization should give the purchaser confidence that the intended quality level is, or will be, achieved in the delivered product or service. When contractually required, this assurance may involve agreed demonstration requirements.[13]

The embodiment of TQM in the United States is the Malcolm Baldrige National Quality Award. This award focuses attention on management systems, processes, and consumer satisfaction as the tools required to achieve product and service excellence. There are three categories of entrants: manufacturing, service, and small business. To win the award, applicants must show excellence in the seven categories shown in Exhibit 3–13.

After 1992, organizational quality results must be demonstrated by entrants who detail their quality "programs' effects in areas such as reducing waste, speeding products to market, improving employee satisfaction and contributing to 'national and community well-being.'"[14] The following News Note provides information on why the Baldrige Award is being embraced by corporate America.

THE QUALITY GOAL

VIDEO VIGNETTE

Athletic Bag Corp. (Blue Chip Enterprises)

Quality Increases Mean Cost Decreases

NEWS NOTE

[T]he Baldrige has become a standard of excellence for quality-improvement at U.S. firms. Winning it signifies that your products or services are among the world's best—an honor that boosts employee morale and vastly improves a company's reputation among customers and shareholders.

"As the country becomes more quality conscious, we'll be able to do two things: replace foreign imports (with U.S.-made goods) . . . and really build our exports," says Commerce Secretary Robert Mosbacher.

U.S. companies still waste billions of dollars on poor quality: retyping memos, repairing finished goods or reworking products in poorly designed plants. (In 1989, IBM paid $2.4 billion on warranties.) If every U.S. firm mastered quality, the gross national product—[climbing in 1990] at less than 1% a year—would soar 7 percentage points or more, says a study by Armand Feigenbaum, a quality consultant and Baldrige Award overseer. "Those figures don't surprise me at all," says Fred Smith (Federal Express chairman). "Quality is not only extremely important to customers. It's also the best way to lower costs."

SOURCE: John Hillkirk and Micheline Maynard, "Baldrige Sets Standard of Excellence," *USA Today* (October 11, 1990), pp. 1B, 2B. Copyright 1990, *USA TODAY*. Reprinted with permission.

---

[13] A. Faye Borthick and Harold P. Roth, "Will Europeans Buy Your Company's Products?" *Management Accounting* (July 1992), pp. 28–29.
[14] Gilbert Fuchsberg, "Baldrige Awards Give More Weight to Results," *Wall Street Journal* (February 24, 1992), p. B1.

Baldrige Quality Award
1996 Criteria–Items

VIDEO
VIGNETTE

Cadillac
(in AME—We're Getting Closer)
and/or Motorola—The First
Baldrige Award (AME)

1996 CATEGORIES/ITEMS	POINT VALUES
1.0 LEADERSHIP	**90**
1.1 Senior Executive Leadership	45
1.2 Leadership System and Organization	25
1.3 Public Responsibility and Corporate Citizenship	20
2.0 INFORMATION AND ANALYSIS	**75**
2.1 Management of Information and Data	20
2.2 Competitive Comparisons and Benchmarking	15
2.3 Analysis and Use of Company-Level Data	40
3.0 STRATEGIC PLANNING	**55**
3.1 Strategy Development	35
3.2 Strategy Deployment	20
4.0 HUMAN RESOURCE DEVELOPMENT AND MANAGEMENT	**140**
4.1 Human Resource Planning and Evaluation	20
4.2 High Performance Work Systems	45
4.3 Employee Education, Training, and Development	50
4.4 Employee Well-Being and Satisfaction	25
5.0 PROCESS MANAGEMENT	**140**
5.1 Design and Introduction of Products and Services	40
5.2 Process Management: Product and Service Production and Delivery	40
5.3 Process Management: Support Services	30
5.4 Management of Supplier Performance	30
6.0 BUSINESS RESULTS	**250**
6.1 Product and Service Quality Results	75
6.2 Company Operational and Financial Results	110
6.3 Human Resource Results	35
6.4 Supplier Performance Results	30
7.0 CUSTOMER FOCUS AND SATISFACTION	**250**
7.1 Customer and Market Knowledge	30
7.2 Customer Relationship Management	30
7.3 Customer Satisfaction Determination	30
7.4 Customer Satisfaction Results	160
TOTAL POINTS	1000

SOURCE: "Malcolm Baldrige National Quality Award 1996 Award Criteria," United States Department of Commerce, Technology Administration, National Institute of Standards and Technology.

Applicants are not judged on financial measures such as profits—in fact, one of the award winners (Wallace Company of Houston, Texas) filed for Chapter 11 bankruptcy after receiving the award. Part of this exclusion of financial measures from consideration is based on the fact that different accounting practices can produce significantly different financial statement results and, therefore, intercompany comparisons may not be appropriate. In addition, because applicants do not have to be publicly held, the same financial information is not available for all.

Japan's equivalent of the Malcolm Baldrige National Quality Award is the Deming Prize. This award, named for the late W. Edwards Deming, has even more rigorous requirements than those for the Baldrige Award. Globally, the quality movement has progressed to the point that certain quality standards have been set, although these are not at the level of either the Baldrige Award or the Deming Prize.

Most large companies view their markets on an international, rather than a domestic, basis. To compete effectively in a global environment, companies must recognize and be willing to initiate compliance with a variety of standards outside their domestic borders. Standards are essentially the international language of trade; they are formalized agreements that define the various contractual, functional, and technical requirements that assure customers that products, services, processes, and/or systems do what they are expected to do.

A primary international guideline for quality standards is the **ISO 9000** series. In 1987, the International Organization for Standardization, based in Geneva, Switzerland, developed a comprehensive list of quality standards known as the ISO 9000 series. The series of three compliance standards (ISO 9001, 9002, and 9003) and two guidance standards (ISO 9000 and 9004) resulted from discussions among quality standards boards of 91 countries. These directives are written in a general manner and prescribe the generic design, material procurement, production, quality control, and delivery procedures necessary to achieve quality assurance.[15] These directives are not product standards and do not imply that companies using them have better products than competitors. The standards articulate what must be done to assure quality, but management must decide how to meet the standards. Exhibit 3–14 indicates the coverage of each of the five standards. At the time of this writing, a new voluntary ISO standard, not part of the 9000 series, dealing with setting guidelines regarding environmental responsibilities, is expected to be issued. It is to be known as ISO 14000.

For some companies, ISO 9000 registration is required for regulated products to be sold in the European Union. Furthermore, the European Union is emphasizing

INTERNATIONAL QUALITY STANDARDS

ISO 9000

EXHIBIT 3–14

Content of ISO 9000 Standards

STANDARD #	CONTENT
9000	Provides guidelines selection and use of the entire ISO standard series and explains basic quality terms and ideas; covers documentation, organizational quality objectives and responsibilities, process assurance, and management review and audit of the quality system
9001	Covers requirements for conformance during product design, production, installation, and servicing; is applicable to architectural, engineering, construction, and manufacturing companies
9002	Provides a model for assuring quality when only production and installation conformance is required; is applicable to companies in which product requirements are stated relative to established designs or specifications (such as chemical, foods, and pharmaceutical companies); ISO 9002 differs from ISO 9001 only because ISO 9001 includes the design function, whereas ISO 9002 does not
9003	Provides a model for assuring quality when only final inspection and testing conformance is required; is applicable to companies (or internal organizational units) that inspect and test the products they supply (such as laboratories)
9004	Provides guidelines related to a company's internal quality management and developing and implementing a quality system; discusses the technical, administrative, and human factors that affect product and service quality

---

[15] The ISO 9000 standards are equivalent to the American Society for Quality Control (ASQC) Q-90 quality series that was issued in 1987. Companies that currently meet the Q-90 standards also meet the ISO 9000 standards.

**N E W S
N O T E**

ISO 9000 Goes to Brazil

Brazilian companies have recognized the importance of registering for international quality standards as a way to penetrate foreign markets and improve competitiveness. By March of [1995], 612 companies in Brazil achieved ISO 9000 registration, the largest number in Latin America. Chemical companies accounted for 20% of the total, with 50 companies registered.

Brazil's chemical industry association, Abiquim, has played a leading role in this process since 1991. José Simanantob, Abiquim's manager of quality, says some multinational players such as Rhodia (Sao Paulo) have started to select suppliers based on ISO 9000 registration. While few firms in the U.S. or Europe limit their business to registered suppliers, this trend is expected to be adopted more generally in Latin America, leading to a domino effect for ISO 9000 registration.

Inmetro, the agency with responsibility for registrar accreditation in Brazil, has accredited several groups, including Instituto Brasileiro de Qualidade Nuclear, Fundacao Vanzolini, American Bureau of Shipping Quality Evaluation, and Bureau Veritas Quality Insurance.

SOURCE: "ISO 'Domino Effect' Spreads South," *Chemical Week* (April 19, 1995), p. 76.

Priority Mfg. (Blue Chip Enterprises)

quality audit

ISO 9000 registration as one of its goals.[16] Unfortunately, there is no international organization that administers the program. Thus, companies seeking ISO registration have to qualify under an internationally accepted registration program that is administered by a national registrar. Examples of such registrars in the United States and Great Britain are, respectively, Underwriters Laboratories and the British Standards Institution. The above News Note demonstrates the spread of and regard for ISO 9000 in Latin America.

After an internal review, a company deciding that it can meet the standards may apply for ISO registration. To be registered, a company must first submit to a quality audit by a third-party reviewer. A **quality audit** involves a review of product design activities (not performed for individual products), manufacturing processes and controls, quality documentation and records, and management quality policy and philosophy. Quality audits to determine compliance are quite expensive, costing between $800 to $3,000 per person-day plus expenses. Audit teams usually consist of between two and six people who work up to ten days between the initial review and follow-up. After registration, teams visit the company biannually to monitor compliance.

Although the costs are high, companies becoming certified believe the benefits are even higher. Externally, companies certified under ISO 9000 will have an important distinguishing characteristic from their noncertified competitors. Additionally, certified companies are listed in a registry of "approved" suppliers, which should increase business opportunities. Internally, certification will help ensure higher process consistency and quality and should help to reduce costs. The cost-benefit relationships of the quality system must be measured, documented, and reported under ISO 9000—all jobs for management accountants.

The ISO standards are not required to do business in the United States, but should be investigated for possible implementation even by companies that do not sell overseas because of the operational and competitive benefits. And, naturally, if a company's competitors are in compliance with and registered under ISO standards, good business sense would indicate the necessity of becoming ISO certified.

[16] James Kolke, "European Union Conformity Assessment," in Fairfax, Virginia, *The ISO 9000 Handbook*, 2nd ed., editor, Robert W. Peach (Irwin Professional Publishing, 1995), p. 344.

Although ISO certification is not required to do business in the U.S., some companies (such as the Baton Rouge Plastic Plant of Exxon Chemical Company) are justifiably proud of their accomplishments and want others to be aware of the quality achievement they have gained.

The ISO standards are also becoming a part of certain U.S. federal rules and regulations. For example, in revising the 1978 Good Manufacturing Practices, the Food and Drug Administration began aligning those standards with ISO 9001 standards by making certain design control and service elements mandatory.

Quality, propelled by changing customer needs and better competition, must be viewed as a moving target; therefore, TQM is inseparable from the concept of continuous improvement. Higher and higher performance standards must be set for everyone in the organization (not just the production people) to provide the sense of working toward a common goal. This philosophy is expressed in the accompanying News Note.

QUALITY AS AN ORGANIZATIONAL CULTURE

Staying Smart Is Their Greatest Challenge

[Consultants Michael Treacy and Fred Wiersema] show that it's not the company with the best product that's going to win—or in other markets, the company with the lowest costs or the one with the best total solution to a customer's problem. Whatever a company does to create customer value, it's not how well it performs today that matters in the long run but how good it is at learning to do it better. For instance, Treacy and Wiersema cite Cott Corp., a beverage company that doesn't make, bottle, or distribute soft drinks. Cott is what Treacy and Wiersema call a customer-intimate company, because it strives to provide ever more comprehensive solutions to its customers' needs. Cott, they write, "uses its knowledge of soft drinks to design and implement sophisticated private-label branding strategies for customers like Wal-Mart and Safeway." Cott consists largely of a bunch of smart people who know how to create and deliver profitable branded retail products, which are what its customers are looking for.

SOURCE: Tom Richman, "What Does Business Really Want from Government?" *The State of Small Business 1995*, p. 96.

NEWS NOTE

V I D E O
VIGNETTE

Portraits in Executive Excellence
(AME)

The behavior of managers and employees comprise the basis for TQM. Consistent and committed top management leadership is the catalyst for moving the company culture toward an esprit de corps in which all individuals, regardless of rank or position, are obsessed with exceeding customer expectations. Such an attitude should also permeate everything a company does, including customer relations, marketing, research and development, product design, production, and information processing. Management can effectively induce change in its organizational culture by providing an environment in which employees know the company cares about them, is responsive to their needs, and will appreciate and reward excellent results. This knowledge goes a long way in motivating employees toward greater cooperation and making them feel trusted, respected, and comfortable. Such employees are more likely to treat customers in a similar manner.

The firm must empower employees to participate fully in the quest for excellence in quality by providing the means by which employees gain pride, satisfaction, and substantive involvement. Encouragement, training, job enhancement, and the proper working environment and tools are what managers must provide. Employees should be recognized with praise and reward for being involved in group problem solving, contributing ideas for improvement, acting as monitors of their own work, and sharing their knowledge and enthusiastic attitudes with their colleagues. The true importance of empowerment is discussed in the following News Note.

With its focus on process and customers, TQM is founded on one very obvious and simple principle: Do the right things right the first time. The heart of this principle is zero defects now and in the future. For example, a non-TQM production policy statement might read: "Do not allow defective production to be greater than one percent of total production." In contrast, total quality management would have the policy statement: "There will be zero defective production." It follows that management's responsibility is to provide employees with the training, equipment, and quality of materials and other resources to meet this objective.

Exhibit 3–15 depicts the quality continuum along which companies move toward achieving world-class status. This continuum indicates that, at the most basic level

N E W S
N O T E

Empowering Employees Is an Ethical Business Practice

Making employees more involved in and responsible for their work activities increases the value of those individuals not only to the organization, but also to themselves and to society as a whole. The organizational benefits gained from empowerment are that employees have a sense of ownership of and work harder toward goals they have set for themselves. Thus, employee involvement automatically promotes a higher degree of effort on the part of the work force. We avoid the basis of the Marxist critique of capitalism: the exploitation and subsequent alienation and rebellion of the worker. Problems will be solved more quickly and, therefore, the cost of errors will be reduced.

Providing training to employees for improving skills and/or decision making results in a person who is a more valuable and productive member of the company and society. Additionally, empowered employees are less likely to become bored and should experience more job satisfaction. Lastly, empowering employees provides a valuable means by which people's "timeless quest to express [themselves] and establish [their] individuality [is] furthered in the face of a world that is becoming more complex and more dependent on technology." Maslow's pinnacle of his hierarchy of need is achieved as well: self-actualization.

SOURCE: Cecily Raiborn and Dinah Payne, "TQM: Just What the Ethicist Ordered," *Journal of Business Ethics* (Vol. 15, Number 9, 1996), p. 969.

SOURCE: Reprinted by permission from Grant Thornton, *Survey of American Manufacturers* (New York, 1992), p. 20. Copyright 1992.

EXHIBIT 3–15

Quality Continuum

of quality assurance, a company simply inspects to find defective products or monitors employees and surveys customers after the fact to find poor service. Implementation of a variety of quality control techniques in the system to eliminate the possibilities of defective products or poor service means that the company has become quality conscious. When the company's (or a division of the company's) quality system has progressed to a high level of sophistication, the company (or division) may choose to compete against others for formal quality recognition. Finally, when the concept of quality has become a distinct element of the organizational culture and tolerances for defective products or poor service are set at zero percent, the company has achieved world-class status and can be viewed as the benchmark for others. But achieving world-class status does not mark an ending point. TQM is not a static concept; when one problem has been solved, another one is always waiting for a solution.

VIDEO
VIGNETTE

Barefoot Grass Lawn Service
(Blue Chip Enterprises)

QUALITY IN NOT-FOR-PROFIT ORGANIZATIONS[17]

Although quality improvements allow businesses to raise profits, it is the decreased cost effect of such improvements that primarily benefits not-for-profit (NFP) organizations. These organizations were formed for one of three purposes: to accomplish a task specified by a governmental entity; to provide a public service; or to influence public-sector or private-sector policy. The organizations are funded either by tax dollars or through contributions, so it is in the public interest that the dollars invested be used in the most effective and efficient manner possible. However, instituting quality improvements in NFP organizations is slightly more complicated than in for-profit ones because of four distinctive characteristics.

First, determining the goals and objectives of a not-for-profit organization may be easier than in a for-profit company, but this characteristic may hinder rather than help the quest for quality. For-profit (FP) organizations typically express their goals in broad, customer-focused terms, which allow expansion into new service areas when opportunities are presented. A not-for-profit firm may have a single, directed focus that hampers its ability to change as the operating environment changes. For example, if the organization's purpose is to find a cure for a specific disease, finding the cure eliminates the need for the organization. Such uncertainty about longevity impedes the NFP organizations' ability to institute long-range plans for quality improvements because, as Raymond Marlow (president of Marlow Industries, a Dallas, Texas, Baldrige-winning company) says, "'You've got to have patience, because it's

[17] The authors are grateful to Dr. Ernest Nordtvedt for his assistance in the preparation of this section.

going to take time to [implement TQM].' He believes that it takes a couple of years before employees can work together smoothly in problem-solving teams."[18]

Second, determining whether goals and objectives have been achieved (measuring performance) is more difficult in NFP organizations than in FP ones. Many goals and objectives in FP companies are measured in quantifiable, often financial, terms. For example, decreasing the cost of producing Part X is a common, measurable goal of a for-profit entity. In a NFP organization, goals may be stated so broadly—to avoid alienating donors—that they may not be measurable at all. Goals such as "to improve the community in which we live" are commendable, but are impossible to measure in any quantifiable way. As noted earlier in the chapter, measurement must be available to know when nonconformance exists. An inability to measure accomplishment obviously makes recognizing achievement significantly more difficult.

Third, judging quality is more difficult in the not-for-profit organization than in the for-profit company. Quality in the FP company is deemed to reflect customer satisfaction, which can be measured by repeat business, new customers, and lack of customer complaints. Quality in the NFP organization must reflect customer/client and donor satisfaction and is subject to individual interpretation among the organization's several constituencies. In the NFP organization, customers/clients often do not pay for a service and will avail themselves of it *regardless* of the level of satisfaction. Donors, who fund the NFP organization's ability to provide the service, may not avail themselves of it and may not know or care about its quality. Thus, the NFP organization may be able to satisfy one group without satisfying the other. This situation creates the inevitable conflict: which of the two groups should receive priority in terms of satisfaction? If the customer/client receives priority, the donors may discontinue support and, thus, cause the service to be eliminated. If the donors receive priority, the customers may stop using the service or find alternatives. This situation may eliminate the need for the service or shift responsibility to another organization supported by different donors who may or may not be able to bear the increased financial burden.

Fourth, because of the more permanent investment base provided by stockholders (and, to some extent, creditors), for-profit organizations frequently have more time to achieve success than do not-for-profit organizations. FP firms can take years to design, test, and produce a new product, but NFP organizations must meet public needs in the present or they will not exist in the future. As mentioned previously, implementing TQM programs takes substantial time; for instance, H. J. Heinz took 8 years to cut its cost of quality by 60 percent. An additional 50 percent reduction is planned for the years 1992 through 1996.[19] Many NFP donors would not continue their contributions over a 12-year period unless service results were being achieved currently. Therefore, the planning horizon (like the definition of customer satisfaction) may be uncertain: even as the NFP organization provides service in the short term, it must focus on the longer-term quality issue of customer satisfaction. Attempts to improve quality often require short-run expenditures, leading to requests for increased donations and causing contribution cutbacks because donors believe the organization does not know how to manage its funds—and the downdraft spirals.

These problematic issues should not be used as reasons to justify why TQM cannot be implemented in NFP organizations. The benefit of reduced costs that is derived from quality improvements should be of equal, if not of more, importance to NFP organizations than to FP companies. For example, a process may be redesigned to improve its efficiency and the quality of the work. As output is received by one employee from another, its quality can be measured by the presence or absence of

---

[18] Michael Barrier, "Small Firms Put Quality First," *Nation's Business* (May 1992), p. 24.
[19] "Quantifying Quality Improvement Efforts Leads to Reduced Costs, Increased Profits," *(Grant Thornton) Manufacturing Issues* (Spring 1991), p. 2.

defects. Just as the reduced costs allow the FP company to hold the line on price increases or to reduce prices, reduced costs in the NFP organization should provide the donors or taxpayers the advantage of holding the line on increased spending for ongoing programs. For donor-based organizations, this advantage could mean the ability to do more for more people than previously; for the government (the largest not-for-profit organization in the United States), this advantage could mean the ability to begin to manage some out-of-control spending.

REVISITING

ITT Sheraton Corporation

The 1980s marked the realization of the "new Sheraton," a worldwide company with a global reputation for service excellence and quality. Under the leadership of John Kapioltas, Sheraton's chairman, president, and chief executive officer, the company received international recognition as an industry innovator.

The 1980s also saw a number of industry initiatives by Sheraton. In 1985, Sheraton became the first international hotel chain to operate a hotel in the People's Republic of China bearing its own name—The Great Wall Sheraton Hotel Beijing. This was followed by the 1986 signing of the first western management agreement in the East Bloc, the Sheraton Sofia Hotel Balkan in Bulgaria.

Serving 25 million guests each year at properties on five continents around the world, ITT Sheraton has properties in more countries under a single brand than any other lodging company.

In the 1990s, ITT Sheraton has focused on improving the quality and service standards of its domestic operations. Over a billion dollars of renovation and construction work at Sheraton properties in North America was completed in 1992. The projects—at hotels in New York City, Toronto, Miami, Dallas, San Francisco, Los Angeles, Hartford, and Kauai—are part of an overall plan to strengthen ITT Sheraton's presence in important business centers across the country. The investment continues, with a host of major projects completed since 1992 at hotels in locations including San Diego, Bal Harbour, Florida, Washington D.C., Chicago, and Los Angeles.

ITT Sheraton is developing a worldwide corporate culture focused on quality. This culture includes formal quality training at all organizational levels, group problem solving by employees comprising multilevel and multifunctional teams, and use of state-of-the-art technology and quality tools and techniques. This corporate culture is dedicated to meeting or exceeding customer needs and to continuously improving service processes. A number of initiatives are underway or are fully implemented to enhance customer satisfaction at ITT Sheraton. These include working desks in guest rooms, in-room computer hook-ups, personalized guest telephone greeting and retrieval messages, virtual elimination of check-in and check-out processes for regular guests choosing these services, a 30-minute room service guarantee, and a number of other business traveler enhancements such as secretarial services, copy and facsimile access, and mailing services.

SOURCE: ITT Sheraton, 1995.

CHAPTER SUMMARY

Continuous quality improvement is essential to survival in the global marketplace. Quality is defined as conformity to requirements as judged by customers. Total quality management is a system involving all company personnel in the pursuit of a continuous improvement process that exceeds customer expectations.

The shared planning and decision making among personnel required by TQM is changing the way managers perform their jobs. Enhanced technology in hardware, production processes, and management systems has made the new quality initiatives possible. Consumers are aware of greater variety by type and quality of products, and they discriminate in their purchases with regard to price, quality, service, and lead time. This intensified competition has motivated producers to adopt a more dynamic attitude about quality improvement and has heightened the use of competitive benchmarking to close any performance gaps.

Quality compliance costs include the costs of prevention and of appraisal. Noncompliance costs are separated into internal and external failure costs. Quality compliance costs are incurred to eliminate the current costs of quality failure and to maintain that zero level in the future.

Productivity is measured by the number of good units generated during a period. Improving quality essentially increases productivity because quality improvement works to remove factors that slow down or halt the production process or that require production redundancy. Eliminating non-value-added activities also increases productivity.

Theoretically, quality can be said to be free if its benefits exceed its costs. However, management should still measure quality costs so that managers have specific information to plan, control, evaluate, and make decisions in a continuous improvement environment.

The Malcolm Baldrige National Quality Award focuses attention on management systems, processes, and consumer satisfaction as the tools to achieve excellence. To compete internationally in the European Union, some companies must comply with the ISO 9000 series of quality standards for regulated products. There are five standards that can serve as guidelines for any company desiring to improve quality.

Assessing quality in a not-for-profit entity is more difficult than in a for-profit firm. Consumers often are not paying for the service and will avail themselves of it regardless of the level of satisfaction. Donors to the NFP may not know of the quality of the organization's services. NFP organizations must perform satisfactorily in the present, or they will not exist in the future. Thus, the NFP organization's planning horizon for quality is shorter than that of the FP company.

KEY TERMS

activity analysis (p. 77)
appraisal cost (p. 85)
benchmarking (p. 80)
control chart (p. 78)
failure cost (p. 85)
grade (p. 80)
ISO 9000 (p. 95)
non-value-added activity (p. 77)
Pareto analysis (p. 89)
prevention cost (p. 85)
process benchmarking (p. 82)

quality (p. 76)
quality audit (p. 96)
quality control (QC) (p. 78)
results benchmarking (p. 81)
statistical process control (SPC)
   (p. 78)
total quality management (TQM)
   (p. 83)
value (p. 80)
value-added activity (p. 77)

Total Quality Costs = Costs of Compliance + Costs of Noncompliance

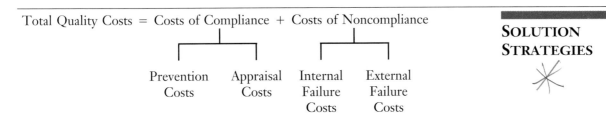

| Prevention Costs | Appraisal Costs | Internal Failure Costs | External Failure Costs |

Costs of noncompliance are inversely related to the costs of compliance. Costs of noncompliance are a direct result of the number of defects.

Dimensions of product quality include:

- Conformity to specifications
- Effective and efficient performance
- Durability
- Ease of use
- Safety
- Comfort of use
- Appeal

TQM leads to greater demand, greater productivity, shorter lead time, lower costs, and greater customer loyalty, which all lead to greater control of pricing.

COST OF QUALITY FORMULAS

Profit Lost by Selling Units as Defects = (Total Defective Units − Number of Units Reworked) × (Profit for Good Unit − Profit for Defective Unit)

$$Z = (D - Y)(P_1 - P_2)$$

Rework Cost = Number of Units Reworked × Cost to Rework Defective Unit

$$R = (Y)(r)$$

Cost of Processing Customer Returns = Number of Defective Units Returned × Cost of a Return

$$W = (D_r)(w)$$

Total Failure Cost = Profit Lost by Selling Units as Defects + Rework Cost + Cost of Processing Customer Returns

$$F = Z + R + W$$

Total Quality Cost = Defect Control Cost + Total Failure Cost

T = (Prevention Cost + Appraisal Cost) + Total Failure Cost

$$T = K + A + F$$

DEMONSTRATION PROBLEM

Foster Company's quality report for April 1997 showed the following information:

Total defective units	1,500
Number of units reworked	900
Number of customer units returned	150
Profit for a good unit	$38
Profit for a defective unit	$22
Cost to rework a defective unit	$ 7
Cost to process a returned unit	$12
Total prevention cost	$15,000
Total appraisal cost	$5,000

Required:
Compute the following:

a. Profit lost by selling unreworked defects
b. Total rework cost
c. Cost of processing customer returns
d. Total failure cost
e. Total quality cost

Solution to Demonstration Problem

a. $Z = (D - Y)(P_1 - P_2) = (1,500 - 900)(\$38 - \$22) = \$9,600$
b. $R = (Y)(r) = (900)(\$7) = \$6,300$
c. $W = (D_r)(w) = (150)(\$12) = \$1,800$
d. $F = Z + R + W = \$9,600 + \$6,300 + \$1,800 = \$17,700$
e. $T = K + A + F = \$15,000 + \$5,000 + \$17,700 = \$37,700$

QUESTIONS

1. Why are high-quality products and services so important in today's global business environment?

2. What is meant by the term *quality?* In defining quality, from what two perspectives may a definition be formulated? Why are both important?

3. In conducting activity analysis, the presence of certain activities indicates low production process quality. List five of these activities.

4. What variables can management manipulate to improve production process quality? How will these changes improve product quality?

5. How can statistical process control techniques be used to evaluate the quality of a production process?

6. "If a company has a high-quality manufacturing process, customers will naturally view the output of that process as high quality." Explain why this statement is true or false.

7. List and explain the eight characteristics of product quality from the perspective of the customer.

8. List and explain the five characteristics of service quality from the perspective of the customer.

9. How does benchmarking allow a company to evaluate the quality of its processes?

10. Describe the eight steps in benchmarking that may be used to improve a specific production process.

11. What is TQM? What are the three important tenets of TQM and why are they important?

12. When consumers compare alternative products and services, one of the characteristics of each alternative that is evaluated is customer service. What are some of the important elements of customer service that consumers may evaluate?

13. What are the two types of costs that comprise the total quality cost of a firm? What are the two subtypes within each type? Given the trade-offs between the two main types of quality costs, is quality ever free? Explain.

14. What are the sources of information for product quality costs within a firm (both financial and nonfinancial)?

15. In the production-sales cycle, what are the four time phases in which quality costs are incurred? How are these costs interrelated through the phases?

16. How can Pareto analysis help focus managerial efforts in reducing the costs of quality-related problems?

17. Describe some additional accounts that can be added to financial records to attempt to better capture the costs of quality in the accounting records. Provide some examples of costs contained in the specified accounts.

18. What is the Malcolm Baldrige National Quality Award? What are the categories of entrants? What are the award categories?

19. Why do countries establish quality standards? Why is it desirable to have a common set of global quality standards?

20. What role is served by the International Organization for Standardization?

21. What are the four stages or levels on the quality continuum? Where is TQM located on the continuum?

22. Why are quality innovations more difficult to implement in governmental and not-for-profit organizations than in profit-oriented firms?

---

23. *(Terminology)* Match the following lettered terms on the left with the appropriate numbered description on the right.

EXERCISES

  a. Value
  b. Quality control
  c. Statistical process control
  d. Quality audit
  e. Quality
  f. Pareto analysis
  g. Grade
  h. Control chart
  i. Benchmarking
  j. Activity analysis

  1. Method to rank causes of variation in a process
  2. Review of product design, manufacturing processes and controls, quality documentation, and records
  3. Technique to identify uncommon variations or errors in a process
  4. Process of classifying activities as value-added or non-value-added
  5. Graphical method of documenting when a process is in or out of control
  6. Different product or service characteristics to satisfy different customer needs
  7. Process of investigating how other firms conduct business
  8. Effect of meeting customer needs at the lowest possible price
  9. Product or service characteristic relating to meeting the most customer needs at the lowest price
  10. Policy and/or practice designed to eliminate poor quality

24. *(True/false)* Mark each of the following statements as true or false and explain why the false statements are incorrect.

    a. The total quality cost is the sum of prevention cost plus failure cost.

    b. Traditional accounting systems have separate accounts to capture quality costs.

    c. Pareto analysis is used to help managers identify areas in which to focus quality-improvement efforts.

    d. As the number of defective products manufactured rises, internal failure costs also rise, but external failure costs are expected to decline.

    e. Higher quality yields lower profits but higher productivity.

    f. Total quality management has production processes as its focus rather than customer satisfaction.

    g. Results benchmarking relies only on comparisons to firms *within* the same industry.

    h. SPC control charts are used to plot the costs of quality over time.

    i. Activity analysis can be used to identify non-value-added activities.

    j. Quality is free.

25. *(Control chart)* Zammilo Pizza's has recently hired several college students to work part-time making pizzas. Bud Zammilo, the owner, has a policy of putting 36 slices of pepperoni on a pizza, but (given diversity in size) he sometimes puts on between 34 and 38. After observing the students for a few days, Bud gathered the following data on number of pepperoni slices:

11:00 A.M. to 5:00 P.M.: 13 pizzas were made containing the following number of pepperoni slices (35, 37, 41, 33, 36, 36, 35, 39, 44, 37, 36, 36, 35)

5:00 P.M. to 11:00 P.M.: 25 pizzas were made containing the following number of pepperoni slices (35, 37, 41, 42, 36, 39, 44, 43, 44, 37, 48, 36, 35, 40, 39, 41, 29, 36, 36, 42, 45, 44, 37, 36, 36)

    a. Prepare a control chart for pepperoni slices.

    b. What information does the chart provide Bud?

26. *(Cost of quality)* Johnson Technology Company has gathered the following data on its quality costs for 1996 and 1997:

Defect Prevention Costs	1996	1997
Quality training	$4,000	$4,750
Quality technology	3,000	4,000
Quality production design	2,000	4,500
External Failure Costs		
Warranty handling	$7,500	$5,000
Customer reimbursements	5,500	3,600
Customer returns handling	3,500	2,000

    a. Compute the percentage change in the two quality cost categories from 1996 to 1997.

    b. Write a brief explanation for the pattern of change in the two categories.

27. *(Cost of quality)* Hanibal Machine Tools Inc.'s accounting system reflected the following costs related to quality for 1997 and 1998:

	1997	1998
Customer refunds for poor product quality	$12,000	$ 9,000
Fitting machines for mistake-proof operations	4,200	6,400
Supply-line management	4,000	5,000
Disposal of waste	22,000	18,000
Quality training	14,000	15,000
Litigation claims	36,000	28,000

    a. Which of these are costs of compliance and which are costs of noncompliance?

    b. Calculate the percentage change in each cost and for each category.

    c. Discuss the pattern of the changes in the two categories.

28. *(Cost of quality)* The Benson Company wants to determine its cost of quality. The company has gathered the following information from records pertaining to June 1997:

Defective units	5,000	Prevention costs	$12,000
Units reworked	4,500	Profit per good unit produced and sold	$30
Defective units returned	200	Profit per defective unit sold	$10
Appraisal costs	$8,000	Cost per unit for customer returns	$12
Cost per unit for rework	$6		

Compute the following:
a. Lost profits from selling defective work
b. Total costs of failure
c. Total quality cost

29. *(Cost of quality)* Rugged Backpack Company has gathered the following information pertaining to quality costs of production for April 1998:

Total defective units	240
Number of units reworked	140
Number of backpacks returned	25
Total prevention cost	$10,000
Total appraisal cost	$12,000
Per-unit profit for defective units	$12
Per-unit profit for good units	$30
Cost to rework defective units	$14
Cost to handle returned units	$18

Using this data, calculate the following:
a. Total cost to rework
b. Profit lost from not reworking all defective units
c. Cost of processing customer returns
d. Total failure costs
e. Total quality cost

---

30. *(Quality characteristics)* Prepare a five-by-eight matrix of the five characteristics of service quality (horizontal axis) and the eight characteristics of product quality (vertical axis). Place a checkmark in the matrix where there is an approximate match in characteristics on both axes. Prepare a brief oral presentation for your classmates explaining the common quality characteristics in your matrix.

31. *(Definition of quality; quality characteristics)* In a team of three, role-play the following individuals who are visiting a car dealership in your community: (1) a 19-year-old college student, (2) a young married man/woman with two children, and (3) an elderly man/woman (postretirement age). Each of you are interested in purchasing a new automobile.
a. How do each of you define quality in an automobile? Explain the reasons for your differences.
b. What vehicle characteristics are important to all of you? Which vehicle characteristics are unique to each of you?

32. *(Quality information system; team activity)* Your company is interested in developing information about quality, but has a traditional accounting system that does not provide such information directly. In a three- or four-person team, prepare a set of recommendations about how to improve the company's information system to eliminate or reduce this deficiency. In your recommendations, also explain in what areas would management have the most difficulty in satisfying its desire for more information about quality and why these areas were chosen.

COMMUNICATION ACTIVITIES

33. *(Cost of quality)* Kleinfeld Aquariums is evaluating its quality control costs for 1997 and preparing plans and budgets for 1998. The 1997 quality costs incurred in the Large Tank Division follow:

Prevention costs	$300,000
Appraisal costs	100,000
Internal failure costs	350,000
External failure costs	100,000
Total	$850,000

Prepare a memo to the company president on the following issues:
   a. Which categories of failure costs would be affected by the decision to spend $150,000 on a new computer-controlled drill press (to replace an old manual drill press)? Why?
   b. If projected external failure costs for 1998 can be reduced 60 percent (relative to 1997 levels) by either spending $50,000 more on appraisal or $80,000 more on prevention, why would the firm opt to spend the $80,000 on prevention rather than the $50,000 on appraisal?

34. *(Control of quality costs; team activity)* The following summary numbers have been taken from a quality cost report of Alabama Millworks Inc. for 1997. The firm manufactures a variety of cast-iron products.

Prevention costs	$3,000,000
Appraisal costs	2,000,000
Internal failure costs	2,000,000
External failure costs	1,000,000
Total quality costs	$8,000,000

The company is actively seeking to identify ways to reduce total quality costs. The company's current strategy is to increase spending in one or more quality cost categories in hopes of achieving greater spending cuts in other quality cost categories. In a team of three or four individuals, prepare an oral presentation to answer the following questions.
   a. Which spending categories are most susceptible to control by managers? Why?
   b. Why is it more logical for the company to increase spending in the prevention cost and appraisal cost categories than in the failure cost categories?
   c. Which cost category is the most likely target for spending reductions? Explain.
   d. How would the adoption of a TQM philosophy affect the focus in reducing quality costs?

35. *(Supplier quality)* Assume that Toyota paid for a full-page advertisement in the *Wall Street Journal*. The ad did not tout Toyota products nor was it in reference to year-end earnings or a new stock issuance. Instead, the ad was to inform readers that "buying quality parts is not a foreign idea to us." The ad named Toyota suppliers and identified their locations. Prepare a brief essay to answer the following questions.
   a. Why would Toyota want other companies to know what suppliers it uses?
   b. Do you think this advertisement had any benefit for Toyota itself? Discuss the rationale for your answer.

36. *(Differences from benchmarks)* For a benchmark, assume that the average firm incurs quality costs in the following proportions:

Prevention	25%
Appraisal	25%
Internal failure	25%
External failure	25%
Total costs	100%

With a partner, explain why the following industries might be inclined to have a spending pattern on quality costs that differs from the benchmark:

a. Pharmaceutical company
b. Department store
c. Computer manufacturer
d. Used-car retailer
e. Lawn service company

---

37. *(Pareto analysis)* Tops Computer Company has identified the following failure costs during 1997:

see p. 89

PROBLEMS

Cost of Type of Failure

MODEL	CPU	INTERNAL DRIVE	EXTERNAL DRIVE	ALL OTHER	TOTAL
Laptop	$ 8,000	$ 7,000	$ 5,000	$ 3,000	$23,000
Desktop	7,000	6,000	12,000	5,000	30,000
Mini	3,000	1,000	8,000	3,000	15,000
Total	$18,000	$14,000	$25,000	$11,000	$68,000

a. Rearrange the above rows in descending order of magnitude based on the total dollars column and prepare a table using Pareto analysis with the following headings:

Model   Dollars   % of Total   Cumulative % of Total

b. Which models account for almost 80 percent of all failure costs?
c. Focusing on the models identified in part b, prepare a table using Pareto analysis to identify the types of failure causing the majority of failure costs. (Hint: Rearrange the cost of failure types in descending order of magnitude.) Use the following headings for your table:

Failure Type   Dollars   % of Total   Cumulative % of Total

d. Describe the problem areas for which to seek preventive measures first. How, if at all, does this answer reflect the concept of leverage?

38. *(Cost of quality)* Lampposts-R-Us, Ltd. manufactures hardwood lampposts for the discriminating homeowner. The firm produced 3,000 lampposts during its first year of operations. At year end, there was no inventory of finished goods. The company sold 2,700 through regular market channels (some after rework), but 300 units were so defective that they had to be sold as scrap. For this first year, the firm spent $30,000 on prevention costs and $15,000 on quality appraisal. There were no customer returns. An income statement for the year follows.

Sales (regular channel)	$270,000	
(scrap)	12,000	$282,000
Cost of Goods Sold		
Original production costs	$150,000	
Rework costs	22,000	
Quality prevention and appraisal	45,000	(217,000)
Gross margin		$ 65,000
Selling and administrative expenses (all fixed)		(90,000)
Net loss		$ (25,000)

a. Compute the total profits lost by the company in its first year of operations by selling defective units as scrap rather than selling the units through regular channels.

b. Compute the total failure costs for the company in its first year.

c. Compute total quality costs incurred by the company in its first year.

d. What evidence indicates the firm is dedicated to manufacturing and selling high-quality products?

39. *(Cost of quality)* Golf courses are demanding in their quest for high-quality carts because of the critical need for lawn maintenance. Ride-in-Style manufactures golf carts and is a recognized leader in the industry for quality products. In recent months, company managers have become more interested in trying to quantify the costs of quality in the company. As an initial effort, the company was able to identify the following 1997 costs, by category, that are associated with quality:

PREVENTION COSTS

Quality training	$15,000
Quality technology	50,000
Quality circles	32,000

APPRAISAL COSTS

Quality inspections	18,000
Test equipment	14,000
Procedure verifications	9,000

INTERNAL FAILURE COSTS

Scrap and waste	6,500
Waste disposal	2,100

EXTERNAL FAILURE COSTS

Warranty handling	9,500
Customer reimbursements/returns	7,600

Managers were also aware that in 1997, 250 of the 8,000 carts that were produced had to be sold as scrap. These 250 carts were sold for $80 less profit per unit than "good" carts. Also, the company incurred rework costs amounting to $6,000 to sell 200 other carts through regular market channels.

a. Using the above data, find Ride-in-Style's 1997 expense for the following:
  1. Lost profits from scrapping the 250 units
  2. Total failure costs
  3. Total quality costs
b. Assume that the company is considering expanding its existing full 5-year warranty to a full 7-year warranty in 1998. How would such a change be reflected in quality costs?

ETHICS AND QUALITY DISCUSSION

40. Use a variety of resources to gather seven definitions of quality.
  a. Compare and contrast each of these definitions, with specific emphasis on whether the definition is conformity- or customer-oriented.
  b. Assume that you are the manager of (1) a restaurant and (2) a microwave oven manufacturer. Prepare definitions of quality to distribute to your employees and discuss how you would measure service/product adherence to those definitions.

41. Institutions of higher education have a variety of internal and external customers. Use a team of three or four individuals to answer the following.
  a. List three internal and two external customers of a college or university.
  b. How would each of the above constituents define quality of product or service? Do any of these views conflict and, if so, how?
  c. Are a college or university's internal customers as important as external customers? Explain the rationale for your answer.

42. By building quality into the process, rather than making quality inspections at the end of the process, certain job functions (such as many quality control inspectors) can be eliminated. Additionally, the installation of automated equipment to monitor product processing could eliminate some line worker jobs.

In a nation with fairly high unemployment, would employers attempting to implement valid quality improvements that resulted in employee terminations be appreciated or condemned? Discuss your answer from the standpoint of a variety of concerned constituencies, including the consumers who purchase the company's products.

43. Assume that you are in charge of a social service agency that provides counseling services to welfare families. The agency's costs have been increasing with no corresponding increase in funding. In an effort to implement some cost reductions, you implement the following ideas:

1. Counselors are empowered to make their own decisions about the legitimacy of all welfare claims.
2. To emphasize the concept of "do it right the first time," counselors are told not to review processed claims at a later date.
3. To discourage "out of control" conditions, an upper and lower control limit of 5 minutes is set on a standard 15-minute time for consultations.

Discuss the ethics as well as the positive and negative effects of each of the ideas listed.

44. Even though revenues to cities in the United States have been rising in the early 1990s, many cities found that they were having great difficulty paying their bills.

But state and local governments can be made to work. There are alternatives to the bulimic spend-and-trim cycles that have plagued them for decades. Look behind the headlines about fiscal crises and rising taxes, and you'll find a growing number of officials quietly embracing concepts that have transformed American industry over the past decade—quality, teamwork, outsourcing, and yes, customer service.

[SOURCE: Ronald Henkoff, "Some Hope for Troubled Cities," *Fortune* (September 9, 1991), p. 121. © 1991 Time Inc. All rights reserved.]

a. How does the concept of civil service for employees mesh with and/or deter the concept of TQM?

b. What instances have you seen in your city or state in which fees or taxes were increased with no increase in service?

c. What instances have you seen in your city or state in which fees or taxes were increased with equitable increases in service?

d. Have there been instances in your city or state in which fees or taxes were reduced because of some governmental program? If so, describe the situation.

e. What are the differences in the incentives offered to workers in private industry and in government to provide high-quality products and services?

45. Sometimes a company, in its efforts to reduce costs, might also reduce quality.

a. What kinds of costs could be reduced in an organization that would almost automatically lower product/service quality?

b. If quality improvements create cost reductions, why would cost reductions not create quality improvements?

c. Are there instances in which cost reductions would create quality improvements?

46. *A Big Three task force has delivered what suppliers across the nation have been waiting for—a single, harmonized quality standard. The single standard, called QS 9000, replaces multiple standards that supplier firms have labored under while proving their abilities to meet automakers' requirements for quality in the design and manufacture of production parts.*

The Automotive Industry Action Group (AIAG) will coordinate QS 9000 training for supplier companies nationally. Training sessions will begin immediately.

[SOURCE: "Automakers Move Closer to a Single Quality Standard," *Purchasing* (November 10, 1994), p. 45.]

    a. What are some advantages to an automaker of having a single industry quality standard?

    b. What are some advantages to automaker customers of having a single industry quality standard?

    c. How would a nation benefit if all major companies in an industry were to subscribe to a single quality standard?

47. *Increasing numbers of U.S. businesses have been seeking to comply with the ISO 9000 standards simply because of real or perceived market forces. Some of the most commonly given reasons for seeking ISO 9000 registration or compliance are:*

- *"Our customers are demanding it, often by putting ISO 9000 into contracts."*
- *"Our customers say they will treat ISO 9000-registered suppliers preferentially."*
- *"Our competitors are achieving registration, so we must also."*
- *"We need to improve quality; ISO 9000 seems like a practical, no-nonsense, and internationally accepted approach."*
- *"Our customers demand quality; ISO 9000 registration makes a statement about our commitment to quality."*
- *"Our European divisions already have ISO 9000 registration, and they are putting pressure on us to conform."*
- *"Our industry seems to be moving toward ISO 9000."*

The rapid growth of ISO 9000 implementation shows that the forces of the marketplace (whether the direct forces at work in regulated industries or the indirect ones that govern the free markets) are an effective influence in getting companies to adopt standards and, more importantly, to use them to improve their processes.

[SOURCE: Stanley A. Marash and Donald W. Marquardt, "Quality Standards and Free Trade," *Quality Progress* (May 1994), p. 29.]

    a. Why do you think customers are insisting that suppliers meet ISO 9000 standards?

    b. Does meeting ISO 9000 standards mean that a supplier's products or services are superior to those of competitors? Elaborate on what such conformance does mean.

    c. Why would the fact that a supplier's industry is moving toward ISO 9000 motivate the supplier to seek registration?

    d. How would complying with ISO 9000 help a company improve quality?

INTERNET ACTIVITIES

48. Find the web site for the University of Illinois (Chicago) Medical Center. Read about the quality initiatives in place at the medical center. What are the major tools the medical center is using to achieve improvements in quality? What is the quality lead team? To whom do the leaders of the quality lead team report? What does the reporting relationship suggest about the importance of quality at the medical center?

49. Find the web page for Collins Printed Circuits of Rockwell Avionics. What products are made by this company? How does the company use statistical process controls to control the quality of output? What is the role of the firm's group testing lab in controlling quality?

50. Find The Benchmarking Exchange on the Internet. What are the top five business processes that are currently the focus of benchmarking by members of The Benchmarking Exchange? How has the ranking changed in the past five years? Why have benchmarking processes related to managing human resources remained so highly ranked over the past five years?

SELECTING, ANALYZING, AND TRACKING COSTS

4

Cost Terminology and Cost Flows

LEARNING OBJECTIVES

After completing this chapter, you should be able to answer these questions:

1. How are costs classified and why are such classifications useful?

2. What assumptions do accountants make about cost behavior and why are these assumptions necessary?

3. How do product and period costs differ and why is this distinction a critical one?

4. How are cost objects and direct costs related?

5. How does the conversion process occur in manufacturing and service companies?

6. What product cost categories exist and what items compose these categories?

7. How does a manufacturing company calculate cost of goods manufactured?

Spanier & Bourne Sailmakers, Inc.

Barry Spanier and Geoff Bourne are two of the most well known and respected sail designers in windsurfing. Their company is located in Kahului on the Hawaiian island of Maui and is known widely as Maui Sails. The firm has earned international recognition for its own sails and for serving as the primary designer of sails and equipment for the world-class Hong Kong manufacturer, Neil Pryde Sails. Spanier & Bourne has been so successful that it was named a "Blue Chip Enterprise" for 1994 by the Blue Chip Enterprise Initiative.

What started out as a sporting activity ultimately turned into a passion for making some of the best sails in the world. Geoff Bourne and Barry Spanier were taking a pleasure cruise on a 38-foot sailboat from New Zealand to the New Hebrides Islands in 1978 when a violent storm shipwrecked and marooned them for 22 days on a small island in the New Zealand waters. During this and other adventures the men developed a strong friendship and respect that ultimately brought them together in the sailmaking business.

They were really intent about what they did even though, in their words, they "didn't have much of a clue about making much money out of it." From the beginning they were trying to make a quality statement about the way sails should be constructed and what was a good quality material setup and what wasn't. They have always taken a lot of pride in their work and have been quite happy with their products.

Making sails, like making almost any other product, requires incurring a combination of materials, labor, and overhead costs. Spanier & Bourne has conducted planning, controlling, and decision-making activities in managing these costs in such a way that sailing and windsurfing enthusiasts have appreciated the value and pricing of the company's products in an abundant and meaningful way: they have become loyal customers.

SOURCES: Interview with Barry Spanier and Geoff Bourne; "Brothers of the Cloth," *Performance Windsurf Report*, (Summer, 1994), p. 20ff; and "Spanier and Bourne Sailmakers," *Real-World Lessons For America's Small Businesses—Insights From The Blue Chip Enterprise Initiative 1994* (1994), pp. 91–92.

As discussed in Chapter 1, every product and service has costs associated with it—the costs of materials, labor, and overhead. **Cost,** a frequently used word in organizations, reflects a monetary measure of the resources given up to attain some objective such as acquiring a good or service. However, like many other words in the English language, the term *cost* must be defined more specifically before "the cost" can be determined. Thus, the term *cost* is seldom used without a preceding adjective to specify the type of cost being considered. Different types of costs are used in different situations. For example, the historical or acquisition cost of an asset is used to prepare a balance sheet, but replacement cost is used to estimate an asset's value for insurance purposes.

cost

Before communicating information effectively to others, accountants must clearly understand the differences among various types of costs, their computations, and their usage. This chapter defines the terminology that is necessary to understand and communicate cost and management accounting information. The chapter also presents cost flows and accumulation in a production environment.

COST CATEGORIES

Cost may be defined in a variety of ways depending on the objectives or information desired. In this text, cost classifications are used to define costs in terms of their relationships to the following four items: (1) time of incurrence, (2) reaction to changes in activity, (3) classification on the financial statements, and (4) impact on decision making. Exhibit 4–1 presents these different cost categories and the types of costs included in each. These categories are not mutually exclusive; a cost may be defined in one way at one time and in another way at a different time. The first three classifications of costs are discussed in this chapter. The costs that relate to decision making are covered at various points throughout the text. At this time, it is merely important to understand that "cost" can have many different meanings.

Costs Associated with Time of Incurrence

historical cost

Costs classified in relationship to the time of incurrence include historical costs, replacement costs, and budgeted costs. **Historical costs** were incurred in the past and are normally used in financial accounting. These costs are objective and verifiable—necessary qualities for income statement and balance sheet valuations. However, historical costs are frequently not as useful for decision making because conditions may have changed since the costs were incurred.

EXHIBIT 4–1

Cost Classification Categories

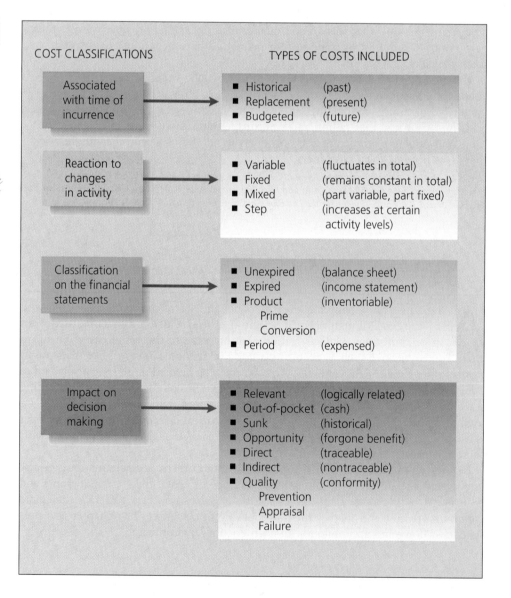

A **replacement cost** is an amount that a firm would currently have to pay to replace an asset or to buy one that performs functions similar to an asset currently held. Several methods may be used to determine the replacement cost of an item, including referencing supplier catalogs and requesting quotes from established markets that deal in similar assets.

replacement cost

An asset's replacement cost may be quite different from its original acquisition price for many reasons. Assume that Spanier & Bourne purchased a plot of land for $25,000 in 1980. The $25,000 is the historical cost of the land and represented an equitable exchange price for the property at that time. If the area surrounding the land has been developed and access to the property has been improved, the land's current replacement cost might be $175,000. But if a nuclear power plant or a hazardous material waste disposal facility has since been built next to the Spanier & Bourne land, the land's replacement cost might be only $4,000. If conditions are essentially the same as when the land was purchased (for example, there have been no changes in the surrounding environment, no new access, no improvements, and no inflation), the land's replacement cost may still be $25,000.

Planned future expenditures are called **budgeted costs.** A budgeted cost could be, but is not necessarily, the same amount as the replacement cost. Assume that Spanier & Bourne needs a new high-speed sewing machine to replace one that was purchased 10 years ago for $30,000. A similar machine now costs $41,000 (the replacement cost). A new, larger-capacity, more efficient machine is available for $48,000. If Spanier & Bourne plans to buy a machine similar to the one it already has, the budgeted cost is equal to the replacement cost of $41,000. If Spanier & Bourne plans to buy the larger machine, the budgeted cost is $48,000, but the replacement cost of the old machine is still $41,000.

budgeted cost

The two cost accounting objectives presented in Chapter 1 were to generate product costs for inventories and other financial accounting purposes and to provide useful information to management. Historical costs are indispensable for the first purpose, because financial statement amounts must be objective and verifiable. Replacement, budgeted, and other versions of current costs are normally more appropriate than historical costs for managerial purposes. Current costs provide more up-to-date information and are more relevant to present problems and alternatives than historical costs. However, replacement and budgeted costs are usually not recorded in the accounting system and typically must be estimated or derived from inference when they are needed.

Cost Reactions to Changes in Activity

Within a period, a particular cost may be observed changing with corresponding changes in some measure of activity. Examples of activity measures include sales, production and/or service volume, machine hours, and number of purchase orders sent. Accountants describe a given cost's behavior pattern according to the way its *total cost* (rather than its unit cost) reacts to changes in a related measure of activity.

However, every cost will change if activity levels are shifted to extremes and given a long enough span of time. Therefore, to properly identify, analyze, and use cost behavior information, a time frame must be specified to indicate how far into the future a cost should be examined, and a particular range of activity must be assumed. For example, the cost of a yard of material for Spanier & Bourne to make a sail might increase by $.05 next year but by $5.00 by the year 2010. The assumed range of activity is referred to as the **relevant range,** which reflects the company's normal operating range. Within the relevant range, the two most common cost behaviors are variable and fixed.

relevant range

A cost that varies *in total* in direct proportion to changes in activity is a **variable cost.** Examples include the costs of materials, wages, and sales commissions. Variable costs can be extremely important in the total profit picture of a company, because every time a product is produced and/or sold or a service is rendered and/or sold, a

variable cost

EXHIBIT 4–2

Economic Representation
of a Variable Cost

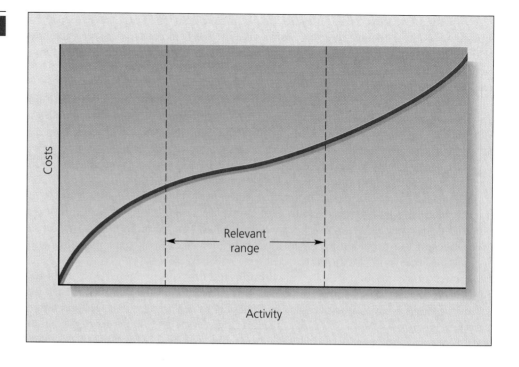

corresponding amount of that variable cost is incurred. Because the total cost varies in direct proportion to the changes in activity levels, a variable cost must be a constant amount *per unit*.

Variable costs are viewed by economists as being curvilinear, as shown in Exhibit 4–2. The cost line slopes upward at a given rate until a range of activity is reached in which the average variable cost rate becomes fairly constant. Within this range, the slope of the cost line becomes less steep because the firm experiences benefits such as discounts on material prices, improved worker skill and productivity, and other operating efficiencies. Beyond this range, the slope becomes quite steep as the entity enters a range of activity in which certain operating factors cause the average variable cost to increase. In this range, the firm finds that costs rise rapidly due to worker crowding, equipment shortages, and other operating inefficiencies.

fixed cost

In contrast, a cost that remains constant *in total* within the relevant range of activity is considered a **fixed cost.** On a per-unit basis, a fixed cost varies inversely with changes in the level of activity. This means that the *per-unit* fixed cost decreases with increases in the activity level, and increases with decreases in the activity level. Fixed costs include supervisors' salaries, depreciation (other than that computed under the units-of-production method), and insurance. However, even fixed costs can be viewed as variable in the long run for the total business. Furthermore, given the discontinuation of production and a sufficient time horizon, these costs and all others can be eliminated.

To illustrate the need for specifying a relevant range of activity, assume that Spanier & Bourne has the cost structure for yards of material purchased and building depreciation shown in the graphs in Exhibit 4–3. The exhibit indicates that actual variable cost for yards of material is curvilinear rather than linear and that, over the long run, several levels of cost exist for building depreciation.

The curves on the cost graph for yards of material purchased reflect pricing policies of suppliers. If Spanier & Bourne's purchasing agent buys less than 1,000 yards at a time, the price per yard is $3.35. If between 1,000 and 2,400 yards are purchased, the price is $3.00 per yard. Quantities over 2,400 yards may be purchased for $2.80 per yard. Because the company always buys between 1,000 and 2,400 yards, this is the relevant range of activity for purchases. The cost of yards of material is variable because total cost will vary in direct proportion to the quantity purchased within the

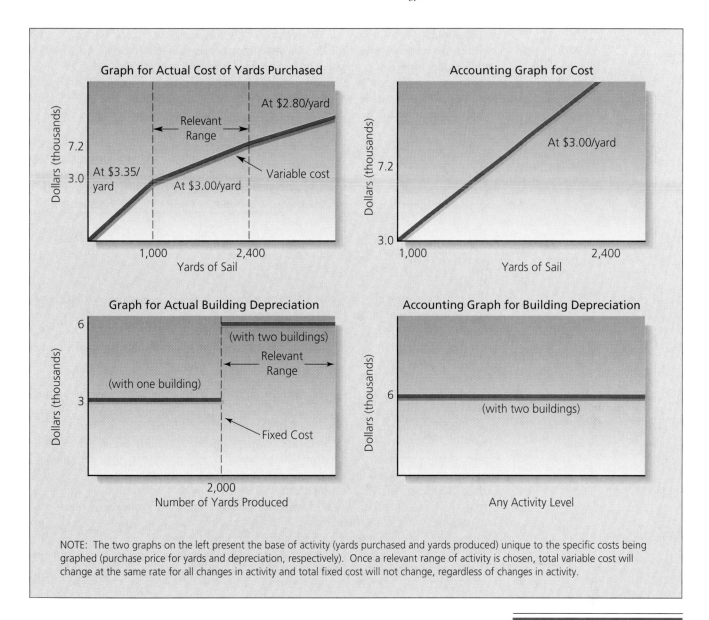

NOTE: The two graphs on the left present the base of activity (yards purchased and yards produced) unique to the specific costs being graphed (purchase price for yards and depreciation, respectively). Once a relevant range of activity is chosen, total variable cost will change at the same rate for all changes in activity and total fixed cost will not change, regardless of changes in activity.

EXHIBIT 4–3

Relevant Range of Activity for Spanier & Bourne

relevant range. If Spanier & Bourne buys 1,500 yards, it will pay $4,500 for its purchases; if it buys 2,000 yards, the cost will be $6,000. In each instance, because both volumes are within the relevant range, the cost remains constant at $3.00 per yard and exemplifies a variable cost that is truly linear over the relevant range.

A decision about the relevant range must also be made for fixed costs. The fixed cost shown in Exhibit 4–3 is for building depreciation. Assume that Spanier & Bourne has determined that one building, depreciated at the straight-line amount of $3,000 per month, can house enough equipment to process up to 2,000 yards of material per month. However, when processing exceeds 2,000 yards, additional facilities will be required. If another similar building is acquired, an additional $3,000 of building depreciation will be incurred per month. Although the company usually purchases yards in quantities of 1,200 to 1,800 at a time, total monthly processing is between 2,200 and 3,000 yards; thus, multiple purchases must be made from the supplier. Processing at this level requires that a second building be used and, therefore, the fixed cost for building depreciation is $6,000 per month.

Although the total cost of depreciation remains constant at $6,000 per month within the relevant range, the depreciation cost per yard of sail material processed is not linear within this relevant range. The fixed cost per unit will decline as the level of activity rises, but a specific percentage increase in the activity level will not result in the same percentage decrease in unit cost. The depreciation cost per yard of material processed is illustrated below, assuming 10 percent increases from a base of 2,500 yards:

PERCENTAGE OF INCREASE IN NUMBER OF YARDS	NUMBER OF YARDS	DEPRECIATION PER YARD	PERCENTAGE OF DECREASE IN DEPRECIATION PER YARD
	2,500	$2.40	
10	2,750	2.18	9.1667
10	3,025	1.98	9.1743
10	3,328	1.80	9.0909

mixed cost

Other costs exist that are not strictly variable or fixed. For example, a **mixed cost** has both a variable and a fixed component. On a per-unit basis, a mixed cost does not fluctuate in direct proportion with changes in activity nor does it remain constant with changes in activity. An example of a mixed cost is electricity that is computed as a flat charge (the fixed component) for basic service plus a stated rate for each kilowatt-hour (kwh) of electricity used (the variable component). Exhibit 4–4 shows a graph for Spanier & Bourne's electricity charge from its power company, which consists of a flat rate of $500 per month plus $.018 per kwh. If Spanier & Bourne uses 80,000 kwhs of electricity in a month, its total electricity bill is $1,940 [$500 + ($.018 × 80,000)]. If 90,000 kwhs are used, the electricity bill is $2,120.

In some businesses and for some items, variable and fixed costs may be "traded" for one another depending on managerial decisions. For example, Spanier & Bourne could decide to install additional automated equipment (generating an additional fixed cost for depreciation) and eliminate the need for some workers who are paid on an hourly basis (a variable cost). Alternatively, the company could decide to out-source some of its production or support functions. Outsourcing is the process of a company using an external provider of a service or manufacturer of a component. Almost all large manufacturers—especially automakers—outsource some of their pro-

EXHIBIT 4–4

Graph of a Mixed Cost

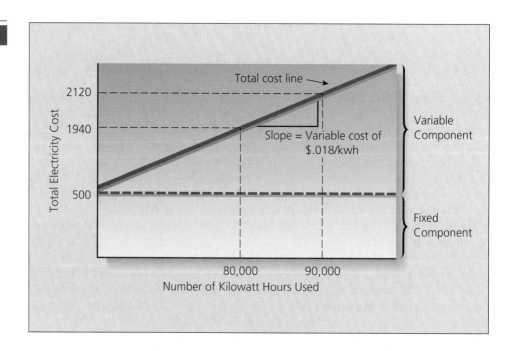

duction operations. For example, Pooler Industries (Muncie, Indiana) is a metal-stamping company that makes between five and ten parts for every American car producer as well as sells to other major companies both domestic and international.

Benefits of outsourcing include:

- Lower cost of raw material, labor, and overhead because supplier enjoys economies of skill and scale
- Reduced investments in physical assets and labor
- Specialized supplier knowledge
- Elimination of problem areas
- Less capital risk and lower break-even points as fixed costs are converted to variable costs
- Perception of outsourcing as a real cost, not a chargeback allocation of a sunk cost[1]

By outsourcing a support function such as data processing, a company might be able to trade its fixed costs of equipment and data processing personnel salaries for a mixed cost. The company providing the data processing service would typically do so for a fixed annual amount plus a charge for the volume of transactions processed. Whether a company exchanges variable for fixed or fixed for mixed costs, shifting costs from one type of cost behavior to another changes the basic cost structure of the company and can have a significant impact on profits.

Companies must be able to recognize when outsourcing is better than providing a function internally. Consider the difficulty encountered by Wieland Furniture when it decided not to outsource the delivery function as presented in the News Note "All Over the Road."

VIDEO
VIGNETTE

NCR (in AME—Managing the Supply Chain) and/or Pooler Industries (Blue Chip Enterprises)

---

[1] Peter Chalos, "Costing, Control, and Strategic Analysis in Outsourcing Decisions," *Journal of Cost Management* (Winter 1995), p. 33.

All Over the Road

The Wieland brothers made furniture. And since it had to be delivered, they thought, "Why not truck it ourselves?" Now they know.

But, says Blaine Wieland of his rationale then, "at the very least I'm seeing the positive side of things. Customers are liking it. I'm loving this repeat-business stuff. Let's add a few more! So we went up to eight trucks."

Somewhere along the way, the Wieland brothers had crossed the line. They were in two businesses now, one unlike the other in a thousand ways.

But then, like visitors and fish in Ben Franklin's aphorism, the beguiling business of trucking started to stink. Exactly when and how are hard to say. Weather was a factor—snow idled the fleet for an extended period, freezing revenues but not expenses. Insurance costs rose unexpectedly. Problems with drivers accumulated.

Realistically, [Blaine Wieland] thinks, his job is now to right the situation. So he's spending at least half of his time on trucking . . . putting in place new procedures that he hopes will allow him to begin backing off by the end of summer.

SOURCE: David Whitford, "All Over the Road," *INC.* (August 1995), pp. 54ff. Reprinted with permission, *INC.* magazine, August 1995. Copyright 1995 by Goldhirsh Group, Inc., 38 Commercial Wharf, Boston, MA 02110.

step cost

Another type of cost shifts upward or downward when activity changes by a certain interval or "step." A **step cost** can be variable or fixed. Step variable costs have small steps and step fixed costs have large steps. For example, a water bill computed as $.002 per gallon for up to 1,000 gallons, $.003 per gallon for 1,001 to 2,000 gallons, $.005 per gallon for 2,001 to 3,000 gallons, and so on is an example of a step variable cost. Bank teller salaries, where one teller is paid $2,400 per month and is needed for every 100 customers received per day by the bank, is an example of a step fixed cost.

Understanding the types of behavior exhibited by costs is necessary to make valid estimates of total costs at various levels of activity. Although all costs do not conform strictly to the above categories, the categories represent the types of cost behavior typically encountered in business. Cost accountants generally separate mixed costs into their variable and fixed components so that behavior of these costs is more readily apparent.[2] This separation allows managers to focus on the two basic types of costs: variable and fixed. When step variable or step fixed costs exist, accountants must choose a specific relevant range of activity that will allow step variable costs to be treated as variable and step fixed costs to be treated as fixed.

By separating mixed costs into their variable and fixed components and by specifying a relevant range for step costs, *accountants force all costs into variable and fixed categories while disregarding economic reality.* A variable cost is *assumed* to be constant per unit within the relevant range, and a fixed cost is *assumed* to be constant in total within the relevant range. These slightly unrealistic treatments of costs can be justified for two reasons. First, the conditions that are assumed approximate reality and, if the company operates only within the relevant range of activity, the cost behaviors selected are appropriate. Second, selection of a constant variable cost per unit and a constant fixed cost in total provides a convenient, stable measurement for use in planning, controlling, and decision making.

predictor

To make these generalizations about variable and fixed costs, accountants need to find a valid predictor for cost changes. A **predictor** is an activity measure that, when changed, is accompanied by consistent, observable changes in a cost item. However, simply because the two items change together does not prove that the predictor causes the change in the other item. For instance, assume that every time the local college football team wins a game, the stock market falls the next business day. If this is consistent, observable behavior, you may use the incident of the local college football winning a game to predict declines in the market—but such wins do not cause stock market changes!

---

[2] A simple method for analyzing a mixed cost is the high-low method discussed in Chapter 5. That chapter also illustrates least squares regression, a more mathematically sophisticated analytical technique.

Find the Driver to Improve the Process

A cost driver is any factor that causes a change in the total cost of an activity. It is, in short, the cause of a cost. Understanding the causal relationship between an activity and its cost enables management to focus improvement efforts on the areas that will produce the best result.

For example, a business process for one company that provides a service to manufacturers that consists of collecting and processing product and demographic information about customers includes the activity of data entry—manually keypunching customer-supplied information into a database. Productivity in this company is measured as a cost per card or the cost per entry of a customer response. Improvement efforts that focused on making data entry clerks (the company's major cost) work better and faster, produced mixed results. [Then] the company instituted a cost driver analysis [which] discovered that, more than any other factor, the design of the card was the root of cost in data entry. Poorly designed cards that were difficult to read slowed the data entry operators. Armed with this information . . . , management focused its improvement efforts on the card design activity, and ultimately achieved performance improvements in the data entry activity.

SOURCE: John A. Miller, "Designing and Implementing a New Cost Management System," *Journal of Cost Management* (Winter 1992), pp. 44–45. Reprinted with permission from *The Journal of Cost Management for the Manufacturing Industry* (Winter 1992), © 1992, Warren Gorham & Lamont, 31 St. James Avenue, Boston, MA 02116. All rights reserved.

Unlike predictors, **cost drivers** are measures of activity that are believed to have a direct cause-effect relationship to a cost. For example, production volume has a direct effect on the total cost of raw material used and can be said to "drive" that cost. Thus, production volume can be used as a valid predictor of that cost. The above News Note illustrates the concept of a cost driver in a service company activity.

cost driver

In most situations, the cause-effect relationship is less clear because costs are commonly caused by multiple factors. For example, quality control costs are affected by a variety of factors such as production volume, quality of materials used, skill level of workers, and level of automation. Although determining which factor actually caused a specific change in quality control cost may be difficult, any of these factors could be chosen to predict that cost if confidence exists about the factor's relationship with cost changes. To be used as a predictor, the factor and the cost need to change together in a foreseeable manner.

Traditionally, a single cost driver has been used to predict all types of costs. Accountants and managers, however, are realizing that single cost drivers do not necessarily provide the most reasonable predictions. This realization has caused a movement toward activity-based costing, which uses different cost drivers to predict different types of costs. Production volume, for instance, would be a valid cost driver for the cost of yards of sail material, but the number of vendors used might be a more realistic driver for Spanier & Bourne's purchasing department costs.[3]

Cost Classifications on the Financial Statements

Two major financial statements prepared by a company are the balance sheet and income statement. The balance sheet is a statement of **unexpired costs** (assets) and equities (liabilities and owners' capital); the income statement is a statement of revenues and **expired costs.** The concept of matching revenues and expenses on the income statement is central to financial accounting. The matching concept provides a basis for deciding when an unexpired cost becomes an expired cost and is moved from an asset category (balance sheet) to an expense or loss category (income statement).

unexpired cost

expired cost

[3] Using multiple cost drivers for illustrative purposes in the text would be unwieldy. Therefore, except when topics such as activity-based costing are being discussed, examples will typically make use of a single cost driver.

Product cost consists of direct material, direct labor, and overhead. In this process, the DM is smoked salmon, the DL is provided by Pat Jackson cutting and arranging the salmon on trays, and the OH is depreciation and electricity on the machinery and equipment in the production area.

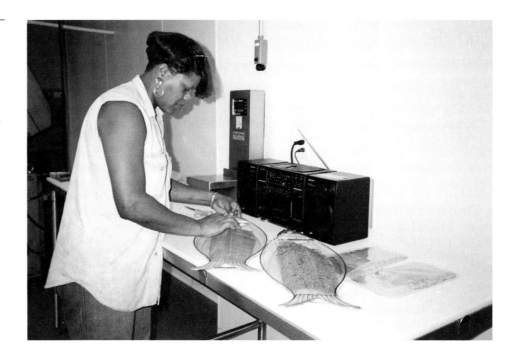

The two categories of expired costs (expenses and losses) differ in that expenses are intentionally incurred in the process of generating revenues, and losses are unintentionally incurred. Examples of expired costs that appear as expenses on the income statement include cost of goods sold, selling expenses, and administrative expenses. Examples of losses include costs expiring from conditions such as fire or flood as well as abnormal production waste.

product cost

period cost

inventoriable cost

In addition to being designated as unexpired or expired costs, many costs can also be classified as either product or period costs. **Product costs** are related to the products or services that directly generate the revenues of an entity; **period costs** are related to other business operations (selling and administrative costs).

Product costs associated with making or acquiring inventory are also called **inventoriable costs.** These costs include the cost of direct materials, direct labor, and overhead. Any readily identifiable part of a product (such as the wood in a table) is a **direct material.** Direct materials may be purchased raw materials, purchased components from contract manufacturers, or manufactured subassemblies. **Direct labor** refers to the time spent by individuals who work specifically on manufacturing a product or performing a service. At Spanier & Bourne, the wages paid to the people cutting and sewing sail material are considered direct labor costs. Any factory or production cost that is indirect to the product or service and, accordingly, does not include direct materials and direct labor is **overhead.** This cost element includes factory supervisors' salaries, depreciation on the sewing machines that are used to make sails, and insurance on the production facilities. Direct materials, direct labor, and overhead are discussed in depth later in the chapter.

direct material

direct labor

overhead

Period costs are generally more closely associated with a particular time rather than with making or acquiring a product or performing a service. Period costs that have future benefit are classified as assets, whereas those deemed to have no future benefit are expensed as incurred. Prepaid insurance on an administration building represents an unexpired period cost; when the premium period passes, the insurance becomes an expired period cost (insurance expense). Salaries paid to the sales force or depreciation on computers in the administrative area are also period costs.

distribution cost

Mention must be made of one specific type of period cost: distribution. A **distribution cost** is any cost incurred to warehouse, transport, or deliver a product or service. Although distribution costs are expensed as incurred, managers should remember that these costs relate directly to products and services and should not adopt

	COST CLASSIFICATION ON	
	BALANCE SHEET	INCOME STATEMENT
	(Unexpired Costs)	*(Expired Costs)*
MERCHANDISING COMPANY		
Product Costs (Inventoriable)—obtained by purchases of merchandise for resale	Merchandise Inventory →	Cost of Goods Sold
Period Costs (Noninventoriable)—obtained by payment or accrual for variety of non-merchandise-related costs	Prepaid Expenses →	Selling & Administrative (S&A) Expenses
MANUFACTURING COMPANY		
Product Costs (Inventoriable)—obtained by purchase of raw materials; converted through incurrence of direct labor and overhead costs; completed and transferred out of the factory; sold	Raw Materials Work in Process → Finished Goods	Cost of Goods Sold
Period Costs (Noninventoriable)—obtained by payment or accrual for variety of non-production-related costs	Prepaid Expenses Nonproduction Assets →	S&A Expenses
SERVICE COMPANY		
Product Costs (Inventoriable)—converted supplies into service function through direct labor and overhead costs; completed service function; acceptance of service by customers	Supplies Work in Process → Completed Services*	Cost of Services Rendered*
Period Costs (Noninventoriable)—obtained by payment or accrual for variety of non-performance-related costs	Prepaid Expenses Nonproduction Assets →	S&A Expenses

*Service companies can have Work in Process and Completed Services on the balance sheet, although most commonly Completed Services would not appear because they generally cannot be warehoused.

EXHIBIT 4–5

Comparison of Product and Period Costs

an "out-of-sight, out-of-mind" attitude about these costs simply because they have been expensed for financial accounting purposes. Distribution costs must be planned for in relationship to product/service volume, and these costs must be controlled for profitability to result from sales. Thus, even though distribution costs are not technically considered part of product cost, they may have a major impact on managerial decision making.[4]

Retailing, manufacturing, and service companies generally all classify the same types of costs as product and period costs, although some of the account titles differ. Exhibit 4–5 compares these costs and account titles.

In a retailing business, typically the only unexpired product cost is the cost of the unsold merchandise that has been purchased for resale (which includes any associated freight charges). In a manufacturing firm, unexpired product costs are classified as (1) raw materials, (2) work in process, or (3) finished goods. Each of these costs is maintained in a separate general ledger account. In both retail and manufacturing companies, product costs expire when the goods are sold and the costs are transferred to Cost of Goods Sold.

In a service company, a work in process inventory account may be maintained to show unexpired costs for projects not yet completed. If necessary, a service company may show a completed services account when projects are finished. However, the latter account is not often shown because most service companies perform services that are transferred to the customer almost immediately upon completion. The total

---

[4] The uniform capitalization rules (unicap rules) of the Tax Reform Act of 1986 caused many manufacturers, wholesalers, and retailers to expand the types and amounts of non-production-area costs that are treated as product costs for tax purposes. The unicap rules require that distribution costs for warehousing be considered part of product cost, but not distribution costs for marketing and customer delivery. The rationale for such treatment is that such warehousing costs are incident to production or acquisition.

cost of performing the service is sent to the income statement as an expired cost (Cost of Services Rendered) at the time the service is transferred.

Exhibit 4–6 summarizes the classifications of costs for financial reporting and provides some additional examples of period costs. Note that when Spanier & Bourne incurs insurance cost for a manufacturing building, that cost is considered overhead and a type of product cost. On the other hand, the insurance cost for Spanier & Bourne's administrative offices is a period cost. If the insurance were prepaid, the expiration of the insurance cost on the manufacturing building would flow into overhead (a product cost), whereas the expiration of the insurance on the administrative offices would flow into a period expense. Only when the products were sold would that insurance cost related to the manufacturing building become expired—as part of Cost of Goods Sold. Thus, the distinction between product and period cost is made primarily on the basis of *where* the cost was incurred rather than the *type* of cost incurred.

The appendix at the end of the chapter presents detailed income statements for each type of business organization. Balance sheets are not shown because the only differences are in the number and titles of inventory accounts.

EXHIBIT 4–6

Cost Classifications for
Financial Reporting

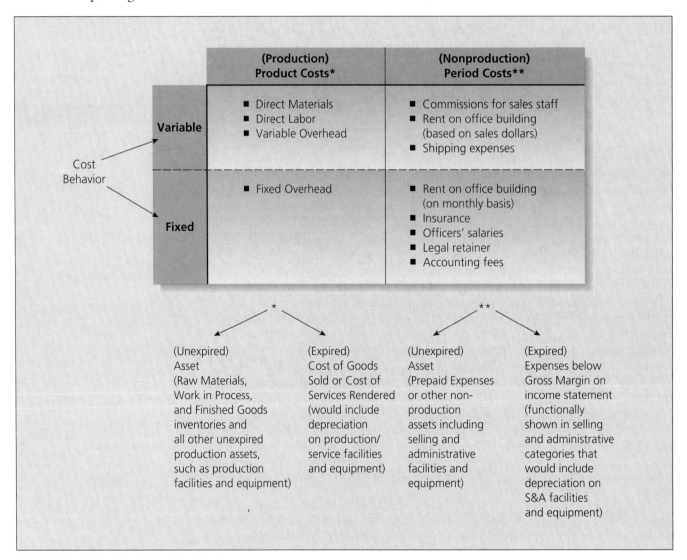

In general, product costs are incurred in the production or conversion area and period costs are incurred in all nonproduction or nonconversion areas.[5] To some extent, all organizations convert (or change) inputs into outputs. Inputs typically consist of materials, labor, and overhead. The outputs of a conversion process include both products and services. Exhibit 4–7 compares the conversion activities of different types of organizations. Note that many service companies engage in a high degree of conversion. Firms of professionals (such as accountants, architects, attorneys, engineers, and surveyors) convert labor and other resource inputs (materials and overhead) into completed jobs (audit reports, building plans, contracts, blueprints, and property survey reports).

Firms that engage in only low or moderate degrees of conversion can conveniently expense insignificant costs of labor and overhead related to conversion. The savings in clerical cost of expensing outweighs the value of any slightly improved information that might result from assigning such costs to products or services. For example, when employees in a grocery store open shipping containers and stock individual packages on shelves, a labor cost for conversion is incurred. Grocery stores, however, do not try to attach the stockpeople's wages to inventory; such labor costs are treated as period costs and are expensed as they are incurred.

In contrast, in high-conversion firms, the informational benefits gained from accumulating the materials, labor, and overhead costs of the output produced significantly exceed the clerical costs of accumulating these costs. For instance, to expense the labor costs incurred for workers constructing a bridge would be inappropriate; these costs are treated as product costs and inventoried as part of the cost of the construction job until the bridge is completed for the client.

For convenience, the term **manufacturer** will be used to refer to any company engaged in a high degree of conversion of raw material input into other tangible output. Manufacturers typically convert raw materials through the use of people and machines to produce large quantities of output that can be physically inspected. The term **service company** will be used to refer to a firm engaged in a high or moderate degree of conversion using a significant amount of labor. The output of a service

THE CONVERSION PROCESS

manufacturer

service company

EXHIBIT 4–7

Degrees of Conversion in Firms

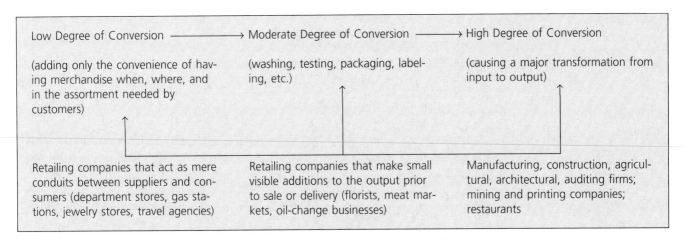

Low Degree of Conversion $\longrightarrow$	Moderate Degree of Conversion $\longrightarrow$	High Degree of Conversion
(adding only the convenience of having merchandise when, where, and in the assortment needed by customers)	(washing, testing, packaging, labeling, etc.)	(causing a major transformation from input to output)
Retailing companies that act as mere conduits between suppliers and consumers (department stores, gas stations, jewelry stores, travel agencies)	Retailing companies that make small visible additions to the output prior to sale or delivery (florists, meat markets, oil-change businesses)	Manufacturing, construction, agricultural, architectural, auditing firms; mining and printing companies; restaurants

[5] It is less common, but possible, for a cost physically incurred outside the production area to be in direct support of production and, therefore, considered a product cost. An example of this situation is the salary of a product cost analyst who is based at corporate headquarters; this cost is part of overhead.

company may be tangible (an audit report) or intangible (health care) and normally cannot be inspected prior to its use. Service firms may be profit-making businesses or not-for-profit organizations.

Firms engaging in only low or moderate degrees of conversion ordinarily have only one inventory account (Merchandise Inventory). In contrast, manufacturers normally use three inventory accounts: (1) Raw Materials, (2) Work in Process (for partially converted goods), and (3) Finished Goods. Service firms will have an inventory account for the supplies used in the conversion process and may have a Work in Process Inventory account, but these firms do not normally have a Finished Goods Inventory account because services typically cannot be warehoused.

Retailers vs. Manufacturers/Service Companies

Retail companies purchase goods in finished or almost finished condition; thus those goods typically need little, if any, conversion before being sold to customers. Costs associated with such inventory are usually easy to determine, as are the valuations for financial statement presentation. In comparison, manufacturers and service companies engage in activities that involve the physical transformation of inputs into finished products and services. The input and conversion costs of manufacturers and service companies must be assigned to output to determine cost of inventory and cost of goods sold or services rendered. Cost accounting provides the structure and process for assigning material and conversion costs to products and services.

Exhibit 4–8 compares the input-output relationships of a retail company with those of a manufacturing/service company. This exhibit illustrates that the primary difference between retail companies and manufacturing/service companies is the absence or presence of the area labeled "the production center." This center involves the conversion of raw material to final products. Input factors flow into the production center and are stored there until the goods or services are completed. If the output is a product, it can be warehoused and/or displayed until it is sold. Service outputs are directly provided to the client commissioning the work.

Technically, conversion does occur in merchandising businesses, but the time, effort, or cost of conversion is not as significant as it is in manufacturing or service companies. Merchandising conversion includes tagging merchandise with sales tickets and adding store-name labels to goods, as is often done at stores such as Neiman Marcus, Marshall Field's, and Macy's. The costs of such activities should theoretically be treated as additional costs of merchandise, and the department adding these costs could be viewed as a "mini" production center. Most often, however, merchandising companies have no designated "production center."

Exhibit 4–8 reflects an accrual-based accounting system in which costs flow from the various inventory accounts on the balance sheet through (if necessary) the production center. The cost accumulation process begins when raw materials or supplies are placed into production. As work progresses on a product or service, costs are accumulated in the firm's accounting records. Accumulating costs in appropriate inventory accounts allows businesses to match the costs of buying or manufacturing a product or providing a service with the revenues generated when the goods or services are sold. At point of sale these product/service costs will flow from an inventory account to cost of goods sold or cost of services rendered on the income statement.

Manufacturers vs. Service Companies

Several differences in accounting for production activities exist between a manufacturer and a service company. A manufacturer must account for raw materials, work in process, and finished goods inventory to maintain control over the production process. An accrual accounting system is essential for such organizations so that the total costs of production can be accumulated as the goods flow through the production process. On the other hand, most service firms need to keep track only of their

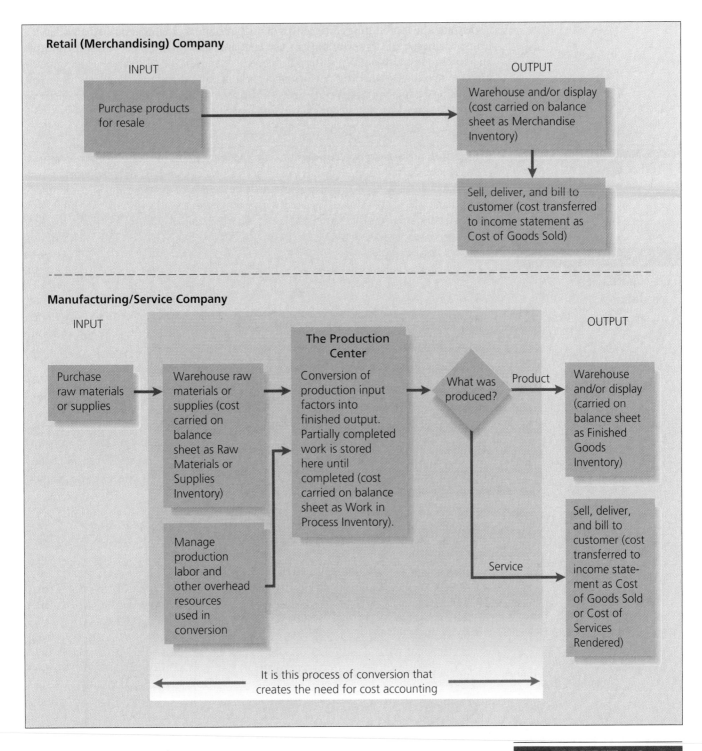

EXHIBIT 4–8

Business Input/Output Relationships

work in process (incomplete jobs). Such accounting is acceptable because service firms normally have few, if any, materials costs other than supplies for work not started. As mentioned earlier, because services generally cannot be warehoused, costs of finished jobs are usually transferred immediately to the income statement to be matched against job revenues, rather than being carried on the balance sheet in a finished goods account.

Despite the accounting differences among retailers, manufacturers, and service firms, each type of organization can use cost and management accounting concepts and techniques, although in different degrees. Managers in all firms engage in planning, controlling, evaluating performance, and making decisions. Thus, management accounting is appropriate for all firms. Cost accounting techniques are essential to all firms engaged in significant conversion activities.

STAGES OF PRODUCTION

Production processing or conversion can be viewed as existing in three stages: (1) work not started (raw materials), (2) work in process, and (3) finished work. Costs are associated with each processing stage. The stages of production in a manufacturing firm and some costs associated with each stage are illustrated in Exhibit 4–9. In the first stage of processing, the cost incurred reflects the prices paid for raw

EXHIBIT 4–9

Stages and Costs of Production

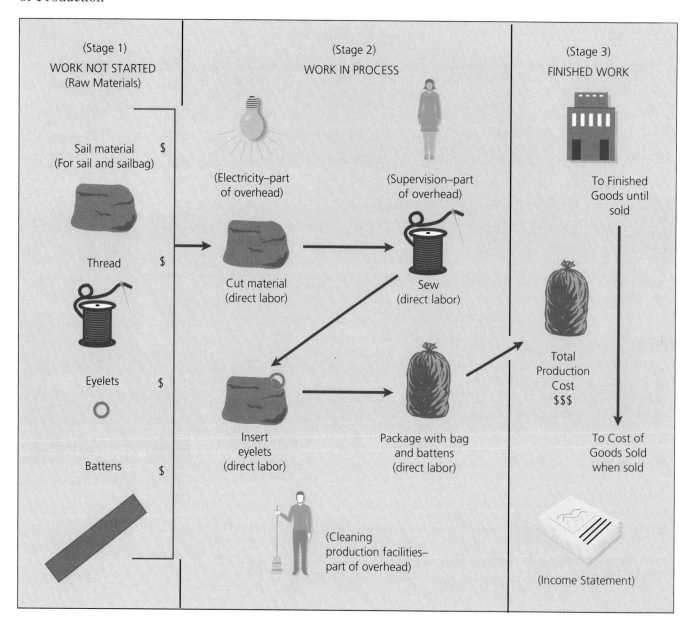

materials and/or supplies. As work progresses through the second stage, accrual-based accounting requires that costs related to the conversion of raw materials or supplies be accumulated and attached to the goods. These costs include the wages paid to people producing the goods as well as overhead charges. The total costs incurred in stages 1 and 2 are equal to the total production cost of goods in the finished goods in stage 3.

Cost accounting provides the means for accumulating the processing costs and allocating the costs to the goods produced. The primary accounts involved in the cost accumulation process are (1) Raw Materials, (2) Work in Process, and (3) Finished Goods. These accounts relate to the three stages of production shown in Exhibit 4–9 and form a common database for cost, management, and financial accounting.

Service firms ordinarily do not have the same degree of cost complexity as manufacturers. The work-not-started stage of processing normally consists of the cost of supplies necessary for performing services. Supplies are inventoried until they are placed into a work-in-process stage. At that point, labor and overhead are added to achieve finished results. Developing the cost of services is extremely important and useful in service-oriented businesses. For instance, cost accounting is very useful in hospitals that need to accumulate the costs incurred by patients during their hospital stays and in architectural firms that need to accumulate the costs incurred for designs and models of individual projects.

The product or service costs accumulated in the inventory accounts are composed of three cost components: direct material, direct labor, and overhead. Each of these components is discussed in depth in the next section. Precise classification of some costs into one of these categories may be difficult and judgment may be required in the classification process.

VIDEO
VIGNETTE

The Real Transformers

Product costs are related to the products or services that generate the revenues of an entity. These costs can be separated into three cost components: direct material, direct labor, and production overhead. To know whether a cost is direct, a **cost object** (anything to which costs attach or are related) must be specified. A cost object can be a product, service, department, division, or territory. Once the cost object is specified, any costs that are distinctly traceable to it are called **direct costs.** Those costs that cannot be traced are called **indirect** (or common) **costs** and are **allocated** or assigned to the cost object using one or more appropriate predictors or arbitrarily chosen bases.[6]

COMPONENTS OF PRODUCT COST

cost object

direct cost

indirect cost

allocate

Direct Material

Any readily identifiable part of a product is called a direct material. Direct material costs theoretically should include the cost of all materials used in the manufacture of a product or performance of a service. For example, in the production of windsurf sails (as depicted in Exhibit 4–9), the costs of the sail material, thread, eyelets, battens, and sail bag theoretically would comprise direct material costs. However, direct costs must be *distinctly and conveniently traceable* to a cost object. The thread cost is not easily traceable or monetarily significant to Spanier & Bourne's production cost. Thus, this cost could be classified and accounted for as an indirect material and included as part of overhead.

In a service business, direct materials are often insignificant or may not be easily traced to a designated cost object. For instance, the automobile policy department

---

[6] Different cost objects may be designated for different decisions. As the cost object changes, the direct and indirect costs may also change. For instance, if a production division is specified as the cost object, the production division manager's salary is direct. If, instead, the cost object is a sales territory and the production division operates in more than one territory, the production division manager's salary is indirect.

in an insurance agency could be designated as a cost object, and the cost of preprinted insurance forms and customer proof-of-insurance cards might be significant enough to trace directly to that department. However, other supplies (pens, paper, envelopes, stationery) used by the department might be relatively inconvenient to trace and thus be treated as overhead.

Therefore, the distinction between direct and indirect costs is not as clear-cut as it may seem. Some costs that may be distinctly traceable would not be conveniently or practically traceable from an accounting standpoint. Such costs are treated and classified as indirect costs.

Direct Labor

Direct labor refers to the individuals who work specifically on manufacturing a product or performing a service. Another perspective of direct labor is that it directly adds value to the final product or service. The person assembling printers at Hewlett-Packard and the nurse at Charity Hospital represent direct labor workers.

Direct labor cost consists of wages or salaries paid to direct labor employees. Such wages and salaries must also be conveniently traceable to the product or service. Direct labor cost should include basic compensation, production efficiency bonuses, and the employer's share of Social Security and Medicare taxes. In addition, if a company's operations are relatively stable, direct labor cost should include all employer-paid insurance costs, holiday and vacation pay, and pension and other retirement benefits.[7]

As with materials, some labor costs that theoretically should be considered direct are treated as indirect. The first reason for this treatment is that specifically tracing the particular labor costs to production may be inefficient. For instance, fringe benefit costs should be treated as direct labor cost, but many companies do not have stable workforces that would allow a reasonable estimate of fringe benefit cost to be developed. Alternatively, the time, effort, and cost such an assignment could require might not be worth the additional accuracy it would provide. Thus, the treatment of employee fringe benefits as indirect costs is based on clerical cost efficiencies. But, when fringe benefit costs are as large as the ones discussed in the accompanying News Note, tracing them to direct labor may provide extremely useful management information.

Second, treating certain labor costs as direct (in the "theoretically" correct manner) may result in erroneous information about product or service costs. Assume that Spanier & Bourne employs 20 workers in its cutting room. These workers are paid $6 per hour and time and a half ($9) for overtime. One week, the employees worked a total of 1,000 hours (or 200 hours of overtime) to complete all production orders. If the overtime premium of $3 per hour were assigned to the sails produced specifically during the overtime hours, these sails would appear to have a labor cost 50 percent greater than items made during regular working hours. Because scheduling is random, the items that *happened* to be completed during overtime hours should not be forced to bear the overtime charges. Therefore, amounts incurred for costs such as overtime or shift premiums are usually considered overhead rather than direct labor cost and are indirectly allocated to all units. Thus, of the total employee labor payroll of $6,600, only $6,000 (1,000 hours × $6 per hour) would be classified as direct labor cost. The remaining $600 (200 hours × $3 per hour) would be considered overhead.

On some occasions, however, costs such as overtime cannot appropriately be considered overhead. If a customer requests a job to be scheduled during overtime hours or is in a rush and requests overtime to be worked, overtime or shift premiums should

[7] Institute of Management Accountants (formerly National Association of Accountants), *Statements on Management Accounting Number 4C: Definition and Measurement of Direct Labor Cost* (Montvale, N.J.: NAA, June 13, 1985), p. 4.

N E W S
N O T E

Employee Health Care Costs Are Skyrocketing

Can anyone still doubt that the U.S. health care system is sick and desperately in need of a cure? Costs are so out of control that the nation's medical bills [in 1992 ran] more than $800 billion. That's 14% of all economic output, a sum as big as the combined GDPs of Canada, Norway, and Sweden.

U.S. employers who provided health care coverage in 1991 spent $3,605 per worker, on average—a total of $196 billion. General Motors alone spent $3.4 billion, or $929 for every car it made. The typical company's medical bill equaled 45% of after-tax profits, an enormous handicap in any race against international competitors who bear no such burden.

SOURCE: Lee Smith, "The Right Cure for Health Care," *Fortune* (October 19, 1992), pp. 88–89. © 1992 Time Inc. All rights reserved.

be considered direct labor and be attached to the job that created the costs. For example, assume that in November, the purchasing agent for Sails-R-Us ordered a shipment of windsurf sails to be delivered in three days for a Christmas catalog promotion. This order caused Spanier & Bourne workers to work overtime to meet the order. Sails-R-Us' bill for the windsurf sails should reflect the overtime charges.

Because production activity was historically performed solely by people, direct labor once represented a primary production cost. Now, in the more highly automated work environments, direct labor often comprises less than 10 to 15 percent of total manufacturing cost. Soon, managers may find that almost all direct labor cost is replaced with a new cost of production—the cost of robots and other fully automated machinery that are used in manufacturing operations. Thus, although labor is an essential element of production, managers should not overstate the importance of labor cost because the proportion of it in products is declining.

Overhead

Overhead is any factory or production cost that is indirect to manufacturing a product or providing a service and, accordingly, does not include direct materials and direct labor. Overhead does include indirect materials and indirect labor as well as any and all other costs incurred in the production area.[8] Companies are finding that as direct labor has become a progressively smaller proportion of product cost in recent years, overhead has become progressively larger in amount and merits much greater attention than in the past.

Overhead costs are categorized as either variable or fixed based on their behavior in response to changes in levels of production volume or some other measure of activity. Variable overhead includes all production overhead costs that change in direct proportion to changes in activity levels. Examples of variable overhead are the cost of indirect materials, the cost of indirect labor paid on an hourly basis (such as wages for forklift operators, material handlers, and others who support the production, assembly, and/or service process), the cost of lubricants used for machine maintenance and floor wax used in the factory lunchroom, and the variable portion of electricity charges (or any other mixed cost) in the factory. Depreciation calculated using either the units-of-production or the service-life method is also a variable overhead cost; this type of depreciation method reflects a decline in machine utility based on usage rather than time passage and is very appropriate in an automated plant.

---

[8] Another term used for overhead is *burden*. Although this is the term under which the definition appears in SMA #2, *Management Accounting Terminology*, the authors believe that this term is unacceptable as it connotes costs that are extra, unnecessary, or oppressive. Overhead costs are essential to the conversion process, but simply cannot be traced directly to output.

Overhead costs can be extremely high for many businesses. These artists in New Orleans' Jackson Square have chosen to eliminate many overhead costs by not maintaining a building or paying for electricity and by minimizing the amount of investment made in equipment that must be depreciated.

Fixed overhead includes all production costs that remain constant within the company's relevant range of activity. Fixed overhead comprises costs such as depreciation (other than that calculated using units-of-production or service-life depreciation) on factory plant assets, factory license fees, factory insurance and property taxes, and some indirect labor costs. Fixed indirect labor cost includes salaries for management personnel such as supervisors, shift superintendents, and the plant manager. The fixed portion of mixed costs (such as maintenance and utilities) incurred in the factory is also part of fixed overhead.

An important type of overhead cost is that of quality. Quality is a managerial concern on two general levels. First, the quality of the product or service as it is perceived by the consumer is an important consideration. On another level, managers are concerned about the quality of the production process. Both levels of quality generate costs that often total 20 to 25 percent of sales.[9] There are two basic categories of quality costs: the cost of control and the cost of failure to control.

The cost of control includes prevention and appraisal costs. As discussed in the previous chapter, prevention costs are incurred to improve quality by preventing product defects and dysfunctional processing from occurring. Amounts spent on implementing training programs, researching customer needs, and acquiring improved production equipment are considered prevention costs. Amounts incurred for monitoring or inspection are called appraisal costs; these costs compensate for mistakes not eliminated through prevention. The second category of quality costs is failure costs, which may be internal (such as scrap and rework) or external (such as product returns due to quality problems, warranty costs, and complaint department costs). Expenditures made for prevention will minimize the costs that will be incurred for appraisal and failure.

In manufacturing, quality costs may be variable in relation to the quantity of defective output; may be step fixed with increases at specific levels of defective output; or may be fixed. For example, scrap and rework costs approach zero if the quantity of defective output is also nearly zero. However, these costs would be extremely high if the number of defective parts produced were high. In contrast, training expenditures are set by management choice and, therefore, would not vary regardless of the quantity of defective output produced in a given time period. As indicated in the

[9] "Measuring the Cost of Quality Takes Creativity," *(Grant Thornton) Manufacturing Issues* (Spring 1991), p. 1.

Understanding Quality Costs

Managers today understand that unsatisfactory quality means poor use of resources and, thus, higher costs. They also know that good quality can even reduce overall product costs.

An understanding of quality cost can help managers identify those areas in the production of goods or services where corrective action will produce major quality improvements and savings. Cost data can be useful in detecting those products that require further engineering and redesign to reduce scrap and reworking cost. Cost data can help identify defective output before materials and labor are committed (and, thus, before costly disassembly and rework become necessary). Finally, quality cost accounting can redirect quality control priorities. For example, cost data can be used in decisions about whether to eliminate inspections at stations where no problems have occurred.

SOURCE: Lawrence P. Carr and Lawrence A. Poneman, "Managers' Perceptions About Quality Costs," *Journal of Cost Management* (Spring 1992), pp. 65–67. Reprinted with permission from *The Journal of Cost Management for the Manufacturing Industry* (Spring 1992), © 1992. Warren Gorham & Lamont, 31 St. James Avenue, Boston, MA 02116. All rights reserved.

accompanying News Note, understanding quality costs will help managers in their control and decision-making functions.

The sum of direct material, direct labor, variable overhead, and fixed overhead costs composes total product cost.[10] Product costs can also be classified as either prime or conversion costs.

Prime and Conversion Costs

The total cost of direct material and direct labor is referred to as **prime cost** because these costs are most convincingly associated with and traceable to a specific product. Historically, the term *prime cost* was equivalent to product cost. There was not a strong consensus on whether to include overhead in the definition of product cost. Because overhead was often difficult to measure, accountants only included direct material and direct labor cost as part of inventoriable cost; thus, these costs were considered to be of primary or prime importance.

According to the Institute of Management Accountants (IMA), **conversion cost** is "the sum of direct labor . . . and factory overhead which is directly or indirectly necessary for transforming raw materials and purchased parts into a salable finished product."[11] In other words, the incurrence of conversion costs causes direct materials to be changed or converted into finished goods. Because direct labor is included as part of both prime cost and conversion cost categories, prime and conversion costs cannot be added to determine product cost.

Exhibit 4–10 shows the typical components of product cost for a manufacturing company. Nevertheless, some companies view product costs in a slightly different manner. Highly automated plants produce goods and change their equipment so rapidly between production activities that the companies are able to meet customer demand while carrying virtually no work in process or finished goods inventory. For these companies, material cost is the major part of product cost and most other costs are fixed rather than variable. There is virtually no labor. Such firms often choose to expense conversion costs. Because these firms have no ending work in process or finished goods, the labor and overhead would have been expensed either through CGS or as a period cost, regardless of the accounting approach taken.

prime cost

conversion cost

VIDEO
VIGNETTE

The Conversion Process and How Federal Express Does It

---

[10] This definition of product cost is the traditionally accepted one and is also referred to as absorption costing. Another product costing method, called variable costing, excludes the fixed overhead component. Absorption and variable costing are compared in depth in Chapter 12.

[11] Institute of Management Accountants (formerly National Association of Accountants), *Statements on Management Accounting Number 2: Management Accounting Terminology* (Montvale, N.J.: NAA, June 1, 1983), p. 24.

EXHIBIT 4–10

Components of
Product Cost

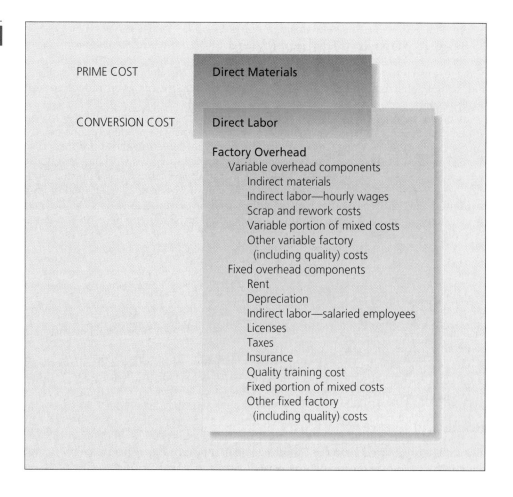

**ACCUMULATION OF
PRODUCT COSTS**

Product costs can be accumulated using either a perpetual or a periodic inventory system. In a perpetual inventory system, all product costs flow through Work in Process to Finished Goods and, ultimately, to Cost of Goods Sold. The perpetual system continuously provides current information for financial statement preparation and for inventory and cost control. Because the costs of maintaining a perpetual system have diminished significantly as computerized production, bar coding, and information processing have become more pervasive, this text will assume that all companies discussed use this inventory method.

The Delightful Sails Corporation is used to illustrate the flow of product costs in a manufacturing organization. The May 1, 1998, inventory account balances for Delightful Sails were as follows: Raw Materials Inventory (all direct), $36,500; Work in Process Inventory, $72,500; and Finished Goods Inventory, $43,700. Delightful Sails uses separate variable and fixed accounts to record the incurrence of overhead. Actual overhead costs are transferred at the end of the month to the Work in Process Inventory account. The following transactions, keyed to the journal entries in Exhibit 4–11, represent Delightful Sails' activity for a month.

During May, Delightful Sails' purchasing agent bought $140,000 of direct materials on account (entry 1), and the warehouse manager transferred $142,000 of materials into the production area (entry 2). Production wages for the month totaled $265,000, of which $218,000 were for direct labor (entry 3). May salary for the production supervisor was $10,000 (entry 4). May utility cost of $14,000 was accrued; analyzing this cost indicated that $8,000 of this amount was variable and $6,000 was fixed (entry 5). Supplies costing $2,600 were removed from inventory and placed into

EXHIBIT 4-11

Delightful Sails
Corporation—May 1998
Journal Entries

(1) Raw Materials Inventory	140,000	
Accounts Payable		140,000
To record cost of direct materials purchased on account.		
(2) Work in Process Inventory	142,000	
Raw Materials Inventory		142,000
To record direct materials transferred to production.		
(3) Work in Process Inventory	218,000	
Variable Overhead Control	47,000	
Salaries & Wages Payable		265,000
To accrue factory wages for direct and indirect labor.		
(4) Fixed Overhead Control	10,000	
Salaries & Wages Payable		10,000
To accrue production supervisor's salary.		
(5) Variable Overhead Control	8,000	
Fixed Overhead Control	6,000	
Utilities Payable		14,000
To record mixed utility cost in its variable and fixed amounts.		
(6) Variable Overhead Control	2,600	
Supplies Inventory		2,600
To record supplies used.		
(7) Fixed Overhead Control	3,500	
Cash		3,500
To record payments for factory property taxes for the period.		
(8) Fixed Overhead Control	86,000	
Accumulated Depreciation—Equipment		86,000
To record depreciation on factory assets for the period.		
(9) Fixed Overhead Control	1,500	
Prepaid Insurance		1,500
To record expiration of prepaid insurance on factory assets.		
(10) Work in Process Inventory	164,600	
Variable Overhead Control		57,600
Fixed Overhead Control		107,000
To record the transfer of actual overhead costs to Work in Process Inventory.		
(11) Finished Goods Inventory	529,100	
Work in Process Inventory		529,100
To record the transfer of work completed during the period.		
(12) Accounts Receivable	730,000	
Sales		730,000
To record the selling price of goods sold on account during the period.		
(13) Cost of Goods Sold	527,000	
Finished Goods Inventory		527,000
To record cost of goods sold for the period.		

EXHIBIT 4-12

Selected T-Accounts for
Delightful Sails

RAW MATERIALS INVENTORY			
Beg. bal.	36,500	(2)	142,000
(1)	140,000		
End. bal.	34,500		

VARIABLE OVERHEAD CONTROL			
(3)	47,000	(10)	57,600
(5)	8,000		
(6)	2,600		

WORK IN PROCESS INVENTORY			
Beg. bal.	72,500	(11)	529,100
(2) DM	142,000		
(3) DL	218,000		
(10) OH	164,600		
End. bal.	68,000		

FIXED OVERHEAD CONTROL			
(4)	10,000	(10)	107,000
(5)	6,000		
(7)	3,500		
(8)	86,000		
(9)	1,500		

FINISHED GOODS INVENTORY			
Beg. bal.	43,700	(13) CGS	527,000
(11) CGM	529,100		
End. bal.	45,800		

COST OF GOODS SOLD		
(13) CGS	527,000	

the production process (entry 6). Also, Delightful Sails paid $3,500 for May's property taxes on the factory (entry 7), depreciated the factory assets $86,000 (entry 8), and recorded the expiration of $1,500 of prepaid insurance on the factory assets (entry 9). Entry 10 shows the transfer of actual overhead to Work in Process Inventory. During May, $529,100 of goods were completed and transferred to Finished Goods Inventory (entry 11). Sales on account in the amount of $730,000 were recorded during the month (entry 12); the goods that were sold had a total cost of $527,000 (entry 13). An abbreviated presentation of the cost flows is shown in selected T-accounts in Exhibit 4–12.

COST OF GOODS MANUFACTURED AND SOLD

costs of goods manufactured

As can be observed from the T-accounts in Exhibit 4–12, the perpetual inventory system provides detailed information about the cost of materials used, goods transferred from work in process, and goods sold. This information is necessary to prepare formal financial statements. However, such detail would not be readily available to a company using the periodic inventory system. Therefore, a schedule of **cost of goods manufactured** (CGM) would need to be prepared as a preliminary step to the determination of cost of goods sold (CGS).[12] CGM is the total production cost of the goods that were completed and transferred to Finished Goods Inventory during the period. This amount is similar to the cost of net purchases in the cost of goods sold schedule for a retailer. Regardless of the inventory method employed, accountants prepare formal schedules of cost of goods manufactured and cost of goods sold for management. These schedules are used to demonstrate the flow of costs and the calculation (or recalculation in the case of a perpetual system) of important amounts contained on the income statement.

Formal schedules of cost of goods manufactured and cost of goods sold are presented in Exhibit 4–13 using the amounts shown in Exhibits 4–11 and 4–12. The schedule of cost of goods manufactured starts with the beginning balance of Work in Process (WIP) Inventory and details all product cost components. The cost of materials used in production during the period is equal to the beginning balance of

[12] A service business prepares a schedule of cost of services rendered.

DELIGHTFUL SAILS CORPORATION
Schedule of Cost of Goods Manufactured
For Month Ended May 31, 1998

Beginning balance of Work in Process, 5/1/98			$ 72,500
Manufacturing costs for the period:			
Raw Materials (all direct):			
Beginning balance	$ 36,500		
Purchases of materials	140,000		
Raw materials available for use	$176,500		
Ending balance	(34,500)		
Total raw materials used		$142,000	
Direct labor		218,000	
Variable overhead			
Indirect labor	$ 47,000		
Utilities	8,000		
Supplies	2,600	57,600	
Fixed overhead			
Supervisor's salary	$ 10,000		
Utilities	6,000		
Factory property taxes	3,500		
Factory asset depreciation	86,000		
Factory insurance	1,500	107,000	
Total current period manufacturing costs			524,600
Total costs to account for			$597,100
Ending balance of Work in Process, 5/31/98			(68,000)
Cost of goods manufactured			$529,100

DELIGHTFUL SAILS CORPORATION
Schedule of Cost of Goods Sold
For Month Ended May 31, 1998

Beginning balance of Finished Goods, 5/1/98	$ 43,700
Cost of Goods Manufactured	529,100
Cost of Goods Available for Sale	$572,800
Ending balance of Finished Goods, 5/31/98	(45,800)
Cost of Goods Sold	$527,000

Raw Materials (RM) Inventory plus raw materials purchased minus the ending balance of RM Inventory. If Raw Materials Inventory includes both direct and indirect materials, the cost of direct material used is assigned to WIP Inventory and the cost of indirect materials used is included in variable overhead. Direct labor cost is added to direct material used in the schedule of cost of goods manufactured. Because direct labor cannot be warehoused, all charges for direct labor during the period are part of WIP Inventory. Variable and fixed overhead costs are added to direct material and direct labor costs to determine total manufacturing costs.

Beginning Work in Process Inventory cost is added to total current period manufacturing costs to obtain a subtotal amount that can be referred to as "total costs to account for." The value of ending WIP Inventory is calculated (through techniques discussed later in the text) and subtracted from the subtotal to provide the cost of goods manufactured during the period. The schedule of cost of goods manufactured allows managers to see the relationships among the various production costs and to trace cost flows through the inventory accounts. It is usually prepared only as an internal schedule and is not provided to external parties.

In the schedule of cost of goods sold, cost of goods manufactured is added to the beginning balance of FG Inventory to find the cost of goods available for sale during the period. The ending FG Inventory is calculated by multiplying a physical unit count times a unit cost. If a perpetual inventory system is used, the actual amount of ending Finished Goods Inventory can be compared to that which *should* be on hand based on the finished goods account balance recorded at the end of the period. Any differences can be attributed to losses that might have arisen from theft, breakage, evaporation, or accounting errors. Ending Finished Goods Inventory is subtracted from the cost of goods available for sale to determine cost of goods sold.

REVISITING

Spanier & Bourne Sailmakers, Inc.

Another major storm played a significant role in the lives of Barry Spanier and Geoff Bourne. This monster storm of 1980 wiped out the boats of most of Spanier & Bourne's customers around Maui. Fortunately, some California windsurfers sailing in the Maui area brought their sails in for repair. This work led to the company having such popularity with windsurfers that international sailboard brands asked for Spanier & Bourne's services in the designing of sails.

Spanier & Bourne has devoted much time and effort in experimenting with sail materials and sail designs to provide the highest quality of sails practical for the windsurfing market. The firm's work has paid off in the marketplace, and its reduced costs and increased profits also reflect excellence in management planning, control, and decision making.

The firm has effectively used the computer in sailmaking. With the help of Sandy Warrick, a talented programmer, the company was able to develop a computerized sail design system. This initiative cut costs and increased sales by speeding up and making the processes of designing new sails and modifying existing models of sails more effective.

Careful attention to design, quality, speed of delivery, and cost are a great recipe for success.

SOURCES: Interview with Barry Spanier and Geoff Bourne; "Brothers of the Cloth," *Performance Windsurf Report*, (Summer, 1994), p. 20ff; and "Spanier and Bourne Sailmakers," *Real-World Lessons For America's Small Businesses—Insights From The Blue Chip Enterprise Initiative 1994* (1994), pp. 91–92.

CHAPTER SUMMARY

This chapter presents a variety of ways that the concept of cost is used by accountants and managers and discusses how costs are classified in a company's accounting system. Major categories of costs are (1) those associated with a particular time of incurrence, (2) those indicating cost behavior, (3) those classified as product or period costs on the financial statements, and (4) those affecting decision making. The first three categories are explained extensively in the chapter; the fourth category is discussed throughout the remainder of the text.

Historical, replacement, and budgeted costs are typically associated with time. Although historical costs are used for external financial statements, replacement and budgeted costs are more often used by managers in conducting their planning, controlling, and decision-making functions. Variable, fixed, mixed, and step costs describe cost behavior within the context of a relevant range. Total variable cost varies directly and proportionately with changes in activity; variable costs are constant on a per-unit basis. Costs that remain constant in total, regardless of changes in activity, are fixed. On a per-unit basis, fixed costs vary inversely with activity changes. Mixed costs are hybrid costs that contain both a fixed and variable component. For product costing and management's uses, mixed costs are analyzed and separated into their variable and fixed components. (This process is discussed in Chapter 5.) Step costs can be variable or fixed, depending on the size of the "step" change (small or large, respectively) that occurs relative to the change in activity. Accountants select a relevant range that allows step variable costs to be treated as variable and step fixed costs to be treated as fixed.

For financial statement purposes, costs are considered to be unexpired and reported on the balance sheet or expired and reported on the income statement. Costs may also be viewed as product or period costs. Product costs are inventoriable and include direct material, direct labor, and variable and fixed manufacturing overhead. These costs expire and become cost of goods sold expense when the products are sold. In contrast, period costs are incurred outside the production area and are usually associated with the functions of selling, administrating, and financing. Period costs are related more to the passage of time than to purchasing or manufacturing a product or rendering a service. Expired period costs are shown on the income statement as expenses or losses.

Costs are also said to be direct or indirect relative to a cost object. The direct material and direct labor costs of production are physically and conveniently traceable to products and are called prime costs. All other costs incurred in the production area are indirect and are referred to as manufacturing overhead.

The extensive activity required to convert raw materials into finished goods is what distinguishes manufacturers and service companies from retailers. This conversion process necessitates that all factory costs be accumulated and reported under accrual accounting as product costs.

An internal management report, known as the cost of goods manufactured schedule, traces the flow of costs into the production area and through conversion into finished goods. This report provides the necessary information to prepare the cost of goods sold section of a manufacturer's income statement.

APPENDIX

Income Statement Comparisons

The income statements of merchandising, service, and manufacturing businesses are the same except for differences in the cost of goods sold section. A merchandising company has only one inventory account and, thus, cost of goods sold reflects changes within the merchandise inventory account. A service company computes the cost of services rendered instead of cost of goods sold. A manufacturing organization has three inventory accounts, and the cost of goods sold section of its income statement depicts the changes in Finished Goods Inventory. A manufacturer supports its cost of goods sold computation with a schedule of cost of goods manufactured for the period. This schedule is not normally presented in the company's external financial statements. Cost of goods manufactured replaces the net purchases amount used by merchandisers. Illustrations of income statements for each type of business follow. Balance sheets are not shown because the only differences are in the number and titles of inventory accounts.

ANDERSON DEPARTMENT STORE

Income Statement
For the Year Ended December 31, 1998

Net Sales			$2,336,000
Cost of Goods Sold			
Merchandise inventory, 1/1/98		$ 369,000	
Cost of purchases		1,616,000	
Total merchandise available for sale		$1,985,000	
Merchandise inventory, 12/31/98		(360,000)	
Cost of goods sold			(1,625,000)
Gross Margin on Sales			$ 711,000
Operating Expenses			
Selling expenses		$ 359,000	
Administrative expenses		251,000	(610,000)
Income from Operations			$ 101,000
Other Income			
Dividend income	$6,800		
Rental income	2,200	$ 9,000	
Other Expenses			
Interest on bonds & notes		(21,000)	(12,000)
Income before Taxes			$ 89,000
Income Taxes			(33,820)
Net Income			$ 55,180
Earnings per share (assume 40,000 shares outstanding)			$1.38

FISHER ACCOUNTING SERVICES

Income Statement
For the Year Ended December 31, 1998

Service Revenue		$1,400,000
Cost of Services Rendered		
Direct labor	$520,000	
Supplies	27,000	
Service department overhead	143,000	(690,000)
Gross Margin on Services		$ 710,000
Operating Expenses		
Selling expenses (similar to items detailed		
for merchandising company)	$105,000	
Administrative expenses (similar to items		
detailed for merchandising company)	312,000	(417,000)
Income from Operations		$ 293,000
Interest Expense		(49,200)
Income before Taxes		$ 243,800
Income Taxes		(92,644)
Net Income		$ 151,156
Earnings per share (assume 40,000 shares outstanding)		$3.78

JAMES MANUFACTURING COMPANY
Income Statement
For the Year Ended December 31, 1998

Sales		$3,600,000
Cost of Goods Sold		
Beginning inventory of finished goods, 1/1/98	$ 72,000	
Cost of goods manufactured (see below)	2,600,000	
Cost of goods available for sale	$2,672,000	
Ending inventory of finished goods, 12/31/98	(66,000)	(2,606,000)
Gross Margin on Sales		$ 994,000
Operating Expenses		
Selling expenses (similar to items detailed for merchandising company)	$ 360,000	
Administrative expenses (similar to items detailed for merchandising company)	216,000	(576,000)
Income from Operations		$ 418,000
Other Expenses		
Interest on notes		(18,000)
Income before Taxes		$ 400,000
Income Taxes		(120,000)
Net Income		$ 280,000
Earnings per share (assume 500,000 shares outstanding)		$.56

JAMES MANUFACTURING COMPANY
Schedule of Cost of Goods Manufactured
For the Year Ended December 31, 1998

Beginning balance of Work in Process Inventory, 1/1/98			$ 240,000
Manufacturing costs for the period:			
Raw Materials (all direct)			
Beginning inventory, 1/1/98	$ 140,000		
Purchases	1,360,000		
Total materials available	$1,500,000		
Ending inventory, 12/31/98	(160,000)		
Direct materials used		$1,340,000	
Direct labor		720,000	
Variable overhead		360,000	
Fixed overhead		140,000	2,560,000
Total costs to account for			$2,800,000
Ending balance of Work in Process Inventory, 12/31/98			(200,000)
Cost of goods manufactured			$2,600,000

KEY TERMS

allocate (p. 131)
budgeted cost (p. 117)
conversion cost (p. 135)
cost (p. 115)
cost driver (p. 123)
cost object (p. 131)
cost of goods manufactured
    (p. 138)
direct cost (p. 131)
direct labor (p. 124)
direct material (p. 124)
distribution cost (p. 124)
expired cost (p. 123)
fixed cost (p. 118)
historical cost (p. 116)

indirect cost (p. 131)
inventoriable cost (p. 124)
manufacturer (p. 127)
mixed cost (p. 120)
overhead (p. 124)
period cost (p. 124)
predictor (p. 122)
prime cost (p. 135)
product cost (p. 124)
relevant range (p. 117)
replacement cost (p. 117)
service company (p. 127)
step cost (p. 122)
unexpired cost (p. 123)
variable cost (p. 117)

SOLUTION STRATEGIES

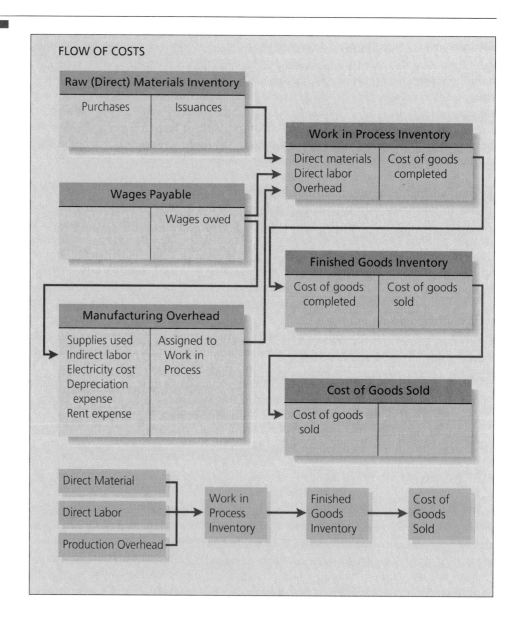

FLOW OF COSTS

Cost of Goods Manufactured

Beginning balance of Work in Process Inventory				XXX
Manufacturing costs for the period:				
Raw materials (all direct)				
Beginning balance		X		
Purchases of materials	+	XXX		
Raw materials available for use		XXX		
Ending balance	−	XXX		
Direct materials used			XXX	
Direct labor		+	XXX	
Variable overhead		+	XXX	
Fixed overhead		+	XXX	
Total current period manufacturing costs			+	XXXX
Total costs to account for				XXXX
Ending balance of Work in Process Inventory			−	XX
Cost of goods manufactured				XXXX

Cost of Goods Sold

Beginning balance of Finished Goods Inventory		XX
Cost of goods manufactured	+	XXXX
Cost of goods available for sale		XXXX
Ending balance of Finished Goods Inventory	−	X
Cost of goods sold		XXXX

Blue Streak Sailmakers had the following account balances as of June 1, 1998:

Raw Materials (direct and indirect) Inventory	$18,600
Work in Process Inventory	27,500
Finished Goods Inventory	35,600

During June the company incurred the following factory costs:

- Purchased $178,000 of raw materials on account.
- Issued $182,000 of raw materials, of which $134,000 were direct materials.
- Factory payroll of $88,000 was accrued; $62,000 was for direct labor and the rest was for supervisors.
- Utility cost was accrued; $6,500 of these costs were variable and $1,500 were fixed.
- Property taxes on the factory were accrued in the amount of $2,200.
- Prepaid insurance of $1,800 on factory equipment expired in June.
- Straight-line depreciation on factory equipment was $40,000.
- Actual overhead was transferred to Work in Process Inventory.
- Goods costing $340,000 were transferred to Finished Goods Inventory.
- Sales on account totaled $700,000.
- Cost of goods sold was $350,000.
- Selling and administrative costs were $280,000 (credit "Various accounts").

Required:

a. Journalize the transactions for June.
b. Prepare a schedule of cost of goods manufactured for June.
c. Prepare an income statement, including a detailed schedule of cost of goods sold.

Solution to Demonstration Problem

a.
(1) Raw Materials Inventory   178,000
          Accounts Payable   178,000

(2) Work in Process Inventory   134,000
       Variable Overhead Control   48,000
          Raw Materials Inventory   182,000

(3) Work in Process Inventory   62,000
       Fixed Overhead Control   26,000
          Salaries and Wages Payable   88,000

(4) Variable Overhead Control   6,500
       Fixed Overhead Control   1,500
          Utilities Payable   8,000

(5) Fixed Overhead Control   2,200
          Property Taxes Payable   2,200

(6) Fixed Overhead Control   1,800
          Prepaid Insurance   1,800

(7) Fixed Overhead Control   40,000
          Accumulated Depreciation—Factory Equipment   40,000

(8) Work in Process Inventory   126,000
          Variable Overhead Control   54,500
          Fixed Overhead Control   71,500

(9) Finished Goods Inventory   340,000
          Work in Process Inventory   340,000

(10) Accounts Receivable   700,000
          Sales   700,000

(11) Cost of Goods Sold   350,000
          Finished Goods Inventory   350,000

(12) Selling & Administrative Expense   280,000
          Various accounts   280,000

b.

BLUE STREAK SAILMAKERS
Cost of Goods Manufactured Schedule
For Month Ended June 30, 1998

Balance of Work in Process Inventory, 6/1/98		$ 27,500
Manufacturing costs for the period:		
Raw Materials		
Beginning balance	$ 18,600	
Purchases of materials	178,000	
Raw materials available for use	$196,600	
Indirect materials used	$48,000	
Ending balance	14,600	(62,600)
Total direct materials used		$134,000
Direct labor		62,000
Variable overhead		
Indirect materials	$48,000	
Utilities	6,500	54,500

Fixed overhead

Indirect labor	$26,000	
Utilities	1,500	
Factory property taxes	2,200	
Factory insurance	1,800	
Factory asset depreciation	40,000	71,500

Total current period manufacturing costs		322,000
Total costs to account for		$349,500
Balance of Work in Process Inventory, 6/30/98		(9,500)
Cost of goods manufactured		$340,000

c.

BLUE STREAK SAILMAKERS
Income Statement
For Month Ended June 30, 1998

Sales		$700,000
Cost of Goods Sold		
Beginning balance of Finished Goods, 6/1/98	$ 35,600	
Cost of Goods Manufactured	340,000	
Cost of Goods Available for Sale	$375,600	
Ending balance of Finished Goods, 6/30/98	(25,600)	
Cost of Goods Sold		(350,000)
Gross Margin		$350,000
Selling & Administrative Expenses		(280,000)
Income from Operations		$ 70,000

QUESTIONS

1. Distinguish among the cost accounting uses of historical costs, replacement costs, and budgeted costs.

2. How does a company determine its relevant range of activity? Of what use to managers is the concept of a relevant range of activity?

3. Why is a cost referred to as variable if it remains constant per unit for all volume levels within the relevant range?

4. Would it be true that fixed costs will never change in an organization? Explain the rationale for your answer.

5. What is the difference between a variable and a mixed cost, given that each changes in total with changes in activity levels?

6. Assume you are the president of your college or university. You are concerned about controlling costs. Discuss at least five campus services that you would be willing to outsource and why you chose those services.

7. Is tuition at your college or university a variable, step, or fixed cost? Justify your answer.

8. How do predictors and cost drivers differ? Why is such a distinction important?

9. What is a product cost? What types of costs are included in product costs for merchandising companies, manufacturers, and service companies?

10. What is a period cost? What types of costs are included in period costs for merchandising companies, manufacturers, and service companies?

11. Can you determine whether a cost is a product or period cost if you simply know for what purpose the cost was incurred (for example, depreciation, wages, property taxes)? If so, indicate how. If not, indicate why not and what other information is needed.

12. Are all product costs unexpired costs and all period costs expired costs? Explain.

13. Discuss why distribution costs would be important to three companies of your choice.

14. What is the process of conversion and why does this process create a need for cost accounting?

15. What are the accounting and reporting implications that accompany the use of a high degree of conversion?

16. What inventory accounts are shown on the balance sheet of a manufacturer and what information is contained in each of these accounts?

17. Why would a service company rarely show a Finished Goods Inventory account on its balance sheet?

18. How is the concept of a direct cost related to that of a cost object?

19. Why are some material and labor costs that should, in theory, be considered direct accounted for as indirect costs?

20. "Prime costs and conversion costs compose product cost; therefore, the sum of these two cost categories is equal to product cost." Is this statement true or false? Explain.

21. A company wants to increase the amount spent on prevention costs. Would such an expenditure increase or decrease product cost? Discuss your answer.

22. Why can it be said that the cost of goods manufactured schedule shows the flow of production costs in a manufacturing company?

23. Why is the amount of cost of goods manufactured different from the amount of cost of goods sold? Could there be a situation in which these amounts are equal? If so, how?

24. (Appendix) Describe the differences among merchandising, service, and manufacturing firms in their respective cost of goods sold accounts.

EXERCISES

25. (Terminology) Match the following lettered terms on the left with the appropriate numbered description on the right.

a. Direct cost	**1.**	An expense or loss
b. Period cost	**2.**	A cost that remains constant on a per-unit basis
c. Prime cost	**3.**	A cost associated with a specific cost object
d. Distribution cost	**4.**	Direct material plus direct labor
e. Variable cost	**5.**	Product cost
f. Fixed cost	**6.**	A cost that varies inversely on a per-unit basis with changes in activity
g. Expired cost	**7.**	A cost primarily associated with the passage of time rather than production activity
h. Inventoriable cost	**8.**	An expected future cost
i. Budgeted cost	**9.**	A cost of transporting a product

26. (Cost classifications) Indicate whether each item listed below is a variable (V), fixed (F), or mixed (M) cost and whether it is a product or service (PT) cost or a period (PD) cost. If some items have alternative answers, indicate the alternatives and the reasons for them.
   a. Wages of forklift operators who move finished goods from a central warehouse to the loading dock.
   b. Paper towels used in factory restrooms.
   c. Insurance premiums paid on the headquarters of a manufacturing company.
   d. Columnar paper used in an accounting firm.
   e. Cost of labels attached to shirts made by a company.

PT/V **f.** Wages of factory maintenance workers.
PT/F **g.** Property taxes on a manufacturing plant.
PO/F **h.** Salaries of secretaries in a law firm.
PT/V **i.** Freight costs of acquiring raw materials from suppliers.
PT/V **j.** Cost of wax to make candles.
PT/V **k.** Cost of radioactive material used to generate power in a nuclear power plant.

27. *(Cost behavior)* Jackson Company produces baseball caps. The company incurred the following costs to produce 2,000 caps last month:

Cardboard for the bills	$ 1,200	V
Cloth materials	2,000	V
Plastic for headband straps	1,500	V
Straight-line depreciation	1,800	F
Supervisors' salaries	4,800	F
Utilities	900	M
Total	$12,200 6.10	

  a. What did each cap component cost on a per-unit basis?
  b. What is the probable type of behavior that each of the costs exhibits?
  c. This month, the company expects to produce 2,500 caps. Would you expect each type of cost to increase or decrease? Why? Why can't the total cost of 2,500 caps be determined?

28. *(Cost behavior)* The Garfield Company manufactures high-pressure garden hoses. Costs incurred in the production process include a rubber material used to make the hoses, steel mesh used in the hoses, depreciation on the factory building, and utilities to run production machinery. Graph the most likely cost behavior for each of these costs and show what type of cost behavior is indicated by each cost.

29. *(Total cost determination with mixed cost)* Accurate & Honest Accounting Services pays $400 per month for a tax software license. In addition, variable charges average $15 for every tax return the firm prepares.
  a. Determine the total cost and the cost per unit if the firm expects to prepare the following number of tax returns in March 1997:
    1. 150
    2. 300
    3. 600
  b. Why does the cost per unit change in each of the three cases above?

30. *(Financial statement classifications)* Everglades Airboats purchased a plastics extruding machine for $100,000 to make boat hulls. During its first operating year, the machine produced 5,000 units and depreciation was calculated to be $12,500 on the machine. The company sold 4,000 of the hulls.
  a. What part of the $100,000 machine cost is expired?
  b. Where would each of the amounts related to this machine appear on the financial statements?

31. *(Product and period costs)* Phylo Company incurred the following costs in August 1997:
  ▪ Paid a 6-month premium for insurance of company headquarters, $12,000.
  ▪ Paid 3 months of property taxes on its factory building, $7,500.
  ▪ Paid a $40,000 bonus to the company president.
  ▪ Accrued $10,000 of utility costs, of which 30 percent was for the headquarters and the remainder for the factory.
  a. What expired period cost is associated with the August information?
  b. What unexpired period cost is associated with the August information?
  c. What product cost is associated with the August information?
  d. Discuss why the product cost cannot be described specifically as expired or unexpired in this situation.

32. *(Company type)* Indicate whether each of the following terms is associated with a manufacturing (Mfg.), a merchandising (Mer.), or a service (Ser.) company. There can be more than one correct answer for each term.
   a. Prepaid rent
   b. Merchandise inventory
   c. Cost of goods sold
   d. Sales salaries expense
   e. Finished goods inventory
   f. Depreciation—factory equipment
   g. Cost of services rendered
   h. Auditing fees expense
   i. Direct labor wages

33. *(Degrees of conversion)* Indicate whether each of the following types of organizations is characterized by a high, low, or moderate degree of conversion.
   a. Bakery in a grocery store
   b. Convenience store
   c. Christmas tree farm
   d. Textbook publisher
   e. Sporting goods retailer
   f. Auto manufacturer
   g. Cranberry farm
   h. Custom print shop
   i. Italian restaurant
   j. Concert ticket seller

34. *(Direct vs. indirect costs)* Modern Cutlery Inc. manufactures kitchen knives. Following are some costs incurred in the factory in 1997 for knife production:

MATERIAL COSTS

Stainless steel	$400,000
Equipment oil and grease	8,000
Plastic and fiberglass for handles	15,000
Wooden knife racks for customer storage	9,200

LABOR COSTS

Equipment operators	$200,000
Equipment mechanics	50,000
Factory supervisors	118,000

   a. What is the direct material cost for 1997?
   b. What is the direct labor cost for 1997?
   c. What is the indirect material and total indirect labor overhead cost for 1997?

35. *(Direct vs. indirect costs)* Mountain State University's College of Business has five departments: Accounting, Finance, Management, Marketing, and Decision Sciences. Each department chairperson is responsible for the department's budget preparation. Indicate whether each of the following costs incurred in the Marketing Department is direct or indirect to the department:
   a. Chairperson's salary
   b. Cost of computer time of campus mainframe used by members of the department
   c. Marketing faculty salaries
   d. Cost of equipment purchased by the department from allocated state funds
   e. Cost of travel by department faculty paid from externally generated funds contributed directly to the department
   f. Cost of secretarial salaries (secretaries are shared by the entire college)
   g. Depreciation allocation of the college building cost for the number of offices used by department faculty
   h. Cost of periodicals/books purchased by the department

36. *(Labor cost classification)* Better Living Inc. produces a variety of household products. The firm operates 24 hours per day with three daily work shifts. The first-shift workers receive "regular pay." The second shift receives a 10 percent pay premium, and the third shift receives a 20 percent pay premium. In addition, when production is scheduled on weekends, the firm pays an overtime premium of 50 percent (based on the pay rate for first-shift employees). Labor premiums are included in overhead. The August 1998 factory payroll is as follows:

Total wages for August for 18,000 hours	$168,000
Normal hourly wage for Shift #1 employees	$8
Total regular hours worked, split evenly among the three shifts	15,000

   a. How many overtime hours were worked in August?
   b. How much of the total labor cost should be charged to direct labor? To overhead?
   c. What amount of overhead was for second- and third-shift premiums? For overtime premiums?

37. *(Prime cost and conversion cost)* Johnson Manufacturing's accounting records showed the following manufacturing costs for 1997:

Direct material	$673,000
Direct labor	241,000
Indirect material	89,500
Indirect labor	176,000
Factory utilities	203,000
Selling and administrative	467,900

   a. What is prime cost for 1997?
   b. What is conversion cost for 1997?
   c. What is total product cost for 1997?

38. *(CGM and CGS)* Leisure Products Company had the following inventory balances at the beginning and end of March 1997:

	3/1/97	3/31/97
Raw Materials Inventory	$12,000	$16,000
Work in Process Inventory	68,000	84,000
Finished Goods Inventory	32,000	24,000

All raw materials are direct to the production process. The following information is also available about March manufacturing costs:

Cost of raw materials used	$128,000
Direct labor cost	162,000
Factory overhead	116,000

   a. Calculate the cost of goods manufactured for March.
   b. Determine the cost of goods sold for March.

39. *(Cost of services rendered)* The following information is related to the Lovejoy Veterinary Clinic for April 1998, the firm's first month in operation:

Veterinarian salaries for April	$12,000
Assistants' salaries for April	4,200
Medical supplies purchased in April	1,800
Utilities for month (80% related to animal treatment)	900
Office salaries for April (20% related to animal treatment)	2,600
Medical supplies on hand at April 30	800
Depreciation on medical equipment for April	600
Building rental (70% related to animal treatment)	700

Compute the cost of services rendered.

40. *(CGM and CGS)* Cathy's Custom Clocks' August 1998 cost of goods sold was $2,300,000. August 31 work in process was 40 percent of the August 1 work in process. Overhead was 225 percent of direct labor cost. During August, $768,500 of direct materials were purchased. Other August information follows:

INVENTORIES	AUGUST 1	AUGUST 31
Direct materials	$ 30,000	$42,000
Work in process	90,000	?
Finished goods	125,000	98,000

a. Prepare a schedule of the cost of goods sold for August.
b. Prepare the August cost of goods manufactured schedule.
c. What was the amount of prime costs incurred in August?
d. What was the amount of conversion costs incurred in August?

COMMUNICATION ACTIVITIES

41. *(Predictors and cost drivers; team activity)* Accountants often use factors that change in a consistent pattern with costs to explain or predict cost behavior.
  a. As a team of three or four, select factors to predict or explain the behavior of the following costs:
    1. Salesperson's travel expenses
    2. Raw material costs at a pizza restaurant
    3. Paper costs in a College of Business
    4. Maintenance costs for a lawn service company
  b. Prepare a presentation of your chosen factors that also addressses whether the factors could be used as cost drivers in addition to predictors.

42. *(Essay)* A portion of the costs incurred by business organizations is designated as direct labor costs. As used in practice, the term *direct labor cost* has a wide variety of meanings. Unless the meaning intended in a given context is clear, misunderstanding and confusion are likely to ensue. If a user does not understand the elements included in direct labor cost, erroneous interpretations of the numbers may occur and could result in poor management decisions.

In addition to understanding the conceptual definition of direct labor cost, management accountants must understand how direct labor cost should be measured.

Write a paper that discusses the following issues:
  a. Distinguish between direct labor and indirect labor.
  b. Discuss why some nonproductive labor time (such as coffee breaks, personal time) can be and often is treated as direct labor, whereas other nonproductive time (such as downtime or training) is treated as indirect labor.
  c. Following are labor cost elements that a company has classified as direct labor, manufacturing overhead, or either direct labor or manufacturing overhead, depending on the situation.
    ▪ Direct labor: Included in the company's direct labor are cost production efficiency bonuses and certain benefits for direct labor workers such as FICA (employer's portion), group life insurance, vacation pay, and workers' compensation insurance.
    ▪ Manufacturing overhead: Included in the company's overhead are costs for wage continuation plans in the event of illness, the company-sponsored cafeteria, the personnel department, and recreational facilities.
    ▪ Direct labor or manufacturing overhead: Included in the "situational" category are maintenance expense, overtime premiums, and shift premiums.
      Explain the rationale used by the company in classifying the cost elements in each of the three presented categories.

d. The two aspects of measuring direct labor costs are (1) the quantity of labor effort that is to be included, that is, the types of hours that are to be counted, and (2) the unit price by which each of these quantities is multiplied to arrive at monetary cost. Why are these considered separate and distinct aspects of measuring labor cost?

(CMA adapted)

43. *(Historical vs. replacement costs; team activity)* The following illustration depicts the cost of rebuilding a 1993 Taurus with Ford replacement parts.

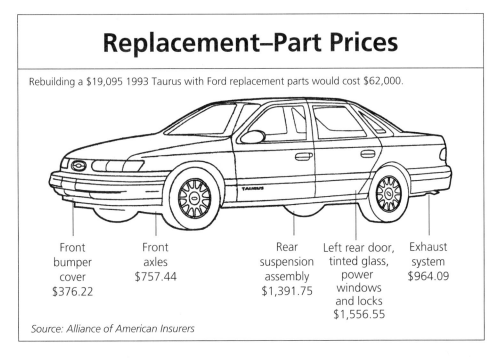

Replacement–Part Prices

Rebuilding a $19,095 1993 Taurus with Ford replacement parts would cost $62,000.

Front bumper cover $376.22	Front axles $757.44	Rear suspension assembly $1,391.75	Left rear door, tinted glass, power windows and locks $1,556.55	Exhaust system $964.09

Source: Alliance of American Insurers

Form a team of three. With each team member representing a different perspective, prepare an oral presentation to discuss the effects of an extremely harsh, snow-laden winter on your business operations (revenues and costs).

a. As the head of Ford's replacement parts division.

b. As a salesperson who must drive his/her automobile for an additional 30,000 miles.

c. As the accountant for a company that provides 30 Tauruses to employees who have limited ability to drive in the snow.

PROBLEMS

44. *(Cost behavior)* Ann's Papers & Pads makes stationery pads. In an average month, the firm produces 200,000 boxes of stationery; each box contains 50 pages of stationery and 40 envelopes. Production costs are incurred for paper, ink, glue, and boxes. The company manufactures this product in batches of 500 boxes of a specific stationery design. The following data have been extracted from the company's accounting records for November 1997:

Cost of paper for each batch	$12
Cost of ink and glue for each batch	2
Cost of 500 boxes for each batch	31
Direct labor for producing each batch	14
Labor costs for each batch design	40

Overhead charges total $20,400 per month; these are considered fully fixed for purposes of cost estimation.

a. What is the cost per box of stationery based on average production volume?

b. If sales volume increases to 300,000 boxes per month, what will be the cost per box (assuming that cost behavior patterns remain the same as in November)?

c. If sales are 300,000 boxes per month but the firm does not want the cost per box to exceed its current level (based on part a above), what amount can the company pay for labor design costs, assuming all other costs are the same as November levels?

d. Assume that Ann's Papers & Pads is now able to sell, on average, each box of stationery at a price of $5.00. If the company is able to increase its volume to 300,000 boxes per month, what sales price per box will generate the same gross margin that the firm is now achieving on 200,000 boxes per month?

e. Would it be possible to lower total costs by producing more boxes per batch, even if the total volume of 200,000 is maintained? Explain.

45. *(Cost behavior)* A company's cost structure may contain numerous different cost behavior patterns. Below are descriptions of several different costs; match these to the appropriate graphs. On each graph, the vertical axis represents cost and the horizontal axis represents level of activity or volume.

Identify, by letter, the graph that illustrates each of the following cost behavior patterns. Graphs may be used more than once.

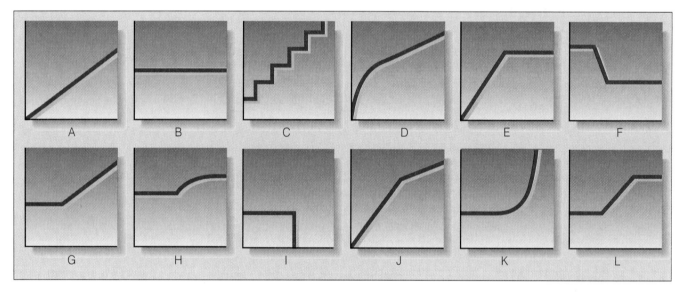

(1) Cost of raw materials, where the cost decreases by 6 cents per unit for each of the first 150 units purchased, after which it remains constant at $2.75 per unit.

(2) City water bill, which is computed as follows:

First 750,000 gallons or less	$1,000 flat fee
Next 15,000 gallons	$0.002 per gallon used
Next 15,000 gallons	$0.005 per gallon used
Next 15,000 gallons	$0.008 per gallon used
Etc.	Etc.

(3) Rent on a factory building donated by the city, where the agreement provides for a fixed-fee payment, unless 250,000 labor hours are worked, in which case no rent needs to be paid.

(4) Cost of raw materials used.

(5) Electricity bill—a flat fixed charge of $250 plus a variable cost after 150,000 kilowatt-hours are used.

(6) Salaries of maintenance workers if one maintenance worker is needed for every 1,000 hours or less of machine time.

(7) Depreciation of equipment using the straight-line method.

(8) Rent on a factory building donated by the county, where the agreement provides for a monthly rental of $100,000 less $1 for each labor hour worked in excess of 200,000 hours. However, a minimum rental payment of $20,000 must be made each month.

(9) Rent on a machine that is billed at $1,000 for up to 500 hours of machine time. After 500 hours of machine time, an additional charge of $1 per hour is paid up to a maximum charge of $2,500 per period.

(AICPA adapted)

46. *(Cost classifications)* Tom Stevens is a house painter who incurred the following costs during June 1998 when he painted three houses. He spent $900 on paint, $40 on mineral spirits, and $75 on brushes. He also bought two pairs of coveralls for $45 each; he wears coveralls only while he works. During the first week of June, Tom placed a $40 ad for his business in the classifieds. He had to hire an assistant for one of the painting jobs; the assistant was paid $12 per hour and worked 25 hours.

Being a very methodical person, Tom kept detailed records of his mileage to and from each painting job. His average operating cost per mile for his van is $.32. He found a $15 receipt in his van for a metropolitan map that he purchased in June. The map is used as a contact file for referral work and for bids that he has made on potential jobs. He also had $15 in receipts for bridge tolls ($1 per trip) for a painting job he did across the river.

Near the end of June, Tom decided to go camping, and he turned down a job on which he had bid $2,800. He called the homeowner long distance (at a cost of $3.60) to explain his reasons for declining the job.

Using the headings below, indicate how each of the June costs incurred by Tom would be classified. Assume that the cost object is a house-painting job.

Type of Cost   Variable   Fixed   Direct   Indirect   Period   Product

47. *(CGM and CGS)* PowerWedge Inc. began business in October of last year. The firm makes a log splitter, a machine that splits logs for more efficient burning in wood stoves and fireplaces. Below are data taken from the firm's accounting records that pertain to its first year of operations.

Direct materials purchased on account	$213,000
Direct materials issued to production	192,000
Direct labor payroll accrued	114,000
Indirect labor payroll paid	45,300
Factory insurance expired	2,700
Factory utilities paid	8,900
Factory depreciation recorded	18,700
Ending Work in Process Inventory (48 units)	32,000
Ending Finished Goods Inventory (30 units)	45,600
Sales on account ($1,060 per unit)	212,000

a. How many units did the company sell in its first year? How many units were manufactured in the first year?

b. What was prime cost for the first year? What was conversion cost?

c. What was the total cost of goods manufactured?

d. What was the per-unit cost of goods manufactured?

e. What was Cost of Goods Sold in the first year?

f. What was the company's first-year gross margin?

48. *(Product and period cost, CGM and CGS)* At the beginning of October 1998, Cristin Corporation had the following account balances:

Raw Materials Inventory	$ 8,000
Work in Process Inventory	13,000
Finished Goods Inventory	5,000

During October, the following transactions took place.

1. Raw materials were purchased on account, $75,000.
2. Direct materials ($21,200) and indirect materials ($2,500) were issued to production.
3. Factory payroll consisted of $50,000 for direct labor employees and $7,000 for indirect labor employees.
4. Office salaries totaled $21,100 for the month.
5. Utilities of $8,700 were accrued; 70 percent of the utilities is for the factory area.
6. Depreciation of $9,000 was recorded on plant assets; 80 percent of the depreciation is related to factory machinery and equipment.
7. Rent of $12,000 was paid on the building. The factory occupies 60 percent of the building.
8. At the end of October, the Work in Process Inventory balance was $8,300.
9. At the end of October, the balance in Finished Goods Inventory was $8,900.
   a. Determine the total amount of product cost and period cost incurred during October 1998.
   b. Compute the cost of goods manufactured for October 1998.
   c. Compute the cost of goods sold for October 1998.
   d. What level of October sales would have generated net income of $22,400?

49. *(CGM and CGS)* Brooke Company produces miniature furniture for dollhouses. The company's Raw Materials Inventory account includes the costs of both direct and indirect materials. Account balances for the company at the beginning and end of August 1997 are shown below:

	AUGUST 1	AUGUST 31
Raw Materials Inventory	$23,300	$17,400
Work in Process Inventory	32,500	29,300
Finished Goods Inventory	18,000	26,200

During the month, Brooke Company purchased $85,000 of raw materials; direct materials used during the period amounted to $68,000. Factory payroll costs for August were $91,300 of which 85 percent was related to direct labor. Overhead charges for depreciation, insurance, utilities, and maintenance totaled $81,200 for August.
a. What amount of prime cost was incurred in August?
b. What amount of conversion cost was incurred in August?
c. Prepare a schedule of cost of goods manufactured.
d. Prepare a schedule of cost of goods sold.

50. *(Journal entries)* Debonaire Clothiers Inc. produces men's suits. The following information has been gathered from the company records for 1998, the first year of company operations. Work in Process Inventory at the end of 1998 was $24,800.

Direct material purchased on account	$330,000
Direct material issued to production	294,000
Direct labor payroll accrued	215,000
Indirect labor payroll paid	62,000
Factory insurance expired	2,500
Factory utilities paid	14,300
Depreciation on factory equipment recorded	21,700
Factory rent paid	84,000
Sales made on account	958,000

The company's gross profit rate for the year was 35 percent.
a. Compute the cost of goods sold for 1998.
b. What was the total cost of goods manufactured for 1998?

c. If net income was $50,295, what were total selling and administrative expenses for the year?

d. Prepare journal entries to record the flow of costs for the year, assuming the company uses a perpetual inventory system.

---

51. *(Missing data)* The Juanita Company suffered major losses in a fire on May 23, 1997. In addition to destroying several buildings, the blaze destroyed the company's work in process for an entire product line. Fortunately, the company was insured. However, the company needs to substantiate the amount of the claim. To this end, the company has gathered the following information that pertains to production and sales of the affected product line:

CASE

1. The company's sales for the first 23 days of May amounted to $230,000. Normally, this product line generates a gross profit equal to 30 percent of sales.
2. Finished Goods Inventory was $29,000 on May 1 and $42,500 on May 23.
3. On May 1, Work in Process Inventory was $48,000.
4. During the first 23 days of May, the company incurred the following costs:

Direct materials used	$76,000
Direct labor	44,000
Manufacturing overhead	42,000

a. Determine the value of Work in Process Inventory that was destroyed by the fire.

b. What other information might the insurance company require? How would management determine or estimate this information?

---

52. An extremely important variable cost per employee is health care provided by the employer. In 1990, the average annual cost per employee was $3,161. This figure is expected to continue to rise each year as more and more expensive technology is used on patients and as the costs of that technology are passed along through the insurance company to the employer. One simple way to reduce these variable costs is to cut back on employee insurance coverage.

ETHICS AND QUALITY DISCUSSION

a. Discuss the ethical implications of reducing employee health care coverage to cut back on the variable costs incurred by the employer.

b. Assume that you are an employer with 500 employees. You are forced to cut back on some insurance benefits. Your coverage currently includes the following items: mental health coverage, long-term disability, convalescent facility care, nonemergency but medically necessary procedures, dependent coverage, and life insurance. Select the two you would eliminate or dramatically reduce and provide reasons for your selections.

c. Prepare a plan that might allow you to "trade" some variable employee health care costs for a fixed or mixed cost.

53. *General Motors Corp., in a move to improve relations with unhappy customers, said it will fix leaky head gaskets on as many as half a million Quad 4 engines. In addition to paying for future repairs, GM said it will reimburse customers who already have had the gasket—which sits between the engine block and the cylinder head—replaced at their own expense. "GM is doing this in the interest of customer satisfaction," the company said.*

GM estimates that about 8% of the half million Quad 4 engines sold from 1987 to 1991 will develop leaky head gaskets. At $550 per car, that would put the cost of the repair campaign at $22 million.

Beginning with the 1992 models, GM switched to a new head gasket in the Quad 4. GM also switched to a new manufacturing procedure to improve head bolt tightening. "We're finding these changes are doubling the life of the head gasket," said a GM spokeswoman.

[SOURCE: Neal Templin, "GM Will Repair Head Gasket on Engines," *Wall Street Journal* (February 16, 1993), p. A4. Reprinted by permission of *The Wall Street Journal*, © 1993 Dow Jones & Company, Inc. All Rights Reserved Worldwide.]

a. Discuss items associated with the leaky gasket that would fall under each of the types of quality costs (prevention, appraisal, and failure).

b. GM quotes a cost of $550 per car to fix the gasket or a total of $22 million. Do you think this estimate reflects the *true* cost of the repairs? Be sure to consider all of the items you mentioned above.

54. *Rising raw material costs are bothering Lancaster Colony these days out in Columbus, Ohio. Soybean oil, a key ingredient in the sauces and dressings that Lancaster's specialty foods division makes for the retail and food-service markets, has been priced sky-high since the end of 1993, thanks to the floods that year in the Midwest. . . . Meanwhile, Lancaster's automotive products division is struggling with the soaring price of aluminum, from which it makes toolboxes and other accessories for light trucks and vans, and with rising prices of synthetic rubber for its car floor mats and of plastic resins for truck bed liners.*

[SOURCE: Lore Croghan, "You Can Always Find More," *Financial World* (July 18, 1995), p. 52. Excerpted from *Financial World*, 1328 Broadway, New York, NY 10001. © Copyrighted 1995 by Financial World Partners. All rights reserved.]

a. Although Lancaster has raised the prices of some of its products, why is such a tactic not a viable option for all products?

b. Why wouldn't the company simply substitute a lower-grade raw material when it was available and less expensive?

c. Lancaster is also seeking out new distribution channels (including catalog sales) in addition to automotive parts stores and mass merchandisers. How might the new distribution systems change the company's variable, fixed, and mixed cost structure?

55. Outsourcing is a frequently used method of cost-cutting or of eliminating organizational activities that are not viewed as core competencies. However, outsourcing also creates new costs and, sometimes, new problems.

Some companies have found themselves locked into long-term contracts with outside suppliers that are no longer competitive. Indeed, multimillion-dollar technology-outsourcing contracts are often so complex that companies are hiring consultants at fees as high as $700,000 simply to evaluate the proposals.

[SOURCE: John A. Byrne, "Has Outsourcing Gone Too Far?" *Business Week* (April 1, 1996), p. 27.]

a. Discuss some benefits and drawbacks to outsourcing the following activities: (1) finance function, (2) data-processing function, and (3) travel arrangements.

b. How might outsourcing of manufacturing functions affect the (1) prevention, (2) appraisal, and (3) failure costs of a company?

c. What effect might outsourcing of each of the activities in part a have on an organization's corporate culture?

INTERNET ACTIVITIES

56. Search the Internet to find information about Amoco Corporation's Decision Support System for Cost Estimation. Find the discussion of the PETS system (project evaluation tool set). Describe the PETS system and the environmental changes that led to its development. What are the major financial tools that comprise PETS?

57. Frequently, corporations issue forecasts of earnings for the upcoming year. Such forecasts require estimations of both costs and revenues. Search the Internet for a discussion of a revision in the earnings forecast of any company. Relative to the original forecast, did the revision indicate earnings would be higher or lower? Discuss the reasons given for the revision in the forecasted earnings.

58. The Securities and Exchange Commission maintains online copies of documents filed by publicly traded companies. This online data source is referred to as EDGAR (Electronic Data Gathering and Retrieval). Pick any industry and select five firms from that industry. For each firm selected, search the EDGAR data base for the firm's latest 10-K filing. Find the income statement in the 10-K and compute the ratio of product costs to sales and the ratio of period costs to sales. Determine whether the ratios vary substantially across the firms. Compute an average for each of these ratios for the five firms that you have selected. Compare your average ratios to those of students who have selected other industries. What causes the ratios to vary across companies and across industries?

CHAPTER

5

Allocating Indirect Costs

LEARNING OBJECTIVES

After completing this chapter, you should be able to answer these questions:

1. Why and how are overhead costs allocated to products and services?

2. How are the high-low method and least squares regression analysis used in analyzing mixed costs?

3. How are flexible budgets used by managers to set predetermined overhead rates?

4. How is underapplied or overapplied overhead treated at the end of a period?

5. What causes underapplied and overapplied overhead?

6. Why are cost pools necessary in large organizations?

7. Why and how are service department costs allocated to producing departments?

8. *(Appendix)* Of what significance are the coefficients of correlation and determination and the standard error of the estimate?

━━━━━━━━━

Antonia's Flowers Inc.

In 1978 Antonia Bellanca moved to East Hampton, on New York's Long Island, where people from Wall Street and the entertainment business like to summer. After three years of scrounging around for work, Bellanca decided to open a flower shop. With a $2,000 loan cosigned by her father in 1981, Bellanca opened Antonia's Flowers. The shop did reasonably well, but business depended entirely on the seasons. Come the fall, the parties stopped and the flower business wilted.

In the summer of 1982, Bellanca decided she wanted a perfume that smelled like her flower shop. Nothing came close. She thought: "Why not make a fragrance to sell in the shop to make it a year-round business?"

Fortunately, Bellanca didn't know much about the cutthroat $3.5 billion (wholesale) perfume industry—that the failure rate of new fragrances is 90% or that companies like L'Oréal and Elizabeth Arden think nothing of spending $10 million to launch a new scent.

Bellanca took a bouquet of freesia to International Flavors & Fragrances Inc., a New York-based scent concocter, and asked the company to re-create its aroma. (IFF doesn't charge to develop prototypes.) After spending most of 1983 sending samples back and forth, IFF finally came up with something Bellanca liked.

Bellanca then attended a party wearing her scent, and several people asked what the fragrance was and where they could buy it. Bellanca took $5,000 from the flower shop's bank account to buy 1,000 perfume bottles and enough freesia-scented eau de toilette to fill them. She priced her Antonia's Flowers scent at $15 a bottle and sold out that summer.

Next, Bellanca got an appointment with Bergdorf Goodman's fragrance buyer who gave Bellanca a $6,000 order but demanded that she contribute $5,000 to help pay for an ad in the *New York Times* and even more for a launch party. She also paid for one of those annoying models who wander the department store floors and spray unsuspecting patrons with the flavor of the month.

The hype didn't seem to help. For weeks the scent failed to sell. With no money left for more model time, Bellanca showed up at Bergdorf's herself in the fall of 1985 to help push the perfume's sales.

SOURCE: Nancy Rotenier, "Flower Girl Makes Good," *Forbes* (September 11, 1995), p. 172. Reprinted by permission of *Forbes* magazine. © Forbes Inc., 1995.

━━━━━━━━━

Antonia Bellanca realized a significant business lesson after the Bergdorf Goodman order: more costs are involved in making and selling perfume than simply the costs of the bottle and the eau de toilette. Any cost of doing business that is not incurred for direct material or direct labor is overhead. Some overhead costs are incurred in the factory or production area; others are incurred in the service and administrative departments.

In the past, a manufacturing company considered direct material and direct labor as the prime production costs; similarly, a retailer's prime costs were inventory purchase prices and sales salaries. Overhead was an "additional" cost that was necessary, but not exceptionally significant. However, in the recent past, many manufacturing firms have invested heavily in automation and many retailers have been pressured by customers to provide more product variety. These changes have significantly increased the amount of production and nonproduction overhead costs incurred. This trend was noticeable even in the 1980s. One survey taken during that time showed that overhead costs represented 35 percent of product cost in the typical U.S. company, although only 26 percent in typical Japanese companies.[1]

[1] Jeffrey G. Miller and Thomas E. Vollman, "The Hidden Factory," *Harvard Business Review* (September–October 1985), pp. 142–150.

Regardless of where costs are incurred, a simple fact exists: for a company to be profitable, the selling prices of its products or services must cover all direct and indirect costs. Direct costs incurred for materials and labor can be easily traced to output and, as such, create few accounting difficulties. In contrast, indirect costs cannot, in many instances, be traced directly to separately distinguishable outputs. To compensate for this situation, accountants often use a process of cost allocation. **Cost allocation** refers to the assignment of an indirect cost to one or more cost objects using some reasonable basis.[2] This chapter discusses the underlying reasons for cost allocations, use of predetermined overhead rates, separation of mixed costs into variable and fixed elements, and various capacity measures that can be used to compute predetermined overhead rates.

cost allocation

WHY INDIRECT COSTS ARE ALLOCATED

A significant number of accounting procedures are based on allocations. Cost allocations can be made over several time periods or within a single time period. For example, in financial accounting, a building's cost is allocated through depreciation charges over the useful or service life. This allocation process is necessary to fulfill the matching principle. In cost accounting, manufacturing overhead costs are allocated within a period to products using predictors or cost drivers. This process reflects application of the cost principle, which requires that all costs of production (or acquisition) attach to the units purchased or produced or to the services rendered.

Indirect costs are allocated to cost objects for three reasons: (1) to determine a full cost of the cost object; (2) to motivate the manager in charge of the cost object to manage it efficiently; and (3) to compare alternative courses of action for management planning, controlling, and decision making.[3] The first reason relates to the valuations that appear on financial statements. Financial accounting has deemed that, under generally accepted accounting principles (GAAP), "full cost" must include allocated production overhead. In contrast, the assignment of nonfactory overhead costs to products is not normally allowed under GAAP.[4] The other two reasons for overhead allocations are related to internal purposes and, thus, no hard-and-fast rules apply to the overhead allocation process.

Regardless of why indirect costs are allocated, the method and basis of the allocation process should be rational and systematic so that the resulting information is useful for product costing and managerial purposes. Traditionally, much of the information generated from satisfying the "full cost" objective was also used for the second and third objectives. However, because the first purpose is externally focused and the others are internally focused, different methods can be used to provide different costs for different needs.

HOW INDIRECT COSTS ARE ALLOCATED

A manufacturer's three product cost elements are direct material, direct labor, and overhead. In an **actual cost system,** actual direct material and direct labor costs are accumulated as incurred in Work in Process Inventory. Actual production overhead costs are accumulated separately in an Overhead Control account and are assigned to Work in Process Inventory at the end of a period or at the completion of production.

actual cost system

Actual cost systems are usually less than desirable because all production overhead information must be available before any cost assignment can be made to products

---

[2] A cost object is defined in Chapter 4 as anything to which costs attach or are related (such as a product or department).

[3] Institute of Management Accountants (formerly National Association of Accountants), *Statements on Management Accounting Number 4B: Allocation of Service and Administrative Costs* (Montvale, N.J.: NAA, June 13, 1985), pp. 9–10.

[4] Although potentially unacceptable for GAAP, certain nonfactory overhead costs must be assigned to products for tax purposes.

or services. Using an actual cost system would mean that the cost of products and services produced, for example, in May could not be calculated until the May electricity bill was received in June.

Predetermined Overhead Rates

An alternative to an actual cost system is a **normal cost system,** which uses actual direct material and direct labor costs and a predetermined overhead (OH) rate or rates to assign overhead cost from an Overhead Control account to Work in Process Inventory. A **predetermined overhead rate** (or overhead application rate) is a budgeted and constant charge per unit of activity that is used to assign overhead to the period's production or services. To calculate a predetermined overhead rate, total budgeted overhead costs at a specific activity level are divided by the related activity level:

normal cost system

predetermined overhead rate

$$\text{Predetermined OH Rate} = \frac{\text{Total Budgeted OH Costs at a Specified Activity Level}}{\text{Volume of Specified Activity Level}}$$

Overhead cost and the related activity measure are typically budgeted for one year "unless the production/marketing cycle of the entity is such that the use of a longer or shorter period would clearly provide more useful information."[5] For example, the use of a longer period would be appropriate in a company engaged in activities such as constructing ships or high-rise office buildings.

Companies should use an activity base that provides a logical relationship between the base and overhead cost incurrence. The activity base that probably first comes to mind is production volume, but this base is reasonable if only one type of product is manufactured or one type of service is rendered. If multiple products or services exist, a summation cannot be made to determine "activity" because of the heterogeneous nature of the items.

Allocating overhead costs of corporate hot air balloons would not be exceptionally complicated. Because there is a definitive relationship between the two, the budgeted annual OH cost would be divided by budgeted number of flights (the activity base) for the year.

[5] Institute of Management Accountants (formerly National Association of Accountants), *Statements on Management Accounting Number 2G: Accounting for Indirect Production Costs* (Montvale, N.J.: NAA, June 1, 1987), p. 11.

Distorted Information Breeds Distorted Decisions

Managers in companies selling multiple products are making important decisions about pricing, product mix, and process technology based on distorted cost information. What's worse, alternative information rarely exists to alert these managers that product costs are badly flawed. Most companies detect the problem only after their competitiveness and profitability have deteriorated.

Distorted cost information is the result of sensible accounting choices made decades ago, when most companies manufactured a narrow range of products. Back then, the costs of direct labor and materials, the most important production factors, could be traced easily to individual products. Distortions from allocating factory and corporate overhead by burden rates on direct labor were minor. And the expense of collecting and processing data made it hard to justify more sophisticated allocation of these and other indirect costs.

Today, product lines and marketing channels have proliferated. Direct labor now represents a small fraction of corporate costs, while expenses covering factory support operations, marketing, distribution, engineering, and other overhead functions have exploded. But most companies still allocate these rising overhead and support costs by their diminishing direct labor base or, as with marketing and distribution costs, not at all.

These simplistic approaches are no longer justifiable—especially given the plummeting costs of information technology. They can also be dangerous. Intensified global competition and radically new production technologies have made accurate product cost information crucial to competitive success.

SOURCE: Reprinted by permission of *Harvard Business Review*. An excerpt from "Measure Costs Right: Make the Right Decisions," by Robin Cooper and Robert S. Kaplan (September–October 1988), p. 96. Copyright © 1988 by the President and Fellows of Harvard College; all rights reserved.

To most effectively allocate overhead to heterogeneous products, a measure of activity must be determined that is common to all output. The base should be a cost driver that directly causes the incurrence of overhead costs. Direct labor hours and direct labor dollars have been commonly used measures of activity; however, as discussed in the News Note on distorted information, the flaws in these bases are becoming more apparent as companies become increasingly automated and managers are made more aware of potential product cost distortions. Using direct labor to allocate overhead costs in automated plants results in extremely high overhead rates because the costs are applied over a smaller number of labor hours (or dollars). Other traditional measures include number of purchase orders and product-related physical characteristics such as tons or gallons.

In automated plants, machine hours may be more appropriate for allocating overhead than either direct labor base. Additionally, innovative new measures for overhead allocation include number or time of machine setups, number of parts, quantity of material handling time, and number of product defects.

Three primary reasons exist for using predetermined overhead rates rather than actual overhead costs in product costing. First, a predetermined rate allows overhead to be assigned during the period to the goods produced or services rendered. If actual overhead is assigned to products or services, total costs cannot be determined until all overhead transactions of the period have occurred. Thus, a predetermined overhead rate increases the timeliness (though reduces the precision) of information.

A second reason to use predetermined overhead rates is to compensate for fluctuations in actual overhead costs that are unrelated to activity. Overhead may vary monthly because of seasonal or calendar factors. For example, factory utility costs may be highest in the summer. If monthly production were constant and actual overhead were assigned to production, the increase in utilities would cause product cost per unit to be higher in the summer than in the rest of the year. Although one such cost difference may not be significant, numerous differences of this type could cause a large distortion in unit cost.

The third reason for using predetermined overhead rates is to overcome the problem of fluctuations in activity levels that have no impact on actual fixed overhead costs. Even if total production overhead were equal each period, changes in activity would cause a per-unit change in cost because of the fixed cost element of overhead.

The Atlanta Division of Davies International is used to illustrate the calculation of a single, plantwide overhead application rate. At the end of 1996, division management budgets its 1997 activity level at 86,000 machine hours and its 1997 manufacturing overhead costs at $559,000. The plantwide predetermined overhead application rate is $6.50 per machine hour:

$$\text{Plantwide OH Rate} = \frac{\text{Budgeted OH}}{\text{Budgeted Activity}} = \frac{\$559,000}{86,000 \text{ MHs}} = \$6.50 \text{ per MH}$$

Departmental Overhead Application Rates

Although single plantwide overhead rates are used by some companies, such a process is generally not adequate. In most companies, work is performed differently in different departments or organizational units. For example, although machine hours may be an appropriate activity base in a highly automated department, direct labor hours (DLHs) may be better for assigning overhead in a labor-intensive department. In the quality control area, number of defects may provide the best allocation base. Thus, because homogeneity is more likely within a department than among departments, separate departmental rates are generally thought to provide managers more useful information than plantwide rates.

To illustrate the differing results obtained by using plantwide and departmental overhead rates, assume that Atlanta Division has two departments: Bottling and Packaging. Bottling is labor intensive; Packaging is highly automated. Because of the differing nature of the activities performed in the two departments, management has determined that direct labor hours most effectively represent the Bottling Department's work and machine hours are appropriate for Packaging. Exhibit 5–1 shows departmental rate computations for the Atlanta Division as well as plantwide rates calculated using either direct labor hours or machine hours.

The amount of overhead applied to company products may be significantly affected by the choice between departmental and plantwide overhead application rates. Consider two perfume products of the Atlanta Division: Peachtree Parfum and Cinnamon Spice. A bottle of Peachtree requires 1 direct labor hour in Bottling and ½ machine hour in Packaging; a bottle of Cinnamon Spice requires ⅕ of a direct labor hour in Bottling and 1.5 machine hours in Packaging. Exhibit 5–2 indicates the overhead that would be applied to each product under three alternative activity bases. If departmental rates are used, product cost more clearly reflects the different amounts and types of machine/labor work performed on the products. If a plantwide rate is

	BOTTLING	PACKAGING
Budgeted annual overhead	$299,800	$259,200
Budgeted annual direct labor hours (DLHs)	40,000	10,000
Budgeted annual machine hours (MHs)	6,000	80,000

Departmental overhead rates:
Bottling (manual): $299,800 ÷ 40,000 DLHs = $7.495 per DLH
Packaging (automated): $259,200 ÷ 80,000 MHs = $3.24 per MH

Total plantwide overhead = $299,800 + $259,200 = $559,000
Plantwide overhead rate (using DLHs): $559,000 ÷ 50,000 DLHs = $11.18 per DLH
Plantwide overhead rate (using MHs): $559,000 ÷ 86,000 MHs = $6.50 per MH

EXHIBIT 5–1

Departmental versus
Plantwide Overhead Rates

EXHIBIT 5–2		TO PEACHTREE PARFUM	TO CINNAMON SPICE
Overhead Application to Products	Overhead assigned: Using departmental rates:		
	Bottling	1($7.495) = $ 7.495	.2($7.495) = $1.499
	Packaging	.5($3.240) = 1.620	1.5($3.240) = 4.860
	Total	= $ 9.115	$6.359
	Using plantwide rate:		
	Based on DLHs	1($11.18) = $11.180	.2($11.18) = $2.236
	Based on MHs	.5($6.50) = $ 3.250	1.5($6.50) = $9.750

used, essentially each product only absorbs overhead from a single department—from Bottling if direct labor hours are used and from Packaging if machine hours are used. Either plantwide rate ignores the dissimilarity of work performed in the two departments.

Consider the situation of Bachman's Inc. (a Minneapolis-based specialty retailer of horticultural products) discussed in the following News Note. The company originally charged a flat-rate fringe benefit allocation to all its stores and departments. Analysis of the drivers of fringe benefit costs helped provide a better allocation process.

Determination of valid unit costs is important because managers must decide whether a "reasonable" profit margin is being made on the goods sold. Although

N E W S N O T E

How Much to Which Area?

[The fringe benefit allocation at Bachman's Inc. had grown to 26.5% of each labor dollar by 1994 and was expected to reach 30% in a few years. The company has nine job types, each being entitled to different benefits.] Our previous studies had shown that full-time regular employees had the highest fringe cost at roughly 36%. Part-time employees (both regular and seasonal) had the lowest rate at approximately 15.5% This study by employee type did not allow us to get accurate numbers by particular divisions or departments. One of the big variables is individuals' use of the company's health insurance. It is a major cost and, to be fair, should be analyzed by each area. Also, unemployment claims vary by department, as do workers' compensation insurance costs. [Following is a discussion of several benefit categories and the new methods of allocating fringe benefit costs. The percentages represent the proportion of total fringe benefit costs.]

Retirement Savings Plan (11.2%): Provided only to nonunion exempt, nonexempt, full-time, part-time, and commissioned employees who have worked at least 1,000 hours and who are employed at year-end. Method of allocation to organizational units: proportion of total eligible employees.

Union Pension (6.3%): Set contribution provided to each union employee. Method of allocation to organizational units: number of union employees in unit.

401K Company Match (2.3%): Matched per department. Method of allocation to organizational units: direct allocation by amount of employee contributions.

FICA-Employer Portion (28.9%): Matched per employee up to FICA limit; salaries of some employees in executive cost center exceeded limit. Method of allocation to organizational units: Flat percentage of 7.65% of each labor dollar except in executive cost center in which adjustments were made for salaries in excess of FICA limit.

State Unemployment (6.4%): Minimum percent on each labor dollar up to a limit plus an adjustment for an experience rating formula based on prior claims. Method of allocation to organizational units: Sorted units by prior claims and job types; applied a minimum rate to each unit; added an additional percentage for units with higher claims.

SOURCE: Dean Lockwood, "Allocating the Cost of Fringe Benefits," *Management Accounting* (November 1994), pp. 51–53. Copyright by Institute of Management Accountants, Montvale, NJ.

	DEPARTMENTAL RATES		PLANTWIDE RATE (DLHs)		PLANTWIDE RATE (MHs)	
Selling price		$23.00		$23.00		$23.00
Direct material	$7.00		$ 7.00		$7.00	
Direct labor	5.00		5.00		5.00	
Overhead	9.12	21.12	11.18	23.18	3.25	15.25
Profit (loss)		$ 1.88		$ (.18)		$ 7.75
Rate of profit		8.2%		n/a		33.7%

EXHIBIT 5–3

Total Product Cost and Profits for Peachtree Parfum

some companies making unique products or having the ability to influence the market can set selling prices, most companies are price takers rather than price makers. Thus, cost may not be a factor in determining selling price, but it is essential in determining profit. If plantwide overhead rates distort product cost, the profit computed on the product may be inaccurate and, thus, cause management to make invalid decisions.

Assume that direct material and direct labor costs for Peachtree Parfum are $7 and $5, respectively. Adding these prime costs to the overhead computed under each method in Exhibit 5–2 gives total product cost. Exhibit 5–3 provides these product costs and the profit or loss that would be indicated if Peachtree Parfum has a selling price of $23 per bottle.

Use of the product costs developed from plantwide rates could cause management to make erroneous decisions about Peachtree Parfum. If the cost figure developed from a plantwide direct labor hour basis is used, management may believe that this product should be discontinued because it is generating a loss per bottle. If the cost figure developed from a plantwide machine hour basis is used, management may think that this fragrance is substantially more successful than it actually is. Such a decision could cause resources to be diverted from other products to increase production of Peachtree Parfum. Assuming that direct labor hours and machine hours are the best possible allocation bases for Bottling and Packaging, respectively, the only cost that gives management the necessary information on which to make resource allocation and product development/elimination decisions is the one produced by using the departmental overhead rates.

Either a departmental or plantwide overhead rate is effective for assigning overhead costs to products and provides a rational and systematic manner of costing products for external financial statement preparation. Three common reasons for using a single overhead rate are clerical ease, cost savings, and elimination of the need to separate overhead costs by cost behavior. However, even using a single rate at a departmental level reduces the applicability and informational content of overhead allocations. Therefore, to focus attention on the fact that variable and fixed overhead costs behave differently and generally result from different causal factors, separate application rates for variable and fixed overhead are encouraged and have been adopted by many companies.

Separate Variable and Fixed Overhead Application Rates

When an application rate does not separate variable and fixed costs, managers do not have the details about cost behavior needed to plan operations, control costs, calculate product costs, and make decisions. Also, cause-and-effect relationships between activity and costs are blurred, which may contribute to an inability to reduce costs or improve productivity. Thus, although clerical cost savings may result from the use of a combined rate, the ultimate cost of poor information may be significantly greater than the savings generated.

Overhead costs are not only caused by numerous different drivers, but also will behave differently with activity changes within the relevant range. Fixed overhead cost is constant in total, but changes inversely per unit with changes in the level of activity. Total variable overhead costs rise in direct proportion to increases in activity, but the per-unit cost does not change. Mixed costs will rise in total with activity changes because of the variable cost element, but the per-unit cost will not remain constant because of the inverse per-unit reaction of the fixed cost element. Thus, the first step in developing separate fixed and variable overhead application rates is to separate any mixed costs into their fixed and variable elements.

SEPARATING MIXED COSTS

As discussed in Chapter 4, accountants assume that costs are linear rather than curvilinear. Because of this assumption, the general formula for a straight line can be used to describe any type of cost within a relevant range of activity. The straight line formula is

$$y = a + bX$$

where y = total cost (dependent variable)

a = fixed portion of total cost

b = variable portion of total cost

X = activity base to which y is being related (the predictor, cost driver, or independent variable)

High-Low Method

high-low method

The **high-low method** analyzes a mixed cost by selecting actual cost observations at two levels of activity and calculating the changes in both activity and cost. Because activities cause costs to change (not the reverse), the observations selected are the highest and lowest activity levels *if these levels are within the relevant range*. Changes in activity and cost are determined by subtracting low values from high values. These changes are then used to calculate the b (variable cost) value in the $y = a + bX$ formula as follows:

$$b = \frac{\text{Cost at High Activity Level} - \text{Cost at Low Activity Level}}{\text{High Activity Level} - \text{Low Activity Level}}$$

$$b = \frac{\text{Change in the Total Cost}}{\text{Change in Activity Level}}$$

The b value is the unit variable cost per measure of activity. This value is multiplied by the activity level to determine the amount of total variable cost contained in total cost at either level of activity.

The fixed portion of a mixed cost is found by subtracting total variable cost from total cost. Because fixed cost is constant at all activity levels within the relevant range, either the high or low level of machine hours can be used to determine the fixed portion of a mixed cost.

Total mixed cost increases or decreases with changes in activity. The change in cost is equal to the change in activity times the unit variable cost; the fixed cost element does not fluctuate with changes in activity. Therefore, any increase or decrease in total cost is because of the increase or decrease in the independent variable. The variable cost per unit of activity reflects the *average* change in unit cost over the relevant range of activity.

Exhibit 5–4 illustrates the high-low method using machine hours and utility cost information for the Packaging Department of the Atlanta Division of Davies International. Information was gathered for the 8 months prior to setting the predetermined overhead rate for 1997. During 1996, the department's normal operating range of activity was between 3,000 and 10,000 machine hours per month. Occasionally, operations may occur at a level outside the relevant range (a rush special

EXHIBIT 5–4

Analysis of Mixed Cost

The following machine hours and utility cost information is available:

MONTH	LEVEL OF ACTIVITY IN MACHINE HOURS	UTILITY COST
March	4,000	$160
April	9,000	320
May	*15,000*	*420 (Outlier)*
June	4,600	175
July	3,000	140
August	8,620	320
September	5,280	210
October	5,000	208

STEP 1: Select the highest and lowest levels of activity within the relevant range and obtain the costs associated with those levels. These levels and costs are 3,000 and 9,000 hours, and $140 and $320, respectively.

STEP 2: Calculate the change in cost compared to the change in activity.

	MACHINE HOURS	ASSOCIATED TOTAL COST
High activity	9,000	$320
Low activity	3,000	140
Changes	6,000	$180

STEP 3: Determine the relationship of cost change to activity change to find the variable cost element.

$$b = \$180 \div 6{,}000 \text{ MH} = \$.03 \text{ per machine hour}$$

STEP 4: Compute total variable cost (TVC) at either level of activity.

$$\text{High level of activity: TVC} = \$.03(9{,}000) = \$270$$

$$\text{Low level of activity: TVC} = \$.03(3{,}000) = \$\ 90$$

STEP 5: Subtract total variable cost from total cost at either level of activity to determine fixed cost.

$$\text{High level of activity: } a = \$320 - \$270 = \$50$$

$$\text{Low level of activity: } a = \$140 - \$\ 90 = \$50$$

STEP 6: Substitute the fixed and variable cost values in the straight-line formula to get an equation that can be used to estimate total cost at any level of activity within the relevant range.

$$y = \$50 + \$.03X$$

where X = machine hours.

order may be taken that requires excess labor or machine time) or there may be distortions of normal cost within the relevant range (a leak in a water pipe goes unnoticed for a period of time). Such nonrepresentative or abnormal observations are called **outliers** and should be disregarded in analyzing a mixed cost. For the Packaging Department, the May observation is an outlier (substantially in excess of normal activity levels) and should not be used in the analysis of utility cost.

One potential weakness of the high-low method is that outliers may be inadvertently used in the calculation. Estimates of future costs calculated from a line drawn

outlier

using such points will not be indicative of actual costs and probably are not good predictions. A second weakness of the high-low method is that it considers only two data points. A more precise method of analyzing mixed costs is least squares regression analysis.

Least Squares Regression Analysis

least squares regression analysis

dependent variable

independent variable

Least squares regression analysis is a statistical technique that analyzes the association (or relationship) between dependent and independent variables. Least squares is used to develop an equation that predicts an unknown value of a **dependent variable** (cost) from the known values of one or more **independent variables** (activity). When multiple independent variables exist, least squares regression also helps to select the independent variable that is the best predictor of the dependent variable. For example, least squares can be used by managers trying to decide whether machine hours, direct labor hours, or pounds of material moved, best explains and predicts changes in a specific overhead cost.

simple regression

multiple regression

Simple regression analysis uses one independent variable to predict the dependent variable. Simple linear regression uses the $y = a + bX$ formula for a straight line. In **multiple regression,** two or more independent variables are used to predict the dependent variable. All examples in this chapter use simple regression and assume that a linear relationship exists between variables so that each one-unit change in the independent variable produces a constant unit change in the dependent variable.[6]

regression line

Least squares mathematically fits the best possible regression line to observed data points. A **regression line** is any line that goes through the means (or averages) of the independent and dependent variables in a set of observations. Numerous straight lines can be drawn through any set of data observations, but most of these lines would provide a poor fit. Least squares regression analysis finds the line of "best fit" for the observed data.

This line of best fit is found by predicting the a and b values in a straight-line formula using the actual activity and cost values (y values) from the observations. The equations necessary to compute b and a values using the method of least squares are as follows:[7]

$$b = \frac{\Sigma xy - n(\bar{x})(\bar{y})}{\Sigma x^2 - n(\bar{x})^2}$$

$$a = \bar{y} - b\bar{x}$$

where $\bar{x}$ = mean of the independent variable

$\bar{y}$ = mean of the dependent variable

n = number of observations

Using the Packaging Department data, the following calculations can be made:

x	y	xy	x^2
4,000	$ 160	$ 640,000	16,000,000
9,000	320	2,880,000	81,000,000
4,600	175	805,000	21,160,000
3,000	140	420,000	9,000,000
8,620	320	2,758,400	74,304,400
5,280	210	1,108,800	27,878,400
5,000	208	1,040,000	25,000,000
39,500	$1,533	$9,652,200	254,342,800

[6] Curvilinear relationships between variables also exist. An example of a curvilinear relationship is that quality defects (dependent variable) tend to increase at an increasing rate in relationship to age of machinery (independent variable). However, because linear relationships are easier to model and more commonly used, this chapter is concerned only with them.

[7] These equations are derived from mathematical computations beyond the scope of this text, but which are found in many statistics books. The symbol Σ means "the summation of."

The mean of x ($\bar{x}$) is 5,642.86 (39,500 ÷ 7) and the mean of y ($\bar{y}$) is $219 ($1,533 ÷ 7). Thus,

$$b = \frac{\$9,652,200 - 7(5,642.86)(\$219)}{254,342,800 - 7(5,642.86)(5,642.86)}$$

$$b = \frac{\$1,001,695.62}{31,449,717.14}$$

$$b = \$.032$$

$$a = \$219 - \$.032(5,642.86)$$

$$a = \$38.43$$

Thus, the b (variable cost) and a (fixed cost) values for the department's utility costs are $.032 and $38.43, respectively.

Using these values, predicted costs (y_c values) can be computed for each actual activity level. The line that is drawn through all of the y_c values will be the line of best fit for the data. Because actual costs do not generally fall directly on the regression line and predicted costs naturally do, there are differences (or deviations) between these two costs at their related activity levels. Although the regression line may not pass through any or all of the actual observation points, this is acceptable because the line has been determined to mathematically "fit" the data.

Exhibit 5–5 illustrates the utility cost and activity level data points for the Packaging Department as they would be plotted on a scattergraph. A **scattergraph** plots all known activity observations and associated costs. Preparation of such a graph prior

scattergraph

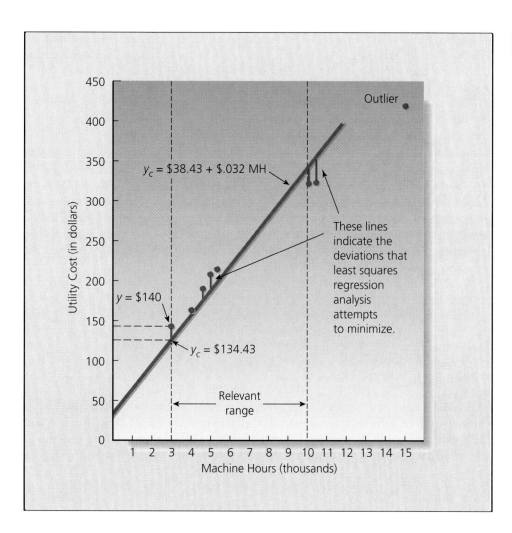

EXHIBIT 5–5

Utility Cost Plotted

to high-low or regression calculations helps verify the linearity of the observations and highlight any outliers in the data set.

The scattergraph in Exhibit 5–5 shows both actual costs (y) as dots on the graph and predicted costs (y_c). The y_c points are directly on the regression line and therefore are not visible. The vertical line segments from the observation points to the regression line are deviations between actual and predicted costs. The amount of a deviation is determined by subtracting the y_c value at an activity level from the related y value. Deviations above the regression line are positive amounts; deviations below the line are negative. The line of best fit minimizes the sum of the squares of the vertical deviations between actual observation points and predicted points on the regression line. Minimizing the sum of the *squared* deviations eliminates the problem of having both positive and negative differences for ($y - y_c$).

High-low and regression analysis help predict (within the relevant range) the value of one variable by using values of another variable. Correlation analysis, which is discussed in the Appendix to this chapter, may be used to indicate how well the known independent variable is suited to predicting the unknown, dependent variable.

USING FLEXIBLE BUDGETS IN SETTING PREDETERMINED OVERHEAD RATES

flexible budget

Before a predetermined overhead rate can be calculated, total overhead costs at various levels of activity must be predicted. A **flexible budget** is a planning document that presents expected costs at different activity levels. In a flexible budget, all costs are treated as either variable or fixed; thus, mixed costs must be separated into their variable and fixed elements using one of the previously discussed methods.

Flexible budgets can be prepared for product or period costs. The activity levels shown on a flexible budget usually cover the contemplated range of activity for the upcoming period. If all activity levels are within the relevant range, costs at each successive level should equal the previous level plus a uniform monetary increment for each variable cost factor. The increment is equal to variable cost per unit of activity times the quantity of additional activity. In some situations, however, a cost component may increase as activity increases within the contemplated range. Such an increase may occur because that cost is a step cost.

Information for the Packaging Department of the Atlanta Division is used to demonstrate the use of cost formulas in preparing flexible budgets. The department's contemplated 1997 activity range is between 70,000 and 90,000 machine hours. Analyzing the individual overhead cost factors has provided the information presented in Exhibit 5–6. This exhibit shows all cost factors in terms of the variable (b) and fixed (a) values of the straight-line formula. There is a fixed cost step increase at 75,000 MHs for insurance charges.

To calculate a predetermined overhead rate, one activity level on the flexible budget must be selected because of the irregular behavior of per-unit fixed costs. Assuming that the Packaging Department has selected 80,000 machine hours as its base activity level, the departmental predetermined overhead rate is $3.24 per machine hour. For each machine hour used in Packaging in 1997, the department's Work in Process Inventory account will be charged with $3.24 of overhead.

Because variable overhead is constant per unit at any level of activity within the relevant range, the level of activity chosen to predict total cost is not important. Note that, at all activity levels shown, the variable cost per machine hour is $2.04. However, because fixed overhead is constant in total, it varies inversely on a per-unit basis with changes in activity. Thus, a particular level of activity or capacity must be specified to calculate the predetermined fixed overhead rate per unit of activity.

capacity

Capacity refers to a measure of production volume or some other activity base.[8] The activity level selected to compute the predetermined overhead rate is often the firm's **expected annual capacity** or anticipated level of activity for the upcoming year. If actual results occur close to expected results, this capacity measure should

expected annual capacity

---

[8] Four production-volume based capacity measures that can be used to compute fixed overhead application rates are discussed in Chapter 11.

	VARIABLE COST PER MH	MACHINE HOURS		
		70,000	80,000	90,000
Variable Costs				
Indirect labor	$ .90	$ 63,000	$ 72,000	$ 81,000
Indirect materials	.44	30,800	35,200	39,600
Variable portion of mixed costs	.70	49,000	56,000	63,000
Total variable cost		$142,800	$163,200	$183,600
Variable cost per hour	$2.04	$2.04	$2.04	$2.04
	FIXED COST			
Fixed Costs				
Rent	$12,500	$ 12,500	$ 12,500	$ 12,500
Depreciation	20,000	20,000	20,000	20,000
Supervisory salaries	40,000	40,000	40,000	40,000
Insurance	2,500	2,500	3,500	3,500
Taxes	8,000	8,000	8,000	8,000
Fixed portion of mixed costs	12,000	12,000	12,000	12,000
Total fixed costs	$95,000	$ 95,000	$ 96,000	$ 96,000
Fixed cost per hour		$1.36	$1.20	$1.07
Total cost		$237,800	$259,200	$279,600
Total cost per hour		$3.40	$3.24	$3.11

EXHIBIT 5–6

Packaging Department
1997 Flexible Budget

One view of capacity in a university is the number of students that can be seated in a classroom. However, oftentimes, the university does not wish to fill a class to "capacity" for a variety of pedagogical reasons.

result in product costs that most closely reflect actual costs.[9] The concept of capacity has traditionally been related to a measure of production activity such as direct labor hours or machine hours. Capacity can also be thought of in terms of *any* measure of activity; for example, the capacity of the purchasing department could be measured by the number of orders issued. Thus, the only reason that the fixed portion of the

[9] Except where otherwise noted in the text, expected annual capacity has been chosen as the basis to calculate the predetermined fixed manufacturing overhead rate because it is believed to be the most prevalent practice. This choice, however, may not be the most effective for planning and control purposes as is discussed further in Chapter 11 in regard to standard cost variances.

predetermined overhead rate is $1.20 per machine hour is because Packaging Department management selected a capacity of 80,000 machine hours. Had any other level of capacity within the relevant range been selected, the fixed portion of the predetermined overhead rate would have differed although the variable portion of the rate would have remained at $2.04 per MH.

APPLYING OVERHEAD TO PRODUCTION

applied overhead

The departmental or variable and fixed predetermined overhead rates are used throughout the year to apply overhead to Work in Process Inventory. Overhead may be applied as production occurs, when goods or services are transferred out of Work in Process Inventory, or at the end of each month. **Applied overhead** is the amount of overhead assigned to Work in Process Inventory as a result of the activity that was used to develop the application rate. Application is made using the *predetermined* rates and the *actual* level of activity.

The cost accountant can record overhead in the accounting system either in separate accounts for actual and applied overhead or in a single account. If actual and applied accounts are separated, the applied account is a contra account to the actual overhead account and is closed against it at year-end. The alternative, more convenient, recordkeeping option is to maintain one general ledger account that is debited for actual overhead costs and credited for applied overhead. This method is used throughout the text.

Additionally, overhead may be recorded in a single overhead account or in separate accounts for the variable and fixed components. Exhibit 5–7 presents the alternative overhead recording possibilities.

If separate rates are used to apply variable and fixed overhead, the general ledger would most commonly contain separate variable and fixed overhead accounts. When separate accounts are used, mixed costs must be separated into their variable and fixed components or assigned to either the variable or the fixed general ledger account. Because overhead costs in an automated factory represent an ever larger part of product cost, the benefits of separating costs according to their behavior are thought to be greater than the time and effort expended to make that separation.

Regardless of the number (combined or separate) or type (plantwide or departmental) of predetermined overhead rates used, actual overhead costs are debited to the appropriate overhead general ledger account(s) and credited to the various sources of overhead costs. Applied overhead is debited to Work in Process Inventory and credited to the overhead general ledger accounts. The amount of applied overhead is only indirectly related to the amount of actual overhead incurred by the

EXHIBIT 5–7

Cost Accounting System Possibilities for Manufacturing Overhead

SEPARATE ACCOUNTS FOR ACTUAL & APPLIED AND FOR VARIABLE & FIXED		COMBINED ACCOUNTS FOR ACTUAL & APPLIED; SEPARATE ACCOUNTS FOR VARIABLE & FIXED	COMBINED ACCOUNT FOR ACTUAL & APPLIED AND FOR VARIABLE & FIXED
VOH Actual	**VOH Applied**	**VOH**	**Manufacturing Overhead**
XXX	YYY	Actual XXX | Applied YYY	Total actual XXX | Total applied YYY
FOH Actual	**FOH Applied**	**FOH**	XX | YY
XX	YY	Actual XX | Applied YY	

company. Actual activity causes actual overhead costs to be incurred and causes overhead to be applied to Work in Process Inventory. Thus, actual and applied overhead costs are both related to actual activity and only by actual activity are they related to each other.

Assume that during January 1997, the Packaging Department incurs 6,000 actual machine hours. Actual variable and fixed overhead costs for the month were $12,600 and $7,400, respectively. Applied variable overhead for the month is $12,240 (6,000 × $2.04) and applied fixed overhead is $7,200 (6,000 × $1.20). The journal entries to record actual and applied overhead for January 1997 are

Variable Manufacturing Overhead	12,600	
Fixed Manufacturing Overhead	7,400	
Various accounts		20,000
To record actual manufacturing overhead.		
Work in Process Inventory	19,440	
Variable Manufacturing Overhead		12,240
Fixed Manufacturing Overhead		7,200
To apply variable and fixed manufacturing overhead		
to WIP.		

At the end of the year, actual overhead will not equal applied overhead. The difference between these two figures is referred to as underapplied or overapplied overhead. **Underapplied overhead** means that the amount of overhead applied to Work in Process Inventory is less than actual overhead; **overapplied overhead** means that the amount of overhead applied to Work in Process Inventory is greater than actual overhead. Underapplied or overapplied overhead must be closed at year-end because the time frame used to determine the overhead rates was one year.

underapplied overhead

overapplied overhead

Disposition of Underapplied and Overapplied Overhead

Disposition of underapplied or overapplied overhead depends on the materiality of the amount involved. If the amount is immaterial, it is closed to Cost of Goods Sold. When overhead is underapplied (debit balance), an insufficient amount of overhead was applied to production and the closing process causes Cost of Goods Sold to increase. Alternatively, overapplied overhead (credit balance) reflects the fact that too much overhead was applied to production, so closing overapplied overhead causes Cost of Goods Sold to decrease. To illustrate this entry, assume that the Packaging Department has an immaterial overhead credit balance at year-end of $3,000. If a combined single overhead account is used, the journal entry to close overapplied overhead is

Manufacturing Overhead	3,000	
Cost of Goods Sold		3,000

If the amount of underapplied or overapplied overhead is significant, it should be allocated among the accounts containing applied overhead: Work in Process Inventory, Finished Goods Inventory, and Cost of Goods Sold. A significant amount of underapplied or overapplied overhead means that the balances in these accounts are quite different from what they would have been if actual overhead costs had been assigned to production. Allocation restates the account balances to conform more closely with actual historical costs as required for external reporting by generally accepted accounting principles. Exhibit 5–8 uses assumed data for the Packaging Department to illustrate the proration of overapplied overhead among the necessary accounts; had the amount been underapplied, the accounts debited and credited in the journal entry would have been reversed.

EXHIBIT 5–8

Proration of Overapplied
Overhead

MANUFACTURING OVERHEAD		ACCOUNT BALANCES	
Actual	$570,000	Work in Process Inventory	$116,400
Applied	600,000	Finished Goods Inventory	203,700
Overapplied	$ 30,000	Cost of Goods Sold	649,900

1. Add balances of accounts and determine proportional relationships:

	BALANCE	PROPORTION	PERCENTAGE
Work in Process	$116,400	$116,400 ÷ $970,000	12
Finished Goods	203,700	$203,700 ÷ $970,000	21
Cost of Goods Sold	649,900	$649,900 ÷ $970,000	67
Total	$970,000		100

2. Multiply percentages times overapplied overhead amount to determine the amount of adjustment needed:

ACCOUNT	PERCENTAGE	×	OVERAPPLIED OH	=	ADJUSTMENT AMOUNT
Work in Process	12	×	$30,000	=	$ 3,600
Finished Goods	21	×	$30,000	=	$ 6,300
Cost of Goods Sold	67	×	$30,000	=	$20,100

3. Prepare journal entry to close manufacturing overhead account and assign adjustment amount to appropriate accounts:

Manufacturing Overhead	30,000	
Work in Process Inventory		3,600
Finished Goods Inventory		6,300
Cost of Goods Sold		20,100

Theoretically, underapplied or overapplied overhead should be allocated based on the amounts of applied overhead contained in each account rather than on total account balances. Total balances contain direct material and direct labor costs that are not related to actual or applied overhead and, thus, could cause distortion. Use of total balances is more common, however, because (1) the theoretical method is complex and requires detailed account analysis, and (2) overhead tends to lose its identity after leaving Work in Process Inventory, thus making determination of the amount of overhead in Finished Goods Inventory and Cost of Goods Sold account balances more difficult.

Causes of Underapplied and Overapplied Overhead

There are three causes of underapplied or overapplied overhead:

1. A difference between actual and budgeted variable cost per unit
2. A difference between actual and budgeted total fixed cost
3. A difference between actual activity and the budgeted capacity used to compute the fixed overhead application rate; only if the company's actual activity level exactly equals the expected activity level will the total budgeted amount of fixed overhead be applied to production

To illustrate the third possibility, assume that the Packaging Department incurred exactly $96,000 in fixed overhead costs in 1997, which equals the amount budgeted in the computation of the FOH rate (Exhibit 5–6). During 1997, the department worked 76,800 machine hours rather than the 80,000 that were budgeted. Fixed overhead would be underapplied by $3,840 as follows:

Actual fixed overhead	$96,000
Applied fixed overhead (76,800 × $1.20)	92,160
Underapplied fixed overhead	$ 3,840

Using this information, the actual departmental FOH rate per machine hour is $1.25 ($96,000 ÷ 76,800). Had 76,800 machine hours been used to calculate the predetermined FOH application rate, there would have been no underapplied overhead. Overhead is underapplied because Packaging used fewer machine hours (76,800) than anticipated (80,000). Every actual hour of machine time caused Work in Process Inventory to receive $1.20 of FOH cost. Because fewer hours than expected were used, a lesser amount (3,200 × $1.20 = $3,840) of fixed cost was applied than was budgeted. Although budgeted and actual FOH are equal, too little overhead was applied to production because activity was less than that on which the predetermined fixed overhead rate was based. Because the capacity measure selected to compute the FOH application rate (or the combined predetermined application rate) can affect the amount of underapplied or overapplied overhead, selection of this base is important in the determination of product costs.

COST ALLOCATION THROUGH COST POOLS

cost pool

Overhead costs should be grouped in cost pools according to a relationship to a similar cost driver. A **cost pool** is simply a collection of monetary amounts. Although overhead can be viewed as a single mass of costs incurred to generate output, all costs are not necessarily incurred in relationship to a single factor. Consider the cost of a factory machine that is used to make five types of products. In many instances, the machine's depreciation is considered part of general factory overhead and allocated on some basis (in many cases, direct labor or machine hours) to all goods produced by the factory, *regardless* of whether those goods were processed by that machine. This single-stage allocation system is illustrated in Exhibit 5–9.

Although all factory overhead costs might be considered one cost pool, these costs can be collected in ways that would more accurately reflect the reason for their incurrence. If similar costs are collected in separate cost pools, their allocation to products is more precise and a more realistic product cost can be calculated and/or managerial decisions can be improved. For instance, plantwide overhead costs such as factory depreciation and insurance, utilities, indirect labor such as janitorial and

---

EXHIBIT 5–9

Single-Stage Allocation of Overhead

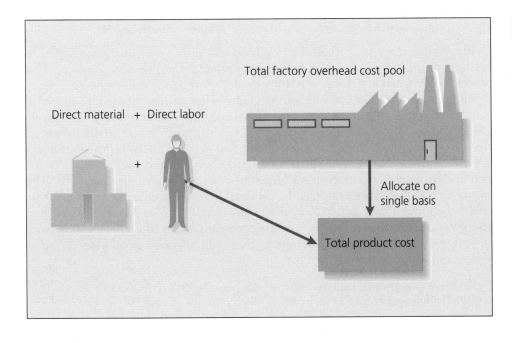

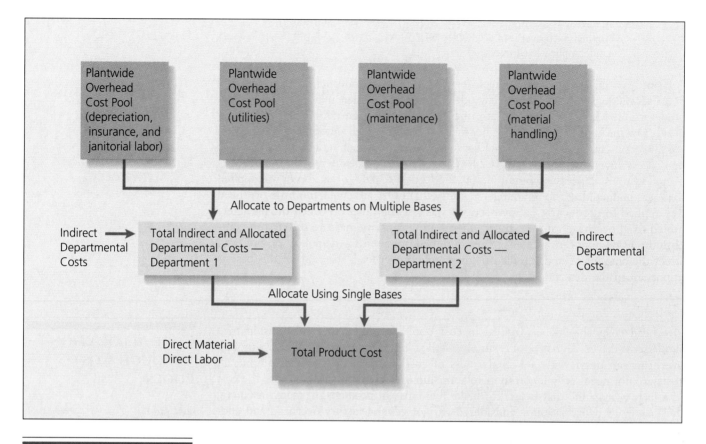

EXHIBIT 5–10

Two-Tier Allocation Pools

maintenance staff, and material handling costs can be assigned using the following bases that reflect the underlying drivers of the costs:

TYPE OF PLANTWIDE COST	ALLOCATION BASE
Plant depreciation and insurance	Square footage
Utilities	Machine hours
Janitorial labor	Square footage
Maintenance	Hours of maintenance time
Material handling	Dollars of material costs

After similar costs are gathered into related cost pools, the costs are assigned to products or services or, possibly, to operation processes and then to products. This process is illustrated in Exhibit 5–10 for a product flowing through two departments.

Multistage assignment can be used to validly assign product or service overhead costs. This process requires costs to be pooled and allocated into other, successively lower-level pools using numerous cost drivers. Such a system, which would have been virtually impossible 20 years ago, can be managed easily today using spreadsheet software. Departments can be divided into processes, and processes can be divided into manufacturing cells or groups of machines that perform similar functions. The cost of each of these layers can then be allocated to lower levels using bases that best reflect the cause of the cost. "Companies must identify drivers for cost centers and cost pools and implement flexible cost management systems to keep allocation bases current and accurate. Understanding the drivers will provide a good basis for monitoring and controlling costs."[10]

[10]Callie Berliner and James A. Brimson (eds.), *Cost Management for Today's Advanced Manufacturing* (Boston, MA: Harvard Business School Press, 1988), p. 100.

Allocating plantwide costs in a more effective manner will help managers better estimate true product costs. "The most important goal for a product cost system is to estimate the long-run costs of producing each product, each salable output, in the company's product line."[11] Use of multiple cost pools for factory overhead allocation will help in reaching this goal. But factory overhead costs are not the only indirect costs incurred in an organization.

As mentioned earlier in the chapter, organizations incur two types of overhead costs: manufacturing-related OH costs and non-manufacturing-related OH costs. Typically, as the number of product lines or the quantity of services increases, so does the need for additional support activities.

An organization's support areas consist of both service and administrative departments. A **service department** is an organizational unit (such as central purchasing, maintenance, engineering, security, or warehousing) that provides one or more specific functional tasks for other internal units. **Administrative departments** perform management activities that benefit the entire organization and include the personnel, legal, payroll, and insurance departments, and organization headquarters. Costs of service and administrative departments are referred to collectively as "service department costs," because corporate administration does service the rest of the company.

Reasons for Service Department Cost Allocations

All service department costs are incurred, in the long run, to support production or service-rendering activities. An organization producing no goods or performing no services has no need to exist; thus, it also would have no need for service departments.

ALLOCATION OF SERVICE DEPARTMENT COSTS

service department

administrative department

At the Hilton Waikoloa Village, boats take hotel guests to and from various locations. This service generates no revenue, but does produce costs that must be covered by room rates at the resort. Do you think all rooms should have an equal overhead allocation or should the rooms in the buildings farthest from the lobby area have higher allocations?

[11] H. Thomas Johnson and Robert S. Kaplan, *Relevance Lost: The Rise and Fall of Management Accounting* (Boston, MA: Harvard Business School Press, 1987), p. 234.

EXHIBIT 5–11

Allocating Service
Department Costs: Pros
and Cons

OBJECTIVE: TO COMPUTE FULL COST

Reasons for:

1. Provides for cost recovery.
2. Instills a consideration of support costs in production managers.
3. Reflects production's "fair share" of costs.
4. Meets regulations in some pricing instances.

Reasons against:

1. Provides costs that are beyond production manager's control.
2. Provides arbitrary costs that are not useful in decision making.
3. Confuses the issues of pricing and costing. Prices should be set high enough for each product to provide a profit margin that should cover all nonproduction costs.

OBJECTIVE: TO MOTIVATE MANAGERS

Reasons for:

1. Instills a consideration of support costs in production managers.
2. Relates individual production unit's profits to total company profits.
3. Reflects usage of services on a fair and equitable basis.
4. Encourages production managers to help service departments control costs.
5. Encourages the usage of certain services.

Reasons against:

1. Distorts production divisions' profit figures because allocations are subjective.
2. Includes costs that are beyond production managers' control.
3. Will not materially affect production divisions' profits.
4. Creates interdivisional ill-will when there is lack of agreement about allocation base or method.
5. Is not cost-beneficial.

OBJECTIVE: TO COMPARE ALTERNATIVE COURSES OF ACTION

Reasons for:

1. Provides relevant information in determining corporatewide profits generated by alternative actions.
2. Provides best available estimate of expected changes in costs due to alternative actions.

Reasons against:

1. Is unnecessary if alternative actions will not cause costs to change.
2. Presents distorted cash flows or profits from alternative actions since allocations are arbitrary.

ADAPTED FROM: Copyright by Institute of Management Accountants (formerly National Association of Accountants), Montvale, NJ, *Statements on Management Accounting Number 4B: Allocation of Service and Administrative Costs* (June 13, 1985), pp. 9–10.

Conversely, as long as operating activities occur, there is a need for service department activity. The conclusion could therefore be drawn that service department costs are merely another form of overhead that must be allocated to revenue-generating departments and, finally, to units of product or service.

The three objectives of cost allocation discussed at the beginning of the chapter are full cost computation, managerial motivation, and managerial decision making. Each of these objectives can be met if service department costs are assigned in a reasonable manner to revenue-producing departments. Such objectives are even met when the revenue-generating (or operating) departments are in the governmental arenas—as indicated in the following News Note. Exhibit 5–11 presents the reasons

Municipal Government Overhead Cost Allocations

NEWS NOTE

Government reformers have long advocated the more complete costing of services. When a government agency knows the full cost of its services, it gains a number of important advantages. First, unwitting subsidies for fee-supported services can be eliminated. Second, more informed choices can be made about whether to contract out a service to the private sector. Third, because work output and work quality can be related to true cost, management can better evaluate organizational efficiency. Finally, departments can better justify their budget requests because they can more accurately explain to policy makers how much work can be done at what cost. The result of all these advantages is a much more efficient public organization, better able to meet the needs of its citizens.

[In governmental operations, Internal Service Funds (ISFs) are used to] account for the financing of goods and services provided by one department to other departments on a fee-for-service basis. [However, many] indirect costs cannot be captured by ISFs. Principal among these are organizationwide support services (e.g., personnel, accounting, legal, purchasing, and auditing) provided to operating departments. These services are often called overhead. Several possible mechanisms exist to recover the cost of organizationwide indirect costs. The California League of Cities, in its definitive handbook on indirect cost allocation, describes in detail [the direct, step, and algebraic methods of allocation].

[The cities listed below have complete cost analysis and allocation systems and their finance officials indicate their uses for such systems.]

CITY	JUSTIFY BUDGET	CONTRACT FOR SERVICES	PRICE SERVICES	EVALUATE PERFORMANCE
Milwaukee, WI	Yes	Yes	Yes	No
Saginaw, MI	Yes	Yes	Yes	Yes
Baltimore, MD	Yes	Yes	Yes	No
Richfield, MN	Yes	Yes	Yes	No
Winston-Salem, NC	Yes	Yes	Yes	Yes
Austin, TX	No	Yes	Yes	No
Lincoln, NE	Yes	Yes	No	No

SOURCE: Charles K. Coe and Elizabethann O'Sullivan, "Accounting for the Hidden Costs: A National Study of Internal Service Funds and Other Indirect Costing Methods in Municipal Governments," *Public Administration Review* (January/February 1992), pp. 59–63. Reprinted with permission from *Public Administration Review* © by the American Society for Public Administration (ASPA), 1120 G Street NW, Suite 700, Washington, DC 20005. All rights reserved.

for and against allocating service department costs in relationship to each allocation objective; some of the positive points follow.

The full cost of a cost object includes all costs that contribute to its existence. Thus, full cost includes all traceable material, labor, and overhead costs incurred by the cost object plus a fair share of allocated costs that support the cost object. If the cost object is defined as a revenue-producing department, the full cost of its operations includes all traceable departmental costs plus an allocated amount of service department costs.[12]

Managers of revenue-producing areas may be made more aware of and sensitive to the support provided by the service areas when full costs are used. This increased sensitivity should motivate operations managers to use support areas in the most

[12] This concept of full cost for revenue-producing departments is recognized to an extent by the Financial Accounting Standards Board in Statement of Financial Accounting Standards No. 14 ("Financial Reporting for Segments of a Business Enterprise"). Based on this statement, certain indirect costs must be allocated to reportable segments on a benefits-received basis. The statement does not, however, allow corporate administrative costs to be allocated to segments. In several pronouncements, the Cost Accounting Standards Board also provides guidance on how to include service and administrative costs in full product cost when attempting to determine a "fair" price to charge under government contracts. For example, CAS 403 ("Allocation of Home Office Expenses to Segment") indicates acceptable allocation bases using benefits-provided or causal relationships; CAS 410 ("Allocation of Business Unit General and Administrative Expenses to Final Cost Objectives") also discusses allocation principles.

cost-beneficial manner and to provide recommendations on service department cost control. In addition, assigning service department costs to revenue-producing divisions and segments allows managers to more effectively compare the performance of their units to independent companies that must incur such costs directly.[13]

The third objective of cost allocation is to help provide a basis for comparing alternative courses of action. Including service department costs with the traceable costs of revenue-producing departments gives an indication of the future differential costs involved in an activity. (A **differential cost** is one that differs in amount among the alternatives being considered.) This comparison is especially useful in and relevant to making decisions about capacity utilization.

differential cost

Meeting one allocation objective may, however, preclude the achievement of another. For example, assignment of full cost to a cost object may not, in some situations, motivate the manager of that cost object. These potential conflicts of objectives may create disagreement as to the propriety of such allocations. If service department costs are to be assigned to revenue-producing areas, a rational and systematic means by which to make the assignment must be developed. Numerous types of allocation bases are available.

Allocation Bases

A rational and systematic allocation base for service department costs should reflect consideration of four criteria. The first criterion is the benefit received by the revenue-producing department from the service department, such as the number of computer reports prepared for each revenue-producing department by the computer department. The second criterion is a causal relationship between factors in the revenue-producing department and costs incurred in the service department; the need for the accounting department to produce paychecks for revenue-department employees illustrates this type of relationship. The third criterion is the fairness or equity of the allocations between or among revenue-producing departments; the assignment of fire and casualty premiums to the revenue-producing departments on the basis of relative fair market values of assets illustrates this type of allocation. The fourth criterion is the ability of revenue-producing departments to bear the allocated costs; this criterion is being used when the operating costs of the public relations department are assigned to revenue-producing departments on the basis of relative revenue dollars.

The benefit received and causal relationship criteria are used most often to select allocation bases, because they are reasonably objective and will produce rational allocations. Fairness is a valid theoretical basis for allocation, but its use may cause dissension because everyone does not have the same perception of what is fair or equitable. The ability-to-bear criterion often results in unrealistic or profit-detrimental actions: managers might manipulate operating data related to the allocation base to minimize service department allocations. For example, the manager of a revenue-producing department that is charged a standard maintenance fee per delivery truck mile might manipulate the mileage logs depending on how well the department is otherwise doing.

Applying the two primary criteria (benefits and causes) to the allocation of service department costs can help to specify some acceptable allocation bases. The allocation base selected should be a valid one because an improper base will yield improper information regardless of how complex or mathematically precise the allocation process appears to be. Exhibit 5–12 lists such bases in order of their frequency of use in industry.

---

[13] The use of a full cost that includes allocated service department costs should be restricted to performance comparisons with entities outside the company. This type of full cost should *not* be used for internal performance evaluations by top management because the division or segment manager has no direct control over the allocated costs.

EXHIBIT 5–12

Appropriate Service/
Administrative Cost
Allocation Bases

TYPE OF COST	ACCEPTABLE ALLOCATION BASES
Research and development	Estimated time or usage, sales, assets employed, new products developed
Personnel functions	Number of employees, payroll, number of new hires
Accounting functions	Estimated time or usage, sales, assets employed, employment data
Public relations and corporate promotion	Sales
Purchasing function	Dollar value of purchase orders, number of purchase orders, estimated time of usage, percentage of material cost of purchases
Corporate executives' salaries	Sales, assets employed, pre-tax operating income
Treasurer's functions	Sales, estimated time or usage, assets or liabilities employed
Legal and governmental affairs	Estimated time or usage, sales, assets employed
Tax department	Estimated time or usage, sales, assets employed
Income taxes	Pre-tax operating income*
Property taxes	Square feet, real estate valuation

* The source lists "net income" as the base of allocation. The authors believe that pre-tax operating income is more realistic because net income has taxes already deducted.

SOURCE: Copyright by Institute of Management Accountants (formerly National Association of Accountants), Montvale, NJ, *Statements on Management Accounting Number 4B: Allocation of Service and Administration Costs* (June 13, 1985), p. 8.

METHODS OF ALLOCATING SERVICE DEPARTMENT COSTS

The allocation process for service department costs is, like that of revenue-producing areas, a process of pooling, allocating, repooling, and reallocating costs. When service departments are considered in the pooling process, the primary pools are composed of all costs of both the revenue-producing and service departments. These costs can be gathered and specified by cost behavior (variable and fixed) or in total. Intermediate pools are then developed in the allocation process. There may be one or more layers of intermediate pools; however, the last layer will consist of only revenue-producing departments. The number of layers and the costs shown in the intermediate pools depend on the type of allocation method selected. The costs of the intermediate pools are then distributed to final cost objects (such as products, services, programs, or functional areas) using specified, rational cost driver allocation bases (such as machine hours, machine throughput time, or number of machine setups).

Allocating the pooled service department costs to revenue-producing departments can be done in three ways: the direct, step, or algebraic method. These methods are listed in order of ease of application, not necessarily in order of soundness of results. The **direct method** assigns service department costs to revenue-producing areas with only one set of intermediate cost pools or allocations. Cost assignment under the direct method is made using one specific cost driver to the intermediate pool; for

direct method

example, personnel department costs are assigned to production departments (the intermediate-level pools) based on the number of people in each production department.

step method

The **step method** of cost allocation considers the interrelationships of the service departments before assigning indirect costs to cost objects. Although a specific base is also used in this method, the step method employs a ranking for the quantity of services provided by each service department to other areas. This **"benefits-provided" ranking** lists service departments in an order that begins with the one providing the most service to all other corporate areas (both non-revenue-producing and revenue-producing areas); the ranking ends with the service department providing the least service to all but the revenue-producing areas. After the ranking is developed, service department costs are sequentially allocated down the list until all costs have been assigned to the revenue-producing areas. This ranking sequence allows the step method to partially recognize reciprocal relationships among the service departments. For example, because the personnel department provides services for all company areas, it might be the first department listed in the ranking and all other areas would receive a proportionate allocation of the personnel department's costs.

benefits-provided ranking

algebraic method

The **algebraic method** of allocating service department costs considers all departmental interrelationships and reflects these relationships in simultaneous equations. These equations provide for reciprocal allocation of service costs among the service departments as well as to the revenue-producing departments. Thus, no benefits-provided ranking is needed and the sequential step approach is not used. The algebraic method is the most complex of all the allocation techniques, but it is also theoretically the most correct and, if relationships are properly formulated, will provide the best allocations.

SERVICE DEPARTMENT COST ALLOCATION ILLUSTRATION

Data for Davies International are used to illustrate the three methods of allocating budgeted service department costs. Davies has two revenue-producing divisions: Atlanta Division (perfumes) and Decatur Division (bath products). The company's service departments are corporate administration, personnel, and maintenance. Budgeted costs of each service department are assigned to each revenue-producing area and are then added to the budgeted overhead costs of those areas to determine an appropriate divisional overhead application rate.

Exhibit 5–13 presents an abbreviated 1997 budget of the direct and indirect costs for each department and division of Davies International. These costs were budgeted using historical information adjusted for expected changes in factors affecting costs such as increases or decreases in volume and personnel from prior periods. Budgeted

EXHIBIT 5–13

Budgeted Departmental and Divisional Costs

	ADMINISTRATION	PERSONNEL	MAINTENANCE	ATLANTA	DECATUR	TOTAL
Initial Departmental Costs						
Direct costs:						
Materials	$ 0	$ 0	$ 0	$ 425,200	$223,200	$ 648,400
Labor	450,000	50,000	120,000	245,400	288,000	1,153,400
Total	$ 450,000	$50,000	$120,000	$ 670,600	$511,200	$1,801,800
Departmental overhead*	550,400	23,250	79,400	559,000	89,200	1,301,250
Total initial departmental costs	$1,000,400	$73,250	$199,400	$1,229,600	$600,400	$3,103,050

* Would be specified by type and cost behavior in actual budgeting process.

	DOLLARS OF ASSETS EMPLOYED	NUMBER OF EMPLOYEES	MACHINE HOURS USED
Administration costs—allocated on dollars of assets employed			
Personnel costs—allocated on number of employees			
Maintenance costs—allocated on machine hours used			
Administration	$ 4,000,000	8	0
Personnel	1,200,000	2	0
Maintenance	2,000,000	6	0
Atlanta Division	10,000,000	25	86,000
Decatur Division	8,000,000	7	21,500

EXHIBIT 5–14

Service Department Allocation Bases

1997 revenues are $2,250,000 for the Atlanta Division and $1,500,000 for the Decatur Division.

Exhibit 5–14 shows the bases that Davies International has chosen for allocating its service department costs. The service departments are listed in a benefits-provided ranking. Davies International's management believes that Administration provides the most service to all other areas of the company; Personnel provides the majority of its services to Maintenance and the revenue-producing areas; and Maintenance provides its services only to the Atlanta and Decatur Divisions (equipment used in other areas is under a lease maintenance arrangement and is not serviced by Davies' Maintenance Department).

Direct Method Allocation

In the direct method of allocation, service department costs are assigned using the specified bases only to the revenue-producing areas. The direct method cost allocation for Davies International is shown in Exhibit 5–15. (All percentages have been rounded to the nearest whole number.)

EXHIBIT 5–15

Direct Allocation of Service Department Costs

	BASE	PROPORTION OF TOTAL BASE	AMOUNT TO ALLOCATE	AMOUNT ALLOCATED
Administration costs ($s of assets employed)				
Atlanta Division	$10,000,000	10* ÷ 18* = 56%	$1,000,400	$ 560,224
Decatur Division	8,000,000	8* ÷ 18* = 44%	$1,000,400	440,176
Total	$18,000,000			$1,000,400
Personnel costs (# of employees)				
Atlanta Division	25	25 ÷ 32 = 78%	$ 73,250	$ 57,135
Decatur Division	7	7 ÷ 32 = 22%	$ 73,250	16,115
Total	32			$ 73,250
Maintenance costs (# of machine hours used)				
Atlanta Division	86,000	86,000 ÷ 107,500 = 80%	$ 199,400	$ 159,520
Decatur Division	21,500	21,500 ÷ 107,500 = 20%	$ 199,400	39,880
Total	107,500			$ 199,400

* In millions

	ATLANTA	DECATUR	TOTAL
Direct costs (a)	$ 670,600	$ 511,200	$1,181,800
Departmental overhead (remaining costs shown in Exhibit 5–13) (b)	$ 559,000	$ 89,200	$ 648,200
Allocated overhead			
From Administration	$ 560,224	$ 440,176	$1,000,400
From Personnel	57,135	16,115	73,250
From Maintenance	159,520	39,880	199,400
Subtotal—allocated costs (c)	$ 776,879	$ 496,171	$1,273,050
Total overhead (for application rate determination) (b + c)	1,335,879	585,371	1,921,250
Total budgeted costs (a + b + c)	$2,006,479	$1,096,571	$3,102,050
Total budgeted revenues	$2,250,000	$1,500,000	$3,750,000
Total budgeted pretax profits	$ 243,521	$ 403,429	$ 646,950

Verification of Allocation

To:	ADMINISTRATION	PERSONNEL	MAINTENANCE	ATLANTA	DECATUR	TOTAL
Initial costs	$1,000,400	$73,250	$199,400			$1,273,050
From: Administration	(1,000,400)			$560,224	$440,176	
Personnel		(73,250)		57,135	16,115	
Maintenance			(199,400)	159,520	39,880	
Totals	$ 0	$ 0	$ 0	$776,879	$496,171	$1,273,050

EXHIBIT 5–16

Direct Method Allocation
to Revenue-Producing
Areas

Use of the direct method of service department allocation produces the total budgeted costs for Atlanta Division and Decatur Division shown in Exhibit 5–16. If budgeted revenues and costs equal actual revenues and costs, Atlanta Division would show a 1997 profit of $243,521 or 11 percent on revenues, and Decatur Division would show a profit of $403,429 or 27 percent.

Step Method Allocation

To apply the step method of allocation, a benefits-provided ranking needs to be specified. This ranking for Davies International was given in Exhibit 5–14. Costs are assigned using an appropriate, specified allocation base to the departments receiving service. Once costs have been assigned from a department, no costs are charged back to that department. Step allocation of Davies International service costs is shown in Exhibit 5–17.

In this case, the amount of service department costs assigned to each revenue-producing area differs only slightly between the step and direct methods. However, in many situations, the difference can be substantial. If budgeted revenues and costs equal actual revenues and costs, the step method allocation process will cause Atlanta Division and Decatur Division to show profits of $213,643 and $433,307, respectively, as follows:

	ATLANTA DIVISION	DECATUR DIVISION
Revenues	$2,250,000	$1,500,000
Direct costs	(670,600)	(511,200)
Indirect departmental costs	(559,000)	(89,200)
Allocated service department costs	(806,757)	(466,293)
Profit	$ 213,643	$ 433,307

	BASE	PROPORTION OF TOTAL BASE	AMOUNT TO ALLOCATE	AMOUNT ALLOCATED
Administration costs ($s of assets employed; 000s omitted)				
Personnel	$ 1,200	1,200 ÷ 21,200 = 6%	$1,000,400	$ 60,024
Maintenance	2,000	2,000 ÷ 21,200 = 9%	$1,000,400	90,036
Atlanta	10,000	10,000 ÷ 21,200 = 47%	$1,000,400	470,188
Decatur	8,000	8,000 ÷ 21,200 = 38%	$1,000,400	380,152
Total	$21,200			$1,000,400
Personnel costs (# of employees)				
Maintenance	6	6 ÷ 38 = 16%	$133,274*	$ 21,324
Atlanta	25	25 ÷ 38 = 66%	$133,274	87,961
Decatur	7	7 ÷ 38 = 18%	$133,274	23,989
Total	38			$ 133,274
Maintenance (# of machine hours used)				
Atlanta	86,000	86,000 ÷ 107,500 = 80%	$310,760**	$248,608
Decatur	21,500	21,500 ÷ 107,500 = 20%	$310,760	62,152
Total	107,500			$310,760

* Personnel costs = Original cost + Allocated from Administration = $73,250 + $60,024 = $133,274
** Maintenance costs = Original cost + Allocated from Administration + Allocated from Personnel = $199,400 + $90,036 + $21,324 = $310,760

Verification of Allocation

To:	ADMINISTRATION	PERSONNEL	MAINTENANCE	ATLANTA	DECATUR	TOTAL
Initial costs	$1,000,400	$ 73,250	$199,400			$1,273,050
From:						
Administration	(1,000,400)	60,024	90,036	$470,188	$380,152	0
Personnel		(133,274)	21,324	87,961	23,989	0
Maintenance			(310,760)	248,608	62,152	0
Totals	$ 0	$ 0	$ 0	$806,757	$466,293	$1,273,050

EXHIBIT 5–17

Step Allocation of Service Department Costs

These profit figures reflect rates of return on revenues of 9 percent and 29 percent, respectively.

The step method is a hybrid allocation method between the direct and algebraic methods. This method is more realistic than the direct method in that it partially recognizes relationships among service departments, but it does not recognize the dual relationships that may exist. A service department is eliminated from the allocation sequence once its costs have been assigned outward. If a service department further down the ranking sequence provides services to departments that have already been eliminated, these benefits are not recognized by the step method cost allocation process.

Algebraic Method Allocation

The algebraic method of allocation eliminates the two disadvantages of the step method in that all interrelationships among departments are recognized and no decision must be made about a ranking order of service departments. The algebraic method involves setting up simultaneous equations to reflect reciprocal relationships among departments. Solving these equations allows costs to flow both into and out of each department.

EXHIBIT 5–18

Interdepartmental
Proportional Relationships

	ADMINISTRATION ($S OF ASSETS EMPLOYED*)		PERSONNEL (# OF EMPLOYEES)		MAINTENANCE (# OF MACHINE HOURS USED)	
	Base	Percent	Base	Percent	Base	Percent
Administration	n/a	n/a	8	18	0	0
Personnel	1,200	6	n/a	n/a	0	0
Maintenance	2,000	9	6	13	n/a	n/a
Atlanta	10,000	47	25	54	86,000	80
Decatur	8,000	38	7	15	21,500	20
Total	21,200	100	46	100	107,500	100

* 000s omitted

The starting point for the algebraic method is a review of the bases used for allocation (shown in Exhibit 5–14) and the respective amounts of those bases for each department. A schedule is created that shows the proportionate usage by each department of the other departments' services. These proportions are then used to develop equations that, when solved simultaneously, will give cost allocations that fully recognize the reciprocal services provided.

The allocation proportions for all departments of Davies International are shown in Exhibit 5–18. Allocation for the Personnel Department is discussed to illustrate how these proportions were derived. The allocation basis for personnel costs is number of employees; there are 46 employees in the organization *exclusive* of those in the Personnel Department. Personnel employees are ignored because costs are being removed from that department and assigned to other areas. Because the Administration Department has eight employees, the proportionate amount of Personnel services used by Administration is 8/46 or 18 percent.

Using the calculated percentages, algebraic equations representing the interdepartmental usage of services can be formulated. The departments are labeled A, P, and M in the equations for Administration, Personnel, and Maintenance, respectively. The initial costs of each service department are shown first in the formulas.

$$A = \$1,000,400 + .18P + .00M$$

$$P = \$\ \ \ 73,250 + .06A + .00M$$

$$M = \$\ \ \ 199,400 + .09A + .13P$$

The above equations are solved simultaneously by substituting one equation into the others, gathering like terms, and reducing the unknowns until only one unknown exists. The value for this unknown is then computed and substituted into the remaining equations. This process is continued until all unknowns have been eliminated.

1. Substituting the equation for A into the equation for P gives the following:

$$P = \$\ 73,250 + .06(\$1,000,400 + .18P)$$

Multiplying and combining terms produces the following results:

$$P = \$73,250 + \$60,024 + .01P$$

$$P = \$133,274 + .01P$$

$$P - .01P = \$133,274$$

$$.99P = \$133,274$$

$$P = \$134,620$$

Costs are allocated based on percentages computed in Exhibit 5–18.

	ADMINISTRATION		PERSONNEL		MAINTENANCE	
	Percent	Amount	Percent	Amount	Percent	Amount
Administration	n/a	n/a	18	$ 24,231	0	$ 0
Personnel	6	$ 61,478	n/a	n/a	0	0
Maintenance	9	92,217	13	17,501	n/a	n/a
Atlanta	47	481,577	54	72,695	80	247,294
Decatur	38	389,360	15	20,193	20	61,824
Total*	100	$1,024,632	100	$134,620	100	$309,118

* Total costs are the solution results of the set of algebraic equations.

EXHIBIT 5–19

Algebraic Solution of
Service Department Costs

2. The value for P is now substituted in the formula for Administration:

$$A = \$1,000,400 + .18(\$134,620)$$

$$A = \$1,000,400 + \$24,232$$

$$A = \$1,024,632$$

3. Substituting the values for A and P into the equation for M gives the following:

$$M = \$199,400 + .09(\$1,024,632) + .13(\$134,620)$$

$$M = \$199,400 + \$92,217 + \$17,501$$

$$M = \$309,118$$

The amounts provided by these equations are used to reallocate costs among all the departments; costs will then be assigned only to the revenue-producing areas. These allocations are shown in Exhibit 5–19.

The $1,024,632 of administration costs are used to illustrate the development of the amounts in Exhibit 5–19. Administration costs are assigned to the other areas based on dollars of assets employed. Exhibit 5–18 indicates that Personnel has 6 percent of the dollars of assets of Davies International; thus, costs equal to $61,478 (.06 × $1,024,632) are assigned to that area. This same process of proration is used for the other departments. Allocations from Exhibit 5–19 are used in Exhibit 5–20 to determine the reallocated costs and finalize the total budgeted overhead of the Atlanta and Decatur Divisions.

By allocating costs in this manner, total costs shown for each service department have increased over the amounts originally given. For example, Administration now shows total costs of $1,024,632 rather than the original amount of $1,000,400. These added "costs" are double-counted in that they arise from the process of service reciprocity. As shown on the line labeled "less reallocated costs" in Exhibit 5–20, these additional double-counted costs are not recognized in the revenue-producing areas for purposes of developing an overhead application rate.

When the company has few departmental interrelationships, the algebraic method can be solved by hand. If a large number of variables are present, this method must be performed by a computer. Because computer usage is now prevalent in all but the smallest organizations, the results obtained from the algebraic method are easy to generate and provide the most rational and appropriate means of allocating service department costs. The chapter demonstration problem includes a computer spreadsheet solution.

Regardless of the method used to allocate service department costs, the final step is to determine the overhead application rates for the revenue-producing areas. Once service department costs have been assigned to production, they are included as part

	TOTAL SERVICE DEPARTMENT COST (FROM EQUATIONS)	ADMINISTRATION	PERSONNEL	MAINTENANCE	ATLANTA	DECATUR
Administration	$1,024,632	$ 0	$61,478	$ 92,217	$ 481,577	$389,360
Personnel	134,620	24,231	0	17,501	72,695	20,193
Maintenance	309,118	0	0	0	247,294	61,824
Total costs	$1,468,370	$24,231	$61,478	$109,718	$ 801,566	$471,377
Less reallocated costs	(195,427)	(24,231)	(61,478)	(109,718)		
Budgeted cost	$1,272,943*	$ 0	$ 0	$ 0		
Departmental overhead costs of revenue-producing areas					559,000	89,200
Total budgeted cost for OH application rate determination					$1,360,566	$560,577

* Off due to rounding.

EXHIBIT 5-20

Final Determination of
Revenue-Producing
Department Overhead
Costs

of production overhead and allocated to products or jobs through normal overhead assignment procedures.

Using the final figures shown in Exhibit 5-20, costs of $1,360,566 and $560,577 for Atlanta Division and Decatur Division, respectively, are divided by an appropriate allocation base to assign both manufacturing and nonmanufacturing overhead to products. For example, assume that Davies International has chosen total ounces of bath products as the overhead allocation base for Decatur Division. If the division expects to produce 750,000 ounces of bath products in 1997, the overhead cost assigned to each ounce would be $.75 or ($560,577 ÷ 750,000).

For simplicity, cost behavior in all departments has been ignored. A more appropriate allocation process would specify different bases in each department for the variable and fixed costs. Such differentiation would not change the allocation process, but would change the results of the three methods (direct, step, or algebraic). Separation of variable and fixed costs would provide better allocation; use of the computer makes this process more practical than it was in the past.

Before any type of allocation is made, management should be certain that the allocation base is reasonable. Allocations are often based on the easiest available measure, such as number of people or number of documents processed. Use of such measures may distort the allocation process.

When service department cost allocations have been made to revenue-producing areas, income figures derived from the use of these amounts should not be used for manager performance evaluations. Any attempt to evaluate the financial performance of a manager of a revenue-producing department should use an incremental, rather than a full allocation, approach. Although full allocation should not be used for performance evaluations, allocating service department costs to revenue-producing areas does make managers more aware of and responsible for controlling service usage. Chapter 19 discusses this type of responsibility in more depth and also covers the concept of setting transfer prices for the provision of services between organizational units.

REVISITING

Antonia's Flowers Inc.

[When Bellanca began demonstrating the perfume herself, customers began buying. Sales were finally really rising] in February 1986; since then Antonia's Flowers has consistently been one of Bergdorf's five top-selling fragrances.

Bellanca now sells 40,000 bottles of eau de toilette annually—along with soap, perfume, shower gel and lotion—to 250 wholesale accounts, including Neiman Marcus, Saks Fifth Avenue and a host of smaller specialty stores.

She prices her basic eau de toilette at $40 for a 1.7-ounce bottle, making it a medium-priced fragrance relative to competitors.

Bellanca shut down the East Hampton flower shop in 1989 to focus solely on perfume, and has been working with IFF noses for two years to develop a second fragrance.

[In 1995] sales of her wholly-owned Antonia's Flowers Inc. are expected to be $1.6 million, with a 30% pretax profit. Overhead is minimal. IFF makes the liquid scent and ships it to Bellanca's New Jersey bottler, which in turn sends the product to a nearby distributor. Bellanca works out of a turn-of-the-century shingled house on Montauk Highway, owned by her husband; her only employees are her office manager, a salesperson and two part-time administrative assistants. She never advertises and rarely does product giveaways. [Thus, Bellanca is well aware that keeping both production and service department overhead low is a key contributor to business success and profits.]

SOURCE: Nancy Rotenier, "Flower Girl Makes Good," *Forbes* (September 11, 1995), p. 173. Reprinted by permission of *Forbes* magazine. © Forbes Inc., 1995.

CHAPTER SUMMARY

This chapter discusses the use of predetermined overhead rates in product costing. A predetermined overhead rate is calculated by dividing the upcoming period's budgeted overhead costs by a selected level of activity. (Budgeted overhead costs at various levels of activity are shown on a flexible budget.) Predetermined overhead rates eliminate the problems caused by delays in obtaining actual cost data, make the overhead allocation process more effective, and allocate a uniform amount of overhead to goods or services based on related production efforts.

The activity base chosen to compute a predetermined overhead rate should be logically related to cost changes and be a direct causal factor of that cost (a cost driver). Units of output are a valid measure only if the company produces a single product.

Departmental rates, rather than a single plantwide base, result in more refined information for product costing and managerial uses. Even within a department, however, related costs should be grouped together and assigned to consecutively lower levels of responsibility through a multistage, multiple cost driver approach. Separate application rates may also be developed for variable and fixed overhead.

To compute variable and fixed overhead rates, mixed costs must be separated into their variable and fixed components, which can be accomplished through the high-low method or least squares regression analysis. The high-low method uses the highest and lowest points of actual activity to determine the unit variable cost included in the mixed cost. Fixed cost is found by subtracting total variable cost from total cost at either the high or low activity level. Least squares regression analysis uses observations of two or more variables to mathematically determine a regression equation for a dependent variable (cost) based on its relationship to a single independent variable (activity).

When a company uses a predetermined overhead rate, underapplied or overapplied overhead results at the end of the year. This amount (if insignificant) should be closed to Cost of Goods Sold or (if significant) allocated among Work in Process Inventory, Finished Goods Inventory, and Cost of Goods Sold.

Management may want to allocate service department costs to revenue-producing areas. The three methods of allocating service department costs are the direct method, step method, and algebraic method. The direct method assigns service department costs only to revenue-producing departments and does not consider services that may be provided by one service department to another. The step method uses a benefits-provided ranking that lists service departments from the one providing the most service to other departments to the one servicing primarily the revenue-producing areas. Costs are assigned from each department in order of the ranking. Once costs have been assigned from an area, they cannot flow back into that area. The algebraic method recognizes the interrelationships among all departments through the use of simultaneous equations. This method provides the best allocation information and is readily adaptable to computer computations.

APPENDIX

Measures of Correlation and Dispersion

correlation analysis

dispersion

The suitability of using specific known (independent) variables to predict an unknown (dependent) variable is important when attempting to determine the driver of a cost. For example, although direct labor hours could be used to estimate maintenance cost, a better cost estimate might be generated by using machine hours, average age of machinery, or number of product changeovers. **Correlation analysis** is a mathematical technique that uses statistical measures of **dispersion** (or variability) to reveal the strength of the relationship between variables. (There are no independent and dependent variables in correlation analysis, only interrelated variables.)

In regression analysis, dispersion is measured as the distance of an actual point from the estimated regression line. Results are said to be highly correlated when little dispersion exists and poorly correlated when dispersion is large. Thus, the degree of correlation is inversely related to the magnitude of dispersion. One measure of dispersion is the coefficient of correlation.

Coefficient of Correlation

coefficient of correlation

The **coefficient of correlation** (r) shows the strength of relative association between two variables. The coefficient of correlation can be viewed as measuring either (1) the relationship or degree of linearity between two variables or (2) the goodness of fit of data to a regression line. The formula is

$$r = \frac{\Sigma[(x - \bar{x})(y - \bar{y})]}{\sqrt{\Sigma[(x - \bar{x})^2 \Sigma(y - \bar{y})^2]}}$$

The coefficient of correlation can range between -1 and $+1$. A positive coefficient indicates that the two variables move in the same direction. Higher values of one variable are associated with higher values of the other. For example, total variable cost is positively correlated with output volume. A negative r value indicates that the two variables move in opposite directions. Fixed cost expressed on a per-unit basis has negative correlation with output.

When all observed points (y values) lie close to the regression line, the unexplained variation in y is small and the correlation coefficient is close to 1 (either positive or negative). As larger deviations of observed values from the regression line occur, the variation becomes larger and the correlation coefficient approaches zero. A coefficient of correlation of $+1$ or -1 indicates a perfect linear relationship, and all actual points lie on the regression line. A coefficient of zero indicates no linear correlation.

Calculations for the coefficient of correlation for the Packaging Department data given in Exhibit 5–4 are shown below. The values of x and y were computed as 5,642.86 and $219, respectively. The r value is found to be .9944, which indicates a high degree of correlation.

$$r = \frac{\$1,001,700}{\sqrt{(31,449,942.86)(\$32,262)}} = .9944$$

Coefficient of Determination

The **coefficient of determination** (r^2) measures the "goodness of fit" of the data to the least squares regression line and indicates what proportion of the total variation in y is explained by the regression model. Variation is measured as the sum of the squares of the deviations from the regression line. The coefficient of determination is simply the coefficient of correlation squared. Thus, the coefficient of determination for the Packaging Department data is .9888, which means that the least squares line for this mixed utility cost explains 98.88 percent of the variation in the utility cost.

coefficient of determination

Both the coefficients of correlation and the coefficients of determination are helpful in determining the strength of the relationship between two or more variables used in predictive formulas. However, because of the process of squaring, the coefficient of determination gives a more conservative picture about the relationship's strength. For example, assume that a coefficient of correlation were found to be .75. It might be assumed that a significant degree of variation could be explained by the regression formula producing this result. However, the coefficient of determination for the same data set is only .562, meaning that only slightly over half the variation is explained by the regression model.

Standard Error of the Estimate

The **standard error of the estimate** (S_e) is a commonly used statistic that indicates the degree of dispersion (or average difference) of actual observations from predicted values. The standard error of the estimate can be calculated using the a and b values from the regression formula as follows:

standard error of the estimate

$$S_e = \sqrt{\frac{\Sigma y^2 - a(\Sigma y) - b(\Sigma xy)}{n - 2}}$$

where n = number of observations

If each actual value of the dependent variable fell on the regression line, the standard error of the estimate would be zero, indicating that the regression equation would provide perfect estimations for that data set. As the standard error of the estimate increases, the strength of the relationship between the two variables declines and the regression equation gives progressively less precise predictions of future results. Using the information from the chapter (pp. 169–170) for the Packaging Department, the standard error of the estimate is

y^2	(FROM THE CHAPTER)
$ 25,600	$a = \$38.43$
102,400	$\Sigma y = \$1,533$
30,625	$\Sigma xy = \$9,652,200$
19,600	$b = \$.032$
102,400	$n = 7$
44,100	
43,264	
$367,989	

$$S_e = \sqrt{\frac{\$367,989 - (\$38.43)(\$1,533) - (\$.032)(\$9,652,200)}{7 - 2}}$$

$$S_e = \sqrt{\frac{\$205.41}{5}} = \$6.41$$

At any level of machine hours, a distribution of the differences between the expected and the actual costs of utilities will have a mean of zero and a standard error of the estimate of $6.41. Thus, the estimates from the regression formula have some variability.

An inverse relationship exists between the quantitative values measured by the standard error of the estimate and the coefficient of determination. The standard error of the estimate measures size of the deviations of expected values from actual observations, whereas the coefficient of determination measures the proportion of variation explained by the regression model. Therefore, smaller deviations give a higher proportion of explanation.

KEY TERMS

actual cost system (p. 162)
administrative department (p. 179)
algebraic method (p. 184)
applied overhead (p. 174)
benefits-provided ranking (p. 184)
capacity (p. 172)
coefficient of correlation (p. 192)
coefficient of determination (p. 193)
correlation analysis (p. 192)
cost allocation (p. 162)
cost pool (p. 177)
dependent variable (p. 170)
differential cost (p. 182)
direct method (p. 183)
dispersion (p. 192)
expected annual capacity (p. 172)
flexible budget (p. 172)

high-low method (p. 168)
independent variable (p. 170)
least squares regression analysis (p. 170)
multiple regression (p. 170)
normal cost system (p. 163)
outlier (p. 169)
overapplied overhead (p. 175)
predetermined overhead rate (p. 163)
regression line (p. 170)
scattergraph (p. 171)
service department (p. 179)
simple regression (p. 170)
standard error of the estimate (p. 193)
step method (p. 184)
underapplied overhead (p. 175)

PREDETERMINED OVERHEAD RATE

$$\text{Predetermined OH Rate} = \frac{\text{Total Budgeted Overhead Costs}}{\text{Total Budgeted Level of Volume or Activity}}$$

(Can be separate variable and fixed rates or a combined rate)

HIGH-LOW METHOD

(Using assumed amounts)

	(INDEPENDENT VARIABLE) ACTIVITY	(DEPENDENT VARIABLE) ASSOCIATED TOTAL COST	=	TOTAL VARIABLE COST (RATE × ACTIVITY)	+	TOTAL FIXED COST
"High" level	14,000	$18,000		$11,200	+	$6,800
"Low" level	9,000	14,000		7,200	+	6,800
Differences	5,000	$ 4,000				

$.80 variable cost per unit of activity

LEAST SQUARES REGRESSION ANALYSIS

The equations necessary to compute b and a values using the method of least squares are as follows:

$$b = \frac{\Sigma xy - n(\bar{x})(\bar{y})}{\Sigma x^2 - n(\bar{x})^2}$$

$$a = \bar{y} - b\bar{x}$$

where $\bar{x}$ = mean of the independent variable

$\bar{y}$ = mean of the dependent variable

n = number of observations

UNDERAPPLIED AND OVERAPPLIED OVERHEAD

Manufacturing Overhead   XXX
    Various accounts   XXX
    Actual overhead is debited to the
    overhead general ledger account.

Work in Process Inventory   YYY
    Manufacturing Overhead   YYY
    Applied overhead is debited to WIP and
    credited to the overhead general ledger
    account.

A debit balance in Manufacturing Overhead at the end of the period is underapplied overhead; a credit balance is overapplied overhead. The debit or credit balance in the overhead account is closed at the end of the period to CGS or prorated to WIP, FG, and CGS.

SERVICE DEPARTMENT COST ALLOCATION

Direct Method

1. Determine rational and systematic allocation bases for each service department.
2. Assign costs from each service department directly to revenue-producing areas using specified allocation bases.

Step Method

1. Determine rational and systematic allocation bases for each service department.
2. List service departments in sequence from the one that provides the most service to all other areas (both revenue- and non-revenue-producing) to the one that provides service to only revenue-producing areas (benefits-provided ranking).
3. Beginning with the first service department listed, allocate the costs from that department to all remaining departments; repeat the process until only revenue-producing departments remain.

Algebraic Method

1. Determine rational and systematic allocation bases for each department.
2. Develop algebraic equations representing the services provided by each department to other service departments and to revenue-producing departments using the allocation bases.
3. Solve the simultaneous equations for the service departments through an iterative process or by computer until all values are known.
4. Allocate costs using allocation bases developed in step 2. Eliminate "reallocated costs" from consideration.

COEFFICIENT OF CORRELATION

$$r = \frac{\Sigma[(x - \bar{x})(y - \bar{y})]}{\sqrt{\Sigma[(x - \bar{x})^2 \Sigma(y - \bar{y})^2]}}$$

STANDARD ERROR OF THE ESTIMATE

$$S_e = \sqrt{\frac{\Sigma y^2 - a(\Sigma y) - b(\Sigma xy)}{n - 2}}$$

DEMONSTRATION PROBLEM

McDonnell Publishing has two production divisions (Textbooks and Fiction) and three service departments (Administration, Personnel, and Public Relations). Budgeted 1998 costs are as follows:

Textbooks	$1,410,000
Fiction	1,688,000
Administration	900,000
Personnel	420,000
Public Relations	480,000

The overhead costs in the Textbook Division can be broken down into their variable and fixed elements as follows:

PURELY VARIABLE OVERHEAD	RATE PER MACHINE HOUR
Indirect labor	$95
Indirect materials	12
Employee fringe benefits	28

PURELY FIXED OVERHEAD	ANNUAL AMOUNT
Supervision	$125,000
Insurance	36,000
Depreciation	83,000
Taxes	24,000
Maintenance	18,000

The division also experienced machine hours (all within the relevant range) and utilities costs for the past 6 months as follows:

	MACHINE HOURS	UTILITIES
November	720	$682
December	920	730
January	810	708
February	680	673
March	860	721
April	640	660

The service departments are listed below in the order of their benefits-provided ranking. Selected potential allocation bases are presented below.

	NUMBER OF EMPLOYEE HOURS	NUMBER OF EMPLOYEES	DOLLARS OF ASSETS EMPLOYED
Administration	14,100	7	$570,000
Personnel	9,200	4	210,000
Public Relations	6,600	3	135,000
Textbooks	16,800	8	600,000
Fiction	20,200	10	900,000

Management thinks that administration costs should be allocated on the basis of employee hours, personnel costs on the basis of number of employees, and public relations costs on the basis of dollars of assets employed.

Required:

a. Using the high-low method, separate the Textbook Division's utility cost into its variable and fixed components.

b. Using the least squares method, separate the Textbook Division's utility cost into its fixed and variable components.

c. Assume the Textbook Division has budgeted 9,200 machine hours for 1998. Compute predetermined variable and fixed application rates for the division's indirect production costs.

d. The Textbook Division incurred 9,340 machine hours and $1,590,000 of actual production overhead costs for 1998. What amount of production overhead was applied in 1998? Did the division have underapplied or overapplied overhead for the year and in what amount?

e. Allocate service department costs using the direct method.

f. Allocate service department costs using the step method.

g. Allocate service department costs using the algebraic method.

h. Given the allocation computed in part g, determine the total predetermined overhead rate that would be used by the Textbook Division for 1998 assuming an expected capacity level of 9,340 machine hours.

Solution to Demonstration Problem

a.
$$b = \frac{\$730 - \$660}{920 - 640} = \frac{\$70}{280} = \$.25$$

$$a = \$730 - (\$.25)(920) = \$500$$

b.

x	y	xy	x^2
720	$ 682	$ 491,040	518,400
920	730	671,600	846,400
810	708	573,480	656,100
680	673	457,640	462,400
860	721	620,060	739,600
640	660	422,400	409,600
4,630	$4,174	$3,236,220	3,632,500

$$\bar{x} = 4,630 \div 6 = 771.67$$

$$\bar{y} = \$4,174 \div 6 = \$695.67$$

$$b = \frac{\$3,236,220 - 6(771.67)(\$695.67)}{3,632,500 - 6(771.67)(771.67)} = \frac{\$15,253.99}{59,652.47} = \$.26 \text{ (rounded)}$$

$$a = \$695.67 - (\$.256)(771.67) = \$498 \text{ (rounded)}$$

c. Variable rate = $95 + $12 + $28 + $.26 = $135.26 per MH
Fixed rate = ($286,000 + $498) ÷ 9,200 MHs = $31.14 per MH

d. Applied OH = 9,340 MHs × ($135.26 + $31.14) = $1,554,176
Underapplied OH = $1,554,176 − $1,590,000 = $35,824

e.

	BASE	PERCENTAGE OF TOTAL BASE	AMOUNT TO ALLOCATE	AMOUNT ALLOCATED
Administration costs (employee hours)				
Textbooks	16,800	45.4	$900,000	$ 408,600
Fiction	20,200	54.6	$900,000	491,400
Totals	37,000	100.0		$ 900,000
Personnel costs (# of employees)				
Textbooks	8	44.4	$420,000	$ 186,480
Fiction	10	55.6	$420,000	233,520
Totals	18	100.0		$ 420,000
Public Relations costs ($s of assets employed)				
Textbooks	$ 600,000	40.0	$480,000	$ 192,000
Fiction	900,000	60.0	$480,000	288,000
Totals	$1,500,000	100.0		$ 480,000
Grand total of allocated departmental costs:				
Textbooks				$ 787,080
Fiction				1,012,920
Total allocated				$1,800,000

f.

	BASE	PERCENTAGE OF TOTAL BASE	AMOUNT TO ALLOCATE	AMOUNT ALLOCATED
Administration costs (employee hours)				
Personnel	9,200	17.4	$900,000	$ 156,600
Public Relations	6,600	12.5	$900,000	112,500
Textbooks	16,800	31.8	$900,000	286,200
Fiction	20,200	38.3	$900,000	344,700
Totals	52,800	100.0		$ 900,000
Personnel costs (# of employees)				
Public Relations	3	14.3	$576,600*	$ 82,454
Textbooks	8	38.1	$576,600*	219,685
Fiction	10	47.6	$576,600*	274,461
Totals	21	100.0		$ 576,600
Public Relations costs ($s of assets employed)				
Textbooks	$ 600,000	40.0	$674,954**	$ 269,982
Fiction	900,000	60.0	$674,954**	404,972
Totals	$1,500,000	100.0		$ 674,954
Grand total of allocated departmental costs:				
Textbooks				$ 775,867
Fiction				1,024,133
Total allocated				$1,800,000

* ($420,000 budgeted for Personnel and $156,600 allocated from Administration costs.)

** ($480,000 budgeted for Public Relations, $112,500 allocated from Administration, and $82,454 from Personnel costs.)

g. McDonnell departmental interrelationships

	ADMINISTRATION (# OF EMPLOYEE HOURS)		PERSONNEL (# OF EMPLOYEES)		PUBLIC RELATIONS ($S OF ASSETS EMPLOYED)	
	Base	Percent	Base	Percent	Base	Percent
Administration	n/a	n/a	7	25	570,000	25
Personnel	9,200	17	n/a	n/a	210,000	9
Public Relations	6,600	13	3	11	n/a	n/a
Textbooks	16,800	32	8	28	600,000	26
Fiction	20,200	38	10	36	900,000	40
Total	52,800	100	28	100	2,280,000	100

$$A = \$900,000 + .25P + .25R$$

$$P = \$420,000 + .17A + .09R$$

$$R = \$480,000 + .13A + .11P$$

Substituting the first equation into the others:

$$P = \$420,000 + .17(\$900,000 + .25P + .25R) + .09R$$
$$\text{and } R = \$480,000 + .13(\$900,000 + .25P + .25R) + .11P$$

Multiplying and combining terms produces the following results:

$$P = \$420,000 + \$153,000 + .0425P + .0425R + .09R$$
$$P = \$573,000 + .0425P + .1325R$$
$$.9575P = \$573,000 + .1325R$$
$$P = \$598,433 + .1384R$$

$$R = \$480,000 + \$117,000 + .0325P + .0325R + .11P$$
$$R = \$597,000 + .1425P + .0325R$$
$$.9675R = \$597,000 + .1425P$$
$$R = \$617,054 + .1473P$$

$$P = \$598,443 + .1384(\$617,054 + .1473P)$$
$$P = \$598,443 + \$85,400 + .0204P$$
$$.9796P = \$683,843P = \$698,084$$

$$R = \$617,054 + .1473(\$698,084)$$
$$R = \$719,882$$

Placing the values of P and R in the original formula, A is calculated as follows:

$$A = \$900,000 + .25(\$698,084) + .25(\$719,882)$$
$$A = \$900,000 + \$174,521 + \$179,971$$
$$A = \$1,254,492$$

These values can now be allocated as follows:

	ADMINISTRATION		PERSONNEL		PUBLIC RELATIONS	
	Percent	*Amount*	*Percent*	*Amount*	*Percent*	*Amount*
Administration	n/a	n/a	25	$174,521	25	$179,971
Personnel	17	$ 213,264	n/a	n/a	9	64,789
Maintenance	13	163,084	11	76,789	n/a	n/a
Textbooks	32	401,437	28	195,464	26	187,169
Fiction	38	476,707	36	251,310	40	287,953
Total*	100	$1,254,492	100	$698,084	100	$719,882

	TEXTBOOKS	FICTION	TOTAL
Administration	$ 401,437	$ 476,707	$ 878,144
Personnel	195,464	251,310	446,774
Public Relations	187,169	287,953	475,122
Total allocation	$ 784,070	$1,015,970	$1,800,040*
Direct costs	1,410,000	1,688,000	3,098,000
Total costs	$2,194,070	$2,703,970	$4,898,040

*Difference due to rounding.

The following spreadsheet is the computer solution to the above set of equations. Note that the precision of the computer spreadsheet program is based on six decimal places and, therefore, yields more accurate results than were provided from a manual computation.

COEFFICIENT MATRIX:

1	0	⟨0.318182⟩	⟨0.285714⟩	⟨0.263158⟩
0	1	⟨0.382576⟩	⟨0.357143⟩	⟨0.394737⟩
0	0	1.000000	⟨0.250000⟩	⟨0.250000⟩
0	0	⟨0.174242⟩	1.000000	⟨0.092105⟩
0	0	⟨0.125000⟩	⟨0.010714⟩	1.000000

MATRIX INVERSE:

1	0	0.447162	0.442040	0.415662
0	1	0.552838	0.557960	0.584338
0	0	1.090723	0.304905	0.300764
0	0	0.204627	1.067169	0.149448
0	0	0.158265	0.152453	1.053608

CALCULATION OF COSTS:

$$\begin{bmatrix} P1 \\ P2 \\ S1 \\ S2 \\ S3 \end{bmatrix} = \begin{bmatrix} 1 & 0 & 0.447162 & 0.442040 & 0.415662 \\ 0 & 1 & 0.552838 & 0.557960 & 0.584338 \\ 0 & 0 & 1.090723 & 0.304905 & 0.300764 \\ 0 & 0 & 0.204627 & 1.067169 & 0.149448 \\ 0 & 0 & 0.158265 & 0.152453 & 1.053608 \end{bmatrix} \times \begin{bmatrix} \$1,410,000 \\ 1,688,000 \\ 900,000 \\ 420,000 \\ 480,000 \end{bmatrix} = \begin{bmatrix} \$2,197,620.36 \\ 2,700,379.64 \\ 1,254,077.52 \\ 704,110.32 \\ 712,200.60 \end{bmatrix}$$

FROM/TO	S1	S2	S3	P1	P2
S1		17.4242%	12.5000%	31.8182%	38.2576%
S2	25.0000%		10.7143%	28.5714%	35.7143%
S3	25.0000%	9.2105%		26.3158%	39.4737%

RELATIVE DISTRIBUTION OF SERVICES:

FROM/TO	S1	S2	S3	P1	P2
Costs	$ 900,000	$ 420,000	$480,000	$1,410,000	$1,688,000
Allocation:					
S1	⟨1,254,078⟩	218,513	156,760	399,025	479,780
S2	176,028	⟨704,110⟩	75,440	201,174	251,468
S3	178,050	65,597	⟨712,200⟩	187,421	281,132
Totals	$ 0	$ 0	$ 0	$2,197,620	$2,700,380

h. Total division overhead rate = $2,194,070 ÷ 9,340 = $234.91 per MH.

---

1. Is allocation of manufacturing overhead to products necessary for external reporting purposes? Internal purposes? Provide explanations for your answers.

2. Compare and contrast a normal cost system and an actual cost system. Relative to an actual cost system, what are the advantages associated with the use of a normal cost system? What are the disadvantages?

3. Discuss the reasons a company would use a predetermined overhead rate rather than apply actual overhead to products or services.

4. Why are departmental overhead rates more useful for managerial decision making than plantwide rates? Separate variable and fixed rates rather than total rates?

5. The high-low method of analyzing mixed costs uses only two observation points: the high and the low points of activity. Are these *always* the best points for prediction purposes? Why or why not?

6. Relative to a set of data observations, what is an outlier? Why is it inappropriate to use outliers to determine the cost formula for a mixed cost?

7. Why would regression analysis provide a more accurate cost formula for a mixed cost than the high-low method?

8. What is a flexible budget? How is it used to predict or budget future costs?

9. When a normal cost system is used, how are costs removed from the Manufacturing Overhead account and charged to Work in Process Inventory?

10. What recordkeeping options are available to account for overhead costs in a normal cost system? Which would be easiest? Which would provide the best information and why?

11. If overhead was materially underapplied for a year, how would it be treated at year-end? Why is this treatment appropriate?

12. What factors may cause overhead to be underapplied or overapplied? Are all of these factors controllable by management? Why or why not?

13. What is a cost pool? Why are multiple cost pools more effective for overhead allocation than single cost pools?

14. Why is a multistage cost allocation system more effective than a single-stage system?

15. Define and give four examples of a service department. How do service departments differ from operating departments?

16. Why are service department costs often allocated to revenue-producing departments? Is such a process of allocation always useful from a decision-making standpoint?

17. How might service department cost allocation create a feeling of cost responsibility among managers of revenue-producing departments?

18. "There are four criteria to use in selecting an allocation base and all four should be applied equally." Discuss the theoretical and practical merits of this statement.

19. How do the direct, step, and algebraic methods of allocating service department costs differ? In what ways are these methods similar?

20. What are the advantages and disadvantages of the direct, step, and algebraic methods of allocating service department costs?

21. Why is a benefits-provided ranking necessary in the step method of allocation but not in the algebraic method?

22. When the algebraic method of allocating service department costs is used, total costs for each service department increase from what they were prior to the allocation. Why does this occur and how are the additional costs treated?

23. How has the evolution of computer technology enhanced the feasibility of using the algebraic method of service department cost allocation?

24. *(Appendix)* How can correlation analysis be used to select an overhead allocation base?

25. *(Appendix)* How is the coefficient of determination related to the coefficient of correlation? Can the coefficient of correlation ever be negative? Can the coefficient of determination ever be negative? Provide justification for your answers.

EXERCISES

26. *(Terminology)* Match the following lettered terms on the left with the appropriate numbered description on the right.

a. Operating department	**1.** Provides a comparison of alternative courses of action
b. Direct method	
c. Cost pool	**2.** Reflects all the service interrelationships among departments
d. Algebraic method	
e. Benefits-provided ranking	**3.** Computes full costs
f. Objectives of allocating service department costs	**4.** Uses the benefits-provided ranking to make allocations
g. Step method	**5.** Indicates the relationships most often used to select an allocation basis
h. Benefits received and causal criteria	**6.** Lists departments in order of services provided to one another
	7. Generates revenue for the organization
	8. Assigns indirect costs directly to revenue-producing areas with no intermediate allocations
	9. Motivates managers
	10. Allows the gathering of related monetary amounts

27. *(High-low method)* Information about Brightman Corporation's utility cost for the first 6 months of 1998 follows. The company's cost accountant wants to use the high-low method to develop a cost formula to predict future charges and believes that the number of machine hours is an appropriate cost driver.

MONTH	MACHINE HOURS	UTILITY EXPENSE	MONTH	MACHINE HOURS	UTILITY EXPENSE
January	68,000	$1,220	April	64,000	$1,195
February	62,000	1,172	May	67,500	1,300
March	66,300	1,014	June	62,500	1,150

  a. What is the cost formula for utility expense?
  b. What would be the budgeted utility cost for September 1998 if 64,750 machine hours are projected?

28. *(High-low method)* The Charlestonian builds tabletop replicas of some of the most famous lighthouses in North America. The company is highly automated and, thus, maintenance cost is a significant organizational expense. The company's owner has decided to use machine hours as a basis for predicting maintenance costs and has gathered the following data from the prior 8 months of operations:

NUMBER OF MACHINE HOURS	MAINTENANCE COSTS
3,000	$980
4,500	690
8,000	510
7,000	600
6,000	550
9,000	440
3,500	840
5,500	600

  a. Using the high-low method, determine the cost formula for maintenance costs.
  b. What aspect of the estimated equation is bothersome? Provide an explanation for this situation.
  c. Within the relevant range, can the formula be reliably used to predict maintenance costs? Can the *a* and *b* values in the cost formula be interpreted as fixed and variable costs? Why or why not?

29. *(Least squares)* Below are data on number of shipments received and the cost of receiving reports for Savannah Supply Company for the first 7 weeks of 1997:

NUMBER OF SHIPMENTS RECEIVED	COST OF RECEIVING REPORT
100	$175
87	162
80	154
70	142
105	185
115	200
120	202

  a. Using the least squares method, develop the equation for predicting weekly receiving report costs based on the number of shipments received.
  b. What is the predicted amount of receiving report costs for a month (assume a month is exactly four weeks) in which 390 shipments are received?

30. *(Scattergraph; least squares)* Richard's Charters operates a fleet of powerboats in Naples, Florida. Richard wants to develop a cost formula for labor costs (a mixed cost). He has gathered the following data on labor costs and two potential predictive bases: number of charters and gross receipts:

MONTH	LABOR COSTS	NUMBER OF CHARTERS	GROSS RECEIPTS
January	$16,000	10	$ 12,000
February	18,400	14	18,000
March	24,000	22	26,000
April	28,400	28	36,000
May	37,000	40	60,000
June	56,000	62	82,000
July	68,000	100	120,000
August	60,000	90	100,000
September	48,000	80	96,000

a. Prepare a scattergraph for labor costs using each of the alternative prediction bases.

b. Using the least squares method, develop a labor cost formula using each prediction base.

31. *(Calculation of flexible budget)* The monthly overhead cost formula for Issac Corporation is currently estimated as $36,000 + $42X, where X represents machine hours. Company management believes operations will expand into a new relevant range in the upcoming year. Fixed costs are expected to rise to $54,000 for any activity level above 5,000 machine hours, and the variable cost rate is expected to drop at 6,000 machine hours by $6 per machine hour due to volume purchasing.

a. Prepare a flexible budget for the 4,500, 5,500, and 6,500 machine hour levels.

b. Calculate total overhead costs per machine hour at each level.

c. If each unit of product requires 2 machine hours, compute the cost per unit if production is set at 4,000 units.

32. *(Flexible budget)* Comet-Comet Enterprises produces glass paperweights, each of which requires one-fourth direct labor hour. The relevant range of activity per month is between 4,000 and 7,000 direct labor hours. The following cost formulas were derived for the company after analyzing cost records:

Direct material	$6.00 per unit
Direct labor	$8.50 per hour
Supervisor salaries	$15,000 per month
Other indirect labor	$6.00 per hour
Utilities	$3,700 plus $.45 per hour
Maintenance	$5,000 plus $.70 per hour
Indirect materials	$.90 per unit
Property taxes and insurance	$6,750 per month
Depreciation (unit of production basis)	$.30 per unit

a. Prepare a flexible budget for Comet-Comet for each 1,000 direct labor hours of activity within the relevant range.

b. Determine the total overhead cost formula for Comet-Comet.

33. *(Predetermined overhead rate)* Porter Enterprises has developed a monthly overhead cost formula of $2,760 + $4 per direct labor hour for 1997. The firm's 1997 expected annual capacity is 24,000 direct labor hours, to be incurred evenly each month. Two direct labor hours are required to make one unit of the company's product.

a. Determine the total overhead to be applied to each unit of product in 1997.

b. Prepare journal entries to record the application of overhead to Work in Process Inventory and the incurrence of $10,430 of actual overhead in a month in which 1,850 direct labor hours were worked.

34. *(Overhead application)* Koontz & Associates applies overhead at a combined rate for fixed and variable overhead of 175% of professional labor costs. During the first 3 months of 1997, the following professional labor costs and actual overhead costs were incurred:

MONTH	PROFESSIONAL LABOR COST	ACTUAL OVERHEAD
January	$270,000	$480,000
February	247,500	427,800
March	255,000	450,000

a. How much overhead was applied to the services provided each month by the firm?

b. What was underapplied or overapplied overhead for each of the 3 months and for the quarter?

35. *(Underapplied or overapplied overhead)* At the end of 1997, Juarez Corporation has the following account balances:

Manufacturing Overhead (credit)	$ 20,000
Work in Process Inventory	128,000
Finished Goods Inventory	32,000
Cost of Goods Sold	240,000

a. Prepare the necessary journal entry to close the overhead account if the balance is considered immaterial.

b. Prepare the necessary journal entry to close the overhead account if the balance is considered material.

c. Which method do you feel is more appropriate for the company and why?

36. *(Underapplied or overapplied overhead)* Rebecca Company uses a normal cost system. At year-end, the balance in the manufacturing overhead control account is a $50,000 debit. Information concerning relevant account balances at year-end are as follows:

	WORK IN PROCESS	FINISHED GOODS	COST OF GOODS SOLD
Direct material	$20,000	$ 40,000	$ 60,000
Direct labor	10,000	20,000	25,000
Factory overhead	20,000	40,000	50,000
	$50,000	$100,000	$135,000

a. What overhead rate was used during the year?

b. Provide arguments to be used for deciding whether to prorate the balance in the overhead account at year-end.

c. Prorate the overhead account balance based on the relative balances of the appropriate accounts.

d. Prorate the overhead account balance based on the relative overhead components of the appropriate account balances.

e. Identify some possible reasons why the company had a debit balance in the overhead account at year-end.

37. *(Direct method)* Clang Corporation allocates its service department costs to its production departments using the direct method. Information for May 1997 follows:

	PERSONNEL	MAINTENANCE
Service department costs	$68,000	$50,000
Services provided to other departments		
Personnel		10%
Maintenance	15%	
Fabricating	45%	60%
Finishing	40%	30%

a. What amount of personnel and maintenance costs should be assigned to Fabricating for May?

b. What amount of personnel and maintenance costs should be assigned to Finishing for May?

38. *(Direct method)* Golden Home Savings Bank has three revenue-generating areas: checking accounts, savings accounts, and loans. The bank also has three service areas: administration, personnel, and accounting. The direct costs per month and the interdepartmental service structure are shown below in a benefits-provided ranking.

DEPARTMENT	DIRECT COSTS	PERCENTAGE OF SERVICE USED BY					
		ADMIN.	PERSONNEL	ACCOUNTING	CHECKING	SAVINGS	LOAN
Administration	$ 90,000		10	10	30	40	10
Personnel	60,000	10		10	30	20	30
Accounting	90,000	10	10		40	20	20
Checking	90,000						
Savings	75,000						
Loans	150,000						

Compute the total cost for each revenue-generating area using the direct method.

39. *(Step method)* Using the information in exercise 38, compute the total cost for each revenue-generating area using the step method.

40. *(Step method)* Perez Inc. is organized in three service departments (Personnel, Administration, and Maintenance) and two revenue-generating departments (Stamping and Assembly). The company uses the step method to allocate service department costs to operating departments. In October 1997, Personnel incurred $60,000 of costs, Administration incurred $90,000, and Maintenance incurred $40,000. Proportions of services provided to other departments for October 1997 follow:

	PERSONNEL	ADMINISTRATION	MAINTENANCE
Personnel		10%	5%
Administration	15%		10%
Maintenance	10%	15%	
Stamping	45%	50%	50%
Assembly	30%	25%	35%

a. Assuming that the departments are listed in a benefits-provided ranking, what amount of Personnel cost should be assigned to each of the other departments for October? Administration costs? Maintenance costs?

b. What is the total service department cost that was assigned to Stamping in October? To Assembly?

c. Explain why the cost allocation is affected by the order in which costs are assigned.

41. *(Algebraic method)* Use the information for Golden Home Savings Bank in exercise 38 to compute the total cost for each revenue-generating area using the algebraic method.

42. *(Algebraic method)* Literary Legends has two revenue-producing divisions (Textbooks and Trade Publications) and two service departments (Administration and Personnel). Direct costs and allocation bases for each of these areas are presented below:

DEPARTMENT	DIRECT COSTS	ALLOCATION BASES	
		Number of Employees	*Dollars of Assets Employed*
Administration	$ 225,000	10	$310,000
Personnel	175,000	5	75,000
Textbooks	1,125,000	50	600,000
Trade Publications	475,000	30	525,000

Company management has decided to allocate administration and personnel costs on the basis of dollars of assets employed and number of employees, respectively. Use the algebraic method to allocate the service department costs and determine the final costs of operating the Textbooks and Trade Publications Departments.

43. *(Appendix)* Katie's Kompany is trying to decide whether tons of material processed or machine hours is the better basis on which to predict and allocate its processing costs. The following data display the historical relationships among these variables for the past 8 years (inflation adjusted).

YEAR	PROCESSING COSTS	TONS OF MATERIAL PROCESSED	MACHINE HOURS
1	$36,000	27.00	1,200
2	42,720	35.00	1,600
3	40,200	32.00	1,325
4	44,020	37.00	1,750
5	38,000	29.00	1,290
6	40,800	33.50	1,510
7	41,800	34.50	1,580
8	34,200	24.25	1,100

   a. Compute the coefficient of correlation and the coefficient of determination between the two candidate bases and the processing costs.

   b. Which base should provide the better predictions? Explain.

44. *(Appendix)* Refer to the information in exercise 43.

   a. Using the least squares method, find the processing cost formula for each of the candidate bases.

   b. Find the standard error of the estimate for each of the bases.

   c. From your answer in part b, which of the bases is a better predictor of processing costs?

---

45. *(Service department allocations)* As a team of three or four, select one of the following types of organizations: hospital or clinic, accounting or law firm, community theater, manufacturer, bank, or utility company. Make an appointment with a manager and interview him/her to learn answers to the following questions. Prepare a written, oral, or video presentation on your findings.

   a. What are the revenue-producing and service departments in the organization?

   b. If service department costs were to be allocated to revenue-producing departments, what would be "reasonable" bases for those allocations and why?

   c. Are service department costs allocated to revenue-producing departments in this organization?

      1. If yes, how and why are the allocations performed? What are some estimated costs and benefits of having allocations?

      2. If no, why are allocations not performed? What are some estimated costs and benefits of not having allocations?

46. *(Cost allocations)* Consider the case of the company that is decentrally organized into five operating divisions. The company pays $150,000 annually to subscribe to the Economic Facts and Projections Hotline (EFPH). This hotline is available via a computer link to all five of the division managers and provides sophisticated information about the U.S. and world economies, demand projections for various industries, interest rate forecasts, and so on, as requested by clients. The company's contract with EFPH specifies that only one division at a time may maintain a computer link with EFPH. Thus, while one division is using the service, other divisions are precluded from using the service. The entire $150,000 cost

COMMUNICATION ACTIVITIES

to subscribe to the service is fixed; there are no variable costs associated with this contract. Write a memo to the company president discussing what considerations should be taken into account in designing a system to allocate the costs of the EFPH contract to the five operating divisions.

47. *(Service department allocations)* Computer Information Services is a computer software consulting company. Its three major functional areas are computer programming, information systems consulting, and software training. Carol Birch, a pricing analyst in the Accounting Department, has been asked to develop total costs for the functional areas. These costs will be used as a guide in pricing a new contract. In computing these costs, Birch is considering three different methods of allocating overhead costs: the direct method, the step method, and the algebraic method. Birch assembled the following data on overhead from the company's two service departments: Information Systems and Facilities.

| | SERVICE DEPARTMENTS | | PRODUCTION DEPARTMENTS | | | |
	INFORMATION SYSTEMS	FACILITIES	COMPUTER PROGRAMMING	CONSULTING	TRAINING	TOTAL
Budgeted overhead	$50,000	$25,000	$75,000	$110,000	$85,000	$345,000
Information Systems* (hours)		300	1,200	600	900	3,000
Facilities** (thousand square feet)	200		400	600	800	2,000

*Allocated on the basis of hours of computer usage.

**Allocated on the basis of floor space.

a. Using computer usage time as the application base for Information Systems and square feet of floor space for Facilities, apply overhead from these service departments to the production departments using (1) the direct method and (2) the step method.

b. Prepare a memo to company management that defines the algebraic method of allocating the costs of service departments and whether this method would be appropriate for Computer Information Services. Also discuss how Computer Information Services might better assign Information Systems' costs.

(CMA adapted)

PROBLEMS

48. *(Analyzing mixed costs)* Erin's Stables determined that the total overhead rate for costing purposes is $6.70 per horse per day (referred to as an "animal day"). Of this, $6.30 is the variable portion. Cost information for two levels of monthly activity within the relevant range are given below:

	4,000 ANIMAL DAYS	6,000 ANIMAL DAYS
Overhead Cost:		
Indirect materials	$ 6,400	$ 9,600
Indirect labor	14,000	20,000
Maintenance	2,600	3,400
Utilities	2,000	3,000
All other	3,800	5,400

a. Determine the fixed and variable values for each of the above overhead items and determine the total overhead cost formula.

b. Assume that the total overhead rate is based on expected annual capacity. What is this level of activity for the company?

c. Determine expected overhead costs at the expected annual capacity.

d. If the company raises its expected capacity to 3,000 animal days above the present level, calculate a new total overhead rate for product costing.

49. *(High-low; least squares regression; scattergraph)* Kemp Industries manufactures screens for residential and commercial applications. The firm has encountered a problem in budgeting utilities expense. The expense is apparently a mixed cost and varies most directly with machine hours worked. However, management does not know the exact relationship between machine hours and utilities expense. The following data have been gathered from recent operations and may help describe the relationship.

MONTH	MACHINE HOURS	UTILITIES EXPENSE
January	1,400	$ 9,000
February	1,700	9,525
March	2,000	10,900
April	1,900	10,719
May	2,300	11,670
June	2,700	13,154
July	2,500	13,000
August	2,200	11,578

   a. How can you tell from the data that utilities expense is a mixed cost?
   b. Prepare a scattergraph. Does the scattergraph indicate utilities expense is a mixed cost?
   c. Use the high-low method to estimate a cost formula for utilities expense.
   d. Use least squares regression to estimate a cost formula for utilities expense.
   e. Does the answer to part c or d provide the better estimate of the relationship between utilities expense and machine hours? Why?

50. *(Scattergraph; high low; least squares)* Shamus Ltd. is analyzing its overhead costs and wants to use direct labor hours as the predictor. The following 18 weeks of information is to be used in developing an overhead cost formula for the company:

WEEK	DLHs	COST	WEEK	DLHs	COST	WEEK	DLHs	COST
1	4,100	$12,000	7	6,550	$13,500	13	5,400	$12,800
2	4,300	12,750	8	6,750	14,000	14	5,650	13,750
3	4,500	13,250	9	7,100	14,000	15	5,800	14,125
4	4,875	12,750	10	4,700	13,125	16	6,000	14,250
5	5,600	13,125	11	5,050	12,500	17	6,850	14,300
6	6,325	13,750	12	5,275	12,300	18	7,050	14,200

   a. Plot the data on a scattergraph and visually fit a linear cost formula.
   b. Compute the cost formula using the high-low method.
   c. Compute the cost formula using the least squares method.
   d. Compare the cost formulas developed in parts a, b, and c.
   e. How much of the variance in overhead is explained by the number of direct labor hours?
   f. Is there a significant relationship between direct labor hours and overhead cost? Explain the rationale for your answer.

51. *(Mixed costs and predetermined overhead rates; two bases, flexible budget)* Les Is Best manufactures fiberglass swimming pools in a two-department process: Production and Installation. Production is highly automated and machine hours are used as the basis for allocating departmental overhead. Installation is labor intensive and uses direct labor hours to apply overhead. Following is cost information at various activity levels for each department:

	MACHINE HOURS (MHs)			
	3,000	*4,000*	*5,000*	*6,000*
PRODUCTION OVERHEAD COSTS:				
Variable	$12,150	$16,200	$20,250	$24,300
Fixed	7,950	7,950	7,950	7,950
Total	$20,100	$24,150	$28,200	$32,250

	DIRECT LABOR HOURS (DLHs)			
	1,000	*2,000*	*3,000*	*4,000*
INSTALLATION OVERHEAD COSTS:				
Variable	$14,250	$28,500	$42,750	$57,000
Fixed	6,150	6,150	6,150	6,150
Total	$20,400	$34,650	$48,900	$63,150

Each pool is estimated to require 500 machine hours in Production and 250 hours of direct labor in Installation. Next month, the company plans to produce and install 11 pools, which is 1 pool beyond the company's expected capacity.

a. Compute the variable and fixed values in the formula $y = a + bX$ for each department.

b. Prepare a flexible budget for next month's variable, fixed, and total overhead costs for each department assuming production is 9, 10, 11, or 12 pools.

c. Calculate the predetermined total overhead cost to be applied to each pool scheduled for production in the coming month if expected annual capacity is used to calculate the predetermined overhead rates.

52. *(Plant vs. department OH rates)* Ogden Manufacturing has two departments: Fabrication and Assembly. Fabrication is composed of 1 worker and 15 machines, and Assembly has 20 workers and few machines. One of the company's products passes through both departments and uses the following quantities of direct labor and machine time:

	FABRICATION	**ASSEMBLY**
	---	---
Machine hours	8.00	.15
Direct labor hours	.02	2.00

Following are the budgeted overhead costs and volumes for each department for the upcoming year:

	FABRICATION	**ASSEMBLY**
	---	---
Estimated overhead	$624,240	$324,000
Estimated machine hours	72,000	9,300
Estimated direct labor hours	4,800	48,000

a. What is the plantwide rate for overhead application based on machine hours for the upcoming year? How much overhead will be assigned to each unit using this rate?

b. The company's auditors inform Ogden that it would be more appropriate to use machine hours as the application base in Fabrication and direct labor hours in Assembly. What would the rates be for each department? How much overhead would have been assigned to each unit of product using departmental rates?

53. *(Multiple cost pools)* Most overhead costs at the Bedford Company can be directly traced to its operating departments: Machining and Assembly. These directly traceable costs are as follows:

	MACHINING	**ASSEMBLY**
	---	---
Indirect labor costs	$200,000	$150,000
Depreciation	800,000	450,000
Other	200,000	400,000

The following companywide costs must be allocated to the two operating departments using the bases indicated:

Depreciation and insurance (square footage)	$2,500,000
Utilities (machine hours)	80,000
Indirect labor (direct labor hours)	450,000

Relevant information for these allocations are as follows:

	SQUARE FEET	MACHINE HOURS	DIRECT LABOR HOURS
Machining	150,000	6,000	80,000
Assembly	100,000	2,000	20,000

In Machining, all overhead costs (direct and allocated) are applied to products based on machine hours; in Assembly, the base used is direct labor hours. Information on the three products produced by the company follows:

	PRODUCT 1	PRODUCT 2	PRODUCT 3
Direct materials—Machining	$15	$14	$18
Direct materials—Assembly	$ 5	$ 3	$ 4
Direct labor hours—Machining	1.2	.8	1.4
Direct labor hours—Assembly	3.0	2.4	4.0
Machine time (hours)—Machining	5.0	6.5	7.0
Machine time (hours)—Assembly	2.5	3.0	3.5
Direct labor wage rate—Machining		$12 per hour	
Direct labor wage rate—Assembly		$10 per hour	

  a. Determine the amount of companywide overhead to be allocated to each of the two departments.
  b. Determine the overhead application rate in each department (be sure to include the companywide allocated overhead).
  c. Determine the cost to produce one unit of each type of product using the overhead application rates developed in part b and the direct labor and material costs presented.
  d. Prepare journal entries to reflect the cost flows for the following:
    1. Assignment of overhead from Machining to 1,500 units of Product 1.
    2. Assignment of overhead from Assembly to 750 units of Product 2.

54. *(Journal entries)* Banff Ltd. applies overhead at the rate of $15 per direct labor hour. The following transactions occurred during May 1997:
    1. Direct material issued to production, $150,000.
    2. Direct labor cost paid, 24,900 hours at $16 per hour.
    3. Indirect labor cost accrued, 7,500 hours at $9 per hour.
    4. Depreciation on factory assets recorded, $37,200.
    5. Supervisors' salaries paid, $15,000.
    6. Indirect materials issued to production, $9,000.
    7. Goods costing $375,000 were completed and transferred to finished goods.

  a. Prepare journal entries for the above transactions using a single overhead account and assuming the Raw Materials Inventory account contains only direct materials.
  b. If Work in Process Inventory had a beginning balance of $55,620, what is the ending balance?
  c. Was overhead underapplied or overapplied for the month? By how much?

55. *(Direct method)* The management of Orlando Community Hospital (OCH) has decided to allocate the budgeted costs of its three service departments (Administration, Public Relations, and Maintenance) to its three revenue-producing programs (Surgery, Inpatient Care, and Outpatient Services). Budgeted information for 1997 follows:

Budgeted costs:	
Administration	$2,000,000
Public Relations	700,000
Maintenance	500,000
Allocation bases:	
Administration	Dollars of assets employed
Public Relations	Number of employees
Maintenance	Hours of equipment operation

	EXPECTED UTILIZATIONS		
	Dollars of Assets Employed	Number of Employees	Hours of Equipment Operation
Administration	$ 740,090	4	1,020
Public Relations	450,100	7	470
Maintenance	825,680	5	1,530
Surgery	1,974,250	10	12,425
Inpatient Care	1,229,250	18	8,875
Outpatient Services	521,500	22	14,200

Using the direct method, allocate the expected service department costs to the revenue-producing areas.

56. *(Step method)* O'Reilly Real Estate classifies its operations into three departments: Commercial Sales, Residential Sales, and Property Management. The owner, Shannen O'Reilly, wants to know the full cost of operating each department. Direct costs of each department, along with several allocation bases associated with each, are as follows:

		AVAILABLE ALLOCATION BASES		
	DIRECT COSTS	Number Employees/ Salespersons	Dollars of Assets Employed	Dollars of Revenue
Administration	$ 750,000	10	$1,240,000	N/A
Accounting	495,000	5	682,000	N/A
Promotion	360,000	6	360,000	N/A
Commercial Sales	5,245,000	21	500,000	$4,500,000
Residential Sales	4,589,510	101	725,000	9,500,000
Property Management	199,200	13	175,000	500,000

The service departments are shown in a benefits-provided ranking. O'Reilly has also selected the following allocation bases: number of employees/salespersons for Administration; dollars of assets employed for Accounting; and dollars of revenue for Promotion.

a. Using the step method, allocate the service department costs to the revenue-generating departments.

b. Which department is apparently the most profitable?

57. *(Comprehensive)* The costs of operating the service departments (Personnel and Administration) at Buxton Architectural are allocated to the revenue-generating departments (Commercial and Residential). The direct and allocated costs are accumulated in the revenue-generating departments and applied to engineering projects. The following data relate to the allocation bases used and the direct costs of the company's departments:

DEPARTMENT	NUMBER OF EMPLOYEES	DOLLARS OF ASSETS EMPLOYED	DIRECT COSTS
Personnel (# of employees)	2	$100,000	$125,000
Administration ($s of assets employed)	3	112,500	375,000
Residential	10	612,500	600,000
Commercial	15	925,000	725,000

a. Use the direct method to allocate the service department costs to the revenue-generating departments. What are the total costs of each revenue-generating department after the allocation?

b. If the benefits-provided ranking is (1) Personnel and (2) Administration, use the step method to allocate the service department costs to the revenue-generating departments. What are the total costs of each revenue-generating department after the allocation?

c. Use the algebraic method to allocate the service department costs to the revenue-generating departments. What are the total costs of each revenue-generating department after the allocation?

58. *(Comprehensive)* Ryan Ltd.'s 1998 annual budget for its three service departments (Administration, Accounting, and Engineering) and its two production departments (Assembly and Finishing) is presented below.

ANNUAL BUDGET ($000 OMITTED)

	Adminis-tration	Accounting	Engineering	Assembly	Finishing	Total
Direct labor	$ 700	$500	$ 900	$2,800	$2,000	$ 6,900
Material	70	200	90	400	1,200	1,960
Insurance	175	50	75	300	220	820
Depreciation	90	70	80	200	150	590
Miscellaneous	30	20	40	60	30	180
Total	$1,065	$840	$1,185	$3,760	$3,600	$10,450
Square feet of floor space	400	300	300	800	1,000	2,800
# of employees	40	25	30	200	150	445
Engineering hours	10	20	15	80	75	200

Assume that expected 1998 activity bases in Assembly and Finishing, respectively, are 24,000 and 20,000 machine hours.

a. Calculate the overhead allocation rate per machine hour in each revenue-producing department using the direct method.

b. Allocate service department costs to the producing departments using the step method. The service departments are listed in the benefits-provided ranking. Allocation bases for each service department's costs are (1) Administration, number of employees; (2) Accounting, floor space; and (3) Engineering, engineering hours. Calculate the overhead allocation rate per machine hour in each revenue-producing department.

c. Calculate the overhead allocation rate per machine hour in each revenue-producing department using the algebraic method.

59. *(Appendix)* Moira Manufacturing has been using direct labor hours as a basis to predict indirect labor costs. Company management has asked the controller's staff to evaluate machine hours as an alternative prediction base because indirect labor costs have been difficult for the company to predict reliably and control. The following data are from the latest 6 months of activity:

MONTH	DIRECT LABOR HOURS	MACHINE HOURS	LABOR COSTS
1	425	3,025	$5,049
2	460	2,750	5,921
3	410	2,973	4,968
4	480	3,264	5,297
5	502	4,167	5,410
6	418	2,897	4,998

a. Using least squares regression, estimate the variable and fixed values for the formula $y = a + bX$ using direct labor hours.

b. Repeat part a using machine hours as the prediction base.

c. Compute the coefficient of correlation, coefficient of determination, and standard error of the estimate for the equation estimated in part a.

d. Repeat part c using the equation estimated in part b.

e. Based on your computations in parts c and d, are direct labor hours or machine hours the better predictor of indirect labor costs? Explain.

60. *(Development of OH rates)* Northcoast Manufacturing Company, a small manufacturer of parts used in appliances, has just completed its first year of operations. The company's controller, Vic Trainor, has been reviewing the actual results for the year and is concerned about the application of factory overhead. Trainor is using the following information to assess operations.

- Northcoast's equipment consists of several machines with a combined cost of $2,200,000 and no residual value. Each machine has an output of five units of product per hour and a useful life of 20,000 hours.
- Selected annual data of Northcoast's operations for the year just ended are as follows:

Products manufactured	650,000 units
Machine utilization	130,000 hours
Direct labor usage	35,000 hours
Labor rate	$15 per hour
Total factory overhead	$1,130,000
Cost of goods sold	$1,720,960
Finished goods inventory (at year-end)	$430,240
Work in process inventory (at year-end)	$0

- Total factory overhead is applied to products on a direct labor cost basis using a predetermined plantwide rate.
- The budgeted activity for the year included 20 employees each working 1,800 productive hours per year to produce 540,000 units of product. The machines are highly automated, and each employee can operate two to four machines simultaneously. Normal activity is for each employee to operate three machines. Machine operators are paid $15 per hour.
- Budgeted factory overhead costs for the past year for various levels of activity are as follows:

	Units of Product		
	360,000	**540,000**	**720,000**
Labor hours	30,000	36,000	42,000
Machine hours	72,000	108,000	144,000
Total factory OH costs:			
Plant supervision	$ 70,000	$ 70,000	$ 70,000
Plant rent	40,000	40,000	40,000
Equipment depreciation	288,000	432,000	576,000
Maintenance	42,000	51,000	60,000
Utilities	144,600	216,600	288,600
Indirect material	90,000	135,000	180,000
Other costs	11,200	16,600	22,000
Total	$685,800	$961,200	$1,236,600

a. Based on Northcoast Manufacturing Company's actual operations for the past year,
   1. determine the dollar amount of total underapplied or overapplied factory overhead and explain why this amount is material.
   2. prepare the appropriate journal entry to close out Northcoast's total factory overhead account.
b. Vic Trainor believes that Northcoast Manufacturing Company should be using machine hours to apply total factory overhead. Using the data given,
   1. determine the dollar amount of total underapplied or overapplied factory overhead if machine hours had been used as the application base.
   2. explain why machine hours would be a more appropriate application base.

(CMA)

61. *(Overhead application)* Rose Bach has recently been hired as controller of Empco Inc., a sheet metal manufacturer. Empco has been in the sheet metal business for many years and is currently investigating ways to modernize its manufacturing process. At the first staff meeting Bach attended, Bob Kelley, the chief engineer, presented a proposal for automating the Drilling Department. Kelley recommended that Empco purchase two robots that would have the capability of replacing the eight direct labor workers in the department.

The cost savings outlined in Kelley's proposal included the elimination of direct labor cost in the Drilling Department plus a reduction of manufacturing overhead cost in the department to zero, because Empco charges manufacturing overhead on the basis of direct labor dollars using a plantwide rate.

The president of Empco was puzzled by Kelley's explanation of cost savings, believing it made no sense. Bach agreed, explaining that as firms become more automated, they should rethink their manufacturing overhead systems. The president then asked Bach to look into the matter and prepare a report for the next staff meeting.

To refresh her knowledge, Bach reviewed articles on manufacturing overhead allocation for an automated factory and discussed the matter with some of her peers. Bach also gathered the historical data presented below on the manufacturing overhead rates experienced by Empco over the years.

DATE	AVERAGE ANNUAL DIRECT LABOR COST	AVERAGE ANNUAL MANUFACTURING OVERHEAD COST	AVERAGE MANUFACTURING OVERHEAD APPLICATION RATE
1950s	$1,000,000	$ 1,000,000	100%
1960s	1,200,000	3,000,000	250
1970s	2,000,000	7,000,000	350
1980s	3,000,000	12,000,000	400
1990s	4,000,000	20,000,000	500

Bach also wanted to have some departmental data to present at the meeting and, using Empco's accounting records, was able to estimate the following annual averages for each manufacturing department in the 1990s:

	CUTTING DEPARTMENT	GRINDING DEPARTMENT	DRILLING DEPARTMENT
Direct labor	$ 2,000,000	$1,750,000	$ 250,000
Manufacturing overhead	11,000,000	7,000,000	2,000,000

a. Disregarding the proposed use of robots in the Drilling Department, describe the shortcomings of the system for applying overhead that is currently used by Empco Inc.

b. Explain the misconceptions underlying Bob Kelley's statement that manufacturing overhead cost in the Drilling Department would be reduced to zero if the automation proposal was implemented.

c. Recommend ways to improve Empco Inc.'s method for applying overhead by describing how it should revise its overhead accounting system:
   1. in the Cutting and Grinding Departments; and
   2. to accommodate the automation of the Drilling Department.

(CMA)

62. *(Direct, step methods)* Amar Supermarkets Corporation operates a chain of three retail stores in a state that permits municipalities to levy an income tax on businesses operating within their respective boundaries. The tax rate is uniform in all of the municipalities that levy the tax and does not vary according to taxable income. Regulations provide that the tax is to be computed on income earned within the particular taxing municipality, after reasonable and consistent allocation of the corporation's general overhead (including service department costs). Amar's general corporate overhead consists of expenses pertaining to the warehouse, central office, advertising, and delivery.

For the year ended December 31, 1997, operating results for each store, before taxes and allocation of corporation overhead, were as follows:

	BIRCH	**MAPLE**	**SPRUCE**	**TOTAL**
Sales	$500,000	$400,000	$300,000	$1,200,000
Cost of sales	280,000	230,000	190,000	700,000
Gross margin	$220,000	$170,000	$110,000	$ 500,000
LOCAL OPERATING EXPENSES:				
Fixed	$ 70,000	$ 60,000	$ 50,000	$ 180,000
Variable	66,000	73,000	31,000	170,000
Totals	$136,000	$133,000	$ 81,000	$ 350,000
Income before corporate overhead and taxes	$ 84,000	$ 37,000	$ 29,000	$ 150,000

For the year ended December 31, 1997, corporation overhead was as follows:

WAREHOUSE AND DELIVERY:

Warehouse depreciation	$10,000	
Warehouse operations	15,000	
Delivery	35,000	$ 60,000

CENTRAL OFFICE:

Advertising	$ 8,000	
Salaries	30,000	
Other	2,000	40,000
Total corporation overhead		$100,000

Delivery expenses vary with distances from the warehouse and number of deliveries to stores. Delivery statistics for 1997 are as follows:

STORE	MILES FROM WAREHOUSE	NUMBER OF DELIVERIES	DELIVERY MILES
Birch	100	150	15,000
Maple	200	50	10,000
Spruce	25	200	5,000

Management has asked the company's cost accountant to evaluate two corporate overhead allocation plans that are being considered, so that operating results under both plans can be compared. In addition, management has decided to expand one of the stores in a plan to increase sales by $80,000. The contemplated expansion is expected to increase local fixed operating costs by $8,000 and to require ten additional deliveries from the warehouse. The accountant has been asked to furnish management with a recommendation as to which store should be selected for the prospective expansion.

a. Rounding off to the nearest whole percent, compute each store's income that would be subject to the municipal tax under the following two plans:

Plan 1—All corporate overhead costs are allocated directly to the stores, using sales as the basis for allocation.

Plan 2—Central office salaries and other central overhead is allocated equally to warehouse operations and to each store.

Then, allocate the resulting warehouse operations costs, warehouse depreciation, and advertising to each store on the basis of sales. Finally, allocate delivery expenses to each store on the basis of delivery miles.

   b. Compute each store's potential increase in relevant expenses, including delivery expenses, but before allocation of other corporation overhead and taxes as a result of the contemplated expansion. Determine which of the three stores should be selected for expansion to maximize corporate net income.

(AICPA adapted)

63. *(Service department allocation)* Columbia Company is a regional office supply chain with 26 independent stores. Each store has been responsible for its own credit and collections. The assistant manager in each store is assigned the responsibility for credit activities including the collection of delinquent accounts because the stores do not need a full-time employee assigned to credit activities. The company has experienced a sharp rise in uncollectibles in the last 2 years. Corporate management has decided to establish a collections department in the home office to be responsible for the collections function companywide. The home office of Columbia Company will hire the necessary full-time personnel. The size of this department will be based on the historical credit activity of all the stores.

   The new centralized collections department was discussed at a recent management meeting. Finding a method to assign the costs of the new department to the stores has been difficult because this type of home office service is somewhat unique. Alternative methods are being reviewed by top management.

   The controller favored using a predetermined rate for charging the costs to the stores. The predetermined rate would be based on estimated costs. The vice president of sales had a strong preference for charging actual costs to the stores. In addition, the basis for the collection charges to the stores was also discussed. The controller identified the following four measures of services or allocation bases that could be used: total dollar sales; average number of past due accounts; number of uncollectible accounts written off; and 1/26 of the cost to each store.

   The executive vice president stated he would like the accounting department to prepare a detailed analysis of the two charging methods (predetermined and actual) and the four service allocation bases.

   a. Evaluate the two methods that could be used to charge the individual stores the costs of Columbia's new collections department in terms of
      1. practicality of application and ease of use; and
      2. ability to control costs.
   b. For each of the service allocation bases identified by the controller,
      1. discuss whether the allocation base is appropriate to use in this situation; and
      2. identify some behavioral problems that might arise as a consequence of adopting the allocation base.

(CMA adapted)

ETHICS AND QUALITY DISCUSSION

64. Haversham Machine Works is bidding on a contract with the government of Bezaire. The contract is a cost-plus situation, with an add-on profit margin of 50 percent. Direct material and direct labor are expected to total $15 per unit. Variable overhead is estimated at $4 per unit. Total fixed overhead to produce the 50,000 units needed by the government is $1,400,000. By acquiring the machinery and supervisory support needed to produce the 50,000 units, Haversham will obtain the actual capacity to produce 80,000 units.

   a. Should the price bid by Haversham include a fixed overhead cost of $28 per unit or $17.50? How were these two amounts determined? Which of these two amounts would be more likely to cause Haversham to obtain the contract? Why?

b. Assume that Haversham set a bid price of $54.75 and obtained the contract. After producing the units, Haversham submitted an invoice to the government of Bezaire for $3,525,000. The minister of finance for the country requests an explanation. Can you provide one?

c. Haversham uses the excess capacity to produce an additional 30,000 units while making the units for Bezaire. These units are sold to another buyer. Is it ethical to present a $3,525,000 bill to Bezaire? Discuss.

d. Haversham does not use the excess capacity while making the units for Bezaire. However, several months after that contract was completed, the company begins production of additional units. Was it ethical to present a $3,525,000 bill to Bezaire? Discuss.

e. Haversham does not use the excess capacity because no other buyer exists for units of this type. Was it ethical to make a bid based on a fixed overhead rate per unit of $54.75? Discuss.

65. One may view the income tax system in the United States as the largest system of cost allocation in the world because the tax system is used to allocate the cost of the government to the people. Assume that the tax system in the United States is mildly progressive in that people who make more money pay relatively larger portions of their income to the government. As discussed in the text, four criteria may be used to identify a basis for cost allocation: benefits received, causal relationships, fairness or equity, and ability to bear.

a. Which of the four allocation criteria justifies a progressive form of income tax as a basis to allocate the costs of government to the people?

b. Identify two alternatives to the income tax system to allocate the costs of government to the people.

c. Is an income tax an ethical basis to allocate governmental costs?

d. What ethical dilemmas are created for citizens (who are also taxpayers) when governmental costs are allocated via an income tax?

66. State prisons often use inmates as "employees" in production operations. Overhead costs in these prison manufacturing environments are generally quite low. For instance, California's Prison Industry Authority pays "roughly 5% of what private competing businesses in the Sacramento area pay for similar space." Unfortunately, however, the prison industries must also cope with some problems that the other businesses may not have, such as unskilled workers and/or illiterate workers, and substantially greater security.

[Facts based on Nina Munk, "Captive Labor, Captive Markets," *Forbes* (August 29, 1994), p. 84.]

a. Discuss the ethics of using prison labor and paying those workers substantially less than the minimum wage to make products for marketplace distribution.

b. In 1993, Cal State Polytechnic University wanted 213 chairs for a computer lab. An outside vendor offered to sell the chairs for $54 each and deliver them in 6 weeks. Under California law, Cal Poly had to buy them from PIA for $92 each and, 8 months after the order, approximately one-fourth of the chairs still had not been delivered. Discuss the rationale of the law requiring state agencies to buy from PIA. Include answers in your discussion as to whether such a law promotes the concepts of (1) total quality management or (2) cost control.

67. In designing an organization, management may want to establish a separate department to be responsible for maintaining/improving the quality of organizational output.

a. What are the advantages and disadvantages associated with allocating the costs of the quality department to producing departments?

b. Assuming such a department is established, what would be some appropriate bases for allocating costs of the quality department to producing departments?

68. *For the distinction of being the world's greatest department store, Harrods faces few rivals. Shoppers rave about the grandeur of the Harrods building, about products not seen just anywhere (a rhinoceros doll for more than $3,700), about halls filled with live music and art. Its financial performance isn't as spectacular.*

[After purchasing Harrods in 1985, owner Mohamed Al Fayed] proceeded to feed £200 million into Harrods—about $298 million, or more than a third the amount that Federated Department Stores Inc. spent to renovate several entire chains, including Bloomingdale's. "Mr. Al Fayed never counts costs," says Harrods spokesman Michael Cole.

That's a good thing, because the renovations didn't bring about any immediate sales boost. But Mr. Al Fayed, heartened by a 14% sales increase through the first nine months of 1993, believes his investment is paying off. At a time when U.S. malls are adding amusement parks and bolstering food offerings, Harrods employs a harpist in one department, pianists in others and a troop of marching bagpipers. The size of the toy department has been quadrupled. There are now 11 restaurants, up from six. Storewide, products include £1,000 clothes hampers, £7,500 dog collars, £8.50 gold-plated toothbrushes.

[SOURCE: Kevin Helliker, "Harrods: Grandeur Comes at Grand Cost," *Wall Street Journal* (December 1, 1993), pp. B1, B6. Reprinted by permission of *The Wall Street Journal*, © 1993 Dow Jones & Company, Inc. All Rights Reserved Worldwide.]

a. Given the information above, discuss why Harrods can charge premium prices for products that are obtainable in other stores in England.

b. Suppliers also pay more to deal with Harrods than with other stores. Why would a supplier such as Estee Lauder or Liz Claiborne agree to terms with Harrods that cut deeply into their profit margins?

c. One thing Harrods is famous for is customer service, employing over 800 more people than the Marshall Fields in Chicago, which is half the size. Discuss some reasons why customer service might be so good at Harrods.

INTERNET ACTIVITIES

69. The National Institute for Consumer Education (College of Education, Eastern Michigan University) maintains an online form to prepare a budget for college spending. The form allows for both income and expense budgeting. The expense budget is divided into fixed and variable (flexible) expenses. Use the form to prepare a budget for your college spending. After you have prepared the expense budgets, determine how much of the total fixed and variable expenses is direct and how much is indirect. Which costs are greater, direct or indirect? Which of the indirect expenses is largest?

70. David M. Griffith & Associates provides a variety of financial services to the public sector. Find the firm's home page and review the services the firm offers to its clients. Then read the materials describing services related to cost allocation plans and indirect cost rate proposals. Considering the materials presented, why would municipalities or other governmental units desire to allocate service department costs to user departments?

71. Find Cost Technology's home page and the discussion of function cost analysis. What is function cost analysis and how does it relate to the topic of cost allocation? How does function cost analysis contribute to product and process design?

Activity-Based Cost Systems for Management

LEARNING OBJECTIVES

After completing this chapter, you should be able to answer these questions:

1. How do product life cycles affect product costing and profitability?

2. What is the focus of activity-based management?

3. Why do non-value-added activities cause costs to increase unnecessarily?

4. How does activity-based costing differ from a traditional cost accounting system?

5. Why must cost drivers be designated in an activity-based costing system?

6. How does the installation of an activity-based costing system affect behavior?

7. *(Appendix)* How can the theory of constraints help in determining production flow?

Lord Corporation

Founded in 1924, Lord Corporation is a worldwide diversified, technology-based company, employing more than 1,700 people and having annual sales of $250+ million. The Industrial Products Division designs, manufactures, and markets products that control vibration, shock, noise, and motion for various transportation markets.

By 1991, the company had made significant investments of time and money to bring the Division to world-class status. Prior to that time, plants were arranged by function, and parts were moved through the manufacturing process from one functional area to the next. Plant cellularizations were introduced in which individual work cells contain entire manufacturing processes—from raw materials to shipment.

While manufacturing was well on its way to becoming world class, accounting's reporting efforts lagged. Reports still were function-focused rather than process-focused. Cost accountants were the bean counters in the back room who sat and crunched numbers all day. The Board of Directors encouraged the CFO to investigate activity-based costing. Considerable time and effort was spent developing an ABC plan for the Chemical Products Division but senior division management, upon hearing the presentation and studying the plan, decided it was an unnecessary accounting exercise.

With hindsight it became clear that the proposal for the Chemical Products Division had three critical mistakes. First, an "outsider" (nonfirm employee) had been assigned to drive the implementation. Second, the divisional departments had not been involved in the plan, making implementation essentially an accounting project. Third, Chemicals was already successful and growing, so there was little incentive to change or adopt ABC.

After consideration, a different Lord division (Industrial Products or IPD) was recruited as an ABC pilot. The atmosphere was different at IPD. Where Chemicals is a simple manufacturing process environment, Industrial is more complicated and has a much more complex overhead structure. IPD was not performing to management's expectations. There was already some discussion of ABC in the division, so management was receptive and more than willing to try and improve performance and provide better product costs.

SOURCE: Alan W. Rupp, "ABC: A Pilot Approach," *Management Accounting* (January 1995), pp. 50–51. Reprinted from *Management Accounting*. Copyright by Institute of Management Accountants, Montvale, NJ.

L ord Corporation, like many other manufacturers, recognized that its accounting reports were not providing managers with the information and details needed to make good business decisions in a global economy. This flaw was caused, first, by the company's new manufacturing process and, second, by the traditional overhead allocation system that was in use. The traditional system discussed in Chapter 5 is geared to satisfy external reporting requirements, but often does a less-than-adequate job of meeting management needs. Lord investigated its cost accounting system and found that some basic changes were necessary. Management concluded that overhead allocations using a minimal number of rates and cost drivers did not provide realistic information for managerial functions.

This chapter presents topics that are at the forefront of managerial accounting literature and result from the intensely competitive nature of the global economy. First, the chapter discusses the concept of costing in reference to product life cycle stages. Second, the chapter presents the reasons that companies now focus on value-added and non-value-added activities, and explains how activities (rather than volume measures) can be used to determine product and service costs and to measure performance. The basics of activity-based costing, as well as some criticisms of this technique, are discussed and illustrated. Finally, the appendix introduces the theory of constraints to show how it can be applied to production activities.

PRODUCT LIFE CYCLES

VIDEO VIGNETTE

Maytag

Product profit margins are typically judged on a period-by-period basis without consideration of the product life cycle. However, products, like people, go through a series of sequential life cycle stages. As mentioned in Chapter 2, the product life cycle is a model depicting the stages through which a product class (not necessarily each product) passes from the time that an idea is conceived until production is discontinued. Those stages are development (which includes design), introduction, growth, maturity, and decline. A sales trend line through each stage is illustrated in Exhibit 6–1. Companies must be aware of where their products are in their life cycles, because in addition to the sales effects, the life cycle stage may have a tremendous impact on costs and profits. The life cycle impact on each of these items is shown in Exhibit 6–2.

Development Stage and Target Costing

From a cost standpoint, the development stage is an important one that is almost ignored by the traditional financial accounting model. Financial accounting requires that development costs be expensed as incurred—even though most studies indicate that decisions made during this stage determine approximately 80 percent to 90 percent of a product's total life cycle costs. That is, the materials and the manufacturing process specifications made during development generally affect production costs for the rest of the product's life.

Although technology and competition have shortened the development stage time tremendously, effective development efforts are critical to a product's profitability over its entire life cycle. Time spent in the planning and development process can often result "in lower production costs, reduced time from the design to manufacture stage, higher quality, greater flexibility, and lower product life cycle cost."[1] All manufacturers are acutely aware of the need to focus attention on the product develop-

EXHIBIT 6–1

Product Life Cycle

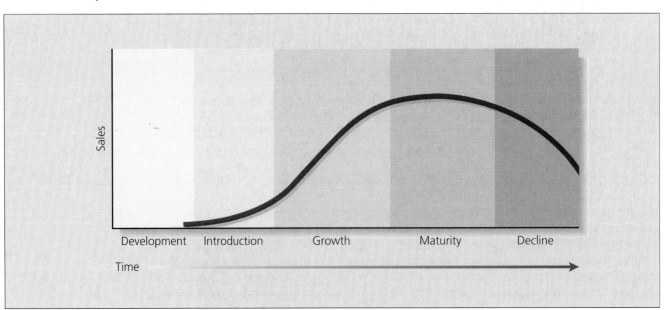

[1] James A. Brimson, "How Advanced Manufacturing Technologies Are Reshaping Cost Management," *Management Accounting* (March 1986), p. 26.

STAGE	COSTS	POSSIBLE APPROACH TO COSTING	SALES	PROFITS
Development	No production costs, but R&D costs very high	Target costing (explained in Ch. 2)	None	None; large loss on product due to expensing of R&D costs
Introduction	Production cost per unit; probably engineering change costs; high advertising cost	Kaizen costing (explained in next section of this chapter)	Very low unit sales; selling price may be high (for early profits) or low (for gaining market share)	Typically losses are incurred partially due to expensing of advertising
Growth	Production cost per unit decreases (due to learning curve and spreading fixed overhead over many units)	Kaizen costing	Rising unit sales; selling price is adjusted to meet competition	High
Maturity	Production cost per unit stable; costs of increasing product mix begin to rise	Standard costing (explained in Ch. 11)	Peak unit sales; reduced selling price	Falling
Decline	Production cost per unit increases (due to fixed overhead being spread over a lower volume)	Standard costing	Falling unit sales; selling price may be increased in an attempt to raise profits or lowered in an attempt to raise volume	May return to losses

EXHIBIT 6–2

Effects of Product Life Cycles on Costs, Sales, and Profits

ment stage, and the performance measure of "time-to-market" is becoming more critical. Exhibit 6–3 provides the average and desired time-to-market statistics for various major automakers. The importance of time-to-market is indicated by the following 1987 survey information for the automobile industry: "For each day of delay in introducing [a generic $10,000 automobile] to the market, the company will lose about $1 million in profits!"[2] If product delays could create such large profit declines in the late 1980s, imagine what kind of impact long lead times will have currently!

Once a product or service idea has been formulated, the market is typically researched to determine the features customers desire. Sometimes, however, such product research is forgone for innovative new products and companies occasionally ignore the market and simply develop and introduce products. For example, "every season Seiko 'throws' into the market several hundred new models of its watches. Those that the customers buy, it makes more of; the others it drops. Capitalizing on the design-for-response strategy, Seiko has a highly flexible design and production process that lets it quickly and inexpensively introduce new products. [The company's] fast, flexible product design process has slashed the cost of failure."[3] Because many products can now be built to specifications, companies can further develop the product to meet customer tastes once it is in the market. Alternatively, flexible manufacturing systems allow rapid changeovers to other designs.

---

[2] David Hall and Jerry Jackson, "Speeding Up New Product Development," *Management Accounting* (October 1992), p. 34.
[3] Willard I. Zangwill, "When Customer Research Is a Lousy Idea," *Wall Street Journal* (March 8, 1993), p. A10.

Time-to-Market for Auto
Manufacturers

AUTOMAKER	CURRENT AVERAGE (MONTHS)	GOAL (MONTHS)	RECORD TIME (MONTHS) (MODEL)
Mazda	21	15–18	17 (Capella)
Toyota	27*	18*	15 (Ipsum, Starlet)
Mitsubishi	24	18	19 (FTO)
Nissan	30	20	Not available
Honda	36*	24*	24* (CR-V)
Chrysler Corporation	29	24	24 (Sebring)
Ford	37	24	18 (European Escort restyling)
GM	46	38	26 (Yukon, Tahoe)

*Includes design time before concept approval.

SOURCES: Automakers; cited in Valerie Reitman and Robert L. Simison, "Japanese Car Makers Speed Up Car Making," *Wall Street Journal* (December 29, 1995), p. B1. Reprinted by permission of *The Wall Street Journal*, © 1995 Dow Jones & Company, Inc. All Rights Reserved Worldwide.

After a product is designed, manufacturers have traditionally determined product costs and set a selling price based, to some extent, on costs. If the market will not bear the resulting selling price (possibly because competitors' prices are lower), the firm either makes less profit than hoped or attempts to lower production costs.

In contrast, since the early 1970s, a technique called target costing has been used by some companies (especially Japanese ones) to view the costing process differently. Target costing develops an "allowable" product cost by analyzing market research to estimate what the market will pay for a product with specific characteristics. Subtracting an acceptable profit margin from the estimated selling price leaves an implied maximum per-unit target product cost, which is compared to an expected product cost. The following News Note describes Toyota's use of target costing in its product

NEWS NOTE

Target Costing Is Useful for Planning at Toyota

Target costing at Toyota begins with a product concept about three years before a new model is introduced. A target cost is calculated for each car model (e.g., Camry or Corolla). A new product concept document is prepared by a new product committee chaired by the chief engineer who is responsible for the car model.

After a new product concept is developed, this committee (with the help of the marketing department) determines an estimated volume and price, which is based on expected market conditions and the added value of the new model over the old model.

Cost considerations play a minor role at best in determining target price. Instead, the committee justifies increased prices by value added to the customer. Current car volumes are used as the baseline for future volume projections, as adjusted for expected market changes.

The target profit is determined by a long-run profitability analysis; it is the desired profit over the life of the product. This total profit is then calculated on a per unit basis. Target cost is determined as the difference between target price and profit. The new product concept is usually released 36 months before production, and the target cost is typically agreed to 33 months before production.

At the same time target cost is being determined, estimated cost is calculated. The engineers and accountants responsible for estimating cost use the current model as the benchmark, then add (or subtract) estimated costs for design changes. The difference between the estimated and target costs represents the amount to be reduced by means of value engineering techniques.

The planning phase culminates with a document containing product specifications, target price, target profit, target cost, [estimated cost, and where cost reductions will occur]. Cost reduction goals are assigned for each production process.

SOURCE: Joseph Fisher, "Implementing Target Costing," *Journal of Cost Management* (Summer 1995), p. 56. Reprinted with permission from *The Journal of Cost Management for the Manufacturing Industry* (Summer 1995), © 1995, Warren Gorham & Lamont, 31 St. James Avenue, Boston MA 02116. All rights reserved.

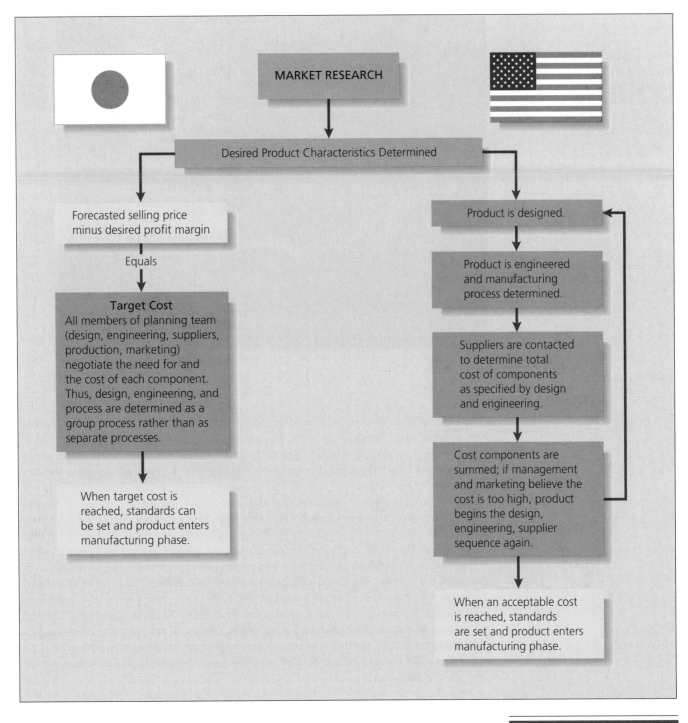

MARKET RESEARCH

Desired Product Characteristics Determined

Forecasted selling price
minus desired profit margin

Equals

Target Cost
All members of planning team
(design, engineering, suppliers,
production, marketing)
negotiate the need for and
the cost of each component.
Thus, design, engineering, and
process are determined as a
group process rather than as
separate processes.

When target cost is
reached, standards can
be set and product enters
manufacturing phase.

Product is designed.

Product is engineered
and manufacturing
process determined.

Suppliers are contacted
to determine total
cost of components
as specified by design
and engineering.

Cost components are
summed; if management
and marketing believe the
cost is too high, product
begins the design,
engineering, supplier
sequence again.

When an acceptable cost
is reached, standards
are set and product enters
manufacturing phase.

EXHIBIT 6–4

Developing Product Costs

planning process. Exhibit 6–4 compares target costing with traditional Western costing.

If the expected cost is greater than the target cost, the company has several alternatives. First, the product design and/or production process can be changed to reduce costs. Preparation of cost tables helps determine how such adjustments can be made. **Cost tables** are databases that provide information about the impact on product costs of using different input resources, manufacturing processes, and design specifications. Second, a less-than-desired profit margin can be accepted. Third, the company can decide that it does not want to enter this particular product market at the current time because it cannot make the profit margin it desires. If, for example, the target costing system at Olympus (the Japanese camera company) indicates that life cycle costs of a product are insufficient to make profitability acceptable, "the product

cost table

In West Point, PA, Merck uses state-of-the-art equipment to conduct a bone densitometry test. However, given the shortening of product life cycles (especially for high-tech products), this piece of equipment could be obsolete in the near future and replaced by something better.

kaizen costing

is abandoned unless there is a strategic reason, such as maintaining a full product line or creating a 'flagship' product, for keeping the product."[4]

Target costing can be applied to services if they are sufficiently uniform to justify the modeling effort required. For example, assume that a copy center wants to offer its customers the opportunity to get passport and other similar "snapshot" photographs. A market survey indicates that the area could sustain an annual 500-order volume and that customers believe $20 is a reasonable fee per service. The center manager believes that a reasonable profit for this service is $7 per customer photo order. Thus, the store has an allowable target cost of $13 per order. The manager will invest in the equipment necessary to provide the new service if he or she believes the indicated volume suggested by market research is sufficient to support the effort.

If a company decides to enter a market, the target cost computed at the beginning of the product life cycle does not remain the final focus. Over the product's life, the target cost is continuously reduced in an effort to spur a process of continuous improvement in actual production cost. **Kaizen costing** involves ongoing efforts to reduce product costs, increase product quality, and/or improve the production process after manufacturing activities have begun. These cost reductions are designed to keep the profit margin relatively stable as the product price is reduced over the product life cycle. Exhibit 6–5 compares target and kaizen costing.

In designing a product to meet an allowable cost, engineers strive to eliminate all nonessential activities from the production process. Such reductions in activities will, correspondingly, reduce costs. The production process and types of components to be used should be discussed among appropriate parties (including engineering, management, accounting, and marketing) in recognition of the product quality and cost desired. Suppliers also may participate in the design phase by making suggestions for modifications that would allow regularly stocked components to be used rather than more costly special-order items.

Properly designed products should require only minimal engineering changes after being released to production. Each time an engineering change is made, one or more

---

[4] Robin Cooper, *When Lean Enterprises Collide* (Boston: Harvard Business School Press, 1995), p. 159.

	TARGET COSTING	KAIZEN COSTING
What?	A procedural approach to determining a maximum allowable cost for an identifiable, proposed product assuming a given target profit margin	A mandate to reduce costs, increase product quality, and/or improve production processes through continuous improvement efforts
Used for?	New products	Existing products
When?	Development stage (includes design)	Primary production stages (introduction and growth; possibly, but not probably, maturity)
How?	Works best through aiming at a specified cost reduction objective; used to set original production standards	Works best through aiming at a specified cost reduction objective; reductions are integrated into original production standards to sustain improvements and provide new challenges
Why?	Extremely large potential for cost reduction because 80% to 90% of a product's life-long costs are embedded in the product during the design and development stages	Limited potential for reducing cost of existing products, but may provide useful information for future target costing efforts
Focus?	All product inputs (materials, labor, and overhead elements) as well as production processes and supplier components	Depends on where efforts will be most effective in reducing production costs; generally begins with the most costly component and (in the more mature companies) ends with overhead components

EXHIBIT 6–5

Differences between Target and Kaizen Costing

of the following problems can occur and create additional costs: production documents must be reprinted; workers must relearn tasks; machine setups must be changed; and parts in stock or currently ordered may be made obsolete. If costs are to be affected significantly, any design changes must be made early in the process—preferably before production begins.

Using target costing requires a shift in the way managers think about the relationships among cost, selling price, and profitability. The traditional attitude has been that a product is developed, production cost is identified and measured, a selling price is set (or a market price is met), and profits or losses result. In target costing, a product is developed, a selling price and desired profit amount are determined, and maximum allowable costs are calculated. By making costs rely on selling prices rather than the opposite, the incurrence of all costs must be justified. Unnecessary costs should be eliminated without reducing quality.

Other Life Cycle Stages

Product introduction is essentially a "start-up" phase. Sales are usually low and selling prices are often set in some relationship to (equal to, above, or below) the market price of similar **substitute goods** or services, if such goods or services are available.

substitute goods

Costs, on the other hand, can be substantial during this life cycle stage. For example, in a 1990 survey, a grocery industry task force determined that on the average, "manufacturers paid $5.1 million to get a new product or line extension on grocery store shelves nationwide. The cheapest [product introduction] studied cost $378,000; the most expensive, $21.2 million."[5] Costs incurred during this stage are typically related to engineering changes, market research, advertising, and promotion.

The growth stage begins when the product has been accepted by the market and begins to show increased sales. Product quality also may improve during this life cycle stage, especially if competitors have improved on original production designs. Prices are fairly stable during the growth stage because many substitutes exist or because consumers have become "attached" to the product and are willing to pay a particular price for it rather than buy a substitute.

In the maturity stage, sales begin to stabilize or slowly decline and firms often compete on the basis of selling price. Costs may be at their lowest level during this period, so profits may be high. Some products remain at this stage seemingly forever.

The decline stage reflects waning sales, and prices may be cut dramatically to stimulate business. Production cost per unit generally increases during this stage because fixed overhead is spread over a smaller production volume.

Life Cycle Costing

Customers are concerned with obtaining a quality product or service for a perceived "reasonable" price. In making such a determination, the consumer views the product from a life cycle perspective. For example, when purchasing a computer, one would investigate not only the original purchase price but also the cost of software, cost of service, length of warranty period, frequency and cost of upgrades, and projected obsolescence period.

From a manufacturing standpoint, because product selling prices (and sales volumes) change over a product's life cycle, target costing requires that profitability be viewed on a long-range rather than period-by-period basis. Thus, producers of goods and providers of services should be concerned about maximizing profits over a product's or service's life cycle because revenues must be generated in excess of total product (not just the current period) costs for a product to be truly profitable.

For financial statement purposes, costs incurred during the development stage *must* be expensed in the period. However, the research and development (R&D) costs that result in marketable products represent a life cycle investment rather than a period expense. Capitalization and product allocation of such costs for managerial purposes would provide better long-range profitability information and a means by which to determine the cost impact of engineering changes on product design and manufacturing process. Thus, companies desiring to focus on life cycle costs and profitability will need to change their *internal* accounting treatments of costs.

life cycle costing

Life cycle costing is the "accumulation of costs for activities that occur over the entire life cycle of a product, from inception to abandonment by the manufacturer and consumer."[6] Manufacturers would base life cycle costing expense allocations on an expected number of units to be sold over the product's life. Each period's internal income statement using life cycle costing would show revenues on a life-to-date basis. This revenue amount would be reduced by total cost of goods sold, total R&D project costs, and total distribution and other marketing costs. If life cycle costing were to be used externally, only annual sales and cost of goods sold would be presented in periodic financial statements. But all preproduction costs would be capitalized, and a risk reserve could be established "to measure the probability that these deferred product costs will be recovered through related product sales."[7]

[5] Richard Gibson, "Marketing—Pinning Down Costs of Product Introductions," *Wall Street Journal* (November 26, 1990), p. B1.
[6] Callie Berliner and James A. Brimson (eds.), *Cost Management for Today's Advanced Manufacturing* (Boston: Harvard Business School Press, 1988), p. 241.
[7] Dennis E. Peavy, "It's Time for a Change," *Management Accounting* (February 1990), p. 34.

Life cycle costing is especially important in industries that face rapid technological or style changes. If substantial money is spent on development, but technology improves faster or customer demand diminishes more rapidly than that money can be recouped from total product sales, was the development investment worthwhile? Periodic external financial statements may make a product appear to be worthwhile because its development costs were initially expensed. But, in total, the company may not even have recovered its original investment. Thus, over the product or service life cycle, companies need to be aware of and attempt to control the *total* costs of making a product or providing a service. One way of creating awareness is to evaluate all activities related to a product or service as value-added or non-value-added.

Product cost determination, although specifically designated as an accounting function, is a major concern of all managers. For example, product costs affect decisions on corporate strategy (Is it profitable to be in this particular market?), marketing (How should this product be priced?), and finance (Should investments be made in additional plant assets to manufacture this product?). In theory, what a product or service costs to produce or perform would not matter if enough customers were willing to buy that product or service at a price high enough to cover costs and provide a reasonable profit margin. In reality, customers usually purchase only something that provides acceptable value for the price being charged.

Management, then, should be concerned about whether customers perceive an equitable relationship between selling price and value. Activity-based management focuses on the activities incurred during the production or performance process as a way to improve the value received by a customer and the resulting profit achieved by providing this value. The concepts covered by activity-based management are shown in Exhibit 6–6 and are discussed in this and other chapters. These concepts help companies to produce more efficiently, determine cost more accurately, and control and evaluate performance more effectively. A primary component of activity-based management is activity analysis, which is the process of studying activities to classify them and to devise ways of minimizing or eliminating non-value-added activities.

ACTIVITY-BASED MANAGEMENT

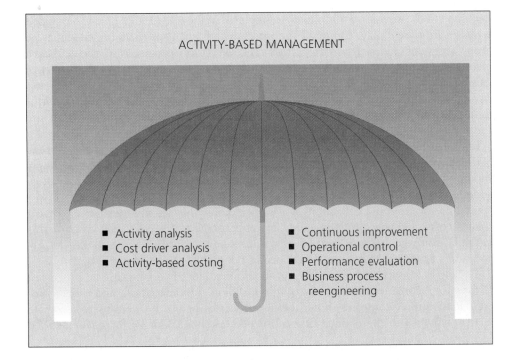

ACTIVITY-BASED MANAGEMENT

- Activity analysis
- Cost driver analysis
- Activity-based costing
- Continuous improvement
- Operational control
- Performance evaluation
- Business process reengineering

EXHIBIT 6–6

The Activity-Based Management Umbrella

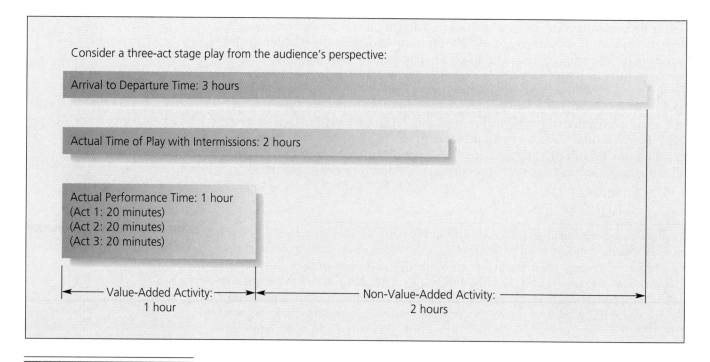

Consider a three-act stage play from the audience's perspective:

Arrival to Departure Time: 3 hours

Actual Time of Play with Intermissions: 2 hours

Actual Performance Time: 1 hour
(Act 1: 20 minutes)
(Act 2: 20 minutes)
(Act 3: 20 minutes)

Value-Added Activity:
1 hour

Non-Value-Added Activity:
2 hours

EXHIBIT 6–7

Value-Added and Non-Value-Added Activities

Value-Added versus Non-Value-Added Activities

activity

In a business context, an **activity** is defined as a repetitive action performed in fulfillment of business functions. If one takes a black-or-white perspective, activities are either value-added or non-value-added. A value-added (VA) activity increases the worth of a product or service to a customer and is one for which the customer is willing to pay. Alternatively, a non-value-added (NVA) activity increases the time spent on a product or service but does not increase its worth. Non-value-added activities are unnecessary from the perspective of the customer, which means they create costs that can be eliminated without affecting the market value or quality of the product or service.

Exhibit 6–7 provides a simplified example of value-added and non-value-added activities in a stage play. Although the intermissions spent in changing costumes or props are value-added from the actors' and directors' perspectives, the audience merely sees a drawn curtain on stage. That time is often considered by the audience (customers) as non-value-added. The two hours spent before and after the play and during intermissions may also be valued-added from certain perspectives, such as those persons managing the concession area, but possibly not from some in the audience.

business-value-added activity

Businesses also experience significant non-value-added time and activities. Some NVA activities are essential to business operations, but customers would not willingly choose to pay for these activities. These activities are known as **business-value-added activities.** For instance, Lord Corporation must prepare invoices as documentation for sales and collections. Customers know this activity must occur, that it creates costs, and that product selling prices must be set to cover the costs of this activity. However, because invoice preparation adds no direct value to Lord Corporation's products, customers would prefer not to have to pay for this activity.

To help in activity analysis, managers should first identify organizational processes. "Processes include production, distribution, selling, administration, and other company functions. A company should define processes before it attempts to associate related activities to the defined process. Processes should not be forced or defined

In a university setting, the time faculty spend in their offices conversing with students is generally value-added. Much of this time is used in helping students better understand material covered in class, discussing career opportunities, or advising about future semesters.

to fit activities; activities should fit processes."[8] Processes are commonly horizontal in nature, overlapping multiple functional areas. For example, any production process also affects engineering, purchasing, warehousing, accounting, personnel, and marketing.

For each distinct process, a **process map** (or detailed flowchart) should be prepared that indicates every step that goes into making or doing something. All steps and all affected areas must be included, not just the obvious ones. For example, storing newly purchased parts would not be on a typical list of "Steps in Making Product X," but when materials and supplies are purchased, they are commonly stored until needed. Storage uses facilities that cost money and requires time to move the items in and out. Each process map is unique and based on the results of a management and employee team's study.

Once the process map has been developed, a **value chart** can be constructed that identifies the stages and time spent in those stages from beginning to end of a process. Time can be consumed in four general ways: processing (or service), inspection, transfer, and idle. The actual time that it takes to perform the functions necessary to manufacture the product or perform the service is the **processing** (or **service**) **time;** this quantity of time is value-added. Performing quality control results in **inspection time,** whereas moving products or components from one place to another constitutes **transfer time.** Lastly, storage time and time spent waiting at a production operation for processing is **idle time.** Inspection time, transfer time, and idle time are all non-value-added. Thus, the **cycle** (or lead) **time** from the receipt of an order to completion of a product or performance of a service is equal to value-added processing time plus non-value-added time.

Although viewing inspection time and transfer time as non-value-added is theoretically correct, few companies can completely eliminate all quality control functions and all transfer time. Understanding the non-value-added nature of these functions, however, should help managers strive to minimize such activities to the extent possible. Thus, companies should view value-added and non-value-added activities as

process map

value chart

processing (service) time

inspection time

transfer time

idle time

cycle time

---

[8] Charles D. Mecimore and Alice T. Bell, "Are We Ready for Fourth-Generation ABC?" *Management Accounting* (January 1995), p. 24.

Assembling									
Operations	Receiving	Quality control	Storage	Move to production	Waiting for use	Setup of machinery	Assembly	Move to inspection	Move to finishing
Average time (days)	2	1	10–15	.5	3	.5	3	.5	.5

Finishing									
Operations	Receiving	Move to production	Waiting for use	Setup of machinery	Finishing	Inspection	Packaging	Move to dockside	Storage	Ship to customer
Average time (days)	.5	.5	5–12	.5	2	.5	.5	.5	1.5	1–4

Total time in Assembling: 21.0 – 26.0 days Assembling value-added time: 3.0 days
Total time in Finishing: 12.5 – 22.5 days Finishing value-added time: 2.5 days
Total processing time: 33.5 – 48.5 days **Total value-added time: 5.5 days**
−Total value-added time: 5.5 – 5.5 days
Total non-value-added time: 28.0 – 43.0 days

Non-Value-Added Activities

Value-Added Activities

EXHIBIT 6–8

Value Chart for Chaix Company

occurring on a continuum and concentrate on attempting to eliminate or minimize those activities that add the most time and cost, and the least value.

Exhibit 6–8 illustrates a value chart for a cleaning product made by the Chaix Company. Note the excessive time consumed by simply storing and moving materials. Value is added to products *only* during the times that production actually occurs; thus, Chaix Company's entire production sequence has only five and one-half days of value-added time.

In some instances, a company may question whether the time spent in packaging is value-added. Packaging is essential for some products but unnecessary for others and, because packaging takes up about a third of the U.S. landfills and creates a substantial amount of cost, companies and consumers are focusing their attention on reducing or eliminating packaging.

Manufacturing Cycle Efficiency

manufacturing cycle efficiency

Dividing value-added processing time by total cycle time provides a measure of efficiency referred to as **manufacturing cycle efficiency** (MCE). (A service company would compute service cycle efficiency by dividing actual service time by total cycle time.) If a company's production time were 3 hours and its total cycle time were 24 hours, its manufacturing cycle efficiency would be 12.5 (3 ÷ 24) percent.

Although the ultimate goal of 100 percent efficiency can never be achieved, typically, value is added to the product only 10 percent of the time from receipt of the parts until shipment to the customer. Ninety percent of the cycle time is waste. A product is much like a magnet. The longer the cycle time, the more the product attracts and creates cost.[9]

[9] Tom E. Pryor, "Activity Accounting: The Key to Waste Reduction," *Accounting Systems Journal* (Fall 1990), p. 38.

Why Reduce Cycle Time?

Reducing cycle time increases profitability through increased sales volume or product profit margin (or both). Achieving manufacturing cycle-time reduction, however, can require significant investment in new technology and changes in operating methods, policies and procedures, or supplier and customer relationships. Management should understand the financial impact of selected cycle-time adjustments before deciding on a course of action.

To assist management in making informed decisions concerning cycle-time activities, a cost-benefit analysis answering the following questions should be part of a cycle-time reduction proposal.

- Will overall cycle-time reduction result in increased throughput?
- What activities consume the most resources, in both time and dollars, within each process?
- What activities within a process can be changed or reduced without compromising throughput? (Throughput is the number of good units or quantity of services produced and sold by an organization within a time period.)
- What will it cost to change or reduce activities that contribute to cycle time?
- What are the realizable cost savings from reduced cycle time for specific activities?

A cycle-time reduction program can translate into improved service and quality when selected non-value-added activities are eliminated. Customer response time can improve without loss of product quality. If higher service and quality are important to the customers, they may pay a higher price for the company's products.

SOURCE: Robert J. Campbell, "Managing Cycle Time," *Management Accounting* (January 1995), pp. 34–35. Reprinted from *Management Accounting*. Copyright by Institute of Management Accountants, Montvale, NJ.

A just-in-time manufacturing process (discussed in Chapter 17) seeks to achieve substantially higher efficiency by producing components and goods at the precise time they are needed by either the next production station or the consumer. Thus, a significant amount of idle time (especially in storage) is eliminated. Raising MCE can also be achieved by installing and using automated technology, such as flexible manufacturing systems. As discussed in the above News Note, the process of and rationale for increasing MCE should be thoroughly considered before implementation.

In a retail environment, cycle time relates to the length of time from ordering an item to selling that item. Non-value-added activities in retail include shipping time from the supplier, receiving delays for counting merchandise, and any storage time between receipt and sale. In a service company, cycle time refers to the time between the service order and service completion. All time spent on activities that are not actual service performance or are nonactivities (such as delays in beginning a job) are considered non-value-added for that job.

Non-value-added activities can be attributed to systemic, physical, and human factors. For example, systemic causes could include a processing requirement that products be manufactured in large batches to minimize setup cost or that service jobs be taken in order of urgency. Physical factors contribute to non-value-added activities because, in many instances, plant and machine layout do not provide for the most efficient transfer of products. This factor is especially apparent in multistory buildings in which receiving and shipping are on the ground floor, but storage and production are on upper floors. People may also be responsible for non-value-added activities because of improper skills or training or the need to be sociable.

Attempts to reduce non-value-added activities should be directed at all of these causes, but it is imperative that the "Willie Sutton" rule be applied. This rule is named for the bank robber who, when asked why he robbed banks, replied, "That's where the money is." The NVA activities that create the most costs should be the ones that management concentrates its efforts on reducing or eliminating. The sys-

NEWS NOTE

Reduction in NVA Time Increases Work Quality and Efficiency

The disbursements department at a major consumer products company identified wait and move time of invoices as non-value-added cost drivers and proposed to eliminate them. Invoices arrived in the disbursements department several times a day. A mail clerk sorted them alphabetically and placed the alphabet segment of invoices in the data entry clerks' mailboxes to which that segment was assigned. The company made an effort to smooth the volume of invoices by dividing the alphabet among the clerks, but, on any given day, predicting the number of invoices that would come in per data entry clerk was impossible. Identifying clerks whose work was completed and who were available to help someone else and clerks who needed help added wait time. Several times a day the data entry clerks left their workstations to go to the mailboxes. Incomplete invoices were returned to the vendor by mail or internal departments by company mail. Up to two weeks could elapse before corrected invoices returned to the system.

Wait and move time virtually were eliminated from the disbursements system when the company implemented an imaging system that smoothed workflow to the clerks. Now all mail is opened by one clerk and screened for items requiring immediate attention. Those items are scanned first and flagged, followed by all other invoices. Data entry clerks or indexers receive work at their terminals on a next-available-invoice basis. Walkaround time is eliminated as is the supervisory time required to match free clerks with overworked ones. Immediate-attention invoices are delivered first so urgent items can't be missed. Incomplete invoices are assigned a voucher number electronically and are faxed internally to a department or externally to a vendor for necessary additions. Corrections now are made in hours or minutes rather than days or weeks.

SOURCE: Charles D. Mecimore and Alice T. Bell, "Are We Ready for Fourth-Generation ABC?" *Management Accounting* (January 1995), pp. 23–24. Reprinted from *Management Accounting*. Copyright by Institute of Management Accountants, Montvale, NJ.

tem must be changed to reflect a new management philosophy regarding performance measures and determination of product cost. Physical factors must be changed as much as possible to eliminate layout difficulties and machine bottlenecks, and people must accept and work toward total quality control. Automated machines and a "lights-out" factory (run by robots with little or no human intervention) are useful to an extent, but people are still necessary for businesses—especially service businesses—to continue. Focusing attention on eliminating non-value-added activities should cause product/service quality to increase and cycle time and cost to decrease. A good example of eliminating NVA activities in a service department is provided in the above News Note.

Although constructing value charts for every product or service would be time-consuming, a few such charts can quickly indicate where a company is losing time and money through non-value-added activities. Using amounts such as depreciation on storage facilities, wages for employees who handle warehousing, and the cost of capital on working capital funds tied up in stored inventory can provide an estimate of the amount by which costs could be reduced through the elimination of non-value-added activities.

COST DRIVER ANALYSIS

Companies engage in many activities that consume resources and, thus, cause costs to be incurred. All activities have cost drivers, defined in Chapter 4 as the factors having direct cause-effect relationships to a cost. Many cost drivers may be identified for an individual business unit. For example, cost drivers for factory insurance are number of employees; value of property, plant, and equipment; and number of accidents or claims during a specified time period. Cost drivers affecting the entire plant include inventory size, physical layout, and number of different products produced. Cost drivers are classified as volume-related (such as machine hours) and non-volume-related, which generally reflect the incurrence of specific transactions (such as setups, work orders, or distance traveled).

A greater number of cost drivers can be identified than should be used for cost accumulation or activity elimination. Management should limit the cost drivers selected to a reasonable number and ascertain that the cost of measuring the driver does not exceed the benefit of using it. A cost driver should be easy to understand, directly related to the activity being performed, and appropriate for performance measurement.[10]

Costs have traditionally been accumulated into one or two cost pools (total factory overhead or variable and fixed factory overhead), and one or two drivers (direct labor hours and/or machine hours) have been used to assign costs to products. These procedures cause few, if any, problems for financial statement preparation. However, the use of single cost pools and single drivers may produce illogical product or service costs for internal managerial use in complex production (or service) environments.

To reflect the more complex environments, the accounting system must first recognize that costs are created and incurred because their drivers occur at different levels.[11] This realization necessitates using **cost driver analysis,** which investigates, quantifies, and explains the relationships of drivers and their related costs. Traditionally, cost drivers were viewed only at the unit level; for example, how many hours of labor or machine time did it take to produce a product or render a service? These drivers create **unit-level costs,** meaning that they are caused by the production or acquisition of a single unit of product or the delivery of a single unit of service. Other drivers and their costs are incurred for broader-based categories or levels of activity. These broader-based activity levels have successively wider scopes of influence on products and product types. The categories are classified as batch, product or process, and organizational or facility levels. Examples of the kinds of costs occurring at the various levels are given in Exhibit 6–9 on the next page.

Costs that are caused by a group of things being made, handled, or processed at a single time are referred to as **batch-level costs.** A good example of a batch-level cost is the cost of setting up a machine. Assume that setting up a machine to cast product parts costs Lord Corporation $400. Two different parts are to be manufactured during the day; therefore, two setups will be needed at a total cost of $800. The first run will generate 1,000 Type A parts; the second run will generate 200 Type B parts. These quantities are specifically needed for production because the company is on a just-in-time production system. If a unit-based cost driver (volume) were used, the total setup cost of $800 would be divided by 1,200 parts, giving a cost per part of $.67. This method would assign the majority of the cost to Type A parts (1,000 × $.67 = $670). However, because the cost is actually created by a batch-level driver, $400 should be spread over 1,000 Type A parts for a cost of $.40 per part and $400 should be spread over 200 Type B parts for a cost of $2 per part. Using a batch-level perspective indicates the commonality of the cost to the units within the batch and is more indicative of the relationship between the activity (setup) and the driver (different production runs).

A cost caused by the development, production, or acquisition of different items is called a **product-level** (or **process-level**) **cost.** To illustrate this level of cost, assume that the engineering department of Lord issued five engineering change orders (ECOs) during May. Of these ECOs, four related to Product R, one related to Product S, and none related to Product T. Each ECO costs $3,000 to issue. During May, the company produced 1,000 units of Product R, 1,500 units of Product S, and 5,000 units of Product T. If ECO costs were treated as unit-level costs, the total ECO cost of $15,000 would be spread over the 7,500 units produced at a cost per

cost driver analysis

unit-level cost

batch-level cost

product-level (process-level) cost

---

[10] Appendix 1 in Chapter 21 provides a detailed list of cost drivers that are appropriate for analyzing cost incurrence as well as performance measures for a variety of areas.

[11] This hierarchy of costs was introduced by Robin Cooper in "Cost Classification in Unit-Based and Activity-Based Manufacturing Cost Systems," *Journal of Cost Management* (Fall 1990), p. 6.

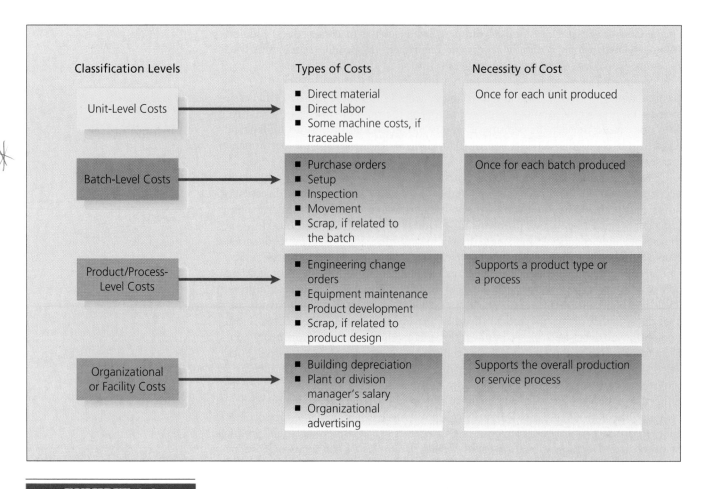

Classification Levels	Types of Costs	Necessity of Cost
Unit-Level Costs	■ Direct material ■ Direct labor ■ Some machine costs, if traceable	Once for each unit produced
Batch-Level Costs	■ Purchase orders ■ Setup ■ Inspection ■ Movement ■ Scrap, if related to the batch	Once for each batch produced
Product/Process-Level Costs	■ Engineering change orders ■ Equipment maintenance ■ Product development ■ Scrap, if related to product design	Supports a product type or a process
Organizational or Facility Costs	■ Building depreciation ■ Plant or division manager's salary ■ Organizational advertising	Supports the overall production or service process

EXHIBIT 6–9

Levels of Costs

organizational-level cost

unit of $2. However, this method inappropriately assigns $10,000 of ECO cost to Product T, which had no engineering change orders issued for it! Using a product/process-level driver (number of ECOs) for ECO costs would assign $12,000 of costs to Product R and $3,000 to Product S. These amounts would be assigned to R and S, but not simply to the current month's production. The ECO cost should be allocated to all current and future R and S units produced while these ECOs are in effect because the products manufactured using the changed design benefit from the costs of the ECOs.

Certain costs at the organizational level are incurred for the singular purpose of supporting continuing facility operations. These **organizational-level costs** are common to many different activities and products or services and can be prorated to products only on an arbitrary basis. Although organizational-level costs theoretically should not be assigned to products at all, some companies attach them to goods produced or services rendered because the amounts are insignificant relative to all other costs.

Accountants have traditionally (and incorrectly) assumed that if costs did not vary with changes in production at the unit level, those costs were fixed rather than variable. In reality, batch-, product/process-, and organizational-level costs are all variable, but they vary for reasons other than changes in production volume. Therefore, to determine a valid estimate of product or service cost, costs should be accumulated at each successively higher level of costs. Because unit-, batch-, and product/process-level costs are all associated with units of products (merely at different levels), these costs can be summed at the product level to match with the revenues generated by product sales. Organizational-level costs are not product related, thus they should only be subtracted in total from net product revenues.

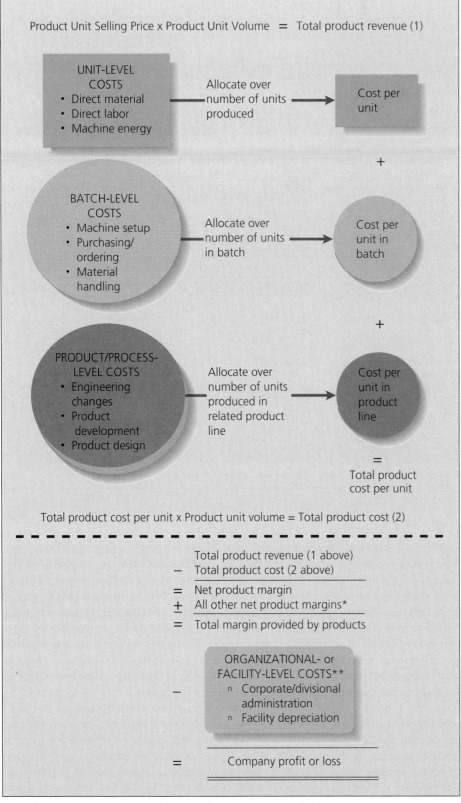

EXHIBIT 6–10

Determining Product
Profitability and Company
Profit

*Calculations are made for each product line using the same method as above.
**Some of these costs may be assignable to specific products or services and would be included in
determining product cost per unit.

Exhibit 6–10 illustrates how costs collected at the unit, batch, and product/process levels can be used to generate a total product cost. Each product cost would be multiplied by the number of units sold and that amount of cost of goods sold would

Total overhead cost = $3,010,500
Total machine hours = 223,000
Overhead rate per machine hour = $13.50

	PRODUCT L (10,000 UNITS)		PRODUCT M (3,000 UNITS)		PRODUCT N (210,000 UNITS)		
	UNIT	TOTAL	UNIT	TOTAL	UNIT	TOTAL	TOTAL
Product revenue	$50.00	$500,000	$45.00	$135,000	$40.00	$8,400,000	$9,035,000
Product costs							
Direct	$20.00	200,000	$20.00	$ 60,000	$ 9.00	$1,890,000	
OH per MH	13.50	135,000	13.50	40,500	13.50	2,835,000	
Total	$33.50	$335,000	$33.50	$100,500	$22.50	$4,725,000	5,160,500
Net income		$165,000		$ 34,500		$3,675,000	$3,874,500

	PRODUCT L (10,000 UNITS)		PRODUCT M (3,000 UNITS)		PRODUCT N (210,000 UNITS)		
	UNIT	TOTAL	UNIT	TOTAL	UNIT	TOTAL	TOTAL
Product revenue	$50	$500,000	$45	$135,000	$40	$8,400,000	$9,035,000
Product costs							
Direct	$20	$200,000	$20	$ 60,000	$ 9	$1,890,000	
Overhead							
Unit-level	8	80,000	12	36,000	6	1,260,000	
Batch-level	9	90,000	19	57,000	3	630,000	
Product-level	3	30,000	15	45,000	2	420,000	
Total	$40	$400,000	$66	$198,000	$20	$4,200,000	4,798,000
Product line income or (loss)		$100,000		$ (63,000)		$4,200,000	$4,237,000
Organizational-level costs							362,500
Net income							$3,874,500

EXHIBIT 6–11

Product Profitability Analysis

be subtracted from total product revenues to obtain a product line profit or loss item. These computations would be performed for each product line and summed to determine net product income or loss from which the unassigned organizational-level costs would be subtracted to find company profit or loss for internal management use. In this model, the traditional distinction (discussed in Chapter 4) between product and period costs can be and is ignored. The emphasis is on refining product profitability analysis for internal management purposes, rather than for external financial statements. Because the product/period cost distinction required by generally accepted accounting principles is not recognized, the model presented in Exhibit 6–10 is not currently acceptable for external reporting.

Data for a sample manufacturing company with three products are presented in Exhibit 6–11 to illustrate the difference in information that would result from recognizing multiple cost levels. Before recognizing that some costs were incurred at the batch, product, and organizational level, the company accumulated and allocated its factory overhead costs among its three products on a machine-hour (MH) basis. Each product requires one machine hour, but Product M is a low-volume, special-order line. As shown in the first section of Exhibit 6–11, cost information indicated that Product M was a profitable product. After analyzing its activities, the company began capturing costs at the different levels and assigning them to products based on appropriate cost drivers. The individual details for this overhead assignment are not shown, but the final assignments and resulting product profitability figures are presented in the second section of Exhibit 6–11. This more refined approach to assigning costs shows that Product M is actually unprofitable.

Costs are incurred because firms engage in a variety of activities, and these activities consume company resources. Accountants have traditionally used a transaction basis to accumulate costs and, additionally, have focused on the cost incurred rather than the source of the cost. However, managers now believe that the "conventional transaction-driven system is costly to administer, fails to control costs, and usually yields erroneous product cost data."[12]

As was the case at Lord Corporation, traditional cost allocations tend to subsidize low-volume, specialty products by misallocating overhead to high-volume, standard products. This problem occurs because costs of the extra activities needed to make specialty products are assigned using the one or very few drivers of traditional costing—and usually those drivers are volume based. Interestingly, as long ago as 1954, William J. Vatter noted that "[j]ust as soon as cost accounting is found inadequate for the needs it is supposed to meet, just as soon as cost accounting does not provide the data which management must have, cost accounting will either change to meet those needs or it will be replaced with something else."[13] The time has come for cost accounting to change by utilizing new bases on which to collect and assign costs. Those bases are the activities that drive or create the costs.

Recognizing that several levels of costs exist, accumulating costs into related cost pools, and using multiple cost drivers to assign costs to products and services are the three fundamental components of activity-based costing (ABC). ABC is a cost accounting system that focuses on the various activities performed in an organization and collects costs on the basis of the underlying nature and extent of those activities. This costing method focuses on attaching costs to products and services based on the activities conducted to produce, perform, distribute, or support those products and services.

As at Lord Corporation, managers in many manufacturing companies are concerned about the product costing information being provided by the traditional cost accounting systems. The general consensus is that product costs currently being developed are useful in preparing financial statements, but are often of limited use for management decision making. Activity-based costing, on the other hand, is useful in companies having the following characteristics:

1. the production or performance of a wide variety of products or services;
2. high overhead costs that are not proportional to the unit volume of individual products;
3. significant automation that has made it increasingly more difficult to assign overhead to products using the traditional direct labor or machine-hour bases;
4. profit margins that are difficult to explain; and
5. hard-to-make products that show big profits and easy-to-make products that show losses.[14]

Companies having the above characteristics may want to reevaluate their cost systems and implement activity-based costing.

Two-Step Allocation

After being recorded in the general ledger and subledger accounts, costs are accumulated in activity center cost pools. An **activity center** is a segment of the production or service process for which management wants a separate report of the costs of activities performed. In defining these centers, management should consider the

ACTIVITY-BASED COSTING

activity center

VIDEO VIGNETTE

An Introduction to Activity-Based Costing

---

[12] Richard J. Schonberger, "World-Class Performance Management," in *Performance Excellence in Manufacturing and Service Organizations*, ed. Peter B. B. Turney (Sarasota, FL: American Accounting Association, 1990), p. 1.

[13] William J. Vatter, "Tailor-making Cost Data for Specific Uses," in *Topics in Managerial Accounting*, ed. L. S. Rosen (Toronto: McGraw-Hill Ryerson Ltd., 1974), p. 194.

[14] Robin Cooper, "You Need a New Cost System When . . . ," *Harvard Business Review* (January–February 1989), pp. 77–82.

following issues: geographical proximity of equipment; defined centers of managerial responsibility; magnitude of product costs; and a need to keep the number of activity centers manageable. Costs having the same driver are accumulated in pools reflecting the appropriate level of cost incurrence (unit, batch, or product/process). The fact that a relationship exists between a cost pool and a cost driver indicates that, if the cost driver can be reduced or eliminated, the related cost should also be reduced or eliminated.

Gathering costs in pools reflecting the same cost drivers allows managers to recognize cross-functional activities in an organization. In the past, some companies may have accumulated overhead in smaller-than-plantwide pools, but this accumulation was typically performed on a department-by-department basis. Thus, the process reflected a vertical-function approach to cost accumulation. But production and service activities are horizontal by nature. A product or service flows *through* an organization, affecting numerous departments as it goes. Using a cost driver approach to develop cost pools allows managers to more clearly focus on the various cost impacts created in making a product or performing a service than was possible traditionally.

activity driver

After accumulation, costs are allocated out of the activity center cost pools and assigned to products and services by use of a second driver. These drivers are often referred to as activity drivers. An **activity driver** measures the demands placed on activities and, thus, the resources consumed by products and services. An activity driver selected often indicates an activity's output. The process of cost assignment is the same as the overhead application process illustrated in Chapter 5. Exhibit 6–12

EXHIBIT 6–12

Tracing Costs in an Activity-Based Costing System

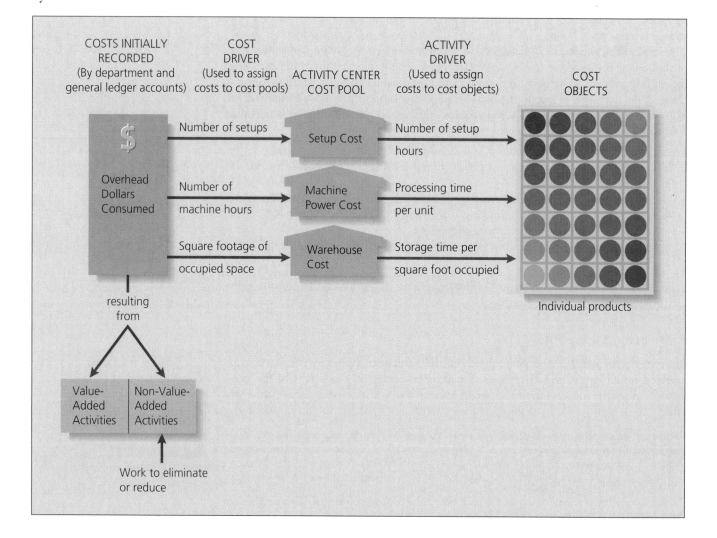

EXHIBIT 6–13

Activity Drivers

ACTIVITY CENTER	ACTIVITY DRIVERS
Accounting	Reports requested; dollars expended
Personnel	Job change actions; hiring actions; training hours; counseling hours
Data processing	Reports requested; transactions processed; programming hours; program change requests
Production engineering	Hours spent in each shop; job specification changes requested; product change notices processed
Quality control	Hours spent in each shop; defects discovered; samples analyzed
Plant services	Preventive maintenance cycles; hours spent in each shop; repair and maintenance actions
Material services	Dollar value of requisitions; number of transactions processed; number of personnel in direct support
Utilities	Direct usage (metered to shop); space occupied
Production shops	Fixed per-job charge; setups made; direct labor; machine hours; number of moves; material applied

SOURCE: Michael D. Woods, "Completing the Picture: Economic Choices with ABC," *Management Accounting* (December 1992), p. 54. Reprinted from *Management Accounting.* Copyright by Institute of Management Accountants, Montvale, NJ.

illustrates this two-step process of tracing costs to products and services in an ABC system.

As noted in Exhibit 6–12, the cost drivers for the collection stage may differ from the activity drivers used for the allocation stage because some activity center costs are not traceable to lower levels of activity. Costs at the lowest (unit) level of activity should be allocated to products by use of volume- or unit-based drivers. Costs incurred at higher (batch and product/process) levels may also be allocated to products by use of volume-related drivers, but the volume measure should include only those units associated with the batch or the product/process—not total production or service volume. Exhibit 6–13 provides some common drivers for various activity centers.

The activity centers and breakdown of overhead costs for one of Lord Corporation's plants are illustrated in Exhibit 6–14. This exhibit indicates the interrelationships within and among functional areas as well as appropriate drivers for cost assignments to products.

Activity-Based Costing Illustrated

An ABC example is shown in Exhibit 6–15 on p. 244. Information is gathered about the activities and costs for a factory maintenance department. Costs are then assigned based on activities to specific products. This department allocates its total personnel cost among the three activities performed in that department based on the number of employees in those areas. This allocation reflects the fact that occurrences of a specific activity, rather than volume of production or service, are indicative of work performed in the department.

This company manufactures Product Z, which is a rather complex unit with relatively low demand. The cost allocated to Product Z with the activity-based costing system is 132 percent higher than the cost allocated with the traditional allocation system ($1.564 to $.675)!

Discrepancies in costs between traditional and activity-based costing methods are not uncommon. Activity-based costing systems indicate that significant resources are consumed by low-volume products and complex production operations. Studies have shown that, after the implementation of activity-based costing, the costs of high-volume, standard products have often been too high and, using ABC, have declined anywhere from 10 to 30 percent. Low-volume, complex specialty product costs tend to increase from 100 to 500 percent, although in some cases these costs have risen

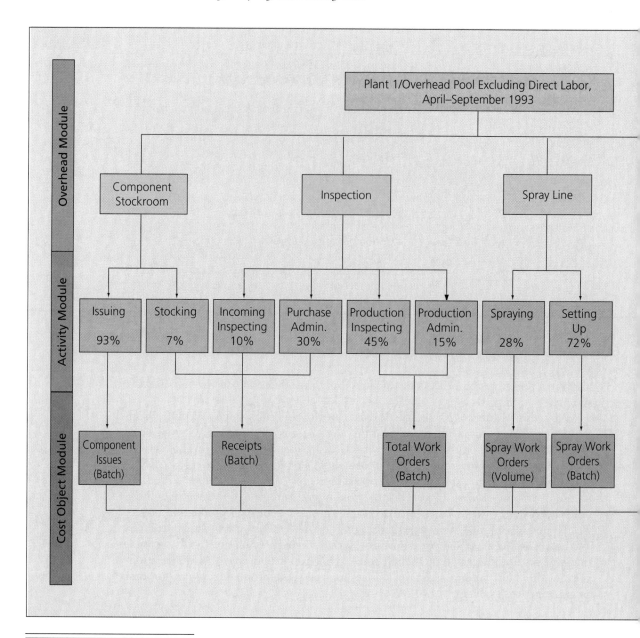

EXHIBIT 6–14

Overhead Pool and
Allocations at Lord
Corporation

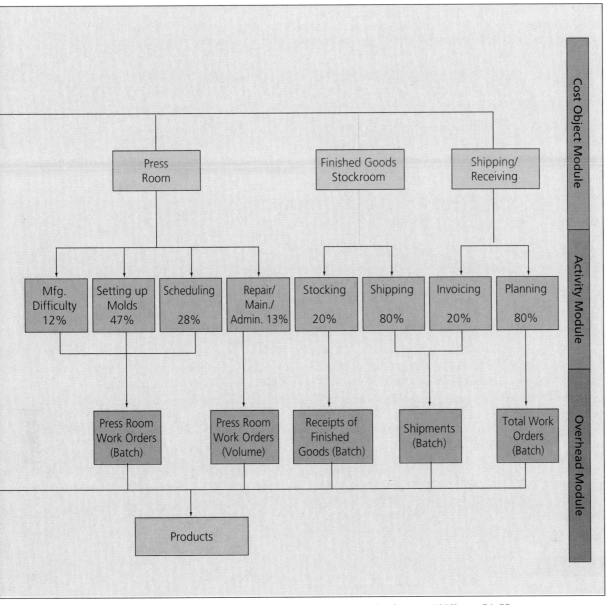

SOURCE: Alan W. Rupp, ''ABC: A Pilot Approach,'' *Management Accounting* (January 1995), pp. 54–55. Reprinted from *Management Accounting.* Copyright by Institute of Management Accountants, Montvale, NJ.

Factory Maintenance Department: The company's conventional system assigns the personnel costs of this department to products using direct labor hours (DLHs); the department has 9 employees and incurred $450,000 of personnel costs in the current year or $50,000 per employee.

ABC ALLOCATION

Stage 1
Trace costs from general ledger and subsidiary ledger accounts to activity center pools according to number of employees:

- Regular maintenance—uses 5 employees; $250,000 is allocated to this activity; second-stage allocation to be based on machine hours (MHs)
- Preventive maintenance—uses 2 employees; $100,000 is allocated to this activity; second-stage allocation to be based on number of setups
- Repairs—uses 2 employees; $100,000 is allocated to this activity; second-stage allocation is based on number of machine starts

Stage 2
Allocate activity center cost pools to products using cost drivers chosen for each cost pool.

1997 activity of second-stage drivers: 500,000 MHs; 5,000 setups; 100,000 machine starts

STEP 1:   Allocate costs per unit of activity of second-stage cost drivers

- Regular maintenance—$250,000 ÷ 500,000 MHs = $.50 per MH
- Preventive maintenance—$100,000 ÷ 5,000 setups = $20 per setup
- Repairs—$100,000 ÷ 100,000 machine starts = $1 per machine start

STEP 2:   Allocate costs to products using quantity of second-stage cost drivers consumed in making these products. The following quantities of activity are relevant to Product Z: 30,000 MHs; 30 setups; 40 machine starts; and 3,000 DLHs out of a total of 200,000 DLHs in 1997. Ten thousand units of Product Z were manufactured during 1997.

ABC Allocation to Product Z = (30,000 × $.50) + (30 × $20) + (40 × $1) = $15,640 for 10,000 units or $1.564 per unit

Traditional Allocation to Product Z = $450,000 ÷ 200,000 DLHs = $2.25 per DLH; (3,000 × $2.25) = $6,750 for 10,000 units or $.675 per unit

---

EXHIBIT 6–15

Illustration of Activity-Based Costing Allocation

by 1,000 percent to 5,000 percent![15] Thus, activity-based costing typically shifts a substantial amount of overhead cost from standard, high-volume products to premium special-order, low-volume products, as shown in Exhibit 6–16. The ABC costs of moderate products and services (those that are neither extremely simple nor complex, nor produced in extremely low or high volumes) tend to remain approximately the same as the costs calculated using traditional costing methods.

Although the preceding discussion addresses costs normally considered product costs, activity-based costing is just as applicable to service department costs. Many companies use an activity-based costing system to allocate corporate overhead costs to their revenue-producing units based on the number of reports, documents, customers, or other reasonable measures of activity.

Short-Term and Long-Term Variable Costs

Short-term variable costs increase or decrease in correspondence with changes in the volume of activity. Costs that do not move in relation to volume have conventionally been accepted as fixed. "Generally [however], as a business expands, costs tend to be

[15] Peter B. B. Turney, *An Introduction to Activity-Based Costing* (ABC Technologies, Inc., 1990), video.

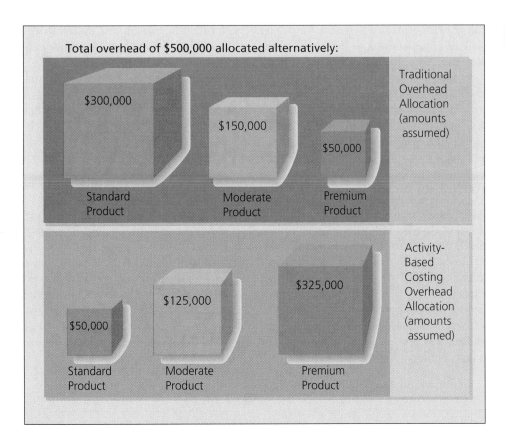

Total overhead of $500,000 allocated alternatively:

$300,000 — Standard Product
$150,000 — Moderate Product
$50,000 — Premium Product

Traditional Overhead Allocation (amounts assumed)

$50,000 — Standard Product
$125,000 — Moderate Product
$325,000 — Premium Product

Activity-Based Costing Overhead Allocation (amounts assumed)

EXHIBIT 6–16

Traditional versus ABC Overhead Allocations

far more variable than they should be, and when it contracts, they are far more fixed than they should be."[16] Professor Robert Kaplan of Harvard University considers the ability of "fixed" costs to change under the "Rule of One," which means that possessing or using more than one unit of a resource is evidence that the resource is variable.[17] Because of this logic, many people have come to view fixed costs as **long-term variable costs,** for which suitable (usually non-volume-related) cost drivers simply need to be identified.

> **long-term variable cost**

Two significant cost drivers that cause long-term variable costs to change, but which traditionally have been disregarded, are product variety and product complexity. **Product variety** refers to the number of different types of products made; **product complexity** refers to the number of components included in a product or the number of processes through which a product flows. Because of the additional overhead support that is needed (such as warehousing, purchasing, setups, and inspections), long-term variable costs tend to increase as the number and types of products increase. Therefore, managers should use these cost drivers in applying ABC when the cost drivers cause significant amounts of overhead.

> **product variety**
>
> **product complexity**

VIDEO VIGNETTE

King Systems Corp. and/or Roscoe Manufacturing (Blue Chip Enterprises)

Horizontal Flow of Activities

ABC permits managers to recognize the horizontal flow of products, services, and activities through an organization. Examining the horizontal flow reveals the many cost impacts that are created by making a product or performing a service. Consider what happens when a plumber, who sets out on a schedule for the day, is contacted and reassigned to an emergency call to a house in which the basement is rapidly

[16] B. Charles Ames and James D. Hlavacek, "Vital Truths About Managing Your Costs," *Harvard Business Review* (January–February 1990), p. 145.
[17] Patrick L. Romano, "Activity Accounting: An Update—Part 2," *Management Accounting* (June 1989), p. 63.

filling with water. The office dispatcher must call other customers either to re-schedule the work or, if necessary, assign a substitute plumber. The dispatcher may also have to send materials, parts, or tools to the plumber at the flooding house.

From an organization's vertical perspective, focusing solely on function, all company personnel performed their respective, regular duties and worked a normal 8-hour day. Such a limited view fails to identify and measure the additional activities and costs caused by the schedule change. ABC refines the costing process to recognize the historically unheeded additional activities, costs, and cost drivers.

Attribute-Based Costing

attribute-based costing

Attribute-based costing (ABC II), an extension of activity-based costing, employs detailed cost-benefit analyses relating to information on customer needs (in terms of performance attributes of a product such as reliability, durability, responsiveness, and so forth) and the costs of the incremental improvements necessary to obtain these attributes. ABC II employs planned costs rather than past costs because, as discussed earlier, such a high percentage of a product's life cycle costs are locked in during the product's development stage. The approach focuses on satisfying customer needs by searching for the optimum enhancement of customer utility through comparisons of alternatives for attribute enhancements relative to the costs of producing those enhancements.[18]

DETERMINING WHETHER ABC IS APPROPRIATE

A vital loss of information may occur in an accounting system that ignores activity and cost relationships. Not every accounting system using direct labor or machine hours as the cost driver is providing inadequate or inaccurate cost information. However, some general clues may alert managers to the need to review the cost data being provided by a conventional accounting system. Some of these clues are more relevant to manufacturing entities, but others are equally appropriate for both manufacturing and service businesses. Consider the following:

For a given organization, is it likely that ABC will produce costs that are significantly different from those that are generated with conventional accounting, and does it seem likely that those costs will be "better"? The factors involved here include:

■ the number and diversity of products or services produced,
■ the diversity and differential degree of support services used for different products,
■ the extent to which common processes are used,
■ the effectiveness of current cost allocation methods,
■ and the rate of growth of period costs.

If information that is considered "better" is generated by ABC, will the new information change the dependent decisions made by the management? The factors involved here are:

■ management's freedom to set prices,
■ the ratio of period costs to total costs,
■ strategic considerations,
■ the climate and culture of cost reduction in the company,
■ and the frequency of analysis that is desirable or necessary.[19]

Two primary underlying assumptions that companies must consider before adopting ABC are that the costs in each cost pool are (1) driven by homogeneous activities

---

[18] For additional information, see Mike Walker, "Attribute Based Costing," *Australian Accountant* (March 1992), pp. 42–45.

[19] T. L. Estrin, Jeffrey Kantor, and David Albers, "Is ABC Suitable for Your Company?" *Management Accounting* (April 1994), p. 40.

and (2) strictly proportional to the activity.[20] If these assumptions are met, the following circumstances may indicate a need to consider using activity-based costing.

With Product Variety and Product Complexity

Product variety is commonly associated with a need to consider activity-based costing. Products may be variations of the same product line (such as Hallmark's different types of greeting cards), or they may be in numerous product families (such as Procter & Gamble's detergents, diapers, fabric softeners, and shampoos). In either case, product additions cause numerous overhead costs to increase. Exhibit 6–17 illustrates the potential for increased overhead with an increase in product variety.

In the quest for product variety, many companies are striving for **mass customization** of products through the use of flexible manufacturing systems. Such personalized production can often be conducted at a relatively low cost. For example, Dell Computer Company in Austin, Texas, allows customers to phone in an order for a computer with the exact features desired to be delivered to the customer's home in one week. Although such customization may please some customers, it does have some drawbacks.

First, there may simply be too many choices. For instance, at GE Fanuc (a Charlottesville, Virginia, manufacturer), customers had to look through several 4-inch-thick binders of components to design a custom-made product—an extremely

mass customization

EXHIBIT 6–17

Product Variety Creates Overhead Costs

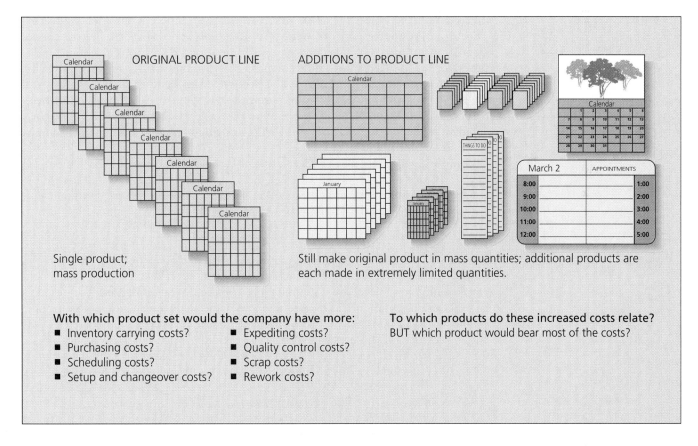

With which product set would the company have more:
- Inventory carrying costs?
- Purchasing costs?
- Scheduling costs?
- Setup and changeover costs?
- Expediting costs?
- Quality control costs?
- Scrap costs?
- Rework costs?

To which products do these increased costs relate?
BUT which product would bear most of the costs?

---

[20] Harold P. Roth and A. Faye Borthick, "Are You Distorting Costs by Violating ABC Assumptions?" *Management Accounting* (November 1991), pp. 39–40.

As product variety increases, so does the cost of overhead. Therefore, companies need to periodically review product offerings to be certain that the products being offered are desired by customers and that those products can be and are priced to cover the total costs of production.

Pareto principle

time-consuming project.[21] Nissan reportedly had 87 different varieties of steering wheels, but customers did not want many of them and disliked having to choose from so many options.[22] Second, mass customization creates a tremendous opportunity for errors. And third, most companies have found that customers, given the wide variety of choices, typically make selections from a rather small percentage of the total. At Toyota, investigation of purchases revealed that 20 percent of the product varieties accounted for 80 percent of the sales.[23] This 20:80 ratio is a fairly common one and is referred to as the **Pareto principle,** after the Italian economist Vilfredo Pareto.[24]

Companies with complex products, services, or processes may want to investigate ways to reduce that complexity. Management may want to review the design of the company's products and processes to standardize them and reduce the number of different components, tools, and processes required. Products should be designed to consider the Pareto principle and take advantage of commonality of parts. Analyzing components will generally reveal that 20 percent of the components are used in 80 percent of the products. If this is the case, then companies need to consider two other factors. First, are the remaining components used in key products? If so, could equal quality be achieved by using the more common parts? If not, can the products be sold for a premium price to cover the costs associated with the use of low-volume components? Second, are the parts specified for use in products purchased by important customers who are willing to pay a premium price for the products? If so, the benefits from the complexity may be worth the cost. However, would customers be equally satisfied if more common parts were used and the product price were

[21] Joe Pine, "Customers Don't Want Choices," *Wall Street Journal* (April 18, 1994), p. A12.

[22] B. Joseph Pine II, Bart Victor, and Andrew C. Boynton, "Making Mass Customization Work," *Harvard Business Review* (September-October 1993), p. 110.

[23] Ibid., p. 108.

[24] Pareto found that about 85 percent of Milan's wealth was held by about 15 percent of the people. The term *Pareto principle* was coined by Joseph Juran in relationship to quality problems. Juran found that a high proportion of such problems were caused by a small number of process characteristics (the vital few), whereas the majority of process characteristics (the trivial many) accounted for only a small proportion of quality problems.

reduced? Complexity is acceptable only if it is value-added from the customer's point of view.

Process complexity may develop over time, or it may exist because of a lack of sufficient planning in product development. Processes are complex when they create difficulties for the people attempting to perform production operations (physical straining, awkwardness of motions, or wasted motions) or for the people using manufacturing machinery (multiple and/or detailed setups, lengthy transfer time between machine processes, recalibration of instruments, and so on). Process complexity reflects numerous non-value-added activities and thus causes time delays and cost increases.

A company can employ simultaneous engineering to reduce both product and process complexity. **Simultaneous** (or **concurrent**) **engineering** refers to a continuous involvement of all primary functions and personnel contributing to a product's origination and production from the beginning of a project. Multifunctional teams design the product by considering customer expectations, vendor capabilities, parts commonality, and production process compatibility. Such an integrated design effort is referred to as a design-for-manufacturability approach. Simultaneous engineering helps companies to shorten the time-to-market for new products and minimize complexity and cost.

simultaneous (concurrent) engineering

Even when simultaneous engineering is used in process development, processes may develop complexity over time. One way to overcome such process complexities is **business process reengineering** (BPR) or process innovation and redesign. BPR's goal is to find and implement radical changes in how things are made or how tasks are performed to achieve substantial cost, service, or time reductions. Emphasizing continuous improvement, BPR ignores "the way it is" and looks instead for "the way it should be." As indicated in the accompanying News Note, BPR may redesign old processes or design new ones to eliminate complexity.

business process reengineering

Many traditional cost systems are not designed to account for information such as how many different parts are used in a product, so management cannot identify products made with low-volume or unique components. Activity-based costing systems are flexible and can gather such details so that persons involved in reengineering efforts have information about relationships among activities and cost drivers. Armed with this data, reengineering efforts can be focused on the primary causes of process complexity and on the causes that create the highest level of waste.

Redesign or Replace?

NEWS NOTE

Process redesign takes the present process and removes waste while reducing cycle time and improving the effectiveness of the process. Process redesign (which is also called focus improvement, since it focuses its efforts on the present process, or process reengineering) can lead to improvements that range from 300 to 1000 percent. Process redesign is the right choice for approximately 70 percent of the business processes.

[In contrast, new process design] takes a fresh look at the objectives of the process. It completely ignores the present process and organizational structure. The approach takes advantage of the latest mechanization, automation, and information techniques available. New process design can lead to improvements that range from 700 to 2000 percent. New process design provides the biggest improvement, though it costs more and takes more time to implement than process redesign. It also has the highest degree of risk; often the new process design approach includes departmental restructuring and is very disruptive to the organization. Most organizations can effectively implement only one change of this magnitude at a time.

SOURCE: H. James Harrington, "Process Breakthrough: Business Process Improvement," *Journal of Cost Management* (Fall 1993), pp. 36, 38. Reprinted with permission from *The Journal of Cost Management for the Manufacturing Industry* (Fall 1993), © 1993, Warren Gorham & Lamont, 31 St. James Avenue, Boston MA 02116. All rights reserved.

With Lack of Commonality in Overhead Costs

Certain products and services create substantially more overhead costs than others. Although some of these additional overhead costs may be caused by product variety or process complexity, others may be related to a variety of support services. For example, some products require significant levels of advertising; some use high cost distribution channels; and some necessitate the use of high-technology machinery. "A software distribution company, for example, discovered that a supposedly profitable high-margin product was generating so many calls to its help line that it was actually a money loser. Dropping that one product improved company profitability by nearly 10%."[25] If only one or two overhead pools are used, overhead related to specific products will be spread over all products. The result will be increased costs for products that are not responsible for the increased overhead.

In addition, some companies' output volumes differ significantly among their products and services. For example, in traditional allocation methods, when "production volumes are fairly similar—say, volume of one product is no more than five times that of any other—product costs will probably be accurate. Accuracy falls off rapidly as the range grows to more than 10 to 1."[26] Similar decreases in accuracy would occur with the other mentioned differences.

With Problems in Current Cost Allocations

If a company has undergone one or more significant changes in its products or processes (such as increased product variety or business process reengineering), managers and accountants need to investigate whether the existing cost system still provides a reasonable estimate of product or service cost. Many companies that have automated their production processes have experienced large reductions in labor and large increases in overhead costs. In such companies, using direct labor as an overhead allocation base produces extraordinarily high application rates. Prior to the introduction of ABC at Harris Semiconductor Sector, the overhead application rate per area ranged from 800 to 1,800 percent of the direct labor costs. This process resulted in 90 percent to 95 percent of all costs being allocated on a "mere 5–10 percent (i.e., direct labor costs) of the cost base."[27] Products made using automated equipment tend to be charged an insufficient amount of overhead, whereas products made using high proportions of direct labor tend to be overcharged.

Traditional cost allocations also generally emphasize the assignment of product costs to products at the same time the majority of period costs are expensed as incurred. Activity-based costing recognizes that some period costs (such as research and development, and distribution) may be distinctly and reasonably associated with specific products and thus should be traced and allocated to those products. This recognition changes the traditional view of product versus period cost.

With Changes in Business Environment

A change in a company's competitive environment may also require better cost information. Increased competition may occur for several reasons: (1) other companies have recognized the profit potential of a particular product or service; (2) the product or service has become cost-feasible to make or perform; or (3) an industry has been deregulated. If many new companies are competing for old business, the best estimate of product or service cost must be available to management so that profit margins and prices can be reasonably set.

Changes in management strategy can also signal a need for a new cost system. For example, if management wants to begin new operations, the cost system must be

VIDEO
VIGNETTE

Reliable Cartage (Blue Chip Manufacturing)

[25] Srikumar S. Rao, "True Cost," *Financial World* (September 25, 1995), pp. 62–63.
[26] Cooper, "You Need a New Cost System When . . . ," p. 80.
[27] Christopher R. Dedera, "Harris Semiconductor ABC: Worldwide Implementation and Total Integration," *Journal of Cost Management* (Spring 1996), p. 44.

capable of providing information on how costs will change. Confirming management's view of costs to the traditional variable versus fixed classifications may not allow such information to be effectively developed. Viewing costs as short-term variable versus long-term variable focuses on cost drivers and on the changes the planned operations will have on activities and costs.

Many companies are currently engaging in kaizen or continuous improvement efforts. As discussed in Chapter 2, kaizen relates to improving the way employees perform their tasks, the level of quality achieved in a product, and the level of organizational service. **Continuous improvement** recognizes the concepts of eliminating non-value-added activities to reduce cycle time, making products (or performing services) with zero defects, reducing product costs on an ongoing basis, and simplifying products and processes. Activity-based costing, by promoting an understanding of cost drivers, allows the non-value-added activities to be identified and their causes eliminated or reduced.

continuous improvement

The choice to implement activity-based costing should mean that management is willing to accept new information and use it to plan, control, and evaluate operating activities. For this to occur, management must have some ability to set prices relative to cost changes, accept alternative business strategies (such as eliminating or expanding product or service offerings) if the new costs should so indicate, and reduce waste where necessary (including downsizing or job restructuring). The following News Note discusses some problems that may occur when there is a lack of management support.

Irrespective of the reason or reasons supporting a change in costing systems, companies now have the ability to implement ABC systems. In the past, such implementation would have been technologically unfeasible. Introduction of the personal computer, ABC software, numerically controlled (NC) machines, and bar coding allows significantly more information to be readily available and cost effective.

We Just Don't Buy It

NEWS NOTE

A lack of buy-in and ownership often manifests itself by the failure of top management to supply their own time, the help of other dedicated people, or the funding needed to implement [an activity-based management project that uses ABC information for decisions].

The defense industry provides a prime example of where lack of top management support can cripple attempts to implement ABM. While many defense companies have had successful pilots that showed the benefits of changing business practices, few have yet led to permanent ABM systems. Why not? Usually because top management has a different view of the business—a view that focuses on viewing costs as required by the Cost Accounting Standards Board and the government procurement regulations.

More than one ABM project has foundered after successful pilot projects out of fear of creating cost and pricing data subject to government disclosure. Top management teams have feared that the government would require cost reductions on contracts for which the ABC cost turns out to be less than the cost using traditional methods and, conversely, would not allow increases on those contracts for which the ABC cost proves to be higher.

While the Defense Contract Audit Agency (DCAA) has encouraged ABC implementations and promised understanding and support, contractors have found it difficult to trust them. Many defense contractors have therefore shifted their focus away from ABC (i.e., for product costing, with all the inherent DCAA risks entailed) toward activity analysis. The goal is thus to reduce overall overhead costs, which is far more appealing to top management.

SOURCE: R. Steven Player and David E. Keys, "Lessons From the ABM Battlefield: Getting Off to the Right Start," *Journal of Cost Management* (Spring 1995), pp. 26–27. Reprinted with permission from *The Journal of Cost Management for the Manufacturing Industry* (Spring 1995), © 1995, Warren Gorham & Lamont, 31 St. James Avenue, Boston MA 02116. All rights reserved.

EXHIBIT 6–18

The Two-Dimensional
ABC Model

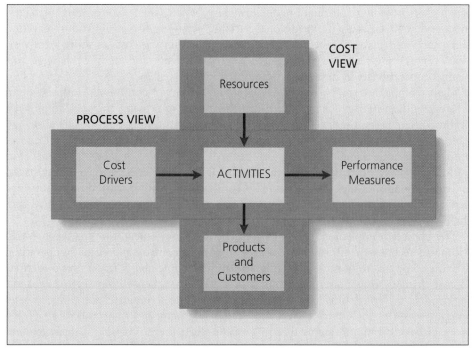

SOURCE: Peter B. B. Turney and Alan J. Stratton, "Using ABC to Support Continuous Improvement,"
Management Accounting (September 1992), p. 47. Reprinted from *Management Accounting.*
Copyright by Institute of Management Accountants, Montvale, NJ.

BENEFITS OF ACTIVITY-BASED COSTING

Activity-based costing promises many benefits for both production and service organizations. The benefits of activity-based costing are twofold: one is improving product costs for managerial decision making; the other is improving the performance measurement process. These two views are illustrated in the model shown in Exhibit 6–18.

The cost perspective highlights the interrelationships among functional areas because costs incurred in one area are often the result of activities in other areas (for instance, the potential relationship of poor product quality or defects to engineering design). Traditional accounting systems concentrate on controlling cost incurrence, whereas activity-based costing focuses on controlling the source (activity) of the cost incurrence. Thus, by concentrating control measurements on causal factors, costs become more controllable because cost reduction efforts can be directed at specific cost drivers. "[H]owever, . . . a reduction in drivers, which results in a reduced dependency on activities, does not lower costs until the excess resources are reduced or redeployed into more productive areas." [28]

Activity-based costing systems reveal that significant resources are consumed by low-volume products and complex production operations. ABC also typically shifts overhead from standard, high-volume products to premium special-order, low-volume products. Activity-based costing, in and of itself, does not change the amount of overhead incurred; however, it does distribute that cost in a more appropriate manner. Finally, ABC does not change the cost accumulation process, but makes that process as well as overhead cost assignment more realistic relative to how and why costs are incurred.

The process view of activity-based costing allows management to focus on value-added and non-value-added activities so that the NVA activities can be reduced or eliminated. ABC provides feedback information related to product design and potential areas for process improvements or waste elimination. This system allows and

[28] Michael R. Ostrenga, "Activities: The Focal Point of Total Cost Management," *Management Accounting* (February 1990), p. 43.

Benefits of ABC Include a Quality Focus

ABC models can play many different roles to support an organization's operational improvement and customer satisfaction programs. First, ABC can provide an attention-getting mechanism for companies not yet indoctrinated into the religion of the lean production paradigm. ABC collects data on activities and business processes that cut across traditional organizational functional boundaries. Often managers can see, for the first time, the cost of nonconformance, the cost of design activities, the cost of new product launches, and the cost of administrative activities, such as processing customer orders, procurement, and handling special requests. The high cost of these activities can stimulate companies to adopt the TQM, JIT, and business process improvement programs that will produce a leaner and more responsive enterprise. The ABC model also produces, for individual products, services, and customers, the bill of activities that describes the cost buildup for these outputs. Managers can see how much of any unexpectedly higher cost arises from inefficient or unnecessary activities. The bill of activities information will indicate the opportunities for cost reduction and profit enhancement from improving quality or reducing the cost of batch and product- or customer-sustaining activities. The existing cost for these activities can provide the justification for new technology or for launching major process improvements.

SOURCE: Robert S. Kaplan, "In Defense of Activity-Based Cost Management," *Management Accounting* (November 1992), p. 60. Reprinted from *Management Accounting.* Copyright by Institute of Management Accountants, Montvale, NJ.

encourages the use of nonfinancial measures of activity and performance. Managerial decisions may be made, such as raising selling prices or discontinuing production of low-volume, specialty output or products that require complex operations. Or managers may reap the benefits of low-volume or complex production through the implementation of high-technology processes. As indicated in the News Note on the benefits of ABC, activity-based costing can even help managers make decisions about instituting quality improvement techniques.

CRITICISMS OF ACTIVITY-BASED COSTING

Realistically assessing new models and accounting approaches for what they can help managers accomplish is always important. However, no currently existing accounting technique or system will provide management with exact cost information for every product or with the information needed to make consistently perfect decisions. Activity-based costing, although it typically provides better information than was generated under the traditional overhead allocation process, is not a panacea for all managerial concerns. The following are some of this method's shortcomings.

First, ABC requires a significant amount of time and, thus, cost to implement. If implementation is to be successful, substantial support is needed throughout the firm. An environment for change must be created that requires overcoming a variety of individual, organizational, and environmental barriers. Individual barriers are typically related to (1) fear of the unknown or shift in status quo, (2) potential loss of status, or (3) a necessity to learn new skills. Organizational barriers are often related to "territorial," hierarchical, or corporate culture issues. Environmental barriers are often built by employee groups (including unions), regulatory agencies, or other stakeholders of interest.

To overcome these barriers, a firm must first recognize that these barriers exist; second, investigate their causes; and, third, communicate information about the "what," "why," and "how" of ABC to all concerned parties. Top management must be involved with and support the implementation process. Lack of commitment or involvement by top management will make any meaningful progress slow and difficult. Additionally, employees and managers must be educated in some nontraditional techniques that include new terminology, concepts, and performance measurements.

Assuming that top management supports the changes in the internal accounting system and that employees are educated about the system, additional time will be required to analyze the activities taking place in the activity centers, trace costs to those activities, and determine the cost drivers.

Another problem with ABC is that it does not conform specifically with generally accepted accounting principles (GAAP). ABC would suggest that some nonproduct costs (such as those in research and development) be allocated to products, whereas certain other traditionally designated product costs (such as factory building depreciation) not be allocated to products. Therefore, most companies have used ABC for internal reporting, while continuing to maintain their general and subsidiary ledger accounts and prepare their external financial statements on the basis of a more "traditional" system—requiring two product costing systems and causing even more costs to be incurred. As ABC systems become more widely accepted, more companies may choose to refine how ABC and GAAP determine product cost to make those definitions more compatible and, thereby, eliminate the need for two costing systems.

One final criticism that has been leveled recently at activity-based costing is that it does not promote total quality management (TQM) and continuous improvement. Dr. H. Thomas Johnson (the Retzlaff Professor of Quality Management at Portland State University) has issued the following cautions:

> [T]he decade of the 1970s ushered in a new competitive environment—call it the global economy—in which accounting information is not capable of guiding companies toward competitiveness and long-term profitability.
>
> Activity-based prescriptions for improved competitiveness usually entail steps that lead to selling more or doing less of what should not be sold or done in the first place. Indeed, activity-based cost information does nothing to change old remote-control, top-down management behavior. Simply because improved cost information becomes available, a company does not change its commitment to mass-produce output at high speed, to control costs by encouraging people to manipulate processes, and to persuade customers to buy output the company has produced to cover its costs. American businesses will not become long-term global competitors until they change the way managers think. No cost information, not even activity-based cost management information, will do that.[29]

Companies attempting to implement ABC as a cure-all for product failures, volume declines, or financial losses will quickly recognize that Professor Johnson is correct. However, companies can implement ABC and its related management techniques in support of and in conjunction with TQM, JIT, and any other world-class methodologies. Companies doing so will provide the customer with the best variety, price, quality, service, and lead time of which they are capable. Not coincidentally, they should find their businesses booming. Activity-based costing and activity-based management are effective in supporting continuous improvement, short lead times, and flexible manufacturing by helping managers

- identify and monitor significant technology costs;
- trace many technology costs directly to products;
- promote achievement of market share through use of target costing;
- identify the cost drivers that create or influence cost;
- identify activities that do not contribute to perceived customer value (i.e., non-value-added activities or waste);
- understand the impact of new technologies on all elements of performance;
- translate company goals into activity goals;
- analyze the performance of activities across business functions;
- analyze performance problems; and
- promote standards of excellence.

In summary, ABC is an improved cost accounting tool that helps managers know how the score is kept so that they can play the game more competitively.

---

[29] H. Thomas Johnson, "It's Time to Stop Overselling Activity-Based Concepts," *Management Accounting* (September 1992), pp. 31, 33.

Lord Corporation

Lord Corporation implemented ABC with a clear objective in mind: to provide better product costs. Had the company chosen a different purpose, different cost pools and cost drivers may have been used. For example, the company selected the number of receipts for each part as the main cost driver; if the objective had been to identify and eliminate non-value-added activities, a good cost driver might have been the number of noncertified suppliers in the supplier base.

The first realization upon analyzing the material overhead pool was that the pool needed to be reorganized. The pilot study showed the Division that part cost was a poor driver of material overhead; the single largest driver for this cost was inspection. (For example, simply moving materials from inspection to stock represented a significant portion of a component's overhead cost.) That's where the need for ABC was driven home to management. In frequent presentations to senior management and corporate officers, the need to beef up our certified supplier program was stressed in order to reduce inspection activities. While the need for such a program was not news to employees who understood how costs were generated, this was the first time the cost of *not* having such a program could be proven.

The ABC approach to costing also sent shock waves through the marketing group. It couldn't understand why low-volume, low-cost parts that once took a flat percentage of their cost as material overhead suddenly jumped 500% to 700%. It only made sense that a 10¢ part should take a penny's worth of overhead, as our old cost system used to show. What ABC revealed was that even those inexpensive parts were being purchased, received, inspected, and stocked in a manner that created significant costs.

Savings that can be attributed directly to ABC are more noticeable in the form of better-priced products than in reductions of manufacturing cost. The ABC results have been used to justify pricing and to discuss with customers a corporate focus on identifying and eliminating costs. Consequently, the Division has been able to improve the bottom line by improving the match between selling price and cost.

The company has focused extensively on one of four approaches for low-volume products:

- Eliminating them from the division,
- Keeping them as part of a larger marketing strategy,
- Outsourcing them to external suppliers who can produce them with fewer overhead costs, and
- Convincing customers who purchase these low-volume parts to buy in larger quantities less frequently.

An extremely important aspect of activity costing is incorporating low-volume parts into a larger marketing strategy. For Lord, there is an ongoing part-by-part analysis to determine which of the approaches above fits each part best. After all, activity costing is a *tool*, not an end-all solution for management.

SOURCE: Alan W. Rupp, "ABC: A Pilot Approach," *Management Accounting* (January 1995), pp. 52–54. Reprinted from *Management Accounting*. Copyright by Institute of Management Accountants, Montvale, NJ.

CHAPTER SUMMARY

Significant changes have taken place in the business environment. These changes have caused concern about the reliability of cost information generated by a system primarily intended to provide product costs for external financial statements. One suggestion for providing better internal user information is to determine product profitability over a product's life cycle rather than on a period-by-period basis. Such a measurement would require a capitalization of product research and development costs and, as such, would not be currently allowable for reporting purposes under generally accepted accounting principles.

Target costing may be combined with life cycle costing to determine an allowable product cost based on an estimated selling price and a desired profit margin. Because sales volume, costs, and profits fluctuate over a product's life cycle, these items would need to be estimated over the entire life rather than on a periodic basis to determine a target cost.

To make profits given the present competitive environment and consumer focus on product price and quality, businesses must find ways to minimize costs. Costs can be reduced without reducing quality by decreasing the number of non-value-added organizational activities. Process mapping can be performed to see all the VA and NVA activities that take place in the production of a product or the performance of a service. Value is added to products only during the times that processing (manufacturing company), performance (service company), or display (retail company) is actually taking place. Inspection time, transfer time, and idle time all add to cycle time and cost, but not to value. The proportion of total cycle time spent in value-added processing is referred to as manufacturing cycle efficiency.

A third category of activities, known as business-value-added activities, also exists. Although customers would not want to pay for these activities, they are necessary to conduct business operations.

In addition to activity analysis, activity-based management is also concerned with finding and selecting activity cost pools and identifying the set of cost drivers that best represent the firm's activities and are the underlying causes of costs. Management should first investigate activities that reflect the major and most significant processes conducted by the company. These activities normally overlap several functional areas and occur horizontally across the firm's departmental lines.

A new method of cost assignment, more compatible with the increased high-technology environment in which business operates, is activity-based costing (ABC). ABC assigns costs to products on the basis of the types and quantities of activities that must be performed to create those products. This costing system accumulates costs for activity centers in multiple cost pools at a variety of levels (unit, batch, product, and organizational) and then allocates these costs using multiple cost drivers (both volume- and non-volume-related). Thus, costs are assigned more accurately, and managers can focus on controlling activities that cause costs rather than trying to control the costs that result from the activities. The use of activity-based costing should provide a more realistic picture of actual production cost than has traditionally been available.

Product and process variety and complexity often cause a business' costs to increase because of increases in non-value-added activities. Simultaneous engineering (using multifunctional teams) can help firms to accelerate the time-to-market of new products and reduce the complexity and costs of these new products and the processes by which they are made.

Business process reengineering is a method of improving or replacing complex processes that already exist. BPR finds and implements radical changes in the way things are made or the way tasks are performed to achieve cost, service, or time reductions.

APPENDIX

The Theory of Constraints

The theory of constraints (TOC) can help management reduce cycle time. The **theory of constraints** indicates that the flow of goods through a production process cannot be at a faster rate than the slowest bottleneck in the process.[30]

Delays in a production environment are caused by human and machine constraints. A **constraint** is anything that confines or limits a person's or machine's ability to perform a project or function. Human constraints can be caused by an inability to understand, react, or perform at some higher rate of speed. These constraints cannot be totally overcome (because humans will never be able to work at the speed of an automated machine), but can be reduced through proper hiring and training. Because the labor content contained in products is declining rapidly as automation increases, constraints caused by machines are often of more concern than human constraints in reducing cycle time.

Machine constraints, also called **bottlenecks,** are points at which the processing levels are sufficiently slow to cause the other processing mechanisms in the network to experience idle time. Bottlenecks cause the processing of an activity to be impeded. Even a totally automated, "lights out" process, will have some constraints, because all machines do not operate at the same speed or handle the same capacity. Therefore, the constraints must be identified and worked around. Exhibit 6–19 provides a simplified illustration of a constraint in a production process. Although Machine 1 can process 100,000 pounds of raw material in an hour, Machine 2 can handle only 50,000 pounds. Of an input of 80,000 pounds, 30,000 pounds of processed material

theory of constraints

constraint

bottleneck

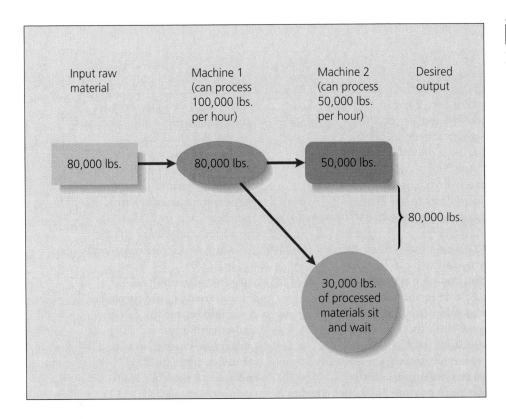

EXHIBIT 6–19

Production Constraint

---

[30] The theory of constraints was introduced to business environments by Eliyahu Goldratt and Jeff Cox in the book *The Goal* (New Haven, CT: North River Press, Inc./Spectrum Publishing Company, Inc., 1986).

must wait at the constraining machine after an hour of processing. The constraint's effect on production is obvious, but the implications are not quite as clear. Managers have a tendency to want to see machines *working*, not sitting idle. Consider what this tendency would mean if the desired output were 500,000 pounds rather than 80,000. If Machine 1 were kept in continual use, all 500,000 pounds would be processed through Machine 1 in 5 hours. However, a backlog of 250,000 pounds [500,000 − 5(50,000)] of processed material would now be in front of Machine 2! All this material would require storage space and create an additional cost of an NVA.

Machine constraints also impact quality control. Managers normally choose quality control points to follow the completion of some particular process. When constraint points are known, quality control points should be placed in front of them.

> Make sure the bottleneck works only on good parts by weeding out the ones that are defective. If you scrap a part before it reaches the bottleneck, all you have lost is a scrapped part. But if you scrap the part after it's passed through the bottleneck, you have lost time that cannot be recovered.[31]

Once constraints are known, the best use of the time they provide should be made. Subsequently, "after having made the best use of the existing constraints, the next step is to reduce their limitations on the system's performance."[32] Options to reduce limitations, such as adding more machines to perform the constraints or processing materials through other machines, should be investigated.

In contrast to activity-based costing, TOC makes the assumption that, except for materials, almost all costs are fixed. Thus, at the outset, TOC and ABC do not view product variety similarly: TOC assumes that product proliferation has no effect on production costs. "This approach works only so long as there is fat in the form of non-value-added activity in the overhead areas. Ultimately product proliferation and increasing activity are likely to create demands for additional overhead resources."[33] In such a case, TOC simply suggests acquiring more capacity (in whatever form is necessary) to remove the constraint.

KEY TERMS

activity (p. 230)
activity center (p. 239)
activity driver (p. 239)
attribute-based costing (ABC II) (p. 246)
batch-level cost (p. 235)
bottleneck (p. 257)
business process reengineering (p. 249)
business-value-added activity (p. 230)
constraint (p. 257)
continuous improvement (p. 251)
cost driver analysis (p. 235)
cost table (p. 225)
cycle time (p. 231)
idle time (p. 231)
inspection time (p. 231)
kaizen costing (p. 226)
life cycle costing (p. 228)

long-term variable cost (p. 245)
manufacturing cycle efficiency (MCE) (p. 232)
mass customization (p. 247)
organizational-level cost (p. 235)
Pareto principle (p. 248)
processing (service) time (p. 231)
process map (p. 231)
product complexity (p. 245)
product-level (process-level) cost (p. 235)
product variety (p. 245)
simultaneous (concurrent) engineering (p. 249)
substitute good (p. 227)
theory of constraints (p. 257)
transfer time (p. 231)
unit-level cost (p. 235)
value chart (p. 231)

[31] Ibid., p. 156.
[32] Robert E. Fox, "The Constraint Theory," in *Cost Accounting for the '90s Responding to Technological Change Proceedings* (Montvale, N.J.: National Association of Accountants, 1988), p. 51.
[33] Eric Noreen, Debra Smith, and James T. Mackey, *The Theory of Constraints and Its Implications for Management Accounting* (Great Barrington, MA: The North River Press, 1995), p. 145.

TARGET COSTING

SOLUTION STRATEGIES

Target Cost = Expected Long-range Selling Price − Desired Profit

Compare predicted total life cycle cost to target cost; if life cycle cost is higher, determine ways to reduce.

MANUFACTURING CYCLE EFFICIENCY

Cycle Time = Processing Time + Inspection Time + Transfer Time + Idle Time

MCE = Value-added Processing Time ÷ Total Cycle Time

ACTIVITY-BASED COSTING

1. Determine the activity centers of the organization.
2. Determine departmental activities and efforts needed to conduct those activities—the cost drivers.
3. Determine departmental resources consumed in conducting activities and allocate to activity centers based on the cost drivers.
4. Determine activities needed to manufacture products or provide revenue-producing services—the activity drivers.
5. Allocate costs to products and services based on activities and cost drivers involved.

Pierre Press prepares two versions of gourmet cookbooks: one is paperback and the other is hand-sewn and leather bound. Management is considering publishing only the higher-quality book. The firm assigns its $500,000 of overhead to the two types of books. The overhead is composed of $200,000 of utilities and $300,000 of quality control inspectors' salaries. Some additional data follow:

DEMONSTRATION PROBLEM

	PAPERBACK	LEATHER BOUND
Revenues	$1,600,000	$1,400,000
Direct costs	$1,250,000	$ 600,000
Production (units)	500,000	350,000
Machine hours	42,500	7,500
Inspections	2,500	12,500

Required:

a. Compute the overhead cost that should be allocated to each type of cookbook using cost drivers appropriate for each type of overhead cost.
b. The firm has used machine hours to allocate overhead in the past. Should Pierre Press stop producing the paperback cookbooks? Explain why management was considering this action and what its decision should be.

Solution to Demonstration Problem

a.

	PAPERBACK	LEATHER BOUND	TOTAL
Machine hours	42,500	7,500	50,000
Rate per MH ($200,000 ÷ 50,000)	× $4	× $4	× $4
Utility cost	$170,000	$ 30,000	$200,000
Number of inspections	2,500	12,500	15,000
Rate per inspection ($300,000 ÷ 15,000)	× $20	× $20	× $20
Quality inspection cost	$ 50,000	$250,000	$300,000
Total traceable overhead costs	$220,000	$280,000	$500,000

b. Income calculation using machine hours to allocate utilities and inspection hours to allocate inspectors' salaries to products.

	PAPERBACK	LEATHER BOUND
Revenue	$1,600,000	$1,400,000
Direct costs	$1,250,000	$ 600,000
Overhead	220,000	280,000
Total costs	$1,470,000	$ 880,000
Margin	$ 130,000	$ 520,000

Using the traditional cost driver (machine hours), the following results had been achieved, given a $10 charge ($500,000 ÷ 50,000) per MH:

	PAPERBACK	LEATHER BOUND
Revenue	$1,600,000	$1,400,000
Direct costs	$1,250,000	$ 600,000
Overhead	425,000	75,000
Total costs	$1,675,000	$ 675,000
Margin	$ (75,000)	$ 725,000

The reason paperbacks were erroneously thought to be unprofitable was caused by the method of allocating overhead. The firm should continue producing paperbacks.

QUESTIONS

1. What are the five stages in the product life cycle and why is each important?

2. Why do costs, sales, and profits change over the product life cycle?

3. What is target costing and how is it useful in assessing a product's total life cycle costs?

4. Does target costing require that profitability be viewed on a period-by-period basis or on a long-term basis? Explain.

5. From a marketing standpoint, why can some companies (such as Seiko and Rubbermaid) introduce products with little or no product research and other companies cannot?

6. Why would a cost table be a valuable tool in designing a new product or service?

7. What is kaizen costing and how does it differ from target costing?

8. Discuss the concept of substitute goods and why these would affect pricing.

9. How would focusing on total life cycle costs call for a different treatment of research and development costs than is made for financial accounting?

10. Define value-added activities and non-value-added activities; compare and give examples of each type.

11. Why are value-added activities defined from a customer viewpoint?

12. What management opportunity is associated with identifying the non-value-added activities in a production process?

13. In a televised football game, what activities are value-added? What activities are non-value-added? Would everyone agree with your choices? Why or why not?

14. How is a process map used to identify opportunities for cost savings?

15. What is manufacturing cycle efficiency (MCE)? What would its value be in an optimized manufacturing environment and why?

16. What is a cost driver and how is it used? Give some examples of cost drivers.

17. Do cost drivers exist in a traditional accounting system? Are they designated as such? How, if at all, does the use of cost drivers differ between a traditional accounting system and an activity-based costing system?

18. What is activity-based costing? How does it differ from traditional product costing approaches?

19. Why do the more traditional methods of overhead assignment "overload" standard, high-volume products with overhead costs, and how does ABC improve overhead assignments?

20. What characteristics of a company would generally indicate that activity-based costing might improve product costing?

21. Why does activity-based costing require that costs be aggregated at different levels?

22. List the benefits of activity-based costing. How could these reduce costs?

23. How does attribute-based costing extend the concept of activity-based costing?

24. *(Appendix)* What is meant by the theory of constraints? How is this concept appropriate for manufacturing and service companies?

25. *(Appendix)* Why should quality control inspection points be placed in front of bottleneck operations?

EXERCISES

26. *(Terminology)* Match the following lettered terms on the left with the appropriate numbered description on the right.

    a. Simultaneous engineering
    b. Target cost
    c. Research and development
    d. Activity driver
    e. Manufacturing cycle efficiency
    f. Non-value-added activities
    g. Cost driver
    h. Activity-based costing
    i. Process map
    j. Value-added activity
    k. Life cycle stages

    1. The process of attaching costs based on activities
    2. A costing system that uses multiple cost drivers
    3. A process of involving all affected personnel from the beginning of a project
    4. Something that causes or influences costs
    5. Development, introduction, growth, maturity, and decline
    6. A flowchart indicating all steps in producing a product or performing a service
    7. Idle time, transfer time, and storage time
    8. Actual production time divided by total cycle time
    9. Expected selling price less desired profit
    10. A cost that would not be expensed under life cycle costing
    11. A means of allocating costs from cost pools to products
    12. Something that increases worth of a product or service

27. *(Target costing)* Headcrafts has developed a new material that has significant potential in the manufacture of sports caps. The firm has conducted significant market research and estimated the following pattern for sales of the new caps:

YEAR	EXPECTED VOLUME	EXPECTED PRICE PER UNIT
1	16,000 units	$7
2	40,000 units	$8
3	70,000 units	$6
4	30,000 units	$5

If the firm desires to net $1.50 per unit in profit, what is the target cost to produce the new caps?

28. *(Target costing)* The marketing department at Bernie Manufacturing has an idea for a new product that is expected to have a life cycle of 5 years. After conducting market research, the company has determined that the product could sell for $250 per unit in the first 3 years of life and $175 per unit for the last 2 years. Unit sales are expected as follows:

Year 1	3,000 units
Year 2	4,500 units
Year 3	4,800 units
Year 4	5,000 units
Year 5	1,500 units

Per-unit variable selling costs are estimated at $30 throughout the product's life; annual fixed selling and administrative costs are expected to be $350,000. Bernie Manufacturing desires a profit margin of 20 percent of selling price per unit.

a. Compute the life cycle target cost to manufacture the product. (Round to the nearest penny.)

b. If the company expects the product to cost $65 to manufacture in the first year, what is the maximum that manufacturing cost can be in the following 4 years? (Round to the nearest penny.)

c. Assume Bernie Manufacturing engineers indicate that the expected manufacturing cost per unit is $70. What actions might the company take to reduce this cost?

29. *(Activity analysis)* Butler Fasteners is investigating the costs of schedule changes in its factory. Following is a list of the activities, estimated times, and average costs required for a single schedule change.

ACTIVITY	ESTIMATED TIME	AVERAGE COST
Review impact of orders	30 min–2 hrs	$ 300
Reschedule orders	15 min–24 hrs	800
—Lost sales		
—Unreliable customer service		
Reschedule production orders	15 min–1 hr	75
Contact production supervisor	5 min	5
—Stop production and change over		
—Generate paperwork to return materials		
Return and locate material (excess inventory)	20 min–6 hrs	1,500
Generate new production paperwork	15 min–4 hrs	500
—Change routings		
—Change bill of materials		
Change procurement schedule	10 min–8 hrs	2,100
—Purchase orders		
—Inventory		
Collect paperwork from the floor	15 min	75
Review new line schedule	15 min–30 min	100
Overtime premiums	3 hrs–10 hrs	1,000
Total		$6,455

a. Which of the above, if any, are value-added activities?

b. What is the cost driver in this situation?

c. How can the cost driver be controlled and the activities eliminated?

30. *(Cycle time and MCE)* The following functions are performed in making salad dressing at Tasty Sensations.

FUNCTION	TIME (MINUTES)
Receiving ingredients	45
Moving ingredients to stockroom	15
Storing ingredients in stockroom	7,200
Moving ingredients from stockroom	15
√ Mixing ingredients	30
√ Cooking ingredients	45
√ Bottling ingredients	90
Moving bottled dressing to warehouse	20
Storing bottled dressing in warehouse	10,080
Moving ingredients from warehouse to trucks	30

a. Calculate the cycle time of this manufacturing process.

b. Calculate the manufacturing cycle efficiency of this process.

c. What could Tasty Sensations do to improve its MCE?

31. *(Identifying cost drivers)* The Lunch Bucket is a highly automated, fast-food restaurant that relies on sophisticated, computer-controlled equipment to prepare and deliver food to customers. Operationally and organizationally, the restaurant operates like other major franchise fast-food restaurants. Determine whether each of the following costs are unit level (U), batch level (B), product/process level (P), or organizational level (O).

a. Store manager's salary

b. Frozen french fries

c. Napkins

d. Oil for the deep-fat fryer

e. Maintenance of the restaurant building

f. Wages of employees who clear and clean tables

g. Electricity expense for the pizza oven

h. Property taxes

i. Depreciation on kitchen equipment

j. Refrigeration of raw materials

32. *(Cost drivers)* For each of the following important costs in manufacturing companies, identify a cost driver and explain why it is appropriate.

a. Equipment maintenance

b. Building utilities

c. Computer operations

d. Quality control

e. Material handling

f. Material storage

g. Factory depreciation

h. Setup cost

i. Engineering changes

j. Advertising expense

k. Freight costs for materials

33. *(Cost allocation using cost drivers)* Abramson Inc. has an in-house legal department whose activities fall into one of three major categories. Recently, operating costs in the department have risen dramatically. Management has decided to implement an activity-based costing system to help control costs and charge in-house users for the legal services provided. The principal expense in the legal department is professional salaries, and the estimated cost of professional salaries associated with each activity follow:

Reviewing supplier or customer contracts	(Contracts)		$400,000
Reviewing regulatory compliance issues	(Regulation)		250,000
Court actions	(Court)		350,000

Management has determined that the appropriate cost allocation base for Contracts is the number of pages in the contract reviewed; for Regulation, the allocation base is the number of reviews; and for Court, the allocation base is professional hours. For 1997, the legal department reviewed 20,000 pages of contracts, responded to 500 regulatory review requests, and logged 3,000 professional hours in court.

a. Determine the allocation rate for each activity in the legal department.

b. How much cost would be charged to a producing department that had 1,000 pages of contracts reviewed, made 15 regulatory review requests, and consumed 250 professional hours in court services during the year?

c. How can the developed rates be used for evaluating output relative to cost incurred in the legal department? What alternative does the firm have to maintaining an internal legal department and how might this choice affect costs?

34. *(Activity-based costing)* Management at Vancouver Ltd. has decided to institute a pilot activity-based costing project in its five-person purchasing department. Annual departmental costs are $473,500. Because finding the best supplier takes the majority of effort in the department, most of the costs are allocated to this area.

ACTIVITY	ALLOCATION MEASURE	NUMBER OF PEOPLE	TOTAL COST
Find best suppliers	Number of telephone calls	3	$300,000
Issue purchase orders	Number of purchase orders	1	100,000
Review receiving reports	Number of receiving reports	1	73,500

During the year, the purchasing department made 150,000 telephone calls, issued 10,000 purchase orders, and reviewed 7,000 receiving reports. Many purchase orders are received in a single shipment.

One product manufactured by Vancouver Ltd. required the following purchasing department activities: 125 telephone calls, 60 purchase orders, and 15 receipts.

a. What amount of purchasing department cost should be assigned to this product?

b. If 200 units of the product are manufactured during the year, what is the purchasing department cost per unit?

35. *(Product profitability)* Innovations manufactures two products: patio lights and commercial pole lights. Patio lights are relatively simple to produce and are made in large quantities. Pole lights must be more customized to individual customer sites. Innovations sells 100,000 patio lights annually and 20,000 pole lights. Revenues and costs incurred for each product are as follows:

	PATIO LIGHTS	POLE LIGHTS
Revenue	$4,000,000	$4,400,000
Direct materials	1,000,000	800,000
Direct labor	600,000	2,000,000
Overhead	?	?

Labor is paid at $20 per hour, manufacturing overhead totals $1,105,000, and administrative expenses equal $806,000.

a. Calculate the profit (loss) on each product if overhead and administrative expenses are assigned to the products using a direct labor hour base.

b. Calculate the profit (loss) on each product if overhead is assigned to products using a direct labor hour base but administrative expenses are deducted from total company income rather than being allocated to products.

c. Does your answer in part a or part b provide the better representation of the profit contributed by each product? Explain.

36. *(Appendix)* Albright Stationers produces commercial calendars in a two-department operation: Department 1 is labor intensive and Department 2 is automated. The average output of Department 1 is 45 units per hour. The units are then transferred to Department 2 where they are finished by a robot. The robot can finish a maximum of 45 units per hour. Albright Stationers needs to complete 180 units this afternoon for an order that has been backlogged for 4 months. The production manager has informed the people in Department 1 that they are to work on nothing else except this order from 1 P.M. until 5 P.M. The supervisor in Department 2 has scheduled the same times for the robot to work on the order. Department 1's activity for each hour of the afternoon follows:

Time	1:00–2:00	2:00–3:00	3:00–4:00	4:00–4:58
Production	44 units	40 units	49 units	47 units

Assume that each unit moves directly from Department 1 to Department 2 with *no* lag time. Did Albright Stationers complete the 180 units by 5:00 P.M.? If not, explain and provide detailed computations.

---

37. *(Product life cycles; team activity)* [*According to Barry Bayus, a marketing professor, the perception that product life cycles are getting shorter is a mistaken one.*] Bayus identified three reasons for the appearance of shortened product life cycles:
    1. *New knowledge is being applied faster. The time between an invention and its first application is decreasing, from 90 years during the 1700s to 20 years from 1901 to 1950.*
    2. *More new products are being introduced. In 1986, for example, the number of new-product introductions was just under 13,000. By 1991, the number had increased to more than 15,000.*
    3. *The time between innovations is decreasing.*

    [SOURCE: Glenn Rifkin, "The Myth of Short Life Cycles," *Harvard Business Review* (July–August 1994), p. 11.]

    a. As a team, investigate the reality or myth of shortened product life cycles. Use all resources (library, Internet, personal) at your disposal.

    b. Prepare a written report on your findings. Also be ready to present this report orally should your team be asked to do so.

38. *(Target costing)* Snowden Corporation is in the process of developing an outdoor power source for various electronic devices used by campers. Market research has indicated that potential purchasers would be willing to pay $175 per unit for this product. Company engineers have estimated first-year production costs would amount to $180 per unit. On this type of product, Snowden would normally expect to earn $10 per unit in profits. Using the concept of target costing, write a memo that (1) analyzes the prospects for this product and (2) discusses possible organizational strategies.

39. *(Value chart)* You are the new controller of a small shop that manufactures special-order desk nameplate stands. As you review the records, you find that all the orders are shipped late; the average process time for any order is 3 weeks; and the time actually spent in production operations is 2 days. The president of the company has called you in to discuss missed delivery dates. Prepare an oral presentation for the executive officers in which you address the following:

a. Possible causes of the problem.

b. How a value chart could be used to address the problem.

40. *(Controlling overhead)* Industrial Paints Inc. has engaged you to help the company analyze and update its costing and pricing practices. The company product line has changed over time from general paints to specialized marine coatings. Although some large orders are received, the majority of business is now generated from products designed and produced in small lot sizes to meet specifically detailed environmental and technical requirements.

The company has experienced tremendous overhead growth, including costs in customer service, production scheduling, inventory control, and laboratory work. Factory overhead has essentially doubled since the shift in product lines. Management believes that large orders are being penalized and small orders are receiving favorable cost (and therefore selling price) treatment.

a. Indicate why the shift in product lines would have caused such major increases in overhead.

b. Is it possible that management is correct in its belief about the costs of large and small orders? If so, why?

c. Write a memo to management suggesting how it might change the cost accounting system to reflect the changes in the business.

41. *(Traditional vs. ABC methods)* Many companies now recognize that their cost systems are inadequate in the context of today's powerful global competition. Managers in companies selling multiple products are making important product decisions based on distorted cost information, as most cost systems designed in the past focused on inventory measurement. To elevate the level of management information, current literature suggests that companies should have as many as three cost systems for (1) inventory measurement, (2) operational control, and (3) activity-based costing.

a. Discuss why the traditional cost information system, developed to value inventory, distorts product cost information.

b. Identify the purpose and characteristics of each of the following cost systems:
   1. Inventory measurement
   2. Activity-based costing

c. Describe the benefits that management can obtain from using activity-based costing.

d. List the steps that a company using a traditional cost system would take to implement activity-based costing.

(CMA adapted)

PROBLEMS

42. *(Life cycle costing)* The Products Development Division of Extralite Cuisine has just completed its work on a new microwave entrée. The marketing group has decided on a very high original price for the entrée, but the selling price will be reduced as competitors appear. Market studies indicate that the following quantities of the product can be sold at the following prices over its life cycle:

YEAR	QUANTITY	SELLING PRICE	YEAR	QUANTITY	SELLING PRICE
1	100,000	$2.50	5	600,000	$2.00
2	250,000	2.40	6	450,000	2.00
3	350,000	2.30	7	200,000	1.90
4	500,000	2.10	8	130,000	1.90

Development costs plus other startup costs for this product will total $600,000. Engineering estimates of direct materials and direct labor costs are $.85 and $.20 per unit. These costs can be held constant for approximately 4 years and in year 5 will each increase by 10 percent. Variable overhead per unit is expected to be

$.25, and fixed overhead is expected to be $100,000 per year. Extralite Cuisine management likes to earn a 20 percent gross margin on products of this type.

a. Prepare an income statement for each year of the product's life, assuming all product costs are inventoried and using 8-year straight-line depreciation of the development and startup costs. What is the cost per unit each year? What rate of gross margin will the product generate each year?

b. Determine the gross margin to be generated by this product over its life. What rate of gross margin is this?

c. Discuss the differences in the information provided by the analyses in parts a and b.

43. *(Identifying non-value-added activities)* Donna Muniz is planning to build a patio in back of her home during her annual vacation. She has prepared the following schedule of how her time on the patio project will be allocated:

Purchase materials	2 hours
Obtain rental equipment	2 hours
Remove sod and level site	10 hours
Build forms for concrete	8 hours
Mix and pour concrete into forms	4 hours
Level concrete and smooth	1 hour
Let dry	24 hours
Remove forms from concrete	1 hour
Return rental tools	1 hour
Clean up	1 hour

a. Identify the value-added activities. How much total time is value-added?

b. Identify the non-value-added activities. How much total time is spent performing non-value-added activities?

c. Calculate the manufacturing cycle efficiency.

44. *(Activity analysis; MCE)* Dan'l Boone Homes constructs log cabin vacation houses in the Tennessee mountains for customers. As the company's consultant, you developed the following value chart:

OPERATIONS	AVERAGE NUMBER OF DAYS
Receiving materials	1
Storing materials	3
Measuring and cutting materials	3
Handling materials	5
Setting up and moving scaffolding	5
Assembling materials	7
Building fireplace	6
Pegging logs	4
Cutting and framing doors and windows	3
Sealing joints	4
Inspecting property (county inspectors)	1

a. What are the value-added activities and their total time?

b. What are the non-value-added activities and their total time?

c. Calculate the manufacturing cycle efficiency of the process.

d. Prepare a one-minute presentation explaining the difference between value-added and non-value-added activities.

45. *(Cost of non-value-added activities)* Refer to the value chart shown in Exhibit 6–8. Jennifer Chaix, the company president, asked her cost accountant for the following information to help determine the total cost of non-value-added activities for one lot of the company's product.

Annual salary for receiving clerks	$25,000
Annual salary for quality control personnel	48,000
Annual salary for materials/product handlers	30,000
Annual salary for setup personnel	28,000

Each unit requires 1 square foot of storage space in a storage building containing 100,000 square feet. Depreciation per year on the building is $125,000 and property taxes and insurance total $35,000. Assume a 365-day year for plant assets and a 240-day year for personnel. Where a range of time is indicated, assume an average. Waiting time cost can be estimated at $50 per batch per day. Each day of delay in customer receipt is estimated to cost $150 per unit per day. The average production lot size is 500 units.

Determine the total cost of non-value-added activities per unit per day for each lot.

46. *(Activity-based costing)* Outdoor Life makes umbrellas, gazebos, and lawn chairs. The company uses a traditional overhead allocation scheme and assigns overhead to products at the rate of $10 per direct labor hour. In 1997, the company produced 100,000 umbrellas, 10,000 gazebos, and 30,000 lawn chairs and incurred $2,000,000 of manufacturing overhead costs. The cost per unit for each product group in 1997 was as follows:

	UMBRELLAS	GAZEBOS	LAWN CHAIRS
Direct materials	$ 4.00	$ 40.00	$ 4.00
Direct labor	6.00	45.00	15.00
Overhead	8.00	60.00	20.00
Total	$18.00	$145.00	$39.00

Because profitability has been lagging and competition has been getting more keen, Outdoor Life is considering implementing an activity-based costing system for 1998. In analyzing the 1997 data, management determined that all $2,000,000 of factory overhead could be assigned to four basic activities: quality control, setups, materials handling, and equipment operation. Data from 1997 on the costs associated with each of the four activities follows:

	QUALITY CONTROL	SETUPS	MATERIALS HANDLING	EQUIPMENT OPERATION	TOTAL
Costs	$100,000	$100,000	$300,000	$1,500,000	$2,000,000

Management determined that it will use the following allocation bases and total 1997 volumes for each allocation base:

ACTIVITY	BASE	VOLUME
Quality control	Number of units produced	280,000
Setups	Number of setups	1,000
Materials handling	Pounds of material used	2,000,000
Equipment operation	Number of machine hours	1,000,000

Volume measures for 1997 for each product and each allocation base were as follows:

	UMBRELLAS	GAZEBOS	LAWN CHAIRS
Number of units	100,000	10,000	60,000
Number of setups	200	400	400
Pounds of material	400,000	1,000,000	600,000
Number of machine hours	200,000	400,000	400,000

a. For 1997, determine the total overhead allocated to each product group using the traditional allocation based on direct labor hours.

b. For 1997, determine the total overhead that would be allocated to each product group if activity-based costing were used. Compute the cost per unit for each product group.

c. Outdoor Life has a policy of setting selling prices based on product costs. How would the sales prices using activity-based costing differ from those obtained using the traditional overhead allocation?

47. *(Activity-based costing)* Goldstein and Marcus Company manufactures two products. Following is a production and cost analysis for each product for the year 1997.

COST COMPONENT	PRODUCT A	PRODUCT B	BOTH PRODUCTS	COST
Units produced	10,000	10,000	20,000	
Raw materials used (units)				
X	50,000	50,000	100,000	$ 800,000
Y		100,000	100,000	$ 200,000
Labor hours used				
Department 1:				$ 681,000
Direct labor ($375,000)	20,000	5,000	25,000	
Indirect labor				
Inspection	2,500	2,500	5,000	
Machine operations	5,000	10,000	15,000	
Setups	200	200	400	
Department 2:				$ 462,000
Direct labor ($200,000)	5,000	5,000	10,000	
Indirect labor				
Inspection	2,500	5,000	7,500	
Machine operations	1,000	4,000	5,000	
Setups	200	400	600	
Machine hours used				
Department 1	5,000	10,000	15,000	$ 400,000
Department 2	5,000	20,000	25,000	$ 800,000
Power used (kw-hours)				$ 400,000
Department 1			1,500,000	
Department 2			8,500,000	
Other activity data:				
Building occupancy				$1,000,000
Purchasing				$ 100,000
Number of purchase orders				
Material X			200	
Material Y			300	
Square feet occupied				
Purchasing			10,000	
Power			40,000	
Department 1			200,000	
Department 2			250,000	

Roberto Lopez, the firm's cost accountant, has just returned from a seminar on activity-based costing. To apply the concepts he has learned, he decides to analyze the costs incurred for Products A and B from an activity basis. In doing so, he specifies the following first and second allocation processes:

FIRST STAGE: ALLOCATIONS TO DEPARTMENTS

COST POOL	COST OBJECT	ACTIVITY ALLOCATION BASE
Power	Departments	Kilowatt-hours
Purchasing	Materials	Number of purchase orders
Building occupancy	Departments	Square feet occupied

SECOND STAGE: ALLOCATIONS TO PRODUCTS

COST POOL	COST OBJECT	ACTIVITY ALLOCATION BASE
Departments:		
Indirect labor	Products	Hours worked
Power	Products	Machine hours
Machinery-related	Products	Machine hours
Building occupancy	Products	Machine hours
Materials:		
Purchasing	Products	Materials used

[SOURCE: From Harold P. Roth and A. Faye Borthick, "Getting Closer to *Real* Product Costs," *Management Accounting* (May 1989), pp. 28–33. Reprinted from *Management Accounting.* Copyright by Institute of Management Accountants, Montvale, NJ.]

a. Determine the total overhead for Goldstein and Marcus Company.

b. Determine the plantwide overhead rate for the company, assuming the use of direct labor hours.

c. Determine the cost per unit of Product A and Product B, using the overhead application rate found in part b.

d. Using activity-based costing, determine the cost allocations to departments (first-stage allocations). Allocate in the following order: Building occupancy, Purchasing, and Power.

e. Using the allocations found in part d, determine the cost allocations to products (second-stage allocations).

f. Determine the cost per unit of Product A and Product B using the overhead allocations found in part e.

48. *(Using ABC to set price)* The budgeted manufacturing overhead costs of Beaver Door Company for 1997 are as follows:

TYPE OF COST	COST AMOUNT
Electric power	$ 500,000
Work cells	3,000,000
Materials handling	1,000,000
Quality control inspections	1,000,000
Product runs (machine setups)	500,000
Total budgeted overhead costs	$6,000,000

For the last 5 years, the cost accounting department has been charging overhead production costs based on machine hours. The estimated budgeted capacity for 1997 is 1,000,000 machine hours.

Phil Stolzer, president of Beaver Door, recently attended a seminar on activity-based costing. He now believes that ABC results in more reliable cost data that, in turn, will give the company an edge in pricing over its competitors. On the president's request, the production manager provided the following data regarding expected 1997 activity for the cost drivers of the preceding budgeted overhead costs.

TYPE OF COSTS	ACTIVITY DRIVERS
Electric power	100,000 kilowatt hours
Work cells	600,000 square feet
Materials handling	200,000 material moves
Quality control inspections	100,000 number of inspections
Product runs (machine setups)	50,000 product runs

Linda Ryan, the VP of Marketing, received an offer to sell 5,000 doors to a local construction company. Linda asks the head of cost accounting to prepare cost estimates for producing the 5,000 doors. The head of cost accounting accumulated the following data concerning production of 5,000 doors:

Direct materials cost	$100,000
Direct labor cost	$300,000
Machine hours	10,000
Direct labor hours	15,000
Electric power—kilowatt-hours	1,000
Work cells—square feet	8,000
Number of materials handling moves	100
Number of quality control inspections	50
Number of product runs (setups)	25

a. What is the predetermined overhead rate if the traditional measure of machine hours is used?

b. What is the manufacturing cost per door as presently accounted for?

c. What is the manufacturing cost per door under the proposed ABC method?

d. If the prior two cost systems will result in different cost estimates, which cost accounting system is preferable as a pricing policy and why?

[SOURCE: Adapted from Nabil Hassa, Herbert E. Brown, and Paula M. Saunders, "Management Accounting Case Study: Beaver Window Inc.," *Management Accounting Campus Report* (Fall 1990). Copyright © 1990 IMA (formerly NAA).]

49. (*Activity driver analysis and decision making*) Thurgood Products is concerned about its ability to control factory labor-related costs. The company has recently finished an analysis of these costs for 1997. Following is a summary of the major categories of labor costs identified by Thurgood's accounting department:

CATEGORY	AMOUNT
Base wages	$42,000,000
Health care benefits	7,000,000
Payroll taxes	3,360,000
Overtime	5,800,000
Training	1,250,000
Retirement benefits	4,600,000
Workers' compensation	800,000

Listed below are some of the potential cost drivers identified by the company for labor-related costs, along with their 1997 volume levels.

POTENTIAL ACTIVITY DRIVER	1997 VOLUME LEVEL
Average number of factory employees	1,400
Number of new hires	200
Number of regular labor hours worked	2,100,000
Number of overtime hours worked	192,000
Total factory wages	$47,800,000
Volume of production in units	8,000,000
Number of production process changes	400
Number of production schedule changes	250

a. For each cost pool, determine the cost per unit of the activity driver using the activity driver that you believe has the closest relationship with the cost pool.

b. Based on your judgments and calculations in part a, which activity driver should receive the most attention from company managers in their efforts to control labor-related costs? How much of the total labor-related cost is attributable to this activity driver?

c. In the contemporary environment, many firms are asking their employees to work record levels of overtime. What activity driver does this practice suggest is a major contributor to labor-related costs? Explain.

50. *(Activity-based costing and pricing)* Covington Community Hospital has found itself under increasing pressure to be accountable for the charges it assesses its patients. Its current pricing system is ad hoc, based on pricing norms for the geographical area, and it only explicitly considers direct costs for surgery, medication, and other treatments. Covington's controller has suggested that the hospital try to improve its pricing policies by seeking a tighter relationship between costs and pricing. This approach would make prices for services less arbitrary. As a first step, the controller has determined that most costs can be assigned to one of three cost pools. The three cost pools follow along with the estimated amounts and activity drivers.

ACTIVITY CENTER	AMOUNT	ACTIVITY DRIVER	QUANTITY
Professional salaries	$900,000	Professional hours	30,000 hours
Building costs	450,000	Square feet used	15,000 square feet
Risk management	320,000	Patients served	1,000 patients

The hospital provides service in three broad categories. The services are listed below with their volume measures for the activity centers.

SERVICE	PROFESSIONAL HOURS	SQUARE FEET	NUMBER OF PATIENTS
Surgery	6,000	1,200	200
Housing patients	20,000	12,000	500
Outpatient care	4,000	1,800	300

a. Determine the allocation rates for each activity center cost pool.
b. Allocate the activity center costs to the three services provided by the hospital.
c. What bases might be used as cost drivers to allocate the service center costs among the patients served by the hospital? Defend your selections.

51. *(Determining product cost)* Pearson Custom Lumber Products has identified activity centers to which overhead costs are assigned. The cost pool amounts for these centers and their selected activity drivers for 1997 are as follows.

ACTIVITY CENTERS	COSTS	ACTIVITY DRIVERS
Utilities	$300,000	60,000 machine hours
Scheduling and setup	273,000	780 setups
Materials handling	640,000	1,600,000 pounds of material

The company's products and other operating statistics follow:

	PRODUCTS		
	A	*B*	*C*
Direct costs	$80,000	$80,000	$90,000
Machine hours	30,000	10,000	20,000
Number of setups	130	380	270
Pounds of materials	500,000	300,000	800,000
Number of units produced	40,000	20,000	60,000
Direct labor hours	32,000	18,000	50,000

a. Determine unit product cost using the appropriate cost drivers for each of the products.
b. Before it installed an ABC system, the company used a conventional costing system and allocated factory overhead to products using direct labor hours. The firm operates in a competitive market and product prices were set as cost plus a 20 percent markup.

   1. Calculate unit costs based on conventional costing.

   2. Determine selling prices based on unit costs for conventional costing and for ABC costs.

   c. Discuss the problems related to setting prices based on conventional costing and explain how ABC improves the information.

52. *(Product complexity)* Tektronix Inc. is a world leader in the production of electronic test and measurement instruments. The company experienced almost uninterrupted growth through the 1970s, but in the 1980s, the low-priced end of the Portables Division product line was challenged by an aggressive low-price strategy of several Japanese competitors. These Japanese companies set prices 25 percent below Tektronix's prevailing prices. To compete, the division would have to reduce costs and increase customer value by increasing operational efficiency.

Steps were taken to implement just-in-time delivery and scheduling techniques, a total quality control program, and people involvement techniques that moved responsibility for problem solving down to the operating level of the division. The results of these changes were impressive: substantial reductions in cycle time, direct labor hours per unit, and inventory levels as well as increases in output dollars per person per day and operating income. The cost accounting system was providing information, however, that did not seem to support the changes.

Total overhead cost for the division was $10,000,000; of this, part (55%) seemed to be related to materials and the remainder (45%) to conversion. Material-related costs pertain to procurement, receiving, inspection, stockroom personnel, etc. Conversion-related costs pertain to direct labor, supervision, and process-related engineering. All overhead was applied on the basis of direct labor.

The division decided to concentrate efforts on revamping the application system for materials-related overhead. Managers believed the majority of materials overhead (MOH) costs were related to the maintenance and handling of each different part number. Other types of MOH costs were costs due to the value of parts, absolute number of parts, and each use of a different part number.

At this time, the division used 8,000 different parts and in extremely different quantities. For example, annual usage of one part was 35,000 units; usage of another part was only 200 units. The division decided that MOH costs would decrease if a smaller number of different parts were used in the products.

   a. Give some reasons that materials overhead (MOH) would decrease if parts were standardized.

   b. Using the numbers given above, develop a cost allocation method for MOH to quantify and communicate the strategy of parts standardization.

   c. Explain how the use of the method developed in part b would support the strategy of parts standardization.

   d. Is any method that applies the entire MOH cost pool on the basis of one cost driver sufficiently accurate for complex products? Explain.

   e. Are MOH product costing rates developed for management reporting appropriate for inventory valuation for external reporting? Why or why not?

[SOURCE: Adapted from Michael A. Robinson, ed., *Cases from Management Accounting Practice*, No. 5 (Montvale, N.J.: National Association of Accountants, 1989), pp. 13–17. Copyright by Institute of Management Accountants (formerly National Association of Accountants), Montvale, NJ.]

53. *(Activity-based costing)* Alaire Corporation manufactures several different types of printed circuit boards; however, two of the boards account for the majority of the company's sales. The first of these boards, a television (TV) circuit board, has been a standard in the industry for several years. The market for this type of board is competitive and, therefore, price sensitive. Alaire plans to sell 65,000 of the TV circuit boards in 1997 at a price of $150 per unit. The second high-volume product, a personal computer (PC) circuit board, is a recent addition to Alaire's product line. Because the PC board incorporates the latest technology, it can be sold at a premium price; the 1997 plans include the sale of 40,000 PC boards at $300 per unit.

Alaire's management group is meeting to discuss strategies for 1997, and the current topic of conversation is how to spend the sales and promotion dollars for next year. The sales manager believes that the market share for the TV board could be expanded by concentrating Alaire's promotional efforts in this area. In response to this suggestion, the production manager said, "Why don't you go after a bigger market for the PC board? The cost sheets that I get show that the contribution from the PC board is more than double the contribution from the TV board. I know we get a premium price for the PC board; selling it should help overall profitability."

Alaire uses a standard cost system, and the following data apply to the TV and PC boards.

	TV BOARD	**PC BOARD**
Direct material	$80	$140
Direct labor	1.5 hours	4 hours
Machine time	.5 hours	1.5 hours

Variable factory overhead is applied on the basis of direct labor hours. For 1997, variable factory overhead is budgeted at $1,120,000, and direct labor hours are estimated at 280,000. The hourly rates for machine time and direct labor are $10 and $14, respectively. Alaire applies a material handling charge at 10 percent of materials cost; this material handling charge is not included in variable factory overhead. Total 1997 expenditures for materials are budgeted at $10,600,000.

Ed Welch, Alaire's controller, believes that before the management group proceeds with the discussion about allocated sales and promotional dollars to individual products, it might be worthwhile to look at these products on the basis of the activities involved in their production. As he explained to the group, "Activity-based costing integrates the cost of all activities, known as cost drivers, into individual product costs rather than including these costs in overhead pools." Welch has prepared the following schedule to help the management group understand this concept.

BUDGETED COST		**COST DRIVER**	**ANNUAL ACTIVITY FOR COST DRIVER**
Material overhead:			
Procurement	$ 400,000	Number of parts	4,000,000 parts
Production scheduling	220,000	Number of boards	110,000 boards
Packaging and shipping	440,000	Number of boards	110,000 boards
	$1,060,000		
Variable overhead:			
Machine setup	$ 446,000	Number of setups	278,750 setups
Hazardous waste disposal	48,000	Pounds of waste	16,000 pounds
Quality control	560,000	Number of inspections	160,000 inspections
General supplies	66,000	Number of boards	110,000 boards
	$1,120,000		

BUDGETED COST		COST DRIVER	ANNUAL ACTIVITY FOR COST DRIVER
Manufacturing:			
Machine insertion	$1,200,000	Number of parts	3,000,000 parts
Manual insertion	4,000,000	Number of parts	1,000,000 parts
Wave soldering	132,000	Number of boards	110,000 boards
	$5,332,000		

REQUIRED PER UNIT		
	TV BOARD	PC BOARD
Parts	25	55
Machine insertions	24	35
Manual insertions	1	20
Machine setups	2	3
Hazardous waste	.02 lb.	.35 lb.
Inspections	1	2

"Using this information," Welch explained, "we can calculate an activity-based cost for each TV board and each PC board and then compare it to the standard cost we have been using. The only cost that remains the same for both cost methods is the cost of direct materials. The cost drivers will replace the direct labor, machine time, and overhead costs in the standard cost."

a. Identify at least four general advantages that are associated with activity-based costing.

b. On the basis of standard costs, calculate the total contribution expected in 1997 for Alaire Corporation's
  1. TV board.
  2. PC board.

c. On the basis of activity-based costs, calculate the total contribution expected in 1997 for Alaire Corporation's
  1. TV board.
  2. PC board.

d. Explain how the comparison of the results of the two costing methods may impact the decisions made by Alaire Corporation's management group.

(CMA)

54. *(Activity-based costing)* Miami Valley Architects Inc. provides a wide range of engineering and architectural consulting services through its three branch offices in Columbus, Cincinnati, and Dayton. The company allocates resources and bonuses to the three branches based on the net income reported for the period. The following presents the results of 1997 performance ($ in thousands).

	COLUMBUS	CINCINNATI	DAYTON	TOTAL
Sales	$1,500	$1,419	$1,067	$3,986
Less: Direct labor	(382)	(317)	(317)	(1,016)
Direct materials	(281)	(421)	(185)	(887)
Overhead	(710)	(589)	(589)	(1,888)
Net income	$ 127	$ 92	$ (24)	$ 195

Overhead items are accumulated in one overhead pool and allocated to the branches based on direct labor dollars. For 1997, this predetermined overhead rate was $1.859 for every direct labor dollar incurred by an office. The overhead pool includes rent, depreciation, taxes, and so on, regardless of which office incurred the expense. This method of accumulating costs forces the offices to absorb a portion of the overhead incurred by other offices.

Management is concerned with the results of the 1997 performance reports. During a review of the overhead, it became apparent that many items of overhead are not correlated to the movement in direct labor dollars as previously assumed. Management decided that applying overhead based on activity-based costing and direct tracing where possible should provide a more accurate picture of the profitability of each branch.

An analysis of the overhead revealed that the following dollars for rent, utilities, depreciation, taxes, and so on, could be traced directly to the office that incurred the overhead ($ in thousands).

	COLUMBUS	CINCINNATI	DAYTON	TOTAL
Direct overhead	$180	$270	$177	$627

Activity pools and activity drivers were determined from the accounting records and staff surveys as follows:

ACTIVITY POOLS		ACTIVITY DRIVER	# OF ACTIVITIES BY LOCATION		
			Columbus	Cincinnati	Dayton
General Administration	$ 409,000	Direct Labor $	382,413	317,086	317,188
Project Costing	48,000	# of Timesheet Entries	6,000	3,800	3,500
Accounts Payable/Receiving	139,000	# of Vendor Invoices	1,020	850	400
Accounts Receivable	47,000	# of Client Invoices	588	444	96
Payroll/Mail Sort & Delivery	30,000	# of Employees	23	26	18
Personnel Recruiting	38,000	# of New Hires	8	4	7
Employee Insurance Processing	14,000	Insurance Claims Filed	230	260	180
Proposals	139,000	# of Proposals	200	250	60
Sales Meetings/Sales Aids	202,000	Contracted Sales	1,824,439	1,399,617	571,208
Shipping	24,000	# of Projects	99	124	30
Ordering	48,000	# of Purchase Orders	135	110	80
Duplicating Costs	46,000	# of Copies Duplicated	162,500	146,250	65,000
Blueprinting	77,000	# of Blueprints	39,000	31,200	16,000
	$1,261,000				

a. What overhead costs should be assigned to each branch based on activity-based costing concepts?

b. What is the contribution of each branch before subtracting the results obtained in part a?

c. What is the profitability of each branch office using activity-based costing?

d. Evaluate the concerns of management regarding the traditional costing technique currently used.

(IMA)

55. *(Activity-based costing and pricing)* Steven Haws owns and manages a commercial cold-storage warehouse. He stores a vast variety of perishable goods for his customers. Historically, he has charged customers using a flat rate of $.04 per pound per month for goods stored. His cold-storage warehouse has 100,000 cubic feet of storage capacity.

In the past 2 years, Haws has become dissatisfied with the profitability of the warehouse operation. Despite the fact that the warehouse remains relatively full, revenues have not kept pace with operating costs. Recently, Haws approached his accountant, Jill Green, about using activity-based costing to improve his understanding of the causes of costs and revise the pricing formula. Green has determined that most costs can be associated with one of four activities. Those activities and their related costs, volume measures, and volume levels for 1997 follow:

ACTIVITY	COST	MONTHLY VOLUME MEASURE
Send/receive goods	$6,000	Weight in pounds—500,000
Store goods	4,000	Volume in cubic feet—80,000
Move goods	5,000	Volume in square feet—5,000
Identify goods	2,000	Number of packages—500

[SOURCE: Adapted from Harold P. Roth and Linda T. Sims, "Costing for Warehousing and Distribution," *Management Accounting* (August 1991), pp. 42–45. Reprinted from *Management Accounting.* Copyright by Institute of Management Accountants, Montvale, NJ.]

a. Based on the activity cost and volume data, determine the amount of cost assigned to the following customers, whose goods were all received on the first day of last month.

CUSTOMER	WEIGHT OF ORDER	CUBIC FEET	SQUARE FEET	NUMBER OF PACKAGES
Jones	40,000	3,000	300	5
Hansen	40,000	2,000	200	20
Assad	40,000	1,000	1,000	80

b. Determine the price to be charged to each customer under the existing pricing plan.
c. Determine the price to be charged using ABC, assuming Haws would base the price on the cost determined in part a plus a markup of 40 percent.
d. How well does Haws's existing pricing plan capture the costs incurred to provide the warehouse services? Explain.

ETHICS AND QUALITY DISCUSSION

56. Many manufacturers are deciding to no longer service small retailers. For example, some companies have policies to serve only customers who purchase $10,000 or more of products from the companies annually. The companies defend such policies on the basis that they allow the companies to better serve their larger outlet, which handle more volume and more diverse product lines.
    a. Relate the concepts in the chapter to the decision of manufacturers to drop small customers.
    b. Are there any ethical implications of eliminating groups of customers that may be less profitable than others?
    c. Does activity-based costing adequately account for all costs that are related to a decision to eliminate a particular customer base? (Hint: Consider opportunity costs such as those related to reputation.)

57. *Evidence suggests that ABM implementations are more likely to succeed in more open organizations. The ground is especially fertile for companies that have a stated interest in becoming world-class competitors and have backed these ambitions up with other initiatives. ABM dovetails with these initiatives, and they reinforce each other. A clear commitment from top management is also essential.*

    [SOURCE: Helen Thorne and Bruce Gurd, "Some Human Aspects of Implementing Activity-Based Management," *Journal of Cost Management* (Fall 1995), p. 51.]

    a. What are some of the "other initiatives" to which the article would be referring?
    b. How might activity-based management and activity-based costing help a company in its quest to achieve world-class status?
    c. Would it be equally important to have top management support if a company was instituting activity-based costing rather than activity-based management? Justify your answer.
    d. Assume you are a member of top management in a large organization. Do you think implementation of ABM or ABC would be more valuable? Explain the rationale for your answer.

58. As the chief executive officer of a large corporation, you have made a decision after discussion with production and accounting personnel to implement activity-based management concepts. Your goal is to reduce cycle time and, thus, costs. A primary way to accomplish this goal is to install highly automated equipment in your plant, which would then displace approximately 60 percent of your workforce. Your company is the major employer in the area of the country where it is located.

    a. Discuss the pros and cons of installing the equipment from the perspective of your (1) stockholders, (2) employees, and (3) customers.

    b. How would you explain to a worker that his/her job is non-value-added?

    c. What alternatives might you have that could accomplish the goal of reducing cycle time but not create economic havoc for the local area?

INTERNET ACTIVITIES

59. Find the IMA (Institute of Management Accountants) home page. Then find and read the article entitled "Practices and Techniques: Implementing Activity-Based Costing." Write a brief summary of the article noting the major considerations in designing the implementation of an ABC system.

60. On the Internet find the Activity Based Cost home page. On this page are discussions of statistical process control, parametric cost analysis, and business process reengineering. Considering the discussion provided, describe how these three tools tie to the concepts of activity based costing and activity based management.

61. Included in the ABC materials provided by the IMA (Institute of Management Accountants) on the Internet is a discussion of ABC for logistics. After reading these materials, discuss how activity-based costing can be used to control and allocate the costs of logistics. In your discussion describe what activities are captured by the word "logistics," what are typical activities for logistics, what are typical cost drivers for logistics, and why logistics costs are a growing concern of businesses today.

PRODUCT COSTING METHOD

7

Job Order Costing

LEARNING OBJECTIVES

After completing this chapter, you should be able to answer these questions:

1. How do job order and process costing systems, and actual, normal, and standard costing valuation methods differ?

2. In what production situations is a job order costing system appropriate and why?

3. What constitutes a "job" from an accounting standpoint?

4. What purposes are served by the basic documents used in a job order costing system?

5. What journal entries are used to accumulate costs in a job order costing system?

6. *(Appendix)* How are standard costs used in a job order costing system?

FM Corporation

FM Corporation of Rogers, Arkansas, custom manufactures a wide variety of products for a diverse set of industries. For example, for the computer industry the company makes housing cases for computers and printers. For the telecommunications industry, the firm makes satellite antenna disks. Other products include waste cans, pallets for materials handling, and seats for ski lifts.

FM Corporation competes using a strategy of producing low volume, diverse products from a standard set of materials, and conversion operations. The usual materials with which the company works include: polypropylene, polystyrene, polyethylene, and engineered resins. The typical conversion operations include materials preparation, injection of resins into molds, curing, and painting. The company makes diverse products using a common set of materials by creating different shapes and functions using a standard set of conversion processes. In short, the company's expertise is in converting plastic resins into a variety of functional products.

To compete successfully, the company must find ways to design products at low cost, minimize waste and inefficiency, control setup costs, and constantly search for ways to improve conversion activities and create value for its customers. The company does not have the economies of scale that are available to the mass producer; consequently, it must find alternative ways to improve efficiencies and remain price competitive.

SOURCES: Anonymous, "FM Updates Its Facility," *Plastics News* (April 15, 1996), p. 68; Bradford McKee, "Ties That Bind Large and Small," *Nations Business* (February 1992), pp. 24–26; Connecticut Mutual Insurance Company and The U.S. Chamber of Commerce in Association with The Blue Chip Enterprise Initiative, *Strengthening America's Competitiveness* (Warner Books, 1991), pp. 89–90.

A t FM Corporation and at other custom manufacturers, most business is conducted on the basis of a competitive bidding process to obtain contracts. In such a process, a company must accurately estimate the costs of making products associated with each bid. Competitive bidding is complicated by the nature of custom manufacturing—each bid may involve unique products. For example, at FM Corporation the only common aspects of all products are the materials used and the conversion processes. Because each bid/order is substantially different from all others, job pricing and cost control cannot be based on an accounting system that aggregates costs across orders. Thus, FM Corporation uses job order costing to accumulate the costs of each job (order) separately from all other jobs.

A primary objective of cost accounting is to determine the cost of an organization's products or services. Just as various methods (first-in, first-out; last-in, first-out; average; specific identification) exist to determine inventory valuation and cost of goods sold for a retailer, different methods are available to value inventory and calculate product cost in a manufacturing or service environment. The method chosen depends on the product or service and the company's conversion processes. A cost flow assumption is required for processes in which costs cannot be identified with and attached to specific units of production.

This chapter begins a sequence of chapters presenting various methods of product costing. The chapter first distinguishes between two primary costing systems (job order and process) and then discusses three methods of valuation that can be used within these systems (actual, normal, and standard). The remainder of the chapter focuses on the job order costing system, such as that used by FM Corporation.

VIDEO
VIGNETTE

FM Corporation (Blue Chip Enterprises)

METHODS OF PRODUCT COSTING

Before the cost of products can be computed, a determination must be made about (1) the product costing system and (2) the valuation method to be used. The product costing system used indicates the cost object and the method of assigning costs to production. The valuation method specifies how product costs will be measured. Companies must have both a cost system and a valuation method; six possible combinations exist (shown in Exhibit 7–1).[1]

Costing Systems

job order costing system

VIDEO
VIGNETTE

Spencer & Jonnatti Architects
(Blue Chip Enterprises)

Job order and process costing are the two primary cost systems. A **job order costing system** is used by entities that make (perform) relatively small quantities or distinct batches of identifiable, unique products (services). For example, job order costing is appropriate for a publishing company that produces educational textbooks, an accountant who prepares tax returns, an architectural firm that designs commercial buildings, and a research firm that performs product development studies. In each instance, the organization produces tailor-made goods or services that conform to specifications designated by the purchaser of those goods or services. Services in general are typically user specific, so job order costing systems are commonly used in such businesses.

The purchaser of goods or services from a job shop can be external or internal contracting parties. External parties include individuals, other businesses, and the government; internal parties include other organizational units within the producing entity. The following News Note indicates how the U.S. Mint manufactures products for sale inside and outside the government. Regardless of whether the relationship

EXHIBIT 7–1

Costing Systems and
Inventory Valuation

COST ACCUMULATION SYSTEM	METHOD OF VALUATION		
	Actual	Normal	Standard
JOB ORDER	Actual DM Actual DL Actual OH (assigned to job after end of period)	Actual DM Actual DL OH applied using predetermined rates at completion of job or end of period (predetermined rates times actual input)	Standard DM and/or Standard DL OH applied using predetermined rates when goods are completed or at end of period (predetermined rates times standard input)
PROCESS	Actual DM Actual DL Actual OH (assigned to job after end of period using FIFO or weighted average cost flow)	Actual DM Actual DL OH applied using predetermined rates (using FIFO or weighted average cost flow)	Standard DM Standard DL Standard OH using predetermined rates (will always be FIFO cost flow)

[1] A third and fourth dimension (cost accumulation and cost presentation) are also necessary in this model. These dimensions relate to the use of absorption or variable costing and are covered in Chapter 12.

Making Money at the Mint

N E W S
N O T E

The U.S. Mint was established by Congress in 1792. It is a complex entity that operates a number of business lines. For example, the Mint produces all U.S. circulating coins (19.2 billion coins in fiscal year 1994), stores the nation's reserves of gold and silver, and manufactures a variety of commemorative coins that are sold to the public. It operates as a bureau of the U.S. Treasury and employs 2,000 people.

To account for its operations, the Mint uses a process costing system to track costs of coins that it produces for the U.S. Treasury. Alternatively, it uses a job order costing system to track costs associated with issues of commemorative coins that are sold directly to the public. On coin sales to the public, the Mint's objective is to make a profit on sales. In 1994, the Mint sold 35 million coins generating $341 million in sales and $10 million in profits.

Like private firms, the Mint relies on accounting data to manage its operations. Its principal accounting reports include a monthly accrued cost summary, a monthly income statement, and a quarterly cost of production report. The income statement is the key tool used to track the success of coin sales to the public.

SOURCE: Michael Kess, "Cost Accounting and Cost Analysis at the U.S. Mint," *Government Accountants Journal* (Summer 1995), pp. 56–61. Reprinted with permission of the Association of Government Accountants.

is internal or external, the purchasing party specifies to the selling party the details of what, when, and how many.

The other primary product costing system, **process costing system,** is used by entities that produce large quantities of homogeneous goods. Process costing is appropriate for companies that mass manufacture products such as bricks, gasoline, detergent, and breakfast cereal. The output of a single process in a mass manufacturer is homogeneous; thus, within a given period, one unit of output cannot be readily identified with specific input costs. This characteristic of process costing systems makes a cost flow assumption necessary. Cost flow assumptions provide a means for accountants to assign costs to products without regard for the actual physical flow of units. Process costing systems (covered in Chapters 8 and 9) allow the use of either a FIFO or weighted average cost flow assumption.

DeBourgh Manufacturing (Blue Chip Enterprises)

process costing system

Valuation Methods

The three valuation methods (shown in Exhibit 7–1) are actual, normal, and standard costing. A company using the actual costs of direct materials, direct labor, and overhead to determine work in process inventory cost is employing an actual cost system. Service businesses that have few customers and/or low volume, such as some advertising agencies or consulting firms, may be able to use an actual cost system. However, because of the reasons discussed in Chapter 4, many companies modify actual cost systems by using predetermined overhead rates rather than actual overhead costs. This combination of actual direct materials and direct labor costs with predetermined overhead rates is called a normal cost system. If the predetermined rate is substantially equivalent to what the actual rate would have been for an annual period, its use provides acceptable and useful costs.

Companies using either job order or process costing may employ standards (or predetermined benchmarks) for costs to be incurred and/or quantities to be used. In a **standard cost system,** unit norms or standards are developed for direct material and direct labor quantities and/or costs. Overhead is applied to production using a predetermined rate that is considered the standard. These standards may then be used to plan for future activities and cost incurrence and to value inventories. Both actual and standard costs are recorded in the accounting records to provide an essential element of cost control—having norms against which actual costs of opera-

standard cost system

variance

tions can be compared. A standard cost system allows companies to quickly recognize deviations or **variances** from normal production costs and to correct problems resulting from excess usage and/or costs. Actual costing systems do not provide this benefit, and normal costing systems cannot provide it in relation to materials and labor.

Because the use of predetermined overhead rates is more common than the use of actual overhead costs, this chapter addresses a job order/normal cost system; the appendix briefly describes some possible job order/standard cost combinations.[2]

JOB ORDER COSTING SYSTEM

job

Product costing is concerned with (1) cost identification, (2) cost measurement, and (3) product cost assignment. In a job order costing system, costs are accumulated individually on a per-job basis. A **job** is a single unit or group of units identifiable as being produced to distinct customer specifications.[3] Each job is treated as a unique cost entity or cost object. Costs of different jobs are maintained in separate subsidiary ledger accounts and are not added together or commingled in those ledger accounts.

The logic of separating costs for individual jobs is shown by the following example. In March, Georgia Plastics produced 1,000 table tops for a Mexican restaurant, 500 display racks for an art exhibitor, and 15,000 sign holders for an international clothing retailer. The quantity of resources used for each project is clearly unique. Each table top required a different amount of material and different set of conversion operations than those required to produce sign holders. Accordingly, Georgia Plastics has no way of determining either a meaningful average cost for the 16,500 units of product. Because job results are heterogeneous and distinctive, the costs of those jobs cannot logistically be averaged.

Exhibit 7–2 provides the Work in Process Inventory control and subsidiary ledger accounts for Georgia Plastics's product costing system. The usual production costs

The costs of constructing this telecommunications tower by PTT on Mt. Santis in the Swiss Alps must be accounted for on a job order basis. Overhead costs are extremely expensive considering the height to which all material and labor must be taken.

[2] Although actual overhead may be assigned to jobs, such an approach would be less customary because total overhead would not be known until the period was over, causing an unwarranted delay in overhead assignment. Activity-based costing can increase the validity of tracing overhead costs to specific products or jobs.

[3] To eliminate the need for repetition, units should be read to mean either products or services because job order costing is applicable to both manufacturing and service companies. For the same reason, *produced* can mean *manufactured* or *performed*.

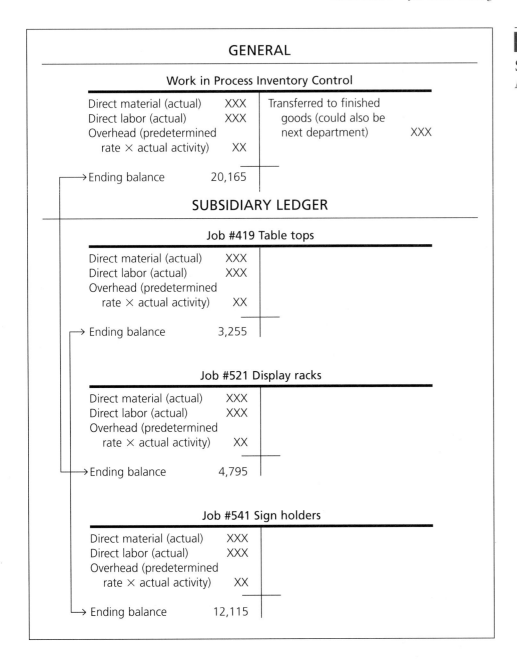

EXHIBIT 7–2

Separate Subsidiary Ledger
Accounts for Jobs

of direct material, direct labor, and overhead are accumulated for each job. Actual direct material and direct labor costs are combined with an overhead cost that is computed as a predetermined overhead rate multiplied by some actual cost driver (such as direct labor hours, cost or quantity of materials used, or number of material requisitions). Normal cost valuation is used because, although actual direct material and direct labor costs are fairly easy to identify and associate with a particular job, overhead costs are usually not traceable to specific jobs and must be allocated to production. For example, Georgia Plastics' March utility costs are related to all jobs worked on during that month. Accurately determining which jobs created the need for a given amount of water, heat, or electricity would be almost impossible.

To help ensure the proper recording of costs, the amounts appearing in the subsidiary ledger accounts are periodically compared with and reconciled to the Work in Process Inventory control account in the general ledger. This reconciliation is indicated by the equality of the assumed ending balances of the subsidiary ledger accounts with the WIP Inventory control account in Exhibit 7–2.

The output of any job can be a single unit or multiple similar or dissimilar units. With multiple outputs, a unit cost may be computed only if the units are similar or if costs are accumulated for each separate unit (such as through an identification number). For example, Conner Peripherals produces compact disk drives to the specifications of a variety of companies including Compaq. Conner can determine the cost per disk drive for each company by accumulating the costs per batch of homogeneous products in different production runs and treating each production run as a separate job. In such cases, production costs of each job batch can be commingled because the units within the batch are not distinguishable and the total cost can be averaged over the number of units produced in the batch to determine a cost per unit. If the output consists of dissimilar units for which individual cost information is not gathered, no cost per unit can be determined although it is still possible to know the total job cost.

JOB ORDER COSTING—DETAILS AND DOCUMENTS

The facts presented in the previous section about a job order costing system provide the necessary foundation to account for individual jobs. A job can be categorized by its stage in its production cycle. There are three stages of production: (1) contracted for but not yet started, (2) in process, and (3) completed.[4]

Because a company using job order costing is making products according to user specifications, jobs might occasionally require unique raw material. Thus, some raw material may not be acquired until a job is under contract and it is known that production will occur. The raw material acquired, although often separately distinguishable and related to specific jobs, is accounted for in a single general ledger control account (Raw Material Inventory) with subsidiary ledger backup. The material may, however, be designated in the storeroom and possibly in the subsidiary records as being "held for use in Job XX." Such designations should keep the material from being used on a job other than the one for which it was acquired.

Material Requisitions

material requisition form

When material is needed to begin a job, a **material requisition form** (shown in Exhibit 7–3) is prepared so that the material can be released from the warehouse and sent to the production area. This source document indicates the types and quantities of materials to be placed into production or used to perform a service job. Such documents are usually prenumbered and come in multicopy sets so that completed copies can be maintained in the warehouse, in the department, and with each job. Completed material requisition forms are important for a company's audit trail because they provide the ability to trace responsibility for material cost and to verify the flow of material from the warehouse to the department for the job receiving the material. These forms release warehouse personnel from further responsibility for issued material and assign responsibility to the requisitioning department.

When material is issued, its cost is released from Raw Material Inventory, and if direct to the job, is sent to Work in Process Inventory. If the Raw Material Inventory account also contains indirect material, the costs of these issuances are assigned to Manufacturing Overhead. Thus, the journal entry will be as follows:

Work in Process Inventory (if direct)	XXX	
Manufacturing Overhead (if indirect)	XXX	
Raw Material Inventory		XXX

When the first direct material associated with a job is issued to production, that job moves to the second stage of its production cycle—being in process. When a job

---

[4] In concept, there could be four categories. The third and fourth categories would distinguish between products completed but not sold and products completed and sold. However, the usual case is that firms using a job order costing system produce only products for which there is a current demand. Consequently, there is usually no inventory of finished products that await sale.

Date _____						No. 341	
Job Number _____			Department _____				
Authorized by _____			Issued by _____				
Received by _____			Inspected by _____				
Item No.	Part No.	Description	Unit of Measure	Quantity Required	Quantity Issued	Unit Cost	Total Cost

Material Requisition Form

enters this stage, cost accumulation must begin using the primary accounting document in a job order system—the job order cost sheet (or job cost record).

Job Order Cost Sheet

The source document that provides virtually all financial information about a particular job is the **job order cost sheet.** The set of job order cost sheets for all uncompleted jobs comprises the Work in Process Inventory subsidiary ledger. Total costs contained in the job order cost sheets for all uncompleted jobs should reconcile the Work in Process Inventory control account balance in the general ledger as shown in Exhibit 7–2.

job order cost sheet

The top portion of a job order cost sheet includes a job number, a description of the task, customer identification, various scheduling information, delivery instructions, and contract price. The remainder of the form details actual costs for material, labor, and applied overhead. The form also might include budgeted cost information, especially if such information had been used to estimate the job's selling price or support a bid price. In bid pricing, budgeted and actual costs should be compared at the end of a job to determine any deviations from estimates.

Exhibit 7–4 illustrates a job order cost sheet for Georgia Plastics. The company has contracted to produce 500 lexan hatch covers, with attachment hardware, for a boat manufacturer. All Georgia Plastics' job order cost sheets include a section for budgeted data so that budget-to-actual comparisons can be made for planning and control purposes. Direct material and direct labor costs are assigned and posted to jobs as work on the job is performed. Direct material information is gathered from the material requisition forms, and direct labor information is found on employee time sheets or employee labor tickets. (Employee time sheets are discussed in the next section.)

Overhead is applied to production at Georgia Plastics based on departmental rates. Each department may have more than one rate. For example, in the Cutting & Forming Department, the 1997 overhead rates are

> Labor-related costs: $15 per direct labor hour
> Machine-related costs: $15.50 per machine hour

Job Number _____602_____

Customer Name and Address:

Gulfcoast Boatworks
9901 Gulfcoast Road
Corpus Christi, TX

Description of Job:

500 lexan hatch covers
Size: 12" × 17"; Product to include
aluminum edge trim and mounting hardware

Contract Agreement Date: 3/25/97
Scheduled Starting Date: 4/5/97
Agreed Completion Date: 6/1/97
Actual Completion Date:
Delivery Instructions: Deliver by rail

Contract Price: $35,250

Cutting & Forming

Direct Material (Est. $12,140) (includes hardware)			Direct Labor (Est. $3,100)			Overhead based on					
						# of labor hours (Est. $1,500)			# of machine hours (Est. $1,240)		
Date	Source	Amount	Date	Source	Amount	Date	Source	Amount	Date	Source	Amount

Edge Polishing
(same format as above but with different OH rates)

Lamination
(same format as above but with different OH rates)

SUMMARY

	Cutting & Forming			Edge Polishing			Lamination	
	Actual	Budget		Actual	Budget		Actual	Budget
Direct material	_____	$12,140		_____	$ 1,200		_____	$ 975
Direct labor	_____	3,100		_____	2,100		_____	1,234
Overhead	_____	1,500		_____	400		_____	450
Overhead	_____	1,240		_____	520		_____	370
Totals	_____	$17,980		_____	$ 4,220		_____	$ 3,029

		Actual	Budget
Final Costs:	Cutting & Forming	_____	$17,980
	Edge Polishing	_____	4,220
	Lamination	_____	3,029
	Totals	_____	$25,229

EXHIBIT 7–4

Georgia Plastics Job
Order Cost Sheet

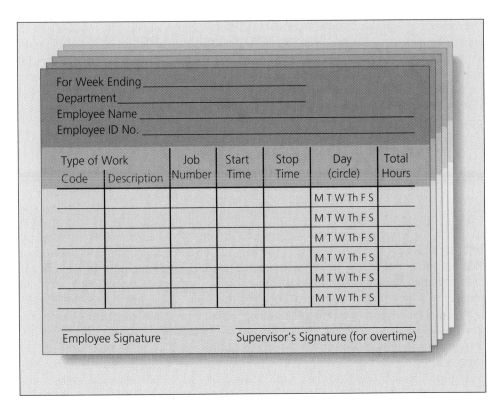

EXHIBIT 7–5

Employee Time Sheet

Employee Time Sheets

An **employee time sheet** (Exhibit 7–5) indicates for each employee the jobs worked on and the direct labor time consumed. These time sheets are most reliable if the employees fill them in as the day progresses. Work arriving at an employee station is accompanied by a tag specifying its job order number. The time work is started and stopped are noted on the time sheet.[5] These time sheets should be collected and reviewed by supervisors to ensure that the information is as accurate as possible.

The time sheet shown in Exhibit 7–5 is appropriate only if employees are asked to record their time and work manually. The time sheet information is the same as that which would be recorded if a computer were used to track employee tasks, as is the norm in larger businesses.

In today's highly automated factories, employee time sheets may not be extremely useful or necessary documents because of the low proportion of direct labor cost to total cost. However, machine time can be tracked through the use of machine clocks or counters in the same way as human labor. As jobs are transferred from one machine to another, the clock or counter can be reset to mark the start and stop times. Machine times can then be equated to employee-operator time. Another convenient way to track employee time is through product bar codes that can be scanned as they pass through individual workstations. At one large Midwest plumbing manufacturer, for example, a bar coding system was implemented for time-and-attendance and shop-floor-control systems. "In less than two years, the company eliminated eleven different forms that were used when time and inspection data were recorded manually. Inspector efficiency improved by 10 to 12 percent, in part because the inspector *never* touched a piece of paper other than a bar code label."[6]

employee time sheet

[5] Alternatives to daily time sheets are job time tickets that supervisors give to employees as they are assigned new jobs and supervisors' records of which employees worked on what jobs for what period of time. The latter alternative is extremely difficult if a supervisor is overseeing a large number of employees or if employees are dispersed through a large section of the plant.

[6] Thomas Tyson, "The Use of Bar Coding in Activity-Based Costing, *Journal of Cost Management* (Winter 1991), pp. 52–53.

Transferring employee time sheet (or alternative source document) information to the job order cost sheet requires a knowledge of employee labor rates. Wage rates are found in employee personnel files. Time spent on the job is multiplied by the employee's wage rate, and the amounts are summed to find total direct labor cost for the period. The summation is recorded on the job order cost sheet. Time sheet information is also used for payroll preparation; the journal entry to record the information is

Work in Process Inventory (if direct)	XXX	
Manufacturing Overhead (if indirect)	XXX	
Salaries and Wages Payable		XXX

cost-plus contract

After these uses, time sheets are filed and retained so they may be referenced if necessary for any future information needs. If total actual labor costs for the job differ significantly from the original estimate, the manager responsible for labor cost control may be asked to clarify the reasons underlying the situation. In addition, if a job is being billed at cost plus a specified profit margin (a **cost-plus contract**), the number of hours worked may be checked by the buyer. This situation is quite common and especially important when dealing with government contracts. Therefore, hours not worked directly on the contracted job cannot be arbitrarily or incorrectly charged to the cost-plus job without the potential for detection. Last, time sheets provide information on overtime hours. Under the Fair Labor Standards Act, overtime must generally be paid at a time-and-a-half rate to all nonmanagement employees when they work more than 40 hours in a week.

Overhead

Overhead costs can be substantial in manufacturing and service organizations. As indicated in the following News Note, the ability to control overhead cost is a major factor in the relative success of accounting firms.

Actual overhead incurred during production is included in the Manufacturing Overhead control account. If actual overhead is applied to jobs, the cost accountant will wait until the end of the period and divide the actual overhead incurred in each

Overhead Costs and the Competitive Structure of the Accounting Industry

[S]ince 1982, about half of the country's midsize accounting firms have either gone out of business or been acquired, says Jay Nisberg, a Ridgefield, Conn., accounting-firm consultant. In five years, middle-tier accounting [firms] will be "as extinct as the dodo," he predicts.

The problems of midsize accounting firms, which typically have as many as 50 partners and 300 employees, underscore a dilemma in many professional fields: They can't offer the numerous services of big competitors [such as the "Big Six"] and don't have the low overhead of tiny ones. Moreover, many accounting firms, big and small, are trying to make up for slow revenue and profit growth—or declines—in the early 1990s compared with their double digit gains in the 1980s . . . .

Big Six firms, under profit pressures themselves, urgently need new clients. Meanwhile, they have vastly expanded the array of services they offer. Since 1982, their total U.S. staffs have climbed 44% to 114,000, and their U.S. partners have increased 24% to 8,270. And small practitioners also "are very hungry for business," says Mr. Nisberg, the consultant. State laws prohibiting accountants from soliciting competitors' clients are disappearing.

SOURCE: Lee Berton, "Squeeze Play: Midsize Accountants Lose Clients to Firms Both Large and Small," *Wall Street Journal* (November 14, 1995), pp. A1, A4. Reprinted by permission of *The Wall Street Journal*, © 1995 Dow Jones & Company, Inc. All Rights Reserved Worldwide.

designated cost pool by a related measure of activity or cost driver. Actual overhead would be applied to jobs by multiplying the actual overhead rate by the actual measure of activity associated with each job.

More commonly, overhead is applied to job order cost sheets using one or more annualized predetermined overhead application rates. Overhead is assigned to jobs by multiplying the predetermined rate by the actual measure of the activity base that was incurred during the period and was associated with each job.

If predetermined rates are used, overhead is applied at the end of the period or at completion of production, whichever is earlier. Overhead is applied at the end of each period so that the Work in Process Inventory account contains costs for all three product elements (direct material, direct labor, and overhead). Overhead is applied to Work in Process Inventory on completion so that a proper product cost can be transferred to Finished Goods Inventory. The journal entry to apply overhead is as follows:

Work in Process Inventory	XXX	
Manufacturing Overhead		XXX

Completion of Production

When a job is completed, its total cost is transferred through a debit to Finished Goods Inventory and a credit to Work in Process Inventory. Job order cost sheets for completed jobs are removed from the WIP subsidiary ledger and become the subsidiary ledger for the Finished Goods Inventory control account. When a job is sold, the cost contained in Finished Goods Inventory for that job is transferred to Cost of Goods Sold. Such a cost transfer presumes the use of a perpetual inventory system, which is common in a job order costing environment because goods are generally easily identified and tracked.

Job order cost sheets for completed jobs are kept in a company's permanent files. A completed job order cost sheet provides management with a historical summary about total costs and, if appropriate, the cost per finished unit for a given job. The cost per unit may be helpful for planning and control purposes as well as for bidding on future contracts. If a job was exceptionally profitable, management might decide to pursue additional similar jobs. If a job was unprofitable, the job order cost sheet may provide indications of areas in which cost control was lax. Such areas are more readily identifiable if the job order cost sheet presents the original, budgeted cost information.

In any job order costing system, the individual job is the focal point. The next section presents a comprehensive job order costing situation using information from Georgia Plastics, the company introduced earlier.

JOB ORDER COSTING ILLUSTRATION

Georgia Plastics sets bid prices based on its costs. Over the long term, the company has a goal of realizing a gross profit equal to 25 percent of the bid price. This level of gross profit is sufficient to generate a reasonable profit after covering selling and administrative costs. In more competitive circumstances, such as when the company has too much unused capacity, bid prices may be set lower to increase the likelihood of successful bids. If the company has little unused capacity, it may set bid prices somewhat higher so that the likelihood of successfully bidding on too many contracts is reduced.

To help in establishing the bid price on the lexan hatch covers, Georgia Plastics' cost accountant provided the vice president of sales with the budgeted cost information shown in Exhibit 7–4. The vice president of sales believed that a bid price slightly above normal levels was possible because of the noncompetitive nature of this particular market. Accordingly, the vice president set the sales price to yield a gross margin of roughly 28.4 percent [($35,250 − $25,229) ÷ $35,250]. This sales price was agreed to by the boat manufacturer in a contract dated March 25, 1997. Georgia Plastics' managers scheduled the job to begin on April 5, 1997, and to be completed by June 1, 1997. The job is assigned the number 602 for identification purposes.

The following journal entries illustrate the flow of costs for the Cutting & Forming Department of Georgia Plastics during April 1997. Several jobs were worked on in Cutting & Forming during that month, including Job #602. In entries 1, 2, and 4 that follow, there is separate WIP inventory accounting for costs related to Job #602 and to other jobs. *In practice, the Work in Process control account for a given department would be debited only once for all costs assigned to it. The details for posting to the individual job cost records would be presented in the journal entry explanations.*

1. During April 1997, material requisition forms #328–360 indicated that $6,325 of raw materials were issued from the warehouse to the Cutting & Forming Department. This amount included $3,182 of direct materials used on Job #602 (issued on April 5 and 18) and $2,172 of direct materials used on other jobs. The remaining $971 of raw materials issued during April were indirect materials.

Work in Process Inventory—Cutting & Forming (Job #602)	3,182	
Work in Process Inventory—Cutting & Forming (other jobs)	2,172	
Manufacturing Overhead—Cutting & Forming (indirect materials)	971	
Raw Material Inventory		6,325
To record direct and indirect materials issued per requisitions during April.		

2. The April time sheets and payroll summaries of the Cutting & Forming Department nonsalaried workers were used to trace direct and indirect labor to that department. Total labor cost for the Cutting & Forming Department for April was $7,400. Job #602 required $651 of direct labor cost during the two biweekly pay periods of April 8 ($170) and April 22 ($481). The remaining jobs in process required $4,244 of direct labor cost, and indirect labor cost for the month totaled $2,505.

Punching in on a time clock provides an employer information on the length of time an employee is at work. However, in a job order costing system, it is also necessary to know what jobs were worked on during the employee's shift. Thus, employee time sheets are essential.

Work in Process Inventory—Cutting & Forming (Job #602)	651	
Work in Process Inventory—Cutting & Forming (other jobs)	4,244	
Manufacturing Overhead—Cutting & Forming (indirect labor)	2,505	
Wages Payable		7,400
To record wages associated with Cutting & Forming during April.		

3. The Cutting & Forming Department incurred overhead costs in addition to indirect materials and indirect labor during April. Factory building and equipment depreciation of $430 was recorded for April. Insurance on the factory building ($360) for the month had been prepaid and had expired. The $450 bill for April factory utility costs was received and would be paid in May. Repairs and maintenance costs of $490 were paid in cash. Overhead costs of $210 for items such as supplies used, supervisors' salaries, and so forth were incurred; these costs are credited to "Various accounts" for illustrative purposes. The following entry summarizes the accumulation of these other actual overhead costs for April.

Manufacturing Overhead—Cutting & Forming	1,940	
Accumulated Depreciation		430
Prepaid Insurance		360
Utilities Payable		450
Cash		490
Various accounts		210
To record actual overhead costs of the Cutting & Forming Department during April exclusive of indirect materials and indirect nonsalaried labor.		

4. Georgia Plastics prepares financial statements at month end. To do so, Work in Process Inventory must include all production costs—direct material, direct labor, and overhead. The company allocates overhead to the Cutting & Forming Work in Process Inventory based on two predetermined overhead rates: $15 per direct labor hour and $15.50 per machine hour. In April the employees committed 21 hours of direct labor time to Job #602, and 30 machine hours were consumed on the job. The other jobs worked on during the month received total applied overhead of $4,425 [140 direct labor hours (assumed) × $15 plus 150 machine hours (assumed) × $15.50].

Work in Process Inventory—Cutting & Forming (Job #602)	780	
Work in Process Inventory—Cutting & Forming (other jobs)	4,425	
Manufacturing Overhead—Cutting & Forming		5,205
To apply overhead to Cutting & Forming work in process for April using predetermined application rates.		

Notice that the amount of actual overhead for April [$971 + $2,505 + $1,940 = $5,416] in the Cutting & Forming Department is not equal to the amount of overhead applied to that department's Work in Process Inventory [$5,205]. This $211 difference is the underapplied overhead for the month. Because the predetermined rates are based on annual estimates, differences in actual and applied overhead will accumulate during the year. Underapplied or overapplied overhead will be closed at year-end (as shown in Chapter 5) to either Cost of Goods Sold (if the amount is immaterial) or to Work in Process Inventory, Finished Goods Inventory, and Cost of Goods Sold (if the amount is material).

The preceding entries for the Cutting & Forming Department would be similar to the entries made in each of the other departments of Georgia Plastics. Direct material and direct labor data are posted to each job order cost sheet on a continuous basis (usually daily); entries are posted to the general ledger control accounts at less frequent intervals (usually monthly).

Job #602 will be worked on by only three departments of Georgia Plastics. Other jobs accepted by the company may involve a different combination of departments. In this company, jobs flow consecutively from one department to the next. In other types of job shops, different departments may work on the same job concurrently. Similar entries for the lexan hatch cover job are made throughout the production process and Exhibit 7–6 shows the completed cost sheet for Job #602 for Georgia Plastics. Note that direct material requisitions, direct labor cost, and applied overhead shown previously in entries 1, 2, and 4 are posted on the job cost sheet. Other entries are not detailed.

When the job is completed, its costs are transferred to Finished Goods Inventory. The journal entries related to completion and sale are as follows:

Finished Goods Inventory—Job #602	25,622	
Work in Process Inventory—Cutting & Forming		18,416
Work in Process Inventory—Edge Polishing		4,130
Work in Process Inventory—Lamination		3,076
Cost of Goods Sold—Job #602	25,622	
Finished Goods Inventory—Job #602		25,622
Accounts Receivable—Gulfcoast Boatworks	35,250	
Sales		35,250

The completed job order cost sheet can be used by managers in all departments to determine how well costs were controlled. The Cutting & Forming Department experienced higher direct material and direct labor costs than budgeted. However, in the Edge Polishing Department, actual direct material and direct labor costs were slightly below budget. Lamination was very close to budget in all categories. Overall, costs were well controlled on this job, because total actual costs were almost identical to the budgeted ones (approximately 1.6 percent above budget).

Managers are interested in controlling costs in each department as well as for each job. Actual direct material, direct labor, and factory overhead costs are accumulated in departmental accounts and are periodically compared to budgets so that managers can respond to significant deviations. Transactions must be recorded in a consistent, complete, and accurate manner to have information on actual costs available for periodic comparisons. Managers may stress different types of cost control in different types of businesses.

The major difference in job order costing for a service organization and a manufacturing firm is that most service organizations use an insignificant amount of materials relative to the value of labor for each job. In such cases, direct material may be treated (for the sake of convenience) as part of overhead rather than accounted for separately. As indicated in the News Note on p. 296, a few service organizations, such as in the medical industry, may use some costly materials. The News Note also presents an interesting managerial issue: the possible substitution of labor for material (medicine).

Accountants in some service companies may need to trace only direct labor to jobs and allocate all other production costs. Allocations of these costs may be accomplished most effectively by using a predetermined rate per direct labor hour or, if wage rates are approximately equal throughout the firm, per direct labor dollar. Other cost drivers may also be used as possible overhead allocation bases.

Job Number _____ _602_____

Customer Name and Address:

Gulfcoast Boatworks
9901 Gulfcoast Road
Corpus Christi, TX

Description of Job:

500 lexan hatch covers
Size: 12" × 17"; Product to include
aluminum edge trim and mounting hardware

Contract Agreement Date: *3/25/97*
Scheduled Starting Date: *4/5/97*
Agreed Completion Date: *6/1/97*
Actual Completion Date: *5/29/97*
Delivery Instructions: *Deliver by rail*

Contract Price: *$35,250*

Cutting & Forming

Direct Material (Est. $12,140) (includes hardware)			Direct Labor (Est. $3,100)			Overhead based on					
						# of labor hours (Est. $1,500)			# of machine hours (Est. $1,240)		
Date	Source	Amount	Date	Source	Amount	Date	Source	Amount	Date	Source	Amount
4/5	MR #344	$ 876	4/8	payroll	$170	4/30	payroll	$315	4/30	machine hour meters	$465
4/18	MR #352	2,306	4/22	payroll	481						

(other similar entries would be made throughout production)

Edge Polishing
(same format as above but with different OH rates)

Lamination
(same format as above but with different OH rates)

SUMMARY

	Cutting & Forming		Edge Polishing		Lamination	
	Actual	Budget	Actual	Budget	Actual	Budget
Direct material	$12,315	$12,140	$ 1,190	$ 1,200	$ 990	$ 975
Direct labor	3,255	3,100	2,050	2,100	1,257	1,234
Overhead	1,575	1,500	390	400	456	450
Overhead	1,271	1,240	500	520	373	370
Totals	$18,416	$17,980	$ 4,130	$ 4,220	$ 3,076	$ 3,029

		Actual	Budget
Final Costs:	Cutting & Forming	$18,416	$17,980
	Edge Polishing	4,130	4,220
	Lamination	3,076	3,029
	Totals	$25,622	$25,229

EXHIBIT 7–6

Georgia Plastics
Completed Job Order
Cost Sheet

Counseling versus Medicine

In an effort to control costs, some health care providers have turned to treating depression with medicine rather than psychology. A recent study analyzed the effects of this shift.

The study discovered that treatment for depression was often provided by the primary care physician rather than a specialist. The primary care physician was likely to treat the depression with tranquilizers rather than with either an antidepressant drug or counseling, and the average cost of treatment was $1,060. The study concluded that if the primary care physician followed expert guidelines in treating depression, costs of treatment would rise, on average, by $370 per patient. However, the patient's functional status would be substantially enhanced. The study found that when depression is treated by a psychiatrist, the average cost of treatment was $3,760 with functional improvement in the range of 32 percent.

The study highlighted one of the interesting aspects of treating depression: the various alternative methods of treatment and the potential substitution of labor for drug costs, and the possible substitution of one type of professional labor for another type. Adding complexity to the cost considerations is the varying level of effectiveness of the alternative treatment combinations.

SOURCE: Ron Winslow, "Technology & Health: Study Challenges Shifting Treatment of Depression to Family Physicians," *Wall Street Journal* (January 4, 1995), p. B8. Reprinted by permission of *The Wall Street Journal*, © 1995 Dow Jones & Company, Inc. All Rights Reserved Worldwide.

JOB ORDER COSTING TO ASSIST MANAGEMENT

Job order costing is useful to managers in planning, controlling, decision making, and evaluating performance. Knowing the costs of individual jobs allows managers to better estimate future job costs and establish realistic bids and selling prices. The use of budgets and standards in a job order costing system provides information against which actual costs can be compared at regular time intervals for control purposes. These comparisons can also furnish some performance evaluation information. The following two examples demonstrate the usefulness of job order costing to managers.

Bradley & Associates

Bradley & Associates is an engineering firm that specializes in concrete structures. The firm has a diverse set of clients and types of jobs. Josh Bradley is the founder and president. Mr. Bradley wanted to know which clients were the most profitable and which were the least profitable. To determine this information, he requested a breakdown of profits per job measured on both a percentage and an absolute dollar basis.

Mr. Bradley discovered that the company did not maintain records of costs per client-job. Costs had been accumulated only by type—travel, entertainment, and so forth. Ms. Tobias, the sales manager, was certain that the largest profits came from the company's largest accounts. A careful job cost analysis found that the largest accounts contributed the most revenue to the firm, but the smallest percentage and absolute dollars of incremental profits. Until the president requested this information, no one had totaled the costs of recruiting each client or the travel, entertainment, and other costs associated with maintaining each client.

A company that has a large number of jobs that vary in size, time, or effort may not know which jobs are responsible for disproportionately large costs. Job order costing can assist in determining which jobs are truly profitable and can help managers to better monitor costs. As a result of the cost analysis, Mr. Bradley changed the company's marketing strategy. The firm began concentrating its efforts on smaller clients who were located in closer proximity to the primary office. These efforts caused profits to substantially increase because significantly fewer costs were incurred for travel and entertainment. A job order costing system was implemented to track the per-period and total costs associated with each client. Unprofitable accounts were dropped, and account managers felt more responsibility to monitor and control costs related to their particular accounts.

Sanford & Son Yacht Company

The Sanford & Son Yacht Company manufactures three types of boats to customer specifications.[7] Before job order costing was instituted, the managers had no means of determining the costs associated with the production of each type of boat. When a customer provided yacht specifications and asked what the selling price would be, managers merely estimated costs in what they felt was a reasonable manner. In fact, during the construction process, no costs were assigned to Work in Process Inventory; all production costs were sent to Finished Goods Inventory.

After implementing a job order costing system, Sanford & Son Yacht Company had better control over its inventory, better inventory valuations for financial statements, and better information with which to prevent part stockouts (not having parts in inventory) and production stoppages. The job order costing system provided managers with information on what work was currently in process and at what cost. From this information, they were better able to judge whether additional work could be accepted and when current work would be completed. Because job order costing assigns costs to Work in Process Inventory, balance sheet figures were more accurate. As material was issued to production, the use of material requisition forms produced inventory records that were more current and reflective of raw material quantities on hand. Finally, the use of a job order costing system gave managers an informed means by which to estimate costs and more adequately price future jobs.

Whether an entity is a manufacturer or service organization that tailors its output to customer specifications, company management will find that job order costing techniques will help in the managerial functions. This cost system is useful for determining the cost of goods produced or services rendered in companies that are able to attach costs to specific jobs. As product variety increases, the size of production lots for many items shrinks, and job order costing becomes more applicable. Custom-made goods may become the norm rather than the exception in an environment that relies on flexible manufacturing systems and computer-integrated manufacturing.

REVISITING

FM Corporation

FM Corporation typifies many firms that use job order costing—diversity of customers and diversity of products. The company's expertise is in the conversion of various types of plastic resins into finished products. To survive, FM has to be able to efficiently produce products in small lot sizes. This requirement mandates that the company be capable of low cost product design and fast, low cost production setups. Accordingly, FM has adopted advanced production and design technology. For example, the firm uses computerized production scheduling and a statistical quality control system. Also, in 1996 the company reorganized its plant layout and added a paint line. The new painting equipment expands the ability of the firm to deliver products to the demands of its customers.

FM Corporation concentrates its sales efforts on finding ways to provide more products to its existing customer base rather than searching for new customers. This approach allows the company to concentrate its sales efforts on delivering increased value to a select group of customers and to have a more complete

[7] This example is based on an article by Leonard A. Robinson and Loudell Ellis Robinson, "Steering a Boat Maker Through Cost Shoals," *Management Accounting* (January 1983), pp. 60–66.

understanding of its customers' needs. This strategy is obviously working for the company as it was recently named supplier of the year by its largest customer. And, the company's customers include America's best: Xerox, Motorola, Abbott Labs, and AT&T.

Because each type of product produced requires a unique set of inputs in terms of material quantity and conversion activities, the costs of producing each type will also be unique. The only way a company like FM Corporation can determine a fair price for each of these diverse products is to have some method of tracking costs to the products produced. A simple averaging of costs across all product types made will provide unacceptable results because the unique production requirements of each product type is ignored by such a method. By using job order costing, costs can be traced to specific products and a sound basis is provided for both pricing products and controlling costs.

SOURCES: Anonymous, "FM Updates Its Facility," *Plastics News* (April 15, 1996), p. 68; Bradford McKee, "Ties That Bind Large and Small," *Nations Business* (February 1992), pp. 24–26; Connecticut Mutual Insurance Company and The U.S. Chamber of Commerce in Association with The Blue Chip Enterprise Initiative," *Strengthening America's Competitiveness* (Warner Books, 1991), pp. 89–90.

CHAPTER SUMMARY

A cost accounting system should be compatible with the manufacturing environment in which it is used. Job order costing and process costing are two traditional cost accounting systems. Job order costing is used in companies that make a limited quantity of products or provide a limited number of services uniquely tailored to customer specifications. This system is especially appropriate and useful for many service businesses, such as advertising, legal, and architectural firms. Process costing is appropriate in production situations in which large quantities of homogeneous products are manufactured on a continuous flow basis.

A job order costing system considers the "job" as the cost object for which costs are accumulated. A job can consist of one or more units of output, and job costs are accumulated in a job order cost sheet. Job order cost sheets for uncompleted jobs serve as the Work in Process Inventory subsidiary ledger. Cost sheets for completed jobs not yet delivered to customers constitute the Finished Goods Inventory subsidiary ledger, and cost sheets for completed and sold jobs compose the Cost of Goods Sold subsidiary ledger.

In an actual or a normal cost job order costing system, direct material and direct labor are traced, respectively, using material requisition forms and employee time sheets, specifically (during the period and for each department) to individual jobs in process. Service companies may not attempt to trace direct material to jobs, but consider the costs of direct material as part of overhead. Tracing is not considered necessary when the materials cost is insignificant in relation to the job's total cost.

In an actual cost system, actual overhead is assigned to jobs. More commonly, however, a normal costing system is used in which overhead is applied using one or more predetermined overhead rates multiplied by the actual activity base(s) incurred. Overhead is applied to Work in Process Inventory at the end of the month or when the job is complete, whichever is earlier.

Job order costing assists management in planning, controlling, decision making, and evaluating performance. It allows managers to trace costs associated with specific current jobs to better estimate costs for future jobs. Additionally, managers using job order costing can better control the costs associated with current production, especially if comparisons with budgets or standards are used. Attachment of costs to jobs is also necessary to price jobs that are contracted on a cost-plus basis. Last, because costs are accumulated by jobs, managers can more readily determine which jobs or types of jobs are most profitable to the organization.

APPENDIX

Job Order Costing Using Standard Costs

The Georgia Plastics example in the chapter illustrates the use of actual historical cost data for direct material and direct labor in a job order costing system. However, using actual direct material and direct labor costs may cause the cost of similar units to fluctuate from period to period or job to job because of changes in component costs. Use of standard costs for direct material and direct labor can minimize the effects of such cost fluctuations in the same way that predetermined rates do for overhead costs.

A standard cost system determines product cost by using, in the inventory accounts, predetermined norms for prices and/or quantities of component elements. After production is complete, the standard production cost is compared with the actual production cost to determine the efficiency of the production process. A difference between the actual quantity, price, or rate and its related standard is called a variance.

Standards can be used in a job order system only if a company typically engages in jobs that produce fairly similar products. One type of standard job order costing system uses standards only for input prices of material and/or rates for labor. This process is reasonable if all output relies on basically the same kinds of material and/ or labor. If standards are used for price or rate amounts only, the debits to Work in Process Inventory become a combination of actual and standard information: actual quantities at standard prices or rates.

Smith Brothers, a house-painting company located on the West Coast, illustrates the use of price and rate standards. Management has decided that, because of the climate, one specific brand of paint (costing $30 per gallon) is the best to use. Painters employed by the company are paid $12 per hour. These two amounts can be used as price and rate standards for Smith Brothers. No standards can be set for the quantity of paint that will be used on a job or the amount of time the job will require, because those items will vary with the quantity and texture of wood on the structure and the size of the structure being painted.

Assume that Smith Brothers paints a house requiring 50 gallons of paint and 80 hours of labor time. The standard paint and labor costs, respectively, are $1,500 (50 × $30) and $960 (80 × $12). Assume Smith Brothers bought the paint when it was on sale, so the actual price paid was $27 per gallon or a total of $1,350. Comparing this price to the standard results in a $150 favorable material price variance (50

Veterinarians can use standard costs to a certain extent in a job order system. For example, the cost of performing tests or providing medications may be standardized by type or size of animal.

gallons at $3 per gallon). If the actual labor rate paid to painters was $11 per hour, there would be an $80 favorable (80 hours at $1 per hour) labor rate variance.

Other job order companies produce output that is homogeneous enough to allow standards to be developed for both quantities and prices for material and labor. Such companies usually use distinct production runs for numerous similar products. In such circumstances, the output is homogeneous for each run, unlike the heterogeneous output of Smith Brothers.

Ace Manufacturing, Inc., is a job order manufacturer that uses both price and quantity material and labor standards. Ace manufactures wooden flower boxes that are retailed through several chains of garden supply stores. The boxes are contracted for on a job order basis, because the retailing chains tend to demand changes in style, color, and size with each spring gardening season. Ace produces the boxes in distinct production runs each month for each retail chain. Price and quantity standards for direct material and direct labor have been established and are used to compare the estimated and actual costs of monthly production runs for each type of box produced.

The standards set for boxes sold to Wolf Creek Mountain Gardens are as follows:

8 linear feet of 1" × 10" redwood plank at $.60 per linear foot

1.4 direct labor hours at $9 per direct labor hour

In June, 2,000 boxes were produced for Wolf Creek. Actual wood used was 16,300 linear feet that was purchased at $.58 per linear foot. Direct labor employees worked 2,700 hours at an average labor rate of $9.10.

From this information, it can be concluded that Ace used 300 linear feet of redwood above the standard quantity for the job [16,300 − (8 × 2,000)]. This usage causes an unfavorable material quantity variance of $180 at the $.60 standard price ($.60 × 300 linear feet). The actual redwood used was purchased at $.02 below the standard price per linear foot, which results in a $326 ($.02 × 16,300) favorable material price variance.

The actual DLHs used were 100 less than standard [2,700 − (1.4 hours × 2,000)], which results in a favorable labor quantity variance of $900 ($9 standard rate × 100 hours). The work crew earned $.10 per hour above standard, which translates to a $270 unfavorable labor rate variance ($.10 × 2,700). A summary of variances follows:

Direct material quantity variance	$ 180 unfavorable
Direct material price variance	(326) favorable
Direct labor quantity variance	(900) favorable
Direct labor rate variance	270 unfavorable
Net variance (cost less than expected)	$(776) favorable

From a financial perspective, Ace controlled its total material and labor costs well on the Wolf Creek job.

Variances can be computed for actual-to-standard differences regardless of whether standards have been established for both quantities and prices or for prices/rates only. Standard costs for material and labor provide the same types of benefits as predetermined overhead rates: more timely information and comparisons against actual amounts.

A predetermined overhead rate is, in essence, a type of standard. It establishes a constant amount of overhead assignable as a component of product cost and eliminates any immediate need for actual overhead information in the calculation of product cost. More is presented on standards and variances in Chapter 11.

Standard cost job order systems are reasonable substitutes for actual or normal costing systems as long as the standard cost systems provide managers with useful information. Any type of product costing system is acceptable in practice if it is effective and efficient in serving the company's unique production needs, provides the information desired by management, and can be implemented at a cost that is reasonable when compared to the benefits to be received. These criteria apply equally well to both manufacturers and service companies.

KEY TERMS

SOLUTION STRATEGIES

BASIC JOURNAL ENTRIES IN A JOB ORDER COSTING SYSTEM:

Raw Material Inventory XXX
    Accounts Payable XXX
To record the purchase of raw materials.

Work in Process Inventory—Dept. (Job #) XXX
Manufacturing Overhead XXX
    Raw Material Inventory XXX
To record the issuance of direct and indirect materials requisitioned for a specific job.

Work in Process Inventory—Dept. (Job #) XXX
Manufacturing Overhead XXX
    Wages Payable XXX
To record direct and indirect labor payroll for production employees.

Manufacturing Overhead XXX
    Various accounts XXX
To record the incurrence of actual overhead costs. (Account titles to be credited must be specified in an actual journal entry.)

Work in Process Inventory—Dept. (Job #) XXX
    Manufacturing Overhead XXX
To apply overhead to a specific job. (This may be actual OH or OH applied using a predetermined rate. Predetermined OH is applied at job completion or end of period, whichever is earlier.)

Finished Goods Inventory (Job #) XXX
    Work in Process Inventory XXX
To record the transfer of completed goods from WIP to FG.

Accounts Receivable YYY
    Sales YYY
To record the sale of goods on account.

Cost of Goods Sold XXX
    Finished Goods Inventory XXX
To record the cost of the goods sold.

DEMONSTRATION PROBLEM

Offshore Solutions is a newly formed firm that conducts research in the Gulf of Mexico for its customers. Organizationally, the firm is composed of two departments: Offshore Operations and Lab Research. The Offshore Operations Department is responsible for gathering test samples and drilling operations on the ocean floor. The Lab Research Department is responsible for analysis of samples and other data gathered by Offshore Operations.

In its first month of operations (March 1998), Offshore Solutions obtained contracts for three research projects:

Job 1: drill, collect, and analyze samples from 10 sites for a major oil company

Job 2: collect and analyze samples for specific toxins off the coast of Louisiana for the U.S. government

Job 3: evaluate 12 existing offshore wells for the presence of oil seepage for a major oil company

Offshore Solutions contracts with its customers on a cost-plus basis; that is, the price charged is equal to costs plus a profit equal to 10 percent of costs. The firm uses a job order costing system based on normal costs. Overhead is applied in the Offshore Operations Department at the predetermined rate of $2,000 per hour of research vessel use (RVH). In the Lab Research Department, overhead is applied at the predetermined rate of $45 per professional labor hour (PLH).

For March 1998, significant transactions are summarized below.

1. Materials and test components were purchased on account: $110,000.
2. Materials were requisitioned for use in the three research projects by the Offshore Operations Department (all of these materials are regarded as direct): Job #1— $40,000; Job #2—$28,000; and Job #3—$10,000. Materials were issued to the Lab Research Department: Job #1—$8,000; Job #2—$6,000; and Job #3— $4,500.
3. The time sheets and payroll summaries indicated the following direct labor costs were incurred:

	OFFSHORE OPERATIONS	LAB RESEARCH
Job #1	$60,000	$56,000
Job #2	50,000	20,000
Job #3	45,000	16,000

4. Indirect research costs were incurred in each department:

	OFFSHORE OPERATIONS	LAB RESEARCH
Labor	$120,000	$10,000
Utilities/Fuel	290,000	5,000
Depreciation	330,000	80,000

5. Overhead was applied based on the predetermined overhead rates in effect in each department. Offshore Operations had 360 RVHs (170 RVHs on Job #1; 90 RVHs on Job #2; and 100 RVHs on Job #3), and Lab Research worked 2,300 PLHs (1,400 PLHs on Job #1; 500 PLHs on Job #2; and 400 PLHs on Job #3) for the year.
6. Job #1 was completed and cash was collected for the agreed upon price of cost plus 10 percent. At the end of the month, Jobs #2 and #3 were only partially complete.
7. Any underapplied or overapplied overhead is assigned to Cost of Goods Sold.

Required:

a. Record the journal entries for transactions 1 through 7.
b. As of the end of March 1998, determine the total cost assigned to Jobs #2 and #3.

Solution to Demonstration Problem

a. 1. Raw Material Inventory   110,000
         Accounts Payable   110,000
       To record purchase of materials.

2. WIP Inventory—Offshore Operations (Job #1)   40,000
   WIP Inventory—Offshore Operations (Job #2)   28,000
   WIP Inventory—Offshore Operations (Job #3)   10,000
      Raw Material Inventory   78,000
      To record requisition and issuance of
      materials to Offshore Operations.

   WIP Inventory—Lab Research (Job #1)   8,000
   WIP Inventory—Lab Research (Job #2)   6,000
   WIP Inventory—Lab Research (Job #3)   4,500
      Raw Material Inventory   18,500
      To record requisition and issuance of
      materials to Lab Research.

3. WIP Inventory—Offshore Operations (Job #1)   60,000
   WIP Inventory—Offshore Operations (Job #2)   50,000
   WIP Inventory—Offshore Operations (Job #3)   45,000
      Wages Payable   155,000
      To record direct labor costs for Offshore
      Operations.

   WIP Inventory—Lab Research (Job #1)   56,000
   WIP Inventory—Lab Research (Job #2)   20,000
   WIP Inventory—Lab Research (Job #3)   16,000
      Wages Payable   92,000
      To record direct labor costs for Lab
      Research.

4. Research Overhead—Offshore Operations   740,000
   Research Overhead—Lab Research   95,000
      Wages Payable   130,000
      Utilities/Fuel Payable   295,000
      Accumulated Depreciation   410,000
      To record indirect research costs.

5. WIP Inventory—Offshore Operations (Job #1)   340,000
   WIP Inventory—Offshore Operations (Job #2)   180,000
   WIP Inventory—Offshore Operations (Job #3)   200,000
      Research Overhead—Offshore Operations   720,000
      To record application of research overhead.

   WIP Inventory—Lab Research (Job #1)   63,000
   WIP Inventory—Lab Research (Job #2)   22,500
   WIP Inventory—Lab Research (Job #3)   18,000
      Research Overhead—Lab Research   103,500
      To record application of research overhead.

6. Finished Goods Inventory*   567,000
      WIP Inventory—Offshore Operations   440,000
      WIP Inventory—Lab Research   127,000
      To record completion of Job #1.

   Cash   623,700
      Research Revenues**   623,700
      To record sale of Job #1.

   Cost of Goods Sold   567,000
      Finished Goods Inventory   567,000

7. Cost of Goods Sold   11,500
        Research Overhead—Lab Research   8,500
                Research Overhead—Offshore Operations   20,000
        To assign underapplied and overapplied
        overhead to cost of goods sold.

* Job #1 costs = $40,000 + $8,000 + $60,000 + $56,000 + $340,000 + $63,000 = $567,000
** Revenue, Job #1 = $567,000 × 1.10 = $623,700

b.

	JOB #2	JOB #3
Direct material—Offshore Operations	$ 28,000	$ 10,000
Direct labor—Offshore Operations	50,000	45,000
Research overhead—Offshore Operations	180,000	200,000
Direct material—Lab Research	6,000	4,500
Direct labor—Lab Research	20,000	16,000
Research overhead—Lab Research	22,500	18,000
Totals	$306,500	$293,500

QUESTIONS

1. When a company produces custom products to the specifications of its customers, why should it not aggregate costs across customer orders to determine the prices to be charged?

2. What production conditions are necessary for a company to use job order costing?

3. What is the alternative to the use of a job order costing system? In what type of production environment would this alternative costing system be found?

4. Identify the three valuation methods discussed in the chapter. What are the differences among these methods?

5. In a job order costing system, what is a job?

6. What are the three stages of production of a job? Of what use is cost information pertaining to completed jobs?

7. What are the principal documents used in a job order costing system and what are their purposes?

8. Why is the material requisition form an important document in a company's audit trail?

9. What is a job order cost sheet, and what information does it contain? How do job order cost sheets relate to control accounts for Work in Process, Finished Goods, and Cost of Goods Sold?

10. Of what use to management are job order cost sheets? Why do some job order cost sheets contain columns for both budgeted and actual costs?

11. "Because the costs of each job are included in the job order cost sheet, they do not need to be recorded in the general ledger." Is this statement true or false, and why?

12. Which document in a job order costing system would show the amount of overtime worked by a specific individual? Explain.

13. Is an actual overhead application rate better than a predetermined overhead rate? Why or why not?

14. What creates underapplied or overapplied overhead when applying overhead to jobs?

15. What is the principal difference between service and manufacturing firms in job order costing?

16. How is the cost of goods sold determined in a company that uses job order costing?

17. *(Appendix)* What differences exist between job order costing based on actual costs and job order costing based on standard costs? Why would a company use a standard cost job order system?

18. *(Appendix)* If a company produces a given type of product only one time, will standard costing be as useful as if the company continually produces the same type of product? Explain.

19. *(Appendix)* How does a firm use information on "variances" in a standard costing system to control costs?

EXERCISES

20. *(Classifying)* For each of the following firms, determine whether it is more likely to use job order or process costing. This firm
    a. does custom printing.
    b. manufactures bottled soft drinks. *proass*
    c. is involved in landscape architecture. *job*
    d. is an automobile repair shop.
    e. provides public accounting services.
    f. manufactures hair spray and hand lotion. *proass*
    g. is a hospital. *job*
    h. cans vegetables and fruits. *process*
    i. mass produces notebook paper. *proass*
    j. provides property management services for a variety of real estate developments. *job*

21. *(Journal entries)* Olson Inc. produces custom-made trash containers for recycling waste. During June 1997, the following information was obtained relating to operations and production:
    1. Direct material purchased on account, $190,000.
    2. Direct material issued to jobs, $163,800.
    3. Direct labor hours incurred, 3,400. All direct factory employees were paid $18 per hour.
    4. Actual factory overhead costs incurred for the month totaled $82,200. This overhead consisted of $18,000 of supervisory salaries, $35,000 of depreciation charges, $7,200 of insurance, $12,500 of indirect material, and $9,500 of utilities. Salaries, insurance, and utilities were paid in cash, and indirect material was removed from the supplies account.
    5. Overhead is applied to production at the rate of $25 per direct labor hour.

    The beginning balances of Raw Material Inventory and Work in Process Inventory were $8,300 and $22,300, respectively. The ending balance in Work in Process Inventory was $4,700.
    a. Prepare journal entries for the above transactions.
    b. Determine the balances in Raw Material Inventory and Work in Process Inventory at the end of the month.
    c. Determine the cost of the goods completed during June. If 2,000 similar units were completed, what was the cost per unit?
    d. What amount of underapplied or overapplied overhead exists at the end of June?

22. *(Journal entries; cost flows)* Prefab Storage produces customized storage buildings that serve the midwest U.S. market. For February 1997, the company incurred the following costs:

Direct material purchased on account		$19,000
Direct material used for jobs		
Job #217	$11,200	
Job #218	1,800	
Other jobs	13,400	26,400

Direct labor costs for month

Job #217	$ 2,600	
Job #218	3,500	
Other jobs	4,900	11,000
Actual overhead costs for February		18,900

The February beginning balance in Work in Process Inventory was $4,200, which consisted of $2,800 for Job #217 and $1,400 for Job #218. The February beginning balance in Direct Material Inventory was $12,300.

Actual overhead is applied to jobs on the basis of direct labor cost. Job #217 was completed and transferred to finished goods during February. It was then sold for cash at 140 percent of cost.

a. Prepare journal entries to record the above information.

b. Determine the February ending balance in Work in Process Inventory and the amount of the balance related to Job #218.

 23. *(Cost flows)* Canadian Steel began operations on March 1, 1997. Its Work in Process Inventory account on March 31 appeared as follows:

WORK IN PROCESS INVENTORY

Direct material	$184,800	Cost of completed jobs	??
Direct labor	128,000		
Applied overhead	115,200		

The company applies overhead on the basis of direct labor cost. Only one job was still in process on March 31. That job had $44,200 in direct material and $31,200 in direct labor cost assigned to it.

a. What was the predetermined overhead application rate?

b. How much cost was transferred out for jobs completed during March?

24. *(Normal versus actual costing)* For fiscal year 1998, Synthetic Solutions estimated it would incur total overhead costs of $1,200,000 and work 40,000 machine hours. During January 1998, the company worked exclusively on one job, Job #1211. It incurred January costs as follows:

Direct material usage		$121,000
Direct labor (1,400 hours)		30,800
Manufacturing overhead:		
Rent	$11,200	
Utilities	15,200	
Insurance	32,100	
Labor	15,500	
Depreciation	23,700	
Maintenance	10,800	
Total OH		108,500

Machine hours worked in January: 3,400

a. Assuming the company uses an actual cost system, compute the January costs assigned to Job #1211.

b. Assuming the company uses a normal cost system, compute the January costs assigned to Job #1211.

c. What is the major factor driving the difference between your answers in parts a and b?

25. *(Cost flows)* Jacob's Well is a small firm that manufactures decorative "wishing wells" for residential and commercial applications. The firm applies overhead to jobs at a rate of 120 percent of direct labor cost. On December 31, 1997, a flood destroyed many of the firm's computerized cost records. Only the following information for 1997 was available from the records:

DIRECT MATERIAL INVENTORY		
Beg. balance $12,300		
Purchases		
?		?
End. balance $4,100		

WORK IN PROCESS INVENTORY		
Beg. balance $28,000		
Direct Mat. ?		?
Direct Lab. 90,000		
Over-head		
$24,000		

FINISHED GOODS INVENTORY		
Beg. balance $45,000		
Goods completed ?	$685,000	
End. balance $42,000		

COST OF GOODS SOLD	
?	

As the accountant of Jacob's Well, you have been asked to find the following:

a. Cost of goods sold for the year.

b. Cost of goods completed during the year.

c. Cost of direct material used during the year.

d. Amount of applied factory overhead during the year.

e. Cost of direct material purchased during the year.

26. *(Departmental overhead rates)* The Lunford Paving Company uses a predetermined overhead rate to apply overhead to jobs, and the company employs a job order costing system. Overhead is applied to jobs in the Mixing Department based on the number of machine hours used, whereas Paving Department overhead is applied on the basis of direct labor hours. In December 1997, the company estimated the following data for its two departments for 1998:

	MIXING DEPARTMENT	PAVING DEPARTMENT
Direct labor hours	1,000	3,500 ✓
Machine hours	7,500 ✓	1,500
Budgeted overhead cost	$60,000	$98,000

a. Compute the predetermined overhead rate that should be used in each department of the Lunford Paving Company.

b. Job #116 was started and completed during March 1998. The job cost sheet shows the following information:

	MIXING DEPARTMENT	PAVING DEPARTMENT
Direct material	$5,800	$700
Direct labor cost	$ 60	$525
Direct labor hours	12	60
Machine hours	80	22

c. Compute the overhead applied to Job #116 for each department and in total.

d. If the company had computed a companywide rate for overhead rather than departmental rates, do you feel that such a rate would be indicative of the actual overhead cost of each job? Explain.

27. *(Job cost and pricing)* Jason Hart is an attorney who employs a job order costing system related to his client engagements. Hart is currently working on a case for Janice Keene. During the first 4 months of 1997, Hart logged 85 hours on the Keene case.

In addition to direct hours spent by Hart, his secretary has worked 14 hours typing and copying 126 pages of documents related to the Keene case. Hart's secretary works 160 hours per month and is paid a salary of $1,800 per month. The average cost per copy is $.04 for paper, toner, and machine rental. Telephone charges for long-distance calls on the case totaled $165.50. Last, Hart has estimated that total office overhead for rent, utilities, parking, and so on, amount to $7,200 per month and that, during a normal month, he is at the office 120 hours.

   a. Hart feels that his time, at a minimum, is worth $40 per hour, and he wishes to cover all direct and allocated indirect costs related to a case. What minimum charge per hour (rounded to the nearest dollar) should Hart charge Keene? (*Hint:* include office overhead.)
   b. All the hours that Hart spends at the office are not necessarily billable hours. In addition, Hart did not take into consideration certain other expenses such as license fees, country club dues, automobile costs, and so on when he determined the amount of overhead per month. Therefore, to cover nonbillable time as well as other costs, Hart feels that billing each client for direct costs plus allocated indirect costs plus 50 percent margin on his time and overhead is reasonable. What will Hart charge Keene in total for the time spent on her case?

28. *(Underapplied or overapplied overhead)* For 1998, Specialty Advertising Products Company applied overhead to jobs using a predetermined overhead rate of $11.60 per machine hour. This rate was derived by dividing the company's total budgeted overhead of $278,400 by the 24,000 machine hours anticipated for the year.

At the end of 1998, the company's manufacturing overhead control account had debits totaling $283,300. Actual machine hours for the year totaled 25,100.

   a. How much overhead should be debited to Work in Process Inventory for 1998?
   b. Is overhead underapplied or overapplied and by how much?
   c. Job #47 consumed 1,400 machine hours during 1998. How much overhead should be assigned to this job for the year?
   d. Describe the disposition of the underapplied or overapplied overhead determined in part b.

29. *(Assigning costs to jobs)* Minnesota Hydraulics uses a job order costing system in which overhead is applied to jobs at a predetermined rate of $1.60 per direct labor dollar. During April 1998, the company spent $6,900 on direct labor related to Job #2144. In addition, the company incurred direct material costs of $24,800 on this job during the month. Budgeted factory overhead for the company for the year was $580,000.

   a. Give the journal entry to apply overhead to all jobs if April's total direct labor cost was $30,100.
   b. How much overhead from part a was assigned to Job #2144?
   c. If Job #2144 had a balance of $14,350 on April 1, what was the balance on April 30?
   d. Demonstrate how the company arrived at the predetermined overhead rate. Include the amount of budgeted direct labor costs for the year in your answer.

30. *(Assigning costs to jobs, cost flows)* Joanna's Custom Designs, an interior decorating firm, uses a job order costing system and applies overhead to jobs using a predetermined rate of 60 percent of direct labor cost. At the beginning of June 1998, Job #918 was the only job in process. Costs of Job #918 included direct

material of $16,500, direct labor of $2,400, and applied overhead of $1,440. During June, the company began work on Jobs #919, #920, and #921 and purchased and issued $34,700 of direct material. Direct labor cost for the month totaled $12,600. Job #920 had not been completed at the end of June, and its direct material and direct labor charges were $6,700 and $1,300, respectively. All the other jobs were completed in June.

  a. What was the total cost of Job #920 as of the end of June 1998?
  b. What was the cost of goods manufactured for June 1998?
  c. If actual overhead for June was $8,700, was the overhead underapplied or overapplied for the month? By how much?

31. *(Assigning costs to jobs)* Joe Show is an advertising consultant. Recently, he has been working with his accountant to develop a formal accounting system. His accountant has suggested the use of a job order costing system to simplify costing procedures. During September, Joe and his staff worked on jobs for the following companies:

	THURSTON COMPANY	BOLLA MANUFACTURING	PLAYSAFE INC.
Direct material cost	$1,500	$2,700	$3,200
Direct labor cost	$900	$3,150	$6,750
Number of ads designed	5	10	15

Joe is able to trace direct material to each job because most of his cost associated with material is related to photography and duplicating. The accountant has told Joe that a reasonable charge for overhead, based on previous information, is $35 per direct labor hour. The normal labor cost per hour is $45.

  a. Determine the total cost for each of the advertising accounts for the month.
  b. Determine the cost per ad developed for each client.
  c. Joe has been charging $1,500 per ad developed. What was his net income for the month, if actual overhead for the month was $9,200?
  d. Do you have any suggestions for Joe about the way he bills his clients for developing ads?

32. *(Appendix)* Sue's Custom Publishing incurred the following direct material costs in November 1998 for high-volume routine print jobs:

Actual unit purchase price	$.025 per sheet
Quantity purchased in November	480,000 sheets
Quantity used in November	480,000 sheets
Standard quantity allowed for good production	460,000 sheets
Standard unit price	$.027 per sheet

Calculate the material price variance and the material quantity variance.

33. *(Appendix)* Atlanta Textiles uses a standard cost system. The company experienced the following results related to direct labor in December 1998:

Actual hours worked	45,500
Actual direct labor rate	$9.25
Standard hours allowed for production	44,200
Standard direct labor rate	$9.75

  a. Calculate the total actual payroll.
  b. Determine the labor rate variance.
  c. Determine the labor quantity variance.

34. *(Appendix)* Allison's Bird Baths employs a job order costing system based on standard costs. For one of its products, a small teak-rimmed concrete bird bath (Product No. 17), the standard costs per unit are as follows:

Direct material	$18
Direct labor	12
Manufacturing overhead	10

a. Record the journal entry for the transfer of direct material into production for 500 units of Product No. 17.

b. Compute the total cost assigned to the 500 units of Product No. 17, and record the journal entry to recognize the completion of the 500 units.

c. Record the journal entries associated with the sale of the 500 units of Product No. 17 for $31,800.

COMMUNICATION ACTIVITIES

35. *(Cost control)* Baltimore Fabricated Steel Products Company produces a variety of steel drums that are used as storage containers for various chemical products. One of the products the firm produces is a 55-gallon drum. In the past year, the company produced this drum on four separate occasions for four different customers. Some financial details of each of the four orders follows.

DATE	JOB NO.	QUANTITY	BID PRICE	BUDGETED COST	ACTUAL COST
Jan. 17	2118	30,000	$150,000	$120,000	$145,000
Mar. 13	2789	25,000	125,000	100,000	122,000
Oct. 20	4300	40,000	200,000	160,000	193,000
Dec. 3	4990	35,000	175,000	140,000	174,000

Baltimore Fabricated Steel Products Company uses a job order costing system and obtains jobs based on competitive bidding. For each project, a budget is developed. As the controller of the company, write a memo to company management describing any problems that you perceive in the data presented and steps to be taken to eliminate the recurrence of these problems.

36. *(Production and marketing environment)* When it comes to tortillas, Mexicans and Americans have distinctly different tastes. Americans are content to purchase mass-produced, prepackaged tortillas from their local grocery stores. Regional and national brands dominate sales. *In Mexico, more than 95 percent of all tortillas are sold in little shops licensed by the government. These outlets, many grinding tortillas on hand-powered conveyor belts, are virtual monopolies in their neighborhoods, with a captive market that so far has resisted modern sales efforts.*

[SOURCE: Joel Millman, "Mexican Tortilla Firms Stage U.S. Bake-Off," *Wall Street Journal* (May 10, 1996), p. A6. Reprinted by permission of *The Wall Street Journal*, © 1996 Dow Jones & Company, Inc. All Rights Reserved Worldwide.]

Assume that you are involved in developing a strategy for your employer, a U.S. food company, to produce tortillas. You are considering competing in both the United States and Mexico. Write a brief report recommending how your company should produce and market tortillas in each country. Also, describe the product costing system that you would recommend for each country.

37. *(Cost manipulation)* Excel Communications is a direct sales marketer of long-distance phone services. The company earns revenues by selling long-distance services to new subscribers. The company is preparing to "go public" through an initial public offering (IPO) of its stock. As with any IPO, the trick for an investment analyst is to determine the value of the stock.

One of the controversial valuation issues for Excel is how to treat the costs the firm incurs to obtain subscribers. *Excel defers a large portion of the costs it incurs to sign up new subscribers—$85 million in the first 2 months of 1996 alone. Excel* *amortizes these costs and revenue over 12 months as a way to "appropriately match revenues and expenses."*

[SOURCE: Jeff D. Opdyke, "Excel's Accounting Methods Raise Red Flags Among IPO Watchers," *Wall Street Journal* (May 8, 1996), p. T2. Reprinted by permission of *The Wall Street Journal*, © 1996 Dow Jones & Company, Inc. All Rights Reserved Worldwide.]

Put yourself into the position of a stock analyst. Write a report for your investor clientele explaining the effect of Excel's accounting methods on its level of reported net income. Be sure to include a discussion of whether this accounting method provides a fair picture of the firm's "economic earnings."

PROBLEMS

38. *(Journal entries)* Waldrip's Custom Awning Company installs awnings on residential and commercial structures. The company had the following transactions for February 1998:
    - Purchased $220,000 in building (raw) material on account.
    - Issued $185,000 of building (direct) material to jobs.
    - Issued $30,000 of building (indirect) material for use on jobs.
    - Accrued wages payable of $297,000, of which $237,000 could be traced directly to particular jobs.
    - Applied overhead to jobs on the basis of 60 percent of direct labor cost.
    - Completed jobs costing $333,000. For these jobs, revenues of $412,000 were collected.

    Make all appropriate journal entries for the above transactions. (*Hint:* There is no finished goods inventory.)

39. *(Journal entries)* Rutherford Custom Concrete uses a job order costing system based on actual costs. The following transactions relate to a single period in which the beginning inventory of Direct Material Inventory was $30,000, of Work in Process Inventory was $75,000, and of Finished Goods Inventory was $63,000.
    - Direct material purchases on account were $210,000.
    - Direct labor cost for the period totaled $197,500 for 25,000 direct labor hours.
    - Actual overhead costs were $172,000.
    - Actual overhead is applied to production based on direct labor hours.
    - The ending inventory of Direct Material Inventory was $12,000.
    - The ending inventory of Work in Process Inventory was $32,000.
    - Of the goods finished during the period, goods costing $295,000 were sold for $383,000.

    Prepare all journal entries for the above transactions and determine the ending balance in Finished Goods Inventory.

40. *(Journal entries, assigning costs to jobs)* Florida Yachts uses a job order costing system. On September 1, 1998, the company had the following account balances:

Raw Material Inventory	$ 332,400
Work in Process Inventory	1,056,300
Cost of Goods Sold	4,732,000

    Work in Process Inventory is the control account for the job cost subsidiary ledger. On September 1, there were three accounts in the job cost ledger with the following balances:

Job #75	$593,200
Job #78	316,800
Job #82	146,300

The following transactions occurred during September:

Sept. 1   Purchased $940,000 of raw material on account.

Sept. 4   Issued $950,000 of raw material as follows: Job #75, $43,800; Job #78, $227,800; Job #82, $396,600; Job #86, $256,200; indirect material, $25,600.

Sept. 15   Prepared and paid the factory payroll for Sept. 1–15 in the amount of $368,500. Analysis of the payroll for Sept. 1–15 reveals the following information as to where labor effort was devoted:

Job #75	4,430 hours	$ 44,300
Job #78	11,160 hours	111,600
Job #82	12,150 hours	121,500
Job #86	5,540 hours	55,400
Indirect wages		35,700

Sept. 16   Florida Yachts applies manufacturing overhead to jobs at a rate of $7.50 per direct labor hour each time the payroll is made.

Sept. 16   Job #75 was completed and accepted by the customer and billed at a selling price of cost plus 25 percent.

Sept. 20   Paid the following monthly factory bills: utilities, $17,200; rent, $38,300; and accounts payable (accrued in August), $91,000.

Sept. 24   Purchased raw material on account, $412,000.

Sept. 25   Issued raw material as follows: Job #78, $74,400; Job #82, $108,300; Job #86, $192,500; and indirect material, $27,200.

Sept. 30   Recorded additional factory overhead costs as follows: depreciation, $206,500; expired prepaid insurance, $35,100; and accrued taxes and licenses, $13,000.

Sept. 30   Recorded the gross salaries and wages for the factory payroll for Sept. 16–30 of $357,200. Analysis of the payroll follows:

Job #78	8,840 hours	$ 88,400
Job #82	11,650 hours	116,500
Job #86	11,980 hours	119,800
Indirect wages		32,500

Sept. 30   Applied overhead for the second half of the month to jobs.

a. Prepare journal entries for the transactions for September 1998.

b. Use T-accounts to post the information from the journal entries in part a to the job cost subsidiary accounts and to general ledger accounts.

c. Reconcile the September 30 balances in the subsidiary ledger with the Work in Process Inventory account in the general ledger.

d. Determine the amount of underapplied or overapplied overhead for September.

 41. (*Journal entries, cost flows*) Custom Office Products Inc. began 1998 with three jobs in process:

	TYPE OF COST			
JOB NO.	DIRECT MATERIAL	DIRECT LABOR	OVERHEAD	TOTAL
147	$ 38,600	$ 45,700	$17,366	$101,666
151	88,300	104,900	39,862	233,062
153	72,700	84,800	32,224	189,724
Totals	$199,600	$235,400	$89,452	$524,452

During 1998, the following transactions occurred:

1. The firm purchased and paid for $266,000 of raw material.

2. Factory payroll records revealed the following:

- Indirect labor incurred was $27,000.
- Direct labor incurred was $301,400 and was associated with the jobs as follows:

JOB NO.	DIRECT LABOR COST
147	$ 8,700
151	4,400
153	10,500
154	68,300
155	72,500
156	47,300
157	89,700

3. Material requisition forms issued during the year revealed the following:
   - Indirect material issued totaled $38,000.
   - Direct material issued totaled $234,200 and was associated with jobs as follows:

JOB NO.	DIRECT MATERIAL COST
147	$ 7,200
151	3,100
153	8,400
154	51,600
155	59,900
156	36,400
157	67,600

4. Overhead is applied to jobs on the basis of direct labor cost. Management budgeted overhead of $120,000 and total direct labor cost of $300,000 for 1998. Actual total factory overhead costs (including indirect labor and indirect material) for the year were $122,200.
5. Jobs #147 through #155 were completed and delivered to customers, C.O.D. The revenue on these jobs was $1,132,387.
a. Prepare journal entries for all of the above events.
b. Determine ending balances for jobs still in process.
c. Determine cost of jobs completed, adjusted for underapplied or overapplied overhead.

42. *(Simple inventory calculation)* Chicago Custom Tools Company manufactures tools and dies for manufacturing firms. Production information for the first week in November 1998 is as follows:

Work in Process Inventory:

	JOB NO.	MATERIAL	LABOR	MACHINE TIME (OVERHEAD)
Nov. 1	411	$950	18 hours	25 hours
	412	620	5 hours	15 hours
Nov. 7	417	310	4 hours	8 hours

Finished Goods Inventory, Nov. 1: $11,900
Finished Goods Inventory, Nov. 7: $ 0

MATERIAL RECORDS

	INV. 11/1	PURCHASES	ISSUANCES	INV. 11/7
Aluminum	$4,150	$49,150	$29,350	$?
Steel	6,400	13,250	17,100	$?
Other	2,900	11,775	12,950	$?

Direct labor hours worked: 340. Labor cost is $15 per direct labor hour. Machine hours worked: 600; Job #411, 175 hours; Job #412, 240 hours; and Job #417, 185 hours.

Overhead for first week in November:

Depreciation	$ 4,500
Supervisor salaries	7,200
Indirect labor	4,175
Insurance	1,400
Utilities	1,125
Total	$18,400

Overhead is charged to production at a rate of $30 per machine hour. Under-applied or overapplied overhead is treated as an adjustment to Cost of Goods Sold at year-end. (All company jobs are consecutively numbered, and all work not in ending Finished Goods Inventory has been completed and sold.)

a. Calculate the value of beginning Work in Process Inventory.
b. What is the value at the end of November of (1) the three material accounts, (2) Work in Process Inventory, and (3) Cost of Goods Sold?

 43. *(Job cost sheet analysis)* As a candidate for a cost accounting position with Aztec Industrial, you have been asked to take a quiz to demonstrate your knowledge of job order costing. Aztec's job order costing system is based on normal costs and overhead is applied based on direct labor cost. The following records pertaining to May have been provided to you.

JOB NO.	DIRECT MATERIAL	DIRECT LABOR	APPLIED OVERHEAD	TOTAL COST
667	$ 5,901	$1,730	$ 1,990	$ 9,621
669	18,312	1,810	2,082	22,204
670	406	500	575	1,481
671	51,405	9,500	10,925	71,830
672	9,615	550	633	10,798

To explain the missing job number, you are informed that Job #668 had been completed in April. You are also told that Job #667 was the only job in process at the beginning of May. At that time, the job had been assigned $4,300 for direct material and $900 for direct labor. At the end of May, Job #671 had not been completed; all others had. You are to provide answers to the following questions:

a. What is the predetermined overhead rate used by Aztec Industrial?
b. What was the total cost of beginning Work in Process Inventory?
c. What was total prime cost incurred for May?
d. What was cost of goods manufactured for May?

44. *(Departmental rates)* The Houston Custom Tile Corporation has two departments: Mixing and Drying. All jobs go through each department, and the company uses a job order costing system. The company applies overhead to jobs based on labor hours in Mixing and on machine hours in Drying. In December 1997, corporate management estimated the following production data for 1998 in setting its predetermined overhead rates:

	MIXING	DRYING
Machine hours	3,600	52,000
Direct labor hours	44,000	6,200
Departmental overhead	$374,000	$494,000

Two jobs completed during 1998 were #2296 and #2297. The job order cost sheets showed the following information about these jobs:

	JOB #2296	JOB #2297
Direct material cost	$4,875	$6,300
Direct labor hours—Mixing	425	510
Machine hours—Mixing	40	45
Direct labor hours—Drying	20	23
Machine hours—Drying	110	125

Direct labor workers are paid $9 per hour in the Mixing Department and $22 per hour in Drying.

a. Compute the predetermined overhead rates used in Mixing and Drying for 1998.
b. Compute the direct labor cost associated with each job for both departments.
c. Compute the amount of overhead assigned to each job in each department.
d. Determine the total cost of Jobs #2296 and #2297.
e. Actual data for 1998 for each department is presented below. What is the amount of underapplied or overapplied overhead for each department for the year ended December 31, 1998?

	MIXING	DRYING
Machine hours	3,700	53,400
Direct labor hours	43,200	6,300
Overhead	$362,000	$512,000

45. *(Comprehensive)* In May 1998, Tucson Construction Company was the successful bidder on a contract to build a pedestrian overpass in Phoenix. The firm utilizes a job order costing system, and this job was assigned Job #515. The contract price for the overpass was $150,000. The owners of Tucson Construction agreed to a completion date of December 15, 1998, for the contract. The firm's engineering and cost accounting departments estimated the following costs for completion of the overpass: $40,000 for direct material, $45,000 for direct labor, and $27,000 for overhead.

   The firm began work on the overpass in August. During August, direct material cost assigned to Job #515 was $10,300 and direct labor cost associated with Job #515 was $15,840. The firm uses a predetermined overhead rate of 60 percent of direct labor cost. Tucson Construction also worked on several other jobs during August and incurred the following costs:

Direct labor (including Job #515)	$84,000
Indirect labor	9,300
Administrative salaries and wages	6,600 ⁻
Depreciation on construction equipment	4,800
Depreciation on office equipment	1,300 ~
Client entertainment (on accounts payable)	1,850 ⁻
Advertising for firm (paid in cash)	1,100 –
Indirect material (from supplies inventory)	3,100
Miscellaneous expenses (design related; to be paid in the following month)	1,700
Accrued utilities (for office, $300; for construction, $900)	1,200

   During August, Tucson Construction completed several jobs that had been in process before the beginning of the month. These completed jobs generated $104,000 of revenues for the company. The related job cost sheets showed costs associated with those jobs of $71,500. At the beginning of August, Tucson Construction had Work in Process Inventory of $45,300.

   a. Prepare a job order cost sheet for Job #515, including all job details, and post the appropriate cost information for August.
   b. Prepare journal entries for the above information.

c. Prepare a Schedule of Cost of Goods Manufactured for August for Tucson Construction Company.

d. Assuming the company pays income tax at a 36 percent rate, prepare an income statement for August.

46. *(Comprehensive)* The Steel Sentinel designs and manufactures perimeter fencing for large retail and commercial buildings. Each order goes through three stages: design, production, and installation. There were three jobs started and completed during the first week in May 1998. There were no jobs in process at the end of April 1998. Information for the three departments for the first week in May follows:

DEPARTMENT

JOB #2019	DESIGN	PRODUCTION	INSTALLATION
Direct labor hours	100	na	70
Machine hours	na	90	na
Direct labor cost	$10,200	$ 4,250	$1,260
Direct material	1,200	14,550	1,300

JOB #2020	DESIGN	PRODUCTION	INSTALLATION
Direct labor hours	85	na	80
Machine hours	na	300	na
Direct labor cost	$ 8,670	$ 7,450	$1,440
Direct material	1,025	33,600	4,600

JOB #2021	DESIGN	PRODUCTION	INSTALLATION
Direct labor hours	90	na	410
Machine hours	na	120	na
Direct labor cost	$ 9,180	$ 2,950	$1,900
Direct material	2,200	29,000	1,300

Overhead is applied using departmental rates. Design and Installation use direct labor cost as the base, with rates of 40 percent and 90 percent, respectively. Production uses machine hours as the base, with a rate of $15 per hour.

Actual overhead in the Design Department for the month was $12,200. Actual overhead costs for the Production and Installation Departments were $7,200 and $3,850, respectively.

a. Determine the overhead to be applied to each job. By how much is the overhead underapplied or overapplied in each department? For the company?

b. Assume no journal entries have been made to Work in Process Inventory. Make all necessary entries to both the subsidiary ledger and general ledger accounts.

c. Calculate the total cost for each job.

47. *(Appendix)* One of the products made by Jersey Logistics is a system to move large oil storage tanks. A single model (Model No. 89) accounts for approximately 60 percent of the company's annual sales. Because the company has produced and expects to continue to produce a significant quantity of this model, the company uses a standard costing system to account for Model No. 89 production costs. The company has a separate plant that is strictly dedicated to Model No. 89 production. The standard costs to produce a single unit follow:

Direct material (14,000 pounds)	$14,000
Direct labor 1,240 hours at $9.50 per hour	11,780
Overhead	19,000
Total standard cost	$44,780

For the 200 units of Model No. 89 produced in 1998, the actual costs were

Direct material (2,400,000 pounds)	$2,650,000
Direct labor	2,520,000
Overhead	3,700,000
Total actual cost	$8,870,000

a. Compute a separate variance between actual and standard cost for direct material, direct labor, and manufacturing overhead for the Model No. 89 units produced in 1998.

b. Is the direct material variance found in part a driven primarily by the price per pound difference between standard and actual or the quantity difference between standard and actual? Explain.

48. *(Appendix)* Laton Mechanical uses a job order costing system. During July 1998, the company worked on two production runs of the same product, a trailer hitch component. These units were included in Jobs #918 and #2002. Job #918 consisted of 1,200 units of the product, and Job #2002 contained 2,000 units. The hitch components are made from 1/2" sheet metal. Because the trailer hitch component is a product that is routinely produced for one of Laton's long-term customers, standard costs have been developed for its production. The standard cost of material for each unit is $4.50; each unit contains 6 pounds of material. The standard direct labor time per unit is 6 minutes for workers earning a rate of $20 per hour. The actual costs recorded for each job were as follows:

	DIRECT MATERIAL	DIRECT LABOR
Job #918	(7,500 pounds) $5,250	(130 hours) $2,470
Job #2002	(11,800 pounds) 9,440	(230 hours) 4,255

a. What is the standard cost of each trailer hitch component?
b. What was the total standard cost assigned to each of the jobs?
c. Compute the variances for direct material and for direct labor for each job.
d. Why should variances be computed separately for each job rather than for the aggregate annual trailer hitch component production?

---

49. *(Comprehensive; job cost sheet)* The Northern Plains Construction Company builds bridges. For the months of October and November 1997, the firm worked exclusively on a bridge spanning the Niobrara River in northern Nebraska. The firm is organized into two departments. The Precast Department builds structural elements of the bridges in temporary plants located near the construction sites. The Construction Department operates at the bridge site and assembles the precast structural elements. Estimated costs for the Niobrara River Bridge for the Precast Department were $150,000 for direct labor, $310,500 for direct material, and $110,000 for overhead. For the Construction Department, estimated costs for the Niobrara River Bridge were $160,000 for direct labor, $50,000 for direct material, and $160,000 for overhead. Overhead is applied on the last day of each month. Overhead application rates for the Precast and Construction Departments are $18 per machine hour and 100 percent of direct labor cost, respectively.

CASES

TRANSACTIONS FOR OCTOBER

Oct. 1 $150,000 of material was purchased (on account) for the Precast Department to begin building structural elements. All of the material issued to production, $130,000, was considered direct material.

Oct. 5 Utilities were installed at the bridge site at a total cost of $15,000.

Oct. 8   Rent was paid for the temporary construction site housing the Precast Department, $4,000.

Oct. 15   Bridge support pillars were completed by the Precast Department and transferred to the construction site.

Oct. 20 $30,000 of machine rental expense was incurred by the Construction Department for clearing the bridge site and digging foundations for bridge supports.

Oct. 24   Additional material costing $285,000 was purchased on account.

Oct. 31   The company paid the following bills for the Precast Department: utilities, $7,000; direct labor, $45,000; insurance, $6,220; and supervision and other indirect labor costs, $7,900. Departmental depreciation was recorded, $15,200. The company also paid bills for the Construction Department: utilities, $2,300; direct labor, $16,300; indirect labor, $5,700; and insurance, $1,900. Departmental depreciation was recorded on equipment, $8,750.

Oct. 31   A check was issued to pay for the material purchased on October 1 and October 24.

Oct. 31   Overhead was applied to production in each department; 2,000 machine hours were worked in the Precast Department in October.

TRANSACTIONS FOR NOVEMBER

Nov. 1   Additional structural elements were transferred from the Precast Department to the construction site. The Construction Department incurred a cash cost of $5,000 to rent a crane.

Nov. 4 $200,000 of material was issued to the Precast Department. Of this amount, $165,000 was considered direct.

Nov. 8   Rent of $4,000 was paid in cash for the temporary site occupied by the Precast Department.

Nov. 15 $85,000 of material was issued to the Construction Department. Of this amount, $40,000 was considered direct.

Nov. 18   Additional structural elements were transferred from the Precast Department to the construction site.

Nov. 24   The final batch of structural elements were transferred from the Precast Department to the construction site.

Nov. 29   The bridge was completed.

Nov. 30   The company paid final bills for the month in the Precast Department: utilities $15,000; direct labor, $115,000; insurance, $9,350; and supervision and other indirect labor costs, $14,500. Depreciation was recorded, $15,200. The company also paid bills for the Construction Department: utilities, $4,900; direct labor, $134,300; indirect labor, $15,200; and insurance, $5,400. Depreciation was recorded on equipment, $18,350.

Nov. 30   Overhead was applied in each department. The Precast Department recorded 3,950 machine hours in November.

Nov. 30   The company billed the state of Nebraska for the completed bridge at the contract price, $1,550,000.

a. Prepare all necessary journal entries for the preceding transactions. For purposes of this problem, it is not necessary to transfer direct material and direct labor from one department into the other.

b. Post all entries to T-accounts.

c. Prepare a job order cost sheet, which includes estimated costs, for the construction of the bridge.

50. *(Comprehensive)* Kids Krafts is a manufacturer of furnishings for infants and children. The company uses a job order cost system. Kids Krafts' Work in Process Inventory on April 30, 1998, consisted of the following jobs:

JOB NO.	ITEMS	UNITS	ACCUMULATED COST
CBS102	Cribs	20,000	$ 900,000
PLP086	Playpens	15,000	420,000
DRS114	Dressers	25,000	1,570,000

The company's finished goods inventory, carried on a FIFO basis, consists of five items:

ITEM	QUANTITY AND UNIT COST	TOTAL COST
Cribs	7,500 units @ $ 64	$ 480,000
Strollers	13,000 units @ $ 23	299,000
Carriages	11,200 units @ $102	1,142,400
Dressers	21,000 units @ $ 55	1,155,000
Playpens	19,400 units @ $ 35	679,000
		$3,755,400

Kids Krafts applies factory overhead on the basis of direct labor hours. The company's factory overhead budget for the year ending May 31, 1998, totals $4,500,000, and the company plans to expend 600,000 direct labor hours during this period. Through the first 11 months of the year, a total of 555,000 direct labor hours were worked, and total factory overhead amounted to $4,273,500.

At the end of April, the balance in Kids Krafts' Material Inventory account, which includes both raw material and purchased parts, was $668,000. Additions to and requisitions from the material inventory during May included the following:

	RAW MATERIAL	PARTS PURCHASED
Additions	$242,000	$396,000
Requisitions:		
Job #CBS102	51,000	104,000
Job #PLP086	3,000	10,800
Job #DRS114	124,000	87,000
Job #STR077 (10,000 strollers)	62,000	81,000
Job #CRG098 (5,000 carriages)	65,000	187,000

During May, Kids Krafts' factory payroll consisted of the following:

JOB NO.	HOURS	COST
CBS102	12,000	$122,400
PLP086	4,400	43,200
DRS114	19,500	200,500
STR077	3,500	30,000
CRG098	14,000	138,000
Indirect	3,000	29,400
Supervision		57,600
		$621,100

The jobs that were completed in and the unit sales for May follow:

JOB NO.	ITEMS	QUANTITY COMPLETED
CBS102	Cribs	20,000
PLP086	Playpens	15,000
STR077	Strollers	10,000
CRG098	Carriages	5,000

ITEMS	QUANTITY SHIPPED
Cribs	17,500
Playpens	21,000
Strollers	14,000
Dressers	18,000
Carriages	6,000

a. Describe when it is appropriate for a company to use a job order costing system.

b. Calculate the dollar balance in Kids Krafts' Work in Process Inventory account as of May 31, 1998.

c. Calculate the dollar amount related to the playpens in Kids Krafts' Finished Goods Inventory as of May 31, 1998.

d. Explain the treatment of underapplied or overapplied overhead when using a job order costing system.

(CMA adapted)

51. *(Missing amounts)* Riveredge Manufacturing Company realized too late that it had made a mistake locating its controller's office and its electronic data processing system in the basement. Because of the spring thaw, the Mississippi River overflowed on May 2 and flooded the company's basement. Electronic data storage was beyond retrieval, and the company had not provided off-site storage of data. Some of the paper printouts were located but were badly faded and only partially legible. On May 3, when the river subsided, company accountants were able to assemble the following factory-related data from the debris and from discussions with various knowledgeable personnel. Data about the following accounts were found:

- Raw Material (includes indirect material) Inventory: Balance April 1 was $4,800.
- Work in Process Inventory: Balance April 1 was $7,700.
- Finished Goods Inventory: Balance April 30 was $6,600.
- Total company payroll cost for April was $29,200.
- Accounts payable balance April 30 was $18,000.
- Indirect material used in April cost $5,800.
- Other nonmaterial and nonlabor overhead items for April totaled $2,500.

Payroll records, kept at an across-town service center that processes the company's payroll, showed that April's direct labor amounted to $18,200 and represented 4,400 labor hours. Indirect factory labor amounted to $5,400 in April.

The president's office had a file copy of the production budget for the current year. It revealed that the predetermined manufacturing overhead application rate is based on planned annual direct labor hours of 50,400 and expected factory overhead of $151,200.

Discussion with the factory superintendent indicated that only two jobs remained unfinished on April 30. Fortunately, the superintendent also had copies of the job cost sheets that showed a combined total of $2,400 of direct material and $4,500 of direct labor. The direct labor hours on these jobs totaled 1,072. Both of these jobs had been started during the current period.

A badly faded copy of April's Cost of Goods Manufactured and Sold schedule showed cost of goods manufactured was $48,000, and the April 1 Finished Goods Inventory was $8,400.

The treasurer's office files copies of paid invoices chronologically. All invoices are for raw material purchased on account. Examination of these files revealed that unpaid invoices on April 1 amounted to $6,100; $28,000 of purchases had been made during April; and $18,000 of unpaid invoices existed on April 30.

a. Calculate the cost of direct material used in April.
b. Calculate the cost of raw material issued in April.
c. Calculate the April 30 balance of Raw Material Inventory.
d. Determine the amount of underapplied or overapplied overhead for April.
e. What is the Cost of Goods Sold for April?

52. *[In 1995, British steelmaker Ispat purchased Kazakstan's largest steel plant.] Little known outside the steel world, Ispat has in recent months assumed a new visibility—as an example of Western companies' problems in the former Soviet Union. Hundreds of its employees come to work drunk; its biggest customer is broke; and Chechen gunmen have been spotted prowling the plant's perimeter, threatening suppliers and hitting customers up for bribes. Despite all their experience in the developing world, the Ispat officials at Karmet "are up against problems we never dreamed about," says Lakshmi Mittal, the company's chairman.*

Since arriving, Ispat has ladled out $11 million for back pay, $31 million to repay debts to raw material suppliers, and $75 million to begin rebuilding the crumbling plant. Overall, the company has pledged to pay $450 million over the next four years, plus an additional $550 million for new technology.

Because the company is the first Karmet owner in years to have any money, it was quickly viewed as a soft target. The local union is seeking a 75% increase in workers' pay, and a Temirtau child-care center is hitting up plant managers for more money.

Soon after Ispat arrived, a man claiming to represent a society for the blind asked the company for donations. If Ispat would donate steel, he said, the society could resell it and raise money. After the company agreed, 68 other societies for the blind turned up. "Karmet in 1995 was not a steel plant. It was looked upon more as a social institution," says Arabinda Tripathy, Ispat's personnel director.

So, Ispat embarked on an ambitious goal—to teach its workers about capitalism. Senior managers get a weeklong course, beginning with the basics of how a market economy works and progressing to discuss how profits are calculated.

[SOURCE: Kyle Pope, "Saga on the Steppes: A Steelmaker Built Up By Buying Cheap Mills Finally Meets Its Match," *Wall Street Journal* (May 2, 1996), pp. A1, A6. Reprinted by permission of *The Wall Street Journal*, © 1996 Dow Jones & Company, Inc. All Rights Reserved Worldwide.]

a. How would the quality considerations in the Temirtau, Kazakstan, steel plant be fundamentally different from quality considerations in a more developed nation?
b. Should the ethical standards of conduct be different for managers in the Temirtau plant than in other plants operated by Ispat? Explain.

53. From William J. Fife Jr., chairman of Giddings & Lewis Inc.: "The labor content of a product today is probably less than 15%. So, I don't care how much I cut [direct] labor, it's not going to get to the bottom line. We have to get at overhead costs."

Today, U.S. firms have some of the highest overhead burdens of all global companies. Much of the higher overhead cost is associated with the tiered management structures prevalent in the United States. The layers of white-collar managers create a tremendous cost disadvantage. The redundant layers of management are associated with the traditional notion that employees need to be supervised to maintain productivity and control quality.

[SOURCE: Adapted from Thane Peterson, "Can Corporate America Get Out From Under Its Overhead?" *Business Week* (May 18, 1992), p. 102.]

a. With appropriate training of blue-collar workers in American industry, how can layers of white-collar managers be eliminated and productivity and quality increased?
b. How does the traditionally hostile relationship between white-collar managers and blue-collar workers place American firms at a disadvantage in the global market relative to countries that have traditionally fostered cooperation among all employees?

ETHICS AND QUALITY DISCUSSION

54. *Cyclemakers Group of Washdyke near Timaru (New Zealand) is lifting its profile locally and overseas in the cycling world through its custom-built bike service.*

Although the prospect of sitting astride a 10-speed may not be everyone's idea of relaxation, at least now they can dictate their choice of seat—or for that matter, their choice of frame, wheels, gears, and the other bits and pieces that Cyclemakers imports from the major branded overseas manufacturers. The company has built simulators so people can try out a range of configurations to see what measurements suit. They can then choose from an enormous range of components of varying sizes and prices including the color and style of the paint job.

"We're doing it at a price not much greater than an off-the-peg production bike because we use a computerised system. The idea has proven very successful here and in Australia. It's not a large percentage of business yet but has provided a lot at the top end," says Bryan Jackson, managing director.

[SOURCE: "Boosting Bike Sales," *NZ Business* (November 1992), p. 33. *NZ Business* is published by Minty's Media Ltd., Private Bag 93218, Parnell, Auckland, N.Z.]

a. Why would Cyclemakers be able to produce custom-made bicycles for almost the same cost as mass-produced ones?

b. Would you expect the quality of the custom-produced bicycles to be higher or lower than the mass-produced ones? Discuss the rationale for your answer.

c. Why would the custom-made bicycles "provide a lot at the top end" (show a high profit margin)?

55. There are two common types of contracts used when private firms contract to provide services to governmental agencies: cost-plus and fixed-price. The cost-plus contract allows the contracting firm to recover the costs associated with providing the product or service plus a reasonable profit. The fixed-price contract provides for a fixed payment to the contractor. When a fixed-price contract is used, the contractor's profits will be based on its ability to control costs relative to the price received.

A *Wall Street Journal* article announced that, in May 1996, Alliant Techsystems Inc. was being investigated for the way that it accounted for its government contracts. Specifically, the company was being investigated because of suspicions that costs related to fixed-price government contracts were being shifted to cost-plus government contracts.

[SOURCE: Andy Pasztor, "Alliant Unit Is Said to Face Criminal Probe," *Wall Street Journal* (May 3, 1996), pp. A3, A6. Reprinted by permission of *The Wall Street Journal*, © 1994 Dow Jones & Company, Inc. All Rights Reserved Worldwide.]

a. Why would a company that conducts work under both cost-plus and fixed-price contracts have an incentive to shift costs from the fixed-price to the cost-plus contracts?

b. From an ethical perspective, do you feel such cost shifting is ever justified? Explain.

INTERNET ACTIVITIES

56. Many software companies produce custom programs for computerized accounting applications. Search the Internet and find two or more companies that make software for job order costing (job costing). Read the ads and descriptions of the job order costing software and identify five of the most important capabilities (or modules) that the software company offers. Write one to two pages describing how these modules might be used in a company that custom manufactures robotic equipment used in manufacturing applications.

57. Search the Internet for pronouncements of the Cost Accounting Standards Board and find CAS #18, "Allocation of Direct and Indirect Costs." Read the pronouncement and write a summary of the most important points. Assuming you work for a firm that contracts with the federal government, how would compliance with this standard affect the design of your firm's job order costing system?

58. Find the home page on the Internet for E & D Plastics. Review the information found there regarding E & D's customers, products, and production processes. Considering this information, describe the core competencies that E & D must possess to be successful.

Process Costing

LEARNING OBJECTIVES

After completing this chapter, you should be able to answer these questions:

1. How is process costing different from job order costing?

2. Why are equivalent units of production used in process costing?

3. How are equivalent units of production determined using the weighted average and FIFO methods of process costing?

4. How are unit costs and inventory values determined using the weighted average and FIFO methods of process costing?

5. How can standard costs be used in a process costing system?

6. Why would a company use a hybrid costing system?

7. *(Appendix)* What alternative methods can be used to calculate equivalent units of production?

Prices Candles

[Each year, many Britons] take a match to an energy source that is home grown and deeply traditional. London-based Prices Candles was originally a family firm, established in the 1830s when there was, understandably, a much larger market in candles. In 1991, the company was acquired from Shell by Richard Simpson, a former corporate financier.

The techniques involved in candle-making have scarcely changed in more than 160 years of operations. Wax—originally tallow but nowadays a by-product of the petroleum industry—arrives in granules or blocks and is melted down. The wicks are made by tying string across rectangular frames which are then dipped in the liquid wax. Once the wax is dry, another coat is applied.

The process has, to some extent, been automated. In one area of the plant, candles are made with the help of a rotary mold and the candles are then chopped up and packaged by machine. As many as 8,000 candles an hour can be manufactured in this way and, while the British candle industry has been devastated by imports, this factory is capable of producing between 20 million and 30 million candles a year.

In spite of the volume of candles produced, the factory is far from hi-tech. The overwhelming images are of wheezing pipes, leaking steam, and vats covered in dried wax.

SOURCE: Tom Rowland, "House of Wax," *(London) Weekend Telegraph* (December 16, 1995), p. 11.

At Prices Candles, the primary products are manufactured in a continuous flow process, and each unit of output is identical to each other unit. Because Prices Candles' production differs so dramatically from the products made by FM Corporation (discussed in Chapter 7), it seems reasonable that the two companies' product costing systems would also differ.

Job order costing is appropriate for companies making products or providing services in limited quantities that conform to customer specifications. In contrast, Prices Candles uses process costing to accumulate and assign costs to units of production. This costing method is also used by manufacturers of bricks, gasoline, paper, and food products, among many other types of firms.

Both job order and process costing systems accumulate costs by cost component in each production department. However, the two systems assign costs to departmental output differently. In a job order system, costs are assigned to specific jobs and then to the units composing the job. Process costing uses an averaging technique to assign the costs directly to the units produced during the period. In both costing systems, unit costs are transferred as goods are moved from one department to the next so that a total production cost can be accumulated.

This chapter presents process costing procedures and illustrates the weighted average and FIFO methods of calculating unit cost in a process costing system. These methods differ only in the treatment of beginning inventory units and costs. Once unit cost is determined, total costs are assigned to the units transferred out of a department and to that department's ending inventory. The chapter also illustrates a standard cost process costing system, which is an often-used simplification of the FIFO process costing system.

Assigning costs to units of production is an averaging process. In the easiest possible situation, a product's actual unit cost is found by dividing a period's departmental production costs by that period's departmental production quantity. This average is expressed by the following formula:

INTRODUCTION TO PROCESS COSTING

$$\text{Unit Cost} = \frac{\text{Sum of Production Costs}}{\text{Production Quantity}}$$

The Numerator

The formula numerator is obtained by accumulating departmental costs incurred in a single period. Because most companies make more than one type of product, costs must be accumulated by product within each department. Costs can be accumulated by using different Work in Process Inventory accounts for each product and for each department through which that product passes. Alternatively, costs can be accumulated using departmental Work in Process Inventory control accounts that are supported by detailed subsidiary ledgers containing specific product information.

Cost accumulation in a process costing system differs from that in a job order costing system in two ways: (1) the *quantity* of production for which costs are accumulated at any one time, and (2) the *cost object* to which the costs are assigned. For example, Prices Candles occasionally contracts to hand-make 6-foot candles for churches and cathedrals. For these orders, the company would use job order costing. The direct material and direct labor costs associated with each 6-foot candle would be accumulated and assigned directly to the buyer's job. After each job is completed, the total material, labor, and allocated overhead costs are known and job cost can be determined.

In contrast, for its traditional candles, Prices Candles would use a process costing system to accumulate periodic costs for each department and each product. Because a variety of sizes, colors, and scents of candles are manufactured each period, the costs assignable to each type of product must be individually designated and attached to the specific production runs. These costs are then assigned to the units worked on during the period.

Exhibit 8–1 presents the source documents used to make initial cost assignments to production departments during a period. Costs are reassigned at the end of the

EXHIBIT 8–1

Cost Flows and Cost Assignment

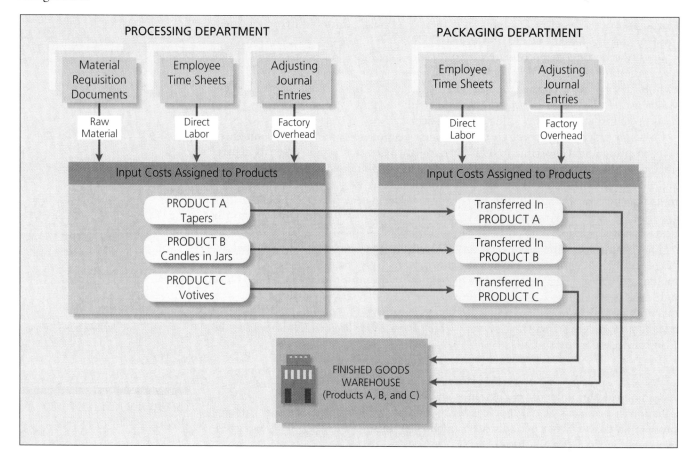

Improving the Relevance of Product Cost Information

In early 1993, Bertch Cabinet Manufacturing implemented substantial changes to its manufacturing operations. The changes involved the implementation of synchronous manufacturing techniques (techniques which are designed to increase throughput and decrease inventory and operating costs). The results of implementing the new manufacturing techniques were impressive and included:

- reduction in lead time from order to delivery of products,
- reduction in production batch size,
- more predictable flows of materials,
- improved placement of inventory buffers relative to production constraints,
- improved worker morale due to increase in on-time deliveries, and
- improved customer satisfaction.

However, the old product costing system failed to meet the information needs of managers in the new manufacturing environment, and Bertch's accountants realized that the accounting system needed to be revised. After some research, the accounting staff designed a system that provided better information to managers in terms of: pricing decisions, job bids, and product mix decisions. The new accounting system was designed to measure throughput and to provide information that allows managers to make decisions that maximize benefits derived from use of the firm's scarce resources. By being aware of changes occurring on the shop floor, the accounting staff was able to design changes to the accounting system that were responsive to the changing information needs of the firm's management.

SOURCE: John B. Macarthur, "From Activity-Based Costing to Throughput Accounting," *Management Accounting*, April 1996, pp. 30, 34, 36–38. Reprinted from *Management Accounting*. Copyright by Institute of Management Accountants, Montvale, NJ.

period (usually each month) from the departments to the units produced. As goods are transferred from one department to the next, the related departmental production costs are also transferred. When products are complete, their costs are transferred from Work in Process Inventory to Finished Goods Inventory.

As in job order costing, the direct material and direct labor components of product cost present relatively few problems for cost accumulation and assignment. Direct material cost can be measured from material requisition slips; direct labor can be determined from employee time sheets and wage rates for the period.

In contrast, overhead is indirectly assigned to output. If total overhead costs are relatively constant from period to period and production volume is relatively steady over time, actual overhead costs provide a fairly uniform production cost and may be used for product costing. If such conditions do not exist, using actual overhead for product costing would result in fluctuating unit costs and, therefore, predetermined application rates are more appropriate.

In both job order costing and process costing systems, firms may change the definitions of cost pools or adopt new schemes for assigning overhead costs to production. Such changes may be desirable as managers find new ways to structure production activities and develop new management methods. The changes in management practices create challenges for accountants in creating accounting systems that provide useful information to managers. The evolution of an accounting system is demonstrated in the above News Note.

The Denominator

The denominator in the unit cost formula represents total departmental production for the period. If all units were 100 percent complete at the end of each accounting period, units could simply be counted to obtain the denominator. But in most production processes, Work in Process (WIP) Inventory exists, which consists of *partially* completed units. Any partially completed ending inventory of the current period becomes the partially completed beginning inventory of the next period. Process costing assigns costs to *both* fully and partially completed units by mathematically converting partially completed units to equivalent whole units.

Units in beginning WIP Inventory were started last period, but will be completed during the current period. This two-period production sequence means that some costs for these units were incurred last period and additional costs will be incurred in the current period. Additionally, the partially completed units in ending WIP Inventory were started in the current period, but will not be completed until next period. Therefore, current period production efforts on ending WIP Inventory units caused some costs to be incurred in this period and more costs will need to be incurred next period.

Physical inspection of the units in ending inventory is needed to determine the proportion of ending WIP Inventory that was completed during the current period. The mathematical complement to this proportion represents the work that needs to be completed next period. Inspection at the end of last period provided information on the proportion of work that needed to be completed this period on beginning inventory.

Equivalent Units of Production

The physical flow of units through a department and the manufacturing effort expended in a department during a period normally occur in the following order:

- Units started in the previous period and finished in the present period.
- Units started in the present period and finished in the present period.
- Units started in the present period and not finished in the present period.

Because of these mixed manufacturing efforts, production cannot be measured by counting whole units. Accountants use a concept known as equivalent units of production to measure the quantity of production achieved during a period.

equivalent units of production

Equivalent units of production (EUP) are an approximation of the number of whole units of output that could have been produced during a period from the actual effort expended during that period. EUP are calculated by multiplying the number of actual but incomplete units produced times the respective percentage degree of completion. The following simple example indicates how equivalent units are calculated. Assume Department 1 of a company had no beginning inventory in May. During May, the department worked on 110,000 units: 100,000 units were completed and 10,000 units were 40 percent complete at the end of the period. The EUP for the period are 104,000 [(100,000 × 100%) + (10,000 × 40%)].

WEIGHTED AVERAGE AND FIFO PROCESS COSTING METHODS

The two methods of accounting for cost flows in process costing are (1) weighted average and (2) FIFO. These methods relate to the manner in which cost flows are assumed to occur in the production process. In a very general way, these process costing approaches can be related to the cost flow methods used in financial accounting.

In a retail business, the weighted average method is used to determine an average cost per unit of inventory. This cost is computed by dividing the total cost of goods available by total units available. Total cost and total units are found by adding purchases to beginning inventory. Costs and units of the current period are not distinguished in any way from those on hand at the end of the prior period. In contrast, the FIFO method of accounting for merchandise inventory separates goods by when they were purchased and at what cost. The costs of beginning inventory are the first costs sent to Cost of Goods Sold; units remaining in the ending inventory are costed at the most recent purchase prices.

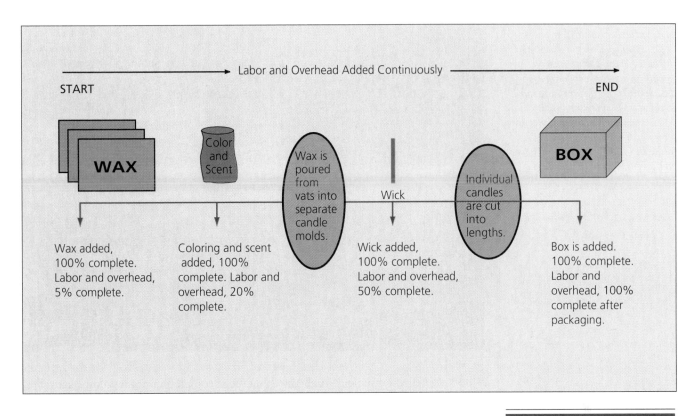

EXHIBIT 8–2

Candle Manufacturing
Process—Production
Department

weighted average method

FIFO method

The use of these methods for costing the production of a manufacturing firm is similar to their use in a retailer. The **weighted average method** computes an average cost per unit of beginning inventory and current period production. The **FIFO method** separates beginning inventory and current period production and their costs so that a current period cost per unit can be calculated. The denominator used in the cost formula to determine unit cost will differ depending on which of the two methods is used.[1]

In almost all cases, some direct material must be introduced at the start of a production process or there would be no need for labor or overhead to be incurred. For example, to make its various products, Prices Candles introduces wax at the start of a process. Any material added at the start of production is 100 percent complete throughout the process *regardless* of the percentage of completion of labor and overhead.

Most production processes require more than one direct material. Additional materials may be added at any point or, possibly, continuously during processing. A material, such as a box, may even be added at the end of processing. At any point within the production process, the product is zero percent complete as to the box although other materials and some labor and overhead may have been incurred.

The production flow of candles in Exhibit 8–2 visually illustrates the need for separate EUP computations for each cost component. The material "wax" is 100 percent complete at any point in the process after the start of production; no additional wax is added later in production. When enough labor and overhead have been

---

[1] Note that the term *denominator* is used here rather than equivalent units of production. Based on its definition, EUP are related to current period productive activity. Thus for any given set of production facts, there is only one true measure of equivalent units produced—regardless of the cost flow assumption used—and that measure is FIFO EUP. However, this fact has been obscured over time due to continued references to the "EUP" computation for weighted average. Thus, the term *EUP* has taken on a generic use to mean "the denominator used to compute the unit cost of production for a period in a process costing system." We use EUP in this generic manner throughout the discussion of process costing.

The production line at this Coca-Cola® plant in Panama illustrates the need for computing separate equivalent units of production for cost elements. Bottles are introduced at the start of processing and are 100% complete throughout. At other points in the process, the bottles are filled with Coke® and capped. Labor and overhead are incurred throughout the process.

added to melt the wax and reach the 20 percent completion point, additional materials (coloring and scent) are added. Prior to 20 percent completion, these materials were zero percent complete; after the 20 percent point, these materials are 100 percent complete. The wick is added at the 50 percent completion point, and the candles are packaged when processing is 99 percent finished, after which the candles are 100 percent complete. Thus, boxes are zero percent complete throughout production; when the candles are packaged, the product is complete and is transferred to the finished goods warehouse or directly to customers.

If 5,000 candles are assumed to be 60 percent complete as to labor and overhead at the end of a period, those candles would be 100 percent complete as to wax, coloring and scent, and wicks, and zero percent complete as to boxes. The EUP calculations would indicate that there are 5,000 EUP for wax, coloring and scent, and wicks, and zero EUP for boxes. The labor and overhead (conversion) components of cost would have an equivalency of 3,000 candles, because the product is 60 percent complete and labor and overhead are added continuously during the process.[2]

When overhead is applied on a direct labor basis, or when direct labor and overhead are added to the product at the same rate, one percentage of completion estimate can be made and used for both conversion cost components. However, because overhead costs are increasingly caused by cost drivers other than direct labor, single computations for "conversion EUP" will be made less often. For example, the cost driver for the utilities portion of overhead cost may be machine hours; the cost driver for the materials handling portion of overhead cost may be pounds of material. The increased use of multiple cost pools and/or activity-based costing concepts makes it less likely that the degrees of completion for the direct labor and overhead components of processing will be equal.

The calculation of equivalent units of production requires that a process cost flow method be specified. A detailed example of the calculations of equivalent units of production and cost assignment under both cost flow methods is presented in the next section.

---

[2] Although the same number of equivalent units results for wax, coloring and scent, and wicks, and for labor and overhead, separate calculations of unit cost may be desirable for each component. These separate calculations would give managers more information for planning and control purposes. Managers must weigh the costs of making separate calculations against the benefits from having the additional information. For illustrative purposes, however, single computations will be made when cost components are at equal percentages of completion.

One purpose of any costing system is to determine a product cost for use on financial statements. When goods are transferred from Work in Process Inventory to Finished Goods Inventory (or another department), a cost must be assigned to those goods. In addition, at the end of any period, a value must be assigned to goods that are only partially complete and still remain in Work in Process Inventory. Exhibit 8–3 outlines the steps necessary to determine the costs assignable to the units completed and to those still in ending inventory at the end of a period in a process costing system. Each of these steps is discussed, and then a complete example is provided for both weighted average and FIFO costing.

The first step is to calculate the total physical units for which the department is responsible or the **total units to account for.** This amount is equal to the total

EUP CALCULATIONS AND COST ASSIGNMENTS

total units to account for

EXHIBIT 8–3

Steps in Process Costing

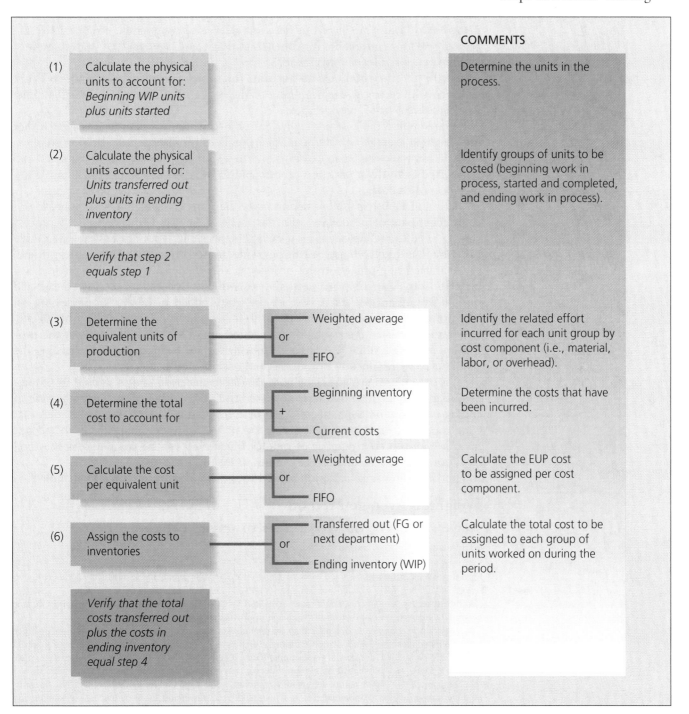

COMMENTS

(1) Calculate the physical units to account for:
Beginning WIP units plus units started

Determine the units in the process.

(2) Calculate the physical units accounted for:
Units transferred out plus units in ending inventory

Identify groups of units to be costed (beginning work in process, started and completed, and ending work in process).

Verify that step 2 equals step 1

(3) Determine the equivalent units of production — Weighted average *or* FIFO

Identify the related effort incurred for each unit group by cost component (i.e., material, labor, or overhead).

(4) Determine the total cost to account for — Beginning inventory + Current costs

Determine the costs that have been incurred.

(5) Calculate the cost per equivalent unit — Weighted average *or* FIFO

Calculate the EUP cost to be assigned per cost component.

(6) Assign the costs to inventories — Transferred out (FG or next department) *or* Ending inventory (WIP)

Calculate the total cost to be assigned to each group of units worked on during the period.

Verify that the total costs transferred out plus the costs in ending inventory equal step 4

number of whole and partial units worked on in the department during the current period: beginning inventory units plus units started.

Second, determine what happened to the units to account for during the period. This step also requires the use of physical units. Units may fit into one of two categories: (1) completed and transferred or (2) partially completed and remaining in ending Work in Process Inventory.[3]

At this point, verify that the total units for which the department was accountable is equal to the total units that were accounted for. If these amounts are not equal, any additional computations will be incorrect.

Third, use either the weighted average or FIFO method to determine the equivalent units of production for each cost component. If all materials are at the same degree of completion, a single materials computation can be made. If multiple materials are used and are placed into production at different points, multiple EUP calculations may be necessary for materials. If overhead is based on direct labor or if these two factors are always at the same degree of completion, a single EUP can be computed for conversion. If neither condition exists, separate EUP schedules must be prepared for labor and overhead.[4]

total cost to account for

Fourth, find the **total cost to account for,** which includes the balance in Work in Process Inventory at the beginning of the period plus all current costs for direct material, direct labor, and overhead.

Fifth, compute the cost per equivalent unit for each cost component using either the weighted average or FIFO equivalent units of production calculated in step 3.

Sixth, use the costs computed in step 5 to assign costs to the units completed and transferred from the production process and to the units remaining in ending Work in Process Inventory.

The Light House is used to demonstrate the steps involved in the computation of equivalent units of production and cost assignment for both methods of process costing. The Light House makes a variety of sizes and types of candles. One candle made by The Light House is 3 inches wide and 6 inches tall. The company views the manufacturing process of this product as a single department with a single direct material: wax. The company treats the costs of coloring and scent as overhead, and the candles are not packaged. Because the wax is added at the start of processing, all inventories are 100 percent complete as to material as soon as processing has begun. Labor and overhead are assumed to be added at the same rate throughout the production process. Exhibit 8–4 presents information for September 1997 regarding the candle maker's production inventories and costs.

Although figures are given for both candles transferred and in ending inventory, providing both of these figures is not essential. The number of candles remaining in ending inventory on September 30 can be calculated by subtracting the candles that were completed and transferred during the period from the total candles to account for. Alternatively, the number of candles transferred can be computed as the total candles to account for minus the candles in ending inventory.

The Light House information is used to illustrate each step listed in Exhibit 8–3.

Weighted Average Method

STEP 1: CALCULATE THE TOTAL UNITS TO ACCOUNT FOR.

Candles in beginning inventory	25,000
Candles started during current period	510,000
Candles to account for	535,000

[3] A third category (spoilage/breakage) does exist. It is assumed at this point that such happenings do not occur. Chapter 9 covers accounting for spoilage in process costing situations.

[4] As discussed in Chapter 5, overhead may be applied to products using a variety of traditional (direct labor hours or machine hours) or nontraditional (such as number of machine setups, pounds of material moved, and/or number of material requisitions) bases. The number of equivalent unit computations that need to be made results from the number of different cost pools and overhead allocation bases established in a company. Some highly automated manufacturers may not have a direct labor category. The quantity of direct labor may be so nominal that it is included in a conversion category and not accounted for separately.

Candles in beginning inventory (40% complete as to labor and conversion)		25,000
Candles started during current period		510,000
Candles completed and transferred to finished goods		523,000
Candles in ending inventory (80% complete as to labor and conversion)		12,000
Cost of beginning inventory:		
Direct material	$ 42,650	
Direct labor	1,400	
Overhead	15,752	$ 59,802
Current period costs:		
Direct material	$433,500	
Direct labor	75,777	
Overhead	263,913	$773,190

EXHIBIT 8–4

Production and Cost Information—September 1997

STEP 2: CALCULATE THE TOTAL UNITS ACCOUNTED FOR.

Candles completed and transferred	523,000
Candles in ending WIP inventory	12,000
Candles accounted for	535,000

The items detailed in this step indicate the categories to which costs will be assigned in the final step. The candles accounted for in step 2 equals the candles to account for in step 1.

STEP 3: DETERMINE THE EQUIVALENT UNITS OF PRODUCTION.

The weighted average EUP computation uses the number of whole candles in beginning inventory and the number of candles started and completed during the period. (**Units started and completed** during a period equals the total units completed during the current period minus the units in beginning inventory.)[5] For The Light House, the candles started and completed in September are 498,000 (523,000 − 25,000). Ending inventory is 100 percent complete as to material, because all material is added at the start of production. The ending inventory is 80 percent complete as to labor and overhead (conversion); one EUP computation can be made because these cost elements were assumed to be added at the same rate throughout the production process. The weighted average computation for equivalent units of production is as follows:[6]

units started and completed

	DM	CONVERSION (LABOR & OVERHEAD)
Beginning inventory (whole candles)	25,000	25,000
Candles started and completed	498,000	498,000
Ending inventory (whole candles × % complete)	12,000	9,600
Equivalent units of production	535,000	532,600

STEP 4: DETERMINE THE TOTAL COST TO ACCOUNT FOR.

The total cost to account for equals beginning inventory cost plus current period costs. Note that information is provided in Exhibit 8–4 on the cost for *each element of production*—direct material, direct labor, and overhead. Production costs can be

[5] Units started and completed can also be computed as the units started during the current period minus the units not finished (or the units in ending inventory).

[6] Different approaches exist to compute equivalent units of production and unit costs under weighted average and FIFO. The models presented in this chapter represent the computations that we have found to be the most readily understood and that best assist students in a clear and unambiguous reconciliation of these two methods. However, two other valid and commonly used approaches for computing and reconciling weighted average and FIFO equivalent units of production and unit costs are presented in the appendix to this chapter.

determined from the departmental Work in Process Inventory accounts and their subsidiary details. These costs come from transfers of direct material from the storeroom, incurrence of direct labor, and either actual or applied overhead amounts. The sum of direct labor and overhead costs is the conversion cost. For The Light House, the total cost to account for is $832,992.

	DM	DL	OH	TOTAL
Beginning inventory cost	$ 42,650	$ 1,400	$ 15,752	$ 59,802
Current period costs	433,500	75,777	263,913	773,190
To account for	$476,150	$77,177	$279,665	$832,992

Total cost is assigned to the goods transferred to Finished Goods Inventory (or, alternatively, to the next department) and to ending Work in Process Inventory in relation to the whole units or equivalent whole units contained in each category.

STEP 5: CALCULATE THE COST PER EQUIVALENT UNIT OF PRODUCTION.

A cost per equivalent unit of production must be computed for each cost component for which a separate calculation of EUP is made. Under the weighted average method, the costs of beginning inventory and the current period are summed for each cost component and averaged over that component's weighted average equivalent units of production. This calculation for unit cost for each cost component at the end of the period is shown below:

$$\text{Unit Cost} = \frac{\text{Beginning Inventory Cost} + \text{Current Period Cost}}{\text{Weighted Average Equivalent Units of Production}}$$

$$= \frac{\text{Total Cost Incurred}}{\text{Total Equivalent Units of Effort}}$$

This computation divides total costs by total units—the common weighted average approach that produces an average component cost per unit. Because labor and overhead are at the same degree of completion, the costs can be combined and shown as a single conversion cost per equivalent unit. The Light House's weighted average calculations for cost per EUP for material and conversion are shown below:

	DIRECT MATERIAL	+	CONVERSION	=	TOTAL
Beginning inventory cost	$ 42,650		$ 17,152		$ 59,802
Current period costs	433,500		339,690		773,190
Total cost per component	$476,150		$356,842		$832,992
Divided by EUP (step 3)	535,000		532,600		
Cost per EUP	$.89		$.67		$1.56

The amounts for the product cost components (material and conversion) are summed to find the total production cost for all whole candles completed during September. For The Light House, this cost is $1.56.

STEP 6: ASSIGN COSTS TO INVENTORIES.

This step assigns total production costs to units of product. Cost assignment in a department involves determining the cost of (1) the goods completed and transferred during the period and (2) the units in ending Work in Process Inventory.

Using the weighted average method, the cost of goods transferred is found by multiplying the total number of units transferred by a cost per unit that combines all the costs of the components or the total cost per EUP. Because this method is based on an averaging technique that combines both prior and current period work, it does not matter in which period the transferred units were started. All units and all costs have been commingled. The total cost transferred for The Light House for September is $815,880 ($1.56 × 523,000).

Ending WIP Inventory cost is calculated based on the equivalent units of production for each cost component. The equivalent units of production for each component are multiplied by the component cost per unit computed in step 5. The cost of ending inventory using the weighted average method (using the previously determined equivalent units) is as follows:

Ending inventory	
Direct material (12,000 × $.89)	$10,680
Conversion (9,600 × $.67)	6,432
Total cost of ending inventory	$17,112

The total costs assigned to units transferred and units in ending inventory must equal the total cost to account for. For The Light House, total cost to account for (step 4) was determined as $832,992, which equals transferred cost ($815,880) plus cost of ending Work in Process Inventory ($17,112).

The steps just discussed can be combined into a **cost of production report.** This document details all manufacturing quantities and costs, shows the computation of cost per EUP, and indicates the cost assignment to goods produced during the period. Exhibit 8–5 shows The Light House's cost of production report using the weighted average method.

cost of production report

EXHIBIT 8–5

Cost of Production Report for Month Ended September 30, 1997 (Weighted Average Method)

PRODUCTION DATA		EQUIVALENT UNITS OF PRODUCTION	
	Whole Units	Direct Material	Conversion
Beginning inventory	25,000*	25,000	10,000
Candles started	510,000		
Candles to account for	535,000		
Beginning inventory completed	25,000	0	15,000
Started and completed	498,000	498,000	498,000
Candles completed	523,000		
Ending WIP inventory	12,000**	12,000	9,600
Candles accounted for	535,000	535,000	532,600

COST DATA			
	Total	Direct Material	Conversion
Cost in beginning inventory	$ 59,802	$ 42,650	$ 17,152
Current period costs	773,190	433,500	339,690
Total cost to account for	$832,992	$476,150	$356,842
Divided by EUP		535,000	532,600
Cost per EUP	$1.56	$.89	$.67

COST ASSIGNMENT			
Transferred (523,000 × $1.56)		$815,880	
Ending inventory			
Direct material (12,000 × $.89)	$10,680		
Conversion (12,000 × 80% × $.67)	6,432	17,112	
Total cost accounted for		$832,992	

*Fully complete as to material; 40% complete as to conversion.
**Fully complete as to material; 80% complete as to conversion.

FIFO Method

Steps 1 and 2 are the same for the FIFO method as for the weighted average method because these two steps involve the use of physical units.

STEP 3: DETERMINE THE EQUIVALENT UNITS OF PRODUCTION.

Under FIFO, the work performed last period is *not* commingled with work of the current period. The EUP schedule for FIFO is

	DM	CONVERSION
Candles in beginning inventory completed in the current period	0	15,000
Candles started and completed	498,000	498,000
Ending inventory (whole candles × % complete)	12,000	9,600
Equivalent units of production	510,000	522,600

Under FIFO, only the work performed on the beginning inventory during the current period is shown in the EUP schedule; this work equals the whole units in beginning inventory times (1 − the percentage of work done in the prior period). No additional material is needed in September to complete the 25,000 candles in the beginning inventory. Because beginning inventory was 40 percent complete as to labor and overhead, the company needs to do 60 percent of the conversion work on the goods in the current period or the equivalent of 15,000 candles (25,000 × 60%).

Except for the different treatment of units in beginning inventory, the remaining figures in the FIFO EUP schedule are the same as for the weighted average method. Thus, the *only* EUP difference between the two methods is equal to the number of candles in beginning inventory times the percentage of work performed in the prior period, as shown below:

	DM	CONVERSION
FIFO EUP	510,000	522,600
Beginning inventory (25,000 units × % work done in prior period; 100% material, 40% conversion)	25,000	10,000
WA EUP	535,000	532,600

STEP 4: DETERMINE THE TOTAL COST TO ACCOUNT FOR.

This step is the same as it was under the weighted average method; the total cost to account for is $832,992.

STEP 5: CALCULATE THE COST PER EQUIVALENT UNIT OF PRODUCTION.

Because cost determination is based on equivalent units of production, different results will be obtained for the weighted average and FIFO methods. The calculations for cost per equivalent unit reflect the difference in quantity that each method uses for beginning inventory. The EUP calculation for FIFO ignores work performed on beginning inventory during the prior period; therefore, the FIFO cost computation per EUP also ignores prior period costs and uses only costs incurred in the current period. The FIFO cost per EUP calculation is

	DIRECT MATERIAL	+	CONVERSION	=	TOTAL
Current period costs	$433,500		$339,690		$773,190
Divided by EUP (step 3)	510,000		522,600		
Cost per EUP	$.85		$.65		$1.50

It is useful to recognize the difference between the two total cost computations. The weighted average total cost of $1.56 is the average total cost of each candle completed during September, *regardless of when production was begun*. The FIFO total cost of $1.50 is the total cost of each candle produced (*both started and completed*) during the period. The $.06 difference is caused by the difference in treatment of beginning work in process costs.

STEP 6: ASSIGN COSTS TO INVENTORIES.

The FIFO method assumes that the units in beginning inventory are the first units completed during the current period and, thus, are the first units transferred. The remaining units transferred during the period were both started and completed in the current period. As shown in the cost of production report in Exhibit 8–6, the two-step computation needed to determine the cost of goods transferred distinctly presents this FIFO logic.

The first part of the cost assignment for units transferred relates to the units that were in beginning inventory. These units had the cost of material and some labor and overhead costs at the start of the period. These costs were not included in the cost per EUP calculations in step 5. The costs to finish these units were incurred in the current period. To determine the total cost of producing the units in beginning

PRODUCTION DATA		EQUIVALENT UNITS OF PRODUCTION	
	Whole Units	Direct Material	Conversion
Beginning inventory	25,000*		
Candles started	510,000		
Candles to account for	535,000		
Beginning inventory completed	25,000	0	15,000
Started and completed	498,000	498,000	498,000
Candles completed	523,000		
Ending inventory	12,000**	12,000	9,600
Candles accounted for	535,000	510,000	522,600

COST DATA			
	Total	Direct Material	Conversion
Cost in beginning inventory	$ 59,802		
Current period costs	773,190	$433,500	$339,690
Total cost to account for	$832,992		
Divided by EUP		510,000	522,600
Current period cost per EUP	$1.50	$.85	$.65

COST ASSIGNMENT			
Transferred			
Beginning inventory cost	$59,802		
Cost to complete:			
Conversion (15,000 × $.65)	9,750	$ 69,552	
Started and completed (498,000 × $1.50)		747,000	
Total cost transferred		$816,552	
Ending inventory			
Direct material (12,000 × $.85)	$10,200		
Conversion (9,600 × $.65)	6,240	16,440	
Total cost accounted for		$832,992	

*Fully complete as to material; 40% complete as to conversion.
**Fully complete as to material; 80% complete as to conversion.

EXHIBIT 8–6

Cost of Production Report for Month Ended September 30, 1997 (FIFO Method)

Southern Shellfish (Harvey, Louisiana) peels thousands of pounds of crawfish to extract and package the tail meat. When completed, the packaged tails are boxed and moved to a refrigeration unit until customer delivery. The production costs are simultaneously moved from Work in Process Inventory to Finished Goods Inventory.

inventory, the beginning inventory costs are added to the current period costs that were needed to complete the goods. Next, the cost of the units started and completed in the current period is computed using current period costs. This cost assignment process is shown for The Light House, which had a beginning September inventory of 25,000 candles and transferred 523,000 candles during the month.

Transferred	
(1) Beginning inventory (prior period costs)	$ 59,802
Completion of beginning inventory:	
Direct material (0 × $.85)	0
Conversion (25,000 × 60% × $.65)	9,750
Total cost of beginning inventory transferred	$ 69,552
(2) Candles started and completed (498,000 × $1.50)	747,000
Total cost transferred	$816,552

The beginning inventory was 100 percent complete as to wax at the beginning of September, therefore, no additional wax needs to be added during the period. Conversion at the start of the month was only 40 percent complete, so 60 percent of the labor and overhead (or 15,000 equivalent units) is added during September at current period costs. The candles started and completed are costed at the total current period FIFO cost of $1.50, because these candles were fully manufactured during the current period.[7]

The process of calculating the FIFO cost of ending Work in Process Inventory is the same as under the weighted average method. Ending work in process cost using FIFO is as follows:

Ending inventory	
Direct material (12,000 × $.85)	$10,200
Conversion (9,600 × $.65)	6,240
Total cost of ending inventory	$16,440

The total cost of the candles transferred ($816,552) plus the cost of the candles in ending inventory ($16,440) equals the total cost to be accounted for ($832,992).

Summary journal entries and T-accounts for The Light House for September are given in Exhibit 8–7. It is assumed that 520,000 candles were sold on account for $2.75 per candle and that a perpetual FIFO inventory system is in use. Assume that The Light House began September with no Finished Goods Inventory. Weighted average amounts are shown where they would differ from FIFO.

[7] Because of FIFO's two-step process to determine cost of units transferred, a question exists as to how to calculate a per-unit cost for the units that were in beginning inventory and those that were started and completed in the current period. The resolution of this question is found in the use of either the strict or the modified FIFO method.

If strict FIFO is used, beginning inventory units are transferred out at their total completed cost; the units started and completed during the current period are transferred at a separate and distinct current period cost. For The Light House, use of strict FIFO means that the 25,000 candles in beginning inventory are transferred at a cost per unit of $2.78 ($69,552 ÷ 25,000). The candles started and completed in September are transferred at the current period cost of $1.50 (computed in step 5). If strict FIFO is used, the costs of these two groups should be reported separately and not added together to get a total transferred cost.

However, unless the difference between the unit costs of beginning inventory units and of units started and completed is significant, there is no need to maintain the distinction. The costs of the two groups can be combined and averaged over all of the units transferred in a process known as the modified FIFO method. For The Light House, modified FIFO assigns an average cost of $1.56 per candle ($816,552 ÷ 523,000) to all candles transferred from the department. Modified FIFO allows the next department or Finished Goods Inventory to account for all units received during the period at the same cost per unit. This method is useful when products are processed through several departments so that the number of separate unit costs to be accounted for does not become excessive.

1. Work in Process Inventory	433,500	
Raw Material Inventory		433,500
To record issuance of materials to production		
(Exhibit 8–4).		
2. Work in Process Inventory	75,777	
Wages Payable		75,777
To accrue wages for direct labor (Exhibit 8–4).		
3. Manufacturing Overhead	263,913	
Various accounts		263,913
To record actual overhead costs (Exhibit 8–4).		
4. Work in Process Inventory	263,913	
Manufacturing Overhead		263,913
To apply actual overhead to production.		
5. Finished Goods Inventory	816,552	
Work in Process Inventory		816,552
To transfer cost of completed candles to		
finished goods (Exhibit 8–6). (Entry would be for		
$815,880 if weighted average were used—		
Exhibit 8–5.)		
6. Cost of Goods Sold	812,052	
Finished Goods Inventory		812,052

EXHIBIT 8–7

Process Costing Journal
Entries and T-accounts

To transfer cost of goods sold, using strict FIFO:

First 25,000 units	$ 69,552
Remaining 495,000 units at $1.50	742,500
	$812,052

(Entry would be for $811,200 if weighted
average were used: 520,000 × $1.56.)

7. Accounts Receivable	1,430,000	
Sales		1,430,000
To record sales on account (520,000 candles ×		
$2.75).		

WORK IN PROCESS INVENTORY

Beginning balance	59,802	Cost of goods	
		manufactured	816,552
Direct material	433,500		
Direct labor	75,777		
Applied overhead	263,913		
Ending balance	16,440		

FINISHED GOODS INVENTORY

Beginning balance	0	Cost of goods sold	812,052
Cost of goods			
manufactured	816,552		
Ending balance			
(3,000 @ $1.50)	4,500		

COST OF GOODS SOLD

September CGS	812,052

PROCESS COSTING IN A MULTIDEPARTMENT SETTING

Most companies have multiple, rather than single, department processing facilities. In a multidepartment processing environment, goods are transferred from a predecessor department to a successor department. For example, if the candles at The Light House were boxed by the dozen, the company's manufacturing activities could be viewed as occurring in two departments: Processing and Packaging.

Manufacturing costs always follow the physical flow of goods. Therefore, the costs of the completed units of predecessor departments are treated as input material costs in successor departments. Such a sequential treatment requires the use of an additional cost component element called "transferred-in" or "prior department cost." This element always has a percentage of completion factor of 100 percent, because the goods would not have been transferred out of the predecessor department if they had not been fully complete. The transferred-in element is handled the same as any other cost element in the calculations of EUP and cost per EUP.

A successor department may add additional raw materials to the units transferred in or may simply provide additional labor with the corresponding incurrence of overhead. Anything added in the successor department requires its own cost element column for calculating equivalent units of production and cost per equivalent unit (unless the additional elements have the same degree of completion, in which case they can be combined).

Occasionally, successor departments may change the unit of measure used in predecessor departments. For example, when The Light House produces candles, the measure in the Processing Department might be number of candles; the measure in the Packaging Department might be number of boxes of candles.

The demonstration problem at the end of the chapter provides a complete example of predecessor and successor department activities.

PROCESS COSTING WITH STANDARD COSTS

Companies may prefer to use standard rather than actual historical costs for inventory valuation purposes. Actual costing requires that a new production cost be computed each production period. Once a production process is established, the "new" costs are often not materially different from the "old" costs. Standards for each cost element can be developed and used as predetermined cost benchmarks to simplify the costing process and eliminate periodic cost recomputations. Standards do need to be reviewed (and possibly revised) at a minimum of once per year to keep the amounts current.

Calculations for equivalent units of production for standard process costing are identical to those of FIFO process costing. Unlike the weighted average method, the emphasis of both standard costing and FIFO are on the measurement and control of current production and current period costs. The weighted average method commingles units and costs of the prior period with those of the current period. This commingling reduces the emphasis on current effort that standard costing is intended to represent and measure.

The use of standard costs allows material, labor, and overhead variances to be measured during the period. To show the differences between using actual and standard process costing, The Light House example is continued. The company's September production and standard cost information is given in Exhibit 8–8. The beginning inventory cost data have been restated from the original to reflect standard costs and to demonstrate the effect of consistent use of standard costs over successive periods. Beginning inventory consisted of 25,000 units that were fully complete as to material and 40 percent complete as to conversion. Therefore, the standard cost of beginning inventory is

Material (25,000 × 100% × $.86)	$21,500
Labor (25,000 × 40% × $.15)	1,500
Overhead (25,000 × 40% × $.48)	4,800
Total	$27,800

EXHIBIT 8–8

Production and Cost Data
(Standard Costing)

Production Data
    Beginning inventory (100%, 40%)   25,000
    Units started   510,000
    Ending inventory (100%, 80%)   12,000

Standard Cost of Production
    Direct material $ .86
    Direct labor   .15
    Overhead   .48
        Total $1.49

Equivalent Units of Production (repeated from Exhibit 8–6):

	DM	CONVERSION
BI (candles × % not complete at start of period)	0	15,000
Candles started and completed	498,000	498,000
EI (candles × % complete at end of period)	12,000	9,600
Equivalent units of production	510,000	522,600

Exhibit 8–9 on the next page presents the cost of production report using The Light House's standard cost information.[8]

When a standard cost system is used, inventories are stated at standard rather than actual costs. Summary journal entries for The Light House's September production, assuming a standard cost FIFO process costing system and amounts from Exhibit 8–9, are as follows.

1. WIP Inventory is debited for $438,600: the standard cost ($428,280) of material used to complete 498,000 units that were started in September plus the standard cost ($10,320) for the material used to produce ending work in process. Raw Material Inventory is credited for the actual cost of the material withdrawn during September ($433,500).

Work in Process Inventory	438,600	
Raw Material Inventory		433,500
Direct Material Variance		5,100
To record issuance of material at		
standard and variance from standard.		

2. WIP Inventory is debited for the standard cost of labor allowed based on the equivalent units produced in September. The EUP for the month reflect the production necessary to complete the beginning inventory (15,000 candles) plus the candles started and completed (498,000) plus the work performed on the ending inventory candles (9,600) or a total of 522,600 EUP. Multiplying this equivalent production by the standard labor cost per candle of $.15 gives a total of $78,390.

Work in Process Inventory	78,390	
Wages Payable		75,777
Direct Labor Variance		2,613
To accrue direct labor cost, assign it to		
WIP Inventory at standard, and record		
direct labor variance.		

[8] Total material, labor, and overhead variances are shown for The Light House in Exhibit 8–9. More detailed variances are presented in Chapter 11 on standard costing. Additionally, variances from actual costs must be closed at the end of a period. If the variances are immaterial, they can be closed to Cost of Goods Sold; otherwise, they should be allocated among the inventory accounts and Cost of Goods Sold.

EXHIBIT 8-9

Cost of Production Report
for Month Ended
September 30, 1997
(Standard Costing)

COSTS TO BE ACCOUNTED FOR				
	DIRECT MATERIAL	DIRECT LABOR	OVERHEAD	TOTAL
Total costs				
BWIP (at standard)	$ 21,500	$ 1,500	$ 4,800	$ 27,900
Current period (actual)	433,500	75,777	263,913	773,190
(1) Total	$455,000	$77,277	$268,713	$801,090
COST ASSIGNMENT (AT STANDARD)				
Transferred				
BI cost*	$ 21,500	$ 1,500	$ 4,800	$ 27,900
Cost to complete				
DL (15,000 × $.15)		2,250		
OH (15,000 × $.48)			7,200	
Total cost to complete				9,450
Started and completed				
DM (498,000 × $.86)	428,280			
DL (498,000 × $.15)		74,700		
OH (498,000 × $.48)			239,040	
Total started and completed				742,020
Ending inventory				
DM (12,000 × $.86)	10,320			
DL (9,600 × $.15)		1,440		
OH (9,600 × $.48)			4,608	
Total WIP ending				16,368
(2) Total standard cost assigned	$460,100	$79,890	$255,648	$795,738
Variances from				
actual (1 − 2)*	(5,100)	(2,613)	13,065	5,352
Total costs accounted for	$455,000	$77,277	$268,713	$801,090

NOTE: Favorable variances are shown in parentheses.
*Beginning work in process is carried at standard costs rather than actual. Therefore, no portion of the variance is attributable to BWIP. Any variance that might have been associated with BWIP was measured and identified with the prior period.

3. Actual factory overhead incurred in September is $263,913.

Manufacturing Overhead	263,913	
Various accounts		263,913
To record actual overhead cost for September.		

4. WIP Inventory is debited for the standard cost of overhead based on the EUP produced in September. Because labor and overhead are consumed at the same rate, equivalent production is the same as in entry 2: 522,600 EUP. Multiplying the EUP by the standard overhead application rate of $.48 per candle gives $250,848.

Work in Process Inventory	250,848	
Manufacturing Overhead Variance	13,065	
Manufacturing Overhead		263,913
To apply overhead to WIP Inventory and record the overhead variance.		

GM Trails Other Automakers in Controlling Labor Cost of Assembly Operations

**N E W S
N O T E**

[GM], the No. 1 auto maker, is pursuing a variety of measures to cut costs, including reducing the number of hours it takes for workers to assemble vehicles and the time it takes to develop them; forcing its inhouse supplier to compete against outside sources for GM business; and pressuring the UAW to improve productivity by eliminating excessive job classifications.

GM's aggressive labor strategy involves more than just reducing the number of hourly workers on its rolls. It goes to the core of the new management's drive to make GM, the auto industry's highest cost producer, at least as competitive as its U.S. rivals.

Reducing hours of assembly per car is a key part of GM's labor strategy. By using fewer parts and smarter engineering as it retools its assembly plants for new launches, GM is slashing by a third the time workers need to build each car.

Seven years ago, it took GM workers an average of 39 hours to build a vehicle. It's now about 30 hours. But at Ford Motor Co., the comparable figure is 25 hours and at Chrysler Corp. it's 27.2.

SOURCE: Rebecca Blumenstein, "GM's Labor Hawks Are Getting Tough With UAW to Fulfill Plans to Cut Costs," *Wall Street Journal* (April 22, 1996), p. A4. Reprinted by permission of *The Wall Street Journal*, © 1996 Dow Jones & Company, Inc. All Rights Reserved Worldwide.

5. Finished Goods Inventory is debited for the total standard cost ($779,270) of all 523,000 candles completed during the month ($1.49 × 523,000).

Finished Goods Inventory	779,270	
Work in Process Inventory		779,270
To transfer standard cost of completed candles to FG Inventory.		

A standard costing system eliminates the need to be concerned about differentiating between the per-unit cost of the beginning inventory units that were completed and the per-unit cost of the units started and completed in the current period. All units flowing out of a department are costed at the standard or "normal" production cost for each cost component: direct material, direct labor, and overhead. Thus, recordkeeping is simplified and variations from the norm are highlighted in the period of incurrence. Standard cost systems are discussed in depth in Chapter 11.

Standard costing not only simplifies the cost flows in a process costing system, it also provides a useful tool to control costs. By developing standards, managers have a benchmark against which actual costs can be compared. Variances serve to identify differences between the benchmark (standard) cost and the actual cost. By striving to control variances, managers control costs. Managers should also compare the costs of their firm to costs incurred by other firms. The above News Note indicates how labor costs in assembly operations is a source of competitive disadvantage for General Motors (GM), relative to its U.S. competitors.

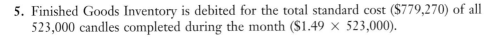

HYBRID COSTING SYSTEMS

Many companies are now able to customize what were previously mass-produced items. In such circumstances, neither job order nor process costing techniques are perfectly suited to attach costs to output. Thus, companies may choose to use a **hybrid costing system** that is appropriate for their particular processing situation. A hybrid costing system combines certain characteristics of a job order system and

hybrid costing system

Car seats are standardized for particular vehicles, but customers may choose leather or cloth in addition to a wide variety of colors. Lear Seating in Dearborn, Michigan, could use a hybrid costing system to account for its mass production of these partially-customized automobile seats.

a process costing system. A hybrid system would be used in a manufacturing environment in which various product lines have different direct materials, but similar processing techniques.

To illustrate the need for hybrid systems, assume you order an automobile with the following options: leather seats, a Bose stereo system and compact disk player, cruise control, and pearlized paint. The costs of all options need to be traced specifically to your car, but the assembly process for all the cars produced by the plant is similar. The job order costing feature of tracing direct materials to specific jobs is combined with the process costing feature of averaging labor and overhead costs over all homogeneous production to derive the total cost of the automobile you ordered. It would be infeasible to try to use a job order costing system to trace labor or overhead cost to your car individually, and it would be improper to average the costs of your options over all the cars produced during the period.

A hybrid costing system is appropriate for companies producing items such as furniture, clothing, or jelly. In each instance, numerous kinds of raw materials could be used to create similar output. A table may be made from oak, teak, or pine; a blouse may be made from silk, cotton, or polyester; and jelly may be made from blackberries, strawberries, or jalapeño peppers. The material cost for a batch run would need to be traced separately, but the production process of the batch is repetitive.

Hybrid costing systems allow accounting systems to portray more accurately the actual type of manufacturing activities in which companies are engaged. Job order costing and process costing are two ends of a continuum and, as is typically the case for any continuum, neither end is necessarily the norm. As flexible manufacturing increases, so will the use of hybrid costing systems.

REVISITING

Prices Candles

Prices Candles occupies a five-and-a-half acre site on which is situated a Victorian factory on the banks of the Thames. As of December 1995, it employed 110 people. Unfortunately, the factory was likely to be closed. Closure would not be caused by the organization's inability to produce the quality and quantity of candles that were desired by customers but rather, to some extent, by an inability to produce at a competitive cost. The company itself is not going out of business, but it will no longer be located at its current site: Gone will be the cobbled alleyways, majestic boiler houses, and cast-iron staircases of one of London's few surviving and functioning examples of Victorian architecture. Prices Candles will be moved to a neat new factory that will cut £500,000 (or approximately $750,000) of overhead from organization costs per year. Owner Simpson has offered to keep the head office staff of 50 people on the south London site and to open a heritage center with candle-making demonstrations. But Prices Candles will take its well-honed mass production processes and its ability to hand-make church and cathedral candles that burn for a year to "an anonymous industrial unit elsewhere."

SOURCE: Tom Rowland, "House of Wax," *(London) Weekend Telegraph* (December 16, 1995), p. 11.

CHAPTER SUMMARY

Process costing is an averaging method used to assign costs to output in manufacturing situations producing large quantities of homogeneous products. A process costing system may use either the weighted average or FIFO method to compute equivalent units of and assign costs to production. The difference between the two methods lies solely in the treatment of the work performed in the prior period on the beginning work in process inventory.

Under the weighted average method, work performed in the prior period is combined with current period work and the total costs are averaged over all units. Using the FIFO method, work performed in the last period on beginning work in process inventory is *not* commingled with current period work nor are costs of beginning work in process added to current period costs to derive unit production cost. With FIFO, current period costs are divided by current period production to generate a unit production cost related entirely to work actually performed in the current period.

Six steps are necessary in deriving and assigning product cost under a process costing system.

1. Calculate the total number of physical units to account for.
2. Calculate the physical units accounted for by tracing the physical flow of units. This step involves identifying the groups to which costs are to be assigned (transferred or remaining in ending inventory).
3. Determine the number of equivalent units of production, either on the weighted average or FIFO basis, for each cost component. The cost components include transferred-in (if multidepartmental), direct material, direct labor, and overhead. In cases of multiple materials having different degrees of completion, each material is considered a separate cost component. If overhead is applied on a direct labor basis or is incurred at the same rate as direct labor, labor and overhead may be combined as one cost component and referred to as "conversion."

4. Determine the total cost to account for, which is the sum of beginning inventory cost and all production costs incurred for the current period.

5. Calculate the cost per equivalent unit of production for each cost component.

6. Assign the costs to the units transferred and the units in ending work in process inventory. The method of cost assignment depends on whether weighted average or FIFO costing is used. The total of the costs assigned to units transferred and to units in ending work in process inventory must equal the total cost to account for.

The FIFO method of process costing can be combined with standard costs so that a "normal" production cost is assigned each period to equivalent units of output. This technique allows managers to quickly recognize and investigate significant deviations from normal production costs.

Hybrid costing systems allow companies to combine the characteristics of both job order and process costing systems. Different direct materials are traced to different outputs using job order costing; direct materials that are common to a batch and conversion activities that are similar for numerous batches of output are accounted for using process costing techniques.

APPENDIX

Alternative Calculations of Weighted Average and FIFO Methods

Various methods exist to allow the computation of equivalent units of production under the weighted average and FIFO methods. One of the most common variations is the following EUP calculation for weighted average:

Units transferred (whole units)

+ Ending work in process (equivalent units)

= Weighted average EUP

Once the weighted average EUP figure is available, the FIFO equivalent units can be quickly derived by subtracting the equivalent units in beginning work in process inventory that had been produced in the previous period:

Weighted average EUP

− Beginning work in process (equivalent units)

= FIFO EUP

This computation is appropriate for the following reason: The weighted average method concentrates on the units that were completed during the period as well as the units that were started but not completed during the period. Unlike FIFO, the weighted average method does not exclude the equivalent units that were in beginning inventory. Thus, to convert from weighted average to FIFO, simply remove the equivalent units produced in the previous period from beginning work in process.

The Light House's September production data presented in the chapter are repeated here to illustrate these alternative calculations for the weighted average and FIFO methods.

Candles in beginning work in process (100% complete as to material; 40% complete as to conversion costs)	25,000
Candles started during the month	510,000
Candles completed during the month	523,000
Candles in ending work in process (100% complete as to material; 80% complete as to conversion costs)	12,000

Using these data, the EUP are computed as follows:

	DM	CONVERSION
Candles transferred	523,000	523,000
+ Ending work in process equivalent units		
(12,000 candles @ 100% and 80% complete)	12,000	9,600
= **Weighted average EUP**	535,000	532,600
− Beginning work in process equivalent units		
produced in previous period (25,000 units @ 100% and		
40% complete)	(25,000)	(10,000)
= **FIFO EUP**	510,000	522,600

The distinct relationship between the weighted average and FIFO costing models can also be used to derive the equivalent units of production calculations. This method begins with the total number of units to account for in the period. From this amount, the EUP to be completed next period are subtracted to give the weighted average EUP. Next, as in the method shown above, the equivalent units completed in the prior period (the beginning Work in Process Inventory) are deducted to give the FIFO equivalent units of production.

Using The Light House data, these computations are

	DM	CONVERSION
Total units to account for	535,000	535,000
− EUP to be completed next period (ending inventory ×		
% *not completed:* 12,000 × 0%; 12,000 × 20%)		(2,400)
= **Weighted average EUP**	535,000	532,600
− EUP completed in prior period (beginning inventory ×		
% *completed last period:* 25,000 × 100%; 25,000 × 40%)	(25,000)	(10,000)
= **FIFO EUP**	510,000	522,600

These alternative calculations can either be used to confirm answers found by using beginning inventory units, units started and completed, and ending inventory units or as a shortcut to initially compute equivalent units of production.

SOLUTION STRATEGIES

STEPS IN PROCESS COSTING COMPUTATIONS

1. Compute the total units to account for (in physical units):

    Beginning inventory in physical units

    + Units started (or transferred in) during period

2. Compute units accounted for (in physical units):

    Units completed and transferred

    + Ending inventory in physical units

3. Compute equivalent units of production per cost component:
   a. Weighted average

$$\begin{array}{l} \text{Beginning inventory in physical units} \\ + \text{ Units started and completed*} \\ + \text{ (Ending inventory} \times \text{ \% complete)} \end{array}$$

   b. FIFO

$$\begin{array}{l} \text{(Beginning inventory} \times \text{ \% } \textit{not} \text{ complete at start of period)} \\ + \text{ Units started and completed*} \\ + \text{ (Ending inventory} \times \text{ \% complete)} \end{array}$$
*Units started and completed = (Units transferred − Units in beginning inventory)

4. Compute total cost to account for:

$$\begin{array}{l} \text{Costs in beginning inventory} \\ + \text{ Costs of current period} \end{array}$$

5. Compute cost per equivalent unit per cost component:
   a. Weighted average

$$\begin{array}{l} \text{Cost of component in beginning inventory} \\ + \text{ Cost of component for current period} \\ = \text{ Total cost of component} \\ \div \text{ EUP for component} \end{array}$$

   b. FIFO

$$\begin{array}{l} \text{Cost of component for current period} \\ \div \text{ EUP for component} \end{array}$$

6. Assign costs to inventories:
   a. Weighted average
     (1) Transferred:
        Units transferred × (Total cost per EUP for all components)
     (2) Ending inventory:
        EUP for each component × Cost per EUP for each component
   b. FIFO
     (1) Transferred:
        + Beginning inventory costs
        + (Beginning inventory × % *not* complete at beginning of period for each component × Cost per EUP for each component)
        + (Units started and completed × Total cost per EUP for all components)
     (2) Ending inventory:
        EUP for each component × Cost per EUP for each component

The Postlewaite Company manufactures briefcases in a two-department process: Forming and Finishing. The Forming Department uses weighted average costing; the cost driver for overhead in this department is unrelated to direct labor. The Finishing Department adds the hardware to the formed cases and uses FIFO costing. Overhead is applied to the cases in this department on a direct labor basis. During April, the following production data and costs have been gathered:

DEMONSTRATION PROBLEM

FORMING DEPARTMENT: UNITS

Beginning work in process (100% complete for material; 40% complete for labor; 30% complete for overhead)	250
Units started	8,800
Ending work in process (100% complete for material; 70% complete for labor; 90% complete for overhead)	400

FORMING DEPARTMENT: COSTS

	MATERIAL	DIRECT LABOR	OVERHEAD	TOTAL
Beginning inventory	$ 3,755	$ 690	$ 250	$ 4,695
Current costs incurred	100,320	63,606	27,681	191,607
Totals	$104,075	$64,296	$27,931	$196,302

FINISHING DEPARTMENT: UNITS

Beginning work in process (100% complete for transferred-in; 15% complete for material; 40% complete for conversion)	100
Units transferred in	8,650
Ending work in process (100% complete for transferred-in; 30% complete for material; 65% complete for conversion)	200

FINISHING DEPARTMENT: COSTS

	TRANS. IN	DIRECT MATERIAL	CONVERSION	TOTAL
Beginning inventory	$ 2,176	$ 30	$ 95	$ 2,301
Current costs incurred	188,570	15,471	21,600	225,641
Totals	$190,746	$15,501	$21,695	$227,942

Required:

a. Prepare a cost of production report for the Forming Department.
b. Prepare a cost of production report for the Finishing Department.

Solution to Demonstration Problem

a.

	Whole Units	EQUIVALENT UNITS OF PRODUCTION		
		Direct Material	Direct Labor	Overhead
Beginning inventory	250	250	100	75
Units started	8,800			
Units to account for	9,050			
BWIP completed	250	0	150	175
Started and completed	8,400	8,400	8,400	8,400
Units completed	8,650			
Ending inventory	400	400	280	360
Units accounted for	9,050			
Weighted average EUP		9,050	8,930	9,010

	Whole Units	EQUIVALENT UNITS OF PRODUCTION		
		Direct Material	Direct Labor	Overhead
	Total			
BWIP costs	$ 4,695	$ 3,755	$ 690	$ 250
Current period costs	191,607	100,320	63,606	27,681
Total costs	$196,302 ←	$104,075	$ 64,296	$27,931
Divided by EUP		9,050	8,930	9,010
Cost per EUP	$21.80	$11.50	$7.20	$3.10

COST ASSIGNMENT

Transferred (8,650 × $21.80)			$188,570	
Ending inventory				
Direct material (400 × $11.50)		$4,600		
Direct labor (280 × $7.20)		2,016		
Overhead (360 × $3.10)		1,116	7,732	
Total cost accounted for			$196,302	

b.

	Whole Units	EQUIVALENT UNITS OF PRODUCTION		
		Transferred-In	Direct Material	Conversion
Beginning inventory	100			
Units started	8,650			
Units to account for	8,750			
BWIP completed	100	0	85	60
Started and completed	8,450	8,450	8,450	8,450
Units completed	8,550			
Ending inventory	200	200	60	130
Units accounted for	8,750			
FIFO EUP		8,650	8,595	8,640
	Total			
BWIP costs	$ 2,301			
Current period costs	225,641	$188,570	$15,471	$21,600
Total costs	$227,942 ←			
Divided by EUP		8,650	8,595	8,640
Cost per EUP	$26.10	$21.80	$1.80	$2.50

COST ASSIGNMENT

Transferred out			
Beginning inventory cost	$2,301		
Cost to complete:			
Transferred-in (0 × $21.80)	0		
Direct material (85 × $1.80)	153		
Conversion (60 × $2.50)	150	$ 2,604	
Started and completed (8,450 × $26.10)		220,545	
Ending inventory			
Transferred-in (200 × $21.80)	$4,360		
Direct material (60 × $1.80)	108		
Conversion (130 × $2.50)	325	4,793	
Total cost accounted for		$227,942	

1. What are the typical characteristics of a company that should employ a process costing system?

2. Why is the process of assigning costs to products essentially an averaging process?

3. How are job order and process costing similar? How do they differ?

4. Why are equivalent units of production used as an output measure in process costing? In your answer, be sure to address the problems created by partially completed inventories.

5. What creates the difference between weighted average and FIFO equivalent units of production? Which EUP calculation more accurately portrays the actual flow of units through a manufacturing process and why?

6. Why is it necessary to calculate separate equivalent units of production for each cost component of a product? Are there times when separate EUP schedules are not necessary and, if so, why?

7. How are units "started and completed" in the current period calculated? Is this figure used in both weighted average and FIFO cost assignment? Why or why not?

8. In which of the six basic steps used in process costing are physical units used and in which are equivalent units of production used? Are there steps in which neither physical nor equivalent units are used? Why or why not?

9. How is the unit cost for each cost component assigned to the units produced during the current period under (a) the weighted average method and (b) the FIFO method?

10. What is the purpose of the cost of production report? How would such a report assist accountants in making entries for a period?

11. Why does the "Transferred" section of the FIFO method cost of production report include multiple computations, whereas the same section for the weighted average report only includes one computation?

12. How does process costing differ in a multidepartmental manufacturing environment from a single-department manufacturing environment? Why does this difference exist?

13. Why are the EUP calculations made for standard process costing the same as the EUP calculations for FIFO process costing?

14. How are inventories accounted for under a standard process costing system? What information is provided to management when inventories are accounted for in this manner?

15. What is a hybrid costing system? Under what circumstances is the use of such a system appropriate?

QUESTIONS

16. *(EUP; weighted average)* Pacioli Pasta uses a weighted average process costing system. All material is added at the start of the production process. Direct labor and overhead are added at the same rate throughout the process. Pacioli's records indicate the following production for February 1997:

Beginning inventory (70% complete as to conversion)	12,000 units
Started during February	17,000 units
Completed during February	26,000 units

Ending inventory for February is 20 percent complete as to conversion.
   a. What are the equivalent units of production for direct material?
   b. What are the equivalent units of production for labor and overhead?

EXERCISES

17. *(EUP; FIFO)* Assume that Pacioli Pasta in exercise 16 uses the FIFO method of process costing.
    a. What are the equivalent units of production for direct material?
    b. What are the equivalent units of production for labor and overhead?

18. *(EUP; weighted average & FIFO)* Pershing Corporation makes toy metal soldiers in a one-department production process. All metal is added at the beginning of the process. Paint for the figures and the plastic bags for packaging are considered indirect materials. The following information is available relative to June 1997 production activities:

    Beginning inventory: 75,000 figures (60% complete as to labor; 85% complete as to overhead)

    Started into production: metal for 250,000 figures; this number of figures were cast during the month

    Ending inventory: 30,000 figures (70% complete as to labor; 90% complete as to overhead)

    a. Compute the EUP for direct material, direct labor, and overhead using weighted average process costing.
    b. Compute the EUP for direct material, direct labor, and overhead using FIFO process costing.
    c. Reconcile the calculations in parts a and b.

19. *(Cost per EUP; weighted average)* Sensational Scents Inc. manufactures candles. In March 1997, company production is 26,800 equivalent units for direct material, 24,400 equivalent units for labor, and 21,000 equivalent units for overhead. During March, direct material and conversion costs incurred are as follows:

Direct material	$ 78,880
Conversion	122,400
Overhead	42,600

    Beginning inventory costs for March were $14,920 for direct material, $36,200 for labor, and $9,900 for overhead. What is the weighted average cost per equivalent unit for the cost components for March?

20. *(Cost per EUP; FIFO)* Assume that Sensational Scents Inc. in exercise 19 had 3,600 EUP for direct material in March's beginning inventory, 4,000 EUP for direct labor, and 3,960 EUP for overhead. What was the FIFO cost per equivalent unit for direct material, labor, and overhead for March?

21. *(Cost per EUP; weighted average & FIFO)* Weeding Edges manufactures concrete garden edging sections. November 1997 production and cost information are as follows:

WA EUP:	Direct material	40,000 sections
	Direct labor	38,000 sections
	Overhead	37,500 sections
FIFO EUP:	Direct material	30,000 sections
	Direct labor	31,000 sections
	Overhead	33,000 sections
BI costs:	Direct material	$ 5,300
	Direct labor	1,580
	Overhead	3,630
Current period costs:	Direct material	$13,500
	Direct labor	8,680
	Overhead	21,120

    All material is added at the beginning of processing.

a. What is the total cost to account for?

b. Using weighted average process costing, what is the cost per equivalent unit for each cost component?

c. Using FIFO process costing, what is the cost per equivalent unit for each cost component?

d. How many units were in beginning inventory and at what percentage of completion was each cost component?

22. *(EUP; cost per EUP; weighted average)* B-Gone manufactures canisters of mace. On October 1, 1997, the company had 4,800 units in beginning Work in Process Inventory that were 100 percent complete as to canisters, 60 percent complete as to other materials, 10 percent complete as to direct labor, and 20 percent complete as to overhead. During October, B-Gone started 22,500 units into the manufacturing process. Ending Work in Process Inventory included 3,600 units that were 100 percent complete as to canisters, 30 percent complete as to other materials, 25 percent complete as to direct labor, and 30 percent complete as to overhead.

Cost information for the month follows:

Beginning inventory:	Canisters	$ 8,175
	Other direct materials	3,393
	Direct labor	1,212
	Overhead	1,038
October costs:	Canisters	$39,600
	Other direct materials	20,148
	Direct labor	61,812
	Overhead	43,734

Prepare a schedule showing B-Gone's October 1997 computation of weighted average equivalent units of production and cost per equivalent unit.

23. *(EUP; cost per EUP; FIFO)* Slip-N-Slide makes skateboards and uses a FIFO process costing system. The company began November with 1,000 boards in process that were 70 percent complete as to material and 85 percent complete as to conversion costs. During the month, 3,800 additional boards were started. On November 30, 800 boards were still in process (60 percent complete as to material and 70 percent complete as to conversion costs). Cost information for November is as follows:

Beginning inventory costs:	Direct material	$13,181
	Conversion	6,732
Current period costs:	Direct material	$71,064
	Conversion	29,309

a. Calculate EUP for each cost component using the FIFO method.

b. Calculate cost per EUP for each cost component.

24. *(Cost assignment; weighted average)* Krantz Inc. uses weighted average process costing. The company's cost accountant has determined the following production and cost per EUP information for May 1997:

Units transferred out during month	256,000
Units in ending inventory (100% complete as to direct material; 80% complete as to direct labor; 95% complete as to overhead)	37,000
Direct material cost per EUP	$3.75
Direct labor cost per EUP	$4.96
Overhead cost per EUP	$5.10

a. What is the cost of the goods transferred during May?

b. What is the cost of the goods in ending inventory at May 31, 1997?

c. What is the total cost to account for during May?

25. *(Cost assignment; FIFO)* In February 1997, Saliba Corporation computed its costs per equivalent unit under FIFO process costing as follows:

Raw materials	$12.75
Packaging	1.50
Direct labor	6.42
Overhead	3.87

The raw materials are all added at the start of processing. Packaging is added at the end of the production process immediately before the units are transferred to the finished goods warehouse.

Beginning inventory cost was $513,405 and consisted of:
- $344,520 raw materials cost for 27,000 EUP
- $95,931 direct labor cost for 14,850 EUP
- $72,954 overhead cost for 18,900 EUP

Saliba transferred a total of 185,000 units to finished goods during February, which left 16,000 units in ending inventory. The EI units were 20 percent complete as to direct labor and 35 percent complete as to overhead.

a. What percentage complete were the beginning inventory units as to raw materials? Packaging? Direct labor? Overhead?

b. What was the total cost of the completed beginning inventory units?

c. What was the cost of the units started and completed in February?

d. What was the cost of February's ending inventory?

26. *(EUP; cost per EUP; cost assignment; FIFO & weighted average)* Technosound Company mass produces miniature speakers for portable CD players. The following T-account presents the firm's cost information for February 1997:

WORK IN PROCESS INVENTORY

2/1 Direct material cost in BI	$ 1,027
2/1 Conversion cost in BI	588
Feb. DM received	11,682
Feb. DL incurred	2,513
Feb. OH applied to production	1,257

The company had 400 units in process on February 1. These units were 40 percent complete as to material and 30 percent complete as to conversion cost. During February, the firm started 1,500 units and ended the month with 150 units still in process. The units in ending WIP Inventory were 20 percent complete as to material and 70 percent complete as to conversion cost.

a. Compute the unit costs for February under the FIFO method for direct material and for conversion costs.

b. Compute the unit costs for February under the weighted average method for direct material and for conversion costs.

c. Determine the total costs transferred to Finished Goods Inventory during February using the FIFO method.

27. *(EUP; weighted average & FIFO; two departments)* Blanchard Metalworks has two processing departments, Fabrication and Assembly. Metal is placed into production in the Fabrication Department, where it is cut, formed, or ground into various components. These components are transferred to Assembly, where they are welded, polished, and hot-dip galvanized with sealant. Following is the production data for these two departments for January 1997:

FABRICATION

Beginning WIP inventory (100% complete as to material; 45% complete as to conversion)	5,000
Units started during month	39,000
Ending WIP inventory (100% complete as to material; 80% complete as to conversion)	6,800

ASSEMBLY

Beginning WIP inventory (0% complete as to sealant; 15% complete as to conversion)	1,500
Units started during month	?
Ending WIP inventory (100% complete as to sealant; 75% complete as to conversion)	4,600

a. Determine the equivalent units of production for each cost component for each department under the weighted average method.

b. Determine the equivalent units of production for each cost component for each department under the FIFO method.

28. *(Standard process costing, variances)* Microtech Products manufactures 3.5-inch preformatted computer disks and uses a standard process costing system. All material is added at the start of production and labor and overhead are incurred equally throughout the process. The standard cost of one disk is

Direct material	$.13
Direct labor	.02
Overhead	.11
Total cost	$.26

The following production and cost data are applicable to September 1997:

Beginning inventory (45% complete)	17,000 units
Started in September	130,000 units
Ending inventory (65% complete)	14,400 units
Current cost of direct material	$18,400
Current cost of direct labor	2,598
Current cost of overhead	15,000

a. What cost is carried as the September beginning balance of Work in Process Inventory?

b. What cost is carried as the September ending balance of Work in Process Inventory?

c. What cost is transferred to Finished Goods Inventory for September?

d. What are the total direct material, direct labor, and overhead variances for September?

29. *(Standard process costing)* Guillermo Company uses a standard FIFO process costing system to account for its tortilla manufacturing process. The tortillas are packaged and sold by the dozen. The company has set the following standards for production of each one-dozen package:

Direct material—ingredients	$.35
Direct material—package	.05
Direct labor	.07
Overhead	.13
Total cost	$.60

On April 1, the company had 7,200 individual tortillas in process; these were 100 percent complete as to ingredients, zero percent complete as to the packaging, and 30 percent complete as to labor and overhead. One hundred forty-four thousand tortillas were started during April and 147,960 were finished. The ending inventory was 100 percent complete as to ingredients, zero percent complete as to the packaging, and 60 percent complete as to labor and overhead.

a. What were the equivalent units of production for April?

b. What was the cost of the packages transferred to Finished Goods Inventory during April?

c. What was the cost of the ending Work in Process Inventory for April?

30. *(Hybrid costing)* Snappy-Jacks Inc. manufactures sports jackets (one size fits most) for sports clubs and other organizations. Each jacket goes through the same conversion process, but customers may select the fabric (dacron, denim, or cotton) to be used. The company uses a standard costing system, and standard costs for each type of jacket follow:

	DACRON	DENIM	COTTON
Material (5 yards)	$10	$ 5	$12
Direct labor (2 hours)	12	12	12
Overhead (based on 1.5 machine hours)	9	9	9
Total	$31	$26	$33

Material is added at the start of production. In May 1997, there was no beginning Work in Process Inventory and 1,500 jackets were started into production. Of these, 200 were dacron, 600 were denim, and 700 were cotton. At the end of May, 300 jackets (50 dacron, 100 denim, and 150 cotton) were not yet completed. The stage of completion for each cost component for the 300 unfinished jackets is as follows:

Material	100% complete
Direct labor	25% complete
Overhead	35% complete

a. Determine the total cost of the jackets completed and transferred to Finished Goods Inventory.

b. Determine the total cost of the jackets in ending Work in Process Inventory.

COMMUNICATION ACTIVITIES

31. *(Concept of EUP)* Cost accountants use the concept of equivalent units of production (EUP) to measure actual production for a period in a process costing environment. Write a memo describing what EUP measures, and why it is necessary to use EUP to determine actual production for a period.

32. *(Production process; team activity)* In a team of three or four, choose a company whose mass-production process you would like to learn. Use library, Internet, and (if possible) personal resources to gather information. Prepare a visual representation (similar to Exhibit 8–2) of that production process. In this presentation, indicate the approximate percentage of completion points at which various materials are added and where/how labor and overhead flow into and through the process. Assume that 1,000 units of product are flowing through your production process and are now at the 60 percent completion point as to labor. Prepare a written explanation about the quantity of direct material equivalent units that are included in the 1,000 units. Also explain how much overhead activity and cost have occurred and why the overhead percentage is the same as or different from the percentage of completion for labor.

PROBLEMS

33. *(EUP; weighted average & FIFO)* Topeka Company produces outdoor brooms. On June 30, 1997, the firm had 3,600 units in process that were 70 percent complete as to material, 40 percent complete as to direct labor, and 30 percent complete as to overhead. During July, 186,000 brooms were started. Records indicate that 184,200 units were transferred to Finished Goods Inventory in July. Ending units in process were 40 percent complete as to material, 25 percent complete as to direct labor, and 10 percent complete as to overhead.

a. Calculate the physical units to account for in July.

b. How many units were started and completed during July?

c. Determine July's EUP for each category using the weighted average method.

d. Determine July's EUP for each category using the FIFO method.

e. Reconcile your answers to parts c and d.

34. *(EUP; weighted average & FIFO)* The Mountain Coal Company mines and processes coal that is sold to four power plants in Northeast Indiana. The company employs a process costing system to assign production costs to the coal it processes. For the third week in March 1997, the firm had a beginning Work in Process Inventory of 50,000 tons of ore that were 100 percent complete as to material and 30 percent complete as to conversion costs. During the week, an additional 200,000 tons of ore were started in process. At the end of the week, 35,000 tons remained in Work in Process Inventory and were 70 percent complete as to material and 60 percent complete as to conversion costs.

    For the third week in March:

    a. Compute the total units to account for.

    b. Determine how many units were started and completed.

    c. Determine the equivalent units of production using the weighted average method.

    d. Determine the equivalent units of production using the FIFO method.

35. *(Weighted average)* Helsinki Products manufactures an electronic language translator. The device can translate seven languages in either direction. Analysis of beginning Work in Process Inventory for February 1997 revealed the following:

800 UNITS	**PERCENT COMPLETE**	**COST INCURRED**
Material	45	$ 8,700
Direct labor	65	3,800
Overhead	40	6,600
Total beginning WIP		$19,100

During February, Helsinki Products started production of another 3,800 translators and incurred $85,380 for material, $23,560 for direct labor, and $65,720 for overhead. On February 28, the company had 400 units in process (70 percent complete as to material, 90 percent complete as to direct labor, and 80 percent complete as to overhead).

    a. Prepare a cost of production report for February using the weighted average method.

    b. Journalize the February transactions.

    c. Prepare T-accounts to represent the flow of costs for Helsinki Products for February. Use "XXX" where amounts are unknown and identify what each unknown amount represents.

36. *(Weighted average)* Junge Enterprises manufactures belt buckles in a single-step production process. To determine the proper valuations for inventory balances and Cost of Goods Sold, you have obtained the following information for October 1997:

	WHOLE UNITS	**COST OF MATERIAL**	**COST OF LABOR**
Beginning work in process	400,000	$ 400,000	$ 630,000
Units started during period	2,000,000	2,600,000	3,990,000
Units transferred to finished goods	1,800,000		

Beginning inventory units were 100 percent complete as to material, but only 80 percent complete as to labor and overhead. The ending inventory units were 100 percent complete as to material and 50 percent complete as to conversion. Overhead is applied to production at the rate of 60 percent of direct labor cost.

a. Prepare a schedule to compute equivalent units of production by cost component assuming the weighted average method.

b. Determine the unit production costs for material and conversion.

c. Prepare a cost of production report for October 1997.

37. *(Weighted average)* You have just been hired as the cost accountant for California Micro, a producer of personal computer cases. This position has been vacant for one month. John Friend, manager of the firm's tax department, has performed some computations for last month's information; however, he confesses to you that he doesn't remember a great deal about cost accounting.

In the production process, materials are added at the beginning of production and overhead is applied to each product at the rate of 70 percent of direct labor cost. There was no Finished Goods Inventory at the beginning of July. A review of the firm's inventory cost records provides you with the following information:

	UNITS	DM COST	DL COST
Work in Process 7/1/97 (70% complete as to labor and overhead)	100,000	$ 750,000	$ 215,000
Units started in production	1,300,000		
Costs for July		4,850,000	3,265,000
Work in Process 7/31/97 (40% complete as to labor and overhead)	400,000		

At the end of July, the cost of Finished Goods Inventory was determined to be $124,033.

a. Prepare schedules for July 1997, to compute the following:

   1. Equivalent units of production using the weighted average method.

   2. Unit production costs for material, labor, and overhead.

   3. Cost of Goods Sold.

b. Prepare the journal entry to record the July transfer of completed goods.

(CPA adapted)

38. *(FIFO cost per EUP)* The following information has been gathered from the records of Snack-On Foods for July 1997. The firm makes a variety of snacks; the information presented here is for a peanut and pretzel mix. Materials are added at the beginning of processing; overhead is applied on a direct labor basis. The mix is transferred to a second department for packaging. Snack-On uses a FIFO process costing system.

Beginning WIP inventory (40% complete as to conversion)	5,000 pounds
Mix started in July	90,400 pounds
Ending WIP inventory (70% complete as to conversion)	4,000 pounds
Materials cost incurred in July	$415,840
Conversion costs incurred in July	$106,030

Beginning inventory cost totaled $13,875. For July 1997, compute the following:

a. Equivalent units of production by cost component.

b. Cost per equivalent unit by cost component.

c. Cost of mix transferred to the packaging department in July.

d. Cost of July's ending inventory.

39. *(Cost assignment; FIFO)* Biltmore Manufacturing is a contract manufacturer for Zesty Dressing. Biltmore uses a FIFO process costing system to account for the production of its salad dressing. All ingredients are added at the start of the process. Zesty provides reusable vats to Biltmore for the completed product to be shipped to Zesty for bottling so Biltmore incurs no packaging costs. June 1997 production and cost information for Biltmore Manufacturing is as follows:

Gallons of dressing in beginning inventory	37,000	
Gallons transferred out during June	243,000	
Gallons of dressing in ending inventory	23,500	
Cost of beginning inventory:		
Direct materials	$ 181,300	
Direct labor	45,695	
Overhead	50,320	
Costs incurred in June:		
Direct materials	$1,131,435	
Direct labor	452,976	
Overhead	770,133	

The beginning and ending inventories had the following degrees of completion for each labor and overhead:

	BEGINNING INVENTORY	ENDING INVENTORY
Direct labor	35%	25%
Overhead	60%	30%

a. How many gallons of dressing ingredients were started in June?
b. What is the total cost of the completed beginning inventory?
c. What is the total cost of goods completed during June?
d. What is the average cost per unit of all goods completed during June?
e. What is the cost of June's ending WIP inventory?

40. *(Weighted average & FIFO)* In a single-process production system, the Gayden Corporation produces fingernails. For August 1997, the company's accounting records reflected the following:

Beginning Work in Process Inventory	
(100% complete as to material; 30% complete as to direct	
labor; 60% complete as to overhead)	6,000 units
Units started during the month	45,000 units
Ending Work in Process Inventory	
(100% complete as to material; 40% complete as to direct	
labor; 70% complete as to overhead	10,000 units

COST COMPONENT	BEGINNING INVENTORY	AUGUST COSTS
Material	$4,980	$45,000
Direct labor	450	21,600
Overhead	3,180	33,300

a. For August, prepare a cost of production report assuming the company uses the weighted average method.
b. For August, prepare a cost of production report assuming the company uses the FIFO method.

41. *(FIFO; second department)* Ottawa Ltd. manufactures porcelain kitchen sinks in a process requiring operations in three separate departments: Molding, Curing, and Finishing. Materials are first introduced in the molding operation and additional material is added during the curing process. The following information is available for the Curing Department for October 1997:

Beginning WIP Inventory (degree of completion: Transferred-in,	
100%; direct material, 80%; direct labor, 40%; overhead,	
30%)	8,000 units
Transferred-in from Molding	40,000 units
Ending WIP Inventory (degree of completion: Transferred-in,	
100%; direct material, 70%; direct labor, 50%; overhead,	
40%)	4,000 units
Transferred to Finishing	? units

COST COMPONENT	BEGINNING INVENTORY	CURRENT PERIOD
Transferred-in	$66,000	$320,000
Direct material	24,960	161,600
Direct labor	6,720	85,600
Overhead	3,580	43,200

Prepare, in good form, a cost of production report for the Curing Department for October 1997.

(CPA adapted)

42. (Two departments; weighted average) The Holiday Spirits Corporation manufactures plastic Christmas trees in two departments: Cutting and Boxing. In the Cutting Department, wire wrapped with green "needles" is placed into production at the beginning of the process and is cut to various lengths depending on the size of the trees being made at that time. The "branches" are then transferred to the Boxing Department where the lengths are separated into the necessary groups to make a tree. These are then placed in boxes and immediately sent to Finished Goods.

    The following data are available related to the August 1997 production in each of the two departments.

		PERCENT OF COMPLETION		
	UNITS	*Transferred-in*	*Material*	*Conversion*
Cutting Department				
Beginning inventory	9,000	N/A	100	30
Started in process	35,000			
Ending inventory	3,600	N/A	100	70
Boxing Department				
Beginning inventory	2,500	100	0	55
Transferred-in	?			
Ending inventory	1,200	100	0	60

	Transferred-in	*Material*	*Conversion*
Cutting Department			
Beginning inventory	N/A	$13,250	$ 5,550
Current period		52,750	80,290
Boxing Department			
Beginning inventory	$9,608	$ 0	$ 550
Current period	?	12,510	20,660

a. Prepare a cost of production report for the Cutting Department assuming a weighted average method.

b. Using the data developed from part a, prepare a cost of production report for the Boxing Department, also using the weighted average method.

43. (Cost flows, multiple departments) Smyrna Corporation produces accent stripes for automobiles in 50-inch rolls. Each roll passes through three departments (stripping, adhesion, and packaging) before it is ready for shipment to automobile dealers and detailing shops. Product costs are tracked by department and assigned using a process costing system. Overhead is applied to production in each department at a rate of 60 percent of the department's direct labor cost. The information below pertains to departmental operations for November 1997.

WORK IN PROCESS—STRIPPING			WORK IN PROCESS—ADHESION		
Beginning	$20,000		Beginning	$70,000	
DM	90,000		Transferred-in	?	
DL	80,000		DM	60,000	$480,000
Overhead	?		DL	?	
			Overhead	?	
Ending	$17,000		Ending	$20,000	

WORK IN PROCESS—PACKAGING			FINISHED GOODS		
Beginning	$150,000		Beginning	$185,000	
Transferred-in	?		CGM	830,000	$720,000
DM	?		Overhead	?	
DL	?				
Overhead	90,000		Ending	?	
Ending	$ 90,000				

a. What was the cost of goods transferred from the Stripping Department to the Adhesion Department for the month?

b. How much direct labor cost was incurred in the Adhesion Department? How much overhead was assigned to production in the Adhesion Department for the month?

c. How much direct material cost was charged to products passing through the Packaging Department?

d. Prepare the journal entries for all interdepartmental transfers of products and the cost of the units sold during November 1997.

44. *(Comprehensive; two departments)* Pet Pens Inc. makes a backyard fencing system for pet owners in a two-stage production system. In Process One, wood is cut and assembled into 6-foot fence sections. In Process Two, the sections are pressure treated to resist the effects of weather and then coated with a wood preservative. The following production and cost data are available for May 1997 (units are 6-foot fence sections):

UNITS	CUTTING PROCESS	PRESSURE PROCESS
Beginning WIP inventory (May 1)	1,300	900
Complete as to material	80%	0%
Complete as to conversion	75%	60%
Units started in May	4,800	?
Units completed in May	?	4,500
Ending WIP inventory (May 31)	1,100	?
Complete as to material	40%	0%
Complete as to conversion	20%	40%

COSTS		
Beginning WIP Inventory		
Transferred-in costs		$ 4,725
Material	$ 2,130	0
Conversion	3,175	1,674
Current costs		
Transferred-in costs		$?
Material	$ 8,800	4,995
Conversion	12,735	13,560

a. Prepare EUP schedules for both the Cutting and Pressure Processes. Use the FIFO method.

b. Determine the cost per equivalent unit for the Cutting Process assuming a FIFO method.

c. Assign costs to goods transferred and to inventory in the Cutting Process on a FIFO basis.

d. Transfer the FIFO costs to the Pressure Process. Determine the cost per equivalent unit in the Pressure Process on a modified FIFO basis.

e. Assign costs to goods transferred and to inventory in the Pressure Process on a modified FIFO basis.

f. Assuming there was no beginning or ending inventory of Finished Goods Inventory for May, what was Cost of Goods Sold for May?

45. *(Standard process costing)* Eye-Guard is a manufacturer of high-quality lenses for sunglasses and ski goggles. Eye-Guard uses a standard process costing system and carries inventories at standard. In July 1997, the following data were available:

	STANDARD COST OF 1 UNIT
Direct material	$ 4.50
Conversion costs	12.50
Total manufacturing cost	$17.00

Beginning WIP inventory	10,000 units (100% DM; 70% Conversion)
Started in July	180,000 units
Completed in July	160,000 units
Ending WIP inventory	? units (100% DM; 60% Conversion)

Actual costs for July	
Direct material	$ 781,000
Conversion	2,045,000
Total actual cost	$2,826,000

a. Prepare an equivalent units of production schedule.
b. Prepare a cost of production report and assign costs to goods transferred and to inventory.
c. Calculate and label the variances and charge them to Cost of Goods Sold.

46. *(Multiproduct; hybrid costing)* Lilliput Industries manufactures a series of three models of molded plastic chairs: Standard (can be stacked), Deluxe (with arms), and Executive (with arms and padding); all are variations of the same design. The company uses batch manufacturing and has a hybrid costing system.

Lilliput has an extrusion operation and subsequent operations to form, trim, and finish the chairs. Plastic sheets are produced by the extrusion operation, some of which are sold directly to other manufacturers. During the forming operation, the remaining plastic sheets are molded into chair seats and the legs are added; the Standard model is sold after this operation. During the trim operation, the arms are added to the Deluxe and Executive models and the chair edges are smoothed. Only the Executive model enters the finish operation where the padding is added. All of the units produced receive the same steps within each operation.

The May production run had a total manufacturing cost of $898,000. The units of production and direct material costs incurred were as follows:

	UNITS PRODUCED	EXTRUSION MATERIALS	FORM MATERIALS	TRIM MATERIALS	FINISH MATERIALS
Plastic sheets	5,000	$ 60,000			
Standard model	6,000	72,000	$24,000		
Deluxe model	3,000	36,000	12,000	$ 9,000	
Executive model	2,000	24,000	8,000	6,000	$12,000
	16,000	$192,000	$44,000	$15,000	$12,000

Manufacturing costs applied during May were as follows:

	EXTRUSION OPERATION	FORM OPERATION	TRIM OPERATION	FINISH OPERATION
Direct labor	$152,000	$60,000	$30,000	$18,000
Factory overhead	240,000	72,000	39,000	24,000

a. For each product produced by Lilliput during May, determine the
  1. unit cost.
  2. total cost.
  Be sure to account for all costs incurred during the month, and support your answer with appropriate calculations.

b. Without prejudice to your answer in part a, assume that 1,000 units of the Deluxe model remained in Work in Process Inventory at the end of the month. These units were 100 percent complete in the trim operation. Determine the value of the 1,000 units of the Deluxe model in Lilliput's Work in Process Inventory at the end of May.

(CMA)

47. *(WA and FIFO)* Whitehall Company makes quality paint sold at premium prices in one production department. Production begins with the blending of various chemicals, which are added at the beginning of the process, and ends with the canning of the paint. Canning occurs when the mixture reaches the 90 percent stage of completion. The gallon cans are then transferred to the Shipping Department for crating and shipment. Labor and overhead are added continuously throughout the process. Factory overhead is applied on the basis of direct labor hours at the rate of $3 per hour.

CASE

Prior to May, when a change in the process was implemented, work in process inventories were insignificant. The change in process enables greater production but results in material amounts of work in process. The company has always used the weighted average method to determine equivalent production and unit costs. Now, production management is considering changing from the weighted average method to the first-in, first-out method.

The following data relate to actual production during May:

COSTS FOR MAY

Work in process inventory, May 1	
Direct material—chemicals	$ 45,600
Direct labor ($10 per hour)	6,250
Factory overhead	1,875
May costs added	
Direct material—chemicals	$228,400
Direct material—cans	7,000
Direct labor ($10 per hour)	35,000
Factory overhead	10,500

UNITS FOR MAY (GALLONS)

Work in process inventory, May 1 (25% complete)	4,000
Sent to Shipping Department	20,000
Started in May	21,000
Work in process inventory, May 31 (80% complete)	5,000

a. Prepare a cost of production report for each cost element for May using the weighted average method.
b. Prepare a cost of production report for each cost element for May using the FIFO method.
c. Discuss the advantages and disadvantages of using the weighted average method versus the FIFO method, and explain under what circumstances each method should be used.

(CMA adapted)

48. Pharmaceutical companies make most drugs in mass-production processes after the products are cleared for sale by the Food and Drug Administration. Additionally, they spend huge amounts of money on research and development; the estimated cost of bringing a drug to market is almost $200 million. However, a study by the Office of Technology Assessment said:

ETHICS AND QUALITY DISCUSSION

[T]he pharmaceutical industry earns at least $36 million more than development costs on each new drug and is able to raise prices for brand name drugs even after they lose patent protection. The surplus return amounts to about 4.3% of the price of each drug over its product life, and the profit margin is two to three percentage points higher than in other industries.

[SOURCE: "Drug Profits Said to Outstrip R&D Costs," *Wall Street Journal* (February 26, 1993), p. B6. Reprinted by permission of *The Wall Street Journal*, © 1993 Dow Jones & Company, Inc. All Rights Reserved Worldwide.]

a. Which of the following types of costs do you think would be the highest for manufacturing pharmaceuticals: material, labor, or overhead? (Remember that past R&D costs cannot currently be included in overhead because they were expensed when incurred.) What kind of costing system would be most applicable to the pharmaceutical industry and why?

b. Is the pharmaceutical industry engaging in life cycle costing as discussed in Chapter 6? If so, how?

c. President Clinton has called drug prices "shocking." Do you believe that pharmaceutical companies should be allowed to earn a significantly higher rate of return than companies in other industries? Why or why not?

d. Is it ethical to charge high prices for drugs that are life-essential for users? For drugs that are non-life-essential? Discuss the rationale for your answer(s).

49. *Quantex makes high-quality steel for specialized applications like ball bearings, camshafts, and tank treads. Most of the armor of Desert Storm rode to victory on Quantex steel.*

The company keeps almost no inventory—a lesson learned from the days when steel produced for the oil patch rusted on its lots. At the company's Fort Smith, Arkansas, facility, every batch of steel is a custom-recipe, sold before it's even cooked in the pot. When cool, it is bar-coded with the owner's name and address.

Mill workers get a bonus based on the amount of steel shipped, minus any defective steel that comes back. That gives them an incentive to make defect-free steel using as few people as possible. Quantex takes about 1.9 man-hours to produce a ton of steel, vs. about four hours for a big integrated mill. Other mini-mill companies are about as efficient as Quantex, but their commodity-grade reinforcing bars sell for roughly $300 a ton, while Quantex specialty steel fetches around $500.

[SOURCE: Peter Nulty, "The Less-Is-More Strategy," *FORTUNE* (December 2, 1991), pp. 102–103. © 1991 Time Inc. All rights reserved.]

a. Discuss the applicability of use to Quantex of a traditional process costing system, a standard process costing system, and a hybrid costing system.

b. What two reasons can be given for such a wide selling price differential for tonnage between Quantex and the other mini-mills? Which of these do you think has more influence on the high selling price and why?

c. Why is quality an extremely important issue for steel producers?

50. As labor markets and product markets become ever more competitive, government programs involving affirmative action and set-asides have increasingly been attacked. U.S. Representative Jan Meyers has led the charge to eliminate the set-aside programs for minority businesses, which are administered by the Small Business Administration (SBA).

"The program has never worked as it was expected to work," said Rep. Meyers, who heads the House Committee on Small Business. Rep. Meyers, a Kansas Republican, said she is especially troubled by the program's practice of awarding contracts without bidding. The SBA confirms that more than 90% of the contracts are awarded without competition.

[SOURCE: Stephanie N. Mehta, "SBA Program for Minorities is Under Attack," *Wall Street Journal* (April 18, 1996), p. B2. Reprinted by permission of *The Wall Street Journal*, © 1996 Dow Jones & Company, Inc. All Rights Reserved Worldwide.]

Thus, for example, minority-owned businesses can obtain federal contracts for construction work without bidding against other businesses.

a. In evaluating the policy of set-asides for minority businesses, address the likely impact of the programs on

1. the cost of contracts to the federal government.

2. the quality of work performed by government contractors.

3. the ability of the minority-owned businesses to successfully compete.

b. Describe the circumstances under which you would find the use of set-asides to be ethically acceptable and ethically unacceptable.

51. In 1996, one of the more hotly contested political issues in the United States was whether the minimum wage should be increased. Proponents of an increase in the minimum wage argue that such an increase is necessary for low-paid employees to maintain a decent standard of living. Opponents of an increase in the minimum wage suggest that an increase in the cost of labor would cause firms to fire employees to control labor cost increases—thereby harming the very group that was intended to be the beneficiary of the wage increase. Analyze the likely effects of an increase in the minimum wage from the perspective of

a. product/service quality and

b. ethical issues.

52. *Every week, hundreds of beer aficionados tour the tiny, run-down brewery of Boston Beer Co., purveyor of the fashionable Samuel Adams beers.*

But all this is just for show. The real stuff is brewing 750 miles away, in the sprawling Cincinnati plant of Hudepohl-Schoenling Brewing Co. Beer-buffs who pay premium prices for Sam Adams might well be surprised to see it bubbling away at the home of such humble brands as Hudy Bold and Little Kings Cream Ale.

About 100 of the nation's thousand or so craft brewers don't make much beer at all. They simply pay another company to make their beer for them, according to their recipe.

Contract brewing, long a behind-the-scenes practice, is now the center of the biggest brawl in the world of beer. The U.S. Bureau of Alcohol, Tobacco and Firearms is weighing whether contract beer should state explicitly on their labels which company brewed them.

[SOURCE: Yumiko Ono, "Who Really Makes That Cute Little Beer? You'd be Surprised," *Wall Street Journal* (April 15, 1996), pp. A1, A8. Reprinted by permission of *The Wall Street Journal*, © 1996 Dow Jones & Company, Inc. All Rights Reserved Worldwide.]

a. Why would "craft brewers" hire other firms to brew their products?

b. How could the practice of subcontracting the brewing be justified on the basis of quality considerations?

c. In your opinion, is subcontracting the actual brewing of the beer an ethical practice in the light of the fact that the practice is not disclosed to the consumer? Explain.

INTERNET ACTIVITIES

53. Find the home page for Deloitte & Touche Consulting Group. From there, find the page discussing developments in the Pharmaceutical/Medical Devices Industry. Read the materials on that page about evolving practices in the industry to improve cost effectiveness of operations. Discuss how the industry's new practices will affect process costing in the pharmaceutical industry. Which cost pools (direct materials, direct labor, manufacturing overhead) will be affected by the emerging practices? Also, address whether any of the evolving practices would be better served by life cycle costing.

54. Find the web page for the "Agile Manufacturing Project at MIT." Discuss the nature of this research project and how the research might affect cost accounting practices in industries that manufacture complex products.

55. Search the Internet to identify a vendor of process costing software. Read the on-line literature provided by the vendor regarding the software. Then, briefly describe the major features of the software in the areas of product costing, cost budgeting, and cost control.

Special Production Issues: Lost Units and Accretion

LEARNING OBJECTIVES

After completing this chapter, you should be able to answer these questions:

1. Why do lost units occur in manufacturing processes?

2. How do normal and abnormal loss of units differ and how is each treated in an EUP schedule?

3. How are the costs of each type of loss assigned?

4. How are losses treated in a job order costing system?

5. How does accretion of units affect the EUP schedule and costs per unit?

6. How are rework costs of defective units treated?

7. What is the cost of quality products?

West Publishing CD-ROM Production

West Publishing is a market leader in legal publications and has more than 6,000 databases primarily in law, medicine, and insurance. The company also publishes about 10,000 different college texts, mostly in business administration, social sciences, and computer science. Company management recognized that the demand for print books (especially those in the legal area) was slowing as CD-ROM versions were gaining popularity. So the company decided to diversify its operations to take advantage of this growing market segment.

CD-ROMs are produced in "clean rooms." The process starts with data and a glass disc. The data are prepared in a manner to conform with ISO 9000 specifications. The optical mastering process begins as a laser beam records the data on a coated glass master and cuts out billions of "peaks and valleys." The finished master is then used to create a niched negative impression of the data pits that can be used to create the "stamper" for CD-ROM replication. The stamper is mounted in an injection molding press where granular, optical-grade polycarbonate is heated and fed into a mold cavity under pressures of 25 to 100 tons. The disc is then cooled and transported robotically to the metalization chamber where the reflective aluminum layer is "spattered" onto the disc and a protective coating is applied. Quality control checks are performed continuously throughout the process, and West's accepted quality level (AQL) is presently 1 defect in 10,000 or .0001 percent.

SOURCES: Steven Lipin, Raju Narisetti, and Solange De Santis, "Thomson to Purchase West Publishing for $3.425 Billion," *Wall Street Journal* (February 27, 1996), p. A3; interview with T. R. Kluge, West Publishing Company CD-ROM Production (March 1996). Reprinted by permission of *The Wall Street Journal*, © 1996 Dow Jones & Company, Inc. All Rights Reserved Worldwide.

L ike West, most companies have established AQLs for their production or service processes. If the percentage of defects is less than the AQL, the company considers that it has performed acceptably. Companies viewed as having world-class status in a particular endeavor seek to continuously tighten the accepted quality level. Thus, producing goods with zero defects and performing services with zero errors are laudable goals and ones toward which domestic and foreign companies are striving. The examples in Chapter 8 assumed that all units to be accounted for have either been transferred or are in ending work in process inventory; however, almost every process produces some units that are spoiled or do not meet production specifications. Phenomena in the production process also may cause the total units accounted for to be less than the total units to account for. In other situations (unrelated to spoiled units), the addition or expansion of materials after the start of the process may cause the units accounted for to be greater than those to be accounted for originally or in a previous department.

This chapter covers these more complex issues of process costing. Spoiled and defective units, reworking of defective units, and accretion require adjustments to the equivalent units of production schedule and cost assignments made at the end of a period. The last section of this chapter discusses controlling quality so that only minimal inferior goods are produced. These issues are of great import to companies considering the results of a February 1996 *Business Week/Harris Poll*, which asked "How would you rate large companies in America on making good products and competing in a global economy?" The answers were as follows: excellent, 14%; pretty good, 44%; only fair, 33%; poor, 9%.[1]

[1] Business Week/Harris Poll, "America, Land of the Shaken," *Business Week* (March 11, 1996), p. 64.

LOSS OF UNITS

shrinkage

economically reworked

defective unit

spoiled unit

normal loss

abnormal loss

Few, if any, processes combine material, labor, and overhead with no loss of units. Some of these losses, such as evaporation, leakage, or oxidation, are inherent in the production process. For example, when Starbucks or Batdorf & Bronson roast coffee beans, approximately 20 percent of the original weight is lost from water evaporation. This situation results in **shrinkage.** Modifying the production process to reduce or eliminate the causes of shrinkage may be difficult, impossible, or simply not cost beneficial.

At other times, errors in the production process (either by humans or machines) cause a loss of units through rejection at inspection for failure to meet appropriate quality standards or designated product specifications. Whether these lost units are considered defective or spoiled depends on their ability to be economically reworked. **Economically reworked** means that (1) the unit can be reprocessed to a sufficient quality level to be salable through normal distribution channels and (2) incremental rework cost is less than incremental revenue from the sale of reworked units. A **defective unit** can be economically reworked, but a **spoiled unit** cannot. This differentiation is determined by an inspector in the producing company.

To illustrate the difference between defective and spoiled units, assume you order a medium-rare steak at a restaurant. You are now the control inspector. If the steak brought to you is rare, it is a defective unit because the chef can cook it longer to bring it up to "product specifications." The incremental revenue is the selling price of the steak; the incremental cost is a few moments of the chef's time. However, if the steak brought to you is well-done, it is a spoiled unit because it cannot be reworked. Therefore, a newly cooked steak would have to be provided.

A **normal loss** of units falls within a tolerance level expected during production. The range of tolerance specified by management creates what is referred to in the opening vignette as the accepted quality level. If West Publishing had set its quality goal as 98 percent of goods produced, the company would have been expecting a normal loss of 2 percent. Any loss in excess of the AQL is an **abnormal loss.** Thus, the difference between normal and abnormal loss is merely one of degree and is determined by management.

A variety of methods may be used to account for units lost during production. Selection of the most appropriate method depends on two factors: (1) the cause of the decrease and (2) management expectations regarding lost units. Understanding why units decreased during production requires detailed knowledge of the manufacturing process. Management's expectations are important to determine the acceptable loss quantities from defects, spoilage, or shrinkage as well as the revenue and cost considerations of defective and spoiled units.

TYPES OF LOST UNITS

In developing the product design, manufacturing process, and product quality, management selects a combination of material, labor, and overhead from the wide resource spectrum available. This combination is chosen to provide the lowest long-run cost per unit *and* to achieve the designated product specifications—including those for quality. In making this resource combination choice, managers recognize that, for most combinations, some degree of production error may occur that will result in lost units. Given the resource choices made by management, the quantity or percentage of lost units to be generated in a given period or production run should be reasonably estimable. This estimate is the normal loss because it is planned for and expected. Normal loss is usually calculated on the basis of good output or actual input.

Some companies may estimate the normal loss to be quite high because the lowest cost material, labor, or overhead support is chosen. For example, assume that Poore Manufacturing Corporation chooses to install the least advanced, lowest cost machinery for production purposes because its workers do not have the educational or technological skills to handle the more advanced equipment. The installed equipment

Aetna Insurance Co. provides an employee literacy program. This program has proven to be cost-beneficial because of fewer employee errors and customer complaints and an increased level of overall service quality.

may have fewer quality checks and, thus, produce more spoiled units than the more advanced equipment. Poore's managers have decided that the costs of upgrading worker skills were greater than the cost of lost units. Such a decision would be in total contrast to the one made by the managers at Delta Wire in Clarksdale, Mississippi. Rather than allow the low education of workers to raise lost unit levels, the company decided to raise the employees' educational levels, as described in the News Note "Increased Education."

Another reason for high estimated normal losses relates not to the resources chosen, but to a problem inherent in the design or production process. In other cases, based on cost-benefit analysis, managers may find that a problem would cost more to eliminate than to tolerate. For example, assume a machine malfunctions once every 100 runs and improperly blends ingredients. The machine processes 50,000 runs each year and the ingredients in each run cost $10. Correcting the problem has been estimated to cost $20,000 per year. Spoilage cost is $5,000 per year (500 spoiled batches $\times$ $10 worth of ingredients) plus a minimal amount of overhead costs. If company employees are aware of the malfunction and catch every improperly blended run, accepting the spoilage is less expensive than correcting the problem.

VIDEO VIGNETTE

Prolight (Blue Chip Enterprises)

Increased Education Causes Reduced Spoilage

Companies across the U.S. are discovering that many of their employees can't meet the demands of high-tech jobs. But a growing number of businesses, including Delta Wire, are trying to do educational makeovers of their own work forces. The company began offering job-specific courses such as statistics to all employees in 1990.

Delta Wire's president, George F. Walker, is bullish about his company's skills-enhancement courses. He says productivity, measured in the amount of usable production vs. material that must be discarded, has jumped 20% since the company started the courses. Customer satisfaction is up, and he points to numerous quality awards that the small company has received.

NEWS NOTE

SOURCE: Helene Cooper, "Carpet Firm Sets Up an In-House School To Stay Competitive," *Wall Street Journal* (October 5, 1992), pp. A1, A5. Reprinted by permission of *The Wall Street Journal,* © 1992 Dow Jones & Company, Inc. All Rights Reserved Worldwide.

EXHIBIT 9–1

The Cost of Unhappy
Customers

Potential Annual Revenue Loss from Dissatisfied Buyers			
IF YOU LOSE	1 customer per day	5 customers per day	10 customers per day
spending $5 weekly	$ 94,900	$ 474,500	$ 949,000
spending $10 weekly	$ 189,800	$ 949,000	$ 1,898,000
spending $50 weekly	$ 949,000	$4,745,000	$ 9,490,000
spending $100 weekly	$1,898,000	$9,490,000	$18,980,000

SOURCE: Customer Service Institute, "The Unhappy Customer," *Black Enterprise* (June 1991), p. 234. Earl G. Graves Publishing Co. Copyright June 1991.

If, alternatively, the spoiled runs are allowed to leave the plant, they may create substantial quality failure costs in the form of dissatisfied customers and/or salespeople who might receive the spoiled product. The accompanying News Note discusses recent problems related to defective room keys and dissatisfied customers. Exhibit 9–1 provides estimates of the cost of unhappy customers. In making their cost-benefit analysis, managers must be certain to quantify *all* the costs (both direct and indirect) involved in spoilage problems.

An abnormal loss is a loss in excess of the normal, predicted tolerance limits. Thus, when an abnormal loss occurs, so does a normal loss (unless zero defects have been set as the AQL). Abnormal losses generally arise because of human or machine error during the production process. For example, if the tolerances on one of West's stampers were set incorrectly, a significant quantity of faulty CDs might be produced before the error was noticed. Abnormal losses are more likely to be preventable than some types of normal losses.

Realistically, units are lost in a production process at a specific point. However, accounting for lost units requires that the loss be specified as being either continuous or discrete. For example, the weight loss in roasting coffee beans and the relatively

continuous loss

discrete loss

continual breakage of fragile glass ornaments can be considered **continuous losses** because they occur fairly uniformly throughout the production process. In contrast, a **discrete loss** is assumed to occur at a specific point. Examples of discrete losses include adding the wrong amount of dye to a vat or sewing a collar on a garment backwards. The units are only deemed lost and unacceptable when a quality check is performed. Therefore, regardless of where in the process the units were truly "lost," the loss point is always deemed to be an inspection point. Thus, units past an inspection point should be good units (relative to the specific characteristics inspected), whereas the units prior to an inspection point may be good or may be defective/spoiled.

Control points can be either built into the system or performed by inspectors. The former requires investments in prevention costs; the latter results in appraisal costs. Both are effective, but prevention is often more efficient because acceptable quality cannot be inspected into a product; it must be a part of the production process. Investments to prevent lost units may relate to either people or machines and both should provide high benefits.

I Want Into (Out Of?) My Room!

NEWS NOTE

Hotels' electronic-lock systems are designed to foil would-be intruders. They do that—and often they do more: They stymie guests trying to get in their own rooms and can even imprison those already inside.

The precise failure rate isn't known. But Chicago-based EMG Associates Inc., which sells and services electronic locks, can attest that it is high. Last year, EMG sold about 5,000 electronic locks—and repaired about 5,500. "Defects are prevalent," says Joshua Alper, president of EMG.

Manufacturers don't deny it. One problem: Quality is getting lost in the rush to meet demand. In only a few years, electronic locks [which cost about $250 a room] have been installed in a third of the nation's 3.2 million hotel rooms, and the pace is quickening because hotels feel the security advantages outweigh inconveniences.

To date, there have been [untold incidents of people being locked out of their rooms, but most] alarming is when guests become prisoners in their rooms—raising the worst-case specters of heart attacks or fires. At best, lock-ins are a nuisance, as was the case for five teenage boys [who were locked in a room while] on a Bible retreat at the Dallas/Fort Worth Airport Hilton. [Hotel engineers had to pry the door open with a crowbar.]

The company that made the malfunctioning lock, Yale Security Inc. of Charlotte, N.C., has gotten out of the electronic-lock business altogether. It says that problems managing that part of its business prompted it to refocus on its core mechanical-lock lines.

SOURCE: Jon Bigness, "Hotel-Room 'Key' Cards Foil Prowlers—and Guests," *Wall Street Journal* (Apr. 12, 1996), p. B1. Reprinted by permission of *The Wall Street Journal*, © 1996 Dow Jones & Company, Inc. All Rights Reserved Worldwide.

In determining how many quality control inspection points (machine or human) to have, management must weigh the costs of having more inspections against the savings resulting from (1) not applying additional material, labor, and overhead to products that are already spoiled or defective (direct savings) and (2) the reduction or elimination of internal and external failure costs (indirect savings). Quality control points should always be placed before any bottlenecks in the production system so that the bottleneck resource is not used to process already defective/spoiled units. Additionally, a process that generates a continuous defective/spoilage loss requires a quality control point at the end of production; otherwise, some defective/spoiled units would not be found and would be sent to customers.

ACCOUNTING FOR LOST UNITS

The method of accounting for the cost of lost units depends on whether the loss is considered normal or abnormal and whether the loss occurred continuously in the process or at a discrete point. Exhibit 9–2 summarizes the accounting for the cost of lost units.

The traditional method of accounting for normal losses is simple. Normal loss cost is considered a product cost and is included as part of the cost of the *good* units resulting from the process. Thus, the cost of the loss is inventoried in Work in Process and Finished Goods Inventories and expensed only when the good units are sold. This treatment has been considered appropriate because normal losses have been viewed as unavoidable costs in the production of good units. If the loss results from shrinkage caused by the production process, such as the weight loss of roasted coffee beans, this treatment seems logical. Alternatively, consider the company producing fragile glass ornaments: if the company allows for the loss by virtue of the level at which accepted quality was set, then management will not receive needed information about the cost of quality losses. To illustrate, if a company instituted a zero-defect policy, there would by definition be no "normal" loss. *All* losses would be outside the tolerance specifications for acceptable quality.

Type	Assumed to Occur	May Be	Cost Handled How?	Cost Assigned To?
Continuous	Uniformly throughout process	Normal	Absorbed by all units in ending inventory and transferred out on an EUP basis	Product
		or		
		Abnormal	Written off as a loss on an EUP basis	Period
Discrete	At inspection point or at end of process	Normal	Absorbed by all units past inspection point on an EUP basis	Product
		or		
		Abnormal	Written off as a loss on an EUP basis	Period

EXHIBIT 9–2

Continuous versus Discrete Losses

method of neglect

The costs of normal shrinkage and normal continuous losses are handled through the **method of neglect,** which simply excludes the spoiled units in the equivalent units schedule. Ignoring the spoilage results in a smaller number of equivalent units of production (EUP) and, by default, raises the cost per equivalent unit. Thus, the cost of lost units is spread proportionately over the good units transferred and those remaining in Work in Process Inventory.

Alternatively, the cost of normal, discrete losses is assigned only to units that have passed the inspection point. Such units should be good units (relative to the inspected characteristic), whereas the units prior to this point may be good or may be defective/spoiled. Assigning loss costs to units that may be found to be defective/spoiled in the next period would not be reasonable.

Regardless of whether defects/spoilage occur in a continuous or discrete fashion, the cost of abnormal losses should be accumulated and treated as a loss in the period in which those losses occurred. This treatment is justified by the cost principle discussed in financial accounting. The cost principle allows only costs that are necessary to acquire or produce inventory to attach to it. All unnecessary costs are written off in the period in which they are incurred. Because abnormal losses are not necessary to the production of good units and the cost is avoidable in the future, any abnormal loss cost is regarded as a period cost. This cost should be brought to the attention of the production manager who should then investigate the causes of the loss to determine how to prevent future similar occurrences. Abnormal loss cost is *always* accounted for on an equivalent unit basis.

ILLUSTRATIONS OF LOST UNITS

To best understand how to account for a process that creates lost goods, it is helpful to know the answers to the following questions:

1. What is the process flow?
2. Where is material added during the process?
3. How are labor and overhead applied? (This answer is usually continuously, but not necessarily at the same rate.)

4. At what stage of completion was the beginning, and is the ending, inventory?

5. Where are the quality control inspection points?

6. How do defective/spoiled units occur? (Continuously or discretely?)

Spin-Out Inc. is used to illustrate several alternative situations regarding the handling of lost units in a process costing environment. Spin-Out produces the protective coating for compact discs in a single department. The coating is then sold to CD manufacturers. All materials are added at the start of the process, and conversion costs are applied uniformly throughout the production process. Recyclable containers are provided by buyers and, therefore, are not a cost to Spin-Out. The company uses the FIFO method of calculating equivalent units.

Situation 1—Normal Loss Only; Loss Occurs Throughout Production Process (Continuous)

During processing, the coating is mechanically blended and cooked, resulting in a normal loss from shrinkage. Any decrease of 10 percent or less of the gallons placed into production for a period is considered normal. The June 1996 data for Spin-Out is given below:

GALLONS

Beginning inventory (60% complete)	2,000
Started during month	15,000
Gallons completed and transferred	13,200
Ending inventory (75% complete)	2,500
Lost gallons (normal)	1,300

COSTS

Beginning inventory:		
Material	$ 15,000	
Conversion	1,620	$ 16,620
Current period:		
Material	$102,750	
Conversion	19,425	
		122,175
Total costs		$138,795

To visualize the manufacturing process for Spin-Out, a flow diagram can be constructed. Such a diagram provides distinct, definitive answers to all of the questions asked at the beginning of this section.

Flow Diagram

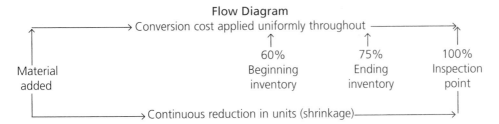

The steps discussed in Chapter 8 on process costing are followed to determine the units accountable for, units accounted for, equivalent units of production, costs accountable for, cost per equivalent unit, and cost assignment. These steps are presented in the cost of production report shown in Exhibit 9–3.

The department is accountable for 17,000 gallons of coating: 2,000 gallons in beginning inventory plus 15,000 gallons started into processing during June. Only 15,700 gallons (13,200 completed and 2,500 in ending inventory) are accounted for prior to considering the processing loss. The 1,300 lost gallons are included in the

EXHIBIT 9–3

Cost of Production Report for Month Ended June 30, 1996 (FIFO method) (Normal continuous shrinkage)

PRODUCTION DATA		EQUIVALENT UNITS	
	WHOLE UNITS	MATERIAL	CONVERSION
Beginning inventory (100%; 60%)	2,000		
+ Gallons started	15,000		
= Gallons to account for	17,000		
Beginning inventory completed (0%; 40%)	2,000	0	800
+ Gallons started and completed	11,200	11,200	11,200
= Total gallons completed	13,200		
+ Ending inventory (100%; 75%)	2,500	2,500	1,875
+ Normal loss	1,300		
= Gallons accounted for	17,000	13,700	13,875

COST DATA			
	TOTAL	MATERIAL	CONVERSION
Beginning inventory costs	$ 16,620		
Current costs	122,175	$102,750	$19,425
Total costs	$138,795		
Divided by EUP		13,700	13,875
Cost per FIFO EUP	$8.90	$7.50	$1.40

COST ASSIGNMENT

Transferred:		
From beginning inventory	$16,620	
Cost to complete: Conversion (800 × $1.40)	1,120	
Total cost of beginning inventory	$17,740	
Started and completed (11,200 × $8.90)	99,680	
Total cost of gallons transferred		$117,420
Ending inventory:		
Material (2,500 × $7.50)	$18,750	
Conversion (1,875 × $1.40)	2,625	21,375
Total costs accounted for		$138,795

schedule of gallons accounted for to balance to the total 17,000 gallons, but these gallons are not extended into the computation of equivalent units of production. Using the method of neglect, these gallons simply "disappear" in the EUP schedule. Thus, the cost per equivalent gallon of the remaining good production of the period is higher for each cost component.

Had the lost gallons been used in the denominator of the cost per EUP computation, the cost per EUP would have been smaller, and the material cost per unit would have been $6.85 ($102,750 ÷ 15,000). Because the lost units do not appear in the Cost Assignment section, their costs must be assigned only to good production. The use of the lower cost per EUP would not allow all of the costs to be accounted for in Exhibit 9–3.

Accounting for normal, continuous shrinkage (or defects/spoilage) is the easiest of all the lost unit computations. There is, however, a theoretical problem with this computation when a company uses weighted average process costing. The units in ending Work in Process Inventory have lost unit cost assigned to them in the current period and will have lost unit cost assigned *again* in the next period. But, even with this flaw, this method provides a reasonable measure of unit cost if the rate of spoilage is consistent from period to period.

Situation 2—Normal Spoilage Only; Spoilage Determined at Final Inspection Point in Production Process (Discrete)

This example uses the same basic cost and unit information given above for Spin-Out Inc. except there are no machine malfunctions. Instead, the coating compound is inspected at the end of the production process. Any spoiled gallons are removed and discarded at inspection; spoilage is usually caused by an improper blending of a batch of coating. Any spoilage of 10 percent or less of the gallons placed into production during the period is considered normal. A production flow diagram is shown below.

In this situation, the spoiled gallons of product *are* included in the equivalent unit schedule. Because the inspection point is at 100 percent completion, all work has been performed on the spoiled gallons and all costs have been incurred to produce those gallons. By including the spoiled gallons at 100 percent completion in the EUP schedule, cost per gallon reflects the cost that *would have been incurred* had all production been good production.

Although quality inspection is often regarded as a non-value-added cost, consumers are generally more than willing to pay for such inspections on foods and pharmaceuticals. Would you want to purchase these items if you knew that a company relied solely on process quality controls and performed no end-of-process inspections?

EXHIBIT 9–4

Cost of Production Report for Month Ended June 30, 1996 (FIFO method) (Normal discrete spoilage)

PRODUCTION DATA		EQUIVALENT UNITS	
	WHOLE UNITS	MATERIAL	CONVERSION
Beginning inventory (100%; 60%)	2,000		
+ Gallons started	15,000		
= Gallons to account for	17,000		
Beginning inventory completed (0%; 40%)	2,000	0	800
+ Gallons started and completed	11,200	11,200	11,200
= Total gallons completed	13,200		
+ Ending inventory (100%; 75%)	2,500	2,500	1,875
+ Normal spoilage (100%; 100%)	1,300	1,300	1,300
= Gallons accounted for	17,000	15,000	15,175

COST DATA			
	TOTAL	MATERIAL	CONVERSION
Beginning inventory costs	$ 16,620		
Current costs	122,175	$102,750	$19,425
Total costs	$138,795		
Divided by EUP		15,000	15,175
Cost per FIFO EUP	$8.13	$6.85	$1.28

COST ASSIGNMENT

Transferred:		
From beginning inventory	$16,620	
Cost to complete: Conversion (800 × $1.28)	1,024	
Total cost of beginning inventory	$17,644	
Started and completed (11,200 × $8.13)	91,056	
Normal spoilage (1,300 × $8.13)*	10,569	
Total cost of gallons transferred (13,200 × $9.04)**		$119,269
Ending inventory:		
Material (2,500 × $6.85)	$17,125	
Conversion (1,875 × $1.28)	2,400	19,525
Total costs accounted for (off due to rounding)		$138,794

*All spoilage cost is assigned to the units transferred.
**For convenience and clerical efficiency, modified FIFO is used. Otherwise, spoilage would have to be allocated to beginning WIP and units started and completed. The $9.04 figure is also computed as the sum of the $8.24 cost [($17,644 + $91,056) ÷ 13,200] per good EUP plus another $.80. This $.80 is the spoilage cost ($10,569) divided by the 13,200 good units transferred.

Cost of the spoiled gallons is assigned solely to the completed units. Because ending Work in Process Inventory has not yet passed the inspection point, this inventory may contain its own normal spoilage that will be detected next period. The cost of production report for Situation 2 is shown in Exhibit 9–4.

Situation 3—Normal Spoilage Only; Spoilage Determined During Production Process (Discrete)

In this example, Spin-Out Inc. inspects the coating compound when the process is 50 percent complete as to conversion. The only difference between this example and the previous one is that, for June, the ending Work in Process Inventory has passed the inspection point. Because of this difference, spoilage cost must be allocated to both the gallons transferred and to ending inventory. Although the ending inventory *could* become spoiled during the remainder of processing, it is either highly unlikely or the cost is so minimal that Spin-Out cannot justify the need for an end-of-process inspection. The flow diagram for this situation follows:

Using the same data as in the two previous situations, Exhibit 9–5 provides the cost per gallon and cost assignment for this situation. Spoiled gallons are extended

(continued)

EXHIBIT 9–5

Cost of Production Report for Month Ended June 30, 1996 (FIFO method) (Normal discrete shrinkage)

PRODUCTION DATA		EQUIVALENT UNITS	
	WHOLE UNITS	MATERIAL	CONVERSION
Beginning inventory (100%; 60%)	2,000		
+ Gallons started	15,000		
= Gallons to account for	17,000		
Beginning inventory completed (0%; 40%)	2,000	0	800
+ Gallons started and completed	11,200	11,200	11,200
= Total gallons completed	13,200		
+ Ending inventory (100%; 75%)	2,500	2,500	1,875
+ Normal spoilage (100%; 50%)	1,300	1,300	650
= Gallons accounted for	17,000	15,000	14,525

COST DATA			
	TOTAL	MATERIAL	CONVERSION
Beginning inventory costs	$ 16,620		
Current costs	122,175	$102,750	$19,425
Total costs	$138,795		
Divided by EUP		15,000	14,525
Cost per FIFO EUP	$8.19	$6.85	$1.34

COST ASSIGNMENT

Transferred:
    From beginning inventory $16,620
    Cost to complete: Conversion (800 × $1.34)   1,072
        Total cost of beginning inventory $17,692
    Started and completed (11,200 × $8.19)   91,728
        Cost prior to proration of spoilage $109,420
    Normal spoilage*   8,051
        Total cost of gallons transferred $117,471
Ending inventory:
    Material (2,500 × $6.85) $17,125
    Conversion (1,875 × $1.34)   2,513
        Cost prior to proration of spoilage $19,638
    Normal spoilage*   1,725
        Total cost of ending inventory   21,363
Total costs accounted for (off due to rounding) $138,834

*Proration of normal spoilage is as follows:

Cost of Production Report
for Month Ended June 30,
1996 (FIFO method)
(Normal discrete shrinkage)

	MATERIAL		CONVERSION	
	EUP	%	EUP	%
Gallons started and completed**	11,200	82	11,200	86
Ending work in process	2,500	18	1,875	14
	13,700	100	13,075	100

Given the above relative EUP percentages, proration of spoilage costs is

Material (1,300 × $6.85)	$8,905
Conversion (650 × $1.34)	871
Cost of normal spoilage to be prorated	$9,776

	MATERIAL	CONVERSION	TOTAL
Gallons started and completed:			
.82 × $8,905	$7,302		
.86 × $ 871		$749	$8,051
Ending work in process:			
.18 × $8,905	1,603		
.14 × $ 871		122	1,725
Total allocations	$8,905	$871	$9,776

**The gallons in beginning WIP were not included in this calculation because beginning WIP
was 100% complete as to material and 60% complete as to conversion. Thus, this inventory
was beyond the inspection point (50%) and no spoilage cost should be assigned to it.

in the EUP schedule at the inspection point degree of completion (100% for material
and 50% for conversion) and affect the cost per gallon. As in Situation 2, the resulting
cost per gallon reflects what the cost *would have been* had all the gallons produced
been good output. Total cost of the spoiled goods is calculated by multiplying the
component cost per gallon by the EUP for each cost component. Total spoilage cost
is then prorated based on the EUP for each cost component between gallons transferred and gallons in ending inventory.

Situation 4—Abnormal Shrinkage (Continuous or Discrete); Some Normal Shrinkage (Continuous)

The final example of Spin-Out Inc. assumes that normal spoilage cannot exceed 5
percent of the gallons placed into production. Additionally, as in Situation 1, the
unit reduction is assumed to occur from shrinkage. The quality control inspection
point is at the end of processing. Because 15,000 gallons were started in June, the
maximum allowable normal shrinkage is 750 gallons (15,000 × 5%). Because the
total reduction in units in June was 1,300 gallons, 550 gallons are considered abnormal shrinkage. Exhibit 9–6 presents the cost of production report for Situation 4.

The approach presented for Situation 4 has one inequity. A portion of the normal
shrinkage is automatically allocated to abnormal shrinkage because the calculation of
EUP allows for the "disappearance" of the normal shrinkage. Cost per gallon is then
computed based on the equivalent units of production. This approach is justified on
the basis of expediency as long as the amount of the allocation of normal shrinkage
to abnormal shrinkage is not considered significant.

Situation 4 is used to illustrate the journal entries necessary to account for shrinkage or spoilage. These entries are as follows:

PRODUCTION DATA		EQUIVALENT UNITS	
	WHOLE UNITS	MATERIAL	CONVERSION
Beginning inventory (100%; 60%)	2,000		
+ Gallons started	15,000		
= Gallons to account for	17,000		
Beginning inventory completed (0%; 40%)	2,000	0	800
+ Gallons started and completed	11,200	11,200	11,200
= Total gallons completed	13,200		
+ Ending inventory (100%; 75%)	2,500	2,500	1,875
+ Normal spoilage	750		
+ Abnormal spoilage (100%; 100%)	550	550	550
= Gallons accounted for	17,000	14,250	14,425

COST DATA			
	TOTAL	MATERIAL	CONVERSION
Beginning inventory costs	$ 16,620		
Current costs	122,175	$102,750	$19,425
Total costs	$138,795		
Divided by EUP		14,250	14,425
Cost per FIFO EUP	$8.56	$7.21	$1.35

COST ASSIGNMENT

Transferred:			
From beginning inventory	$16,620		
Cost to complete: Conversion (800 × $1.35)	1,080		
Total cost of beginning inventory	$17,700		
Started and completed (11,200 × $8.56)	95,872		
Total cost of gallons transferred		$113,572	
Ending inventory:			
Material (2,500 × $7.21)	$18,025		
Conversion (1,875 × $1.35)	2,531	20,556	
Abnormal loss (550 × $8.56)		4,708	
Total costs accounted for (off due to rounding)		$138,836	

EXHIBIT 9–6

Cost of Production Report for Month Ended June 30, 1996 (FIFO method) (Abnormal shrinkage; normal continuous shrinkage)

Work in Process Inventory	122,175	
Raw Material Inventory		102,750
Wages Payable (and/or other appropriate accounts)		19,425
To record current period costs.		

Finished Goods Inventory	113,572	
Work in Process Inventory		113,572
To record cost transferred from the department.		

Loss from Abnormal Spoilage	4,708	
Work in Process Inventory		4,708
To remove cost of abnormal spoilage from Work in Process Inventory.		

The accounts debited and credited in the first journal entry would be the same for Situations 1, 2, and 3. The dollar amount of the second entry would change for each of Situations 1, 2, and 3 to reflect the appropriate "cost transferred" figure shown in the respective cost of production report. The third journal entry above is made only when abnormal defects/spoilage occurs.

All illustrations to this point have used FIFO process costing. If the weighted average method were used, the difference would appear (as discussed in Chapter 8) only in the treatment of beginning inventory and its related costs. Lost units would be handled as illustrated in each exhibit shown for Situations 1 through 4. Exhibit 9–7 illustrates the weighted average method for the data used in Exhibit 9–6.

A summary of the treatment of various types of lost units in a process costing system is shown in Exhibit 9–8.

DEFECTIVE UNITS

The preceding examples have all presumed that the lost units were valueless. However, some goods that do not meet quality specifications are merely defective rather than spoiled. Such units are either reworked to meet product specifications or sold as irregulars. Rework cost is a product or period cost depending on whether the rework is considered to be normal or abnormal.

If the rework is normal and actual costing is used, the rework cost is added to the current period's work in process costs for good units and assigned to all units completed. In companies using predetermined overhead application rates, normal rework cost should be estimated and included as part of the estimated factory overhead cost used in computing the overhead application rates. In this way, the overhead application rate will be large enough to cover rework costs. When actual rework costs are incurred, they are assigned to the Manufacturing Overhead account.

If rework is abnormal, the costs should be accumulated and assigned to a loss account. The units are included in the EUP schedule for the period and only actual production (not rework) costs will be considered in determining unit cost.[2]

Reworked units may be irregular and have to be sold at less than the normal selling price. Production cost of irregular items should be transferred to a special inventory account and should not be commingled with the production costs of good units. When the net realizable value (selling price minus cost to rework and sell) is less than total cost, the difference is referred to as a deficiency. If the number of defective units is normal, the deficiency should be treated as part of the production cost of good units. If some proportion of the defective units is considered an abnormal loss, that proportion of the deficiency should be written off as a period cost.

Accounting for defective units is illustrated by the August 1996 manufacturing data of Spin-Out Inc. During August, the company produced 17,900 good gallons and 100 defective gallons of coating component. The 100 gallons were considered defective because the traditional silver coloration of the product was, instead, dark gray. Total production costs other than rework were $160,200. The 100 defective gallons can be reworked at a total cost of $140 (or $1.40 per gallon) by mixing the defective gallons with a chemical lightening additive. The cost of the additive itself is only $.05 per gallon, so all rework costs are assumed to be related to direct labor. The chemical additive is also gaseous and will cause no increase in the number of gallons of the coating compound. Entries for defective units are shown in Exhibit 9–9 on page 382. This exhibit uses this information to show a variety of circumstances involving defective goods.

---

[2] If the company is using a standard costing system, then standard costs will be considered in determining unit cost.

PRODUCTION DATA		EQUIVALENT UNITS	
	WHOLE UNITS	MATERIAL	CONVERSION
Beginning inventory (100%; 60%)	2,000	2,000	1,200
+ Gallons started	15,000		
= Gallons to account for	17,000		
Beginning inventory completed (0%; 40%)	2,000	0	800
+ Gallons started and completed	11,200	11,200	11,200
= Total gallons completed	13,200		
+ Ending inventory (100%; 75%)	2,500	2,500	1,875
+ Normal spoilage	750		
+ Abnormal spoilage (100%; 100%)	550	550	550
= Gallons accounted for	17,000	16,250	15,625

COST DATA			
	TOTAL	MATERIAL	CONVERSION
Beginning inventory costs	$ 16,620	$ 15,000	$ 1,620
Current costs	122,175	102,750	19,425
Total costs	$138,795	$117,750	$21,045
Divided by EUP		16,250	15,625
Cost per FIFO EUP	$8.60	$7.25	$1.35

COST ASSIGNMENT

Transferred (13,200 × $8.60)		$113,520
Ending inventory:		
Material (2,500 × $7.25)	$18,125	
Conversion (1,875 × $1.35)	2,531	20,656
Abnormal loss (550 × $8.60)		4,730
Total costs accounted for (off due to rounding)		$138,906

EXHIBIT 9–7

Cost of Production Report for Month Ended June 30, 1996 (Weighted average method) (Abnormal shrinkage; normal continuous shrinkage)

	NORMAL	ABNORMAL
CONTINUOUS	Do not include equivalent lost units in EUP schedule. Units effectively "disappear"; unit costs of good production are increased.	Must include equivalent lost units in EUP schedule. Assign cost to lost units and charge as loss of period.
DISCRETE	Must include equivalent lost units in EUP schedule. Assign cost to lost units. Determine point of ending work in process: a. if before inspection point, assign cost of lost units only to units transferred. b. if after inspection point, prorate cost of spoiled units between units transferred and units in ending inventory.	Must include equivalent lost units in EUP schedule. Assign cost to lost units and charge as loss of period.

EXHIBIT 9–8

Summary of Handling Lost Units in a Process Costing System

<table>
<tr><td>

EXHIBIT 9–9

Entries for Defective Units

</td><td>

Good production: 17,900 gallons
Defects: 100 gallons
Cost of production other than rework: $160,200
Cost of rework: $140 or $1.40 per gallon

1. Rework is normal; actual costing is used; reworked gallons can be sold at normal selling price
   Work in Process Inventory   140
       Wages Payable   140
   Cost per acceptable gallon = $8.91 ($160,340 ÷ 18,000)
2. Rework is normal; predetermined OH rate is used (rework estimated); reworked gallons can be sold at normal selling price
   Manufacturing Overhead   140
       Wages Payable   140
   Cost per acceptable gallon = $8.90 ($160,200 ÷ 18,000)
3. Rework is abnormal; reworked gallons can be sold at normal selling price
   Loss from Defects   140
       Wages Payable   140
   Cost per acceptable gallon = $8.90 ($160,200 ÷ 18,000)
4. Reworked gallons are irregular; can only be sold for $7; actual costing is used.

Normal production cost ($8.90 × 100)	$ 890
Cost of rework	140
Total cost of defective units	$1,030
Total sales value of defective units (100 × $7)	700
Total deficiency	$ 330

</td></tr>
</table>

If defects are normal:

Inventory—Defects	700	
Work in Process Inventory	140	
Wages Payable		140
Work in Process Inventory		700

The deficiency ($330) remains with the good units; cost per acceptable gallon is $8.92:
[($160,200 + $140 − $700) ÷ 17,900]

If defects are abnormal:

Inventory—Defects	700	
Loss from Defects	330	
Wages Payable		140
Work in Process Inventory		890

The deficiency is assigned as a period loss; cost per acceptable gallon is $8.90:
[($160,200 − $890) ÷ 17,900]

DEFECTS/SPOILAGE IN JOB ORDER COSTING

The previous examples are related to spoilage issues in a process costing environment. In a job order situation, the accounting treatment of spoilage depends on two issues: (1) Is spoilage generally incurred for most jobs or is it specifically identified with a particular job? (2) Is the spoilage normal or abnormal?

Generally Anticipated on All Jobs

net cost of normal spoilage

If normal spoilage is anticipated on all jobs, the predetermined overhead application rate should include an amount for the **net cost of normal spoilage,** which is equal to the cost of spoiled work less the estimated disposal value of that work. This approach assumes that spoilage is naturally inherent and unavoidable in the production of good jobs, and its estimated cost should be proportionately assigned among the good jobs produced.

Assume that Spin-Out produces a special coating compound for several CD manufacturers. Each production run is considered a separate job because each manufacturer indicates the particular coating specifications it requires. Regardless of the job, there is always some shrinkage because of the mixing process. In computing the predetermined overhead rate related to the custom coatings, the following estimates are made:

Overhead costs other than spoilage		$121,500
Estimated spoilage unit cost	$10,300	
Sales of improperly mixed coatings to foreign distributors	(4,300)	6,000
Total estimated overhead		$127,500
Estimated gallons of production during the year		÷ 150,000
Predetermined overhead rate per gallon		$.85

During the year, Spin-Out Inc. accepted a job (#73) from West Publishing to manufacture 500 gallons of coating. Direct material cost for this job was $4,660, direct labor cost totaled $640, and applied overhead was $425 ($.85 × 500 gallons), giving a total cost for the job of $5,725. Spin-Out Inc. put 500 gallons of coating into production. Five gallons (or 1 percent) of the coating compound were made defective during the production process when a worker knocked some dye meant for another job into a container of the coating. The actual cost of the defective mixture was $57.25 (.01 × $5,725) and it can be sold for $14. The entry below is made to account for the actual defect cost:

Disposal Value of Defective Work	14.00	
Manufacturing Overhead	43.25	
Work in Process Inventory—Job #73		57.25
To record disposal value of defective work incurred on Job #73 for West Publishing.		

The estimated cost of spoilage was originally included in determining the predetermined overhead rate. Therefore, as actual defects or spoilages occur, the disposal value of the nonstandard work is included in an inventory account (if salable), and the net cost of the normal nonstandard work is charged to the Manufacturing Overhead account as is any other actual overhead cost.

Specifically Identified with a Particular Job

If defects or spoilages are not generally anticipated, but are occasionally experienced on specific jobs *because of job-related characteristics*, the estimated cost should *not* be included in setting the predetermined overhead application rate. Because the cost of defects/spoilage attaches to the job, the disposal value of such goods reduces the cost of the job that created those goods. If no disposal value exists for the defective/spoiled goods, that cost remains with the job that caused the defects/spoilage.

Assume that Spin-Out did not typically experience spoilage in its production process. The company's predetermined overhead would have been calculated as $.81 per gallon ($121,500 ÷ 150,000). Thus, the total cost for the West Publishing job would have been $5,705 [$4,660 + $640 + ($.81 × 500)]. Five gallons of the batch were dyed yellow at the request of West Publishing. After checking the color, West rejected the five gallons and changed the tinting formula slightly. The five gallons could be sold for $14; this amount would reduce the cost of the West Publishing job as shown in the following entry:

Disposal Value of Defective Work	14	
Work in Process Inventory—Job #73		14
To record disposal value of defective work incurred on Job #73 for West Publishing.		

The production cost of any new mixture will be assigned a new job number.

Abnormal Spoilage

The cost of abnormal losses (net of any disposal value) should be written off as a period cost. The following entry assumes that Spin-Out normally anticipates some lost units on its custom orders and that the estimated cost of those units was included in the development of a predetermined overhead application rate. Assume that on Job #286, the cost of defective units was $395, but there was $35 of disposal value associated with those units. Of the remaining $360 of cost, $240 was related to normal defects and $120 was related to abnormal defects.

Disposal Value of Defective Work	35	
Manufacturing Overhead	240	
Loss from Abnormal Spoilage	120	
Work in Process Inventory—Job #286		395
To record reassignment of cost of defective and spoiled work on Job #286.		

The first debit represents the defective goods' disposal value; the debit to Manufacturing Overhead is for the net cost of normal spoilage. The debit to Loss from Abnormal Spoilage is for the portion of the net cost of spoilage that was not anticipated in setting the predetermined application rate.

ACCRETION

accretion

Accretion refers to an increase in units or volume because of the addition of material in successor departments or to factors (such as heat) that are inherent in the production process.[3] For example, adding filler to beef in preparing packages of ground meat causes the pounds of product to increase just as cooking pasta increases the volume of product.

If materials are added in a single department, the number of equivalent units computed for that department compensates for this increase from the beginning to the end of processing. When accretion occurs in successor departments in a multi-department process, the number of units transferred into the department and the related cost per unit must be adjusted. For instance, assume that one coating made by Spin-Out Inc. requires processing in two departments. Department 2 adds a compound to increase the scratch-resistant properties of the mixture produced in Department 1. The gallons of compound added increase the total gallons of mixture that were transferred out of Department 1 and decrease the transferred-in cost per unit.

The production of this heavy-duty coating is used to illustrate the accounting for accretion of units in a successor department. Department 1 mixes the primary coating ingredients in large vats and sends the mixture to Department 2, which adds the scratch-resistant compound and remixes the coating. The coating is poured into 50-gallon containers that are shipped to buyers. Spoilage occurs in Department 2 when too much compound is added to the coating mixture. The spoilage is detected when the mixture is transferred from the vats to the containers. Spoilage is never containerized. Spoilage is considered normal as long as it does not exceed 1 percent of the gallons transferred into Department 2 from Department 1.

October production information for Department 2 is given below. For this product, assume that Spin-Out Inc. uses weighted average process costing. The units in beginning inventory were 100 percent complete as to the compound, zero percent

---

[3] Not all additions of material in successor departments cause an increase in units. Adding bindings to books in a second department does not increase the number of books printed and transferred from the prior department. When the material added in a successor department does not increase the number of units, it is accounted for as shown in Chapter 8.

complete as to the container, and 25 percent complete as to conversion costs. Ending inventory is 100 percent complete as to the compound, zero percent complete as to the container, and 70 percent complete as to conversion.

Gallons in beginning inventory	1,000
Gallons transferred in	21,000
Gallons of compound added	5,000
Gallons in ending inventory	1,200
Units completed (50-gallon containers)	512

Note that the measure for completed production is containers rather than gallons. Because each container represents 50 gallons, the actual gallons completed are 25,600 (50 × 512). To handle this change in measuring units, either the incoming gallons must be reported as containers or the completed containers must be reported as gallons. The cost of production report for October (Exhibit 9–10) is prepared using gallons as the measurement unit, and assumed cost information is supplied in the exhibit.

EXHIBIT 9–10

Department 2 Cost of Production Report for the Month Ended October 31, 1996 (Weighted average method)

PRODUCTION DATA	WHOLE UNITS	EQUIVALENT UNITS			
		TRANSFERRED IN	COMPOUND	CONTAINER	CONVERSION
Beginning inventory (gals.)	1,000	1,000	1,000	0	250
Transferred in (gals.)	21,000				
Compound added (gals.)	5,000				
Gallons to account for	27,000				
BI completed	1,000	0	0	1,000	750
Started and completed	24,600	24,600	24,600	24,600	24,600
Total gallons completed	25,600				
Ending inventory (70%)	1,200	1,200	1,200	0	840
Normal spoilage	200	200	200	0	200
Gallons accounted for	27,000	27,000	27,000	25,600	26,640

COST DATA	TOTAL	TRANSFERRED IN	COMPOUND	CONTAINER	CONVERSION
BI costs	$ 8,415	$ 7,385	$ 840	$ 0	$ 190
Current costs	331,455	189,715	22,110	99,840	19,790
Total costs	$339,870	$197,100	$22,950	$99,840	$19,980
Divided by EUP		27,000	27,000	25,600	26,640
Cost per EUP	$12.80	$7.30	$.85	$3.90	$.75

COST ASSIGNMENT

Transferred:		
Cost of good units (25,600 × $12.80)	$327,680	
Cost of spoilage:		
Transferred in (200 × $7.30)	1,460	
Compound (200 × $.85)	170	
Conversion (200 × $.75)	150	
Total cost transferred		$329,460
Ending inventory:		
Transferred in (1,200 × $7.30)	$ 8,760	
Compound (1,200 × $.85)	1,020	
Conversion (840 × $.75)	630	10,410
Total costs accounted for		$339,870

Several items need to be noted about this exhibit. First, the number of spoiled gallons was determined by subtracting the total gallons completed plus the gallons in ending inventory from the total gallons for which the department was responsible. Because spoilage was less than 1 percent of the gallons transferred into Department 2, it was all considered normal. Second, the $197,100 cost transferred from Department 1 was related to 22,000 gallons of mixture: the gallons in beginning inventory plus those transferred during the period. Thus, the original cost of each gallon was approximately $8.96 ($197,100 ÷ 22,000). With the addition of the compound in Department 2, the transferred-in cost per gallon declined to $7.30. Third, spoilage is assignable only to the completed units because the ending inventory has not yet reached the discrete point of inspection (transference to containers). Finally, the average cost of each 50-gallon container completed is approximately $643.48 ($329,460 ÷ 512).

CONTROLLING QUALITY TO MINIMIZE LOST UNITS

Up to this point, the chapter has focused on the ways to account for lost units in the production process. The fact is, if there were no lost units (from shrinkage, defects, or spoilage), there would be no need to account for them. The control aspect in quality control requires knowledge of three questions in addition to the six questions posed earlier in the chapter. These three questions are

1. What do the lost units actually cost?
2. Why do the lost units occur?
3. How can the lost units be controlled?

Many companies find it difficult, if not impossible, to answer the question of what lost units (or the lack of quality) cost. A direct cause of part of this difficulty is the use of the traditional method of assigning the cost of normal losses to the good units produced. By excluding lost units from the extensions in the equivalent units schedule, the cost of those units is effectively "buried" and hidden in magnitude from managers. In a job order costing environment, if the cost of lost units is included in calculating the predetermined overhead rate, that cost is also being hidden and ignored. In service organizations, the cost of "lost units" may be even more difficult to determine because those lost units are, from a customer viewpoint, poor service. After such service, the customer simply may not do business with the organization again. Such an opportunity cost is not processed by the accounting system. Thus, in all instances, a potentially significant dollar amount is unavailable for investigation as to its planning, controlling, and decision-making ramifications.

As to the second question, managers may be able to pinpoint the reasons for lost units or poor service but may also have two perspectives of those reasons that instinctively allow for a lack of control. First, managers may believe that the cause creates only a "minimal" quantity of lost units; such an attitude creates the allowance of an "accepted quality level" with some tolerance for error. These error tolerances are built into the system and become justifications for problems. Production is "graded on a curve" that allows for a less-than-perfect result.

Incorporating error tolerances into the production/performance system and combining such tolerances with the method of neglect results in managers not being provided with the information necessary to determine how much spoilage cost is incurred by the company. Therefore, although believing that the quantity and cost of lost units are "minimal," the managers do not have historical or even estimated accounting amounts on which to base such a conclusion. If managers were aware of the costs, they could make more informed decisions about whether to ignore it or try to correct its causes. The accompanying News Note discusses the possible range of costs from having units that need rework.

In other instances, managers may believe that the quantity of lost units is uncontrollable. In some cases, this belief is accurate. For example, the shrinkage of coffee beans during roasting is virtually uncontrollable. Or, when a printing press converts

What Does That "Bad" Unit Cost?

Various costs are incurred when products fall outside specification limits. These include out-of-pocket costs such as costs of inspection and rework.

If the product can be sold as a first-quality unit after the rework, these out-of-pocket costs are the total costs of variability. If the reworked unit cannot be sold as a first-quality unit, then the cost of variability also may include an opportunity cost. The opportunity cost will be relevant if the second-quality item replaces a sale for a first-quality item. In this case, the opportunity cost of variability is the difference between the contribution margin of the first-quality product and the actual contribution margin.

If a product falls outside the specification limits, cannot be reworked, and must be scrapped, then the cost of variability includes the materials, labor, and other costs incurred in producing the product. In addition, any cost incurred in disposing of the product also is a cost of variability. [These concepts are illustrated in the following example.]

Sales price per first-quality unit	$50
Sales price per second-quality unit	45
Variable production cost per unit	20
Normal contribution margin (SP − VC) per unit	30
Rework cost per unit	12
Disposal cost per unit	5

CONDITION	VARIABLE PRODUCTION COST	REWORK COST	DISPOSAL COST	LOST CONTRIBUTION MARGIN	TOTAL UNIT COST
Unit is reworked and sold for $50		$12			$12
Unit is reworked and sold for $5		12		5	17
Unit cannot be reworked and has no disposal cost	$20			30	50
Unit cannot be reworked and has a $5 disposal cost	20		$5	30	55

The total cost of variability for this product can be calculated by multiplying the unit cost by the number of nonconforming units. If 1,240 units were produced during the month, the cost of variability could range from a low of $14,880 ($12 × 1,240) if the units are reworked and sold as first-quality units to a high of $68,200 ($55 × 1,240) if the units cannot be reworked and must be disposed of at a cost of $5 per unit.

SOURCE: Harold P. Roth and Thomas L. Albright, "What Are the Costs of Variability?" *Management Accounting* (June 1994), pp. 52–53. Reprinted from *Management Accounting.* Copyright by Institute of Management Accountants, Montvale, NJ.

from one job to the next, some number of pages are consistently misprinted. The number is not large and process analysis has proven that the cost of attempting to correct this production defect would be significantly greater than the savings resulting from the correction. But in most production situations and almost every service situation, the cause of lost units or poor service is controllable. Managers only need to determine the cause of the problem and institute corrective action.

Defects and spoiled units were originally controlled through a process of inspecting goods or, in the case of service organizations, surveying customers. Now companies are deciding that if quality is *built* into the process, there will be less need for inspections or surveys because defects/spoilage and poor service will be minimized. The goal is, then, process *control* rather than output *inspection or observation.*

As explained in Chapter 3, companies implementing quality programs to minimize defects/spoilage or poor service often employ a tool called statistical process control (SPC) to analyze their processes for situations that are "out of control." As discussed in the accompanying News Note, this technique uses graphs and/or control charts to understand and reduce fluctuations in processes until they are under control.

SPC requires that persons or machines involved in problem areas select a relevant measure of performance and track that performance measurement over time. The resulting control chart provides information on the circumstances existing when a problem arises. Analyzing this chart in relation to the benchmark or standard and to the amount of variation expected in a stable (controlled) process provides process control information that lets the company improve its performance.

SPC allows the individuals involved with the process to become the quality control points and helps to eliminate the need for quality inspections. Thus, the "accepted quality level" can be raised, and the defects can be significantly reduced. For instance, Senco Products, located in Cincinnati, Ohio, has a goal of zero defects in the manufacture of its industrial fastening systems. Such a target is not that unusual for companies competing in world-class environments.

The development, implementation, and interpretation of an SPC system requires a firm grasp on statistics and is well beyond the scope of this text. However, cost and management accountants must recognize the usefulness of such a tool in deter-

SPC Charts Help Evaluate the Quality of Activities

N E W S
N O T E

In general, an SPC chart is a graph that shows the measurements of some characteristic of interest. The characteristic may be a quantitative variable (e.g., weight, length, or thickness) or it may be a qualitative attribute (e.g., whether a product is defective).

SPC charts are used to identify points that differ from the process average and to discover shifts in the process. If the points on a control chart are randomly scattered around the center line and they fall within the upper and lower control limits, the process is considered to be in statistical control. An out-of-control condition is indicated if points fall outside the control limits or if *runs* exist in the data. (A run is a trend—i.e., a series of consecutive points above or below the center line.) By analyzing the conditions existing when an out-of-control signal occurs, an investigator attempts to discover the source of the variation and then determine a remedy.

SPC charts are appropriate for measuring and evaluating many different types of processes. Generally, they can be used in any repetitive situation where either a quantitative variable or qualitative attribute is measurable. Many manufacturing processes can be analyzed using SPC. . . . [H]owever, SPC charts can also be used in other functional areas including accounting, finance, and marketing. [For example,] repetitive activities in the finance and accounting areas include processing payroll, accounts payable, and accounts receivable.

SOURCE: Thomas L. Albright and Harold P. Roth, "Controlling Quality on a Multidimensional Level," *Journal of Cost Management* (Spring 1993), pp. 30–31. Reprinted with permission from *The Journal of Cost Management for the Manufacturing Industry* Spring 1993, © 1993, Warren Gorham & Lamont, 31 St. James Avenue, Boston, MA 02116. All rights reserved.

mining why problems occur. This knowledge allows cost and management accountants to better track the costs flowing into the problem areas, estimate the opportunity costs associated with the problems, and perform a more informed cost-benefit analysis about problem correction.

In conclusion, the important managerial concern regarding spoilage is in *controlling* it rather than *accounting for* spoilage costs. Quality control programs can be implemented to develop ideas on product redesign for quality, determine where quality control problems exist, decide how to measure the costs associated with those problems, and assess how to correct the problems. If quality is defined in an organization as zero lost units (excepting those caused by inherent shrinkage), all defects/spoilage will be accounted for as an abnormal cost of production or service. Such accounting would mean that defect/spoilage costs would no longer be hidden from managerial eyes through the use of the method of neglect discussed earlier in the chapter.

REVISITING

West Publishing CD-ROM Production

West began its analysis of developing an internal CD-ROM factory in 1993. Because of the need for the environmentally controlled "clean room" factory, initial capital investment was extremely high—about $2,000,000. But West management analyzed the cost-benefit relationships of the production process by investigating the cost savings that would arise from internal production rather than external purchase, the greater ability to control quality, the reduction in turnaround time, and the higher security created for proprietary information.

The company actually began making CD-ROMs in mid-1995 and produces approximately 100,000 discs per month. (Actual capacity is significantly higher and will be utilized in the near future.) Disc spoilage can occur from a wide range of causes and at numerous points during production. Because the process is almost fully automated and one operator oversees the replication line, spoilage tends to be machine-related. Thus, it makes sense that the quality checks are built into the production system and are performed robotically. However, the final quality control analysis is performed on an independent testing system by the replication operator.

The CD-ROM production process is continuously being refined in a spirit of continuous improvement to lower the defect rate. Although 100 defective discs per million represents a high-quality process, it pales in comparison to, for example, Motorola's goals. As early as 1994, some Motorola factories had raised quality levels so high that defects were no longer counted on a per million basis, but rather on a per billion basis! West isn't daunted by such statistics: the company approaches all its business enterprises with an eye toward achieving world-class status, knowing that goal is a continuously moving target.

SOURCE: Interview with T. R. Kluge, West Publishing CD-ROM Production (March 1996).

CHAPTER SUMMARY

This chapter covers the accounting treatment for shrinkage, defective and spoiled units, and accretion of units in a process costing system. Management typically specifies a certain level of shrinkage/defects/spoilage that will be tolerated as normal if a loss of units is commonly anticipated. If lost units exceed that expectation, the excess is considered an abnormal loss. Normal losses are product costs, and abnormal losses are period costs.

To account for the cost of lost units, the location of the loss within the process must be known in addition to knowing whether the quantity of lost units is normal or abnormal. If the loss point is continuous, the period's good production absorbs the cost of the lost units. This treatment is handled in the cost of production report by not extending the lost units to the equivalent units columns. If the loss point is discrete, lost units are included in the EUP schedule at their unit equivalency at the quality control point. If ending inventory has reached the inspection point, the cost of the lost units is allocated both to units transferred from the department and units in ending inventory. If ending inventory has not yet reached the quality control inspection point, the lost unit cost attaches only to the units transferred.

In a job order costing system, the cost of anticipated defects/spoilage is estimated and included in setting the predetermined overhead rate. This approach allows expected cost of lost units to be assigned to all jobs. When lost units occur, any disposal value of those units is carried in a separate inventory account; the net cost of defects/spoilage is debited to Manufacturing Overhead. If lost units do not generally occur in a job order system, any normal defects/spoilage associated with a specific job is carried as part of that job's cost; the disposal value of such units reduces the cost of the specific job.

Treatment of the rework cost for defective units depends on whether the rework is normal or abnormal. If rework is normal, the cost is considered to be a product cost and either (1) increases actual costs in the cost schedule or (2) is considered in setting an overhead application rate and charged to overhead when incurred. If rework is abnormal, the cost is assigned to the period as a loss.

Adding material to partially completed units may increase the number of units. If the material addition occurs in a successor department, a new transferred-in cost per unit must be calculated using the increased number of units. If units of measure change between the start and end of production, a consistent measuring unit must be used in the cost of production report to properly reflect production of the period.

Accounting for spoiled and defective units is essential when total quality does not exist. The traditional methods of accounting for spoilage often "bury" the cost of poor quality by spreading that cost over good output. Managers should attempt to compute the costs of spoiled or defective units and search for ways to improve product quality, reduce product cost, and increase the company's competitive market position.

abnormal loss (p. 368)
accretion (p. 384)
continuous loss (p. 370)
defective unit (p. 368)
discrete loss (p. 370)
economically reworked (p. 368)

method of neglect (p. 372)
net cost of normal spoilage (p. 382)
normal loss (p. 368)
shrinkage (p. 368)
spoiled unit (p. 368)

KEY TERMS

Lost units are *always* shown with other whole units under "Units accounted for" in the cost of production report.

SOLUTION STRATEGIES

CONTINUOUS NORMAL LOSS

1. Lost units are *not* extended to EUP schedule.
2. All good production (both fully and partially completed) absorb the cost of the lost units through higher per-unit costs.

CONTINUOUS ABNORMAL LOSS

1. All units are appropriately extended to EUP schedule.
2. Cost of lost units is assigned as period loss.

DISCRETE NORMAL LOSS

1. Normal loss is appropriately extended to the EUP schedule.
2. Determine whether ending inventory has passed inspection point.
   a. If no, cost of lost units is assigned only to the good production that was transferred.
   b. If yes, cost of lost units is prorated between units in ending WIP Inventory and units transferred out based on
      (1) (weighted average) total costs contained in each category prior to proration, or
      (2) (FIFO) current costs contained in each category prior to proration.

DISCRETE ABNORMAL LOSS

1. Abnormal loss is appropriately extended to the EUP schedule.
2. Cost of lost units is assigned as period loss.

NORMAL REWORK

1. *(Actual cost system)* Add rework costs to original material, labor, and overhead costs and spread over all production.
2. *(Normal and standard cost systems)* Include cost of rework in estimated overhead when determining standard application rate. Assign actual rework costs to Manufacturing Overhead.

ABNORMAL REWORK

Accumulate rework costs separately and assign as period loss.

ACCRETION IN SUCCESSOR DEPARTMENTS

An increase in units requires that the per-unit transferred-in cost be reduced in the successor department based on the new, larger number of units.

DEMONSTRATION PROBLEM

Marc Huber Enterprises incurs spoilage continuously throughout the manufacturing process. All materials are added at the beginning of the process, and the inspection point is at the end of the production process. June 1996 operating statistics are as follows:

Pounds		
Beginning inventory (75% complete)		2,000
Started in June		10,000
Completed and transferred		9,500
Ending inventory (70% complete)		1,000
Normal spoilage		900
Abnormal spoilage		?
Costs		
Beginning inventory		
Material	$117,780	
Conversion	47,748	$ 165,528
Current period		
Materials	$546,000	
Conversion	325,500	871,500
Total costs		$1,037,028

Required:

a. Prepare a cost of production report using the weighted average method.
b. Prepare a cost of production report using the FIFO method.
c. Using the information from part b, prepare the journal entry to recognize the abnormal loss from spoilage.

Solution to Demonstration Problem

a.

Marc Huber Enterprises

Cost of Production Report

(Continuous spoilage—normal & abnormal; weighted average method)

For the Month Ended June 30, 1996

PRODUCTION DATA		EQUIVALENT UNITS	
	WHOLE UNITS	MATERIAL	CONVERSION
Beginning inventory (100%; 75%)	2,000	2,000	1,500
+ Pounds started	10,000		
= Pounds to account for	12,000		
Beginning inventory completed (0%; 25%)	2,000	0	500
+ Pounds started and completed	7,500	7,500	7,500
= Total pounds completed	9,500		
+ Ending inventory (100%; 70%)	1,000	1,000	700
+ Normal spoilage	900		
+ Abnormal spoilage (100%; 100%)	600	600	600
= Pounds accounted for	12,000	11,100	10,800

COST DATA			
	TOTAL	MATERIAL	CONVERSION
Beginning inventory costs	$ 165,528	$117,780	$ 47,748
Current costs	871,500	546,000	325,500
Total costs	$1,037,028	$663,780	$373,248
Divided by EUP		11,100	10,800
Cost per WA EUP	$94.36	$59.80	$34.56

COST ASSIGNMENT

Transferred (9,500 × $94.36)		$ 896,420
Ending inventory:		
Material (1,000 × $59.80)	$59,800	
Conversion (700 × $34.56)	24,192	83,992
Abnormal loss (600 × $94.36)		56,616
Total costs accounted for		$1,037,028

b.

Marc Huber Enterprises

Cost of Production Report

(Continuous spoilage—normal & abnormal; FIFO method)

For the Month Ended June 30, 1996

PRODUCTION DATA		EQUIVALENT UNITS	
	WHOLE UNITS	MATERIAL	CONVERSION
Beginning inventory (100%; 75%)	2,000		
+ Pounds started	10,000		
= Pounds to account for	12,000		
Beginning inventory completed (0%; 25%)	2,000	0	500
+ Pounds started and completed	7,500	7,500	7,500
= Total pounds completed	9,500		
+ Ending inventory (100%; 70%)	1,000	1,000	700
+ Normal spoilage	900		
+ Abnormal spoilage (100%; 100%)	600	600	600
= Pounds accounted for	12,000	9,100	9,300

COST DATA

	TOTAL	MATERIAL	CONVERSION
Beginning inventory costs	$ 165,528		
Current costs	871,500	$546,000	$325,500
Total costs	$1,037,028		
Divided by EUP		9,100	9,300
Cost per FIFO EUP	$95	$60	$35

COST ASSIGNMENT

Transferred:			
From beginning inventory	$165,528		
Cost to complete: Conversion (500 × $35)	17,500		
Total cost of beginning inventory	$183,028		
Started and completed (7,500 × $95)	712,500		
Total cost of pounds transferred		$ 895,528	
Ending inventory:			
Material (1,000 × $60)	$ 60,000		
Conversion (700 × $35)	24,500	84,500	
Abnormal loss (600 × $95)		57,000	
Total costs accounted for		$1,037,028	

c.

Loss from Abnormal Spoilage	57,000	
Work in Process Inventory		57,000
To remove cost of abnormal spoilage from Work in Process Inventory account.		

QUESTIONS

1. Differentiate among shrinkage, spoilage, and defects.

2. What are some reasons a company would set a "tolerated" loss level? How might such a level be set?

3. List five examples (similar to the steak illustration in the text) in which a unit would be considered (a) defective and (b) spoiled.

4. What is the difference between a normal and an abnormal loss?

5. Why would abnormal losses be more likely to be preventable than some types of normal losses?

6. How does a continuous loss differ from a discrete loss?

7. When does a discrete loss actually occur? When is it assumed to occur for accounting purposes? Why are these not necessarily at the same point?

8. Why is the cost of an abnormal loss considered a period cost? How is its cost removed from Work in Process Inventory?

9. What is meant by the term *method of neglect?* When is this method used?

10. How does using the method of neglect affect the cost of good production in a period?

11. In a job order costing system, spoilage may be incurred in general for all jobs or it may be related to a specific job. What differences do these circumstances make in the treatment of spoilage?

12. In a production process what is accretion? How does it affect the cost of the units transferred in from a predecessor department?

13. The Mixing Department of Leeward Company transferred 100,000 gallons of material to the Baking Department during July. The cost per gallon transferred out shown on Mixing's cost of production report was $2.50. On Baking's cost of production report for the same period, the cost per gallon for material transferred in was $2.00. Why might the cost have changed?

14. How are costs of reworking defective units treated if the defects are considered normal? Abnormal?

15. A company has an AQL for defects of 5 percent of units started during the period. Current period loss was 3 percent. Why should management attempt to measure the cost of this loss rather than simply include it as part of the cost of good production?

16. How do statistical process control techniques contribute to the control of spoilage costs?

17. (*Terminology*) Match the following lettered terms on the left with the appropriate numbered definition on the right.

EXERCISES

   a. Spoiled unit
   b. Normal loss
   c. Economically reworked
   d. Abnormal loss
   e. Defective unit
   f. Method of neglect
   g. Accretion

   1. Allowing the production of unacceptable units to increase the cost of good production
   2. Results in the decrease in the transferred-in cost per unit
   3. Results from having good production of less than the AQL
   4. A unit that is discarded upon inspection
   5. A unit that can be reworked
   6. An expected decline in units in the production process
   7. Additional processing that results in net incremental revenue

18. (*Cost-benefit analysis*) Jim Logan, plant manager at UNO Manufacturing, is investigating spoilage created by a machine that prints packing boxes for computers and other large, fragile items. At the beginning of each production run, fifty boxes are misprinted either because of miscoloration or misalignment. These boxes must be destroyed. The variable production cost per box is $5.50. The machine averages 300 setups for production runs each year.

A regulator is available that will correct the problem. Jim is trying to decide whether to purchase the regulator.

   a. At what cost for the regulator would the benefit of acquisition not exceed the cost? What other factors should Jim consider in addition to the purchase price of the regulator?
   b. If each setup produces an average of 1,000 boxes, what is the increased cost per good box that is caused by the spoiled units?
   c. UNO Manufacturing runs 12 batches per year for Fok Corporation, which makes very specialized equipment in limited quantities. Thus, each batch contains only 20 boxes. If UNO Manufacturing is passing its spoilage cost on to customers based on batch costs, might Fok Corporation be willing to buy the regulator for UNO Manufacturing if the regulator costs $3,000? Justify your answer.
   d. Why are the cost-per-box answers in parts b and c so different?

19. *(Normal vs. abnormal spoilage; WA)* Albuquerque Electronics uses a weighted average process costing system for its production process in which all material is added at the beginning of production. Company management has specified that the normal loss cannot exceed 7 percent of the units started in a period. All losses are caused by shrinkage. March processing information follows:

Beginning inventory (10% complete—conversion)	7,000 units
Started during March	60,000 units
Completed during March	52,000 units
Ending inventory (60% complete—conversion)	10,000 units

  a. How many total units are there to account for?
  b. How many units should be treated as normal loss?
  c. How many units should be treated as abnormal loss?
  d. What are the equivalent units of production for direct material? For conversion?

20. *(EUP computations; normal and abnormal loss)* The Bangor factory of New England Chemical produces environmental chemicals in processes in which spoilage takes place on a continual basis. Management considers normal spoilage to be 0.5 percent or less of gallons of material placed into production. The following operating statistics are available for September 1997 for the chemical XZP:

Beginning inventory (20% complete as to material; 30% complete as to conversion)	8,000 gallons
Started during September	180,000 gallons
Ending inventory (60% complete as to material; 70% complete as to conversion)	4,000 gallons
Spoiled	1,400 gallons

  a. How many gallons were transferred out?
  b. How much normal spoilage occurred?
  c. How much abnormal spoilage occurred?
  d. What are the FIFO equivalent units of production for materials? For conversion costs?
  e. How are costs associated with the normal spoilage handled?
  f. How are costs associated with the abnormal spoilage handled?

21. *(EUP computation; normal and abnormal loss; FIFO)* Southern Foods manufactures corn meal in a continuous, mass-production process. Corn is added at the beginning of the process. Losses are few and occur only when foreign materials are found in the corn meal. Inspection occurs at the 95 percent completion point as to conversion.

  During March, a machine malfunctioned and dumped salt into 18,000 pounds of corn meal. This abnormal loss occurred when conversion was 70 percent complete on those pounds of product. The error was immediately noticed, and those pounds of corn meal were pulled from the production process. An additional 1,000 pounds of meal were detected as unsuitable at the inspection point. These lost units were considered well within reasonable limits.

  March production data are shown below:

Beginning work in process (85% complete)	50,000 pounds
Started during the month	425,000 pounds
Ending work in process (25% complete)	10,000 pounds

  a. Determine the number of equivalent units for direct material and for conversion assuming a FIFO cost flow.
  b. If the costs per equivalent unit are $2.50 and $4.50 for direct material and conversion, respectively, what is the cost of ending inventory?
  c. What is the cost of abnormal loss? How is this cost treated in March?

22. *(EUP computation; normal and abnormal loss; cost per EUP; FIFO)* Luminations uses a FIFO process costing system to account for its candle production process. Wax occasionally forms imperfectly in molds and, thus, spoilage is viewed as continuous. The accepted quality level is 92 percent of the pounds of wax placed in production. All wax is entered at the beginning of the process. July 1996 data follow:

Beginning inventory (100% complete as to material; 30% complete as to conversion)	9,000 pounds
Started during month	30,000 pounds
Transferred	31,500 pounds
(315,000 candles; there are 10 wax candles obtained from a pound of wax)	
Ending inventory 100% complete as to material; 20% complete as to conversion)	5,400 pounds
Loss	? pounds

The following costs are associated with July production:

Beginning inventory:		
Material	$3,600	
Conversion	2,700	$ 6,300
Current period:		
Material	$9,207	
Conversion	8,964	18,171
Total costs		$24,471

a. Prepare the production data segment of Luminations' cost of production report for July 1996.

b. Compute the cost per equivalent unit for each cost component.

c. Assign July costs to the appropriate units.

23. *(Cost assignment; WA)* Zero-Bounce manufactures automobile springs. Its production equipment is fairly old, and one bad unit is typically produced for every 20 good units. The bad units cannot be reworked and must be discarded. Spoilage is determined at an end-of-process inspection point. Zero-Bounce uses a weighted average process costing system and adds all material at the beginning of the process. The following data have been gathered from the accounting records for October 1997:

Beginning inventory (60% complete as to conversion)	4,000 units
Units started	20,000 units
Ending inventory (30% complete as to conversion)	3,000 units
Good units completed	20,000 units

	MATERIAL	CONVERSION	TOTAL
Beginning inventory	$ 12,492	$ 9,927	$ 22,419
Current period	112,548	63,000	175,548
Total costs	$125,040	$72,927	$197,967

a. Prepare an EUP schedule.

b. Determine the cost of the normal spoilage and allocate that cost to the appropriate inventory.

24. *(Rework)* Slick Shine Inc. manufactures two-gallon tubs of car wax for body shops. The company uses an actual cost, process costing system. All material is added at the beginning of production; labor and overhead are incurred evenly through the process. Defective units are identified through inspection at the end of the production process. The following information is available for March 1998:

Beginning inventory (30% complete as to conversion)	750 units
Started during month	17,250 units
Completed during month	15,000 units
Defective units (100% complete as to conversion)	1,800 units
Ending inventory (70% complete as to conversion)	1,200 units

Actual March production costs (including those for beginning inventory) were $126,000 for direct material and $40,572 for conversion. In addition, rework cost to bring the 1,800 units up to specifications was $3,150 for material and $1,323 for conversion.

a. Determine the equivalent units of production using the weighted average method.

b. Assume that the rework is normal. Determine the cost per good unit for direct material and conversion.

c. Assume that the rework is normal. How would the rework cost be handled in a normal (rather than actual) costing system?

d. Assume that the rework is abnormal. Determine the cost per good unit for direct material and conversion. How is the rework cost recorded for financial statement purposes?

25. *(Controlling losses)* For each of the following types of production losses or poor service, indicate whether prevention (P) or appraisal (A) techniques would provide the most effective control mechanism. Explain why you made your choice.

a. Putting pages in upside down in a book.

b. Bolting the wrong parts together.

c. Shrinkage from cooking.

d. Breaking glasses when they are being boxed.

e. Paying an account payable twice.

f. Bringing the wrong meal to a restaurant customer.

COMMUNICATION ACTIVITIES

26. *(Process improvement)* Use library, Internet, or personal resources to find three companies (such as Delta Wire) that instituted workforce education programs and, thereby, reduced the number of lost units. Prepare a 5- to 7-minute oral presentation about your companies' programs and their benefits.

27. *(Requirements; team activity)* Every job has certain requirements, and quality is defined by meeting those requirements. In some cases, however, people make decisions to override requirements. In a team of three or four, choose four requirements for your class (or for a job held by one of you). Prepare a memo that would explain to your teacher (or your boss) the following:

a. The requirements you have chosen and why you think the teacher (boss) made those requirements.

b. The conditions under which your team would decide to override the requirements.

c. Why you believe that overriding the requirements would be appropriate in the conditions you have specified.

d. The potential for problems that may arise by overriding the requirements.

28. *(Normal discrete spoilage, weighted average)* The Potato Division of Global Foods Company processes potatoes. In the process, raw potatoes are sequentially cleaned, skinned, cooked, and canned. Spoilage amounting to less than 12 percent of the total pounds of potatoes that are introduced to the cleaning operation is considered normal (in this case, normal spoilage is to include the weight of the potato peels). Inspection occurs when the products are 50 percent complete. Information that follows pertains to operations in the Potato Division for January 1997:

Beginning WIP inventory (30% complete)	500,000 pounds
Started	13,500,000 pounds
Transferred	11,400,000 pounds
Ending WIP inventory (40% complete)	750,000 pounds

a. Compute the amount of spoilage in January. How much of the spoilage was normal?

b. Compute the equivalent units of production assuming the weighted average method is used.

c. Prepare a memo explaining why you might expect some (1) accretion in the canning operation and (2) some shrinkage other than the weight of the peels in one or more of the operations.

---

29. *(Shrinkage; WA)* Department 1 of Tastee Patties cooks ground beef for hamburger patties. The patties are then transferred to Department 2 where they are placed on buns, boxed, and frozen. The accepted level of shrinkage in Department 1 is 10 percent of the pounds started. Tastee Patties uses a weighted average process costing system and has the following production and cost data for Department 1 for August 1997:

PROBLEMS

Beginning inventory (80% complete as to conversion)	1,000 pounds
Started	125,000 pounds
Transferred to Department 2 (550,000 patties)	110,000 pounds
Ending inventory (30% complete as to conversion)	3,000 pounds
Beginning inventory cost of ground beef	$ 1,020
August cost of ground beef	$106,710
Beginning inventory conversion cost	$ 195
August conversion cost	$ 27,630

a. What is the total shrinkage (in pounds)?

b. How much of the shrinkage is classified as normal? How is it treated for accounting purposes?

c. How much of the shrinkage is classified as abnormal? How is it treated for accounting purposes?

d. What is the total cost of the patties transferred to Department 2? Cost of ending inventory? Cost of abnormal spoilage?

e. How might Tastee Patties reduce its shrinkage loss? How, if at all, would your solution(s) affect costs?

30. *(Discrete spoilage; WA)* Sara Fims Inc. makes stuffed angels in a mass-production process. Parachute cloth and stuffing are added at the beginning of the production process; the angels are packaged in sky-blue boxes at the end of production. Conversion costs for the highly automated process are incurred evenly throughout processing. The angels are inspected at the 95 percent completion point prior to being boxed. Defective units of more than 1 percent of the units started are considered abnormal.

The company uses a weighted average process costing system. April 1997 production and cost data for Sara Fims Inc. follow:

Beginning inventory (40% complete as to conversion)	5,000
Started	70,000
Ending inventory (70% complete as to conversion)	6,000
Total defective units	400
Beginning inventory cloth and stuffing cost	$ 21,900
Beginning inventory conversion cost	$ 7,680
April cloth and stuffing cost	$315,600
April box cost	$ 75,460
April conversion cost	$270,404

a. How many units were completed in April?

b. How many of the defective units are considered a normal loss? An abnormal loss?

c. What is the per-unit cost of the completed units? What would the per-unit cost of the completed units have been if the 400 units had been good units at their same stages of completion at the end of the period?

d. What is the total cost of ending inventory?

31. *(Normal and abnormal discrete spoilage; WA)* Payne Tools manufactures one of its products in a two-department process. A separate work in process account is maintained for each department, and Payne Tools uses a weighted average process costing system. The first department is Forming; the second is Grinding. At the end of production in Grinding, a quality inspection is made and then packaging is added. Overhead is applied in the Grinding Department on a machine-hour basis. Production and cost data for the Grinding Department for October 1997 follow:

PRODUCTION DATA

Beginning inventory (complete: labor, 30%; overhead, 40%)	2,000 units
Transferred in from Forming	49,800 units
Normal spoilage (discrete—found at the end of processing during quality control)	650 units
Abnormal spoilage (found at end of processing during quality control)	350 units
Ending inventory (complete: labor, 40%; overhead, 65%)	1,800 units
Transferred to finished goods	? units

COST DATA

Beginning inventory:		
Transferred in	$ 6,050	
Material (label and package)	0	
Direct labor	325	
Overhead	750	$ 7,125
Current period:		
Transferred in	$149,350	
Material (label and package)	11,760	
Direct labor	23,767	
Overhead	50,932	235,809
Total cost to account for		$242,934

a. Prepare a cost of production report for the Grinding Department for October.

b. Prepare the journal entry to dispose of the cost of abnormal spoilage.

32. *(Normal and abnormal spoilage; WA)* Ozark Furniture produces coffee tables in a two-department process: Cutting/Assembly and Lamination. Varnish is added in the Lamination Department when the goods are 60 percent complete as to overhead. Spoiled units are found on inspection at the end of production. Spoilage is considered discrete.

PRODUCTION DATA FOR SEPTEMBER 1997

Beginning inventory (80% complete as to labor, 70% complete as to overhead)	2,000 units
Transferred in during month	14,900 units
Ending inventory (40% complete as to labor, 20% complete as to overhead)	3,000 units
Normal spoilage (found at final quality inspection)	200 units
Abnormal spoilage (found at 30% completion as to labor and 15% as to overhead; the sanding machine was misaligned and scarred the tables)	400 units

The remaining units were transferred to finished goods.

COST DATA FOR SEPTEMBER 1997

Beginning Work in Process Inventory:

Prior department costs	$ 15,020	
Varnish	1,900	
Direct labor	4,388	
Overhead	11,044	$ 32,352

Current period costs:

Prior department costs	$137,080	
Varnish	14,030	
Direct labor	46,000	
Overhead	113,564	310,674
Total costs to account for		$343,026

Determine the proper disposition of the September costs for the Lamination Department using the weighted average method; include journal entries.

33. *(Normal and abnormal discrete spoilage; FIFO method)* Use the Ozark Furniture information from problem 32. Determine the proper disposition of the September costs of the Lamination Department using the FIFO method; include journal entries.

34. *(Normal and abnormal discrete spoilage; FIFO)* Hinkley Company produces hinges. Completed hinges are inspected at the end of production. Any spoilage in excess of 2 percent of the completed units is considered abnormal. Material is added at the start of production. Labor and overhead are incurred evenly throughout production.

Hinkley's July 1997 production and cost data follow:

Beginning inventory (50% complete)	5,600
Transferred in	74,400
Good units completed	70,000
Ending inventory (1/3 complete)	7,500

	MATERIAL	CONVERSION	TOTAL
Beginning inventory	$ 6,400	$ 1,232	$ 7,632
Current period	74,400	31,768	106,168
Total	$80,800	$33,000	$113,800

Calculate the equivalent units schedule, prepare a FIFO cost of production report, and assign all costs.

35. *(Normal and abnormal discrete spoilage; WA)* Use the Hinkley Company data as given in problem 34. Prepare a July 1997 cost of production report using the weighted average method.

36. *(Cost assignment)* Data below summarize operations for Lawn Gro Company. The company makes five-gallon containers of herbicide. All material is added at the beginning of the process.

COSTS	MATERIAL	CONVERSION	TOTAL
Beginning inventory	$ 30,000	$ 3,600	$ 33,600
Current period	885,120	335,088	1,220,208
Total costs	$915,120	$338,688	$1,253,808

UNITS

Beginning inventory (30% complete—conversion)	6,000 units
Started	180,000 units
Completed	152,000 units
Ending inventory (70% complete—conversion)	20,000 units
Normal spoilage	4,800 units

Spoilage is detected at inspection when the units are 60 percent complete.

a. Prepare an EUP schedule using the weighted average method.

b. Determine the cost of goods transferred out, ending inventory, and abnormal spoilage.

37. *(Cost assignment)* Tons of Shade employs a weighted average process costing system for its products. One product passes through three departments (Molding, Assembly, and Finishing) during production. The following activity took place in the Finishing Department during March 1997:

Units in beginning inventory	4,200
Units transferred in from Assembly	42,000
Units spoiled	2,100
Good units transferred out	33,600

The equivalent units and the costs per equivalent unit of production for each cost factor are as follows:

Cost of prior departments	$5.00
Raw material	1.00
Conversion	3.00
Total cost per EUP	$9.00

Raw material is added at the beginning of processing in Finishing without changing the number of units being processed. Work in process inventory was 70 percent complete as to conversion on March 1 and 40 percent complete as to conversion on March 31. All spoilage was discovered at final inspection. Of the total units spoiled, 1,680 were within normal limits.

a. Calculate the equivalent units of production.

b. Determine the cost of units transferred out of Finishing.

c. Determine the cost of ending Work in Process Inventory.

d. The portion of the total transferred-in cost associated with beginning Work in Process Inventory amounted to $18,900. What is the current period cost that was transferred in from Assembly to Finishing?

e. Determine the cost associated with abnormal spoilage for the month. How would this amount be accounted for?

(CMA adapted)

38. *(Comprehensive; weighted average)* Caunitz Company produces mops. Department 1 winds and cuts cotton into mop heads and transfers these to Department 2 where the mop head is twisted and attached to a handle. Cotton is added at the beginning of the first process, and the handle is added at the end of the second process.

Normal losses in Department 1 should not exceed 5 percent of the units started; losses are determined at an inspection point at the end of the production process. The AQL in Department 2 is 10 percent of the mop heads transferred in; losses are found at an inspection point located 70 percent of the way through the production process.

The following production and cost data are available for January 1997.

	PRODUCTION RECORD (IN UNITS)	
	DEPT. ONE	DEPT. TWO
Beginning inventory	6,000	3,000
Started or transferred in	150,000	?
Ending inventory	18,000	15,000
Spoiled units	9,000	6,000
Transferred out	?	111,000

COST RECORD

Beginning inventory:		
Preceding department	n/a	$ 6,690
Material	$ 3,000	0
Conversion	2,334	504
Current period:		
Preceding department	n/a	230,910*
Material	36,000	740
Conversion	208,962	52,920

*This is *not* the amount derived from your calculations. Use this amount so that you do not carry forward any possible cost errors from Department 1.

The beginning and ending inventory units in Department 1 are, respectively, 10 percent and 60 percent complete as to conversion. In Department 2, the beginning and ending units are, respectively, 40 percent and 80 percent complete as to conversion.

Using the weighted average method, determine a cost of production report for each department for January 1997.

39. *(Comprehensive; FIFO method)* Use the information for Caunitz Company from problem 38 to prepare a FIFO cost of production report for each department for January 1997.

40. *(Comprehensive; weighted average and FIFO)* Kansas Company mines salt in central Kansas. Approximately 30 percent of the mined salt is processed into table salt. Kansas Company uses a process costing system for the table salt operation. Processing takes place in two departments. Department 1 uses FIFO costing, and Department 2 uses weighted average. The cost of the processed salt transferred from Department 1 to Department 2 is averaged over all the units transferred.

Salt is introduced into the process in Department 1. Spoilage occurs continuously through the department and normal spoilage should not exceed 10 percent of the units started; a unit is 50 pounds of salt.

Department 2 packages the salt at the 75 percent completion point; this material does not increase the number of units processed. A quality control inspection takes place when the goods are 80 percent complete. Spoilage should not exceed 5 percent of the units transferred in from Department 1.

The following production and cost data are applicable to Kansas Company's table salt operations for May 1997:

DEPARTMENT 1 PRODUCTION DATA

Beginning inventory (65% complete)	5,000
Units started	125,000
Units completed	110,000
Units in ending inventory (40% complete)	14,000

DEPARTMENT 1 COST DATA

Beginning inventory:		
Material	$ 7,750	
Conversion	11,500	$ 19,250
Current period:		
Material	$190,400	
Conversion	393,225	583,625
Total costs to account for		$602,875

DEPARTMENT 2 PRODUCTION DATA

Beginning inventory (90% complete)	40,000
Units transferred in	110,000
Units completed	120,000
Units in ending inventory (20% complete)	22,500

DEPARTMENT 2 COST DATA

Beginning inventory:

Transferred in	$204,000	
Material	120,000	
Conversion	21,600	$ 345,600

Current period:

Transferred in	$568,500*	
Material	268,875	
Conversion	55,395	892,770
Total costs to account for		$1,238,370

*This may not be the same amount determined for Department 1; ignore any difference and use this figure.

a. Compute the equivalent units of production in each department.

b. Determine the cost per equivalent unit in each department and compute the cost transferred out, cost in ending inventory, and cost of spoilage (if necessary).

41. *(Defective units and rework)* Terrell Corporation produces plastic pipe and accounts for its production process using weighted average process costing. Material is added at the beginning of production. The company applies overhead to products using machine hours. Terrell Corporation used the following information in setting its predetermined overhead rate for 1997:

Expected overhead other than rework	$425,000
Expected rework costs	37,500
Total expected overhead	$462,500
Expected machine hours for 1997	50,000

During 1997, the following production and cost data were accumulated:

Total good production completed	2,000,000 feet of pipe
Total defects	40,000 feet of pipe
Ending inventory (35% complete)	75,000 feet of pipe

Total (beginning inventory and current period) cost of direct material	$3,750,000
Total (beginning inventory and current period) cost of conversion	$5,650,000
Cost of reworking defects	$ 37,750

Terrell Corporation sells pipe for $3.50 per foot.

a. Determine the overhead application rate for 1997.

b. Determine the cost per pipe-foot for production in 1997.

c. Assume that the rework is normal and those units can be sold for the regular selling price. How will Terrell Corporation account for the $37,750 of rework cost?

d. Assume that the rework is normal, but the reworked pipe is irregular and can only be sold for $2.50 per foot. Prepare the journal entry to establish the inventory account for the reworked pipe. What is the total cost per unit for the good output completed?

e. Assume that 20 percent of the rework is abnormal and that all reworked output is irregular and can be sold for only $2.50 per foot. Prepare the journal entry to establish the inventory account for the reworked pipe. What is the total cost per foot for the good output completed during 1997?

42. *(Job order costing; rework)* Michaels Rigging manufactures pulley systems to customer specifications and uses a job order system. A recent order from Barnett Company was for 10,000 pulleys, and the job was assigned number BA468. The job cost sheet for #BA468 revealed the following:

WIP—JOB #BA468

Direct material	$20,400
Direct labor	24,600
Overhead	18,400
Total	$63,400

Final inspection of the 10,000 pulleys revealed that 230 of the pulleys were defective. In correcting the defects, an additional $950 of cost was incurred ($250 for direct material and $700 for direct labor). After the defects were cured, the pulleys were included with the nondefective units and shipped to the customer.

a. Assuming the rework costs are normal but specific to this job, show the journal entry to record incurrence of the rework costs.

b. Assuming the company has a predetermined overhead rate that includes normal rework costs, show the journal entry to record incurrence of the rework costs.

c. Assuming the rework costs are abnormal, show the journal entry to record incurrence of the rework costs.

---

43. *(Normal and abnormal spoilage; WA method)* APCO Company manufactures various lines of bicycles. Because of the high volume of each type of product, the company employs a process cost system using the weighted average method to determine unit costs. Bicycle parts are manufactured in the Molding Department and transferred to the Assembly Department where they are partially assembled. After assembly, the bicycle is sent to the Packing Department.

CASE

Cost-per-unit data for the 20-inch dirt bike has been completed through the Molding Department. Annual cost and production figures for the Assembly Department are presented below.

PRODUCTION DATA

Beginning inventory (100% complete as to transferred-in; 100% complete as to assembly material; 80% complete as to conversion)	3,000 units
Transferred in during the year (100% complete as to transferred-in)	45,000 units
Transferred to Packing	40,000 units
Ending inventory (100% complete as to transferred-in; 50% complete as to assembly material; 20% complete as to conversion)	4,000 units

COST DATA	TRANSFERRED-IN	DIRECT MATERIAL	CONVERSION
Beginning inventory	$ 82,200	$ 6,660	$ 11,930
Current period	1,237,800	96,840	236,590
Totals	$1,320,000	$103,500	$248,520

Damaged bicycles are identified on inspection when the assembly process is 70 percent complete; all assembly material has been added at this point of the process. The normal rejection rate for damaged bicycles is 5 percent of the bicycles reaching the inspection point. Any damaged bicycles above the 5 percent quota are considered to be abnormal. All damaged bikes are removed from the production process and destroyed.

a. Compute the number of damaged bikes that are considered to be
   1. a normal quantity of damaged bikes.
   2. an abnormal quantity of damaged bikes.

    b. Compute the weighted average equivalent units of production for the year for

       1. bicycles transferred in from the Molding Department.

       2. bicycles produced with regard to assembly material.

       3. bicycles produced with regard to assembly conversion.

    c. Compute the cost per equivalent unit for the fully assembled dirt bike.

    d. Compute the amount of the total production cost of $1,672,020 that will be associated with the following items:

       1. Normal damaged units

       2. Abnormal damaged units

       3. Good units completed in the Assembly Department

       4. Ending Work in Process Inventory in the Assembly Department

    e. Describe how the applicable dollar amounts for the following items would be presented in the financial statements:

       1. Normal damaged units

       2. Abnormal damaged units

       3. Completed units transferred to the Packing Department

       4. Ending Work in Process Inventory in the Assembly Department

    f. Determine the cost to APCO Company of normal spoilage. Discuss some potential reasons for spoilage to occur in this company. Which of these reasons would you consider important enough to correct and why? How might you attempt to correct these problems?

(CMA adapted)

ETHICS AND QUALITY DISCUSSION

44. FulRange Inc. produces complex printed circuits for stereo amplifiers. The circuits are sold primarily to major component manufacturers, and any production overruns are sold to small manufacturers at a substantial discount. The small manufacturer segment appears to be very profitable because the basic operating budget assigns all fixed expenses to production for the major manufacturers, the only predictable market.

A common product defect that occurs in production is a "drift," caused by failure to maintain precise heat levels during the production process. Rejects from the 100 percent testing program can be reworked to acceptable levels if the defect is drift. However, in a recent analysis of customer complaints, George Wilson, the cost accountant, and the quality control engineer have ascertained that normal rework does not bring the circuits up to standard. Sampling shows that about one-half of the reworked circuits fail after extended, high-volume amplifier operation. The incidence of failure in the reworked circuits is projected to be about 10 percent over 1 to 5 years of operation.

Unfortunately, there is no way to determine which reworked circuits will fail because testing does not detect this problem. The rework process could be changed to correct the problem, but the cost-benefit analysis for the suggested change in the rework process indicates that it is not practicable. FulRange's marketing analyst feels that this problem will have a significant impact on the company's reputation and customer satisfaction if it is not corrected. Consequently, the board of directors would interpret this problem as having serious negative implications for the company's profitability.

Wilson has included the circuit failure and rework problem in his report for the upcoming quarterly meeting of the board of directors. Due to the potential adverse economic impact, Wilson has followed a long-standing practice of highlighting this information.

After reviewing the reports to be presented, the plant manager and her staff were upset and indicated to the controller that he should control his people better. "We can't upset the board with this kind of material. Tell Wilson to tone that down. Maybe we can get it by this meeting and have some time to work on it. People who buy those cheap systems and play them that loud shouldn't expect them to last forever."

The controller called Wilson into his office and said, "George, you'll have to bury this one. The probable failure of reworks can be referred to briefly in the oral presentation, but it should not be mentioned or highlighted in the advance material mailed to the board."

Wilson feels strongly that the board will be misinformed on a potentially serious loss of income if he follows the controller's orders. Wilson discussed the problem with the quality control engineer, who simply remarked, "That's your problem, George."

a. Discuss the ethical considerations that George Wilson should recognize in deciding how to proceed in this matter.

b. Explain what ethical responsibilities should be accepted in this situation by
   1. the controller.
   2. the quality control engineer.
   3. the plant manager and her staff.

c. What should George Wilson do in this situation? Explain your answer.

(CMA)

45. Read the News Note on page 573 Joseph Pereira and Joseph Rebello in Chapter 13. The company states that only 4 lots (118,000 vials) were sold that were contaminated with relatively benign bacteria. However, in January 1995, Copley informed the court that it is possible that there may be over 10,000 adverse reaction reports.

    a. In the health-care industry, why does the matter of quality control involve ethical considerations as well as cost considerations?

    b. For this company, are the standards of quality set internally or externally? Explain.

    c. Why do you think Copley might be slow to improve its quality control procedures?

    d. If Copley tracks spoilage costs, do you think its recorded costs of spoiled products would be higher or lower than those of the most quality-conscious drug makers? Explain.

    e. If operating in such a manner is profitable for Copley, what does this suggest about the penalties for poor quality control in the generic drug industry?

46. *The IRS collects and accounts for over $1 trillion in revenue each year. Yet it is estimated another $100 billion of tax owed each year is not collected. In addition, millions of unnecessary taxpayer contacts are made annually requiring countless hours of taxpayers' time.*

    Taxpayer service also leaves much to be desired. The General Accounting Office (GAO) reported that while IRS staffers correctly answered 89% of questions posed by test callers in 1993 (up from 88% in 1992), three out of four calls during filing season were not answered at all.

    Individual taxpayers sometimes are the beneficiaries of IRS quality problems. In 1992, the IRS sent out erroneous tax refunds in excess of $175 million to more than 270,000 filers.

    [SOURCE: Al Y. S. Chen and Roby B. Sawyers, "TQM at the IRS," *Journal of Accountancy* (July 1994), p. 77. Reprinted with permission from *The Journal of Accountancy.* Copyright © 1994 by American Institute of CPAs. Opinions of the authors are their own and do not necessarily reflect policies of the AICPA.]

    a. Because the IRS cannot really "lose" customers, why would the organization worry about customer service?

    b. Other than the direct monetary effects of quality problems, what indirect costs do IRS mistakes have on its customers?

c. The IRS is interested in adopting TQM. Provide at least five suggestions that might reduce quality problems at the IRS and what the benefits of those suggestions would be. (Do not suggest a change in the tax code because that is out of the Service's control.)

INTERNET ACTIVITIES

47. Find the home page for Interkinetics Corporation. Identify and discuss the services offered by this firm to manufacturers that might be useful to improve the quality of production processes, improve the yield of processes, and reduce waste and defective products.

48. Find the home page for Precision Machined Products Association. From there, find in the reports issued by the association a discussion of "Screw Machining Skill Standards Update." Discuss the purposes of the associations's skill standards initiative and how such industry-level initiatives can affect spoilage rates and the quality of production.

49. Search the Internet for information regarding the PCS Software Package which was developed under the auspices of the Canadian government. The software was designed for sewing factories. Discuss the capabilities of the software and how it could be utilized by a small firm to monitor quality and costs of production.

CHAPTER

10

Cost Allocation for Joint Products and By-Products

LEARNING OBJECTIVES

After completing this chapter, you should be able to answer these questions:

1. How are the outputs of a joint process classified?

2. At what point in a joint process are joint products identifiable?

3. What management decisions must be made before a joint process is begun?

4. How are joint costs allocated to products?

5. How are by-products treated in job order costing?

6. How should not-for-profit organizations account for joint costs?

Kraft Foods, Inc.

Kraft Foods, Inc. was formed as a company in 1989, but its history goes back centuries. It is a company with many different roots and founders, all sharing a commitment to quality, a willingness to take risks and a spirit of innovation. Among the products now sold by Kraft Foods, Inc. are so many "firsts" and innovations that the history of the company is almost a history of the food industry. [The company today is a combination] of three predecessor companies: Kraft (established 1903), General Foods (established 1895), and Oscar Mayer (established 1883).

The history of the KRAFT brand can be traced to 1903, when with $65 in capital, a rented wagon and a horse named Paddy, J. L. Kraft started purchasing cheese at Chicago's Water Street wholesale market and reselling it to local merchants. Within a short time, four of J. L. Kraft's brothers joined him in the business, and in 1909 they incorporated as J. L. Kraft & Bros. Co. In 1914 J. L. Kraft and his brothers purchased their first cheese factory in Stockton, Illinois, and in 1915 they began producing process cheese in 3–1/2 and 7–3/4-ounce tins. J. L. Kraft's method of producing process cheese was so revolutionary, in 1916 he obtained a patent for it and in 1917 the company started supplying cheese in tins to the U.S. Government for the armed forces in World War I.

Oscar F. Mayer was a Bavarian immigrant who started his career in 1873 at the age of 14 as a "butcher's boy" in a Detroit meat market. By 1883 he had saved up enough money to lease a failing Chicago meat market. With the help of his brothers Gottfried and Max, he made the business such a success that the landlord refused to renew the lease when it came up for renewal in 1888. So in that year Oscar Mayer and his brothers started again from scratch, this time building their own meat market just down the street from the original leased market. With the Mayer brothers' attention to quality and customer service, their customers followed them and their original landlord was soon out of business.

Early company specialties were "Old World" sausages and Westphalian hams, soon followed by bacon and wieners. The company's concern for quality was so strong that in 1906, Oscar Mayer & Co. was among the first to volunteer to join the newly created federal meat inspection program. In 1919 the company made its first major expansion, with the purchase of a processing plant in Madison, Wisconsin. The plant quickly proved to be a profitable, efficient operation and eventually Madison became the corporate headquarters. [Oscar Mayer is involved with conducting and accounting for several joint processes that result in joint products and by-products. These processes are concerned with butchering, processing, and packing various livestock products. A few of these are mentioned above.]

SOURCE: *A Brief History of Kraft Foods, Inc.*, Corporate Affairs Office, Kraft Foods, Inc., Three Lakes Drive, Northfield, IL 60093–2753, pp. 1–4.

Almost every company produces and sells more than one type of product. Although companies may engage in multiple production processes to manufacture a variety of products, they may also engage in a single process to simultaneously generate various different outputs such as those at Oscar Mayer (meat packers cut, segment, process, and package meats from a side of beef). In a like manner, the refining of crude oil may produce gasoline, motor oil, heating oil, and kerosene. A single process in which one product cannot be manufactured without producing others is known as a **joint process.** Such processes are common in the

joint process

joint cost

extractive, agricultural, food, and chemical industries. The costs incurred for materials, labor, and overhead during a joint process are referred to as the **joint cost** of the production process.

This chapter discusses joint processes, their related product outputs, and the accounting treatment of joint cost. Outputs of a joint process are classified based on their revenue-generating ability, and joint cost is allocated, using either a physical or monetary measure, only to the primary products of a joint process. Although joint cost allocations are necessary to determine financial statement valuations, such allocations should *not* be used in internal decision making.

Joint costs may also be incurred in service businesses and not-for-profit organizations. Such costs in these organizations are often for advertisements that publicize different product lines or locations, or ads for different purposes, such as public service information and requests for donations. Joint costs of not-for-profit firms are covered in the last section of this chapter.

OUTPUTS OF A JOINT PROCESS

joint product

A joint process simultaneously produces more than one product line. The product lines resulting from a joint process and having a sales value are referred to as (1) joint products, (2) by-products, and (3) scrap. **Joint products** are the *primary* outputs of a joint process; each joint product individually has substantial revenue-generating ability. Joint products are the primary reason management undertakes the production process yielding them. These products are also called primary products, main products, or coproducts.

Joint products do not necessarily have to be totally different products; the definition of joint products has been extended to include similar products of differing quality that result from the same process. For example, when computer memory chips are fabricated, the output will all have the same design, but some will have more memory density than others.

by-product

scrap

waste

In contrast, **by-products** and **scrap** are *incidental* outputs of a joint process. Both are salable, but their sales values alone would not be sufficient for management to justify undertaking the joint process. By-products are viewed as having a higher sales value than scrap. A final output from a joint process is **waste,** which is a residual output that has no sales value. A normal amount of waste may create a production

The locale in which sales occur may, in part, help a meat processing company specify which cuts will be classified as joint products, by-products, scrap, or waste.

Love, Love Me Doo

N E W S
N O T E

Manure may not seem romantic, but 150 sweethearts received gifts of Love Me Doo for Valentine's Day last year. It was a holiday offering from the Memphis-based Zoo-Doo Compost Company. Most zoos sell manure as a novelty product that generates more publicity than cash. But every pound customers buy is a pound that the zoo doesn't have to cart away.

The Zoo-Doo Compost Company helps zoos understand the costs and opportunities involved with their occupants' by-products. "Many zoos don't even know how much manure they are producing or the cost of disposing of it," explains president and founder Pierce Ledbetter. Disposal costs are often lost in layers of city budgets, and when zoo management uncovers the actual amount, "they are shocked."

Zoo-Doo has two basic markets: the novelty market and serious organic gardeners. So far, novelty sales have been the largest, with 160 zoo stores and 700 additional retail outlets carrying Zoo-Doo. "It's a symbol of creative recycling, and we infuse a lot of humor," says Ledbetter. "Some people actually use it, but most buy it as a gag gift." He anticipates that this market will be short-lived, but generate a high level of sales.

SOURCE: Susan Krafft, "Love, Love Me Doo," *American Demographics* (June 1994), p. 15. *American Demographics* magazine © 1994. Reprinted with permission.

cost that cannot be avoided in some industries. Alternatively, many companies have learned either to minimize their production waste by changing their processing techniques or to reclassify waste as a by-product or scrap through selling it to generate some minimal amount of revenue.

A product classification may be changed by a company over time because of changes in technology, consumer demand, or ecological factors. Some products originally classified as by-products are reclassified as joint products, whereas some joint products are reduced to the by-product category. Even products originally viewed as scrap or waste may be upgraded to a joint product status. Years ago, for example, the sawdust and chips produced in a lumber mill were considered waste and discarded. These items are now processed further to produce particle board used in making inexpensive furniture. Therefore, depending on the company, sawdust and chips may be considered a joint product or a by-product. The News Note entitled "Love, Love Me Doo" provides an unusual example of innovative waste usage.

Classification of joint process output is based on the judgment of company managers, normally after considering the relative sales values of the outputs. Classifications are unique to each company engaged in the joint process. For example, East Company and West Inc. each engage in the same joint production process that produces three chemicals: X, Y, and Z. East Company classifies all three chemicals as joint products, whereas West Inc. classifies Chemicals Y and Z as joint products and Chemical X as a by-product. These classifications could have resulted from the fact that East has the facilities to refine Chemical X beyond the joint process, but West does not have such facilities. Further refining provides Chemical X with a substantially higher sales value per unit than selling the chemical as it exits the joint process.

Joint products are typically produced in companies using mass production processes and, thus, a process costing accounting method.[1] The outputs of a corn processing plant, for example, may include corn on the cob and whole-kernel corn (joint products), partial corn kernels (by-product) used for corn meal and grits, inferior kernels (scrap) for sale to producers of animal food, and husks, corn silk, and cobs (waste)

THE JOINT PROCESS

[1] For simplicity, Chapters 8 and 9 on process costing included examples only of single-product processes.

EXHIBIT 10–1

Illustration of Joint Process
Output

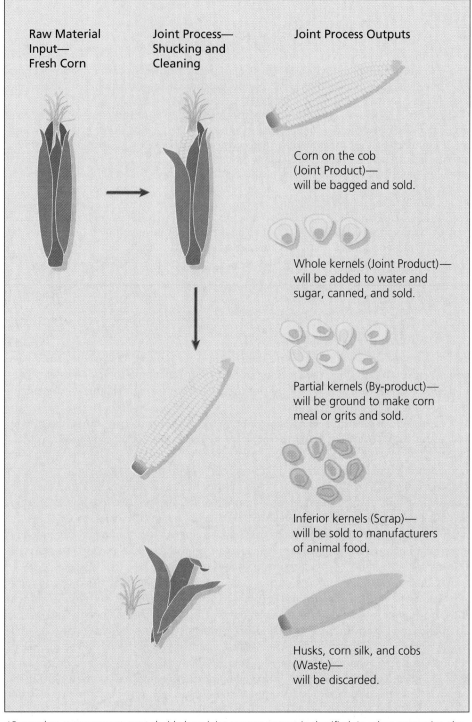

Raw Material
Input—
Fresh Corn

Joint Process—
Shucking and
Cleaning

Joint Process Outputs

Corn on the cob
(Joint Product)—
will be bagged and sold.

Whole kernels (Joint Product)—
will be added to water and
sugar, canned, and sold.

Partial kernels (By-product)—
will be ground to make corn
meal or grits and sold.

Inferior kernels (Scrap)—
will be sold to manufacturers
of animal food.

Husks, corn silk, and cobs
(Waste)—
will be discarded.

*Remember, management must decide how joint process output is classified. In other companies, the
cobs and husks could be sold to other companies as filler in those companies' products.

that are discarded. Exhibit 10–1 illustrates the output of such a joint process. The
point at which joint process outputs are first identifiable as individual products is
called the **split-off point.** A joint process may have one or more split-off points,
depending on the number and types of output produced. Output may be sold at the
split-off point if a market exists for products in that condition. Alternatively, some
or all of the products may be processed further after exiting the joint process.

Joint cost includes all costs incurred up to the split-off point for direct material,
direct labor, and overhead. Joint cost is allocated, at the split-off point, to *only* the
joint products because these products are the reason that management undertook the

split-off point

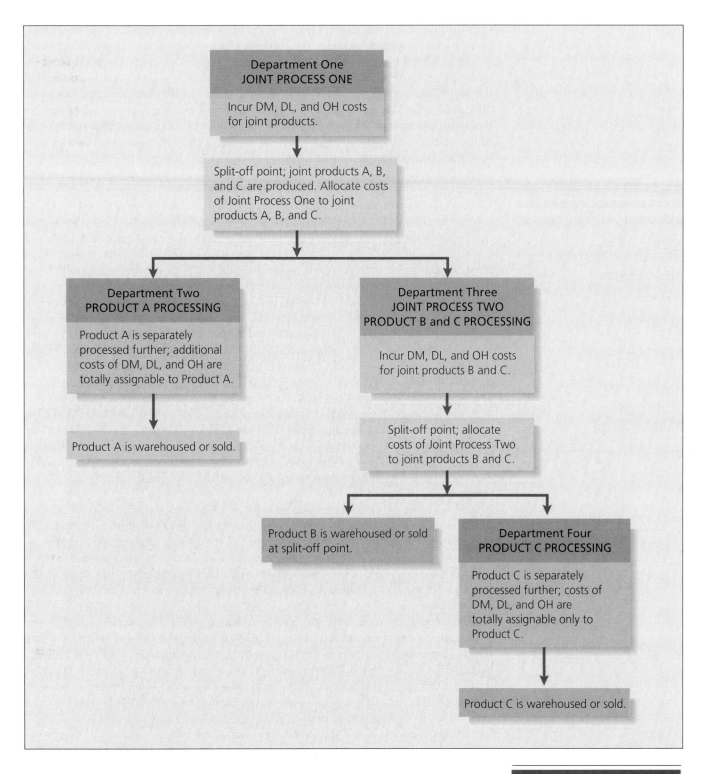

Department One
JOINT PROCESS ONE

Incur DM, DL, and OH costs
for joint products.

Split-off point; joint products A, B,
and C are produced. Allocate costs
of Joint Process One to joint
products A, B, and C.

Department Two
PRODUCT A PROCESSING

Product A is separately
processed further; additional
costs of DM, DL, and OH are
totally assignable to Product A.

Product A is warehoused or sold.

Department Three
JOINT PROCESS TWO
PRODUCT B and C PROCESSING

Incur DM, DL, and OH costs
for joint products B and C.

Split-off point; allocate
costs of Joint Process Two
to joint products B and C.

Product B is warehoused or sold
at split-off point.

Department Four
PRODUCT C PROCESSING

Product C is separately
processed further; costs of
DM, DL, and OH are
totally assignable only to
Product C.

Product C is warehoused or sold.

EXHIBIT 10–2

Model of a Joint Process

production process. Allocation is necessary because of the cost principle. Joint cost is a necessary and reasonable cost of producing the joint products and, therefore, should be attached to them. But although necessary for valuation purposes for financial statements, *the joint cost allocation to joint products is not relevant to decision making.* Once the split-off point is reached, the joint cost has already been incurred and is a **sunk cost** that cannot be changed no matter what future course of action is taken.

sunk cost

If any of the joint process outputs are processed further, additional costs after split-off will be incurred. Any costs after split-off are assigned to the separate products for which those costs are incurred. Exhibit 10–2 depicts a joint process with multiple split-off points and the allocation of costs to products. For simplicity, all the output of this joint process is primary output; there are no by-products, scrap, or waste. Note that some of the output of Joint Process One (joint products B and C) becomes part of the direct material for Joint Process Two. The joint cost allocations will follow products B and C into Joint Process Two for accounting purposes, but these allocated costs should not be used in making decisions about further processing in that department or in Department 4. Such decisions should be made after considering only whether the additional revenues to be gained from further processing are greater than the additional costs of further processing.

MANAGEMENT DECISIONS REGARDING JOINT PROCESSES

Certain decisions need to be made by company managers before committing resources to a joint production process. First, total expected revenues from the sale of the joint process output must be estimated and compared to total expected processing costs of the output. If the revenues are expected to exceed the costs, management must then consider other potential costs. Because the joint process results in a "basket" of products, managers must be aware that some of the joint process output may require additional processing to make it salable. Once joint process costs have been incurred, they become sunk costs *regardless* of whether the output is salable at the end of the joint process or at what amount. Thus, management must consider total joint costs plus separate processing or selling costs expected to be incurred at or after the end of the joint process in making the decision to commit resources to the joint process.

If total anticipated revenues from the "basket" of products exceed the anticipated joint and separate costs, the second management decision must be made. Managers must compare the net income from this use of resources to that which would be provided by all other alternative uses of company resources. If joint process net income is greater than would be provided by other uses, management would decide that this joint production process is the best use of capacity and would begin production.

The next two decisions are made at split-off. The third decision is to determine how the joint process output is to be classified. Some output will be primary; other output will be considered by-product, scrap, or waste. This classification decision is necessary for the joint cost to be allocated, because *joint cost is only assigned to joint products.* However, before allocation, joint cost may be reduced by the value of the by-products and scrap. Determination of by-product and scrap value is discussed later in the chapter.

The fourth decision is the most complex. Management must decide whether any (or all) of the joint process output will be sold (if marketable) at split-off or whether it will be processed further. If primary products are marketable at split-off, further processing should only be undertaken if the value added to the product, as reflected by the incremental revenue, exceeds the incremental cost. If a primary product is not marketable at split-off, additional costs *must* be incurred to make that product marketable. For nonprimary output, management must also estimate whether the incremental revenue from additional processing will exceed additional processing cost. If there is no net incremental benefit, the nonmarketable output should be disposed of without further processing after the split-off point.

To illustrate a further-processing decision, assume that a whole chicken has a selling price of $.15 per pound at split-off, but the minimum selling price for chicken parts after further processing is $.19 per pound. If the additional processing cost is less than $.04 per pound, the $.04 incremental revenue ($.19 − $.15) exceeds the incremental cost and additional processing should occur. Note that the joint cost is *not* used in this decision process. The joint cost is a sunk cost after it has been incurred, and the only relevant items in the decision to process further are the incremental revenue and incremental cost.

Exhibit 10–3 presents the four management decision points in a joint production process. In making decisions at any potential point of sale, managers must have a

EXHIBIT 10–3

Decision Points in a Joint
Production Process

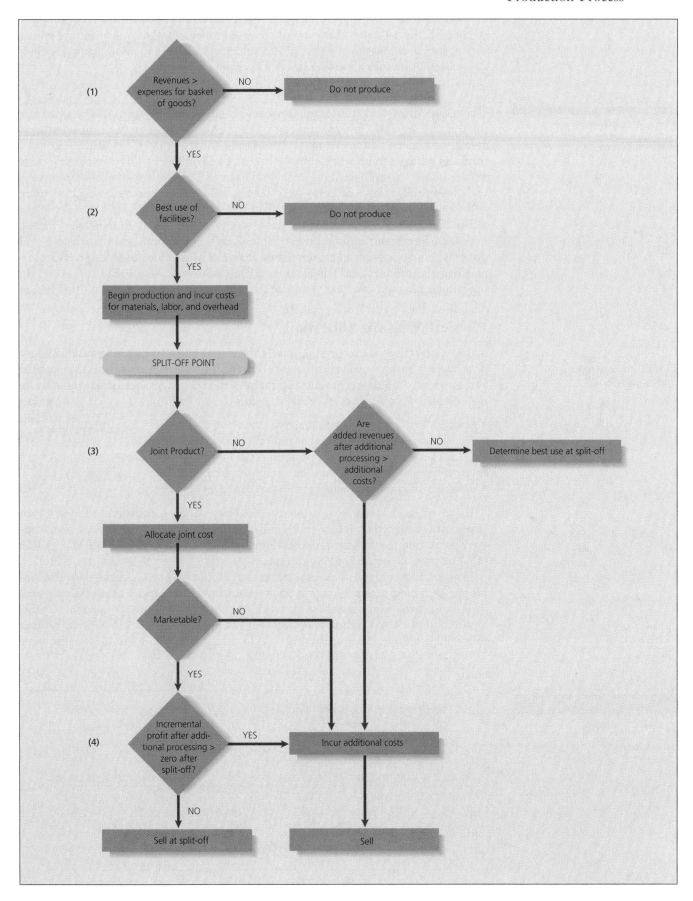

valid estimate of the selling price of each type of joint process output. Expected selling prices should be based on both cost and market factors. In the long run, assuming demand exists, the selling prices and volumes of products must be sufficient to cover their total costs. However, immediate economic influences on setting selling prices, such as competitors' prices and consumers' sensitivity to price changes, cannot be ignored in estimating selling prices and forecasting revenues.

ALLOCATION OF JOINT COST

The Tasty Meats Company is used to demonstrate alternative methods of allocating joint processing cost. Because the consumer market for large portions of large farm animals is limited, Tasty Meats processes sides of beef into three distinct primary products during a joint process: steaks, roasts, and hamburger. (The remaining parts are considered by-products.) All joint products may be sold at split-off. Alternatively, each beef product may be processed further, which will create additional separate costs for the products. Steaks may be processed further to produce steak sandwiches; roasts can be processed further to make special cuts; and hamburger meat can be processed further to be used as part of a sausage mixture. Certain marketing and disposal costs for advertising, commissions, and transportation are incurred regardless of when the products are sold. Assumed information on Tasty Meats' processing operations and joint products for October 1997 is presented in Exhibit 10–4.

Physical Measure Allocation

An easy, objective way to prorate joint cost at the split-off point is through the use of a physical measure. **Physical measurement allocation** uses a common physical characteristic of the joint products as the proration base. All joint products must be measurable by the same characteristic, such as

physical measurement allocation

- tons of ore in the mining industry,
- linear board feet in the lumber milling industry,
- barrels of oil in the petroleum refining industry,
- tons of meat, bone, and hide in the meat packing or processing industry, or
- number of computer chips in the semiconductor industry.

Using physical measurement allocation, Tasty Meats Company's $5,200,000 of joint cost is assigned as shown in Exhibit 10–5. For Tasty Meats, physical measurement allocation would assign a cost of approximately $582.31 ($5,200,000 ÷ 8,930 tons) per ton of beef, regardless of type.

Physical measurement allocation treats each unit of output as equally desirable and assigns the same per-unit cost to each. Also, unlike monetary measures, physical measures provide an unchanging yardstick of output. A ton of output produced from a process 8 years ago is the same measurement as a ton produced from that process today. Physical measures are useful in allocating joint cost to products that have

EXHIBIT 10–4

Basic Joint Cost Information

Joint processing cost for period: $5,200,000					
(1)	(2)	(3)	(4)	(5)	(6)
		SALES PRICE PER TON	COST PER TON IF SOLD AT	SEPARATE COST PER TON IF	FINAL SALES PRICE
JOINT PRODUCTS	TONS OF PRODUCTION	AT SPLIT-OFF	SPLIT-OFF*	PROCESSED FURTHER	PER TON
Steaks	3,720	$2,700	$200	$100	$3,200
Roasts	2,430	1,680	100	100	1,800
Hamburger	2,780	1,176	50	60	1,500
*These selling costs will also be incurred if product is processed further.					

| Cost per Physical Measure = Total Joint Cost ÷ Total Units of Physical Measurement | | | |
| = $5,200,000 ÷ 8,930 tons = $582.31 (rounded) | | | |
JOINT PRODUCT	TONS	COST PER TON	TOTAL ALLOCATED COST
Steaks	3,720	$582.31	$2,166,193
Roasts	2,430	$582.31	1,415,013
Hamburger	2,780	$582.31	1,618,822
Total	8,930		$5,200,028*

*Off due to rounding of cost per ton.

EXHIBIT 10–5

Joint Cost Allocation Based on Physical Measurement

extremely unstable selling prices. These measures are also necessary in rate-regulated industries that use cost to determine selling prices. For example, assume that a rate-regulated company has the right to set selling price at 20 percent above cost. It is circular logic to allocate joint cost based on selling prices that were set based on cost to produce the output.

A major disadvantage of allocating joint cost based on a physical measure is that the revenue-generating ability of individual joint products is ignored. Products that weigh the most or that are produced in the largest quantity will receive the highest proportion of joint cost allocation—regardless of their ability to bear that cost when they are sold. In the case of Tasty Meats, each ton of hamburger has been assigned a cost of $582.31. However, computations will demonstrate that hamburger generates the lowest gross profit of the three joint products and yet is being assigned the same joint cost per ton as the more desirable steaks and roasts.

The process of refining crude oil at this petrochemical plant generates a variety of joint products. One way of assigning the joint cost is on the basis of physical quantities of the outputs.

Monetary Measure Allocation

All commonly used allocation methods employ a process of proration. Because of the simplicity of the physical measure allocation process, a detailed proration scheme was unnecessary. However, the following steps can be used to prorate joint cost to joint products in the more complex monetary measure allocations:

1. Choose a monetary allocation base.
2. List the values that comprise the base for each joint product.
3. Sum the values in step 2 to obtain a total value for the list.
4. Divide each individual value in step 2 by the total in step 3 to obtain a numerical proportion for each value. The sum of these proportions should total 1.00 or 100 percent.[2]
5. Multiply the joint cost by each proportion to obtain the amount to be allocated to each product.
6. Divide the prorated joint cost for each product by the number of equivalent units of production for each product to obtain a cost per EUP for valuation purposes.

The primary benefit of monetary measure allocations over physical measure allocations is that the former recognize the relative ability of each product to generate a profit at sale. A problem with monetary measure allocations is that the basis used is not constant or unchanging. Because of fluctuations in the general and specific price levels, a dollar's worth of output today is different from a dollar's worth of output from the same process 5 years ago. However, accountants customarily ignore price level fluctuations when recording or processing data, so this particular flaw of monetary measures is not usually viewed as significant.

Three of the many monetary measures that can be used to allocate joint cost to primary output are presented in this text. These measures are sales value at split-off, net realizable value at split-off, and approximated net realizable value at split-off.

sales value at split-off allocation

SALES VALUE AT SPLIT-OFF   The **sales value at split-off allocation** assigns joint cost to joint products based solely on relative sales values of the products at the split-off point. Thus, to use this method, all joint products must be marketable at split-off. Exhibit 10–6 shows how Tasty Meats' joint cost is assigned to production using the sales value at split-off allocation method. Under this method, the low selling price per ton of hamburger, relative to the other joint products, results in a lower allocated cost per ton than resulted from the physical measure allocation technique.

EXHIBIT 10–6

Joint Cost Allocation Based on Sales Value at Split-Off

JOINT PRODUCT	TONS	SELLING PRICE	REVENUE	DECIMAL FRACTION	JOINT COST	AMOUNT ALLOCATED	COST PER TON
Steaks	3,720	$2,700	$10,044,000	.58	$5,200,000	$3,016,000	$810.75
Roasts	2,430	1,680	4,082,400	.23	$5,200,000	1,196,000	$492.18
Hamburger	2,780	1,176	3,269,280	.19	$5,200,000	988,000	$355.40
Total	8,930		$17,395,680	1.00		$5,200,000	

[2] Decimal fractions rounded to two places are used throughout the chapter for presentation purposes and to highlight the proportion of the total joint cost allocated to each joint product. Greater precision may be obtained by simply dividing each step 2 value by the step 3 value, leaving the result in the calculator, and multiplying that resulting value by the total joint cost.

This process uses a weighting technique based on both quantity produced and selling price of production.

NET REALIZABLE VALUE AT SPLIT-OFF   The **net realizable value at split-off allocation** method assigns joint cost based on the joint products' proportional net realizable values at the point of split-off. Net realizable value is equal to product sales revenue at split-off minus any costs necessary to prepare and dispose of the product. This method also requires that all joint products be marketable at the split-off point, but it considers the additional costs that must be incurred at split-off to realize the estimated sales revenue. The costs at split-off point for Tasty Meats' products are shown in the fourth column of Exhibit 10–4. The net realizable value of each product is computed by subtracting the cost at split-off from the selling price at split-off. The $5,200,000 joint cost is then assigned based on each product's relative proportion of total net realizable value (Exhibit 10–7). This method provides an allocated product cost that considers the disposal costs that would be necessitated if the product were to be sold at split-off.

net realizable value at split-off allocation

APPROXIMATED NET REALIZABLE VALUE AT SPLIT-OFF   Often, some or all of the joint products are not salable at the split-off point. For these products to be sold, additional processing must take place after split-off, causing additional costs to be incurred. Because of this lack of marketability at split-off, neither the sales value nor the net realizable value approach can be used. **Approximated net realizable value at split-off allocation** requires that a simulated net realizable value at the split-off point be calculated. This approximated value is computed on a per-product basis as final sales price minus incremental separate costs. **Incremental separate costs** refer to all costs that are incurred between the split-off point and the point of sale. The approximated net realizable values are then used to proportionately distribute joint cost. An underlying assumption in this method is that the incremental revenue from further processing is equal to or greater than the incremental cost of further processing and selling. Using the information in Exhibit 10–4, approximated net realizable values at split-off are determined for each product processed by Tasty Meats:

approximated net realizable value at split-off allocation

incremental separate cost

JOINT PRODUCTS	FINAL PER TON SELLING PRICE	PER TON SEPARATE COSTS AFTER SPLIT-OFF	APPROXIMATED NET REALIZABLE VALUE AT SPLIT-OFF
Steaks	$3,200	$300	$2,900
Roasts	1,800	200	1,600
Hamburger	1,500	110	1,390

Further processing should be undertaken only if the incremental revenues will exceed the incremental costs. These computations are shown as follows:

EXHIBIT 10–7

Joint Cost Allocation Based on Net Realizable Value at Split-Off

JOINT PRODUCT	TONS	UNIT NET REALIZABLE VALUE PER TON	TOTAL NET REALIZABLE VALUE	DECIMAL FRACTION	JOINT COST	AMOUNT ALLOCATED	COST PER TON
Steaks	3,720	$2,500	$ 9,300,000	.57	$5,200,000	$2,964,000	$796.77
Roasts	2,430	1,580	3,839,400	.24	$5,200,000	1,248,000	$513.58
Hamburger	2,780	1,126	3,130,280	.19	$5,200,000	988,000	$355.40
Total	8,930		$16,269,680	1.00		$5,200,000	

JOINT PRODUCTS	FINAL SALES PRICE	SALES PRICE AT SPLIT-OFF	COST PER TON AT SPLIT-OFF	COST PER TON AFTER SPLIT-OFF
Steaks	$3,200	$2,700	$200	$300
Roasts	1,800	1,680	100	200
Hamburger	1,500	1,176	50	110

JOINT PRODUCTS	INCREMENTAL REVENUE	INCREMENTAL COST	DIFFERENCE
Steaks	$500	$100	$400
Roasts	120	100	20
Hamburger	324	60	264

The previous information shows that Tasty Meats will be better off if all of the joint products are processed further than if they are sold at split-off. For all products, the incremental revenues from further processing exceed the incremental costs beyond split-off. The same conclusion can be reached by comparing the net realizable values at split-off with the approximated net realizable values at split-off as follows:

JOINT PRODUCTS	NET REALIZABLE VALUE AT SPLIT-OFF	APPROXIMATED NET REALIZABLE VALUE AT SPLIT-OFF	DIFFERENCE
Steaks	$2,500	$2,900	$400
Roasts	1,580	1,600	20
Hamburger	1,126	1,390	264

The decisions made about further processing affect the values used to allocate joint cost in the approximated net realizable sales value method. If one or more products will not be processed further because it is uneconomical to do so, the value base used for allocation of joint cost will be a mixture of actual and approximated net realizable values at split-off. Products that will not be processed further will be valued at their actual net realizable values at split-off; products that will be processed further are valued at approximated net realizable values at split-off. However, using a mixed base was unnecessary in this case because all products are to be processed further. Tasty Meats' $5,200,000 joint cost is allocated among the products as shown in Exhibit 10–8.

Each of the above physical and monetary measures allocates a different amount of joint cost to products and results in a different per-unit cost for each product. Each method has advantages and disadvantages. For most companies, approximated net realizable value at split-off provides the best joint cost assignment. This method is the most flexible in that no requirements exist about similar measurement bases (pounds, tons, etc.) or actual marketability at split-off. It is, however, more complex than the other methods, because estimations must be made about additional processing costs and potential future sales values.

The values obtained from the approximated net realizable value at split-off allocation method are used to illustrate cost flows in a joint cost environment. Tasty

EXHIBIT 10–8

Joint Cost Allocation Based on Approximated Net Realizable Value at Split-Off

JOINT PRODUCTS	TONS	APPROXIMATED NET REALIZABLE VALUE PER TON	TOTAL APPROXIMATED NET REALIZABLE VALUE	DECIMAL FRACTION	JOINT COST	AMOUNT ALLOCATED	COST PER TON
Steaks	3,720	$2,900	$10,788,000	.58	$5,200,000	$3,016,000	$810.75
Roasts	2,430	1,600	3,888,000	.21	$5,200,000	1,092,000	449.38
Hamburger	2,780	1,390	3,864,200	.21	$5,200,000	1,092,000	392.81
Total	8,930		$18,540,200	1.00		$5,200,000	

Meats has four production departments: (1) Meat Processing, (2) Steak Sandwich Production (using selected cuts of steak), (3) Fine Cuts Production (using roasts), and (4) Sausage Production (using hamburger). Work performed in the second, third, and fourth departments creates the finished, further-processed products. Tasty Meats uses FIFO costing and had the following finished goods inventories at the beginning of October:

Steak sandwiches	380 tons @ $850 per ton	$323,000
Fine Cuts	240 tons @ $560 per ton	134,400
Sausage	280 tons @ $420 per ton	117,600

During October, the company incurred separable costs for steaks, roasts, and sausage of $372,000, $243,000, and $166,800, respectively. All the products that were started into processing in October were also completed during that month. The company sold the following quantities of products in October:

PRODUCT	QUANTITY	SALES PRICE PER TON	TOTAL SALES PRICE (CASH)
Steak sandwiches	3,972 tons	$3,200	$12,710,400
Fine Cuts	2,440 tons	1,800	4,392,000
Sausage	3,000 tons	1,500	4,500,000

The October 1997 journal entries for Tasty Meats Company are shown in Exhibit 10–9. The ending balances of Tasty Meats' three finished goods accounts are computed as follows:

	TONS		
	Sandwiches	*Fine Cuts*	*Sausage*
Beginning inventory	380	240	280
Tons completed[a]	3,948	2,430	3,058
Tons available	4,328	2,670	3,338
Tons sold	3,972	2,440	3,000
Ending inventory	356	230	338
Times FIFO unit costs	$858.16[b]	$549.38[c]	$411.64[d]
EI valued at FIFO costs	$305,504.96	$126,357.40	$139,134.32

[a]As per the explanation to entry 4 in Exhibit 10–9, the tonnage of sandwiches and sausage increased due to adding ingredients.
[b]($3,016,000 + $372,000) ÷ 3,948 tons = $858.16
[c]($1,092,000 + $243,000) ÷ 2,430 tons = $549.38
[d]($1,092,000 + $166,800) ÷ 3,058 tons = $411.64

These ending inventory unit values represent *approximate* actual costs of production.

Prorating joint cost provides necessary inventory valuations for manufacturing companies. However, the allocation process may be influenced by the net realizable values of the other possible output of a joint process—by-products and scrap.

EXHIBIT 10–9

Journal Entries for October 1997

(1) Work in Process Inventory—Meat Processing	5,200,000	
Supplies Inventory		185,714
Wages Payable		3,900,000
Manufacturing Overhead		1,114,286
To record joint process costs incurred in October 1997; credit amounts are assumed.		*continued*

EXHIBIT 10–9

Journal Entries for
October 1997
(continued)

(2) Work in Process Inventory—Sandwiches 3,016,000
Work in Process Inventory—Fine Cuts 1,092,000
Work in Process Inventory—Sausage 1,092,000
    Work in Process Inventory—Meat
    Processing 5,200,000
To allocate the joint cost incurred in Meat
Processing to the joint products.

(3) Work in Process Inventory—Sandwiches 372,000
Work in Process Inventory—Fine Cuts 243,000
Work in Process Inventory—Sausage 166,800
    Various accounts 781,800
To record separate costs for further process-
ing incurred in the Sandwich, Fine Cuts, and
Sausage Production Departments. (Actual
costs are assumed to equal estimated sepa-
rate costs shown in Exhibit 10–4.)

(4) Finished Goods Inventory—Sandwiches 3,388,000
Finished Goods Inventory—Fine Cuts 1,335,000
Finished Goods Inventory—Sausage 1,258,800
    Work in Process Inventory—Sandwiches 3,388,000
    Work in Process Inventory—Fine Cuts 1,335,000
    Work in Process Inventory—Sausage 1,258,800
To transfer 3,948 tons of steak sandwiches,
2,430 tons of fine cuts, and 3,058 tons of
sausage to Finished Goods Inventory (cost
per ton: Sandwiches, $858.16; Fine Cuts,
$549.38; and Sausage, $411.64). The tonnage increased in the Sandwiches and Sausage Departments over that in Exhibit 10–8
due to the addition of other ingredients.

(5) Cash 21,602,400
    Sales 21,602,400
To record cash sales: Sandwiches,
$12,710,400; Fine Cuts, $4,392,000; Sausage, $4,500,000.

(6) Cost of Goods Sold 5,985,808
    Finished Goods Inventory—Sandwiches 3,405,511
    Finished Goods Inventory—Fine Cuts 1,343,036
    Finished Goods Inventory—Sausage 1,237,261
To record cost of goods sold on a FIFO basis:
Sandwiches (380 tons × $850) + (3,592
tons × $858.16); Fine Cuts (240 tons ×
$560) + (2,200 tons × $549.38); Sausage
(280 tons × $420) + (2,720 tons ×
$411.64)

(7) Selling Expenses 1,188,400
    Cash 1,188,400
To record selling expenses ($200 × 3,972)
+ ($100 × 2,440) + ($50 × 3,000). (Actual costs are assumed to equal estimated
selling costs shown in Exhibit 10–4.)

Because the distinction between by-products and scrap is one of degree, we have chosen to discuss them together by presenting several of the many treatments found in practice. The appropriate choice of method depends on the magnitude of the net realizable value of the by-products/scrap and the need for additional processing after split-off. As the sales value of the by-product/scrap increases, so does the need for inventory recognition. Sales value of the by-products/scrap is generally recorded under either the (1) net realizable value approach or (2) realized value approach. These approaches are discussed in the following sections using additional data for Tasty Meats Company, which considers bonemeal as a by-product. Data for November 1997 are shown in Exhibit 10–10.

ACCOUNTING FOR BY-PRODUCTS AND SCRAP

Net Realizable Value Approach

Use of the **net realizable value** (or offset) **approach** requires that the net realizable value of the by-product/scrap be treated as a reduction in the joint cost of manufacturing primary products. This method is normally used when the net realizable value of the by-product or scrap is expected to be significant.

net realizable value approach

Under the net realizable value approach, an inventory value is recorded that equals the selling price of the by-product/scrap produced minus the related processing, storing, and disposing costs. Any income remaining after covering these costs is used to reduce the joint cost of the main products. Any loss generated by the by-product/scrap is added to the cost of the main products. The credit for this Work in Process Inventory debit may be to one of two accounts. First, under the indirect method, Cost of Goods Sold for the joint products is reduced when the by-product/scrap is generated and joint products are sold:

Work in Process Inventory—Bonemeal	42,500	
Cost of Goods Sold—Main Products		42,500

When additional costs are incurred:

Work in Process Inventory—Bonemeal	7,500	
Various accounts		7,500

When by-product is completed:

Finished Goods Inventory—Bonemeal	50,000	
Work in Process Inventory—Bonemeal		50,000

When by-product is sold:

Cash (or Accounts Receivable)	50,000	
Finished Goods Inventory—Bonemeal		50,000

Total purchases for month: 10,000 tons of beef

Bonemeal (by-product) included in purchases: 500 tons
Selling price of bonemeal: $100 per ton
Processing costs per ton of bonemeal: $10 for labor and $5 for overhead
Net realizable value per ton of bonemeal: $85

EXHIBIT 10–10

November 1997 Data for By-Product

This technique may result in a slight mismatching of costs if by-products are created in a different period from when joint products are sold. Also, inventory values for the main products will be slightly overstated.

Alternatively, under the direct method, the work in process (WIP) joint cost of the primary products is reduced by the net realizable value of the by-product/scrap produced. Reducing WIP joint cost causes the costs of the primary products to be lowered for both cost of goods sold and inventory purposes. Thus, the only change in the above journal entries would be on the date the by-product was generated. The direct approach journal entry at that time is

Work in Process Inventory—Bonemeal	42,500	
Work in Process Inventory—Main Products		42,500

The major advantage of the direct approach is timing. The reduction in main products' joint cost is accomplished simultaneously with production of the main products. The disadvantage of this approach is that it is less conservative than waiting to record revenues until the by-product or scrap is actually sold, as does the realized value approach presented in the next section.

By-products and scrap may have sales potential beyond that currently known to management. Although reducing joint cost by the net realizable value of by-products/scrap is the traditional method of accounting for these goods, it is not necessarily the best method for managerial decision making, as indicated in the following remarks by John Fertakis:

> [T]he typical accounting methods used are not geared toward providing information useful to their management. By-products are treated as either having no assignable cost or as having costs equal to their net sales value. Either procedure is difficult to justify except on the grounds of expediency.
>
> If management considers the by-product as a resource in its own right, it should be subject to the same economic factors and analyses as joint products, though perhaps on a lesser scale.[3]

The net realizable value method does not indicate the sales dollars, expenses, or profits from the by-product/scrap and, thus, does not provide sufficient information to induce management to maximize the inflows from by-product/scrap disposal.

[3] John P. Fertakis, "Responsibility Accounting for By-Products and Industrial Wastes," *Journal of Accountancy* (May 1986), p. 138ff.

Realized Value Approach

Under the **realized value** (or other income) **approach,** no value is recognized for the by-products/scrap until they are sold. This method is the simplest approach to accounting for by-products/scrap. Several reporting techniques can be used with the realized value approach. One presentation shows total sales price of the by-product/scrap on the income statement under an "Other Revenue" caption. Costs of additional processing or disposal of the by-product/scrap are included with the cost of producing the main products. This presentation provides little useful information to management because the costs of producing the by-products/scrap are not matched with the revenues generated by those items.

realized value approach

For the Tasty Meats Company, the entries under the "Other Revenue" method are as follows when labor and overhead costs are incurred:

Work in Process Inventory—Joint Products	5,000	
Manufacturing Overhead	2,500	
Various accounts		7,500
To record the labor cost of		
grinding to WIP Inventory and of overhead		
charges for bonemeal (all included in the cost of		
joint products).		

At point of sale:

Cash (or Accounts Receivable)	50,000	
Other Revenue		50,000
To record sale of bonemeal.		

Another presentation shows by-product/scrap revenue on the income statement net of additional costs of processing and disposal. This method presents the net by-product revenue as an enhancement of net income in the period of sale under an "Other Income" caption. Such a presentation allows management to recognize the dollar benefit added to company income by managing the costs and revenues related to the by-products/scrap. The entries for the processing and sale of the by-products/scrap under this method for the Tasty Meats Company are as follows when labor and overhead costs are incurred:

Work in Process Inventory—Bonemeal	7,500	
Various accounts		7,500
To record the labor cost of grinding and		
overhead charges for bonemeal; this assumes that		
overhead charges are applied to WIP (with a		
corresponding credit to Manufacturing Overhead		
included in the various accounts).		

At point of sale:

Cash (or Accounts Receivable)	50,000	
Work in Process Inventory—Bonemeal		7,500
Other Income		42,500
To record sale of bonemeal net of processing/		
disposal costs.		

Because the "Other income" method matches by-product/scrap revenue with related storage, further processing, transportation, and disposal costs, this method provides detailed information on financial responsibility and accountability for disposition, provides better control, and may improve performance. Managers are

(a)
Net Realizable Approach: Reduce CGS

Sales		$7,200,000
Cost of Goods Sold		
Beginning FG	$ 400,000	
CGM	3,600,000	
CGA	$4,000,000	
Ending FG	(380,000)	
Unadjusted CGS	$3,620,000	
NRV of By-Product	(42,500)	(3,577,500)
Gross Margin		$3,622,500
Operating Expenses		2,600,000
Income from Principal Operations		$1,022,500
Other Income		
Commissions		80,000
Income before Income Taxes		$1,102,500

(b)
Net Realizable Approach: Reduce CGM

Sales		$7,200,000
Cost of Goods Sold		
Beginning FG	$ 400,000	
CGM ($3,600,000 −		
$42,500)	3,557,500	
CGA	$3,957,500	
Ending FG [assumed		
to be smaller than		
under (a)]	(375,380)	(3,582,120)
Gross Margin		$3,617,880
Operating Expenses		(2,600,000)
Income from Principal Operations		$1,017,880
Other Income		
Commissions		80,000
Income before Income Taxes		$1,097,880

(c)
Net Realized Value Approach: Increase Revenue

Sales		$7,200,000
Other Revenue		
By-Product Sales		50,000
Total Revenue		$7,250,000
Cost of Goods Sold		
Beginning FG	$ 400,000	
CGS (Main Products)	3,500,000	
CGS (Processing By-		
Product)	7,500	
CGA	$4,007,500	
Ending FG	(380,000)	(3,627,500)
Gross Margin		$3,622,500
Operating Expenses		(2,600,000)
Income from Principal Operations		$1,022,500
Other Income		
Commissions		80,000
Income before Income Taxes		$1,102,500

(d)
Net Realized Value Approach: Present as Other Income

Sales		$7,200,000
Cost of Goods Sold		
Beginning FG	$ 400,000	
CGM	3,600,000	
CGA	$4,000,000	
Ending FG	(380,000)	(3,620,000)
Gross Margin		$3,580,000
Operating Expenses		(2,600,000)
Income from Principal Operations		$ 980,000
Other Income		
Commissions	$ 80,000	
By-Product Sales (NRV)	42,500	122,500
Income before Income Taxes		$1,102,500

EXHIBIT 10–11

Comparative Income Statement By-Product Presentations

more apt to look for new or expanded sales potential because the net benefits of doing so are shown directly on the income statement.

Other alternative presentations include showing the realized value from the sale of the by-product/scrap as (1) an addition to gross margin, (2) a reduction of the cost of goods manufactured, or (3) a reduction of the cost of goods sold. The major advantage of these simplistic approaches is that of clerical efficiency.

Regardless of whether a company uses the net realizable value or the realized value approach, the specific method used to account for by-products/scrap should be established *before* the joint cost is allocated to the primary products. Exhibit 10–11 presents four comparative income statements using different methods of accounting for by-product income for the *Tasty Meats Company*. Some assumed amounts have been included to provide complete income statements.

By-products, scrap, and waste are created in all types of businesses, not just manufacturing. Managers may not see the need to determine the cost of these secondary types of products. However, as discussed in Chapters 3 and 9 in relation to the cost of quality, the importance of this cost information has only recently been recognized.

> Scrap material represents a source of revenue that has not been fully exploited. Unless companies can establish the value of their scrap, they will be indecisive about expending the capital (time and effort) needed to recover the revenue.[4]

The following examples illustrate organizations that have made the utmost of their scrap/waste. Arizona Record Destruction pulverizes confidential documents such as payroll records, credit card receipts, and legal briefs for customers. The remains are then sold for $50 per 1,000-pound bale to ranchers and horse trainers, who use the material as bedding for horse stalls. It has been a good source of extra revenue for Arizona Record and using the shredded documents is more environmentally conscious than using similarly priced wood shavings.[5] Many plastics producers routinely recycle their own plant scrap by grinding it up and compressing the flakes into pellets that work almost as well as original plastic. GE even buys back scrap from plants that purchase GE products. This buy-back plan allows GE to know the quality of the plastic being purchased that is then recycled into new products for GE to sell.[6]

Although joint products normally are not associated with job order costing systems, these systems may have by-products or scrap. Either the realized value approach or the net realizable value approach can be used with regard to the timing of recognition of the value of by-product/scrap.

The value of by-product/scrap in a job order system is appropriately credited to either manufacturing overhead or to the specific jobs in process. The former account is credited if by-product/scrap value is generally created by a significant proportion of all jobs undertaken. In contrast, if only a few or specific jobs generate a disproportionate amount of by-product/scrap, then individual jobs should be credited with the value because they directly generated the by-product/scrap.

To illustrate, assume that Tasty Meats occasionally prepares special meat-based foods for several large institutional clients. Recently, the company received an order for 15,000 beef potpies from the Greenville Junior High School. As the potpies are prepared, some scrap meat and vegetables are generated. During October 1997, Tasty Meats sold $180 of scraps to the Purrfect Catfood Corporation. The entry to record the sale, using the realized value approach, is

Cash	180	
Manufacturing Overhead		180

In contrast, assume that Tasty Meats Company seldom has salable scrap on its jobs. However, during October 1997, Tasty Meats contracted with the Keesler Veterans Hospital to prepare 50,000 frozen chicken croquettes. Specific raw material had to be acquired for the job because Tasty Meats normally does not process chicken. Thus, all raw material costs will be charged directly to the Keesler Veterans Hospital. As the chicken is prepared for the order, some scraps are generated that can be sold to the Purrfect Catfood Corporation for $450. Because the cost of the material is directly related to this job, the sale of the scrap from that raw material also relates to the specific job. Under these circumstances, the production of the scrap is recorded (using the net realizable value approach) as follows:

Scrap Inventory—Chicken	450	
Work in Process Inventory—Keesler Veterans Hospital		450

BY-PRODUCTS OR SCRAP IN JOB ORDER COSTING

---

[4] Donald Rogoff, "Scrap into Profits: How to Fully Exploit Scrap as a Revenue Source," *Journal of Accountancy* (February 1987), p. 113.

[5] Anthony J. Michels, "Animals Do Their Bit for Recycling, the Olympics, and Alternative Energy," *Fortune* (July 27, 1992), p. 14.

[6] Stratford P. Sherman, "Trashing a $150 Billion Business," *Fortune* (August 28, 1989), p. 94.

In this case, the net realizable value approach is preferred because of the timing of recognition. To affect the specific job cost that caused an unusual incidence and amount of scrap, the by-product/scrap may need to be recognized upon production; otherwise, the job may be completed before a sale of the by-product/scrap can be made.

Manufacturing processes are generally thought of as creating the need to allocate costs. However, some costs incurred in service businesses and not-for-profit organizations may be allocated among product lines, organizational locations, or types of activities performed by the organizations.

JOINT COSTS IN SERVICE AND NOT-FOR-PROFIT ORGANIZATIONS

Service and not-for-profit organizations may incur joint costs for advertising multiple products, printing multipurpose documents, or holding multipurpose events. For example, not-for-profit entities often issue brochures containing information about the organization, its purposes, and its programs; simultaneously, these documents make an appeal for funds.

If a service business decides to allocate a joint cost, either a physical or monetary allocation base can be chosen. Joint costs in service businesses often relate to advertisements rather than to processes. For example, a local carpet cleaning store may advertise a sale and list all store locations in a single newspaper ad. The ad cost could be allocated equally to all the locations or be based on sales volume for each location during the period of the sale. Alternatively, a laundry service may wash several customers' clothes in the same load. The cost of the load could be allocated based on the number of pieces or the pounds of clothes washed for each customer.

Service businesses may decide that allocating joint costs is not necessary. Not-for-profit organizations, however, are *required* under American Institute of Certified Public Accountants (AICPA) Statement of Position (SOP) 78–10 to categorize their expenses as either "program" or "support" costs.[7] Program costs are necessary for the accomplishment of the organization's specific objectives. Support costs arise from purposes other than the charitable objective; such costs include administrative and fund-raising expenses.

Because regulations exist as to the classification of nonprofit expenses, any joint cost of multipurpose communications must be allocated between program and support activities. A valid multipurpose communication is one that clearly demonstrates that a non-fund-raising purpose has been enhanced by the communication in addition to the request for funds. If a communication does not qualify, the cost is not eligible for allocation between program and support activities.

The AICPA did not provide definitive guidelines on how to allocate joint costs of multipurpose communications in SOP 87–2.[8] This statement indicated that cost accounting techniques are available to assist in such a process. For example, the directors of the not-for-profit organization, and the auditors associated with it, may decide that an allocation can be made based on the proportional amount of space or time in the communication that is devoted to program activities compared to fund-raising activities. Regardless of the allocation method used, the SOP requires that a footnote disclosure be made that indicates the total amount of the allocated cost and the amounts assigned to each category. This disclosure allows external users to recalculate the allocation in another manner should they choose to do so. The requirement for such disclosure implies that users have different attitudes about costs incurred in not-for-profits as compared with for-profit businesses. In for-profit businesses, external users of financial statements are typically unconcerned as to how joint costs are allocated.

[7] AICPA Accounting Standards Division, *Statement of Position 78–10: Accounting Principles and Reporting Practices for Certain Nonprofit Organizations* (December 31, 1978), p. 29, para. 86.
[8] AICPA Accounting Standards Division, *Statement of Position 87–2: Accounting for Joint Costs of Informational Materials and Activities of Not-for-Profit Organizations that Include a Fund-Raising Appeal* (August 21, 1987).

REVISITING

Kraft Foods, Inc.

Kraft continued to grow and prosper and during World War II. Kraft Cheese Company earned the U.S. Government's first Army-Navy "E" award for excellence in the food industry. At the government's request, the company produced preserved butter spreads and tinned cheeses for the armed forces.

Meanwhile, through the years, Oscar Mayer rose to a leadership position in the processed meat industry, partly by the creation of innovative packaging that increased the shelf life of its products. Extended shelf life enabled Oscar Mayer to expand the distribution of its products across the country.

For nearly a century Oscar Mayer remained an independent company owned primarily by descendants of the Mayer brothers. In 1981 Oscar Mayer stockholders elected to sell their company to General Foods Corporation. In 1985, General Foods was acquired by Philip Morris Companies, which also acquired Kraft, Inc. in 1988, and merged the two companies in 1989 to form Kraft General Foods.

Over the years, Oscar Mayer has continued to improve its joint processes and joint products. For example, in 1950, the company introduced "slice-pak," the meat processing industry's first vacuum-sealed package for meat products. This innovation, along with others, affected not only product quality but also joint process and joint product costs and the accounting thereof.

In January 1995 the merged divisions of the former General Foods and Kraft Foods, Inc. were reorganized into a single operating company, Kraft Foods, Inc., with 12 divisions: Pizza, Foodservice management, Bakery, Kraft Foods-Canada, Beverages, Kraft Cheese, Oscar Mayer, Maxwell House, Dinners, Post, Enhancers and Desserts.

SOURCES: Adapted from *A Brief History of Kraft Foods, Inc.* (pp. 1–5) and *Kraft Foods, Inc. Historical Timeline* (pp. 11, 13), Corporate Affairs Office, Kraft Foods, Inc., Three Lakes Drive, Northfield, IL 60093–2753.

CHAPTER SUMMARY

Multiple products from a joint process are defined (based on market value) as joint products, by-products, and scrap. A residual product that has no market value is called waste. Joint process cost is allocated only to joint products. However, before the allocation is made, the joint cost may be reduced by the net realizable value of by-products and/or scrap. Costs incurred after the split-off point(s) are traced directly to the products with which those costs are associated.

A multiple product setting has three decision points: (1) before the joint process is started, (2) at a split-off point, and (3) after a split-off point. At any of these points, management should consider further processing only if it believes that the incremental revenues from proceeding will exceed the incremental costs of proceeding. How joint cost was allocated is irrelevant to these decisions because the joint cost is considered sunk and, therefore, unrecoverable.

All the commonly used techniques for allocating joint process cost to the joint products use proration. Allocation bases are classified as either physical or monetary. Physical measures provide an unchanging yardstick of output over time and treat each unit of product as equally desirable. Monetary measures, because of inflation, are a changing yardstick of output over time, but these measures consider the different market values of the individual joint products.

The realized value approach to accounting for by-products and scrap ignores the value of such output until it is sold. At that time, either revenue is recorded or the selling price is used to reduce the joint cost of production. Alternatively, when by-products or scrap are generated, the net realizable value of the by-products/scrap at the split-off point can be recorded in a special inventory account, and the production cost of the primary products can be reduced. Additional processing costs for the by-products/scrap are debited to the special inventory account. Regardless of the approach used, if joint cost is to be reduced by the value of the by-products/scrap, the method and value to be used must be determined before allocating the net joint processing cost to the primary products.

Joint costs are also incurred in service businesses and not-for-profit organizations for some types of processes or for things such as communications instruments (brochures, media advertisements) that serve multiple purposes. Service businesses may allocate joint costs if they so desire. Not-for-profits must allocate all expenses between program and support activities based on some reasonable measure, such as percentage of space or time.

KEY TERMS

approximated net realizable value at split-off allocation (p. 421)
by-product (p. 412)
incremental separate cost (p. 421)
joint cost (p. 412)
joint process (p. 411)
joint product (p. 412)
net realizable value approach (p. 425)
net realizable value at split-off allocation (p. 421)

physical measurement allocation (p. 418)
realized value approach (p. 427)
sales value at split-off allocation (p. 420)
scrap (p. 412)
split-off point (p. 414)
sunk cost (p. 415)
waste (p. 412)

SOLUTION STRATEGIES

ALLOCATION OF JOINT COST

Joint cost is allocated only to joint products; however, joint cost may be reduced by the value of by-products/scrap before the allocation process begins.

For physical measure allocation: Divide joint cost by the products' total physical measurements to obtain a cost per unit of physical measure.

For monetary measure allocation:

1. Choose an allocation base.
2. List the values that comprise the allocation base for each joint process.
3. Sum the values in step 2.
4. Calculate the decimal fraction of value of the base to the total of all values in the base. The decimal fractions so derived should add to 100 percent or 1.00.
5. Multiply the total joint cost to be allocated by each of the decimal fractions to separate the total cost into prorated parts.
6. Divide the prorated joint cost for each product by the number of equivalent units of production for each product to obtain a cost per EUP for valuation purposes.

Allocation bases, measured at the split-off point, by which joint cost is prorated to the joint products include the following:

TYPE OF MEASURE	ALLOCATION BASE
Physical output	Physical measurement of units of output (e.g., tons, feet, barrels, liters)
Monetary:	Currency units of value:
Sales value	Revenues of the several products
Net realizable value	Net realizable value of the several joint products
Approximated net realizable value	Approximated net realizable value of the several joint products (may be a hybrid measure)

DEMONSTRATION PROBLEM

Sunshine Quarries incurred $130,000 of production cost in 1997 in a joint process to extract two joint products, X and Z. The following are data related to 1997 operations:

(1)	(2)	(3)	(4)	(5)	(6)
			PER TON	PER TON	
		SALES	SEPARATE	SEPARATE	PER TON
		PRICE PER	COSTS IF	COSTS IF	FINAL
JOINT	TONS OF	TON AT	SOLD AT	PROCESSED	SALES
PRODUCTS	PRODUCTION	SPLIT-OFF	SPLIT-OFF	FURTHER	PRICE
X	48	$1,200	$ 20	$170	$1,550
Z	20	1,600	150	200	2,000

Required:

a. Allocate the joint process cost to X and Z using tons as the allocation base.
b. Allocate the joint process cost to X and Z using the sales value at split-off.
c. Allocate the joint process cost to X and Z using the net realizable value at split-off.
d. Allocate the joint process cost to X and Z using the approximated net realizable value at split-off.

Solution to Demonstration Problem

a. $130,000 ÷ 68 tons = $1,911.76 per ton

PRODUCT	TONS OF PRODUCTION	COST PER TON	ALLOCATION OF JOINT COST
X	48	$1,911.76	$ 91,765
Z	20	1,911.76	38,235
Total	68		$130,000

b.

PRODUCT	TONS OF PRODUCTION	SALES PRICE AT SPLIT-OFF	SALES VALUE	DECIMAL FRACTION	JOINT COST	ALLOCATION OF JOINT COST
X	48	$1,200	$57,600	.64	$130,000	$ 83,200
Z	20	1,600	32,000	.36	$130,000	46,800
Total	68		$89,600	1.00		$130,000

c.

PRODUCT	TONS OF PRODUCTION	PER TON NRV AT SPLIT-OFF	TOTAL NRV AT SPLIT-OFF	DECIMAL FRACTION	JOINT COST	ALLOCATION OF JOINT COST
X	48	$1,180	$56,640	.66	$130,000	$ 85,800
Z	20	1,450	29,000	.34	$130,000	44,200
Total	68		$85,640	1.00		$130,000

d.

PRODUCT	TONS OF PRODUCTION	PER TON APPROXIMATED NRV	TOTAL APPROXIMATED NRV	DECIMAL FRACTION	JOINT COST	ALLOCATION OF JOINT COST
X	48	$1,380	$ 66,240	.65	$130,000	$ 84,500
Z	20	1,800	36,000	.35	$130,000	45,500
Total	68		$102,240	1.00		$130,000

QUESTIONS

1. What is a joint production process? Give several examples of joint processes.

2. What are joint products, by-products, and scrap? How do they differ? Which of these product categories provides the greatest incentive or justification to produce?

3. How does management determine into which category to classify each type of output from a joint process?

4. When do the multiple products of a joint process gain separate identity?

5. How are separate costs distinguished from joint costs?

6. To which types of joint process output is joint cost allocated? Why?

7. What are the decision points associated with multiple products? By what criteria would management assess whether to proceed at each point?

8. What is cost allocation and why is it necessary in a joint process?

9. What are the two primary methods used to allocate joint cost to joint products? Compare the advantages and disadvantages of each.

10. Why is it sometimes necessary to use an approximated rather than actual net realizable value at split-off to allocate joint cost? How is this approximated value calculated?

11. Describe two common approaches used to account for by-products.

12. When are by-product or scrap costs considered in setting the predetermined overhead rate in a job order costing system? When are they not considered?

13. Why must "not-for-profits" allocate joint costs of multipurpose documents or events between "program" and "support" costs?

14. *(Terminology)* Match the following lettered terms on the left with the appropriate numbered description on the right.

a. Monetary measure allocation
b. Joint process
c. Physical measure allocation
d. Waste
e. Sales value at split-off method
f. Proration
g. Scrap
h. Net realizable value
i. Sunk cost
j. By-product
k. Split-off point
l. Joint product
m. Joint cost
n. Incremental separate costs
o. Approximated sales value at split-off method
p. Realized value approach

1. Proration of joint cost on nonmonetary basis
2. Proration of joint cost on basis of dollar values
3. Employed by all commonly used allocation methods
4. Cost incurred to produce several products at the same time in one process
5. Residual output with no sales value
6. Production process yielding more than one product
7. Has sales value less than that of a by-product
8. Proration of joint cost on the basis of relative sales values of joint products at split-off
9. Material, labor, and overhead incurred in a joint process
10. Additional costs incurred between split-off point and sale
11. A cost that cannot change, no matter what course of future action is taken
12. Incidental output with value greater than scrap
13. Primary output of a joint process
14. Point at which outputs first become identifiable as individual products
15. No recognition of by-product value until sale
16. Selling price less costs to complete and dispose

15. *(Physical and sales value allocations)* Bright Academy runs two night programs for adults. During 1998, the following operating data were generated:

	HOME MANAGEMENT	CAREER ENHANCEMENT
Class hours taught	5,000	3,000
Hourly tuition	$5	$12

The general ledger accounts show $38,500 for direct instructional costs and $5,500 for overhead associated with these two programs. The Board of Trustees wants to know the cost of each program.

a. Determine the cost of each program using a physical measurement base.
b. Determine the cost of each program using the sales value method.
c. Make a case for each allocation method required above.

16. *(Processing beyond split-off)* Post Food Processors makes three products in a single joint process. For 1997, the firm processed all three products beyond the split-off point. The following data are generated for the year.

JOINT PRODUCT	FINAL REVENUES	INCREMENTAL SEPARATE COSTS
Candied Peaches	$72,000	$28,000
Peach Jelly	64,000	48,000
Peach Jam	27,000	15,000

Analysis of 1997 market data reveals that these three products could have been sold at split-off for $50,000, $40,000, and $10,000 respectively.

a. Evaluate, based on hindsight, management's production decisions in 1997.

b. How much additional profit could the company have generated in 1997 with better ability to forecast prices?

17. *(Net realizable value method)* Jackson Processing produces three joint products in a single process. The joint cost is $25,000.

PRODUCT	UNITS PRODUCED	UNIT COSTS AT SPLIT-OFF	SELLING PRICE
X	8,000	$ .75	$4.00
Y	9,000	1.00	4.25
Z	500	.10	.40

a. Allocate the joint cost based on net realizable value at split-off. If necessary, use the net realizable value method for accounting for any by-products.

b. Determine the value of the inventory, assuming the following finished goods inventories:

PRODUCT	UNITS
X	500
Y	1,000
Z	74

18. *(Approximated net realizable value method)* Hanna Chemical Company makes three products that can either be sold or processed further and then sold. The costs associated with the Hanna joint process is $60,000.

PRODUCT	UNITS OF OUTPUT	SALES PRICES AT SPLIT-OFF	SEPARATE COSTS AFTER SPLIT-OFF	FINAL SALES PRICE
Chemical 1	7,500	$3.00	$1.00	$4.25
Chemical 2	10,000	2.00	.50	3.00
Chemical 3	12,500	2.00	.75	3.00

Per unit, Chemical 1 weighs 3 pounds, Chemical 2 weighs 2 pounds, and Chemical 3 weighs 3 pounds. Assume that all additional processing is undertaken.

a. Allocate the joint cost based on the units of output, weight, and approximated net realizable value at split-off.

b. Assume all products are additionally processed and completed. At the end of the period, the inventories are as follows: Chemical 1—500 units; Chemical 2—1,000 units; Chemical 3—1,500 units. Determine the values of the inventories based on answers obtained in part a.

19. *(Processing beyond split-off and cost allocations)* Sunshine Products has a joint process that makes three products. Joint cost for the process is $30,000.

PRODUCT	UNITS OF OUTPUT	PER UNIT SELLING PRICE AT SPLIT-OFF	INCREMENTAL PROCESSING COSTS	FINAL SELLING PRICES
Alpha	5,000	$2.00	$1.50	$3.00
Beta	10,000	1.00	2.00	6.00
Gamma	250	1.50	.20	1.80

Alpha, Beta, and Gamma weigh 10 pounds, 6 pounds, and 2 pounds, respectively.

a. Determine which products should be processed beyond the split-off point.

b. Determine whether Gamma should be treated as a joint product or a by-product. Allocate the joint processing cost based on units produced, weight, and approximated net realizable value at split-off. If necessary, use the net realizable value method in accounting for any by-products.

20. *(Physical measure allocation)* Gruenfeld Chemical Company uses a joint process to manufacture two chemicals. During October 1997, the company incurred $10,000,000 of joint production cost in producing 12,000 tons of Chemical A and 8,000 tons of Chemical B (a ton is equal to 2,000 pounds). Joint cost incurred by the company is allocated on the basis of tons of chemicals produced. Gruenfeld Chemical is able to sell Chemical A at the split-off point for $.50 per pound, or the chemical can be processed further at a cost of $1,500 per ton and then sold for $1.25 per pound. There is no opportunity for the company to further process Chemical B.

a. What amount of joint cost is allocated to Chemical A and to Chemical B?

b. If Chemical A is processed further and then sold, what is the incremental effect on Gruenfeld Chemical Company's net income? Should the additional processing be performed?

21. *(Monetary measure allocation)* Wallace Realty has two operating divisions: Leasing and Sales. In March 1998, the firm spent $100,000 for general company promotions (as opposed to advertisements promoting specific properties). Wilma Hingle, the corporate controller, is now faced with the task of fairly allocating the promotion costs to the two operating divisions.

Wilma has reduced the potential bases for allocating the promotion costs to two alternatives: the expected revenue to be generated for each division from the promotions, or the expected profit to be generated in each division from the promotion.

The promotions are expected to have the following effects on the two divisions:

	LEASING	SALES
Increase in revenue	$400,000	$800,000
Increase in net income before allocated promotion costs	150,000	100,000

a. Allocate the total promotion costs to the two divisions using change in revenue.

b. Allocate the total promotion costs to the two divisions using change in net income before joint cost allocation.

c. Which of the two approaches is most appropriate? Explain.

22. *(Net realizable value allocation)* Arizona Mining Limited had the following gem output during October 1997: 1 diamond, 1 carat; multiple rubies, 10 carats; and multiple opals, 20 carats. This production was determined at the split-off point, and the output had to be processed further before the company could sell it. The joint cost amounted to $16,000, and the total additional costs after split-off and the final per-carat selling prices are as follows:

	ADDITIONAL PROCESSING COSTS	FINAL SELLING PRICES
Diamond	$15,000	$43,000
Rubies	5,000	8,000
Opals	1,000	2,000

Using the approximated net realizable value at split-off method, allocate the joint cost to the joint products.

23. *(Sales value allocation)* Vaca Dairy produces milk and sour cream from a joint process. During November, the company produced 120,000 quarts of milk and 160,000 pints of sour cream. Sales value at split-off point was $50,000 for the milk and $110,000 for the sour cream. The milk was assigned $21,600 of the joint cost.

   a. Using the sales value at split-off approach, what was the total joint cost for November?

   b. Assume, instead, that the joint cost was allocated based on units (quarts) produced. What was the total joint cost incurred in November?

24. *(Sell or process further)* A certain joint process yields two joint products, A and B. The joint cost for May 1998 is $80,000, and the sales value of the output at split-off is $120,000 for Product A and $100,000 for Product B. Management is trying to decide whether to process the products further. If the products are processed beyond split-off, the final sales value will be $180,000 for Product A and $140,000 for Product B. The additional costs of processing are expected to be $70,000 for A and $34,000 for B.

   a. Should management process the products further? Show computations.

   b. Were any revenues and/or costs irrelevant to the decision? If so, what were they?

25. *(By-products and cost allocation)* Carlsbad Petroleum has a joint process that yields three products: A, B, and C. The company allocates the joint cost to the products on the basis of pounds of output. A particular joint process run cost $125,000 and yielded the following output by weight:

PRODUCT	WEIGHT IN POUNDS
A	4,800
B	13,000
C	4,200

The run also produced by-products having a total net realizable value of $15,000. The company recognizes by-product inventory at the time of production. Allocate the joint cost to the joint products.

26. *(Sell or process further)* New England Weavers produces three products (precut fabrics for hats, shirts, and pants) from a joint process. Joint cost is allocated on the basis of relative sales value at split-off. Rather than sell the products at split-off, the company has the option to complete each of the products. Information related to these products is shown below:

	HATS	SHIRTS	PANTS	TOTAL
Number of units produced	5,000	8,000	3,000	16,000
Joint cost allocated	$ 87,000	?	?	$180,000
Sales values at split-off point	?	?	$ 40,000	$300,000
Additional costs of processing further	$ 13,000	$ 10,000	$ 39,000	$ 62,000
Sales values after all processing	$150,000	$134,000	$105,000	$389,000

   a. What amount of joint cost should be allocated to the shirts and pants products?

   b. What are the sales values at split-off for hats and shirts?

   c. Which products should be processed further? Show computations.

   d. If 4,000 shirts are processed further and sold for $67,000, what is gross profit on the sale?

27. *(By-products and cost allocation)* Classic Productions produced two movies (joint products) in 1997 in its Seattle facilities. The company also generated revenue from admissions paid by fans touring the movie production sets. Classic regards the net income from tours as a by-product of movie production. The firm accounts for this income as a reduction in the joint cost before that joint cost is allocated to movies. The following information pertains to the two movies:

PRODUCTS	TOTAL RECEIPTS	SEPARATE COSTS
Movie 1	$ 4,000,000	$ 2,400,000
Movie 2	27,000,000	18,600,000
Tours	300,000	140,000

The joint cost incurred to produce the two movies was $8,000,000. Joint cost is allocated based on net realizable value.

a. How much of the joint cost is allocated to each movie?

b. How much profit was generated by each movie?

28. *(Accounting for by-products)* Alabama Mills Company manufactures various wood products that yield sawdust as a by-product. The only costs associated with the sawdust are selling costs of $5 per ton sold. The company accounts for sales of sawdust by deducting sawdust's net realizable value from the major product's cost of goods sold. Sawdust sales in 1997 were 12,000 tons at $40 each. If Alabama Mills changes its method of accounting for sawdust sales to show the net realizable value as other revenue (presented at the bottom of the income statement), how would its gross margin be affected?

29. *(Accounting for by-products)* A by-product, produced from processing the joint products of frozen potato patties and potatoes for dehydration, is potato skins. These potato skins can be frozen and sold to restaurants for use in preparing appetizers. The additional processing and disposal costs associated with such by-product sales are $.30 per pound of skins. During May 1998, the Flagler Potato Processors produced and sold 45,000 pounds of potato skins for $23,850. In addition, joint cost for its dehydrated potatoes and frozen potato patties totaled $60,000, and 80 percent of all joint production was sold for $79,000. Nonfactory operating expenses for May were $7,600.

a. Prepare an income statement for Flagler Potato Processors if sales of the by-product are shown as other revenue and its additional processing and disposal costs are shown as additional cost of goods sold of the joint products.

b. Prepare an income statement for Flagler Potato Processors if the net realizable value of the by-product is shown as other income.

c. Prepare an income statement for Flagler Potato Processors if the net realizable value of the by-product is subtracted from the joint cost of the main products.

d. Which of the above presentations do you think would be most helpful to managers and why?

30. *(Accounting for by-products)* Providence EDP provides computing services for its commercial clients. Records for clients are maintained on both computer files and paper files. After 7 years, the paper records are sold for recycling material. The net realizable value of the recycled paper is treated as a reduction to operating overhead. Data pertaining to operations for 1997 follow:

Estimated operating overhead	$400,500
Estimated CPU time (hours)	35,000
Estimated net realizable value of recycled paper	$ 20,400

During 1997, the following actual data were recorded:

Operating overhead	$399,500
Actual CPU time	34,200
Net realizable value of recycled paper	$ 21,500

a. What was the company's estimated predetermined overhead rate?

b. What journal entry should the company make to record the sale of the recycled paper?

c. What was the company's underapplied or overapplied overhead for 1997?

31. *(Accounting for scrap)* Artistic Lites restores antique stained glass windows. Regardless of the job, there is always some breakage or improper cuts. This scrap can be sold to amateur stained glass hobbyists. The following estimates are made in setting the predetermined overhead rate for 1998:

Overhead costs other than breakage		$124,100
Estimated cost of scrap	$8,800	
Estimated sales value of scrap	(2,400)	6,400
Total estimated overhead		$130,500

Artistic Lites expects to incur approximately 15,000 direct labor hours during 1998.

One job that Artistic Lites worked on during 1998 was a stained glass window of a family crest; the job took 63 hours. Direct materials cost $420; direct labor is costed at $20 per hour. The actual cost of the scrap on this job was $55; this scrap was sold for $18.
  a. What predetermined overhead rate was set for 1998?
  b. What was the cost of the family crest stained glass window?
  c. What journal entry is made to record the cost and selling value of the scrap from the family crest stained glass window?

32. *(Scrap, job order costing)* Madison Architects offers a variety of architectural services for its commercial construction clients. For each major job, architectural models of the completed structures are built for use in presentations to clients. The firm tracks all costs using a job order costing system. At the completion of the job, the architectural models can be sold to an arts and crafts retailer. The firm uses the realized value method of accounting for the sale of the models. The sales value of each model is credited to the cost of the specific job for which the model was built. During 1998, the model for the Coulson Building was sold for $2,750.
  a. Using the realized value approach, give the entry to record the sale.
  b. Independent of your answer to part a, assume instead that the sales value of the models is not credited to specific jobs. Give the entry to account for the sale of the Coulson Building model.

33. *(Net realizable value versus realized value)* Indicate whether each item listed below is associated with the (1) realized value approach or (2) the net realizable value approach.
  a. Has the advantage of better timing.
  b. Ignores value of by-product/scrap until it is sold.
  c. Is simplest.
  d. Is used to reduce the cost of main products when by-products are produced.
  e. Credits either cost of goods sold of main products or the joint cost when the by-product inventory is recorded.
  f. Presents proceeds from sale of by-products as other revenue or other income.
  g. Is appropriate if the by-product's net realizable value is small.
  h. Is less conservative.
  i. Is the most clerically efficient.
  j. Should be used when the by-product's net realizable value is large.

34. *(Not-for-profit, program, and support cost allocation)* The Grand Rapids Opera Company is preparing a small pamphlet that will provide information on the types of opera, opera terminology, and storylines of some of the more well-known operas. In addition, there will be a request for funds to support the Opera Company at the end of the brochure. The company has tax-exempt status and operates on a not-for-profit basis.

The cost of designing and printing 100,000 copies of the pamphlet is $360,000. One page out of twelve is devoted to soliciting funding; however, 98% of the time spent in the design stage was on developing and writing the opera information.

a. If space is used as the allocation measure, how much of the pamphlet's cost should be assigned to program activities? To support activities?

b. If design time is used as the allocation measure, how much of the pamphlet's cost should be assigned to program activities? To support activities?

---

35. *(Joint process outputs and allocation methods)* Provide five examples of businesses that engage in joint processes. For each of these businesses, describe the following:

a. The various outputs, classified as joint products, by-products, scrap, or waste.

b. Your recommendation of the most appropriate methods of allocating joint costs to the output you have described in part a. Express, in nontechnical terms, your justification for each of your recommendations.

36. *(Joint process decision making)* Tim Burns has been asked by his aged uncle to take over the family butcher shop. Tim knows that you are majoring in accounting—he majored in art—and asks you to help him understand the butcher shop business. He wants you to do the following:

a. Explain, in nontechnical terms, what questions about joint processes must be answered by someone who manages a butcher shop. Also, provide the points in a joint process at which these questions should be addressed.

b. Describe, in your own words, the proper managerial use of joint cost; also, describe whether joint cost can be used inappropriately and the basis on which you think a particular use is inappropriate.

c. Compare and contrast the various categories of outputs generated by a joint process.

37. *(By-product accounting method selection)* Your company engages in joint processes that produce significant quantities and types of by-products. You have been requested by the chairman of your company's Board of Directors to give a report to the board regarding making a good choice of accounting methods for by-products. Develop a set of criteria for making such a choice and provide reasons that each of the criteria has been selected. On the basis of your criteria, along with any additional assumptions you may wish to provide about the nature of your company, recommend a particular method of accounting for by-products and explain why you consider it to be better than the alternatives.

38. *(Net realizable value allocation)* Star Communications is a regional television network. The firm has three service groups: Sports, News, and Entertainment. Joint production costs (costs incurred for facilities, administration, and so forth) for May 1997 were $16,000,000. The revenues and separate production costs of each group for May follow:

	SPORTS	NEWS	ENTERTAINMENT
Revenues	$18,000,000	$15,000,000	$95,000,000
Separate costs	17,000,000	8,000,000	55,000,000

a. What amounts of joint cost are allocated to each service group using the net realizable value approach? Compute the profit for each group after the allocation.

b. What amount of joint cost is allocated to each service group if the allocation is based on revenues? Compute the profit for each group after the allocation.

c. Assume you are head of the Sports Group. Would the difference in allocation bases create significant problems for you when you report to Star Communications' Board of Directors? Develop a short presentation to make to the board if the allocation base in part b is used to determine group relative profitability. Be certain to discuss important differences in revenues and cost figures between the Sports and Entertainment Groups.

COMMUNICATION ACTIVITIES

39. (*Allocation of joint cost*) Nova Scotia Fish Processors produces three products from a common input. The three products are fish meat, fish oil, and fish meal. For April 1998, the firm produced the following average quantities of each product from each pound of fish processed:

PRODUCT	OBTAINED FROM EACH POUND OF FISH
Fish meat	8 ounces
Fish oil	4 ounces
Fish meal	2 ounces
Total	14 ounces

Note that 2 ounces of each pound (1 pound = 16 ounces) of fish processed is waste that has no market value. In April, the firm processed 50 tons of fish (one ton is equal to 2,000 pounds) of fish. Joint cost amounted to $95,200. On average, each pound of fish meat sells for $3; each pound of fish oil sells for $4; and each pound of fish meal sells for $2.

a. Allocate the joint cost using weight as the basis.

b. Allocate the joint cost using sales value as the basis.

c. Discuss the advantages and disadvantages of your answers to parts a and b.

PROBLEMS

40. (*Journal entries*) Lady Chic Cosmetics uses a joint process to make two main products: Elegance (a perfume) and Sooosoft (a skin lotion). Two departments, Mixing and Cooking, are used, but the products do not become separable until they have been through the cooking process. After cooking, the perfume is removed from the vats and bottled without further processing. The residue remaining in the vats is then blended with aloe and lanolin to become the lotion.

In the Mixing Department, these costs were incurred during October 1997:

Direct material	$28,000
Direct labor	7,560
Manufacturing overhead applied	4,250

In the Cooking Department, costs incurred during October 1997, before separation of the joint products, were

Direct material	$6,100
Direct labor	2,150
Manufacturing overhead applied	3,240

In that same month, the Cooking Department incurred separable costs for each of the products as follows:

Elegance Perfume (bottles only)	$2,120
Sooosoft Lotion:	
Direct material	1,960
Direct labor	3,120
Manufacturing overhead applied	4,130

Neither department had beginning Work in Process Inventory balances, and all work started in October was completed in that month. The joint costs are allocated to perfume and lotion on the basis of approximated net realizable values at split-off. For October, the approximated net realizable values at split-off were $158,910 for perfume and $52,970 for lotion.

a. Prepare journal entries for the Mixing and Cooking Departments for October 1997.

b. Determine the joint cost allocated to, and the total cost of, Elegance and Sooosoft.

c. Diagram the flow of costs for Lady Chic Cosmetics for these two products.

41. (*Joint cost allocation; by-product; income determination*) East Lansing Financial Services has two main service lines: commercial loans and residential mortgages. As a by-product of these two main services, the firm also generates some revenue from selling credit life insurance. Joint cost for producing the two main services includes expenses for facilities, legal support, equipment, record keeping, and administration. The joint service cost incurred during May 1997 was $145,000.

These costs are to be allocated on the basis of total revenues generated from each main service.

The following table presents the results of operations and revenues for May:

SERVICE	NUMBER OF LOANS	TOTAL REVENUES
Commercial loans	30	$189,750
Residential mortgages	70	140,250
Credit life insurance	65	6,500

Management accounts for the credit life insurance on a realized value basis. When commissions on credit life insurance are received, management has elected to present the proceeds as a reduction in the Cost of Services Rendered for the main services.

Separate costs for the two main services for May were $25,000 and $18,000, respectively, for commercial loans and residential mortgages.

a. Allocate the joint costs.

b. Determine the income for each main service and the company's overall gross margins for May 1997.

42. (*Joint cost allocation; scrap*) Virginia Textiles produces terrycloth products for hotels. The company buys the fabric in 60-inch-width bolts. In the first process, the fabric is set up, cut, and separated into pieces. Setup can either be for robes and bath towels or for hand towels and washcloths.

During June, the company set up and cut 3,000 robes and 6,000 bath towels. Because of the irregular pattern of the robes, scrap is produced in the process and is sold to various institutions (prisons, hospitals, etc.) for rags at $1.25 per pound. June production and cost data for Virginia Textiles are as follows:

Fabric used, 12,500 feet at $1.75 per foot	$21,875
Labor, joint process	$ 5,000
Overhead, joint process	$ 4,900
Pounds of scrap produced	1,800

Virginia Textiles assigns the joint processing cost to the robes and towels based on an approximated net realizable value at split-off. The final selling prices for robes and bath towels are $20 and $11 per unit, respectively. Costs after split-off are $8.40 and $2.30, respectively, for the robes and the towels. The selling price of the scrap is treated as a reduction of joint cost.

a. Determine the joint cost to be allocated to the joint products for June. Prepare the journal entry necessary at the point of split-off.

b. How much joint cost is allocated to the robes in June? To the bath towels?

c. What amount of cost for robes is transferred to Finished Goods Inventory for June? What amount of cost for towels is transferred to Finished Goods Inventory for June?

43. (*Joint products; by-product*) Indian River Mangoes runs a fruit-packing business in southern Florida. The firm buys mangoes by the truckload in season. The fruit is then separated into three categories according to its condition. Group 1 is suitable for selling *as is* to supermarket chains and specialty gift stores. Group 2 is suitable for slicing and bottling in light syrup to be sold to supermarkets. Group 3 is considered a by-product and is sold to another company that processes it into jelly. The firm has two producing departments: (1) Receiving and Separating; and (2) Slicing and Bottling.

A particular truckload cost the company $1,500 and yielded 1,500 mangoes in Group 1, 2,000 mangoes in Group 2, and 500 mangoes in Group 3. The labor to separate the fruit into categories was $300, and the company uses a predetermined overhead application rate of 50 percent of direct labor cost. Only Group 2 has any significant additional processing cost, estimated at $220, but each group has boxing and delivery costs as follows:

Group 1	$150
Group 2	220
Group 3	50

The final sales revenue of Group 1 is $3,000, of Group 2 is $1,500, and of Group 3 is $450.

a. Determine the sum of the material, labor, and overhead costs associated with the joint process.

b. Allocate the total joint cost using the approximated net realizable value at split-off method, assuming that the by-product is recorded when realized and is shown as other income on the income statement.

c. Prepare the entries for parts a and b assuming that the by-product is sold for $450 and that all costs were incurred as estimated.

d. Allocate the total joint cost using the approximated net realizable value at split-off method, assuming that the by-product is recorded using the net realizable value approach and that the joint cost is reduced by the net realizable value of the by-product.

e. Prepare the entries for parts a and d, assuming that the estimated realizable value of the by-product is $400.

44. *(Process costing; joint cost allocation; by-product)* The Evans Hair Salon provides hair styling services and sells a variety of cosmetic and hair-care products. The firm also generates some revenue from the sale of hair, which is periodically swept from the floor of the styling salon.

The net realizable value of hair is accounted for as a reduction in the joint cost assigned to the Styling Services and Cosmetic Products. Hair sells for $3 per pound. The cost of packaging the hair is $.25 per pound, and selling costs of the hair are $.15 per pound. The following information is available for 1998 on the inventory of Cosmetic Products (the firm does not produce these products; they are purchased):

Beginning inventory	$ 35,000
Ending inventory	21,500
Purchases	181,350

Joint cost is to be allocated to Styling Services and Cosmetic Products based on approximated net realizable values (revenues less separate costs). For 1998, total revenues were $753,000 from Styling Services and $289,000 from Cosmetic Products. The following joint costs were incurred:

Rent	$38,000
Insurance	21,000
Utilities	3,800

Separate costs were as follows for 1998:

	STYLING SERVICES	COSMETIC PRODUCTS
Labor	$431,000	$24,000
Supplies	98,000	700
Equipment depreciation	65,000	1,200
Administration	113,000	3,700

For the year, 5,020 pounds of hair were collected and sold.

a. What is the total net realizable value of hair that is applied to reduce the joint cost assigned to Styling Services and to Cosmetic Products?

b. What is the joint cost to be allocated to Styling Services and Cosmetic Products?

c. What is the approximated pretax realizable value of each main product or service for 1998?

d. How much joint cost is allocated to each main product or service?

e. Determine the net income produced by each main product or service.

45. (*Joint cost allocation; by-product*) The Farmers' Delight Company produces tomato paste and tomato sauce from a joint process. In addition, second-stage processing of the tomato sauce creates a residue mixture of tomato peels and seeds (simply referred to as P&S) as a by-product. P&S is sold for $.08 per gallon to Pavlov's Doggy Products for that company's use in Canine Delight Chow. Distribution expenses for P&S total $110.

In May 1997, 140,000 pounds of tomatoes are processed in the first department; the cost of this input is $44,200. An additional $33,700 is spent on conversion costs. There are 56,000 gallons of output from Department 1. Thirty percent of this output is transferred as tomato paste to Department 2, and 70 percent of the output is transferred to Department 3. Of the input to Department 3, 20 percent will result in P&S and 80 percent will result in tomato sauce. Joint cost is allocated to tomato paste and sauce on the basis of approximated net realizable values at split-off.

The tomato paste in Department 2 is processed at a total cost of $9,620; the tomato sauce in Department 3 is processed at a total cost of $6,450. The net realizable value of P&S is accounted for as a reduction in the separate processing costs in Department 3. Selling prices per gallon are $5.25 and $3.45 for tomato paste and tomato sauce, respectively.

a. How many gallons leaving Department 1 are sent to Department 2 for further processing? To Department 3?

b. How many gallons leave Department 3 as P&S? As tomato sauce?

c. What is the net realizable value of P&S?

d. What is the total approximated net realizable value of the tomato paste? The tomato sauce?

e. What amount of joint cost is assigned to each main product?

f. If 85 percent of the final output of each main product is sold during May and Farmers' Delight had no beginning inventory of either product, what is the value of the ending inventory of tomato paste and tomato sauce?

46. (*By-product/joint product journal entries*) Midwest Wheat Farms is a 5,000-acre wheat farm. The growing process yields two principal products: wheat and straw. Wheat is sold for $3.50 per bushel (assume a bushel of wheat weighs 60 pounds). Without further processing, the straw sells for $30 per ton (a ton equals 2,000 pounds). If the straw is processed further, it is baled and then sells for $45 per ton. In 1998, total joint cost to the split-off point (harvest) was $175 per acre.

The farm produced 70 bushels of wheat per acre and 1 ton of straw per acre. If all of the straw were processed further, processing costs (baling) for the straw would amount to $50,000.

Prepare the 1998 journal entries for straw, if straw is

a. transferred as a by-product at sales value to storage without further processing, with a corresponding reduction of wheat's production costs.

b. further processed as a by-product and transferred to the warehouse at net realizable value, with a corresponding reduction of the manufacturing costs of the product wheat.

c. further processed and transferred to finished goods, with joint cost being allocated between wheat and straw based on relative sales value at the split-off point.

(*CPA adapted*)

47. (*Ending inventory valuation; joint cost allocation*) Emerson Meat Packers experienced the operating statistics in the following table for its joint meat cutting process during March 1997, its first month of operations. The costs of the joint process were direct material, $24,400; direct labor, $8,200; and overhead, $4,100. Products X, Y, and Z are main products; B is a by-product. The company's policy is to recognize the net realizable value of any by-product inventory at split-off and reduce the total joint cost by that amount. Neither the main products nor the by-product *require* any additional processing or disposal costs, although management may consider additional processing.

PRODUCTS	WEIGHT IN POUNDS	SALES VALUES AT SPLIT-OFF	UNITS PRODUCED	UNITS SOLD
X	4,300	$66,000	3,220	2,720
Y	6,700	43,000	8,370	7,070
Z	5,400	11,200	4,320	3,800
B	2,300	2,300	4,600	4,000

a. Calculate the ending inventory values of each joint product based on (1) relative sales value and (2) pounds.

b. Discuss the advantages and disadvantages of each allocation base for (1) financial statement purposes and (2) decisions about the desirability of processing the joint products beyond the split-off point.

48. *Some waste, scrap, or by-product materials have little value. In fact many such materials represent liabilities for companies because the materials require companies to incur significant disposal costs. Alternatively, some companies have historically found "cheap" ways to dispose of such materials. For example, on Friday, April 2, 1993, residents of Brazos County, Texas, stumbled across 19 cans of industrial waste that were scattered along the banks of the Navasota River. The cans were labeled "lacquer thinner," but the actual contents, which were leaking into the ground and the river, were not immediately known. The cans appeared to have been thrown from a vehicle traveling over a nearby road. Some cans were heavily dented, some were capped with rags, and all of them appeared to be scattered in a random pattern. State and county officials worked most of Saturday, April 3, cleaning up the site.*

[SOURCE: Chuck Squatriglia, "Solvent Cans Dumped near Navasota River," *Bryan/College Station Eagle* (April 4, 1993), p. A9. Reprinted courtesy of *The Bryan/College Station Eagle*.]

a. Comment on whether this method of disposing of industrial waste is a "cheap" alternative.

b. Discuss the ethical and legal implications of disposing of industrial waste in this manner.

c. What actions can people take to reduce these kinds of incidents?

d. Ethically, what obligation does the vendor/manufacturer of these industrial materials have to the industrial consumer of the materials?

49. *Gypsum waste is created from manufacturing phosphorous fertilizer. Pure gypsum is better known as the wallboard used in interior walls of buildings; gypsum waste is contaminated with low levels of potentially toxic heavy metals and some radioactive elements. Freeport-McMoRan owns two fertilizer plants producing the waste material. Early in 1990, the company completed a $6 million experimental plant to recycle gypsum waste into an environmentally safe, synthetic aggregate that could be used in building materials. The aggregate from the recycling plant is a rocklike cinder that the company hopes to use as an additive to concrete and in roadbeds.*

[SOURCE: Based on James O'Byrne, "Protests Inspired $6 Million Plant to Recycle Gypsum," *(New Orleans) Times-Picayune* (March 4, 1990), p. B1. © The Times-Picayune Publishing Corporation.]

a. Which of the methods of accounting for by-products/scrap discussed in the chapter would allow Freeport-McMoRan to know whether recycling gypsum waste is cost beneficial? Why is this information available from this particular method?

b. Discuss the ethics of the recycling plan begun by the company.

c. Discuss the potential profitability of the recycling plan.

d. The gypsum waste cannot be dumped into the Mississippi River. Currently there are stacks of gypsum waste more than a mile long and 80 feet high. If the waste is not recycled, how would you suggest eliminating it? How would you estimate the costs and benefits of your plan compared with the costs and benefits of the recycling plan?

50. *In the late 1980's two unlikely organizations, the Environmental Protection Agency and Amoco, agreed to form a joint venture to produce two unlikely joint products, regulation and cost savings. The substance of the joint venture was a study of pollution at the Yorktown, Virginia, oil refinery of Amoco. Initially, communication between employees of the two groups was stiff and cautious, and miscommunication frequently resulted from differing definitions of words such as "risk." After a time, the two groups learned to work together and (perhaps) grudgingly became more appreciative of the other's problems and concerns.*

Ultimately, it appears the project will be very fruitful for both parties. The EPA has learned that many of the requirements it has placed on oil refineries do little to protect the environment and much to increase the costs of operating the refinery. For example, it had required Amoco to build a $41 million enclosed canal to control benzene vapors. In the testing that was conducted in the joint project, it was discovered that the benzene vapors in this part of the operation were 20 times smaller than expected. Also, the EPA has identified areas of the oil refinery operation that produce substantial amounts of pollution that the EPA has historically ignored. For example, at the loading docks in Yorktown, the team estimated that 1.6 million pounds of pollutants are pumped into the atmosphere annually. No EPA rules address this area of the operation. Perhaps the greatest lesson learned by the EPA is that it should refocus its efforts on identifying and controlling pollution rather than mandating the type and extent of equipment that must be used by industry.

[SOURCE: Caleb Solomon, "What Really Pollutes? Study of a Refinery Proves an Eye-Opener," *Wall Street Journal* (March 29, 1993), pp. A1, A6. Reprinted by permission of the *The Wall Street Journal*, © 1993 Dow Jones & Company, Inc. All Rights Reserved Worldwide.]

a. Potentially, how will the quality of Amoco's operations be affected by the joint venture?

b. Potentially, how will the quality of the EPA's operations be affected by the joint venture?

c. Why would the EPA have been reluctant to participate in the joint venture?

d. Comment on the ethical considerations in a joint venture that involves a regulator and one of its regulated groups.

INTERNET ACTIVITIES

51. Find the home page for Kraft Foods. On its home page the company provides much information regarding its philosophies, product lines, strategy, production and distribution systems. Review the information provided. Then, discuss how an operating environment, such as that at Kraft in which there are many joint production processes, creates unique opportunities for new product innovation. Also, discuss the characteristics of employees that would be important in such an environment.

52. Find the home page of AT&T. Review news announcements provided that discuss the recent breakup of the company into three independent firms. Given that if the firm would have maintained its operations as a single business, more opportunities for new services would presumably have been available from merging its many technologies, why did the firm break up into three independent companies?

53. Search the Internet for associations that promote the sale of beef or pork products. One or more of the associations will provide information on the many applications of beef and pork by-products. Review these materials and write a brief summary of how various by-products of beef or pork production benefit many other industries.

CHAPTER

11

Standard Costing

LEARNING OBJECTIVES

After completing this chapter, you should be able to answer these questions:

1. Why are standard cost systems used?

2. How are standards for material, labor, and overhead set?

3. What documents are associated with standard cost systems and what information do those documents provide?

4. How are material, labor, and overhead variances calculated and recorded?

5. How can variance analysis be used for control and performance evaluation purposes?

6. How will standard costing be affected if a company uses a single conversion element rather than the traditional labor and overhead elements?

7. *(Appendix)* How do multiple material and labor categories affect variances?

Anglo-American Trading Partners (ATP)

In 1993, ATP was formed in New Orleans, Louisiana, to provide a seafood production operation previously unavailable in the southern United States: a smoking facility for salmon. The owners of ATP and their families have extensive backgrounds in seafood processing and salmon smoking. Prior to the introduction of salmon "farms," Atlantic salmon was only available from February to September, with the largest catches from June to August. With the advent of farms, the average catch of Atlantic salmon in Scotland is about 1,300 tons per season; Norway harvests more than this amount each week.

After doing in-depth market research, the owners of ATP decided that a smoking facility would be a viable business venture. ATP has set detailed specifications for the salmon purchased in regard to flesh oil content and meat and skin coloration; compliance with these specifications is required of the company's suppliers. Salmon is bought primarily from suppliers in Scotland and Chile, although back-up suppliers are available on demand in Norway, Ireland, and other producing areas.

In designing the smoking facility, ATP set two primary goals: (1) that the products would be made to the highest standards of both quality and hygiene and (2) that production efficiency would be paramount. Linking these goals means that production activity can flow rapidly through the operation but that the product is protected and monitored continuously for quality, temperature, texture, and so forth. The production process takes five days:

Day 1: Fresh salmon fillets are hand salted; variation in size dictates that some fillets will require more salt than others.

Day 2: Fillets are washed to eliminate excess salt and refrigerated to allow the salt level to equalize throughout the fillet.

Day 3: Fillets are dried and cold smoked for a minimum of 12 hours.

Day 4: Fillets are chilled, but never frozen, prior to slicing.

Day 5: Fillets are sliced to a thickness of 2.5 mm at a controlled angle, making each slice identical; slices are vacuum packed in 2-pound units.

Given the refrigeration and smoking requirements, both completed and partially completed salmon fillets are held in inventory at any time. Processing costs for a period must be assigned to all production of the period, whether that production is complete or in process.

SOURCE: Interview with Eric Skrmetta and Jon Bard, ATP owners, 1996.

In producing ATP's smoked salmon, Eric Skrmetta and Jon Bard are adamant about salmon quality and standardization of the production process. Product consistency can occur only if there are standards or benchmarks for both the materials and the process. Additionally, performance can be evaluated only by comparing it against some predetermined measure. Without a predetermined performance measure, there is no way to know what is expected. And, without making a comparison between the actual result and the predetermined measure, there is no way to know whether expectations were met and no way for managers to exercise control.

Organizations develop and use standards for almost all tasks. For example, businesses set standards for employee sales expenses; hotels set standards for housekeeping tasks and room service delivery; casinos set standards for revenue to be generated per square foot of playing space. Because of the variety of organizational activities and information objectives, no single form of standard cost system is appropriate for all situations. Some systems use standard prices, but not standard quantities; other systems (especially in service businesses) use labor, but not material, standards.

This chapter discusses a traditional standard cost system that requires price and quantity standards for each cost component: direct material (DM), direct labor (DL), and factory overhead (OH). Discussion is provided on how standards are developed, how variances are calculated, and what information can be gained from detailed variance analysis. Journal entries used in a standard cost system are also presented. The appendix expands the presentation by covering the mix and yield variances that may arise from using multiple materials or groups of labor.

DEVELOPMENT OF A STANDARD COST SYSTEM

standard cost

Although standard cost systems were initiated by manufacturing companies, these systems can also be used by service and not-for-profit organizations. In a standard cost system, both standard and actual costs are recorded in the accounting records. This dual recording provides an essential element of cost control: having norms against which actual operations can be compared. Standard cost systems make use of **standard costs,** which are the budgeted costs to manufacture a single unit of product or perform a single service. Developing a standard cost involves judgment and practicality in identifying the material and labor types, quantities, and prices as well as understanding the kinds and behaviors of organizational overhead.

A primary objective in manufacturing a product is to minimize unit cost while achieving certain quality specifications. Almost all products can be manufactured with a variety of inputs that would generate the same basic output and output quality. The input choices that are made affect the standards that are set.

Some possible input resource combinations are not necessarily practical or efficient. For instance, a work team might consist only of craftspersons or skilled workers, but such a team might not be cost-beneficial if there were a large differential in the wage rates of skilled and unskilled workers. Or, although providing high-technology equipment to an unskilled labor population is possible, to do so would not be an efficient use of resources, as indicated in the following situation:

> A company built a new $250 million computer-integrated, statistical process controlled plant to manufacture a product whose labor cost was less than 5% of total product cost. Unfortunately, 25% of the work force was illiterate and could not handle the machines. The workers had been hired because there were not enough literate workers available to hire. When asked why the plant had been located where it was, the manager explained: "Because it has one of the cheapest labor costs in the country."[1]

Once management has established the desired output quality and determined the input resources needed to achieve that quality at a reasonable cost, quantity and price standards can be developed. Standards should be developed by a group composed of representatives from cost accounting, industrial engineering, personnel, data processing, purchasing, and management. To ensure credibility of the standards and to motivate people to operate as close to the standards as possible, it is especially important to involve the managers and workers whose performance will be compared to the standards. The discussion of the standard setting process begins with material.

Material Standards

The first step in developing material standards is to identify and list the specific direct materials used to manufacture the product. This list is often available on the product specification documents prepared by the engineering department prior to

[1] Thomas A. Stewart, "Lessons from U.S. Business Blunders," *Fortune* (April 23, 1990), pp. 128, 129.

In This Case, Material Specifications Requires Customer Knowledge

N E W S
N O T E

[At Southern Mattress Company, president Betsy] Birdsong acknowledged people don't get excited about buying bedding. It's a $100 to $2,300 purchase that no one even sees. But considering the amount of time spent in bed, it's an invaluable asset, and looks are important. [So Southern offers 40 different models.]

Certain fabrics sell better in some markets than in others. A crazy quilt pattern doesn't sell in Mississippi but Louisiana customers choose it often. For the really picky, there is a seasonal mattress—with plushy quilted pillow covering—that is wool on one side for winter and cashmere on the other for summer.

Colors are important, too. Teal green used to be "in." Now it is blue. And in some markets, such as Dallas, the hot item is white bedding. For those who favor the natural look, there is the 100 percent cotton covered mattress, which looks more like a duvet cover almost too pretty for a covering.

SOURCE: Mary Judice, "No Sleepy Business," *(New Orleans) Times-Picayune* (June 9, 1995), p. C1. © The Times-Picaynne Publishing Corporation.

initial production. In the absence of such documentation, material specifications can be determined by observation in the production area, inquiry of production personnel, inspection of material requisitions, and review of the cost accounts related to the product. Three things must be known about the material inputs: what types of inputs are used; what quantity of inputs are used; and what quality of inputs are used. As indicated in the above News Note, a knowledge of the customer market is also helpful in specifying material.

In making quality decisions, managers should seek the advice of materials experts, engineers, cost accountants, marketing personnel, and sometimes suppliers. Many cost-benefit trade-offs exist in making quality decisions. In most cases, as the material grade rises, so does cost; decisions about material inputs usually attempt to balance the relationships of cost, quality, and projected selling prices with company objectives. The resulting trade-offs affect material mix, material yield, finished product quality and quantity, overall product cost, and product salability. Thus, quantity and cost estimates become direct functions of quality decisions. Given the quality selected for each component, physical quantity estimates of weight, size, volume, or other measure can be made. These estimates can be based on results of engineering tests, opinions of managers and workers using the material, past material requisitions, and review of the cost accounts.

Specifications for materials, including quality and quantity, are compiled on a **bill of materials.** Even companies that do not have formal standard cost systems are likely to develop bills of materials for products simply as guides for production activity. Exhibit 11–1 illustrates a bill of materials for a pound of smoked oysters produced by Captain's Cannery, an illustrative company. When converting quantities on the bill of materials into costs, allowances are often made for normal waste of components.[2] For example, 19 ounces of oysters are considered the *minimum* quantity necessary to make one pound of smoked oysters because, during smoking, oysters lose approximately 85 percent of their weight. In setting a standard for the oysters, however, the company has decided to include an additional 1 ounce allowance for possible other shrinkage. Thus, 20 ounces of oysters has been set as the standard for a one-pound (16-ounce) package of smoked oysters.

bill of materials

[2] Although such allowances are often made, they do not result in the most effective use of a standard cost system. Problems arising from their inclusion are discussed later in the chapter.

EXHIBIT 11-1

Smoked Oysters Bill of
Materials

| Product: 1 pound smoked oysters | | Revision Date: 8/1/96 | |
| Product Number: 10 | | Standard Lot Size: 2,500 pounds | |

Component ID#	Quantity Required	Description	Comments
OY-15	20 ounces	Oysters, medium size	Clean and steam cooked; selected by size and texture
B-06	1 vat	Brine mixture	Brine reading: 10% saturation
50-65	10 gallons	Soya oil	100% pure
VP-25	1 bag	Vacuum pack	8"L X 12"W

After the standard quantities are developed, prices for each component must be determined. Prices should reflect desired quality, reliability and physical proximity of suppliers, quantity discounts allowed, and freight and receiving costs. Although not always able to *control* prices, given adequate lead time and resources, purchasing agents are the most likely persons to *influence* prices. These individuals know what suppliers are available and attempt to choose suppliers providing the most appropriate material in the most reasonable time span at the most reasonable cost. The purchasing agent also is most likely to have expertise about the company's purchasing habits. Incorporating this information in price standards should allow a more thorough analysis by the purchasing agent at a later time as to the causes of any significant differences between actual and standard prices.

When all quantity and price information is available, component quantities are multiplied by unit prices to obtain the total cost of each component. (Remember, the *price paid* for the material becomes the *cost* of the material.) These totals are summed to determine the total standard material cost of one unit of product.

Labor Standards

Development of labor standards requires the same basic procedures as those used for material. Each production operation performed by either workers (such as bending, reaching, lifting, moving material, and packing) or machinery (such as drilling, cooking, and attaching parts) should be identified. In specifying operations and movements, activities such as cleanup, setup, and rework need to be considered. Although not strictly part of the production process, these actions may be necessary and will affect the time realistically needed to produce the units. All unnecessary movements by workers and of material should be disregarded when time standards are set. As motion observations are made, the standards development team should evaluate the factory layout as to suitability for minimizing unnecessary motions.[3] Exhibit 11–2 indicates that a manufacturing worker's day is not spent in entirely productive work.

[3] Plant layout and space utilization are covered in more depth in Chapter 17.

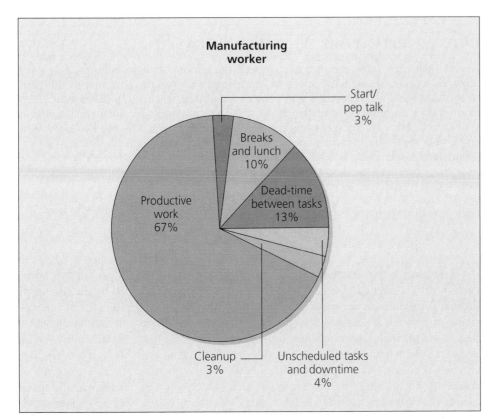

EXHIBIT 11–2

Where Did the Day Go?

Labor rate standards reflect skill levels and production location. The low wage rate provided to these sweatshop clothing workers in Singapore may cause total product cost to be minimized, but would a truly ethical company engage in such a practice?

NEWS NOTE

Don't Carry Your Mistakes Forward

[Using historical information for standards is] seldom specific enough and never provides targets. If you have operated inefficiently and spent too much in the past, you simply build all those costs and problems and deficiencies into the system. That kind of cost accounting is really an obstacle to improving productivity because it accepts and rewards inefficiency. If you are going to improve, you need to know how much you *should* be spending, not just how much you've spent in the past. That means going over every product, looking at every part, examining every process and operation, breaking each down into its individual components and then coming up with standard costs for everything you do.

SOURCE: Jack Stack, *The Great Game of Business* (New York: Currency Doubleday, 1992), p. 101.

To develop usable standards, quantitative information for each production operation must be obtained. Time and motion studies may be performed by the company; alternatively, times developed from industrial engineering studies for various movements can be used.[4] A third way to set a time standard is to use the average time needed to manufacture a product during the past year. Such information can be calculated from employees' past time sheets. A problem with this method is that historical data may include past inefficiencies. To compensate for the problems of observed or historical data, management and supervisory personnel normally make subjective adjustments to the available data. The above News Note provides further insight into the rationale for not using historical information.

operations flow document   After all labor tasks are analyzed, an **operations flow document** can be prepared that lists all operations necessary to make one unit of product (or perform a specific service). A simplified operations flow document is shown in Exhibit 11–3 for a pound of smoked oysters produced in the Smoking Department of Captain's Cannery. Details of the process are as follows.

Approximately 2,500 pounds of clean and steamed oysters are brine salted for 10 minutes. After brining, the oysters are washed to remove the excess brine. The oysters are chilled for 4 hours to allow the brine to equalize through the meat. Soya oil is added to coat the oysters, which are placed on racks and smoked for 3 hours. After smoking, the oysters are moved to the Packaging Department, cooled, vacuum packed, and blast frozen.

When products are manufactured individually, the operations flow document shows the time necessary to produce each unit. In a flow process that produces goods in batches (such as smoked oysters), individual times cannot be specified accurately. The time to make a single pound of oysters is not 1/2,500 of the time that it would take to make the standard batch of 2,500 pounds because the brining, oiling, and smoking are performed for mass quantities.

Labor rate standards should reflect the employee wages and the related employer costs for fringe benefits, FICA (Social Security), and unemployment taxes. In the simplest situation, all departmental personnel would be paid the same wage rate if, for example, wages are job specific or tied to a labor contract. If employees performing the same or similar tasks are paid different wage rates, a weighted average rate (total wage cost per hour divided by the number of workers) must be computed and used as the standard. Differing rates could be caused by employment length or skill level.

---

[4] In performing internal time and motion studies, observers need to be aware that employees may engage in "slow down" tactics when they are being clocked. The purpose of such tactics is to establish a longer time as the standard, which would make employees appear more efficient when actual results are measured. Or employees may slow down simply because they are being observed and want to be sure they are doing the job correctly.

EXHIBIT 11–3

Operations Flow
Document

Product: 1 pound smoked oysters   Revision Date: 8/1/96
Product Number: 10   Standard Lot Size: 2,500 pounds
     (10 employees)

Operation ID#	Department	Standard Time	Description of Task
50	*Smoking*	*20 min.*	*Moving oysters and placing in vat*
21	Smoking	5/6 hour (L)	Add brine to vats
31		1 hour (M)	
50	*Smoking*	*10 min.*	*Brining period*
22	Smoking	10 hours (L)	Rinse brine from oysters
32		1 hour (M)	
50	*Smoking*	*240 min.*	*Cooling period*
23	Smoking	31 hours (L)	Add soya oil and coat oysters
33		3.1 hours (M)	
24	Smoking	5 hours (L)	Lay oysters on racks for smoking
50	*Smoking*	*180 min.*	*Smoking and cooling period*
50	*Packaging*	*15 min.*	*Moving oysters on conveyor*
45	Packaging	32.5 hours (L)	Package oysters in vacuum bags
35		3.3 hours (M)	
36	Packaging	1 hour (M)	Blast freeze

Note: All operations with ID# 50 require more or wait time, but no labor.
(L) designates labor time; (M) designates machine time.

Overhead Standards

Overhead standards are simply the predetermined factory overhead application rates discussed in Chapters 5 and 6. To provide the most appropriate costing information, overhead should be assigned to separate cost pools based on the cost drivers and allocations to products should be made using different activity drivers. For ease of calculations, the Smoking Department of Captain's Cannery example uses two cost pools: variable overhead and fixed overhead. The allocation base for variable overhead is number of machine hours; the allocation base for fixed overhead is total move and wait time (operation ID #50 on the operations flow document). In Packaging, the company uses a single departmental overhead rate based on direct labor hours.

After the bill of materials, operations flow document, and predetermined overhead rates per activity measure have been developed, a **standard cost card** is prepared. This document (shown in Exhibit 11–4) summarizes all the standard quantities and costs needed to complete one 2,500-unit lot of 1-pound bags of smoked oysters. Standard cost information is used to assign costs to inventory accounts. Both actual and standard costs are recorded in a standard cost system, although it is the standard (rather than actual) costs of production that are debited to Work in Process Inventory.[5] Any difference between an actual and a standard cost is called a variance.

standard cost card

---

[5] The standard cost of each cost element (direct material, direct labor, variable overhead, and fixed overhead) is said to be *applied* to the goods produced. This terminology is the same as that used when overhead is assigned to inventory based on a predetermined rate.

EXHIBIT 11–4

Standard Cost Card

Product: 1–pound bag of smoked oysters
Product Number: 10
Standard Lot Size: 2,500 pounds

DIRECT MATERIAL

ID#	Unit Price	Total Quantity	Departments Smoking Costs	Packaging Cost	Cost per Pound
OY-15	$ 5.00 per lb.	3,125 lbs.*	$15,625		$6.25
B-06	25.00 per vat	1 vat	25		.01
SO-65	10.00 per gal.	10 gal.	100		.04
VP-25	.05 per bag	2,500 bags		$250.00	.05
Direct Material Total					$6.35

DIRECT LABOR

ID#	Avg. Wage per Hour	Hours	Smoking Costs	Packaging Cost	Cost per Pound
21	$14.25	5/6	$ 11.88		
22	14.25	10.0	142.50		
23	14.25	31.0	441.75		
24	14.25	5.0	71.25		$.27
45	13.80	32.5	$667.38	$448.50	.18
Direct Labor Total					$.45

PRODUCTION OVERHEAD

Cost Driver	Standard Time	Predetermined Overhead Rate	Total Cost	Cost per Pound
Smoking Department				
Machine Hours	5.1 hours	$122 per MH for VOH	$ 622.20	$ .25
Move/Wait Time	7.5 hours	$180 per hour for FOH	1,350.00	.54
Packaging Department				
Direct Labor Hours	32.5 hours	$5.30 per DLH for all OH	172.25	.07
Overhead Total				$ .86

Total cost = $6.35 + $.45 + $.86 = $7.66

*Each 1–pound bag has a requirement of 20 ounces of oysters: 2,500 lot size X 20 ounces = 50,000 ounces; 50,000 ÷ 16 ounces = 3,125 pounds.

A **total variance** is the difference between total actual cost incurred and total standard cost applied to the output produced during the period. This variance can be diagrammed as follows:

Total variances do not provide useful information for determining why cost differences occurred. To help managers in their control objectives, total variances are subdivided into price and usage components. The total variance diagram can be expanded to provide a general model indicating the two subvariances as shown in Exhibit 11–5.

A price variance reflects the difference between what was paid for inputs and what should have been paid for inputs. A usage variance shows the difference between the quantity of actual input and the quantity of standard input allowed for the actual output of the period. The quantity difference is multiplied by a standard price to provide a monetary measure that can be recorded in the accounting records. Usage variances focus on the efficiency of results or the relationship of input to output.

The basic diagram moves from the *actual* price of *actual* input on the left to the *standard* price of *standard* input quantity on the right. The middle measure of input is a hybrid of *actual* quantity and *standard* price. The change from input to output reflects the fact that a specific quantity of production input will not necessarily produce the standard quantity of output. The far right column uses a measure of output known as the **standard quantity allowed.** This quantity measure translates the actual production output into the standard input quantity *that should have been needed* to achieve that output. The monetary amount shown in the right-hand column is computed as the standard quantity allowed times the standard price of the input.

standard quantity allowed

The price variance portion of the total variance is measured as the actual input quantity multiplied by the difference between the actual and standard prices:

$$\text{Price Element} = (AP - SP)(AQ)$$

Actual Price of Actual Production Input AP × AQ	Standard Price of Actual Production Input SP × AQ	Standard Price of Standard Quantity of Production Output SP × SQ

(Price Component)
Price or Rate Variance

(Usage Component)
Quantity or Efficiency Variance

Total Variance

where AP = Actual material price or average actual labor rate
      AQ = Actual quantity of material or actual labor hours
      SP = Standard material price or average standard labor rate
      SQ = Standard quantity of material or standard labor hours
           allowed for the actual quantity of production achieved

EXHIBIT 11–5

General Variance Model
with Subvariances

The usage variance portion of the total variance is determined by measuring the difference between actual and standard quantities at the standard price:

$$\text{Usage Element} = (AQ - SQ)(SP)$$

The following sections illustrate variance computations for each cost element.

MATERIAL AND LABOR VARIANCE COMPUTATIONS

The standards for producing one lot of smoked oysters in the Smoking Department of Captain's Cannery are shown at the top of Exhibit 11–6. For simplicity and because of the immaterial amounts, Captain's Cannery has decided to consider the brine and soya oil shown on the bill of materials in Exhibit 11–1 as indirect materials. In addition, because all workers in the Smoking Department are paid the same wage rate, the labor standards for these operations are combined.

Also shown in Exhibit 11–6 are the actual quantity and cost data for October 1996. This standard and actual cost information are used to compute the October variances.

Material Variances

Using the model and inserting information concerning oyster prices and quantities used in production provides the following computations:

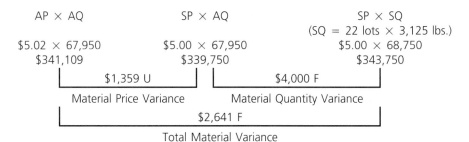

AP × AQ	SP × AQ	SP × SQ
		(SQ = 22 lots × 3,125 lbs.)
$5.02 × 67,950	$5.00 × 67,950	$5.00 × 68,750
$341,109	$339,750	$343,750

$1,359 U — Material Price Variance

$4,000 F — Material Quantity Variance

$2,641 F — Total Material Variance

EXHIBIT 11–6

Smoking Department Standard and Actual Production and Cost Data

Material standard:	
3,125 pounds of oysters at $5 per pound	$15,625.00
Labor standard:	
46 hours and 50 minutes at $14.25 per hour	667.38
Variable overhead standard:	
5.1 hours at $122 per MH	622.20
($122 = Budgeted monthly VOH of $14,640 ÷ Budgeted activity of 120 MHs)	
Fixed overhead standard:	
7.5 hours at $180 per hour of move/wait time	1,350.00
($180 = Budgeted monthly FOH of $31,500 ÷ Budgeted activity of 175 hours)	
Total standard Smoking Department cost for 1 lot (2,500 pounds) of smoked oysters	$18,264.58
Actual data for October:	
Number of lots produced (55,000 pounds)	22 lots
Pounds of oysters purchased	68,900
Pounds of oysters used	67,950
Price per pound of oysters purchased	$5.02
Direct labor hours incurred in Smoking Department	1,020
Total direct labor cost in Smoking Department	$14,637
Total variable overhead cost in Smoking Department	$19,200
Machine hours incurred in Smoking Department	107
Total fixed overhead cost in Smoking Department	$29,900
Hours of move/wait time incurred in Smoking Department	160

If the actual price or quantity amounts are larger than the standard price or quantity amounts, the variance is unfavorable (U); if the standards are larger than the actuals, the variance is favorable (F).

The **material price variance** (MPV) indicates whether the amount paid for material was below or above the standard price. For Captain's Cannery, the price paid for oysters was $5.02, whereas the standard was $5.00. The unfavorable MPV of $1,359 can also be calculated as [($5.02 − $5.00)(67,950) = ($.02)(67,950) = $1,359]. The variance sign is positive because the actual price paid is greater than the standard allowed.

material price variance

The **material quantity variance** (MQV) indicates whether the actual quantity used was below or above the standard quantity allowed for the actual output. This difference is multiplied by the standard price per unit of material. Captain's Cannery used 800 fewer pounds of oysters than the standard allowed, resulting in a favorable material quantity variance [(67,950 − 68,750)($5.00) = (−800)($5.00) = −$4,000]. In this instance, the variance sign is negative because actual quantity is less than standard.

material quantity variance

The total material variance ($2,641 F) can be calculated by subtracting the total standard cost of output ($343,750) from the total actual cost of input ($341,109). The total variance also represents the summation of the individual variances: [$1,359 + (−$4,000)] = −$2,641 (a favorable variance).

Point of Purchase Material Variance Model

A total variance for a cost component is *generally* equal to the sum of the price and usage subvariances. An exception to this rule occurs when the quantity of material purchased is not the same as the quantity of material placed into production. Because the material price variance relates to the purchasing (not production) function, the point of purchase model calculates the material price variance using the quantity of materials *purchased* rather than the quantity of materials *used*. The general model can be altered slightly to isolate the variance as close to the source as possible and provide more rapid information for management control purposes.

As noted in Exhibit 11–6, Captain's Cannery purchased 68,900 pounds of oysters during October. Using this information, rather than the 67,950 pounds used, the material price variance is calculated as

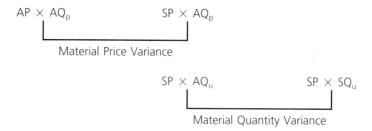

This change in the general model is shown below, using subscripts to indicate actual quantity purchased (p) and used (u).

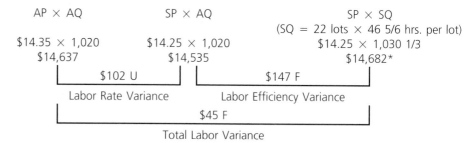

The material quantity variance is still computed on the basis of the actual quantity used. Thus, the MQV remains at $4,000 F. Because the price and quantity variances have been computed using different bases, they should not be summed and no total material variance can be meaningfully determined.

Labor Variances

The model for and computations of the labor variances for Captain's Cannery are as follows:

AP × AQ	SP × AQ	SP × SQ
		(SQ = 22 lots × 46 5/6 hrs. per lot)
$14.35 × 1,020	$14.25 × 1,020	$14.25 × 1,030 1/3
$14,637	$14,535	$14,682*
$102 U		$147 F
Labor Rate Variance		Labor Efficiency Variance
	$45 F	
	Total Labor Variance	

*Rounded to the nearest whole dollar.

labor rate variance

    The **labor rate variance** (LRV) shows the difference between the actual wages paid to labor for the period and the standard wages for all hours worked. The actual wage rate per hour is calculated by dividing total October labor cost ($14,637) by the number of hours worked (1,020). The LRV can also be computed as [($14.35 − $14.25)(1,020) = ($.10)(1,020) = $102 U]. Multiplying the standard labor rate by the difference between the actual hours worked and the standard hours allowed for

labor efficiency variance

the production achieved results in the **labor efficiency variance** (LEV): [(1,020 − 1,030 1/3)($14.25) = (− 10 1/3)($14.25) = − $147].
    The efficiency variance may also be viewed as being composed of two elements (quality and efficiency) that should be accounted for separately. The preceding computation "has been criticized for motivating managers to ignore quality concerns to avoid unfavorable efficiency variances."[6] Thus, reductions in labor time and the resulting "favorable" efficiency variances may be obtained by producing defective or poor quality units.

[6] Carole Cheatham, "Updating Standard Cost Systems," *Journal of Accountancy* (December 1990), p. 59.

For example, the standard wage rate for workers in the Smoking Department is $14.25 per hour. These workers can produce one lot of smoked oysters in 46 5/6 hours. In November, 30 lots were made in 1,320 hours (or an average of 44 hours per lot). The standard time allowed for production is 1,405 hours. The traditionally calculated labor efficiency variance is [$14.25 (1,320 − 1,405)] or $1,211 F. However, assume that 6 of the lots produced were unacceptable.

Captain's Cannery management wants to know the cost of producing the unacceptable 6 lots. Because each lot took an average of 44 hours to produce, the quality variance related to labor can be computed as follows: 6 × 44 × $14.25 = $3,762 U. The true efficiency variance for the 24 good lots is

Actual hours for good lots (24 × 44)	1,056
Standard hours allowed for good lots (24 × 46 5/6)	1,124
Reduction in hours used	68
Standard cost per hour	× $14.25
"True" efficiency variance	$969 F

The $2,793 U difference between these two amounts ($3,762 U − $969 F) could be referred to as the labor production variance:

Actual cost to produce 24 good lots (1,320 hours × $14.25)	$18,810
Standard cost to produce 24 good lots (1,124 hours × $14.25)	(16,017)
Labor production variance	$ 2,793 U

These calculations can be expressed in model form as follows:

	$SP \times AH_a$			$SP \times SH_a$		$SP \times SH_g$
good ($14.25 × 1,056)	$15,048	←$969 F →	($14.25 × 1,124)	$16,017.00		$16,017
bad ($14.25 3 264)	3,762	←$242.25 F→	($14.25 3 281)	4,004.25		0
	$18,810	←—— $1,211.25 ——→		$20,021.25	←$4,004.25 U→	$16,017

$2,793 U

Labor Production Variance

where AH_a = actual hours for all lots

SH_a = standard hours for all lots

SH_g = standard hours for good lots

Note that the two italicized variances ($242.25 F and $4,004.25 U) compose the true amount of the quality variance ($3,762). The favorable "efficiency" variance arose, in part, because workers produced the unacceptable units in a less-than-standard-allowed time.

OVERHEAD VARIANCES

In developing overhead application rates, a company must specify an operating level of capacity. Capacity refers to any measure of activity. Alternative measurement bases include theoretical, practical, normal, and expected capacity. Because total variable overhead changes in direct relationship with changes in activity and fixed overhead *per unit* changes inversely with changes in activity, a specific activity level must be chosen to determine budgeted overhead costs.

The estimated maximum potential activity for a specified time is the **theoretical capacity.** This measure assumes that all factors are operating in a technically and humanly perfect manner. Theoretical capacity disregards realities such as machinery breakdowns and reduced or stopped plant operations on holidays. Reducing theoretical capacity by ongoing, regular operating interruptions (such as holidays, downtime, and start-up time) provides the **practical capacity** that could be achieved during regular working hours. Consideration of historical and estimated future production levels and the cyclical fluctuations provides a **normal capacity** measure that encompasses the long-run (5 to 10 years) average activity of the firm. This measure

theoretical capacity

practical capacity

normal capacity

NEWS
NOTE

Use of Practical Capacity Can Highlight Low Usage of Resources

Practical capacity should be used as the relevant capacity level because it reveals the cost of unused resources. The concept of unused resources makes a distinction between the cost of resources *available* for manufacturing and the cost of resources acually *used* for that purpose.

The cost of supplying the productive resources is largely fixed in the short-run, does not vary with usage, and provides information relevant for predicting near-term spending. The cost of resources used provides information relevant for predicting changes in resource requirements as a function of changes in demand, technology, and product design. The difference between these two costs is called the cost of unused resources.

By using the practical capacity available in determining the fixed [overhead] rate, the cost of each unit produced contains only the cost of the resource used and, unlike the cost computed using [expected activity], does not include the cost of unused resources. Hence, each identical item of production is assigned the same cost, regardless of the number of such items produced or the number of changes in the product mix.

In addition, using practical capacity highlights the fact that some capacity is idle. [Note: Idle capacity is indicated by the size of the underapplied overhead at the end of the period. This concept is discussed later in the chapter.] Since world-class manufacturing must be flexible enough to respond to changing market conditions, corporate management must be informed when its facilities are not being used efficiently so that appropriate action can be taken.

SOURCE: Marinus DeBruine and Parvez R. Sopariwala, "The Use of Practical Capacity for Better Management Decisions," *Journal of Cost Management* (Spring 1994), pp. 26–27. Reprinted with permission from *The Journal of Cost Management for the Manufacturing Industry* Spring 1994, © 1994, Warren Gorham & Lamont, 31 St. James Avenue, Boston, MA 02116. All rights reserved.

represents a reasonably attainable level of activity, but will not provide costs that are most similar to actual historical costs. Thus, many firms use expected annual capacity as the selected measure of activity. Expected capacity is a short-run concept that represents the anticipated level of the firm for the upcoming period. If actual results are close to budgeted results (in both dollars and volume), this measure should result in product costs that most closely reflect actual costs. However, the above News Note provides a perspective on valid reasons why practical capacity (rather than expected activity) may be a more appropriate base to calculate a predetermined overhead rate.

The predetermined variable and fixed overhead rates shown in Exhibit 11–6 were calculated by the Smoking Department of Captain's Cannery using a capacity of 120 machine hours per month and 175 hours of move/wait time, respectively. At those levels of capacity, total variable overhead was budgeted at $14,640 per month and total fixed overhead was budgeted at $31,500.

The use of separate variable and fixed overhead application rates and accounts allows separate price and usage variances to be computed for each type of overhead. Such a four-variance approach provides managers with the greatest detail and, thus, the greatest flexibility for control and performance evaluation.

Variable Overhead

The general variance analysis model can be used to calculate the price and usage subvariances for variable overhead (VOH) as follows:

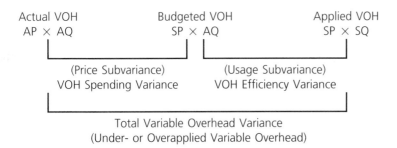

Actual VOH cost is debited to the Variable Manufacturing Overhead account; applied VOH reflects the standard overhead application rate multiplied by the standard quantity of activity for the actual output of the period. Applied VOH is debited to Work in Process Inventory and credited to Variable Manufacturing Overhead. The total VOH variance is the balance in the variable overhead account at year-end and equals the amount of underapplied or overapplied VOH.

Using the information in Exhibit 11–6, the variable overhead variances for the Smoking Department are calculated as follows:

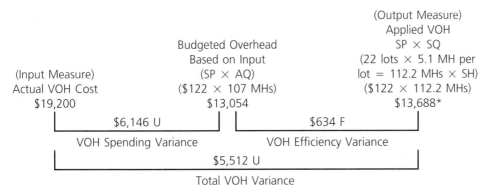

*Rounded to the nearest whole dollar.

The difference between actual VOH and budgeted VOH based on actual input is the **variable overhead spending variance.** Variable overhead spending variances are often caused by price differences—paying higher or lower prices than the standard prices allowed. Such fluctuations may occur because, over time, changes in variable overhead prices have not been reflected in the standard rate. For example, average indirect labor wage rates or utility rates may have changed since the predetermined variable overhead rate was computed. Managers usually have little control over prices charged by external parties and should not be held accountable for variances arising because of such price changes. In these instances, the standard rates should be adjusted.

Another possible cause of the VOH spending variance is waste or shrinkage associated with production resources (such as indirect materials). For example, deterioration of materials during storage or from lack of proper handling may be recognized only after those materials are placed into production. Such occurrences usually have little relationship to the input activity basis used, but they do affect the VOH spending variance. If waste or spoilage is the cause of the VOH spending variance, managers should be held accountable and encouraged to implement more effective controls.

The difference between budgeted VOH at actual input activity and applied VOH at standard input allowed is the **variable overhead efficiency variance.** This variance quantifies the effect of using more or less actual input than the standard allowed for

variable overhead spending variance

variable overhead efficiency variance

the production achieved. When actual input exceeds standard input allowed, production operations are considered to be inefficient. Excess input also indicates that a larger VOH budget is needed to support the additional input.

Fixed Overhead

The total fixed overhead (FOH) variance is divided into its price and usage subvariances by inserting *budgeted* fixed overhead as a middle column into the general model as follows:

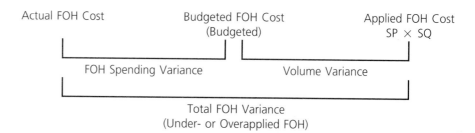

In the model, the left column is simply labeled "actual cost" and is not computed as a price times quantity measure because FOH is generally acquired in lump sums rather than on a per-unit basis. Actual FOH cost is debited to Fixed Manufacturing Overhead. Budgeted FOH is a constant amount throughout the relevant range; thus, *the middle column is a constant figure regardless of the actual quantity of input or the standard quantity of input allowed.* This concept is a key element in computing FOH variances. The budgeted amount of fixed overhead can also be presented analytically as the result of multiplying the standard FOH application rate by the capacity measure that was used to compute that standard rate.

The difference between actual and budgeted FOH is the **fixed overhead spending variance.** This amount normally represents a weighted average price variance of the multiple components of FOH, although it can also reflect mismanagement of resources. The individual FOH components are detailed in the flexible budget, and individual spending variances should be calculated for each component.

As with variable overhead, applied FOH is related to the standard application rate and the standard hours allowed for the actual output. In regard to fixed overhead, the standard input allowed for the achieved production level measures capacity utilization for the period. Applied fixed overhead is debited to Work in Process Inventory and credited to Fixed Manufacturing Overhead.

The fixed overhead **volume variance** is the difference between budgeted and applied fixed overhead. The volume variance is caused solely by producing at a level that differs from that used to compute the predetermined overhead rate. The volume variance occurs because, by using an application rate per unit of activity, FOH cost is treated as if it were variable even though it is not.

Although capacity utilization is controllable to some degree, managers have the least influence and control over the volume variance, especially in the short run. So the volume variance is also called the **noncontrollable variance.** This lack of influence is usually not too important. What is important is whether managers exercise their ability to adjust and control capacity utilization properly. The degree of capacity utilization should *always* be viewed in relationship to inventory and sales. Managers must understand that underutilization of capacity is not always an undesirable condition. It is significantly more appropriate for managers to regulate production than to produce goods that will end up in inventory stockpiles. Unneeded inventory production, although it serves to utilize capacity, generates substantially more costs for materials, labor, and overhead (including storage and handling costs). The positive impact that such unneeded production will have on the volume variance is insignificant because this variance is of little or no value for managerial control purposes.

fixed overhead spending variance

volume variance

noncontrollable variance

The difference between actual FOH and applied FOH is the total fixed overhead variance and is equal to the amount of underapplied or overapplied fixed overhead.

Inserting the data from Exhibit 11–6 for the Smoking Department into the model gives the following:

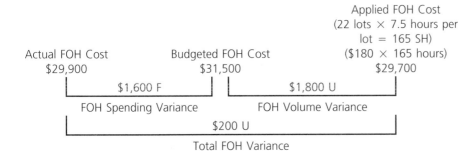

The reason the Smoking Department's FOH application rate is $180 per hour of move/wait time is that a capacity level of 175 hours per month was chosen. Had any other capacity level been chosen, the rate would have differed, even though the total amount of budgeted monthly fixed overhead ($31,500) would have remained the same. *If any level of capacity other than that used in determining the application rate is used to apply FOH, a volume variance will occur.* For example, if the department had chosen 165 hours as the denominator level of activity to set the predetermined FOH rate, there would be no volume variance for October. If any number of hours less than 165 had been chosen as the denominator level of activity, the volume variance for October would have been favorable.

Management is usually aware, as production occurs, of the physical level of capacity utilization even if a volume variance is not reported. The volume variance, however, translates the physical measurement of underutilization or overutilization into a dollar amount. An unfavorable volume variance indicates less-than-expected utilization of capacity. If available capacity is currently being utilized at a level below (or above) that which was anticipated, managers are expected to recognize that condition, investigate the reasons for it, and (if possible and desirable) initiate appropriate action. Managers can sometimes influence capacity utilization by modifying work schedules, taking measures to relieve any obstructions to or congestion of production activities, and carefully monitoring the movement of resources through the production process. Preferably, such actions should be taken before production rather than after it. Efforts made after production is completed may improve next period's operations, but will have no impact on past production.

Alternative Overhead Variance Approaches

If the accounting system does not distinguish between variable and fixed costs, a four-variance approach is unworkable. Use of a combined (variable and fixed) overhead rate requires alternative overhead variance computations. A one-variance approach calculates only a **total overhead variance** as the difference between total actual overhead and total overhead applied to production. The amount of applied overhead is determined by multiplying the combined rate by the standard input activity allowed for the actual production achieved. The one-variance model is diagrammed as follows:

total overhead variance

Like other total variances, the total overhead variance provides limited information to managers. Two-variance analysis is performed by inserting a middle column in the one-variance model as follows:

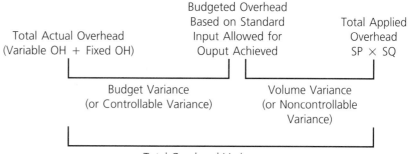

The middle column provides information on the expected total overhead cost based on the standard input allowed for the output produced. This amount represents total budgeted variable overhead at the standard hours allowed plus budgeted fixed overhead, which is constant across all activity levels in the relevant range.

budget variance

controllable variance

  The **budget variance** equals total actual overhead minus budgeted overhead based on the standard input allowed for this period's production. This variance is also referred to as the **controllable variance** because managers are somewhat able to control and influence this amount during the short run. The difference between total applied overhead and budgeted overhead based on the standard input allowed for the output achieved is the volume variance.

  A modification of the two-variance approach provides a three-variance analysis. Inserting another column between the left and middle columns of the two-variance model separates the budget variance into spending and efficiency variances. The new column represents the flexible budget based on the actual *input* level of activity. The three-variance model is as follows:

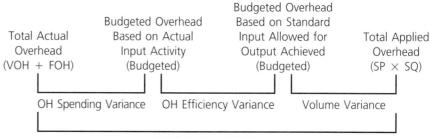

overhead spending variance

overhead efficiency variance

  The spending variance shown in the three-variance approach is a total **overhead spending variance.** It is equal to total actual overhead minus total budgeted overhead at the actual hours of activity. The **overhead efficiency variance** is related solely to variable overhead and is the difference between total budgeted overhead at the actual input activity and total budgeted overhead at the standard input allowed (output activity). This variance measures, at standard cost, the approximate amount of variable overhead caused by using more or fewer inputs than standard for the actual production. The sum of the overhead spending and overhead efficiency variances of the three-variance analysis is equal to the budget variance of the two-variance analysis. The volume variance amount is the same as that calculated using the two-variance or the four-variance approach.

  If variable and fixed overhead are applied using the same base, the one-, two-, and three-variance approaches will have the interrelationships shown in Exhibit 11–7. (The demonstration problem at the end of the chapter shows computations for each

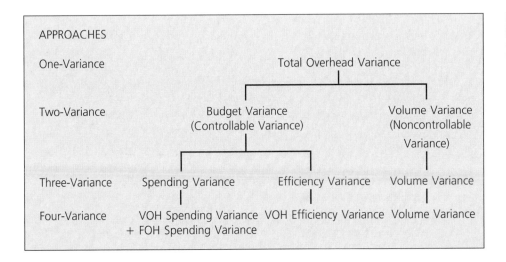

EXHIBIT 11–7

Interrelationships of
Overhead Variances

of the overhead variance approaches.) Managers should select the method that provides the most useful information and that conforms to the company's accounting system. As more companies begin to recognize the existence of multiple cost drivers for overhead and to use multiple bases for applying overhead to production, computation of the one-, two-, and three-variance approaches will diminish.

Journal entries using the Captain's Cannery information for October 1996 are given in Exhibit 11–8 on the next page. This exhibit uses the 68,900 pounds of oysters purchased to account for the material price variance. The following explanations apply to the numbered journal entries.

**STANDARD COST
SYSTEM JOURNAL
ENTRIES**

1. The debit to Raw Material Inventory is for the standard price of the actual quantity of oysters purchased. The credit to Accounts Payable is for the actual price of the actual quantity of oysters purchased. The debit to the variance account reflects the unfavorable material price variance.

2. The debit to Work in Process Inventory is for the standard price of the standard quantity of material allowed, whereas the credit to Raw Material Inventory is for the standard price of the actual quantity of material used in production. The credit to the Material Quantity Variance account reflects the overuse of materials valued at the standard price per pound.

3. The debit to Work in Process Inventory is for the standard hours allowed to produce 22 lots of smoked oysters multiplied by the standard wage rate. The Wage Payable credit is for the actual amount of direct labor wages paid during the period. The debit to the Labor Rate Variance account reflects the unfavorable rate differential. The Labor Efficiency Variance credit reflects the less-than-standard hours allowed incurred by direct labor multiplied by the standard wage rate.

4. During the period, actual costs incurred for the various variable and fixed overhead components are debited to the manufacturing overhead accounts. These costs are caused by a variety of transactions including indirect material and labor usage, depreciation, and utility costs.

5. Overhead is applied to production using the predetermined rates multiplied by the standard input allowed. Overhead application is recorded at completion of production or at the end of the period, whichever is earlier. The difference between actual debits and applied credits in each overhead account represents the total variable and fixed overhead variances and is also the underapplied or overapplied overhead of the period.

EXHIBIT 11-8

Journal Entries for October

(1) Raw Materials Inventory	344,500	
Material Purchase Price Variance	1,378	
Accounts Payable		345,878

To record the purchase of 68,900 pounds of oysters at $5.02 per pound.

(2) Work in Process Inventory	343,750	
Raw Materials Inventory		339,750
Material Quantity Variance		4,000

To record the issuance and usage of 67,950 pounds of oysters to produce 22 lots.

(3) Work in Process Inventory	14,682	
Labor Rate Variance	102	
Wages Payable		14,637
Labor Efficiency Variance		147

To record the usage of 1,020 hours of direct labor time at a wage rate of $14.35 per hour to produce 22 lots.

(4) Variable Manufacturing Overhead	19,200	
Fixed Manufacturing Overhead	29,900	
Various accounts		49,100

To record actual variable and fixed overhead costs incurred.

(5) Work in Process Inventory	43,388	
Variable Manufacturing Overhead		13,688
Fixed Manufacturing Overhead		29,700

To apply variable overhead to production at $122 per MH and fixed overhead at $180 per hour of move/wait time for 22 lots.

(6) VOH Spending Variance	6,146	
VOH Efficiency Variance		634
Variable Manufacturing Overhead		5,512

To close the variable overhead account.

(7) FOH Volume Variance	1,800	
FOH Spending Variance		1,600
Fixed Manufacturing Overhead		200

To close the fixed overhead account.

6. & 7. These entries assume an end-of-month closing of the Variable Manufacturing Overhead and Fixed Manufacturing Overhead accounts. The balances in the accounts are reclassified to the appropriate variance accounts. This entry is provided for illustration only. This process would typically *not* be performed at month-end, but rather at year-end, because an annual period is used to calculate the overhead application rates.

Note that all unfavorable variances have debit balances and favorable variances have credit balances. Unfavorable variances represent excess production costs; favorable variances represent savings in production costs. Standard production costs are shown in inventory accounts (which have debit balances); therefore, excess costs are also debits.

Although standard costs are useful for internal reporting, they are acceptable only when the financial statement figures are substantially equivalent to those that would have resulted from using an actual cost system. If standards are realistically achievable and current, this equivalency should exist. Using standard costs for financial statements should provide fairly conservative inventory valuations because the effects of excess prices and/or inefficient operations are eliminated.

At year-end, adjusting entries must be made to eliminate standard cost variances. The entries depend on whether the variances are, in total, insignificant or significant. If the combined impact of the variances is immaterial, unfavorable variances are closed as debits to Cost of Goods Sold; favorable variances are credited to Cost of Goods Sold. Thus, unfavorable variances have a negative impact on operating income because of the higher-than-expected costs, whereas favorable variances have a positive effect on operating income because of the lower-than-expected costs. Although the year's entire production may not have been sold yet, this variance treatment is based on the immateriality of the amounts involved.

In contrast, large variances are prorated at year-end among ending inventories and Cost of Goods Sold. This proration disposes of the variances and presents the financial statements in a manner that approximates the use of actual costing. Proration is based on the relative size of the account balances. Disposition of significant variances is similar to the disposition of large amounts of underapplied or overapplied overhead shown in Chapter 5.

To illustrate the disposition of significant variances, assume that there is a $10,000 unfavorable (debit) year-end balance in the Material Purchase Price Variance account of Captain's Cannery. Other relevant year-end account balances are as follows:

Raw Material Inventory	$ 245,630
Work in Process Inventory	140,360
Finished Goods Inventory	350,900
Cost of Goods Sold	2,772,110
Total of affected accounts	$3,509,000

The theoretically correct allocation of the material purchase price variance would use actual material cost in each account at year-end. However, as was mentioned in Chapter 5 with regard to overhead, after the conversion process has begun cost elements within account balances are commingled and tend to lose their identity. Thus, unless a significant misstatement would result, disposition of the variance can be based on the proportions of each account balance to the total, as shown below:

Raw Material Inventory	7%	($ 245,630 ÷ $3,509,000)
Work in Process Inventory	4%	($ 140,360 ÷ $3,509,000)
Finished Goods Inventory	10%	($ 350,900 ÷ $3,509,000)
Cost of Goods Sold	79%	($2,772,110 ÷ $3,509,000)

Applying these percentages to the $10,000 material price variance gives the amounts shown in the following journal entry to assign to the affected accounts:

Raw Material Inventory ($10,000 × .07)	700	
Work in Process Inventory ($10,000 × .04)	400	
Finished Goods Inventory ($10,000 × .10)	1,000	
Cost of Goods Sold ($10,000 × .79)	7,900	
Material Purchase Price Variance		10,000
To dispose of the material price variance at		
year-end.		

All variances other than the material price variance occur as part of the conversion process. Raw material *purchases* are not part of conversion, but raw material *used* is. Therefore, the remaining variances are prorated only to Work in Process Inventory, Finished Goods Inventory, and Cost of Goods Sold.

The preceding discussion about standard setting, variance computations, and year-end adjustments indicates that a substantial commitment of time and effort is required to implement and use a standard cost system. Companies are willing to make such a commitment for a variety of reasons.

WHY STANDARD COST SYSTEMS ARE USED

"A standard cost system has three basic functions: collecting the actual costs of a manufacturing operation, determining the achievement of that manufacturing operation, and evaluating performance through the reporting of variances from standard."[7] These basic functions result in six distinct benefits of standard cost systems.

Clerical Efficiency

A company using standard costs usually discovers that less clerical time and effort are required than in an actual cost system. In an actual cost system, the accountant must continuously recalculate changing actual unit costs. In a standard cost system, unit costs are held constant for some period. Costs can be assigned to inventory and cost of goods sold accounts at predetermined amounts per unit regardless of actual conditions.

Motivation

Standards are a way to communicate management's expectations to workers. When standards are achievable and when workers are informed of rewards for standards attainment, those workers are likely to be motivated to strive for accomplishment. The standards used must require a reasonable amount of effort on the workers' part.

Planning

Planning generally requires estimates about the future. Managers can use current standards to estimate what future quantities and costs should be. These estimates should help in the determination of purchasing needs for material, staffing needs for labor, and capacity needs related to overhead that, in turn, will aid in planning for company cash flows. In addition, budget preparation is simplified if standard costs are available because a standard is, in fact, a budget for one unit of product or service. Standards are also used to provide the cost basis needed to analyze relationships among costs, sales volume, and profit levels of the organization.

Controlling

variance analysis

The control process begins with the establishment of standards that provide a basis against which actual costs can be measured and variances calculated. **Variance analysis** is the process of categorizing the nature (favorable or unfavorable) of the differences between actual and standard costs and seeking explanations for those differences. A well-designed variance analysis system captures variances as early as possible, subject to cost-benefit assessments. The system should help managers determine who or what is responsible for each variance and who is best able to explain it. An early measurement and reporting system allows managers to monitor operations, take corrective action on problems, evaluate performance, and motivate workers to achieve standard production.

In implementing control, managers must recognize that they are faced with a specific scarce resource—their time. They must distinguish between situations to ignore and those to investigate. To make this distinction, managers establish upper and lower limits of acceptable deviations from standard. These limits are similar to tolerance limits used by engineers in the development of statistical process control charts. If variances are small and within an acceptable range, no managerial action is

[7] Richard V. Calvasina and Eugene J. Calvasina, "Standard Costing Games That Managers Play," *Management Accounting* (March 1984), p. 49. Although the authors of the article only specified manufacturing operations, these same functions are equally applicable to service businesses.

EXHIBIT 11–9

Illustration of Management by Exception Concept

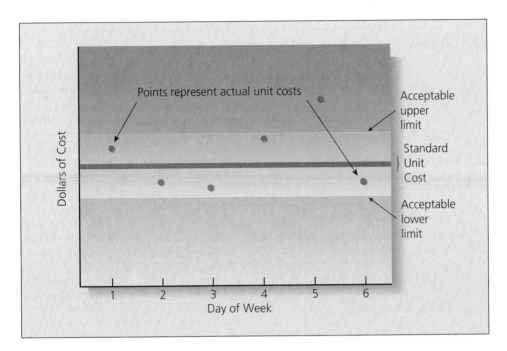

required. If an actual cost differs significantly from standard, the manager responsible for the cost is expected to determine the variance cause(s). If the cause(s) can be found and corrective action is possible, such action should be taken so that future operations will adhere more closely to established standards.

The setting of upper and lower tolerance limits for deviations allows managers to implement the management by exception concept, as illustrated in Exhibit 11–9. In the exhibit, the only significant deviation from standard occurred on Day 5, when the actual cost exceeded the upper limit of acceptable performance. An exception report should be generated on this date so that the manager will investigate the underlying variance causes.

Variances large enough to fall outside the acceptability ranges often indicate trouble. However, a variance does not reveal the cause of the trouble or the person or group responsible. To determine variance causes, managers must investigate significant variances through observation, inspection, and inquiry. Such an investigation will involve the time and effort of people at the operating level as well as accounting personnel. Operations personnel should be alert in spotting variances as they occur and record the reasons for the variances to the extent they are discernable. For example, operating personnel could readily detect and report causes such as machine downtime or material spoilage.

One important point needs to be made about the control uses of variances. An extremely favorable variance is not necessarily a good variance. Although the "favorable" designation may often equate to good, an extremely favorable variance could mean an error was made when the standard was set or that a related, offsetting unfavorable variance exists. For example, if low-grade material is purchased, a favorable price variance may exist, but additional quantities of the material may be used to overcome defective production. An unfavorable labor efficiency variance could also result because a longer time was spent on completing a job because a substantial number of defective units were produced as a result of using the inferior materials. Not only are the unfavorable variances incurred, but internal quality failure costs are also generated. Another common situation begins with labor rather than material. Using lower-paid workers will result in a favorable rate variance, but may cause excessive usage of raw materials. Managers must constantly be aware that relationships exist and not analyze variances in isolation.

When to Investigate Variances

Variance investigation policies [for materials and labor at large companies] are moving away from pure judgment and toward the use of structured or formalized exception procedures.

[One] explanation is that the results are being driven by manufacturing innovations that lead to shorter production runs and shorter product life cycles. In such an environment, monthly variance reports may be so untimely as to be virtually useless. In a flexible manufacturing environment, production runs can be extremely short—only days or perhaps even hours. To provide timely feedback in an environment where the nature of operations and the products being produced change rapidly, more accounts and greater reporting frequency are required.

[Another] explanation relates to the increasing globalization of markets rather than to the characteristics or individual operating policies of the firm. When competing internationally, companies face more competitors, are less likely to be the lowest-cost producers, and face more uncertainties than in domestic markets. . . . By reducing production cost surprises, intensified management accounting (in the frequency of reports and the details of variance composition) can compensate for these additional uncertainties.

SOURCE: Bruce R. Gaumnitz and Felix P. Kollaritsch, "Manufacturing Variances: Current Practice and Trends," *Journal of Cost Management* (Boston: Warren Gorham Lamont, Spring 1991), pp. 63–64. Reprinted with permission from *The Journal of Cost Management for the Manufacturing Industry* Spring 1991, © 1991, Warren Gorham & Lamont, 31 St. James Avenue, Boston, MA 02116. All rights reserved.

EXHIBIT 11–10

Time Period Covered by
Variance Reports

| | RAW MATERIAL | | | | DIRECT LABOR | | | |
| | Currently | | Five Years Ago | | Currently | | Five Years Ago | |
	No.	%	No.	%	No.	%	No.	%
Year	0	0	0	0	0	0	1	0.8
Quarter	3	2.5	4	3.3	2	1.7	2	1.7
Month	72	60.0	85	70.9	48	40.3	60	50.4
Week	16	13.3	16	13.3	32	26.9	32	26.9
Day	26	21.7	13	10.8	31	26.1	22	18.5
Hour or less	3	2.5	2	1.7	6	5.0	2	1.7
Total companies responding	120	100.0	120	100.0	119	100.0	119	100.0

SOURCE: Bruce R. Gaumnitz and Felix P. Kollaritsch, "Manufacturing Variances: Current Practice and Trends," *Journal of Cost Management* (Spring 1991), p. 60. Reprinted with permission from *The Journal of Cost Management for the Manufacturing Industry* Spring 1991, © 1991, Warren Gorham & Lamont, 31 St. James Avenue, Boston, MA 02116. All rights reserved.

The time frame for which variance computations are made is being shortened, as is indicated in the News Note "When to Investigate Variances." Exhibit 11–10 provides the results of a limited survey conducted with controllers of manufacturing companies using standard cost systems. Monthly variance reporting is still the most common, but the movement toward shorter reporting periods is obvious. As more companies integrate various world-class concepts such as total quality management and just-in-time production into their operations, there will be more frequent reporting of variances. Proper implementation of such concepts requires that managers be continuously aware of operating activities and recognize (and correct) problems as soon as they arise.

Decision Making

Standard cost information facilitates many decisions. For example, managers can compare a standard cost with a quoted price to determine whether an item should be manufactured in-house or be purchased. Use of actual cost information in such a decision could be inappropriate because the actual cost may fluctuate from period to period. Also, in making a decision on a special price offering to purchasers, managers can use standard product cost to determine the lower limit of the price to offer. In a similar manner, if a company is bidding on contracts, it must have some idea of estimated product costs. Bidding too low and receiving the contract could cause substantial operating income (and, possibly, cash flow) problems; bidding too high might be uncompetitive and cause the contract to be awarded to another company.

Performance Evaluation

When top management receives summary variance reports highlighting the operating performance of subordinate managers, these reports are analyzed for both positive and negative information. Top management needs to know when costs were and were not controlled and by which managers. Such information allows top management to provide essential feedback to subordinates, investigate areas of concern, and make performance evaluations about who needs additional supervision, who should be replaced, and who should be promoted. For proper performance evaluations to be made, the responsibility for variances must be traced to specific managers.[8]

When standards are established, appropriateness and attainability should be considered. Appropriateness, in relation to a standard, refers to the basis on which the standards are developed and how long they are expected to last. Attainability refers to management's belief about the degree of difficulty or rigor that should be incurred in achieving the standard.

CONSIDERATIONS IN ESTABLISHING STANDARDS

Appropriateness

Although standards are developed from past and current information, they should reflect relevant technical and environmental factors expected during the time in which the standards are to be applied. Consideration should be given to factors such as material quality, normal material ordering quantities, expected employee wage rates, degree of plant automation, facility layout, and mix of employee skills. Management should not think that, once standards are set, they will remain useful forever. Current operating performance is not comparable to out-of-date standards. Standards must evolve over the organization's life to reflect its changing methods and processes. Out-of-date standards produce variances that do not provide logical bases for planning, controlling, decision making, or evaluating performance. Consider what needed to happen to production standards at Alexander Doll Company based on the discussion in the News Note on the next page.

Attainability

Standards provide a target level of performance and can be set at various levels of rigor. The level of rigor affects motivation, and one reason for using standards is to motivate employees. Standards can be classified as expected, practical, and ideal. Depending on the type of standard in effect, the acceptable ranges used to apply the management by exception principle will differ. This difference is especially notable on the unfavorable side.

   Expected standards are set at a level that reflects what is actually expected to occur. Such standards anticipate future waste and inefficiencies and allow for them.

---

[8] Cost control relative to variances is discussed in greater depth in Chapter 16. Performance evaluation is discussed in greater depth in Chapters 20 and 21.

NEWS
NOTE

Implementing Kaizen Reduces Time Standards

[In 1995, Alexander Doll Company, in New York City, was in bankruptcy. A decision was made to apply kaizen principles to the company's production of collectible dolls.] Beginning with the company's small production line for baby dolls, a cross-functional team was established to evaluate problems with the production line. The team observed 25 operations and measured each with a stopwatch.

Operations were spread out over three floors, causing extra handling that wasted time and damaged the dolls. "We physically moved the operation [within the building] and combined everything in one location" on one floor, says William Schwartz, director of Alexander Doll and a vice president of TBM Consulting Group Inc.

The results: The distance each doll traveled from the beginning to the end of the process was reduced from 630 feet to 40 feet. The time required to complete a doll went from 90 days to 90 minutes. The square footage used for the line was reduced from 2,010 to 980. And productivity increased from eight dolls per person per day to 25.

SOURCE: Roberta Maynard, "A Company Is Turned Around Through Japanese Principles," *Nation's Business* (February 1996), p. 9. Reprinted by permission, *Nation's Business*, February 1996. Copyright 1996, U.S. Chamber of Commerce.

As such, expected standards are not of significant value for motivation, control, or performance evaluation. If a company uses expected standards, the ranges of acceptable variances should be extremely small (and, commonly, favorable) because the actual costs should conform closely to standards.

practical standard

Standards that can be reached or slightly exceeded approximately 60 to 70 percent of the time with reasonable effort are called **practical standards.** These standards allow for normal, unavoidable time problems or delays such as machine downtime and worker breaks. Practical standards represent an attainable challenge and traditionally have been thought to be the most effective at inducing the best worker performance and at determining the effectiveness and efficiency of workers at performing their tasks. Both favorable and unfavorable variances result from the use of such moderately rigorous standards.

ideal standard

Standards that provide for no inefficiency of *any* type are called **ideal standards.** Ideal standards encompass the highest level of rigor and do not allow for normal operating delays or human limitations such as fatigue, boredom, or misunderstanding. Unless a plant is entirely automated (and then the possibility of human or power failure still exists), ideal standards are impossible to attain. Attempts to apply such standards have traditionally resulted in discouraged and resentful workers who, ultimately, ignore the standards. Variances from ideal standards will always be unfavorable and were commonly not considered useful for constructive cost control or performance evaluation. Such a perspective has, however, begun to change.

CHANGES IN STANDARDS USAGE

In using variances for control and performance evaluation, many accountants (and, often, businesspeople in general) believe that an incorrect measurement is being used. For example, material standards generally include a factor for waste, and labor standards are commonly set at the expected level of attainment even though this level compensates for downtime and human error. Usage of standards that are not aimed at the highest possible (ideal) level of attainment are now being questioned in a business environment concerned with world-class operations.

Use of Ideal Standards and Theoretical Capacity

Recently there has been a significant amount of Japanese influence on management philosophy and production techniques. Just-in-time (JIT) production systems and total quality management (TQM) both evolved as a result of an upsurge in Japanese productivity. These two world-class concepts are inherently based on a notable exception to the traditional disbelief in the use of ideals in standards development and use. Rather than including waste and inefficiency in the standards and then accepting additional waste and spoilage deviations under a management by exception principle, JIT and TQM both begin from the premises of zero defects, zero inefficiency, and zero downtime. Consider the fact that 70 percent of Nissan's Japanese suppliers achieve a quality standard of 10 or fewer defective parts per million—compared to only 47 percent of the company's European suppliers.[9] Under JIT and TQM, ideal standards become expected standards and there is no (or only a minimal allowable) level of acceptable deviation from standards.

When the standard permits a deviation from the ideal, managers are allowing for inefficient uses of resources. Setting standards at the tightest possible level results in the most useful information for managerial purposes as well as the highest quality products and services at the lowest possible cost. If no inefficiencies are built into or tolerated in the system, deviations from standard should be minimized and overall organizational performance improved. Workers may, at first, resent the introduction of standards set at a "perfection" level, but it is in their and management's best long-run interest to have such standards.

If theoretical standards are to be implemented, management must be prepared to go through a four-step "migration" process. First, teams should be established to determine current problems and the causes of those problems. Second, if the causes relate to equipment, the facility, or workers, management must be ready to invest plant and equipment items, equipment rearrangements, or worker training so that the standards are amenable to the operations. (Training is essential if workers are to perform at the high levels of efficiency demanded by theoretical standards.) If problems are related to external sources (such as poor quality materials), management must be willing to change suppliers and/or pay higher prices for higher grade input. Third, because the responsibility for quality has been assigned to workers, management must also empower those workers with the authority to react to problems. "The key to quality initiatives is for employees to move beyond their natural resistance-to-change mode to a highly focused, strategic, and empowered mind-set. This shift unlocks employees' energy and creativity, and leads them to ask 'how can I do my job even better today?'"[10] Fourth, requiring people to work at their maximum potential demands recognition and means that management must provide rewards for achievement.

In the same vein, a company that wants to be viewed as a world-class competitor may want to use theoretical capacity in setting fixed overhead rates. If a company were totally automated or if people consistently worked to their fullest potential, such a measure would provide a reasonable overhead application rate. Thus, any underapplied overhead resulting from a difference between theoretical and actual capacity would indicate capacity that should be either used or eliminated; it could also indicate human capabilities that have not been fully developed. If a company uses theoretical capacity as the defined capacity measure, any end-of-period underapplied overhead should be viewed as a period cost and closed to a loss account (such as "Loss from Inefficient Operations") on the income statement. Showing the capacity potential and the use of the differential in this manner should attract managerial attention to the inefficient and ineffective use of resources.

Whether setting standards at the ideal level and using theoretical capacity to determine FOH applications will become norms of non-Japanese companies cannot be determined at this time. However, we expect that attainability levels will move away from the expected or practical and closer to the ideal. This conclusion is based on the fact that a company whose competitor produces goods based on the highest possible standards must also use such standards to compete on quality and to meet

[9] John Griffiths, "Nissan in Project to Help Suppliers Raise Standards," *(London) Financial Times* (December 13, 1995), p. 10.
[10] Sara Moulton, Ed Oakley, and Chuck Kremer, "How to Assure Your Quality Initiative Really Pays Off," *Management Accounting* (January 1993), p. 26.

cost (and, thus, profit margin) objectives. Higher standards for efficiency automatically mean lower costs because of the elimination of non-value-added activities such as waste, idle time, and rework.

Adjusting Standards

Standards have generally been set after comprehensive investigation of prices and quantities for the various cost elements. These standards were almost always retained for at least one year and, sometimes, for multiple years. Currently, the business environment (which includes suppliers, technology, competition, product design, and manufacturing methods) changes so rapidly that a standard may no longer be useful for management control purposes throughout a year.

Company management needs to consider whether to incorporate rapid changes in the environment into the standards during the year in which *significant* changes occur. Ignoring the changes is a simplistic approach that allows the same type of cost to be recorded at the same amount all year. Thus, for example, any material purchased during the year would be recorded at the same standard cost regardless of when the purchase was made. This approach, although making recordkeeping easy, eliminates any opportunity to adequately control costs or evaluate performance. Additionally, such an approach could create large differentials between standard and actual costs, making standard costs unacceptable for external reporting.

Changing the standards to reflect price or quantity changes would make some aspects of management control and performance evaluation more effective and others more difficult. For instance, budgets prepared using the original standards would need to be adjusted before appropriate actual comparisons could be made against them. Changing standards also creates a problem for recordkeeping and inventory valuation. At what standard cost should products be valued—the standard in effect when they were produced or the standard in effect when the financial statements are prepared? Although production-point standards would be more closely related to actual costs, many of the benefits discussed earlier in the chapter might be undermined.

If possible, management may wish to consider combining these two choices in the accounting system. The original standards can be considered "frozen" for budget purposes and a revised budget prepared using the new current standards. The difference between these budgets would reflect variances related to business environment cost changes. These variances could be designated as uncontrollable (such as those related to changes in the market price of raw material) or internally initiated (such as changes in standard labor time resulting from employee training or equipment rearrangement). Comparing the budget based on current standards with actual costs would provide variances that would more adequately reflect internally controllable causes, such as excess material and/or labor time usage caused by inferior grade purchases.

Price Variance Based on Purchases versus on Usage

The price variance computation has traditionally been based on purchases rather than on usage. This choice was made so as to calculate the variance as quickly as possible relative to the cost incurrence. Although calculating the price variance for material at purchase point allows managers to see the impact of buying decisions more rapidly, such information may not be most relevant in a just-in-time environment. Buying materials in quantities that are not needed for current production requires that the materials be stored and moved—both non-value-added activities. The trade-off in price savings would need to be measured against the additional costs to determine the cost-benefit relationship of such a purchase.

Additionally, computing a price variance on purchases, rather than on usage, may reduce the probability of recognizing a relationship between a favorable material price variance and an unfavorable material usage variance. If the favorable price variance resulted from the purchase of low-grade material, the effects of that purchase will not be known until the material is actually used.

The determination of whether to use a material price variance based on purchases or usage is a management decision and should reflect the environment in which the company operates. Both variances could be computed and the information used at different times. If, however, a just-in-time inventory system is implemented by the manufacturer and material variances are virtually eliminated, there is little need to compute the traditional material price and usage variances. Reasons for the elimination of material variances are discussed more thoroughly in Chapter 17.

Decline in Direct Labor

As the proportion of product cost related to direct labor declines, the necessity for direct labor variance computations is minimized. Direct labor may simply become a part of a conversion cost category, as noted in Chapter 4. Alternatively, the increase in automation often relegates labor to an indirect category because workers become machine overseers rather than product producers. The chapter suggested that the labor efficiency variance could contain a subvariance related to quality as well as one simply related to hours of effort. The News Note "Did the Employee or the Machine Create the Variance?" provides another alternative segmentation of the labor efficiency variance.

Did the Employee or the Machine Create the Variance?

**N E W S
N O T E**

In an automated environment, the traditional labor efficiency variance should be divided into two new variances: *an employee labor efficiency variance* and a *machine labor efficiency variance*. In such an environment, employee efficiency has two different aspects. One aspect is directly related to the employee's skill and industriousness; the other is directly related to the equipment's state of readiness. Recognizing these aspects separately will allow the control system to direct management's attention to the real source of problems (the employee or the machine configuration).

Dividing the traditional labor efficiency variance into the two new variances requires the establishment of a *ratio standard* for employee labor hours to machine hours for each piece of equipment. The new variances also require two other items of information for each machine in the machine cluster:
1. Actual machine hours devoted by each machine to production in each accounting period; and
2. Actual hours devoted by the employee to each machine during the accounting period.

The new employee labor efficiency variance is calculated as: (Budgeted Employee Wages for Actual Hours) minus (Budgeted Employee Wages for Required Employee Hours) or (Standard Wage Rate × Actual Employee Hours) − (Standard Wage Rate × Actual Machine Hours × Ratio Standard). This variance indicates whether the employee devoted more (or fewer) hours to the machine than were required for the actual production.

The machine labor efficiency variance is calculated as: (Budgeted Employee Wages for Required Employee Hours) minus (Allowed Employee Labor Cost for Actual Production) or (Standard Wage Rate × Standard Machine Time Allowed for Actual Production × Ratio Standard). This variance reflects the additional (or reduced) costs of employee labor that was caused by the machine's having been operated more (or fewer) hours than were allowed based on the number of units produced.

SOURCE: Adapted from Alan S. Levitan and Sidney J. Baxendale, "Analyzing the Labor Efficiency Variance to Signal Process Engineering Problems," *Journal of Cost Management* (Boston: Warren Gorham Lamont, Summer 1992), pp. 63–72. Reprinted with permission from *The Journal of Cost Management for the Manufacturing Industry* Summer 1992, © 1992, Warren Gorham & Lamont, 31 St. James Avenue, Boston, MA 02116. All rights reserved.

CONVERSION COST AS AN ELEMENT IN STANDARD COSTING

Conversion cost consists of direct labor and manufacturing overhead. The traditional view of separating product cost into three categories (direct material, direct labor, and overhead) is appropriate in a labor-intensive production setting. However, in more highly automated factories, direct labor cost generally represents only a small part of total product cost. In such circumstances, one worker might oversee a large number of machines and often deal with troubleshooting machine malfunctions more than with converting raw material into finished products. These new conditions mean that workers' wages are more closely associated with indirect, than direct, labor.

Many companies have responded to the condition of large overhead costs and small direct labor costs by adapting their standard cost systems to provide for only two elements of product cost: direct material and conversion. In these situations, conversion costs are likely to be separated into their variable and fixed components. Conversion costs may also be separated into direct and indirect categories based on the ability to trace such costs to a machine rather than to a product. Overhead may be applied using a variety of cost drivers including machine hours, cost of material, number of production runs, number of machine setups, or throughput time.

Variance analysis for conversion cost in automated plants normally focuses on the following: (1) spending variances for overhead costs; (2) efficiency variances for machinery and production costs rather than labor costs; and (3) volume variance for production. These types of analyses are similar to the traditional three-variance overhead approach. In an automated system, managers are likely to be able to better control not only the spending and efficiency variances, but also the volume variance. The idea of planned output is essential in a just-in-time system. Variance analysis under a conversion cost approach is illustrated in Exhibit 11–11. Regardless of the method by which variances are computed, managers must analyze those variances and use them for cost control purposes to the extent that such control can be exercised.

Assume that the Smoking Department of Captain's Cannery is fully automated and direct labor is not needed. However, in this example, two highly trained employees monitor all processes by physical and computer observation. These employees are considered indirect labor and are paid a total of $8,925 per month. Variable factory overhead information remains unchanged from Exhibit 11–6.

Because all direct labor is eliminated and no additional variable overhead is involved, the analysis of variable conversion costs shows the same computations as those used to analyze variable overhead. On the other hand, the following analysis

Chrysler has an extremely automated assembly line. One worker can run this entire central control panel, thus eliminating the majority of direct labor cost. Only utilizing direct material and conversion cost categories for standard costing would be very appropriate in such a situation.

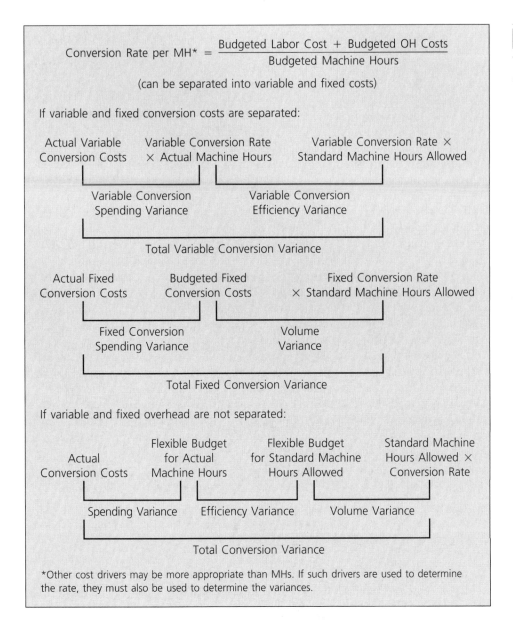

EXHIBIT 11–11

Variances under
Conversion Approach

of fixed conversion costs reflects the newly assumed addition of $8,925 of indirect labor salaries. Assume that the actual amount of indirect labor cost was $9,050; thus, the new actual amount of fixed conversion cost is $29,900 (from Exhibit 11–6) plus the new $9,050.

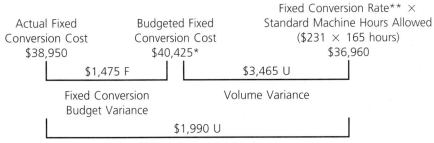

*Original $31,500 of budgeted fixed overhead costs + new $8,925 of salaries
**Fixed Conversion Rate = ($40,425 budgeted fixed conversion cost ÷ 175 hours of move/wait time)
  = $231

REVISITING

Anglo-American Trading Partners (ATP)

In a new-venture enterprise such as ATP, cost awareness and cost control are essential operational elements. Eric Skrmetta and Jon Bard are deeply aware of the competitive environment of food product sales. Costs must be monitored continuously so that profitability remains reasonable.

For direct material costs, the price paid for seafood may vary dramatically by season unless contracts are negotiated; additionally, direct material cost composes the highest proportion of total product cost for many seafood processors. ATP guarantees a fairly stable price by virtue of long-term contracts with suppliers who are in compliance with ATP's quality specifications. The process of smoking salmon has only limited labor involvement, so the direct labor cost per pound can also be viewed as a standard. One large overhead cost for ATP is the depreciation of machinery and equipment, a stable per-month cost. ATP's smoking facility was designed and built directly to specifications by another affiliated company; this interrelationship of organizations allowed ATP to be influential in assessing the cost-benefit relationships of the processing equipment. The other primary overhead cost is that of electricity, a noncontrollable cost that fluctuates in direct response to weather conditions in south Louisiana. Utility cost can, however, be estimated with some degree of accuracy for an annual period. Thus, given the types of costs it has, ATP can easily use a standard cost system for its smoked salmon production activities—allowing company owners a costing method that accounts for completed and partial production in a manner that indicates cost departures from norms.

SOURCE: Interview with Eric Skrmetta and Jon Bard, ATP owners, 1996.

CHAPTER SUMMARY

A standard cost is computed as a standard quantity multiplied by a standard price. In a true standard cost system, standards are derived for quantities and prices of each product component and for each product. A standard cost card provides information about a product's standards for components, processes, quantities, and costs. The material and labor sections of the standard cost card are derived from the bill of materials and the operations flow document, respectively.

A variance is any difference between an actual and a standard cost. A total variance is composed of a price and a usage subvariance. The material subvariances are the price and the quantity variances. The material price variance can be computed on either the quantity of material purchased or the quantity of material used in production. This variance is computed as the quantity measure selected multiplied by the difference between the actual and standard prices. The material quantity variance is the difference between the standard price of the actual quantity of material used and the standard price of the standard quantity of material allowed for the actual output.

The two labor subvariances are the rate and efficiency variances. The labor rate variance indicates the difference between the actual rate paid and the standard rate allowed for the actual hours worked during the period. The labor efficiency variance compares the number of hours actually worked against the standard number of hours allowed for the level of production achieved and multiplies this difference by the standard wage rate.

If separate variable and fixed overhead accounts are kept (or if this information can be generated from the records), two subvariances can be computed for both the variable and fixed overhead cost categories. The subvariances for variable overhead are the VOH spending and VOH efficiency variances. The VOH spending variance is the difference between actual variable overhead cost and budgeted variable overhead based on the actual level of input. The VOH efficiency variance is the difference between budgeted variable overhead at actual activity level and variable overhead applied on the basis of standard input quantity allowed for the production achieved.

The fixed overhead subvariances are the FOH spending and volume variances. The fixed overhead spending variance is equal to actual fixed overhead minus budgeted fixed overhead. The volume variance compares budgeted fixed overhead to applied fixed overhead. Fixed overhead is applied based on a predetermined rate using a selected measure of capacity. Any output capacity utilization actually achieved (measured in standard input quantity allowed), other than the level selected to determine the standard rate, will cause a fixed overhead volume variance to occur.

Depending on the detail available in the accounting records, a variety of overhead variances may be computed. If a combined variable and fixed overhead rate is used, companies may use a one-, two-, or three-variance approach. The one-variance approach provides only a total overhead variance as the difference between actual and applied overhead. The two-variance approach provides information on a budget and a volume variance. The budget variance is calculated as total actual overhead minus total budgeted overhead at the standard input quantity allowed for the production achieved. The volume variance is calculated in the same manner as under the four-variance approach. The three-variance approach calculates an overhead spending variance, overhead efficiency variance, and a volume variance. The spending variance is the difference between total actual overhead and total budgeted overhead at the actual level of activity worked. The efficiency variance is the difference between total budgeted overhead at the actual activity level and total budgeted overhead at the standard input quantity allowed for the production achieved. The volume variance is computed in the same manner as it was using the four-variance approach.

Actual costs are required for external reporting, although standard costs may be used if they approximate actual costs. Adjusting entries are necessary at the end of the period to close the variance accounts. Standards provide a degree of clerical efficiency and assist management in its planning, controlling, decision making, and performance evaluation functions. Standards can also be used to motivate employees if the standards are seen as a goal of expected performance.

A standard cost system should allow management to identify significant variances as close to the time of occurrence as feasible and, if possible, to help determine the variance cause. Significant variances should be investigated to decide whether corrective action is possible and practical. Guidelines for investigation should be developed using the management by exception principle.

Standards should be updated periodically so that they reflect actual economic conditions. Additionally, they should be set at a level to encourage high-quality production, promote cost control, and motivate workers toward production objectives.

Automated manufacturing systems will have an impact on variance computations. One definite impact is the reduction in or elimination of direct labor hours or costs for overhead application. Machine hours, production runs, and number of machine setups are examples of more appropriate activity measures than direct labor hours in an automated factory. Companies may also design their standard cost systems to use only two elements of production cost: direct material and conversion. Variances for conversion under such a system focus on machine or production efficiency rather than on labor efficiency.

APPENDIX

Mix and Yield Variances

The Captain's Cannery example in the chapter used only one type of material and one category of labor in the production of the company's product. Most companies, however, use a combination of many materials and various classifications of direct labor to produce goods. In such settings, the material and labor variance computations presented in the chapter are insufficient.

When a company's product uses more than one material, a goal is to combine those materials in such a way as to produce the desired product quality in the most cost-beneficial manner. Sometimes, materials may be substituted for one another without affecting product quality. In other instances, only one specific material or type of material can be used. For example, a furniture manufacturer might use either oak or maple to build a couch frame and still have the same basic quality. A perfume manufacturer, however, may be able to use only a specific fragrance oil to achieve a desired scent.

Labor, like materials, can be combined in many different ways to make the same product. Some combinations will be less expensive than others; some will be more efficient than others. Again, all potential combinations may not be viable: unskilled laborers would not be able to properly cut Baccarat or Waterford crystal.

Management desires to achieve the most efficient use of labor inputs. As with materials, some amount of interchangeability among labor categories is assumed. Skilled labor is more likely to be substituted for unskilled because interchanging unskilled labor for skilled labor is often not feasible. However, it may not be cost effective to use highly skilled, highly paid workers to do tasks that require little or no training. A rate variance for direct labor is calculated in addition to the mix and yield variances.

mix

Each possible combination of materials or labor is called a **mix.** Management's standards development team sets standards for materials and labor mix based on experience, judgment, and experimentation. Mix standards are used to calculate mix and yield variances for materials and labor. An underlying assumption in product mix situations is that there is potential for substitution among the material and labor components. If this assumption is invalid, changing the mix cannot improve the yield and may even prove wasteful. In addition to mix and yield variances, price and rate variances are still computed for materials and labor.

Captain's Cannery has begun packaging a frozen 1-pound "Gumbo-combo" that contains crab, shrimp, and oysters. This new product is used to illustrate the computations of mix and yield variances. To some extent, one ingredient may be substituted for the other. In addition, it is assumed that the company now uses two direct labor categories (A and B). There is a labor rate differential between these two categories. Exhibit 11–12 provides standard and actual information for the company for December 1996.

Materials Price, Mix, and Yield Variances

materials mix variance

materials yield variance

As stated earlier in the chapter, a material price variance shows the dollar effect of paying prices that differ from the raw material standard. The **materials mix variance** measures the effect of substituting a nonstandard mix of materials during the production process. The **materials yield variance** is the difference between the actual total quantity of input and the standard total quantity allowed based on output; this

EXHIBIT 11–12

Standard and Actual
Information for December
1996

Materials standards for one lot (200 1-pound packages):
  Crab: 60 pounds at $7.20 per pound $ 432
  Shrimp: 90 pounds at $4.50 per pound   405
  Oysters: 50 pounds at $5.00 per pound   250
    Total   200 pounds $1,087

Labor standards for one lot (200 1-pound packages):
  Category A workers: 20 hours at $10.50 per hour $210
  Category B workers: 10 hours at $14.30 per hour   143
    Total   30 hours $353

Actual production and cost data for December:
  Production: 40 lots
  Materials:
    Crab: Purchased and used   2,285.7 pounds at $7.50 per pound
    Shrimp: Purchased and used   3,649.1 pounds at $4.40 per pound
    Oysters: Purchased and used   2,085.2 pounds at $4.95 per pound
      Total   8,020.0 pounds
  Labor:
    Category A   903 hours at $10.50 per hour ($9,481.50)
    Category B   387 hours at $14.35 per hour ($5,553.45)
      Total   1,290 hours

difference reflects standard mix and standard prices. The sum of the materials mix and yield variances equals a material quantity variance similar to the one shown in the chapter; the difference between these two variances is that the sum of the mix and yield variances is attributable to multiple ingredients rather than to a single one. A company can have a mix variance without experiencing a yield variance.

In the Captain's Cannery example, the standard mix of materials is 30 percent (60 pounds of 200 pounds per lot) crab, 45 percent shrimp, and 25 percent oysters. The **yield** of a process is the quantity of output resulting from a specified input. For Captain's Cannery, the yield from 60 pounds of crab, 90 pounds of shrimp, and 50 pounds of oysters is one lot of 200 1-pound packages. Computations for the price, mix, and yield variances are given below in a format similar to the one shown in the chapter:

yield

Captain's Cannery used 8,020 total pounds of ingredients to make 40 lots. The standard quantity necessary to produce this quantity of Gumbo-combo is 8,000 total pounds of ingredients. The actual mix of crab, shrimp, and oysters was 28.5 percent, 45.5 percent, and 26.0 percent, respectively:

Crab   (2,285.7 pounds out of 8,020) = 28.5%
Shrimp   (3,649.1 pounds out of 8,020) = 45.5%
Oysters   (2,085.2 pounds out of 8,020) = 26.0%

EXHIBIT 11-13

Computations for Materials Mix and Yield Variances

(1) Total actual data (mix, quantity, and prices):

Crab—2,285.7 pounds at $7.50	$17,142.75	
Shrimp—3,649.1 pounds at $4.40	16,056.04	
Oysters—2,085.2 pounds at $4.95	10,321.74	$43,520.53

(2) Actual mix and quantity; standard prices:

Crab—2,285.7 pounds at $7.20	$16,457.04	
Shrimp—3,649.1 pounds at $4.50	16,420.95	
Oysters—2,085.2 pounds at $5.00	10,426.00	$43,303.99

(3) Standard mix; actual quantity; standard prices:

Crab—30% × 8,020 pounds × $7.20	$17,323.20	
Shrimp—45% × 8,020 pounds × $4.50	16,240.50	
Oysters—25% × 8,020 pounds × $5.00	10,025.00	$43,588.70

(4) Total standard data (mix, quantity, and prices):

Crab—30% × 8,000 pounds × $7.20	$17,280.00	
Shrimp—45% × 8,000 pounds × $4.50	16,200.00	
Oysters—25% × 8,000 pounds × $5.00	10,000.00	$43,480.00

Computations necessary for the materials variances are shown in Exhibit 11–13. These amounts are then used to compute the variances.

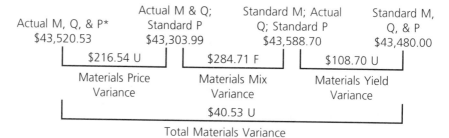

*Note: M = mix, Q = quantity, and P = price

The above computations show a single price variance being calculated for materials. To be more useful to management, separate price variances can be calculated for each material used. For example, the material price variance for crab is $685.71 U ($17,142.75 − $16,457.04), for shrimp $364.91 F ($16,056.04 − $16,420.95), and for oysters $104.26 F ($10,321.74 − $10,426.00). The savings on the shrimp and oysters was less than the added cost for the crab, so the total price variance was unfavorable. Also, less than the standard proportion of the most expensive ingredient (crab) was used, so it is reasonable that there would be a favorable mix variance. The company also experienced an unfavorable yield because total pounds of material allowed for output (8,000) was less than actual total pounds of material used (8,020).

Labor Rate, Mix, and Yield Variances

The two labor categories used by Captain's Cannery are unskilled (A) and skilled (B). When preparing the labor standards, the development team establishes the labor categories required to perform the various tasks and the amount of time each task is expected to take. During production, variances will occur if workers are not paid the standard rate, do not work in the standard mix on tasks, or do not perform those tasks in the standard time.

The labor rate variance is a measure of the cost of paying workers at other than standard rates. The **labor mix variance** is the financial effect associated with chang-

labor mix variance

---

(1) Total actual data (mix, hours, and rates):
      Category A—903 hours at $10.50 $9,481.50
      Category B—387 hours at $14.35   5,553.45 $15,034.95

(2) Actual mix and hours; standard rates:
      Category A—903 hours at $10.50 $9,481.50
      Category B—387 hours at $14.30   5,534.10 $15,015.60

(3) Standard mix; actual hours; standard rates:
      Category A—2/3 × 1,290 × $10.50 $9,030.00
      Category B—1/3 × 1,290 × $14.30   6,149.00 $15,179.00

(4) Total standard data (mix, hours, and rates):
      Category A—2/3 × 1,200 × $10.50 $8,400.00
      Category B—1/3 × 1,200 × $14.30   5,720.00 $14,120.00

EXHIBIT 11–14

Computations for Labor Mix and Yield Variances

ing the proportionate amount of higher- or lower-paid workers in production. The **labor yield variance** reflects the monetary impact of using more or fewer total hours than the standard allowed. The sum of the labor mix and yield variances equals the labor efficiency variance. The diagram for computing labor rate, mix, and yield variances is as follows:

labor yield variance

Actual Mix ×	Actual Mix ×	Standard Mix ×	Standard Mix ×
Actual Hours ×	Actual Hours ×	Actual Hours ×	Standard Hours ×
Actual Rate	Standard Rate	Standard Rate	Standard Rate

   Labor Rate Variance   Labor Mix Variance   Labor Yield Variance

Standard rates are used to make both the mix and yield computations. For Captain's Cannery, the standard mix of A and B labor shown in Exhibit 11–12 is 2/3 and 1/3 (20 hours to 10 hours), respectively. The actual mix is 70 percent (903 of 1,290) (A) and 30 percent (387 of 1,290) (B). Exhibit 11–14 presents the labor computations for Captain's Cannery. Because standard hours to produce one lot of Gumbo-combo were 20 and 10, respectively, for categories A and B labor, the standard hours allowed for the production of 40 lots are 1,200 (800 of A and 400 of B). Using the amounts from Exhibit 11–12, the labor variances for Captain's Cannery are calculated in diagram form:

		Standard M;	
	Actual M & H;	Actual H;	
Actual M, H, & R*	Standard R	Standard R	Standard M, H, & R
$15,034.95	$15,015.60	$15,179.00	$14,120.00

    $19.35 U $163.40 F $1,059 U

  Labor Rate Variance Labor Mix Variance Labor Yield Variance

             $914.95 U

         Total Labor Variance

*Note: M = mix, H = hours, and R = rate

As with material price variances, separate rate variances can be calculated for each class of labor. Because category A does not have a labor rate variance, the total rate variance relates to category B.

The company has saved $163.40 by using the actual mix of labor rather than the standard. A higher proportion of the less-expensive class of labor (category A) than specified in the standard mix was used. One result of substituting a greater proportion of lower-paid workers seems to be that an unfavorable yield occurred because total actual hours (1,290) were greater than standard (1,200).

Because there are trade-offs in mix and yield when component qualities and quantities are changed, management should observe the integrated nature of price, mix, and yield. The effects of changes of one element on the other two need to be considered for cost efficiency and output quality. If mix and yield can be increased by substituting less-expensive resources *while still maintaining quality*, managers and product engineers should change the standards and the proportions of components. If costs are reduced but quality maintained, selling prices could also be reduced to gain a larger market share.

KEY TERMS

bill of materials (p. 451)
budget variance (p. 466)
controllable variance (p. 466)
expected standard (p. 473)
fixed overhead spending variance (p. 464)
ideal standard (p. 474)
labor efficiency variance (p. 460)
labor mix variance (p. 484)
labor rate variance (p. 460)
labor yield variance (p. 485)
material price variance (p. 459)
material quantity variance (p. 459)
materials mix variance (p. 482)
materials yield variance (p. 482)
mix (p. 482)
noncontrollable variance (p. 464)
normal capacity (p. 461)

operations flow document (p. 454)
overhead efficiency variance (p. 466)
overhead spending variance (p. 466)
practical capacity (p. 461)
practical standard (p. 474)
standard cost (p. 450)
standard cost card (p. 455)
standard quantity allowed (p. 457)
theoretical capacity (p. 461)
total overhead variance (p. 465)
total variance (p. 457)
variable overhead efficiency variance (p. 463)
variable overhead spending variance (p. 463)
variance analysis (p. 470)
volume variance (p. 464)
yield (p. 483)

SOLUTION STRATEGIES

ACTUAL COSTS

Direct Material: Actual Price × Actual Quantity Purchased or Used
$$DM: AP \times AQ = AC$$

Direct Labor: Actual Price (Rate) × Actual Quantity of Hours Worked
$$DL: AP \times AQ = AC$$

STANDARD COSTS

Direct Material: Standard Price × Standard Quantity Allowed
$$DM: SP \times SQ = SC$$

Direct Labor: Standard Price (Rate) × Standard Quantity of Hours Allowed
$$DL: SP \times SQ = SC$$

Standard Quantity Allowed: Standard Quantity of Input (SQ) × Actual Quantity of Output Achieved

VARIANCES IN FORMULA FORMAT

The following abbreviations are used:

AFOH = actual fixed overhead

AM = actual mix

AP = actual price or rate

AQ = actual quantity or hours

AVOH = actual variable overhead

BFOH = budgeted fixed overhead (remains at constant amount regardless of activity level as long as within the relevant range)

SM = standard mix

SP = standard price

SQ = standard quantity

TAOH = total actual overhead

$$\text{Material price variance} = (AP \times AQ) - (SP \times AQ)$$
$$\text{Material quantity variance} = (SP \times AQ) - (SP \times SQ)$$
$$\text{Labor rate variance} = (AP \times AQ) - (SP \times AQ)$$
$$\text{Labor efficiency variance} = (SP \times AQ) - (SP \times SQ)$$

Four-variance approach:

Variable OH spending variance = AVOH − (VOH rate × AQ)
Variable OH efficiency variance = (VOH rate × AQ) − (VOH rate × SQ)
Fixed OH spending variance = AFOH − BFOH
Fixed OH volume variance = BFOH − (FOH rate × SQ)

Three-variance approach:

Spending variance = TAOH − [(VOH rate × AQ) + BFOH]
Efficiency variance = [(VOH rate × AQ) + BFOH)] −
   [(VOH rate × SQ) + BFOH]
Volume Variance = [(VOH rate × SQ) + BFOH] − [(VOH rate × SQ) +
   (FOH rate × SQ)] (This is equal to the fixed OH volume variance
   of the four-variance approach.)

Two-variance approach:

Budget variance = TAOH − [(VOH rate × SQ) + BFOH]
Volume variance = [(VOH rate × SQ) + BFOH] − [(VOH rate × SQ) +
   (FOH rate × SQ)] (This is equal to the fixed OH volume variance
   of the four-variance approach.)

One-variance approach:

$$\text{Total OH variance} = TAOH - (\text{Combined OH rate} \times SQ)$$

MULTIPLE MATERIALS:

$$\text{Material price variance} = (AM \times AQ \times AP) - (AM \times AQ \times SP)$$
$$\text{Materials mix variance} = (AM \times AQ \times SP) - (SM \times AQ \times SP)$$
$$\text{Materials yield variance} = (SM \times AQ \times SP) - (SM \times SQ \times SP)$$

MULTIPLE LABOR CATEGORIES:

$$\text{Labor rate variance} = (AM \times AQ \times AP) - (AM \times AQ \times SP)$$
$$\text{Labor mix variance} = (AM \times AQ \times SP) - (SM \times AQ \times SP)$$
$$\text{Labor yield variance} = (SM \times AQ \times SP) - (SM \times SQ \times SP)$$

VARIANCES IN DIAGRAM FORMAT

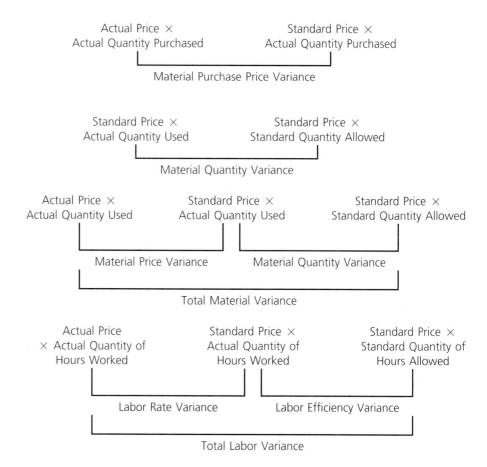

Actual Price ×
Actual Quantity Purchased

Standard Price ×
Actual Quantity Purchased

Material Purchase Price Variance

Standard Price ×
Actual Quantity Used

Standard Price ×
Standard Quantity Allowed

Material Quantity Variance

Actual Price ×
Actual Quantity Used

Standard Price ×
Actual Quantity Used

Standard Price ×
Standard Quantity Allowed

Material Price Variance   Material Quantity Variance

Total Material Variance

Actual Price
× Actual Quantity of
Hours Worked

Standard Price ×
Actual Quantity of
Hours Worked

Standard Price ×
Standard Quantity of
Hours Allowed

Labor Rate Variance   Labor Efficiency Variance

Total Labor Variance

Overhead four-variance approach:

Variable Overhead

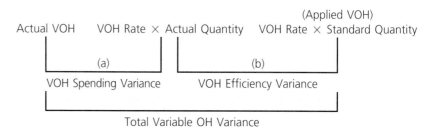

Actual VOH   VOH Rate × Actual Quantity

(Applied VOH)
VOH Rate × Standard Quantity

(a)   (b)

VOH Spending Variance   VOH Efficiency Variance

Total Variable OH Variance

Fixed Overhead

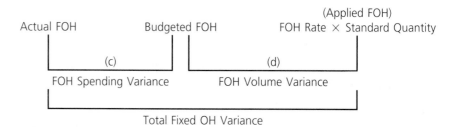

Actual FOH   Budgeted FOH

(Applied FOH)
FOH Rate × Standard Quantity

(c)   (d)

FOH Spending Variance   FOH Volume Variance

Total Fixed OH Variance

Overhead one-, two-, and three-variance approaches:

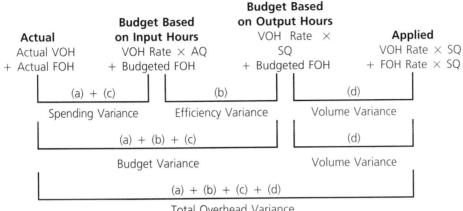

MULTIPLE MATERIALS:

MULTIPLE LABOR CATEGORIES:

Cassidy Toys makes "Slinkos," a plastic, battery-operated toy. The standard material, labor, and overhead costs are as follows:

Direct material: 8 ounces @ $.40 per ounce (or $6.40 per pound)	$3.20
Direct labor: 6 minutes @ $6.60 per hour	.66
Variable overhead: 10 minutes of machine time @ $12.00 per hour	2.00
Fixed overhead: 10 minutes of machine time @ $18.00 per hour	3.00

DEMONSTRATION PROBLEM

The overhead application rates were developed using a practical capacity of 360,000 units per year. Production is assumed to occur evenly throughout the year.

During May 1996, the company produced 31,500 toys. Actual data for May 1996 are as follows:

Direct material purchased: 16,200 pounds @ $7.36 per pound

Direct material used: 15,790 pounds (all from May's purchases)

Total labor cost: $20,587.50 for 3,050 hours

Variable overhead incurred: $61,880 for 5,200 hours of machine time

Fixed overhead incurred: $93,080 for 5,200 hours of machine time

Required:

Calculate the following:

a. Material price variance based on purchases
b. Material quantity variance
c. Labor rate variance
d. Labor efficiency variance
e. Variable overhead spending and efficiency variances
f. Fixed overhead spending and volume variances
g. Overhead variances using a three-variance approach
h. Overhead variances using a two-variance approach
i. Overhead variance using a one-variance approach

Solution to Demonstration Problem

a.

$$AP \times AQ_p \qquad\qquad SP \times AQ_p$$
$$\$7.36 \times 16{,}200 \qquad \$6.40 \times 16{,}200$$
$$\$119{,}232 \qquad\qquad \$103{,}680$$
$$\$15{,}552 \text{ U}$$
$$\text{MPV}$$

b. $SQ = (31{,}500 \times 8 \text{ ounces}) \div 16 \text{ ounces} = 15{,}750 \text{ pounds}$

$$SP \times AQ_u \qquad\qquad SP \times SQ$$
$$\$6.40 \times 15{,}790 \qquad \$6.40 \times 15{,}750$$
$$\$101{,}056 \qquad\qquad \$100{,}800$$
$$\$256 \text{ U}$$
$$\text{MQV}$$

c. & d. $AR = \$20{,}587.50 \div 3{,}050 \text{ hours} = \$6.75 \text{ per hour}$

$SQ = (31{,}500 \times 6 \text{ minutes}) \div 60 \text{ minutes} = 3{,}150 \text{ hours}$

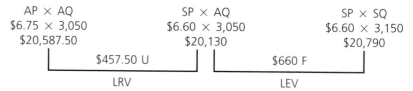

$$AP \times AQ \qquad\qquad SP \times AQ \qquad\qquad SP \times SQ$$
$$\$6.75 \times 3{,}050 \qquad \$6.60 \times 3{,}050 \qquad \$6.60 \times 3{,}150$$
$$\$20{,}587.50 \qquad\qquad \$20{,}130 \qquad\qquad \$20{,}790$$
$$\$457.50 \text{ U} \qquad\qquad\qquad \$660 \text{ F}$$
$$\text{LRV} \qquad\qquad\qquad\qquad \text{LEV}$$

e. $SQ = (31{,}500 \times 10 \text{ minutes}) \div 60 \text{ minutes} = 5{,}250 \text{ hours}$

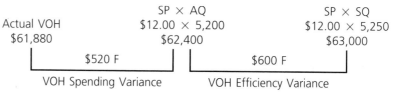

$$\qquad\qquad SP \times AQ \qquad\qquad SP \times SQ$$
$$\text{Actual VOH} \qquad \$12.00 \times 5{,}200 \qquad \$12.00 \times 5{,}250$$
$$\$61{,}880 \qquad\qquad \$62{,}400 \qquad\qquad \$63{,}000$$
$$\$520 \text{ F} \qquad\qquad\qquad \$600 \text{ F}$$
$$\text{VOH Spending Variance} \qquad \text{VOH Efficiency Variance}$$

f. $BFOH = (360{,}000 \text{ toys per year} \times 10 \text{ minutes}) \div 60 \text{ minutes} = 60{,}000 \text{ MHs}$
per year; $60{,}000 \text{ MHs} \times \$18 \text{ per hour} = \$1{,}080{,}000 \text{ annual FOH};$
$\$1{,}080{,}000 \div 12 \text{ months} = \$90{,}000 \text{ per month}$

$SQ = (31{,}500 \times 10 \text{ minutes}) \div 60 \text{ minutes} = 5{,}250 \text{ hours}$

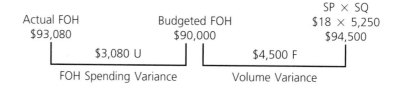

$$\qquad\qquad\qquad\qquad\qquad\qquad\qquad SP \times SQ$$
$$\text{Actual FOH} \qquad \text{Budgeted FOH} \qquad \$18 \times 5{,}250$$
$$\$93{,}080 \qquad\qquad \$90{,}000 \qquad\qquad \$94{,}500$$
$$\$3{,}080 \text{ U} \qquad\qquad\qquad \$4{,}500 \text{ F}$$
$$\text{FOH Spending Variance} \qquad\qquad \text{Volume Variance}$$

g., h., and i. Combined overhead application rate = $12 + $18 = $30 per MH
SQ = (31,500 × 10 minutes) ÷ 60 minutes = 5,250 hours

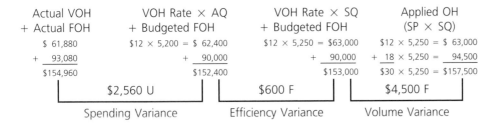

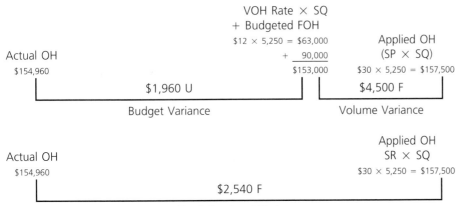

1. What are the three primary uses of a standard cost system? In a business that routinely manufactures the same products or performs the same services, why would standards be helpful?

2. The standards development team should be composed of what experts? Why are these people included?

3. Discuss the development of standards for a material. How is the quality standard established for a material?

4. What is a standard cost card? What information is contained on it? How does it relate to a bill of materials and an operations flow document?

5. Why are the quantities shown in the bill of materials not always the same quantities that are shown in the standard cost card?

6. A total variance may be calculated for each cost component of a product. Into what variances can this total be separated and to what does each relate? (Discuss separately for material and labor.)

7. What is meant by the term *standard hours allowed?* Does the term refer to inputs or outputs?

8. Why are the overhead spending and overhead efficiency variances said to be controllable? Is the volume variance controllable? Why or why not?

9. How are actual and standard costs recorded in a standard cost system?

10. "Unfavorable variances will always have debit balances, whereas favorable variances will always have credit balances." Is this statement true or false? Why?

11. How are immaterial variances closed at the end of an accounting period? How are significant variances closed at the end of an accounting period? Why is there a difference in treatment?

12. What is meant by the process of "management by exception?" How is a standard cost system helpful in such a process?

13. Discuss the three types of standards with regard to the level of rigor of attainment. Why are some companies currently adopting the most rigorous standard?

14. Why may traditional methods of setting standards lead to less than desirable material resource management and employee behavior?

15. Why do managers care about the utilization of capacity? Are they controlling costs when they control utilization?

16. How are variances used by managers in their efforts to control costs?

17. Fixed overhead costs are generally incurred in lump-sum amounts. What implications does this have for control of fixed overhead?

18. Can combined overhead rates be used for control purposes? Are such rates more or less appropriate than separate overhead rates? Why or why not?

19. Which overhead variance approach (two-variance, three-variance, or four-variance) provides the most information for cost control purposes?

20. Why are some companies replacing the two traditional cost categories of direct labor and manufacturing overhead with a "conversion cost" category?

21. How has automation affected standard costing? How has automation affected the computation of variances?

22. (Appendix) What variances can be computed for direct material and direct labor when some materials or labor inputs are substitutes for others? What information does each of these variances provide?

EXERCISES

23. (Direct material variances) Leisure Furniture makes wrought iron table and chair sets. During April 1996, the purchasing agent bought 17,600 pounds of scrap iron at $.89 per pound. Each set requires a standard quantity of 70 pounds at a standard cost of $.85 per pound. During April, the company used 16,940 pounds and produced 250 sets.
   a. For April, compute the direct material price variance (based on the quantity purchased) and the direct material quantity variance.
   b. Identify the titles of individuals in the firm who would be responsible for each of the variances.
   c. Identify some potential explanations for the variances computed in part a.

24. (Direct material variances) In August 1996, Westwego Company's costs and amounts of paper consumed in manufacturing its 1997 Executive Planner and Calendar were as follow:

Actual unit purchase price	$.16 per page
Standard quantity allowed for good production	195,800 pages
Actual quantity purchased during August	230,000 pages
Actual quantity used in August	200,000 pages
Standard unit price	$.15 per page

   a. Calculate the total cost of purchases for August.
   b. Compute the material price variance (based on quantity purchased).
   c. Calculate the material quantity variance.

25. *(Direct labor variances)* Prefab Construction Inc. builds standard prefabricated wooden frames for apartment walls. The standard quantity of direct labor is 3.5 hours for each frame at an average standard hourly wage of $14.50. During May 1996, the company produced 520 frames. The payroll records indicated that the carpenters worked 1,950 hours and earned $27,885.
   a. What were the standard hours allowed for May construction?
   b. Calculate the direct labor variances.

26. *(Direct labor variances)* In auditing the inventory account of a client, the accounting firm of Porter & Co., CPAs, set the following standard: 200 hours at an hourly rate of $24.50. The firm actually worked 190 hours auditing inventory. The total labor variance for the inventory audit was $40 unfavorable.
   a. Compute the total actual payroll.
   b. Compute the labor efficiency variance.
   c. Compute the labor rate variance.
   d. Offer a brief explanation that is consistent with the two variances.

27. *(Direct material and direct labor variances)* Lisa Scamponi Ltd. produces evening bags. In December 1996, Ms. Scamponi, president of the company, received the following information from Antonio Buffa, the new controller, in regard to November production:

Production during month	1,200 handbags
Actual cost of material purchased and used	$4,767.18
Standard material allowed	1/3 square yard per bag
Material quantity variance	$594 U
Actual hours worked	2,520
Standard labor time per handbag	2 hours
Labor rate variance	$630 F
Standard labor rate per hour	$7
Standard price per yard of material	$8

Ms. Scamponi asked Mr. Buffa to provide her with the following specific information:
   a. The standard quantity of material allowed for November production
   b. The standard direct labor hours allowed for November production
   c. The material price variance
   d. The labor efficiency variance
   e. The standard prime (direct material and direct labor) cost to produce one bag
   f. The actual cost to produce one bag in November
   g. An explanation for the difference between standard and actual cost. Be sure the explanation is consistent with the pattern of the variances.

28. *(Missing information for materials and labor)* For each of the independent cases, fill in the missing figures.

	CASE A	CASE B	CASE C	CASE D
Units produced	800	?	240	1,500
Standard hours per unit	3	.8	?	?
Standard hours allowed	?	600	480	?
Standard rate per hour	$7	?	$9.50	$6
Actual hours worked	2,330	675	?	4,875
Actual labor cost	?	?	$4,560	$26,812.50
Labor rate variance	$466F	$1,080F	$228U	?
Labor efficiency variance	?	$780U	?	$2,250U

29. *(Four-variance approach; journal entries)* For 1996, Phelps Manufacturing has set 120,000 direct labor hours as the annual capacity measure for computing its predetermined variable overhead rate. At that level, budgeted variable overhead costs are $540,000. The company has decided to apply fixed overhead on the basis of machine hours. Total budgeted annual machine hours are 6,600 and annual budgeted fixed overhead is $118,800. Both machine hours and fixed overhead costs are expected to be incurred evenly each month.

During March 1996, Phelps incurred 9,800 direct labor hours and 500 machine hours. Variable and fixed overhead were, respectively, $42,350 and $10,500. The standard times allowed for March production were 9,910 direct labor hours and 480 machine hours.

a. Using the four-variance approach, determine the overhead variances for March 1996.

b. Prepare all journal entries for Phelps Manufacturing for March 1996.

30. *(Computation of all variances)* The manager of the Automobile Registration Division of the State of Louisiana has determined that it typically takes 30 minutes for the department's employees to register a new car. The following predetermined overhead costs are applicable to Orleans Parish. Fixed overhead, computed on an estimated 4,000 direct labor hours, is $8 per DLH. Variable overhead is estimated at $3 per DLH.

During July 1996, 7,600 cars were registered in Orleans Parish, taking 3,700 direct labor hours. For the month, variable overhead was $10,730 and fixed overhead was $29,950.

a. Compute overhead variances using a four-variance approach.

b. Compute overhead variances using a three-variance approach.

c. Compute overhead variances using a two-variance approach.

31. *(Missing data, three-variance approach)* The flexible budget formula for total overhead for the Compass Division of Maritime Products Company is $360,000 + $8 per direct labor hour. The combined overhead rate is $20 per direct labor hour. The following data have been recorded for the year:

Actual total overhead for 1997	$580,000
Total overhead spending variance	$ 16,000 U
Volume variance	$ 24,000 U

Use a three-variance approach to determine the following:

a. Number of standard hours allowed

b. Actual hours of direct labor worked

32. *(Variances and cost control)* Windfall Company applies overhead on a direct labor hour basis. Each unit of product requires 5 direct labor hours. Overhead is applied on a 30 percent variable and 70 percent fixed basis; the overhead application rate is $16 per hour. Standards are based on a normal monthly capacity of 5,000 direct labor hours.

During September 1996, Windfall produced 1,010 units of product and incurred 4,900 direct labor hours. Actual overhead cost for the month was $80,000.

a. What were standard hours allowed for September?

b. What is total annual budgeted fixed overhead cost?

c. What is the controllable overhead variance?

d. What is the noncontrollable overhead variance?

33. *(Journal entries)* Thurston Custom Floors had the following balances in its trial balance at year-end 1996:

	DEBIT	CREDIT
Direct Material Inventory	$ 36,600	
Work in Process Inventory	43,920	
Finished Goods Inventory	65,880	
Cost of Goods Sold	585,600	
Material Price Variance	7,250	
Material Quantity Variance		$10,925
Labor Rate Variance		1,200
Labor Efficiency Variance	4,390	
VOH Spending Variance		3,600
VOH Efficiency Variance	200	
FOH Spending Variance	650	
Volume Variance	1,375	

Assume that the variances, taken together, are believed to be significant. Prepare the journal entries to dispose of the variances.

34. *(Variances and conversion cost category)* Kansas Brass makes small brass statues. Until recently, the company used a standard cost system and applied overhead to production based on direct labor hours. The company automated its facilities in March 1996 and revamped its accounting system so that there are only two cost categories: direct material and conversion costs. Estimated variable conversion costs for April 1996 were $85,000, and estimated fixed conversion costs were $38,000; machine hours were estimated at 10,000 for April. Expected output for April was 5,000 statues. In April, the firm actually used 9,000 machine hours in making 4,800 statues. The firm incurred conversion costs totaling $115,000; $75,000 of this amount was variable cost.
   a. Using the four-variance approach, compute the variances for conversion costs in April.
   b. Evaluate the effectiveness of the firm in controlling costs in April.

35. *(Appendix)* Salem Corporation produces 12-ounce cans of mixed pecans and cashews. Standard and actual information is shown below.

Standard quantities and costs (12-oz. can):

Pecans: 6 ounces at $3.00 per pound	$1.125
Cashews: 6 ounces at $4.00 per pound	1.500

Actual quantities and costs for February 1996 when production was 18,000, 12-oz. cans:

Pecans: 7,473 pounds at $2.90 per pound

Cashews: 6,617 pounds at $4.25 per pound

Determine the materials price, mix, and yield variances.

36. *(Appendix)* Apex Mechanical Systems is a mechanical engineering firm. The firm employs both engineers and draftspeople. The average hourly rates are $40 for engineers and $20 for draftspeople. For one project, the standard was set at 750 hours of engineer time and 1,250 hours of draftsperson time. Actual hours worked on this project were:

Engineers—1,000 hours at $42.50 per hour

Draftspeople—1,000 hours at $21.00 per hour

Determine the labor rate, mix, and yield variances for this project.

37. *(Developing standard cost card and discussion)* The Frozen Fruitcup Company is a small producer of fruit-flavored frozen desserts. For many years, Frozen Fruitcup products have had strong regional sales on the basis of brand recognition; however, other companies have begun marketing similar products in the area, and price competition has become increasingly important. Tanya Morse, the company's controller, is planning to implement a standard cost system for Frozen Fruitcup and has gathered considerable information from her coworkers on production and material requirements for the company's products. Morse believes that the use of standard costing will allow the firm to improve cost control and make better pricing decisions.

Frozen Fruitcup's most popular product is raspberry sherbet. The sherbet is produced in 10-gallon batches, and each batch requires 6 quarts of good raspberries. The fresh raspberries are sorted by hand before they enter the production process. Because of imperfections in the raspberries and normal spoilage, 1 quart of berries is discarded for every 4 quarts of acceptable berries. The standard direct labor time is 3 minutes for the sorting that is required to obtain 1 quart of acceptable raspberries. The acceptable raspberries are then blended with the other ingredients; blending requires 12 minutes of direct labor time per batch. During blending, there is some loss of material. After blending, the sherbet is packaged in quart containers. Morse has gathered the following cost information.

- Frozen Fruitcup purchases raspberries at a cost of $.80 per quart.
- All other ingredients cost a total of $.45 per gallon.
- Direct labor is paid at the rate of $9.00 per hour.
- The total cost of material and labor required to package the sherbet is $.38 per quart.

a. Develop the standard cost for the direct cost components of a 10-gallon batch of raspberry sherbet. The standard cost should identify the standard quantity, the standard rate, and the standard cost per batch for each direct cost component of a batch of raspberry sherbet.

b. As part of the implementation of a standard cost system at the company, Morse plans to train those responsible for maintaining the standards on how to use variance analysis. She is particularly concerned with the causes of unfavorable variances.

   1. Discuss the possible causes of unfavorable material price variances, and identify the individual(s) who should be held responsible for these variances.

   2. Discuss the possible causes of unfavorable labor efficiency variances, and identify the individual(s) who should be held responsible for these variances.

(CMA)

38. *(Behavioral implications of standard costing)* Contact a local company that uses a standard cost system. Make an appointment with a manager at that company to interview him or her on the following issues.

- The characteristics that should be present in a standard cost system to encourage positive employee motivation.
- How a standard cost system should be implemented to positively motivate employees.
- What "management by exception" is and how variance analysis often results in "management by exception."
- How employee behavior could be adversely affected when "actual to standard" comparisons are used as the basis for performance evaluation.

Prepare a paper and an oral presentation based on your interview.

39. *(Variances and cost control)* Hillsdale Inc. planned to produce at the 4,000-unit level for its single type of product. Because of unexpected demand, the firm actually operated at the 4,400-unit level. The company's flexible budget appears as follows:

	3,000 UNITS	**4,000 UNITS**	**5,000 UNITS**
OVERHEAD COSTS:			
Variable	$12,000	$16,000	$20,000
Fixed	8,000	8,000	8,000
Total	$20,000	$24,000	$28,000

ACTUAL COSTS INCURRED IN PRODUCING THE 4,400 UNITS:

Variable	$17,160
Fixed	8,200
Total	$25,360

The production manager was upset because the company planned to incur $24,000 of costs and actual costs were $25,360. Prepare a memo to the production manager regarding the following questions.

a. Was it correct to compare the $25,360 to the $24,000 for cost control purposes?

b. Analyze the costs and explain where the company did well and/or did poorly in controlling its costs.

40. *(Standard setting; team project)* As a four-person team, choose an activity that is commonly performed every day, such as taking a shower/bath, preparing a meal, or doing homework. Have each team member time himself/herself performing that activity for 2 days and then develop a standard time for the team. Now have the team members time themselves performing the same activity for the next 5 days.

a. Using an assumed hourly wage rate of $6, calculate the labor efficiency variance for your team.

b. Prepare a list of reasons for the variance.

c. How could some of the variance causes be avoided?

41. *(Cost control evaluation)* The Costa Mesa Concrete Company makes precast concrete steps for use with manufactured housing. The plant had the following 1996 budget based on expected production of 3,200 units:

	STANDARD COST	**AMOUNT BUDGETED**
Direct material	$22.00	$ 70,400
Direct labor	12.00	38,400
VARIABLE OVERHEAD:		
Indirect material	4.20	13,440
Indirect labor	1.75	5,600
Utilities	1.00	3,200
FIXED OVERHEAD:		
Supervisory salaries		40,000
Depreciation		15,000
Insurance		9,640
Total		$195,680

Cost per unit = $195,680 ÷ 3,200 = $61.15

Actual production for 1996 was 3,500 units, and actual costs for the year were as follows:

Direct material used	$ 80,500
Direct labor	42,300

VARIABLE OVERHEAD:

Indirect material	14,000
Indirect labor	6,650
Utilities	3,850

FIXED OVERHEAD:

Supervisory salaries	41,000
Depreciation	15,000
Insurance	8,800
Total	$212,100

Cost per unit = $212,100 ÷ 3,500 = $60.60

The plant manager, John Wessly, whose annual bonus includes (among other factors) 20 percent of the net favorable cost variances, states that he saved the company $1,925 [($61.15 − $60.60) × 3,500]. He has instructed the plant cost accountant to prepare a detailed report to be sent to corporate headquarters comparing each component's actual per-unit cost with the per-unit amounts set forth above in the annual budget to prove the $1,925 cost savings.

a. Is the actual-to-budget comparison proposed by Wessly an appropriate one? If Wessly's comparison is not appropriate, prepare a more appropriate comparison.

b. How would you, as the plant cost accountant, react if Wessly insisted on his comparison? Suggest what alternatives are available to you.

42. *(Appendix)* Wisnowski & Coffin has three labor classes: secretaries, paralegals, and attorneys. The standard wage rates are shown in the standard cost system as follows: secretaries, $11 per hour; paralegals, $18 per hour; and attorneys, $44 per hour. The firm has established a standard of .5 hours of secretarial time and 2 hours of paralegal time for each hour of attorney time in probate cases. The actual direct labor hours worked on probate cases and the standard hours allowed for the work accomplished for one month in 1996 were as follows:

	ACTUAL DLHS	STANDARD HOURS FOR OUTPUT ACHIEVED
Secretarial	500	500
Paralegal	1,800	2,000
Attorney	1,100	1,000

a. Calculate the amount of the direct labor efficiency variance for the month and decompose the total into the following components:
   1. Direct labor mix variance
   2. Direct labor yield variance

b. Prepare a memo addressing whether management used an efficient mix of labor.

(CMA adapted)

PROBLEMS

43. *(Material and labor variances)* Savannah Boat Company uses a standard cost system for materials and labor in producing fishing boats. Production requires three materials: fiberglass, paint, and a prepurchased trim package. The standard costs and quantities for materials and labor are as follows:

STANDARDS FOR 1 FISHING BOAT

1,200 pounds of fiberglass @ $.80 per pound	$ 960
2 quarts gel coat paint @ $60.00 per gallon	30
1 trim package	165
40 hours of labor @ $12.00 per hour	480
Prime standard cost	$1,635

During July 1996, the company had the following actual data related to the production of 100 boats:

MATERIAL PURCHASED:

Fiberglass—130,000 pounds @ $.79 per pound
Paint—60 gallons @ $55.50 per gallon
Trim packages—100 @ $175 per package

MATERIAL USED:

Fiberglass—125,000 pounds
Paint—54 gallons
Trim packages—105

DIRECT LABOR USED:

4,250 hours @ $11.50 per hour

Calculate the material and labor variances for Savannah Boat Company for July 1996. Base the material price variance on the quantity of material purchased.

44. *(Variance calculation and journal entries)* Quebec Ltd. makes small plastic toys. Following are standard quantities and standard costs for material and labor.

	STANDARD QUANTITY	STANDARD COST
Material	1/4 pound	$2 per pound ($.50 per unit of output)
Labor	12 minutes	$8 per hour ($1.60 per unit of output)

During October 1996, 100,000 toys were produced. The purchasing agent bought 29,000 pounds of material during the month at $1.88 per pound. October payroll for the factory revealed direct labor cost of $165,240 on 20,400 direct labor hours. During the month, 24,800 pounds of raw material were used in production.

a. Compute material and labor variances, basing the material price variance on the quantity of material purchased.
b. Assuming a perpetual inventory system, prepare general journal entries for the month.

45. *(Incomplete data)* Freeport Surgical Supply manufactures latex surgical gloves. It takes .85 square feet of latex to manufacture a pair of gloves. The standard price for material is $.60 per square foot. Most processing is done by machine; the only labor required is for operators, who are paid $10.50 per hour. The machines can produce 400 pairs of gloves per hour.

During one week in May, Freeport Surgical produced 20,000 pairs of gloves and experienced a $180 unfavorable material quantity variance. The company had purchased 2,000 more square feet of material than it used in production that week, producing a favorable price variance of $946. Based on 42 total actual labor hours to produce the gloves, a $21 favorable total labor variance was generated.

Determine the following amounts:
a. Standard quantity of material allowed
b. Actual quantity of material used
c. Actual quantity of material purchased
d. Actual price of material purchased

e. Standard hours allowed for production
f. Labor efficiency variance
g. Labor rate variance
h. Actual labor rate

46. *(Incomplete data)* Nevada Learning Aids makes wooden lap desks. A small fire on October 1 partially destroyed the books and records relating to September's production. The charred remains of the standard cost card appears below.

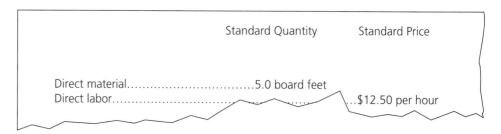

	Standard Quantity	Standard Price
Direct material	5.0 board feet	
Direct labor		$12.50 per hour

From other fragments of records and several discussions with employees, you learn the following:
1. The standard quantity of material used in September was 4,000 board feet.
2. The September payroll for direct labor was $19,220 based on 1,550 actual hours worked.
3. The production supervisor distinctly remembered being held accountable for 50 more hours of direct labor than should have been worked. She was upset because top management failed to consider that she saved several hundred board feet of material by creative efforts that required extra time.
4. The purchasing agent's files showed that 4,300 board feet had been purchased and consumed in September for $2.05 per board foot. She was proud of the fact that this price was $.05 below standard cost per foot.

a. How many units were produced during September?
b. Calculate all variances for direct material and direct labor for September.
c. What is the standard number of hours allowed for the production of each unit?
d. Prepare general journal entries reflecting direct material and direct labor activity and variances for September, assuming a standard cost, perpetual inventory system.

47. *(Adjusting standards)* Maui Muumuus manufactures traditional Hawaiian dresses. The company was started early in 1990, and the following standards for materials and labor were developed at that time:

Materials	3 yards at $6 per yard
Labor	1.5 hours at $10 per hour

In May 1996, Maui Muumuus hired a new cost accountant, Sally Rogers. At the end of May, Sally was reviewing the variances calculated for the month and was amazed to find that standards had never been revised since the company started. Actual data for May 1996 for material and labor are as follows:

Materials	Purchased, 50,000 yards at $7.00
	Used in production of 17,200 muumuus, 50,000 yards
Labor	17,800 hours at $13.50 per hour

Since 1990, material prices have risen 4 percent each year. However, the company can now buy at 94 percent of regular price due to the increased volume of purchases. Labor contracts have specified a 5 percent cost-of-living adjustment for each year, beginning in 1991. Because of revising the plant layout and purchasing some more efficient machinery, the labor time per muumuu has decreased by one-third; also, direct material waste has been reduced from 1/4 yard to 1/8 yard per muumuu.

a. Determine the material and labor variances based on the standards originally designed for the company.

b. Determine the new standards against which Sally should measure the May 1996 results. (Round adjustments annually to the nearest penny.)

c. Compute the variances for material and labor using the revised standards.

48. *(Calculation of four variances)* Deidra's Hattery utilizes a standard cost system. Data for October are presented below:

STANDARD COST PER UNIT (1 UNIT TAKES 1 HOUR)	
Direct materials	$ 4.00
Direct labor	7.00
Variable overhead	2.00
Fixed overhead	4.00
Total	$17.00

The fixed overhead charge is based on an expected monthly capacity of 5,000 units, but due to a fire on the production floor, the company only produced 3,500 units. Actual variable overhead was $8,000 and actual fixed overhead was $19,000. The company recorded 4,000 direct labor hours for the month.

a. Compute and compare the actual overhead cost per unit with the expected overhead cost per unit.

b. Calculate overhead variances using the four-variance method.

49. *(Four-variance approach; journal entries)* Brimson Lumber produces picnic tables, swings, and benches and uses direct labor hours to apply overhead. Standard hours allowed for each product are as follows:

Picnic table:	10 standard direct labor hours
Swing:	3 standard direct labor hours
Bench:	12 standard direct labor hours

The standard variable overhead rate is $4 per direct labor hour; the standard fixed overhead application rate at expected annual capacity is $2 per direct labor hour. Expected capacity on a monthly basis is 3,000 direct labor hours.

Production for June 1996 was 100 picnic tables, 400 swings, and 60 benches. Actual direct labor hours incurred were 3,020. Actual variable overhead was $11,900, and actual fixed overhead was $6,100 for the month.

a. Prepare a variance analysis using the four-variance approach. (*Hint:* Convert the production of each type of product into standard hours allowed for all work accomplished for the month.)

b. Prepare journal entries for (1) incurring overhead costs, (2) applying overhead costs, and (3) closing the variance accounts (assume *immaterial* variances).

c. Evaluate the effectiveness of managers in controlling costs.

50. *(Variance analysis with unknowns)* ATTENTION Products manufactures a neon lamp sign with the following standard conversion costs:

Direct labor (2 hours @ $6 per hour)	$12
Factory overhead (10,000 DLH expected capacity)	
Variable (2 hours @ $4 per hour)	8
Fixed (2 hours @ $2 per hour)	4
Total unit conversion cost	$24

The following data are given for December, when 8,000 standard labor hours were used:

Labor rate variance	$ 4,500 U
Labor efficiency variance	6,000 U
Actual variable overhead	$32,300
Actual total overhead	$60,000

Calculate the answers for the following unknowns:
a. Total applied factory overhead
b. Volume variance
c. Variable overhead spending variance
d. Variable overhead efficiency variance
e. Actual fixed overhead
f. Number of units manufactured

51. *(Combined overhead rates)* Vancouver Production manufactures a down-filled sleeping bag with the following standard cost information for 1996:
   - Each sleeping bag requires 3 hours of machine time to produce.
   - Variable overhead: $3 per machine hour
   - Fixed overhead: $2.50 per machine hour; calculated as total budgeted overhead divided by expected annual capacity of 50,000 machine hours

   PRODUCTION STATISTICS FOR 1996 WERE:

Number of sleeping bags produced	21,000 units
Actual machine hours	62,200 hours
Variable overhead cost incurred	$189,710
Fixed overhead cost incurred	$132,200

   a. Using a combined overhead rate, calculate variances according to the two-variance approach.
   b. Using a combined overhead rate, calculate variances according to the three-variance approach.

52. *(Comprehensive)* Zenith Corporation manufactures metal screen doors for commercial buildings. The standard costs per screen door follow:

   DIRECT MATERIALS:

Aluminum	4 sheets at $2	$ 8
Copper	3 sheets at $4	12
Direct labor	7 hours at $8	56
Variable overhead	5 machine hours at $3	15
Fixed overhead	5 machine hours at $2	10

   Overhead rates were based on normal monthly capacity of 6,000 machine hours.

   During November, 850 doors were produced. This was below normal levels due to the effects of a labor strike that occurred during union contract negotiations. Once the dispute was settled, the company scheduled overtime to try to catch up to regular production levels. The following costs were incurred in November:

   MATERIAL:

   Aluminum: 4,000 sheets purchased at $2; used 3,500 sheets
   Copper: 3,000 sheets purchased at $4.20; used 2,600 sheets

   DIRECT LABOR:

   Regular time: 5,200 hours at $8.00 (precontract settlement)
   Regular time: 900 hours at $8.50 (postcontract settlement)

   VARIABLE OVERHEAD:

   $11,700 (based on 4,175 machine hours)

   FIXED OVERHEAD:

   $9,300 (based on 4,175 machine hours)

Determine the following:

a. Total material price variance
b. Total material usage (quantity) variance
c. Labor rate variance
d. Labor efficiency variance
e. Variable overhead spending variance
f. Variable overhead efficiency variance
g. Fixed overhead spending variance
h. Fixed overhead volume variance
i. Budget variance

53. *(Comprehensive; all variances; all methods)* Degas Painting Services Inc. paints interiors of residences and commercial structures. The firm's management has established cost standards based on the amount of area to be painted.

Direct material ($18 per gallon of paint): $1.50 per 100 square feet

Direct labor: $2 per 100 square feet

Variable overhead: $0.60 per 100 square feet

Fixed overhead (based on 600,000 square feet per month): $1.25 per 100 square feet

Management has determined that 400 square feet can be painted by the average worker each hour. During May 1996, the company painted 600,000 square feet of wall and ceiling space. The following costs were incurred:

Direct material (450 gallons purchased and used)	$ 8,550.00
Direct labor (1,475 hours)	12,242.50
Variable overhead	3,420.00
Fixed overhead	7,740.00

a. Compute the direct material variances.
b. Compute the direct labor variances.
c. Use a four-variance approach to compute overhead variances.
d. Use a three-variance approach to compute overhead variances.
e. Use a two-variance approach to compute overhead variances.
f. Reconcile your answers for parts c through e.
g. Discuss other cost drivers that could be used as a basis for measuring activity and computing variances for this company.

54. *(Variance disposition)* Ito Manufacturing had the following variances at year-end 1996:

Material price variance	$ 7,800 U
Material quantity variance	8,300 F
Labor rate variance	1,750 F
Labor efficiency variance	12,300 U
Variable overhead spending variance	1,000 U
Variable overhead efficiency variance	600 F
Fixed overhead spending variance	2,200 F
Volume variance	5,600 U

In addition, the inventory and cost of goods sold account balances were as follows at year-end 1996:

Raw Material Inventory	$112,931
Work in Process Inventory	304,759
Finished Goods Inventory	221,221
Cost of Goods Sold	908,089

a. Assuming that all variances are insignificant, prepare the journal entry at December 31 to dispose of them.
b. After posting your entry in part a, what is the balance in Cost of Goods Sold?

c. Assuming that all variances are significant, prepare the necessary journal entries at December 31 to dispose of them.

d. What will be the balance in each of the inventory accounts and cost of goods sold account?

55. *(Conversion cost variances)* Guillermo Company budgeted $720,000 of variable conversion costs and $180,000 of fixed conversion costs for May 1996. When the budget was developed, Guillermo estimated 144,000 machine hours would be required to make 48,000 units of product. During May, 152,000 machine hours were worked and the firm incurred $752,400 of variable conversion costs and $187,000 of fixed conversion costs. Fifty thousand units were produced in May.

a. Calculate the four conversion cost variances assuming separation of fixed and variable costs is maintained.

b. Calculate the three conversion cost variances assuming fixed and variable costs are combined.

56. *(Appendix)* Dominic's three-topping 18-inch frozen pizzas are produced by Lira Enterprises in Newark, New Jersey. The company uses a standard cost system. The three toppings (in addition to cheese) for each pizza are onions, olives, and mushrooms. To some extent, discretion may be used to determine the actual mix of these toppings. The company has two classes of labor, and discretion may be used to some extent to determine the mix of the labor inputs. The standard cost card for a pizza follows:

Onions: 3 ounces at $.10 per ounce

Olives: 3 ounces at $.35 per ounce

Mushrooms: 3 ounces at $.50 per ounce

Labor category 1: 5 minutes at $12 per hour

Labor category 2: 6 minutes at $8 per hour

During May 1996, Lira Enterprises produced 12,000 pizzas and used the following inputs:

Onions:	2,000 pounds
Olives:	3,000 pounds
Mushrooms:	2,000 pounds
Labor category 1:	1,300 hours
Labor category 2:	1,000 hours

During the month there were no deviations from standards on material prices or labor rates.

a. Determine the materials quantity, mix, and yield variances.

b. Determine the labor efficiency, mix, and yield variances.

c. Prepare the journal entries to record the above mix and yield variances.

57. *(Appendix)* Jackson Products makes NOTAM, a new health food. For a 50-pound batch, the standard costs for materials and labor are as follows:

	QUANTITY	UNIT PRICE	TOTAL
Wheat	25 pounds	$ .20 per pound	$5.00
Barley	25 pounds	$ .10 per pound	2.50
Corn	10 pounds	$ .05	.50
Skilled labor	.8 hours	$12.00 per hour	9.60
Unskilled labor	.2 hours	$ 8.00 per hour	1.60

During June, the following materials and labor were used in producing 600 batches of NOTAM:

Wheat	18,000 pounds at $.22 per pound
Barley	14,000 pounds at $.11 per pound
Corn	10,000 pounds at $.04 per pound
Skilled labor	400 hours at $12.25 per hour
Unskilled labor	260 hours at $8.00 per hour

a. Calculate the materials quantity, mix, and yield variances.
b. Calculate the labor efficiency, mix, and yield variances.

CASES

58. *(Standards revision)* NuLathe Company produces a component for aircraft manufacturers. A standard cost system has been used for years with good results. Unfortunately, NuLathe's original direct material source went out of business. The new source produces a similar but higher quality material. The price per pound from the original source averaged $7; the price from the new source is $7.77. The new material reduces scrap and, thus, reduces the use of direct material from 1.25 to 1.00 pounds per unit. In addition, direct labor is reduced from 24 to 22 minutes per unit because there is less scrap labor and machine setup time.

The direct material problem was occurring at the same time that labor negotiations resulted in an increase of over 14 percent in hourly direct labor costs. The average rate rose from $12.60 per hour to $14.40 per hour. Production of the main product requires a high level of labor skill. Because of a continuing shortage in that skill area, an interim wage agreement had to be signed.

NuLathe started using the new direct material on April 1, the same date that the new labor agreement went into effect. However, the company is still using standards that were set at the beginning of the calendar year. The direct material and direct labor standards for the turbo engine component are as follows:

Direct material	1.2 pounds at $6.80 per pound	$ 8.16
Direct labor	20 minutes at $12.30 per DLH	4.10
Standard prime cost per unit		$12.26

Howard Foster, cost accounting supervisor, had been examining the following April 30 performance report.

PERFORMANCE REPORT			
STANDARD COST VARIANCE ANALYSIS FOR APRIL 1996			
STANDARD	PRICE VARIANCE	QUANTITY VARIANCE	ACTUAL
DM $ 8.16	($.97 × 1.0) $.97 U	($6.80 × .2) $1.36 F	$ 7.77
DL 4.10	[$2.10 × (22/60)] .77 U	[$12.30 × (2/60)] .41 U	5.28
$12.26			$13.05

COMPARISON OF 1996 ACTUAL COSTS		
	1ST QUARTER	% INCREASE
	COSTS	APRIL COSTS	(DECREASE)
DM	$ 8.75	$ 7.77	(11.2)
DL	5.04	5.28	4.8
	$13.79	$13.05	(5.4)

Jane Keene, assistant controller, came into Foster's office and Foster said, "Jane, look at this performance report! Direct material price increased 11 percent and the labor rate increased over 14 percent during April. I expected greater variances, yet prime costs decreased over 5 percent from the $13.79 we experienced during the first quarter of this year. The proper message just isn't coming through."

"This has been an unusual period," said Keene. "With all the unforeseen changes, perhaps we should revise our standards based on current conditions and start over."

Foster replied, "I think we can retain the current standards but expand the variance analysis. We could calculate variances for the specific changes that have occurred to direct material and direct labor before we calculate the normal price and quantity variances. What I really think would be useful to management right now is to determine the impact the changes in direct material and direct labor had in reducing our prime costs per unit from $13.79 in the first quarter to $13.05 in April—a reduction of $.74."

a. Discuss the advantages of (1) immediately revising the standards and (2) retaining the current standards and expanding the analysis of variances.

b. Prepare an analysis that reflects the impact of the new direct material and new labor contract on reducing NuLathe's prime costs per unit from $13.79 to $13.05. The analysis should show the changes in prime costs per unit that are caused by (1) the use of new direct materials and (2) the new labor contract. This analysis should be in sufficient detail to identify the changes due to direct material price, direct labor rate, the effect of direct material quality on direct material usage, and the effect of direct material quality on direct labor usage.

(CMA adapted)

59. *(Variances and variance responsibility)* Childsafe Product Corporation began operations in 1995. In 1996, the company manufactured only one product, a hand-painted toy horse. The 1996 standard cost per unit is as follows:

Material: one pound plastic at $2.00	$ 2.00
Direct labor: 1.6 hours at $4.00	6.40
Variable overhead cost	3.00
Fixed overhead cost	1.45
	$12.85

The overhead cost per unit was calculated from the following annual overhead cost budget for 60,000 units.

VARIABLE OVERHEAD COST:

Indirect labor—30,000 hours at $4.00	$120,000	
Supplies (oil)—60,000 gallons at $.50	30,000	
Allocated variable service department costs	30,000	
Total variable overhead cost		$180,000

FIXED OVERHEAD COST:

Supervision	$ 27,000	
Depreciation	45,000	
Other fixed costs	15,000	
Total fixed overhead cost		87,000
Total budgeted overhead cost at 60,000 units		$267,000

Following are the charges to the manufacturing department for November, when 5,000 units were produced:

Material (5,300 pounds at $2.00)	$10,600
Direct labor (8,200 hours at $4.10)	33,620
Indirect labor (2,400 hours at $4.10)	9,840
Supplies (oil) (6,000 gallons at $.55)	3,300
Allocated variable service department costs	3,200
Supervision	2,475
Depreciation	3,750
Other fixed costs	1,250
Total	$68,035

The Purchasing Department normally buys about the same quantity as is used in production during a month. In November, 5,200 pounds of material were purchased at a price of $2.10 per pound.

a. Calculate the following variances from standard costs for the data given:
   1. Materials purchase price
   2. Materials quantity
   3. Direct labor rate
   4. Direct labor efficiency
   5. Overhead budget

b. The company has divided its responsibilities so that the Purchasing Department is responsible for the price at which materials and supplies are purchased. The Manufacturing Department is responsible for the quantities of materials used. Does this division of responsibilities solve the conflict between price and quantity variances? Explain your answer.

c. Prepare a report detailing the overhead budget variance. The report, which will be given to the Manufacturing Department manager, should show only that part of the variance that is her responsibility and should highlight the information in ways that would be useful to her in evaluating departmental performance and when considering corrective action.

d. Assume that the departmental manager performs the timekeeping function for this manufacturing department. From time to time analyses of overhead and direct labor variances have shown that the manager has deliberately misclassified labor hours (i.e., listed direct labor hours as indirect labor hours and vice versa) so that only one of the two labor variances is unfavorable. It is not feasible economically to hire a separate timekeeper. What should the company do, if anything, to resolve this problem?

(CMA)

60. *In the mid-1940s, a young man named Donald Roy was working on a Ph.D. at the University of Chicago. As part of his dissertation project, Mr. Roy posed (anonymously) for eleven months as a radial-drill operator at a steel-processing plant. Workers in this plant were paid on a piece-rate basis (with a minimum hourly base pay of 85 cents) for all of the jobs (parts) they worked on. Some of the most interesting behaviors that Mr. Roy observed involved games the employees played based on their perceptions of the fairness of piece rates. If the employees perceived that the piece rates were set too low (required too much output per hour to exceed the base rate) they would engage in work slowdowns. Thus, they would receive the base rate pay of 85 cents per hour rather than the piece rate pay. The company's cost of components produced when employees engaged in slowdowns was consequently higher than the piece rate cost. The slowdown was essentially a way to express discontentment with the piece rate and implied to management a need to revise the piece rate pay. Communication among employees ensured that, with respect to a certain part, all employees participated in the slowdown. Other jobs were recognized by employees as "gravy jobs." On these jobs, the piece rates were sufficiently high to allow employees to easily exceed the base rate pay without exerting significant effort. On these jobs, employees carefully monitored each*

ETHICS AND QUALITY DISCUSSION

other so that no employee generated income substantially above the base rate of 85 cents per hour. The fear was that managers would revise the piece rate if employees generated too much hourly income from the piece rate pay.

[SOURCE: Donald Roy, "Quota Restriction and Goldbricking in a Machine Shop," *American Journal of Sociology* (March 1952), pp. 427–442. Published by the University of Chicago Press.]

a. Why would it be difficult in the environment described by Donald Roy to develop credible standards of performance?

b. Was the behavior of the employees ethical?

c. Is it ethical for managers to revise piece rate pay when it becomes obvious that standards can be easily met or beat?

d. How does honest communication between managers and workers help avoid the problems described by Donald Roy?

61. The chapter mentions that two trends in American industry are establishing higher standards (perhaps ideal standards) as benchmarks for evaluating actual results and adopting just-in-time (JIT) production systems and total quality management (TQM).

There is a growing body of evidence to support the notion that successful adopters of JIT have higher quality production processes than nonadopters. One of the more interesting studies conducted to date examined supplier/consumer relationships among U.S. firms. The study found that the highest quality output was generated by the supplier firm when both the supplier firm and the consumer firm utilized JIT production techniques. The lowest quality output was generated in relationships where neither the supplier, nor the consumer, utilized JIT production techniques.

[SOURCE: M. Frank Barton, Surendra P. Agrawal, and L. Mason Rockwell, Jr., "Meeting the Challenge of Japanese Management Concepts," *Management Accounting* (September 1988), pp. 49–53. Reprinted from *Management Accounting*. Copyright by Institute of Management Accountants, Montvale, NJ.]

a. Why is lack of quality (e.g., substantial number of reworks) in the production process a less tolerable problem in JIT firms than other firms?

b. Based on your understanding of JIT, why is there a need for more communication between supplier and consumer firms when JIT production systems are used by one or both firms?

c. How could the communication mentioned in part b lead to higher quality production?

d. Which would be of greater concern to a firm practicing JIT, an unfavorable direct material price variance or an unfavorable direct material efficiency variance (assume they are of equal magnitude)? Explain.

62. Tim Zeff is a plant manager who has done a good job of controlling some overhead costs during the current period and a poor job of controlling others. Tim's boss has asked him for a variance report for the period.

a. Discuss the ethics of using a two-variance approach to report the overhead variances rather than a three- or four-variance approach.

b. If Tim does not provide his boss with detailed information on the individual cost components and their related variances, can the boss judge Tim's performance during the period? Defend your answer.

63. *At a time when nearly 9 million people can't find jobs, other Americans are putting in the most overtime since the government started keeping records in the 1950s. With factory workers averaging 4.2 hours of overtime per week, the Bureau of Labor Statistics says more than a tenth of all work done in the nation's factories is performed on overtime.*

"If we could go back to the amount of overtime worked in 1982, we would create 3 million new jobs without increasing the federal deficit," said John Zalusky, an economist at the AFL-CIO. He said many workers are putting in extra hours against their wishes.

One reason employers are going the overtime route, economists say, is that overtime pay doesn't cost much extra. Fringe benefits, representing as much as 40 percent of labor costs, are mostly covered by the first 40 hours worked. And the overtime hours generally are worked by employers' most skilled and productive people. Beyond that, using overtime avoids the cost of hiring and training new workers, finding space for them and dealing with the added paperwork. Because of all those factors, Zalusky calculates that paying a skilled worker time-and-a-half actually costs employers only about 3 percent extra.

[SOURCE: Mike Feinsliber, "Employers Paying Overtime Instead of Hiring," *(New Orleans) Times-Picayune* (March 18, 1993), p. C-2. © The Times-Picayune Publishing Corporation.]

a. How does overtime pay affect direct labor cost? Variable overhead?

b. Obviously, paying overtime to already employed workers makes better financial business sense than does hiring additional workers. If, however, workers would prefer not to work overtime but do so to maintain their jobs, how does overtime affect the ethical contract between employers and employees?

c. What effects might overtime have on job efficiency? On job effectiveness (such as quality of production)?

d. Would you be in favor of limiting allowable hours of overtime in order to have more individuals employed? Discuss this question from the standpoint of the government, the employer, a currently employed worker, and an unemployed individual.

64. As of 1983, Medicare began reimbursing hospitals according to Diagnostic Related Groups (DRGs). Each DRG has a specified standard length of stay. If a patient leaves the hospital early, the hospital is favorably financially impacted, but a patient staying longer than the specified time costs the hospital money.

a. From the hospital administrator's point of view, would you want favorable "length of stay" variances? How might you go about trying to obtain such variances?

b. From a patient's point of view, would you want favorable "length of stay" variances? Answer this question from the point of view of a patient who has had minor surgery and from the point of view of a patient who has had major surgery.

c. Would favorable "length of stay" variances necessarily equate to high-quality care?

65. *National standards for U.S. schools covering 13 subjects have been devised by educators in the arts, mathematics, history, English and the sciences. . . . Academic professional groups, meanwhile, have been so wary of offending minorities, and so protective of teachers' academic freedoms, that they have often come up with guidelines that are awash in generalities and impossible to codify into a curriculum.*

An analysis last year by the American Federation of Teachers found that only 13 states had developed standards clear enough to be translated into actual classroom curriculum. The others have standards that "are too vague for teachers to use them, for parents to understand them," says AFT president Albert Shanker.

The report also found that only seven states plan to require students to meet the standards to graduate. "In most states, students won't in any way be affected by whether or not they can meet the standards," the report said.

The AFT found that most states developed their standards without reviewing what high-achieving countries such as Japan, Germany and France require of students. According to the AFT, at least a quarter of all secondary-school students in Germany, France, England and Japan pass at least one advanced exam in mathematics, science or other subjects. In the U.S., only 5% of students pass one of the advanced-placement exams that can give them college credit; but the exams aren't required, and there is no penalty for failure.

[SOURCE: Gary Putka and Steve Stecklow, " 'A' for Effort: Educators Try to Set Standards—Again," *Wall Street Journal* (March 26, 1996), p. B1. Reprinted by permission of *The Wall Street Journal*, © 1996 Dow Jones & Company, Inc. All Rights Reserved Worldwide.]

a. Research the education standards in your home state or country and prepare a report on them. Do you think these standards are measurable? Why or why not?

b. Why do standards, regardless of the purpose for which they are set, need to be tied to consequences?

c. Assume you have been elected state governor on an education reform platform. The state has in place some objective and measurable education standards. How would you tie these standards to consequences? What costs to the state's taxpayers would be associated with such consequences?

d. Consider the following: Scott Paper spent $400,000 screening 14,176 job applicants to hire 174. Of the 10,000 people who passed the initial screening, 4,000 failed a standardized English and high school algebra test. [SOURCE: Raju Narisetti, "Manufacturers Decry a Shortage of Workers While Rejecting Many," *Wall Street Journal* (September 8, 1995), p. A4.] Scott was looking for employees to perform numerous tasks previously handled by managers, and the jobs had a starting salary of $29,000. Do you think that educational standards would help a company like Scott Paper find qualified employees? Explain.

INTERNET ACTIVITIES

66. Find the Internet site for Kaizen Works, Inc. or another firm that provides consulting services regarding kaizen techniques. Review the array of services provided by such a firm. How could these services be utilized by a manufacturing firm to reduce unfavorable standard cost variances that are realized in a production process?

67. Find the Internet site for PRO:MAN software. Write a short paper on the main features of the software and how such features would be useful to a manufacturing firm that uses a standard costing system.

68. Find the homepage for ADVANCE Screw Products Corporation. Review the materials there and then briefly describe the types of products produced by the company and its production processes. Next, write a one page essay in which you present an argument as to whether this company would be a good candidate for adoption of a standard costing system.

COST
PLANNING

Variable Costing and Cost-Volume-Profit Analysis

LEARNING OBJECTIVES

After completing this chapter, you should be able to answer these questions:

1. What are the cost accumulation and cost presentation approaches to product costing?

2. What are the differences between absorption and variable costing?

3. How do changes in sales and/or production levels affect net income as computed under absorption and variable costing?

4. How can cost-volume-profit (CVP) analysis be used by a company?

5. How does CVP analysis differ between single-product and multiproduct firms?

6. How are margin of safety and operating leverage concepts used in business?

7. What are the underlying assumptions of CVP analysis?

8. *(Appendix)* How are break-even charts and profit-volume graphs constructed?

The Procter & Gamble Company

William Procter, an emigrant from England, quickly established himself as a candle maker. James Gamble, an emigrant from Ireland, apprenticed himself to a soap maker. The two might never have met had they not married sisters, Olivia and Elizabeth Norris, whose father convinced his new sons-in-law to become business partners. In 1837, as a result of Alexander Norris' suggestion, a bold new enterprise was born: Procter & Gamble.

In that year they began selling their soap and candles. Once a staple of the company's product line, candles declined in popularity with the invention of the electric light bulb. The company discontinued candle manufacturing in the 1920s.

James Norris Gamble, son of the founder and a trained chemist, developed an inexpensive white soap equal to high-quality, imported castiles. Inspiration for the soap's name—Ivory—came to Harley Procter, the founder's son, as he read the words "out of ivory palaces," in the Bible one Sunday in church.

Today, the firm markets more than 300 brands in over 140 countries around the world. It employs over 99,000 people, and has net sales of $33.4 billion. In the words of the Chairman of the Executive Committee of the Board, Edwin Artzt, in the 1995 *Annual Report*, "Volume growth, driven by innovation and lower prices, is an important contributor to higher earnings. An essential element of this has been sharp cost control throughout the organization—which we have pursued aggressively for the past several years."

[Observe here that Mr. Artzt has tied the relationship among *cost*, *volume*, and *price* together along with innovation as an element of *quality* to create better values for consumers as well as higher earnings for Procter & Gamble's constituents. To have the information to relate cost, volume, and profit (or CVP), the firm's accounting system must be able to provide the necessary dimensions of cost for management to be able to plan, control, and solve problems regarding the production, delivery, and sale of its products.]

SOURCE: *Procter & Gamble History*, pp. 1–3, and *Facts About Procter & Gamble*, p. 1, both provided by the Procter & Gamble Company General Offices, Two Procter & Gamble Plaza, Cincinnati, Ohio, 45202-3314 and the Procter & Gamble Company 1995 *Annual Report*, pp. 4–5. © The Procter & Gamble Company. Reprinted by permission.

This chapter discusses the cost accumulation and cost presentation approaches to product costing. The **cost accumulation** approach determines which manufacturing costs are recorded as part of product cost. Although one approach to cost accumulation may be appropriate for external reporting, that approach is not necessarily appropriate for internal decision making. The **cost presentation** approach focuses on how costs are shown on external financial statements or internal management reports. Accumulation and presentation procedures are accomplished using one of two methods: absorption costing or variable costing. Each method uses the same basic data, but structures and processes the data differently. Either method may be used in job order or process costing and with actual, normal, or standard costs.

Absorption costing is the traditional approach to product costing. Variable costing facilitates the use of models for analyzing break-even point, cost-volume-profit relationships, margin of safety, and the degree of operating leverage. Use of these models is explained in this chapter after presentation of absorption costing and variable costing.

cost accumulation

cost presentation

AN OVERVIEW OF THE TWO METHODS

absorption costing

full costing

functional classification

variable costing

Absorption costing treats the costs of all manufacturing components (direct material, direct labor, variable overhead, and fixed overhead) as inventoriable or product costs in accordance with generally accepted accounting principles (GAAP). Absorption costing is also known as **full costing.** This method has been used consistently in the previous chapters that dealt with product costing systems and valuation. In fact, the product cost definition given in Chapter 4 specifically fits the absorption costing method. Under absorption costing, costs incurred in the nonmanufacturing areas of the organization are considered period costs and are expensed in a manner that properly matches them with revenues. Exhibit 12–1 depicts the absorption costing model.

Absorption costing presents expenses on an income statement according to their functional classifications. A **functional classification** is a group of costs that were all incurred for the same principal purpose. Functional classifications include categories such as cost of goods sold, selling expense, and administrative expense.[1]

In contrast, **variable costing** is a cost accumulation method that includes only *variable* production costs (direct material, direct labor, and variable overhead) as product or inventoriable costs. Under this method, fixed manufacturing overhead is

EXHIBIT 12–1

Absorption Costing Model

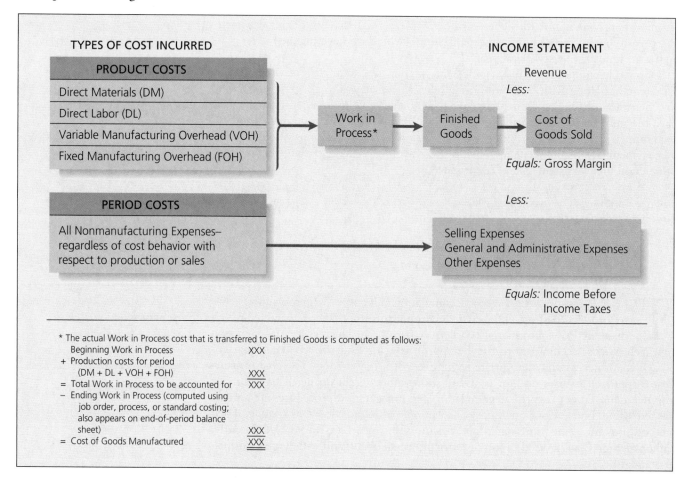

[1] Under FASB Statement 34, certain interest costs may be capitalized during a period of asset construction. If a company is capitalizing or has capitalized interest costs, these costs will not be shown on the income statement, but will become a part of fixed asset cost. The fixed asset cost is then depreciated as part of fixed overhead. Thus, although interest is typically considered a period cost, it may be included as fixed overhead and affect the overhead application rate.

treated as a period cost. Like absorption costing, variable costing treats costs incurred in the organization's selling and administrative areas as period costs. Variable costing income statements typically present expenses according to cost behavior (variable and fixed), although they may also present expenses by functional classifications within the behavioral categories. Variable costing has also been known as **direct costing.** Exhibit 12–2 presents the variable costing model.

direct costing

Two basic differences can be seen between absorption and variable costing. The first difference is the way fixed overhead (FOH) is treated for product costing purposes. Under absorption costing, FOH is considered a product cost; under variable costing, it is considered a period cost. Absorption costing advocates contend that products cannot be made without the capacity provided by fixed manufacturing costs and so these costs are product costs. Variable costing advocates contend that the fixed manufacturing costs would be incurred whether or not production occurs and, therefore, cannot be product costs because they are not caused by production. The second difference is in the presentation of costs on the income statement. Absorption costing classifies expenses by function, whereas variable costing categorizes expenses first by behavior and may further classify them by function.

EXHIBIT 12–2

Variable Costing Model

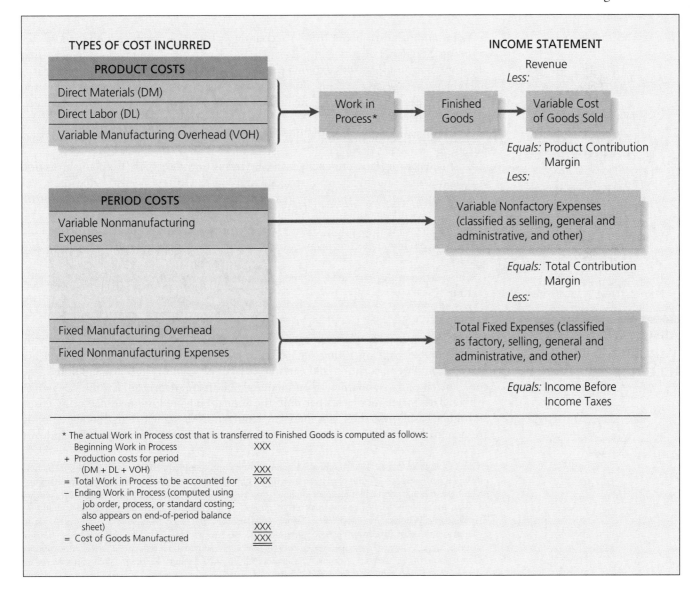

Variable costing allows costs to be separated by cost behavior on the income statement or internal management reports. Cost of goods sold, under variable costing, is more appropriately called variable cost of goods sold (VCGS), because it is composed *only* of variable production costs. Sales (S) minus variable cost of goods sold is called **product contribution margin** (PCM) and indicates how much revenue is available to cover all period expenses and potentially to provide net income.

product contribution margin

Variable, nonmanufacturing period expenses (VNME), such as a sales commission set at 10 percent of product selling price, are deducted from product contribution margin to determine the amount of **total contribution margin** (TCM). Total contribution margin is the difference between total revenues and total variable expenses. This amount indicates the dollar figure available to "contribute" to the coverage of all fixed expenses, both manufacturing and nonmanufacturing. After fixed expenses are covered, any remaining contribution margin provides income to the company. A variable costing income statement is also referred to as a contribution income statement. A formula representation of a variable costing income statement follows:

total contribution margin

$$S - VCGS = PCM$$
$$PCM - VNME = TCM \longrightarrow \text{Fixed Expenses}$$
$$\longrightarrow \text{Profit Before Taxes}$$

Major authoritative bodies of the accounting profession, such as the Financial Accounting Standards Board and Securities and Exchange Commission, believe that absorption costing provides external parties with a more informative picture of earnings than does variable costing. By specifying that absorption costing must be used to prepare external financial statements, the accounting profession has, in effect, disallowed the use of variable costing as a generally accepted inventory method for external reporting purposes. Additionally, the IRS requires absorption costing for tax purposes.[2]

Cost behavior (relative to changes in activity) is not observable from an absorption costing income statement or management report. However, cost behavior is extremely important for a variety of managerial activities including cost-volume-profit analysis, relevant costing, and budgeting.[3] Although companies prepare external statements on an absorption costing basis, *internal* financial reports distinguishing costs by behavior are often prepared to facilitate management decision making and analysis.

The next section provides a detailed illustration using both absorption and variable costing.

ABSORPTION AND VARIABLE COSTING ILLUSTRATIONS

Swift Company makes a single product, the Bright Smile Dental Kit. Swift Company is a 3-year-old firm operating out of the owner's home. Data for this product are used to compare absorption and variable costing procedures and presentations. The company employs standard costs for material, labor, and overhead. Exhibit 12–3 gives the standard production costs per unit, the annual budgeted nonmanufacturing costs, and other basic operating data for Swift Company. All standard and budgeted costs are assumed to remain constant over the three years 1996 through 1998 and, for

[2] The Tax Reform Act of 1986 requires all manufacturers and many wholesalers and retailers to include many previously expensed indirect costs in inventory. This method is referred to as "super-full absorption" or uniform capitalization. The uniform capitalization rules require manufacturers to assign to inventory all costs that directly benefit or are incurred because of production, including some general and administrative costs. Wholesalers and retailers, which previously did not need to include any indirect costs in inventory, now must inventory costs for items such as off-site warehousing, purchasing agents' salaries, and repackaging. However, the material in this chapter is not intended to reflect "super-full absorption."

[3] Cost-volume-profit analysis is discussed subsequently in this chapter. Relevant costing is covered in Chapter 13 and budgeting is discussed in Chapter 14.

EXHIBIT 12–3

Basic Data for 1996, 1997, and 1998

Sales price per unit	$3.00
Standard variable cost per unit:	
Direct material	$1.020
Direct labor	.750
Variable manufacturing overhead	.090
Total variable manufacturing cost per unit	$1.860

Standard Fixed Factory Overhead Rate = $\dfrac{\text{Budgeted Annual Fixed Factory Overhead}}{\text{Budgeted Annual Capacity in Units}}$

$$\text{FOH rate} = \frac{\$8{,}010}{30{,}000} = \$.267$$

Total absorption cost per unit:	
Standard variable manufacturing cost	$1.860
Standard fixed manufacturing overhead (BFOH)	.267
Total absorption cost per unit	$2.127

Budgeted nonproduction expenses:	
Variable selling expenses per unit	$.12
Fixed selling and administrative expenses	$1,170

Total budgeted nonproductive expenses = ($.12 per unit sold + $1,170)

	1996	1997	1998	TOTAL
Actual units made	30,000	29,000	31,000	90,000
Actual unit sales	30,000	27,000	33,000	90,000
Change in FG inventory	0	+2,000	−2,000	0

simplicity, the company is assumed to have no Work in Process Inventory at the end of a period.[4] Also, all actual costs are assumed to equal the budgeted and standard costs for the years presented. The bottom section of Exhibit 12–3 compares actual unit production with actual unit sales to determine the change in inventory for each of the three years.

The company determines its standard fixed manufacturing overhead application rate by dividing estimated annual FOH by expected annual capacity. Total estimated annual fixed manufacturing overhead for Swift is $8,010 and expected annual production is 30,000 units. These figures provide a standard FOH rate of $.267 per unit. Fixed manufacturing overhead is typically under- or overapplied at year-end when a standard, predetermined fixed overhead rate is used rather than actual FOH cost.

Under- or overapplication is caused by two factors that can work independently or simultaneously. These two factors are cost differences and utilization differences. If actual FOH cost differs from expected FOH cost, a fixed manufacturing overhead spending variance is created. If actual capacity utilization differs from expected utilization, a volume variance arises.[5] The *independent* effects of these differences are as follows:

[4] Actual costs can also be used under either absorption or variable costing. Standard costing was chosen for these illustrations because it makes the differences between the two methods more obvious. If actual costs had been used, production costs would vary each year and such variations would obscure the distinct differences caused by the use of one method, rather than the other, over a period of time. Standard costs are also treated as constant over time to more clearly demonstrate the differences between absorption and variable costing and to reduce the complexity of the chapter explanations.

[5] These variances are covered in depth in Chapter 11.

$$\text{Actual FOH Cost} > \text{Expected FOH Cost} = \text{Underapplied FOH}$$

$$\text{Actual FOH Cost} < \text{Expected FOH Cost} = \text{Overapplied FOH}$$

$$\text{Actual Utilization} > \text{Expected Utilization} = \text{Overapplied FOH}$$

$$\text{Actual Utilization} < \text{Expected Utilization} = \text{Underapplied FOH}$$

In most cases, however, both costs and utilization differ from estimates. When this occurs, no generalizations can be made as to whether FOH will be under- or over-applied. Assume that Swift Company began operations in 1996. Production and sales information for the years 1996 through 1998 are shown in Exhibit 12–3.

Because the company began operations in 1996, that year has a zero balance for beginning Finished Goods Inventory. The next year, 1997, also has a zero beginning inventory because all units produced in 1996 were also sold in 1996. In 1997 and 1998, production and sales quantities differ, which is a common situation because production frequently "leads" sales so that inventory can be stockpiled for a later period. The illustration purposefully has no beginning inventory and equal cumulative units of production and sales for the 3 years to demonstrate that, regardless of whether absorption or variable costing is used, the cumulative income before taxes will be the same ($64,260 in Exhibit 12–4) under these conditions. Also, for any particular year in which there is no change in inventory levels from the beginning of the year to the end of the year, both methods will result in the same net income. An example of this occurs in 1996 as is demonstrated in Exhibit 12–4.

Because all actual production and operating costs are assumed to be equal to the standard and budgeted costs for the years 1996 through 1998, the only variances presented are the volume variances for 1997 and 1998. These volume variances are

---

EXHIBIT 12–4

Absorption and Variable Costing Income Statements for 1996, 1997, and 1998

ABSORPTION COSTING PRESENTATION

	1996	1997	1998	TOTAL
Sales ($3 per unit)	$90,000	$81,000	$99,000	$270,000
CGS ($2.127 per unit)	(63,810)	(57,429)	(70,191)	(191,430)
Std GM	$26,190	$23,571	$28,809	$ 78,570
Volume Variance (U)	0	(267)	267	0
Adjusted Gross Margin	$26,190	$23,304	$29,076	$ 78,570
Operating Expenses				
Selling and administrative	(4,770)	(4,410)	(5,130)	(14,310)
Income before Tax	$21,420	$18,894	$23,946	$ 64,260

VARIABLE COSTING PRESENTATION

	1996	1997	1998	TOTAL
Sales ($3 per unit)	$90,000	$81,000	$99,000	$270,000
Variable CGS ($1.86 per unit)	(55,800)	(50,220)	(61,380)	(167,400)
Product Contribution Margin	$34,200	$30,780	$37,620	$102,600
Variable Selling Expenses				
($.12 × units sold)	(3,600)	(3,240)	(3,960)	(10,800)
Total Contribution Margin	$30,600	$27,540	$33,660	$ 91,800
Fixed Expenses				
Manufacturing	$ 8,010	$ 8,010	$ 8,010	$ 24,030
Selling and administration	1,170	1,170	1,170	3,510
Total fixed expenses	$ (9,180)	$ (9,180)	$ (9,180)	$ (27,540)
Income before Tax	$21,420	$18,360	$24,480	$ 64,260
Differences in Income before Tax	$　　0	$　534	$ (534)	$　　0

Under absorption costing, all costs of direct materials, direct labor, and production overhead would be assigned to McDonald's various products to determine product cost. Variable costing, however, would exclude fixed overhead (such as the depreciation on the equipment shown here) from product cost and consider this element as a period cost.

immaterial and are reflected as adjustments to the gross margins for 1997 and 1998 in Exhibit 12–4.

Volume variances under absorption costing are calculated as standard fixed overhead (SFOH) of $.267 multiplied by the difference between expected capacity (30,000 kits) and actual production. For 1996, there is no volume variance because expected and actual production are equal. For 1997, the volume variance is $267 unfavorable, calculated as [$.267 × (29,000 − 30,000)]. For 1998, it is $267 favorable, calculated as [$.267 × (31,000 − 30,000)]. Variable costing does not have a volume variance because fixed manufacturing overhead is not applied to units produced but is written off in its entirety as a period expense.

In Exhibit 12–4, income before tax for 1997 for absorption costing exceeds that of variable costing by $534. This difference is caused by the positive change in inventory (2,000 shown in Exhibit 12–3) to which the absorption SFOH of $.267 per unit has been assigned (2,000 × $.267 = $534). This $534 is the fixed manufacturing overhead added to absorption costing inventory and therefore not expensed in 1997. Critics of absorption costing refer to this phenomenon as one that creates illusionary or **phantom profits.** Phantom profits are temporary absorption-costing profits caused by producing more inventory than is sold. When sales increase to eliminate the previously-produced inventory, the phantom profits disappear. In contrast, all fixed manufacturing overhead, including the $534, is expensed in its entirety in variable costing.

phantom profit

Exhibit 12–3 shows that in 1998, inventory decreased by 2,000 kits. This decrease, multiplied by the SFOH ($.267), explains the $534 by which 1998 absorption costing income falls short of variable costing income on Exhibit 12–4. This is because the fixed manufacturing overhead written off in absorption costing through the cost of goods sold at $.267 per kit for all units sold in excess of production (33,000 − 31,000 = 2,000) results in the $534 by which absorption costing income is lower than variable costing income in 1998.

Variable costing income statements are more useful internally for planning, controlling, and decision making than absorption costing statements. To carry out their functions, managers need to understand and be able to project how different costs will change in reaction to changes in activity levels. Variable costing, through its emphasis on cost behavior, provides that necessary information.

The income statements in Exhibit 12–4 show that absorption and variable costing tend to provide different income figures in some years. Comparing the two sets of statements illustrates that the difference in income arises solely from which production component costs are included in or excluded from product cost for each method.

If no beginning or ending inventories exist, cumulative total income under both methods will be identical. For the Swift Company over the three-year period, 90,000 dental kits are produced and 90,000 kits are sold. Thus, all the costs incurred (whether variable or fixed) are expensed in one year or another under either method. The income difference in each year is solely caused by the timing of the expensing of fixed manufacturing overhead.

COMPARISON OF THE TWO APPROACHES

Whether absorption costing income is greater or less than variable costing income depends on the relationship of production to sales. In all cases, to determine the effects on income, it must be assumed that variances from standard are immaterial and that unit product costs are constant over time. Exhibit 12–5 shows the possible relationships between production and sales levels and the effects of these relationships on income.

These relationships are as follows:

- If production is equal to sales, absorption costing income will equal variable costing income.
- If production is greater than sales, absorption costing income is greater than variable costing income. This result occurs because some fixed manufacturing overhead cost is deferred as part of inventory cost on the balance sheet under

EXHIBIT 12–5

Production/Sales Relationships and Effects*

where P = Production and S = Sales
AC = Absorption Costing and VC = Variable Costing

	Absorption vs. Variable Income Statement Income before Taxes	Absorption vs. Variable Balance Sheet Ending Inventory
P = S	AC = VC No difference from beginning inventory $FOH_{EI} - FOH_{BI} = 0$	No additional difference $FOH_{EI} = FOH_{BI}$
P > S (Stockpiling inventory)	AC > VC By amount of fixed OH in ending inventory minus fixed OH in beginning inventory $FOH_{EI} - FOH_{BI} = +$ amount	Ending inventory increased (by fixed OH in additional units because P > S) $FOH_{EI} > FOH_{BI}$
P < S (Selling off beginning inventory)	AC < VC By amount of fixed OH released from balance sheet beginning inventory $FOH_{EI} - FOH_{BI} = -$ amount	Ending inventory difference reduced (by fixed OH from BI charged to cost of goods sold) $FOH_{EI} < FOH_{BI}$

*The effects of the relationships presented here are based on two qualifying assumptions:
  (1) that unit costs are constant over time; and
  (2) that any fixed cost variances from standard are written off when incurred rather than being prorated to inventory balances.

Income Manipulation Not Possible under Variable Costing

Conceptually, variable costing has always given a more realistic income. Any "full" method of costing (absorption costing or activity-based costing) permits management to manipulate income by adjusting inventory. A company can increase income by producing more units and thus deferring more fixed costs of this period. In this way it even is possible for a company to report a profit when its sales are lower than the breakeven point. If planned income is more than sufficient in the current period, production could be reduced so that fewer fixed costs could be deferred. Accordingly, income can be reported higher or lower than in the previous period even if unit sales, prices, and costs are the same. Variable costing would eliminate this avenue for income manipulation. It is a purer system because costs are charged off as incurred.

SOURCE: Robert W. Koehler, "Triple-Threat Strategy," *Management Accounting* (October 1991), p. 34. Reprinted from *Management Accounting*. Copyright by Institute of Management Accountants, Montvale, NJ.

absorption costing, whereas the total amount of fixed manufacturing overhead cost is expensed as a period cost under variable costing.

- If production is less than sales, income under absorption costing is less than income under variable costing. In this case, absorption costing expenses all of the current period fixed manufacturing overhead cost and releases some fixed manufacturing overhead cost from the beginning inventory where it had been deferred from a prior period.

This process of deferring and releasing fixed overhead costs in and from inventory makes income manipulation possible under absorption costing, as discussed in the News Note on income manipulation. For this reason, some people believe that variable costing might be more useful for external purposes than absorption costing. For internal reporting, variable costing information provides managers with information about the behavior of the various product and period costs. This information can be used in computing break-even point and analyzing a variety of cost-volume-profit relationships.

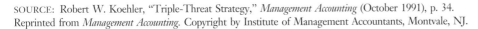

Examining shifts in costs and volume and their resulting effects on profit is called **cost-volume-profit** (CVP) **analysis.** This analysis is applicable in all economic sectors, including manufacturing, wholesaling, retailing, and service industries. CVP can be used by managers to plan and control more effectively because it allows them to concentrate on the relationships among revenues, costs, volume changes, taxes, and profits. The CVP model can be expressed through a formula or graphically, as illustrated in the chapter appendix. All costs, regardless of whether they are product, period, variable, or fixed, are considered in the CVP model. The analysis is usually performed on a companywide basis. The same basic CVP model and calculations can be applied to a single- or multiproduct business. That CVP analysis is not a new tool is indicated in the News Note "A Gunfighter with the Soul of a Management Accountant" on the next page.

CVP analysis has wide-range applicability. It can be used to determine a company's **break-even point** (BEP), which is that level of activity, in units or dollars, at which total revenues equal total costs. At breakeven, the company's revenues simply cover its costs; thus, the company incurs neither a profit nor a loss on operating activities. Companies, however, do not wish merely to "break even" on operations. The break-even point is calculated merely to establish a point of reference. Knowing BEP,

DEFINITION AND USES OF CVP ANALYSIS

cost-volume-profit analysis

break-even point

NEWS
NOTE

A Gunfighter with the Soul of a Management Accountant

Most people today know Wyatt Earp as one of the most respected and feared lawmen of the Old West. He helped bring law and order to Dodge City and Wichita, the toughest of frontier towns. He became the stuff of legend at the O.K. Corral in Tombstone, Arizona, where he joined his brothers Morgan and Virgil, and his friend, Doc Holliday, in a deadly face-to-face gun battle with the notorious Clanton gang. Wyatt survived and lived to old age, never having been grazed by a bullet.

Wyatt's earlier career pursuits, though perhaps just as dangerous, are not as well known: teamster, gambler, and buffalo hunter. In fact, during the period 1871–74, he made quite a tidy profit in buffalo hunting using methods that were revolutionary at the time. He developed his methods by observing what more experienced hunters were doing and making improvements—improvements aimed at ensuring that his hunts were more efficient and profitable. In doing so, Wyatt made efficient use of cost-volume-profit analysis, a key analytical tool for the 20th century management accountant. Wyatt's approach was surprisingly sophisticated for its time and circumstances.

SOURCE: Thomas L. Barton, William G. Shenkir, and John E. Hess, "Wyatt Earp, Frontier Accountant," *The CPA Journal* (June 1995), p. 48.

managers are better able to set sales goals that should generate income from operations rather than produce losses. CVP analysis can also be used to calculate the sales volume necessary to achieve a desired target profit. Target profit objectives may be stated as either a fixed or variable amount on a before- or after-tax basis. Because profit cannot be achieved until the break-even point is reached, the starting point of CVP analysis is BEP.

THE BREAK-EVEN POINT

Finding the break-even point first requires an understanding of company revenues and costs. A short summary of revenue and cost assumptions is presented at this point to provide a foundation for CVP analysis. These assumptions, and some challenges to them, are discussed in more detail at the end of the chapter.

- *Relevant range:* A primary assumption is that the company is operating within the relevant range of activity specified in determining the revenue and cost information used in each of the following assumptions.[6]
- *Revenue:* Revenue per unit is assumed to remain constant; fluctuations in per-unit revenue for factors such as quantity discounts are ignored. Thus, total revenue fluctuates in direct proportion to level of activity or volume.
- *Variable costs:* On a per-unit basis, variable costs are assumed to remain constant. Therefore, total variable costs fluctuate in direct proportion to level of activity or volume. Note that assumed variable cost behavior is the same as assumed revenue behavior. Variable production costs include direct material, direct labor, and variable overhead; variable selling costs include charges for items such as commissions and shipping. Variable administrative costs may exist in areas such as purchasing.
- *Fixed costs:* Total fixed costs are assumed to remain constant and, as such, per-unit fixed cost decreases as volume increases. (Fixed cost per unit would increase as volume decreases.) Fixed costs include both fixed manufacturing overhead and fixed selling and administrative expenses.

[6] Relevant range is the range of activity over which a variable cost per unit will remain constant and a fixed cost will remain fixed in total.

	TOTAL	PER UNIT	PERCENTAGE
Sales		$90,000	$3.00	100
Variable Costs:			
Production	$55,800		$1.86	62
Selling	3,600		.12	4
Total Variable Cost		(59,400)	$1.98	66
Contribution Margin		$30,600	$1.02	34
Fixed Costs:			
Production	$ 8,010		
Selling and administrative	1,170		
Total Fixed Cost		(9,180)	
Income before Income Taxes		$21,420	

EXHIBIT 12–6

Income Statement for 1996

- *Mixed costs:* Mixed costs must be separated into their variable and fixed elements before they can be used in CVP analysis. Any method (such as regression analysis) that validly separates these costs in relation to one or more predictors may be used. After being separated, the variable and fixed cost components of the mixed cost take on the assumed characteristics mentioned above.

An important amount in break-even and CVP analysis is **contribution margin** (CM), which may be defined on either a per-unit or total basis. Contribution margin per unit is the difference between the selling price per unit and the sum of variable production, selling, and administrative costs per unit. Unit contribution margin is constant because revenue and variable cost have been defined as remaining constant per unit. Total contribution margin is the difference between total revenues and total variable costs for all units sold. This amount fluctuates in direct proportion to sales volume. On either a per-unit or total basis, contribution margin indicates the amount of revenue remaining after all variable costs have been covered.[7] This amount contributes to the coverage of fixed costs and the generation of profits.

Data needed to compute the break-even point and perform CVP analysis are given in the income statement shown in Exhibit 12–6 for Swift Company.

contribution margin

The formula approach to break-even analysis uses an algebraic equation to calculate the exact break-even point. In this analysis, sales, rather than production activity is the focus for the relevant range. The equation represents the variable costing income statement presented in the first section of the chapter and shows the relationships among revenue, fixed cost, variable cost, volume, and profit as follows:

FORMULA APPROACH TO BREAK EVEN

$$R(X) - VC(X) - FC = P$$

where R = revenue (selling price) per unit

X = number of units

$R(X)$ = total revenue

VC = variable cost per unit

$VC(X)$ = total variable cost

FC = total fixed cost

P = profit

[7] Contribution margin refers to the total contribution margin discussed in the preceding section of the chapter rather than product contribution margin. Product contribution margin is simply the difference between revenues and total variable *production* costs for the cost of goods sold.

Because the above equation is simply a formula representation of an income statement, P can be set equal to zero so that the formula indicates a break-even situation. At the point where P = $0, total revenues are equal to total costs and break-even point (BEP) in units can be found by solving the equation for X.

$$R(X) - VC(X) - FC = \$0$$
$$R(X) - VC(X) = FC$$
$$(R - VC)(X) = FC$$
$$X = FC \div (R - VC)$$

Break-even point volume is equal to total fixed cost divided by (revenue per unit minus the variable cost per unit). Using the operating statistics shown in Exhibit 12–6 for Swift Company ($3.00 selling price per kit, $1.98 variable cost per kit, and $9,180 of total fixed costs), break-even point for the company is calculated as

$$\$3.00(X) - \$1.98(X) - \$9,180 = \$0$$
$$\$3.00(X) - \$1.98(X) = \$9,180$$
$$(\$3.00 - \$1.98)(X) = \$9,180$$
$$X = \$9,180 \div (\$3.00 - \$1.98)$$
$$X = 9,000 \text{ kits}$$

Revenue minus variable cost is contribution margin. Thus, the formula can be shortened by using the contribution margin to find BEP.

$$(R - VC)(X) = FC$$
$$(CM)(X) = FC$$
$$X = FC \div CM$$

where CM = contribution margin per unit

Swift's contribution margin is $1.02 per kit ($3.00 − $1.98). The calculation for BEP using the abbreviated formula is $9,180 ÷ $1.02 or 9,000 kits.

Break-even point can be expressed either in units or dollars of revenue. One way to convert a unit break-even point to dollars is to multiply units by the selling price per unit. For Swift, break-even point in sales dollars is $27,000 (9,000 kits × $3.00 per kit).

Another method of computing break-even point in sales dollars requires the computation of a **contribution margin** (CM) **ratio.** The CM ratio is calculated as contribution margin divided by revenue and indicates what proportion of revenue remains after variable costs have been covered. For each dollar of revenue, the contribution margin ratio represents that portion of the revenue dollar remaining to go toward covering fixed costs and increasing profits. The CM ratio can be calculated using either per-unit or total revenue minus variable cost information. Subtracting the CM ratio from 100 percent gives the **variable cost** (VC) **ratio,** which represents the variable cost proportion of each revenue dollar.

The contribution margin ratio allows the break-even point to be determined even if unit selling price and unit variable cost are not known. Dividing total fixed cost by CM ratio gives the break-even point in sales dollars. The derivation of this formula is as follows:

$$\text{Sales} - [(VC\%)(\text{Sales})] = FC$$
$$(1 - VC\%)\text{Sales} = FC$$
$$\text{Sales} = FC \div (1 - VC\%)$$
$$\text{because } (1 - VC\%) = CM\%$$
$$\text{Sales} = FC \div CM\%$$

VIDEO
VIGNETTE

Pacific Paper Tube Inc. (Blue Chip Enterprises)

contribution margin ratio

variable cost ratio

where VC% = the % relationship of variable cost to sales
      CM% = the % relationship of contribution margin to sales

Thus, the variable cost ratio plus the contribution margin ratio is equal to 100 percent.

The contribution margin ratio for Swift Company is given in Exhibit 12–6 as 34 percent ($1.02 ÷ $3.00). The company's computation of dollars of break-even sales is $9,180 ÷ .34 or $27,000. The BEP in units can be determined by dividing the BEP in sales dollars by the unit selling price or $27,000 ÷ $3.00 = 9,000 kits.

The break-even point provides a starting point for planning future operations. Managers want to earn operating profits rather than simply cover costs. Substituting an amount other than zero for the profit (P) term in the break-even formula converts break-even analysis to cost-volume-profit analysis.

CVP analysis requires the substitution of known amounts in the formula to determine an unknown amount. The formula mirrors the income statement when known amounts are used for selling price per unit, variable cost per unit, volume of units, and fixed costs to find the amount of profit generated under given conditions. Because CVP analysis is concerned with relationships among the elements comprising continuing operations, in contrast with nonrecurring activities and events, *profits,* as used in this chapter, refer to operating profits before extraordinary and other non-operating, nonrecurring items.

A more pervasive and significant application of CVP analysis is to set a desired target profit and focus on the relationships between it and known income statement amounts to find an unknown. A common unknown in such applications is volume because managers want to know what quantity of sales needs to be generated to produce a particular amount of profit.

Selling price is not assumed to be as common an unknown as volume because selling price is often market-related and not a management decision variable. Additionally, because selling price and volume are often directly related, and certain costs are considered fixed, managers may use CVP to determine how high variable cost may be and still allow the company to produce a desired amount of profit. Variable cost may be affected by modifying product specifications or material quality or by

USING COST-VOLUME-PROFIT ANALYSIS

When it first opened, Euro Disneyland was concerned about profitability. Like other theme parks, Euro Disneyland has a substantial amount of fixed costs and the market must be willing to accept the established ticket price. Thus, control of total variable cost is the primary factor that can fluctuate in performing CVP analysis.

being more efficient or effective in the production, service, and/or distribution process(es). Profits may be stated as either a fixed or variable amount and on either a before- or after-tax basis. The following examples continue use of the Swift Company data using different amounts of target profit.

Fixed Amount of Profit

Because contribution margin represents the amount of sales dollars remaining after variable costs are covered, each dollar of CM generated by product sales goes first to cover fixed costs and then to produce profits. *After the break-even point is reached, each dollar of contribution margin is a dollar of profit.*

BEFORE TAX Profits are treated in the break-even formula as additional costs to be covered. The inclusion of a target profit changes the formula from a break-even to a CVP equation.

$$R(X) - VC(X) - FC = PBT$$
$$R(X) - VC(X) = FC + PBT$$
$$X = (FC + PBT) \div (R - VC)$$

or

$$X = (FC + PBT) \div CM$$

where PBT = fixed amount of profit before taxes

Swift's management wants to produce a before-tax profit of $12,750. To do so, the company must sell 21,500 kits that will generate $64,500 of revenue. These calculations are shown in Exhibit 12–7.

AFTER TAX Income tax represents a significant influence on business decision making. Managers need to be aware of the effects of income tax in choosing a target profit amount. A company desiring to have a particular amount of net income must first determine the amount of income that must be earned on a before-tax basis, given the applicable tax rate. The CVP formulas that designate a fixed after-tax net income amount are

$$PBT = PAT + [(TR)(PBT)] \text{ and}$$
$$R(X) - VC(X) - FC = PAT + [(TR)(PBT)]$$

EXHIBIT 12–7

CVP Analysis—Fixed
Amount of Profit
Before Tax

In units:

PBT desired = $12,750

$$R(X) - VC(X) = FC + PBT$$
$$CM(X) = FC + PBT$$
$$(\$3.00 - \$1.98)X = \$9,180 + \$12,750$$
$$\$1.02X = \$21,930$$
$$X = \$21,930 \div \$1.02 = 21,500 \text{ kits}$$

In sales dollars:

$$Sales = (FC + PBT) \div CM \text{ ratio}$$
$$= \$21,930 \div .34 = \$64,500$$

where PAT = fixed amount of profit after tax
     PBT = fixed amount of profit before tax
      TR = tax rate

PAT is further defined so that it can be integrated into the original CVP formula:

$$PAT = PBT - [(TR)(PBT)] \text{ or}$$

$$PBT = PAT \div (1 - TR)$$

Substituting into the formula,

$$R(X) - VC(X) = FC + PBT$$

$$(R - VC)(X) = FC + [PAT \div (1 - TR)]$$

$$CM(X) = FC + [PAT \div (1 - TR)]$$

Assume the managers at Swift Company want to earn $12,240 of profit after tax and the company's marginal tax rate is 20 percent. The number of kits and dollars of sales needed are calculated in Exhibit 12–8.

Variable Amount of Profit

Managers may wish to state profits as a variable amount so that, as units are sold or sales dollars increase, profits will increase at a constant rate. Variable amounts of profit may be stated on either a before- or after-tax basis. Profit on a variable basis can be stated either as a percentage of revenues or a per-unit profit. The CVP formula must be adjusted to recognize that profit (P) is related to volume of activity.

BEFORE TAX   This example assumes that the variable amount of profit is related to the number of units sold. The adjusted CVP formula for computing the necessary unit volume of sales to earn a specified variable amount of profit before tax per unit is

$$R(X) - VC(X) - FC = P_uBT(X)$$

where P_uBT = variable amount of profit per unit before tax

In units:
 	
PAT desired = $12,240; tax rate = 20%
 	
          PBT = PAT ÷ (1 − TR)
          PBT = $12,240 ÷ (1 − .20)
               = $12,240 ÷ .80
               = $15,300 necessary profit before tax
        and
      CM(X) = FC + PBT
   $1.02X = $9,180 + $15,300
   $1.02X = $24,480
        X = $24,480 ÷ $1.02 = 24,000 kits
 	
In sales dollars:
 	
      Sales = (FC + PBT) ÷ CM ratio
            = ($9,180 + $15,300) ÷ .34
            = $24,480 ÷ .34 = $72,000

EXHIBIT 12–8

CVP Analysis—Fixed Amount of Profit after Tax

EXHIBIT 12–9

CVP Analysis—Variable
Amount of Profit
Before Tax

In units:

$$P_uBT \text{ desired} = 16\% \text{ on sales revenues}$$

$$P_uBT = .16(\$3.00) = \$.48$$

$$CM(X) - P_uBT(X) = FC$$

$$\$1.02X - \$.48X = \$9,180$$

$$X = \$9,180 \div \$.54$$

$$X = 17,000 \text{ kits}$$

In sales dollars, the following relationships exist:

	PER KIT	PERCENTAGE
Selling price	$ 3.00	100
Variable costs	(1.98)	(66)
Variable profit before tax	(.48)	(16)
"Adjusted" contribution margin	$ .54	18

$$\text{Sales} = FC \div \text{"Adjusted" CM ratio*}$$

$$= \$9,180 \div .18 = \$51,000$$

*Note that it is not necessary to have per-unit data; all computations can be made with percentage information only.

Moving all the Xs to the same side of the equation and solving for X (volume) gives the following:

$$R(X) - VC(X) - P_uBT(X) = FC$$

$$CM(X) - P_uBT(X) = FC$$

$$X = FC \div (CM - P_uBT)$$

The variable profit is treated in the CVP formula as if it were an additional variable cost to be covered. This treatment effectively "adjusts" the original contribution margin and contribution margin ratio. When setting the desired profit as a percentage of selling price, the profit percentage cannot exceed the contribution margin ratio. If it does, an infeasible problem is created because the "adjusted" contribution margin is negative. In such a case, the variable cost percentage plus the desired profit percentage would exceed 100 percent of the selling price, and such a condition cannot occur.

Assume that the president of Swift Company wants to know what level of sales (in kits and dollars) would be required to earn a 16 percent before-tax profit on sales. The calculations shown in Exhibit 12–9 provide the answers to these questions.

AFTER TAX   Adjustment to the CVP formula to determine variable profits on an after-tax basis involves stating profits in relation to both the volume and the tax rate. The algebraic manipulations are:

$$R(X) - VC(X) - FC = P_uAT(X) + [(TR)(P_uBT(X))]$$

where P_uAT = variable amount of profit per unit after tax

EXHIBIT 12–10

CVP Analysis—Variable Amount of Profit After Tax

In units:

$$P_uAT \text{ desired} = 16\% \text{ of revenue} = .16(\$3.00) = \$.48; \text{ tax rate} = 20\%$$

$$P_uBT(X) = [\$.48 \div (1 - .20)]X$$

$$P_uBT(X) = (\$.48 \div .80)X = \$.60X \text{ profit needed before tax}$$

$$CM(X) - P_uBT(X) = FC$$

$$\$1.02X - \$.60X = \$9,180$$

$$\$.42X = \$9,180$$

$$X = \$9,180 \div \$.42 = 21,857 \text{ kits (rounded)}$$

	PER KIT	PERCENTAGE
Selling price	$3.00	100
Variable costs	(1.98)	(66)
Variable profit before tax	(.60)	(20)
"Adjusted" contribution margin	$ .42	14

$$\text{Sales} = FC \div \text{"Adjusted" CM ratio}$$

$$= \$9,180 \div .14 = \$65,571 \text{ (rounded)}$$

P_uAT is further defined so that it can be integrated into the original CVP formula:

$$P_uAT(X) = P_uBT(X) - [(TR)(P_uBT(X))]$$

$$P_uAT(X) = P_uBT(X)[(1 - TR)]$$

$$P_uBT(X) = [P_uAT \div (1 - TR)](X)$$

Thus, the following relationship exists:

$$R(X) - VC(X) = FC + [P_uAT \div (1 - TR)](X)$$

$$R(X) - VC(X) = FC + P_uBT(X)$$

$$CM(X) = FC + P_uBT(X)$$

$$CM(X) - P_uBT(X) = FC$$

$$X = FC \div (CM - P_uBT)$$

Swift wishes to earn a profit after tax of 16 percent on revenue and has a 20 percent tax rate. The necessary sales in units and dollars are computed in Exhibit 12–10.

All the preceding illustrations of CVP analysis were made using a variation of the formula approach. Solutions were not accompanied by mathematical proofs. The income statement model is an effective means of developing and presenting solutions and/or proofs for solutions to CVP applications.

THE INCOME STATEMENT APPROACH

The income statement approach to CVP analysis allows accountants to prepare pro forma (budgeted) statements using available information. Income statements can be used to prove the accuracy of computations made using the formula approach to CVP analysis, or the statements can be prepared merely to determine the impact of various sales levels on profit after tax (net income). Because the formula and income statement approaches are based on the same relationships, each should be able to

EXHIBIT 12–11

Income Statement Approach to CVP—Proof of Computations

Previous computations:
Break-even point: 9,000 kits
Fixed profit ($12,750) before tax: 21,500 kits
Fixed profit ($12,240) after tax: 24,000 kits
Variable profit (16% on revenues) before tax: 17,000 kits
Variable profit (16% on revenues) after tax: 21,857 kits

R = $3.00 per kit; VC = $1.98 per kit; FC = $9,180;
tax rate = 20% for Exhibits 12–8 and 12–10

	BASIC DATA	EX. 12–7	EX. 12–8	EX. 12–9	EX. 12–10
Kits sold	**9,000**	**21,500**	**24,000**	**17,000**	**21,857**
Sales	$27,000	$64,500	$72,000	$51,000	$65,571
Total variable costs	(17,820)	(42,570)	(47,520)	(33,660)	(43,277)
Contribution margin	$ 9,180	$21,930	$24,480	$17,340	$22,294
Total fixed costs	(9,180)	(9,180)	(9,180)	(9,180)	(9,180)
Profit before tax	$ 0	$12,750	$15,300	$ 8,160*	$13,114
Taxes (20%)			(3,060)		(2,623)
Profit after tax (NI)			$12,240		$10,491**

*Desired profit before tax = 16% on revenue; .16 × $51,000 = $8,160
**Desired profit after tax = 16% on revenue; .16 × $65,571 = $10,491

prove the other.[8] Exhibit 12–11 proves each of the computations made in Exhibits 12–7 through 12–10 for Swift Company.

The answers provided by break-even or cost-volume-profit analysis are valid only in relation to specific selling prices and cost relationships. Changes that occur in the company's selling price or cost structure will cause a change in the break-even point or in the sales needed to obtain a desired profit figure. However, the effects of revenue and cost changes on a company's break-even point or sales volume can be determined through incremental analysis.

INCREMENTAL ANALYSIS FOR SHORT-RUN CHANGES

The break-even point may increase or decrease, depending on the particular changes that occur in the revenue and cost factors. Other things being equal, the break-even point will increase if there is an increase in the total fixed cost or a decrease in the unit (or percentage) contribution margin. A decrease in contribution margin could arise because of a reduction in selling price, an increase in variable cost per unit, or a combination of the two. The break-even point will decrease if there is a decrease in total fixed cost or an increase in unit (or percentage) contribution margin. A change in the break-even point will also cause a shift in total profits or losses at any level of activity.

incremental analysis

Incremental analysis is a process focusing only on factors that change from one course of action or decision to another. As related to CVP situations, incremental analysis is based on changes occurring in revenues, costs, and/or volume. Following are some examples of changes that may occur in a company and the incremental computations that can be used to determine the effects of those changes on the break-even point or profits. In most situations, incremental analysis is sufficient to determine the feasibility of contemplated changes and a complete income statement need not be prepared.

[8] The income statement approach can be readily adapted to computerized spreadsheets, which can be used to quickly obtain the results of many different combinations of the CVP factors.

The basic facts related to Swift Company presented in Exhibit 12–6 are continued. All of the following examples use before-tax information to simplify the computations. After-tax analysis would require the application of a (1 − tax rate) factor to all profit figures.

CASE #1   The company wishes to earn a before-tax profit of $5,100. How many kits does it need to sell?

The incremental analysis relative to this question addresses the number of kits *above* the break-even point that must be sold. Because each dollar of contribution margin after BEP is a dollar of profit, the incremental analysis focuses only on the profit desired:

$$\$5,100 \div \$1.02 = 5,000 \text{ kits above BEP}$$

Because the BEP has already been computed as 9,000 kits, the company must sell a total of 14,000 kits.

CASE #2   Swift Company estimates that it can sell an additional 3,600 kits if it spends $765 more on advertising. Should the company incur this extra fixed cost? The contribution margin from the additional kits must first cover the additional fixed cost before profits can be generated.

Increase in contribution margin	
(3,600 kits × $1.02 CM per kit)	$3,672
− Increase in fixed cost	(765)
= Net incremental benefit	$2,907

Because the net incremental benefit is $2,907, the advertising campaign would result in an additional $2,907 in profits and, thus, should be undertaken.

An alternative computation is to divide $765 by the $1.02 contribution margin. The result indicates that 750 kits would be required to cover the additional cost. Because the company expects to sell 3,600 kits, the remaining 2,850 kits would produce a $1.02 profit per kit or $2,907.

CASE #3   The company estimates that, if the selling price of each kit is reduced to $2.70, an additional 2,000 kits per year can be sold. Should the company take advantage of this opportunity? Current sales volume, given in Exhibit 12–6, is 30,000 kits.

If the selling price is reduced, the contribution margin per unit will decrease to $.72 per kit ($2.70 SP − $1.98 VC). Sales volume will increase to 32,000 kits (30,000 + 2,000).

Total new contribution margin	
(32,000 kits × $.72 CM per kit)	$23,040
− Total fixed costs (unchanged)	(9,180)
= New profit before taxes	$13,860
− Current profit before taxes	
(from Exhibit 12–6)	(21,420)
= Net incremental loss	$(7,560)

Because the company will have a lower before-tax profit than is currently being generated, the company should not reduce its selling price based on this computation. Swift should investigate the possibility that the reduction in price might, in the long run, increase demand to more than the additional 2,000 kits per year and, thus, make the price reduction more profitable.

CASE #4   Swift Company has an opportunity to sell 10,000 kits to a department store for $2.50 per kit. The kits will be packaged and sold under the department store's own label. Packaging costs will increase by $.14 per kit, but no other variable selling costs will be incurred by the company. If the opportunity is accepted, a $500 commission will be paid to the salesperson calling on this department store. This sale will not interfere with current sales and is within the company's relevant range of activity. Should Swift make this sale?

The new total variable cost per kit is $2.00 ($1.98 total current variable costs + $.14 additional variable packaging cost − $.12 current variable selling costs). The $2.50 selling price minus the $2.00 new total variable cost provides a contribution margin of $.50 per kit sold to the department store.

Total contribution margin provided by this sale (10,000 kits × $.50 CM per kit)	$5,000
− Additional fixed cost (commission) related to this sale	(500)
= Net incremental benefit	$4,500

The total contribution margin generated by the sale is more than enough to cover the additional fixed cost. Thus, the sale produces a net incremental benefit to the firm in the form of increased profits and, therefore, should be made.

Similar to all proposals, this one should be evaluated on the basis of its long-range potential. Is the commission a one-time payment? Will sales to the department store continue for several years? Will such sales not affect regular business in the future? Is such a sale within the boundaries of the law?[9] If all these questions can be answered "yes," Swift should seriously consider this opportunity. In addition to the direct department store sales potential, referral business might also arise to increase sales.

The contribution margin or incremental approach will often be sufficient to decide on the monetary merits of proposed or necessary changes. In making decisions, however, management must also consider the qualitative and long-run effects of the changes. Additional considerations include production throughput, changes in future capacity requirements, ability to control quality, ability to make timely delivery, demographics, availability of raw materials, and price and quality of raw materials. The above examples all assume a single-product company, but most businesses do not produce and/or sell a single product. The next section of the chapter deals with the more realistic, multiproduct entity.

CVP ANALYSIS IN A MULTIPRODUCT ENVIRONMENT

VIDEO VIGNETTE

Wilamette International Travel (Blue Chip Enterprises)

Companies typically produce and sell a variety of products, some of which may be related (such as dolls and doll clothes or sheets, towels, and bedspreads). To perform CVP analysis in a multiproduct company, one must assume either a constant product sales mix or an average contribution margin ratio. The constant mix assumption can be referred to as the "bag" (or "basket") assumption. The analogy is that the sales mix represents a bag of products that are sold together. For example, whenever some of Product A is sold, a set amount of Products B and C are also sold. Use of an assumed constant mix allows the computation of a weighted average contribution margin ratio for the bag of products being sold. Without the assumption of a constant sales mix, break-even point cannot be calculated nor can CVP analysis be used effectively.[10]

In a multiproduct company, the CM ratio is weighted on the quantities of each product included in the "bag" of products. This weighting process means that the contribution margin ratio of the product making up the largest proportion of the bag has the greatest impact on the average contribution margin of the product mix.

The Swift Company example is continued. Because of the success of the dental kits, company management has decided to also produce breath freshener packs. The vice president of marketing estimates that, for every three kits sold, the company will

[9] The Robinson-Patman Act addresses the legal ways companies may price their goods for sale to different purchasers.
[10] Once the constant percentage contribution margin in a multiproduct firm is determined, all situations regarding profit points can be treated in the same manner as they were earlier in the chapter. One must remember, however, that the answers reflect the "bag" assumption.

EXHIBIT 12–12

CVP Analysis—Multiple
Products

	DENTAL KITS		FRESH BREATH PACKS	
Product Cost Information				
Selling price	$3.00	100%	$1.00	100%
Total variable cost	(1.98)	66%	(.46)	46%
Contribution margin	$1.02	34%	$ .54	54%

Total fixed costs = $9,180 previous + $2,340 new = $11,520

	KITS		PACKS	TOTAL	PERCENTAGE
Number of products	3		1		
Revenue per product	$3.00		$1.00		
Total revenue per "bag"		$9.00		$1.00 $10.00	100
Variable cost per product	(1.98)		(.46)		
Total variable per "bag"		(5.94)		(.46) (6.40)	(64)
Contribution margin—product	$1.02		$ .54		
Contribution margin—"bag"		$3.06		$ .54 $ 3.60	36

BEP in units (where B = "bags" of products)

$$CM(B) = FC$$

$$\$3.60B = \$11,520$$

$$B = 3,200 \text{ bags}$$

Note: Each "bag" consists of 3 kits and 1 pack; therefore, it will take 9,600 kits and 3,200 packs to break even, assuming the constant 3:1 mix.
BEP in sales dollars (where CM ratio = weighted average CM per "bag"):

$$B = FC \div CM \text{ ratio}$$

$$B = \$11,520 \div .36$$

$$B = \$32,000$$

Note: The break-even sales dollars also represent the assumed constant sales mix of $9.00 of sales of kits to $1.00 of sales of packs to represent a 90% to 10% ratio. Thus, the company must have $28,800 ($32,000 × 90%) in sales of kits and $3,200 in sales of packs to break even.

Proof of the above computations using the income statement approach:

	KITS	PACKS	TOTAL
Sales	$28,800	$3,200	$32,000
Variable costs	(19,008)	(1,472)	(20,480)
Contribution margin	$ 9,792	$1,728	$11,520
Fixed costs			(11,520)
Income before taxes			$ 0.00

sell one pack of breath fresheners. Therefore, the "bag" of products has a 3:1 ratio. The company will incur an additional $2,340 in fixed costs related to plant assets (depreciation, insurance, and so forth) needed to support a higher relevant range of production. Exhibit 12–12 provides relevant company information and shows the break-even computations.

Any shift in the proportion of sales mix of products will change the weighted average contribution margin and, as such, the break-even point. If the sales mix shifts toward products with lower contribution margins, there will be an increase in the BEP and a decrease in profits unless there is a corresponding increase in total revenues. A shift toward higher margin products without a corresponding decrease in

EXHIBIT 12–13

Effects of Product Mix
Shift

	KITS		PACKS	TOTAL	PERCENTAGE
Number of products	2.5		1.5		
Revenue per product	$3.00		$1.00		
Total revenue per "bag"		$7.50		$1.50	$9.00	100.0
Variable cost per product	(1.98)		(.46)		
Total variable per "bag"		(4.95)		(.69)	(5.64)	(62.7)
Contribution margin—product	$1.02		$ .54		
Contribution margin—"bag"		$2.55		$ .81	$3.36	37.3

BEP in units (where B = "bag" or mix of products)

$$CM(B) = FC$$

$$\$3.36B = \$11,520$$

$$B = 3,429 \text{ "bags" to break even}$$

Actual results: 3,200 "bags" with a sales mix ratio of 2.5 kits to 1.5 packs; thus, the company sold 8,000 kits and 4,800 packs.

	8,000 KITS	4,800 PACKS	TOTAL
Sales	$24,000	$4,800	$28,800
Variable costs	(15,840)	(2,208)	(18,048)
Contribution margin	$ 8,160	$2,592	$10,752
Fixed costs			(11,520)
Net loss			$ (768)

revenues will cause a lower break-even point and increased profits. As illustrated by the financial results shown in Exhibit 12–13, a shift toward the product with the lower contribution margin (breath freshener packs) causes a higher break-even point and lower profits (in this case, a loss). This exhibit assumes that Swift sells 3,200 "bags" of product, but the mix was not in the exact proportions assumed in Exhibit 12–12. Instead of a 3:1 ratio, the sales mix was 2.5:1.5 kits to packs. A loss of $768 resulted because the company sold a higher proportion of the packs, which have a lower contribution margin than the kits.

MARGIN OF SAFETY

margin of safety

When making decisions about various business opportunities and changes in sales mix, managers often consider the size of the company's **margin of safety (MS).** The margin of safety is the excess of a company's budgeted or actual sales over its break-even point. It is the amount that sales can drop before reaching the break-even point and, thus, it provides a measure of the amount of "cushion" from losses.

The margin of safety can be expressed as units, dollars, or a percentage. The following formulas are applicable:

Margin of safety in units = Actual units − Break-even units

Margin of safety in dollars = Actual sales in $ − Break-even sales in $

Margin of safety % = Margin of safety in units or $Actual sales in units or $

The break-even point for Swift (using the original, single-product data) is 9,000 units or $27,000 of sales. The income statement for the company presented in Exhibit 12–6 shows actual sales for 1996 of 30,000 kits or $90,000. The margin of safety for Swift is quite high, because it is operating far above its break-even point (see Exhibit 12–14).

In units: 30,000 actual − 9,000 BEP = 21,000 kits

In sales $: $90,000 actual − $27,000 BEP = $63,000

Percentage: 21,000 ÷ 30,000 = 70%

or

$63,000 ÷ $90,000 = 70%

EXHIBIT 12–14

Margin of Safety

The margin of safety calculation allows management to determine how close to a danger level the company is operating and, as such, provides an indication of risk. The lower the margin of safety, the more carefully management must watch sales figures and control costs so that a net loss will not be generated. At low margins of safety, managers are less likely to take advantage of opportunities that, if incorrectly analyzed or forecasted, could send the company into a loss position.

OPERATING LEVERAGE

Another measure that is closely related to the margin of safety and also provides useful management information is the company's degree of operating leverage. The relationship of a company's variable and fixed costs is reflected in its **operating leverage.** Typically, highly labor-intensive organizations, such as Burger King and Connecticut Mutual Life Insurance Company, have high variable costs and low fixed costs and, thus, have low operating leverage. (An exception to this rule is a sports team, which is highly labor-intensive, but the labor costs are fixed rather than variable.)

Conversely, organizations that are highly capital intensive (such as American Airlines) or automated (such as Allen-Bradley) have a cost structure that includes low variable and high fixed costs, providing high operating leverage. Because variable costs are low relative to selling prices, the contribution margin is high. However, the high level of fixed costs means that the break-even point also tends to be high. If selling prices are predominantly set by the market, volume has the primary impact on profitability. As they become more automated, companies will face this type of cost structure and become more dependent on volume to add profits. Thus, a company's **cost structure,** or the relative composition of its fixed and variable costs, strongly influences the degree to which its profits respond to changes in volume.

Companies with high operating leverage have high contribution margin ratios. Although such companies have to establish fairly high sales volumes to initially cover fixed costs, once those costs are covered, each unit sold after breakeven produces large profits. Thus, a small increase in sales can have a major impact on a company's profits.

The **degree of operating leverage** (DOL) measures how a *percentage* change in sales from the current level will affect company profits. In other words, it indicates how sensitive the company is to sales volume increases and decreases. The computation providing the degree of operating leverage factor is

Degree of Operating Leverage = Contribution Margin ÷ Profit before Tax

This calculation assumes that fixed costs do not increase when sales increase.

Assume that Swift Company is currently selling 20,000 kits. Exhibit 12–15 provides the income statement that reflects this sales level. At this level of activity, the company has an operating leverage factor of 1.818. If the company increases sales by 20 percent, the change in profits is equal to the degree of operating leverage multiplied by the percentage change in sales or 36.36 percent. If sales decrease by the same 20 percent, there is a negative 36.36 percent impact on profits. Exhibit 12–15 confirms these computations.

EXHIBIT 12–15

Degree of Operating
Leverage

	(20,000 KITS) CURRENT	(24,000 KITS) 20% INCREASE	(16,000 KITS) 20% DECREASE
Sales	$60,000	$72,000	$48,000
Variable costs ($1.98 per kit)	(39,600)	(47,520)	(31,680)
Contribution margin	$20,400	$24,480	$16,320
Fixed costs	(9,180)	(9,180)	(9,180)
Profit before tax	$11,220	$15,300*	$ 7,140**

Degree of operating leverage:

Contribution margin ÷ Profit before tax
($20,400 ÷ $11,220)   1.818
($24,480 ÷ $15,300)   1.600
($16,320 ÷ $ 7,140)   2.286

*Profit increase = $15,300 − $11,220 = $4,080 (or 36.36% of the original profit)
**Profit decrease = $7,140 − $11,220 = $(4,080) (or −36.36% of the original profit)

The relationship between the margin of safety and degree of operating leverage is shown below:

$$\text{Margin of Safety \%} = 1 \div \text{Degree of Operating Leverage}$$

$$\text{Degree of Operating Leverage} = 1 \div \text{Margin of Safety \%}$$

The degree of operating leverage *decreases* the farther a company moves from its break-even point. Thus, when the margin of safety is small, the degree of operating leverage is large. In fact, at breakeven, the degree of operating leverage is infinite because any increase from zero is an infinite percentage change. If a company is operating close to the break-even point, each percentage increase in sales can make a dramatic impact on net income. As the company moves away from break-even sales, the margin of safety increases, but the degree of operating leverage declines.

This relationship is proved in Exhibit 12–16 using the 20,000-kit sales level information for Swift. Therefore, if one of the two measures is known, the other can be easily calculated.

UNDERLYING ASSUMPTIONS OF CVP ANALYSIS

CVP analysis is a short-run model that focuses on relationships among several items—selling price, variable costs, volume, fixed costs, and profits. This model is a useful planning tool that can provide information on the impact on profits when changes are made in the cost structure or in sales levels. However, the CVP model, like other human-made models, is an abstraction of reality and, as such, does not reveal all the forces at work. It reflects reality but does not duplicate it. Although limiting the accuracy of the results, several important but necessary assumptions are made in the CVP model. These assumptions follow.

EXHIBIT 12–16

Margin of Safety and
Degree of Operating
Leverage Relationship

Margin of Safety % = Margin of Safety in Units ÷ Actual Sales in Units
= [(20,000 − 9,000) ÷ 20,000] = .55 or 55%

Degree of Operating Leverage = Contribution Margin ÷ Profit before Tax
= $20,400 ÷ $11,220 = 1.818

Margin of Safety = (1 ÷ DOL) = (1 ÷ 1.818) = .55 or 55%

Degree of Operating Leverage = (1 ÷ MS %) = (1 ÷ .55) = 1.818

1. All revenue and variable cost behavior patterns are constant per unit and linear within the relevant range.
2. Total contribution margin (total revenue − total variable costs) is linear within the relevant range and increases proportionally with output. This assumption follows directly from assumption 1.
3. Total fixed cost is a constant amount within the relevant range.
4. Mixed costs can be *accurately* separated into their fixed and variable elements. Although accuracy of separation may be questioned, reliable estimates can be developed from the use of regression analysis or the high-low method (discussed in Chapter 5).
5. Sales and production are equal; thus, there is no material fluctuation in inventory levels. This assumption is necessary because of the allocation of fixed costs to inventory at potentially different rates each year. This assumption requires that variable costing information be available. Because both CVP and variable costing focus on cost behavior, they are distinctly compatible with one another.
6. There will be no capacity additions during the period under consideration. If such additions were made, fixed (and, possibly, variable) costs would change. Any changes in fixed or variable costs would violate assumptions 1 through 3.
7. In a multiproduct firm, the sales mix will remain constant. If this assumption were not made, no weighted average contribution margin could be computed for the company.
8. There is either no inflation or, if it can be forecasted, it is incorporated into the CVP model. This eliminates the possibility of cost changes.
9. Labor productivity, production technology, and market conditions will not change. If any of these changes occur, costs would change correspondingly and selling prices might change. Such changes would invalidate assumptions 1 through 3.

These assumptions limit not only the volume of activity for which the calculations can be made, but also the time frame for the usefulness of the calculations to that period for which the specified revenue and cost amounts remain constant. Changes in either selling prices or costs will require that new computations be made for break-even and product opportunity analyses.

The nine assumptions listed above are the traditional ones associated with cost-volume-profit analysis. An additional assumption must also be noted in regard to the distinction of variable and fixed costs. Accountants have generally assumed that cost behavior, once classified, remained constant over periods of time as long as operations remained within the relevant range. Thus, for example, once a cost was determined to be "fixed," it would be fixed next year, the year after, and 10 years from now.

It is more appropriate to regard fixed costs as, instead, long-term variable costs. Over the long run, through managerial decisions, companies can lay off supervisors and sell plant and equipment items. Fixed costs are not fixed forever. In fact, in many companies, overhead costs considered to be fixed "have been the most variable and rapidly increasing costs."[11] Part of this "misclassification" has been caused by im-properly specifying the drivers of the costs. As companies become less focused on production and sales volumes as cost drivers, they will begin to recognize that "fixed costs" only exist under a short-term reporting period perspective.

Such a reclassification simply means that the cost drivers of the long-term variable costs will have to be specified in the break-even and CVP analyses. The formula will need to be expanded to include these additional drivers, and more information and a longer time frame will be needed to make the calculations. No longer will sales volume necessarily be the overriding nonmonetary force in the computations.

These adjustments to the CVP formula will force managers to take a long-run, rather than a short-run, view of product opportunities. Such a perspective could produce better organizational decisions. As the time frame is extended, both the time value of money and life-cycle costing become necessary considerations. Additionally,

[11] Robin Cooper and Robert S. Kaplan, "How Cost Accounting Distorts Product Costs," *Management Accounting* (April 1988), p. 27.

the traditional income statement becomes less useful for developing projects that will take several years to mature. A long-run perspective is important in a variety of circumstances, such as when variable or fixed costs arise only in the first year that a product or service is provided to customers.

QUALITY AND COSTS

VIDEO
VIGNETTE

Hewlett-Packard (in AME—On the Road) and/or Task Lighting (Blue Chip Enterprises)

One important long-run change that may create significant short-run costs is the implementation of a total quality management (TQM) program. A TQM program, as discussed in Chapter 3, generally causes prevention costs to increase. These costs probably will not be recouped in the short run by the decreases in appraisal and failure costs. However, in the long run, appraisal and failure costs should decline and the higher-quality goods produced might command higher selling prices and sell better than the lower-quality goods produced before the TQM program. Thus, the three primary factors in determining a company's profits (costs, price, and volume) are intimately related to a fourth factor: quality. Quality considerations are primarily concerned with improving or maintaining customer satisfaction. As the News Note on keeping customers indicates, satisfying customers over the long run has beneficial effects on the first of these three primary factors.

It would seem that the costs of ensuring quality should, in the long run, outweigh the costs of having poor quality. Implementation of a TQM program could cause higher variable costs (in the form of higher-quality materials) or fixed costs (for plant assets and training). Other costs (such as those attributable to rework, redesign, and product failure) should fall after a period of time. Higher variable costs will not necessarily result in a lower contribution margin because of the possibility of higher selling prices. Higher fixed costs may only be incurred for the short-run, returning to lower levels after the implementation program is completed.

NEWS NOTE

The Longer You Keep a Customer, the Less It Costs You

It may be obvious that acquiring a new customer entails certain one-time costs for advertising, promotions, and the like. In credit cards, for example, companies spend an average of $51 to recruit a new customer and set up the new account. But there are many more pieces to the profitability puzzle.

As purchases rise, operating costs decline. Checking customers' credit histories and adding them to the corporate database is expensive, but those things need be done only once. Also, as the company gains experience with its customers, it can serve them more efficiently. One small financial consulting business that depends on personal relationships with clients has found that costs drop by two-thirds from the first year to the second because customers know what to expect from the consultant and have fewer questions or problems.

Also, companies with long-time customers can often charge more for their products or services. Many people will pay more to stay in a hotel they know or to go to a doctor they trust than to take a chance on a less expensive competitor.

Yet another economic boon from long-time customers is the free advertising they provide. One of the leading home builders in the United States, for example, has found that more than 60% of its sales are the result of referrals.

These cost savings and additional revenues combine to produce a steady stream of profits over the course of the customer's relationship with the company. While the relative importance of these effects varies from industry to industry, the end result is that longer term [service-satisfied] customers generate increasing profits.

When Boeing began planning for the development of the 777 plane, company management reviewed the issues of cost components and quality of output. Management concluded that it was cost-effective to invest heavily in fixed costs by installing computer-driven machinery and, thereby, reduce not only direct labor cost but (possibly more importantly) reduce the cost of waste from cutting the plane's sections. The result: higher product quality, not only on prototypes, but on final models.

Recall that CVP behavior patterns were required to be stable for the model to produce valid results. If the CVP component elements are sensitive to continuous quality improvement efforts, they must be reevaluated frequently enough to compensate for changes that have occurred. Updating the CVP factors and their relationships for the impact of quality initiatives will help ensure the measurement of longer-run valid results.

Although efforts to improve quality may take some time to produce noticeable results, it is widely believed that continuous quality improvement will increase sales volume and productivity, lower costs, and support management's ability to adjust product and service prices. As mentioned in the previous sections, when managers analyze break-even computations or product opportunities, managers should consider both quantitative and qualitative information. In addition, managers should consider the potential benefits generated by focusing their attention more on the long run and less on the short run.

REVISITING

The Procter & Gamble Company

Consider the Procter & Gamble Company "Statement of Purpose":

- We will provide products of superior quality and value that best fill the needs of the world's consumers.
- We will achieve that purpose through an organization and a working environment which attracts the finest people; fully develops and challenges our individual talents; encourages our free and spirited collaboration to drive the business ahead; and maintains the Company's historic principles of integrity and doing the right thing.
- Through the successful pursuit of our commitment, we expect our brands to achieve leadership share and profit positions and that, as a result, our business, our people, our shareholders, and the communities in which we live and work, will prosper.

[Note the word *value* that refers to delivering comparable or better quality than the competition for a lower price. Of course, in the long run, a company can only charge lower prices if it has lower costs or will accept lower profit margins. Also, the terms *leadership share* and *profit positions* imply the interplay among cost, volume, and profit.]

John Pepper, Chairman of the Board and Chief Executive, talks about the firm's future in the 1995 *Annual Report:* "First and foremost, we need to win with consumers even more consistently. That means delivering better value—with better products at a better price—in every category. . . . That's why the company's second focus area—broader, deeper cost control—is so essential. . . . The third focus area is globalization—particularly fast, effective expansion of proven success models.

"Creating and expanding these models has driven the growth of core businesses such as Shampoo, Laundry and Feminine Protection—businesses in which P & G is now the world's leader."

In remarks to financial analysts made in Cincinnati, Ohio, in November 1995, Durk Jager, President and Chief Operating Officer, elaborated on cost control: "First, we have three major areas for cost control. These are our Total Delivered Costs of our products, or TDC as we call it. TDC includes raw material, packaging, manufacturing, and distribution costs. Secondly, we have our Marketing costs, and third, we have administrative costs. Control of all three is critical.

". . . We plan to drive up capacity utilization, we will use our raw and packaging materials more efficiently, and we will further reduce working capital. Simplification, standardization, and mechanization will play a major role in achieving these goals."

SOURCES: *Remarks to Financial Analysts,* Cincinnati, Ohio (November 1, 1995), p. 15 and *Facts About Procter & Gamble,* p. 1—both provided by the Procter & Gamble Company General Offices, Two Procter & Gamble Plaza, Cincinnati, Ohio; and The Procter & Gamble Company 1995 *Annual Report,* pp. 6–7. © The Procter & Gamble Company. Reprinted by permission.

CHAPTER SUMMARY

Cost accumulation and cost presentation are two dimensions of product costing. Cost accumulation determines which costs are treated as product costs, whereas cost presentation focuses on how costs are shown on the financial statements or internal management reports.

Absorption and variable costing are two production costing methods that differ in regard to product cost composition and income statement presentation. Under absorption costing, all manufacturing costs, both variable and fixed, are treated as product costs. The absorption costing method presents nonmanufacturing costs according to functional areas on the income statement, whereas the variable costing method presents both nonmanufacturing and manufacturing costs according to cost behavior on the income statement.

Variable costing computes product costs by including only the variable costs of production (direct material, direct labor, and variable manufacturing overhead). Fixed manufacturing overhead is viewed as a period expense in the period of occurrence by variable costing. Variable costing is not considered to be an acceptable method of inventory valuation for preparing external reports or filing tax returns.

Absorption costing income differs from variable costing income for any period in which production and sales volumes differ. This difference reflects the amount of fixed manufacturing overhead that is either attached to, or released from, inventory in absorption costing as opposed to being immediately expensed in variable costing.

Management planning includes planning for prices, volumes, fixed and variable costs, contribution margins, and break-even point. The interrelationships of these factors are studied when applying cost-volume-profit (CVP) analysis. Management should understand these interrelationships and combine them effectively and efficiently for company success.

The CVP model reflects linear relationships that can be used to calculate the level of sales volume necessary to achieve target profit objectives. CVP can also be used to compute break-even point (BEP), at which total contribution margin is equal to total fixed costs. Contribution margin equals sales minus all variable costs. BEP can be calculated using a cost-volume-profit formula that reflects basic income statement relationships. The BEP will change if the company's selling price(s) or costs change. Because most companies do not wish to operate at breakeven, CVP analysis extends the break-even point computation through the introduction of profit. The sales necessary to generate a desired amount of profit are computed by adding the desired profit to fixed costs and dividing that total by contribution margin. Profit may be stated as a fixed or a variable amount on a before- or after-tax basis. After fixed costs are covered, each dollar of contribution margin generated by company sales will produce a dollar of before-tax profit.

In a multiproduct firm, all break-even and cost-volume-profit analyses are performed using an assumed constant sales mix of products. This sales mix is referred to as the "bag" assumption. Use of the bag assumption requires the computation of a weighted average contribution margin (and, thus, contribution margin ratio) for the "bag" of products being sold by the company. Answers to break-even or CVP computations are in units or dollars of "bags" of products; these bag amounts can be converted to individual products by using the sales mix relationship.

The margin of safety (MS) of a firm indicates how far (in units, sales dollars, or a percentage) a company is operating from its break-even point. A company's degree of operating leverage (DOL) shows what percentage change in profit would occur given a specified percentage change in sales from the current level. The MS percentage is equal to $(1 \div \text{DOL})$ and the DOL is equal to $(1 \div \text{MS\%})$.

CVP analysis enhances a manager's ability to beneficially influence current operations and to predict future operations, thereby reducing the risk of uncertainty. The model is, however, based on several assumptions that limit its ability to reflect reality. Managers may also wish to begin viewing the CVP relationships more on a long-range basis than the currently held short-range viewpoint.

APPENDIX

Graphic Approaches to Breakeven

Solutions to break-even problems are determined in this chapter using an algebraic formula. Sometimes, however, the cost accountant may wish to present information to managers in a more visual format, such as graphs. Exhibit 12–17 graphically presents each income statement item for Swift Company original data (see Exhibit 12–6), to provide visual representations of the behavior of revenue, costs, and contribution margin.

While illustrating individual behaviors, the graphs presented in Exhibit 12–17 are not very useful for determining the relationships among the various income statement categories. A **break-even chart** can be prepared to graph the relationships among revenue, volume, and the various costs. The break-even point on a break-even chart is located at the point where the total cost and total revenue lines cross.

break-even chart

Two approaches can be used to prepare break-even charts: the traditional approach and the contemporary approach. A third graphical presentation, the profit-volume graph, is closely related to the break-even chart.

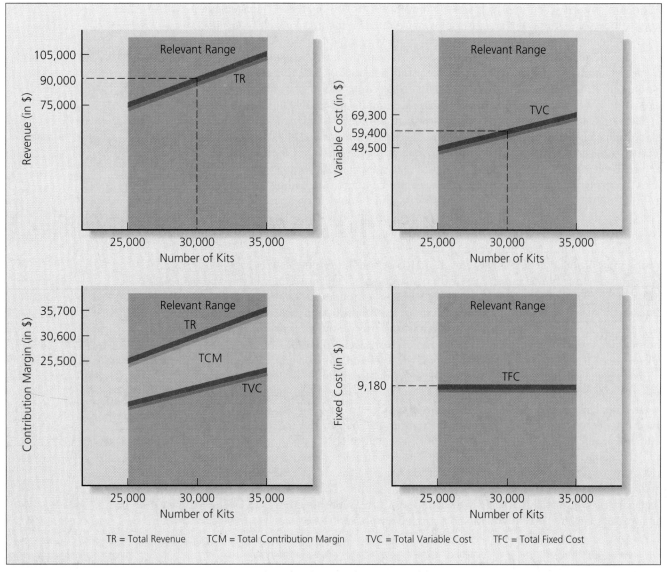

EXHIBIT 12–17

Graphical Presentation of
Income Statement Items

Note: Linear functions are always assumed for total revenue, total variable cost, and total fixed cost. These functions are reflected in the basic assumptions given on p. 523.

TRADITIONAL APPROACH

The traditional approach to graphical break-even analysis focuses on the relationships among revenues, costs, and profits (losses). This approach does *not* show contribution margin. A traditional break-even chart for Swift Company is prepared as follows.

Step 1: Label each axis and graph the cost lines. The total fixed cost is drawn horizontal to the *x*-axis (volume). The variable cost line begins at the point where the total fixed cost line intersects the *y*-axis. The slope of the variable cost line is the per-unit variable cost. The resulting line represents total cost. The distance between the fixed cost and the total cost lines indicates total variable cost at each activity volume level.

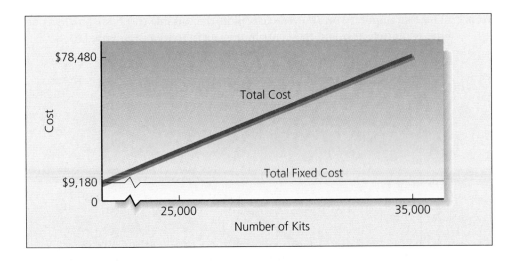

Step 2: Chart the revenue line, beginning at zero dollars. The break-even point is located at the intersection of the revenue line and the total cost line. The vertical distance to the right of the BEP and between the revenue and total cost lines represents profits; the distance between the revenue and total cost lines to the left of the break-even point represents losses. If exact readings could be taken on the graph, the break-even point for Swift Company would be $27,000 of sales or 9,000 kits.

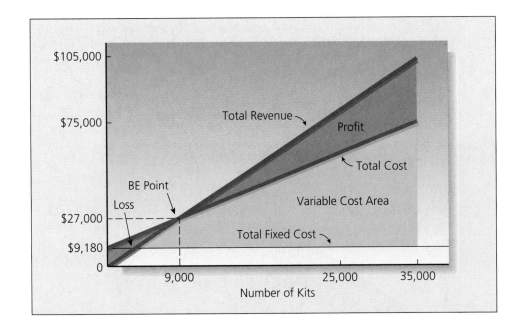

The contribution margin provided by each level of sales volume is not apparent on the traditional break-even chart. Because contribution margin is so important in CVP analysis, another graphical approach can be used. The contemporary approach specifically presents CM in the break-even chart. The preparation of a contemporary break-even chart is detailed in the following steps.

CONTEMPORARY APPROACH

Step 1: The contemporary break-even chart plots the variable cost first. The revenue line is plotted next and the contribution margin area is indicated.

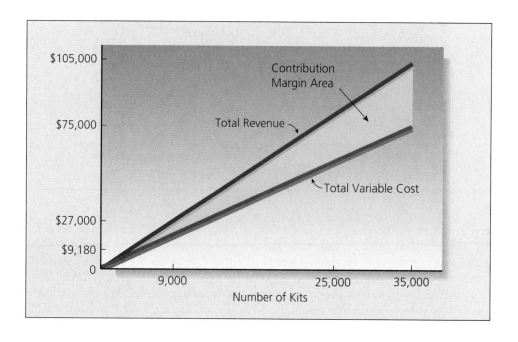

Step 2: Total cost is graphed by adding a line parallel to the total variable cost line. The distance between the total cost line and the variable cost line is the amount of fixed cost. The break-even point is located where the revenue and total cost lines intersect. Breakeven for Swift Company is again shown at $27,000 of sales and 9,000 kits.

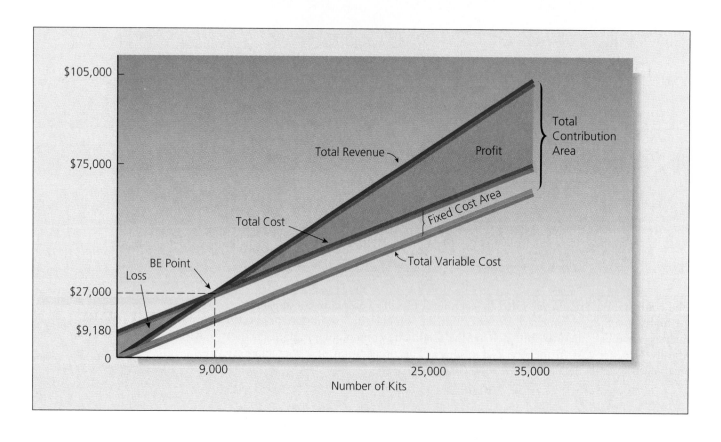

The contemporary graphic approach allows the following important observations to be made.

1. Contribution margin is created by the excess of revenues over variable costs. If variable costs are greater than revenues, no quantity of volume will ever allow a profit to be made.
2. Total contribution margin is always equal to total fixed cost plus profit or minus loss.
3. Before profits can be generated, contribution margin must exceed fixed costs.

The **profit-volume** (PV) **graph** reflects the amount of profit or loss associated with each level of sales. The horizontal axis on the PV graph represents sales volume and the vertical axis represents dollars. Amounts shown above the horizontal axis are positive and represent profits; amounts shown below the horizontal axis are negative and represent losses.

Two points are located on the graph: total fixed costs and break-even point. Total fixed costs are shown on the vertical axis below the sales volume line as a negative amount. If no products were sold, fixed costs would still be incurred and a loss of the entire amount would result. The location of the break-even point may be determined algebraically or by using a break-even chart. Break-even point in units is shown on the horizontal axis because there is zero profit/loss at that point. The last step in preparing the PV graph is to draw a profit line that passes between and extends through the two located points. Using this line, the amount of profit or loss for any sales volume can be read from the vertical axis. The profit line is really a contribution margin line and the slope of the line is determined by the unit contribution margin. The line shows that no profit is earned until the contribution margin covers the fixed costs.

The PV graph for Swift Company is shown in Exhibit 12–18. Total fixed costs are $9,180 and break-even point is 9,000 kits. The profit line reflects the original Exhibit 12–6 income statement data indicating a profit of $21,420 at a sales level of 30,000 kits.

PROFIT-VOLUME GRAPH

profit-volume graph

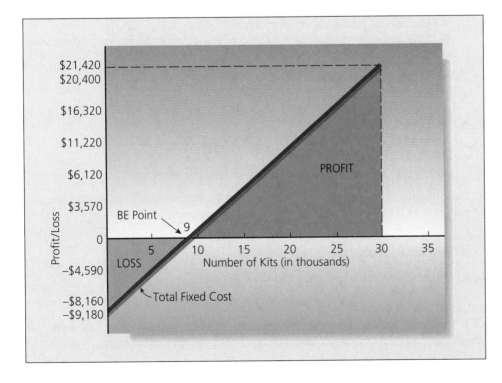

EXHIBIT 12–18

Profit-Volume Graph

The graphic approaches to breakeven provide detailed visual displays of break-even point. They do not, however, provide a precise solution because exact points cannot be determined on a graph. A definitive computation of break-even point can be found algebraically using the formula approach or a computer software application.

KEY TERMS

absorption costing (p. 514)	full costing (p. 514)
break-even chart (p. 541)	functional classification (p. 514)
break-even point (p. 521)	incremental analysis (p. 530)
contribution margin (p. 523)	margin of safety (p. 534)
contribution margin ratio (p. 524)	operating leverage (p. 535)
cost accumulation (p. 513)	phantom profit (p. 519)
cost presentation (p. 513)	product contribution margin (p. 516)
cost structure (p. 535)	profit-volume graph (p. 545)
cost-volume-profit analysis (p. 521)	total contribution margin (p. 516)
degree of operating leverage (p. 535)	variable costing (p. 514)
direct costing (p. 515)	variable cost ratio (p. 524)

SOLUTION STRATEGIES

ABSORPTION AND VARIABLE COSTING

1. Which method is being used (absorption or variable)?
   a. If absorption:
      - What is the fixed manufacturing overhead application rate?
      - What denominator capacity was used in determining the fixed manufacturing overhead application rate?
      - Is production equal to the denominator capacity used in determining the fixed manufacturing overhead application rate? If not, there is a fixed overhead volume variance that must be properly assigned to cost of goods sold and, possibly, inventories.
      - What is the cost per unit of product? (DM + DL + VOH + FOH)
   b. If variable:
      - What is the cost per unit of product? (DM + DL + VOH)
      - What is total fixed manufacturing overhead? Assign to income statement in total as a period expense.

2. What is the relationship of production to sales?
   a. Production = Sales
      Absorption Costing Income = Variable Costing Income
   b. Production > Sales
      Absorption Costing Income > Variable Costing Income
   c. Production < Sales
      Absorption Costing Income < Variable Costing Income

3. Dollar Difference between Absorption Costing Income and Variable Costing Income = FOH Application Rate × Change in Inventory Units

COST-VOLUME-PROFIT

The basic equation for break-even and CVP problems is

$$\text{Total Revenue} - \text{Total Cost} = \text{Profit}$$

CVP problems can also be solved by using a numerator/denominator approach. All numerators and denominators and the types of problems each relate to are listed below. The formulas relate to both single- and multiproduct firms, but results for multiproduct firms are per bag and can be converted to units of individual products.

PROBLEM SITUATION	NUMERATOR	DENOMINATOR
Simple BEP in units	FC	CM
Simple BEP in dollars	FC	CM%
CVP with lump-sum profit in units	FC + P	CM
CVP with lump-sum profit in dollars	FC + P	CM%
CVP with variable profit in units	FC	$CM - P_u$
CVP with variable profit in dollars	FC	$CM\% - P_u\%$

where   FC = fixed cost

CM = contribution margin per unit

CM% = contribution margin percentage

P = total profit (on a before-tax basis)

P_u = profit per unit (on a before-tax basis)

$P_u\%$ = profit percentage per unit (on a before-tax basis)

To convert after-tax profit to before-tax profit, divide after-tax profit by (1 − tax rate).

MARGIN OF SAFETY

Margin of Safety in Units = Actual units − Break-even units

Margin of Safety in Dollars = Actual sales in $ − Breakeven sales $

Margin of Safety % = Margin of safety in units or $ ÷ Actual sales in units or $

DEGREE OF OPERATING LEVERAGE

Degree of Operating Leverage = Contribution margin ÷ Profit before tax

Predicted Profit = [1 + (DOL × Percent change in sales)] × Current profit

---

Samson Company's management is interested in seeing the company's absorption costing income statements for 1997 and 1998 (the first two years of operation) recast using variable costing. The company incurred total fixed manufacturing overhead of $80,000 each year and produced 25,000 and 20,000 units, respectively, each year. The absorption costing statements based on FIFO costing follow.

DEMONSTRATION PROBLEM

	1997	1998
Net sales (a)	$300,000	$330,000
Cost of goods sold (b)	(124,000)	(150,000)
Gross margin	$176,000	$180,000
Operating expenses (c)	(82,500)	(88,500)
Income before tax	$ 93,500	$ 91,500

(a) Net sales:		
20,000 units @ $15	$300,000	
22,000 units @ $15		$330,000

(b) Cost of goods sold:		
Beginning inventory	$ 0	$ 31,000
Cost of goods manufactured*	155,000	140,000
Goods available for sale	$155,000	$171,000
Ending inventory**	(31,000)	(21,000)
Cost of goods sold	$124,000	$150,000

	1997	1998
(c) Analysis of operating expenses:		
Variable	$ 50,000	$ 55,000
Fixed	32,500	33,500
Total	$ 82,500	$ 88,500

*CGM

25,000 units @ $6.20 (of which $3 are variable)	$155,000	
20,000 units @ $7.00 (of which $3 are variable)		$140,000

**EI

5,000 units @ $6.20	$ 31,000	
3,000 units @ $7.00		$ 21,000

Required:

a. Recast the 1997 and 1998 income statements on a variable costing basis.
b. Reconcile income for each year between absorption and variable costing.

Solution to Demonstration Problem

a.

	1997	1998
Net sales	$300,000	$330,000
Variable cost of goods sold	(60,000)	(66,000)
Product contribution margin	$240,000	$264,000
Variable operating expenses	(50,000)	(55,000)
Total contribution margin	$190,000	$209,000
Fixed costs		
Manufacturing	$ 80,000	$ 80,000
Operating	32,500	33,500
Total fixed costs	$112,500	$113,500
Income before tax	$ 77,500	$ 95,500

b.

Reconciliation 1997:	
Absorption costing income before tax	$93,500
− Fixed manufacturing overhead in ending inventory ($3.20 × 5,000)	(16,000)
Variable costing income before tax	$77,500
Reconciliation 1998:	
Absorption costing income before tax	$91,500
+ Fixed manufacturing overhead released from beginning inventory ($3.20 × 5,000)	16,000
− Fixed manufacturing overhead deferred in ending inventory ($4.00 × 3,000)	(12,000)
Variable costing income before tax	$95,500

QUESTIONS

1. In what ways does absorption costing differ from variable costing?
2. What is the difference between absorption and variable costing in the treatment of fixed overhead?
3. What is a functional classification of costs? What is a behavioral classification of costs?

4. Which product costing alternative, variable or absorption, is generally required for external reporting? Why?

5. How do the income statement formats for variable and absorption costing differ?

6. Why does the variable costing approach provide more useful information for making internal decisions?

7. Why is income under absorption costing higher (lower) than under variable costing in years when production exceeds (is below) sales?

8. What is the break-even point? Why is calculating break-even point the starting point for cost-volume-profit analysis?

9. What is contribution margin and why does it fluctuate in direct proportion with sales volume?

10. Why is the formula for a variable costing income statement the basis for break-even or cost-volume-profit analysis?

11. If a product's fixed costs increase and its selling price and variable costs remain constant, what will happen to (a) contribution margin and (b) break-even point?

12. How can contribution margin be used to calculate break-even point in both units and dollars?

13. What is the contribution margin ratio? How is it used to calculate the break-even point?

14. A company is in the 40 percent tax bracket. Why is desired profit after tax divided by 60 percent to determine the needed before-tax profit amount?

15. What is meant by the "bag" or "basket" assumption and why is it necessary in a multiproduct firm? What additional assumption must be made in multiproduct CVP analysis that doesn't pertain to a single-product CVP situation?

16. What is operating leverage? How does it pertain to CVP analysis? What is the margin of safety? How does it apply to CVP analysis?

17. *(Appendix)* What are the purposes of a break-even chart? What is the difference between the traditional approach and the contemporary approach to preparing a break-even chart? Between a break-even chart and a profit-volume graph?

EXERCISES

18. *(Ending inventory valuation; absorption vs. variable costing)* Princeton Products Company produces leather wallets. In July 1997, the company manufactured 25,000 wallets. July sales were 23,400 wallets. The cost per wallet for the 25,000 wallets produced was

Direct material	$3.00
Direct labor	2.00
Variable overhead	1.00
Fixed overhead	1.50
Total	$7.50

There was no beginning inventory for July.
a. What is the value of ending inventory using absorption costing?
b. What is the value of ending inventory using variable costing?
c. Which accounting method, variable or absorption, would have produced the higher net income for July?

19. *(Absorption vs. variable costing)* The following data were taken from records of the Lucky Lady Vacuum Cleaner Company. The company uses variable costing. The data relate to the company's first year of operation.

Units produced:	20,000
Units sold:	17,500
Variable cost per unit:	
Direct material	$38
Direct labor	17
Variable overhead	7
Variable selling costs	12
Fixed costs:	
Selling and administrative	$750,000
Manufacturing	250,000

How much higher (or lower) would the company's first-year net income have been if the company had used absorption costing rather than variable costing? Show computations.

20. *(Production cost; absorption vs. variable costing)* The Clean-N-Brite Dish Soap Company began business in 1996. Production for the year was 100,000 bottles of dish soap, and sales were 98,000 bottles. Costs incurred during the year were

Chemicals used	$28,000
Direct labor	13,000
Variable overhead	24,000
Fixed overhead	12,000
Variable selling expenses	5,000
Fixed selling and administrative expenses	14,000
Total actual costs	$96,000

a. What was the actual production cost per bottle under variable costing? Under absorption costing?
b. What was variable Cost of Goods Sold for 1996 under variable costing?
c. What was Cost of Goods Sold for 1996 under absorption costing?
d. What was the value of ending inventory under variable costing? Under absorption costing?
e. How much fixed overhead was charged to expense in 1996 under variable costing? Under absorption costing?

21. *(Net income; absorption vs. variable costing)* Modmodems manufactures high-speed modems. Throughout 1997, unit variable cost remained constant and fixed overhead was applied at the rate of $4 per unit. Income before tax using the variable costing method was $86,000 for July 1997. Beginning and ending inventories for July were 17,000 and 15,000 units, respectively.
a. Calculate income before tax under absorption costing assuming no variances.
b. Assume that the company's beginning and ending inventories were 15,000 and 18,000 units, respectively. Calculate income before tax under absorption costing.

22. *(Standard costing; variable and absorption costing)* Olympic Star Company manufactures athletes' foot powder. The company uses a standard costing system. Following are data pertaining to the company's operations for 1996:

Production for the year	180,000 units
Sales for the year (sales price per unit, $1.25)	195,000 units
Beginning 1996 inventory	35,000 units

STANDARD COSTS TO PRODUCE 1 UNIT:

Direct material	$.15
Direct labor	.10
Variable overhead	.05
Fixed overhead	.15

SELLING AND ADMINISTRATIVE COSTS:

Variable (per unit sold)	$.14
Fixed (per year)	$120,000

Fixed manufacturing overhead is assigned to units of production based on a predetermined rate using a normal production capacity of 200,000 units per year.

a. What is the estimated annual fixed manufacturing overhead?

b. If estimated fixed overhead is equal to actual fixed overhead, what is the amount of under- or overapplied overhead in 1996 under absorption costing? Under variable costing?

c. What is the product cost per unit under absorption costing? Under variable costing?

d. How much expense will be charged against revenues in 1996 under absorption costing? Under variable costing?

e. Will pretax income be higher under absorption or variable costing? By what amount?

23. *(Cost and revenue behavior)* The following financial data have been determined from analyzing the records of Frisco Electronics (a one-product firm):

Contribution margin per unit	$20
Variable costs per unit	$16
Annual fixed costs	$275,000

How do each of the following measures change when product volume goes up by one unit at Frisco Electronics?

a. Total revenue

b. Total costs

c. Profit before tax

24. *(Break-even point)* Albany Manufacturing has the following revenue and cost functions:

Revenue = $50 per unit

Costs = $216,750 + $25 per unit

What is the break-even point in units? In dollars?

25. *(Incremental sales)* Orlando Company has annual sales of $5,000,000 with variable expenses of 60 percent of sales and fixed expenses per month of $80,000. By how much will annual sales have to increase for Orlando Company to have pretax income equal to 30 percent of sales?

26. *(CVP, taxes)* Helen Smith has a small plant that makes playhouses. She sells them to local customers at $3,000 each. Her costs are as follows:

COSTS	PER UNIT	TOTAL
Direct material	$1,200	
Direct labor	400	
Variable overhead	150	
Variable selling	50	
Fixed production overhead		$200,000
Fixed general, selling, and administrative		80,420

Helen is in a 35 percent tax bracket.

a. How many playhouses must she sell to earn $247,507 after taxes?

b. What level of revenue is needed to yield an after-tax income equal to 20 percent of sales?

27. *(Operating leverage, margin of safety)* One of the products produced by California Vineyards is the Arizona Cooler. The selling price per package is $4.50, and variable cost of production is $2.70. Total fixed costs per year are $316,600. The company is currently selling 200,000 packages per year.
    a. What is the margin of safety in units?
    b. What is the degree of operating leverage?
    c. If the company can increase sales in units by 30 percent, what percentage increase will it experience in income? Prove your answer using the income statement approach.
    d. If the company increases advertising by $41,200, sales in units will increase by 15 percent. What will be the new break-even point? The new degree of operating leverage?

28. *(Miscellaneous)* Compute the answers to each of the following *independent* situations.
    a. Happy Toys sells two products, S and T. The sales mix of these products is 2:4, respectively. S has a contribution margin of $10 per unit, and T has a contribution margin of $5 per unit. Fixed costs for the company are $90,000. What would be the total units of T sold at the break-even point?
    b. Jones Company has a break-even point of 2,000 units. At breakeven, variable costs are $3,200 and fixed costs are $800. If the company sells one unit over breakeven, what will be the pretax income of the company?
    c. Chocolate Delights sells boxed candy for $5 per box. The fixed costs of the company are $108,000. Variable costs amount to 40 percent of selling price. What amount of sales (in units) would be necessary for Chocolate Delights to earn a 25 percent pretax profit on sales?
    d. Bellfast Company has a break-even point of 1,400 units. The company is currently selling 1,600 units for $65 each. What is the margin of safety for the company in units, sales dollars, and percentage?

29. *(CVP, multiproduct)* Peak Performance Wholesalers sells sports products. The Little League Division handles both bats and gloves. Historically, the firm has averaged three bats sold for each glove sold. Each bat has a $4 contribution margin and each glove has a $5 contribution margin. The fixed costs of operating the Little League Division are $200,000 per year. Each bat sells for $10 on average and each glove sells for $15 on average. The corporatewide tax rate for the company is 40 percent.
    a. How much revenue is needed to break even? How many bats and gloves would this represent?
    b. How much revenue is needed to earn a pretax profit of $90,000?
    c. How much revenue is needed to earn an after-tax profit of $90,000?
    d. If the Little League Division earns the revenue determined in part b above, but in doing so sells two bats for each glove, what would the pretax profit (or loss) be? Why is this amount *not* $90,000?

COMMUNICATION ACTIVITIES

30. *(Fixed overhead as a product cost)* A significant difference between absorption costing and variable costing centers around the debate of whether fixed manufacturing overhead is justified as a product cost. Because your professor is scheduled to address a national professional meeting at the same time your class would ordinarily meet, the class has been divided into teams to confront selected issues. Your team's assignment is to prepare a report arguing both sides of the issue stated above. You are also expected as a team to draw your own conclusion and so state it in your report along with the basis for your conclusion.

31. *(CVP model and the long run)* A colleague of yours alleged to your company's Board of Directors that CVP is a short-run oriented model and is therefore of limited usefulness. Because you have used it many times in making presentations to the board, the CEO has asked you to evaluate the perspective voiced by your colleague and prepare a report addressing the contention for the board. In a second request, the CEO has asked you to prepare a separate report for internal management's use addressing how the CVP model could be adapted to become more useful for making long-run decisions. The CEO challenges you to create such an adaptation. Prepare these two reports.

32. *(Cost structure and its implications)* A group of prospective investors has asked your help in understanding the comparative advantages and disadvantages of building a company that is either labor-intensive or, in contrast, one that uses significant cutting-edge technology and is therefore capital-intensive. Prepare a report addressing the issues. Include discussions regarding cost structure, BEP, CVP, MS, DOL, risk, customer satisfaction, and the relationships among these constructs.

33. *(Convert variable to absorption)* Philip Barnes, vice president of marketing for Atlantic Gifts, has just received the November 1997 income statement, shown below, which was prepared on a variable costing basis. The firm uses a variable costing system for internal reporting purposes.

Atlantic Gifts
Income Statement
For the Month Ended November 30, 1997
($000 omitted)

Sales		$4,800
Variable standard cost of goods sold		(2,400)
Product contribution margin		$2,400
Fixed expenses		
Manufacturing (at budget)	$1,000	
Manufacturing spending variance	0	
Selling and administrative	800	(1,800)
Income before tax		$ 600

The controller attached the following notes to the statements:

The unit sales price for November averaged $48.

The standard unit manufacturing costs for the month were:

Variable cost	$24
Fixed cost	10
Total cost	$34

The unit rate for fixed manufacturing costs is a predetermined rate based on a normal monthly production of 100,000 units. Production for November was 5,000 units in excess of sales, and the November ending inventory consisted of 8,000 units.

a. The vice president of marketing is not comfortable with the variable cost basis and wonders what income before tax would have been under the prior basis (absorption costing).

   1. Present the November income statement on an absorption costing basis.

   2. Reconcile and explain the difference between the variable costing and the absorption costing income figures.

b. Explain the features associated with variable cost income measurement that should be attractive to the vice president of marketing.

(CMA adapted)

34. (*Break-even point*) A company is currently using break-even analysis, but the president is uncertain as to the uses of this analytical tool.

a. Define break-even point for the president and explain how it is computed.

b. Discuss the major uses of break-even analysis.

(*AICPA adapted*)

35. (*Appendix*) Fit and Trim had the following income statement for 1997.

Sales (15,000 gallons @ $8)		$120,000
Variable Costs		
Production (20,000 gallons @ $3)	$60,000	
Selling (20,000 gallons @ $.50)	10,000	(70,000)
Contribution Margin		$ 50,000
Fixed Costs		
Production	$22,000	
Selling and administrative	4,000	26,000
General		
Income before Taxes		$ 24,000
Income Taxes (40%)		(9,600)
Net Income		$ 14,400

a. Prepare a CVP graph, in the traditional manner, to reflect the relations among costs, revenues, profit, and volume.

b. Prepare a CVP graph, in the contemporary manner, to reflect the relations among costs, revenues, profit, and volume.

c. Prepare a profit-volume graph.

d. Prepare a short explanation for company management about each of the graphs.

PROBLEMS

36. (*Convert variable to absorption*) Jenny Lowe started a new business in 1996 to produce portable, climate-controlled shelters. The shelters have many applications in special events and sporting activities. Jenny's accountant prepared the following variable costing income statement after the first year to help her in making decisions.

Jenny Lowe Enterprises
Income Statement
For the Year Ended December 31, 1996

Sales (1,500 shelters @ $2,500)		$3,750,000
Variable cost of goods sold:		
Beginning inventory	$ -0-	
Cost of goods manufactured (1,750 @ $1,300)	2,275,000	
Cost of goods available for sale	$2,275,000	
Less ending inventory (250 @ $1,300)	(325,000)	(1,950,000)
Product contribution margin		$1,800,000
Less variable selling and administrative		
expenses (1,500 @ $180)		(270,000)
Total contribution margin		$1,530,000
Less fixed expenses:		
Fixed factory overhead	$1,500,000	
Fixed selling and administrative expenses	190,000	(1,690,000)
Net loss		$ (160,000)

During the year, the following variable production costs per unit were recorded: direct material, $800; direct labor, $300; and overhead, $200.

Ms. Lowe was upset about the net loss because she had wanted to borrow funds to expand capacity. Her friend who teaches accounting at a local university suggested that the use of absorption costing could change the picture.

a. Prepare an absorption costing pretax income statement.

b. Explain the source of the difference between the net income and the net loss figures under the two costing systems.

c. Would it be appropriate to present an absorption costing income statement to the local banker in light of Ms. Lowe's knowledge of the net loss determined under variable costing? Explain.

d. Assume that during the second year of operations, Ms. Lowe's company produced 1,750 shelters, sold 1,850, and experienced the same total fixed costs.

   1. Prepare a variable costing pretax income statement.

   2. Prepare an absorption costing pretax income statement.

   3. Explain the difference between the incomes for the second year under the two systems.

37. *(Income statements, variance)* Alabama Electronic makes a heating element that is used in several kitchen appliances. The company produces and sells approximately 800,000 elements per year. The projected unit cost data for 1998 follows; the company uses standard full absorption costing and writes off all variances to Cost of Goods Sold.

	VARIABLE	**FIXED**
Direct material	$1.50	-0-
Direct labor	1.20	-0-
Variable overhead	.40	-0-
Fixed overhead		$110,000
Selling and administrative	4.00	145,000

The fixed overhead application rate is $.14 per unit.

a. Calculate the per-unit inventory cost for variable costing.

b. Calculate the per-unit inventory cost for absorption costing.

c. The projected income before tax from variable costing is $230,000 at production and sales of 800,000 units and 790,000 units, respectively. Projected beginning and ending finished goods inventories are 20,000 and 30,000 units, respectively. Calculate the projected income before tax using absorption costing.

38. *(Comprehensive)* New York Fashions produces and sells cotton vests. The firm uses variable costing for internal management purposes and absorption costing for external purposes. At the end of each year, financial information must be converted from variable costing to absorption costing to satisfy external requirements.

At the end of 1996, it was anticipated that sales would rise 20 percent from 1996 levels for 1997. Therefore, production was increased from 20,000 to 24,000 units to meet this expected demand. However, economic conditions kept the sales level at 20,000 for both years. The following data pertain to 1996 and 1997:

	1996	1997
Selling price per unit	$ 40	$ 40
Sales (units)	20,000	20,000
Beginning inventory (units)	2,000	2,000
Production (units)	20,000	24,000
Ending inventory (units)	2,000	?
Unfavorable labor, material, and variable overhead variances (total)	$ 5,000	$ 4,000

Standard variable costs per unit for 1996 and 1997 were

Material	$ 4.50
Labor	7.50
Overhead	3.00
Total	$15.00

Annual fixed costs for 1996 and 1997 (budgeted and actual) were

Production	$117,000
Selling and administrative	125,000
Total	$242,000

The overhead rate under absorption costing is based on practical capacity of 30,000 units per year. All variances and under- or overapplied overhead are taken to Cost of Goods Sold. All taxes are to be ignored.

a. Present the income statement based on variable costing for 1997.

b. Present the income statement based on absorption costing for 1997.

c. Explain the difference, if any, in the income figures. Assuming no Work in Process Inventory, give the entry necessary to adjust the book figure to the financial statement figure, if one is necessary.

d. The company finds it worthwhile to develop its internal financial data on a variable cost basis. What advantages and disadvantages are attributed to variable costing for internal purposes?

e. Many accountants believe that variable costing is appropriate for external reporting and many oppose its use for external reporting. What arguments for and against the use of variable costing can you think of for its use in external reporting?

(CMA adapted)

39. *(Income statements for 2 years, both methods)* Modernage manufactures portable telephones. The following data from the company are available for 1997 and 1998:

	1997	1998
Selling price per unit	$ 170	$ 170
Number of units sold	20,000	24,000
Number of units produced	25,000	22,000
Beginning inventory (units)	15,000	20,000
Ending inventory (units)	20,000	?

Standard costs per unit for 1997 and 1998 were

Direct material	$20.00	
Direct labor	60.00	
Variable overhead	20.00	
Fixed overhead	30.00	(based on budget of $750,000 and normal capacity of 25,000 units)
Variable sales commission	20.00	

In addition, selling and administrative fixed costs were $190,000. All variances are charged or credited to Cost of Goods Sold.

Prepare income statements under absorption and variable costing for the years ended 1997 and 1998. Reconcile the differences in income between the methods. (Ignore taxes.)

 40. *(CVP decision alternatives)* John Thomas owns a small travel agency. His revenues are based on commissions earned as follows:

Airline bookings	10% commission
Rental car bookings	15% commission
Hotel bookings	20% commission

Monthly fixed costs include advertising ($1,100), rent ($900), utilities ($250), and other costs ($2,200). There are no variable costs.

During a normal month, John records the following items, which are subject to the above commission structure:

Airlines	$24,000
Cars	3,000
Hotels	7,000
Total	$34,000

John is concerned because his monthly income is so small.
a. What is John's normal monthly income?
b. John can increase his airline bookings by 40 percent with an increase in advertising of $600. Should he increase advertising?
c. John's friend Tim has asked him for a job in the travel agency. Tim has proposed that he be paid 40 percent of whatever additional commissions he can bring to the agency plus a salary of $300 per month. John has estimated Tim can generate the following additional bookings per month:

Airlines	$4,000
Cars	1,000
Hotels	4,000
Total	$9,000

  Hiring Tim would also increase other fixed costs by $300 per month. Should John accept Tim's offer?
d. John hired Tim and in the first month Tim generated an additional $8,000 of bookings for the agency. The bookings, however, were all airline tickets. Was the decision to hire Tim a good one? Why or why not?

41. *(Retail merchant CVP)* Baker Optical Shop has been in operation for several years. Analysis of the firm's recent financial statements and records reveal the following:

Average selling price per pair of glasses	$70
Variable expenses per pair:	
Lenses and frames	$28
Sales commission	12
Variable overhead	8
Annual fixed costs:	
Selling expenses	$18,000
Administrative expenses	48,000

The company's effective tax rate is 40 percent. Sara Baker, company president, has asked you to help her answer the following questions about the business.
a. What is the break-even point in pairs of glasses? In dollars?
b. How much revenue must be generated to produce $80,000 of pretax earnings? How many pairs of glasses would this level of revenue represent?
c. How much revenue must be generated to produce $80,000 of after-tax earnings? How many pairs of glasses would this represent?
d. What amount of revenue would be necessary to yield an after-tax profit equal to 20 percent of revenue?
e. Baker is considering adding a lens-grinding lab, which will save $6 per pair of glasses in lens cost, but will raise annual fixed costs by $8,000. She expects to sell 5,000 pairs of glasses. Should she make this investment?
f. A marketing consultant told Baker that she could increase the number of glasses sold by 30 percent if she would lower the selling price by 10 percent and spend $20,000 on advertising. She has been selling 3,000 pairs of glasses. Should she make these two related changes?

42. *(CVP single product—comprehensive)* Louis Mouse Technology makes a special low-cost mouse for computers. Each mouse sells for $25 and annual production and sales are 120,000 units. Costs for each mouse are as follows:

Direct material	$ 6.00
Direct labor	3.00
Variable overhead	.80
Variable selling expenses	2.20
Total variable cost	$12.00
Total fixed overhead	$589,550

a. Calculate the unit contribution margin in dollars and the contribution margin ratio for the product.

b. Determine the break-even point in number of mice.

c. Calculate the dollar break-even point using the contribution margin ratio.

d. Determine Louis Mouse Technology's margin of safety in units, in sales dollars, and as a percentage.

e. Compute Louis Mouse Technology's degree of operating leverage. If sales increase by 25 percent, by what percentage would before-tax income increase?

f. How many mice must the company sell if it desires to earn $996,450 in before-tax profits?

g. If Louis Mouse Technology wants to earn $657,800 after tax and is subject to a 20 percent tax rate, how many units must be sold?

h. How many units would the company need to sell to break even if its fixed costs increased by $7,865? (Use original data.)

i. Louis Mouse Technology has received an offer to provide a one-time sale of 4,000 mice to a network of computer superstores. This sale would not affect other sales or their costs, but the variable cost of the additional units will increase by $.60 for shipping and fixed costs will increase by $18,000. The selling price for each unit in this order would be $20. Based on quantitative measurement, should the company accept this offer? Show your calculations.

43. *(CVP, DOL, MS—two quarters, comprehensive)* Presented below is information pertaining to the first and second quarters of 1998 operations of the Greg Company:

	QUARTER	
	FIRST	**SECOND**
Units:		
Production	35,000	30,000
Sales	30,000	35,000
Expected activity level	32,500	32,500
Unit selling price	$75.00	$75.00
Unit variable costs:		
Direct material	34.50	34.50
Direct labor	16.50	16.50
Factory overhead	7.80	7.80
Operating expenses	5.70	5.70
Quarterly fixed costs:		
Factory overhead	$97,500.00	$97,500.00
Operating expenses	21,400.00	21,400.00

Additional information:

■ There were no finished goods at January 1, 1998.

■ Greg writes off any quarterly underapplied or overapplied overhead as an adjustment of Cost of Goods Sold.

- Greg's income tax rate is 35 percent.
- **a.** Prepare an absorption costing income statement for each quarter.
- **b.** Prepare a variable costing income statement for each quarter.
- **c.** Calculate each of the following for 1998, if 130,000 units were produced and sold:
  - **1.** Unit contribution margin
  - **2.** Contribution margin ratio
  - **3.** Total contribution margin
  - **4.** Net income
  - **5.** Degree of operating leverage
  - **6.** Annual break-even unit sales volume
  - **7.** Annual break-even dollar sales volume
  - **8.** Annual margin of safety as a percentage

44. *(Multiproduct firm)* Family Publishing produces and sells two book products: an encyclopedia set and a dictionary set. The company sells these book sets in a ratio of three encyclopedia sets to five dictionary sets. Selling prices for the encyclopedia and dictionary sets are, respectively, $1,200 and $240; respective variable costs are $480 and $160. The company's fixed costs are $1,800,000 per year. Compute the volume of sales of each type of book set needed to
    - **a.** break even.
    - **b.** earn $800,000 of income before tax.
    - **c.** earn $800,000 of income after tax, assuming a 30 percent tax rate.
    - **d.** earn 12 percent on sales revenue in before-tax income.
    - **e.** earn 12 percent on sales revenue in after-tax income, assuming a 30 percent tax rate.

45. *(Comprehensive; multiproduct)* Jim's Flooring makes three types of flooring products: tile, carpet, and parquet. Cost analysis reveals the following costs (expressed on a per-square-yard basis) are expected for 1997:

	TILE	CARPET	PARQUET
Direct material	$5.20	$3.25	$8.80
Direct labor	1.80	.40	6.40
Variable overhead	1.00	.15	1.75
Variable selling expenses	.50	.25	2.00
Variable administrative expenses	.20	.10	.30
Fixed overhead		$760,000	
Fixed selling expenses		240,000	
Fixed administrative expenses		200,000	

Per-yard expected selling prices are: tile, $16.40; carpet, $8.00; and parquet, $25.00. In 1996, sales were as follows and the mix is expected to continue in 1997:

	TILE	CARPET	PARQUET
Square yards	18,000	144,000	12,000

Review of recent tax returns reveals an expected tax rate of 40 percent.
- **a.** Calculate the break-even point for the coming year.
- **b.** How many square yards of each product are expected to be sold at the break-even point?
- **c.** Assume that the company desires a pretax profit of $800,000. How many square yards of each type of product would need to be sold to generate this profit level? How much revenue would be required?
- **d.** Assume that the company desires an after-tax profit of $680,000. Use the contribution margin percentage approach to determine the revenue needed.
- **e.** If the company actually achieves the revenue determined in part d above, what is Jim's Flooring's margin of safety in (1) dollars and (2) percentage?

46. (*Appendix*) The Charleston Social Club (CSC) has provided you with the following monthly cost and fee information: monthly membership fee per member, $25; variable cost per member per month, $12; fixed cost per month, $1,800. Costs are extremely low because almost all services and supplies are provided by volunteers.

   a. Prepare a traditional break-even chart for CSC.

   b. Prepare a contemporary break-even chart for the CSC.

   c. Prepare a profit-volume graph for the CSC.

   d. Indicate which of the above you would use in giving a speech to the membership in order to solicit volunteers to help with a fund-raising project. Assume at this time there are only 120 members belonging to the CSC.

CASES

47. (*Absorption costing versus variable costing*) Indiana Metalworks builds camshafts for car manufacturers. Company sales have increased yearly as the company gains a reputation for reliable and quality products. The company manufactures dies to customer specifications and it uses a job order cost system. Factory overhead is applied to the jobs based on direct labor hours, using the absorption costing method. Under- or overapplied overhead is treated as an adjustment to Cost of Goods Sold. The company's inventory balances and income statements for the last 2 years are presented below.

INVENTORY BALANCES	12/31/96	12/31/97	12/31/98
Raw material	$22,000	$30,000	$10,000
Work in process			
Costs	$40,000	$48,000	$64,000
Direct labor hours	1,335	1,600	2,100
Finished goods			
Costs	$25,000	$18,000	$14,000
Direct labor hours	1,450	1,050	820

1997–1998 COMPARATIVE INCOME STATEMENTS

	1997		1998	
Sales		$840,000		$1,015,000
Cost of goods sold				
Finished goods, 1/1	$ 25,000		$ 18,000	
Cost of goods manufactured	548,000		657,600	
Total available	$573,000		$675,600	
Finished goods, 12/31	(18,000)		(14,000)	
CGS before overhead adjustment	$555,000		$661,600	
Underapplied factory overhead	36,000		14,400	
CGS		(591,000)		(676,000)
Gross profit		$249,000		$ 339,000
Selling expenses	$ 82,000		$ 95,000	
Administrative expenses	70,000		75,000	
Total operating expenses		(152,000)		(170,000)
Operating income		$ 97,000		$ 169,000

The same predetermined overhead rate was used in applying overhead to production orders in both 1997 and 1998. The rate was based on the following estimates:

Fixed factory overhead	$ 25,000
Variable factory overhead	$155,000
Direct labor hours	25,000
Direct labor cost	$150,000

In 1997 and 1998, actual direct labor hours expended were 20,000 and 23,000, respectively. The cost of raw material put into production was $292,000 in 1997 and $370,000 in 1998. Actual fixed overhead was $37,400 for 1997 and $42,300 for 1998, and the planned direct labor rate was equal to the actual direct labor rate.

For both years, all of the reported administrative costs were fixed. The variable portion of the reported selling expenses result from a commission of 5 percent of sales revenue.

a. For the year ended December 31, 1998, prepare a revised income statement using the variable costing method.

b. Prepare a numerical reconciliation of the difference in operating income between the 1998 absorption and variable costing statements.

c. Describe both the advantages and disadvantages of using variable costing.

(CMA adapted)

48. *(Absorption costing versus variable costing)* Williams Company, a wholly owned subsidiary of Jonah, Inc., produces and sells three main product lines. The company employs a standard cost accounting system for recordkeeping purposes. At the beginning of 1996, the president of Williams Company presented the budget to the parent company and accepted a commitment to contribute $15,800 to Jonah's consolidated profit in 1996. The president has been confident that the year's profit would exceed the budget target, because the monthly sales reports that he has been receiving have shown that sales for the year will exceed budget by 10 percent. The president is both disturbed and confused when the controller presents an adjusted forecast as of November 30, 1996, indicating that profit will be 11 percent under budget. The two forecasts are presented below:

	1/1/96	11/30/96
Sales	$268,000	$294,800
Cost of sales at standard*	(212,000)	(233,200)
Gross margin at standard	$ 56,000	$ 61,600
(Under-) overapplied fixed overhead	-0-	(6,000)
Actual gross margin	$ 56,000	$ 55,600
Selling expenses	$ 13,400	$ 14,740
Administrative expenses	26,800	26,800
Total operating expenses	$(40,200)	$(41,540)
Earnings before tax	$ 15,800	$ 14,060

*Includes fixed manufacturing overhead of $30,000.

There have been no sales price changes or product mix shifts since the 1/1/96 forecast. The only cost variance on the income statement is the underapplied manufacturing overhead. This amount arose because the company produced only 16,000 standard machine hours (budgeted machine hours were 20,000) during 1996 as a result of a shortage of raw material while the company's principal supplier was closed for a strike. Fortunately, Williams Company's finished goods inventory was large enough to fill all sales orders received.

a. Analyze and explain why the profit has declined in spite of increased sales and effective control over costs.

b. What plan, if any, could Williams Company adopt during December to improve its reported profit at year-end? Explain your answer.

c. Illustrate and explain how Williams Company could adopt an alternative internal cost reporting procedure that would avoid the confusing effect of the present procedure.

d. Would the alternative procedure described in part c be acceptable to Jonah, Inc., for financial reporting purposes? Explain.

49. *(CVP analysis)* Susan Katz owns the Holiday Litter Box, a luxury hotel for dogs and cats. The capacity is 40 pets: 20 dogs and 20 cats. Each pet has an air-conditioned room with a window overlooking a garden. Soft music is played continuously. Pets are awakened at 7 A.M., served breakfast at 8 A.M., fed snacks at 3:30 P.M., and receive dinner at 5 P.M. Hotel services also include airport pickup, daily bathing and grooming, night lighting in each suite, carpeted floors, and daily play visits by pet "babysitters."

Pet owners are interviewed about their pets' health-care requirements, likes and dislikes, diet, and other needs. Reservations are essential and health must be documented by each pet's veterinarian. The costs of operating the pet hotel are substantial. The hotel's original cost was $85,000. Depreciation is $6,000 per year. Other costs of operating the hotel include:

Labor costs	$18,000 per year plus $.25 per animal per day
Utilities	$ 8,900 per year plus $.05 per animal per day
Miscellaneous costs	$ 4,000 per year plus $.30 per animal per day

In addition to these costs, costs are incurred for food and water for each pet. These costs are strictly variable and (on average) run $2.00 per day for dogs and $.75 per day for cats.

a. Assuming that the hotel is able to maintain an average annual occupancy of 75 percent in both the cat and the dog units (based on a 360-day year), determine the minimum daily charge that must be assessed per animal day to generate $12,000 of income before taxes.

b. Assume that the price Susan charges cat owners is $10 per day and the price charged to dog owners is $12 per day. If the sales mix is 1 to 1 (one cat day of occupancy for each dog day of occupancy) compute the following:

1. The break-even point in total occupancy days.

2. Total occupancy days required to generate $20,000 of income before tax.

3. Total occupancy days to generate $20,000 of after-tax income; Susan's personal tax rate is 35 percent.

c. Susan is considering adding an animal training service for guests to complement her other hotel services. Susan has estimated the costs of providing such a service would largely be fixed. Because all of the facilities already exist, Susan would merely need to hire a dog trainer. She estimates a dog trainer could be hired at a cost of $25,000 per year. If Susan decides to add this service, how much would her daily charges have to increase (assume equal dollar increases to cat and dog fees) to maintain the break-even level you computed in part b?

50. *(CVP analysis)* Security Airlines is a small local carrier in the Northwest. All seats are coach and the following data are available.

Number of seats per plane	120
Average load factor (percentage of seats filled)	75%
Average full passenger fare	$70
Average variable cost per passenger	$30
Fixed operating costs per month	$1,200,000

a. What is break-even point in passengers and revenues?

b. What is break-even point in number of flights?

c. If Security raises its average full passenger fare to $85, it is estimated that the load factor will decrease to 60 percent. What will be the break-even point in number of flights?

d. The cost of fuel is a significant variable cost to any airline. If fuel charges increase by $8 per barrel, it is estimated that variable cost per passenger will rise to $40. In this case, what would be the new break-even point in passengers and in number of flights? (Refer back to original data.)

e. Security has experienced an increase in variable cost per passenger to $35 and an increase in total fixed costs to $1,500,000. The company has decided to raise the average fare to $80. What number of passengers are needed to generate an after-tax profit of $400,000 if the tax rate is 40 percent?

f. (Use original data.) Security is considering offering a discounted fare of $50, which the company feels would increase the load factor to 80 percent. Only the additional seats would be sold at the discounted fare. Additional monthly advertising costs would be $80,000. How much pretax income would the discounted fare provide Security if the company has 40 flights per day, 30 days per month?

g. Security has an opportunity to obtain a new route. The company feels it can sell seats at $75 on the route, but the load factor would be only 60 percent. The company would fly the route 15 times per month. The increase in fixed costs for additional crew, additional planes, landing fees, maintenance, etc., would total $100,000 per month. Variable cost per passenger would remain at $30.

1. Should the company obtain the route?

2. How many flights would Security need to earn pretax income of $50,500 per month on this route?

3. If the load factor could be increased to 75 percent, how many flights would be needed to earn pretax income of $50,500 per month on this route?

4. What qualitative factors should be considered by Security in making its decision about acquiring this route?

51. Lucy Clark is the sales representative for a heavy construction equipment manufacturer. She is compensated by a moderate fixed salary plus a 5 percent bonus on sales. Lucy is aware that some of the higher-priced items earn the company a lower contribution margin and some of the lower-priced items earn the company a higher contribution margin. She learned this information from the variable costing financial statements provided by the company.

Lucy has recently started pushing sales of only the high-priced items by generously entertaining receptive customers and offering them gifts through the company's promotion budget. She feels that management has not given her adequate raises in the 20 years she has been with the company and now she is too old to find a better job.

a. Is what Lucy doing legal?

b. What are the ethical issues involved in the case from Lucy's standpoint?

c. Are there ethical issues in the case from company management's standpoint?

d. What do you believe Lucy should do? Why?

52. Missouri Chemical Company's new president has learned that, for the past 4 years, the company has been dumping its industrial waste into the local river and falsifying reports to authorities about the levels of suspected cancer-causing materials in that waste. The plant manager says that there is no proof that the waste causes cancer and there are only a few fishing villages within a hundred miles down-river. If the company has to treat the substance to neutralize its potentially injurious effects and then transport it to a legal dump site, the company's variable and fixed costs would rise to a level that might make the firm uncompetitive. If the company loses its competitive advantage, 10,000 local employees could become unemployed and the town's economy could collapse.

ETHICS AND QUALITY DISCUSSION

   a. What kinds of variable and fixed costs can you think of that would increase (or decrease) if the waste were treated rather than dumped? How would these costs affect product contribution margin?
   b. What are the ethical conflicts the president faces?
   c. What rationalizations can you detect that have been devised by plant employees?
   d. What options and suggestions can you offer the president?

53. Women often receive reports of positive Pap smears when, in actuality, the results are negative. Newspaper accounts detail an industry utilizing overworked, undersupervised, poorly paid technicians to perform Pap smear tests. Some labs allow workers to analyze up to four times as many specimens per year as experts recommend for accuracy. Workers may be paid $.45 to analyze a smear when patients are charged $35.
   a. Discuss the cost-volume-profit relationships that exist in this case.
   b. Discuss the ethics of the laboratories' owners who allow technicians to be paid piecework for such analysis work.
   c. Discuss the ethics of the workers who rush through Pap smear analyses.

54. High-quality raw materials are typically associated with high prices. Jane Phipps of Fresh From Texas, however, was quick to point out that such a situation does not exist in the vegetable market. "When floods or droughts occur in California, Texas, Florida, and Arizona, prices for inferior products skyrocket. On the other hand, when the weather is great, produce is plentiful, the quality is great, and prices are low," she said.

   If you were in the business of wholesaling produce to grocery stores, would you buy the low-quality produce from the farms and package and resell it to your customers or would you refuse to handle the low-quality produce because you have a reputation for high quality products to uphold? Discuss the pros and cons of each position before selecting the choice you would make.

55. *Recently, health professionals and others have taken notice of actions by pharmaceutical giant Eli Lilly & Co. to increase the volume of sales for its antidepressant drug, Prozac. Critics suggest the company has launched a major advertising program and sponsored other efforts to induce greater consumer demand for this prescription medication. At the heart of the issue is an expenditure of several million dollars by Lilly to sponsor ads that urge people who think that they might be depressed to see their doctor.*

   The American Psychological Association says such advertisements will encourage patients to see their primary-care physician, rather than a psychologist (who cannot prescribe medicine) to address their depression. Primary-care physicians would be more likely than mental health professionals to rely strictly on medication to treat depression. Critics suggest that Prozac is already overprescribed and that it is an appropriate treatment for only about 1/3 of its current users.

   Lilly has countered the criticism by suggesting that the ads it sponsored were not intended to promote its drug Prozac, but were instead intended to promote awareness of mental health.

   According to the Mental Health Association, the advertising campaign is expected to reach 93% of American adults.

   [SOURCE: Elyse Tanouye, "Critics See Self-Interest in Lilly's Funding of Ads Telling the Depressed to Get Help," *Wall Street Journal* (April 15, 1993), p. B1. Reprinted by permission of the *The Wall Street Journal*, © 1993 Dow Jones & Company, Inc. All Rights Reserved Worldwide.]

   a. How could Lilly's advertising have been construed by critics as being intended to increase the volume of Prozac sales?
   b. Discuss the ethics of using advertising to generate demand for prescription drugs.
   c. Would the advertising be more or less ethical if it were directed at health-care professionals rather than consumers? Discuss.
   d. Discuss whether advertising of medical products, including drugs, should be more strictly regulated by government agencies.

56. Read the opening vignette of this chapter which describes the early years of Procter & Gamble. Then, find the web homepage for the company. Scan the information on the homepage noting the breadth of operations in terms of product offerings and geographical coverage. How would conducting CVP analysis be different in the company today relative to conducting the analysis in the company's early years?

57. Search the web using the search term "parametric cost analysis." Write a brief report in which you describe parametric cost analysis and how it could be used in CVP analysis.

58. A significant trend in business today is increasing use of outsourcing. Search web sites with the objective of gaining an understanding for the vast array of outsourcing services that are available. Prepare a presentation in which you discuss the extensive use of outsourcing today and how outsourcing could be used as a tool to manage a firm's cost structure, and as a tool in CVP planning.

INTERNET ACTIVITIES

CHAPTER

13 Relevant Costing

LEARNING OBJECTIVES

After completing this chapter, you should be able to answer these questions:

1. What factors are relevant in making decisions and why?

2. How do opportunity costs affect decision making?

3. What are sunk costs and why are they not relevant in making decisions?

4. What are the relevant financial considerations in outsourcing?

5. How can management make the best use of a scarce resource?

6. How does sales mix pertain to relevant costing problems?

7. How are special prices set and when are they used?

8. How is segment margin used to determine whether a product line should be retained or eliminated?

9. *(Appendix)* How is a linear programming problem formulated?

KPMG Peat Marwick

The successful management of business activity requires vigilance over all costs. Managers must be aware that costs that were relatively trivial in prior years can become significant in the present or future. This aptly describes one of the most significant costs of American businesses today: litigation.

For large accounting firms, litigation settlements and liability insurance can consume large percentages of income. For example, such costs consume about 8 percent of revenues for the "Big Six" accounting firms operating in Britain and 12 percent of revenues for the U.S. operations of these firms. The recent response of KPMG Peat Marwick (a member of the Big Six) to such litigation costs is noteworthy. This global financial services firm abandoned its traditional partnership organizational form for alternative organizational forms that offer its partners greater protection against lawsuits. An unattractive feature of the partnership form in today's litigious environment is that the partners' personal assets, as well as the assets of the partnership, are at risk in lawsuits. In the event the partnership is a loser in a legal action, after the assets of the partnership have been exhausted, the personal assets of the partners can be taken to satisfy lawful claims. The risks of the partnership organization are greatly magnified by statutes allowing joint and several liability. This means that accounting firms (and their partners), which have relatively "deep pockets," can be held liable for damages that are disproportionately large relative to their errors or omissions simply because they have greater ability to pay.

In the United Kingdom, KPMG has incorporated its operations as a limited liability company (LLC). In the United States, its operations have been organized as a limited liability partnership (LLP). Both of these organizational forms provide greater protection of the partners' personal assets in legal actions. The protection of the partners' personal assets under these organizational forms more closely resembles that available to corporations.

In the United States, all the Big Six firms have switched to the LLP form; in Britain, KPMG was the first to move to the LLC form, but the others are considering a similar action.

SOURCES: Adapted from Frances McNair and Edward Milam, "The Limited Liability Company: An Idea Whose Time Has Come," *Management Accounting* (December 1994), pp. 30–33; Anonymous, "British Accountants' Liability: Big Six PLC," *Economist* (October 7, 1995), pp. 87–88. Reprinted from *Management Accounting*. Copyright by Institute of Management Accountants, Montvale, NJ.

A s discussed in prior chapters, managers are charged with the responsibility of managing organizational resources effectively and efficiently relative to the organization's goals and objectives. Managers of accounting firms, including those of KPMG, determined that discontinuing use of the general partnership organizational form is an efficient and effective action to control the legal costs and risks of their firms. In coming to this conclusion, KPMG considered the costs and benefits of alternative actions such as greater insurance coverage and curtailment of services.

Accounting information can improve, but not perfect, management's understanding of the consequences of decision alternatives. To the extent that accounting information can reduce management's uncertainty about economic facts, outcomes, and relationships involved in various courses of action, such information is valuable for decision-making purposes.

As discussed in Chapter 12, many decisions can be made using incremental analysis. This chapter continues that discussion by introducing **relevant costing**, which

relevant costing

is an approach that focuses managerial attention on a decision's relevant (or pertinent) facts. Relevant costing techniques are applied in virtually all business decisions in both short-term and long-term contexts. This chapter examines their application to several common types of business decisions: replacing an asset, making or buying a product or part, allocating scarce resources, accepting specially priced orders, and determining the appropriate sales/production mix. The discussion of decision tools applied to some longer-term decisions is deferred to Chapter 18. In general, these decisions require a consideration of costs and benefits that are mismatched in time; that is, the cost is incurred currently but the benefit is derived in future periods.

In making a choice among the alternatives available, managers need to consider all relevant costs and revenues associated with each alternative. One of the most important concepts discussed in this chapter is the relationship between time and relevance. As the decision time horizon becomes shorter, fewer costs and revenues are relevant because only a limited set of them is susceptible to change by short-term management actions. Over the long term, virtually all costs can be influenced by management actions. Regardless of whether the decision is short- or long-term, all decision making requires

> relevant information at the point of decision; the knowledge of how to analyze that information at the point of decision; and enough time to do the analysis.
>
> In today's corporations, oceans of data drown most decision makers. Eliminating irrelevant information requires the knowledge of what is relevant, the knowledge of how to access and select appropriate data, and the knowledge of how best to prepare the data by sorting and summarizing it to facilitate analysis. This is the raw material of decision making.[1]

THE CONCEPT OF RELEVANCE

For information to be relevant, it must possess three characteristics. It must (1) be associated with the decision under consideration, (2) be important to the decision maker, and (3) have a connection to or bearing on some future endeavor.

Association with Decision

Costs or revenues are relevant when they are logically related to a decision and vary from one decision alternative to another. Cost accountants can assist managers in determining which costs are relevant to decisions at hand. To be relevant, a cost or revenue item must be differential or incremental. These synonymous terms refer to an additional or extra amount associated with some action. Thus, **incremental revenue** is the additional revenue resulting from a contemplated sale or provision of a service, and **incremental cost** is the additional cost of producing or selling the same contemplated good or service.

incremental revenue

incremental cost

To the extent possible and practical, relevant costing compares the differential revenues and differential costs of alternative decisions. Although incremental costs can be variable or fixed, a general guideline is that most variable costs are relevant and most fixed costs are not. The logic of this guideline is that as sales or production volume change, within the relevant range, variable costs change, but fixed costs do not. As with most generalizations, there are some exceptions that must be acknowledged in the decision-making process.

The difference between the incremental revenue and the incremental cost of a particular alternative is the positive or negative incremental benefit of that course of action. Management can compare the incremental benefits of alternatives to decide on the most profitable (or least costly) alternative or set of alternatives. Such a comparison may sound simple; it often is not. The concept of relevance is an inherently individual determination, and the quantity of information available to make decisions is increasing. The challenge is to get information that identifies relevant costs and benefits.

[1] Edward G. Mahler, "Perform as Smart as You Are," *Financial Executive* (July-August 1991), p. 18.

If executives once imagined they could gather enough information to read the business environment like an open book, they have had to dim their hopes. The flow of information has swollen to such a flood that managers are in danger of drowning; extracting relevant data from the torrent is increasingly a daunting task.[2]

Some relevant factors, such as sales commissions or prime costs of production, are easily identified and quantified because they are integral parts of the accounting system. Other factors may be relevant and quantifiable, but are not part of the accounting system. Such factors cannot be overlooked simply because they may be more difficult to obtain or may require the use of estimates. For instance, an opportunity cost represents the benefits forgone because one course of action is chosen over another. These costs are extremely important in decision making, but are not included in the accounting records.

An example of a relevant opportunity cost involving forgone sales follows. Assume that managers at an electronics manufacturer are considering dropping a printer product line and renting out the facilities in which that product line is currently being made. The company presently sells 5,000 units annually with a contribution margin of $100 each. The annual rental income from the leased facilities is expected to be $250,000, and renting the facilities will cause fixed expenses to decline by $390,000. The opportunity cost of choosing to rent the facilities is the forgone profit on the discontinued product line of $500,000 (5,000 units × $100 contribution margin).

Importance to Decision Maker

The need for specific information depends on how important that information is relative to the objectives that a manager wants or needs to achieve. Moreover, if all other factors are equal, more precise information is given greater weight in the decision-making process. However, if the information is extremely important, but less precise, the manager must weigh importance against precision. The following News Note illustrates both the need for qualitative information and the legal and

N E W S
N O T E

Stopping the Thieving Hotel Guest

One of the problems that has continually plagued the hotel/motel industry is loss of property to theft by guests. The costs of these thefts are difficult to control because too-aggressive anti-theft measures drive customers away and reduce revenues. Further, some anti-theft measures may involve ethical decisions regarding the rights of guests.

For example, consider measures taken by the Sheraton New York Hotel and Towers in Manhattan. . . . the battle against petty crime has turned to a combination of high-tech gadgetry and employee tattletales. According to hotel security officials, the 300 maids have been trained to peek into rooms, even if the guest is still packing up. The maids won't confront anyone, but they are supposed to report any major missing item to the front desk. As an incentive, the hotel says it has occasionally rewarded an employee with a $25 bonus or a free dinner.

"It's not Big Brother," says the director of security. "It's just making room attendants more responsible for the room."

It has all come to this, hotels say, because petty theft is turning into grand larceny. Analysts estimate that the industry is losing more than $100 million a year to thieves.

SOURCE: Jacqueline Simmons, "Hotels Snoop to Stop Guests' Thievery of Everything That Isn't Nailed Down," *Wall Street Journal* (March 17, 1995), pp. B1, B13. Reprinted by permission of *The Wall Street Journal* © 1995 Dow Jones & Company, Inc. All Rights Reserved Worldwide.

[2] Amitai Etzioni, "Humble Decision Making," *Harvard Business Review* (July-August 1989), p. 122.

ethical duties of managers to weigh important but imprecise, qualitative information against company profits.

Bearing on the Future

Information can be *based* on past or present data, but it can be relevant only if it pertains to a future decision choice. All managerial decisions are made to affect future events, so the information on which decisions are based should reflect future conditions. The future may be the short-run (2 hours from now or next month) or the long-run (3 years from now).

Future costs are the only costs that can be avoided, and a longer time horizon equates to more costs that are controllable, avoidable, and relevant. *Only information that has a bearing on future events is relevant in decision making.* But people too often forget this adage and try to make decisions using inapplicable data. One common error is trying to use a previously purchased asset's acquisition cost or book value in current decision making. This error reflects the misconception that sunk costs are relevant costs.

SUNK COSTS

Costs incurred in the past for the acquisition of an asset or a resource are called sunk costs. They cannot be changed, no matter what future course of action is taken because past expenditures are not recoverable, regardless of current circumstances.

After an asset or resource is acquired, managers may find that it is no longer adequate for the intended purposes, does not perform to expectations, is technologically out-of-date, or is no longer marketable. A decision, typically involving two alternatives, must then be made: keep or dispose of the old asset. In making this decision, a current or future selling price may be obtained for the old asset, but such a price is the result of current or future conditions and does not "recoup" an historical cost. The historical cost is not relevant to the decision.

Although asset-acquisition decisions are covered in depth in Chapter 18, these decisions provide an excellent introduction to the concept of relevant information. The following illustration makes some simplistic assumptions regarding asset acquisitions, but is used to demonstrate why sunk costs are not relevant costs.

Assume that Latin Cellular Technologies purchases a statistical process control system for $2,000,000 on January 6, 1997. This system (referred to as the "original" system) is expected to have a useful life of 5 years and no salvage value. Five days later, on January 11, Trisha Black, vice president of production, notices an advertisement for a similar system for $1,800,000. This "new" system also has an estimated life of 5 years and no salvage value; its features will allow it to perform as well as the original system, and in addition, it has analysis tools that will save $50,000 per year in operating costs over the original system. On investigation, Ms. Black discovers that the original system can be sold for only $1,300,000. The data on the original and new statistical process control systems are shown in Exhibit 13–1.

EXHIBIT 13–1

Latin Cellular Technologies: Statistical Process Control System Decision

	ORIGINAL SYSTEM (PURCHASED JAN. 6)	NEW SYSTEM (AVAILABLE JAN. 11)
Cost	$2,000,000	$1,800,000
Life in years	5	5
Salvage value	$ 0	$ 0
Current resale value	$1,300,000	Not applicable
Annual operating cost	$ 105,000	$ 55,000

Latin Cellular Technologies has two options: (1) use the original system or (2) sell the original system and buy the new system. Exhibit 13–2 presents the costs Ms. Black should consider in making her asset replacement decision—that is, the relevant costs. As shown in the computations in Exhibit 13–2, the $2,000,000 purchase price of the original system does not affect the decision process. This amount was "gone

Alternative (1): Use original system		
Operating cost over life of original system		
($105,000 × 5 years)		$525,000
Alternative (2): Sell original system and buy new system		
Cost of new system	$1,800,000	
Resale value of original system	(1,300,000)	
Effective net outlay for new system	$ 500,000	
Operating cost over life of new system		
($55,000 × 5 years)	275,000	
Total cost of new system		(775,000)
Benefit of keeping the old system		$250,000
The alternative, incremental calculation follows:		
Savings from operating the new system for 5 years		$250,000
Less: Effective incremental outlay for new system		(500,000)
Incremental advantage of keeping the old system		$250,000

EXHIBIT 13–2

Relevant Costs Related to Latin Cellular Technologies' Alternatives

forever" when the company bought the system. However, if the company sells the original system, it will be able to effectively reduce the net cash outlay for the new system to $500,000 because it will generate $1,300,000 from selling the old system. Using either system, Latin Cellular Technologies will spend money over the next 5 years for operating costs, but it will spend $250,000 less using the new system ($50,000 savings per year × 5 years).

The common tendency is to include the $2,000,000 cost of the old system in the analysis. However, this cost is not differential between the decision alternatives. If Latin Cellular Technologies keeps the original system, that $2,000,000 will be deducted as depreciation expense over the system's life. Alternatively, if the system is sold, the $2,000,000 will be charged against the revenue realized from the sale of the system. Thus, the $2,000,000 loss, or its equivalent in depreciation charges, is the same in magnitude whether the company retains the original or disposes of it and buys the new one. Because the amount is the same under both alternatives, it is not relevant to the decision process.

Ms. Black must condition herself to make decisions given her set of *future* alternatives. The relevant factors in deciding whether to purchase the new system are

1. cost of the new system ($1,800,000);
2. current resale value of the original system ($1,300,000); and
3. annual savings of the new system ($50,000) and the number of years (5) such savings would be enjoyed.[3]

This preceding example demonstrates the difference between relevant and irrelevant costs, including sunk costs. The next section shows how the concepts of relevant costing, incremental revenues, and incremental costs are applied in making some common managerial decisions.

RELEVANT COSTS FOR SPECIFIC DECISIONS

Managers routinely choose a course of action from alternatives that have been identified as feasible solutions to problems. In so doing, managers weigh the costs and benefits of these alternatives and determine which course of action is best. Incremental revenues, costs, and benefits of all courses of action are measured against a baseline alternative. In making decisions, managers must provide for the inclusion of any inherently nonquantifiable considerations. Inclusion can be made by attempting to quantify those items or by simply making instinctive value judgments about nonmonetary benefits and costs.

In evaluating courses of action, managers should select the alternative that provides the highest incremental benefit to the company. In some instances, all alternatives result in incremental losses, and managers must choose the one that creates the smallest incremental loss. One course of action that is often used as the baseline case is the "change nothing" option.

Although other alternatives have certain incremental revenues and incremental costs associated with them, the "change nothing" alternative has a zero incremental benefit because it represents the current conditions. In some situations involving specific government regulations or mandates, a "change nothing" alternative does not exist. For example, if a company were polluting river water and a duly-licensed governmental regulatory agency issued an injunction against it, the company (assuming it wishes to continue in business) would be forced to correct the pollution problem. The company could delay the installation of pollution control devices at the risk of fines or closure. Such fines would be incremental costs that would need to be considered; closure would create an opportunity cost amounting to the income that

---

[3] In addition, two other factors that were not discussed are also important: the potential tax effects of the transactions and the time value of money. The authors have chosen to defer consideration of these items to Chapter 18, which covers capital budgeting. Because of the time value of money, both systems were assumed to have zero salvage values at the end of their lives—a fairly unrealistic assumption.

Drug Maker Is Tardy in Decision to Recall Drug

**N E W S
N O T E**

[When a manufacturer believes that it has created a defective product, it has at least two courses of action: recall the product or do nothing. In making this decision, the manufacturer must consider the consequences of the alternatives. For products that affect human health, the consequences can be severe.]

On Jan. 13, 1994, a day after his lungs collapsed, Jeffory Flower died in his mother's arms. He was nine years old.

In the prior year, Jeffory, who had cerebral palsy and asthma, had been admitted to the hospital 12 times for pneumonia, says his mother, Michele Hommerbocker. Soon after returning home each time, she says, his condition worsened.

Although she was baffled then, Ms. Hommerbocker eventually concluded that his asthma medicine played a role. When Jeffory was in the hospital, she says, he was given a brand-name inhalant, and his pneumonia abated. But at home in Oroville, Calif., where he inhaled a less-costly generic version of it mandated by his parents' health plan, she says, the pneumonia always returned.

Many other patients thrived on the brand-name drug, Proventil, and degenerated on the generic version, Albuterol, according to plaintiffs in suits against Albuterol's maker. The company, Copley Pharmaceutical Inc., of Canton, Mass., recalled the drug in January 1994 after finding bacterial contamination in it. The suits, most of them consolidated in federal court in Cheyenne, Wyo., allege that about 100 people died from Albuterol use.

Food and Drug Administration records, and Copley documents, some of them obtained from plaintiff's lawyers, show that questions about the company's ability to make Albuterol bacteria-free began before it reached the market and continued throughout the 20 months it was sold. The FDA-approved recipe called for three ingredients to kill bacteria. But Copley now concedes it never used two of the three and never told the FDA it wasn't doing so.

SOURCE: Joseph Pereira and Joseph Rebello, "Production Problems at Generic-Drug Firm Lead to Serious Claims," *Wall Street Journal* (February 2, 1995), pp. A1, A6. Reprinted by permission of *The Wall Street Journal*, © 1995 Dow Jones & Company, Inc. All Rights Reserved Worldwide.

would have been generated had sales continued. Managers must make these types of decisions using a "now-versus-later" attitude, and as shown in the above News Note, may determine that "now" is better for both financial and public relations reasons.

Rational decision-making behavior includes a comprehensive evaluation of the monetary effects of all alternative courses of action. The chosen course should be one that will make the business better off. Decision choices can be evaluated using relevant costing techniques.

Make-or-Buy Decisions

A daily question faced by managers is whether the right components will be available at the right time to ensure production. Additionally, the components must be of the appropriate quality and obtainable at a reasonable price. Traditionally, companies assured themselves of component availability and quality by doing their own manufacturing. However, in recent years there is a growing trend of "outsourcing" a greater percentage of required materials, components, and services.

This **make-or-buy decision** (or outsourcing decision) is made only after a proper analysis that compares internal costs with cost to purchase, and assesses the best uses of the available facilities. Consideration of a "make" option automatically implies that the company has the available capacity for that purpose or has considered the cost of obtaining the necessary capacity. Relevant information for this type of decision includes both quantitative and qualitative factors.

make-or-buy decision

VIDEO
VIGNETTE

Hewlett-Packard (in AME—On the Road)

RELEVANT QUANTITATIVE FACTORS

Incremental production costs for each unit
Unit cost of purchasing from outside supplier (price less any discounts available plus
   shipping, etc.)
Number of available suppliers
Production capacity available to manufacture components
Opportunity costs of using facilities for production rather than for other purposes
Quantity of space available for storage
Costs associated with carrying inventory
Increase in throughput generated by buying components

RELEVANT QUALITATIVE FACTORS

Reliability of source(s) of supply
Ability to control quality of unit when purchased from outside
Nature of the work to be subcontracted (such as the importance of the part to the
   whole)
Impact on customers and markets
Future bargaining position with supplier(s)
Perceptions regarding possible future price changes
Perceptions about current product prices (are the prices appropriate or, in some cases
   with international suppliers, is product dumping involved?)

EXHIBIT 13-4

Latin Cellular
Technologies—Make-or-
Buy Cost Information

	PRESENT MANUFACTURING COST PER CASE	RELEVANT COST TO MANUFACTURE PER CASE
Direct material	$1.70	$1.70
Direct labor	2.00	2.00
Variable factory overhead	.40	.40
Fixed factory overhead*	.40	.10
Total unit cost	$4.50	$4.20
Quoted price from supplier	$4.10	

*Of the $.40 fixed factory overhead, only $.10 is actually caused by case production and could
be avoided if the firm chooses to not produce cases. The remaining $.30 of fixed factory
overhead is allocated indirect (common) costs that would continue even if case production
ceases.

Exhibit 13–3 presents factors that should be considered in a make-or-buy decision. Several of the quantitative factors [such as incremental prime (direct material and direct labor) production cost per unit and purchase price quoted by the supplier] are known with a high degree of certainty. Other factors, such as the variable overhead per unit and the opportunity cost associated with production facilities, must be estimated. The qualitative factors should be evaluated by more than one individual so personal biases do not cloud valid business judgment.

Exhibit 13–4 provides information about a case for cellular telephones produced by Latin Cellular Technologies and used in the company's line of pocket phones. The total cost to manufacture one case is $4.50. The company can purchase the case from a chemical products company for $4.10 per unit. Latin Cellular Technologies' cost accountant is preparing an analysis to determine whether the company should make the cases or buy them from the outside supplier.

Production of each case requires a cost outlay of $4.10 per unit for material, labor, and variable overhead. In addition, $.10 of the fixed overhead is considered direct product cost because it specifically relates to the manufacture of cases. This $.10 is

Walker Manufacturing (Virginia) makes mufflers for Nissan. This outsourcing decision was determined by comparing the relevant cost (including opportunity cost) of internal production to total purchase cost. After a quantitative analysis is made, qualitative factors such as supplier reliability and parts quality are also evaluated.

an incremental cost because it could be avoided if cases were not produced. The remaining fixed overhead ($.30) is not relevant to the make-or-buy decision. This amount is a common cost incurred because of general production activity, unassociated with the cost object (cases). Therefore, because this portion of the fixed cost would continue under either alternative, it is not relevant.

The relevant cost for the "make" alternative is $4.20—the cost that would be avoided if the product were not made. This amount should be compared to the $4.10 cost quoted by the supplier under the "buy" alternative. Each amount is the incremental cost of making and buying, respectively. All else being equal, management should choose to purchase the cases rather than make them, because $.10 will be saved on each case that is purchased rather than made. Relevant costs are those costs that are avoidable by choosing one decision alternative over another, regardless of whether they are variable or fixed. In a make-or-buy decision, variable production costs are relevant. Fixed production costs are relevant if they can be avoided when production is discontinued.

The opportunity cost of the facilities being used by production is also relevant in a make-or-buy alternative. If a company chooses to buy a product rather than to make it, an alternative purpose may exist for the facilities now being used for manufacturing. If a more profitable alternative is available, management should consider diverting the capacity to this use.

Assume that Latin Cellular Technologies has an opportunity to rent the physical space now used to produce cases for $80,000 per year. If the company produces 500,000 cases annually, there is an opportunity cost of $.16 per unit ($80,000 ÷ 500,000 cases) from using, rather than renting, the production space. The existence of this cost makes the "buy" alternative even more attractive.

The opportunity cost is added to the production cost because the company is forgoing this amount by choosing to make the cases. Sacrificing potential revenue is as much a relevant cost as is the incurrence of expenses. Exhibit 13–5 shows calculations relating to this decision on both a per-unit and a total cost basis. Under either format, the comparison indicates that there is a $.26 per-unit advantage to purchasing over producing.

Another opportunity cost associated with making is the increased plant throughput that is sacrificed to make a component. Assume that case production uses a resource that has been determined to be a bottleneck in the manufacturing plant. Management calculates that plant throughput can be increased by 4 percent per year on all products if the cases are bought rather than made. This increase in throughput would

EXHIBIT 13-5

Latin Cellular
Technologies' Opportunity
Costs and Make-or-Buy
Decision

	MAKE	BUY
PER UNIT:		
Direct production costs	$4.20	
Opportunity cost (revenue)	.16	
Purchase cost		$4.10
Cost per case	$4.36	$4.10

	MAKE	BUY	DIFFERENCE IN FAVOR OF PURCHASING
IN TOTAL:			
Revenue from renting capacity	$ 0	$ 80,000	$ 80,000
Cost for 500,000 cases	(2,100,000)	(2,050,000)	50,000
Net cost	$(2,100,000)	$(1,970,000)	$130,000*

*The $130,000 represents the net purchase benefit of $.26 per unit multiplied by the 500,000 units to be purchased during the year.

provide an estimated additional annual contribution margin (with no incremental fixed costs) of $210,000. Dividing this amount by the 500,000 cases currently being produced results in a $.42 per-unit opportunity cost related to making. When added to the production costs of $4.20, the true cost of manufacturing cases becomes $4.62.

Based on the information in Exhibit 13–5 (even without the inclusion of the throughput opportunity cost), Latin Cellular Technologies' cost accountant should inform company management that it is more economical to buy cases for $4.10 than to manufacture them. This analysis is the typical starting point of the decision process—determining which alternative is preferred based on the *quantitative* considerations. Managers then use judgment to assess the decision's qualitative aspects.

Assume that Latin Cellular Technologies' purchasing agent read in the newspaper that the supplier being considered was in poor financial condition and there was a high probability of a bankruptcy filing. In this case, management would likely decide to continue producing rather than purchase the cases from this supplier. In this instance, quantitative analysis supports the purchase of the units, but qualitative considerations suggest this would not be a wise course of action because the stability of the supplying source is questionable.

This additional consideration also indicates that there are many potential long-run effects of a theoretically short-run decision. If Latin Cellular Technologies had stopped case production and rented its production facilities to another firm, and the supplier had gone bankrupt, the company could be faced with high start-up costs to revitalize its case production process. This was essentially the situation faced by Stoneyfield Farm, a New Hampshire-based yogurt company. Stoneyfield Farm subcontracted its yogurt production and one day, found its supplier bankrupt—creating an inability to fill customer orders. It took Stoneyfield two years to acquire the necessary production capacity and regain market strength.

This long-run view is also expressed in Chapter 6 where it is suggested that the term *fixed cost* is really a misnomer. These costs should be referred to as long-run variable costs because, although they do not vary with volume in the short run, they *do* vary in the long run. As such, they are relevant for long-run decision making. For example, assume a part or product is manufactured (rather than purchased) and the company expects demand for that item to increase in the next few years. At a future time, the company may be faced with a need to expand capacity and incur additional "fixed" capacity costs. These long-run costs would, in turn, theoretically cause product cost to increase because of the need to allocate the new overhead to production. To suggest that products made before capacity is added would cost less than those made afterward is a short-run view. The long-run viewpoint would consider both the current and "long-run" variable costs over the product life cycle. However, as indicated in the following News Note, many major firms expect prices charged by their suppliers to change over time. Many firms actively engage in cooperative efforts with suppliers to control costs and reduce prices.

Make-or-buy decisions are not confined to manufacturing entities. Many service organizations must also make these kinds of choices. For example, accounting and law firms must decide whether to prepare and present in-house continuing education programs or to outsource such programs to external organizations or consultants. Private schools must determine whether to have their own buses or use independent contractors. Doctors investigate the differences in cost, quality of results, and convenience to patients between having blood samples drawn and tested in the office or in a separate lab facility. These examples demonstrate that the term *make* in make-or-buy decisions does not necessarily require converting a raw material to a finished component. Outsourcing can include product and process design activities, accounting and legal services, utilities, engineering, and employee health services.

Make-or-buy decisions consider the opportunity costs of facilities. If capacity is occupied in one way, it cannot be used at the same time for another purpose. Limited capacity is only one type of scarce resource that managers need to consider when making decisions.

Scarce Resources Decisions

scarce resource

Managers are frequently confronted with the short-run problem of making the best use of **scarce resources** that are essential to production activity, but are available only in limited quantity. Scarce resources create constraints on producing goods or providing services and can include machine hours, skilled labor hours, raw materials, and (as mentioned above) production capacity. Management may, in the long run, obtain a greater quantity of a scarce resource. For instance, additional machines could be purchased to increase availability of machine hours. However, in the short run, management must make the most efficient use of the scarce resources it has currently.

Ford Sets Expectations for Its Suppliers' Future Costs

NEWS NOTE

Ford has asked its 250 biggest suppliers world-wide to join in a "collaborative effort" to cut costs of parts 5% a year from 1996 through 1999, a company spokesman said. In 1994, Ford spent $50 billion with suppliers; a spokesman said the figure would most likely increase somewhat this year, but he didn't have an estimate.

. . . A major thrust of the cost-cutting effort is to cut complexity by reducing the number of alternative components used on Ford vehicles. For example, Ford aims to cut the number of types of car horns it uses to three from 30, the number of types of batteries to 14 from 40, and the number of types of steering wheels to 11 from 50.

Industry analysts and consultants say Ford's campaign is necessary to put the auto maker's costs in line with those of competitors'—and to meet its own goals. In the first quarter, Ford's profit margin was 4.2%, down from a year-earlier profit margin of 4.5% and well off the company's stated goal of a 5% return on sales.

SOURCE: Robert L. Simison, "Ford Sets Goal of Keeping Overall Costs At '95 Level to 2000, Cutting Parts Prices," *Wall Street Journal* (May 9, 1995), p. A4. Reprinted by permission of *The Wall Street Journal*, © 1995 Dow Jones & Company, Inc. All Rights Reserved Worldwide.

Determining the best use of a scarce resource requires managerial recognition of company objectives. If the objective is to maximize company contribution margin and profits, a scarce resource is best used to produce and sell the product having the highest contribution margin *per unit of the scarce resource.* This strategy assumes that the company is faced with only one scarce resource.

Exhibit 13–6 presents information on two products being manufactured by the Latin Cellular Technologies company. The company's scarce resource is a computer chip that is purchased from a supplier. Each cellular telephone requires three chips and each beeper requires a single chip. Currently, the firm has access to only 5,100 chips per month to make either beepers or cellular telephones or some combination of both. Demand is unlimited for both products, and there are no variable selling, general, or administrative costs related to either product.

The beeper's $150 selling price minus its $115 variable cost provides a contribution margin of $35 per unit. The cellular telephone's contribution margin per unit is $120 ($400 selling price minus $280 variable cost). Fixed annual overhead related to these two product lines totals $120,000 and is allocated to products for purposes of inventory valuation. Fixed overhead, however, does not change with production levels within the relevant range and, accordingly, is not relevant in a short-run scarce resource decision.

Because fixed overhead per unit is not relevant in the short run, unit contribution margin rather than unit gross margin is the appropriate measure of profitability of the two products.[4] Unit contribution margin is divided by the input quantity of the scarce resource (in this case, computer chips) to obtain the contribution margin per unit of scarce resource. The last line in Exhibit 13–6 shows the $35 contribution margin per chip for the beeper compared to $40 for the cellular telephones. Thus, it is more profitable for Latin Cellular Technologies to produce cellular telephones than beepers.

At first glance, it would appear that the cellular telephone would be, by a substantial margin, the more profitable of the two products because its contribution margin per unit ($120) is significantly higher than that of the beeper ($35). However, because the cellular telephone requires three times as many chips as the beeper, only a slightly greater amount of contribution margin per chip is generated by the production of the cellular telephones. If these were the only two products made by Latin Cellular Technologies and the company wanted to achieve the highest possible profit, it would dedicate all chips to the production of cellular telephones. Such a strategy would provide a total contribution margin of $204,000 per month [(5,100 ÷ 3) × $120], if all units produced were sold.

EXHIBIT 13–6		BEEPERS	CELLULAR TELEPHONE
Latin Cellular Technologies—Beepers and Telephone Product Information	Selling price per unit (a)	$150	$400
	Variable production cost per unit:		
	Direct material	$ 45	$ 80
	Direct labor	25	115
	Variable overhead	45	85
	Total variable cost (b)	$115	$280
	Unit contribution margin (c) = [(a) − (b)]	$ 35	$120
	Divided by chips required per unit (d)	÷ 1	÷ 3
	Contribution margin per chip [(c) ÷ (d)]	$ 35	$ 40

[4] Gross margin (or gross profit) is unit selling price minus total production cost per unit. Total production cost includes allocated fixed overhead.

When one limiting factor is involved, the outcome of a scarce resource decision will indicate that a single type of product should be manufactured and sold. Most situations, however, involve several limiting factors that compete with one another in the process of striving to attain business objectives. One method used to solve problems that have several limiting factors is **linear programming** (LP).[5]

linear programming

In addition to considering the monetary effects related to scarce resource decisions, managers must remember that all factors cannot be readily quantified and the qualitative aspects of the situation must be evaluated in addition to the quantitative ones. For example, before choosing to produce only cellular telephones, Latin Cellular Technologies' managers would need to assess the potential damage to the firm's reputation and markets if the company limited its product line to a single item. Such a choice severely restricts its customer base and is especially important if the currently manufactured products are competitively related. For example, if Hewlett-Packard began making only HP DeskJet 500 printers, many printer buyers who would not find that model appropriate for their needs would purchase their printers from another company.

Concentrating on a single product can also create market saturation or company stagnation. Some products, such as refrigerators and Rolex watches, are purchased infrequently or in single units. Making such a product limits the company's opportunity for repeat business. And, if the company concentrates on the *wrong* single product (such as buggywhips or Hoola Hoops), that exclusionary choice can be the beginning of the end for the company.

In some cases, the revenues and expenses of a group of products must be considered as a set of decisions in allocating scarce resources. For example, multiple products may be complementary or one product may be sold as part of a package with other products, cannot be used effectively without another, or will be the key to revenue generation in future periods. To illustrate these possibilities, consider the following products: Cross' well-known ballpoint pen and mechanical pencil sets; dining room tables and dining room chairs produced by Drexel Heritage Furniture; and the Barbie "family" of products made by Mattel, Inc. Would it be reasonable for Cross to make only pens, Drexel Heritage to make only tables, or Mattel to make only Barbie dolls? In the case of Mattel, company management would probably choose to manufacture Barbie dolls even if they produced zero contribution so that profits could be earned on Barbie accessories.

Thus, company management may decide that production and sale of some number of less profitable products is necessary to maintain either customer satisfaction or sales of other products. Production mix translates on the revenue side into sales mix, which is addressed in the next section.

Sales Mix Decisions

Managers continuously strive to achieve a variety of company objectives such as profit maximization, improvement of the company's relative market share, and generation of customer goodwill and loyalty. These objectives are accomplished by selling products or performing services. Regardless of whether the company is a retailer, manufacturer, or service organization, **sales mix** refers to "the relative quantities of the products that make up the total sales of a company."[6] Some important factors affecting the sales mix of a company are product selling prices, sales force compensation, and advertising expenditures. A change in one or all of these factors may cause a company's sales mix to shift.

sales mix

---

[5] Linear programming techniques are useful in determining the appropriate amount of scarce resources to allocate to less-profitable products. Linear programming techniques are discussed briefly in the appendix to the chapter and are covered in depth in most management science courses.

[6] Institute of Management Accountants (formerly National Association of Accountants), *Statements on Management Accounting Number 2: Management Accounting Terminology* (Montvale, N.J.: June 1, 1983), p. 94.

EXHIBIT 13–7

Latin Cellular
Technologies—Pager
Product Information

	STUDENT	COMMERCIAL	ADVANCED
Unit selling price	$100	$150	$180
Unit costs:			
Variable costs:			
Direct material	$ 33	$ 45	$ 58
Direct labor	12	25	32
Variable factory overhead	15	25	30
Total variable production cost	$ 60	$ 95	$120
Product contribution margin	$ 40	$ 55	$ 60
Less variable selling expense*	(10)	(15)	(18)
Contribution margin per unit**	$ 30	$ 40	$ 42

Total annual fixed costs:	
Production	$2,700,000
Selling and administrative	1,300,000
Total	$4,000,000

*The only variable selling expense is for sales commissions, which are always set at 10 percent of the selling price per unit.
**The machine time is one hour to produce any of the pager types. Thus, the contribution margin per machine hour is the same as the contribution margin per unit.

Information on Latin Cellular Technologies' pocket pager line is presented in Exhibit 13–7 and is used to illustrate the effects of the three factors mentioned above on sales mix. The product line includes Student, Commercial, and Advanced pagers, each having different features and aimed at a different market segment.

SALES PRICE CHANGES AND RELATIVE PROFITABILITY OF PRODUCTS
Managers must continuously monitor the relative selling prices of company products, in respect both to each other and to competitors' prices. This process may provide information that causes management to change one or more selling prices. Factors that might influence price changes include fluctuations in demand or production/distribution cost, economic conditions, and competition. Any shift in the selling price of one product in a multiproduct firm will normally cause a change in sales mix of that firm because of the economic law of demand elasticity with respect to price.[7]

Latin Cellular Technologies' management has set profit maximization as the primary corporate objective. Such a strategy does not necessarily translate to maximizing unit sales of the product with the highest selling prices and minimizing unit sales of the product with the lowest selling price. The product with the highest selling price per unit does not necessarily yield the highest contribution margin per unit or per dollar of sales. In Latin Cellular Technologies' case, the pager with the highest selling price (the Advanced model) yields the highest unit contribution margin of the three products but the lowest contribution margin as a percentage of sales. It is more profit-beneficial to sell a dollar's worth of the Student Pager than a dollar's worth of either Commercial or Advanced models. A dollar of sales of the Student Pager yields $.30 of contribution margin; this compares to $.27 for the Commercial Pager and $.23 for the Advanced Pager.

If profit maximization is a company's goal, management should consider the sales volume and unit contribution margin of each product. Total company contribution

[7] The law of demand elasticity indicates how closely price and demand are related. Product demand is highly elastic if a small price reduction generates a large demand increase. If demand is less elastic, large price reductions are needed to bring about moderate sales volume increases. In contrast, a small price increase results in a large drop in demand if demand is highly elastic.

	UNIT CONTRIBUTION MARGIN (FROM EXHIBIT 13–7)	CURRENT SALES VOLUME IN UNITS	INCOME STATEMENT INFORMATION
Student Pagers	$30	82,000	$2,460,000
Commercial Pagers	$40	39,000	1,560,000
Advanced Pagers	$42	29,000	1,218,000
Total contribution margin of product sales mix			$5,238,000
Fixed costs (from Exhibit 13–7)			(4,000,000)
Product line income at present volume and sales mix			$1,238,000

EXHIBIT 13–8

Latin Cellular Technologies—Relationship Between Contribution Margin and Sales Volume

margin is the sum of the contribution margins provided by all the products' sales. Exhibit 13–8 provides information on sales volumes and indicates the respective total contribution margins of the three types of pagers. Although Student Pagers do not have the highest contribution margin per unit, they do generate the largest total contribution margin in this product line for Latin Cellular Technologies because of their sales volume. To maximize profits from this product line, company management must maximize total contribution margin rather than per-unit contribution margin.

A product's sales volume is almost always intricately related to its selling price. Generally, when the selling price of a product or service is increased and demand is elastic with respect to price, demand for that product decreases.[8] Thus, if Latin Cellular Technologies' management, in an attempt to increase profits, raises the price of the Student Pager to $120, there should be some decline in demand. Assume that consultation with the marketing research personnel indicates that such a price increase would cause demand for that product to drop from 82,000 to 50,000 pagers per period. Exhibit 13–9 shows the effect of this pricing decision on the pager product line income of Latin Cellular Technologies.

Even though the contribution margin per unit of the Student Pager increased, the total dollar contribution margin generated by sales of that product declined because of the decrease in sales volume. This example assumed that customers did not switch their purchases from Student Pagers to other Latin Cellular Technologies' products when the price of the Student Pager was raised. When prices of some products in a product line remain fixed while others are changed, customers may substitute the purchase of one product for another. Switching within the company was ignored in this instance, but some customers would likely purchase one of the more expensive pagers after the price of the Student Pager is increased. For example, customers might believe that the difference in quality between the Student and Commercial Pagers is worth the $30 (rather than $50) price difference and make such a purchasing switch.

In making decisions to raise or lower prices, the relevant quantitative factors include (1) prospective or new contribution margin per unit of product; (2) both short-term and long-term changes in product demand and production volume because of the price change; and (3) best use of the company's scarce resources. Some relevant qualitative factors involved in pricing decisions are (1) impact of changes on customer goodwill toward the company; (2) customer loyalty toward company products; and (3) competitors' responses to the firm's new pricing structure.[9] As demonstrated in the following News Note, changes in the competitive environment create opportunities to produce new products. Exploiting such opportunities leads to changes in the sales mix.

---

[8] Such a decline in demand would generally not occur when the product in question has no close substitutes or is not a major expenditure in consumers' budgets.

[9] In regard to this last item, consider what occurs when one airline raises or lowers its fares between cities. It typically does not take very long for all the other airlines flying that route to adjust their fares accordingly. Thus, any competitive advantage is only for a short time span.

EXHIBIT 13–9

Latin Cellular
Technologies—
Relationship Between
Selling Price and Demand

	UNIT CONTRIBUTION MARGIN	NEW SALES VOLUME IN UNITS	INCOME STATEMENT INFORMATION
Student Pager	$48*	50,000	$2,400,000
Commercial Pager	$40	39,000	1,560,000
Advanced Pager	$42	29,000	1,218,000
Total contribution margin of product sales mix			$5,178,000
Fixed costs			(4,000,000)
Product line income at new volume of sales			$1,178,000

*New selling price of $120 minus [total variable production costs of $60 plus variable selling expense of $12 (10% of new selling price)].

When pricing proposed new products, a long-run view of the product's life cycle should be taken. This view would include assumptions about consumer behavior, competitor behavior, pace of technology changes, government posture, environmental concerns, size of the potential market, and demographic changes. These considerations would affect product price estimates at the various stages in the product's life cycle. Then, as discussed in Chapter 6, these estimates would be averaged to obtain the starting point in the process of target costing.

COMPENSATION CHANGES   Many companies compensate their salespeople by paying a fixed rate of commission on gross sales dollars. This approach motivates salespeople to sell the highest-priced product rather than the product providing the highest contribution margin to the company. If the company has a profit-maximization objective, a commission policy of a percentage of sales may not be effective in achieving that objective.

Assume Latin Cellular Technologies has a price structure for its pagers as indicated in Exhibit 13–10 (p. 584): Student, $120; Commercial, $150; and Advanced, $180. The company has a current policy of paying sales commissions equal to 10 percent of selling price. This commission structure encourages sales of the Advanced pagers, rather than the Commercial or Student pagers. The company is considering a new compensation structure for its sales force. The new structure would provide for a base salary to all salespeople, which would total $875,000 per period.[10] In addition, the salespeople would be paid a 12 percent commission on product contribution margin (selling price minus total variable *production* costs). The per-unit product contribution margins of the pager are $60, $55, and $60, respectively, for Student, Commercial, and Advanced pagers. The new compensation policy should motivate sales personnel to sell more of the products that produce the highest commission, which would correspondingly be the company's most profitable products.[11]

Exhibit 13–10 compares Latin Cellular Technologies' total contribution margin using the original sales mix and commission with total contribution margin provided under a newly assumed sales mix and the new salesperson compensation structure. The new structure increases profit because sales are shifted from the lower contribution margin pager toward the more profitable pagers. The sales personnel also benefit from the new compensation structure as their combined incomes is slightly higher than under the original structure.

[10] The revised compensation structure should allow the sales personnel to achieve the same income as before the change given a similar level of effort.

[11] This statement relies on the assumption that the salespersons' efforts are more highly correlated with unit sales than dollar sales. If the salespersons' efforts are more highly correlated with dollar sales, the commission structure should encourage sales of products with higher contribution margin ratios.

Change in Legal Liability Law Creates New Opportunity for Cessna

[Cessna, an aircraft manufacturer based in Wichita, Kansas, recently announced that it intends to hire 1,500 employees to restart production of small, single-engine aircraft.] Huge numbers of the planes were once made in the U.S., but manufacturing virtually halted in the mid-1980s following post-crash lawsuits alleging faulty production.

The main impetus behind Cessna's restart is the federal General Aviation Revitalization Act, passed last year, which limits lawsuits involving airplanes more than 18 years old and protects makers from serious liability exposure.

Cessna said it will invest at least $30 million over the next three years to build a new Kansas plant and will refurbish another to restart production.

Single-engine plane production reached a record at Cessna in 1977 with 8,893 planes, the company said. By the early 1980s, even as liability claims hurt the industry, Cessna still employed 14,000 workers and turned out thousands of airplanes. But by 1986, the number of workers had dropped to less than 4,000 and production of single-engine planes fell to zero.

The aircraft maker hopes that pent-up demand from a variety of customers, including pleasure and business pilots, will allow it to sell 2,000 of these planes annually by 1998.

SOURCE: Barbara Carton, "Cessna Says It Will Make More Small Airplanes," *Wall Street Journal* (March 14, 1995), pp. B1, B9. Reprinted by permission of *The Wall Street Journal*, © 1995 Dow Jones & Company, Inc. All Rights Reserved Worldwide.

Fixed expenses would not be considered in setting compensation structures unless those expenses were incremental relative to the new policy or to changes in sales volumes. The new base salaries were an incremental cost of Latin Cellular Technologies' proposed compensation plan.

ADVERTISING BUDGET CHANGES   Shifts in the sales mix may also be effected by either adjusting the advertising budgets respective to each company product or increasing the company's total advertising budget. This section continues using the data for Latin Cellular Technologies from Exhibit 13–9 and examines a proposed increase in the company's total advertising budget.

Latin Cellular Technologies' advertising manager, Barry Fostwick, has proposed increasing the advertising budget from $60,000 to $140,000 per year. Mr. Fostwick thinks the increased advertising will result in the following additional unit sales during the coming year: Student, 1,000; Commercial, 750; and Advanced, 500.

If the company spends the additional $80,000 for advertising, will the additional 2,250 units of sales produce larger profits than Latin Cellular Technologies is currently experiencing on this product line? The original fixed costs, as well as the contribution margin generated by the old sales level, are irrelevant to the decision. The relevant items are the increased sales revenue, increased variable costs, and increased fixed cost—the incremental effects of the change. The difference between incremental revenues and incremental variable costs is the incremental contribution margin from which the incremental fixed cost is subtracted to provide the incremental benefit (or loss) of the decision.[12]

Exhibit 13–11 shows calculations of the expected increase in contribution margin if the increased advertising expenditure is made. The $99,000 of additional contribution margin exceeds the $80,000 incremental cost for advertising, indicating company management should increase its advertising by $80,000.

[12] This same type of incremental analysis is shown in Chapter 12 in relation to CVP computations.

Old Policy—Commissions equal 20 percent of selling price

	PRODUCT CONTRIBUTION MARGIN	−	COMMISSION	=	CONTRIBUTION MARGIN AFTER COMMISSION	×	VOLUME	=	TOTAL CONTRIBUTION MARGIN
Student	$60		(.10 × $ 120) or $12		$48		50,000		$2,400,000
Commercial	55		(.10 × $ 150) or 15		40		39,000		1,560,000
Advanced	60		(.10 × $ 180) or 18		42		29,000		1,218,000
Total contribution margin for product sales									$5,178,000

New Policy—Commissions equal 12 percent of product contribution margin per unit and incremental base salaries of $875,000.

	PRODUCT CONTRIBUTION MARGIN	−	COMMISSION	=	CONTRIBUTION MARGIN AFTER COMMISSION	×	VOLUME	=	TOTAL CONTRIBUTION MARGIN
Student	$60		(.12 × $60) or $7.20		$52.80		60,000		$3,168,000
Commercial	55		(.12 × $55) or 6.60		48.40		18,000		871,200
Advanced	60		(.12 × $60) or 7.20		52.80		40,000		2,112,000
Total contribution margin for product sales									$6,151,200
Less sales force base salaries									(875,000)
Contribution margin adjusted for sales force base salaries									$5,276,200

EXHIBIT 13–10

Latin Cellular Technologies—Impact of Change in Commission Structure

Increased advertising may cause changes in the sales mix or in the number of units sold. By targeting advertising efforts at specific products, either of these changes can be effected. Sales can also be affected by opportunities that allow companies to obtain business at a sales price that differs from the normal price.

Special Order Decisions

special order decision

A **special order decision** requires that management compute a reasonable sales price for production or service jobs outside the company's normal realm of operations. Special order situations include jobs that require a bid, are taken during slack periods, or are made to a particular buyer's specifications. Typically, the sales price quoted on a special order job should be high enough to cover the job's variable and incremental fixed costs and to generate a profit. Moreover, as discussed in Chapter 6, overhead costs tend to rise with increases in product variety and product complexity. The increases are typically experienced in receiving, inspection, order processing, and inventory carrying costs. Activity-based costing techniques allow managers to more accurately determine these incremental costs and, thereby, properly include them in analyzing special orders.

Sometimes companies will depart from the above price-setting routine and "low-ball" bid jobs. A low-ball bid may cover only costs and produce no profit or may even be below cost. The rationale of low-ball bids is to obtain the job and have the opportunity to introduce company products or services to a particular market segment. Special pricing of this nature may provide work for a period of time, but it cannot be continued over the long run. To remain in business, a company must set selling prices to cover total costs and provide a reasonable profit margin.[13]

Another type of special pricing job is that of private-label orders in which the buyer's name (rather than the seller's) is attached to the product. Companies may

---

[13] An exception to this general rule may occur when a company produces related or complementary products. For instance, an electronics company may sell a video game at or below cost and allow the ancillary software program sales to be the primary source of profit.

	STUDENT	COMMERCIAL	ADVANCED	TOTAL
New volume	51,000	39,750	29,500	120,250
Old volume	50,000	39,000	29,000	(118,000)
Increase in volume	1,000	750	500	2,250
Contribution margin per unit	× $48	× $40	× $42	
Incremental contribution margin	$48,000	$30,000	$21,000	$ 99,000
Incremental fixed cost of advertising				(80,000)
Incremental benefit of increased advertising expenditure				$ 19,000

EXHIBIT 13–11

Latin Cellular Technologies—Analysis of Increased Advertising Cost

accept these jobs during slack periods to more effectively use available capacity. Fixed costs are typically not allocated to special order, private-label products. Some variable costs (such as sales commissions) may be reduced or eliminated by the very nature of the private-label process. The prices on these special orders are typically set high enough to cover the actual variable costs and thereby contribute to overall profits.

Special prices may also be justified when orders are of an unusual nature (because of the quantity, method of delivery, or packaging) or because the products are being tailor-made to customer instructions. Lastly, special pricing may be used when goods are produced for a one-time job, such as an overseas order that will not affect domestic sales.

Assume that Latin Cellular Technologies has been given the opportunity to bid on a special order for 50,000 private-label beepers for a major electronics retailer. Company management wants to obtain the order as long as the additional business will provide a satisfactory contribution to profit. Latin Cellular Technologies has available production capacity that is not currently being used, and necessary components and raw materials can be obtained from suppliers. Also, the company has no immediate opportunity to apply its currently unused capacity in another way, so there is no opportunity cost.

Exhibit 13–12 presents information that management has gathered to determine a price to bid on the beepers. Direct materials and components, direct labor, and *variable* factory overhead costs are relevant to setting the bid price because these costs will be incurred for each beeper produced. Although all variable costs are normally relevant to a special pricing decision, the variable selling expense is irrelevant in this instance because no sales commission will be paid on this sale. Fixed manufacturing overhead and fixed selling and administrative expenses are not expected to increase because of this sale, so these expenses are not included in the pricing decision.

Using the available cost information, the relevant cost for determining the bid price for each beeper is $35 (direct materials and components, direct labor, and variable overhead). This cost is the *minimum* price at which the company should sell one beeper. Any price higher than $35 will provide the company some profit on the sale.

Assume that Latin Cellular Technologies' beeper line is currently experiencing a $220,000 net loss and that company managers want to set a bid price that would cover the net loss and create a $50,000 before-tax profit. In this case, Latin Cellular Technologies would spread the total $270,000 desired contribution margin over the 50,000 unit special order at $5.40 per beeper. This decision would give a bid price of $40.40 per beeper ($35 variable cost + $5.40). However, *any* price above the $35 variable cost will contribute toward reducing the $220,000 product line loss.

In setting the bid price, management must decide how much profit it would consider reasonable on the special order. Assume Latin Cellular Technologies' usual selling price for a beeper is $65 and each sale provides a normal profit margin of $7 per beeper or 12 percent (rounded) of the $58 total cost. Setting the bid price for the special order at $39.20 would cover the variable production costs of $35 and provide a normal 12 percent profit margin on the incremental unit cost. This com-

EXHIBIT 13–12

Latin Cellular
Technologies—Beeper
Product Information

PER-UNIT COST FOR ONE BEEPER:	NORMAL COSTS	RELEVANT COSTS
Direct materials and components	$22	$22
Direct labor	8	8
Variable overhead	5	5
Variable selling expense (commission)	6	0
Total variable cost	$41	$35
Fixed factory overhead (allocated)	14	
Fixed selling and administrative expense	3	
Total cost per beeper	$58	

putation illustrates a simplistic cost-plus approach to pricing, but ignores both product demand and market competition. Latin Cellular Technologies' bid price should also reflect these considerations. In addition, company management should consider the effect that the additional job will have on the activities engaged in by the company and whether these activities will create additional, unforeseen costs.

When setting a special order price, management must consider the qualitative issues as well as the quantitative ones. For instance, will setting a low bid price cause this customer (or others) to believe that a precedent has been established for future prices? Will the contribution margin on a bid, set low enough to acquire the job, earn a sufficient amount to justify the additional burdens placed on management or employees by this activity? Will the additional production activity require the use of bottleneck resources and reduce company throughput? How, if at all, will special order sales affect the company's normal sales? If the job is scheduled during a period of low business activity (off-season or recession), is management willing to take the business at a lower contribution or profit margin simply to keep a trained workforce employed and maintain skill levels?

Robinson-Patman Act

A final management consideration in special pricing decisions is the **Robinson-Patman Act,** which prohibits companies from pricing the same product at different levels when those amounts do not reflect related cost differences. Cost differences must result from actual variations in the cost to manufacture, sell, or distribute a product because of differing methods of production or quantities sold.

ad hoc discount

Companies may, however, give **ad hoc discounts,** which are price concessions that relate to real (or imagined) competitive pressures rather than to location of the merchandising chain or volume purchased. Such discounts are not usually subject to detailed justification, because they are based on a competitive market environment. Although ad hoc discounts do not require intensive justification under the law, other types of discounts do because they may reflect some type of price discrimination. Prudent managers must understand the legalities of special pricing and the factors that allow for its implementation. For merchandise that is normally stocked, the only support for pricing differences is a difference in distribution costs.

In making pricing decisions, managers typically first analyze the market environment, including the degree of industry competition and competitors' prices. Then, managers normally consider full production cost in setting normal sales prices. Full production cost includes an allocated portion of fixed costs of the production process, which in a multiproduct environment, could include common costs of production relating to more than one type of product. Allocations of common costs can distort the results of operations shown for individual products.

Product Line Decisions

Operating results of multiproduct environments are often presented in a disaggregated format that shows results for separate product lines within the organization or

division. In reviewing these disaggregated statements, managers must distinguish relevant from irrelevant information regarding individual product lines. If all costs (variable *and* fixed) are allocated to product lines, a product line or segment may be perceived to be operating at a loss when actually it is not. Such perceptions may be caused by the commingling of relevant and irrelevant information on the statements.

Exhibit 13–13 presents basic earnings information for Latin Cellular Technologies Consumer Products Division, which manufactures three product lines—cellular phones, pagers and beepers, and cameras.

The format of the information given in the exhibit makes it appear that the Pagers and Beepers and Camera lines are each operating at a net loss ($40,000 and $155,000, respectively). Managers reviewing such results might reason that the firm would be $195,000 more profitable if both products were eliminated. Such a conclusion may be premature because of the mixing of relevant and irrelevant information in the income statement presentation.

All fixed expenses have been allocated to the individual product lines in Exhibit 13–13. Such allocations are traditionally based on one or more measures of "presumed" equity, such as square footage of the manufacturing plant occupied by each product line, number of machine hours incurred for production of each product line, or number of employees directly associated with each product line. In all cases, however, allocations may force fixed expenses into specific product line operating results even though some of those expenses may not have actually been incurred for the benefit of the specific product line.

In Exhibit 13–14, the fixed expenses of the Consumer Products Division are segregated into three subcategories: (1) those that are avoidable if the particular product line is eliminated (these expenses may also be referred to as attributable expenses); (2) those that are directly associated with a particular product line but are unavoidable; and (3) those that are incurred for the company as a whole (common expenses) and that are allocated to the individual product lines. The latter two subcategories are irrelevant to the question of whether to eliminate a product line. An unavoidable expense will merely be shifted to another product line if the product line with which it is associated is eliminated. Common expenses will be incurred regardless of which

EXHIBIT 13–13

Consumer Products
Division of Latin Cellular
Technologies Product Line
Income Statements

	CELLULAR PHONES	PAGERS AND BEEPERS	CAMERAS	TOTAL
Sales	$4,000,000	$800,000	$1,000,000	$5,800,000
Total direct variable expenses	(1,400,000)	(570,000)	(600,000)	(2,570,000)
Total contribution margin	$2,600,000	$230,000	$ 400,000	$3,230,000
Total fixed expenses	(2,100,000)	(270,000)	(555,000)	(2,925,000)
Net income (loss)	$ 500,000	$(40,000)	$ (155,000)	$ 305,000

FIXED EXPENSES ARE DETAILED BELOW:

	CELLULAR PHONES	PAGERS AND BEEPERS	CAMERAS	TOTAL
(1) Avoidable fixed expenses	$1,200,000	$242,000	$ 230,000	$1,672,000
(2) Unavoidable fixed expenses	600,000	8,000	200,000	808,000
(3) Allocated common expenses	300,000	20,000	125,000	445,000
Total	$2,100,000	$270,000	$ 555,000	$2,925,000

product lines are eliminated. An example of a common cost is the insurance premium on a manufacturing facility that houses all product lines.

If both the Pagers and Beepers and Cameras lines are eliminated, total company profit will decline by $158,000. This amount represents the combined lost segment margin of the two product lines—$12,000 negative for Pagers and Beepers and $170,000 positive for Cameras. **Segment margin** represents the excess of revenues over direct variable expenses and avoidable fixed expenses. It is the amount remaining to cover unavoidable direct fixed expenses and common expenses, and to provide profits.[14] The segment margin figure is the appropriate one on which to base the continuation or elimination decision because it measures the segment's contribution to the coverage of indirect and unavoidable expenses. The decrease in total income that would result with only one product line can be shown in the following alternative computations. With only one product line (Cellular Phones), Consumer Products would experience a total net income of $147,000, computed as follows:

segment margin

Current net income	$ 305,000
Increase in income due to elimination of Pagers and Beepers (segment margin)	12,000
Decrease in income due to elimination of Cameras (segment margin)	(170,000)
New net income	$ 147,000

[14] It was assumed here that all common expenses are fixed expenses; this is not always the case. Some common costs could be variable, such as expenses of processing purchase orders or computer time-sharing expenses for payroll or other corporate functions.

EXHIBIT 13–14

Consumer Products
Division of Latin Cellular
Technologies Segment
Margin Income Statements

	CELLULAR PHONES	PAGERS AND BEEPERS	CAMERAS	TOTAL
Sales	$4,000,000	$800,000	$1,000,000	$5,800,000
Total direct variable expenses	(1,400,000)	(570,000)	(600,000)	(2,570,000)
Total contribution margin	$2,600,000	$230,000	$ 400,000	$3,230,000
(1) Avoidable fixed expenses	(1,200,000)	(242,000)	(230,000)	(1,672,000)
Segment margin	$1,400,000	$(12,000)	$ 170,000	$1,558,000
(2) Unavoidable fixed expenses	(600,000)	(8,000)	(200,000)	(808,000)
Product line result	$ 800,000	$(20,000)	$ (30,000)	$ 750,000
(3) Allocated common expenses	(300,000)	(20,000)	(125,000)	(445,000)
Net income (loss)	$ 500,000	$(40,000)	$ (155,000)	$ 305,000

This new net income can be proved by the following computation:

Total contribution margin of Cellular Phones	$2,600,000
Minus avoidable fixed expenses of Cellular Phones product line	(1,200,000)
Segment margin of Cellular Phones	$1,400,000
Minus *all* remaining unavoidable and allocated expenses shown on	
Exhibit 13–14 ($808,000 + $445,000)	(1,253,000)
Remaining income with one product line	$ 147,000

Based on the information shown in Exhibit 13–14, the Consumer Products Division should eliminate the Pagers and Beepers product line because it is generating a negative segment margin, and therefore, is not generating enough revenue to cover its relevant expenses. If this product line were eliminated, total company profit would increase by $12,000, the amount of the negative segment margin.

In classifying product line costs, managers should be aware that some costs may appear to be avoidable but are actually not. For example, the salary of a supervisor working directly with a product line appears to be an avoidable fixed cost if the product line is eliminated. However, if these individuals have significant experience, they are often retained and transferred to other areas of the company even if product lines are cut. Determinations such as these need to be made before costs can be appropriately classified in product line elimination decisions.

Depreciation on factory equipment used to manufacture a specific product is an irrelevant cost in product line decisions. Even if the equipment will be kept in service and used to produce other products, the depreciation expense is unavoidable and irrelevant to the decision. But, if the equipment can be sold, the selling price is relevant to the decision because it would increase the marginal benefit of the decision to discontinue the product line.

Before making spontaneous decisions to discontinue a product line, management should carefully consider what it would take to "turn the product line around" and the long-term ramifications of the elimination decision. For example, elimination of a product line shrinks market assortment, which may cause some customers to seek other suppliers that maintain a broader market assortment. And, as in other relevant costing situations, a decision to eliminate a product line has qualitative as well as quantitative factors that must be analyzed.

Management's task is to effectively and efficiently allocate its finite stock of resources to accomplish its chosen set of objectives. A cost accountant needs to learn what uses will be made of the information requested by managers to make certain that the relevant information is provided in the appropriate form. Managers must have a reliable quantitative basis on which to analyze problems, compare viable solutions, and choose the best course of action. Because management is a social rather than a natural science, there are no fundamental "truths" and few problems are susceptible to black-or-white solutions. Relevant costing is a process of making human approximations of the costs of alternative decision results.

VIDEO
VIGNETTE

Financial Services Corp. and/or Cortland Line Company and/or Northwest Distribution (Blue Chip Enterprises)

REVISITING

KPMG Peat Marwick

The opening vignette discussed how KPMG changed from operating as a general partnership to newer organizational forms that have become available as a result of recent U.S., state, and international laws. The change to new organizational forms reduced the potential cost of litigation to KPMG.

However, even with the switch to new organizational forms, KPMG Peat Marwick chairman Jon Madonna noted that his company's litigation woes were hardly solved: "Our switch to an LLP does not change the need for litigation reform. Frivolous litigation facing the accounting profession continues to increase dramatically and unreasonably raises the cost of doing business, not only for firms like us, but also for our clients and their shareholders."

Also, by switching to the LLC form in Britain, KPMG will now be forced to open its books to the public, something it had not been required to do when it was operating as a partnership. Additionally, it must hire one of its competitors to audit its accounts and attest to their fair presentation. One further disadvantage is that the company will now face a greater tax burden.

The reorganizing still makes financial sense. It is a rational action by KPMG management to control legal costs so the firm can remain financially viable. The reorganization makes recruiting easier also because new employees recognize that their personal assets are now exposed to less risk than under the general partnership arrangement if those employees advance to the partner level.

SOURCE: Anonymous, "US Firms Go for LLPs," *Accountancy* (September 1994), p. 11.

CHAPTER SUMMARY

Relevant information is logically related and pertinent to a given decision. Relevant information may be both quantitative and qualitative. Variable costs are generally relevant to a decision; they are irrelevant only when they cannot be avoided under any possible alternative or when they do not differ across alternatives. Direct avoidable fixed costs are also relevant to decision making. Sometimes costs give the illusion of being relevant when they actually are not. Examples of such irrelevant costs include sunk costs, arbitrarily allocated common costs, and nonincremental fixed costs.

Relevant costing compares the incremental revenues and/or costs associated with alternative decisions. Managers use relevant costing to determine the incremental benefits of decision alternatives. One decision is established as a baseline against which the alternatives are compared. In many decisions the alternative of "change nothing" is the obvious baseline case.

Common situations in which relevant costing techniques are applied include asset replacements, make-or-buy decisions, scarce resource allocations, special price determinations, sales mix distributions, and retention or elimination of product lines. The following points are important to remember:

1. In an asset replacement decision, costs paid in the past are not relevant to a decision being made currently; these are sunk costs and should be ignored.
2. In a make-or-buy decision, include the opportunity costs associated with the buy alternative; nonproduction potentially allows management an opportunity to make plant assets and personnel available for other purposes.
3. In a decision involving a single scarce resource, if the objective is to maximize company contribution margin and profits, then production and sales should be focused toward the product with the highest contribution margin per unit of the scarce resource.
4. In a special order decision, the minimum selling price a company should charge is the sum of all the incremental costs of production and sale on the order.
5. In a sales mix decision, changes in selling prices and advertising will normally affect sales volume and change the company's contribution margin ratio. Tying sales commissions to contribution margin will motivate salespeople to sell products that will most benefit the company's profits.
6. In a product line decision, product lines should be evaluated based on their segment margins rather than on net income. Segment margin captures the change in corporate net income that would occur if the segment were discontinued.

Quantitative analysis is generally short-range in perspective. After analyzing the quantifiable factors associated with each alternative, a manager must assess the merits and potential risks of the qualitative factors involved to select the best possible course of action. Some of these qualitative factors (such as the community economic impact of closing a plant) may present long-range planning and policy implications. Other qualitative factors may be short-range in nature, such as competitor reactions. Managers must decide the relevance of individual factors based on experience, judgment, knowledge of theory, and use of logic.

APPENDIX

Linear Programming

There are factors that restrict the immediate attainment of almost any objective. For example, assume that the objective of the board of directors at Washington Hospital is to aid sick people during the coming year. Factors restricting the attainment of that objective include number of beds in the hospital, size of the hospital staff, hours per week the staff is allowed to work, and number of charity patients the hospital can accept. Each factor reflects a limited or scarce resource, and Washington Hospital must find a means of achieving its objective by efficiently and effectively allocating its limited resources.

Managers are always concerned with allocating scarce resources among competing uses. If a company has only one scarce resource, managers will schedule production or other measures of activity in a way that maximizes the use of the scarce resource. Most situations, however, involve several limiting factors that compete with one another during the process of striving to attain business objectives. Solving problems having several limiting factors requires the use of **mathematical programming,** which refers to a variety of techniques used to allocate limited resources among activities to achieve a specific goal or purpose. This appendix provides an introduction to linear programming, which is one form of mathematical programming.[15]

mathematical programming

BASICS OF LINEAR PROGRAMMING

Linear programming (LP) is a method used to find the optimal allocation of scarce resources in a situation involving one objective and multiple limiting factors.[16] The objective and restrictions on achieving that objective must be expressible as linear equations.[17] The equation that specifies the objective is called the **objective function;** typically, the objective is to maximize or to minimize some measure of performance. For example, a company's objective could be to maximize contribution margin or to minimize product cost.

objective function

A constraint is any type of restriction that hampers management's pursuit of the objective. Resource constraints involve limited availability of labor time, machine time, raw materials, space, or production capacity. Demand or marketing constraints restrict the quantity of product that can be sold during a time period. Constraints can also be in the form of technical product requirements. For example, management may be constrained in the production requirements for frozen meals by caloric or vitamin content. A final constraint in all LP problems is a **nonnegativity constraint.** This constraint specifies that there cannot be negative values of physical quantities. Constraints are specified in mathematical equations and represent the limits imposed on optimizing the objective function.

nonnegativity constraint

[15] This chapter discusses some basic linear programming concepts; it is not an all-inclusive presentation. Any standard management science text should be consulted for an in-depth presentation of the subject.
[16] Finding the best allocation of resources when multiple goals exist is called goal programming. This topic is not addressed in this text.
[17] If the objective and/or restrictions cannot be expressed in linear equations, the technique of nonlinear programming must be used. No general method has been developed that can solve all types of nonlinear programming problems.

feasible solution

Almost every allocation problem has multiple **feasible solutions** that do not violate any of the problem constraints. Different solutions generally give different values for the objective function, although in some cases, a problem may have several solutions that provide the same value for the objective function. Solutions may be generated that contain fractional values. If solutions for variables must be restricted to whole numbers, **integer programming** techniques must be used to add additional constraints to the problem. The **optimal solution** to a maximization or minimization goal is the one that provides the best answer to the allocation problem. Some LP problems may have more than one optimal solution.

integer programming

optimal solution

FORMULATING A LP PROBLEM

Two common situations for applying linear programming techniques are scheduling production and combining ingredients. Management's goal in determining production mix in a multiproduct environment is to find the mix of products that, when sold, will maximize the company's contribution margin (the goal). The goal in determining the mix of ingredients for a specific product is to find that mix providing the specified level of quality at the minimum variable cost.

Each LP problem contains a dependent variable, two or more independent (or decision) variables, and one or more constraints. A **decision variable** is an unknown item for which the problem is being solved. The first and most important step in solving linear programming problems is setting up the information in mathematical equation form. The objective function and each of the constraints must be identified. The objective function is frequently stated such that the solution will either maximize contribution margin or minimize variable costs. Basic objective function formats for maximization and minimization problems are shown below:

decision variable

MAXIMIZATION PROBLEM

Objective Function: $\text{MAX CM} = \text{CM}_1 X_1 + \text{CM}_2 X_2$

MINIMIZATION PROBLEM

Objective Function: $\text{MIN VC} = \text{VC}_1 X_1 + \text{VC}_2 X_2$

where CM = contribution margin

CM_1 = contribution margin per unit of the first product

CM_2 = contribution margin per unit of the second product

X_1 = number of units of the first product

X_2 = number of units of the second product

VC = variable cost

VC_1 = variable cost per unit of the first product

VC_2 = variable cost per unit of the second product

Resource constraints are usually expressed as inequalities.[18] The following is the general formula for a less-than-or-equal-to resource constraint:

Resource Constraint(1): $A_1 X_1 + A_2 X_2 \leq \text{Resource 1}$

input-output coefficients

The coefficients (A_1 and A_2) are **input-output coefficients** that indicate the rate at which each decision variable uses up or depletes the scarce resource.

Machine hours is an example of a resource constraint. Assume that Latin Cellular Technologies has only 10,000 machine hours available to produce television remote control units and automobile-entry remote control units. One-half machine hours

---

[18] It is also possible to have strict equality constraints. For example, in producing a 10-pound bag of dog food, ingredients could be combined in a variety of ways, but total weight is required to be equal to 10 pounds.

FILE CABINET (X₁)

Contribution margin per unit: $25
Labor hours to manufacture one unit: 3
Machine hours to assemble one unit: 2
Cubic feet of warehouse space per unit: 8

PORTABLE SHELF (X₂)

Contribution margin per unit: $9
Labor hours to manufacture one unit: 2
Machine hours to assemble one unit: 1
Cubic feet of warehouse space per unit: 3

CONSTRAINTS

Total labor time available each month: 2,100 hours
Total machine time available each month: 850 hours
Warehouse cubic feet available: 4,000

are required to produce a television remote control unit and .25 hours are needed for one automobile-entry unit. The resource constraint is shown as

$$.5X_1 + .25X_2 \leq 10,000$$

where X_1 = number of television remote control units

   X_2 = number of automobile-entry remote control units

If Latin Cellular Technologies manufactured only one of the two types of products, it could produce 20,000 (10,000 ÷ .5) television control units or 40,000 (10,000 ÷ .25) automobile-entry units. In manufacturing both products, the company must recognize that producing one television control unit precludes manufacturing two automobile-entry units. The mix of units to be produced will be determined by the contribution margin of each product and the other constraints under which the company operates.

All of the general concepts of formatting a linear programming problem are shown in the following maximization problem using data for the Office Storage Company. Office Storage sells two office storage products: file cabinets and portable shelves. Information on these products and the constraints that must be considered are provided in Exhibit 13–15. Office Storage managers want to know the mix of products to produce and sell that will generate the maximum contribution margin. The company is producing the items for future sale and must store them for the near term in its warehouse. For Office Storage Company, the problem is composed of the following factors: (1) the objective is to maximize contribution margin (CM); (2) the decision variables are the file cabinet (X_1) and portable shelves (X_2); and (3) the constraints are labor time, machine time, and warehouse storage space.

Equations used to express objective functions should indicate the purpose of the problem and how that purpose is to be realized. Office Storage Company's purpose (objective) is to maximize its contribution margin by producing and selling the combination of file cabinets and portable shelves that provide contribution margins of $25 and $9, respectively. The objective function is stated as

$$\text{MAX CM} = 25X_1 + 9X_2$$

The inequalities constraints indicate the demands made by each decision variable on scarce resource availability. Total labor time for producing the two products must be less than or equal to 2,100 hours per month. It is possible that all labor time will not be used each month. Each file cabinet and portable shelf produced takes 3 and 2 labor hours, respectively. The labor constraint is expressed as

Office Storage Company
LP Problem Statement

Objective Function: MAX CM = $25X_1 + 9X_2$

Constraints (Subject to):
$3X_1 + 2X_2 \leq 2,100$ (labor time in hours)
$2X_1 + 1X_2 \leq 850$ (machine time in hours)
$8X_1 + 3X_2 \leq 4,000$ (warehouse storage space)
$X_1 \geq 0$ (nonnegativity of file cabinets)
$X_2 \geq 0$ (nonnegativity of portable shelves)

$$3X_1 + 2X_2 \leq 2,100$$

Expressing the machine time constraint equation is similar to that of the labor time constraint. Each file cabinet requires 2 hours of machine time and each portable shelf requires 1 hour. Total machine time available per month is 850 hours. This resource constraint is

$$2X_1 + 1X_2 \leq 850$$

The file cabinets and portable shelves produced cannot exceed available warehouse storage space. Each file cabinet consumes substantially more space than each portable shelf. The production constraint is expressed as

$$8X_1 + 3X_2 \leq 4,000$$

Although not shown in Exhibit 13–15, nonnegativity constraints exist for this problem. The nonnegativity constraints simply state that production of either product cannot be less than zero units. Nonnegativity constraints are shown as

$$X_1 \geq 0$$

$$X_2 \geq 0$$

The mathematical formulae needed to solve the Office Storage Company LP production problem are shown in Exhibit 13–16. Next, a method for solving the problem must be chosen.

SOLVING A LP PROBLEM

Linear programming problems may be solved by a graphical approach or the simplex method. Graphs are simple to use and provide a visual representation of the problem. The computer-adaptable simplex method is a more efficient means to handle complex linear programming problems. Graphical methods of solving linear programming problems are useful only when there are two decision variables and few constraints or two constraints and few decision variables. Graphs also illustrate the process of solving a LP problem. Such illustrations are helpful in visualizing how the simplex method works.

The graphical method of solving a linear programming problem consists of five steps:

1. State the problem in terms of a linear objective function and linear constraints.
feasible region
2. Graph the constraints and determine the feasible region. The **feasible region** is the graphical space contained within and on all of the constraint lines.
vertex
3. Determine the coordinates of each corner **(vertex)** of the feasible region.
4. Calculate the value of the objective function at each vertex.
5. Select the optimal solution. The optimal solution for a maximization problem is the one with the highest objective function value. The optimal solution in a minimization problem has the lowest objective function value.

Without intending to elaborate on its construction, Exhibit 13–17 shows the constraint lines labeled and the various corner values determined and presented. The feasible region is shaded, and one can see that its corners are A-B-C. Only the

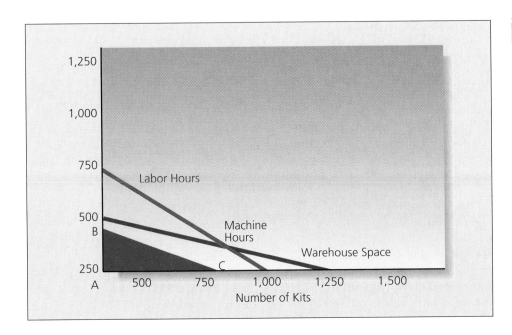

EXHIBIT 13–17

Office Storage Company
Production Constraints

machine hours constraint is binding; the other two constraints are redundant. The total contribution margin at each corner is calculated as follows:

Corner	VALUES X_1	X_2	
A	0	0	CM = $25(0) + $9(0) = $0
B	425	0	CM = $25(425) + $9(0) = $10,625
C	0	850	CM = $25(0) + $9(850) = $7,650

Inspection reveals that contribution margin is at its highest ($10,625) at point B. The corners that are not part of the feasible region are not evaluated because they do not satisfy all the constraints of the problem.

The **simplex method** is an iterative (sequential) algorithm that solves multivariable, multiconstraint linear programming problems. An **algorithm** is a logical step-by-step problem-solving technique (generally utilizing a computer) that continuously searches for an improved solution from the one previously computed. The simplex method does not check every feasible solution. It only checks those occurring at the corners of the feasible region because the optimal solution is always at a corner. Because corners always represent the extremities of the feasible region, a corner is where the maximum or minimum value of the objective function is always located.

The simplex method begins with a mathematical statement of the objective function and constraints. The inequalities in the constraints must be expressed as equalities to solve the problems algebraically. Expressing inequalities as equalities is accomplished by introducing slack or surplus variables (S) into constraint equations. A **slack variable** represents the unused amount of a resource at any level of operation. The amount of the slack variable can range from zero to the total amount of the constrained resource. Slack variables are associated with less-than-or-equal-to (≤) constraints and are added to the left side of the constraint equation. A **surplus variable** represents overachievement of a minimum requirement and is associated with greater-than-or-equal-to (≥) constraints. Surplus variables are subtracted from the left side of a constraint equation. The formulae for Office Storage Company shown in Exhibit 13–16 are repeated below with the inclusion of slack variables (S_1, S_2, and S_3) for each constrained resource. There are no surplus variables for Office Storage Company because all constraints are less-than-or-equal-to constraints.

simplex method

algorithm

slack variable

surplus variable

Objective Function: MAX CM = $25X_1 + 9X_2$

Constraints (Subject to):

$$3X_1 + 2X_2 + S_1 = 2,100 \text{ (labor time in hours)}$$

$$2X_1 + 1X_2 + S_2 = 850 \text{ (machine time in hours)}$$

$$8X_1 + 3X_2 + S_3 = 4,000 \text{ (warehouse storage in cubic feet)}$$

Solving a linear programming problem using the simplex method requires either the use of matrix algebra or a computer.

KEY TERMS

ad hoc discount (p. 586)
algorithm (p. 595)
decision variable (p. 592)
feasible region (p. 594)
feasible solution (p. 592)
incremental cost (p. 568)
incremental revenue (p. 568)
input-output coefficients (p. 592)
integer programming (p. 592)
linear programming (p. 579)
make-or-buy decision (p. 573)
mathematical programming (p. 591)

nonnegativity constraint (p. 591)
objective function (p. 591)
optimal solution (p. 592)
relevant costing (p. 567)
Robinson-Patman Act (p. 586)
sales mix (p. 579)
scarce resource (p. 577)
segment margin (p. 588)
simplex method (p. 595)
slack variable (p. 595)
special order decision (p. 584)
surplus variable (p. 595)
vertex (p. 594)

SOLUTION STRATEGIES

General rule of decision making: Choose the alternative that yields the greatest incremental benefit (or provides the smallest incremental loss).

Incremental (additional) revenues
− Incremental (additional) costs
= Incremental benefit (positive or negative)

RELEVANT COSTS

Direct material

Direct labor

Variable production overhead

Variable selling expenses related to *each* alternative (may be greater or less than under the "change nothing" alternative)

Avoidable fixed production overhead

Avoidable fixed selling/administrative costs (if any)

Opportunity cost of choosing some other alternative (will either increase the cost of this alternative or reduce the cost of the other alternative)

SINGLE SCARCE RESOURCE

1. Determine the scarce resource.
2. Determine the production per unit of the scarce resource.
3. Determine the contribution margin per unit of the scarce resource.
4. Multiply production (2) times contribution margin (3) to obtain total contribution margin provided by the product per unit of the scarce resource. Production and sale of the product with the highest contribution margin per unit of scarce resource will maximize profits.

PRODUCT LINES

Sales
− Direct variable expenses
= Product line contribution margin
− Avoidable fixed expenses
= Segment (product line) margin*
− Sunk direct fixed expenses
= Product line operating results
*Make decision to retain or eliminate based on this line item.

Hands-On Enterprises produces a revolutionary, ergonomically correct keyboard for PC-compatible computers. The firm has been making the electronic controller for the keyboard, and the costs incurred to make each controller unit are

DEMONSTRATION PROBLEM

Direct material	$14
Direct labor	6
Variable overhead	9
Fixed overhead	10

Of the per-unit fixed overhead, $7 could be avoided if the firm did not make the controller. Another company has offered to sell an equivalent controller to Hands-On for $38. Hands-On produces 20,000 controller units annually.

Required (consider each requirement to be independent of the other requirements):

a. Should Hands-On make or buy the component? Show calculations.
b. Hands-On's vice president, James Palm, estimates that the company can rent out the facilities used to make the controller units for $60,000 annually. What should the company do? Show calculations.
c. What are some of the qualitative factors that should be considered if Hands-On is contemplating purchasing the controller component?

Solution to Demonstration Problem

a. Relevant cost of making:

Direct material	$14
Direct labor	6
Variable overhead	9
Fixed overhead	7
Total	$36
Cost to purchase	$38

Therefore, Hands-On should continue to make the controller component.

b. $60,000 Rental Income ÷ 20,000 Components = $3 Opportunity Cost Per Unit

Relevant cost to produce	$36
Opportunity cost	3
Total	$39

This total exceeds the cost to purchase. Therefore, Hands-On should purchase the item.

c. Some qualitative factors include the following:
- Future control by Hands-On of quality, supply, cost, and price of the controller
- Supplier's long-run chances of being in business
- Existence and number of other suppliers
- Impact on customers and markets

QUESTIONS

1. Define a relevant cost. For a hospital considering the purchase of a new X-ray machine, what would be examples of the relevant costs of the purchase decision? What would be one of the alternatives to purchasing the X-ray machine?

2. What are the characteristics of a relevant cost? Why are future costs not always relevant? Are all relevant costs found in accounting records? Explain.

3. What is an opportunity cost? In a make-or-buy decision, what opportunity cost may be associated with the production facilities?

4. Which are more important in decision making: quantitative or qualitative factors? Why? How can qualitative factors be explicitly considered in making a decision?

5. Can a particular cost be relevant for one purpose, but not for other purposes? Give three examples where this would be the case.

6. Are sunk costs ever relevant in decision making? If so, give one or more examples. If not, explain why.

7. You are considering the sale of your old stereo system. According to your records, you paid $500 for the stereo system. The current market value of the stereo is $150. A new stereo of the same make and model could be purchased today for $375. Which of these figures is relevant to your decision to sell or keep the stereo system? If any figures are not relevant, explain why.

8. Kelly O'Riley, owner of Juanita's Mexican Cafe, is trying to decide whether to make tortillas or buy them from a supplier, Ricardo's Super Mercado. Kelly has come to you for advice. What factors would you tell him to consider in making his choice?

9. What is a scarce resource? Why will the resource that is most scarce in an organization be likely to change from time to time?

10. Suggest possible alternatives to basing sales commissions on the sales revenue generated by each salesperson. What would be the benefits and drawbacks of your methods to the salesperson and to the company?

11. Why is the effect of a sales price change on volume partly determined by the elasticity of demand for the product?

12. What is the special order decision? What are typical circumstances that lead to the need to make this decision?

13. What are differences among avoidable fixed costs, sunk direct fixed costs, and common fixed costs? Which are relevant and which are irrelevant in the decision to keep or eliminate a particular product line?

14. Lazlow Optical Manufacturing produces a line of single-reflex cameras. Corporate records reveal that one of the mid-priced cameras is producing a negative segment margin. Before discontinuing production of the camera, what factors should Lazlow's managers consider?

15. Are segment margin or product line operating results more important in product line decisions? Why?

16. (Appendix) Why is linear programming used in business organizations?

17. (Appendix) What are two typical objective function expressions that are stated in terms of accounting information?

18. (Appendix) What are nonnegativity constraints in the linear programming model? Why is it not necessary that they be specified for every linear programming problem?

19. (Appendix) What is the difference between a feasible solution and an optimal solution?

20. (Appendix) "Resource constraints are always inequalities." Is this statement true or false? Why?

21. (Appendix) What is the difference between a slack variable and a surplus variable? Can each exist in the same linear programming problem? If so, discuss how; if not, discuss why.

22. *(Relevant costs)* Assume that you are about to graduate from your university. You are currently trying to decide whether to apply for graduate school or enter the job market. To help make the decision, you have gathered the following data:

Costs incurred for the bachelor's degree:	$62,000
Additional costs to get a master's degree:	$41,000
Estimated starting salary with B.A.:	$32,300
Estimated starting salary with M.A.:	$38,400
Estimated time to complete master's degree:	2 years
Estimated time from the present to retirement:	40 years

    a. Which of the above factors are relevant to your decision?
    b. What is the opportunity cost associated with earning the master's degree? What is the total cost to obtain the master's degree?
    c. What other factors should you consider before making a decision?

23. *(Relevant costs)* Prior to the 1996 NBA finals, a Houston area clothes retailer purchased 25,000 T-shirts that read: Houston Rockets—Three-Peaters. The company paid, on average, $12.50 for each of these custom T-shirts. With Houston losing early in the playoffs, the department store is now stuck with 15,000 of the T-shirts. The first 10,000 T-shirts were sold during the playoffs at an average price of $21. The company has learned from one of its suppliers that each shirt could be reworked at a cost of $4 per shirt (which involves removing the words "Three-Peaters" from each shirt). The company could then sell each shirt for $10. Alternatively, the company can sell the shirts for $3 each to a clothes wholesaler.

    a. Which costs are sunk in this decision?
    b. What are the relevant costs of each decision alternative, and what should the company do?

24. *(Asset-replacement decision)* Certain production equipment used in Hatare's Canadian plant have become obsolete relative to current technology. The company is considering whether it should keep its existing equipment or purchase new equipment. To aid in this decision, the company's controller gathered the following data.

	OLD EQUIPMENT	NEW EQUIPMENT
Original cost	$134,000	$198,000
Remaining life	5 years	5 years
Accumulated depreciation	$ 79,000	$ 0
Annual cash operating costs	$ 34,000	$ 8,000
Current salvage value	$ 44,000	NA
Salvage value in 5 years	$ 0	$ 0

    a. Identify any sunk costs listed in the data.
    b. Identify any irrelevant (nondifferential) future costs.
    c. Identify all relevant costs to the equipment replacement decision.
    d. What are the opportunity costs associated with the alternative of keeping the old equipment?
    e. What is the incremental cost to purchase the new equipment?
    f. What qualitative considerations should be taken into account before making any decision?

25. *(Asset-replacement decision)* Lawton Energy Company purchased new computer scheduling software on April 1, 1998, for $40,000 to manage its production. On May 15, 1998, a representative of a computerized manufacturing technology company demonstrated new software that was clearly superior to that purchased by the firm earlier in the year. The price of this software is $70,000. Corporate managers estimate that the new software would save the company $6,000 annually in schedule-related costs compared with the recently installed software.

Both software systems should last 10 years (the expected life of the computer hardware) and have no salvage value at that time. The company can sell its existing software for $20,000 if it chooses to purchase the new system. Should the company keep and use the software purchased earlier in the year or buy the new software?

26. *(Make-or-buy decision)* Bozeman Plastics manufactures plastic housings for computer printers. One of the parts required to manufacture a printer case is a metal latch. Currently Bozeman produces all metal latches that it requires (60,000 units annually). The company's management is considering purchasing the part from an external vendor, Arlington Mechanical. The following data are available for making the decision:

Cost per unit to manufacture:
Direct material	$.20
Direct labor	.17
Variable overhead	.09
Fixed overhead—applied	.14
Total cost	$.60

Cost per unit to buy:
Purchase price	$.49
Freight charges	.01
Total cost	$.50

a. Assuming all of Bozeman's internal production costs are avoidable if it purchases rather than makes the latch, what would be the net annual cost advantage to Bozeman of purchasing?

b. Assume that some of Bozeman's fixed overhead costs could not be avoided if it purchases rather than makes the latches. How much of the fixed overhead must be avoidable for the company to be indifferent between making and buying the component?

27. *(Make-or-buy decision)* Edson Automotive Accessories produces bumpers for pickup trucks, which are sold on a wholesale basis to new-car retailers. The average sales price of a bumper is $75. Normal annual sales volume is 50,000 units, which is maximum production capacity. At this capacity, the company's costs per unit are as follows:

Direct material	$28	(including mounting hardware, which is $6 per unit)
Direct labor	8	
Overhead (2/3 is fixed)	18	
Total	$54	

A key component in the production of bumpers is the mounting hardware that is used to attach the bumpers to the vehicles. Luhr's Metal Stamping has offered to sell Edson as many mounting units as the company needs for its bumper production. The offering price is $8 per unit. If Edson accepts the offer, the released facilities (that are used to produce mounting hardware) could be used to produce an additional 2,400 bumpers. What alternative is more desirable and by what amount? [Assume the company is currently operating at its capacity of 50,000 units.]

28. *(Make-or-buy decision)* The Pneu Shoe Company manufactures various types of shoes for sports and recreational use. Several types of shoes require a built-in air pump. Presently, the company makes all the air pumps it requires for production. However, management is evaluating an offer from Aire Supply Company to provide air pumps at a cost of $6 each. Pneu Shoe Company management has estimated that the variable production costs of the air pump

are $5 per unit. The firm also estimates that it could avoid $40,000 per year in fixed costs if it purchased rather than produced the air pumps.

a. If Pneu Shoe Company requires 20,000 pumps per year, should it make them or buy them from Aire Supply Company?

b. If Pneu Shoe Company requires 60,000 pumps per year, should it make them or buy them?

c. Assuming all other factors are equal, at what level of production would the company be indifferent between making and buying the pumps?

29. *(Allocation of scarce resource)* Because the plant of its major competitor burned to the ground on July 4, Detroit Wheel Company has found itself operating at peak capacity. The firm makes two automotive components, wheel rims and jacks. At this time, the company can sell as many of each product as it can make, but it takes twice as long in machine hours to make a jack as it does to make wheel rims. The firm's machines can be run only 120,000 hours per month. Data on each product follow:

	WHEELS	JACKS
Sales	$15	$28
Variable costs	12	23
Contribution margin	$ 3	$ 5
Machine hours required	2	4

Fixed costs run $70,000 per month.

a. How many of each product should the company make? Explain your answer.

b. What qualitative factors would you consider in making this product mix decision?

30. *(Allocation of scarce resources)* John Henry received his accounting degree in 1972. Since receiving his degree, Mr. Henry has obtained significant experience in a variety of job settings. His skills include auditing, income and estate taxation, and business consulting. Mr. Henry currently has his own practice and his skills are in such demand that he limits his practice to taxation issues. Most of his engagements are one of three types: individual income taxation, estate taxation, or corporate taxation. Below are data pertaining to the revenues and costs of each tax area (per tax return).

	INDIVIDUAL	ESTATE	CORPORATE
Revenue	$350	$1,200	$750
Variable costs	$ 50	$ 200	$150
Hours per return required of Mr. Henry	2	8	5

Fixed costs of operating Mr. Henry's office are $40,000 per year. Mr. Henry has such significant demand for his work that he must ration his time. He desires to work no more than 2,500 hours in the coming year. He can allocate his time such that he works only on one type of tax return or on any combination of the three types.

a. How should Mr. Henry allocate his time in the coming year to maximize his income?

b. Based on the optimal allocation, what is Mr. Henry's projected pretax income for the coming year?

c. What other factors should Mr. Henry consider in allocating his time?

31. *(Special order decision)* Really Wired produces 18-gauge barbwire, which is retailed through farm supply companies. Presently, the company has the capacity to produce 2,000 tons of wire per year. The firm is operating at 85 percent of annual capacity, and at this level of operations the cost per ton of wire is as follows:

Direct material	$160
Direct labor	40
Variable overhead	25
Fixed overhead	80
Total	$305

The average sales price for the output produced by the firm is $400 per ton. The firm has been approached by an Australian company about supplying 200 tons of wire for a new game preserve. The company has offered Really Wired $240 per ton for the order (FOB Really Wired's plant). No production modifications would be necessary to fulfill the order from the Australian company.

a. What costs are relevant to the decision to accept this special order?

b. What would be the dollar effect on pretax income if this order is accepted?

32. *(Special order decision)* Been Framed produces high-quality picture frames. Each frame is hand-made and hand-finished using the finest materials available. The firm has been operating at capacity for the past 3 years (1,000 frames per year). Based on the capacity level operations, the firm's costs per frame are as follows:

Direct material	$125
Direct labor	135
Variable overhead	35
Fixed overhead	60
Total cost	$355

All selling and administrative expenses incurred by the firm are fixed. The firm has generated an average selling price of $550 for its frames.

Recently, an art gallery approached Sam Spade, the president of Been Framed, about supplying the art gallery with three special frames. These frames would be approximately two times as large as the typical frame the company now makes. Mr. Spade has estimated that the following per-unit costs would be incurred to make the three frames:

Direct material	$425
Direct labor	465
Variable overhead	80
Total direct costs	$970

To accept the art gallery order, the firm would have to sacrifice production of 25 regular units.

a. Identify all the relevant costs that Mr. Spade should consider in deciding whether he will accept the art gallery's order.

b. Assume the art gallery offers a total of $3,400 for the three frames. How would Been Framed's pretax income be affected by the acceptance of this offer?

33. *(Sales mix decision)* Poodle Pound provides two types of services to dog owners: grooming and training. All company personnel can perform either service equally well. To expand sales and market share, the Poodle Pound's manager, Golden Retriever, relies heavily on radio and billboard advertising. For 1997, advertising funding is expected to be very limited. Information on projected operations for 1997 follows:

	GROOMING	TRAINING
Revenue per billable hour	$ 15	$ 25
Variable cost of labor/hour	$ 5	$ 10
Material cost per billable hour	1	2
Allocated fixed costs per year	$100,000	$90,000
Projected billable hours for 1997	10,000	8,000

a. What is Poodle Pound's projected pretax profit or (loss) for 1997?

b. If $1 spent on advertising could increase either Grooming revenue by $20 or Training revenue by $20, on which service should the advertising dollar be spent?

c. If $1 spent on advertising could increase Grooming billable time by 1 hour or Training billable time by 1 hour, on which service should the advertising dollar be spent?

34. *(Sales mix decision)* One of the products produced and sold by Denver Chemical Company is a 90-quart cold drink cooler. The company's projections for this product for 1999 follow.

Sales price per unit	$72
Variable production costs	$42
Variable selling costs	$8
Fixed production costs	$450,000
Fixed selling and administration costs	$150,000
Projected volume	90,000 units

a. Compute the projected pretax profit to be earned on the cooler during 1999.

b. Corporate management estimates that unit volume could be increased by 20 percent if the sales price were decreased by 10 percent. How would such a change affect the profit level projected in part a?

c. Rather than cutting the sales price, management is considering holding the sales price at the projected level and increasing advertising by $200,000. Such a change would increase volume by 25 percent. How would the level of profit under this alternative compare with the profit projected in part a?

35. *(Product line decision)* North American Toy Company's operations are separated into two geographical divisions: the United States and Mexico. The operating results of each division for 1998 are shown below:

	UNITED STATES	MEXICO	TOTAL
Sales	$3,600,000	$1,800,000	$5,400,000
Variable costs	(2,370,000)	(1,044,000)	(3,414,000)
Contribution margin	$1,230,000	$ 756,000	$1,986,000
Fixed costs:			
Direct	(450,000)	(240,000)	(690,000)
Segment margin	$ 780,000	$ 516,000	$1,296,000
Fixed costs:			
Corporate	(900,000)	(450,000)	1,350,000
Operating income (loss)	$ (120,000)	$ 66,000	$ (54,000)

Corporate fixed costs are allocated to the divisions based on relative sales. Assume that all direct fixed costs of a division could be avoided if the division were eliminated. Because the U.S. Division is operating at a loss, the president is considering eliminating it.

a. If the U.S. Division had been eliminated at the beginning of the year, what would pretax income have been for North American Toy Company?

b. Recast the income statements into a more meaningful format than the one shown above. Why would total corporate operating results go from a $54,000 loss to the results determined in part a above?

36. *(Product line decision)* The management of Montgomery Steel Corporation produces three products: wire, tubing, and sheet metal. The company is currently contemplating the elimination of the tubing product line because it is showing a pretax loss. An annual income statement follows.

MONTGOMERY STEEL CORPORATION
INCOME STATEMENT
FOR YEAR ENDED AUGUST 1, 1998
(IN THOUSANDS)

PRODUCT	WIRE	TUBING	SHEET METAL	TOTAL
Sales	$2,200	$1,600	$1,800	$5,600
Cost of sales	(1,400)	(1,000)	(1,080)	(3,480)
Gross margin	$ 800	$ 600	$ 720	$2,120
Avoidable fixed and variable costs	$ 630	$ 725	$ 520	$1,875
Allocated fixed costs	90	80	105	275
Total fixed costs	$ 720	$ 805	$ 625	$2,150
Operating income (loss)	$ 80	$ (205)	$ 95	$ (30)

    a. Should corporate management drop the tubing product line? Support your answer with appropriate schedules.

    b. How would the pretax profit of the company be affected by the decision?

37. *(Appendix)* The contribution margins for three different products are $9.50, $5.00, and $1.50. State the objective function in equation form to maximize the contribution margin.

38. *(Appendix)* The variable costs for four different products are $.65, $.93, $1.39, and $.72. State the objective function in equation form to minimize the variable costs.

39. *(Appendix)* Carolina Textiles makes three items: pants, shorts, and shirts. The contribution margins are $3.25, $2.05, and $2.60 per unit, respectively. The manager must decide what mix of clothes to make. He has 800 labor hours and 4,000 yards of material available. Additional information for labor and material requirements are given below.

	SEWING TIME	FABRIC NEEDED
Pants	2.0 hours	3.0 yards
Shorts	1.5 hours	1.0 yards
Shirts	2.5 hours	1.5 yards

Write the objective function and constraints for the clothes manufacturer.

40. *(Appendix)* Janet Terwilliger is a college student and has set a budget of $120 per month for food. She wants to get a certain level of nutritional benefits from the food she has selected to buy. The table below lists the types of food she may buy, along with the nutritional information per serving of that food.

	CARBOHYDRATES	PROTEIN	POTASSIUM	CALORIES	COST
Pizza	38 g.	10 g.	-0-	500	$3.99
Tuna fish	1 g.	13 g.	-0-	60	1.29
Cereal	35 g.	7 g.	120 mg.	190	.93
Macaroni and cheese	23 g.	3 g.	110 mg.	110	2.12
Spaghetti	42 g.	8 g.	100 mg.	210	3.42
Recommended daily allowance	50 g.	10 g.	100 mg.	2,000	

Write the objective function and constraints to minimize the cost and yet meet the recommended daily nutritional allowances.

41. *(Relevant vs. sunk costs)* Your friend, Bill Hawkins, purchased a new combination phone and answering machine just prior to the start of this school term. He paid $95 for the equipment. Shortly after the start of the semester, during a party at his apartment, Bill's answering machine was crushed by an errant "flying plant." Returning the equipment to his retailer, Bill was informed that the estimated cost of repairs was $45.

Bill, pondering the figures, was ready to conclude that repairs should be made; after all, he had recently paid $95 for the equipment. However, before making a decision, Bill decided to ask for your advice, knowing that you were enrolled in an accounting course this term.

a. Using concepts learned from this chapter, prepare a brief oral presentation for Bill that outlines factors Bill should consider in making his decision.

b. Follow the presentation in part a with a brief oral presentation of the options Bill should consider in making his decision. Start by defining a base case against which alternatives may be compared.

42. *(Time and relevant costs)* The following are costs associated with a product line of Turnbull Mechanical Systems. The costs reflect capacity-level production of 45,000 units per year.

Variable production costs	$45
Fixed production costs	27
Variable selling costs	12
Fixed selling and administrative costs	16

Prepare a written presentation showing how time affects relevant costs for a product line. Begin with the point in time at which the product and production facilities are in the planning stage. Then, show how the set of relevant costs changes (1) after acquisition of the production facilities but before actual production commences, and (2) after production of products is complete but before the units are sold.

43. *(Relevant costs)* An analysis of GM's labor costs at its parts plant in Dayton, Ohio, provides evidence of one source of the firm's competitive problems. Its UAW employees are provided fringe benefits that cost, on average, about $16 per labor hour. Fringe benefits provided include full health-care coverage (no deductibles or co-payments), vision care, dental care, full pension after 30 years, life insurance, disability benefits, legal services, and supplemental unemployment benefits. Add to the $16 cost per hour of fringe benefits about $18 per hour in base pay, plus an additional increment for profit sharing, and the total cost of the average laborer is about $43 an hour.

[SOURCE: Adapted from Nichole M. Christian, "Rich Benefits Plan Gives GM Competitors Cost Edge," *Wall Street Journal* (March 21, 1996), pp. B1, B4. Reprinted by permission of *The Wall Street Journal*, © 1996 Dow Jones & Company, Inc. All Rights Reserved Worldwide.]

Assume you have been hired as a cost analyst by GM management. Write a report offering specific suggestions as to actions GM can take to control its parts and components costs.

44. *(Asset-replacement decision)* The manager, Diane Blocker, of the Plastics Fabrication Division of Balsom Chemical Corporation, has heard about a new extruding machine on the market that could replace one of her existing machines. The manufacturer has suggested to Ms. Blocker that the new machine would save $200,000 per year in the costs of operations. Ms. Blocker's controller compiled additional information as follows.

COMMUNICATION ACTIVITIES

PROBLEMS

OLD MACHINE:

Original cost new	$750,000
Present book value	500,000
Annual cash operating costs	500,000
Market value now	100,000
Market value in 5 years	0
Remaining useful life	5 years

NEW MACHINE:

Cost	$900,000
Annual cash operating costs	300,000
Market value in 5 years	0
Useful life	5 years

a. Based on financial considerations alone, should Ms. Blocker purchase the new machine? Show computations to support your answer.

b. What qualitative factors should Ms. Blocker consider before making a decision about purchasing the new machine?

45. *(Asset-replacement decision)* Grist Energy Company provides electrical services to several rural Alabama counties. The company's efficiency has been greatly affected by changes in technology. Most recently, the company is considering replacement of its main steam turbine. The existing turbine was put in place in the 1970s, but has become somewhat obsolete. Although the system's operation is very reliable, it is much less efficient than newer turbines that are computer controlled. The company has gathered financial information pertaining to the new and old technologies. The following information was presented by the controller to corporate management:

	OLD TURBINE	NEW TURBINE
Original cost	$6,000,000	$4,000,000
Market value now	$ 400,000	—
Remaining life	8 years	8 years
Quarterly operating costs	$ 800,000	$ 100,000
Salvage value in 8 years	0	0
Accumulated depreciation	$2,000,000	—

a. Identify the costs that are relevant to the company's equipment replacement decision.

b. Determine which alternative is better from a financial perspective. Provide your own computations based on relevant costs only.

c. For this part only, assume that the cost of the new technology is unknown. What is the maximum amount that Grist could pay for the new technology and be no worse off financially?

46. *(Make-or-buy decision)* The Closet Organizer Company manufactures vinyl-clad wire baskets that are used as components in modular storage systems. Each basket requires two to six standard fasteners to attach it to other modular components or structural members of closets. Historically, the company has produced the fasteners. The costs to produce a fastener (based on capacity operation of 4,000,000 units per year) are

Direct materials	$.03
Direct labor	.01
Variable factory overhead	.01
Fixed factory overhead	.03
Total	$.08

The fixed factory overhead includes $80,000 of depreciation on equipment for which there is no alternative use and no market value. The balance of the fixed factory overhead pertains to the salary of the production supervisor. Although the supervisor of fastener production has a lifetime employment contract, she has skills that could be used to displace another manager (the supervisor of floor maintenance) who draws a salary of $15,000 per year but is due to retire from the company.

The Moulson Fastener Corporation has recently approached Closet Organizer Company with an offer to supply all required fasteners at a price of $.065 per unit. Anticipated sales demand for the coming year will require 4,000,000 fasteners.

a. Identify the costs that are relevant in this make-or-buy decision.

b. What is the total annual advantage or disadvantage (in dollars) of buying the fasteners rather than making them?

c. What qualitative factors should be taken into account in this make-or-buy decision?

47. *(Make-or-buy decision)* Larson Building Systems manufactures steel buildings for agricultural and commercial applications. Currently, the company is trying to decide between two alternatives regarding a major overhead door assembly for the company's buildings. The alternatives are

#1: Purchase new equipment at a cost of $5,000,000. The equipment would have a 5-year life and no salvage value. Larson Building Systems uses straight-line depreciation and allocates that amount on a per-unit-of-production basis.

#2: Purchase the door assemblies from an outside vendor who will sell them for $240 each under a 5-year contract. Larson's present cost of producing the door assemblies is given below. The costs are based on current and normal activity of 50,000 units per year.

Direct material	$139
Direct labor	66
Variable overhead	43
Fixed overhead*	36
Total	$284

*The fixed overhead includes $7 supervision cost, $9 depreciation, and $20 general company overhead.

The new equipment would be more efficient than the old and would reduce direct labor costs and variable overhead costs by 25 percent. Supervisory costs of $350,000 would be unaffected. The new equipment would have a capacity of 75,000 units per year. The space occupied by subassembly production could be leased by Larson to another firm for $114,000 per year if the company decides to buy from the outside vendor.

a. Show an analysis, including relevant unit and total costs, for each alternative. Assume 50,000 subassemblies are needed each year.

b. How would your answer differ if 60,000 subassemblies were needed?

c. How would your answer differ if 75,000 subassemblies were needed?

d. In addition to quantitative factors, what factors should be considered?

48. *(Sales mix with scarce resources)* Old Time Furniture makes three unique wood products: desks, chairs, and footstools. These products are made wholly by hand; there is no electric machinery or hydraulic machinery used in production. All products are made by skilled craftspeople who have been trained to make all three products. Because it takes about a year to train each craftsperson, labor is a fixed production constraint over the short term. For 1999, the company expects to have available 24,000 labor hours. The average hourly labor rate is $25. Data regarding the current product line follow.

	DESKS	CHAIRS	FOOTSTOOLS
Selling price	$900	$680	$240
Variable costs:			
Direct material	$220	$160	$ 60
Direct labor	300	275	75
Variable overhead	180	120	41
Variable selling	20	15	10
Fixed costs:			
Factory	$150,000		
Selling & administrative	75,000		

The company is in the 40 percent tax bracket.

a. If the company can sell an unlimited amount of any of the products, how many of each product should it make? What pretax income will the company earn given your answer?

b. How many of each product must the company make if it has a policy of devoting no more than 50 percent of its available skilled labor capacity to any one product and at least 20 percent to every product? What pretax income will the company earn given your answer?

c. Given the nature of the three products, is it reasonable to believe that there are market constraints on the mix of products that can be sold? Explain.

49. *(Sales mix decisions)* Arizona Fashions produces silk scarves and handkerchiefs, which sell for $40 and $10, respectively. The company currently sells 100,000 units of each type with the following operating results:

SCARVES

Sales (100,000 × $40)		$4,000,000
Variable costs:		
Production (100,000 × $22)	$2,200,000	
Selling (100,000 × $6)	600,000	(2,800,000)
Contribution margin		$1,200,000
Fixed costs:		
Production	$ 400,000	
Selling and administrative	180,000	(580,000)
Income from Scarves		$ 620,000

HANDKERCHIEFS

Sales (100,000 × $10)		$1,000,000
Variable costs:		
Production (100,000 × $5)	$ 500,000	
Selling (100,000 × $1)	100,000	(600,000)
Contribution margin		$ 400,000
Fixed costs:		
Production	$ 100,000	
Selling & administrative	80,000	(180,000)
Income from Handkerchiefs		$ 220,000

Corporate management has expressed its disappointment with the income being generated from the sales of these two products. Managers have asked for your help to analyze alternative plans that have been formulated to improve operating results.

1. Change the sales commission to 9 percent of sales price less variable production costs for each product rather than the current 5 percent of selling price. The marketing manager believes that the sales of Scarves will decline by 5,000 units, but the sales of Handkerchiefs will increase by 15,000 units.

2. Increase the advertising budget for Scarves by $15,000. The marketing manager believes this will increase the sales of Scarves by 18,000 units but will decrease the sales of the Handkerchiefs by 9,000 units.

3. Raise the price of the Handkerchiefs by $2 per unit and the Scarves by $4 per unit. The marketing manager believes this will cause a decrease in the sales of Scarves by 5,000 units and a decrease in Handkerchiefs of 10,000 units.

a. Determine the effects on income of each product line and the company in total if each of these alternative plans is put into effect.

b. What is your recommendation to the management of Arizona Fashions?

50. *(Product line decision)* Paulson Fresh Meats sells two major lines of products, fish and chicken, to grocery chains and food wholesalers. Income statements showing revenues and costs of 1997 for each product line follow.

	FISH	CHICKEN
Sales	$ 4,000,000	$ 1,800,000
Cost of merchandise sold	$(2,400,000)	$(1,300,000)
Commissions to salespeople	(400,000)	(150,000)
Delivery costs	(600,000)	(120,000)
Depreciation on equipment	(200,000)	(100,000)
Salaries of division managers	(80,000)	(75,000)
Allocated corporate costs	(100,000)	(100,000)
Net Income (loss)	$ 220,000	$ (45,000)

Management is concerned about the profitability of chicken sales and is considering the possibility of dropping the line. Management estimates that the equipment currently used to process chickens could be rented to a competitor for $85,000 annually. If the chicken product line is dropped, allocated corporate costs will decrease from a total of $200,000 to $185,000; and, all employees, including the manager of the product line, would be dismissed. The depreciation would be unaffected by the decision, but $105,000 of the delivery costs charged to the chicken line could be eliminated if the chicken product line is dropped.

a. Recast the above income statements in a format that provides more information in making this decision regarding the chicken product line.

b. What is the net advantage or disadvantage (change in total company pretax profits) of continuing sales of chicken?

c. Should the company be concerned about losing sales of fish products if it drops the chicken line? Explain.

51. *(Product line changes)* You have been engaged to assist the management of Circle X Farm Products in arriving at certain decisions. Circle X has its home office in Arkansas and leases production facilities in Arkansas, Louisiana, and Mississippi, which produce a fertilizer spreader designed for residential use. The management of Circle X has provided you with a projection of operations for 1998, the forthcoming year, as follows:

	TOTAL	ARKANSAS	LOUISIANA	MISSISSIPPI
Sales	$8,800,000	$4,400,000	$2,800,000	$1,600,000
Fixed costs:				
Factory	$2,200,000	$1,120,000	$ 560,000	$ 520,000
Administration	700,000	420,000	220,000	60,000
Variable costs	2,900,000	1,330,000	850,000	720,000
Allocated home office costs	1,000,000	450,000	350,000	200,000
Total	$6,800,000	$3,320,000	$1,980,000	$1,500,000
Pretax profit from operations	$2,000,000	$1,080,000	$ 820,000	$ 100,000

The sales price per unit is $50.

Due to the marginal results of operations in Mississippi, Circle X has decided to cease operations and sell that factory's machinery and equipment by the end of 1998. Managers expect proceeds from the sale of these assets will exceed the assets' book values by enough to cover termination costs.

However, Circle X would like to continue serving its customers in that area if it is economically feasible and is considering one of the following three alternatives:

1. Expand the operations of the Louisiana factory by using space presently idle. This move would result in the following changes in that factory's operations:

	PERCENTAGE INCREASE OVER FACTORY'S CURRENT OPERATIONS
Sales	50
Fixed costs:	
Factory	20
Administration	10

Under this proposal, variable costs would be $16 per unit sold.

2. Enter into a long-term contract with a competitor who will serve that area's customers. This competitor would pay Circle X a royalty of $8 per unit based on an estimate of 30,000 units being sold.

3. Close the Mississippi factory and not expand the operations of the Louisiana factory.

To assist the management of Circle X Farm Products in determining which alternative is more economically feasible, prepare a schedule computing Circle X's estimated pretax profit from total operations that would result from each of the following methods:

a. Expansion of the Louisiana factory.

b. Negotiation of a long-term contract on a royalty basis.

c. Shutdown of the Mississippi operations with no expansion at other locations. Note: Total home office costs of $500,000 will remain the same under each situation.

(CPA adapted)

52. *(Comprehensive)* GreenX Glass Recyclers has processing plants in Delaware and Florida. Both plants use recycled glass to produce jars that are used in food canning by a variety of food processors. The jars sell for $20 per hundred units. Budgeted revenues and costs for the year ending December 31, 1998, are

	(000 OMITTED)		
	DELAWARE	**FLORIDA**	**TOTAL**
Sales	$2,200	$4,000	$6,200
Variable production costs:			
Direct material	$ 550	$1,000	$1,550
Direct labor	660	1,000	1,660
Factory overhead	440	700	1,140
Fixed factory overhead	700	900	1,600
Fixed regional promotion costs	100	100	200
Allocated home office costs	110	200	310
Total costs	$2,560	$3,900	$6,460
Operating income (loss)	$ (360)	$ 100	$ (260)

Home office costs are fixed and are allocated to manufacturing plants on the basis of relative sales levels. Fixed regional promotional costs are discretionary advertising costs needed to obtain budgeted sales levels.

Because of the budgeted operating loss, GreenX is considering the possibility of ceasing operations at its Delaware plant. If GreenX were to cease operations at its Delaware plant, proceeds from the sale of plant assets would exceed their book value and exactly cover all termination costs; fixed factory overhead costs of $50,000 would not be eliminated. GreenX is considering the following three alternative plans:

PLAN A: Expand Delaware's operations from its budgeted 11,000,000 units to a budgeted 17,000,000 units. It is believed that this can be accomplished by increasing Delaware's fixed regional promotional expenditures by $120,000.

PLAN B: Close the Delaware plant and expand Florida's operations from the current budgeted 20,000,000 units to 31,000,000 units to fill Delaware's budgeted production of 11,000,000 units. The Delaware region would continue to incur promotional costs to sell the 11,000,000 units. All sales and costs would be budgeted through the Florida plant.

PLAN C: Close the Delaware plant and enter into a long-term contract with a competitor to serve the Delaware region's customers. This competitor would pay GreenX a royalty of $2.50 per 100 units sold. GreenX would continue to incur fixed regional promotional costs to maintain sales of 11,000,000 units in the Delaware region.

a. Without considering the effects of implementing Plans A, B, and C, compute the number of units that must be produced and sold by the Delaware plant to cover its fixed factory overhead costs and fixed regional promotional costs.

b. Prepare a schedule by plant, and in total, computing GreenX's budgeted contribution margin and operating income resulting from the implementation of Plan A, Plan B, and Plan C.

(CPA adapted)

CASES

53. *(Sales and profit improvement)* Bold and Brassy is a retail organization that sells upscale clothing to professional women in the Northeast. Each year, store managers, in consultation with their supervisors, establish financial goals, and then actual performance is captured by a monthly reporting system.

One sales district of the firm, District A, contains three stores. This district has historically been a very poor performer. Consequently, its supervisor has been searching for ways to improve the performance of her three stores. For the month of May, the district supervisor has set performance goals with the managers of Stores 1 and 2 who will receive bonuses if certain performance measures are exceeded. The manager of Store 3 decided not to participate in the bonus scheme. Because the district supervisor is unsure what type of bonus will encourage better performance, the manager of Store 1 will receive a bonus based on sales in excess of budgeted sales of $570,000, and the manager of Store 2 will receive a bonus based on net income in excess of budgeted net income. The company's net income goal for each store is 12 percent of sales. The budgeted sales for Store 2 are $530,000.

Other pertinent data for May follow:

- At Store 1, sales were 40 percent of total District A sales, whereas sales at Store 2 were 35 percent of total District A sales. The cost of goods sold at both stores was 42 percent of sales.

- Variable selling expenses (sales commissions) were 6 percent of sales for all stores and districts.

- Variable administrative expenses were 2.5 percent of sales for all stores and districts.

- Maintenance cost includes janitorial and repair services and is a direct cost for each store. The store manager has complete control over this outlay; however, this cost should not be below 1 percent of sales.

- Advertising is considered a direct cost for each store and is completely under the control of the store manager. Store 1 spent two-thirds of District A's total outlay for advertising, which was ten times more than Store 2 spent on advertising.

- The rental expenses at Store 1 are 40 percent of District A's total, whereas Store 2 incurs 30 percent of District A's total.
- District A expenses are allocated to the stores based on sales.

a. Which store, Store 1 or Store 2, would appear to be generating the most profit under the new bonus scheme?

b. Which store, Store 1 or Store 2, would appear to be generating the most revenue under the new bonus scheme?

c. Why would Store 1 have incentive to spend so much more on advertising than Store 2?

d. Which store manager has the most incentive to spend money on regular maintenance? Explain.

e. Which bonus scheme appears to offer the most incentive to improve the profit performance of the district in the short term? Long term?

(CMA adapted)

54. *(Plant closing decision)* Elephant Industries is a multiproduct company with several manufacturing plants. The Dole Plant manufactures and distributes two household cleaning and polishing compounds, regular and heavy duty, under the HouseSafe label. The forecasted operating results for the first 6 months of 1998, when 100,000 cases of each compound are expected to be manufactured and sold, are presented in the following statement:

HOUSESAFE COMPOUNDS—DOLE PLANT
FORECASTED RESULTS OF OPERATIONS
FOR THE SIX-MONTH PERIOD ENDING JUNE 30, 1998
($000 OMITTED)

	REGULAR	HEAVY DUTY	TOTAL
Sales	$2,000	$3,000	$5,000
Cost of sales	(1,600)	(1,900)	(3,500)
Gross profit	$ 400	$1,100	$1,500
Selling and administrative expenses			
Variable	$ 400	$ 700	$1,100
Fixed*	240	360	600
Total selling and administrative			
expenses	$ 640	$1,060	$1,700
Income (loss) before taxes	$ (240)	$ 40	$ (200)

*The fixed selling and administrative expenses are allocated between the two products on the basis of dollar sales volume on the internal reports.

The regular compound sold for $20 a case and the heavy-duty compound sold for $30 a case during the first 6 months of 1998. The manufacturing costs by case of product are presented in the following schedule.

	COST PER CASE	
	REGULAR	HEAVY DUTY
Raw material	$ 7.00	$ 8.00
Direct labor	4.00	4.00
Variable manufacturing overhead	1.00	2.00
Fixed manufacturing overhead*	4.00	5.00
Total manufacturing cost	$16.00	$19.00
Variable selling and administrative costs	$ 4.00	$ 7.00

*Depreciation charges are 50 percent of the fixed manufacturing overhead of each line.

Each product is manufactured on a separate production line. Annual normal manufacturing capacity is 200,000 cases of each product. However, the plant is capable of producing 250,000 cases of regular compound and 350,000 cases of heavy-duty compound annually.

The schedule below reflects the consensus of top management regarding the price/volume alternatives for the HouseSafe products for the last 6 months of 1998. These are essentially the same alternatives management had during the first 6 months of 1998.

REGULAR COMPOUND		HEAVY-DUTY COMPOUND	
Alternative Prices (per case)	Sales Volume (in cases)	Alternative Prices (per case)	Sales Volume (in cases)
$18	120,000	$25	175,000
20	100,000	27	140,000
21	90,000	30	100,000
22	80,000	32	55,000
23	50,000	35	35,000

Top management believes the loss for the first 6 months reflects a tight profit margin caused by intense competition. Management also believes that many companies will be forced out of this market by next year and profits should improve.

a. What unit selling price should Elephant Industries select for each of the HouseSafe compounds for the remaining 6 months of 1998? Support your answer with appropriate calculations.

b. Without prejudice to your answer to part a, assume that the optimum price/ volume alternatives for the last 6 months were a selling price of $23 and volume level of 50,000 cases for the regular compound and a selling price of $35 and volume of 35,000 cases for the heavy-duty compound.

   1. Should Elephant Industries consider closing down its operations until 1999 to minimize its losses? Support your answer with appropriate calculations.

   2. Identify and discuss the qualitative factors that should be considered in deciding whether the Dole Plant should be closed down during the last 6 months of 1998.

(CMA adapted)

55. *(Special order decision)* Adrian Pipe Company, located in southern Kentucky, manufactures a variety of industrial valves and pipe fittings that are sold to customers in nearby states. Currently, the company is operating at 70 percent of capacity and is earning a satisfactory return on investment.

   Management has been approached by Glascow Industries Ltd. of Scotland with an offer to buy 120,000 units of a pressure valve. Glascow Industries manufactures a valve that is almost identical to Adrian Pipe's pressure valve; however, a fire in Glascow Industries' valve plant has shut down its manufacturing operations. Glascow needs the 120,000 valves over the next 4 months to meet commitments to its regular customers; the company is prepared to pay $19 each for the valves, FOB shipping point.

   Adrian Pipe Company's product cost, based on current attainable standards, for the pressure valve is

Direct material	$ 5
Direct labor	6
Manufacturing overhead	9
Total cost	$20

   Manufacturing overhead is applied to production at the rate of $18 per standard direct labor hour. This overhead rate is made up of the following components:

Variable factory overhead	$ 6
Fixed factory overhead—direct	8
Fixed factory overhead—allocated	4
Applied manufacturing overhead rate	$18

Additional costs incurred in connection with sales of the pressure valve include sales commissions of 5 percent and freight expense of $1 per unit. However, the company does not pay sales commissions on special orders that come directly to management.

In determining selling prices, Adrian Pipe Company adds a 40 percent markup to product cost. This provides a $28 suggested selling price for the pressure valve. The Marketing Department, however, has set the current selling price at $27 to maintain market share.

Production management believes that it can handle the Glascow Industries order without disrupting its scheduled production. The order would, however, require additional fixed factory overhead of $12,000 per month in the form of supervision and clerical costs.

If management accepts the order, 30,000 pressure valves will be manufactured and shipped to Glascow Industries each month for the next 4 months. Shipments will be made in weekly consignments, FOB shipping point.

a. Determine how many additional direct labor hours would be required each month to fill the Glascow Industries order.

b. Prepare an incremental analysis showing the impact of accepting the Glascow Industries order.

c. Calculate the minimum unit price that Adrian Pipe Company's management could accept for the Glascow Industries order without reducing net income.

d. Identify the factors, other than price, that Adrian Pipe Company should consider before accepting the Glascow Industries order.

(CMA)

ETHICS AND QUALITY DISCUSSION

56. In Japan, the decision to stop production of a product or to close down a plant has different cost consequences than in the United States. One principal difference is that Japanese managers are much less likely to fire workers who are displaced by an event such as a plant closing. Japanese managers would simply try to move the displaced workers to active plants. However, this concept of permanent or lifetime employment can be awkward to manage when economic times become difficult and prudent financial management suggests that activities, including employment, be scaled back to cut costs. One Japanese company has found an interesting solution:

Nissan Motor Co., in a sign that its severe slump may be worsening, is taking the unusual step of loaning some of its idle factory workers to a rival auto maker.

Nissan said it will assign 250 of its production employees to work for six months at factories run by Isuzu Motors Ltd., a 37% owned affiliate of General Motors Corp.

Nissan's spokesman, Koji Okuda called the move an attempt to deal with the company's sharp drop in auto output in Japan. In May, Nissan's Japanese auto production fell 26% from a year earlier. "Demand is low," Mr. Okuda said. "We have to adjust our operations."

[SOURCE: Michael Williams, "Nissan Will Loan Workers to Rival Amid Low Demand," *Wall Street Journal* (June 24, 1994), p. A4. Reprinted by permission of *The Wall Street Journal*,© 1994 Dow Jones & Company, Inc. All Rights Reserved Worldwide.]

a. What specific types of costs might Nissan have considered relevant in its decision to loan employees to Isuzu?

b. Why would Isuzu be interested in hiring, on a temporary basis, workers of Nissan?

c. What are the likely impacts of this arrangement on quality of the output at Isuzu? The quality of output at Nissan?

57. Carter's Computers manufactures computers and all components. The purchasing agent informed the company owner, Abraham Carter, that another company has offered to supply keyboards for Carter's computers at prices below the variable costs at which Carter can make them. Incredulous, Mr. Carter hired an industrial consultant to explain how the supplier could offer the keyboards at less than Carter's variable costs. It seems that the competitor supplier is suspected by the consultant of using many illegal aliens to work in that plant. These people are poverty-stricken and will take such work at substandard wages. The purchasing agent and the plant manager feel that Carter should buy the keyboards from the competitor supplier as "no one can blame us for his hiring practices and will not even be able to show that we knew of those practices."

   a. What are the ethical issues involved in this case?

   b. What are the advantages and disadvantages of buying from this competitor supplier?

   c. What do you think Mr. Carter should do and why?

58. In 1982, Ford Motor Company officials went to the test track to evaluate a prototype of their new Bronco II, a sports utility vehicle. One of the officials was the head of automotive safety, another was his superior. These two officials, along with Ford's top lawyer, witnessed something that surely sent shivers up their spines—while rounding a corner, a front wheel of the Bronco II lifted off the ground; a clear indication of its instability.

   The Ford Bronco II went into production in January 1983. As of early 1993, 260 people have died in Bronco IIs in accidents involving the vehicle flipping over. Also, more than 100 lawsuits relating to the Bronco II have been settled by Ford. Ford settled all but two of these lawsuits out of court. Of the two that went to court, Ford won one and lost one. Court testimony in the cases that went to trial revealed the following facts:

   1. Ford knew in 1981 that it could make the vehicle considerably more stable by switching to a wider chassis, but it didn't do so because that would have cost valuable time in getting the product to market; it was in a race with GM and GM's S-10 Blazer to get to market.

   2. Ford's safety changes following the test track incident were largely superficial.

   3. Ford's tests after the Bronco II was available to the market continued to indicate that the vehicle was prone to tip or roll over on sharp turns.

   4. More that 50 safety-related documents regarding early rollover tests and suggestions for design improvements were inadvertently destroyed by Ford.

   [SOURCE: Adapted from Milo Geyelin and Neal Templin, "Ford Attorneys Played Unusually Large Role in Bronco II's Launch," *Wall Street Journal* (January 5, 1993), pp. A1, A6. Reprinted by permission of *The Wall Street Journal*, © 1993 Dow Jones & Company, Inc. All Rights Reserved Worldwide.]

   a. Discuss whether it was ethical of Ford Motor Company to bring the Bronco II to market, given the company's knowledge about the vehicle's safety problems.

   b. In making the decision to bring the vehicle to market in 1983, rather than make safety design changes and bring it to market later, what relevant costs did Ford possibly overlook?

   c. What action could the head of automotive safety at Ford have taken to induce Ford to revise the design of the Bronco II before bringing it to market?

59. *In 1987 EEOC's [Equal Employment Opportunity Commission] local field office wrote me a letter saying they had reason to believe I didn't have enough women "food servers" and "busers." No woman had complained against me. So the EEOC advertised in the local paper to tell women whose job applications we had rejected—or even women who had just thought of applying—that they could be entitled to damages. Twenty-seven women became plaintiffs in a lawsuit against me. The EEOC interviewed me for hours to find out what kind of person I was. I told them in Sicily where I came from I learned to respect women. I supplied them with hundreds of pounds* *of paper. I had to hire someone full time for a year just to respond to EEOC demands. Six months ago I finally settled. I agreed to pay $150,000 damages and as jobs open up, to hire the women on the EEOC's list. Even if they don't know what spaghetti looks like! I have to advertise twice a year even if I have no openings, just to add possible female employees to my files. I also had to hire an EEOC-approved person to teach my staff how not to discriminate. I employ 12 food servers in these two restaurants. Gross sales, around $2 million. How much did it all cost me? Cash outlay, about $400,000.*

What the government's done to me—devastating. I wouldn't wish it on my worst enemy."
Thomas Maggiore
Phoenix, Arizona

[SOURCE: Peter Brimelow and Leslie Spencer, "When Quotas Replace Merit, Everybody Suffers," *Forbes* (February 15, 1993), pp. 80–82 ff. Reprinted by permission of *Forbes* magazine. © Forbes, Inc., 1994.]

a. Do you think Mr. Maggiore's cash outlay of $400,000 includes all of the costs he incurred because of the EEOC regulation? Try breaking down the various costs that he may have incurred into three categories: direct costs, indirect costs, and opportunity costs.

b. Are hiring policies based on quotas ethical? How do quota systems affect the economic viability of American firms?

c. If EEOC regulations are intended to right past wrongs, should EEOC guidelines apply differently to immigrant Americans than to second-, third-, and fourth-generation Americans. (Consider, for example, that any immigrant that falls into a protected class qualifies for all U.S. quota programs just like an American whose great-great-great-grandfather was a slave.)

d. How can quota systems have an effect on the quality of American products?

INTERNET ACTIVITIES

60. Search the Internet for technology aids (software programs) to group decision making. After reviewing the features of some available decision making aids, discuss how such aids might help or hinder the making of decisions based on only *relevant* information.

61. Search the Internet for discussions and promotions regarding outsourcing services. Write a summary describing the variety of services that are now available to firms that wish to outsource functions.

62. Assume that you work for a firm that is about to launch a new product line of digital cameras and that you are responsible for devising a strategy to promote and sell the product line through the Internet. Describe how you would use the Internet to promote and market the new product line.

The Master Budget

LEARNING OBJECTIVES

After completing this chapter, you should be able to answer these questions:

1. Why is budgeting important?

2. How are strategic and tactical planning related to budgeting?

3. What is the starting point of a master budget and why?

4. How are the various schedules in a master budget prepared?

5. How do the schedules of the master budget relate to one another?

6. Why is the cash budget so important in the master budgeting process?

7. *(Appendix)* What are the advantages and disadvantages of imposed budgets? Participatory budgets?

8. *(Appendix)* How does a budget manual facilitate the budgeting process?

Binney & Smith, Inc.

The Binney & Smith story began in 1864 when Joseph Binney, an Englishman, started a chemical company in Peekskill, New York. Called the Peekskill Chemical Works, it made such products as lampblack, charcoal, and red oxide, which was used to paint the red barns dotting America's landscape.

In 1885, Joseph's son, Edwin Binney, and nephew, C. Harold Smith, took over the control of the company and formed the partnership of Binney & Smith, which operated until 1902, the date of incorporation. In 1984, Binney & Smith became a wholly owned subsidiary of Hallmark Cards, Inc., the world's largest greeting card manufacturer.

Crayola is a registered trademark of Binney & Smith. Crayola products are sold in more than 80 countries from the island of Iceland to the tiny Central American nation of Belize. They are packaged in 11 languages and come in three sizes: regular, jumbo, and So Big, and seven styles: glitter, scented, fabric, wipe-off, washable, anti-roll, and hexagonal shaped. Crayola crayons are primarily made from paraffin wax and colored pigments by essentially the same formula as that of the original crayons made in 1903. Improvements and minor adjustments have taken place over the past 90 years, but the crayon formula is as guarded today as it was then.

After being molded, crayons are placed in an automated labeling machine that wraps and glues on the labels. The crayons are then fed into packing machines that collate the colors into different assortments. If all the regular size crayons made in one year were melted, the resulting bands of color would circle the Earth over four and a half times. [This is big business! Although the firm offers a large variety of other successful products (primarily markers, paints, and activity kits), it is easy to see that, even with just crayons, preparing the master budget is an extremely important, complex endeavor for company management and accountants.]

SOURCE: Binney & Smith, Inc., Consumer Affairs Office, 1100 Church Lane, P.O. Box 431, Easton, PA 18044–0431.

In virtually any endeavor, intelligent behavior involves visualizing the future, imagining what results one wishes to occur, and determining the activities and resources required to achieve those results. If the process is complex, the means of obtaining results should be written. Writing out complex plans is necessary because of the human tendency to forget and the difficulty of mentally processing many facts and relationships at the same time.

Planning is the cornerstone of effective management, and effective planning requires that managers must predict, with reasonable precision, the key variables that affect company performance and conditions. These predictions provide management with a foundation for effective problem solving, control, and resource allocation. Planning (especially in financial terms) is important when future conditions are expected to be approximately the same as current ones, but it is critical when conditions are expected to change.

During the strategic planning process, managers attempt to agree on company goals and objectives and how to achieve them. Typically, goals are stated as desired abstract achievements (such as "to become a market leader for a particular product"). Objectives are desired quantifiable results for a specified time (such as "to have $1,000,000 in sales next year"). Achievement of a company's desired goals and objectives requires complex activities, uses diverse resources, and necessitates formalized planning.

A plan should include qualitative narratives of goals, objectives, and means of accomplishment. However, if plans were limited to qualitative narratives, comparing

VIDEO
VIGNETTE

Minnesota Twins

budgeting

budget

actual results to expectations would only allow generalizations, and no measurement of how well the organization met its specified objectives would be possible. The process of formalizing plans and translating qualitative narratives into a written, quantitative format is called **budgeting.** The end result of this process is a **budget,** which expresses an organization's *commitment* to planned activities and resource acquisition and use.

> A budget is more than a forecast. A forecast is a prediction of what may happen and sometimes contains prescriptions for dealing with future events. A budget, on the other hand, involves a commitment to a forecast to make an agreed-on outcome happen.[1]

This chapter covers the budgeting process and preparation of the master budget. Although budgeting is important for all organizations, the process becomes exceedingly complex in entities that have significant pools of funds and resources.

THE BUDGETING PROCESS

Budgeting is an important part of an organization's entire planning process. As with other planning activities, budgeting helps provide a focused direction or a path chosen from many alternatives. Management generally indicates the direction chosen through some accounting measure of financial performance, such as net income, earnings per share, or sales level expressed in dollars or units. Such accounting-based measures provide specific quantitative criteria against which future performance (also recorded in accounting terms) can be compared. Thus, a budget is a type of standard, allowing variances to be computed. Budgets can also help identify potential problems in achieving specified organizational goals and objectives. By quantifying potential difficulties and making them visible, budgets can help stimulate managers to think of ways to overcome those difficulties before they are realized. As indicated in the following News Note, the planning process has become interdisciplinary, and cross-

NEWS NOTE

Budgeting for Multiple Objectives

A decision-support system can provide management with a powerful tool to aid in planning and budgeting. In today's complex business environment, management must make decisions using not only financial measures, but also nonfinancial performance measures such as minimizing defects and throughput while maximizing customer satisfaction. In response to this environment, the planning process has become interdisciplinary and involves cross-functional teamwork. Financial management, corporate management, and product marketing and sales have targeted goals, and the planning process must balance their varied agendas. This challenge often calls for a multiple-objective planning environment.

The solution to this problem involves operating decisions that include product sales, production, and use of scarce resources. For management, optimizing these objectives means increased performance evaluations and salary and bonus determinations. The beauty of the decision-support system is that it promotes goal congruence so that what is good for managers also is good for the company.

Moreover, the decision-support system enables management to view complex planning and budgeting problems in terms of its objectives and not get swamped by the detailed operating decisions necessary to implement the alternative plans. Also, the decision-support system is iterative and is designed to search a narrower and narrower set of feasible alternative plans, enabling management to select a satisfactory plan of action. This final plan is not optimal with respect to all the objectives, but it is satisfactory in that management has approved any trade-offs.

SOURCE: James Godfrey, Robert Leitch, and Ralph Steuer, "Budgeting for Multiple Objectives," *Management Accounting* (January 1996), p. 38. Reprinted from *Management Accounting.* Copyright by Institute of Management Accountants, Montvale, NJ.

---

[1] Neil C. Churchill, "Budget Choice: Planning vs. Control," *Harvard Business Review* (July–August 1984), p. 150.

functional teams are used to balance the various agendas of functional management throughout the firm.

A well-prepared budget can also be an effective device to communicate objectives, constraints, and expectations to all organizational personnel. Such communication promotes understanding of what is to be accomplished, how those accomplishments are to be achieved, and the manner in which resources are to be allocated. Determination of resource allocations is made, in part, from a process of obtaining information, justifying requests, and negotiating compromises. Participation in the budgeting process helps to produce a spirit of cooperation, motivate employees, and instill a feeling of teamwork. Employee participation is needed to effectively integrate necessary information from various sources as well as to obtain individual managerial commitment to the resulting budget.

The budget indicates the resource constraints under which managers must operate for the upcoming budget period. Thus, the budget becomes the basis for controlling activities and resource usage. Most managers in U.S. companies make periodic budget-to-actual comparisons that allow them to determine how well they are doing, assess variance causes, and implement rational and realistic changes that can, among other benefits, create greater budgetary conformity.

Although budgets are typically expressed in financial terms, they must begin with nonquantitative factors. The budgeting and planning processes are concerned with all organizational resources—raw materials, inventory, supplies, personnel, and facilities—and can be viewed from a long-term or a short-term perspective.

Managers who plan on a long-range basis (5 to 10 years) are engaged in **strategic planning.** This process is generally performed by top-level management with the assistance of several key staff members. The result is a statement of long-range organizational goals and the strategies and policies that will help achieve those goals. Strategic planning is not concerned with day-to-day operations, although the strategic plan is the foundation on which short-term planning is based.

Managers engaging in strategic planning should identify **key variables** or critical factors believed to be direct causes of the achievement or nonachievement of organizational goals and objectives. Key variables can be internal (under the control of management) or external (normally noncontrollable by management). Exhibit 14–1 provides the results of one study about the most critical external factors in determining the strategic plans of manufacturing companies. One conclusion from the survey was that a "firm's long-term success is dependent on the integration of the forces in its environment into its own planning process so that the firm *influences* its own destiny instead of constantly *reacting* to environmental forces."[2] The following News Note on p. 623 advocates spending more time evaluating external factors for better forecasting.

After identifying key variables, management should gather information related to them. Much of this information is historical and qualitative and provides a useful starting point for tactical planning activities. **Tactical planning** determines the specific objectives and means by which strategic plans will be achieved. Some tactical plans, such as corporate policy statements, exist for the long term and address repetitive situations. Most tactical plans, however, are short term (1 to 18 months); they are considered "single-use" plans and have been developed to address a given set of circumstances or for a specific time.

The annual budget is an example of a single-use tactical plan. Although a budget is typically prepared for a 1-year period, shorter period (quarterly and monthly) plans should also be included for the budget to work effectively. A well-prepared budget translates a company's strategic and tactical plans into usable guides for company activities. Exhibit 14–2 illustrates the relationships among strategic planning, tactical planning, and budgeting.

Both strategic and tactical planning require that information regarding the economy, environment, technological developments, and available resources be incorpo-

strategic planning

V I D E O
VIGNETTE

Sonic Corp. (Blue Chip Enterprises)
key variable

tactical planning

---

[2] James F. Brown, Jr., "How U.S. Firms Conduct Strategic Planning," *Management Accounting* (February 1986), p. 55.

EXHIBIT 14–1

External Factors to Include in Strategic Plans

SOURCE: James F. Brown, Jr., "How U.S. Firms Conduct Strategic Planning," *Management Accounting* (February 1986), p. 55. Reprinted from *Management Accounting.* Copyright by Institute of Management Accountants, Montvale, NJ.

Organizational Characteristics
- Market share
- Quality of products
- Discretionary cash flow/gross capital investment

Market and Consumer Behavior
- Market segmentation
- Market size
- New market development
- Buyer loyalty

Industry Structure
- Rate of technological change in products or processes
- Degrees of product differentiation
- Industry price/cost structure
- Economies of scale

Supplier
- Major changes in availability of raw materials

Social, Economic and Political Factors
- GNP trend
- Interest rates
- Energy availability
- Government established and legally enforceable regulations

EXHIBIT 14–2

Relationships Among Planning Processes

WHO?	WHAT?	HOW?	WHY?
Top management	Strategic planning	Statement of organizational mission, goals, and strategies; long range (5–10 years)	Establish a long-range vision of the organization and provide a sense of unity of and commitment to specified purposes
Top management and mid-management	Tactical planning	Statement of organizational plans; short range (1–18 months)	Provide direction for achievement of strategic plans; state strategic plans in terms on which managers can act; furnish a basis against which results can be measured
Top management, mid-management, and operational management	Budgeting	Quantitative and monetary statements that coordinate company activities for a year or less	Allocate resources effectively and efficiently; indicate a commitment to objectives; provide a monetary control device

External View Needed for Strategic Planning

Now that companies have re-engineered, consultants are pushing them to beef up study of the outside world. The Futures Group, Glastonbury, Conn., says managers who spend more time evaluating external factors such as their competitors, the U.S. market climate and emerging technology, can better manage and forecast business than those who focus on internal factors, such as budgets. Its poll of 100 companies finds that extrovert managers graded their long-term planning higher than did introverts.

One such company that is thinking externally is Monsanto Co. in St. Louis, a maker of agricultural products, chemicals and food products. Greg Griffin, head of finance for the company's crop protection business, says employees created four different "worlds" and began "war-gaming" with external forces such as U.S. farm policy and global views on technology. Monsanto plans to apply the planning techniques to other departments.

SOURCE: Pamela Sebastian, "Business Bulletin—An Exterior View May Be What Some Companies Need in Their Strategic Planning," *Wall Street Journal* (December 14, 1995), p. 1. Reprinted by permission of *The Wall Street Journal*, © 1995 Dow Jones & Company, Inc. All Rights Reserved Worldwide.

rated into the setting of goals and objectives. This information is used to adjust the previously gathered historical information for any changes in the key variables for the planning period. The planning process also demands that, as activity takes place and plans are implemented, a monitoring system be in place to provide feedback so that the control function can be operationalized.

Management reviews the budget prior to approving and implementing it to determine whether the forecasted results are acceptable. The budget may indicate that results expected from the planned activities do not achieve the desired objectives. In this case, planned activities are reconsidered and revised so that they more effectively achieve the desired outcomes expressed during the tactical planning stage. After a budget is accepted, it is implemented and considered a standard against which performance can be measured. Managers operating under budget guidelines should be provided copies of all appropriate budgets. These managers should also be informed that their performance will be evaluated by comparing actual results to budgeted amounts. Feedback should generally be made by budget category for specific times, such as 1 month.

Once the budget is implemented, the control phase begins, which includes making actual-to-budget comparisons, determining variances, investigating variance causes, taking necessary corrective action, and providing feedback to operating managers. Feedback (both positive and negative) is essential to the control process and, to be useful, must be provided in a timely manner.

The preceding discussion details a budgeting process but, like many other business practices, budgeting may be unique to individual countries. For example, the lengthy and highly specific budgeting process used by many U.S. companies differs dramatically from that used by many Japanese companies. Japanese companies view the budget more as a device to help focus on achieving group and firm-level targets than as a control device by which to gauge individual performance.

Regardless of the budgeting process, the result is what is known as a master budget. This budget is actually a comprehensive *set* of budgets and budgetary schedules as well as pro forma organizational financial statements.

THE MASTER BUDGET

The master budget is composed of both operating and financial budgets as shown in Exhibit 14–3. An **operating budget** is expressed in both units and dollars. When an operating budget relates to revenues, units are those expected to be sold and dollars reflect selling prices. When an operating budget relates to cost items, units are those expected to be consumed and dollars reflect costs.

operating budget

Components of a Master
Budget

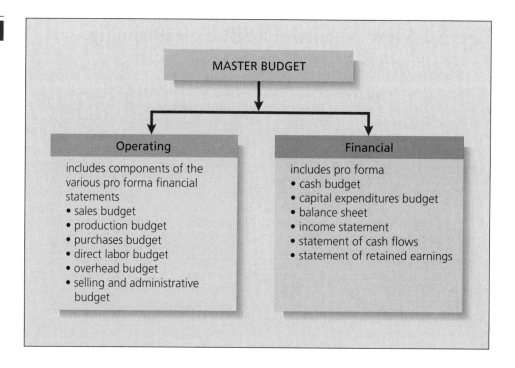

financial budget

Monetary details from the operating budgets are aggregated to prepare **financial budgets** indicating the funds to be generated or consumed during the budget period. Financial budgets include the organization's cash and capital budgets as well as its projected or pro forma financial statements. These budgets are the ultimate focal points for top management.

The master budget is prepared for a specific period and is static in the sense that it is based on a single level of output demand.[3] Expressing the budget on a single output level is necessary to facilitate the many time-consuming financial arrangements that must be made before beginning operations for the budget period. Such arrangements include making certain that an adequate number of personnel are hired, needed production and/or storage space is available, and suppliers, prices, delivery schedules, and quality of resources are confirmed.

The sales demand level selected for use in the master budget preparation affects all other organizational components. Because of the budgetary interrelationships illustrated in Exhibit 14–4, all the departmental components must interact in a coordinated manner. A budget developed by one department is often an essential ingredient in developing another department's budget.

The budgetary process shown in Exhibit 14–4 begins with the Sales Department's estimates of the types, quantities, and timing of demand for the company's products. The budget is typically prepared for a year and then subdivided into quarterly and monthly periods. A production manager combines sales estimates with additional information from Purchasing, Personnel, Operations, and Capital Facilities; the combined information allows the production manager to specify the types, quantities, and timing of products to be manufactured. The accounts receivable area uses sales es-

---

[3] Some companies engage in contingency planning that provides for multiple budgeting paths. Emerson Electric, for example, uses a technique they refer to as ABC budgeting in which the A budget applies to the most likely scenario, the B budget to a possible lower level of activity, and so on. As a result, company managers can react with previously considered plans in the event of business environment changes. [Charles F. Knight, "Emerson Electric: Consistent Profits, Consistently," *Harvard Business Review* (January–February 1992), p. 65.]

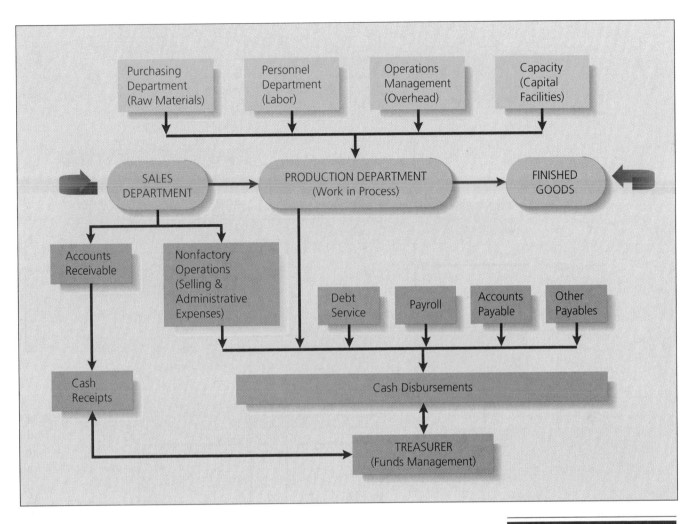

EXHIBIT 14–4

The Budgetary Process
in a Manufacturing
Organization

timates, in conjunction with estimated collection patterns, to determine the amounts and timing of cash receipts. For the treasurer to properly manage the organization's flow of funds, cash receipts and cash disbursements information must be matched from all areas so that cash is available when, and in the quantity, it is needed.

Note that some information must flow back into a department from which it began. For example, the Sales Department must receive finished goods information to know whether goods are in stock (or can be produced) before selling products. In addition, the treasurer must *receive* continual information on cash receipts and disbursements as well as *provide* information to various organizational units on funds availability so that proper funds management can be maintained.

If top management encourages participation by lower-level managers in the budgeting process, each department either prepares its own budget or provides information for inclusion in a budget. Exhibit 14–5 presents an overview of the component budget preparation sequence of the master budget, indicates which departments are responsible for which budget's preparation, and illustrates how the budgets interface with one another. The master budget begins with a sales budget based on expected demand. Production and cash flows are planned using the chosen sales level, and ultimately pro forma financial statements are prepared. The information flow is visible from Exhibit 14–5, but the quantitative and monetary implications are not. Therefore, the next section of the chapter is devoted to the preparation of a master budget.

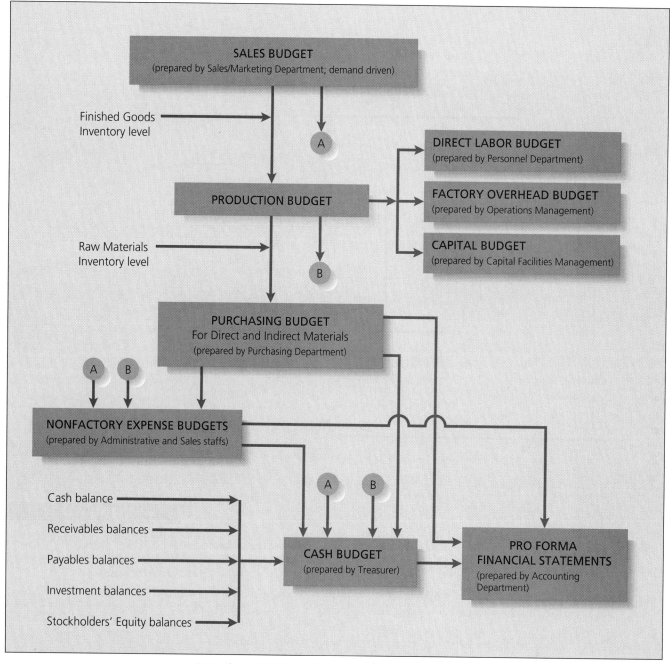

Note: The circled letters reflect a flow of information as an output of one area and an input of another.

EXHIBIT 14–5

The Master Budget: An Overview

THE MASTER BUDGET ILLUSTRATED

This illustration will use information from Happy Times, a small company that has been in business for several years. The company, which produces jumbo-size crayons for small children, is preparing its 1997 budget and has estimated total annual sales at 900,000 crayons. Although annual sales would be detailed on a monthly basis, the Happy Times illustration focuses only on the budgets for the first quarter of 1997. The process of developing the master budget is the same regardless of whether the time frame is one year or one quarter.

ASSETS			LIABILITIES AND STOCKHOLDERS' EQUITY		
Current Assets			Current Liabilities		
Cash		$ 6,000	Accounts Payable		$ 4,330
Accounts Receivable	$ 24,000		Dividends Payable (payment		
Less Allowance for Uncollectibles	(432)	23,568	scheduled for March 31)		25,000
			Total Current Liabilities		$ 29,330
Inventories					
Raw Material (31,800 ounces)	$ 636				
Finished Goods (4,000 units)	748	1,384			
Total Current Assets		$ 30,952			
Plant Assets			Stockholders' Equity		
Property, Plant, and Equipment	$370,000		Common Stock	$180,000	
Less Accumulated Depreciation	(90,000)	280,000	Retained Earnings	101,622	
			Total Stockholders' Equity		281,622
			Total Liabilities and		
Total Assets		$310,952	Stockholders' Equity		$310,952

EXHIBIT 14–6

Balance Sheet—December 31, 1996

The December 31, 1996, balance sheet presented in Exhibit 14–6 provides account balances needed to begin preparation of the master budget. The December 31, 1996, balances are really estimates rather than actual figures because the budget process for 1997 must begin significantly before December 31, 1996. The company's budgetary time schedule depends on many factors, including its size and degree of forecasting sophistication. Assume that Happy Times begins its budgeting process in November 1996, when the 1997 sales forecast is received by management or the budget committee.

To properly budget international sales, companies need to be aware of such things as consumer spending patterns and product preferences. Forecasts need to be detailed by product, region, selling price, and timing of sales.

Sales Budget for the Three
Months and Quarter
Ending March 31, 1997

	JANUARY	FEBRUARY	MARCH	TOTAL FOR QUARTER	APRIL*
Sales in units	80,000	70,000	75,000	225,000	64,000
Sales in dollars	$40,000	$35,000	$37,500	$112,500	$32,000

*Information for April is needed for subsequent computations.

Sales Budget

The sales budget is prepared in both units and sales dollars. The selling price set for 1997 is $.50 per crayon, regardless of sales territory or customer. Monthly demand and its related revenue impact for the first 4 months of 1997 are shown in Exhibit 14–7. Dollar sales figures are computed by multiplying sales quantities by product selling prices. April information is presented because some elements of the March budget require the following month's information.

The accompanying News Note about budgeting for international sales indicates the importance of analyzing the characteristics associated with the market when preparing a sales budget. Although such analysis is important domestically, it is critical for companies such as Dawson/Berg that has international operations.

**NEWS
NOTE**

The Complexities of Budgeting International Sales

Budgeting is impacted by conditions tied to a multinational's international business operations. Multinationals must be aware of and respond to the conditions of each market they service, including the level of economic development, degree of government price control, cost of sales in each market, product pricing decisions for each market (e.g., standard mark-up, market prices), available channels of distribution and promotion, and import/export controls.

Dawson/Berg Corporation is a multinational entity that does business in several areas of the world. In preparing its sales budget, the following analysis might occur:

REGION/COUNTRY	DOMINANT AND DISTINCTIVE MARKET CHARACTERISTICS
Canada	North American Free Trade Agreement
Denmark	Strong local competition
Eastern Europe	Recent democratization and uncertain trade regulations
European Union	EC92 economic integration
France	Price controls
Germany	New and uncertain situation caused by the reunification of the country
Japan	Complex distribution system
Pacific Rim	New area with many developing countries offering a growing consumer base
United States	Specific market penetration is desired in highly segmented market

[Factors requiring consideration may] arise from a specific nation's characteristics [or] from international forces. Whatever their origin, [t]he existence of these differences indicates that marketing strategies and the resulting sales budget cannot be transplanted merely from domestic operations to a foreign operation.

SOURCE: Adapted from Paul V. Mannino and Ken Milani, "Budgeting for an International Business," *Management Accounting* (February 1992), p. 39. Reprinted from *Management Accounting*. Copyright by Institute of Management Accountants, Montvale, NJ.

Production Budget

The production budget follows from the sales budget and uses information regarding the type, quantity, and timing of units to be sold. Sales information is used in conjunction with beginning and ending inventory information so that managers can schedule necessary production. The following formula provides the computation for units to be produced:

Number of units to be sold (from sales budget)	XXX
+ Number of units desired in ending inventory	XXX
= Total units needed during period	XXX
− Number of units in beginning inventory	(XXX)
= Units to be produced	XXX

The number of units desired in ending inventory is determined and specified by company management. Desired ending inventory balance is generally a function of the quantity and timing of demand in the upcoming period as related to the firm's capacity and speed to produce particular units. Frequently, management stipulates that ending inventory be equal to a given percentage of the next period's projected sales. Other alternatives include a constant amount of inventory, a build-up of inventory for future high-demand periods, or near-zero inventory under a just-in-time system. The decision about ending inventory levels results from the consideration of whether a firm wants to have constant production with varying inventory levels or variable production with constant inventory levels. Managers should consider the high costs of stockpiling inventory before making a decision about how much inventory to keep on hand.

Demand for Happy Times's products is relatively constant, but the company's most active sales season is in the fall. The company's ending finished inventory policy for December through March is that FG inventory equal 5 percent of the next month's sales. Considering this policy and using the sales information from Exhibit 14–7, the production budget shown in Exhibit 14–8 is prepared.

The January beginning inventory balance is 4,000 units that were on hand at December 31, 1996, which represents 5 percent of January's estimated sales of 80,000 units. Desired March ending inventory is 5 percent of April sales of 64,000 (given in Exhibit 14–7). Happy Times does not have any work in process inventory because all units placed into production are assumed to be fully completed each period.[4]

Purchases Budget

Direct materials are essential to production and must be purchased each period in sufficient quantities to meet production needs. In addition, the quantities of direct

	JANUARY	FEBRUARY	MARCH	TOTAL
Sales in units (from Exhibit 14–7)	80,000	70,000	75,000	225,000
+ Desired ending inventory	3,500	3,750	3,200	3,200
= Total needed	83,500	73,750	78,200	228,200
− Beginning inventory	(4,000)	(3,500)	(3,750)	(4,000)
= Units to be produced	79,500	70,250	74,450	224,200

EXHIBIT 14–8

Production Budget for the Three Months and Quarter Ending March 31, 1997

---

[4] Most manufacturing entities do not produce only whole units during the period. Normally, partially completed beginning and ending work in process inventories will exist. These inventories create the need to use equivalent units of production when computing the production budget.

	JANUARY	FEBRUARY	MARCH	QUARTER
Units to be produced (from Exhibit 14–8)	79,500	70,250	74,450	224,200
+ EI (10% of next month's production)*	7,025	7,445	6,450	6,450
= Total whole units needed	86,525	77,695	80,900	230,650
− Beginning inventory	(7,950)**	(7,025)	(7,445)	(7,950)
Finished units for which purchases are required	78,575	70,670	73,455	222,700
WAX PURCHASES				
Finished units	78,575	70,670	73,455	222,700
Ounces needed per unit	× 4	× 4	× 4	× 4
Total ounces to be purchased	314,300	282,680	293,820	890,800
× Price per ounce	× $.02	× $.02	× $.02	× $.02
Total cost of wax purchases	$ 6,286	$ 5,654	$ 5,876	$17,816

*April production is expected to be 64,500 units.

**BI of RM was 31,800; each unit requires 4 ounces, so there was enough RM for 7,950 units or 10% of the following month's production.

EXHIBIT 14–9

Purchases Budget for the Three Months and Quarter Ending March 31, 1997

material purchased must be in conformity with the company's desired ending inventory policies. Happy Times' management ties its policy for ending inventories of direct materials to its production needs for the following month. Because of occasional difficulty in obtaining the quality of materials needed, Happy Times' ending inventories of direct materials from December through March equal 10 percent of the quantities needed for the following month's production. Companies may have different policies for the direct materials associated with different products or for different seasons of the year. For example, a company may maintain only a minimal ending inventory of a direct material that is consistently available in the quantity and quality desired. Alternatively, if a material is difficult to obtain at certain times of the year (such as certain components for food preparation), a company may stockpile that material for use in future periods.

The purchases budget is first stated in whole units of finished products and then converted to direct material component requirements and dollar amounts. Production of a Happy Times crayon requires only one direct material: four ounces of colored wax. (Cost of the paper wrapper is insignificant and treated as part of overhead.) Material cost has been estimated by the purchasing agent as $.02 per ounce of wax. Exhibit 14–9 shows Happy Times' purchases cost for each month of the first quarter of 1997. Note that beginning and ending inventory quantities are expressed first in terms of crayons and then converted to the appropriate quantity measure (ounces of wax). The total budgeted cost of direct material purchases for the quarter is $17,816 ($6,286 + $5,654 + $5,876).

Personnel Budget

Given expected production, the Engineering and Personnel Departments can work together to determine the necessary labor requirements for the factory, sales force, and office staff. Labor requirements are stated in total number of people, specific number of types of people (skilled laborers, salespeople, clerical personnel, and so forth), and production hours needed for factory employees. Labor costs are computed from items such as union labor contracts, minimum wage laws, fringe benefit costs, payroll taxes, and bonus arrangements. The various personnel amounts will be shown, as appropriate, in either the direct labor budget, manufacturing overhead budget, or selling and administrative budget.

	JANUARY	FEBRUARY	MARCH	TOTAL
Units of production	79,500	70,250	74,450	224,200
× Standard hours allowed	.01	.01	.01	.01
= Total hours allowed	795	702.5	744.5	2,242
× Average wage rate (including fringe cost)	× $6	× $6	× $6	× $6
= Direct labor cost	$ 4,770	$ 4,215	$ 4,467	$ 13,452

EXHIBIT 14–10

Direct Labor Budget for the Three Months and Quarter Ending March 31, 1997

Direct Labor Budget

Happy Times' management has reviewed the staffing requirements and has developed the direct labor cost estimates shown in Exhibit 14–10 for the first quarter of 1997. Factory direct labor costs are based on the standard hours of labor needed to produce the number of units shown in the production budget. The average wage rate includes both the direct labor payroll rate and the payroll taxes and fringe benefits related to direct labor (because these items usually add between 25 and 30 percent to the base labor cost). All compensation is paid in the month in which it is incurred. Assume that Happy Times is too small to be affected by minimum wage requirements.

Overhead Budget

Another production cost that management must estimate is overhead. Exhibit 14–11 presents Happy Times' monthly cost of each overhead item for the first quarter of 1997. The company has determined that machine hours is the best predictor of overhead costs.

In estimating overhead, all fixed and variable costs must be specified and mixed costs must be separated into their fixed (a) and variable (b) components. Each overhead amount shown is calculated using the $y = a + bX$ formula discussed in Chapter 5. For example, March maintenance cost is the fixed amount of $175 plus ($.30 times 1,240 estimated hours of machine time) or $175 + $372 = $547. Both total cost and cost net of depreciation are shown in the budget. The net of depreciation cost is expected to be paid in cash during the month and will affect the cash budget.

	Value of (fixed) a	Value of (variable) b	JANUARY	FEBRUARY	MARCH	TOTAL
Estimated machine hours (X) (assumed)			1,325	1,171	1,240	3,736
FOH item:						
Depreciation	$ 600	$ —	$ 600	$ 600	$ 600	$ 1,800
Indirect material	—	.20	265	234	248	747
Indirect labor	1,000	.50	1,663	1,585	1,620	4,868
Utilities	100	.20	365	334	348	1,047
Property tax	100	—	100	100	100	300
Insurance	50	—	50	50	50	150
Maintenance	175	.30	573	526	547	1,646
Total cost (y)	$2,025	$1.20	$3,616	$3,429	$3,513	$10,558
Total cost net of depreciation			$3,016	$2,829	$2,913	$ 8,758

EXHIBIT 14–11

Overhead Budget for the Three Months and Quarter Ending March 31, 1997

Selling and Administrative
Budget for the Three
Months and Quarter
Ending March 31, 1997

		Value of		JANUARY	FEBRUARY	MARCH	TOTAL
Predicted sales (from Exhibit 14–7)				$40,000	$35,000	$37,500	$112,500
	(fixed) a	(variable) b					
S&A:							
Supplies	$ —	$.010		$ 400	$ 350	$ 375	$ 1,125
Depreciation	200	—		200	200	200	600
Miscellaneous	100	.001		140	135	138	413
Compensation							
Salespeople	1,000	.040		2,600	2,400	2,500	7,500
Administrative	2,000			2,000	2,000	2,000	6,000
Total cost (y)	$3,300	$.051		$5,340	$ 5,085	$ 5,213	$ 15,638
Total cost (net of depreciation)				$ 5,140	$ 4,885	$ 5,013	$ 15,038

Capital Budget for the
Three Months and Quarter
Ending March 31, 1997

	JANUARY	FEBRUARY	MARCH	TOTAL
Acquisition—computer	$0	$23,000	$0	$23,000
Cash payment for computer	$0	$23,000	$0	$23,000

Selling and Administrative (S&A) Budget

Selling and administrative expenses can be predicted in the same manner as overhead costs. Exhibit 14–12 presents the first quarter 1997 Happy Times S&A budget. Note that sales figures rather than production levels are the activity measure in preparing this budget. The company has two salespeople who receive $500 per month plus a 4 percent commission on sales. Administrative salaries total $2,000 per month.

Capital Budget

The budgets included in the master budget focus on the short-term or upcoming fiscal period. Managers, however, must also assess such long-term needs as plant and equipment purchases and budget for those expenditures in a process called **capital budgeting.** The capital budget is prepared separately from the master budget, but because expenditures are involved, capital budgeting does affect the master budgeting process.[5]

capital budgeting

As shown in Exhibit 14–13, Happy Times's managers have decided that a $23,000 computer to control the automation of the production machinery will be purchased and paid for in February. The computer will be placed into service when installation is complete in April 1997 after software has been written and adapted to the company's machinery. Depreciation on the computer will not be included in the overhead calculation until installation is complete.

Cash Budget

After the preceding budgets have been developed, a cash budget can be constructed. The cash budget may be the most important schedule prepared during the budgeting process because, without cash, a company cannot survive.

[5] Capital budgeting is discussed in depth in Chapter 18.

The following model can be used to summarize cash receipts and disbursements in a way that assists managers to devise appropriate financing measures to meet company needs.

Rosario, Barlets & Talamo (Blue Chip Enterprises)

CASH BUDGET MODEL

Beginning cash balance	XXX
+ Cash receipts (collections)	XXX
= Cash available for disbursements exclusive of financing	XXX
− Cash needed for disbursements (purchases, direct labor, overhead, S&A, taxes, bonuses, etc.)	(XXX)
= Cash excess or deficiency (*a*)	XXX
− Minimum desired cash balance	(XXX)
= Cash needed or available for investment or repayment	XXX

Financing methods:

± Borrowing (repayments)	XXX	
± Issue (reacquire) capital stock	XXX	
± Sell (acquire) investments or plant assets	XXX	
± Receive (pay) interest or dividends	XXX	
Total impact (+ or −) of planned financing (*b*)		XXX
= Ending cash balance (*c*), where [(*c*) = (*a*) ± (*b*)]		XXX

The cash budget is one of the most important components of the master budget. Because the sales forecast is on an accrual basis, a company must estimate a cash receipts pattern for its credit sales customers to know when actual funds will be available to make a variety of payments.

EXHIBIT 14-14

Happy Times Collection
Pattern for Sales

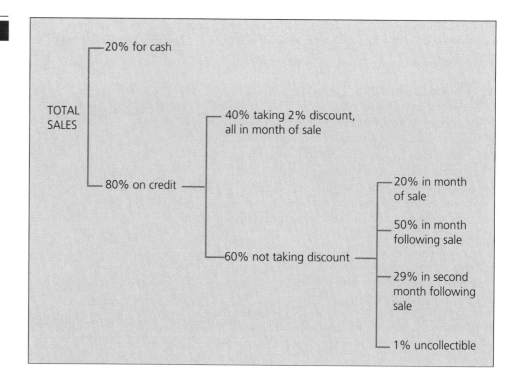

CASH RECEIPTS AND ACCOUNTS RECEIVABLE   Once sales dollars have been determined, managers translate revenue information into cash receipts through the use of an expected collection pattern. This pattern considers the collection patterns experienced in the recent past and management's judgment about changes that could disturb current collection patterns. For example, changes that could weaken current collection patterns include recessionary conditions, increases in interest rates, less strict credit granting practices, or ineffective collection practices.

In specifying collection patterns, managers should recognize that different types of customers pay in different ways. Any sizable, unique category of clientele should be segregated. Happy Times has two different types of customers: cash customers who never receive a discount and credit customers. Of the credit customers, wholesalers are allowed a 2 percent cash discount; retailers are not allowed the discount. Happy Times has determined from historical data that the collection pattern diagrammed in Exhibit 14–14 is applicable to its customers. Of each month's sales, 20 percent will be for cash and 80 percent will be on credit. The 40 percent of the credit customers who are allowed the discount pay in the month of the sale. Collections from the remaining credit customers are as follows: 20 percent in the month of sale; 50 percent in the month following the sale; and 29 percent collected in the second month following the sale. One percent of credit sales not taking a discount are uncollectible.

Using the sales budget, information on November and December 1996 sales, and the collection pattern, management can estimate cash receipts from sales during the first 3 months of 1997. Management must have November and December sales information because collections for credit sales extend over 3 months, meaning that collection of some of the previous year's sales occur early in the current year. Happy Times' November and December sales were $44,000 and $46,000, respectively. Projected monthly collections in the first quarter of 1997 are shown in Exhibit 14–15. The individual calculations relate to the alternative collection patterns and corresponding percentages presented in Exhibit 14–14. All amounts have been rounded to the nearest dollar.

	JANUARY	FEBRUARY	MARCH	TOTAL	DISC.	UNCOLL.
FROM:						
November 1996 sales:						
$44,000(.8)(.6)(.29)	$ 6,125			$ 6,125		
$44,000(.8)(.6)(.01)						$211
December 1996 sales:						
$46,000(.8)(.6)(.5)	11,040			11,040		
$46,000(.8)(.6)(.29)		$ 6,403		6,403		
$46,000(.8)(.6)(.01)						221
January 1997 sales:						
$40,000(.2)	8,000			8,000		
$40,000(.8)(.4)(.98)	12,544N			12,544	$256	
$40,000(.8)(.6)(.2)	3,840			3,840		
$40,000(.8)(.6)(.5)		9,600		9,600		
$40,000(.8)(.6)(.29)			$ 5,568	5,568		
$40,000(.8)(.6)(.01)						192
February 1997 sales:						
$35,000(.2)		7,000		7,000		
$35,000(.8)(.4)(.98)		10,976N		10,976	224	
$35,000(.8)(.6)(.2)		3,360		3,360		
$35,000(.8)(.6)(.5)			8,400	8,400		
March 1997 sales:						
$37,500(.2)			7,500	7,500		
$37,500(.8)(.4)(.98)			11,760N	11,760	240	
$37,500(.8)(.6)(.2)			3,600	3,600		
Totals	$41,549	$37,339	$36,828	$115,716	$720	$624

"N" stands for "Net of discount." To determine the gross amount, divide the net amount by .98 (i.e., 100% − 2%).

The amounts for November and December collections can be reconciled to the December 31, 1996, balance sheet (Exhibit 14–6), which indicated an Accounts Receivable balance of $24,000. This amount appears in the collection schedule as follows:

DECEMBER 31, 1996, BALANCE IN ACCOUNTS RECEIVABLE:

January collections of November sales	$ 6,125
Estimated November bad debts	211
January collections of December sales	11,040
February collections of December sales	6,403
Estimated December bad debts	221
December 31, 1996, balance in Accounts Receivable	$24,000

January 1997 sales of $40,000 are used to illustrate the collection calculations in Exhibit 14–15. The first line (for January) represents cash sales of 20 percent of total sales, or $8,000. The next two lines represent the 80 percent of the customers who buy on credit. The first of these lines represents the 40 percent of credit customers who take the discount, computed as follows:

Sales to credit customers (80% of $40,000)		$32,000
Sales to customers allowed discount (40% × $32,000)		$12,800
− Discount taken by customers (.02 × $12,800)		256
= Net collections from customers allowed discount		$12,544

The second of these two lines relates to the remaining 20 percent of credit customers who paid in the month of sale but were not allowed the discount. The remaining amounts in Exhibit 14–15 are computed similarly.

Once the cash collections schedule is prepared, balances for Accounts Receivable, Allowance for Uncollectibles, and Sales Discounts can be projected. (These T-accounts for Happy Times follow.) These amounts will be used to prepare pro forma quarter-end 1997 financial statements. All sales are initially recorded as Accounts Receivable. Immediate cash collections are then deducted from the Accounts Receivable balance.

Note that the estimated uncollectible accounts from November 1996 through March 1997 have not been written off as of the end of the first quarter of 1997. Companies continue to make collection efforts for a substantial period before accounts are acknowledged as truly worthless. Thus, these receivables may remain on the books 6 months or more from the sale date. When accounts are written off, Accounts Receivable and the Allowance for Uncollectibles will both decrease; however, there will be no income statement impact relative to the write-off.

ACCOUNTS RECEIVABLE

12/31/96 Balance (Exhibit 14–6)	24,000	Collections in January from beginning A/R ($6,125 + $11,040)	17,165
January 1997 sales (Exhibit 14–7)	40,000	Cash sales in January (Exhibit 14–15)	8,000
		Credit collections subject to discount (cash received, $12,544)	12,800
		Credit collections not subject to discount	3,840
February 1997 sales (Exhibit 14–7)	35,000	Collections in February from beginning A/R	6,403
		Cash sales in February (Exhibit 14–15)	7,000
		Collections in February from January sales	9,600
		Credit collections subject to discount (cash received, $10,976)	11,200
		Credit collections not subject to discount	3,360
March 1997 sales (Exhibit 14–7)	37,500	Cash sales in March (Exhibit 14–15)	7,500
		Collections in March from January sales	5,568
		Collections in March from February sales	8,400
		Credit collections subject to discount (cash received, $11,760)	12,000
		Credit collections not subject to discount	3,600
3/31/97 Balance	20,064		

ALLOWANCE FOR UNCOLLECTIBLE ACCOUNTS

12/31/97 Balance (Exhibit 14–6)	432
January estimate (Exhibit 14–15)	192
February estimate [$35,000(80%)(60%)(1%)]	168
March estimate [$37,500(80%)(60%)(1%)]	180
3/31/97 Balance	972

SALES DISCOUNTS

January discounts	256
February discounts	224
March discounts	240
3/31/97 Balance	720

CASH DISBURSEMENTS AND ACCOUNTS PAYABLE   Using the purchases information from Exhibit 14–9, management can prepare a cash disbursements schedule for Accounts Payable. All raw material purchases are made on account by Happy Times. The company pays for 40 percent of each month's purchases in the month of purchase. These purchases are from suppliers who allow Happy Times a 2 percent discount for prompt payment. The remaining suppliers allow no discounts, but require payments be made within 30 days from the purchase date. Thus, the remaining 60 percent of each month's purchases are paid in the month following the month of purchase.

Exhibit 14–16 presents the first quarter 1997 cash disbursements information for purchases. The December 31, 1996, Accounts Payable balance of $4,330 (Exhibit 14–6) represents 60 percent of December purchases of $7,217. All amounts have been rounded to whole dollars.

EXHIBIT 14–16

Cash Disbursements for Accounts Payable for the Three Months and Quarter Ending March 31, 1997

	JANUARY	FEBRUARY	MARCH	TOTAL	DISCOUNT
PAYMENT FOR PURCHASES OF:					
December 1996	$4,330			$ 4,300	
January 1997 (from Exhibit 14–9)					
$6,286(.40)(.98)	2,464N			2,464	$ 50
$6,286(.60)		$3,772		3,772	
February 1997 (from Exhibit 14–9)					
$5,654(.40)(.98)		2,216N		2,216	45
$5,654(.60)			$3,393	3,393	
March 1997 (from Exhibit 14–9)					
$5,876(.40)(.98)			2,303N	2,303	47
Total disbursements for A/P	$6,794	$5,988	$5,696	$18,478	$142

"N" stands for "Net of discount." The total amount of gross purchases being paid for in the month of purchase is the sum of the net of discount payment plus the amount shown on the same line in the Discount column.

Accounts payable activity is summarized in the following T-account. The March 31 balance represents 60 percent of March purchases that will be paid during April.

ACCOUNTS PAYABLE

		12/31/96 Balance (Exhibit 14–6)	4,330
January payments for December purchases (Exhibit 14–16)	4,330	January purchases (Exhibit 14–9)	6,286
January payments for January purchases subject to discount (cash paid, $2,464)	2,514		
February payments for January purchases (Exhibit 14–16)	3,772	February purchases (Exhibit 14–9)	5,654
February payments for February purchases subject to discount (cash paid, $2,216)	2,261		
March payments for February purchases (Exhibit 14–16)	3,393	March purchases (Exhibit 14–9)	5,876
March payments for March purchases subject to discount (cash paid, $2,303)	2,350		
		3/31/97 Balance	3,526

PURCHASES DISCOUNTS

January discounts	50
February discounts	45
March discounts	47
3/31/97 Balance	142

Given the cash receipts and disbursements information for Happy Times, the cash budget model is used to formulate the cash budget shown in Exhibit 14–17. The company has established $6,000 as its desired minimum cash balance. There are two primary reasons for having a desired minimum cash balance: one is internal; the other is external. The first reason reflects the uncertainty associated with the budgeting process. Because managers cannot budget with absolute precision, a "cushion" is maintained to protect the company from potential errors in forecasting collection and payment schedules. The second reason is the company's banks may require a minimum cash balance in relation to an open line of credit.

For simplicity, it is assumed that any investments or sales of investments are made in end-of-month $1,000 increments. Interest on company investments at 12 percent per annum or 1 percent per month is added to the company's bank account at month's end.

Exhibit 14–17 indicates that Happy Times has a $27,829 excess of cash available over disbursements in January. Such an excess, however, does not consider the need for the $6,000 minimum balance. Thus, the company has $21,829 available. It used $21,000 of that amount to purchase temporary investments at the end of January.

In February, Happy Times again will have enough cash to meet its desired minimum cash balance and, by liquidating $3,000 of its investments, pay for the computer. In March, there is enough excess cash available, coupled with the liquidation of another $6,000 of investments, to pay the $25,000 dividend which is due in March.

	JANUARY	FEBRUARY	MARCH	TOTAL
Beginning cash balance	$ 6,000	$ 6,829	$ 6,461	$ 6,000
Cash collections (Exhibit 14–15)	41,549	37,339	36,828	115,716
Cash available exclusive of financing	$ 47,549	$ 44,168	$ 43,289	$121,716
DISBURSEMENTS:				
Accounts payable (for purchases, Exhibit 14–16)	$ 6,794	$ 5,988	$ 5,696	$ 18,478
Direct labor (Exhibit 14–10)	4,770	4,215	4,467	13,452
Overhead (Exhibit 14–11)*	3,016	2,829	2,913	8,758
S&A expenses (Exhibit 16–12)*	5,140	4,885	5,013	15,038
Total disbursements	$ 19,720	$ 17,917	$ 18,089	$ 55,726
Cash excess (inadequacy)	$ 27,829	$ 26,251	$ 25,200	$ 65,990
Minimum balance desired	(6,000)	(6,000)	(6,000)	(6,000)
Cash available (needed)	$ 21,829	$ 20,251	$ 19,200	$ 59,990
FINANCING:				
Borrowings (repayments)	$ 0	$ 0	$ 0	$ 0
Issue (reacquire) stock	0	0	0	0
Sell (acquire) investments	(21,000)	3,000	6,000	(12,000)***
Sell (acquire) plant assets	0	(23,000)	0	(23,000)
Receive (pay) interest**		210	180	390
Receive (pay) dividends			(25,000)	(25,000)
Total impact of planned financing	$(21,000)	$(19,790)	$(18,820)	$(59,610)
Ending cash balance	$ 6,829	$ 6,461	$ 6,380	$ 6,380

EXHIBIT 14–17

Cash Budget for the Three Months and Quarter Ending March 31, 1997

*These amounts are the net of depreciation figures.

**Interest is calculated assuming a 12 percent annual rate (1 percent per month) and that investments and disposals of investments are made at the end of the month in $1,000 increments.

***This is the net result of investments and disposals of investments.

Budgeted Financial Statements

The final step in the budgeting process is the development of budgeted (pro forma) financial statements for the period. These financial statements reflect the results that will be achieved if the estimates and assumptions used for all previous budgets actually occur. Such statements allow management to determine whether the predicted results are acceptable. If they are not acceptable, management has the opportunity to change and adjust items prior to the beginning of the period. When expected net income is not considered reasonable, management may investigate the possibility of raising selling prices or finding ways to decrease costs. Any specific changes considered by management may have related effects that must be included in the revised

EXHIBIT 14–18

Pro Forma Cost of Goods
Manufactured Schedule
for Quarter Ending
March 31, 1997

Beginning work in process inventory		$ 0
Cost of raw material used:		
Beginning balance (Exhibit 14–6)	$ 636	
Net purchases (from Accounts Payable and Purchases Discounts, p. 638)	17,674	
Total raw material available	$18,310	
Ending balance of RM (Note A)	(516)	
Cost of raw material used	$17,794	
Direct labor (Exhibit 14–10)	13,452	
Factory overhead (Exhibit 14–11)	10,558	
Total costs to be accounted for		41,804
Ending work in process inventory		(0)
Cost of goods manufactured		$41,804

Note A:	WAX
Ending balance (Exhibit 14–9) required for FG	6,450
Ounces per unit	× 4
Total ounces of RM required	25,800
Price per ounce	× $.02
Ending balance of RM	$ 516

projections. For example, raising selling prices may decrease volume. Alternatively, reductions in costs from using lower-grade materials could affect spoilage during production or cause a decline in demand. With the availability of the computer, changes in budget assumptions and their resultant effects can be simulated quickly and easily.

COST OF GOODS MANUFACTURED SCHEDULE   Management must prepare a schedule of cost of goods manufactured before an income statement can be prepared. This schedule is necessary to determine cost of goods sold. Using information from previous budgets, the Happy Times' budgeted cost of goods manufactured schedule is shown in Exhibit 14–18. Because there were no beginning or ending work in process inventories, cost of goods manufactured is equal to the manufacturing costs of the period. Had work in process inventory existed, the computations would be more complex and have involved the use of equivalent units of production.

INCOME STATEMENT   The projected income statement for Happy Times for the first quarter of 1997 is presented in Exhibit 14–19. This statement uses much of the information previously developed in determining the revenues and expenses for the period.

BALANCE SHEET   On completion of the income statement, a March 31, 1997, balance sheet (Exhibit 14–20, p. 642) can be prepared.

STATEMENT OF CASH FLOWS   The information found on the income statement, balance sheet, and cash budget is also used to prepare a Statement of Cash Flows

Sales (Exhibit 14–7)			$112,500
Less: Sales discounts (p. 637)			(720)
Net sales			$111,780
Cost of goods sold:			
Finished goods—12/31/96			
(Exhibit 14–6)		$ 748	
Cost of goods manufactured			
(Exhibit 14–18)		41,804	
Cost of goods available for sale		$ 42,552	
Finished goods—3/31/97 (Note A)		(598)	41,954
Gross margin			$ 69,826
Expenses:			
Bad debts expense (Note B)		$ 540	
S&A expenses (Exhibit 14–12)		15,638	16,178
Income from operations			$ 53,648
Other revenue—Interest earned			390
Income before income taxes			$ 54,038
Income taxes (assumed rate of 40%)			(21,615)
Net income			$ 32,423

Note A:		
Beginning finished goods		4,000
Production (Exhibit 14–8)		224,200
Units available for sale		228,200
Sales (Exhibit 14–7)		(225,000)
Ending finished goods		3,200
Cost per unit:		
Material	$.080	
Conversion (assumed)	.107	× $ .187
Cost of ending inventory		$ 598

Note B:		
Total sales	$112,500	
× % credit sales	× .80	
Credit sales	$ 90,000	
× % not taking discount	× .60	
× Potential bad debts	$ 54,000	
× % estimated uncollectible	× .01	
Estimated bad debts	$ 540	

(SCF). This statement can assist managers in judging the company's ability to handle fixed cash outflow commitments, adapt to adverse changes in business conditions, and undertake new commitments. Further, because the SCF identifies the relationship between net income and net cash flow from operations, it assists managers in judging the quality of the company's earnings.

Whereas the cash budget is essential to current cash management, the budgeted SCF gives managers a more global view of cash flows by rearranging them into three distinct major activities (operating, investing, and financing). Such a rearrangement permits management to judge whether the specific anticipated flows are consistent with the company's strategic plans.

In addition, the SCF would incorporate a schedule or narrative about significant noncash transactions if any have occurred, such as an exchange of stock for land, that are disregarded in the cash budget.

EXHIBIT 14–20

Pro Forma Balance Sheet,
March 31, 1997

ASSETS

Current Assets		
Cash (Exhibit 14–17)		$ 6,380
Accounts Receivable (p. 636)	$ 20,064	
Less Allowance for Uncollectibles (p. 637)	(972)	19,092
Inventory		
Raw Material (Exhibit 14–18, Note A)	$ 516	
Finished Goods (Exhibit 14–19, Note A)	598	1,114
Investments (Exhibit 14–17)		12,000
Total Current Assets		$ 38,586
Plant Assets		
Property, Plant, and Equipment (Note A)	$393,000	
Less Accumulated Depreciation (Note B)	(92,400)	300,600
Total Assets		$339,186

LIABILITIES AND STOCKHOLDERS' EQUITY

Current Liabilities		
Accounts Payable (p. 638)		$ 3,526
Income Taxes Payable (Exhibit 14–19)		21,615
Total Current Liabilities		$ 25,141
Stockholders' Equity		
Common Stock	$180,000	
Retained Earnings (Note C)	134,045	314,045
Total Liabilities and Stockholders' Equity		$339,186

Note A:
Beginning balance	
(Exhibit 14–6)	$370,000
Purchased new computer	23,000
Ending balance	$393,000

Note B:
Beginning balance	
(Exhibit 14–6)	$ 90,000
Factory depreciation	
(Exhibit 14–11)	1,800
S&A depreciation	
(Exhibit 14–12)	600
Ending balance	$ 92,400

Note C:
Beginning balance	
(Exhibit 14–6)	$101,622
Net income (Exhibit 14–21)	32,423
Ending balance	$134,045

The operating section of the SCF on either a direct or an indirect basis is acceptable for external reporting. The direct basis uses pure cash flow information (cash collections and cash disbursements) for operating activities. The operating section for a SCF prepared on an indirect basis begins with net income and makes reconciling adjustments to arrive at cash flow from operations. Exhibit 14–21 provides a Statement of Cash Flows for Happy Times using the information from the cash budget in Exhibit 14–17; the second, indirect presentation of the operating section uses the information from the income statement in Exhibit 14–19 and the balance sheets in Exhibits 14–6 and 14–20.

Operating Activities:		
Cash collections		
from sales (Exhibit 14–17)		$115,716
Interest earned (Exhibit 14–17)		390
Total		$116,106
Cash payments		
For inventory:		
Raw materials (Exhibit 14–17)	$18,478	
Direct labor (Exhibit 14–17)	13,452	
Overhead (Exhibit 14–17)	8,758	(40,688)
For nonfactory costs:		
Salaries and wages (Exhibit 14–12)	$13,500	
Supplies (Exhibit 14–12)	1,125	
Other S&A expenses (Exhibit 14–12)	413	(15,038)
Net cash inflow from operating activities		$60,380
Investing Activities:		
Purchase of plant asset (Exhibit 14–13)	$ 23,000	
Short-term investment (Exhibit 14–17)	12,000	
Net cash outflow from investing activities		(35,000)
Financing Activities:		
Dividends (Exhibit 14–17)	$ 25,000	
Net cash outflow from financing activities		(25,000)
Net increase in cash		$ 380
Alternative (Indirect) Basis for Operating Activities:		
Net income		$32,423
+ Depreciation (Exhibit 14–11 and Exhibit 14–12)	$ 2,400	
+ Decrease in Accounts Receivable ($23,568 − $19,092)	4,476	
+ Decrease in total inventory ($1,384 − $1,114)	270	
+ Increase in Taxes Payable ($21,615 − $0)	21,615	
− Decrease in Accounts Payable ($4,330 − $3,526)	(804)	27,957
= Net cash inflow from operating activities		$60,380

Happy Times generates both a large cash flow from operations ($60,380 from Exhibit 14–21) and a high net income per net sales dollar (29 percent). This strong showing by both measures suggests that Happy Times has high-quality earnings. Both cash flow from operations and net income are necessary for long-run business success. Happy Times's management is doing an effective job in pricing the company's product and an efficient job in controlling costs.

A well-prepared budget provides the following benefits:

CONCLUDING COMMENTS

1. a detailed path for managers to follow to achieve organizational goals;
2. an allocation of resources among departments;
3. a means by which managerial performance can be judged;
4. a device to allow employee participation and influence;
5. a means by which troublesome or hard-to-control cost areas can be noted;
6. a realization of the dynamic nature of departmental interrelationships;
7. improved planning and decision making;

8. "more timely responses to changing environmental conditions; and

9. an enhanced understanding of the factors important to the operations of the business."[6]

Because of its fundamental nature in the budgeting process, demand must be predicted as accurately and with as many details as possible. Sales forecasts should indicate type and quantity of products to be sold, geographic locations of the sales, types of buyers, and when the sales are to be made. Such detail is necessary because different products require different production and distribution facilities, different customers have different credit terms and payment schedules, and different seasons or months may necessitate different shipping schedules or methods.

Estimated sales demand has a pervasive impact on the master budget. To arrive at a valid prediction, managers use as much information as is available and may combine several estimation approaches. Combining prediction methods provides managers with a means to confirm estimates and reduce uncertainty. Some ways of estimating future demand are (1) canvassing sales personnel for a subjective consensus, (2) making simple extrapolations of past trends, (3) using market research, and (4) employing statistical and other mathematical models.

Care should be taken to use realistic, rather than optimistic or pessimistic, forecasts of revenues and costs. Computer models can be developed that allow repetitive computer simulations to be run after changes are made to one or more factors. These simulations permit managers to review results that would be obtained under various circumstances.

continuous budgeting

The master budget is normally prepared for a year and detailed by quarters and months within those quarters. Some companies use a process of **continuous budgeting,** which means that an ongoing 12-month budget is presented by successively adding a new budget month (12 months into the future) as each current month expires. The accompanying News Note gives an example of the rationale for doing this. Such a process allows management to work, at any time, within the present 1-month component of a full 12-month annual budget. Continuous budgets make the planning process less sporadic. Rather than having managers "go into the budgeting period" at a specific time, they are continuously involved in planning and budgeting.

If actual results differ from plans, management should find the causes of the differences and then consider budget revisions. Arrangements usually cannot be made rapidly enough to revise the current month's budget. However, under certain circumstances and if they so desire, managers may be able to revise future months' budgets. If actual performance is substantially less than what was expected, the budget may or may not be adjusted, depending on the variance causes. If the causes are beyond the organization's control and are cost related, management may decide to revise budget cost estimates upward to be more realistic. If the causes are internal (such as the sales staff not selling the product), management may leave the budget in its original form so that the lack of operational control is visible in the comparisons.

If actual performance is substantially better than expected, alterations may also be made to the budget, although management may decide not to alter the budget so that the positive performance is highlighted. Regardless of whether the budget is revised, managers should commend those individuals responsible for the positive performance and communicate the effects of such performance to other related departments. For example, if the sales force has sold significantly higher quantities of product than expected (at the expected selling price), production and purchasing will need to be notified to increase the number of units manufactured and raw material purchased.

[6] Gadis J. Dillon, "Getting the Most from Your Forecasting System," *Management Accounting* (April 1984), p. 32.

Continuous Budgeting at the HON Company

Survival in today's competitive environment means that businesses must be flexible and innovative, largely through development of new products and services, while simultaneously improving productivity and customer service. But building the effects of innovation into the annual budget can be difficult because actions and outcomes often are evolutionary and only become known as the year progresses. Under these conditions it is understandable that the annual budget is not an effective control tool because revenue and spending targets are based on operating conditions different from those actually encountered.

Standard cost accounting systems are not helpful either when budgeting for continuous change because of built-in contradictions. One shortcoming of standard costs for companies seeking continuous improvement, for example, is that they presuppose the goal is to optimize efficiency within a given state of operating conditions rather than to strive for ongoing improvement. Consequently, when production processes undergo continuous change, standards developed annually for static conditions no longer offer meaningful targets for gauging their success.

The HON Company, the largest maker of mid-priced office furniture in the United States and Canada, has overcome these obstacles through use of a continuous three-month budget cycle. The budget has become the integral planning and control device for achieving two strategic objectives: ongoing new product and service development and rapid continuous improvement. The budget also serves as an important vehicle for ensuring that the corporate culture is unified in its understanding of—and commitment to—strategic objectives.

SOURCE: Ralph Drtina, Steve Hoeger, and John Schaub, "Continuous Budgeting at The HON Company," *Management Accounting* (January 1996), pp. 20–21. Reprinted from *Management Accounting.* Copyright by Institute of Management Accountants, Montvale, NJ.

When budgets are used for performance evaluations, management often encounters the problem of **budget slack.** Budget slack is the intentional underestimation of revenues and/or overestimation of expenses. Slack can be incorporated into the budget during the participation process; slack is not often found in imposed budgets (discussed in the chapter appendix). Having budget slack allows subordinate managers to achieve their objectives with less effort than would be necessary without the slack. Slack also creates problems because of the significant interaction of the budget factors. If sales volumes are understated, problems can arise in the production, purchasing, and personnel areas. One way that top management can try to reduce slack is by tying actual performance to the budget through a bonus system. Operating managers are rewarded with large bonuses for budgeting relatively high performance levels and achieving those levels. If performance is set at a low or minimal level, achievement of that performance is either not rewarded or only minimally rewarded. Top management must be aware that budget slack has a tremendous negative impact on organizational effectiveness and efficiency.

budget slack

Managers may want to consider expanding their budgeting process to recognize the concepts of activities and cost drivers. Jeffrey A. Schmidt, a vice president in the management consulting firm of Towers Perrin, has suggested that management convert its traditional budget "into an activity budget, which discloses how much the company spends on specific tasks and the types of resources it devotes to them. An activity budget is created by mapping the line items in the conventional budget to a list of activities (responding to customer complaints, requisitioning new parts, etc.)."[7] Such a budget presentation would provide a focus on the costs of non-value-added activities and make managers more aware of why costs are being incurred and

[7] Jeffrey A. Schmidt, "Is It Time to Replace Traditional Budgeting?" *Journal of Accountancy* (June 1992), p. 104.

how much is being spent on non-value-added activities. Armed with such knowledge, managers could make more informed decisions about what activities to eliminate and why *seemingly* fixed costs continue to rise over time.

REVISITING

Binney & Smith, Inc.

Binney & Smith has slowly expanded its range of colors and streamlined its production methods. Crayola crayons are now available in a total of 96 colors. Today, more than two billion Crayola crayons are produced each year. Sales volume in 1995 was $535 million and the firm employed 2,600 people.

In Spring 1996, Binney & Smith celebrated the making of the 100 billionth Crayola crayon. The average child in the United States will wear down 730 crayons by his 10th birthday. According to a Yale University study, the scent of Crayola crayons is 18th among the 20 most recognizable to American adults. Coffee and peanut butter are one and two.

The firm is proud of its customer focus and the technological superiority of its high-performing and innovative products. From developing the industry-leading washable technology to creating innovative modeling compounds and glow-in-the-dark Silly Putty, Binney & Smith makes sure its products remain on the cutting edge of fun and creativity.

Binney & Smith has manufacturing facilities in the U.S., Canada, Mexico, England, and Germany. It also has international sales and marketing facilities in numerous countries around the world. [Effective budgeting is essential for the successful planning, coordinating, and controlling operations of this magnitude.]

SOURCE: Binney & Smith, Inc., Consumer Affairs Office, 1100 Church Lane, P.O. Box 431, Easton, PA 18044–0431.

CHAPTER SUMMARY

Planning is the process of setting goals and objectives and translating them into activities and resources required for accomplishment within a specified time horizon. Budgeting is the quantifying of a company's financial plans and activities. Budgets facilitate communication, coordination, and teamwork.

A master budget is the comprehensive set of projections for a specific budget period, culminating in a set of pro forma financial statements. It is composed of operating and financial budgets and is usually detailed by quarters and months. Some companies prepare continuous budgets by successively adding a new budgetary month, 12 months into the future, as each current month expires.

Sales demand is the proper starting point for the master budget. Once sales demand is determined, the cost accountant forecasts revenues, production quantities and costs, and cash flows for the firm's activities for the upcoming period. These expectations reflect the firm's inflows and outflows of resources.

When preparing a budget, managers must remember that organizational departments interact with each other, and the budget for one department may form the basis of or have an effect on the budgets in other departments. Actual operating results can be compared to budget figures to measure how effectively and efficiently organizational goals were met. Significant unfavorable variances dictate that managers either attempt to alter the behavior of personnel or alter the budget if it appears to be unrealistic; significant favorable variances most likely will not cause the budget to be adjusted, but rather will cause communication to affected departments on possible consequences (such as increased production needs indicated by a favorable difference in sales demand). Regardless of whether variances are unfavorable or favorable, feedback to operating personnel is an important part of the budgeting process.

Approaches to Budgeting and the Budget Manual

Budgeting requires the integration of a complex set of facts and projections with human relationships and attitudes. Throughout the budgeting literature, it has been noted that "the appropriate budgetary system and its implementation techniques are dependent upon organizational structure, management strategies, corporate goals and objectives, leadership style of top management, and employee attitudes."[8] In other words, one system of budgeting is not right for all organizations.

Imposed versus Participatory Budgets

The budgeting process can be represented by a continuum with *imposed budgets* on one end and *participatory budgets* on the other. Because the original goal of budgeting was monetary control, most budgets were imposed on the individuals who had to work within those budgets. **Imposed budgets** are prepared by top management with little or no input from operating personnel. After the budget is developed, operating personnel are informed of the budget goals and constraints. Exhibit 14–22 indicates

imposed budget

EXHIBIT 14–22

Imposed Budgets

BEST TIMES TO USE

- In start-up organizations
- In extremely small businesses
- In times of economic crises
- When operating managers lack budgetary skills or perspective
- When the organizational units require precise coordination of efforts

ADVANTAGES

- Increase probability that organization's strategic plans are incorporated in planned activities
- Enhance coordination among divisional plans and objectives
- Utilize top management's knowledge of overall resource availability
- Reduce the possibility of input from inexperienced or uninformed lower-level employees
- Reduce the time frame for the budgeting process

DISADVANTAGES

- May result in dissatisfaction, defensiveness, and low morale among individuals who must work under them
- Reduce the feeling of teamwork
- May limit the acceptance of the stated goals and objectives
- Limit the communication process between employees and management
- May create a view of the budget as a punitive device
- May result in unachievable budgets for international divisions if the local operating and political environment is not adequately considered
- May stifle initiative of lower-level managers

---

[8] Mary T. Soulier, "A Psychological Model of the Budgetary Process," *Woman CPA* (January 1980), p. 3.

If allowed to participate in the budget process, employees are more likely to strive to meet budget targets. Participation is essential in companies with wide-spread operations because imposed budgets could probably not take advantage of the decentralized managers' knowledge of local conditions.

participatory budget

when imposed budgets are effective and provide some distinct benefits; the disadvantages of imposed budgets are also listed.

At the other end of the continuum, a **participatory budget** is developed through joint decision making by top management and operating personnel. It was only in the last half century that the dissatisfaction caused by imposed budgets was first recognized and the idea of participation by various management levels was introduced. The degree to which lower-level operating management is allowed to participate in budget development usually depends on top management's awareness of and agreement with the advantages of the participation process.

From the standpoint of operational managers, participation could be viewed on a spectrum from having a right to merely comment on budgets before top management implements them to having the ultimate right to *set* budgets. Neither end of that spectrum is totally desirable. Simply commenting on the handed-down budget still reflects an imposed budgeting system, whereas each individual manager setting his or her own budget disregards the fact that cooperation and communication among areas is essential to the functioning of a cohesive organization.

The benefits and disadvantages of participatory budgets are listed in Exhibit 14–23. One of the primary benefits of this type of budgeting process is that people who have participated in budget development are normally more committed to the budget's success than if the budget is imposed. Currently, most business budgets are prepared through a coordinated effort of input from operating personnel and revision by top management.

Cost accountants play a major role in the budgetary process. As members of management's staff, cost accountants assist top management by designing and communicating budgetary forms, procedures, and schedules for responsible personnel. Historical financial information is also provided by cost accountants so that participating managers can make effective projections. Cost accountants analyze, review, and summarize the projections and prepare budgeted financial statements for top management's consideration.

BEST TIMES TO USE

- In well-established organizations
- In extremely large businesses
- In times of economic affluence
- When operating managers have strong budgetary skills and perspectives
- When the organizational units are quite autonomous

ADVANTAGES

- Obtain information from those persons most familiar with the needs and constraints of organizational units
- Integrate knowledge that is diffused among various levels of management
- Lead to better morale and higher motivation
- Provide a means to develop fiscal responsibility and budgetary skills of employees
- Develop a high degree of acceptance of and commitment to organizational goals and objectives by operating management
- Are generally more realistic
- Allow organizational units to coordinate with one another
- Allow subordinate managers to develop operational plans that conform to organizational goals and objectives
- Include specific resource requirements
- Blend overview of top management with operating details
- Provide a social contract that expresses expectations of top management and subordinates

DISADVANTAGES

- Require significantly more time
- May create a level of dissatisfaction with the process approximately equal to that occurring under imposed budgets if effects of managerial participation are negated by top management changes
- May be unachievable because managers are ambivalent about participating or unqualified to participate
- May motivate managers to introduce "slack" into the budget
- May support "empire building" by subordinates
- May start the process earlier in the year when there is more uncertainty about the future year

EXHIBIT 14–23

Participatory Budgets

Budget Manuals

To be useful, a budget requires a substantial amount of time and effort by the persons who prepare it. This process can be improved by the availability of an organizational **budget manual,** which is a detailed set of information and guidelines about the budgetary process. The manual should include

budget manual

1. statements of the budgetary purpose and its desired results;
2. a listing of specific budgetary activities to be performed;
3. a calendar of scheduled budgetary activities;
4. sample budgetary forms; and
5. original, revised, and approved budgets.

The statements of budgetary purpose and desired results communicate the reasons behind the process. These statements should flow from general to specific details. An example of a general statement of budgetary purpose is: "The Cash Budget provides a basis for planning, reviewing, and controlling cash flows from and for various activities; this budget is essential to the preparation of a Statement of Cash Flows." Specific statements could include references to minimum desired cash balances and periods of intense cash needs.

Budgetary activities should be listed by position rather than person because the responsibility for actions should be assigned to the individuals holding the designated positions at the time the budget is being prepared. The manual's activities section should indicate who has the final authority for revising and approving the budget. Budget approval may be delegated to a budget committee or reserved by one or several members of top management.

The budget calendar helps coordinate the budgetary process; it should indicate a timetable for all budget activities and be keyed directly to the activities list. The timetable for the budget process is unique to each organization. The larger the organization, the more time that will be necessary to gather and coordinate information, identify weak points in the process or the budget itself, and take corrective action. The calendar should also indicate control points for the upcoming periods at which budget-to-actual comparisons are made and feedback is provided to managers responsible for operations.

Sample forms are extremely useful because they provide for consistent presentations of budget information from all individuals, making summarization of information easier and quicker. The sample forms should be easy to understand and may include standardized worksheets that allow managers to update historical information to arrive at budgetary figures. This section of the budget manual may also provide standard cost tables for items on which the organization has specific guidelines or policies. For example, in estimating employee fringe benefit costs, the company rule of thumb may be 25 percent of base salary. Or, if company policy states that each salesperson's per diem meal allowance is $30, meal expenses would be budgeted as estimated travel days multiplied by $30.

The final section of the budget manual contains the budgets generated during the budgeting process. Numerous budgets probably will be submitted and revised prior to actual budget implementation. Understanding this revision process and why changes were made is helpful for future planning. The final approved master budget is included in the budget manual as a control document.[9]

KEY TERMS

budget (p. 620)
budgeting (p. 620)
budget manual (p. 649)
budget slack (p. 645)
capital budgeting (p. 632)
continuous budgeting (p. 644)
financial budget (p. 624)

imposed budget (p. 647)
key variable (p. 621)
operating budget (p. 623)
participatory budget (p. 648)
strategic planning (p. 621)
tactical planning (p. 621)

SOLUTION STRATEGIES

SALES BUDGET

    Units of sales
$\times$ Selling price per unit
$=$ Dollars of sales

[9] In the event of changes in economic conditions or strategic plans, the "final" budget may be revised during the budget period.

PRODUCTION BUDGET

    Units of sales
+ Units desired in ending inventory
− Units in beginning inventory
= Units to be produced

PURCHASES BUDGET

    Units to be produced
+ Units desired in ending inventory
− Units in beginning inventory
= Units to be purchased

DIRECT LABOR BUDGET

    Units of production
× Standard time allowed per unit
= Standard labor time allowed
× Per hour direct labor cost
= Total direct labor cost

OVERHEAD BUDGET

    Predicted activity base
× VOH rate per unit of activity
= Total variable OH cost
+ Fixed OH cost
= Total OH cost

SELLING AND ADMINISTRATIVE BUDGET

    Predicted sales dollars (or other variable measure)
× Variable S&A rate per dollar (or other variable measure)
= Total variable S&A cost
+ Fixed S&A cost
= Total S&A cost

SCHEDULE OF CASH COLLECTIONS FOR SALES

    Dollars of credit sales for month
× Percent collection for month of sale
= Credit to A/R for month's sales
− Allowed and taken sales discounts
= Receipts for current month's credit sales
+ Receipts from cash sales
+ Current month's cash receipts for prior months' credit sales
= Cash receipts for current month

SCHEDULE OF CASH PAYMENTS FOR PURCHASES

Units to be purchased

$\times$ Cost per unit

$=$ Total cost of purchases

$\times$ Percent payment for current purchases

$=$ Debit to A/P for month's purchases

$-$ Purchase discounts taken

$=$ Cash payments for current month's purchases

$+$ Cash purchases

$+$ Current month's payments for prior months' purchases

$=$ Cash payments for A/P for current month

CASH BUDGET

Beginning cash balance

$+$ Cash receipts (collections)

$=$ Cash available for disbursements

$-$ Cash needed for disbursements:
   Cash payments for A/P for month
   Cost of compensation
   Total cost of overhead minus depreciation
   Total S&A cost minus depreciation

$=$ Cash excess or deficiency

$-$ Minimum desired cash balance

$=$ Cash needed or available for investment or financing
   Cash excess or deficiency

$+$ or $-$ various financing methods

$=$ Ending cash balance

DEMONSTRATION PROBLEM

Martins' March 31, 1997, balance sheet includes the following:

Cash	$15,000 debit
Accounts Receivable	46,000 debit
Allowance for Uncollectible Accounts	1,022 credit
Merchandise Inventory	6,133 debit

The firm's management has designated $15,000 as the firm's monthly minimum cash balance. Other information about Martins follows:

- Revenues of $100,000 and $120,000 are expected for April and May, respectively. All goods are sold on account.
- The collection pattern for Accounts Receivable is 55 percent in the month of sale, 44 percent in the month following the sale, and 1 percent uncollectible.
- Cost of goods sold approximates 60 percent of sales revenues.
- Management wants to end each month with 10 percent of that month's cost of sales in Merchandise Inventory.
- All Accounts Payable for inventory are paid in the month of purchase.
- Other monthly expenses are $13,000, which includes $2,000 of depreciation, but does not include bad debt expense.

Required:

a. Forecast the April cash collections.
b. Forecast the April and May cost of purchases.
c. Prepare the cash budget for April including the effects of financing (borrowing or investing).

Solution to Demonstration Problem

a.

APRIL COLLECTIONS	
From March ($46,000 − $1,022)	$44,978
From April ($100,000 × .55)	55,000
Total	$99,978

b.

	APRIL	MAY
Sales	$100,000	$120,000
Cost of goods (60%)	$ 60,000	$ 72,000
Add desired ending balance	6,000	7,200
Total needed	$ 66,000	$ 79,200
Less beginning balance	(6,133)	(6,000)
Cost of purchases	$ 59,867	$ 73,200

c. **APRIL CASH BUDGET**

Beginning cash		$ 15,000
April collections		99,978
Total cash available before financing		$114,978
Disbursements:		
Purchase of merchandise	$59,867	
Other monthly expenses ($13,000 − $2,000)	11,000	
Total disbursements		(70,867)
Cash excess or inadequacy (*a*)		$ 44,111
Less minimum cash balance desired		(15,000)
Cash available or needed		$ 29,111
Financing:		
Acquire investment (*b*)		(29,111)
Ending cash balance (*c*); (*c* = *a* − *b*)		$ 15,000

---

1. Why do businesses formalize their plans in writing?
2. Outline the basic budgeting process.
3. Why is a budget considered a communication device?
4. Managers formulate strategic plans that have time horizons of 5 to 10 years. Why do managers also formulate shorter-term plans?
5. What major factors are taken into account in formulating an organization's strategic plan?
6. How are budgets used as both planning and control tools?
7. The master budget contains both operational and financial budgets. What is the difference between an operating budget and a financial budget? How do they relate to each other?
8. It is said that the master budget is "demand driven." What does this mean?
9. Explain how managers estimate collections from sales. Why is this information important in the budgeting process?

QUESTIONS

10. How are the production budgets and materials purchasing budgets similar? How are they different? When is each used?

11. In estimating the overhead budget, why is it necessary to separate overhead into its variable and fixed components?

12. Why is the cash budget so important to an organization? If the cash budget identifies a period in which a cash shortage is expected, what actions can a firm take?

13. Why would a company wish to maintain a minimum cash balance?

14. How does the cash budget interact with the sales budget and planned accounts receivable?

15. Why is it useful to complete the budgeting process with a presentation of pro forma financial statements?

16. How are the budgeted Statement of Cash Flows and the cash budget similar? How are they different?

17. What benefits should arise from a process of continuous budgeting?

18. What is budget slack? What induces managers to build slack into their budgets?

19. *(Appendix)* Why is employee participation in developing the budget important to an organization?

20. *(Appendix)* What are the various sections of the budget manual and why is each section necessary?

EXERCISES

21. *(Production schedule)* The projected sales, in units, for Jacobs Company by month for the first four months were

January	10,000
February	15,000
March	20,000
April	24,000

Inventory of finished goods on December 31 was 8,000 units. The company desires to have an ending inventory each month equal to one-half of next month's estimated sales.

Determine the company's production requirements for each month of the first quarter.

22. *(Production budget)* The sales budget for Carson Company shows the following sales projections (in units) for the quarters of the calendar year of 1997:

January–March	270,000
April–June	340,000
July–September	245,000
October–December	275,000
Total	1,130,000

Sales for the first quarter of 1998 are expected to be 295,000 units. Finished Goods Inventory at the end of each production period is scheduled to equal 30 percent of the next quarter's budgeted sales in units. The company is expected to be in compliance with this policy as of December 31, 1996. Develop a quarterly production budget for 1997. Include a column to show total expected production for 1997.

23. *(Materials purchasing budget)* Catskill Ski Company has projected sales of 21,480 ski boots in September. Each pair of boots requires 2 1/2 linear feet of leather. The beginning inventory of leather and boots, respectively, are 2,500 yards and 1,154 pairs. Catskill Ski wants to have 9,000 yards of leather and 3,800 pair of boots at the end of September due to high sales projections for the winter months. The leather comes in standard widths. Therefore, to convert linear feet to yards, divide by 3. If Catskill has no beginning or ending Work in Process Inventory, how many yards of leather must the company purchase in September?

24. *(Materials purchasing budget)* Alberta Culvert Company has budgeted sales of 200,000 feet of its concrete culvert products for June 1997. Each foot of product requires 12 pounds of concrete ($.10 per pound) and 15 pounds of gravel ($.03 per pound). Actual beginning inventories and projected ending inventories are shown below.

	JUNE 1	JUNE 31
Finished Goods Inventory (in feet)	25,000	10,500
Concrete (in pounds)	82,000	68,600
Gravel (in pounds)	65,300	92,500

   a. How many pounds of concrete does Alberta Culvert plan to purchase in June? What will be the cost of that purchase?
   b. How many pounds of gravel does Alberta Culvert plan to purchase in June? What will be the cost of that purchase?

25. *(Production and related schedules)* The Walker Company manufactures and sells two products: plastic boxes and plastic trays. Estimated needs for a unit of each are

	BOXES	TRAYS
Material A	2 pounds	1 pound
Material B	4 pounds	4 pounds
Direct labor	2 hours	2 hours

Overhead is applied on the basis of $2 per direct labor hour.

The estimated sales by product for 1997 are:

	BOXES	TRAYS
Sales	42,000	24,000

The beginning inventories are expected to be as follows:

Material A	4,000 pounds
Material B	6,000 pounds
Boxes	1,000 units
Trays	500 units

The desired inventories are one month's production requirements, assuming constant sales throughout the year.

   Prepare the following information:
   a. Production schedule
   b. Purchases budget in units
   c. Direct labor budget in hours
   d. Overhead to be charged to production

26. *(Cash collections)* Primrose Printers is developing its first-quarter monthly cash budget for 1997 and is having difficulty determining its expected cash collections. On investigation, the following actual and expected sales information was revealed:

NOVEMBER	DECEMBER	JANUARY	FEBRUARY	MARCH
$41,500	$38,000	$29,500	$34,000	$39,500

Tracing collections from prior-year monthly sales and discussions with the credit manager helped develop a profile of collection behavior patterns.

Of a given month's sales, 40 percent are typically collected in the month of sale. Because the company terms are 1 percent EOM [end of month], net 30, all collections within the month of sale are net of the 1 percent discount. Thirty percent of a given month's sales are collected in the month following the sale. The remaining 30 percent are collected in the second month following the month of the sale. Bad debts are negligible and should be ignored.

a. Prepare a schedule of cash collections for Primrose Printers by month for January, February, and March.

b. Calculate the Accounts Receivable balance at March 31.

27. *(Cash budget)* The Accounts Receivable balance at October 1, 1997, for Terra Engineering was $606,900. Of that balance, $450,000 represents remaining Accounts Receivable from September billings. The normal collection pattern for the firm is 20 percent of billings in the month of service, 55 percent in the month after service, and 22 percent in the second month following service. The remaining billings are uncollectible. October billings are expected to be $700,000.

a. What were August billings for Terra Engineering?

b. What amount of September billings are expected to be uncollectible?

c. What are projected cash collections in October 1997 for the firm?

28. *(Cash collections/accounts receivable)* Edison Utilities is developing a forecast of June 1998 cash receipts from sales. Total sales for June 1998 are expected to be $650,000. Of each month's sales, 75 percent is expected to be on credit. The Accounts Receivable balance at May 31 is $171,000 of which $135,000 represents the remainder of May credit sales. There are no receivables from months prior to April 1998. Edison has an established collection pattern for credit sales of 60 percent in the month of sale, 25 percent in the month following the sale, and 15 percent in the second month following the sale. Edison has no uncollectible accounts.

a. What were total sales for April 1998?

b. What were credit sales for May 1998?

c. What are projected cash collections for June 1998?

d. What will be the balance of Accounts Receivable at June 30, 1998?

29. *(Cash balance)* Thompson Hardware has prepared a forecast for May 1997. Some of the projected information follows:

Income after tax	$250,000
Accrued Income Tax Expense	72,000
Increase in Accounts Receivable for month	41,000
Decrease in Accounts Payable for month	18,300
Depreciation Expense	71,200
Estimated Bad Debts Expense	13,100
Dividends declared	20,000

Using the above information, what is the company's projected increase in cash for May 1997?

30. *(Cash disbursements)* In trying to decide whether it was feasible for the company to acquire treasury stock during May 1997, Jon Hardtack, president of Rocky Mountain Bootery, Inc., requested information on projected cash disbursements for that month. He received the following information from his new accountant:

Sales for May	$2,000,000
Gross profit on sales	40%
Wages expense for May	$ 412,500
Other cash expenses for May	$ 235,250
Decrease in Accounts Payable during May	$ 40,000
Decrease in Merchandise Inventory during May	$ 33,750

Not understanding how the above information could help him compute cash disbursements, Mr. Hardtack asked the accountant to show how cash disbursements can be computed from these figures. If all significant data are given, what are projected cash disbursements for May?

31. *(Cash budget)* The accountant for Heavenly Pizza prepared the following cash budget for the third quarter of 1997. When the owner was reviewing it, he was eating a deep-dish pizza loaded with extra cheese. Some of the topping inadvertently spilled onto the page and smeared the figures. Complete the missing numbers on the cash budget, assuming that the accountant has projected a minimum cash balance at the start of each month of $2,500. All borrowings, repayments, and investments are made in even $500 amounts.

	JULY	AUGUST	SEPTEMBER	TOTAL
Beginning cash balance	$ 4,500	$?	$?	$?
Cash receipts	8,200	10,100	?	?
Total cash available	$?	$13,000	$19,500	$39,400
Cash disbursements:				
Payments on account	$?	$ 3,900	$ 5,700	$?
Wages expense	5,000	?	6,100	17,200
Overhead costs	4,000	4,600	?	13,000
Total disbursements	$10,300	$?	$16,200	$?
Cash excess (inadequacy)	$?	$?	$?	$?
Minimum cash balance	(2,500)	(2,500)	?	?
Cash available (needed)	$?	$(4,100)	$?	$(4,200)
Financing:				
Borrowings (repayments)	$ 500	$?	$ (500)	$?
Acquire (sell) investments	0	0	?	?
Receive (pay) interest	0	0	?	(50)
Ending cash balance	$ 2,900	$?	$?	$ 2,750

32. *(Various budgets)* The following are four independent situations.
   a. Bryan Frozen Foods is planning to produce two products: frozen dinners and frozen desserts. Sales of frozen dinners are expected to be 200,000 units at $4 per unit; projected sales for frozen desserts are 400,000 units at $3 per unit. Variable costs are 70 percent and 80 percent of sales for dinners and desserts, respectively. What are total fixed costs if Bryan expects net income to be $425,000?
   b. Douglas Company is projecting sales of $20,000,000 and total fixed manufacturing costs of $4,000,000 for 1997. The company estimates that variable manufacturing costs will be 40 percent of sales. Assuming no change in inventory, what is the company's projected Cost of Goods Sold?
   c. The Classic Cosmetics Company has projected the following information for October 1998:

Sales	$800,000
Gross profit (based on sales)	25%
Increase in Merchandise Inventory in October	$ 60,000
Decrease in trade Accounts Payable for October	$ 24,000

   What are expected cash disbursements for inventories for October 1998?
   d. Juanita's Clocks' preliminary forecast for its product in 1997 is as follows:

Selling price per unit	$ 20
Unit sales	200,000
Variable costs	$1,200,000
Fixed costs	$ 600,000

In preparing the above forecast, Juanita included no advertising expenditures. Based on a market study conducted in December 1996, the firm estimated that it could increase the unit selling price by 15 percent and increase unit sales volume by 10 percent if $200,000 were spent on advertising. If Juanita's Clocks adjusts its forecast by these amounts, what is the projected operating income for 1997?

(CPA adapted)

33. *(Projected income statement)* Last year's income statement for Federico Company is presented below:

Sales (50,000 × $10)		$500,000
Cost of goods sold:		
Direct materials	$200,000	
Direct labor	100,000	
Overhead	50,000	(350,000)
Gross profit		$150,000
Expenses		
Selling	$ 60,000	
Administrative	40,000	(100,000)
Net income before taxes		$ 50,000

Sales are expected to decrease by 10 percent, and material and labor costs are expected to increase by 10 percent. Overhead is applied to production based on a percentage of direct labor costs. Ten thousand dollars of selling expenses are considered fixed. The balance varies with sales dollars. All administrative costs are fixed.

Management desires to earn 5 percent on sales this year and will adjust the unit selling price, if necessary. Develop a pro forma income statement for the year for Federico Company that incorporates the indicated changes.

34. *(Budgeted income, cash, and accounts receivable)* In preparing its budget for July 1997, Management Consultants Company has the following accounts receivable information available:

Accounts Receivable at June 30	$700,000
Estimated credit sales for July	800,000
Estimated collections in July for credit sales in July and prior months	640,000
Estimated write-offs in July for uncollectible credit sales	32,000
Estimated provision for uncollectible accounts for credit sales in July	24,000

a. What is the projected balance of Accounts Receivable at July 31, 1997?
b. Which of the above amounts (if any) will affect the cash budget?
c. Which of the above amounts (if any) will affect the pro forma income statement for July?

(CPA adapted)

35. *(Pro forma income statement)* Greenville Novelty Wholesale Store has prepared the following budget information for May 1998:
- Sales of $300,000. All sales are on account and a provision for bad debts is made monthly at 3 percent of sales.
- Inventory was $70,000 on April 30 and an increase of $10,000 is planned for May.
- All inventory is marked to sell at cost plus 50 percent.
- Estimated cash disbursements for selling and administrative expenses for the month are $40,000.
- Depreciation for May is projected at $5,000.

Prepare a pro forma income statement for Greenville Novelty Wholesale Store for May 1998.

(CPA adapted)

36. *(Pro forma income)* Sara Tucker, president of Westcoast Bungee Cords, is considering buying a new piece of equipment for her plant. This piece of equipment will increase her fixed overhead by $300,000 per year, but reduce her variable expenses per unit of production by 35 percent. Budgeted sales of bungee cords for 1998 are 120,000 feet at an average selling price of $25 per foot. Variable expenses are currently 75 percent of selling price and fixed costs total $400,000 per year. Assuming that Sara acquires the new piece of equipment, answer the following questions.
   a. What is the projected variable cost per foot of cord?
   b. What are the projected fixed costs per year?
   c. What is the expected operating profit if actual sales are equal to budgeted sales?
   d. Should Sara acquire the equipment?

COMMUNICATION ACTIVITIES

37. *(Key variables)* A consultant mentioned to Alpha Company's CEO that key variables are significant if the company is to control its destiny. The CEO has asked you to prepare a brief memo explaining what the consultant meant.

38. *(Continuous budgeting)* You own a small boat manufacturing company. At a recent manufacturers' association meeting, you overheard one of the other company owners saying how he liked using a continuous budgeting process. Discuss what you believe are the advantages and disadvantages of continuous budgeting for your company in a report to your top management group.

39. *(Planning versus control)* Your colleague, who loves riddles, has asked you the following question: "Is planning an extension of control or is control an extension of planning?" Prepare a reply.

40. *(Cash collections)* *The Girl Scouts Councils around the United States rely principally on annual cookie sales for the income to support their activities. In 1993, the San Francisco Council found itself with record levels of bounced checks from cookie customers. Bad checks for 1993 amounted to $35,000, as compared to only $21,000 for 1992. Other California Councils experienced similar increases in rubber checks.*

   [SOURCE: Dan Reed, "Cookie Buyers Stiff Girl Scouts," *The (New Orleans) Times-Picayune* (April 18, 1993), p. A-15. © The Times-Picayune Publishing Corporation.]

   a. How could the Girl Scouts Councils protect themselves against the possibility of receiving bad checks?
   b. The Girl Scouts organization seemed to be surprised by the level of bad checks received in 1993. How could the Councils improve their planning process to predict the amount of bad checks that will be received in a given year?

41. *(Budgeting process)* *Budgets require a certain amount of negotiation among managers as part of the budget process. The time spent in these negotiations, however, can become excessive. Executives should ask whether the time spent by managers on budget activities really benefits the company. Consider the case of the mid-level manager at a large company who spent one day each month on budget activities. She devoted an additional 10 working days each year to the annual budgeting process—a total of 22 working days per year, or approximately one working month per year! Did the budget contribute enough additional profits to compensate for the loss of one month of the manager's time?*

   [SOURCE: Germain B. Böer, "Making Accounting a Value-Added Activity," *Management Accounting* (August 1991), pp. 37–38. Published by Institute of Management Accountants, Montvale, N.J.]

    a. Discuss your perceptions as to how these "budgeting days" would affect the quality of the other work that was within the scope of this mid-level manager.

    b. If one considers the time spent by the manager in this situation to be a "cost" of participatory budgeting, what are the benefits that potentially offset this cost?

    c. How can budget participation have a positive effect on the quality of products produced by firms?

PROBLEMS

42. *(Production and purchases budgets)* Purely Entertainment has prepared the following unit sales forecast for 1997:

	JANUARY–JUNE	JULY–DECEMBER	TOTAL
Sales	380,000	420,000	800,000

Estimated ending finished goods inventories are 30,000 units at December 31, 1996; 76,000 units at June 30; and 90,000 units at December 31, 1997.

    In manufacturing each unit of this product, Purely Entertainment uses 5 pounds of Material A and 3 gallons of Material B. The company carries no Work in Process Inventory. Direct material ending inventories are projected as follows:

	DECEMBER 31,1996	JUNE 30, 1997	DECEMBER 31, 1997
Material A (in pounds)	200,000	250,000	300,000
Material B (in gallons)	140,000	160,000	200,000

Prepare a production and purchases budget for 1997.

43. *(Production, purchases, cash disbursements)* Boston Tea Company has budgeted sales of 200,000 cans of iced tea mix during June 1997 and 375,000 cans during July. Production of the mix requires 14 ounces of tea and 2 ounces of sugar. Beginning inventories of tea and sugar are as follows:

Iced tea mix	4,300 cans of finished product
Tea	2,750 pounds
Sugar	600 pounds

    Boston Tea Company generally carries an inventory of 3 percent of the following month's needs for finished goods. Raw materials are stocked in relation to finished goods ending inventory. Assuming the desired ending inventory stock is achieved, answer the following questions.

    a. How many cans of iced tea mix need to be produced in June?

    b. How many ounces of tea need to be purchased in June? (There are 16 ounces in a pound.)

    c. How many pounds of sugar need to be purchased in June?

    d. If tea and sugar cost $4.50 and $.30 per pound respectively, what dollar amount of purchases is budgeted for June?

    e. If Boston Tea Company normally pays for 30 percent of its budgeted purchases during the month of purchase and takes a 2 percent discount, what are budgeted cash disbursements for June purchases during June?

44. *(Production, purchases, and cash budgets)* Pop's Tops makes one style of men's hats. Sales and collections for the first 3 months of 1998 are expected to be

	JANUARY	FEBRUARY	MARCH	TOTAL
Sales quantity	3,200	2,600	3,700	9,500
Revenue	$57,600	$46,800	$66,600	$171,000
Collections	$58,080	$48,960	$62,640	$169,680

The December 31, 1997, balance sheet revealed the following selected balances: Cash, $18,760; Raw Materials Inventory, $3,812.50; Finished Goods Inventory, $10,500; and Accounts Payable, $3,800. The Raw Materials Inventory balance represents 457.50 yards of felt and 12,200 inches of ribbon. The Finished Goods Inventory consists of 800 hats.

During the first quarter of 1998, management expects that all work started within a month will be finished within that month, so no work in process is anticipated.

Management plans to have enough hats on hand at the end of each month to satisfy 25 percent of the subsequent month's sales. In this regard, the company predicts both production and sales of 3,600 hats in April.

Each hat requires 3/4 of a yard of felt and 20 inches of ribbon. Felt costs $7 per yard and ribbon costs $.05 per inch. Ending inventory policy for raw materials is 20 percent of the next month's production.

The company normally pays for 80 percent of a month's purchases of raw materials in the month of purchase (on which it takes a 2 percent cash discount). The remaining 20 percent is paid in full in the month following the month of purchase.

The cost of direct labor is budgeted at $3 per hat produced and is paid in the month of production. Total out-of-pocket factory overhead can be predicted as $5,200 per month plus $2.25 per hat produced. Total nonfactory cash costs are equal to $2,800 per month plus 10 percent of sales revenue. All factory and nonfactory cash expenses are paid in the month of incurrence. In addition, the company plans to make an estimated quarterly tax payment of $5,000 and pay executive bonuses of $15,000 in January 1998.

The management of Pop's Tops wishes to have a minimum of $12,000 of cash at the end of each month. If the company has to borrow funds, it will do so in $1,000 multiples at the beginning of a month at a 12 percent annual interest rate. Loans are to be repaid at the beginning of a month in multiples of $1,000. Interest is only paid when a repayment is made.

a. Prepare a production budget by month and in total for the first quarter of 1998.

b. Prepare a raw materials purchases budget by month and in total for the first quarter of 1998.

c. Prepare a schedule of cash payments for purchases by month and in total for the first quarter of 1998. The Accounts Payable balance on December 31, 1997, represents the unpaid 20 percent of December purchases.

d. Prepare a combined payments schedule for factory overhead and nonfactory cash costs for each month and in total for the first quarter of 1998.

e. Prepare a cash budget for each month and in total for the first quarter of 1998.

45. *(Cash budget)* The January 31, 1996, balance sheet of Jane's Trophies follows:

ASSETS		LIABILITIES AND STOCKHOLDERS' EQUITY		
Cash	$ 12,000	Accounts Payable		$ 58,400
Accounts Receivable (Net of Allowance for Uncollectibles of $2,000)	34,000			
Inventory	52,400	Common Stock	$90,000	
Plant Assets (Net of Accumulated Depreciation of $60,000)	36,000	Retained Earnings (Deficit)	(14,000)	76,000
Total Assets	$134,400	Total Liabilities and Stockholders' Equity		$134,400

Additional information about the company includes the following:
- Expected sales for February and March are $120,000 and $130,000, respectively.
- The collection pattern from the month of sale forward is 50 percent, 48 percent, and 2 percent uncollectible.
- Cost of goods sold is 75 percent of sales.
- Purchases each month are 55 percent of the current month's sales and 45 percent of the next month's projected sales. All purchases are paid for in full in the month following purchase.
- Other cash expenses each month are $21,500. The only noncash expense each month is $4,000 of depreciation.

a. What are budgeted cash collections for February 1997?
b. What will be the Inventory balance at February 28, 1997?
c. What will be the projected balance in Retained Earnings at February 28, 1997?
d. If the company wishes to maintain a minimum cash balance of $8,000, how much will be available for investment or need to be borrowed at the end of February 1997?

46. *(Cash budget)* Bill's Department Store typically makes 50 percent of its sales on credit. Sales are billed twice monthly, on the 10th of the month for the last half of the prior month's sales and on the 20th of the month for the first half of the current month's sales. All sales are made with terms of 2/10, n/30. Based on past experience, Accounts Receivable are collected as follows:

Within the discount period	80%
On the 30th day	18%
Uncollectible	2%

Sales for May 1997 were $600,000 and projected sales for the next four months are

June	$800,000
July	700,000
August	800,000
September	600,000

Bill's average profit margin on its products is 30 percent of selling price.

Bill's purchases merchandise for resale to meet the current month's sales demand and to maintain a desired monthly ending inventory of 25 percent of the next month's sales. All purchases are on account with terms of n/30. Bill's pays for one-half of a month's purchases in the month of purchase and the other half in the month following the purchase. All sales and purchases occur evenly throughout the month.

a. How much cash can Bill's plan to collect from Accounts Receivable during July 1997?
b. How much cash can Bill's plan to collect in September 1997 from sales made in August?
c. What will be the budgeted dollar value of Bill's inventory on August 31, 1997?
d. How much merchandise should Bill's plan to purchase during June 1997?
e. What are Bill's budgeted cash payments for merchandise during August 1997?

(CMA adapted)

47. *(Cash budget)* Bixby Manufacturing has incurred substantial losses for several years and has decided to declare bankruptcy. The company petitioned the court for protection from creditors on March 31, 1995, and submitted the following balance sheet:

Bixby Manufacturing
Balance Sheet
March 31, 1996

	Book Value	Liquidation Value
Assets:		
Accounts Receivable	$100,000	$ 50,000
Inventories	90,000	40,000
Plant Assets (Net)	150,000	160,000
Totals	$340,000	$250,000

The liabilities and stockholders' equity of Bixby at this date are

Accounts Payable—General Creditors	$600,000
Common Stock	60,000
Retained Earnings Deficit	(320,000)
Total	$340,000

Bixby's management informed the court that the company has developed a new product and that a prospective customer is willing to sign a contract for the purchase of 10,000 units of this product during the year ending March 31, 1997, 12,000 units during the year ending March 31, 1998, and 15,000 units during the year ending March 31, 1999, at a firm price of $90 per unit for all units. This product can be manufactured using Bixby's present facilities. Monthly production with immediate delivery is expected to be uniform within each year. Receivables are expected to be collected during the calendar month following sales. Unit production costs of the new product are estimated as follows:

Direct materials	$20
Direct labor	30
Variable overhead	10

Fixed costs of $130,000 (excluding depreciation) are estimated per year. Purchases of direct materials will be paid during the calendar month following purchase. Fixed costs, direct labor, and variable overhead will be paid as incurred. Inventory of direct materials will be equal to 60 days' usage. After the first month of operations, 30 days' usage will be ordered each month.

The general creditors have agreed to reduce their total claims to 60% of their March 31, 1996, balances under the following conditions:

■ Existing accounts receivable and inventories are to be liquidated immediately, with the proceeds turned over to the general creditors.
■ The reduced balance of accounts payable is to be paid as cash is generated from future operations, but in no event later than March 31, 1998. No interest will be paid on these obligations.

Under this proposed plan, the general creditors would receive $110,000 more than the current liquidation value of Bixby's assets. The court has engaged you to determine the feasibility of this plan.

Ignoring any need to borrow and repay short-term funds for working capital purposes, prepare a cash budget for the years ending March 31, 1997 and 1998, showing the cash expected to be available to pay the claims of the general creditors, payments to general creditors, and the cash remaining after payment of claims.

(CPA)

48. *(Budgeted sales and S&A; other computations)* Exotic Statues has projected Cost of Goods Sold for June 1997 of $925,000. Of this amount, $60,000 represents fixed overhead costs. Total variable costs for the company each month average 70 percent of sales. The company's cost to retail (CGS to sales) percentage is 60 percent and the company normally shows a 15 percent rate of net income on

sales. All purchases and expenses (except depreciation) are paid in cash: 55 percent in the month incurred and 45 percent in the following month. Depreciation is $20,000 per month.

a. What are Exotic Statues' expected sales for June?

b. What are Exotic Statues' expected variable selling and administrative costs for June?

c. What is Exotic Statues' normal contribution margin ratio?

d. What are Exotic Statues' total fixed costs?

e. Exotic Statues normally collects 45 percent of its sales in the month of sale and the rest in the next month. What are cash receipts and disbursements related only to June's transactions?

49. *(Pro forma results)* The Rabb Company is attempting to set a new selling price for its single product, a metal file cabinet, for the upcoming year. The current variable cost is $40 per unit and total fixed costs are $2,000,000. Fixed manufacturing costs are 80 percent of total fixed costs and are allocated to the product based on the number of units produced. There are no variable selling or administrative costs. Variable and fixed costs are expected to increase by 15 percent and 8 percent, respectively, next year. Estimated production and sales are 200,000 units. Selling price is normally set at full production cost plus 25 percent.

a. What is the expected full production cost per unit of Rabb's file cabinets for next year?

b. What is the expected selling price of the product?

c. What is pro forma income before tax using the selling price computed in part b?

d. What would be the required selling price for the company to earn income before tax equal to 25 percent of sales?

50. *(Comprehensive)* Better Appliance Company produces and sells two kitchen appliances: Mixers and Doughmakers. In July 1996, Better's budget department gathered the following data to meet budget requirements for 1997.

1997 PROJECTED SALES

PRODUCT	UNITS	PRICE
Mixers	60,000	$ 50
Doughmakers	40,000	120

1997 INVENTORIES (UNITS)

PRODUCT	EXPECTED 1/1/97	DESIRED 12/13/97
Mixers	15,000	20,000
Doughmakers	4,000	5,000

To produce one unit of each product, the following major internal components are used (in addition to the plastic housing for products, which is subcontracted in a subsequent operation):

COMPONENT	MIXER	DOUGHMAKER
Motor	1	1
Beater	2	4
Fuse	2	3

Projected data for 1997 with respect to components are as follows:

COMPONENT	ANTICIPATED PURCHASE PRICE	EXPECTED INVENTORY 1/1/97	DESIRED INVENTORY 12/31/97
Motor	$15.00	2,000	3,600 pounds
Beater	$ 1.25	21,000	24,000 pounds
Fuse	$ 2.00	6,000	7,500 units

Projected direct labor requirements for 1997 and rates are as follows:

PRODUCT	HOURS PER UNIT	RATE PER HOUR
Mixers	2	$7
Doughmakers	3	$9

Overhead is applied at a rate of $5 per direct labor hour.

Based on the above projections and budget requirements for 1997 for Mixers and Doughmakers, prepare the following budgets for 1997:

a. Sales budget (in dollars).
b. Production budget (in units).
c. Internal components purchases budget (in quantities).
d. Internal components purchases budget (in dollars).
e. Direct labor budget (in dollars).

(CPA adapted)

51. *(Master budget preparation)* Cheyenne Chemical Company manufactures a red industrial dye. The company is preparing its 1997 master budget and has presented you with the following information.

1. The December 31, 1996, balance sheet for the company is shown below.

Cheyenne Chemical Company
Balance Sheet
December 31, 1996

Assets			**Liabilities and Stockholders' Equity**		
Cash		$ 5,080	Notes Payable		$ 25,000
Accounts Receivable		26,500	Accounts Payable		2,148
Raw Materials Inventory		800	Dividends Payable		10,000
Finished Goods Inventory		2,104	Total Liabilities		$ 37,148
Prepaid Insurance		1,200	Common Stock $100,000		
Building	$300,000		Paid-in Capital 50,000		
Accumulated			Retained		
Depreciation	(20,000)	280,000	Earnings 128,536		278,536
			Total Liability and Stock-		
Total Assets		$315,684	holders' Equity		$315,684

2. The Accounts Receivable balance at 12/31/96 represents the remaining balances of November and December credit sales. Sales were $70,000 and $65,000, respectively, in those two months.

3. Estimated sales in gallons of dye for January through May 1997 are shown below.

January	8,000
February	10,000
March	15,000
April	12,000
May	11,000

Each gallon of dye sells for $12.

4. The collection pattern for accounts receivable is as follows: 70 percent in the month of sale; 20 percent in the first month after the sale; 10 percent in the second month after the sale. Cheyenne Chemical expects no bad debts and no customers are given cash discounts.

5. Each gallon of dye has the following standard quantities and costs for direct materials and direct labor:

1.2 gallons of direct materials (some evaporation occurs during	
processing) @ $.80 per gallon	$ .96
1/2 hour of direct labor @ $6 per hour	3.00

Variable overhead is applied to the product on a machine-hour basis. It takes 5 hours of machine time to process 1 gallon of dye. The variable overhead rate is $.06 per machine hour; VOH consists entirely of utility costs. Total annual fixed overhead is $120,000; it is applied at $1.00 per gallon based on an expected annual capacity of 120,000 gallons. Fixed overhead per year is composed of the following costs:

Salaries	$78,000
Utilities	12,000
Insurance—factory	2,400
Depreciation—factory	27,600

Fixed overhead is incurred evenly throughout the year.

6. There is no beginning inventory of Work in Process. All work in process is completed in the period in which it is started. Raw Materials Inventory at the beginning of the year consists of 1,000 gallons of direct materials at a standard cost of $.80 per gallon. There are 400 gallons of dye in Finished Goods Inventory at the beginning of the year carried at a standard cost of $5.26 per gallon: Direct Materials, $.96; Direct Labor, $3.00; Variable Overhead, $.30; and Fixed Overhead, $1.00.

7. Accounts Payable relates solely to raw materials. Accounts payable are paid 60 percent in the month of purchase and 40 percent in the month after purchase. No discounts are given for prompt payment.

8. The dividend will be paid in January 1997.

9. A new piece of equipment costing $9,000 will be purchased on March 1, 1997. Payment of 80 percent will be made in March and 20 percent in April. The equipment will have no salvage value and has a useful life of 3 years.

10. The note payable has a 12 percent interest rate; interest is paid at the end of each month.

11. Cheyenne Chemical's management has set a minimum cash balance at $5,000. Investments and borrowings are made in even $100 amounts. Investments will earn 9 percent per year.

12. The ending inventory of Finished Goods Inventory should be 5 percent of the next month's needs. This is not true at the beginning of 1997 due to a miscalculation in sales for December. The ending inventory of raw materials should be 5 percent of the next month's needs.

13. Selling and administrative costs per month are as follows: salaries, $18,000; rent, $7,000; and utilities, $800. These costs are paid in cash as they are incurred.

Prepare a master budget for each month of the first quarter of 1997 and pro forma financial statements as of the end of the first quarter of 1997.

CASES

52. *(Preparing and analyzing a budget)* Harvey & Company, a local accounting firm, has a formal budgeting system. The firm is comprised of five partners, two managers, four seniors, two secretaries, and two bookkeepers. The budgeting process has a bottom-line focus; i.e., the budget and planning process continues to iterate and evolve until an acceptable budgeted net income is obtained. The determination of an acceptable level of net income is based on two factors: (1) the amount of salary the partners could generate if they were employed elsewhere, and (2) a reasonable return on the partners' investment in the firm's net assets.

For 1998, after careful consideration of alternative employment opportunities, the partners agreed that the best alternative employment would generate the following salaries:

Partner 1	$150,000
Partner 2	225,000
Partner 3	110,000
Partner 4	90,000
Partner 5	125,000
Total	$700,000

The second input to determination of the desired net income level is more complex. This part of the desired net income is based on the value of the net assets owned by the accounting firm. The partners have identified two major categories of assets: tangible assets and intangible assets. The partners have agreed that the net tangible assets are worth $230,000. The intangible assets, consisting mostly of the accounting practice itself, are worth 1.1 times gross fees billed in 1997. In 1997, the firm's gross billings were $1,615,000. The partners have also agreed that a reasonable rate of return on the net assets of the accounting firm is 12 percent. Thus, the partners' desired net income from return on investment is as follows:

Tangible assets	$ 230,000
Intangible assets ($1,615,000 × 110%)	1,776,500
Total investment	$2,006,500
Times rate of return	× .12
Equals required dollar return	$ 240,780

The experience of the accounting firm indicates that other operating costs are incurred as follows:

FIXED EXPENSES (PER YEAR):

| Salaries (other than partners) | $300,000 |
| Overhead | 125,000 |

VARIABLE EXPENSES:

| Overhead | 15% of gross billings |
| Client service | 5% of gross billings |

[SOURCE: Adapted from Jerry S. Huss, "Better Budgeting for CPA Firms," *Journal of Accountancy* (November 1977), pp. 65–72.]

a. Determine the minimum level of gross billings that would allow the partners to realize their net income objective. Prepare a budget of costs and revenues at that level.

b. If the partners believe that the level of billings you have projected in part a is not feasible given the time constraints at the partner, manager, and senior levels, what changes can they make to the budget to preserve the desired level of net income?

53. *(Preparing a cash budget)* Collegiate Management Education (CME), Inc., is a nonprofit organization that sponsors a wide variety of management seminars throughout the Southwest. In addition, it is heavily involved in research into improved methods of teaching and motivating college administrators. The seminar activity is largely supported by fees, and the research program is supported from membership dues.

CME operates on a calendar year basis and is finalizing the budget for 1997. The following information has been taken from approved plans, which are still tentative at this time:

SEMINAR PROGRAM

Revenue—The scheduled number of programs should produce $12,000,000 of revenue for the year. Each program is budgeted to produce the same amount of revenue. The revenue is collected during the month the program is offered. The programs are scheduled during the basic academic year and are not held during June, July, August, and December. Twelve percent of the revenue is generated in each of the first 5 months of the year and the remainder is distributed evenly during September, October, and November.

Direct expenses—The seminar expenses are made up of three types:

- Instructors' fees are paid at the rate of 70 percent of seminar revenue in the month following the seminar. The instructors are considered independent contractors and are not eligible for CME employee benefits.
- Facilities fees total $5,600,000 for the year. They are the same for each program and are paid in the month the program is given.
- Annual promotional costs of $1,000,000 are spent equally in all months except June and July when there is no promotional effort.

RESEARCH PROGRAM

Research grants—The research program has a large number of projects nearing completion. The main research activity this year includes feasibility studies for new projects to be started in 1998. As a result, the total grant expense of $3,000,000 for 1997 is expected to be paid out at the rate of $500,000 per month during the first 6 months of the year.

SALARIES AND OTHER CME EXPENSES

- Office lease—Annual amount of $240,000 paid monthly at the beginning of each month.
- General administrative expenses—$1,500,000 annually or $125,000 per month. These are paid in cash as incurred.
- Depreciation expense—$240,000 per year.
- General CME promotion—annual cost of $600,000, paid monthly.
- Salaries and benefits are as follows:

NUMBER OF EMPLOYEES	MONTHLY CASH SALARY	TOTAL ANNUAL SALARIES
1	$50,000	$ 50,000
3	40,000	120,000
4	30,000	120,000
15	25,000	375,000
5	15,000	75,000
22	10,000	220,000
50		$960,000

Employee benefits amount to $240,000 or 25 percent of annual salaries. Except for the pension contribution, the benefits are paid as salaries are paid. The annual pension payment of $24,000, based on 2.5 percent of total annual salaries, is due on April 15, 1997.

OTHER INFORMATION

- Membership income—CME has 100,000 members who each pay an annual fee of $100. The fee for the calendar year is invoiced in late June.
- The collection schedule is as follows: July, 60 percent; August, 30 percent; September, 5 percent; and June, 5 percent.
- Capital expenditures—The capital expenditures program calls for a total of $510,000 in cash payments to be spread evenly over the first 5 months of 1997.
- Cash and temporary investments at January 1, 1997, are estimated at $750,000.

a. Prepare a budget of the annual cash receipts and disbursements for 1997.

b. Prepare a cash budget for CME for January 1997.

c. Using the information developed in parts a and b, identify two important operating problems of CME.

(CMA adapted)

54. *(Revising and analyzing an operating budget)* The Mason Agency, a division of General Service Industries, offers consulting services to clients for a fee. The corporate management at General Service is pleased with the performance of the Mason Agency for the first 9 months of the current year and has recommended that the division manager of the Mason Agency, Ramona Howell, submit a revised forecast for the remaining quarter, because the division has exceeded the annual year-to-date plan by 20 percent of operating income. An unexpected increase in billed hour volume over the original plan is the main reason for this gain in income. The original operating budget for the first three quarters for the Mason Agency is presented below.

1997 OPERATING BUDGET

	1ST QUARTER	2ND QUARTER	3RD QUARTER	TOTAL 9 MONTHS
Revenue:				
Consulting fees				
Management consulting	$315,000	$315,000	$315,000	$ 945,000
EDP consulting	421,875	421,875	421,875	1,265,625
Total	$736,875	$736,875	$736,875	$2,210,625
Other revenue	10,000	10,000	10,000	30,000
Total	$746,875	$746,875	$746,875	$2,240,625
Expenses:				
Consultant salaries	$386,750	$386,750	386,750	$1,160,250
Travel and entertainment	45,625	45,625	45,625	136,875
Administrative	100,000	100,000	100,000	300,000
Depreciation	40,000	40,000	40,000	120,000
Corporate allocation	50,000	50,000	50,000	150,000
Total	$622,375	$622,375	$622,375	$1,867,125
Operating income	$124,500	$124,500	$124,500	$ 373,500

When comparing the actuals for the first three quarters to the original plan, Howell analyzed the variances and will reflect the following information in her revised forecast for the fourth quarter.

The division currently has 25 consultants on staff, 10 for management consulting and 15 for EDP consulting, and has hired three additional management consultants to start work at the beginning of the fourth quarter to meet the increased client demand.

The hourly billing rate for consulting revenues will remain at $90 per hour for each management consultant and $75 per hour for each EDP consultant. However, due to the favorable increase in billing hour volume when compared to the plan, the hours for each consultant will be increased by 50 hours per quarter. New employees are equally as capable as current employees and will be billed at the same rates.

The budgeted annual salaries and actual annual salaries, paid monthly, are the same at $50,000 for a management consultant and 8 percent less for an EDP consultant. Corporate management has approved a merit increase of 10 percent at the beginning of the fourth quarter for all 25 existing consultants, but the new consultants will be compensated at the planned rate.

The planned salary expense includes a provision for employee fringe benefits amounting to 30 percent of the annual salaries; however, the improvement of some corporatewide employee programs will increase the fringe benefit allocation to 40 percent.

The original plan assumes a fixed hourly rate for travel and other related expenses for each billing hour of consulting. These are expenses that are not reimbursed by the client, and the previously determined hourly rate has proven to be adequate to cover these costs.

Other revenues are derived from temporary rentals and interest income and remain unchanged for the fourth quarter.

Administrative expenses have been favorable at 7 percent below the plan; this 7 percent savings on fourth-quarter expenses will be reflected in the revised plan.

Depreciation for office equipment and microcomputers will stay constant at the projected straight-line rate.

Due to the favorable experience for the first three quarters and the division's increased ability to absorb costs, the corporate management at General Service Industries has increased the corporate expense allocation by 50 percent.

a. Prepare a revised operating budget for the fourth quarter for the Mason Agency that Ramona Howell will present to General Service Industries. Be sure to furnish supporting calculations for all revised revenue and expense amounts.

b. Discuss the reasons why an organization would prepare a revised forecast.

c. Discuss your feelings about the 50 percent increase in corporate expense allocations.

(CMA adapted)

ETHICS AND QUALITY DISCUSSION

55. *The Chicago Archdiocese of the Catholic Church was mired in a $47 million deficit in 1989. Contributions to the various churches were declining and costs were skyrocketing. A committee recommended that numerous layoffs be made and that parishes be required to "submit three year budgets and quarterly financial reports. Pastors exceeding their budgets are called in for consultation and urged to cut expenses [in an effort to begin] implementing basic business practices. Such changes helped to slice the deficit by 40% to $29 million [in 1990]."*

[SOURCE: Kevin Kelly, "Chicago's Catholic Church: Putting Its House in Order," *Business Week* (June 10, 1991), p. 61.]

a. Why should not-for-profits (including churches) need to prepare detailed budgets and be required to follow them?

b. Consider some instances in the past involving various churches that were striving to achieve certain specified financial goals. What impact did those financial targets have on the ethical behavior of the ministers and some board members of those churches?

c. Would there be certain instances in which pastors who exceeded their budgeted expenses should not be urged to cut those expenses? Discuss the rationale for your answer.

56. *Chambers Development Co.'s founder, John G. Rangos Sr., demanded results no matter where they came from. "Go find the rest of it," he told an executive in 1990 after the executive said profit would fall short of projections.*

The charade collapsed [on June 20, 1991] when an outside audit disclosed that in every year since Chambers went public in 1985, the company reported strong profits but actually lost money. Now, a chastened Chambers, once hailed on Wall Street as a waste-management star, has restated net income for each of the past seven years to reduce its reported profits by $362 million on an after-tax basis.

Mr. Rangos and his two sons hold a sizable equity stake in the company. Former and current managers describe Mr. Rangos as a man obsessed with making his garbage company a star and insistent on managers meeting his lofty profit goals.

[SOURCE: Gabriella Stern, "Audit Report Shows How Far Chambers Would Go for Profits," *Wall Street Journal* (October 21, 1992), p. A1. Reprinted by permission of *The Wall Street Journal,* © 1992 Dow Jones & Company, Inc. All Rights Reserved Worldwide.]

a. Discuss whether it is more likely that Chambers Development used an imposed or participatory budgeting process. Explain the rationale for your answer.

b. How might it have been possible for managers to "find" additional profits? Why would such "found profits" not have been discovered by the auditors?

c. Why would the managers be willing to "find" the additional profits?

d. At some point should the ethics of the managers have outweighed the notion of budget performance responsibility? Why?

57. *Many managers believe that, if all amounts in their budgets are not spent during a period, they will lose allocations in future periods and that little or no recognition will result from cost savings. The figure below indicates results of a survey of IMA members about the motivating factors behind budgeting issues.*

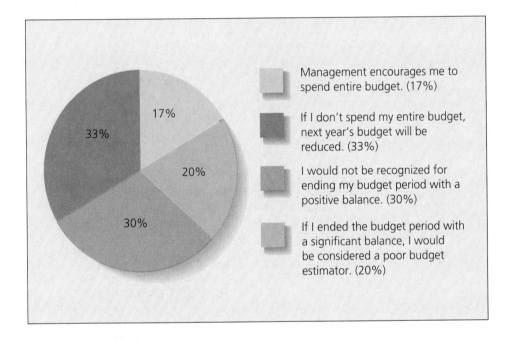

[SOURCE: Gerald L. Finch and William Mihal, "Spend It or Lose It," *Management Accounting* (March 1989), p. 45. Reprinted from *Management Accounting*. Copyright by Institute of Management Accountants, Montvale, NJ.]

Discuss the behavioral and ethical issues involved in a spend-it or-lose-it attitude. Include in your discussion the issue of negotiating budget allocation requests prior to the beginning of the period.

58. Find the web page for the BMA Group. Review the services offered by the firm and write a summary of how the services might be utilized by a retailer to improve its planning and budgeting processes.

59. Find the budget for the U.S. government on the web. Read the portion of the budget that discusses the assumptions on which the budget is based. Write a report summarizing the five most important assumptions (in your opinion) and the likely effects of an error in each assumption on the budgetary amounts.

60. Find the web page for the International Red Cross. Review the variety of activities in which this organization is currently involved. What would be the greatest challenges in budgeting for such an organization? What actions has the organization taken to deal with its budgeting challenges?

INTERNET ACTIVITIES

COST
CONTROL

CHAPTER

15

Introduction to Cost Management Systems

LEARNING OBJECTIVES

After completing this chapter, you should be able to answer the following questions:

1. Why do organizations have management control systems?

2. What is a cost management system and what are its primary goals?

3. What major factors influence the design of a cost management system?

4. Why are organizational form, structure, and culture important considerations in designing a cost management system?

5. How do the internal and external operating environments affect the cost management system?

6. What three groups of elements affect the design of a cost management system and how are these elements used?

7. How is gap analysis used in the implementation of a cost management system?

Group Michelin

Michelin's history is closely linked to that of the pneumatic tire and the company has innovated constantly since the registration of its first patent in 1889. The invention of the radial tire by Michelin in 1946 is seen as a major technological revolution in the transport industry. . . .

Michelin's growth in the last 30 years has taken it from tenth world ranking in 1960 to number one [in 1989], with approximately 19% of the world tire sales in 1994. In the same period, Group tire output has multiplied by six. . . .

[The company] specializes in the manufacture of tires and inner tubes for passenger cars, trucks, motorcycles, bicycles, aircraft, earthmoving equipment and agricultural vehicles. . . . Over the years, by improving the quality of its basic materials, by improving manufacturing processes and through innovations in tire architecture, tread pattern and design, Michelin has constantly developed the use of the radial technique, enlarging the range of its applications and with a product diversification to meet the needs of all types of users. . . .

As of 1995, Michelin had:

- 115,000 employees
- Commercial offices in 170 countries
- 70 factories in 15 countries in Africa, Asia, Europe, North America and South America
- Technology Centers for research (France, Japan, and the U.S.A.) and Testing Centers (France, Japan, Spain, and the U.S.A.)
- 5 rubber plantations in Brazil and Nigeria
- Daily worldwide production of 698,000 tires; 100,700 inner tubes; 1,065 tons of steel; 4 million kilometers of cable; 46,000 wheels; and 60,000 maps and guides

SOURCE: Michelin, *1995 Annual Report*, pp. 4, 5, and 7.

Top management of Group Michelin is aware that a system of cost management and other control systems need to evolve as a business grows and becomes more complex. Information systems that are too centralized to provide relevant information to individual business segment managers will not allow needed organizational changes to occur and new strategies to be investigated and pursued.

This chapter introduces concepts relevant to the design of a cost management system as an integral part of an organization's overall management information and control systems. An emphasis is placed on the main factors that determine the structure and success of a cost management system, factors that influence the design of such a system, and the elements that comprise the system.

The next section provides a broad introduction to management information and control systems. It provides a foundation and context for understanding the roles of the cost management system.

INTRODUCTION TO MANAGEMENT INFORMATION AND CONTROL SYSTEMS

management information system

management control system

EXHIBIT 15–1

Information Flows and Types of Information

A cost management system is part of an overall management information and control system. Exhibit 15–1 illustrates the types of information needed in an organization for individuals to perform their managerial functions. The exhibit also demonstrates the demand from external parties for information from the firm. This text defines a **management information system** (MIS) as a structure of interrelated elements that collects, organizes, and communicates data to managers so they may plan, control, evaluate performance, and make decisions. The emphasis in an MIS is satisfying internal demands for information rather than external demands. In most modern organizations, part or all of the MIS is computerized for ease of access to information, reliability of input and processing, and ability to simulate outcomes of alternative situations. Managers use internally and externally generated information to govern their organizations.

Because one of the managerial functions requiring information is control, the MIS is part of the **management control system** (MCS). As illustrated in Exhibit 15–2, a control system has the following four primary components:

1. A *detector* or *sensor*, which is a measuring device that identifies what is actually happening in the process being controlled.
2. An *assessor*, which is a device for determining the significance of what is happening. Usually, significance is assessed by comparing the information on what is actually happening with some standard or expectation of what should be happening.

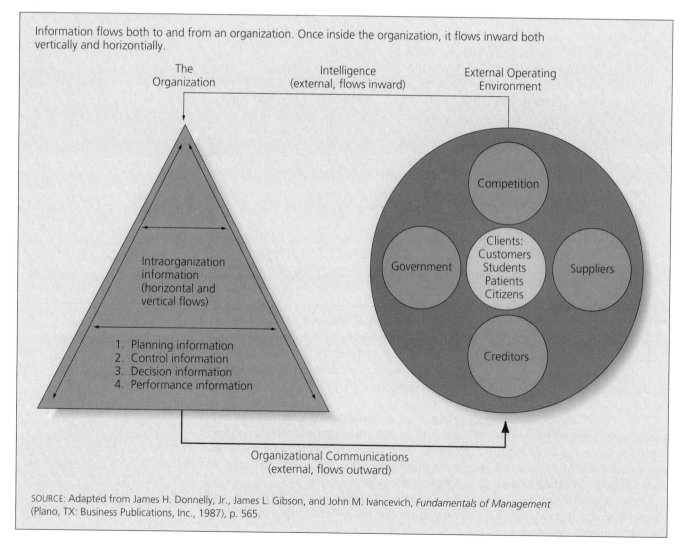

Information flows both to and from an organization. Once inside the organization, it flows inward both vertically and horizontially.

The Organization

Intelligence (external, flows inward)

External Operating Environment

Intraorganization information (horizontal and vertical flows)

1. Planning information
2. Control information
3. Decision information
4. Performance information

Competition

Clients: Customers Students Patients Citizens

Government

Suppliers

Creditors

Organizational Communications (external, flows outward)

SOURCE: Adapted from James H. Donnelly, Jr., James L. Gibson, and John M. Ivancevich, *Fundamentals of Management* (Plano, TX: Business Publications, Inc., 1987), p. 565.

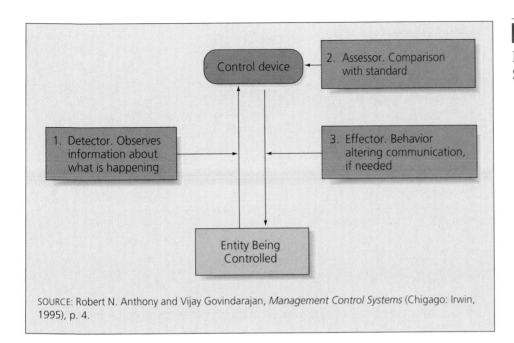

EXHIBIT 15–2

Elements of a Control System

SOURCE: Robert N. Anthony and Vijay Govindarajan, *Management Control Systems* (Chigago: Irwin, 1995), p. 4.

3. An *effector*, which is a device that alters behavior if the assessor indicates the need for doing so. This device is often called "feedback."
4. A *communications network*, which transmits information between the detector and the assessor and between the assessor and the effector.[1]

It is through these system elements that information about actual organizational occurrences is gathered, comparisons are made against plans, changes are effected when necessary, and communications are provided among appropriate parties. For example, source documents (detectors) gather information about sales that is compared to the budgets (assessor). If sales revenues are below the budget, management *may* issue (communications network) a variance report (effector) to encourage the sales staff to increase volume.

However, even given the same information, different managers may take different actions because of alternative interpretations of the information. In this respect, a management control system is not merely mechanical; it requires judgment. Thus, a management control system may be referred to as a black box: an operation whose exact nature cannot be observed.[2] Regardless of the specific actions taken, a management control system should serve to guide a company in designing and implementing strategies such that organizational goals and objectives are achieved.

Most businesses have a variety of control systems in place. For example, a control system may reflect a set of procedures for screening potential suppliers or employees, a set of criteria to evaluate potential and existing investments, or a statistical control process to monitor and evaluate quality. Another important part of the management information and control systems is the cost management system.

A **cost management system** (CMS) consists of a set of formal methods developed for planning and controlling an organization's cost-generating activities relative to its goals and objectives. The evolutionary stages of development for cost management systems are depicted in Exhibit 15–3. Although specific eras are listed for each stage, all stages of development can currently be found in organizations. For instance, infant systems are often found in new organizations or organizations that have not found

DEFINING A COST MANAGEMENT SYSTEM

cost management system

[1] Robert N. Anthony and Vijay Govindarajan, *Management Control Systems* (Chicago: Irwin, 1995), p. 3.
[2] Ibid., p. 6.

EXHIBIT 15–3

Stages of Cost
Management Systems

INFANT SYSTEMS (1900–1920)

Are appropriate when a company

- lacks formal controls
- does not calculate real product costs
- relies on physical inventories to maintain financial systems integrity

TRADITIONAL SYSTEMS (1920–1960)

Are appropriate when a company

- has few product or process changes
- produces few products or services
- is highly labor-intensive

INTEGRATED INFORMATION SYSTEMS (1960–1980)

Are appropriate when a company

- has moderate product or technology changes
- can make use of the available software relative to the company's manufacturing process
- has trained people to operate the system
- has managers who support the integration of operations

COST MANAGEMENT SYSTEMS (1980–FUTURE)

Are appropriate when a company

- incorporates both financial and nonfinancial measures in its performance measurement system
- integrates managerial and operating activities
- links operating position to strategic goals
- links technology, human behavior, and information systems
- desires cost elimination rather than cost allocation
- engages in intergroup coordination and coordinated management
- reflects changing technologies and customer values

SOURCE: Adapted from Robert McIlhattan, "The Path to Total Cost Management," in *Emerging Practices in Cost Management,* ed. Barry J. Brinker (Boston: Warren, Gorham & Lamont, 1990), p. 178. Reprinted with permission from *Emerging Practices in Cost Management,* © 1990, Warren, Gorham & Lamont of the RIA Group, 31 St. James Avenue, reserved.

---

a need to develop their information and control systems; the most advanced systems are found in enterprises that are confronting high-quality, worldwide competition.

A CMS should help managers

- identify the cost of resources consumed in performing significant activities of the firm (accounting models and practices);
- determine the efficiency and effectiveness of the activities performed (performance measurement);
- identify and evaluate new activities that can improve the future performance of the firm (investment management); and
- accomplish the three previous objectives in an environment characterized by changing technology (manufacturing processes).[3]

The information generated from the CMS should benefit all functional areas of the entity, not just accounting. Thus, the system should integrate the areas shown in

---

[3] Reprinted by permission of the publishers from *Cost Management for Today's Advanced Manufacturing* by Callie Berliner and James A. Brimson, eds. (Cambridge, Mass.: Harvard Business School Press, 1988), p. 10. Copyright © 1988 by the President and Fellows of Harvard College.

EXHIBIT 15–4

An Integrated Cost
Management System

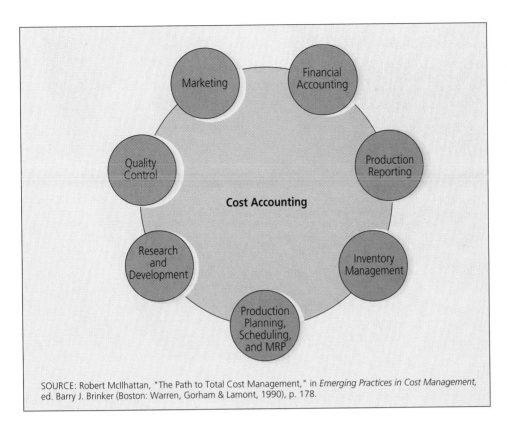

SOURCE: Robert McIlhattan, "The Path to Total Cost Management," in *Emerging Practices in Cost Management*, ed. Barry J. Brinker (Boston: Warren, Gorham & Lamont, 1990), p. 178.

Exhibit 15–4 and should "improve the quality, content, relevance, and timing of cost information that managers use for [either strategic or tactical] decision making."[4]

Crossing all functional areas, a cost management system can be viewed as having six primary goals: (1) develop reasonably accurate product costs, especially through the use of cost drivers; (2) assess product/service life cycle performance; (3) improve understanding of processes and activities; (4) control costs; (5) measure performance; and (6) allow the pursuit of organizational strategies.

First and foremost, a CMS should provide the means to develop reasonably accurate product or service costs. This requires that the system be designed to use cost driver information to trace costs to products and services. The system need not be "the most accurate one, but one which matches benefits of additional accuracy with expenses of achieving additional accuracy. The best system will report approximate but inaccurate product costs, with the degree of approximation determined by the organization's competitive, product, and process environment."[5] Traceability has been made easier by improved information technology, including bar coding.

The product/service costs generated by the cost management system are the input to managerial processes. These costs are used to plan, prepare financial statements, assess individual product/service profitability and period profitability, establish prices for cost-plus contracts, and create a basis for performance measurements. If the input costs generated by the CMS are not reasonably accurate, the output of the preceding processes will be inappropriate for control and decision-making purposes.

Although product/service profitability may be calculated periodically as a requirement for external reporting, the financial accounting system does not reflect life cycle information. The cost management system should provide information about the life

[4] Steven C. Schnoebelen, "Integrating an Advanced Cost Management System into Operating Systems (Part 2)," *Journal of Cost Management* (Spring 1993), p. 60.
[5] Robin Cooper and Robert S. Kaplan, *The Design of Cost Management Systems* (Englewood Cliffs, NJ: Prentice-Hall, 1991), p. 4.

In most large companies, the management information systems are computerized. To be useful, these systems must provide rapid access to relevant and reliable data that can be analyzed and processed into information for numerous purposes and, for UPS, in numerous locations.

cycle performance of a product or service. Without life cycle information, managers will not have a basis to relate costs incurred in one stage of the life cycle to costs and profitability of other stages. For example, managers may not recognize that strong investment in the development and design stage of the life cycle could provide significant rewards in later stages by minimizing engineering change order costs and potential internal and external failure costs. Further, if development/design cost is not traced to the related product or service, managers may not be able to recognize organizational investment "disasters." Lastly, companies engaging in target costing must set the allowable cost based on life cycle, rather than period-by-period, relationships among price, profit margin, and cost.

A cost management system should help managers comprehend business processes and organizational activities. Only by understanding how an activity is accomplished and the reasons for cost incurrence can managers make cost-beneficial improvements in the production and processing systems. Managers of a company desiring to implement new technology or adopt a just-in-time system must recognize what costs and benefits will flow from such actions; these assessments can be made only if the managers understand how the processes and activities will differ after the change. Process understanding helps managers become aware of the generation of unit, batch, product/process, and organizational costs. Process understanding also may help managers achieve better cost control by viewing certain costs as "long-term variable" as opposed to "short-term fixed."

Cost control was the original purpose served by creating a cost accounting system, and given the current global competitive environment, it is still an important function of cost management systems. A cost can be controlled only when the related activity is monitored, the cost driver is known, and the information is available. For example, if units are spoiled in a process, the CMS should provide information on spoilage quantity and cost rather than "burying" that information in the cost of good production. Additionally, the cost management system should allow managers to understand the process so that the underlying drivers of the spoilage can be determined. Armed with this information, managers can compare the costs of fixing the process with the benefits to be provided.

The information generated from a cost management system should help managers measure and evaluate performance. As indicated in the accompanying News Note, financial and nonfinancial measurements in a CMS can be captured at different or-

The System Captures the Measures

N E W S N O T E

An automotive supplier recently designed a new plan that incorporates the latest thinking in manufacturing and management strategy. The plant will employ an all-salaried work force. The company developed a comprehensive set of performance measurements not only to meet traditional management objectives but to serve as feedback to factory employees. The performance measurements include product-line profitability, cost of quality, first-run capability, inventory turnover, total cost performance, and cost variances. Report hierarchies have been developed, and reports are individually targeted to each level of management or worker.

SOURCE: Michael W. Grady, "Is Your Cost Management System Meeting Your Needs?" in *Emerging Practices in Cost Management*, ed. Barry J. Brinker (Boston: Warren, Gorham & Lamont, 1990), p. 152. Reprinted with permission from *Emerging Practices in Cost Management*, © 1990, Warren, Gorham & Lamont of the RIA Group, 31 St. James Avenue, reserved.

ganizational levels and can be combined and used for different purposes. The measurements may be used to evaluate human or equipment performance and future investment opportunities.

Lastly, to maintain a competitive position in an industry, a firm must generate information necessary to define and implement its organizational strategies. As discussed in Chapter 2, strategy is the link between an organization's goals and objectives and the activities actually conducted by the organization. In the current global market, firms must be certain that such a linkage exists. Information provided by a CMS allows managers to perform strategic analyses on issues such as determining core competencies and organizational constraints from a cost-benefit perspective, assessing the positive and negative financial and nonfinancial factors of investment and operational plans, and engaging in employee empowerment by using open-book management techniques. Thus, the cost management system is essential to the generation of information for effective strategic resource management.

The world of business competition is dynamic. Creative managers are constantly creating new business practices and innovative approaches to competition. This type of environment requires that cost management systems be designed to be responsive to evolutionary management practices.

In designing and revising a cost management system, managers and accountants must be attuned to the unique characteristics of their firms. A generic cost management system cannot be "pulled off the shelf" and applied to any organization. Each firm warrants a cost management system that is tailored to its situation. However, some overriding factors are important in designing a cost management system. These factors are depicted in Exhibit 15–5 and described in this section.

DESIGNING A COST MANAGEMENT SYSTEM

Organizational Form, Structure, and Culture

An entity's legal nature reflects its **organizational form.** Selecting the organizational form is one of the most important decisions made by business owners because that choice affects the cost of raising capital, cost of operating the business (including taxation issues), and possibly, cost of litigating. In recent years, the available organizational form alternatives have increased remarkably.

The most popular form for large, publicly traded businesses is the corporation. However, smaller businesses or cooperative ventures between large businesses also use general partnerships, limited partnerships, limited liability partnerships (LLPs), and limited liability companies (LLCs). These latter two forms have recently emerged as a result of new federal, state, and international legislation. Both the LLP and LLC provide more protection for a partner's personal assets than a general partnership in the event of litigation that leads to firm liquidation. Accordingly, LLPs and LLCs may offer better control for legal costs than general partnerships.

organizational form

EXHIBIT 15–5

Design of a Cost
Management System

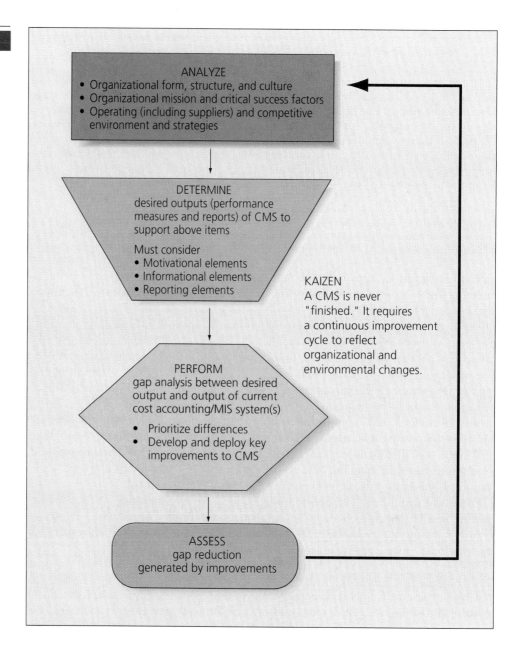

Organizational form also helps determine who has the statutory authority to make decisions for the firm. In a general partnership, all partners are allowed to make business decisions as a mere incidence of ownership. Alternatively, in a corporation, individual shareholders must act through a board of directors, who in turn, typically rely on professional managers. This ability to "centralize" authority is regarded as one of the primary advantages of the corporate organizational form, and to some extent, is available in limited partnerships, LLPs, and LLCs.

Once the organizational form is selected, top managers are responsible for creating a structure that is best suited to achieving the firm's goals and objectives. **Organizational structure** refers to how authority and responsibility for decision making are distributed in the entity.[6] Top managers make judgments about how to organize subunits and the extent to which authority will be decentralized. Although the current competitive environment is conducive to strong decentralization, top managers usually retain authority over operations that can be performed more economically centrally because of economies of scale. For example, financing, personnel, and certain

organizational structure

[6] Organizational structure is discussed in detail in Chapters 1 and 2.

accounting functions may be maintained "at headquarters" rather than being delegated to organizational subunits.

In designing the organizational structure, top managers normally will try to group subunits either geographically or by similar missions or natural product clusters. These aggregation processes provide effective cost management because of proximity or similarity of the units under a single manager's control.

For example, relative to similarity of mission, Chapter 2 introduced three generic missions (build, harvest, and hold) for business subunits. Subunits pursuing a build mission are using more cash than they are generating. Such subunits are investing cash with an expectation of future returns. At the other extreme, subunits pursuing a harvest mission are expected to generate excess cash and have a much shorter investment horizon. If one manager were responsible for subunits that represented both build and harvest missions, it would be difficult for top management to design proper incentives and performance evaluation measures for the subunit manager or to evaluate his or her cost management effectiveness and efficiency. Different cost management tools are used for different subunit missions. If a specific cost management tool is to be applied to an entire subunit, the potential for making poor decisions in the subunit is increased if there is a mix of missions across that subunit's components.

The extent to which managers decentralize also determines who will be accountable for cost management and organizational control. An information system must provide relevant and timely information to persons who are making decisions that have cost control implications, and a control system must be in place to evaluate the quality of those decisions.

An entity's culture also plays an important role in setting a cost management system. Organizational culture refers to the underlying set of assumptions about the entity and the goals, processes, practices, and values that are shared by its members. To illustrate the effect of organizational culture on the cost management system, consider AT&T prior to its divestiture: it was an organization characterized by "bureaucracy, centralized control, nepotism, a welfare mentality in which workers were 'taken care of,' strong socialization processes, [and] little concern for efficiency. . . ."[7] In such a culture, the requirements of a cost management system would have been limited because few individuals needed information, decisions were made at the top of the organization, and cost control was not a consideration because costs were passed along through the rate structure to customers. After divestiture, the company's culture changed to embrace decentralized decision making, cost efficiency, and individual responsibility and accountability; supporting such a changed culture requires different types, quantities, and distributions of cost management information.

The values-based aspects of organizational culture are also extremely important in assessing the cost management system. For example, one part of Birmingham Steel Corporation's mission statement is "to be the lowest cost, highest quality manufacturer of steel products in the markets served."[8] Without a well-designed cost management system, Birmingham Steel could not evaluate how well it is progressing toward the accomplishment of that mission. Thus, the cost management system is instrumental in providing a foundation for companies with an organizational culture that emphasizes total quality management.

Organizational Mission and Critical Success Factors

Knowledge of the organization's mission and critical success factors (CSFs) is a key consideration in the design of a cost management system. The mission provides a long-term goal toward which the organization wishes to move. If the mission that the entity wishes to achieve is unknown, it does not matter what information is generated by the cost management system—or any other information system!

---

[7] Thomas S. Bateman and Scott A. Snell, *Management Building Competitive Advantage* (Chicago: Irwin, 1996), p. 268.
[8] Birmingham Steel Corporation, *1995 Annual Report*, p. 1.

The Jackson Laboratory, located in Bar Harbor, Maine, has a mission of being a world leader in mammalian genetics research. In working to achieve this mission, the Lab has over 1,700 different strains and stocks of mice—making it the only supplier of many strains of mice to research around the globe.

In pursuing the business mission, companies may avoid or confront competition. For example, companies may try to avoid competition by attempting to be more adept in some way than other entities. The generic paths a company may take to avoid competition include compression of competitive scope, differentiation, or cost leadership.[9] A company deciding to compress its competitive scope simply focuses on a narrow market segment to the exclusion of others.

differentiation

Differentiation involves avoiding competition by distinguishing a product or service from that of competitors through adding enough value (including quality and/or features) that customers are willing to pay a higher price. Differentiation can be "based on the product itself, the delivery system by which it is sold, the marketing approach, or other factors."[10] This strategy allows the maker to earn higher-than-average rates of return. The accompanying News Note indicates how Hewlett-Packard, an American firm, used Japanese tactics to implement a differentiation strategy in the inkjet printer market.

cost leadership

The third way to avoid competition is to establish a position of **cost leadership** by becoming the low-cost producer or provider. Competition is held in abeyance because prices can be set that emphasize the cost efficiencies. In this strategy, competitors are generally forced to differentiate their products/services from the cost leader because they cannot compete on the basis of price.

In the current global environment, maintaining a competitive advantage under a scope compression, differentiation, or cost leadership strategy is often difficult. Competitors are becoming adept at duplicating the specific competencies that gave rise to the original competitive advantage. For many companies, the key to success in the future may be to confront competition by identifying and exploiting temporary opportunities for advantage. In a **confrontation strategy** the companies "still try to differentiate their products by introducing new features, or try to develop a price leadership position by dropping prices, . . . [but the companies] assume that their competitors will rapidly bring out products that are equivalent and match any price changes."[11] Although it may be necessary, a confrontation strategy is, by its very nature, less profitable for companies than differentiation or cost leadership.

confrontation strategy

critical success factor

Clarification of mission can be served by identifying the organization's **critical success factors** (CSFs), which are dimensions of operations that are so important

[9] Michael Porter, *Competitive Advantage: Creating and Sustaining Superior Performance* (New York: Free Press, 1985), p. 17.
[10] Richard J. Palmer, "Strategic Goals and Objectives and the Design of Strategic Management Accounting Systems," *Advances in Management Accounting* (Vol. 1, 1992), p. 187.
[11] Robin Cooper, *When Lean Enterprises Collide* (Boston: Harvard Business School Press, 1995), p. 11.

Do It the Japanese Way!

NEWS NOTE

A few years ago, U.S. companies were ruing Japan's unbeatable speed to market and economies of scale in many industries, and printers were a prime example: Japan made four out of five personal-computer printers that Americans bought in 1985. But now many American and Japanese companies are trading places, a shift confirmed by an annual global survey that reported . . . that the U.S. has replaced Japan as the world's most competitive economy for the first time since 1985.

H-P [Hewlett-Packard Co.] is one of the most dramatic of an increasing number of U.S. take-back stories, in technologies including disk drives, cellular phones, pagers and computer chips.

Among other things, the H-P story dispels common myths about the relative strengths of the U.S. and Japan, showing how big U.S. companies, under proper leadership, can exploit American creativity while using their huge resources to deploy "Japanese" tactics. H-P used its financial might to invest heavily in a laboratory breakthrough, then kept market share by enforcing rules that are gospel in Japan: Go for mass markets, cut costs, sustain a rapid fire of product variations and price cuts, and target the enemy.

When H-P started thinking of entering the printer market, it realized it couldn't unseat the dominant Japanese makers, such as Seiko Epson Corp. and Oki Electric Industry Co., without a technological advance. Japan had a lock on the mass market with low-cost, well-engineered dot matrix printers, which form relatively rough letters.

The seeds for the H-P breakthrough had been nurtured by engineers in a converted janitor's closet at a Vancouver, Wash., plant. . . . The discovery evolved into the "thermal" inkjet.

Based on decisions made in the hinterlands, H-P engineers adopted two Japanese tactics: They filed a blizzard of patents to protect their design and frustrate rivals, and embarked on a process of continual improvement to solve the ink jet's problems.

Dot matrix, the biggest section of the market, had serious flaws—poor print quality and color. Epson, the No. 1 player, had a soft underbelly: No competitive inkjet and the distraction of an expensive and failing effort to sell a PC. "We said, 'Maybe this is a good time to attack,' " Mr. Snyder [head of H-P's PC inkjet business] says.

H-P did so with the obsessive efficiency of a Japanese company. A week later, H-P teams were wearing "Beat Epson" football jerseys. The company began tracking Epson's market share, studying its marketing practices and public financial data, surveying loyal Epson customers and compiling profiles of Epson's top managers. Engineers tore apart Epson printers for ideas on design and manufacturing: a tactic the Japanese often use.

Among the findings: Epson's marketers got stores to put their printers in the most prominent spots; Epson used price cuts as tactical weapons to fend off challengers; consumers liked Epson machines for their reliability; Epson's printers were built to be manufactured easily. H-P responded, demanding that stores put its inkjet printers alongside Epson's. It tripled its warranty to three years and redesigned printers with manufacturing in mind.

This has allowed H-P to carry out a vital strategy: When a rival attacks, hit back quickly and hard. When Canon was about to introduce a color inkjet printer last year, H-P cut the price of its own version before its rival had even reached the market. The black-and-white printer, priced at $995 in 1988 listed for $365 [in 1994].

SOURCE: Stephen Kreider Yoder, "How H-P Used Tactics of the Japanese to Beat Them at Their Own Game," *Wall Street Journal* (September 8, 1994), pp. A1, A6. Reprinted by permission of *The Wall Street Journal*, © 1994 Dow Jones & Company, Inc. All Rights Reserved Worldwide.

to an organization's survival that, with poor performance in these areas, the entity would cease to exist. Most organizations would consider timeliness, quality, customer service, efficiency and cost control, and responsiveness to change as five critical success factors. Once managers have gained consensus on an entity's CSFs, the cost management system can be designed to (1) gather information related to measurement of those items and (2) generate output about those CSFs in forms that are useful to interested parties.

EXHIBIT 15–6

Average Sales per
Employee by Industry (in
thousands)

INDUSTRY	YEAR 1974	YEAR 1994	PERCENTAGE INCREASE
Agriculture and forestry	$ 96	$172	79
Air transportation	46	140	204
Computers	40	245	513
Grocery stores	67	139	107
Hotels and motels	24	42	75
Mining	71	190	168
Petroleum refining	222	716	223
Pharmaceuticals	50	123	146
Plastics	37	116	214
Restaurants	27	40	48
Steel works	67	271	304
Telephone and telegraph	54	168	211
Textiles	40	127	218
Trucking	59	145	146

SOURCE: COMPUSTAT (an electronic data source published by Standard and Poors).

Operating and Competitive Environment and Strategies

Once the organizational "big picture" has been established, managers can assess internal specifics related to the design of a cost management system. A primary consideration is the firm's cost structure or relative proportions of variable and fixed costs. Traditionally, cost structure has been defined in terms of variable and fixed costs relative to production or sales volume. These definitions are being revised in consideration of the concepts of batch, product/process level, and long-term variable costs.

The percentage of fixed or long-term variable costs within organizational cost structures has dramatically increased in recent years largely because of the increased use of technology. Many of these costs are associated with plant, equipment, and infrastructure investments that provide the capacity to produce goods and services. Higher proportions of these costs are most evident in industries that depend on technology for competing on the bases of quality and price. Manufacturing and service firms have been more able to leverage technology than most retailing businesses because of the greater extent of their conversion processes. This leveraging ability is indicated by the data for selected industries shown in Exhibit 15–6.[12] Sales per employee has been viewed traditionally as a measure of organizational productivity. Technology acquisition in conjunction with employee training are regarded as principal sources of productivity improvement.

The cost management implications of this shift in cost structure are significant. Most importantly, fewer costs are susceptible to short-run control so cost management efforts are increasingly directed toward the longer term. Also, managing fixed costs is partly a matter of capacity management: high capacity utilization (if accompanied by high sales volumes) allows a firm to reduce its per-unit fixed costs in pursuing a low-cost producer strategy.

A second implication of the increased proportion of fixed or long-term variable costs relates to a firm's flexibility to respond to changing short-term conditions. When these costs have increased because of higher levels of technology investment, a firm has less flexibility to take short-term actions to effect a change in the cost levels. Additionally, most efforts to change costs in the short term will have long-term consequences.[13]

[12] These data are not adjusted for inflation.
[13] Many of the new fixed costs would be regarded as "committed" rather than "discretionary." See Chapter 16 for additional details.

EXHIBIT 15–7

Actions to Substantially
Reduce Product Costs

- Develop new production processes
- Capture learning curve and experience effects
- Increase capacity utilization
- Use focused factory arrangement
    reduces coordination costs
- Design for manufacturability
    reduces assembly time
    reduces training costs
    reduces warranty costs
    reduces required number of spare parts
- Design for logistical support
- Design for reliability
- Design for maintainability
- Adopt advanced manufacturing technologies
    reduces inventory levels
    reduces required production floor space
    reduces defects, rework, and quality costs

SOURCE: Adapted from Gerald I. Susman, "Product Life Cycle Management," *Journal of Cost Management* (Summer 1989), pp. 8–22. Reprinted with permission from *The Journal of Cost Management for the Manufacturing Industry* (Summer 1989), © 1989, Warren Gotham & Lamont, 31 St. James Avenue, Boston MA 02116. All rights reserved.

In pursuing either a differentiation or cost leadership strategy, the management of an increasingly fixed or long-term variable cost structure requires beating competitors to the market with new products. The importance of timeliness is illustrated in the following quote:

> There are numerous innovations which maximized a market window to achieve phenomenal success—Polaroid is a case in point. Equally, there have been numerous high quality products that arrived too late, either because the market had been acquired by a competitor, or because the need no longer existed. By the time Head began to produce oversized tennis racquets, Prince had cornered the market.[14]

Being first to market may allow a company to set a price that provides the opportunity to obtain a large market share, which may result in an industry position of cost leadership. Alternatively, the leading edge company may set a product price that provides a substantial per-unit profit for all sales generated before competitors are able to offer alternative products. Rapid time-to-market requires a short development stage in the product life cycle.[15]

The auto industry is one in which time-to-market offers substantial advantages. For example, General Motors "aims to cut its costs of bringing new cars and light trucks to market 25% by 1997 by speeding up its product-development activities."[16] Chrysler Corporation and Dassault Systemes of France have developed a computer-aided design system that will slash approximately 20 percent off the factory time needed to retool to produce a new model.[17] Timeliness to customers can also refer to delivery time. Ford Motor, for instance, wants to cut 15 days off the time it takes to get a new car to buyers after their orders have been placed.[18]

Reducing time-to-market is one way a company can reduce costs. Other ways are listed in Exhibit 15–7—most of these actions are associated with the earlier stages of

[14] Simon Cooper, "There Is No Point Putting a Wind Spoiler on the Back of a Turtle," *CMA Magazine* (February 1996), p. 4.
[15] The concept of product life cycle is introduced in Chapter 2 and explained in detail in Chapter 6.
[16] Robert L. Simison, "GM Plans to Speed Vehicle Development and Reduce Such Costs 25% by 1997," *Wall Street Journal* (August 11, 1995), p. A2.
[17] Neal Templin, "Chrysler Co-Designs a Computer-Aided Manufacturing Plan," *Wall Street Journal* (August 2, 1995), p. B3.
[18] Earle Eldridge, "Ford Hopes to Speed Up Car Deliveries," *USA Today* (February 2, 1996), p. B1.

Product Life Cycles Affect Cost Management Information

Product lives are becoming shorter and shorter. Many electronic products measure life cycles in months instead of years. This means that accountants must produce product costs quickly to meet management needs. Accountants will not have the luxury of spending a year to develop a product cost for a product that has a life of only nine months. They will have to develop systems that rapidly roll out product costs.

In this environment, the accountant will focus on developing a "minimalist" product cost. This product cost includes the absolute minimum amount of cost—e.g., the costs of raw materials and components. This minimalist cost will serve as the building block for creating financial analyses for managers.

In a quick response environment, speedy analysis takes precedence over complete costing of products. . . . Product cost provides only part of the picture for the manager in a quick response setting. The manager needs cost models that rapidly predict the cost or cash-flow impact of changes in operations, products, or distribution systems. A cost model that includes parameters for the strategic and operational tools managers use to steer the organization toward some goal enables managers to instantly assess the profit impact of changes in any of these leverage points. These cost models will require management accountants to learn about the strategies and alternatives managers routinely consider so that the strategies and different possibilities can be incorporated into cost models.

SOURCE: Germain Böer, "Management Accounting Beyond the Year 2000," *Journal of Cost Management* (Winter 1996), p. 48. Reprinted with permission from *The Journal of Cost Management for the Manufacturing Industry* (Winter 1996), © 1996, Warren Gorham & Lamont, 31 St. James Avenue, Boston, MA 02116. All rights reserved.

the product life cycle. Thus, as has been previously mentioned, product profitability is largely determined by an effective design and development process.

Getting products to market quickly and profitably requires a compromise between the advantages associated with speed of product innovation and with superior product design. Rapid time-to-market may mean that a firm incurs costs associated with design flaws (such as the costs of engineering changes orders) that could have been avoided if more time were allowed for the product's development. Also, if a flawed product is marketed, external failure costs will likely be incurred for returns, warranty work, or customer "badwill" regarding the firm's reputation for product quality.

Time-to-market is important because of the competitive advantages it offers and because of the compressed product life cycles. Both of these factors have a significant affect on cost management systems as discussed in the above News Note.

Another aspect of an organization's operating environment is supplier relations. Many companies that have formed strategic alliances with suppliers have found such relationships to be effective cost control mechanisms. For example, by involving suppliers early in the design and development stage of new products, a better design for manufacturability will be achieved and the likelihood of meeting target costs will be improved. Additionally, if companies and suppliers are linked through an electronic data interchange system, the capabilities and functions of that system must be considered in designing the CMS.

Another operating environment consideration in designing a cost management system is the need to integrate the organization's current information systems. The "feeder" systems (such as payroll, inventory valuation, budgeting, and costing) that are in place should be evaluated to determine answers to the following questions:

- What data are being gathered and in what form?
- What outputs are being generated and in what form?
- How do the current systems interact with one another and how effective are those interactions?
- Is the current chart of accounts appropriate for the cost management information desired?

■ What significant information issues (such as yield, spoilage, and cycle time) are not presently being addressed by the information system and could those issues be integrated into the current feeder systems?

With knowledge of the above information, management must analyze the cost-benefit trade-offs that relate to the design of the cost management system. As the costs of gathering, processing, and communicating information decrease, or as the quantity and intensity of competition increase (possibly forcing a confrontation strategy), more sophisticated cost management systems are required. Additionally, as companies focus on customer satisfaction and expand their product or service offerings, more sophisticated cost management systems are needed. In these conditions, the generation of "better" cost information is essential to long-run organizational survival and profitability.

Even with appropriate information systems in place, managers might fail to make decisions that are consistent with organizational strategies. Proper incentives and reporting systems must be incorporated into the CMS for managers to make appropriate decisions.

A cost management system is composed of a set of three primary elements or components: motivational elements, informational elements, and reporting elements. Some cost management system elements are detailed in Exhibit 15–8. The elements as a whole must be internally consistent, and the individually selected elements must be consistent with the strategies and missions of the subunits. Different aspects of these elements may be used for different purposes. For example, numerous measures of performance can be specified but only certain measures will be appropriate for specific purposes.

ELEMENTS OF A COST MANAGEMENT SYSTEM

Motivational Elements

Performance measurements are chosen so as to be consistent with organizational goals and objectives, and to "drive" managers toward designated achievements. These measurements, which are discussed in depth in Chapters 20 and 21, may be quan-

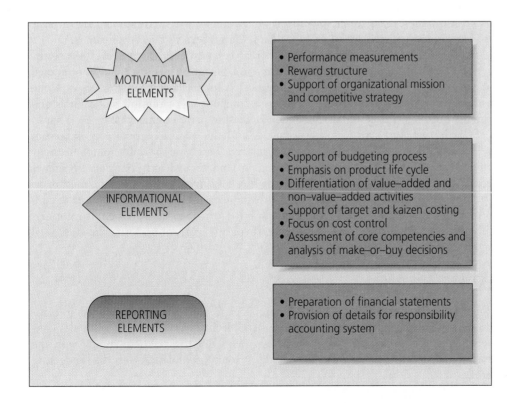

EXHIBIT 15–8

Cost Management System Elements

titative or nonquantitative, financial or nonfinancial, and short term or long term. For example, if a subunit is expected to generate a specified dollar amount of profit for the year, the performance measure has been set to be quantitative, financial, and short term. A longer-term performance measure might be an average increase in profit or change in stock price over a 5 to 10 year period.

The performance measurement system should be designed to encourage managers to act in the best interest of the organization and their subunits, and in support of the organizational missions and competitive strategies. Once defined, the criteria used to measure performance should be linked to the organizational incentive system because it tends to be true that "you get what you measure." This linkage sends the message to managers that they will be rewarded in line with the quality of their organizational and subunit decisions, and thereby, their contributions to achieving the organizational missions.

In addition to performance measures, different forms of rewards have different incentive effects and can reflect different time orientations. In general, longer-term incentives encourage managers to be more long-term oriented in their decisions, and shorter-term incentives encourage managers to be focused on the near future.

To illustrate, cash is the most obvious reward that can be used to reward short-term performance. All managers receive some compensation in cash so they may pay ordinary living expenses. However, once a manager receives a cash reward, its value is not dependent on future performance. In contrast, a stock option that is not exercisable until a future time provides a manager with an incentive to be more concerned about long-term performance. The ultimate value of the stock option is determined in the future when it is exercised rather than on the date it is received. Thus, the option's value is related more to long-term than to short-term organizational performance.

Performance rewards for top management may consist of both short-term and long-term incentives. Normally, a major incentive is performance-based pay that is tied to the firm's stock price. The rewards for subunit managers should be based on the specific subunit's mission. Managers of subunits charged with a build mission should receive long-term incentives. These managers need to be concerned about long-term success and be willing to make short-term sacrifices for long-term gains. Alternatively, managers of subunits charged with a harvest mission must be more oriented to the short term. These subunits are expected to squeeze as much cash and profit as possible from their operations. Accordingly, incentives should be in place to encourage their managers to have a short-term focus in decision making.

profit sharing

Profit sharing refers to compensation that is contingent on the level of organizational profit generated. This type of pay is a powerful incentive and is now used in virtually every U.S. industry. As is indicated in the accompanying News Note, even the medical industry is undergoing a competitive revolution as hospitals and health professionals try to survive under increasing price competition.

Selection of performance measurements and the reward structure is important because managers evaluate decision alternatives based on how the outcomes may affect the selected performance (measurement and reward) criteria. Because higher performance equates to a larger reward, the cost management system must have specified performance "yardsticks" and provide measurement information to the appropriate individuals for evaluation purposes. Performance measurement is meaningful only in a comparative or relative sense. Typically, current performance is assessed relative to past or expected performance.

Informational Elements

The accounting function in an organization is expected to support managers in planning, controlling, performance evaluation, and decision making. All these roles converge in a system designed for cost management. Relative to the planning role, the cost management system should provide a sound foundation for the budgeting process.

Costs Are Lower When They Affect "My" Pocket!

Doctors, who normally complain about HMO cost crackdowns, turn out to cut costs even more when they form their own managed-care practices and share in profits.

That's one conclusion of a new study that analyzes the performance of six physician-owned medical groups in California under a controversial payment system called capitation that is gaining popularity in markets across the U.S.

The six medical groups get most of their revenues through capitation arrangements under which they agree to manage a full spectrum of medical needs—including hospital care—of their enrolled patients for a flat fee per month for each member. Typically, the practices pocket the difference between the cost of medical services provided and the capitated payment, but they are at financial risk for any care that exceeds that revenue.

The study found that under these financial incentives, hospital use in the six medical groups in 1994 averaged 139 days per 1,000 members, about 40% lower than the 1993 average of 232 days per 1,000 members of commercial health maintenance organizations in California.

The report didn't determine whether patients of the medical practice group fared better or worse as a result of the lower rate of services.

SOURCE: Ron Winslow, "Doctors Cut Costs More When They Own Managed-Care Practices, Share Profits," *Wall Street Journal* (December 21, 1995), p. B2. Reprinted by permission of *The Wall Street Journal*, © 1995 Dow Jones & Company, Inc. All Rights Reserved Worldwide.

Budgets provide both a specification of expected achievement as well as a benchmark against which to compare actual performance. A CMS, like a traditional cost accounting system, should be able to provide the financial information needed for budget preparation. But, in addition, a well-designed CMS will disclose the cost drivers for activities so that more useful simulations of alternative scenarios can be made. The same system can highlight any non-value-added activities in the budgeting process so that these can be reduced or eliminated. This helps reduce the time needed for budget preparation. "By reducing the length of the budgeting cycle and making the process more efficient, the informational benefit of semiannual or quarterly budgeting may become practical."[19]

As competitive advantage becomes more and more difficult to maintain, firms must place greater emphasis on management of the product life cycle. In such an environment, firms often use innovative tools (including benchmarking and reverse engineering, cost/value analysis, kaizen costing and target costing, and process cost management) first developed by the Japanese to provide information relevant to assessing their competitive positions. As discussed earlier in this chapter, most actions available to managers to control costs are concentrated in the earliest stages of the product life cycle. Accordingly, information relevant to managing costs must be focused on decisions made during those stages—that information will be provided by a well-designed and integrated cost management system.

The life cycle of many products will become shorter as firms become more and more adept at duplicating their competitors' offerings. In the future, managers will confront the fact that products will spend less time in the maturity stage of the product life cycle. In this competitive environment, firms will be forced to find ways to continue to squeeze cash from their mature products to support development of new products. Additionally, the future will place greater emphasis on a firm's ability to adapt to changing competitive conditions. Flexibility will be an important organizational attribute and will cause managers to change the emphasis of control systems as shown in Exhibit 15–9.

To provide information relevant to product design and development, the accounting information system must be able to relate resource consumption and cost to alternative product and process designs. Computer simulation models are useful in

[19] Schnoebelen, "Integrating an Advanced Cost Management System," p. 63.

Shift in Control Emphasis in Future Competitive Environment

	FROM		TO
Strategic Focus	Achieving financial results: sales, costs, and profits	→	Achieving critical success factors: low cost, high quality, sales mix variety, on-time delivery, and high capacity usage
Product Sales	Submitting bids and taking orders	→	Developing partnerships and creating sales opportunities
Budgeting	Developing annual plans	→	Ongoing planning and frequent budget revisions
Culture	Meeting project expectations	→	Learning and improving upon processes

SOURCE: Adapted from Ralph E. Drtina and Gary A. Monetti, "Controlling Flexible Business Strategies," *Journal of Cost Management* (Fall 1995), pp. 42–49. Reprinted with permission from *The Journal of Cost Management for the Manufacturing Industry* (Fall 1995), © 1995, Warren Gorham & Lamont, 31 St. James Avenue, Boston, MA 02116. All rights reserved.

relating products to activities.[20] In addition to focusing information on the front end of the product life cycle, the capital budget is becoming an increasingly important tool in cost management, especially relative to new technology acquisition decisions. Decisions made with regard to capital investments affect the future cost structure of firms, and hence, the extent to which short-term actions can effect a change in the level of total costs.

In regard to its control roles, a cost management system is useful for variance, cost behavior, and process value analysis; cost driver and value-added/non-value-added activity identification; and cost-to-value chain linkages. The CMS should be able to generate information that supports product development efforts for target costing purposes and business process reengineering actions for kaizen costing purposes.

Lastly, the system should produce cost information with minimal distortions from improper or inaccurate allocations, or from improper exclusions. Improper allocations could be related to assignment of joint costs to joint products or organizational-level costs to products and services. Inaccurate allocations or assignments could occur from using unit-level drivers to assign batch or product/process-level costs. Improper exclusions usually relate to the influence of financial accounting, such as the mandate to expense product development or distribution costs. If the system minimizes these cost distortions, the cost assignments are more relevant for control purposes and for internal decision making.

The information required to support decisions depends on the unique situational factors of the firm and its subunits. The information system must allow the decision maker to evaluate how alternative decision choices would affect the items that are used to measure and evaluate the decision maker's performance.

Techniques, such as relevant costing, quality cost management, job order and process costing, and cost-volume-profit analysis discussed in earlier chapters, relate to the role of cost information in decision making. Many decisions involve comparing the benefit received from some course of action (such as serving a given customer)

[20] Using computer models is an element of process cost management. For more details, see Thomas G. Greenwood and James M. Reeve, "Process Cost Management," *Journal of Cost Management* (Winter 1994), pp. 4–19.

The Need to Assess Customer Profitability

NEWS NOTE

Big accounting firms say they have begun dropping risky audit clients to lower their risk of lawsuits for allegedly faulty audits. New companies, which have a particularly high chance of failure, are affected most, because almost nothing triggers lawsuits against accountants faster than company failures.

But established companies are getting the ax, too. KPMG Peat Marwick, the fourth-biggest U.S. accounting firm, is currently dropping 50 to 100 audit clients annually, up from only zero to 20 five years ago, says Robert W. Lambert, the firm's new director of risk management. "When a client we audit goes bust," he says, "it costs us a bundle in court if we're sued by investors, whether we win or lose the case."

Mr. Lambert says that legal costs were "staggering" for a lawsuit filed in a federal court in Texas alleging a faulty review of a bank's books by Peat. The bank was taken over by the federal government in 1992 after big losses. The jury ruled in Peat's favor in 1993, but the firm had to spend $7 million defending itself "even though the fee for the job was only $15,000," Mr. Lambert says.

Lawrence Weinbach, managing partner of Arthur Andersen & Co., another leading accounting firm, says his organization has either dropped or declined to audit more than 100 companies over the past two years. "When the company has a risky profile and its stock price is volatile, we're just not going to jump in and do the audit and invite a lawsuit," says Mr. Weinbach.

. . . Litigation settlement costs of the Big Six accounting firms now exceed $1 billion a year. The firms say that even after insurance reimbursement, these costs equal 12% of their annual audit and accounting revenue.

SOURCE: Lee Berton, "Big Accounting Firms Weed Out Risky Clients," *Wall Street Journal* (June 26, 1995), p. B1, B6. Reprinted by permission of *The Wall Street Journal*, © 1995 Dow Jones & Company, Inc. All Rights Reserved Worldwide.

to the costs of the action (costs of providing services). Only if they are given cost data that contain minimal distortion can managers make valid cost-benefit assessments.

Activity-based cost information tends to exemplify cost data having minimal cost distortions, and thus, provides an approach to relate costs to organizational benefits received from incurrence of the costs. Based on the relationship of costs to benefits, managers take actions to improve the yield (revenue) realized from cost incurrence. The above News Note indicates how "Big Six" accounting firms are responding to certain groups of customers whose revenue contribution relates poorly to the costs the accounting firms incur to provide them with accounting and auditing services.

Reporting Elements

The reporting elements of a cost management system refer to methods of providing information to persons in evaluative roles. First and foremost, the CMS must be effective in generating fundamental financial statement information including inventory valuation and cost of sales information. This information is not necessarily the same as that being used for internal planning, control, performance evaluation, or decision-making purposes. But, if the feeder systems to the CMS have been appropriately integrated and the system itself has been designed to minimize distortions, generating an "external" product or service cost will cause the system no difficulties. However, if system design has been faithful to these two criteria, a "second" cost may not be needed, as discussed in the News Note on the next page.

In addition to financial statement valuations, the reporting elements of the cost management system must address internal needs of a **responsibility accounting system.** This system provides information to top management about the performance of an organizational subunit and its manager.[21] For each subunit, the responsibility accounting system separately tracks costs and, if appropriate, revenues.

responsibility accounting system

[21] Responsibility accounting concepts are discussed in detail in Chapters 19 through 21.

We Probably Only Need One Cost

Because of [differences in the underlying nature] of the new product costs and a sense of loyalty to the old product costs, a company may decide to use two sets of product costs. The "official" cost would be the cost used for external reporting, and the new ABC cost would be used for internal reporting and to support management decisions. Although this approach is possible, it has definite drawbacks, including the following:

- Product costing is, by nature, a relatively difficult concept to understand, especially for nonfinancial managers. Most managers would agree that one set of product costs is difficult enough to understand, let alone two.
- Two sets of product costs could result in two sets of financial results for budgets, estimates, closings, and simulations. Which cost would be believed? Managers might want to choose the costs that give them the best results for a certain decision. Total confusion might ensue, and the credibility of the system would almost certainly be questioned.
- This policy runs completely counter to current thinking about reengineering to simplify processes, eliminate inefficiency, and reduce non-value-added activity. Having two sets of product costs breeds complexity throughout the company, from accounting reconciliations to decision making.

A primary purpose of an integrated advanced cost management system (ACMS) is to provide improved information for business decisions. Revised product costs using ABC and the new cost information about business events or processes should fulfill this objective. Accordingly, during the design of an integrated ACMS, a decision should be made to use ABC product costs as the "official" costs to serve both internal and external reporting needs.

SOURCE: Steven C. Schnoebelen, "Integrating an Advanced Cost Management System Into Operating Systems (Part 2)," *Journal of Cost Management* (Spring 1993), p. 65. Reprinted with permission from *The Journal of Cost Management for the Manufacturing Industry* (Spring 1993), © 1993, Warren Gorham & Lamont, 31 St. James Avenue, Boston, MA 02116. All rights reserved.

Performance reports are useful only to the extent that the measured performance of a given manager or subunit can be compared to a meaningful baseline. The normal baseline is a measure of expected performance, which can be denoted in financial terms, such as budgetary figures, or in nonfinancial terms, such as throughput, customer satisfaction measures, lead time, capacity utilization, and research and development activities. By comparing expected and actual performance, top managers are able to determine which managers and subunits performed according to expectations and which exceeded or failed to meet expectations. Using this information that has been processed and formulated by the cost management system, top managers link decisions about managerial rewards to performance.

The movement toward decentralization has increased the importance of an effective reporting system. With decentralization, top managers must depend on the reporting system to keep all organizational subunits striving to achieve their subunit missions and organizational goals and objectives. A cost management system is not designed to "cut" costs. It exists to ensure that a satisfactory yield (revenue) is realized from the incurrence of costs. Accordingly, cost management begins with an understanding that different costs are incurred for different purposes. Some costs are incurred to yield immediate benefit; others are expected to yield a benefit in the near or distant future.

Only by linking costs to activities and activities to strategies can the yield on costs be understood. Thus, to achieve effective cost management, managers should start by sorting organizational activities according to their strategic roles. This logic suggests that organizational management is made easier by decomposing operations into subunits. By so doing, top managers can assign responsibility and accountability for

A good cost management system will allow comparisons to be made to both internal and external benchmarks. By linking costs, activities, and strategies, managers and empowered employees are more able to understand the reasons behind the incurrence of costs.

distinct subunit missions to a particular manager. In turn, by creating the correct incentives for each subunit manager, top management will have set the stage for each subunit manager to act in the best interest of the overall organization. This linkage is the start of a process that focuses the attention of a specific subunit manager on a set of costs and activities that uniquely relate to the subunit's organizational mission.

For subunit managers to be effective in managing costs, each must be provided with relevant information. Because the nature and time horizon of decisions made by managers vary across subunits, each manager requires unique information. Accountants face the task of providing information to each subunit manager that is tailored to the particular context. In addition to information about decision alternatives, managers need to know how the alternatives are likely to affect their expected rewards.

A reporting system provides a comparison of expected performance to actual performance for each manager. It is on the basis of this comparison that the relative rewards of subunit managers are determined. Accordingly, this is a key source of motivation for subunit managers to act in the best interest of the organization.

Optimal organizational performance is realized only if there is consistency for each subunit across the elements of motivation, information, and reporting. Managers of subunits with a build mission need information tailored to their competitive strategies and focused on the early stages of the product life cycle. Their incentives to manage costs need to be relatively long term, and their reward structures should emphasize success in product development and design. Alternatively, subunit managers of mature businesses need more information pertaining to short-term competition. Their reward and reporting structures should emphasize near term profit and cash flow.

Because most businesses have a CMS in place, CMS design and implementation issues typically relate to the modification of existing systems.

CMS
IMPLEMENTATION

Once the organization and its subunits have been assessed and the structure of the cost management system determined, the current information system(s) should be evaluated. A gap analysis is necessary to compare the information that is needed to the information that is currently available, or how well desired outputs coincide with current outputs. Any difference represents a "gap" to be overcome.

In many situations, eliminating all system gaps is impossible in the short term, potentially because of software or hardware capability or availability. Methods of reducing or eliminating the gaps, including all related technical requirements and changes to existing feeder systems, should be specified in detail. These details should be expressed, qualitatively and quantitatively, in terms of costs and benefits.

In the event of limited resources, top management may then prioritize the differences as to which gap issues to address and in which order. As system implementation proceeds, management should assess the effectiveness of the improvements and evaluate the need for other improvements. Once the CMS has been established, previously identified gaps may become irrelevant or may rise in rank of priority. It is only through continuous improvement efforts that the cost management system will provide an ongoing, viable network of information to users.

REVISITING

Group Michelin

Through its industrial and commercial companies Michelin has set up an extensive and diversified sales organization worldwide, complete with appropriate facilities for storage and delivery. In some companies, particularly in Asia, the commercial organization is managed through joint ventures. . . .

Continuous contact with tire users provides the company with a valuable source of information and feedback, enabling it to adapt to market trends and to guide its research activities. . . .

With the acquisition of Uniroyal Goodrich in 1990, Michelin was able to reach a critical size in North America, as was already the case in Europe. From then the problem was to improve profitability and reduce indebtedness and an organization by geographic area was introduced. The changed organization enabled the necessary restructuring to be done: employee numbers dropped from 145,000 to 115,000, debt levels were cut by 7 billion francs, mainly from cash flow, and profitability was improved. In order to speed up the improvement it was decided at the beginning of 1996 to introduce a new organization.

The new setup is designed to meet two major requirements: the need to provide specific products, responding more quickly to meet increased segmentation of market demand, and to create centers of responsibility per product category.

In order to achieve this, the company has been structured in Tactical Operating Units (Unités Opérationelles Tactiques—UOT). For a defined segment of the market each UOT will combine marketing, product development, manufacturing and sales. The UOT thus becomes a "business unit," more responsive and accountable for the chain of added value for the customers in its market segment.

The UOTs are grouped under nine product categories: passenger car and light truck; truck; earthmover; agricultural; two-wheel; aircraft; suspension systems; tourism services; and primary products. The international nature of vehicle and of tire markets requires a cohesive approach in the various continents, for example in product development or in commercial operations. Those responsible for the product categories and UOTs will ensure this coherence and thus provide a new interlocking element in Group management. . . .

SOURCE: Michelin, *1995 Annual Report*, pp. 5–7.

CHAPTER SUMMARY

As first discussed in Chapter 1, cost accounting's role in management accounting is to provide information for managers' planning, controlling, performance evaluation, and decision-making needs. This chapter discusses the role of accountants and accounting information in developing a formal system of cost management.

A cost management system is a part of a firm's information and control systems. A management information system is a structure that organizes and communicates data to managers. Control systems exist to guide organizations to achievement of their goals and objectives. They have four primary components: detectors, assessors, effectors, and a communications network.

A cost management system consists of a set of formal methods developed for planning and controlling an organization's cost-generating activities relative to its goals and objectives. This system serves multiple purposes: develop product costs, assess product/service profitability, improve understanding of how processes affect costs, facilitate cost control, measure performance, and implement organizational strategies.

A generic, off-the-shelf cost management system is not effective. As in the design of any control system, managers must be sensitive to the unique aspects of their organizations. Three sets of factors that should specifically be taken into account in designing a control system are the organizational form, structure, and culture; organizational mission and critical success factors; and the competitive environment.

A cost management system must be designed using elements from three groups of management control tools. The selected elements of the system should be internally consistent and be consistent with the missions of the individual subunits. The three groups of control tools are motivational elements, informational elements, and reporting elements.

The motivational elements exist to provide managers the incentive to take the actions that are in the best interest of their subunits and the overall organization. Managers are motivated to do the right thing when the rewards they receive for their efforts are linked to the quality of decisions they make on behalf of the organization and their specific subunits.

The informational elements provide managers with relevant data. Accountants play a primary role in information management and are charged with maintaining an information system that is useful in performance measurement of managers and subunits and in making managerial decisions. To compete in the global environment, firms are developing new techniques to provide information relevant to assessing their competitive positions. These techniques include benchmarking and reverse engineering, cost/value analysis, kaizen costing and target costing, and process cost management.

The reporting elements exist to provide information regarding managerial performance. For accounting, this is sometimes referred to as the "scorekeeping" role. A responsibility accounting system provides information to top management about the performance of an organizational subunit and its manager.

Gap analysis is the key to identifying differences (gaps) between the ideal cost management system and the existing system. By prioritizing the order in which gaps are to be closed, managers can proceed in an orderly manner with updating the cost management system. Because business processes are constantly evolving, the cost management system must be continuously evaluated and updated so that it provides the information and motivation that managers currently require.

APPENDIX

Cost Management System Conceptual Design Principles

"In 1986, Computer Aided Manufacturing-International, Inc. (CAM-I) formed a consortium of progressive industrial organizations, professional accounting firms, and government agencies to define the role of cost management in the new advanced manufacturing environment."[22] One outcome of this consortium was a conceptual framework of principles (listed in Exhibit 15–10) for designing a cost management

EXHIBIT 15–10

CMS Conceptual Design Principles

COST PRINCIPLES

- Identify costs of non-value-added activities to improve use of resources.
- Recognize holding costs as a non-value-added activity traceable directly to a product.
- Significant costs should be directly traceable to management reporting objectives.
- Separate cost centers should be established for each homogeneous group of activities consistent with organizational responsibility.
- Activity-based cost accumulation and reporting will improve cost traceability.
- Separate bases for allocations should be developed to reflect causal relations between activity costs and management reporting objectives.
- Costs should be consistent with the requirement to support life-cycle management.
- Technology costs should be assigned directly to products.
- Actual product cost should be measured against target cost to support elimination of waste.
- Cost-effective approaches for internal control should be developed as a company automates.

PERFORMANCE MEASUREMENT PRINCIPLES

- Performance measures should establish congruence with a company's objectives.
- Performance measures should be established for significant activities.
- Performance measures should be established to improve visibility of cost drivers.
- Financial and nonfinancial activities should be included in the performance measurement system.

INVESTMENT MANAGEMENT PRINCIPLES

- Investment management should be viewed as more than the capital budgeting process.
- Investment management decisions should be consistent with company goals.
- Multiple criteria should be used to evaluate investment decisions.
- Investments and attendant risks should be considered interrelated elements of an investment strategy.
- Activity data should be traceable to the specific investment opportunity.
- Investment management decisions should support the reduction or elimination of non-value-added activities.
- Investment management decisions should support achieving target cost.

SOURCE: Reprinted by permission of the publishers from *Cost Management for Today's Advanced Manufacturing* by Callie Berliner and James A. Brimson, eds. (Cambridge, Mass.: Harvard Business School Press, 1988), pp. 13–18. Copyright © 1988 by the President and Fellows of Harvard College.

[22] Berliner and Brimson, *Cost Management*, p. vii.

system. If a CMS provides the suggested information relating to costs, performance measurements, and investment management, that system will be relevant to management's decisionmaking needs. Although compatible with existing cost accounting systems, the set of principles as a whole suggests a radical departure from traditional practices. The practices focus management attention on organizational activities, product life cycles, integrating cost management and performance measurement, and integrating investment management and strategic management.

confrontation strategy (p. 684)
cost leadership (p. 684)
cost management system (p. 677)
critical success factor (p. 684)
differentiation (p. 684)
management control system (p. 676)

management information system (p. 676)
organizational form (p. 681)
organizational structure (p. 682)
profit sharing (p. 690)
responsibility accounting system (p. 693)

1. Why is an effective management information system a key element of an effective management control system?

2. What are the benefits of a computerized MIS relative to a manual MIS?

3. What are the four components of a control system? To what devices would each of these relate in one of an automobile's systems?

4. Why would an organization have multiple control systems in place?

5. Exhibit 15–3 identifies life cycle stages of cost management systems and assigns those stages to historical eras. However, the text also notes that all of these stages are found in business today. Why would all firms not have advanced to the final life cycle stage?

6. How can a cost management system help in investment management activities?

7. Identify examples of useful information that could be provided to a cost management system by each of the functional areas shown in Exhibit 15–4.

8. Why would management be willing to accept inaccurate costs from the cost management system? What sacrifices would be necessary to obtain accurate costs?

9. What are examples of costs that a cost management system might treat differently for internal and external purposes? Why would these treatments be appropriate?

10. How can an integrated cost management system help managers understand and evaluate the effectiveness and efficiency of business processes?

11. Why might activity-based costing be viewed as a fundamental part of a truly integrated cost management system?

12. Is cost control the primary purpose of a cost management system? Discuss the rationale for your answer.

13. Why do different performance measurements exist at different organizational levels? What are the benefits and problems associated with having such differences?

14. What information could be generated from a cost management system that would help an organization ascertain its core competencies?

15. Describe characteristics of organizations in which (a) centralized and (b) decentralized control would be effective.

16. Would you prefer to work as an employee in an organization that had (a) centralized or (b) decentralized control? Discuss the reasons for your answer.

17. List five types of cost management information that would be most useful to an organizational subunit that was engaged in a (a) build, (b) harvest, and (c) hold mission.

18. Discuss ways in which organizational culture could be used as a control mechanism.

19. Compare the description in the chapter of AT&T prior to divestiture with the former Soviet Union prior to perestroika. How has the culture of each of these entities changed over time? How would these changes affect the types of information needed by managers/leaders?

20. Discuss the three generic strategies a company may pursue to avoid competition. What benefits would be gained from each strategy?

21. What do you believe are the critical success factors of your college or university? Why did you choose these?

22. What benefits are gained by an organization that has a high level of variable costs and a low level of fixed costs? A high level of fixed costs and low level of variable costs?

23. How has technology increased the level of fixed (or long-term variable) costs in companies?

24. How might the cost management system of an organization that has a high level of variable costs and a low level of fixed costs differ from that of an organization with a high level of fixed costs and a low level of variable costs?

25. Why can "dollar sales per employee" be viewed as a measure of organizational productivity? What actions can managers take to increase productivity?

26. Give three examples of industries in which time-to-market is critical. Give three examples of industries in which time-to-market is almost irrelevant. Discuss the reasons for importance or lack thereof in each industry.

27. What are feeder systems and why are they important in the design of a cost management system?

28. Which is most important in the design of a cost management system: motivational elements, informational elements, or reporting elements? Discuss the rationale for your answer.

29. "A firm cannot be successful unless short-term profits are achieved." Is this statement true or false? Why?

30. Provide three examples from your academic career of the accuracy of the statement "you get what you measure."

31. How does the nature of the performance reward provided affect the incentives of a manager to be either short-term or long-term oriented in making decisions?

COMMUNICATION ACTIVITIES

32. (*Organizational form*) As a team of three, or as individuals, write a paper that compares and contrasts the corporate, general partnership, limited partnership, LLP, and LLC forms of business. At a minimum, include in your discussion issues related to the following: formation, capital generation, managerial authority and responsibility, taxation, ownership liability, and implications for success in mission and objectives.

33. *(Role of accounting information)* In a team of three, prepare an oral presentation discussing how accounting information can help and hinder an organization's progress toward its mission and objectives. Be sure to differentiate between the effects of what you perceive as "traditional" versus "nontraditional" accounting information.

34. *(Manual versus computerized information system)* Divide a team of four into two groups (a "pro" and a "con" group) of two. Prepare a debate on the following statement: To be useful, an information system must be computerized. Summarize the arguments of both sides and decide which argument was most persuasive and why.

35. *(Organizational culture)* Write a paper describing the organizational culture at a job you have held or at the college or university that you attend. Be sure to include a discussion of the value system and how it was communicated to new employees or new students.

CASES

36. *(Marketing strategy) Robert L. Wehling, Procter & Gamble's senior vice president for advertising and market research, would like to wean Americans off coupons.*

    His relentless cost-control efforts, which P&G began in the manufacturing area in 1993, have led to moves to eliminate couponing, increase print advertising and curb growth in P&G's marketing spending.

    In fact, fewer than 2% of the 291.9 billion coupons that companies distributed in 1995 were redeemed. . . .

    P&G has been plowing back savings from cost-cutting initiatives into lowering prices on most of its 300 brands. Since 1992–93, the list prices on P&G brands, excluding coffee, have declined by $1 billion. Prices on diapers and detergents have particularly declined.

    In February, P&G eliminated all promotional coupons in three New York state markets—in a test that many industry watchers doubted could be successfully expanded nationwide because coupons are such an integral part of American consumer's psyche.

    Until P&G came along, no company had risked eliminating all coupons in a big geographical market, despite the growing consensus among major marketers that coupons are expensive and turn brand-loyal customers into bargain hunters who select brands based on short-term price promotions.

    P&G spent $3.3 billion in 1995 on advertising. Its popular brand names include Tide, Vicks, Cover Girl, and Pringles.

    [SOURCE: Raju Narisetti, "P&G Ad Chief Plots Demise of the Coupon," *Wall Street Journal* (April 17, 1996), pp. B1, B5A. Reprinted by permission of *The Wall Street Journal*, © 1996 Dow Jones & Company, Inc. All Rights Reserved Worldwide.]

    a. What costs and benefits likely were considered by P&G in its decision to consider discontinuing the use of coupons to promote its products?
    b. What is P&G apparent market strategy in deciding to lower prices? Explain.
    c. What risks should P&G consider before discontinuing the use of coupons nationwide?

37. *(Interaction of costs and quality) In Digital Equipment Corp.'s 1994 reorganization, its second in as many years, the company eliminated hundreds of sales and marketing jobs in its health-industries group, which had been bringing in $800 million of annual revenue by selling computers to hospitals and other health-care providers world-wide.*

    Digital says it cut [costs and positions] because it had to act fast. It was losing about $3 million a day, and its cost of sales was much higher than that of its rivals. Robert B. Palmer, the chief executive officer of the Maynard, Mass., company, saw across-the-board cuts in all units, regardless of profitability, as the way to go. . . .

    But in the health-industries group, the cutbacks imposed unexpected costs. Digital disrupted longstanding ties between its veteran salespeople and major customers by transferring their accounts to new sales divisions. It also switched hundreds of smaller accounts to outside distributors without notifying the customers.

At the industry's annual conference, "I had customers coming up to me and saying, 'I haven't seen a Digital sales rep in nine months. Whom do I talk to now?'" recalls Joseph Lesica, a former marketing manager in the group who resigned last year. "That really hurt our credibility. I was embarrassed."

Resellers of Digital computers, who account for most of its health-care sales, also complained about diminished technology and sales support. "There were months when you couldn't find anybody with a Digital badge," complains an official at one former reseller who had been accustomed to Digital sales reps accompanying him on customer calls. "They walked away from large numbers of clients." Adds Richard Tarrant, chief executive of IDX Systems Corp., a Burlington, Vt. reseller that used to have an exclusive arrangement with Digital: "Now, they're just one of several vendors we use."

Many Digital customers turned to International Business Machines Corp. [IBM] and Hewlett-Packard Co. and so did some employees of Digital's downsized health-care group. Mr. Lesica says some laid-off workers went to Hewlett-Packard and quickly set about bringing Digital clients with them. "That's another way [Digital] shot itself in the foot," he says.

[SOURCE: Alex Markels and Matt Murray, "Call It Dumbsizing: Why Some Companies Regret Cost-Cutting," *Wall Street Journal* (May 4, 1996), pp. A1, A6. Reprinted by permission of *The Wall Street Journal*, © 1996 Dow Jones & Company, Inc. All Rights Reserved Worldwide.]

a. What is the implied mission (build, hold, or harvest) of the health-industries group of Digital? Explain.

b. Describe the circumstances in which across-the-board cuts in spending represent a rational approach to cost management.

c. When Digital decided to cut costs, what were the apparent criteria used to determine which costs were cut? What evidence is there that Digital employs activity-based costing concepts?

d. How could a better, integrated cost management system have helped Digital avoid the adverse effects of its cost-cutting efforts?

38. *(Organizational strategy and cost management)* Flatland Metals Company produces steel products for a variety of customers. One division of the company is Residential Products Division. This division was created in the late 1940s and its principal products since that time have been galvanized steel components used in garage door installations. The division has been continuously profitable since 1950 and in 1996 generated profits of $10 million on sales of $300 million.

However, over the past 10 years, growth in the division has been slow; profitability has become stagnant, and few new products have been developed, although the garage door components market has matured. The president of the company, John Stamp, has asked his senior staff to evaluate the operations of the Residential Products Division and to make recommendations for changes that would improve its operations. The staff uncovered the following facts:

■ Tracinda Green, age 53, has been president of the division for the past 15 years.

■ Ms. Green receives a compensation package that includes a salary of $175,000 annually plus a cash bonus based on achievement of the budgeted level of annual profit.

■ Growth in sales in the residential metal products industry has averaged 12 percent annually over the past decade. Most of the growth has occurred in ornamental products used in residential privacy fencing.

■ Nationally, the division's market share in the overall residential metal products industry has dropped from 12 percent to 7 percent during the past 10 years, and it has dropped from 40 percent to 25 percent for garage door components.

■ The division maintains its own information systems. The systems in use today are mostly the same systems that were in place 15 years ago; however, some of the manual systems have been computerized (e.g., payroll, accounts payable, accounting).

■ The division has no customer service department. A small sales staff solicits and takes orders by phone from national distribution chains.

- The major intradivision communication tool is the annual operating budget. No formal statements have been prepared in the division regarding strategies, mission, values, goals and objectives, or identifying core competencies or critical success factors.

Given the introductory paragraphs and the facts from the staff of the company's president, identify the major problems in the Residential Products Division and develop recommendations to address the problems you have identified.

39. *(Cost and quality management)* A joke making the rounds in Philadelphia-area doctors' lounges goes like this:

> Leonard Abramson, chief executive officer of U.S. Healthcare Inc., the big health-maintenance company, dies and goes to heaven, where he tells God what a great place it is. "Don't get too comfortable," God advised, "You're only approved for a three-day stay."

That's the kind of cost control that the messianic Mr. Abramson understands. In the past 2 years, U.S. Healthcare has slashed the fees it pays to specialists and hospitals by 12 percent to 20 percent and sometimes more, these providers say. In the past year, it has cut members' days in hospitals by 11 percent. Increasingly, it asks specialists and hospitals to assume the financial risk for procedures that cost more than anticipated.

U.S. Healthcare is widely considered one of the country's toughest HMO companies, and one of the most innovative. It keeps 30 cents of every premium dollar to pay for salaries, marketing, administration, and shareholder dividends, nearly 10 cents more than the industry average. It zealously tracks the performance of doctors and hospitals, paying more to those whose quality scores are high. It is earning robust profits—up 99 percent in the past 24 months—while rocking the tradition-bound health-care markets along the East Coast.

"Unless you change the culture of the community you're working in, you're not changing health care," Mr. Abramson declares.

In the health-care community, U.S. Healthcare has both staunch supporters and critics. Consider the following additional information:

- Last year, Mr. Abramson earned $9.8 million in salary, bonuses, and stock options. Critics suggest this is excessive pay and takes resources that could otherwise have been applied to benefit patients. Mr. Abramson says, in a free-market economy, large rewards flow to those who provide superior performance.
- Critics claim U.S. Healthcare selects service providers based on price rather than quality.
- The company pays doctors to take training courses, such as one in breast cancer screening techniques.
- The company has an information system that allows it to rank hospitals according to infection rates of urology patients, by the length of stay for coronary-bypass surgery, or by the number of babies delivered by cesarean. The company shows the comparative data to its service providers and uses it as leverage in negotiations.
- The company is increasingly using performance-based pay contracts for its service providers.
- All of U.S. Healthcare's HMOs have earned 3-year accreditation from the National Committee for Quality Assurance; this is the best performance of any U.S. managed-care company.

[SOURCE: Adapted from Ron Winslow, "HMO Juggernaut: U.S. Healthcare Cuts Costs, Grows Rapidly, and Irks Some Doctors; A Few Patients Are Slighted, Squeezed, Specialists Say; But Firm Also Gets Praise; How Katie Avoids Hospital," *Wall Street Journal* (September 6, 1994), p. A1. Reprinted by permission of *The Wall Street Journal*, © 1994 Dow Jones & Company, Inc. All Rights Reserved Worldwide.]

Examine the preceding information and determine your opinion as to whether U.S. Healthcare is developing superior methods of delivering health care to U.S. citizens, or alternatively, uses its market power and information resources to exploit members and service providers. Support your conclusion with arguments by applying concepts provided in the chapter to the information provided in this case.

40. *(Cost management and product life cycle)* Ford Motor Co. reported a 58% drop in its fourth-quarter profit as a result of the heavy costs of launching new vehicles. And officials predicted that similar costs will continue to depress earnings through the first half of this year.

In the fourth quarter, Ford launched its Taurus sedan, its biggest-selling car, at the same time it was preparing for the debut of its F-series pickup trucks. The two vehicle lines account for sales of more than one million vehicles each year.

In the first half of 1996, Ford also plans to introduce a new version of its Escort small car, another of Ford's top sellers.

"The time to make changes is when you are strong," said David Mc-Cammon, Ford's vice-president for finance. He said the auto maker still managed to finish 1995 with $12.4 billion in cash despite a drop in full-year reported profit of 22%.

[SOURCE: Adapted from Oscar Suris, "Ford's Net Declined 58% in 4th Period," *Wall Street Journal* (February 1, 1996), pp. A3, A4. Reprinted by permission of *The Wall Street Journal*, © 1996 Dow Jones & Company, Inc. All Rights Reserved Worldwide.]

a. Why would Ford Motor's reported profits for 1995 have dropped because of the launching of new vehicles?
b. How would Ford Motor's reported profit have differed from that reported if the company used life cycle costing techniques to account for the costs of launching new products?
c. Explain what David McCammon meant when he said, "The time to make changes is when you are strong."
d. By management's willingness to proceed with launching new products even though doing so lowers reported profits for the current year, what can be inferred about the motivational elements in Ford's cost management system?

ETHICS AND QUALITY DISCUSSION

41. When a machine tried out for her job reading electricity meters earlier this year, Vicki Barsczak hoped it would fail. It didn't.

So, in April, Kansas City Power & Light Co., her employer, became the first big U.S. utility to begin installing a tiny electronic device in each of its 420,000 meters. The automatic reader, which broadcasts data on electricity usage every few minutes, is dooming Ms. Barsczak's $15-an-hour job—and probably those of all of the nation's 35,000 human meter readers.

She admits to feeling "animosity toward this inanimate object."

The number of people displaced by technology—modern-day John Henrys—is becoming legion. Automation has been shrinking manufacturing payrolls for years, but now it is spreading rapidly into the much-larger service sector. Smart machines and networks born of a marriage of computing and communications are raising service productivity, but also destroying many jobs, destabilizing others and constraining growth in new jobs.

Since services provide most of the jobs in any mature economy, the new information networks raise doubts about the commonly held belief that technology always creates more jobs than it destroys.

[SOURCE: Adapted from Pascal Zachary, "Service Productivity Is Rising Fast—and So Is the Fear of Lost Jobs," *Wall Street Journal* (June 8, 1995), pp. A1, A10. Reprinted by permission of *The Wall Street Journal*, © 1995 Dow Jones & Company, Inc. All Rights Reserved Worldwide.]

a. One of the critical success factors of most companies is quality output. Often, new technology is acquired for the sake of improving efficiency and quality. However, when new technology is installed, it often displaces existing employees. Knowledge of the impact of technology acquisitions on employment may make employees fearful of new technology and distrustful of management. In turn, the lack of trust may impair quality initiatives, including the very quality initiatives for which new technology is sought.

What actions can managers take in acquiring new technology to maintain the loyalty of workers and maintain or improve the overall quality of operations?

b. What are the ethical responsibilities of managers to workers in instances where new technology displaces existing workers?

42. *[John] Strazzanti is the president of Com-Corp Industries, a $13 million, 100 employee metal-stamping shop he incorporated in Cleveland in 1980. He'd started out as a machine operator with a tool-and-die manufacturer, rapidly climbing the ladder to become general manager of another stamping company. Along the way, he didn't just dream about what he'd change if he were a company president. He figured out ways to make his dreams a reality.*

[Dateline] Cleveland, 1977. Packie Presser was vice-president of the notoriously demanding local chapter of the teamsters' union. The chapter controlled a metal-stamping plant where Strazzanti had just been promoted from floor supervisor to general manager. Strazzanti recalls:

"Two coworkers marched into my office. It was a hot summer day; they had had a few beers at lunch and were fired up. They worked hard in the warehouse and saw the engineers working in the air-conditioning and getting paid a lot more. They didn't think it was fair and wanted more money. I knew I was in a no-win situation. If I told them I thought they were being paid fairly, that's what they expected; they were going to argue, and they weren't going to be happy with the results. If I gave them more money, I was being unfair to everybody else.

"So I took out a legal pad and I told them to write down whatever they wanted to be paid. Thirty days from that date, they would get that pay—with one caveat. During the 30 days, I would shop for replacements for them. If I could get highly qualified people to work for anything less than that number, they would have to take a hike. They asked for time to think about it and never came back with a number.

"A lot of these guys think that if a company fills an order for a million dollars, it earns a million dollars in profit. I realized that if workers understood how a company earned a profit and how it had to be competitive, a lot of the resentment between managers and employees could be eliminated. And they needed to understand that if they improved their job skills, they could receive a higher wage."

[SOURCE: Anonymous, "If I Were President . . . ," *Inc.* (April 1995), pp. 56–61. Reprinted with permission, *Inc.* magazine, April 1995. Copyright 1995 by Goldhirsh Group, Inc., 38 Commercial Wharf, Boston, MA 02110.]

a. How does the sharing of information in an organization contribute to the empowerment of employees in a decentralized organizational structure to enhance their performance and that of the organization?

b. In a decentralized organization, how does the sharing of information allow employees to better understand their organizational roles relative to the roles of others?

c. In a decentralized organization, how does quality control depend on widespread distribution of information?

43. Some people may view an organization's culture as a mechanism to eliminate diversity in the workplace. Is it ethical to attract and retain only individuals who accept an organization's culture and value system? In responding, be sure to discuss the positive and negative aspects of "conformity" as part of organizational culture.

44. Use Internet resources to compare and contrast the organizational cultures and operating performance of three of the following pairs of organizations:
   a. Delta Air Line and Southwest Airlines
   b. Exxon and Royal Dutch Shell
   c. Nordstroms and Wal-Mart
   d. Haggar and Levi Strauss
   e. IBM and Dell Computer

Which of the pair is the better operating performer? Discuss whether you believe that organizational culture has any relationship to operating performance and your reasons for that belief.

45. Use Internet resources to find a company (regardless of where it is domiciled) whose managers have chosen to: (a) avoid competition through compression of competitive scope, (b) avoid competition through differentiation, (c) avoid competition through cost leadership, and (d) confront competitors head-on. Prepare an analysis of each of these companies' strategies and discuss your perception of how well that strategy has worked.

46. Management Sciences for Health is a not-for-profit organization that exists to improve the quality of healthcare delivered in the United States, and to improve the manner in which decisions are made in health care organizations. Find the home page for this organization. Read the materials describing the organizational role of a management information system in a health-care firm. Based on these materials, describe how a management information system is intended to benefit a health-care organization. What are major components of a modern management information system in the health-care industry?

CHAPTER

16

Cost Control for Noninventory Costs

LEARNING OBJECTIVES

After completing this chapter, you should be able to answer these questions:

1. Why is cost consciousness important to all members of an organization?

2. How are costs determined to be committed or discretionary?

3. How are the benefits of expenditures for discretionary costs measured?

4. When are standards applicable to discretionary costs?

5. How does a budget help control discretionary costs?

6. *(Appendix)* How is program budgeting used in not-for-profit entities?

7. *(Appendix)* Why is zero-base budgeting useful in cost control?

Volkswagen

In Wolfsburg, Germany, Jens Neumann's starkly modern office looks out on an apparently endless maze of factory buildings where Volkswagens are being assembled many floors below. The scene is as dreary as Volkswagen's performance in recent years. But Neumann, VW's chief strategist as well as a member of the board of management, is cheery and enthusiastic . . . [discussing] an entirely new VW Beetle, designed and developed in Simi Valley, Calif., to be introduced in the U.S. by 2000, that he says "will revitalize the spirit of Volkswagen."

Volkswagen is already showing signs of revitalization after three painful years of restructuring under its new chairman, Ferdinand Piëch, a former Audi man. [Although finally generating positive pretax earnings after a loss of $1.4 billion in 1993,] Neumann says that the company is still maybe five years away from the 6.5% to 8% operating margins it enjoyed in the Eighties.

Like Piëch, a former Audi man, Neumann outlines VW's strategy and its progress to date. The key operating statistic to keep an eye on, he says, is the point at which plant capacity for a given brand generates enough revenue to cover fixed capital and labor costs. As recently as 1992, for example, this break-even point was a suicidal 107% for the VW brand itself, which means that VW would have had to operate at 107% of capacity to cover fixed costs and begin to make a profit. In other words, VW could never break even.

Enter Piëch. By 1994, VW had lowered its costs enough so that its break-even was 91% of capacity, still worrisome but at least tenable. Neumann says the goal is to reach 60% to 70% by 2000, a level that would protect VW from losses in a recession.

It is encouraging to look at the cost-cutting progress elsewhere in the company. At Audi, the 1992 break-even of 78% had improved impressively to 59% by 1994, making Audi the chief profit center for VW. Skoda, a small Czech automaker that Volkswagen acquired after Communist rule ended in 1989, improved its break-even from 98% in 1992 to 65% in 1994.

In contrast, [the break-even at Seat, the Spanish subsidiary] has risen from 72% in 1992 to 94% in 1994, but that's because the new plant in Martorell, Spain, came on line. [Seat's capacity is 525,000 cars per year, but it] is producing only 300,000 to 310,000. Still, the new plant should bring significant new efficiencies once it's running at capacity.

SOURCE: Robert Stowe England, "Hard Day's Night," *Financial World* (January 30, 1996), pp. 48–49. Excerpted from *Financial World*. Copyrighted 1996. All rights reserved.

The automobile industry is highly competitive, and an ability to manufacture products and operate administrative and service departments efficiently is required for continued existence and expansion. VW's concentration on break-even points reflects a management awareness of the critical nature of fixed costs relative to contribution margin. Because its products are differentiated from other automobiles, Volkswagen does not have to be *the* low-cost industry producer. However, effective cost control will help the company achieve its target profit margins.

Previous chapters present a variety of ways to control costs. For example, flexible budgets can be developed to monitor and control product and period costs. Direct material and direct labor cost control are often tied to the development and implementation of a standard cost system. Use of a variable costing system tends to focus on the costs that are more susceptible to control by managers in the short run.

cost control system

This chapter focuses on three major topics related to cost control. First, discussion is provided on **cost control systems,** which are the formal and/or informal activities designed to analyze and evaluate how well expenditures are managed during a period. The second topic is control over costs (such as advertising) that management sets each period at specified levels. Because the benefits of these costs are often hard to measure, they may be more difficult to control than costs that relate either to the long-term plant asset investments or to "permanent" organizational personnel. Third, methods of using budgets to help in cost control are discussed. The chapter appendix considers two alternative budgeting methods: program budgeting, which is often used in governmental and not-for-profit entities, and zero-base budgeting, which can be effective in some cost control programs.

COST CONTROL SYSTEMS

The cost control system is an integral part of the overall organizational decision support system. The cost control system focuses on intraorganizational information and contains the detector, assessor, effector, and network components discussed in Chapter 15. Relative to the cost management system, the cost control system provides information for planning and for determining the efficiency of activities while they are being planned and after they are performed, as indicated in Exhibit 16–1.

Managers alone cannot control costs. An organization is composed of many individuals whose attitudes and efforts should help determine how an organization's costs may be controlled. Cost control is a continual process that requires the support of *all* employees at *all* times. Thus, a good control system encompasses not only the functions shown in Exhibit 16–1, but also the ideas about cost consciousness shown in Exhibit 16–2. **Cost consciousness** refers to a companywide employee attitude toward the topics of cost understanding, cost containment, cost avoidance, and cost reduction. Each of these topics is important at a different stage of the control system.

cost consciousness

Cost Understanding

Control requires that a set of expectations exist. Thus, cost control is first exercised when the budget is prepared. However, budgets cannot be prepared without an understanding of the reasons underlying period costs changes, and cost control cannot be achieved without understanding why costs may differ from the budgeted amounts.

VIDEO VIGNETTE

Commercial Blueprint and/or The Pro Image (Blue Chip Enterprises)

COST CHANGES DUE TO COST BEHAVIOR   Costs may change from previous periods or differ from budget expectations for many reasons. Some costs change

EXHIBIT 16–1

Functions of an Effective Cost Control System

CONTROL POINT	REASON	COST CONTROL METHOD
Before an event	Preventive; reflects planning	Budgets; standards; policies concerning approval for deviations; expressions of quantitative and qualitative objectives
During an event	Corrective; ensures that the event is being pursued according to plans; allows management to correct problems as they occur	Periodic monitoring of ongoing activities; comparison of activities and costs against budgets and standards; avoidance of excessive expenditures
After an event	Diagnostic; guides future actions	Feedback; variance analysis; responsibility reports (discussed in Chapter 19)

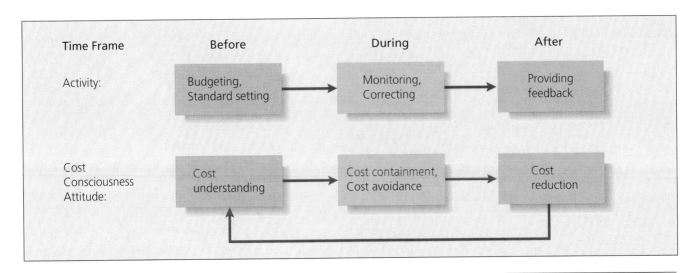

Time Frame	Before	During	After
Activity:	Budgeting, Standard setting	Monitoring, Correcting	Providing feedback
Cost Consciousness Attitude:	Cost understanding	Cost containment, Cost avoidance	Cost reduction

EXHIBIT 16–2

Cost Control System

because of their underlying behavior. Total variable or mixed cost increases or decreases with, respectively, increases or decreases in activity. If the current period's actual activity differs from a prior period's or the budgeted activity level, total actual variable or mixed cost will differ from that of the prior period or that in the budget. For example, Volkswagen's payroll processing costs will vary in proportion to the number of paychecks produced during a period. A flexible budget can compensate for such differences by providing expected costs at any activity level. By using a flexible budget, managers can then make valid budget-to-actual cost comparisons to determine whether costs were properly controlled.

In addition to the reactions of variable and mixed costs to changes in activity, other factors such as inflation/deflation, supply/supplier cost adjustments, and quantity purchased can cause costs to differ from those of prior periods or the budget. In considering these factors, remember that an external *price* becomes an internal *cost* when a good or service is acquired.

COST CHANGES DUE TO INFLATION/DEFLATION   Fluctuations in the value of money are called general price-level changes. When the general price level changes, the prices of goods and services also change. General price-level changes affect almost all prices approximately equally and in the same direction, if all other factors are constant. The statistics in Exhibit 16–3 represent the annual rates of inflation from 1970 through 1995 in the United States using the Consumer Price Index (CPI) as a measure. Thus, a company having office supplies expense of $10,000 in 1970 would expect to have approximately $39,300 of office supplies expense in 1995, *for the same basic "package" of supplies.* However, some economists believe the CPI is out of date and may overstate inflation by up to 1.5 percentage points annually.[1]

Some companies include price-escalation clauses in sales contracts to cover the inflation occurring from order to delivery. Such escalators are especially prevalent in industries having production activities that require substantial time. For instance, the airplane manufacturing industry uses escalators that averaged 3 + percent per year from 1989 to 1995.[2]

COST CHANGES DUE TO SUPPLY/SUPPLIER COST ADJUSTMENTS   The relationship between the availability of a good or service and the demand for that item affects its selling price. If supply is low but demand is high, the selling price of the item increases. The higher price often stimulates greater production, which, in turn,

When inflation hits an economy, it's as if part of an individual's or organization's money goes up in flames. It is almost impossible to control costs when they rise in conjunction with a loss in purchasing power.

[1] James Worsham, "A Guide for Comparing Expenses By Year," *Nation's Business* (February 1996), p. 8.
[2] Howard Banks, "Moment of Truth," *Forbes* (May 22, 1995), p. 56.

EXHIBIT 16–3

Cumulative Rate
of Inflation

YEAR	INDEX	YEAR	INDEX	YEAR	INDEX	YEAR	INDEX
1970	3.93	1977	2.52	1983	1.53	1990	1.17
1971	3.76	1978	2.34	1984	1.47	1991	1.12
1972	3.65	1979	2.10	1985	1.42	1992	1.09
1973	3.43	1980	1.85	1986	1.39	1993	1.05
1974	3.09	1981	1.68	1987	1.34	1994	1.03
1975	2.83	1982	1.58	1988	1.29	1995	1.00
1976	2.68			1989	1.23		

SOURCE: U.S. Bureau of Labor Statistics; cited in "How Costs Have Changed." Reprinted by permission, *Nation's Business* (February 1996), p. 8. Copyright 1996, U.S. Chamber of Commerce.

increases supply. In contrast, if demand falls but supply remains constant, the price falls. This reduced price should motivate lower production, which lowers supply. Therefore, price is consistently and circularly influenced by the relationship of supply and demand. Price changes resulting from independent causes are specific price-level changes, and these may move in the same or opposite direction as a general price-level change.

To illustrate, gasoline prices soared in the spring of 1996 because of two supply-related factors. First was a harsh winter that caused refineries to reduce gasoline and increase heating oil production. Second, several refineries had problems that caused shutdowns, which also reduced supply in the third week of April from 7.5 million barrels a day to 7.29 million barrels a day.[3]

Specific price-level changes may also be caused by advances in technology. As a general rule, as suppliers advance the technology of producing a good or performing a service, its cost to producing firms declines. Assuming competitive market conditions, such cost declines are often passed along to consumers of that product or service in the form of lower selling prices. Consider the following: "You receive one of those little greeting cards that plays 'Happy Birthday' when you open it. Casually toss it into the trash, and you've just discarded more computer processing power than existed in the entire world before 1950."[4] This is a simple example of the interaction of increasing technology and decreasing selling prices and costs.

Alternatively, when suppliers incur additional production or performance costs, they typically pass such increases on to their customers as part of specific price-level changes. Such costs may be within or outside the control of the supplier. For example, an agreement in 1994 by General Motors to pay up to 12 percent more for steel may cause GM automobiles to increase in price.[5] The price of dynamic random-access memories (DRAMs) increased after an explosion at the Japanese Sumitomo Chemical plant, which made a large portion of the world's supply of the plastic resin used to cover the DRAMs. Increased costs for employee health-care benefits are commonly passed along in the form of higher selling prices for that company's products or services.

The quantity of suppliers of a product or service can also affect selling prices. As the number of suppliers increases in a competitive environment, price tends to fall. Likewise, a reduction in the number of suppliers will, all else remaining equal, cause prices to increase. A change in the number of *suppliers* is not the same as a change in the quantity of *supply*. If the supply of an item is large, one normally expects a low price; however, if there is only one supplier, the price can remain high because of supplier control. Consider that combating illnesses commonly requires the use of various medications. When drugs are first introduced under patent, the supply may

[3] "They're Back: High Gas Costs Fuel Carpools," *(New Orleans) Times-Picayune* (April 26, 1996), p. C-3.
[4] John Huey, "Waking Up to the New Economy," *Fortune* (June 27, 1994), p. 37.
[5] Erle Norton, "GM Agrees to Pay As Much As 12% More in Supply Pacts with Major Steelmakers," *Wall Street Journal* (December 8, 1994), p. A2.

Discounted Footwear? Not Reeboks.

[In May 1995], the Federal Trade Commission, along with all 50 state attorneys general, announced an agreement with Reebok International Ltd. settling government charges that Reebok and its Rockport Co. subsidiary tried to fix the prices of their footwear with retailers.

According to the FTC's director of competition, William Baer, Reebok coerced retailers into agreeing to keep prices above certain levels. Some retailers raised prices by as much as 30% to stay in line with what they assumed was a minimum retail price, said Mr. Baer, because they feared Reebok would cut off their supplies or not fill orders.

[A]nalysts say that athletic-footwear manufacturers routinely pressure retailers to sell their shoes at suggested retail prices. "But Reebok was one of the few in the industry to ever put such a policy in writing," said Rich Wilner, athletics editor for Footwear News, a trade publication.

In the fall of 1992, Reebok insisted through what was called a Centennial Plan that retailers keep prices inflated during certain brisker shopping periods of the year. . . . It was around that time that a number of disgruntled retailers approached federal regulators to discuss the industry's practice.

In the proposed consent decree Reebok and Rockport didn't admit guilt, but agreed not to try to set or control the prices at which retailers sell or advertise their brands—and not to threaten retailers with suspension or termination if they don't go along with suggested prices. In their settlement with the states, the companies also agreed to pay $9.5 million. About $1.5 million of that will cover the cost of the litigation, and the rest will be distributed among the states to improve public and nonprofit athletic facilities and services. . . . [The companies did] entered into the consent decree "to avoid the considerable expense of protracted litigation."

SOURCE: Viveca Novak and Joseph Pereira, "Reebok and FTC Settle Price-Fixing Charges," *Wall Street Journal* (May 5, 1995), p. B1. Reprinted by permission of *The Wall Street Journal*, © 1995 Dow Jones & Company, Inc. All Rights Reserved Worldwide.

be readily available, but the selling price is high, because there is only a single source. As patents expire and generics become available, selling prices decline because more suppliers can produce the item. For example, when the patents on Syntex Corporation's antiarthritis drugs Naprosyn and Anaprox expired in December 1993, two-thirds of the prescriptions filled within a month were filled with generic versions and the price plummeted more than 80 percent.[6]

In some cases, all other factors are not equal, and the quantity of suppliers may not affect the selling price of a good or service. Firms may unethically conspire to engage in **price fixing** or setting an item's price at a specified level. Buyers must purchase the good or service at the specified price because no suppliers are offering the item at a lower price. Price fixing may be vertical or horizontal.

price fixing

Vertical price fixing (also known as resale price maintenance) involves agreements by businesses and their distributors to control the prices at which products may be sold to consumers. In 1993, a 1985 policy that allowed manufacturers to fix retail prices with distributors was rescinded, making all vertical price fixing illegal.[7] Companies may set suggested retail selling prices for items, but any attempts to prohibit retailers from selling below those prices are considered antitrust activities. The accompanying News Note discusses a recent price-fixing settlement between Reebok and the Federal Trade Commission (FTC). And, in May 1996, the FTC alleged price-fixing charges against Toys 'R' Us, saying the company struck "agreements

vertical price fixing

---

[6] Elyse Tanouye, "Price Wars, Patent Expirations Promise Cheaper Drugs," *Wall Street Journal* (March 24, 1994), p. B1.

[7] Joe Davidson, "Rules Allowing Manufacturers to Fix Prices with Distributors Are Rescinded," *Wall Street Journal* (August 11, 1993), p. A3.

with manufacturers as early as 1989 under which toy makers would not sell to warehouse clubs the same toys they sold to Toys 'R' Us."[8]

In **horizontal price fixing,** competitors attempt to regulate prices by agreeing on either a selling price or the quantity of goods that may be produced or offered for sale. Airlines, oil and credit card companies, the NCAA, and eight Ivy League schools and M.I.T. have all been accused of horizontal price fixing. In 1994, the United States and Canada filed the first joint criminal antitrust prosecution against several Japanese companies that controlled the thermal fax paper market; the Justice Department will collect almost $6.5 million in settlement.[9]

Sometimes, cost increases are caused by increases in taxes or regulatory requirements. For example, paper manufacturers are continually faced with more stringent clean air, clean water, and safety legislation. Complying with these regulations increases costs for paper companies. The companies can (1) pass along the costs as price increases to maintain the same income level, (2) decrease other costs to maintain the same income level, or (3) experience a decline in net income. To illustrate, in 1995, airlines were required to pay a new federal fuel tax that added $22 million to Delta Air Lines' costs for the quarter ending December 31, 1995.[10]

COST CHANGES DUE TO QUANTITY PURCHASED   Firms are normally given quantity discounts, up to some maximum level, when they make purchases in bulk. Therefore, a cost per unit may change because quantities are purchased in lot sizes differing from those of previous periods or those projected. Involvement in group purchasing arrangements can make quantity discounts easier to obtain. For example, in the spring of 1993, seventeen institutions in the Council of Independent Colleges in Virginia negotiated as a group to obtain long-distance telephone services. A bid from MCI dropped the cost of service from $.21 per minute to as little as $.07 per minute and the institutions expected a total savings of $5 + million over the 3-year life of the contract.[11]

The preceding reasons indicate why costs change. Minimizing the upward trends means controlling costs.

Cost Containment

To the extent possible, period-by-period increases in per-unit variable and total fixed costs should be *minimized* through a process of **cost containment.** Cost containment is not possible for inflation adjustments, tax and regulatory changes, and supply and demand adjustments because these forces occur outside the organizational structure. Additionally, in most Western companies, adjustments to prices resulting from factors within the supply chain are not controlled by managers.

Japanese companies may not have the same view of supply-chain cost containment techniques. In some circumstances, a significant exchange of information occurs among members of the supply chain, and members of one organization may actually be involved in activities designed to reduce costs of another organization. For example, Citizen Watch Company has long set target cost reductions for external suppliers. If suppliers could not meet the target, they would be assisted by Citizen engineers in efforts to meet the target the following year.[12]

In the United States, some interorganizational arrangements of this kind do exist. For instance, an agreement between Baxter International (a hospital supply company) and BJC Health System allows Baxter access to BJC's hospital computer information database. The information obtained is used by Baxter "to measure more precisely

---

[8] Darlene Superville, "Toys 'R' Us Fixed Prices, FTC Says," *(New Orleans) Times-Picayune* (May 23, 1996), p. C-1.

[9] Yi-Hsin Chang, "Two Firms to Pay Almost $6.5 Million to Settle Charges on Fax Paper Pricing," *Wall Street Journal* (July 15, 1994), p. C17.

[10] Martha Brannigan and Eleena De Lisser, "A Slimmer Delta Still Loves to Fly, but Does It Show?" *Wall Street Journal* (January 26, 1996), p. B3.

[11] Julie L. Nicklin, "Cost-Cutting Consortia," *Chronicle of Higher Education* (April 6, 1994), p. A52.

[12] Robin Cooper, *Citizen Watch Company, Ltd.* (Boston: Harvard Business School Case No. 194–033).

Price Isn't Everything

All too often companies fail to operate their purchasing function in strategically consistent ways. They go after transaction price reduction instead of purchasing for maximum value or minimum total cost.

A recent example of this price "mentality" creating an undesirable situation was with a large multinational organization. In this particular case, the organization was relying heavily on the support of a technologically-capable supplier to help develop a new product. The supplier invested months in this development effort—at no cost to the multinational. However, when the product moved into production and the purchasing department finally became involved in the process, the key raw materials were sent out for bid. The supplier which had helped with the development quoted a reasonable price, but it was not the lowest. As a result of purchasing's focus on price, the supplier lost the contract. The multinational obtained a lower price for the raw materials, but lost part of the technical capabilities needed for future product development. Furthermore, once into production, the alternative supplier's product fell short of the manufacturing yield expectations set during the development phase.

SOURCE: Steven Mehltretter, "Strategic Sourcing Means Just That—Sourcing Strategically," *CMA Magazine* (February 1996), p. 6. Reprinted from an article appearing in *CMA Magazine*, with permission of The Society of Management Accountants of Canada.

the types of procedures conducted and the exact amount of supplies needed."[13] Although not based on interorganizational agreements, "Ford has asked its 250 biggest suppliers world-wide to join in a 'collaborative effort' to cut costs of parts 5% a year from 1996 through 1999."[14]

However, costs that rise because of reduced competition, seasonality, and quantities purchased are subject to cost containment activities. A company should look for ways to cap the upward changes in these costs. For example, purchasing agents should be aware of new suppliers for needed goods and services and determine which, if any, of those suppliers can provide needed items in the quantity, quality, and time desired. Comparing costs and finding new sources of supply can increase buying power and reduce costs.

If bids are used to select suppliers, the purchasing agent should remember that a bid is merely the first step in negotiating. Although a low bid may eliminate some competition from consideration, additional negotiations between the purchasing agent and the remaining suppliers may result in a purchase cost even lower than the bid amount, or concessions (such as faster and more reliable delivery) can be obtained. However, purchasing agents must remember that the supplier offering the lowest bid amount is not necessarily the best supplier to choose. One aspect of this point is emphasized in the above News Note.

Reduced costs can often be obtained when long-term or single-source contracts are signed. For example, Ochsner Hospital in New Orleans has several limited (between one and three) source relationships for office and pharmaceutical supplies, food, and sutures. Most of these suppliers also provide just-in-time delivery. For instance, operating room (OR) supplies are ordered based on the next day's OR schedule. Two hours later, individual OR trays containing specified supplies for each operation are delivered by the vendor. By engaging in supplier relationships of this kind, Ochsner has not only introduced volume purchasing discounts but also effected timely delivery with total quality control.[15]

A company may circumvent seasonal cost changes by postponing or advancing purchases of goods and services. However, such purchasing changes should not mean

[13] Thomas M. Burton, "Baxter Reaches Novel Supply Pact with Duke Hospital," *Wall Street Journal* (July 15, 1994), p. B2.

[14] Robert L. Simison and Oscar Suris, "Ford Sets Goal of Keeping Overall Costs at '95 Level to 2000, Cutting Parts Prices," *Wall Street Journal* (May 9, 1995), p. A4.

[15] 1994 Interview with Graham Cowie, Oschner Medical Institutions.

EXHIBIT 16–4

Labor Costs for
Selected Processes

PROCESS	MEASURE	AVERAGE	WORLD-CLASS
Payables	Invoice	$2.90	$0.71
Receivables	Remittance	0.71	0.01
Travel and expense	Expense report	7.60	1.29
Fixed assets	Asset tracked	5.90	0.16
Payroll	Paycheck	3.00	0.95

SOURCE: Christine A. Gattenio, "How to Benchmark the Performance of Your Finance Function," *CMA Magazine* (April 1996), p. 23. Reprinted from an article appearing in *CMA Magazine*, with permission of The Society of Management Accountants of Canada.

buying irresponsibly or incurring excessive carrying costs. Economic order quantities, safety stock levels, and materials requirements planning as well as the just-in-time philosophy should be considered when making purchases. These concepts are discussed in the next chapter.

As to services, employees could repair rather than replace items that have seasonal cost changes. For example, maintenance workers might find that a broken heat pump can be repaired and used for the spring months so that it would not have to be replaced until summer when the purchase cost is lower.

Cost Avoidance and Reduction

Cost containment can prove very effective if it can be implemented. In some instances, although cost containment may not be possible, cost avoidance might be. **Cost avoidance** means finding acceptable alternatives to high-cost items and/or not spending money for unnecessary goods or services. Avoiding one cost may require that an alternative, lower cost be incurred. For example, some companies have decided to self-insure for many workers' compensation claims rather than paying high insurance premiums. Self-insurance does create costs for posting a bond or letter or credit to state regulators and also for claims that are made, but companies with approximately $200,000 in annual workers' compensation costs may be better off with self-insurance.[16] Gillette avoids substantial costs by warehousing and shipping Oral-B toothbrushes, Braun coffeemakers, Right Guard deodorant, and Paper Mate ballpoint pens together because all these products share common distribution channels.[17]

cost avoidance

cost reduction

Closely related to cost avoidance, **cost reduction** refers to lowering current costs. Benchmarking is especially important in this area so that companies can become aware of costs that are in excess of what is necessary. For example, Exhibit 16–4 indicates the average and world-class labor cost for a variety of processes. The exhibit indicates that most companies have substantial opportunities for cost reduction activities.

As discussed in Chapter 2 relative to core competencies, companies may also reduce costs by outsourcing rather than maintaining internal departments. Data processing and the financial and legal functions are prime targets for outsourcing in many companies. Distribution is also becoming a highly viable candidate for outsourcing, because "for many products, distribution costs can be as much as 30% to 40% of a product's cost."[18] The following News Note discusses Volkswagen's use of outsourcing in its new General Pacheco plant in Buenos Aires.

When considering cost reduction strategies, company management needs to consider the ramifications of those strategies. Although it may be "easy" to reduce certain costs, the results may not be the most appropriate. For instance, the proportion

[16] Jill Andresky Fraser, ed. "The Case for Self-Insurance," *Inc.* (May 1994), p. 154.
[17] Pablo Galarza, "Nicked and Cut," *Financial World* (April 8, 1996), p. 38.
[18] Rita Koselka, "Distribution Revolution," *Forbes* (May 25, 1992), p. 58.

Interestingly, the Outsourcing Here Is Within the Plant!

Gabriel Fernandez works on the assembly line at Volkswagen AG's new plant. But Mr. Fernandez, who makes doors for the company's Golf model sedan, isn't a VW employee. Instead, as part of a radical experiment aimed at slicing the costs of making cars, Mr. Fernandez works for Metalurgica Romet SA, one of a dozen companies VW has contracted with to run operations and to build big chunks of its vehicles at the General Pacheco plant.

When the 480 car-a-day General Pacheco plant is fully operational in July, VW workers will be directly responsible for building only the chassis, powertrain and a few other parts. They'll also remain in charge of safety engineering and quality control. But suppliers will do the rest, from assembling car-instrument panels or feeding workers their lunch. VW has even hired Australian transport company TNT Ltd. to handle logistics operations.

By using this system, VW will cut the time it spends making a car to between 30 and 32 hours (compared with about 16 hours for higher-volume plants of big auto makers around the world), from nearly 70 hours at its old Argentine facility.

[The manufacturing process is designed in a modular fashion] to have as few parts as possible handled on the assembly line. Take doors, for instance. At General Pacheco, they are fitted to the chassis, go through the rustproofing and paint shops, and then are detached and carried to another part of the plant, where Mr. Fernandez and his team from supplier Metalurgica Romet put in windows, locks, even speakers. The fully assembled door is then conveyed back to the main line, where it is bolted in by a VW worker.

SOURCE: Jonathan Friedland, "VW Puts Suppliers on Production Line," *Wall Street Journal* (February 15, 1996), p. A11. Reprinted by permission of *The Wall Street Journal*, © 1996 Dow Jones & Company, Inc. All Rights Reserved Worldwide.

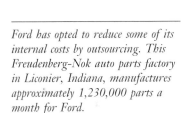

Ford has opted to reduce some of its internal costs by outsourcing. This Freudenberg-Nok auto parts factory in Liconier, Indiana, manufactures approximately 1,230,000 parts a month for Ford.

of small companies providing "medical benefits to at least some retirees plunged to 35% in 1994 from 50% in 1993."[19] Although this cost reduction activity may have short-run profit benefits for the companies, one must question the overall economic impact of such choices as well as the impact on the individuals.

[19] Stephanie N. Mehta, "Many Small Companies Drop Retiree Health Benefits," *Wall Street Journal* (August 22, 1995), p. B2.

Sometimes money must be spent to generate cost savings. Accountants may opt to use videotaped rather than live presentations to reduce the cost of continuing education programs. Some of the larger firms (such as Arthur Andersen) have their own in-house studios and staffs. Although the cost of producing a tape is high, the firms feel the cost is justified because many copies can be made and used in multiple presentations over time by all the offices. Other firms bring in specialists or use satellite or two-way interactive television to provide continuing education hours to their employees.

Some companies are also beginning to look outside for information about how and where to cut costs. Consulting firms, such as Fields & Associates (Burlingame, California), review files for duplicate payments and tax overpayments. Fields "recovered about $1 million for Intel Corp. in two years, in exchange for part of the savings."[20]

A starting point for determining appropriate cost reduction practices is to focus on the activities that are creating costs. As discussed in Chapter 6 on activity-based management, reducing or eliminating non-value-added activities will cause the associated costs to be reduced or eliminated. Activities must be analyzed so that those adding no value are uncovered and the cost reduction that can occur with the elimination of such activities is recognized. Volkswagen Canada has instituted an effective activity-based costing system that is used, in part, to highlight areas that increase product costs and areas where costs need to be cut. The ABC system is part of a full-blown activity-based management system that provides information in support of total quality management process reengineering activities, cost-of-quality computations, and resource utilization decisions. Such information is designed to "help VW [Canada] to achieve its goal of becoming the ultimate, cost-conscious, world-class, customer-focused supplier" [to Volkswagen and other third-party original equipment manufacturers.][21]

Although many companies believe that eliminating jobs and labor are effective ways to reduce costs, the following quote provides a more appropriate viewpoint:

> Cutting staffs to cut costs is putting the cart before the horse. The only way to bring costs down is to restructure the work. This will then result in reducing the number of people needed to do the job, and far more drastically than even the most radical staff cutbacks could possibly do. Indeed, a cost crunch should always be used as an opportunity to rethink and to re-design operations.[22]

In fact, sometimes cutting costs by cutting people merely creates other problems. The people who are cut may have been performing a value-added activity; and by eliminating the people, a company may reduce its ability to do necessary and important tasks.

This point can be illustrated by the following example. After downsizing by about 3,000 workers in 1994, Delta Air Lines decided to "put about 665 baggage handlers, fuelers, gate agents and ticket counter employees back to work by the end of the summer [of 1996]: the company was responding to customer complaints about service levels.[23] Thus, the cost reduction was not proportionate to the potential for revenue reduction from dissatisfied flyers.

Use of part-time rather than full-time employees is another cost reduction technique. When temporaries (temps) are used, companies do not have to pay payroll taxes, fringe benefits, or Social Security taxes. Thus, although temps often cost more per hour than full-time workers, total cost may be reduced. If the amount of work in an area fluctuates substantially, part-time employees can be hired for peak periods. Businesses are also hiring temps to work on special projects, provide expertise in a

[20] Jeffrey A. Tannenbaum, "Entrepreneurs Thrive by Helping Big Firms Slash Costs," *Wall Street Journal* (November 10, 1993), p. B2.

[21] Jim Gurowka, "ABC, ABM, and the Volkswagen Saga," *CMA Magazine* (May 1996), p. 32.

[22] Peter Drucker, "Permanent Cost Cutting," *Wall Street Journal* (January 11, 1991), p. A8.

[23] The Associated Press, "Customers' Gripes Force Delta to Rehire Workers," *(New Orleans) Times-Picayune* (February 2, 1996), p. C-6.

How Much Care Would You Want an Aide to Give You?

NEWS NOTE

When hospital executives want cost-cutting advice, they increasingly turn to the consulting firm of APM Inc. But to many nurses, APM is an enemy.

At issue is one of APM's most frequent recommendations: that hospitals change their "nursing skills mix" to rely less on higher-paid and better-trained nurses and more on lower-paid aides to perform routine tasks. APM claims it can save money without affecting patient care; many nurses disagree.

"We view APM as the nemesis of health care," says Rose Ann DeMoro, president of the California Nurses Association. "They're out selling cost-savings models that have been used in the industrial sector. The problem is they look at the patient as a bunch of parts, rather than as a whole human being."

The showdown typifies the turmoil associated with hospitals' efficiency campaigns. Many of America's 5,300 hospitals say they must trim expenses as they lose business to outpatient services and cope with insurers' demands for discounts to hospitals' prices. But cost cutting can bring labor clashes and a hail of questions about whether patient care is at risk.

At many hospitals, 75% or more of patient care is provided by registered nurses, who have at least two to four years of training. They make appreciably more than licensed practical nurses, who generally have 12 to 14 months of training, and often make double the pay of unlicensed aides or orderlies.

Because of the cost differentials, APM advises hospitals to redesign work teams to rely more on lower-paid aides for simple duties, like making beds. This workplace reengineering can mean big savings. In California, hospitals can save as much as $25,000 a year for each nurse's job converted to an aide's job.

More controversy may lie ahead as some hospitals try to expand the work that lower-paid aides can perform. Among those tasks are drawing blood, gathering data for medical charts or bandaging incisions after surgery—duties that nurses may not want to leave in the hands of less-trained personnel.

SOURCE: George Anders, "Nurses Decry Cost-Cutting Plan that Uses Aides to Do More Jobs," *Wall Street Journal* (January 20, 1994), p. B1. Reprinted by permission of *The Wall Street Journal*, © 1994 Dow Jones & Company, Inc. All Rights Reserved Worldwide.

specific area, or fill in until the "right" full-time employee can be found for a particular position.

Companies are beginning to view their personnel needs from a **strategic staffing** perspective. This outlook requires departments to analyze their personnel needs by considering long-term objectives and determining a specific combination of permanent and temporary employees or highly skilled and less skilled employees who offer the best opportunity to meet those needs. However, as the above News Note indicates, some differences of opinion exist about the appropriate level of strategic staffing.

Companies can also reduce costs by using permanent part-time employees. The airline industry provides an excellent example of how part-time employees can be beneficial. Airlines often hire permanent part-time ground personnel because of the "bunching" nature of the airline schedule (early morning, midday, and early evening flights). Use of these part-timers has dramatically reduced airline fringe benefit costs.

On-the-job training is an important component in instilling cost consciousness within an organization's quest for continuous improvement. Giving training to personnel throughout the firm is an effective investment in human resources because workers can apply the concepts and skills they are learning directly to the jobs they are doing.

Managers may adopt the five-step method of implementing a cost control system shown in Exhibit 16–5. First, the type of costs incurred by an organization must be understood. Are the costs under consideration fixed or variable, product or period?

strategic staffing

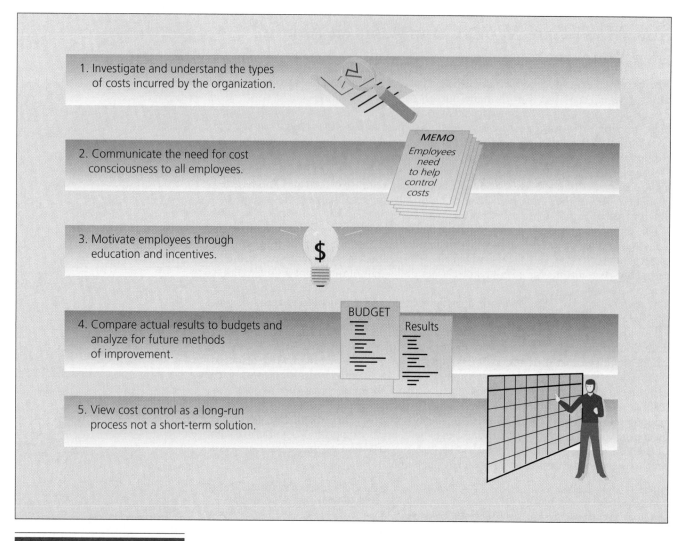

1. Investigate and understand the types of costs incurred by the organization.

2. Communicate the need for cost consciousness to all employees.

MEMO
Employees need to help control costs

3. Motivate employees through education and incentives.

$

4. Compare actual results to budgets and analyze for future methods of improvement.

BUDGET   Results

5. View cost control as a long-run process not a short-term solution.

EXHIBIT 16–5

Implementing a Cost Control System

What cost drivers affect those costs? Does management view the costs as committed or discretionary? Second, the need for cost consciousness must be communicated to all employees for the control process to be effective. Employees must be aware of which costs need to be better controlled and why cost control is important to both the company and the employees themselves. Third, employees must be educated in cost control techniques, encouraged to provide ideas on how to control costs, and motivated by incentives to embrace the concepts. The incentives may range from simple verbal recognition to monetary rewards to time off with pay. Managers must also be flexible enough to allow for changes from the current method of operation. Fourth, reports must be generated indicating actual results, budget-to-actual comparisons, and variances. These reports must be evaluated by management as to why costs were or were not controlled in the past. Such analysis may provide insightful information about cost drivers so that the activities causing costs to be incurred may be better controlled in the future. And last, the cost control system should be viewed as a long-run process, not a short-run solution. "To be successful, organizations must avoid the illusion of short-term, highly simplified cost-cutting procedures. Instead, they must carefully evaluate proposed solutions to insure that these are practical, workable, and measure changes based on realities, not illusions."[24]

Following these five steps will provide an atmosphere conducive to controlling costs to the fullest extent possible as well as deriving the most benefit from the costs that are incurred. Costs to be incurred should have been compared to the benefits

[24] Mark D. Lutchen, "Cost Cutting Illusions," *Today's CPA* (May/June 1989), p. 46.

expected to be achieved before cost incurrence took place. The costs should also have been incorporated into the budgeting system because costs cannot be controlled *after* they have been incurred. Future costs, on the other hand, may be controlled based on information learned about past costs. Cost control should not cease at the end of a fiscal period or because costs were reduced or controlled during the current period. However, distinct differences exist in the cost control system between committed and discretionary costs.

Managers are charged with planning and controlling the types and amounts of costs necessary to conduct business activities. Many activities required to achieve business objectives involve fixed costs. All fixed costs (and the activities that create them) can be categorized as either committed or discretionary. The difference between the two categories is primarily the time period for which management binds itself to the activity and the cost.

The costs associated with basic plant assets or with the personnel structure that an organization must have to operate are known as **committed costs.** The amount of committed costs is normally dictated by long-run management decisions involving the desired level of operations. Committed costs include depreciation, lease rentals, and property taxes. Such costs cannot be reduced easily even during temporarily diminished activity.

One method of controlling committed costs involves comparing the expected benefits of having plant assets (or human resources) with the expected costs of such investments. Managers must decide what activities are needed to attain company objectives and what (and how many) assets are needed to support those activities. Once the assets are acquired, managers are committed to both the activities and their related costs for the long run. However, regardless of how good an asset investment appears to be on the surface, managers need to understand how committed fixed costs could affect income in the event of changes in operations.

Assume the managers at Munich Glass are considering an investment of $1,000,000 in an automated glass cutter. The machine will be depreciated at the rate of $200,000 per year. The company's cost relationships indicate that variable costs are 45 percent of revenues, giving a contribution margin of 55 percent. Exhibit 16–6 illustrates the potential effects of this long-term commitment on net income under three condi-

COMMITTED FIXED COSTS

committed cost

EXHIBIT 16–6

Risk Related to Committed Costs

	CURRENT LEVEL OF OPERATIONS	(a) CURRENT LEVEL OF REVENUES AND INCREASE IN DEPRECIATION	(b) INCREASE IN REVENUES OF 20% AND INCREASE IN DEPRECIATION	(c) DECREASE IN REVENUES OF 20% AND INCREASE IN DEPRECIATION
Revenues	$5,000,000	$5,000,000	$6,000,000	$4,000,000
Variable costs	(2,250,000)	(2,250,000)	(2,700,000)	(1,800,000)
Contribution margin	$2,750,000	$2,750,000	$3,300,000	$2,200,000
Fixed costs	(2,400,000)	(2,600,000)	(2,600,000)	(2,600,000)
Net income	$ 350,000	$ 150,000	$ 700,000	$ (400,000)

Each change from the original income level to the new income level is explained as the change in the contribution margin minus the increase in fixed costs:

Change to (a) = Increase in CM − Increase in FC = $0 − $200,000 = $(200,000)

Change to (b) = Increase in CM − Increase in FC = $550,000 − $200,000 = $350,000

Change to (c) = Decrease in CM − Increase in FC = $(550,000) − $200,000 = $(750,000)

tions: maintenance of current revenues, a 20 percent increase in revenues, and a 20 percent decrease in revenues.

Note that the $200,000 increase in depreciation expense affects the income statement more significantly when sales decline than when sales increase. This effect is caused by the operating leverage factor discussed in Chapter 12. Companies that have fairly high contribution margins can withstand large increases in fixed costs as long as revenues increase. However, these same companies feel greater effects of decreases in revenue because the margin available to cover fixed costs erodes so rapidly. As the magnitude of committed fixed costs increases, so does the risk of incurring an operating loss in the event of a downturn in demand. Therefore, managers must be extremely careful about the level of fixed costs to which they commit the organization.

A second method of controlling committed costs involves comparing actual and expected results from plant asset investments. During this process, managers are able to see and evaluate the accuracy of their cost and revenue predictions relative to the investment. This comparison is called a postinvestment audit and is discussed in Chapter 18.

An organization cannot operate without some basic levels of plant and human assets. Considerable control can be exercised over the process of determining how management wishes to define *basic* and what funds will be committed to those assets. The benefits from committed costs can generally be predicted and are commonly compared with actual results in the future.

DISCRETIONARY COSTS

discretionary cost

In contrast to a committed cost, a **discretionary cost** is one "that a decision maker must periodically review to determine if it continues to be in accord with ongoing policies."[25] A discretionary fixed cost is one that reflects a management decision to fund a particular activity at a specified amount *for a specified period of time*. Discretionary costs relate to company activities that are important but are viewed as optional. Discretionary cost activities are usually service oriented and include employee travel, repairs and maintenance, advertising, research and development, and employee training and development. There is no "correct" amount at which to set funding for discretionary costs, and there are no specific activities whose costs are always considered discretionary (or discretionary fixed) in all organizations. In the event of cash flow shortages or forecasted operating losses, discretionary fixed costs may be more easily reduced than committed fixed costs.

Discretionary costs, then, are generated by unstructured activities that vary in type and magnitude from day to day and whose benefits are often not measurable in monetary terms. For example, in 1996, McDonald's decided to spend more than $200 million to promote its quarter-pound Arch Deluxe hamburger and several other adult entrees.[26] How can McDonald's know whether this advertising campaign actually created a demand for these products? Similarly, Oscar Mayer spent $2.5 million to back Super Bowl XXX's half-time show and air a new TV ad.[27] How will Oscar Mayer know whether this ad sold more bologna to customers? Expenditures of this magnitude require that management have some idea of the benefits that are expected, but measuring results is often difficult. Management can employ market research in trying to gain knowledge of the effectiveness of advertising and other promotional tools.

[25] Institute of Management Accountants (formerly National Association of Accountants), *Statements on Management Accounting Number 2: Management Accounting Terminology* (Montvale, N.J.: June 1, 1983), p. 35.
[26] Bruce Horovitz and Dottie Enrico, "Chain Hoping Grown-Up Chow Boosts Sales," *USA Today* (May 9, 1996), p. 1A.
[27] Michael Hiestand, "Name of Game Is Sponsorships," *USA Today* (January 26, 1996), p. 15E.

Just as discretionary cost activities vary, the quality of performance may also vary according to the tasks involved and the skill levels of the persons performing them. Because of these two factors—varying activities and varying quality levels—discretionary costs are not usually susceptible to the precise measures available to plan and control variable production costs or the cost-benefit evaluation techniques available to control committed fixed costs. Because the benefits of discretionary cost activities cannot be assessed definitively, these activities are often among the first to be cut when profits are lagging. Thus, proper planning for discretionary activities and costs may be more important than subsequent control measures. Control after the planning stage is often restricted to monitoring expenditures to ensure conformity with budget classifications and preventing managers from overspending their budgeted amounts.

Budgeting Discretionary Costs

Budgets, described in Chapter 14 as both planning and controlling devices, serve to officially communicate a manager's authority to spend up to a predetermined amount **(appropriation)** or rate for each budget item. Budget appropriations serve as a basis for comparison with actual costs. Accumulated expenditures in each budgetary category are periodically compared with appropriated amounts to determine whether funds have been under- or overexpended.

appropriation

Before top management can address the issue of discretionary costs, company goals must be translated into specific objectives and policies that management believes will contribute to organizational success. Then, management needs to budget the type and funding levels of discretionary activities that will accomplish those objectives. Funding levels should be set only after discretionary cost activities have been prioritized and cash flow and income expectations for the coming period have been reviewed. Management tends to be more generous in making discretionary cost appropriations during periods of strong economic outlook for the organization than in periods of weak economic outlook.

Discretionary costs are generally budgeted on the basis of three factors: the related activity's perceived significance to the achievement of objectives and goals; the upcoming period's expected level of operations; and managerial negotiations in the budgetary process. For some discretionary costs, managers are expected to spend the full amount of their appropriations within the specified time frame. For other discretionary cost activities, the "less is better" adage is appropriate.

As an example of "less is *not* better," consider the cost of preventive maintenance. This cost can be viewed as discretionary, but reducing it could result in diminished quality, production breakdowns, or machine inefficiency. Although the benefits of maintenance expenditures cannot be precisely quantified, most managers would believe that incurring less maintenance cost than budgeted is not a positive type of cost control. In fact, spending (with supervisory approval) more than originally appropriated might be necessary or even commendable—assuming that positive results (such as a decline in quality defects) were obtained. Such a perspective illustrates the perception mentioned earlier that cost control should be a long-run process rather than a short-run concern.

Alternatively, spending less than budgeted on travel and entertainment (while achieving the desired results) would probably be considered positive performance, but requesting travel and entertainment funds in excess of budget appropriations might be considered irresponsible.

In developing discretionary cost budgets, top management often relies on the advice of specialists or project managers. Information from such specialists is an important input to the process because these people have more detailed knowledge of the specific discretionary cost area, legitimate reasons for funding, and potential benefits (at least qualitatively) to be derived from the expenditures. Top management should be aware, though, that specialists sometimes provide biased advice. To dissuade specialists from seeking excessive appropriations, a corporate officer with adequate technical knowledge of the service functions may be added to the administrative team. This officer would have the responsibility of working with the specialists in the planning and control of discretionary cost budgets.

Managers may view discretionary activities and costs as though they were committed. A discretionary expenditure may be budgeted on an annual basis as a function of planned volume of company sales. Once this appropriation has been justified, management's intention may be that it is not to be reduced within that year regardless of whether actual sales are less than planned sales. A manager who states that a particular activity's cost will not be reduced during a period has chosen to view that activity and cost as committed. This viewpoint does not change the underlying discretionary nature of the item. In such circumstances, top management must have a high degree of faith in the ability of lower-level management to perform the specified tasks in an efficient manner.

However, if revenues, profits, or cash flows are reduced, funding for discretionary expenditures should be evaluated not simply in reference to reduced operations, but relative to activity priorities. Eliminating the funding for one or more discretionary activities altogether may be possible while maintaining other funding levels at the previously determined amounts. For instance, if a company experiences a downturn in demand for its product, the discretionary cost budget for advertising is often reduced—a potentially illogical reaction. Instead, increasing the advertising budget and reducing the corporate executives' travel budget might be more appropriate.

Discretionary cost activities involve services that vary significantly in type and magnitude from day to day. The output quality of discretionary cost activities may also vary according to the tasks and skill levels of the persons performing the activities. Because of these two factors (varying service levels and quality), discretionary costs are generally not susceptible to the precise planning and control measurements that are available for variable production costs or to the cost-benefit evaluation techniques available for committed fixed costs.

Part of the difference in management attitude between committed and discretionary costs has to do with the ability to measure the benefits provided by those costs. Whereas benefits of committed fixed costs can be measured on a before-and-after basis (through the capital budgeting and postinvestment audit processes), the benefits from discretionary fixed costs are often not distinctly measurable in terms of money.

Discretionary Cost Activity	Surrogate Measure of Results
Preventive maintenance	• Reduction in number of equipment failures • Reduction in unplanned downtime • Reduction in frequency of production interruptions caused by preventable maintenance activities
Advertising	• Increase in unit sales in the two weeks after an advertising effort relative to the sales two weeks prior to the effort • Number of customers referring to the ad • Number of coupons clipped from the ad and redeemed
University admissions recruiting trip	• Number of students met who requested an application • Number of students from area visited who requested to have ACT/SAT scores sent to the university • Number of admissions that year from that area
Prevention and appraisal quality activities	• Reduction in number of customer complaints • Reduction in number of warranty claims • Reduction in number of product defects discovered by customers
Staffing law school indigent clinic	• Number of clients served • Number of cases effectively resolved • Number of cases won
Executive retreat	• Proportion of participants still there at end of retreat • Number of useful suggestions made • Values tabulated from an exit survey

EXHIBIT 16–7

Nonmonetary Measures of Output from Discretionary Costs

Measuring Benefits from Discretionary Costs

Because benefits from some activities traditionally classified as discretionary cannot be adequately measured, companies often assume that the benefits—and, thus, the activities—are unimportant. Many of the activities previously described as discretionary (repairs, maintenance, R&D, and employee training) are critical to a company's position in a world-class environment. These activities, in the long run, produce quality products and services; therefore, before reducing or eliminating expenditures in these areas, managers should attempt to more appropriately recognize and measure the benefits of these activities.

The value of discretionary costs should be estimated using nonmonetary, surrogate measures. Devising such measures often requires substantial time and creativity. Exhibit 16–7 presents some useful surrogate measures for determining the effectiveness of various types of discretionary costs. Some of these measures are verifiable and can be gathered quickly and easily; others are abstract and require a longer time horizon before they can be obtained. The News Note about Motorola indicates why the measure of a discretionary cost must often be stated as a nonmonetary, rather than a monetary, one.

The amounts spent on discretionary activities reflect resources that are consumed by an activity that should provide some desired monetary or surrogate output. Comparing input costs and output results can help to determine whether a reasonable cost-benefit relationship exists between the two. Managers can judge this cost-benefit relationship by how efficiently inputs (represented by costs) were used and how ef-

The Amount of Money Spent Is Not the Proper Measure

The first step to increasing white-collar productivity may be figuring out how to measure it. Motorola used to chart the productivity of its communications-sector employee recruiting department by the amount of money the recruiters spent to sign up each new hire. The goal was to spend less per hire each year. Yes, productivity went up steadily, but without regard to the quality of the people who were joining the company. Notes Bill Smith, a Motorola quality manager and VP: "If you hired an idiot for 39 cents you would meet your goal."

Motorola has completely revamped the way it calculates the effectiveness of its employees. In the office, as in the factory, the company emphasizes quality. The recruiting department is now measured by how well its recruits subsequently do at Motorola. Did they turn out to be well qualified for the job or did they need a lot of remedial training? Were they hired at the right salary or did they leave six months later for a higher-paying job at another company? Judged by such standards, the department decided to increase its spending per new hire.

SOURCE: Ronald Henkoff, "Make Your Office More Productive," *Fortune* (February 25, 1991), p. 76. © 1991 Time Inc. All rights reserved.

fectively those resources (again represented by costs) achieved their purposes. These relationships can be seen in the following model:

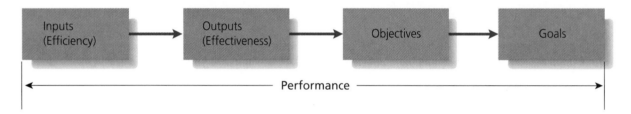

The degree to which a satisfactory relationship occurs when comparing outputs to inputs reflects the efficiency of the activity. Thus, efficiency is a yield concept and is usually measured by a ratio of output to input. For instance, one measure of automobile efficiency is miles driven per gallon of fuel consumed. The higher the number of miles per gallon, the greater the efficiency.

Comparing actual output results to desired results indicates the effectiveness of an activity or how well the objectives of the activity were achieved. When a valid output measure is available, efficiency and effectiveness can be determined as follows:

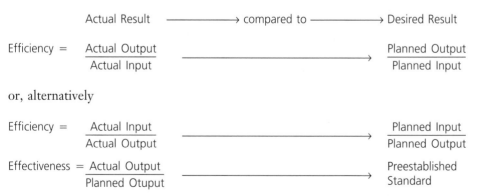

A reasonable measure of efficiency can exist only when inputs and outputs can be matched in the same period and when a credible causal relationship exists between them. These two requirements make measuring the efficiency of discretionary costs very difficult. First, several years may pass before output occurs from some discretionary cost expenditures. Consider, for example, the length of time between making expenditures for research and development or a drug rehabilitation program and the time at which results of these types of expenditures are visible. Second, there is frequently a dubious cause-effect relationship between discretionary cost inputs and resulting outputs. For instance, assume that you clip out and use a cents-off coupon for Crest toothpaste from the Sunday paper. Can Procter & Gamble be certain that it was the advertising coupon that caused you to buy the product, or might you have purchased the toothpaste anyway?

Effectiveness, on the other hand, is determined for a particular period by comparing the results achieved with the results desired. Determination of an activity's effectiveness is unaffected by whether the designated output measure is stated in monetary or nonmonetary terms. But management can only subjectively attribute some or all of the effectiveness of the cost incurrence to the results. Subjectivity is required because the comparison of actual output to planned output is not indicative of a perfect causal relationship between activities and output results. *Measurement of effectiveness does not require the consideration of inputs, but measurement of efficiency does.*

Assume that last month Munich Glass increased its quality control training expenditures and, during that period, defective output dropped by 12 percent. The planned decrease in defects was 15 percent. Although management was 80 percent effective (.12 ÷ .15) in achieving its goal of decreased defects, that result was not necessarily related to the quality control program expenditures. The decline in defects may have been caused partially or entirely by such factors as use of higher grade raw materials, more skilled production employees, or more properly maintained production equipment. Management, therefore, does not know for certain whether the quality control training program was the most effective way in which to decrease production defects.

The efficiency relationship between discretionary costs and their desired results is inconclusive at best, and the effectiveness of such costs can only be inferred from the relationship of actual to desired output. Because many discretionary costs result in benefits that must be measured on a nondefinitive and nonmonetary basis, exercising control of these costs during activities or after they have begun is difficult. Therefore, planning for discretionary costs may be more important than subsequent control measures. Control after the planning stage is often relegated to monitoring discretionary expenditures to ensure conformity with budget classifications and preventing managers from overspending their budgeted amounts.

Control of discretionary costs is often limited to a monitoring function. Management compares actual discretionary expenditures with standards or budgeted amounts to determine variances in attempting to understand the cause-effect relationships of discretionary activities.

CONTROLLING DISCRETIONARY

Control Using Engineered Costs

Some discretionary activities are repetitive enough to allow the development of standards similar to those for manufacturing costs. Such activities result in **engineered costs,** which are costs that have been found to bear observable and known relationships to a quantifiable activity base. Such costs may be treated as either variable or fixed. Discretionary cost activities that can fit into the engineered cost category are usually geared to a performance measure related to work accomplished. Budget appropriations for engineered costs are based on the static master budget level. However, control can be exerted through the use of flexible budgets if the expected level of activity is not achieved.

To illustrate the use of engineered costs, assume that Munich Glass has found that quality control can be treated as an engineered cost. Taken as a whole, quality control inspections are similar enough to allow management to develop a standard inspection time. Company management, in a cost reduction effort, is willing to contract with

engineered cost

part-time qualified quality control inspectors who will be paid on an hourly basis. Munich Glass has found that inspection of each product averages slightly less than 4 minutes. Thus, each inspector should be able to perform approximately 15 inspections per hour. From this information, the company can obtain a fairly valid estimate of what inspection costs should be based on a particular activity level and can compare actual cost against the standard cost each period. The activity base of this engineered cost is the number of inspections performed.

In April, Munich Glass management predicts that 26,250 inspections will be performed and, thus, 1,750 inspection hours should be provided. If the standard average hourly pay rate for inspectors is $10, the April budget is $17,500. In April, 25,575 inspections are made at a cost of $17,034 for 1,670 actual hours. Using the generalized cost analysis model for variance analysis presented in Chapter 11, the following calculations can be made:

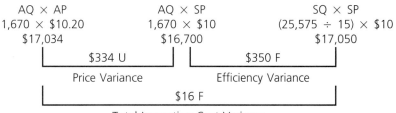

The price variance shows that, on average, Munich Glass paid $.20 more per hour for inspectors during April than was planned. The favorable efficiency variance results from using fewer hours than standard; however, recall that the standard requires only 15 inspections per hour even though the average inspection is expected to take "slightly less" than 4 minutes. Thus, a favorable variance is not surprising. A "generous" standard was set by Munich Glass to reinforce the importance of making high-quality inspections regardless of the time taken.

The preceding analysis is predicated on the company being willing and able to hire the exact number of inspection hours needed. If Munich Glass has to employ only full-time employees on a salary basis, analyzing inspection costs in the above manner is not very useful. In this instance, quality inspection cost becomes a discretionary fixed cost and Munich Glass may prefer the following type of fixed overhead variance analysis:

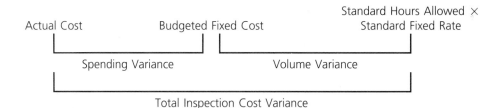

In a third type of analysis, it is assumed that part-time help will be needed in addition to the full-time staffing, and the flexible budget is used as the center column measure in the following diagram. Assume the following facts: (1) there are three full-time inspectors, each earning $1,600 per month and working 160 hours per month; (2) the standard hourly rate for part-time help is $10; (3) the standard quantity of work is 15 inspections per hour; (4) 25,575 inspections were made during the month; and (5) actual payroll for 1,670 total hours was $4,800 for full-time inspectors and $12,269 for part-time inspectors who worked 1,190 hours. Munich Glass prepares a flexible budget for its fixed inspection cost at $4,800 (3 × $1,600) based on a normal processing volume of 7,200 inspections and $10 per hour for part-time workers. The following variances can be computed:

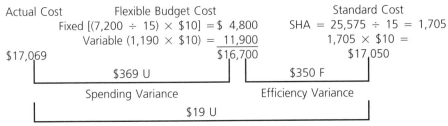

Actual Cost	Flexible Budget Cost	Standard Cost

Fixed [(7,200 ÷ 15) × $10] = $ 4,800   SHA = 25,575 ÷ 15 = 1,705
Variable (1,190 × $10) = 11,900   1,705 × $10 =
$17,069 $16,700 $17,050
          $369 U $350 F
     Spending Variance   Efficiency Variance
                    $19 U
          Total Inspection Cost Variance

The unfavorable spending variance was incurred because part-time employees had to be hired at approximately $.31 more per hour than standard [($12,269 ÷ 1,190) − $10]. The favorable efficiency variance reflects above-normal productivity (1,705 standard hours allowed − 1,670 actual hours). To determine the implications of these figures, Munich Glass management would need to know which employees did and did not perform 15 inspections per hour. Management can evaluate an individual's productivity to ascertain whether it is within preestablished control limits. If productivity is outside those limits, management should seek the causes and work with the employee to improve performance.

The method of variance analysis and, thus, cost control must be appropriate to the cost category and management information needs. Regardless of the variance levels or the explanations provided, managers should always consider whether the activity itself and, therefore, the cost incurrence was sufficiently justified. For example, assume that $76,000 is spent on the salary of an additional systems analyst in the Systems Department. During the year, systems activities take place, but there is no measurable output such as systems modifications or a new system. Before determining that the discretionary cost expenditure was justified, top management should review the systems manager's activity reports for the analysts in the department. The discretionary expenditure would not be considered effective if the new analyst spent a significant portion of the period doing menial tasks. In other words, postincurrence audits of discretionary costs are important in determining the value of the expenditure.

Control Using the Budget

Once discretionary cost budget appropriations have been made, monetary control is effected through the use of budget-to-actual comparisons in the same manner as for other costs in the budget. Actual results are compared to expected results and explanations should be provided for variances. Explanations for variances can often be found by recognizing cost consciousness attitudes. The following illustration involving two discretionary cost activities provides a budget-to-actual comparison that demonstrates employee cost consciousness.

Munich Glass and several other companies outsource their payroll processing activities to Garmish Services. That company has prepared the condensed budget shown in Exhibit 16–8 for the first quarter of 1997. Ms. Brenda Joyner, the controller

Revenues:		
Processing fees (250,000 × $1.55)		$387,500
Expenses:		
Employee training	$18,500	
Maintenance	50,000	
Utilities	20,072	
Wages and fringe benefits	78,000	
Salaries and fringe benefits	59,000	
Depreciation	37,700	(263,272)
Operating Income before Tax		$124,228

EXHIBIT 16–8

Budget—First
Quarter 1997

EXHIBIT 16-9

Actual Results—First
Quarter 1997

Revenues:		
Processing fees (286,000 × $1.55)		$443,300
Expenses:		
Employee training	$19,200	
Maintenance	57,500	
Utilities	21,435	
Wages and fringe benefits	84,500	
Salaries and fringe benefits	60,200	
Depreciation	43,700	(286,535)
Operating Income before Tax		$156,765

for Garmish Services, estimates 250,000 paychecks will be processed during that period; the company charges its clients $1.55 per check processed.

In pursuing a strategy of total quality and continuous improvement, Garmish Service's management has chosen to fund employee training to improve employee and customer satisfaction. Maintenance is also considered a discretionary cost and is budgeted at $.20 per check processed. Office costs include utilities, phone service, supplies, and delivery. These costs are variable and are budgeted at $38.60 for each hour that the firm operates. Garmish Services operates 8 hours per day, 5 days per week, and there are 13 weeks in the budget quarter. Wages are for the 12 employees who are paid $12.50 per hour. Salaries and fringe benefits are for management level personnel and, like depreciation, are fixed amounts.

Ms. Joyner collected the revenue and expense data shown in Exhibit 16–9 during the first quarter of 1997. Because of computer downtime during the quarter, Garmish Services needed to stay open 2 extra hours on 10 different nights. Additional contracts were responsible for the majority of the increase in additional checks processed.

After reviewing the actual results, the company's board of directors requested a budget-to-actual comparison from Ms. Joyner and explanations for the cost variances. Because every cost was higher than budgeted, the board was of the opinion that costs had not been properly controlled. Ms. Joyner prepared the comparison presented in Exhibit 16–10 and provided the following explanations for the variances. Each explanation is preceded by the related budget item number.

1. The discretionary cost for employee training was increased because the company took advantage of an unforeseen opportunity to obtain Covey's "Seven Habits of Highly Effective People" training for its employees. Additionally, employees received training on a new electronic data interchange (EDI) system that Garmish Services installed. *Comment: These explanations reflect an understanding of long-term variable cost behavior and of the long-run quality considerations of having well-trained employees.*

2. Maintenance cost was increased by management after reviewing the increased activity and wear and tear on equipment. *Comment: This explanation also reflects an understanding of long-run quality considerations. In this situation, the company incurs the additional cost to maintain client satisfaction with the company's service. The increased maintenance cost indicates a situation in which management agrees that an expenditure above the original discretionary cost appropriation is reasonable and beneficial to the organization.*

3. The utility cost was influenced by two factors: the additional 20 hours of operation and an increase in local utility rates, which caused Garmish Service's costs to rise $.30 per operating hour. *Comment: The first part of the explanation reflects an understanding of the nature of variable costs: additional hours worked caused additional costs to be incurred. The second part of the explanation reflects an understanding of the nature of specific price-level adjustments. The increase in utility rates could possibly have been caused by inflation, an increase in demand with no corresponding increase in supply, or additional utility regulatory costs being passed along to the utility's customers.*

	BUDGET ITEM #	ORIGINAL BUDGET	BUDGET BASED ON ACTUAL RESULTS	ACTUALS	VARIANCES
Revenues:					
Processing fees		$387,500	$443,300	$443,300	$ 0
Expenses:					
Training	(1)	$ 18,500	$ 18,500	$ 19,200	(700)
Maintenance	(2)	50,000	57,200	57,500	(300)
Utilities	(3)	20,072	21,006*	21,435	(429)
Wages &	(4)	78,000	78,000	84,500	(6,500)
fringes					
Salaries &	(5)	59,000	59,000	60,200	(1,200)
fringes					
Depreciation	(6)	37,700	37,700	43,700	(6,000)
Total expenses		$263,272	$271,406	$286,535	$(15,129)
Operating					
Income					
before Taxes		$124,228	$171,894	$156,765	

*This amount is based on the assumption that the rate increase was not an unforeseen event: (8 hours × 5 days × 13 weeks) + 20 hours = 540 hours × $38.90 = $21,006.

EXHIBIT 16–10

Budget-to-Actual Comparison for First Quarter 1997

4. The increase in wages was caused by three factors: 20 additional operating hours, time-and-a-half pay for overtime, and the hiring of one additional employee for the last 4 weeks of the quarter. The newest employee did not work any overtime. The company had a total of 540 hours of operation:

12 people × 540 hours × $12.50 per hour	$81,000
1 person × (8 hours per day × 5 days per week × 4 weeks) × $12.50	2,000
12 people × 20 hours of overtime × $6.25 per hour	1,500
Total wages cost	$84,500

Comment: These cost changes reflect the nature of variable costs. Had the company known overtime would be needed, those costs could have been budgeted.

5. A new purchasing agent was hired at the beginning of the quarter at $4,800 more per year than the one who was replaced. *Comment: Increases in salaries are typically caused either by inflation or supply and demand relationships for professional staff.*

6. The depreciation increase was related to the purchase and installation of the new EDI system. The purchase was made with board approval when a competitor went bankrupt during the quarter and had a distress liquidation sale. The purchase of such equipment had been included in the capital budget for the end of 1997, not during the first quarter. *Comment: Acquiring the EDI technology is a good example of the cost containment concept. Garmish Services wanted to buy the equipment and had an opportunity to buy it at a substantial savings, but earlier than anticipated. This purchase created an unfavorable cost variance for depreciation in the first quarter, but it shows an instance of planning, foresight, and flexibility. The long-run benefits of this purchase are twofold. First, a favorable variance will be shown in the capital budget when the cost of this equipment is compared to the expected cost. Second, in future periods, the budgeted committed cost for depreciation will be less than it would have been had the purchase not been made at this time.*

Note that the variance computations in Exhibit 16–10 are based on comparisons between a revised budget that uses actual checks processed as the cost driver and the actual revenues/costs incurred. When comparing budgeted and actual expenditures, managers must be careful to analyze variances using an equitable basis of comparison. These variance computations illustrate the use of the flexible budgeting concepts presented in Chapter 5. Comparisons between the original budget and actual results for the variable cost items would not have been useful for control purposes because variable costs automatically rise with increases in cost driver activity.

Suppose Garmish Services's board also wanted a better understanding of why the original budget indicated an operating income before taxes of $124,228, but the actual results showed $156,765—an increase of $32,537. A set of comparisons of each cost line of the original budget with its counterpart actual cost indicates an increase in expenses of $23,263. Revenue can be analyzed in the following manner:

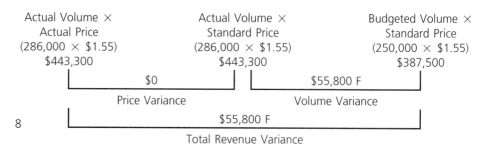

The $55,800 favorable variance for revenue is assigned completely to the 36,000 unit increase in checks processed over budget as there was no change in the per-check price. Thus, the increase in income from the original budget is ($55,800 − $23,263) or $32,537. The standard costing models presented in Chapter 11 can be adapted if further analysis of expenses is desired. For the immediate purpose of explaining the increase in operating income before tax, the report shown in Exhibit 16–10 coupled with the previous explanations should suffice.

Garmish Services was more profitable by $32,537 than originally planned. With the explanations presented to the board of directors, it does appear that costs were relatively well controlled. The larger variances were based on rational management decisions to incur greater-than-planned costs.

REVISITING

Volkswagen

[One important part of VW's progress in cutting costs] has been Piëch's effort to reduce the number of platforms, or basic auto frames, on VW assembly lines from 16 to four . . . [which] can gradually reduce Volkswagen's overall cost base by "several billion deutschemarks." Design and engineering costs are reduced since fewer platforms are being made. And the increased volume of production of fewer types of parts lowers their unit costs. While reengineering and cost cutting have reduced the time needed to make a Golf from over 40 hours in 1993 to about 32 [in early 1996], the new Polo is being designed under the four-platform strategy and takes only about 16 to 17 hours to build, according to Neumann. VW's goal is to lower that to less than 10 hours to match the efficiency of the best Japanese companies.

The four-platform strategy also allows Volkswagen more design flexibility, permitting a new emphasis on style . . . [and allowing products to] be tailored more closely to the tastes of local markets. Neumann calls this process of standardizing platforms and increasing the range of product offerings "glocalization," a combination of globalizing the production and localizing the product offering.

Lucrative as the new strategy is proving, however, most analysts doubt that Volkswagen can raise its operating margins from 1994's 0.5% to 8% by 2000 [primarily because of] German wages. They are the world's highest in the auto industry and Volkswagen has thus far been unable to eliminate some 30,000 redundant workers [partially in concession to the unions] for lower overtime pay and increased labor flexibility.

For most companies, shifting production overseas would be a solution to such overstaffing problems. But Volkswagen is committed to maintaining a large German manufacturing base. Neumann says Volkswagen has a "social responsibility" to keep as many German jobs as it can.

So VW has had to be creative in its cost cuts. Its latest labor agreement includes further concessions in return for firmer job guarantees. And VW won union approval to sell selected components to third parties as a means of absorbing excess labor.

The trouble with all these imaginative solutions, however, is that as Volkswagen improves its productivity, more and more workers will become redundant. This growing labor surplus, if not otherwise absorbed, could leave Volkswagen vulnerable in the next downturn.

SOURCE: Robert Stowe England, "Hard Day's Night," *Financial World* (January 30, 1996), pp. 49–50. Excerpted from *Financial World* Copyrighted 1996. All rights reserved.

CHAPTER SUMMARY

Cost control over expenditures is essential to an organization's long-run success. An effective cost control system encompasses efforts before, during, and after a cost is incurred. Regardless of the type of cost involved, managers and employees must exercise attitudes of cost consciousness to provide the best means of cost control. Cost consciousness reflects cost understanding, cost containment, cost avoidance, and cost reduction.

Fixed costs may be classified as either committed or discretionary. Committed fixed costs relate to long-run investments in plant assets or personnel. Discretionary costs are annually appropriated for the conduct of activities that could be temporarily reduced without impairing the firm's capacity to function.

Costs are incurred to provide results, but measuring the outputs generated by cost inputs is not always easy. Comparing inputs to actual outputs reflects efficiency, whereas comparing actual outputs to desired results reflects effectiveness. Efficiency plus effectiveness indicates performance.

Budgeting is a primary tool in planning and controlling discretionary costs. Budget appropriations provide authorization for spending and the bases against which actual costs are compared. Managers should clearly state and adhere to an overall management philosophy so that expenditures for discretionary items can be budgeted to achieve results that fit within this philosophy. Managers must avoid making expenditures for discretionary activities that may be conducted efficiently, but for which the results are of dubious effectiveness. To obtain effective cost control, care must be taken to use appropriate levels of activity for budget-to-actual comparisons.

Difficulty is often encountered with discretionary fixed costs because many of these costs are incurred to provide service-type activities that are often considered optional in the short run. Additionally, the outputs of discretionary cost activities often are not measurable in dollars. Surrogate measures of the outputs provided by discretionary costs can be developed; however, even when surrogate measures are used, ascribing a cause-effect relationship between the result and the current amounts of input costs may be questionable.

Some discretionary costs, such as quality control costs, may be conducive to treatment as engineered costs. Engineered costs are those that are routine and structured enough to allow for the computation of standards. One aspect of control over engineered costs can be provided by performing variance analysis similar to that used for variable manufacturing overhead.

Program and Zero-Base Budgeting

In addition to the traditional master and flexible budgets, two other types of budgets (program and zero-base) are useful for cost control in certain types of organizations. Program budgeting focuses on the relationship of benefits to cost expenditures; zero-base budgeting requires that all budgeted amounts be justified.

Program Budgeting

program budgeting

The problems of controlling discretionary costs have been particularly acute in governmental and other not-for-profit entities. These organizations' activities produce results that are often difficult to measure in monetary terms or that may take several years to be measured (although the related activities must continue to be funded annually). Thus, relating outputs to inputs is often extremely difficult. **Program budgeting** is an approach that relates resource inputs to service outputs.[28]

Program budgeting generally starts by defining objectives in terms of output results rather than in terms of quantity of input activities. For instance, an input measure of an executive development program would be the number of courses each person must complete by year-end. An output measure would state the objective in terms of expected improvement rates on executive annual performance evaluations. Once output results have been defined in some measurable terms, effectiveness can be measured.

The process of program budgeting requires a thorough analysis of the alternative activities that may achieve an organization's objectives. Such an analysis includes projecting both quantitative and qualitative costs and benefits for each alternative. Then, those alternatives are selected that, in the judgment of top management, yield a satisfactory result at a reasonable cost. These choices are translated into budget appropriations to be acted on by the manager(s) responsible for the related programs.

Program budgeting requires the use of detailed surrogate measures of output and necessitates answers to the following questions.

1. When should results be measured? Because many not-for-profit programs are effective only after some period of time, multiple measurements are necessary to determine effectiveness. When should these measures begin to be made and how often should they be made thereafter?
2. What results should be chosen as output measures? Many not-for-profit programs have multiple results. For example, the institution of reading programs for illiterate adults can reduce unemployment rates, overall crime statistics, welfare dollars provided, and so forth. Should a determination be made of which results are more important than others or should all results be given equal weight?
3. What program actually caused the result? There are questions about the legitimacy of cause-effect relationships when measuring the results of not-for-profit programs. For example, did an adult literacy program reduce the unemployment statistics or was that reduction more appropriately deemed a result of money spent for job placement programs?
4. Did the program actually affect the target population? An adult literacy program may be aimed at the unemployed. If the majority of persons who attended the program already had jobs, the program had no impact on the target group. However, the program could still be considered effective if the participants increased their job skills and employment levels.

Program budgeting is useful in government and not-for-profit organizations as well as for service activities in for-profit businesses. This process can help managers

---

[28] Program and performance budgeting have often been used as interchangeable terms. The Municipal Finance Officers Association has suggested that the term *program budgeting* be used when dealing with one function regardless of the number of organizational units involved and *performance budgeting* be used when dealing with the inputs and outputs of a single organizational unit.

TRADITIONAL BUDGETING	ZERO-BASE BUDGETING
Starts with last year's funding appropriation	Starts with a minimal (or zero) figure for funding
Focuses on money	Focuses on goals and objectives
Does not systematically consider alternatives to current operations	Directly examines alternative approaches to achieve similar results
Produces a single level of appropriation for an activity	Produces alternative levels of funding based on fund availability and desired results

EXHIBIT 16–11

Differences Between Traditional Budgeting and Zero-Base Budgeting

evaluate and control discretionary costs, avoid excessive cost expenditures, and make certain that expenditures are used for programs and activities that generate the most beneficial results.

Zero-Base Budgeting

Traditional budgeting is often limited in its usefulness as a cost control tool because poor budgeting techniques are used. For instance, many managers prepare budgets by beginning with the prior year's funding levels and treat these appropriations as given and essential to operations. Decisions are then made about whether, and by what percentage, to raise existing appropriations. Such an approach has often resulted in what is known as the "creeping commitment syndrome" in which activities are funded without systematic annual regard for priorities or alternative means for accomplishing objectives.

Zero-base budgeting (ZBB) is a comprehensive budgeting process that systematically considers the priorities and alternatives for current and proposed activities in relation to organizational objectives. Annual justification of programs and activities is required to have managers rethink priorities within the context of agreed-upon objectives. ZBB does not necessarily mean that each operation is specified from a zero-cost base, because this would be unrealistic and extreme. However, ZBB requires that managers reevaluate all activities at the start of the budgeting process to make decisions about which activities should be continued, eliminated, or funded at a lower level. Some basic differences between traditional budgeting and zero-base budgeting are shown in Exhibit 16–11.

ZBB is difficult to implement because of the significant effort needed to investigate the causes of prior costs and justify the purposes of budgeted costs. To be workable, it also requires a wholehearted commitment by the organization's personnel. Without the time, effort, and commitment, ZBB should not be attempted. With these ingredients, an organization can be more effective in planning and controlling costs.

zero-base budgeting

SOLUTION STRATEGIES

Efficiency: Relationship of input and output

$$\text{Actual Yield Ratio} = \text{Actual Output} \div \text{Actual Input}$$

or

$$\text{Actual Input} \div \text{Actual Output}$$

$$\text{Desired Yield Ratio} = \text{Planned Output} \div \text{Planned Input}$$

or

$$\text{Planned Input} \div \text{Planned Output}$$

Effectiveness: Relationship of actual output and desired output

Efficiency + Effectiveness = Performance

Cost Variances

Comparison of actual costs with budgeted costs—allows management to compare discrepancies from the original plan

Comparison of actual costs with budgeted costs at actual activity level—allows management to determine how well costs were controlled; uses a flexible budget

Variance analysis using standards for discretionary costs—allows management to compute variances for routine, structured discretionary costs

For discretionary costs susceptible to engineered cost treatment:

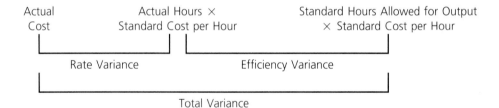

For discretionary costs that are managed as lump-sum fixed costs:

For discretionary costs involving both fixed and variable elements:

Donelon Manufacturing just purchased a plastic extruding machine and ran the machine 35 hours during the first week. Management wants to know the efficiency and effectiveness of the machine. The production supervisor has provided you with the following statistics:

Planned output	50 pounds per hour
Power usage planned	100 kwh per running hour
Actual output	1,800 pounds
Actual power used	3,400 kwh

Required:

a. Calculate the planned output for 35 operating hours.
b. Calculate the degree of effectiveness of the machine in its first week.
c. Calculate planned efficiency for the machine.
d. Calculate the actual efficiency of the machine in its first week.
e. Comment on the machine's performance.

Solution to Demonstration Problem

a. Planned output: 35 hours $\times$ 50 pounds = 1,750 pounds of output
b. Degree of effectiveness: Actual output $\div$ Planned output = 1,800 pounds $\div$ 1,750 pounds = 103 percent
c. Planned efficiency: Planned input $\div$ Planned output = 100 kwh $\div$ 50 pounds = 2 kwh per pound
d. Actual efficiency: Actual input $\div$ Actual output = 3,400 kwh $\div$ 1,800 pounds = 1.89 kwh per pound
e. The performance of the machine is better than expected. The machine exceeded both effectiveness and efficiency expectations.

1. How does the cost control system interact with the overall cost management system?

2. When is cost control for any specific organizational activity exercised? Why are these points of cost control important?

3. What factors can cause costs to change? Which of these are subject to cost containment and which are not? What creates the difference in controllability?

4. Compare and contrast general and specific price-level changes.

5. How do horizontal and vertical price fixing differ? What makes them similar? Why are such practices not only illegal, but also unethical?

6. How might members of the supply chain be helpful in an organization's quest for cost containment activities?

7. "A company will always experience reduced costs if long-term or single-source contracts are signed." Is this statement true or false? Discuss the rationale for your answer.

8. How are cost avoidance and cost reduction related? How do they differ?

9. What are some reasons supporting the use of temporaries in what used to be full-time labor positions? What are some reasons against such usage?

10. Why should activity-based management be considered an integral part of cost control?

11. Differentiate between committed and discretionary costs. Could a cost be considered discretionary by one firm and committed by another? If so, discuss and give an example. If not, discuss why not.

12. Are all discretionary costs fixed? Justify your answer. If not, provide an example to prove your point.

13. Is an investment in expensive, automated technology wise in an industry characterized by wide variations in demand? What if that industry were highly competitive? Provide underlying reasons for your answers.

14. What issues does management need to consider when setting the budget appropriations for discretionary costs?

15. Why are income levels generally more important considerations for budget decisions about discretionary costs than for committed costs?

16. Why is it difficult to measure the output of activities funded by discretionary costs?

17. What are surrogate measures of output and how are they used in conjunction with discretionary costs?

18. Define efficiency and effectiveness and distinguish one from the other. Why is measuring the efficiency of discretionary costs often difficult? Explain how effectiveness of discretionary cost activities can be measured.

19. Why does performance encompass the spectrum from organizational goals to inputs to outputs?

20. What is an engineered cost? How can engineered costs be used in controlling some discretionary costs?

21. What types of discretionary costs are subject to control as engineered costs? Provide several examples.

22. How can variance analysis be used to investigate the control of engineered costs?

23. Is a budget-to-actual comparison essential in the control of discretionary costs? Provide reasoning for your answer.

24. Why is the budget used for planning purposes not necessarily the best budget to use for evaluating cost control?

25. (Appendix) Compare and contrast a programmed budget, a zero-base budget, and a traditional budget.

26. (Appendix) What problems are encountered in using program budgeting? Why might such problems arise?

27. (Appendix) What problems are encountered in using zero-base budgeting? Why might such problems arise?

28. (Appendix) How does zero-base budgeting assist in planning and controlling discretionary costs?

EXERCISES

29. (Matching) Match the following lettered terms on the left with the appropriate numbered description on the right.

a. Engineered cost
b. Effectiveness
c. Discretionary cost
d. Committed cost
e. Appropriation
f. Cost containment
g. Cost avoidance
h. Cost consciousness
i. Efficiency

1. An attitude regarding cost understanding, cost containment, cost avoidance, and cost reduction
2. A cost incurred to provide physical or organizational capacity
3. A measure of input-output yield
4. Any cost that bears an observable and known relationship to an activity base
5. A process of finding acceptable alternatives for high-priced items and not buying unnecessary goods or services
6. A maximum allowable expenditure

7. An assessment of how well a firm's goals and objectives were achieved
8. A fixed cost incurred to fund an activity for a specified period of time
9. A process by which unit variable costs and total fixed costs are not allowed to increase from prior periods

30. *(Cost control activities)* The firm of Rezac & Gibson, CPAs, hires full- and part-time clerical employees. Full-time clerical staff can be hired for $27,500 per year; fringe benefit costs for each full-time employee amount to 20 percent of base salary. R&G pays part-time clerical employees $20 per hour, but does not provide any fringe benefits. If, however, a part-time employee has worked for the firm for over 1,600 hours by year-end, he/she receives a $2,000 bonus.
    a. Does the firm's policy of hiring part-time clerical staff represent an example of cost containment, cost avoidance, or cost reduction? Explain.
    b. For a given clerical position, at what level of annual hours worked should the firm consider hiring full-time clerical staff rather than part-time?

31. *(Cost control activities)* Ms. Renwick has just been appointed as the new director of Youth Hot-Line, a not-for-profit organization that operates a phone bank for individuals experiencing emotional difficulties. The phones are staffed by qualified social workers and psychologists who are paid on an hourly basis. Ms. Renwick took the following actions in the first week at Youth Hot-Line. Indicate whether the actions represent cost understanding, cost containment, cost avoidance, or cost reduction. Some actions may have more than one implication; if they do, indicate the reason.
    a. Increased the budget appropriation for advertising of the Hot-Line.
    b. Exchanged the more expensive pushbutton, cream-colored designer telephones for regular, pushbutton desk telephones.
    c. Eliminated the call-forwarding feature installed on all telephones because Youth Hot-Line will now be staffed 24 hours a day.
    d. Eliminated two paid clerical positions and replaced these individuals with volunteers.
    e. Ordered blank notepads for the counselors to keep by their phones; the old notepads (stock now depleted) had the Youth Hot-Line logo and address printed on them.
    f. Negotiated a new contract with the telephone company; Youth Hot-Line will now pay a flat rate of $100 per month, regardless of the number of telephones installed by the Hot-Line. The previous contract charged the organization $10 for every telephone. At the time that contract was signed, Youth Hot-Line only had ten telephones. With the increased staff, Ms. Renwick plans to install at least five additional telephones.

32. *(Committed versus discretionary costs)* Following is a list of committed and discretionary costs:

Annual audit fees	Internal audit salaries
Annual report preparation and printing	Marketing research
Building flood insurance	Preventive maintenance
Charitable contributions	Property taxes
Corporate advertising	Quality control inspection
Employee continuing education	Research and development salaries
Office equipment depreciation	Research and development supplies
Interest on bonds payable	Secretarial pool salaries

    a. Classify each of the above costs as *normally* being either committed (C) or discretionary (D).

b. Which of the above costs may be either committed or discretionary based on management philosophy?

c. For the expenses marked discretionary in part a, provide a monetary or non-monetary surrogate output measure. For each output measure, briefly discuss any objections that may be raised to it.

33. *(Committed versus discretionary costs)* Choose letter C (for committed cost) or D (for discretionary cost) to indicate which type of cost each of the sentences below best relates. Explain the rationale for your choice.

  a. Control is first provided during the capital budgeting process.

  b. Examples include advertising, research and development, and employee training.

  c. This type of cost cannot be easily reduced even during temporary slowdowns in activity.

  d. There is usually no "correct" amount at which to set funding levels.

  C **e.** Examples include depreciation, lease rentals, and property taxes.

  D **f.** This type of cost often provides benefits that are not monetarily measurable.

  D **g.** Temporary reductions can usually be made without impairing the firm's long-range capacity or profitability.

  C **h.** This cost is primarily affected by long-run decisions regarding desired capacity levels.

  D **i.** It is often difficult to ascribe outcomes as being closely correlated with this type of cost.

  j. This cost usually relates to service-type activities.

34. *(Effectiveness measures)* St. Francis Hospital has used funds during 1996 for the following purposes. Provide nonmonetary, surrogate measures that would help evaluate the effectiveness of the monies spent.

  a. Sent two cost accounting staff members to seminars on activity-based costing.

  b. Installed a kidney dialysis machine.

  c. Built an attached parking garage for the hospital.

  d. Redecorated the main lobby.

  e. Placed a full-page advertisement in the local Yellow Pages.

  f. Acquired new software to track patient charges and prepare itemized billings.

35. *(Surrogate measures of output)* The Coast Casino and Hotel has established performance objectives for each major operational area for the budget year. Following are some of the major objectives that were established for the budget year 1997. For each objective, identify a surrogate measure of performance.

  a. Increase volume of customer traffic at the gaming tables.

  b. Decrease the labor cost per beverage served to customers.

  c. Increase the length of stay per hotel guest.

  d. Attract more out-of-state visitors and reduce the number of in-state visitors.

  e. Increase convention business.

  f. Increase the quality of room-cleaning services.

  g. Increase the relative amount of gaming revenue generated by the slot machines.

36. *(Effectiveness and efficiency measures)* The president at Perdido Bay University has formed a new department to recruit top out-of-state students. The department's funding for 1996 is $400,000 and the department was given a goal of recruiting 300 new nonresident students. By year-end 1996, the department had been credited with recruiting 325 new students. The department actually consumed $460,000 in its recruiting efforts.

  a. How effective was the newly-formed department? Show calculations.

  b. How efficient was the department? Show calculations.

 37. *(Engineered cost variances)* Orangeburg Courier employs three drivers who are paid an average of $8 per hour for regular time and $12 for overtime. A pickup and delivery requires, on average, one hour of driver time. Drivers are paid for

a 40-hour week because they must be on call all day. One driver stands by for after-hour deliveries.

Analyze the labor costs for one week in which the company made 105 daytime deliveries and 12 after-hour deliveries. The payroll for drivers for that week was $1,140. The employees worked 120 hours regular time and 15 hours overtime.

38. *(Engineered cost variances)* Management at Huron Manufacturing has estimated that each quality control inspector should be able to make an average of 12 inspections per hour. Retired factory supervisors are excellent quality control inspectors because of their familiarity with the products and processes in the plant. Huron management has decided to staff the quality control program with these individuals and has set $9 as the standard hourly rate. During the first month of the new program, 12,560 inspections were made and the total pay to the inspectors was $9,964 for 1,030 hours of work.
    a. Perform a variance analysis for management on the quality control labor cost.
    b. Assume that management could hire four full-time inspectors for a monthly salary of $2,500 each and hire part-timers for the overflow. Each full-time inspector would work 170 hours per month. How would total cost of this alternative compare to the cost of a 1,030-hour month at the standard rate of $9?

39. *(Revenue variances)* The manager of a lumber mill has been asked to explain to the company president why sales of scrap firewood were above budget by $2,100. He requests your help. On examination of budget documents, you discover that budgeted revenue from firewood was $37,500 based on expected sales of 1,875 cords of wood at $20 per cord. Further investigation reveals that 1,800 cords were actually sold at an average price of $22. Prepare an analysis of firewood sales and explain what happened.

40. *(Revenue variances)* "Babies Doing Funny Stuff" is a videotape series that is marketed to day care centers and parents. The series has been found to make babies who watch it extremely content and quiet. In 1996, Angels Ltd., maker of the tapes, sold 400 of the series for $60 per package. In preparing the 1997 budget, company management estimated a 15 percent increase in sales volume because the price was to be reduced by 10 percent. At the end of 1997, company management is disappointed that actual revenue is only $24,440 although 470 packages of the series were sold.
    a. What was the expected revenue for 1997?
    b. Calculate the price and volume variances for Angels Ltd.

41. *(Budgeting concepts; includes appendix)* Select the letter of the budget category from the list below that best corresponds to items a through j.

T = traditional budgeting
Z = zero-base budgeting
P = program budgeting
B = both zero-base and program budgeting

a. Requires annual justification of programs and activities.
b. Is concerned with alternative approaches to achieve similar results.
c. Begins by defining objectives in terms of output results rather than quantity of input activities.
d. Requires developing and assessing decision packages.
e. Treats prior year's funding levels as given and essential to operations.
f. Is particularly well suited to budgeting for discretionary cost expenditures.
g. Produces alternative levels of funding based on fund availability and desired results.
h. Requires the use of detailed surrogate measures of output.
i. Focuses more on monetary levels of appropriations rather than goals, objectives, and outputs.
j. Results in the "creeping commitment syndrome."

42. *(Cost changes)* Alyssa Enterprises has been in existence since 1990. The company board of directors is interested in how well certain office costs have been controlled over the past 5 years. Following are several cost categories and the related 1990 and 1995 expenditures:

COST CATEGORY	1990 COST	1995 COST
Wages and fringe benefits	$160,000	$125,000
Supplies	50,000	85,000
Equipment depreciation	36,000	58,000
Utilities	4,800	6,600

Over this 5-year period, Alyssa Enterprises has downsized from eight office staff to five and made substantial investments in computer hardware and software.

a. Use the above information and information in Exhibit 16–3 to prepare an alternative comparison for the board of directors relative to the office costs in these 2 years.

b. Write a detailed memo to provide explanations of the cost changes.

43. *(Variance analysis)* Cost control in the Personnel Office of Lancaster Supply Corporation is evaluated based on engineered cost concepts. The office incurs both variable and fixed costs. The variable costs are largely driven by the amount of employee turnover in Lancaster Supply. For 1996, budgeted costs in the Personnel Office were

Fixed $200,000
Variable   400,000 (based on projected turnover of 1,000 employees)

For 1996, actual costs in the Personnel Office were

Fixed $210,000
Variable   450,000 (actual turnover of 1,050 employees)

Using traditional variance analysis, evaluate the control of fixed and variable costs in the Personnel Office of Lancaster Supply. Does this method of evaluation encourage the Personnel Office managers to hire low-quality workers? Explain.

44. *(Cost consciousness; team activity)* All organizations seek to be aware of and control costs. In a team of three or four, choose one of the following industries and do research to identify methods that have been used to control costs. Prepare a written presentation that discusses the various methods of cost control, dollars of costs saved (if available), and your perceptions of the positive and negative implications of each of the cost control methodologies. You may choose a particular company within the industry should you so desire.

a. Airlines

b. Automobile manufacturers

c. Hospitals

d. Colleges and universities

e. Government entities

45. *(Cost control)* Recently, the California State University system placed a purchase order (PO) for a book published by a small New Canaan, Conn., company, The Information Economics Press. The following is a copy of the letter the Press sent back to the California procurement officer:
  We have your eight page PO#940809 for one copy of our book "The Politics of Information Management." We are unable to fill your $49 order for the following reasons:

▪ In the Purchase Order Terms and Conditions you wish us to waive any infringement of our copyrighted materials by officers, agents and employees of the California State University. We cannot agree to make available a valuable Copyright for the price of a book.

▪ You will withhold all payments or make a 38% withholding in order to file a year-end 1099 form. We are unable to handle the paperwork of a separate 1099 for every book we sell. That would double our paperwork.

▪ You are requiring us to file a Vendor Data Record (form 204) which is largely identical with your Vendor Information form. Filing both forms takes excessive amounts of time.

- *We are a small business, and therefore you require that we submit a copy of the OSMB Small Business Certification. We do not have an OSMB Certification and we do not know where to get one.*

- *Your attachment to form 204 specifies that I obtain a determination with regard to my being classified either as resident or non-resident subject to California tax withholdings, to be reclaimed by filing at year-end California tax returns. We do not plan to make any tax filings in California.*

- *Your contract rider contains a Privacy Statement on unspecified disclosures that makes us liable for penalties of up to $20,000.*

- *As a condition of our filling out the order you are asking us to post statements notifying all employees of compliance with Code Section 8355 and certifying as to our adopting a four point Drug-Free Awareness program that complies with California law. Deviations are punishable as perjury under the laws of the State of California. Please note our firm has only two employees, who do not take even an aspirin.*

- *Your Minority/Women Business Enterprise Self Certification Form 962 requires detailed statistics on ethnic characteristics of our firm, defining each ethnic group according to their stated geographic origins. To assist in making such distinctions you provide a check-list of ethnic identity of the owners of this firm, leaving us by default with only one open choice, Caucasian, which you do not define. My husband and I do not know of any ancestors who may have ever been in the proximity of the Caucasian mountains, and therefore we are unable to comply with your requirement to identify our ethnic origin according to your geographic rules.*

We therefore suggest that you purchase our book at a bookstore.

Mona Frankel
Publisher

[SOURCE: Mona Frankel, "Just Go to the Bookstore and Buy One," *Wall Street Journal* (October 18, 1994), p. A20. Reprinted by permission of *The Wall Street Journal*, © 1994 Dow Jones & Company, Inc. All Rights Reserved Worldwide.]

   a. What cost control strategy was the author of the preceding letter employing in her decision to reject the book order? Explain.

   b. What appears to be the source of most of the complexity associated with the purchase order? Explain.

   c. What does the letter suggest about the opportunity for improved cost control in the California State University purchasing system? Explain.

46. *(Cost control and financial records)* Turbo Propulsion is a medium-sized manufacturing plant in a capital-intensive industry. The corporation's profitability is very low at the moment. As a result, investment funds are limited and hiring is restricted. These consequences of the corporation's problems have placed a strain on the plant's repair and maintenance program. The result has been a reduction in work efficiency and cost control effectiveness in the repair and maintenance area.

   The assistant controller proposes the installation of a maintenance work order system to overcome these problems. This system would require a work order to be prepared for each repair request and for each regular maintenance activity. The maintenance superintendent would record the estimated time to complete a job and send one copy of the work order to the department in which the work was to be done. The work order would also serve as a cost sheet for a job. The actual cost of the parts and supplies used on the job as well as the actual labor costs incurred in completing the job would be recorded directly on the work order. A copy of the completed work order would be the basis of the charge to the department in which the repair or maintenance activity occurred.

   The maintenance superintendent opposes the program on the grounds that the added paperwork will be costly and nonproductive. The superintendent states that the departmental clerk who now schedules repairs and maintenance activities is doing a good job without all the extra forms the new system would require. The real problem, in the superintendent's opinion, is that the department is understaffed.

   a. Discuss how such a maintenance work order system would aid in cost control.

   b. Explain how a maintenance work order system might assist the maintenance superintendent in getting authorization to hire more mechanics.

(CMA)

47. *(Price fixing; team activity)* At the end of 1995 and in early 1996, numerous articles were written on the Archer-Daniels-Midland (ADM) price-fixing scandal. Use library or other resources to investigate the facts of this case. One good preliminary source is "Checks, Lies and Videotape," by Ronald Henkoff in the October 30, 1995, issue of *Fortune.*

Prepare a four-part paper or presentation to cover the following issues:
a. Company background
b. Claims and charges made against the company
c. Details of the settlement of the suit
d. Company status from time of the settlement to the present

PROBLEMS

48. *(Cost consciousness)* Meri and Jerry Smith are preparing their household financial budget for December. They have started with their November budget and are adjusting it to reflect the difference between November and December in planned activities. The Smiths are expecting out-of-town guests for 2 weeks over the holiday season. The following describe the budgetary changes from November to December that are contemplated by the Smith family:
a. Increase the grocery budget by $135.
b. Decrease the commuter transportation budget by $50 to reflect the days off from work.
c. Change food budget to reflect serving pizza rather than steak and lobster each weekend.
d. Budget an extra $70 for utilities.
e. Reduce household maintenance budget by $60 to reflect the fact that outside maid services will not be needed over the holiday period.
f. Buy generic breakfast cereal rather than name-brand due to the quantity the guests will consume.
g. Buy paper plates rather than run the dishwasher.
h. Buy the institutional-size packages of paper plates rather than smaller-size packages.
i. Budget the long-distance phone bill at $50 less because there will be no need to call the relatives who will be visiting.
j. Budget movie rentals for $3 per tape rather than spend $7 per person to go to the movies.
k. Postpone purchasing needed work clothes until January.
l. Budget funds to repair the car. Meri plans to use part of her vacation time to make the repairs herself rather than take the car to a garage in January.

Indicate whether each of the above items is indicative of cost understanding (CU), cost containment (CC), cost avoidance (CA), or cost reduction (CR). Some items may have more than one answer.

49. *(Use of temporaries)* Temporary or part-time employees may be used rather than full-time employees in each of the following situations:
a. To teach undergraduate accounting courses at a university.
b. To serve as security guards.
c. To staff a health clinic in a rural area.
d. To write articles for a monthly technical magazine.
e. To clean the house when the regular maid is ill.
f. To answer questions on a tax help-line during tax season.
g. To work in department stores during the Christmas rush.
h. To do legal research in a law firm.
i. To perform quality control work in a car manufacturing plant.
j. To do seamstress work in a custom dress shop.
k. To work as a clerk/cashier in a small retail store. The store is a mom-and-pop operation and the clerk is the only employee in the store when he/she works.

Indicate the potential advantages and disadvantages of the use of temporaries in each of the above situations. These advantages and disadvantages can be viewed from the standpoint of the employer or the user of the employer's products or services.

50. *(Efficiency standards)* Hong Nguyen has been asked to monitor the efficiency and effectiveness of a newly installed machine. The specialized machine has been guaranteed by the manufacturer to produce 3,900 engine gaskets per kilowatt-hour (kwh). The rate of defects on production is estimated at 1.5 percent. The machine is equipped with a device to measure the number of kwhs used. During the first month of use, the machine produced 695,000 gaskets, of which 8,950 were flawed, and it used 175 kwhs.

    a. What is the efficiency standard for flawless output?

    b. Calculate the achieved efficiency for the first month and briefly comment on it.

    c. Determine the achieved effectiveness and briefly comment on it.

    d. Assume that the company was charged $1.60 per kwh during the first month this machine was in service. Estimate the company's savings or loss in power costs because of the machine's efficiency level in the first month of operations.

    e. If you were a customer buying this company's gaskets for use in automobile production, what amount of quality control would you want the company to have and why?

51. *(Effectiveness/efficiency)* Top management of RX Hospital Administrators observed that the budget for the EDP department had been growing far beyond what was anticipated for the past several years. Each year, the EDP manager would demonstrate that increased usage by the company's non-EDP departments would justify the enlarged appropriations. The administrative vice president commented that she was not surprised because user departments were not charged for the EDP department services and EDP department personnel were creative and eager to continue expanding services.

    Review of the current year's statistics of the EDP department revealed the following:

Budgetary appropriation	$500,000, based on 2,000 hours of run time; $400,000 of this appropriation is related to fixed costs
Actual department expenses	Variable $87,750 (incurred for 1,950 hours of run time)
	Fixed $402,000

    a. Did the EDP manager stay within his appropriation? Show calculations.

    b. Was the EDP department effective? Show calculations. Comment.

    c. Was the EDP department efficient? Show calculations. (*Hint:* Treat variable and fixed expenses separately.)

    d. Using the formulas for analyzing variable and fixed costs, calculate the variances incurred by the EDP department.

    e. Propose a rate per hour to charge user departments for EDP services. Do you think charging users will affect the demand for services by user departments? Why or why not?

52. *(Efficiency versus effectiveness)* The health-care industry has recently found itself in a new era that is characterized by cost competition. As a result of the new emphasis on cost management, many existing practices are being revised or dropped. Following are changes that have been made by specific health-care providers. For each change mentioned, indicate whether the change is intended to control cost through increased efficiency or increased effectiveness. Also indicate whether the change represents cost understanding, cost containment, cost avoidance, or cost reduction. Discuss your justification for each answer.

a. Before entering the hospital for chemotherapy, a patient's health-care provider required her to drink more than 2 quarts of water at home. By doing so, a day's stay in the hospital for hydration was avoided.

b. By administering an antibiotic within 2 hours of each operation, a hospital reduced the postoperative infection rate from 1.8 percent of patients to .4 percent of patients.

c. Some surgeons have started removing the drainage tubes from heart-bypass patients 24 hours after the operation rather than 48 hours after the operation. The change reduces the length of the typical hospital stay.

d. Doctors at a major hospital tightened scheduling requirements for blood analysis so that results were obtained on the same day that the blood was drawn. The change allowed many patients to be dismissed immediately.

e. A hospital began a practice of paying about $130 per average dose of a new antinausea drug to be administered to chemotherapy patients. The drug allowed vomiting to be controlled much faster and the patient to be more comfortable and dismissed a day earlier.

[SOURCE: Facts based on Ron Winslow, "Health-Care Providers Try Industrial Tactics to Reduce Their Costs," *Wall Street Journal* (November 3, 1993), pp. A1, A5.]

53. *(Budget-to-actual comparison)* Iroquois Falls Products evaluates performance in part through the use of flexible budgets. Selling expense budgets at three activity levels within the relevant range are shown below.

ACTIVITY MEASURES:

	15,000	17,500	20,000
Unit sales volume			
Dollar sales volume	$15,000,000	$17,500,000	$20,000,000
Number of orders processed	1,500	1,750	2,000
Number of salespersons	100	100	100

MONTHLY EXPENSES:

Advertising and promotion	$ 1,500,000	$ 1,500,000	$ 1,500,000
Administrative salaries	75,000	75,000	75,000
Sales salaries	90,000	90,000	90,000
Sales commissions	450,000	525,000	600,000
Salesperson travel	200,000	225,000	250,000
Sales office expense	445,000	452,500	460,000
Shipping expense	650,000	675,000	700,000
Total	$ 3,410,000	$ 3,542,500	$ 3,675,000

The following assumptions were used to develop the selling expense flexible budgets:

- The average size of the company's sales force during the year was planned to be 100 people.
- Salespersons are paid a monthly salary plus commission on gross dollar sales.
- The travel costs have both a fixed and a variable element. The fixed portion is related to the number of salespersons, whereas the variable portion tends to fluctuate with gross dollars of sales.
- Sales office expense is a mixed cost with the variable portion related to the number of orders processed.
- Shipping expense is a mixed cost with the variable portion related to the number of units sold.

A sales force of 90 persons generated a total of 1,600 orders resulting in a sales volume of 16,000 units during November. The gross dollar sales amounted to $14.9 million. The selling expenses incurred for November were as follows:

Advertising and promotion	$1,450,000
Administrative salaries	80,000
Sales salaries	92,000
Sales commissions	460,000
Salesperson travel	185,000
Sales office expense	500,000
Shipping expense	640,000
Total	$3,407,000

a. Explain why the selling expense flexible budget would not be appropriate for evaluating the company's November selling expense, and indicate how the flexible budget would have to be revised.

b. Determine the budgeted variable cost per salesperson and variable cost per sales order for the company.

c. Prepare a selling expense report for November that the company can use to evaluate its control over selling expenses. The report should have a line for each selling expense item showing the appropriate budgeted amount, the actual selling expense, and the monthly dollar variation.

d. Determine the actual variable cost per salesperson and variable cost per sales order processed for the company.

e. Comment on the effectiveness and efficiency of the salespersons during November.

(CMA adapted)

54. *(Appendix)* Hans Flims is the controller of Bavaria Labs, a manufacturer and distributor of generic prescription pharmaceuticals. He is currently preparing the annual budget and reviewing the current business plan. The business unit managers of Bavaria Labs prepare and assemble the detailed operating budgets, with technical assistance from the corporate accounting staff. The final budgets are then presented by the business unit managers to the corporate executive committee for approval. The corporate accounting staff reviews the budgets for adherence to corporate accounting policies, but not for reasonableness of the line items within the budget.

Flims is aware that the upcoming year for Bavaria may be a difficult one due to the expiration of a major patent and the loss of a licensing agreement for another product line. He also knows that during the budgeting process, budget slack is created in varying degrees throughout the organization. He believes this slack has a negative effect on the overall business objectives of Bavaria Labs and should be eliminated where possible.

a. Define budget slack.

b. Explain the advantages and disadvantages of budget slack for (1) the business unit manager who must achieve the budget and (2) corporate management.

c. Hans Flims is considering implementing zero-base budgeting at Bavaria Labs. Define zero-base budgeting. Describe how zero-base budgeting could be advantageous to Bavaria Labs in controlling budget slack. Discuss the disadvantages Bavaria Labs might encounter from using zero-base budgeting.

(CMA)

CASES

55. *(Cost control)* The following graph indicates where each part of the dollar that a student pays for a new college textbook goes.

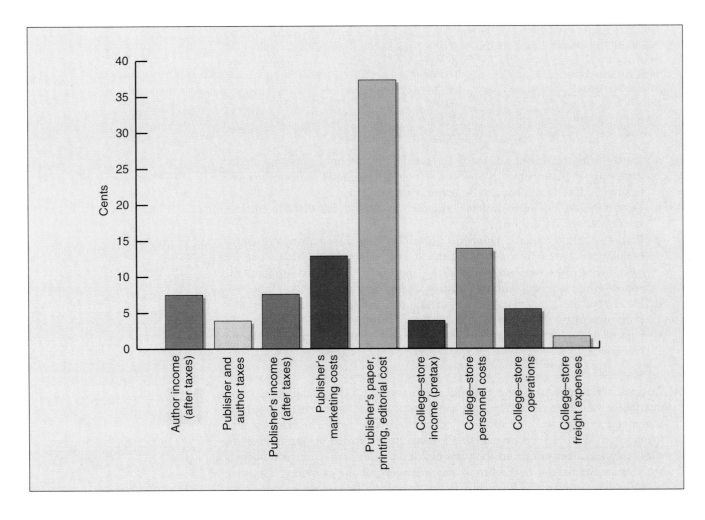

[SOURCE: Association of American Publishers and National Association of College Stores, "Where Does the Textbook Dollar Go?," *The Chronicle of Higher Education* (September 22, 1995), p. A51.]

Students are frustrated with the cost of their textbooks, but most publishers would say that the selling prices have merely kept pace with inflation. Buying used books is an option, but publishers say that used books simply drive up the cost of future texts: if the publisher cannot sell as many of the new edition as are printed, the price is raised "to compensate for decreased sales volume, and the cycle starts again." Publishers also must cover the costs of many nonsalable supplements that are requested by faculty such as instructor's manuals, solutions manuals, transparency acetates, videos, and test banks (hard copy and electronic). Additionally, as the books become "fancier" with multiple colors, photographs, and periodical cites, costs also increase. Write a paper that does the following:

a. Provides suggestions for ways the college/university bookstore could control costs.

b. Provides suggestions for ways the publisher could control costs.

c. Provides suggestions for ways students can legally control textbook expenditures (i.e., substantial reproduction of the text is illegal).

d. Discusses why college textbooks today are so different from college textbooks of 20 years ago. Are these differences cost beneficial from your perspective?

56. *(Analyzing cost control)* The financial results for the Continuing Education Department of BusEd Corporation for November 1997 are presented in the schedule at the end of the case. Mary Ross, president of BusEd, is pleased with the final results but has observed that the revenue and most of the costs and expenses of this department exceeded the budgeted amounts. Barry Stein, vice president of the Continuing Education Department, has been requested to provide an explanation of any amount that exceeded the budget by 5 percent or more.

Stein has accumulated the following facts to assist in his analysis of the November results:

- The budget for calendar year 1997 was finalized in December 1996, and at that time, a full program of continuing education courses was scheduled to be held in Chicago during the first week of November 1997. The courses were scheduled so that eight courses would be run on each of the five days during the week. The budget assumed that there would be 425 participants in the program and 1,000 participant days for the week.
- BusEd charges a flat fee of $150 per day of course instruction, so the fee for a three-day course would be $450. BusEd grants a 10 percent discount to persons who subscribe to its publications. The 10 percent discount is also granted to second and subsequent registrants for the same course from the same organization. However, only one discount per registration is allowed. Historically, 70 percent of the participant day registrations are at the full fee of $150 per day, and 30 percent of the participant day registrations receive the discounted fee of $135 per day. These percentages were used in developing the November 1997 budgeted revenue.
- The following estimates were used to develop the budgeted figures for course-related expenses.

Food charges per participant day (lunch/coffee breaks)	$27
Course materials per participant	$8
Instructor fee per day	$1,000

- A total of 530 individuals participated in the Chicago courses in November 1997, accounting for 1,280 participant days. This number included 20 persons who took a new, two-day course on pension accounting that was not on the original schedule; thus, on two of the days, nine courses were offered, and an additional instructor was hired to cover the new course. The breakdown of the course registrations were as follows:

Full fee registrations	704
Discounted fees	
Current periodical subscribers	128
New periodical subscribers	128
Second registrations from the same organization	320
Total participant day registrations	1,280

- A combined promotional mailing was used to advertise the Chicago program and a program in Cincinnati that was scheduled for December 1997. The incremental costs of the combined promotional price were $5,000, but none of the promotional expenses ($20,000) budgeted for the Cincinnati program in December will have to be incurred. This earlier-than-normal promotion for the Cincinnati program has resulted in early registration fees collected in November as follows (in terms of participant days):

Full fee registrations	140
Discounted registrations	60
Total participant day registrations	200

- BusEd continually updates and adds new courses, and includes $2,000 in each monthly budget for this purpose. The additional amount spent on course development during November was for an unscheduled course that will be offered in February for the first time.

Barry Stein has prepared the following quantitative analysis of the November 1997 variances:

BusEd Corporation
STATEMENT OF OPERATIONS
CONTINUING EDUCATION DEPARTMENT
FOR THE MONTH ENDED NOVEMBER 30, 1997

	BUDGET	ACTUAL	FAVORABLE (UNFAVORABLE) DOLLARS	FAVORABLE (UNFAVORABLE) PERCENT
Revenue				
Course fees	$145,500	$212,460	$ 66,960	46.0
Expenses				
Food charges	$ 27,000	$ 32,000	$ (5,000)	(18.5)
Course materials	3,400	4,770	(1,370)	(40.3)
Instructor fees	40,000	42,000	(2,000)	(5.0)
Instructor travel	9,600	9,885	(285)	(3.0)
Staff salaries and benefits	12,000	12,250	(250)	(2.1)
Staff travel	2,500	2,400	100	4.0
Promotion	20,000	25,000	(5,000)	(25.0)
Course development	2,000	5,000	(3,000)	(150.0)
Total expenses	$116,500	$133,305	$(16,805)	(14.4)
Revenue over expenses	$ 29,000	$ 79,155	$ 50,155	172.9

BusEd Corporation
ANALYSIS OF NOVEMBER 1997 VARIANCES

Budgeted revenue		$145,500
Variances:		
Quantity variance [(1,280 − 1,000) × $145.50]	$40,740 F	
Mix variance [($143.25 − $145.50) × 1,280]	2,880 U	
Timing difference ($145.50 × 200)	29,100 F	66,960 F
Actual revenue		$212,460
Budgeted expenses		$116,500
Quantity variances		
Food charges [(1,000 − 1,280) × $27]	$ 7,560 U	
Course materials [(425 − 530) × $8]	840 U	
Instructor fees (2 × $1,000)	2,000 U	10,400 U
Price variances		
Food charges [($27 − $25) × 1,280]	$ 2,560 F	
Course materials [($8 − $9) × 530]	530 U	2,030 F
Timing differences		
Promotion	$ 5,000 U	
Course development	3,000 U	8,000 U
Variances not analyzed (5% or less)		
Instructor travel	$ 285 U	
Staff salaries and benefits	250 U	
Staff travel	100 F	435 U
Actual expenses		$133,305

After reviewing Barry Stein's quantitative analysis of the November variances, prepare a memorandum addressed to Mary Ross explaining the following:

a. The cause of the revenue mix variance
b. The implication of the revenue mix variance
c. The cause of the revenue timing difference
d. The significance of the revenue timing difference
e. The primary cause of the unfavorable total expense variance
f. How the favorable food price variance was determined
g. The impact of the promotion timing difference on future revenues and expenses
h. Whether or not the course development variance has an unfavorable impact on the company

(CMA)

57. *Ferdows and De Meyer argue that long-term cost improvement is the result of having first achieved improvement in quality, then dependability, and finally speed. There is a cumulative effect by which prior gains influence current gains, a process that can be illustrated as a pile of sand with four layers: quality at the bottom and cost at the top (see figure). [The sand represents management effort and resources.] Increases in quality help increase dependability; then gains in both quality and dependability spur gains in speed. Finally, the cumulative effects of these prior gains result in cost efficiency gains.*

Ferdows and De Meyer also point out that, due to the shape of the pile of sand, achieving a small gain in cost requires successively larger gains for the other aspects of performance (e.g., a 10 percent cost gain may require a 15 percent gain in speed, a 25 percent gain in dependability, and a 40 percent gain in quality). The implication is that long-term successful cost reduction is achieved indirectly—through gains made in other strategically important areas. Thus, the cost reduction strategy should be deeply embedded in the firm's competitive strategy.

[SOURCE: Michael D. Shields and S. Mark Young, "Effective Long-Term Cost Reduction: A Strategic Perspective," *Journal of Cost Management* (Spring 1992), pp. 20–21. Reprinted with permission from *The Journal of Cost Management for the Manufacturing Industry* (Spring 1992), © 1992, Warren Gorham & Lamont, 31 St. James Avenue, Boston MA 02116. All rights reserved.]

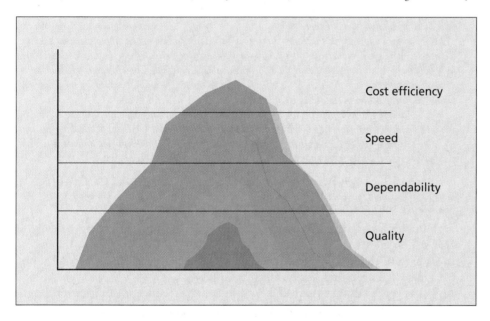

Cost efficiency

Speed

Dependability

Quality

[SOURCE: Reprinted from "Lasting Improvements in Manufacturing Performance: In Search of a New Theory," *Journal of Operations Management* (April 1990), p. 175, by Karsa Ferdows and Arnoud De Meyer, with kind permission of Elsevier Science–NL, Sara Burgerhartstraat 25, 1055 KV Amsterdam, The Netherlands.]

a. How does the depiction of cost control in the figure relate to the concept of activity-based management?

b. If the relation between cost and quality is as depicted in the figure, how does the quality level of the production process serve as a constraint on organizational profitability?

c. What does the figure suggest about the prospects of competing via a strategy of offering low-cost/low-quality products?

58. *The cost of "people" constitutes 75 percent to 80 percent of the total costs of operating a public accounting firm. In periods of economic contractions (such as the late 1980s and early 1990s), accounting firms have to look to cut labor costs to keep costs in line with decreasing revenues. Many firms have resorted to the restricted use of part-time employees who can be laid off during the slack periods in the year. Part-timers include college interns, and parents with young children who only want to work during the busy season. Firms have also resorted to the use of paraprofessionals, individuals with two-year degrees in business.*

[SOURCE: Don Istvan, "Cost Cutting: A Survival Plan," *Accounting Today* (November 11, 1991), p. 26. Reprinted by permission from *Accounting Today*. Copyright Lebhar-Friedman, Inc., 425 Park Avenue, New York, NY 10022.]

a. Discuss the use of part-timers and paraprofessionals from the perspective of controlling costs.

b. How could the use of part-timers and paraprofessionals impair the quality of work performed by public accounting firms?

c. How could the use of part-timers and paraprofessionals affect the effectiveness and efficiency with which work is performed in public accounting firms?

59. *For Caesar O'Neal, a nausea-free day is priceless. But for the hospital treating the 6-foot-8-inch University of Florida football player for liver cancer, the price of delivering that relief is becoming troublesome.*

Mr. O'Neal has been getting massive chemotherapy, including a round last fall that left him vomiting so much that he nearly quit treatment. After that crisis, doctors gave him Zofran, a powerful antinausea drug. Now chemotherapy isn't so frightening, Mr. O'Neal says as he sits on his bed sipping Gatorade. Instead of suffering anguish after each treatment, he can enjoy small pleasures such as video games, big meals or chats with relatives.

But Zofran is one of the most expensive drugs around—and a hot issue as hospitals and drug makers clash over the cost of medications. A standard 32-milligram dose of Zofran—less than a single teardrop—costs hospitals $143. Factor in expenses for stocking it and having nurses administer it intravenously, and each use of Zofran can turn into a $300 patient charge. By weight, gem-quality diamonds are cheaper.

Many doctors and nurses, however, think they can slash Zofran costs without making patients feel worse. "We may be overusing the drug," says Robert Benjamin, an oncologist who treats Mr. O'Neal at the University of Texas M.D. Anderson Cancer Center in Houston. He and other doctors around the U.S. think Glaxo's official package inserts, though approved by the Food and Drug Administration, overstate the Zofran dose that many patients need.

M.D. Anderson is seeking to trim its spending on costly antinausea drugs such as Zofran by 10% this year. Other teaching hospitals, in Boston, New York and Chicago, are looking for cuts of 25% to 50%—mostly by drafting new treatment standards that lean on doctors to shrink dosages or try less costly substitutes.

[SOURCE: George Anders, "Costly Medicine Meets Its Match: Hospitals Just Use Lower Doses," *Wall Street Journal* (August 1, 1994), pp. A1, A6. Reprinted by permission of *The Wall Street Journal*, © 1994 Dow Jones & Company, Inc. All Rights Reserved Worldwide.]

a. What cost control strategy are health administrators attempting to employ for Zofran?

b. What are the ethical considerations in cutting drug costs by cutting doses and switching to less costly substitutes?

c. What is the ethical responsibility of the pharmaceutical manufacturer in setting the prescribed doses for medicines it develops?

60. *Kirsh Guilory pumped out Cajun music, vendors hawked Creole crafts, but the crawfish delicacies dished out along food row at the New Orleans Jazz and Heritage Festival were not from the bayous and backwaters of Louisiana. The Chinese have taken over the crawfish pies, etouffee, file gumbo and most other crawfish dishes served at the festival. Captured, cooked, peeled and processed with low-cost labor in China, the crawfish from overseas are too cheap to pass up, say the merchants who sell food at the fest.*

"I had to go to the Chinese tails," said Clark Hoffpauer, whose festival specialty is crawfish etouffee. "They're at least $2 a pound cheaper, and when you talk 1,700 pounds, that's quite a bit of change. I'd rather use Louisiana crawfish. After all, this is about Louisiana heritage, but business is business."

[SOURCE: Mary Foster, "China Syndrome," *(New Orleans) Times-Picayune* (May 3, 1996), p. C-1. © The Times-Picayune Publishing Corporation.]

a. Is "business is business" a true statement? Discuss the concept of this statement relative to costs, to employment, and to tradition.

b. Provide some examples in which you would believe that the quality of a product and/or the ethics of a company would be enhanced if management considered all of the stakeholders in an organization in addition to costs when making a "business is business" decision.

61. Obtain a copy of "Can the Savoy Cut Costs and Be the Savoy?" by Janet Guyon (*Wall Street Journal*, October 25, 1994, p. B1). After reading of the services offered by that hotel, answer in detail the question asked in the title of the article. Can you think of other similar situations in regard to cost-cutting abilities?

INTERNET ACTIVITIES

62. Search the Internet to find information regarding the U.S. Republican Party's *Contract with America*. Read the available information about the purpose of the contract with America movement. Then, prepare an oral presentation which addresses how zero-base budgeting could be used to achieve some of the goals of the movement.

63. There are many firms that provide services to support advertising and marketing functions of businesses. One such firm is B/R/S Group, Inc. Find the homepage for this company and read the materials provided there describing the services offered by the company. Then, prepare an oral report in which you describe how a firm could utilize the services of B/R/S Group, Inc. as an aid to control its advertising or promotion expenses.

64. Many large firms, such as General Electric (GE), have a center or department that is primarily responsible for the internal R & D function. Find GE's homepage and the materials that describe the GE Research and Development Center. Prepare a written report in which you discuss how concepts presented in this chapter could be applied at GE to control the costs of operating the research center.

Control of Inventory and Production

LEARNING OBJECTIVES

After completing this chapter, you should be able to answer these questions:

1. How are economic order quantity and reorder point determined and used?

2. Why do managers use ABC inventory control systems?

3. How does materials requirements planning differ from the economic order quantity model?

4. How do push and pull systems of production control work?

5. What is the just-in-time philosophy and how does it affect production?

6. How would the traditional cost accounting system change if a JIT inventory system were adopted?

7. *(Appendix)* Why does a company carry safety stock and how is the amount estimated?

Boeing Company

When Boeing set out to build its new 777 commercial airplane, the company broke some of its most sacred materials handling traditions. And nowhere are those changes more evident than at the company's new $200 million plant in Tacoma that builds tail sections for the new two-engine aircraft.

"This facility is designed to take every advantage of new or existing materials handling technology to bring down manufacturing costs and cycle times," says Ken Bailey, manufacturing center director.

Traditional facilities rely almost exclusively on overhead cranes to handle work-in-process (WIP). Inventory levels and materials handling costs are high while WIP flow in the facility is cumbersome.

All of that changes for the production of tails for the 777. This is a just-in-time plant designed to minimize WIP and cut cycle times by 65%.

Parts and tools are pulled through the system only when requested by workers. Automatic guided vehicles [AGVs] are teamed with overhead handling equipment to meet the needs of workers. In addition, smart materials handling kept floor space requirements to just 480,000 square feet, saving millions of dollars in building construction costs.

"Innovative materials handling systems are the key to our pull manufacturing system," says Bailey.

Getting to this point required extensive teamwork by departments used to working independently, says Rick Boston, manager of materials handling systems.

. . . The flow of WIP in the just-in-time plant is U-shaped with parts manufacturing on one side and assembly on the other. Three giant autoclaves separate clean room manufacturing from final manufacturing and assembly. AGVs are teamed with monorail track and lowerators in manufacturing while overhead cranes dominate handling operations in assembly.

Using computer terminals at their workstations, workers request delivery of parts by AGV. All routing decisions over the 8,000 feet of guidepath are under computer control; however, workers use hand-held radio control units with start/stop control to ensure total safety when moving the 43-foot tools. When production is at full rate, the vehicles will make 350 moves during a 15-hour production day. The system moves parts the shortest route between workstations.

SOURCE: Gary Forger, "Boeing Slashes Costs and Time with JIT," *Modern Materials Handling* (August 1, 1994).

In recent years, some people have questioned whether some segments of American industry are as productive and efficient as their counterparts in Japan, Germany, or other parts of the world. Many U.S. companies are concentrating on ways to improve productivity and utilization of available technology. These efforts are often directed toward reducing the costs of producing and carrying inventory.

The amount spent on inventory may be the largest investment, other than plant assets, made by a company. Investment in inventory, though, provides no return until that inventory is sold. This chapter deals with ways for companies to minimize their monetary commitments to inventory. These techniques include economic order quantity (EOQ), materials requirements planning (MRP), the just-in-time (JIT) inventory philosophy and its accounting implications, flexible manufacturing systems (FMS), and computer-integrated manufacturing (CIM). The appendix to this chapter covers the concepts of order point and safety stock.

BUYING AND CARRYING INVENTORY

In manufacturing organizations, one basic cost is for raw materials. Although possibly not the *largest* production cost, raw material purchases cause a continuous cash outflow each period. Similarly, retailers invest a significant proportion of their assets in merchandise purchased for sale to others. Profit margins in both types of organizations can benefit from reducing or minimizing inventory investment, assuming that demand for products could still be met. The term *inventory* is used in this section to refer to any of the following: raw material, work in process, finished goods, indirect materials (supplies), or merchandise inventory.

Good inventory management relies largely on cost-minimization strategies. As indicated in Exhibit 17–1, the basic costs associated with inventory are (1) purchasing/production, (2) ordering/setup, and (3) carrying/not carrying goods in stock. The **purchasing cost** for inventory is the quoted purchase price minus any discounts allowed plus shipping charges. For a manufacturer, production cost refers to the costs associated with purchasing direct material, paying for direct labor, incurring traceable overhead, and absorbing allocated fixed manufacturing overhead. Purchasing/production cost is the amount to be recorded in the appropriate inventory account (Raw Material Inventory, Work in Process Inventory, Finished Goods Inventory, or Merchandise Inventory).

purchasing cost

EXHIBIT 17–1

Categories of Inventory Costs

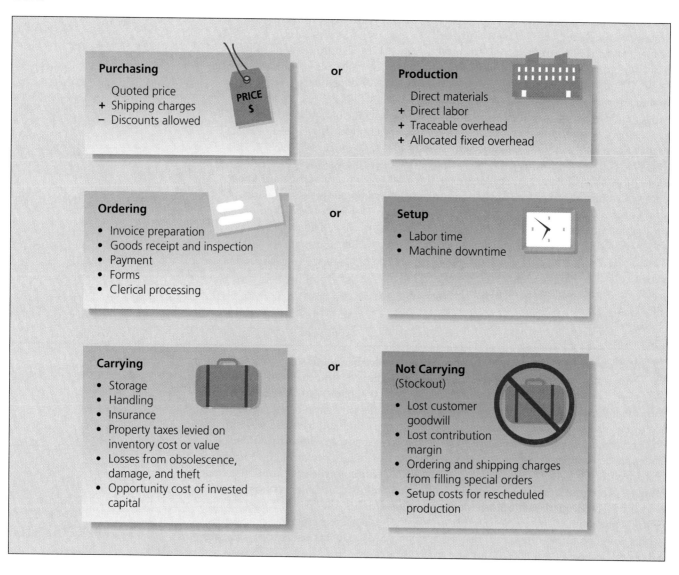

Purchasing		Production
Quoted price + Shipping charges − Discounts allowed	**or**	Direct materials + Direct labor + Traceable overhead + Allocated fixed overhead

Ordering		Setup
• Invoice preparation • Goods receipt and inspection • Payment • Forms • Clerical processing	**or**	• Labor time • Machine downtime

Carrying		Not Carrying (Stockout)
• Storage • Handling • Insurance • Property taxes levied on inventory cost or value • Losses from obsolescence, damage, and theft • Opportunity cost of invested capital	**or**	• Lost customer goodwill • Lost contribution margin • Ordering and shipping charges from filling special orders • Setup costs for rescheduled production

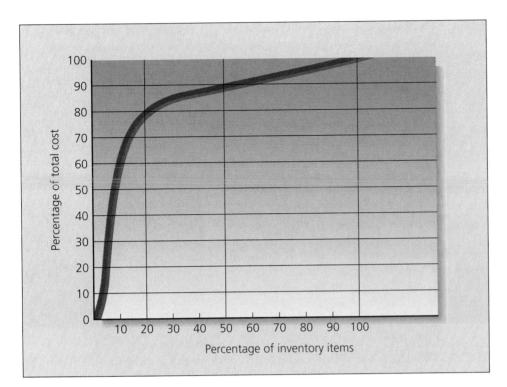

EXHIBIT 17–2

ABC Inventory Analysis

Unit cost commonly affects the degree of control maintained over an inventory item. As unit cost increases, internal controls (such as inventory access) are typically tightened and a perpetual inventory system is more often used. Recognition of cost-benefit relationships may result in an **ABC analysis** of inventory, which separates inventory into three groups based on annual cost-to-volume usage.[1]

ABC analysis

Items having the highest value are referred to as A items; C items represent the lowest dollar volume usage. All other inventory items are designated as B items. Exhibit 17–2 provides the results of a typical ABC inventory analysis—20 percent of the inventory items (A items) accounts for 80 percent of the cost; an additional 30 percent of the items (B items), taken together with the first 20 percent (the A items), account for 90 percent of the cost; and the remaining 50 percent of the items (C items) accounts for the remaining 10 percent of the cost.

Once inventory is categorized as A, B, or C, management can determine the best inventory control method for items in each category. A-type inventory should require a perpetual inventory system and would be a likely candidate for just-in-time purchasing techniques that minimize the funds tied up in inventory investment. The highest control procedures would be assigned to these items. Such a treatment reflects the financial accounting concept of materiality.

Items falling into the C category may need only periodic inventory procedures and may use a two-bin or red-line system. Under a **two-bin system,** one container (or stack) of inventory is available for production needs. When production begins to use materials in the second bin, a purchase order is placed to refill the first bin. In a **red-line system,** a red line is painted on the inventory container at a point deemed to be the point at which to reorder. Both systems require that production needs and estimates of receipt-time from suppliers be fairly accurate. Having the additional container or stack of inventory on hand is considered to be reasonable based on the insignificant dollar amount of investment involved with C category items. The degree of control placed on C items will probably be minimal because of the lack of materiality of the inventory cost. The type of inventory system (perpetual or periodic)

two-bin system

red-line system

[1] ABC inventory analysis should not be confused with activity-based costing (also ABC), which is covered in depth in Chapter 6.

The cost of a stockout can be extremely expensive if a company does not accurately forecast its purchasing needs. This textile mill was forced to completely shut down when no raw materials were available.

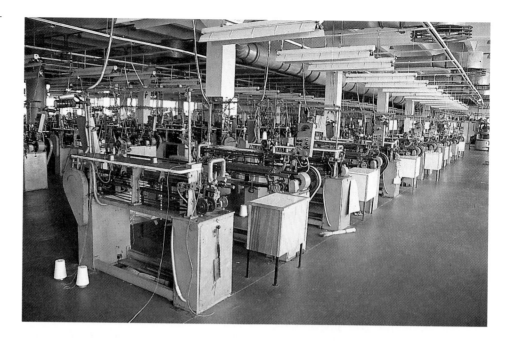

and level of internal controls associated with items in the B category will depend on management's judgment. Such judgment will be based on cruciality of the item to the production process, quickness of response time of suppliers, and estimates of benefits to be gained by increased accounting or access controls. Computers and bar coding have made additional controls over inventory easier and more cost beneficial.

ordering cost

Incremental, variable costs associated with preparing, receiving, and paying for an order are called **ordering costs** and include the cost of forms and a variety of clerical costs. Ordering costs are traditionally expensed as incurred by retailers and wholesalers, although under an activity-based costing system these costs could be traced to the ordered items as an additional direct cost. Retailers incur ordering costs for all their merchandise inventory. In manufacturing companies, ordering costs are incurred for raw material purchases. If the company intends to produce rather than order a part, direct and indirect **setup costs** (instead of ordering costs) would be created as equipment is readied for each new production run. Setup would necessitate costs for changing dies or drill heads, recalibrating machinery, and resetting tolerance limits for quality control apparatuses.

setup cost

carrying cost

Inventory **carrying costs** are the variable costs of carrying one inventory unit in stock for one year. Carrying costs are incurred for storage, handling, insurance, property taxes based on inventory cost or value, and possible losses from obsolescence or damage. In addition, carrying cost should include an amount for opportunity cost. When a firm's capital is invested in inventory, that capital is unable to earn interest or dividends from alternative investments. Inventory is one of the many investments made by an organization and should be expected to earn the same rate of return as other investments. Some Japanese managers have referred to inventory as a *liability*. One can readily understand that perspective considering that carrying costs, which can be estimated using information from various budgets, special studies, or other analytical techniques, "can easily add 20 percent to 25 percent per year to the initial cost of inventory."[2] The News Note on the next page indicates the materiality of carrying costs for Boeing.

stockout

Although carrying inventory *in excess* of need generates costs, a fully depleted inventory can also generate costs. A **stockout** occurs when a company does not have inventory available on request. The cost of having a stockout is not easily determin-

[2] Bill Moseley, "Boosting Profits and Efficiency: The Opportunities Are There," *(Grant Thornton) Tax & Business Adviser* (May/June 1992), p. 6.

Boeing's Inventory Costs Were Flying High

The most obvious place for managers to find savings in Boeing's commercial aircraft operations [is in] its nearly $8 billion of inventory. Boeing turns over its stock a little more than twice a year, compared with ten times a year or higher for world-class manufacturers in other industries. By streamlining workflows and eliminating excesses, Boeing aims to shrink the time needed to manufacture a plane from more than a year to just six months by 1998. If inventories are cut in half as a result, *Fortune's* estimates based on current production levels, that [change] would translate into an annual saving of $400 million in financing costs and as much as $600 million in storage, handling, and transportation.

The company used to rationalize its bulging warehouses by invoking the incredible complexity of its products; each 747 has more than three million parts, not counting fasteners. What's more, no two orders are exactly alike. Boeing prided itself on being able to satisfy each buyer. Explains Patrick Day, head of the plant that makes ducts for pneumatic, hydraulic, and fuel systems: "In the past, the idea was not to delay a $100 million plane for lack of a $2,000 part. It was just-in-case management instead of just-in-time."

[T]he inventory-cutting campaign, launched in 1990, had [by 1993] pared Boeing's [inventory] by some $700 million, or about 9%.

SOURCE: Shawn Tully, "Can Boeing Reinvent Itself?" *Fortune* (March 8, 1993), p. 68. © 1993 Time Inc. All rights reserved.

able, but some of the costs involved include lost customer goodwill, lost contribution margin from not being able to make a sale, additional ordering and shipping charges incurred from special orders, and possibly lost customers. For a manufacturer, another important stockout cost is incurred for production adjustments arising from not having inventory available. If a necessary raw material is not on hand, the production process must be rescheduled or stopped, which in turn may cause the incurrence of additional setup costs before resuming production. Consider the magnitude of the parts shortage in the News Note below.

All inventory-related costs must be evaluated when purchasing or production decisions are made. The costs of ordering and carrying inventory offset each other when estimating the economic order quantity.

Ford to Suspend Some Production
Due to Parts Snag

Ford Motor Co. said it will suspend production at six car and light truck plants in the U.S., Canada and Mexico next week because of shortages of parts.

Ford said the shutdowns, which will cost it 20,600 units of production, were caused by a parts-supply problem, but a spokesman declined to say what parts are involved or what the problem is. The suspension comes at a time when the vehicle market has been soft, and the closings affect plants that build vehicles that are in excess supply.

The loss of production will hurt Ford's third-quarter earnings, which analysts already have been projecting will include red ink for North American auto operations. . . . The closings will temporarily idle 12,950 hourly workers.

SOURCE: Angeloi B. Henderson and Andrea Puchalsky, "Ford to Suspend Some Production Due to Parts Snag," *Wall Street Journal* (September 15, 1995), p. A1. Reprinted by permission of *The Wall Street Journal*, © 1995 Dow Jones & Company, Inc. All Rights Reserved Worldwide.

ECONOMIC ORDER QUANTITY

economic order quantity

Companies making purchasing (rather than production) decisions often compute the **economic order quantity** (EOQ), which represents the least costly number of units to order. The EOQ indicates the optimal balance between ordering and carrying costs by mathematically equating total ordering costs to total carrying costs. Purchasing managers should first determine which supplier can offer the appropriate quality of goods at the best price in the most reliable manner. *After* the supplier is selected, the most economical inventory quantity to order—at a single time—is determined. The EOQ formula is

$$EOQ = \sqrt{\frac{2QO}{C}}$$

where EOQ = economic order quantity in units

Q = estimated annual quantity used in units
   (can be found in the annual purchases budget)

O = estimated cost of placing one order

C = estimated cost to carry one unit in stock for one year

Note that unit purchase cost is not included in the EOQ formula. Purchase cost relates to the question of from whom to buy, which is considered separately from the question of how many to buy. Inventory unit purchase cost does not affect the other EOQ formula costs except to the extent that opportunity cost is calculated on the basis of investment.

Calculating EOQ

Monitronics, Inc., manufactures a variety of computer devices for automobiles. The company purchases a universal type of bracket by which the computer devices can be attached; therefore, an adequate inventory must be available for Monitronic's continuing production needs. The company's purchasing manager has found several suppliers who can consistently provide the proper quality of brackets at a cost of $.60 each. Exhibit 17–3 provides information for use in calculating economic order quantity and uses a flexible budget to show the total costs of purchasing 700,000 brackets per year in various order sizes. This exhibit reflects the following traditional formula for determining total inventory costs:

[(Annual Demand × Ordering Cost) ÷ Order Quantity]
+ (Order Quantity × Carrying Cost) ÷ 2
= Total Inventory Cost

Ordering cost for Monitronics includes the cost of purchase order forms and apportioned amounts for various clerical, telephone, and receiving department charges. Six

---

EXHIBIT 17–3

Yearly Costs of Purchasing Computer Device Brackets

Annual quantity needed (Q) = 700,000
Ordering cost (O) = $8 per order
Carrying cost (C) = $.20 per unit

SIZE OF ORDER	5,000	6,000	7,000	8,000	9,000
Average inventory	2,500	3,000	3,500	4,000	4,500
Number of orders	140	116.67	100	87.5	77.78
Annual ordering cost	$1,120	$ 933*	$ 800	$ 700	$ 622*
Annual carrying cost	500	600	700	800	900
Total cost	$1,620	$1,533	$1,500	$1,500	$1,522

*Rounded.

cents of the $.20 per unit carrying cost is an opportunity cost, representing a forgone 10 percent rate of return on the $.60 per unit of funds invested in inventory. The remaining $.14 of carrying costs are for previously mentioned items such as storage, handling, and insurance.

Average inventory is one-half of the order size, because the EOQ model assumes that orders will be filled exactly when needed. Such a delivery schedule means that, before the order arrives, the inventory on hand is fully depleted. When the order arrives, inventory level is equal to the order size. Therefore, average inventory is half of any given order size or [(0 + order size) ÷ 2]. The number of times an order must be placed depends on how many units are ordered at a time. The total number of orders equals total annual quantity of units needed divided by the order size. Exhibit 17–3 indicates that, as order size increases, the number of orders and the total annual ordering cost decline. However, at the same time, total annual cost of carrying inventory increases because more units are being held in inventory at any given point. Alternatively, smaller order sizes reduce carrying cost, but increase annual ordering cost. Total annual costs for Monitronics decline through an order size of 7,000 to 8,000 brackets; then they begin to rise. These relationships are graphed in Exhibit 17–4.

Monitronics's most economical order size for brackets is between 7,000 and 9,000 units. This quantity range can be determined both from the amounts shown in Exhibit 17–3 and the graph in Exhibit 17–4. The precise economic order quantity of 7,484 units can be found using the EOQ formula:

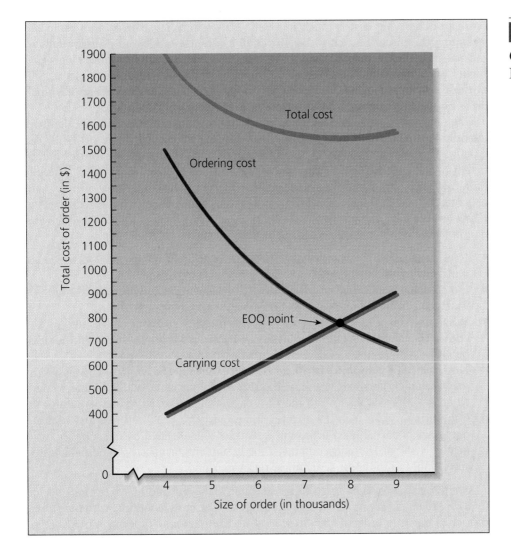

EXHIBIT 17–4

Graphical Analysis of Economic Order Quantity

$$EOQ = \sqrt{\frac{2(700,000)(\$8)}{\$.20}}$$

$$= \sqrt{\frac{\$11,200,000}{\$.20}}$$

$$= \sqrt{56,000,000} = 7,484 \text{ (rounded up)}$$

The total annual cost to place and carry orders of 7,484 units is $1,496.64, calculated as follows:

Average inventory (7,484 ÷ 2)	3,742
Number of orders (700,000 ÷ 7,484)	93.53*
Ordering cost (93.53 × $8)	$ 748.24
Carrying cost (3,742 × $.20)	748.40
Total cost (excluding $.60 per unit purchase cost)	$1,496.64

*This numerical result involves a partial (.53) order. In reality, a firm would order either 93 or 94 times. The precise result of 93.53 orders is used here to demonstrate the equality (except for a slight rounding difference) of total ordering cost and total carrying cost at the EOQ.

Note that, as mentioned previously, the total ordering cost and total carrying cost are equal (except for slight differences caused by rounding) at the EOQ point. Although the mathematical proof of this equality is beyond the scope of this text, the equality relationship is nonetheless an important point of this technique.

Managers must remember when they use the EOQ formula that the formula contains *estimated* values. The estimate of ordering cost is often fairly precise, but the estimate of carrying cost is much more subjective. Carrying cost is often estimated as simply the direct financing cost of holding inventory. Such an estimate fails to include indirect costs such as those related to additional space requirements and higher obsolescence. In most instances, though, small errors in estimating costs will not cause a major impact on total cost. Exhibit 17–5 illustrates the effect of a small error on the total assumed ordering and carrying costs of Monitronics.

Comparing the total ordering cost ($1,496.94) for the 7,484 unit economic order quantity with the total ordering cost ($1,500 or $1,522 from Exhibit 17–3) for the 7,000 or 9,000 units shows that the total annual cost of ordering quantities immediately around the EOQ point does not vary significantly for Monitronics. There is only a $25.06 cost difference between ordering the economic order quantity and ordering 1,516 additional units. Because the cost of ordering quantities close to the EOQ level is not significantly different, management should consider the following questions before placing all orders at the EOQ level:

- Is storage space a limited resource? If so, it would be advantageous to order fewer units each time.
- How critical is the item to production? If it is extremely critical, it is more advantageous to order in larger quantities.
- What would be the effect of a stockout on customer goodwill? If this item is not critical to maintaining customer loyalty and positive image, smaller quantities may be more appropriate.
- How critical is cash flow? If projected cash availability is limited or if the incremental cost of borrowing or holding cash is high, it is most appropriate to purchase in quantities as close to the EOQ as possible to minimize expenditures.
- Can units be ordered in the quantity indicated? The EOQ formula may indicate purchases in partial units or in unit quantities not provided by the supplier (who may only sell in 100-unit containers, for example). Quantities should be adjusted accordingly to the most economical purchase option.

At different times, answers to these questions may vary and managers may decide to place orders of varying quantities. But, to minimize costs associated with inventory, the actual quantity ordered should be close to the economic order quantity.

EXHIBIT 17–5

Estimation Error in EOQ Formula

ORIGINAL ESTIMATES:

Annual quantity needed = 700,000
Ordering cost = $8.00 per order
Carrying cost = $.20 per unit
EOQ = 7,484 units
Assume that an error exists in the estimated ordering cost. The actual ordering cost is $9 per order. All other factors are appropriate. The actual total cost of buying in an EOQ of 7,484 units using the correct ordering cost of $9 is determined as follows:

Number of orders (700,000 ÷ 7,484) = 93.53
Average inventory (7,484 ÷ 2) = 3,742

Ordering cost (93.53 × $9)	$ 841.77
Carrying cost (3,742 × $.20)	748.40
Total actual cost of purchasing an EOQ of 7,746 units	$1,590.17

To recalculate both EOQ and total costs based on $9, the following results are obtainable:

$$EOQ = \sqrt{\frac{2QO}{C}} = \sqrt{\frac{2(700,000)(\$9)}{\$.20}} = 7,938 \text{ (rounded up)}$$

Number of orders (700,000 ÷ 7,938) = 88.18

Average inventory (7,938 ÷ 2) = 3,969

Ordering cost (88.18 × $9)	$ 793.62
Carrying cost (3,969 × $.20)	793.80
Total cost	$1,587.42

Thus, an error of $1 in estimating the ordering cost results in a total cost difference of only $2.75 ($1,590.17 − $1,587.42) over one year!

Economic Production Run

In a manufacturing company, managers are concerned with how many units to produce in addition to how many units (of raw material) to buy. The EOQ formula can be modified to calculate the appropriate number of units to manufacture in an **economic production run** (EPR). This estimate reflects the production quantity that minimizes the total costs of setting up a production run and carrying a unit in stock for one year. The only change in the EOQ formula is that the terms of the equation are redefined as manufacturing, rather than purchasing, costs. The formula is

economic production run

$$EPR = \sqrt{\frac{2QS}{C}}$$

where   EPR = economic production run quantity
    Q = estimated annual quantity produced in units
    S = estimated cost of setting up a production run
    C = estimated cost of carrying one unit in stock for one year

Another product manufactured by Monitronics is a wiring harness to attach automobile computer devices. A total of 162,000 units of this product are made each year. Setup cost for harness production run is $40 and the annual carrying cost for each harness is $4. The economic production run quantity is:

$$EPR = \sqrt{\frac{2(162,000)(\$40)}{\$4}} = \sqrt{\frac{\$12,960,000}{\$4}} = 1,800 \text{ units}$$

Like the answer provided by the EOQ model, the cost differences among various run sizes around the EPR may not be significant. If such costs are insignificant, management would have a range of acceptable, economical production run quantities.

The critical element in using either an EOQ or EPR model is to properly identify costs. Identifying all the relevant inventory costs (especially carrying costs) is very difficult, and some costs (such as those for facilities, operations, administration, and accounting) traditionally viewed as irrelevant fixed costs may, in actuality, be long-term relevant variable costs. The EOQ model also does not provide any direction for managers attempting to control all the separate costs that collectively comprise purchasing and carrying costs. By only considering trade-offs between ordering and carrying costs, the EOQ model does not lead managers to consider inventory management alternatives that may simultaneously reduce both categories of costs.

Additionally, as companies significantly reduce the necessary setup time (and thus cost) for operations and move toward a "stockless" inventory policy, a more comprehensive cost perspective will indicate a substantially smaller cost per setup and a substantially larger annual carrying cost. For instance, if the setup and carrying cost information given for Monitronics were reversed, the EPR would be only 180 units. Using either a new perspective of variable cost or minimizing setup cost will provide much lower economic order or production run quantities than indicated in the past.

Although the basic EOQ model determines what inventory quantity to order, it also ignores relationships among inventory items. For example, Monitronics might require three metal mounting bolts and two computer chips for each automobile computer device produced. If the EOQs for bolts and chips were computed independently, this interrelationship might be overlooked. Monitronics might find that, when 14,000 chips were on hand, there were only 2,000 mounting bolts. Computer techniques known as MRP or MRP II address this problem with the EOQ model by considering component interrelationships in the ordering process.

MATERIALS REQUIREMENTS PLANNING

materials requirements planning

VIDEO VIGNETTE

J.R. Clarkson Co. (Blue Chip Enterprises)

manufacturing resource planning

Materials requirements planning (MRP) is a computer-based information and simulation system for the ordering and/or production scheduling of items, the quantity demands of which are dependent on those of other items. This system was developed to answer the question of what items are needed, how many of them are needed, and when they are needed. A depiction of the interrelationships of the MRP system elements is shown in Exhibit 17–6. The MRP begins with a master production schedule (MPS) based on budgeted sales information. The MRP computer model then accesses the product's bill of materials to determine all the components needed for production. Quantities needed are compared to current inventory balances. If purchases are necessary, the model accesses information about component part interdependencies and supplier shipping times to determine the quantity and time to order, and ultimately generates a time-sequenced component purchases schedule. This schedule allows users to reduce inventory by eliminating the holding of unneeded parts. At J. R. Clarkson (Sparks, Nevada), for instance, MRP implementation reduced inventory by 30 percent.

The MPS is also integrated with the operations flow documents to project each work center's workload resulting from the master schedule. Workloads are compared to the center's capacity to determine whether meeting the master schedule is feasible. Potential bottlenecks are identified so that changes in input factors (such as the quantity of a particular component) can be made, and the MRP program is run again. This process is reiterated until the schedule compensates for all potential bottlenecks in the production system.

A fully integrated MRP system, known as MRP II **(manufacturing resource planning),** plans production jobs using MRP and also provides a basis for both strategic and tactical planning. MRP II involves top management, marketing, and finance in determining the master production schedule. Manufacturing is primarily responsible for carrying out the master schedule, but availability of appropriate resources and sales support are essential to making the plan work.

EXHIBIT 17-6

Schematic of
an MRP System

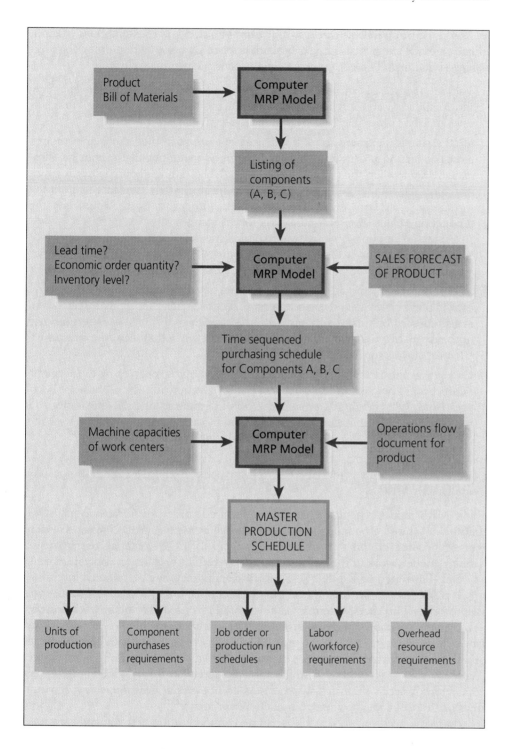

Thousands of companies are currently using MRP or MRP II, and many have achieved significant benefits through lowering inventory levels, using labor and facilities more efficiently, and eliminating wasted activities in all facets of operations. In addition, companies report improved customer service arising from the elimination of erratic production and back orders.

MRP and MRP II are complex models that rely on strong technical support from computer hardware and software specialists as well as detailed inputs. If these factors do not exist in an organization, the MRP models cannot be effectively implemented. And, although many positive effects can be shown by the adoption of an MRP system, MRP also has its problems. Some problems are caused by the fact that MRP models are based on several less-than-realistic assumptions. (These assumptions are not unique to MRP and can also cause difficulties when they are used in other decision-making situations.) These "problem" assumptions include the following:

1. The bill of materials and operations flow documents are assumed to be complete and totally accurate. If they are not, small inconsistencies or distortions in quantities or labor times may become cumulatively significant over time.

2. MRP assumes that there are no bottleneck operations in the factory even though most production processes include one or more operations that cannot be eliminated. (Remember, the process is run successively until the bottlenecks are eliminated on the computer model—which does not necessarily eliminate them in the workplace.) The best way to determine what bottlenecks exist is to go into the production facility and see where inventory is stacking up.

   This assumption often provides unrealistic schedules of processing. MRP compensates for this lack of realism by building excess lead time and inventories into the model—creating additional costs for the company.

3. MRP is based on the EOQ model and uses fixed estimates for annual usage, carrying and ordering costs, and lead time. These estimates may be imprecise and actual cost factors may be quite volatile. Although individually such errors may not make a significant difference in the EOQ/EPR/MRP models, the cumulative effect of such errors could be substantial.

4. Current inventory levels are assumed to be the amounts reflected by the accounting records. These records can be incorrect for a variety of reasons, such as shortages from theft, breakage, or human errors in counting or recording. In fact, a recent survey of manufacturing companies indicated that only 4.4 percent of the respondents had no inventory adjustments during the most recent year.[3]

5. MRP assumes that the system will be in effect and used at all times. Managers, however, often use less formalized systems to achieve objectives and may not fully implement MRP.

The MRP models extend the use of the economic order quantity concept. EOQ indicates the most economical quantity to order at a time. MRP indicates which items of inventory to order at what point in time. Like EOQ, materials requirements planning models work in the traditional **push system** of production control. In such a system (illustrated in Exhibit 17–7), work centers may buy or produce inventory not currently needed because of lead time or economic order or production quantity requirements. This excess inventory is stored until it is needed by other work centers.

To reduce the cost of carrying inventory until future needs require it, many companies have begun to implement **pull systems** of production control (depicted in Exhibit 17–8). In these systems, parts are delivered or produced only as they are needed by the work center for which they are intended. Although some minimal storage must exist by necessity, work centers do not produce to compensate for lead times or to meet some economic production run model.

Because the need for prompt and accurate communication between company and supplier is essential in a pull system, many companies are eliminating paper and telephone communication processes and relying instead on **electronic data interchange** (EDI). EDI refers to the computer-to-computer transfer of information in virtual real time using standardized formats developed by the American National Standards Institute. In addition to the cost savings obtained from reduced paperwork and data entry errors, EDI users experience more rapid transaction processing and response time than can occur using traditional communication channels. Workers and teams of workers can also reduce time to perform activities and consume fewer resources by cooperating and conferring on cross-functional interface activities as discussed in the next section.

VIDEO
VIGNETTE

Aquathin Corp. (Blue Chip
Enterprises)

push system

pull system

electronic data interchange

---

[3] Il-Woon Kim and Arjan T. Sadhwani, "Is Your Inventory Really All There?" *Management Accounting* (July 1991), p. 37.

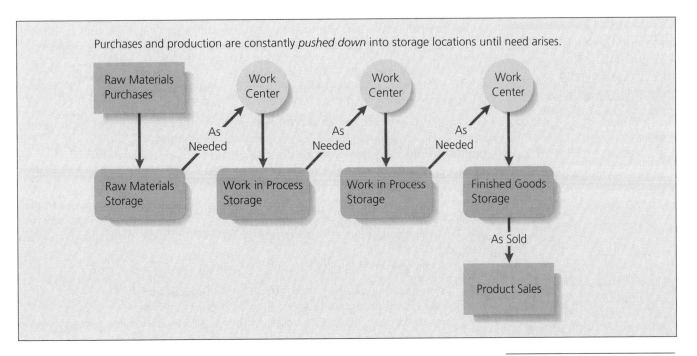

Purchases and production are constantly *pushed down* into storage locations until need arises.

EXHIBIT 17–7

Push System of
Production Control

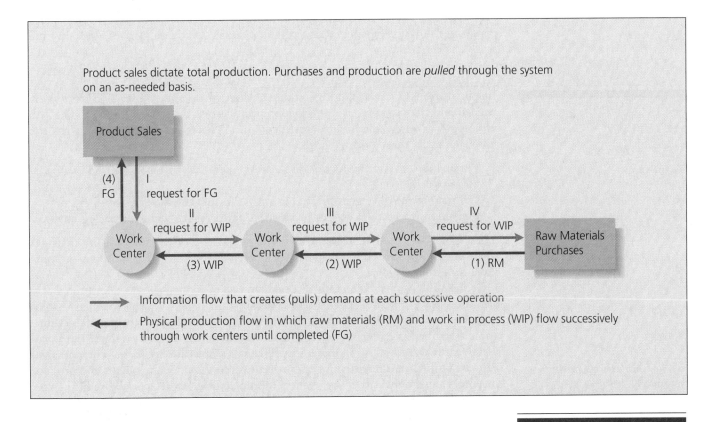

Product sales dictate total production. Purchases and production are *pulled* through the system
on an as-needed basis.

EXHIBIT 17–8

Pull System of
Production Control

THREE MOST IMPORTANT RELATIONSHIPS IN THE VALUE CHAIN

Every company has a set of upstream suppliers and a set of downstream customers. In a one-on-one context, these parties can be depicted in the following model:

| UPSTREAM SUPPLIER | —— | THE COMPANY | —— | DOWNSTREAM CUSTOMER |

It is at the interfaces of these relationships where real opportunities for improvements exist. By building improved cooperation, communication, and integration, the entities within the value chain can treat each other as extensions of themselves. In so doing, they can enjoy gains in quality, throughput, and cost efficiency. Non-value-added activities can be reduced or eliminated and performance of value-added activities can be enhanced. Shared expertise and problem solving can be very beneficial. Products and services can be provided faster and with fewer defects, and activities can be performed more effectively and reliably with fewer deficiencies and less redundancy.

Consider the following opportunities for improvement between each entity:

- Improved communication of requirements and specifications
- Greater clarity in requests for products or services
- Improved feedback regarding unsatisfactory products or services
- Improvements in planning, controlling, and problem solving
- Shared managerial and technical expertise, supervision, and training

All of these opportunities are also available to individuals and groups within an organization. Within the company, each employee or group of employees has both an upstream supplier and a downstream customer that form the context of an intraorganizational value chain. When employees see their internal suppliers and customers as extensions of themselves and work to exploit the opportunities for improvement, teamwork will be significantly enhanced. Improved teamwork helps companies in their implementation of pull systems, which are part of a just-in-time work environment.

JUST-IN-TIME SYSTEMS

just-in-time

Just-in-time (JIT) is a philosophy about when to do something. The *when* is as needed and the *something* is a production, purchasing, or delivery activity. The JIT philosophy is applicable in all departments of all types of organizations. It has the following as its three primary goals:

1. Elimination of any production process or operation that does not add value to the product/service
2. Continuous improvement in production/performance efficiency
3. Reduction in the total cost of production/performance while increasing quality

These goals are totally consistent with and supportive of the total quality management program discussed in Chapter 3. The elements of the JIT philosophy are outlined in Exhibit 17–9.

Because JIT is most commonly discussed in regard to manufacturing or production activities, this is a logical starting point. Just-in-time manufacturing has many names including zero-inventory production systems (ZIPS) and kanban (pronounced kahn-

kanban

bahn). (**Kanban** is Japanese for card. The manufacturing system originated in Japan where cards were used to indicate a work center's need for additional components.)

just-in-time manufacturing system

A **just-in-time manufacturing system** attempts to acquire components and produce inventory units only as they are needed, minimize product defects, and reduce cycle/setup times for acquisition and production.

Production has traditionally been dictated by the need to smooth operating activity over a period of time. Although allowing a company to maintain a steady workforce and continuous machine utilization, smooth production often creates products that must be stored until future sales arise. In addition, although smooth production

EXHIBIT 17–9

Elements of a
JIT Philosophy

- Quality is essential at all times; work to eliminate defects and scrap.
- Employees often have the best knowledge of ways to improve operations; listen to them.
- Employees generally have more talents than are being used; train them to be multiskilled and increase their productivity.
- Ways to improve operations are always available; constantly look for them, being certain to make fundamental changes rather than superficial ones.
- Creative thinking doesn't cost anything; use it to find ways to reduce costs before making expenditures for additional resources.
- Suppliers are essential to operations; establish and cultivate good relationships with suppliers and use, if possible, long-term contracts.
- Inventory is an asset that generates no revenue while it is held in stock. Thus, it can be viewed as a "liability"; eliminate it to the extent possible.
- Storage space is directly related to inventories; eliminate it in response to the elimination of inventories.
- Long cycle times cause inventory buildup; keep cycle times as short as possible by using frequent deliveries.

works well with the EOQ concept, managers recognize that EOQ is based on estimates and therefore a stock of parts is maintained (as Boeing did) "just in case" they are needed. Traditionally, companies filled warehouses with products that were not currently in demand, while often failing to meet promised customer delivery dates. The cause of this dysfunctional behavior was the preoccupation with spreading overhead over a maximum number of products being produced. This obsession unwittingly resulted in much unwanted inventory, huge inventory carrying costs, and other operations problems to be subsequently discussed.

Thus, raw material and work in process inventories historically have been maintained at levels that were considered sufficient to cover up inefficiencies in acquisition and/or production. Exhibit 17–10 depicts these inefficiencies or problems as "rocks" in a stream of "water" that represents inventory. The traditional philosophy is that the water level should be kept high enough for the rocks to be so deeply submerged that there will be "smooth sailing" in production activity. This technique is intended to avoid the original problems, but it creates a new one. By covering up the problems, the excess "water" adds to the difficulty of making corrections. The JIT manufacturing philosophy is to lower the water level, expose the rocks, and eliminate them to the extent possible. The shallower stream will then flow more smoothly and rapidly than the deep river.

CHANGES NEEDED TO IMPLEMENT JIT MANUFACTURING

Implementation of a just-in-time system in a manufacturing firm does not occur overnight. It took Toyota over 20 years to develop the system and realize significant benefits from it. But JIT techniques are becoming better known and more easily implemented and it is now possible for a company to have a system in place and be recognizing benefits in a fairly short time.

In a world where managers work diligently to produce improvements of a percentage point or two, some numbers just do not look real. Coleman Company of Wichita, Kansas, previously needed 2 months of inventory to provide giant retailers such as Wal-Mart and Kmart with a shipment of camping stoves or lanterns. As of 1991, Coleman could make and ship a new order in a week. In 1989, the company offered 20 models of ice coolers in 3 color combinations; in 1991, it sold 140 models in 12 color combinations. Coleman cut inventory costs by $10 million, reduced scrap 60 percent, and raised productivity 35 percent. What on earth happened? In a word: speed. In 1990, Coleman adopted a just-in-time inventory system.[4]

[4] Brian Dumaine, "Earning More By Moving Faster," *Fortune* (October 7, 1991), pp. 89–90, 94.

Depiction of Traditional
and JIT Production
Philosophies

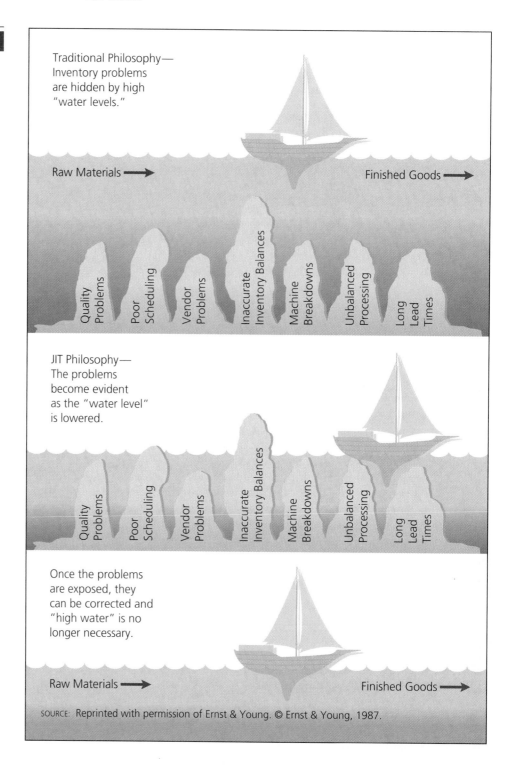

Traditional Philosophy—
Inventory problems
are hidden by high
"water levels."

Raw Materials →   Finished Goods →

Quality Problems · Poor Scheduling · Vendor Problems · Inaccurate Inventory Balances · Machine Breakdowns · Unbalanced Processing · Long Lead Times

JIT Philosophy—
The problems
become evident
as the "water level"
is lowered.

Quality Problems · Poor Scheduling · Vendor Problems · Inaccurate Inventory Balances · Machine Breakdowns · Unbalanced Processing · Long Lead Times

Once the problems
are exposed, they
can be corrected and
"high water" is no
longer necessary.

Raw Materials →   Finished Goods →

SOURCE: Reprinted with permission of Ernst & Young. © Ernst & Young, 1987.

The most impressive benefits from JIT, though, are normally reached only after the system has been operational for 5 to 10 years. Coleman President Bob Ring agrees; he thinks the company has not even scratched the surface of possible gains. Implementing JIT is not easy and takes time and perseverance. Further, JIT must have strong backing and resource commitment from top management. Without these ingredients, considerable retraining, and backing of all levels of company personnel, implementing JIT cannot succeed.

JIT and activity-based management (ABM) are similar because they are both aimed at reducing operating and producing costs and the time, space, and energy necessary for effective and efficient operations and production. Both processes center on the planning, control, and problem solving of activities. Also, both include quality and continuous improvement as prime considerations.

For just-in-time production to be effective, certain modifications must be made in purchasing, supplier relationships, distribution, product design, product processing, and plant layout. JIT depends on employees and suppliers being able to compress the time, distance, resources, activities, and interactions needed to produce a company's products and services. The methods currently being used successfully by many companies are discussed below.

Purchasing Considerations

When applying JIT to purchasing, managers must first recognize that the lowest quoted purchase price is not necessarily the lowest cost. Suppliers should be screened to systematically consider other factors. If other costs such as the failure costs of poor quality (machine downtime, labor idle time, rework, and scrap) are considered, the lowest price could become the most expensive. Additionally, the vendor willing to quote the lowest price may not be willing to make frequent small-quantity deliveries, sign a long-term contract, or form a strategic alliance with the JIT firm.

Long-term contracts are negotiated with suppliers and continuance of those contracts is based on delivery reliability. Vendors missing a certain number of scheduled deliveries by more than a specified number of hours are dismissed. Vendor agreements are made in which components are delivered "ready for use" without packaging, eliminating the need for the JIT manufacturer to unpack components; other agreements may specify that goods will be received from suppliers in modular form, so that less subassembly work is required in the assembly plant.

Suppliers may be requested to bar code raw materials sent to a JIT company so that inventory management techniques are improved. Bar coding allows raw material inventory records to be updated more quickly, raw material to be processed by receiving more precisely, work in process to be tracked more closely, and finished goods shipments to be quickly made and all with incredible accuracy. Bar code technology is continually improving and one company, Symbol Technologies of Bohemia, New York, has developed a two-dimensional bar code that will allow storage of about two pages of text or 100 times the information currently available on a bar code. Bar codes of the future will be able to track products even more effectively and efficiently through the plant.

V I D E O
VIGNETTE

Motorola (in AME—On the Road)

V I D E O
VIGNETTE

NCR (in AME—Managing the Supply Chain)

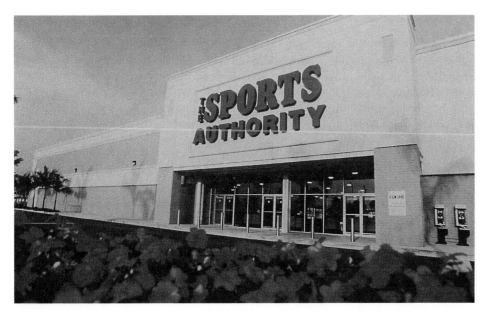

To manage the inventory at the Sports Authority, chief executive Jack Smith wisely invested in computer systems that monitor store inventory daily. The systems use EDI to automatically transmit orders to suppliers who, in turn, ship directly to the stores without the need for a distribution center.

Although bar codes on purchased goods will improve recordkeeping and inventory management, even that would not be necessary if the ideal JIT purchase quantity of one unit could be implemented. Such a quantity is typically not a feasible ordering level, although Allen-Bradley (and some other highly automated, flexible manufacturers) can produce in such a lot size. Thus, the closer a company can get to a lot size of one, the more effective the JIT system is. This reduction in ordering levels means more frequent orders and deliveries. Some automobile companies, for example, have some deliveries made every 2 hours! Thus, vendors chosen by the company should be located close to the company to minimize both shipping costs and delivery time. The ability to obtain suppliers close to the plant is easy in a country the size of Japan. Such an objective is not so readily accomplished in the United States where a plant can be located in New Jersey and a critical parts vendor in California. However, air express companies help to make just-in-time more practical.

Focused Factory Arrangements

focused factory arrangement

Focused factory arrangements are often adopted to connect a vendor more closely to a JIT manufacturer's operations. Such an arrangement means that a vendor agrees to provide a limited number of products according to specifications or to perform a limited number of unique services for the JIT company. The supplier may be an internal division of the same organization or an external party. Focused factory arrangements may also involve relocation or plant modernization by the vendor, and financial assistance from the JIT manufacturer may be available to recoup such investments. In addition, the vendor benefits from long-term supply contracts.

Major reliance on a single customer can be difficult, especially for small vendors. A decline in the business of the primary customer or demands for lower prices can be disastrous for the focused factory. To maintain customers, some companies are submitting to vendor certification processes.

B Machine Products Inc. and/or National Customer Engineering (Blue Chip Enterprises)

Vendor Certification

The optimal JIT situation would be to have only one vendor for any given item. Such an ideal, however, creates the risk of not having alternative sources (especially for critical parts) in the event of vendor business failure, production strikes, unfair pricing, or shipment delays. Thus, it is often more feasible and realistic to limit the number of vendors to a few that are selected and company-certified as to quality and reliability. The company then enters into long-term relationships with these suppliers, who become pseudo "partners" in the process. Vendor certification is becoming more and more popular. For example, Allen-Bradley, a world-class electronics manufacturer, has been named the preferred automation controls supplier to Ford's Automotive Components Group network of more than 30 manufacturing plants worldwide.

The Bernd Group and/or Den-Con Tool Co. (Blue Chip Enterprises)

Vendor certification requires substantial efforts on the purchasing company's part, such as obtaining information on the supplier's operating philosophy, costs, product quality, and service. People from various areas must decide on the factors by which the vendor will be rated; these factors are then weighted as to relative importance. Rapid feedback should be given to potential suppliers so that they can, if necessary, make changes prior to the start of the relationship or, alternatively, to understand why the relationship will not occur.

Allen-Bradley (in AME—On the Road)

To illustrate the type of document necessary for such a rating process, Exhibit 17–11 provides Digital Equipment Corporation's vendor service rating form. This form does not consider factors such as supplier quality or delivery; these criteria are covered by different rating scales. Evaluations of new and infrequent suppliers are more difficult because of the lack of experience by which the purchasing company vendor analysis team can make informed judgments.

Characteristics of Vendor	Vendor		
Excellent = 5 points; Average = 4 points; Below average = 2 points	A	B	C
1. Personnel Capabilities: a. Caliber and availability of sales and technical personnel. b. Is management progressive? c. Technical knowledge of supervision. d. Cooperation on changes and problems. e. Technical field service availability. f. Labor relations.			
2. Facilities Capabilities: a. Capability for anticipated volume. b. Latest technology and equipment. c. Excess production capacity. d. Geographical location. e. Financial capacity to stand behind product failures. f. Investing capital in the organization.			
3. R&D Capabilities: a. New product development. b. Alerted for future needs? c. Does the vendor update the buyer with the latest techniques?			
4. Product Service Capability: a. Offers emergency assistance? b. Does vendor provide consultation for potential troubles? c. What type of warranty is furnished? d. Is the vendor willing to accept responsibility? e. What is the vendor's record for reliability in past dealings?			
Total service points			

EXHIBIT 17–11

Digital Equipment Corporation Vendor Service Rating

SOURCE: Narenda S. Patel, "Source Surveillance and Vendor Evaluation Plan," *Quality Costs: Ideas and Applications,* A. Grimm, ed. (Milwaukee, Wis.: American Society for Quality Control, 1987).

Working with fewer vendors on a long-term basis provides the opportunity to continuously improve quality and substantially reduce costs. "By forming partnerships with all members of the supply chain, we can eliminate redundancies in warehousing, packaging, labeling, transportation, inventories, etc., that will provide continuous savings instead of one-time inventory buy-backs or other current industry gimmicks and fads," says Fred Ricker, a vice president at Owens & Minor, a Baylor University Medical Center (Dallas, Texas) certified supplier.[5]

Product Design

Products need to be designed to use the fewest number of parts and parts should be standardized to the greatest extent possible. For example, at Harley-Davidson, engines and their components were traditionally designed without regard for manufacturing efficiency. Harley was making two similar crankpins, one having an oil hole drilled at a 45-degree angle, and the other at a 48-degree angle. (A crankpin is a

VIDEO VIGNETTE

Harley-Davidson (in AME— Managing the Supply Chain)

[5] "Baylor University Medical Center Teams Up with O&M," *(Owens & Minor, Inc.) Community Post* (Fall 1991), p. 3.

EXHIBIT 17–12

Development of Product
Cost Commitment

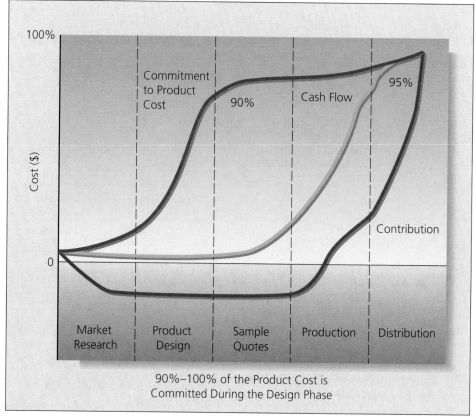

90%–100% of the Product Cost is
Committed During the Design Phase

SOURCE: Charles N. Porter, Coopers & Lybrand, *Cost Management in the New Manufacturing Environment* (Presentation, 1989).

cylindrical bar that attaches a connecting rod to a crank in an engine.) Repositioning the machines to make these different crankpins required about 2 hours. Engineers designed a common angle on both parts and common tools for drilling the holes, which cut changeover time for that process to 3 minutes.[6] Another company discovered that it used 29 different types of screws to manufacture a single product. Downtime was excessive because screwdrivers were continuously being passed among workers. Changing to all the same type screws significantly reduced production time.

Parts standardization does not have to result in identical finished products. Many companies (such as Ford Motor Company) are finding that they can produce a great number of variations in finished products from just a few basic models. Many of the variations can be made toward the end of the production process so that the vast proportion of parts and tasks are standardized and are added before the latter stages of production when the variations take place. Such differentiation can be substantially aided by flexible manufacturing systems and computer-integrated manufacturing.

Products should be designed for the quality desired and should require only a minimal number of engineering changes after the design is released for production. Approximately 90 to 100 percent of all product costs are preestablished by the production team when the stage of product design is only 25 percent to 50 percent completed (see Exhibit 17–12). It is often helpful to have vendors' engineers participate in the design phase or simply to provide the vendor with product specifications and allow the vendor company to draft the design for approval.

If costs are to be significantly affected, any design changes must be made early in the process. Each time an engineering change is made, one or more of the following problems occurs, creating additional costs: the operations flow document must be reprinted; workers must relearn tasks; machine dies or setups must be changed; and

VIDEO
VIGNETTE

North Valley Precision (Blue
Chip Enterprises)

[6] John Van, "Leaks No Longer Stain Harley-Davidson Name," *Chicago Tribune* (November 4, 1991), Sec. 1, p. 6.

parts currently ordered or in stock may be made obsolete. Regardless of whether a company embraces JIT, time that is spent doing work that adds no value to the production process should be viewed as wasted. Effective activity analysis eliminates such non-value-added work and its unnecessary cost.

From another point of view, good product design should address all concerns of the intended consumers, even the degree of recyclability of the product. For example, "BMW's plant is equipped to receive and take apart used-up models, remanufacture them, and then send them back into the marketplace."[7] Thus, companies are considering remanufacturing as part of their design and processing capabilities.

Product Processing

In the production processing stage, one primary JIT consideration is reduction of machine setup time. Reduction of setup time allows processing to shift between products more often and at a lower cost. The costs of reducing setup time are more than recovered by the savings derived from reducing downtime, WIP inventory, and materials handling as well as increasing safety, flexibility, and ease of operation.

Most companies implementing rapid tool-setting procedures have been able to obtain setup times of 10 minutes or less. Such companies use a large number of low-cost setups rather than the traditional processing approach of a small number of more expensive setups. Under JIT, setup cost is considered almost purely variable rather than fixed, as it was in the traditional manufacturing environment. One way to reduce machine setup time is to have workers perform as many setup tasks as possible while the machine is on-line and running. All unnecessary movements by either workers or materials should be eliminated. Teams similar to pit-stop crews at auto races can be used to perform setup operations, with each team member handling a specialized task. Based on past results, it appears that with planning and education, setup times can be reduced by 50 percent or more.

Another essential part of product processing is the institution of high quality standards because JIT has the goal of zero defects. Under just-in-time systems, quality is determined on a continual basis rather than at quality control checkpoints. Continuous quality is achieved by first ensuring vendor quality at point of purchase and also by having workers and machines (such as optical scanners or chutes for size dimensions) monitor quality while production is in process. Controlling quality on an ongoing basis can significantly reduce the costs of obtaining good quality. The JIT philosophy recognizes that it is less costly not to make mistakes than to correct them after they are made. Unfortunately, as mentioned in Chapters 3 and 11, quality control costs and costs of scrap are frequently buried in the standard cost of production, which often makes such costs hard to ascertain.

Standardizing work is an important aspect of any process. This means that work is conducted according to standard procedures without variation, by every worker, every time. Such standard procedures are devised to produce the most efficient way to conduct the tasks to which they relate. Planning, supervising and training are more efficiently and effectively conducted when work has been standardized. Standard work also provides the ability to improve processes. As Dr. W. Edwards Deming so aptly demonstrated during his many courses on TQM, it is nearly impossible to improve an unstable process because there is too much variation in it to ascribe cause and effect to modifications which might be made.

Plant Layout

Most manufacturing plants are still designed in conformity with functional areas. For a JIT system to work effectively, the physical plant must be conducive to the flow of goods and organization of workers and to increasing the value added per square foot of plant space. Manufacturing plants should be designed to minimize material

---

[7] Sandra Vandermerwe and Michael Oliff, "Corporate Challenges for an Age of Reconsumption," *Business Edge* (May 1992), p. 26.

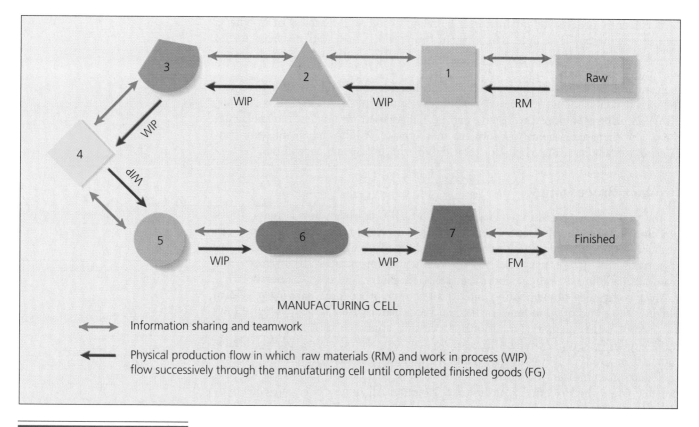

MANUFACTURING CELL

⟷ Information sharing and teamwork

⟵ Physical production flow in which raw materials (RM) and work in process (WIP) flow successively through the manufaturing cell until completed finished goods (FG)

EXHIBIT 17–13

Depiction of a Manufacturing Cell

manufacturing cell

handling time, lead time, and movement of goods from raw material input to completion of the finished product. This goal often means establishing linear or U-shaped production groupings of workers or machines, commonly referred to as **manufacturing cells.** A manufacturing cell is depicted in Exhibit 17–13. This streamlined design allows for more visual controls to be instituted for problems such as excess inventory, production defects, equipment malfunctions, and out-of-place tools. It also allows for greater teamwork and quicker exchange of vital information.

Exhibit 17–14 illustrates the flow of three products through a factory before and after the redesign of factory floor space. In the "before" diagram, processes were grouped together by function and products flowed through the plant depending on what type of processing needed to be performed. If the company uses JIT and a cellular design, substantial storage is eliminated because goods should only be ordered as needed. (All storage is not eliminated, because the company needs to maintain some minimal level of stock.) Products also flow through the plant more rapidly. Product 2 can use the same flow as Product 1, but skip the cell's grinding process.

When plant layout is redesigned to incorporate manufacturing cells, an opportunity arises for workers to broaden their skills and deepen their involvement in the

multiprocess handling

VIDEO VIGNETTE

Northern Telecom (in AME— Self-Directed Work Teams)

process because of **multiprocess handling.** Workers are trained to monitor numerous machines and thereby become more flexible and less bored because they are performing a variety of tasks rather than a single one. Being able to oversee an entire process may prompt employee suggestions on improvement techniques that would not have been visible had the employee been working on a single facet of the process.[8]

[8] The average American company receives about one suggestion per year from every seven employees. On the other hand, the Japanese companies of Mitsubishi, Canon, and Pioneer Electronic Corp. receive, respectively, an average of 100, 70, and 60 suggestions. [Lloyd Shearer, "Parade's Special Intelligence Report," *Parade Magazine* (May 19, 1991), p. 8.]

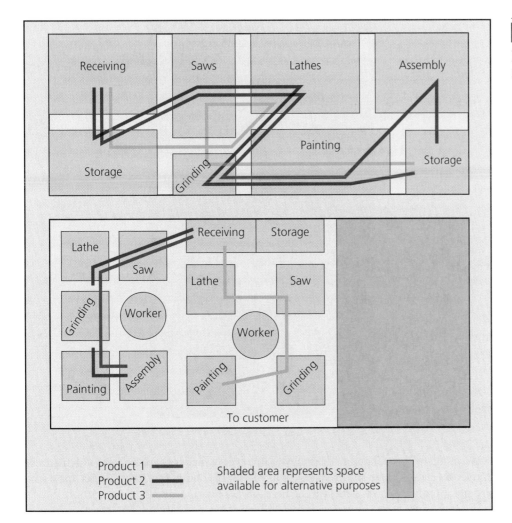

EXHIBIT 17–14

Factory Floor
Space Redesign

Highly automated equipment may run without direct labor involvement, but it will still require monitoring. For instance, some equipment stops automatically when a given situation arises. The "situation" may be positive (a specified quantity of production has been reached) or negative (a quality defect has been indicated). Toyota refers to the usage of such equipment in a factory environment as **autonomation** to distinguish it from automated factories in which the machinery is not programmed to stop when specified situations arise. Because machines "know" the certain conditions they are expected to sense, workers are able to oversee several machines concurrently. A worker's responsibility may be to monitor all those machines operating in a single manufacturing cell.

autonomation

Automated equipment and a cellular plant layout, coupled with computer hardware and software technology and new manufacturing systems and philosophies such as JIT and activity-based management, have allowed many manufacturers to change their basic manufacturing philosophy. Traditionally, most manufacturing firms employed long production runs to make thousands of identical models of the same products; this process was encouraged by the idea of economies of scale. After each run, the machines would be stopped and a slow and expensive setup would be made for the next massive production run to begin. Now, an entirely new generation of manufacturing processing known as flexible manufacturing systems (FMSs) is being developed.

**FLEXIBLE
MANUFACTURING
SYSTEMS AND
COMPUTER-
INTEGRATED
MANUFACTURING**

Mass customization allows production of dolls at My Twinn. Although all dolls are a standard 23 inches, company artisans select the appropriate face shape, skin tone, eyes, and hair color and style from photographs of the recipient—right down to adding freckles, if necessary.

As indicated in Chapter 1, an FMS involves a network of robots and material conveyance devices monitored and controlled by computers that allows for rapid production and responsiveness to changes in production needs. Two or more FMSs connected via a host computer and an information networking system are generally referred to as **computer-integrated manufacturing** (CIM). Exhibit 17–15 contrasts the dimensions of a traditional manufacturing system with an FMS. Although an FMS is typically associated with short-volume production runs, many companies (such as Allen-Bradley and Cummins Engine) have also begun to use CIM for high-volume lines.

FMSs are used in modular factories and are able to customize output on request for customers. Customization can be accomplished because of the ability to introduce new products quickly, produce small lot sizes, make rapid machine and tool setups,

computer-integrated manufacturing

VIDEO VIGNETTE

Lonestar-SW Mailing Service (Blue Chip Enterprises)

EXHIBIT 17–15

Comparison of Traditional Manufacturing and FMS

FACTOR	TRADITIONAL MANUFACTURING	FMS
Product variety	Few	Basically unlimited
Response time to market needs	Slow	Rapid
Worker tasks	Specialized	Diverse
Production runs	Long	Short
Lot sizes	Massive	Small
Performance rewards basis	Individual	Team
Setups	Slow and expensive	Fast and inexpensive
Product life cycle expectations	Long	Short
Work area control	Centralized	Decentralized
Technology	Labor intensive	Technology intensive
Information requirements	Batch based	On line, real time
Worker knowledge of technology	Low to medium	High

Flexible Systems Mean Frequent Changes

N E W S
N O T E

Flexibility is an explicit goal at Toshiba, whose $35.5 billion in sales in 1991 came from products as diverse as appliances and computers, light bulbs and power plants. Okay, so the slogan "synchronize production in proportion to customer demand" probably made a few hearts leap when Toshiba workers first heard it in 1985. The idea, explains Toshiba President Fumio Sato, is to push Toshiba's two dozen factories to adapt faster to markets. Says Sato: "Customers wanted choices. They wanted a washing machine or a TV set that was precisely right for their needs. We needed variety, not mass production."

Sato hammered home his theme in an almost nonstop series of factory visits. The key to variety: finding ways to make money from ever shorter production runs. Sato urged managers to reduce setup times, shrink lead time, and learn to make more products with the same equipment and people. He says: "Every time I go to a plant I tell the people, 'Smaller lot!'"

[Toshiba's computer factory in Ome is referred to as] an "intelligent works" because a snazzy computer network links office, engineering, and factory operations, providing just-in-time information as well as just-in-time parts. Ome workers assemble nine different word processors on the same line and, on an adjacent one, 20 varieties of laptop computers. Usually they make a batch of 20 before changing models, but Toshiba can afford lot sizes as small as ten.

Workers have been trained to make each model but don't need to rely on memory. A laptop at every post displays a drawing and instructions, which change when the model does. Product life-cycles for low-end computers are measured in months these days, so the flexible lines allow the company to guard against running short of a hot model or overproducing one whose sales have slowed.

When it comes to hardware for flexible manufacturing, the Japanese lead is, if anything, widening. Okuma Corp., which makes the world's broadest machine-tool product line, sells 14 flexible manufacturing systems in Japan for every one it exports to America. Though U.S. purchases of industrial robots are at record highs, Japan has already installed 390,000 to America's 45,000.

SOURCE: Thomas A. Stewart, "Brace for Japan's Hot New Strategy," *Fortune* (September 21, 1992), pp. 64, 74. © 1992 Time Inc. All rights reserved.

and communicate and process large amounts of information. Information is transferred through an electronic network to the computers that control the robots performing most of the production activities. On-line, real-time production flow control using fiber optics and local area networks makes the system function.

Companies are able to quickly and inexpensively stop producing one item and start producing another. This ability to make quick and inexpensive production changes and to operate at great speed permits a company to build a large assortment of products and thereby offer its customers a wide variety of high-quality products while minimizing product costs. In effect, machines are able to make other machines and can do so with little human intervention. The system can operate in a "lights-out" environment and never tire. The News Note "Flexible Systems Mean Frequent Changes" discusses Toshiba's flexible manufacturing system in Ome, Japan.

The need for direct labor is diminished in such a technology-intensive environment. The workers who remain in a company employing an FMS must be more highly trained than those working in traditional manufacturing environments and find themselves handling a greater variety of tasks than the narrowly specialized workers of earlier manufacturing eras. The manufacturing cells are managed by persons with greater authority and responsibility. This increase in control occurs because production and production scheduling changes happen so rapidly on the shop floor that an FMS relies on immediate decisions by persons who "live there" and have a grasp of the underlying facts and conditions.

The FMS works so fast that moving products along and out of the way of other products is sometimes a problem. Japan's Nissan Motor Company's new FMS facility on Kyushu Island replaced the time-honored conveyor belt with a convoy of little yellow intelligent motor-driven dollies that "tote cars at variable speeds down the assembly line sending out a stream of computer-controlled signals to coach both robots and workers along the way."[9]

ACCOUNTING IMPLICATIONS OF JIT

There are significant accounting implications for companies adopting a just-in-time inventory and/or flexible manufacturing system. A primary accounting impact occurs in variance analysis. Because it is primarily historical in nature, the main goal of a traditional standard cost accounting system is variance reporting. The reports allow the variances to be analyzed for cause-effect relationships to eliminate future similar problems.

Variances Under JIT

Variance reporting and analysis in JIT systems essentially disappears. Because most variances first appear in a *physical* (rather than financial) fashion, JIT mandates that variances be recognized on the spot so that causes can be ascertained and, if possible, promptly removed. JIT workers are trained and expected to monitor quality and efficiency continually *while production occurs* rather than just at the end of production. Furthermore, if the firm is using statistical process controls, workers can predict the impending occurrence of production defects and take measures to prevent them from ever actually occurring. Therefore, the number and monetary significance of end-of-period variances being reported for managerial control should be limited.

Under a JIT system, long-term price agreements have been made with vendors, so material price variances should be minimal. The JIT accounting system should be designed so that purchase orders cannot be cut for an amount greater than the designated price without manager approval.[10] In this way, the variance amount and its cause are known in advance, providing an opportunity to eliminate the excess expenditure before it occurs. Calls can be made to the vendor to negotiate the price, or other vendors can be contacted for quotes.

The ongoing use of specified vendors also provides the ability to control material quality. It is becoming relatively common around the world for companies to require that their vendors maintain quality standards and submit to quality assurance audits. Because raw material quality is expected to be better controlled, little or no material quantity variances should be caused by substandard material. If usage standards are accurate, there should be virtually no favorable usage variance of material during production. Unfavorable use of material should be promptly detected because of ongoing machine and/or human observation of processing. When an unfavorable variance occurs, the JIT system is stopped and the error causing the unfavorable material usage is corrected to minimize material quantity variances.

One type of quantity variance is not caused by errors but by engineering changes (ENCs) made to the product specifications. A JIT system has two comparison standards: an annual standard and a current standard. Design modifications would change the current standard, but not the annual one. Such a procedure allows comparisons to be made that indicate the cost effects of having engineering changes implemented after a product has begun to be manufactured. A material quantity variance caused by an ENC is illustrated in Exhibit 17–16. In the illustration, the portion of the total quantity variance caused by the engineering change ($46,800 U) is shown separately from that caused by efficiency ($9,360 F). Labor, overhead, and/or conversion can also have ENC variances.

[9] Clay Chandler and Joseph B. White, "It's Hello Dollies at Nissan's New 'Dream Factory'," *Wall Street Journal* (July 6, 1992), p. 1.
[10] This same procedure can be implemented under a traditional standard cost system as well as under a JIT system. It is, however, less common to find in a traditional system, but is a requirement under JIT.

Annual standard:	8 feet of material M @ $5.10		$40.80		
	5 feet of material N @ $7.70		38.50		
			$79.30		
Current standard:	7 feet of material M @ $5.10		$35.70		
	6 feet of material N @ $7.70		46.20		
			$81.90		
Production during month:	18,000 units				
Usage during month:	129,600 feet of material M @ $5.10		$ 660,960		
	104,400 feet of material N @ $7.70		803,880		
	Total cost of materials used		$1,464,840		
Material quantity variance:					
18,000 × 7 × $5.10			$ 642,600		
18,000 × 6 × $7.70			831,600		
Material cost at current standard			$1,474,200		
Actual material cost			1,464,840		
Material quantity variance			$ 9,360 F		
Engineering change variance for material:					
18,000 × 8 × $5.10			$ 734,400		
18,000 × 5 × $7.70			693,000		
Materials cost at annual standard			$1,427,400		
Materials cost at current standard			1,474,200		
ENC variance (material)			$ 46,800 U		

EXHIBIT 17–16

Material Variances
Under a JIT System

Labor variances in a just-in-time system should be minimal if standard rates and times have been set appropriately. Labor time standards should be carefully evaluated after the implementation of a JIT production system. If the plant is not entirely automated, redesigning the physical layout and minimizing any non-value-added labor activities should decrease the direct labor time component.

Another accounting change that may occur in a JIT system is the use of a "conversion" category for purposes of cost control rather than separate labor and overhead categories. This category becomes more useful as factories reduce the direct labor cost component through continuous improvements and, possibly, automation. A standard departmental or manufacturing cell conversion cost per unit of product (or per hour of production time per manufacturing cell) may be calculated rather than individual standards for labor and overhead. Denominators in each case would be practical or theoretical capacity in either units or hours.[11] For example, if time were used as the base, the conversion cost for a day's production would be equal to the number of units produced multiplied by the standard number of production hours multiplied by the standard cost per hour. Variances would be determined by comparing actual cost to the designated standard.

In addition to minimizing and adjusting the variance calculations, a JIT system can have a major impact on inventory accounting. Companies employing JIT production processes would no longer need a separate raw material inventory classification because material would be acquired only when and as production occurs. Instead, JIT companies could use a Raw and In Process (RIP) Inventory account.

[11] Practical or theoretical capacity is the appropriate measure of activity because the goal of JIT is virtually continuous processing. In a highly automated plant, these capacities more closely reflect world status than does expected annual capacity.

Backflush Costing

throughput

The focus of accounting in a JIT system is on the plant's output (**throughput**) to the customer.[12] Because each sequential area is dependent on the previous area, any problems will quickly cause the system to stop the production process. Individual daily accounting for the costs of production will no longer be necessary because all costs should be at standard and variations will be observed and corrected almost immediately.

Additionally, fewer costs need to be allocated to products because more costs can be traced directly to their related output in a JIT system. Costs are incurred in specified cells on a per-hour or per-unit basis. Energy is a direct production cost in a comprehensive JIT system because there should be a minimum of downtime by machines or unplanned idle time for workers. Virtually the only costs still being allocated are costs associated with the structure (building depreciation, rent, taxes, and insurance) and machinery depreciation. The reduction of allocations provide more useful measures of cost control and performance evaluation than have been traditionally available.

backflush costing

Backflush costing is a streamlined cost accounting method that speeds up, simplifies, and minimizes accounting effort in an environment that minimizes inventory balances, requires few allocations, uses standard costs, and has minimal variances from standard. During the period, this costing method records purchases of raw material and accumulates actual conversion costs. Then, either at completion of production or on the sale of goods, an entry is made to allocate the total costs incurred to cost of goods sold and to finished goods inventory using standard production costs.

The backflush costing system journal entries related to one of Monitronics' products are illustrated in Exhibit 17–17. The product's standard production cost is $137.40. The company has a long-term contract with its direct material supplier to supply raw material at $42 per unit, so there is no material price variance upon purchase. Beginning inventories for June are assumed to be zero.

The following selected T-accounts summarize the activity presented in Exhibit 17–17:

RAW AND IN PROCESS INVENTORY				CONVERSION COSTS			
(1)	1,281,000	(4)	4,122,000	(2)	2,868,000	(3)	2,862,000
(3)	2,862,000						
Bal.	21,000						

FINISHED GOODS INVENTORY				COST OF GOODS SOLD			
(4)	4,122,000	(5)	4,094,520	(5)	4,094,520		
Bal.	27,480						

ACCOUNTS RECEIVABLE			SALES		
(5)	6,556,000			(5)	6,556,000

Three alternatives are also possible for the Exhibit 17–17 entries. First, if Monitronics' production time were extremely short, it might not journalize raw material purchases until completion of production. In that case, the entry [in addition to recording entries (2) and (5) in Exhibit 17–17] to replace entries (1), (3), and (4) would be

---

[12] A company may wish to measure output of each manufacturing cell or work center rather than plant throughput. Such measurements may indicate problems in a given area, but do not correlate with the JIT philosophy of the team approach, plantwide attitude, and total cost picture.

EXHIBIT 17–17

Backflush Costing

Monitronics' standard production cost per unit:

Direct material	$ 42.00
Conversion	95.40
Total cost	$137.40

No beginning inventories exist.

(1) Purchased $1,281,000 of direct material in June:

Raw and In Process Inventory	1,281,000	
Accounts Payable		1,281,000

Purchased material at standard cost under
a long-term agreement with supplier.

(2) Incurred $2,868,000 of conversion costs in June:

Conversion Costs	2,868,000	
Various accounts		2,868,000

Recorded conversion costs; various accounts include
Wages Payable for direct and indirect labor,
Accumulated Depreciation, Supplies, etc.

(3) Applied conversion costs to RIP for 30,000 units completed:

Raw and In Process Inventory (30,000 × $95.40)	2,862,000	
Conversion Costs		2,862,000

(4) Transferred 30,000 units of production in June:

Finished Goods (30,000 × $137.40)	4,122,000	
Raw and In Process Inventory		4,122,000

(5) Sold 29,800 units on account in June for $220:

Cost of Goods Sold (29,800 × $137.40)	4,094,520	
Finished Goods		4,094,520
Accounts Receivable (29,800 × $220)	6,556,000	
Sales		6,556,000

Ending Inventories:

Raw and In Process Inventory ($4,143,000 − $4,122,000)	$21,000
Finished Goods Inventory ($4,122,000 − $4,094,520)	$27,480

In addition, there are underapplied conversion costs of $6,000 ($2,868,000 − $2,862,000).

Raw and In Process Inventory	21,000	
Finished Goods Inventory	4,122,000	
Accounts Payable		1,281,000
Conversion Costs		2,862,000

If goods were shipped immediately to customers upon completion, Monitronics could use a second alternative in which the entries to complete and sell would be combined. It would replace entries (3), (4), and the first entry in (5) in Exhibit 17–17. Entries (1), (2), and the second entry in (5) in Exhibit 17–17 would still be needed.

Finished Goods Inventory	27,480	
Cost of Goods Sold	4,094,520	
Raw and In Process Inventory		1,260,000
Conversion Costs		2,862,000

The third alternative reflects the ultimate JIT system, in which only one entry [other than recording entry (2) in Exhibit 17–17] is made. For Monitronics, this entry would be

Raw and In Process Inventory	21,000	
(minimal overpurchases)		
Finished Goods Inventory (minimal overproduction)	27,480	
Cost of Goods Sold	4,094,520	
Accounts Payable		1,281,000
Conversion Costs		2,862,000

Implementation of the just-in-time philosophy can cause significant cost reductions and productivity improvements. But, even within a single company, all inventory situations do not necessarily have to be on a just-in-time system. The costs and benefits of any inventory control system must be evaluated before management should install the system. The use of JIT, however, does allow workers as well as managers to concentrate on providing quality service to customers.

JIT IN NONMANUFACTURING SITUATIONS

Although a JIT manufacturing system can only be adopted by a company actually producing a product, other just-in-time systems can be employed by nonmanufacturers. An all-encompassing view of JIT covers a variety of policies and programs that are implemented to continuously improve the use of company human and mechanical resources. Thus, just-in-time is a type of management control system having a distinct underlying philosophy of which inventory minimization is only one element. In addition to being used by manufacturers, the JIT philosophy can be adopted within the purchasing and delivery departments of any organization involved with inventory, such as retailers, wholesalers, and distributors.

Many of the just-in-time techniques do not require a significant investment in new equipment but depend, instead, on the attitude of company management and the involvement of the organization's people and their willingness to work together and trust one another. People working under a JIT system must be open to change and question established routines and procedures. All of an employee's talents, not just a limited few, should be used by the company. Creative abilities have sometimes been overlooked or neglected in the workplace. The "Five Whys" News Note discusses a valuable technique to enhance the creative thought process.

JIT emphasizes that there is always room for workplace improvement, whether in floor space design, training and education, equipment and technology, vendor relationships, or any one of a multitude of other items. Managers and employees should be continuously alert to the possibilities for lowering costs while increasing quality and service. But JIT is more than a cost-cutting endeavor or a matter of reducing personnel; it requires good human resources management. Exhibit 17–18 provides a seven-step action plan for implementing JIT in an organization. In many respects, JIT really requires management to act with common sense.

EXHIBIT 17–18

Seven Steps to Implement JIT

1. Determine how well products, materials, or services are delivered now.
2. Determine what customers consider superior service and set priorities accordingly.
3. Establish specific priorities for distribution (and possibly purchasing) functions to meet customer needs.
4. Collaborate with and educate managers and employees to refine objectives and to prepare for implementation of JIT.
5. Execute a pilot implementation project and evaluate its results.
6. Refine the JIT delivery program and execute it companywide.
7. Monitor progress, adjust objectives over time, and always strive for excellence.

SOURCE: Gene R. Tyndall, "Just-in-Time Logistics: Added Value for Manufacturing Cost Management," *Journal of Cost Management* (Spring 1989), pp. 57–59. Reprinted with permission from *The Journal of Cost Management for the Manufacturing Industry* (Spring 1989), © 1989, Warren Gorham & Lamont, 31 St. James Avenue, Boston MA 02116. All rights reserved.

"Five Whys" Approach to Problem Analysis

Rather than looking at problems as problems, it is more productive to consider problems as opportunities for improvement. Problems are the raw materials for improvement. Asking "Why?" five times is an attempt to challenge traditional thinking and accepted habits. The "five whys" approach gets to the root cause of a problem. Once the root cause is resolved, the problem will not occur again.

Here is an example of the use of the "five whys" approach:

Problem. A machine went down because of an electrical problem.

Why did the machine go down? Because the fuse blew out.
Why did the fuse blow out? Because the fuse was the wrong size.
Why was the fuse the wrong size? Because the electrician made a mistake.
Why did the electrician make a mistake? Because the supply room issued the wrong fuse.
Why did the supply room issue the wrong fuse? Because the stocking bin for the fuses was mislabeled.

Solution. Relabel the stocking bin with the correct fuse size. Check all the other bins to assure accuracy.

As this example points out, the root cause of the machine's going down was a mislabeled bin in the supply room. Simple as it may seem, without repeatedly asking "Why?," the root cause of the problem might never have been discovered. Since the root cause was not identified, this problem would have occurred again sometime in the future. Asking a person "Why?" five times can cause conflict and be considered antagonistic; however, this is a risk that must be taken to prevent the recurrence of a problem.

SOURCE: Mark C. DeLuzio, "The Tools of Just-In-Time," *Journal of Cost Management* (Summer 1993), pp. 19–20. Reprinted with permission from *The Journal of Cost Management for the Manufacturing Industry* (Summer 1993), © 1993, Warren Gorham & Lamont, 31 St. James Avenue, Boston MA 02116. All rights reserved.

REVISITING

Boeing Company

In just a year and a half, Boeing Commercial Airplane Group's efforts to cut its production cycle time have saved more than $1 billion in inventory costs alone, BCAG President Ron Woodard reported.

Cycle time—whose clock starts ticking when the company begins to custom-tailor an aircraft for a customer and ends with delivery—was as high as 18 months. But by "changing processes, doing things concurrently instead of serially, working with suppliers and systematically attacking the long lead times," he said, Boeing has cut that down to 12 months for all four of its mature jetliner programs.

"Our target is six months by the end of 1996 for the 737 and 757, and eight months for the 767 and 747, and eventually the 777," Woodard told reporters at BCAG's Seattle offices.

But he allowed that those levels will be harder to reach. "We picked a lot of the low-hanging fruit to get to 12 months," he said.

. . . "In the past, we spent a lot of effort and time tracking many different indicators, not all of which mattered to our customers," Woodard said, "So now we're concentrating on these four: unit cost, cycle time, defects and customer satisfaction—with ambitious targets for each of them."

In unit costs, for example, BCAG's goal is to "hold them flat," Woodard said, while the rate of defects, which require rework on the line, should be cut in half within three years. Customer satisfaction will be measured by a combination of warranty claims, and feedback from customers on how responsive Boeing is in addressing warranty issues and other factors.

SOURCE: "Boeing Saves More Than $1 Billion in Inventory Thanks to Cycle-time Cuts," *Aerospace Daily* (April 13,1994). Copyright 1994 The McGraw-Hill Companies.

CHAPTER SUMMARY

Costs associated with inventory can be significant for any company and sound business practices seek to limit the amount of those costs. The process of classifying inventory into ABC categories allows management to establish controls relative to the cost of inventory items. Two-bin and red-line systems are appropriate for inventory items in the C category because of the limited financial investment.

Inventory costs include the costs of purchasing, ordering, carrying, and not carrying inventory. The economic order quantity (EOQ) model determines the purchase order size that minimizes, in total, the costs of ordering and carrying inventory. This model can also be adapted to find the most economical production run.

Because the EOQ model ignores relationships among product components, another model known as MRP (materials requirements planning) can be used to generate master production and time-sequenced purchasing schedules. MRP uses the lead time, EOQ, and inventory level of each component together with the sales forecast, bill of materials, operations flow document, and machine capacity information to schedule a smooth production flow minimizing the effects of bottlenecks. MRP II (manufacturing resource planning) implements MRP on a companywide basis, including input from top management levels.

MRP is a push system of production control dictated by lead times and EOQ requirements. Purchased and produced goods must be stored until needed. In contrast, a pull system of production control (such as just-in-time manufacturing) involves the purchase and/or production of inventory only as the need arises. Storage is basically eliminated except for a minimal level of safety stock.

The goals of a just-in-time system are to eliminate non-value-added processes, continuously improve efficiency, and reduce costs while increasing quality. The JIT philosophy can be applied to some extent to any company having inventories. JIT requires that purchases be made in small quantities and deliveries be frequent. Production lot sizes are minimized so that many different products can be made on a daily basis. Products are designed for quality and component parts are standardized to the extent possible. Machine setup time is reduced so that production runs can be easily shifted between products. Plant layout emphasizes manufacturing cells, and the operating capabilities of all factory equipment are considered in order to eliminate the need for or buildup of buffer inventories between operations.

A special type of just-in-time company is one that engages in flexible manufacturing. Flexible manufacturing systems are so fast and versatile that products can be tailored to customer requests with only an insignificant delay in production time in most instances.

The institution of a JIT system has accounting implications. Variances should be negligible, but their occurrence should be recognized earlier in the process so that causes may be found and corrective action taken quickly. Because few raw materials would be stocked (because they are only acquired as needed in production) and work in process time should be short, JIT companies may use a merged raw material and work in process inventory classification. The traditional categories of direct labor and overhead may be combined and accounted for under the single category of conversion cost, and a greater number of costs will be directly traceable to production under a JIT system. Backflush accounting techniques may be used that reduce the number of journal entries currently needed to trace production costs through the process.

APPENDIX

Order Point and Safety Stock

The economic order quantity or production run model indicates how many units to order or produce. But managers are also concerned with the **order point**. This quantity reflects the level of inventory that triggers the placement of an order for additional units. Determination of the order point is based on three factors: usage, lead time, and safety stock. **Usage** refers to the quantity of inventory used or sold each day. The **lead time** for an order is the time it takes from the placement of an order to when the goods arrive or are produced. Many times companies can project a constant, average figure for both usage and lead time. The quantity of inventory kept on hand by a company in the event of fluctuating usage or unusual delays in lead time is called **safety stock.**

order point

usage

lead time

safety stock

If usage is entirely constant and lead time is known with certainty, the order point is equal to daily usage multiplied by lead time:

$$\text{Order Point} = \text{Daily Usage} \times \text{Lead Time}$$

As an example, assume that Monitronics, Inc., produces robot controllers for sale to industrial companies. Monitronics uses 500 computer chips per day, and the supplier can have the chips to Monitronics in 4 days. When the stock of chips reaches 2,000 units, Monitronics should reorder.

The order point formula minimizes the dollars a company has invested in its inventory. Orders would arrive at precisely the time the inventory reached zero. This formula, however, does not take into consideration unusual events such as variations in production schedules, defective products being provided by suppliers, erratic shipping schedules of the supplier, or late arrival of units shipped. To provide for these kinds of events, managers carry a "buffer" safety stock of inventory to protect the company from stockouts. When a safety stock is maintained, the order point formula becomes:

$$\text{Order Point} = (\text{Daily Usage} \times \text{Lead Time}) + \text{Safety Stock}$$

Safety stock size should be determined based on how crucial the item is to production or to the retail business, the item's purchase cost, and the amount of uncertainty related to both usage and lead time.

One way to estimate the quantity of safety stock is to allow one factor to vary from the norm. For example, either excess usage during normal lead time or normal usage during an excess lead time can be considered in the safety stock calculation. Assume that Monitronics never uses more than 600 controller chips in one day. One estimate of the necessary safety stock is 400 units, computed as follows:

Maximum daily usage	600 units
Normal daily usage	500 units
Excess usage	100 units
Lead time	× 4 days
Safety stock	400 units

Using this estimate of safety stock, Monitronics would reorder chips when 2,400 units (2,000 original order point + 400 safety stock) were on hand.

EXHIBIT 17–19

Delayed Shipment and
Impact on Production

	ORDER POINT DAY 1	DAY 2	DAY 3	DAY 4	DAY 5	DAY 6
Inventory	2,400					
Usage	(600)					
Inventory		1,800				
Usage		(600)				
Inventory			1,200			
Usage			(600)			
Inventory				600		
Usage				(600)		
Inventory					0	
Usage					**No production possible**	
Inventory arrives						7,500

It is possible that several adverse events could occur simultaneously. For example, Monitronics could be using the maximum number of chips each day and a one-day shipping delay occurs. Assume that the economic order quantity for Monitronics is 7,500 units. Even with a safety stock of 400 units, the one-day shipping delay will cause Monitronics to stop production, as illustrated in Exhibit 17–19. The amounts shown on the lines labeled "Inventory" are as of 8:00 A.M. Thus, on Day 1, the purchasing agent for Monitronics orders 7,500 chips because the reorder point of 2,400 units has been reached. If the order had been received in the normal lead time, it would have arrived at 8:00 A.M. on Day 5. The fact that the order was delayed one day means that Monitronics has no chips on hand for Day 5 and, therefore, production is stopped.

Instead of estimating that only one factor can be out of the ordinary, the cost accountant can approximate the safety stock needed by using probabilities and weighing the cost of carrying safety stock against the cost of having a stockout. The cost of carrying safety stock is equal to the cost of carrying other units of inventory. This cost was estimated in computing economic order quantity. The cost of having a stockout is based on the concerns expressed earlier in the chapter—lost profits, lost customer goodwill, and production adjustments. As the safety stock increases, the probability of a stockout decreases. Stockout probability estimates can be based on historical data for usage and lead time. Such probabilities are related to each purchase order, and it is possible to have a stockout before every order arrives.

Assume that Monitronics has estimated its stockout cost for computer chips to be $200 and the cost of carrying one chip in stock for one year is $1. The largest portion of the cost associated with carrying chips in stock is the opportunity cost of having funds invested in inventory rather than being used for another purpose. Computation of Monitronics' optimal safety stock of 400 to 800 units is shown in Exhibit 17–20.

Mathematical determination of economic order quantity and optimal quantity of safety stock helps a company control its investment in inventory. However, such models are only as valid as the estimates used in the formula. For example, projections of costs such as lost customer goodwill may be extremely difficult. In some cases, the degree of inaccuracy may not be important; in other cases, it may be critical.[13]

[13] Sensitivity analysis can indicate which estimates have the most significant impact on proper inventory planning. Sensitivity analysis is a means of determining the effect that a change in an independent variable will have on a dependent variable. One application of sensitivity analysis in relation to safety stock is the evaluation of the effects that a change in the rate of return expected on investments would have on the opportunity cost of carrying inventory and thus on the optimal size of inventory orders and safety stock.

EXHIBIT 17–20

Optimal Safety Stock
for Computer Chips

Cost of stockout = $200 per occurrence
Cost of carrying safety stock = $1 per unit per year
Number of orders per year = 20

UNITS OF SAFETY STOCK	PERCENT PROBABILITY OF STOCKOUT
50	65
100	50
200	30
400	20
800	10
1,200	5

COST OF CARRYING SAFETY STOCK

NUMBER OF UNITS	×	COST OF CARRYING	=	TOTAL COST
50		$1		$ 50
100		1		100
200		1		200
400		1		400
800		1		800
1,200		1		1,200

COST OF NOT CARRYING SAFETY STOCK

NUMBER OF UNITS	PERCENT PROBABILITY OF STOCKOUT	×	NUMBER OF PURCHASE ORDERS PER YEAR	=	WEIGHTED PROBABILITY OF STOCKOUT	×	COST OF STOCKOUT	=	TOTAL COST
50	65		20		13		$200		$2,600
100	50		20		10		200		2,000
200	30		20		6		200		1,200
400	20		20		4		200		800
800	10		20		2		200		400
1,200	5		20		1		200		200

Optimal safety stock will minimize the cost of carrying and not carrying safety stock units:

NUMBER OF UNITS	TOTAL COST OF CARRYING	+	TOTAL COST OF NOT CARRYING	=	SUMMATION
50	$ 50		$2,600		$2,650
100	100		2,000		2,100
200	200		1,200		1,400
400	400		800		1,200*
800	800		400		1,200*
1,200	1,200		200		1,400

*Low point in summation of costs indicates an optimal safety stock in the range of 400 to 800 units.

KEY TERMS

ABC analysis (p. 757)
autonomation (p. 777)
backflush costing (p. 782)
carrying cost (p. 758)
computer-integrated manufacturing
  (CIM) (p. 778)
economic order quantity (EOQ)
  (p. 760)
economic production run (EPR)
  (p. 763)
electronic data interchange (EDI)
  (p. 766)
focused factory arrangement (p. 772)
just-in-time (JIT) (p. 768)
just-in-time manufacturing system
  (p. 768)
kanban (p. 768)
lead time (p. 787)

manufacturing cell (p. 776)
manufacturing resource planning
  (MRP II) (p. 764)
materials requirements planning
  (MRP) (p. 764)
multiprocess handling (p. 776)
ordering cost (p. 758)
order point (p. 787)
pull system (p. 766)
purchasing cost (p. 756)
push system (p. 766)
red-line system (p. 757)
safety stock (p. 787)
setup cost (p. 758)
stockout (p. 758)
throughput (p. 782)
two-bin system (p. 757)
usage (p. 787)

SOLUTION STRATEGIES

ECONOMIC ORDER QUANTITY

$$EOQ = \sqrt{\frac{2QO}{C}}$$

where   EOQ = economic order quantity in units
        Q = estimated annual quantity used in units
        O = estimated cost of placing one order
        C = estimated cost to carry one unit in stock for one year

ECONOMIC PRODUCTION RUN

$$EPR = \sqrt{\frac{2QS}{C}}$$

where   EPR = economic production run quantity
        Q = estimated annual quantity produced in units
        S = estimated cost of setting up a production run
        C = estimated cost of carrying one unit in stock for one year

ORDER POINT:

Order Point = (Daily Usage × Lead Time) + Safety Stock

MATERIAL AND LABOR VARIANCES UNDER JIT

Two standards may exist:

1. an annual standard (set and held constant for the year)
2. a current standard (based on design modifications or engineering changes)

Generally firms will have minimal, if any, material price variances because prices are set by long-term contracts. A labor rate variance may exist and would be calculated in the traditional manner.

MATERIAL QUANTITY VARIANCE

> Actual material cost
> − Materials cost at current standard
> Material quantity variance

ENGINEERING CHANGE VARIANCE FOR MATERIALS

> Material cost at annual standard
> − Material cost at current standard
> ENC variance (material)

LABOR EFFICIENCY VARIANCE

> (Actual labor hours × current standard rate)
> − (Standard labor hours × current standard rate)
> Labor efficiency variance

ENGINEERING CHANGE VARIANCE FOR LABOR

(would exist only if a change occurred in the mix of labor used to manufacture the product or through the automation of processes)

> (Standard labor hours × annual standard rate)
> − (Standard labor hours × current standard rate)
> ENC variance (labor)

DEMONSTRATION PROBLEM

Physionics, Inc., prepares compact discs (CDs) with tutorials in physics to be sold in bookstores on college campuses. John Hanson, company president, has been wondering how many blank CDs to buy at a time, and when an order should be placed. He wants a safety stock of 140 CDs and has estimated that his company uses 9,000 CDs annually. Ordering cost is $6.40 per order and carrying cost per CD in inventory is $2. The studio operates 300 days a year. It takes 7 days from placement of an order to arrival of the CDs.

Required:

a. Determine the EOQ.
b. Calculate the order point.
c. Disregard the 140 unit safety stock. Assume that the studio estimates the following:

Cost of a stockout	$32 per occurrence
Cost of carrying a CD in stock for a year	$2
Number of orders per year	38

Estimated stockout probabilities:

UNITS OF SAFETY STOCK	PERCENT PROBABILITY OF STOCKOUT
50	70
100	45
200	25
300	10
400	5

Estimate the optimal safety stock for the company.

Solution to Demonstration Problem

a.
$$EOQ = \sqrt{\frac{2(9,000)(\$6.4)}{\$2}} = 240 \text{ CDs}$$

b. Order point = (Daily Usage × Lead Time) + Safety Stock
= [(9,000 ÷ 300) × 7] + 140 = 350 CDs

c.   Cost of Carrying Safety Stock

NUMBER OF UNITS	×	COST OF CARRYING	=	TOTAL COST
50		$2		$100
100		2		200
200		2		400
300		2		600
400		2		800

Cost of Not Carrying Safety Stock

NUMBER OF UNITS	PERCENT PROBABILITY OF STOCKOUT	×	NUMBER OF PURCHASE ORDERS PER YEAR	=	WEIGHTED PROBABILITY OF STOCKOUT	×	COST OF STOCKOUT	=	TOTAL COST
50	70		38		26.6		$20		$532
100	45		38		17.1		20		342
200	25		38		9.5		20		190
300	10		38		3.8		20		76
400	5		38		1.9		20		38

Optimal safety stock will minimize the cost of carrying and not carrying safety stock units:

NUMBER OF UNITS	TOTAL COST OF CARRYING	+	TOTAL COST OF NOT CARRYING	=	SUMMATION
50	$100		$532		$632
100	200		342		542*
200	400		190		590
300	600		62		662
400	800		38		838

*Optimal safety stock is approximately 100 units.

1. What are the three basic costs of carrying inventory? How do the ordering cost and carrying costs relate to one another?

2. What is the ABC method of inventory analysis? Why do A items and C items warrant different inventory control methods? What are some methods that may be employed to control C items?

3. How and why is the cost of capital used in economic order quantity computations?

4. What is a stockout? What costs are associated with a stockout?

5. Why is the purchasing cost not part of the EOQ formula?

6. After the EOQ point is found, what qualitative factors may be considered in determining the actual order quantity?

7. You own a manufacturing company and your friend Joe owns a retail appliance store. Joe is concerned about how many VCRs to order at a time. You proceed to tell him about using economic production runs at your company. How do EPRs relate to Joe's concerns? What adjustments must he make to the formula you use?

8. What deficiency of the EOQ and safety stock models does MRP (materials requirements planning) overcome and how does MRP do this?

9. Can MRP be effectively implemented without a computer system? Why or why not?

10. MRP produces a time-sequenced schedule for component requirements and a time-phased projection of workloads for various work centers as a result of a given master schedule. What do these workloads determine and how is this information used?

11. What are some of the problems associated with MRP and why do these problems occur?

12. Discuss the differences between push and pull systems of production. Are MRP and JIT push or pull systems?

13. What are the primary goals of a JIT philosophy and how does JIT attempt to achieve these goals?

14. What kinds of changes need to occur in a production environment to effectively implement JIT? Why are these changes necessary?

15. "JIT cannot be implemented as effectively in the United States as it can be in Japan." Discuss the rationale behind this statement.

16. How can the JIT philosophy be used by nonmanufacturers?

17. Describe the production system found in a "lights-out" environment.

18. How would switching from a traditional manufacturing system to a flexible manufacturing system affect a firm's inventory and production control systems?

19. In what areas of accounting can a company implementing a JIT manufacturing system expect changes? Why will such changes arise? Why is backflush costing used in JIT environments?

20. *(Appendix)* How are economic order quantity and order point related?

21. *(Appendix)* What is safety stock and why is it necessary?

EXERCISES

22. *(Terminology)* Match the following lettered terms on the left with the appropriate numbered description on the right.

a. Pull system
b. Order point
c. Stockout
d. Materials requirements planning
e. Safety stock
f. Multiprocess handling
g. Autonomation
h. Throughput
i. Lead time
j. Push system
k. Flexible manufacturing system
l. Just-in-time

1. The average delay in days between the time a purchase order is initiated and when the company receives delivery
2. A system in which inventory is produced before it is needed and placed in storage until needed
3. Output of the entire plant
4. The situation of not having a product or component available when it is needed
5. A manufacturing environment in which machinery is programmed to stop work when specified situations arise
6. The use of machines and robots to perform the production process
7. The broadening of worker involvement to include monitoring all machines in a manufacturing cell
8. A system that generates an interrelated purchase order and production schedule
9. A buffer supply of inventory that minimizes the possibility of running out of a product or component
10. A system in which purchases and production are made only on an as-needed basis
11. A philosophy that focuses on value-added activities
12. The inventory level at which a purchase order is to be issued

23. *(Carrying costs)* Determine the carrying costs for an item costing $4.30, given the following per-unit cost information:

Storage cost	$.04
Handling cost	.03
~~Production labor cost~~	~~.80~~
Insurance	.02
Opportunity cost	10% of investment

24. *(EOQ)* Hawk Company wants to determine its economic order quantity for a T-bracket. The company supplies you with the following information:

✓ Annual units of the T-bracket used	3,000
Per unit cost of the T-bracket	$14.50
✓ Cost of each order	$12.00
✓ Annual cost of stocking 1 unit of the T-bracket	$ .60 — *carrying cost.*

Determine the economic order quantity.

25. *(Ordering)* Based on the EOQ associated with the following data, determine the total annual ordering cost.

Annual demand	20,000 units
Ordering cost	$5.25 per order
Carrying cost	$0.84 per unit

26. *(Cost classification)* For each of the following costs, indicate whether it would be considered an ordering cost (O), a carrying cost (C), or a cost of not carrying (N) inventory. For any costs that do not fit these categories, indicate N/A.

   1. Telephone call to supplier
   2. Stationery and purchase order forms
   3. Purchasing agent's salary
   4. Purchase price of product
   5. Goodwill of customer lost due to unavailability of product
   6. Postage on purchase order
   7. Freight-in cost on product
   8. Insurance on products on hand
   9. Wages of receiving clerks
   10. Preparing and issuing checks to suppliers
   11. Contribution margin lost due to unavailability of product
   12. Storage costs for products on hand
   13. Quantity discounts on products ordered
   14. Opportunity cost of funds invested in inventory
   15. Property taxes on warehouses
   16. Handling costs for products on hand
   17. Excess ordering and shipping charges for rush orders of standard product lines
   18. Spoilage of products awaiting use

27. *(Carrying cost)* Katbites manufactures a variety of pet food products from dried seafood "pellets." The firm has determined that its EOQ is 20,000 pounds of pellets. Based on the EOQ, the firm's annual ordering costs for pellets is $12,700. Given this information, what is the firm's annual carrying cost of pellets? Explain.

28. *(Multiproduct EOQs)* A pharmacy carries three types of face cream: Wrinkle Free, Skin-so-Tight, and Smooth & Sweet. Determine the economic order quantity for each, given the following information:

PRODUCT	ORDER COST	CARRYING COST	DEMAND
Wrinkle Free	$4.30	$1.90	1,200
Skin-so-Tight	$6.25	$1.45	1,000
Smooth & Sweet	$3.70	$1.25	900

29. *(Product demand)* Compute the annual estimated demand if the economic order quantity for a product is 78 units; carrying cost is $.65 per unit; and ordering cost is $3.042 per order.

30. *(EPR)* Lars Gonzalez has taken a new job as production superintendent in a plant that makes briefcases. He is trying to determine how many cases to produce on each production run. Discussions reveal that last year the plant made 2,500 such cases, and this level of demand is expected for the coming year. The setup cost of each run is $200, and the cost of carrying a case in inventory for a year is estimated at $5.

   a. Calculate the economic production run (EPR) and the total cost associated with it.
   b. Recalculate the EPR and total cost if the annual cost of carrying a case in inventory is $10 and the setup cost is $20.

31. *(EPR)* Johns Company manufactures parts to be sold to other companies. Part #48 has the following data related to its production:

Annual quantity produced in units	3,200
Cost of setting up a production run	$200
Cost of carrying one unit in stock for a year	$ 2

Calculate the economic production run for Part #48.

32. *(EPR)* Gazelle Equipment Company requires 10,000 castings a year for use in assembling lawn and garden tractors. The foundry can produce 30,000 castings a year. The cost associated with setting up the production line is $25, and the carrying cost per unit is $2 annually. Lead time is 60 days.
   a. Find the production quantity that minimizes cost.
   b. Calculate the total cost of setting up for and carrying costing, based on the answer to part a for a year.

33. *(EOQ, number of orders)* Marianne May is a wholesale distributor of videotapes. She sells approximately 9,000 tapes every year. She estimates that it costs $.25 per tape to carry inventory for 12 months and it costs $15 each time she orders tapes from the factory.
   a. How many tapes should she order to minimize costs?
   b. Based on the order size computed in part a, how many orders will she need to place each year?
   c. Based on your answer to part b, at what time interval will Marianne be placing orders for videotapes?

34. *(EOQ, sensitivity analysis)* Bill Bennett owns and operates a gift shop near Niagra Falls. His estimated annual demand for Niagra Falls coffee mugs is 12,000 units. His ordering costs are $15 per order, and his carrying costs are $.25 per mug.
   a. What is the economic order quantity for mugs?
   b. If the ordering cost rises by $2.50 per order, what will be the new EOQ for mugs?
   c. If the carrying cost rises to $.35 per unit per year, what will be the new EOQ? (Use the original data except for carrying costs.)
   d. Discuss the reasons that rising order cost and rising carrying cost cause a different reaction in the size of the economic order quantity.

35. *(JIT variances)* Smith Company uses a JIT system. The following standards are related to materials A and B, which are used to make one unit of the company's final product:

ANNUAL MATERIAL STANDARDS:		CURRENT MATERIAL STANDARDS:	
6 pounds of material A @ $2.25	$13.50	7 pounds of material A @ $2.25	$15.75
8 pounds of material B @ $3.40	27.20	7 pounds of material B @ $3.40	23.80
	$40.70		$39.55

The current material standards differ from the original because of an engineering change made near the end of March. During April, the company produced 3,000 units of its final product and used 22,000 pounds of material A and 20,500 pounds of material B. All material is acquired at the standard cost per pound.
   a. Calculate the material variance and the ENC materials variance.
   b. Explain the effect of the engineering change on product cost.

36. *(JIT variances)* Tom Sawyer uses a JIT system in his manufacturing firm, which makes "Purrr," for cats. Tom provides you with the following standards for a can of "Purrr":

ANNUAL MATERIAL STANDARDS:	
5 ounces of component X @ $.10	$.50
1 ounce of component Y @ $.25	.25
	$.75

CURRENT MATERIAL STANDARDS:

4 ounces of component X @ $.10	$.40
2 ounces of component Y @ $.25	.50
	$.90

The standards were changed because of a nutritional (engineering) adjustment. Production during June was 60,000 cans of "Purrr." Usage of raw materials (all purchased at standard costs) was 250,000 ounces of component X and 108,000 ounces of component Y.

a. Calculate the material quantity variance for each component.

b. Calculate the engineering change variance for each component.

c. Why would a company implement an engineering change that increases the standard production cost by 20 percent?

37. *(Backflush costing)* Crosby Manufacturing uses backflush costing to account for an electronic meter it makes. During October 1998, the firm produced 16,000 meters, of which it sold 15,800. The standard cost for each meter is

Direct material	$20
Conversion costs	44
Total cost	$64

Assume that the firm had no inventory on October 1. The following events took place in October:

1. Purchased $320,000 of direct material.
2. Incurred $708,000 of conversion costs.
3. Applied $704,000 of conversion costs to Raw and In Process Inventory.
4. Finished 16,000 meters.
5. Sold 15,800 meters for $100 each.

a. Prepare journal entries using backflush costing with a minimum number of entries.

b. Post the amounts in part a to T-accounts.

c. Explain any inventory account balances.

38. *(Appendix)* Bobbie Brown manages a printing company in Seattle, Washington. She has been wondering how many reams of letter-size paper to order at a time and when to reorder paper. She says that she wants a safety stock of 500 reams and that she uses 93,750 reams annually. Further analysis reveals that the cost of placing an order is about $12, the cost of carrying one ream of paper in stock is estimated at $1 annually, and order lead time is 5 days. The printing company operates 300 days each year.

a. Calculate the economic order quantity.

b. Calculate the order point.

39. *(Appendix)* Billy Blades is a hockey player living in Los Angeles. Billy, a Canadian, deeply misses Calgary Spring Water and must have it imported. Billy drinks 5 bottles of Calgary Spring Water a day. It takes 4 days for him to receive the water after he orders it because Tim Green must drive to Canada to get it.

a. If Tim Green picks up 15 cases of Calgary Spring Water (24 bottles per case) for Billy each time he goes to Canada, at what point should Billy send Tim Green to Canada to buy more Calgary Spring Water to ensure against a stockout?

b. Using your answer to part a, if Billy might drink a maximum of 7 bottles of water per day, what should his safety stock level be? What would be his order point assuming that level of safety stock?

COMMUNICATION ACTIVITIES

40. *(Impact of technology or ordering)* A plant manager and her controller were discussing the plant's inventory control policies one day. The controller suggested to the plant manager that the ordering policies needed to be reviewed because of new technology that had been put in place in the plant's purchasing department. Among the changes that had been implemented in the plant were (1) installation of computerized inventory tracking, (2) installation of electronic data interchange capabilities with the plant's major suppliers, and (3) installation of in-house facilities for electronic fund transfers.

   a. As technology changes, why should managers update ordering policies for inventory?

   b. Write a memo to the plant manager describing the likely impact of the changes made in this plant on the EOQ of material input?

41. *(Excessive inventory)* The director of supply management at Turner Machine Works has contracted for $1 million of spare parts that are currently unneeded. His rationale for the contract was that the parts were available for purchase at a significantly reduced price. The company just hired a new president who, on learning about the contracts, stated that the parts contracts should be canceled because the parts would not be needed for at least a year. The supply director informed the president that the penalties for canceling the contracts would cost more than letting the orders go through. How would you respond to this situation from the standpoint of the president? From the standpoint of the supply director?

42. *(EOQ larger than needed)* Assume that your company uses 1,000 units of Part Q per day. The economic order quantity for Part Q is 1,050 units and the part can be ordered daily. Discuss the "ripple effect" throughout all areas (purchasing, production, warehouse management, and accounting) of the company from ordering the extra 50 units.

43. *(Potential causes of procurement problems)* Logan Logging Company began implementing a just-in-time inventory system several months ago. The production and purchasing managers, however, have not seen any dramatic improvements in throughput. They have decided that the problems are related to their suppliers. The suppliers (there are 3) seem to send the wrong materials at the wrong times. Prepare an oral discussion of the problems that might exist in this situation. Be certain to address in your discussion the following items: internal and external communications; possible engineering changes and their impacts; number, quality, and location of suppliers; and length of system implementation.

44. *(JIT for a restaurant)* Choose a fast-food restaurant and prepare a report showing how JIT can be used to improve operations.

45. *(Cases in which JIT will not work)* Everyone in your company seems excited about the suggestion that the firm implement a JIT system. Being a cautious person, your company president has asked you to write a report describing situations in which JIT will not work. Prepare such a report.

PROBLEMS

46. *(Identification of carrying, ordering costs)* Wilson Industries has been evaluating its policies with respect to control of costs of metal tubing, one of the firm's major component materials. The firm's controller has gathered the following financial data, which may be pertinent to controlling costs associated with the metal tubing:

ORDERING COSTS

Annual salary of purchasing department manager	$41,500
Depreciation of equipment in purchasing department	$22,300
Cost per order for purchasing department supplies	$.30
Typical phone expense per order placed	$3.20
Monthly expense for heat and light in purchasing department	$400

CARRYING COSTS

Annual depreciation on materials storage building	$15,000
Annual inventory insurance premium (per dollar of inventory value)	$.05
Annual property tax on materials storage building	$2,500
Obsolescence cost per dollar of average annual inventory	$.07
Annual salary of security officer assigned to the materials storage building	$18,000

a. Which of the ordering costs would Wilson's controller take into account in using the EOQ model? Explain.

b. Which of the carrying costs would Wilson's controller take into account in using the EOQ model? Explain.

47. *(Missing data, EOQ)* The following represent five independent situations from which one amount is missing. Compute the missing figures for each of the cases.

	ANNUAL QUANTITY	CARRYING COST	ORDERING COST	EOQ
a.	450	$1.00	$?	45
b.	?	7.00	5.00	70
c.	?	1.50	1.25	225
d.	1,400	.75	4.20	?
e.	135	?	3.00	30

48. *(Estimate errors)* A company has computed its economic order quantity based on the following estimates: annual demand, 75,000 units; ordering cost, $4.25 per order; and carrying cost, $.75 per unit. However, management has now learned that these estimates were wrong. Ordering cost is $3.60 per order and carrying cost is $.90 per unit.

a. Compute the EOQ based on the original costs and the revised costs.

b. Compute the annual ordering and carrying costs based on the original EOQ and the original costs.

c. Compute the annual ordering and carrying costs based on the revised EOQ and revised costs.

d. Assuming the revised costs are the correct ones, compare the costs of ordering and carrying the first EOQ to the costs of ordering and carrying the revised EOQ.

49. *(EPR)* The Town and Country Nursery grows and sells a tremendous variety of household and outdoor plants. The firm also grows and sells garden vegetables. One of the more popular vegetables grown by the firm is a red onion. The company sells approximately 30,000 pounds of red onions per year. Two of the major inputs in the growing of onions are seeds and fertilizer. Due to the poor germination rate, 2 seeds must be purchased for each onion plant grown (a mature onion plant provides .5 pound of onion). Also, .25 pounds of fertilizer are required for each pound of onion produced. The following information summarizes costs pertaining to onions, seeds, and fertilizer. Carrying costs for onions are expressed per pound of onion; carrying costs for seeds are expressed per seed; and for fertilizer, carrying costs are expressed per pound of fertilizer. To plant onions, the company incurs a cost of $50 to set up the planter and the fertilizing equipment.

	ONIONS	SEEDS	FERTILIZER
Carrying cost	$ .25	$ .01	$ .05
Ordering cost	—	$4.25	$8.80
Setup cost	$50.00	—	—

a. What is the economic production run for onions?

b. How many production runs will Town and Country make for onions annually?

c. What are the economic order quantities for seeds and fertilizer?

    d. How many orders will be placed for seeds? For fertilizer?

    e. What is the total annual cost of ordering, carrying, and setting up for onion production?

    f. How is the planting of onions similar to and different from a typical factory production run?

    g. Are there any inconsistencies in your answers to parts a through c that need to be addressed? Explain.

50. *(EOQ, sensitivity analysis)* Janet Monet wanted to know what the economic order quantity for an important component would be. Upon your inquiry, she estimated annual usage to be 6,000 units, cost of each order to be $15, and cost of carrying each unit to be $.20 annually.

    a. Calculate the economic order quantity. What is the total cost associated with this EOQ?

    b. Suppose that Janet is worried and, upon inquiry, she says each element she estimated may be only 90 percent of the actual amount. Recalculate EOQ and total cost using the revised estimates.

51. *(Just-in-time features)* Given the features below concerning just-in-time systems, indicate by letter which of the three categories apply to the following items. If more than one category applies, indicate with an additional letter.

D = desired intermediate result of using JIT
U = ultimate goal of JIT
T = technique associated with JIT

    a. Reducing setup time

    b. Reducing total cost of producing and carrying inventory

    c. Using focused factory arrangements

    d. Designing products to minimize design changes after production starts

    e. Monitoring quality on a continuous basis

    f. Using manufacturing cells

    g. Minimizing inventory stored

    h. Measuring variances caused by engineering changes

    i. Using autonomation processes

    j. Pulling purchases and production through the system based on sales demand

52. *(JIT journal entries)* Keller Production Company has implemented a just-in-time inventory system for the production of its insulated wire. Inventories of raw material and work in process are so small that Keller uses a Raw and In Process account. In addition, almost all labor operations are automated and Keller has chosen to cost products using standards for direct material and conversion. The following production standards are applicable at the beginning of 1997 for one roll of insulated wire:

Direct material (100 yards @ $2.00)	$200
Conversion (4 machine hours @ $35)	140
Total cost	$340

The conversion cost of $35 per machine hour was estimated on the basis of 500,000 machine hours for the year and $17,500,000 of conversion costs. The following activities took place during 1997:

1. Raw material purchased and placed into production totaled 12,452,000 yards. All except 8,000 yards were purchased at the standard price of $2 per yard. The other 8,000 yards were purchased at a cost of $2.06 per yard due to the placement of a rush order. The order was approved in advance by management. All purchases are on account.

2. From January 1 to February 28, Keller manufactured 20,800 rolls of insulated wire. Conversion costs incurred to date totaled $3,000,000. Of this amount, $600,000 was for depreciation, $2,200,000 was paid in cash, and $200,000 was on account.

3. Conversion costs are applied to the Raw and In Process account from January 1 to February 28 on the basis of the annual standard.

4. The Engineering Department issued a change in the operations flow document effective March 1, 1997. The change decreased the machine time to manufacture one roll of wire by 5 minutes per roll. However, the standard raises the quantity of direct material to 100.4 yards per roll. The Accounting Department requires that the annual standard be continued for costing the Raw and In Process Inventory for the remainder of 1997. The effects of the engineering changes should be shown in two accounts: Material Quantity Engineering Change Variance and Machine Hours Engineering Change Variance.

5. Total production for the remainder of 1997 was 103,200 rolls of wire. Total conversion costs for the remaining 10 months of 1997 were $14,442,000. Of this amount, $4,000,000 was depreciation, $9,325,000 was paid in cash, and $1,117,000 was on account.

6. The standard amount of conversion cost is applied to the Raw and In Process Inventory for the remainder of the year.

(Note: Some of the journal entries for the following items are not explicitly covered in the chapter. This problem challenges students in the accounting effects of the implementation of a JIT system.)

a. Prepare entries for items 1, 2, 3, 5, and 6 above.

b. Determine the increase in material cost due to the engineering change related to direct material.

c. Prepare a journal entry to adjust the Raw and In Process Inventory account for the engineering change cost found in part b.

d. Determine the reduction in conversion cost due to the engineering change related to machine time.

e. Prepare a journal entry to reclassify the actual conversion costs by the savings found in part d above.

f. Making the entry in part e raises conversion costs to what they would have been if the engineering change related to machine time had not been made. Are conversion costs under- or overapplied and by what amount?

g. Assume the reduction in machine time could not have been made without the corresponding increase in material usage. Is the net effect of these engineering changes cost beneficial? Why?

53. *(Appendix)* Elke Ginter operates a health-food bakery that uses specially ground flour in its products. The bakery operates 360 days a year. Elke finds that she seems to order either too much or too little flour and asks for your help. After some discussion, you find she does not have any idea of when or how much to order. An examination of her records and Elke's answers to further questions reveal the following information:

Annual usage of flour	14,000 pounds
Average number of days delay between initiating and receiving an order	12
Estimated cost per order	$8.00
Estimated annual cost of carrying a pound of flour in inventory	$.25
Estimated cost of a stockout	$150.00

POUNDS OF FLOUR IN SAFETY STOCK	PERCENT PROBABILITY OF STOCKOUT
33	70
66	55
99	40
132	20
165	10
198	1
231	.1
264	.05

a. Calculate the economic order quantity for flour.
b. Calculate the optimal safety stock (in pounds) for flour.
c. Calculate the appropriate order point.

54. *(Appendix)* L'Orange Computer Systems acquires its keyboards to make microcomputers from an external supplier. Management is wondering what its safety stock should be and obtains the following information:

Cost of a stockout = $250 per occurrence
Cost of carrying safety stock = $16 per unit annually
Number of orders per year = 24

The following probabilities are associated with various safety stock sizes:

UNITS OF SAFETY STOCK	PROBABILITY OF STOCKOUT
50	60
100	35
150	20
200	10
250	2

a. Calculate the cost of carrying the various safety stock sizes.
b. Calculate the cost of not carrying the various safety stock sizes.
c. Calculate the combined costs from parts a and b and identify the size of safety stock that results in the lowest combined cost.

CASES

55. *(Using EOQ for cash/securities management)* Chemcon Corporation sells various industrial supplies used for general-purpose cleaning. Approximately 85 percent of its sales are to not-for-profit and governmental institutions. These sales are on a contract basis with an average contract length of 2 years. Al Stanly, Chemcon's treasurer, wants to initiate a system that will maximize the amount of time Chemcon holds its cash in the form of marketable securities. Chemcon currently has $9 million of securities that have an expected annual earnings rate of 8 percent. Chemcon is expecting a cash drain over the next 12-month period. Monthly cash outflows are expected to be $2,650,000, but inflows are only expected to be $2,500,000. The cost of either buying or selling securities is $125 per transaction. Stanly has heard that the EOQ inventory model can be applied to cash management. Therefore, he has decided to employ this model to determine the optimal value of marketable securities to be sold to replenish Chemcon's cash balance.

a. Use the EOQ model in the chapter to
   (1) explain the costs Al Stanly is attempting to balance in this situation, and
   (2) calculate the optimal dollar amount of marketable securities Stanly should sell when Chemcon needs to replenish its cash balance.
b. Without prejudice to your solution in part a(2), assume that the optimal dollar amount of marketable securities to be sold is $60,000.

(1) Calculate the average cash balance in Chemcon's checking account that will be on hand during the course of the year.

(2) Determine the number of times during the year that Stanly will have to sell securities.

c. Describe two different economic circumstances applicable to Chemcon that would render its use of the EOQ inventory model inappropriate as a cash management model.

(CMA adapted)

56. *(Managing procurement for products with short life cycles)* The Smith Company manufactures various electronic assemblies that it sells primarily to computer manufacturers. Smith's reputation has been built on quality, timely delivery, and products that are consistently on the cutting edge of technology. Smith's business is fast-paced. The typical product has a short life; the product is in development for about a year and in the growth stage, with sometimes spectacular growth, for about a year. Each product then experiences a rapid decline in sales as new products become available.

Smith's competitive strategy requires a reliable stream of new products to be developed each year. This is the only way that the company can overcome the threat of product obsolescence. Although the products go through the first half of the product life cycle like products in other industries, they don't go through the second half of the product life cycle in a similar manner. Smith's products never reach the mature product or declining product stage. Toward the end of the growth stage, products just die as new ones are introduced.

a. In the competitive market facing Smith Company, what would be key considerations in production and inventory control?

b. How would the threat of immediate product obsolescence affect Smith's practices in purchasing product components and materials?

c. How would the threat of product obsolescence affect the EPR for a typical product produced by Smith Company?

(CMA adapted)

57. For nearly a decade since its forced divestiture, AT&T has been fighting to maintain market share and profitability in the telecommunications industry. In some cases, the quality of services offered by AT&T appears to be falling. Consider, for example, these facts.

- The company's market share of the corporate long distance market is estimated to have fallen from 80% in 1989 to 55% in 1993.
- AT&T's long distance network, after operating reliably for many decades, has failed four times in the past few years. One outage closed down air traffic control on the east coast and interrupted transaction processing on Wall Street. Three of the four failures were blamed on worker and management carelessness.

Some attribute AT&T's failures to its efforts to down-size and become more efficient and more profitable. Critics claim the down-sizing is affecting not only the firm's costs but the quality of its services. As a result of the cost cutting, the company has been slow in responding to customer service needs and has resorted to the use of independent contractors in some customer servicing roles.

ETHICS AND QUALITY DISCUSSION

[SOURCE: Adapted from John J. Keller, "Some AT&T Clients Gripe That Cost Cuts Are Hurting Service," *Wall Street Journal* (January 24, 1992), pp. A1, A4. Reprinted by permission of *The Wall Street Journal*, © 1992 Dow Jones & Company, Inc. All Rights Reserved Worldwide.]

a. How would production control (or service control) at AT&T differ from production control in a typical factory?

b. In trying to improve the efficiency of its operations, is it possible that AT&T has lowered the quality of its operations? Explain.

c. Could the downsizing and cost cutting at AT&T create an endless downward spiral? Explain.

d. How could AT&T adopt a JIT service approach to improve its response time and the quality of its efforts in servicing its customers?

58. You are the owner of Peterson Company, which provides a significant product component to the Gund Firm. The manager at Gund has asked you for a discount on the components you are providing. Since becoming a major supplier for Gund, your firm has spent $26,000,000 in plant layout changes, quality improvements, and equipment purchases to provide the type of product and the delivery schedule requested by Gund. The only way in which you could provide the price break is to lower your quality control standards. The lowered quality control standards would save the company approximately $5,000,000 annually for the next 3 years.

a. Discuss your response to Gund Firm.

b. Is it ethical to make a product at lower than the best possible quality that you have already achieved? Why or why not?

INTERNET ACTIVITIES

59. Find the home pages of Boeing Company and Coca Cola. Read materials presented for each company discussing the companies' operations. Prepare a written report in which you compare and contrast the production operations of the companies. In your report, identify and discuss the management techniques that would be appropriate for managing inventory and production in each company.

60. Bar coding technology has revolutionized inventory and production management. Search the web for advertisements of bar coding technology vendors. Then, after selecting a small business in your area, prepare a written report in which you discuss how specific bar coding technologies could be adopted by that firm to improve its operations. Make certain that you address the nature of the improvements that would be expected from the adoption of each bar coding application.

61. There exists a large volume of software to aid manufacturing companies in managing inventory and production. Search the web for promotional materials from vendors of such software (such as Syspro Value-Added Manufacturing). Read a sample of the descriptions of the production and inventory management software. Prepare an oral report to be presented to the board of directors of a small yard-care equipment manufacturer (manufactures mowers, trimmers, rakes, etc.) as to how installation of one or more of the inventory management software modules could be used to provide better information for management of production activities and inventories.

DECISION
MAKING

CHAPTER

18

Capital Budgeting

LEARNING OBJECTIVES

After completing this chapter, you should be able to answer these questions:

1. Why do most capital budgeting methods focus on cash flows?

2. What is measured by the payback period?

3. How are the net present value and profitability index of a project measured?

4. How is the internal rate of return on a project computed? What does it measure?

5. What are the underlying assumptions and limitations of each capital project evaluation method?

6. How and why should management conduct a post-investment audit of a capital project?

7. How do taxation and depreciation methods affect cash flows?

8. How do managers rank investment projects?

9. How is risk considered in capital budgeting analysis?

10. *(Appendix 1)* How are present values calculated?

11. *(Appendix 2)* What are the advantages and disadvantages of the accounting rate of return?

12. *(Appendix 3)* How can the risk of a capital project be measured on a statistical basis?

INTRODUCING

Genentech, Inc.

One of the oldest companies in one of the newest industries is Genentech, Inc. Founded in 1976, Genentech was one of the first companies formed for the purpose of pursuing market applications of emerging biotechnology. When the company was formed, it had no products and it had no established markets to serve. Currently, the company produces five products that generated sales of more than $600 million in 1995. All of the products serve the medical industry, and they consist of two products that treat deficiencies in growth hormones of children, a product that dissolves blood clots, a product that treats an inherited deficiency in the immune system, and one that is used to combat cystic fibrosis.

The challenges of maintaining solvency and a competitive position in this industry are enormous. Survival of Genentech depends on a critical balance between achieving current profits and investing for future growth. In 1995, Genentech reported a net income of $146 million (16% of revenue). Also in 1995, Genentech invested $363 million (40% of revenue) in research and development activities to create new products and technologies. The company has approximately 15 products with potential commercial applications under development.

SOURCES: Internet home page of Genentech, Inc. (http://www.gene.com/ae/backgrounder.html); 1995 Annual Report of Genentech, Inc.

Choosing the assets in which an organization will invest is one of the most important business decisions of managers. In almost every organization, investments must be made in some short-term working-capital assets, such as merchandise inventory, supplies, and raw materials. Organizations must also invest in **capital assets** that are used to generate future revenues; cost savings; or distribution, service, or production capabilities. A capital asset may be a tangible fixed asset (such as a piece of machinery or a building) or an intangible asset (such as a capital lease or a patent). The research and development activities of Genentech resulted in the issuance of 397 new patents in 1994 alone.[1]

capital asset

Financial managers, assisted by cost accountants, are responsible for capital budgeting. Capital budgeting is "a process for evaluating proposed long-range projects or courses of future activity for the purpose of allocating limited resources."[2] The process includes planning for and preparing the capital budget as well as reviewing past investments to assess and enhance the effectiveness of the process. The capital budget presents planned annual expenditures for capital projects for the near term (tomorrow to 5 years from now) and summary information for the long term (6 to 10 years). The capital budget is a key instrument in implementing organizational strategies.

Capital budgeting involves comparing and evaluating alternative **projects** within a budgetary framework. A variety of criteria are applied by managers and accountants to evaluate the feasibility of alternative projects. Although financial criteria are used to assess virtually all projects, today more firms are also using nonfinancial criteria. The nonfinancial criteria are critical to the assessment of activities that have financial benefits that are difficult to quantify. For example, high-technology investments and investments in research and development (R & D) are often difficult to evaluate using only financial criteria. One firm in the biotechnology industry uses nine criteria to evaluate the feasibility of R & D projects. These criteria are presented in Exhibit 18–1.

project

[1] 1994 annual report of Genentech, Inc.
[2] Institute of Management Accountants (formerly National Association of Accountants), *Statements on Management Accounting Number 2: Management Accounting Terminology* (Montvale, N.J.: June 1, 1983), p. 14.

EXHIBIT 18–1

Project Evaluation
Criteria—R & D Projects

1. Potential for proprietary position.
2. Balance between short-term and long-term projects and payoffs.
3. Potential for collaborations and outside funding.
4. Financial rate of return on investment.
5. Need to establish competency in an area.
6. Potential for spin-off projects.
7. Strategic fit with the corporation's planned and existing technology, manufacturing capabilities, marketing and distribution systems.
8. Impact on long-term corporate positioning.
9. Probability of technical success.

SOURCE: Suresh Kalahnanam and Suzanne K. Schmidt, "Analyzing Capital Investments in New Products," *Management Accounting* (January 1996), pp. 31–36. Reprinted from *Management Accounting.* Copyright by Institute of Management Accountants, Montvale, NJ.

VIDEO
VIGNETTE

Mall of America and/or Delta Air
Lines and/or First Bank

By evaluating potential capital projects using a portfolio of criteria, managers can be confident that all possible costs and contributions of projects have been considered. Additionally, the multiple criteria allow for a balanced evaluation of short- and long-term benefits, the fit with existing technology, and the roles of projects in both marketing and cost management. For this biotechnology company, the use of multiple criteria ensures that projects will be considered from the perspectives of strategy, marketing, cost management, quality, and technical feasibility. Although use of multiple criteria makes the evaluation of projects inherently subjective as trade-offs are contemplated among the criteria, the approach ensures a balanced consideration of potential projects. As indicated in the following News Note, the biotech company experienced difficulty in the past in identifying a structured approach to evaluating capital projects.

Note that one of the criteria in Exhibit 18–1 is financial rate of return on investment. Providing information about the financial returns of potential capital projects is one of the important tasks of cost accountants. This chapter discusses a variety of techniques that are used in businesses to evaluate the potential financial costs and contributions of proposed capital projects. Several of these techniques are based on an analysis of the amounts and timing of project cash flows.

**NEWS
NOTE**

Project Evaluation Structure

To successfully screen and select capital projects, firms must have a formal approach to identify and evaluate alternative projects. Additionally, managers must be careful to include individuals with expertise in all areas affected by new investments. For Cyto Technologies,* this has been an historical challenge.

In the past, the project selection process at Cyto lacked a structured approach. Projects were selected with just sketchy ideas about financial numbers and rough ideas of payback periods. Increasing competition and the higher cost of capital have forced Cyto to change its approach. A project approval team (PAT) was set up three years ago to provide structure for the project development and evaluation process. The PAT consists of five constant members (the heads of manufacturing, quality assurance, finance and accounting, research and development, and marketing) and two rotating members (one each from marketing and R&D). This team oversees the allocation of resources to new projects in alignment with the company's objectives.

_____

* This is a fictional name used to protect the identity of the company.

SOURCE: Suresh Kalahnanam and Suzanne K. Schmidt, "Analyzing Capital Investments in New Products," *Management Accounting* (January 1996) pp. 31–36. Reprinted from *Management Accounting.* Copyright by Institute of Management Accountants, Montvale, NJ.

Capital budgeting investment decisions can be made using a variety of techniques including payback period, net present value, profitability index, internal rate of return, and accounting rate of return. All but the last of these methods focus on the amounts and timing of **cash flows** (receipts or disbursements of cash). Cash receipts include the revenues from a capital project that have been earned and collected, savings generated by the project's reductions in existing operating costs, and any cash inflow from selling the asset at the end of its useful life. Cash disbursements include asset acquisition expenditures, additional working-capital investments, and costs for project-related direct materials, direct labor, and overhead.

Any investment made by an organization is expected to earn some type of return, such as interest, cash dividends, or operating income. Because interest and dividends are received in cash, accrual-based operating income must be converted to a cash basis for comparison purposes. Remember that accrual accounting recognizes revenues when earned, not when cash is received, and recognizes expenses when incurred regardless of whether a liability is created or cash is paid. Converting accounting income to cash flow information puts all investment returns on an equivalent basis.

Interest cost is a cash outflow associated with debt financing and is not part of the project selection process. The funding of projects is a financing, not an investment, decision. A **financing decision** is a judgment regarding the method of raising capital to fund an investment. Financing is based on the entity's ability to issue and service debt and equity securities. On the other hand, an **investment decision** is a judgment about which assets to acquire to achieve an entity's stated objectives. Cash flows generated by the two types of decisions should not be combined. Company management must justify the acquisition and use of an asset *prior* to justifying the method of financing that asset.

Including receipts and disbursements caused by financing with other project cash flows conceals a project's true profitability because financing costs relate to the total entity. The assignment of financing costs to a specific project is often arbitrary, which causes problems in comparing projects that are to be acquired with different financing sources. In addition, including financing effects in an investment decision creates a problem in assigning responsibility. Investment decisions are typically made by divisional managers, or by top management after receiving input from divisional managers. Financing decisions are typically made by an organization's treasurer in conjunction with top management.

Cash flows from a capital project are received and paid at different points in time over the project's life. Some cash flows occur at the beginning of a period, some during the period, and some at the end. To simplify capital budgeting analysis, most analysts assume that all cash flows occur at a specific, single point in time—either at the beginning or end of the time period in which they actually occur. The following example illustrates how cash flows are treated in capital budgeting situations.

USE OF CASH FLOWS IN CAPITAL BUDGETING

cash flow

financing decision

investment decision

CASH FLOWS ILLUSTRATED

Assume that a variety of capital projects are being considered by EastBay Biotechnology Company, a small biotech company located in Oklahoma City. One investment being considered by EastBay is a research project that would lead to a patent for a new biotechnology product, a hormone that would enhance growth of new skin in burn patients. The idea for this biotechnology application was generated by basic research activities conducted by the firm in past years.

As is common with most firms that depend on research and development for their survival, product research is often conducted in stages or phases. The phases range from early, basic research to more focused and refined applied research. If a product demonstrates potential based on technical feasibility and market prospects in early stages, it undergoes additional testing in later stages. For example, Genentech recognizes five phases of formal product development. These are displayed in Exhibit 18–2 along with the products the company has in each phase.

EXHIBIT 18–2	

Product Pipeline of Genentech, Inc.

PRECLINICAL DEVELOPMENT

Anti-VEGE Antibody
Lymphotoxin

PHASE 1

Thrombopoietin
Oral IIb/IIIa Antagonist
Second Generation t-PA

PHASE 2

Nerve Growth Factor
Insulin-like Growth Factor (IGF-I)
Anti-IgE Humanized Monoclonal Antibody
gp 120

PHASE 3

Anti-HER2 Humanized Monoclonal Antibody
Actimmune
IDEC C2B8

AWAITING REGULATORY APPROVAL

Nutropin
Activase

EastBay's expected research and development costs and expected revenues of the skin growth product appear in Exhibit 18–3. EastBay has no intention of marketing the product directly; instead its management intends to license the product to an established pharmaceutical company.

EXHIBIT 18–3	

Research and Development Investment—Skin Growth Hormone (dollars in thousands)

CASH OUTFLOWS:

Research and development costs:	$7,000 (to be incurred immediately)
	4,200 (to be incurred in 1 year)
Clinical tests:	1,200 (payable in 1 year)

Royalty collection fee (2% of gross royalties collected)

Year 2	$50
Year 3	68
Year 4	98
Year 5	82
Year 6	44
Year 7	38

CASH INFLOWS:

Gross royalty to be earned by year:

Year 2	$2,500
Year 3	3,400
Year 4	4,900
Year 5	4,100
Year 6	2,200
Year 7	1,900

Note: After year 7, it is expected that competitive products will render the patent on the skin hormone product worthless.

This detailed information can be simplified to a net cash flow for each year. For EastBay, the project generates a net negative flow in the first year and net positive cash flows thereafter. This cash flow information for EastBay can be illustrated through the use of a timeline.

A **timeline** visually illustrates the points in time when cash flows are expected to be received or paid, making it a helpful tool for analyzing cash flows of a capital investment proposal. Cash inflows are shown as positive amounts on a timeline and cash outflows are shown as negative amounts.

The following timeline represents the cash flows from EastBay's potential investment in the skin growth hormone.

End of period	0	1	2	3	4	5	6	7
Inflows	$ 0	$ 0	+$2,500	+$3,400	+$4,900	+$4,100	+$2,200	+$1,900
Outflows	−$7,000	−$5,400	− 50	− 68	− 98	− 82	− 44	− 38
Net cash flow	−$7,000	−$5,400	+$2,450	+$3,332	+$4,802	+$4,018	+$2,156	+$1,862

On a timeline, the date of initial investment represents time point 0 because this investment is made immediately. Each year after the initial investment is represented as a full time period, and periods only serve to separate the timing of cash flows. Nothing is presumed to happen *during* a period. Thus, for example, cash inflows each year from royalties earned are shown as occurring at the end of, rather than during, the time period. A less conservative assumption would show the cash flows occurring at the beginning of the period.

The information on timing of net cash flows is an input to a simple and often-used capital budgeting technique called **payback period**. This method measures the time required for a project's cash inflows to equal the original investment. At the end of the payback period, a company has recouped its investment.

In one sense, payback period measures a dimension of project risk by focusing on the timing of cash flows. The assumption is that the longer it takes to recover the initial investment, the greater is the project's risk because cash flows in the more distant future are more uncertain than relatively current cash flows. Another reason for concern about long payback periods relates to capital reinvestment. The faster capital is returned from an investment, the more rapidly it can be invested in other projects.

Payback period for a project having unequal cash inflows is determined by accumulating cash flows until the original investment is recovered. Thus, using the information shown in Exhibit 18–3 and the timeline presented earlier, the skin growth hormone's payback period must be calculated using a yearly cumulative total of inflows as follows:

YEAR	AMOUNT	CUMULATIVE TOTAL
1	− $5,400	− $5,400
2	+ 2,450	− 2,950
3	+ 3,332	+ 382
4	+ 4,802	+ 5,184
5	+ 4,018	+ 9,202
6	+ 2,156	
7	+ 1,862	

Because $5,184 will be received by the end of the fourth year, $1,816 more ($7,000 − $5,184) is needed to recover the original $7,000 investment. The $4,018 inflow in the fifth year is assumed to occur evenly throughout the year. Therefore, it should take approximately .45 ($1,816 ÷ $4,018) of the fifth year to cover the rest of the original investment, giving a payback period for this project of 4.45 years (or slightly more than 4 years and 5 months).

annuity

When the cash flows from a project are equal each period (an **annuity**), the payback period is determined as follows:

$$\text{Payback Period} = \frac{\text{Investment}}{\text{Annuity}}$$

Assume for a moment that the skin growth hormone being considered by EastBay requires an initial investment of $10,000 and is expected to generate equal annual cash flows of $4,000 in each of the next 5 years. In this case, the payback period would be equal to the $10,000 net investment cost divided by $4,000 or 2.5 years (2 years and 6 months).

Company management typically sets a maximum acceptable payback period as one of the financial evaluation criteria for capital projects. If EastBay has set 5 years as the longest acceptable payback period, this project would be acceptable under that criterion. Most companies, though, use payback period as only one way of financially judging an investment project. After being found acceptable in terms of payback period, a project is subjected to evaluation by other financial capital budgeting techniques. A second evaluation is usually performed because the payback period method ignores three things: inflows occurring after the payback period has been reached, the company's desired rate of return, and the time value of money. These issues are incorporated into the decision process by using discounted future cash flows.

DISCOUNTING FUTURE CASH FLOWS

discounting

present value

discount rate

cost of capital

Money has a time value associated with it; this value is created because interest is paid or received on money.[3] For example, the receipt of $1,000 today has greater value than the same sum received one year from today because money held today can be invested to generate a return that will cause it to accumulate to more than $1,000 in one year. This phenomenon encourages the use of discounted cash flow techniques in most capital budgeting situations.

Discounting future cash flows means reducing them to present value amounts by removing the portion of the future values representing interest. This "imputed" amount of interest is based on two considerations: the length of time until the cash flow is received or paid and the rate of interest assumed. After discounting, all future values associated with a project are stated in a common base of current dollars, also known as their **present values.** Cash receipts and disbursements occurring at the beginning of a project (time 0) are already stated in their present values and do not need to be discounted.

Information on capital projects involves the use of estimates; therefore, having the best possible estimates of all cash flows (such as initial project investment) is extremely important. Care should be taken also to include all potential future inflows and outflows. To appropriately discount cash flows, managers must estimate the rate of return on capital required by the company in addition to the project's cost and cash flow estimates. This rate of return is called the **discount rate** and is used to determine the imputed interest portion of future cash receipts and expenditures. The discount rate should equal or exceed the company's **cost of capital** (COC)[4], which is the weighted average cost of the various sources of funds (debt and stock) that comprise a firm's financial structure.[5] For example, if a company has a COC of 10 percent, it costs an average of 10 percent of each capital dollar annually to finance investment projects. To determine whether a capital project is a worthwhile investment, this company should generally use a *minimum* rate of 10 percent to discount its projects' future cash flows.

---

[3] The time value of money and present value computations are covered in Appendix 1 of this chapter. These concepts are essential to understanding the rest of this chapter; be certain they are clear before continuing.

[4] Cost of capital computations are discussed in Chapter 2.

[5] All examples in this chapter use an *assumed* discount rate or cost of capital. The computations required to find a company's cost of capital rate are discussed in any principles of finance text.

With so many different interest rates in the marketplace, how does a company choose the one to use in discounting future cash flows? That choice will be affected by the organization's cost of capital and managerial judgment as to project risk.

The rate of return for government securities (such as treasury bills) can be seen as riskless. Thus, if a company were analyzing an investment with almost no risk, did not have to borrow funds to make the investment, and had no alternative investment possibilities, the T-bill rate could be used as the minimum rate of return rather than the cost of capital. However, as project risk increases and there is a need to borrow funds to make the investment, the minimum acceptable rate of return should also rise.

Some managers believe that the discount rate used for these higher-risk capital budgeting decisions should reflect the **opportunity cost of capital.** This COC rate is the highest rate of return that *could* be earned from the most attractive, alternative capital project available. Using the opportunity COC to discount project cash flows reflects the benefits that could have been realized from the forgone opportunity. Although use of the opportunity cost of capital has theoretical merit, its application would require that management calculate a rate of return on *all* available alternative projects. Because such a calculation is generally not feasible, most companies use the overall cost of capital as the discount rate.

opportunity cost of capital

A distinction must be made between cash flows representing a return *of* capital and those representing a return *on* capital. A **return of capital** simply means recovery of the original investment or the return of principal, whereas a **return on capital** represents income and equals the discount rate multiplied by the investment amount. For example, $1 invested in a project that yields a 10 percent rate of return will grow to a sum of $1.10 in one year. Of the $1.10, $1 represents the return of capital and $.10 represents the return on capital. The return on capital is computed for each period of the investment life. For a company to be better off by making an investment, a project must produce cash inflows that exceed the investment made and the cost of capital. To determine whether a project meets a company's desired rate of return, one of several discounted cash flow methods can be used.

return of capital

return on capital

DISCOUNTED CASH FLOW METHODS

Three discounted cash flow techniques are the net present value method, the profitability index, and the internal rate of return. Each of these methods is defined and illustrated in the following subsections.

Net Present Value Method

net present value method

The **net present value method** determines whether the rate of return on a project is equal to, higher than, or lower than the desired rate of return. Each cash flow from the project is discounted to its present value using the rate specified by the company as the desired rate of return. The total present value of all cash outflows of an investment project subtracted from the total present value of all cash inflows yields the **net present value** (NPV) of the project. Exhibit 18–4 presents net present value calculations, assuming the use of a 9 percent discount rate. The data are taken from Exhibit 18–3.

net present value

The factors used to compute the net present value are obtained from the present value tables provided in Appendix A at the end of the text. Each lump-sum cash flow uses a factor from Table 1 (PV of $1) for 9 percent and the appropriate number of years designated for the cash flow. Table 2 in Appendix A is used to discount annuities rather than single cash flows and its use is demonstrated in later problems.

The net present value of the skin growth hormone is $999,000. The NPV represents the net cash benefit or net cash cost to a company acquiring and using the proposed asset. *If the NPV is zero, the actual rate of return on the project is equal to the desired rate of return. If the NPV is positive, the actual rate is greater than the desired rate. If the NPV is negative, the actual rate is less than the desired rate of return. Note that the exact rate of return is not indicated under the NPV method, but its relationship to the desired rate can be determined.* If all estimates about the investment are correct, the skin growth hormone being considered by EastBay will provide a rate of return greater than 9 percent.

Had EastBay chosen any rate other than 9 percent and used that rate in conjunction with the same facts, a different net present value would have resulted. For example, if EastBay set 14 percent as the discount rate, a negative $947,000 NPV would have resulted for the project (see Exhibit 18–5). Net present values at other selected discount rates are given in this exhibit also. The computations for these values are made in a manner similar to those at 9 percent and 14 percent. (To indicate your understanding of the NPV method, you may want to prove these computations.)

The table in Exhibit 18–5 indicates that the NPV is not a single, unique amount, but is a function of several factors. First, changing the discount rate while holding the amounts and timing of cash flows constant affects the NPV. Increasing the discount rate causes the NPV to decrease; decreasing the discount rate causes NPV to increase. Second, changes in estimated amounts and/or timing of cash inflows and outflows affect the net present value of a project. Effects of cash flow changes on the NPV depend on the changes themselves. For example, decreasing the estimate of

---

EXHIBIT 18–4

Net Present Value Calculation for Skin Growth Hormone

NET PRESENT VALUE (IN THOUSANDS)	
Initial research cost: −$7,000 × 1.0000	−$7,000
Year 1 cash outflows: (−$4,200 − $1,200) × .9174	− 4,954
Year 2 net cash flow: ($2,500 − $50) × .8417	+ 2,062
Year 3 net cash flow: ($3,400 − $68) × .7722	+ 2,573
Year 4 net cash flow: ($4,900 − $98) × .7084	+ 3,402
Year 5 net cash flow: ($4,100 − $82) × .6499	+ 2,611
Year 6 net cash flow: ($2,200 − $44) × .5963	+ 1,286
Year 7 net cash flow: ($1,900 − $38) × .5470	+ 1,019
Net Present Value	+$ 999

EXHIBIT 18–5

Net Present Value
Calculation for Skin
Growth Hormone

```
DISCOUNT RATE = 14%

NET PRESENT VALUE (IN THOUSANDS)

Initial research cost: − $7,000 × 1.0000            − $7,000
Year 1 cash outflows: (− $4,200 − $1,200) × .8772   −  4,737
Year 2 net cash flow: ($2,500 − $50) × .7695        +  1,885
Year 3 net cash flow: ($3,400 − $68) × .6750        +  2,249
Year 4 net cash flow: ($4,900 − $98) × .5921        +  2,843
Year 5 net cash flow: ($4,100 − $82) × .5194        +  2,087
Year 6 net cash flow: ($2,200 − $44) × .4556        +    982
Year 7 net cash flow: ($1,900 − $38) × .3996        +    744
      Net Present Value                             − $  947
```

For various other discount rates:

DISCOUNT RATE	NET PRESENT VALUE (IN THOUSANDS)
2%	+ $4,813
6%	+ 2,450
11%	+ 157
17%	− 1,888
20%	− 2,698

cash outflows causes NPV to increase; reducing the stream of cash inflows causes NPV to decrease. When amounts and timing of cash flows change in conjunction with one another, the effects of the changes are determinable only with calculation.

The net present value method, although not providing the actual rate of return on a project, provides information on how that rate compares with the desired rate. This information allows managers to eliminate from consideration any project producing a negative NPV because it would have an unacceptable rate of return. The NPV method can also be used to select the best project when choosing among investments that can perform the same task or achieve the same objective.

The net present value method should not, however, be used to compare independent projects requiring different levels of initial investment. Such a comparison favors projects having higher net present values over those with lower net present values *without regard to the capital invested* in the project. As a simple example of this fact, assume that EastBay could spend $200,000 on Machine A or $40,000 on Machine B. Machine A's and B's net present values are $4,000 and $2,000, respectively. If only NPVs were compared, the company would conclude that Machine A was a "better" investment because it has a larger NPV. However, Machine A provides an NPV of only 2 percent ($4,000 ÷ $200,000) on the investment, whereas Machine B provides a 5 percent ($2,000 ÷ $40,000) NPV on its investment. Logically, organizations should invest in projects that produce the highest return *per investment dollar*. Comparisons of projects with uneven investments can be made by using a variation of the NPV method known as the profitability index.

Profitability Index

The **profitability index** (PI) is a ratio comparing the present value of a project's net cash inflows to the project's net investment. The PI is calculated as

profitability index

$$PI = \frac{\text{Present Value of Net Cash Flows}}{\text{Net Investment}}$$

The present value of net cash flows equals the PV of future cash inflows minus the PV of future cash outflows. The PV of net cash inflows represents an output measure of the project's worth, whereas the net investment represents an input measure of the project's cost. By relating these two measures, the profitability index gauges the efficiency of the firm's use of capital. The higher the index, the more efficient is the capital investment.

The following information illustrates the calculation and use of a profitability index. EastBay is considering two investments: a lab machine costing $720,000 and a product patent costing $425,000. Corporate managers have computed the present values of the investments by discounting all future expected cash flows at a rate of 12 percent. Present values of the expected net cash inflows are $900,000 for the lab machine and $580,000 for the product patent. Dividing the PV of the net cash inflows by initial cost gives the profitability index for each investment. Subtracting asset cost from the present value of the net cash inflows provides the NPV. Results of these computations are shown below.

	PV OF INFLOWS	COST	PROFITABILITY INDEX	NPV
Lab machine	$900,000	$720,000	1.25	$180,000
Product patent	580,000	425,000	1.36	155,000

Although the lab machine's net present value is higher, the profitability index indicates that the product patent is a more efficient use of corporate capital.[6] The higher PI reflects a higher rate of return on the product patent than on the lab machine. The higher a project's PI, the more profitable is that project per investment dollar.

If a capital project investment is made to provide a return on capital, the profitability index should be equal to or greater than 1.00, the equivalent of an NPV equal to or greater than 0. Like the net present value method, the profitability index does not indicate the project's expected rate of return. However, another discounted cash flow method, the internal rate of return, provides the expected rate of return to be earned on an investment.

Internal Rate of Return

internal rate of return

A project's **internal rate of return** (IRR) is the discount rate that causes the present value of the net cash inflows to equal the present value of the net cash outflows. It is the project's expected rate of return. If the IRR is used to determine the NPV of a project, the NPV is zero.

Consider the following formula to determine net present value:

NPV = − Investment + PV of Cash Inflows − PV of Cash Outflows other than the investment

NPV = − Investment + Cash Inflows (PV Factor) − Cash Outflows (PV Factor)

Capital project information should include the amounts of the investment, cash inflows, and cash outflows. Thus, the only missing data in the above formula are the present value factors. These factors can be calculated and then found in the present value tables. The interest rate with which the factors are associated is the internal rate of return.

The internal rate of return is most easily computed for projects having equal annual net cash flows. When an annuity exists, the NPV formula can be restated as follows:

NPV = − Net Investment + PV of Annuity Amount

= − Net Investment + (Cash Flow Annuity Amount × PV Factor)

---

[6] Two conditions must exist for the profitability index to provide better information than the net present value method. First, the decision to accept one project must require that the other project be rejected. The second condition is that availability of funds for capital acquisitions is limited.

	CASH FLOW
Cost of equipment (time 0)	− $25,000
Installation cost (time 0)	− 10,471
Operating savings* (time 1–5)	+ 9,000

*From savings in insurance costs.

EXHIBIT 18–6

Information Pertaining to
Alarm Project

The investment and annual cash flow amounts are known from the expected data and net present value is known to be zero at the IRR. The IRR and its present value factor are unknown. To determine the internal rate of return, substitute known amounts into the formula, rearrange terms, and solve for the unknown (the PV factor):

$$\text{NPV} = -\text{Net Investment} + (\text{Annuity} \times \text{PV Factor})$$

$$0 = -\text{Net Investment} + (\text{Annuity} \times \text{PV Factor})$$

$$\text{Net Investment} = (\text{Annuity} \times \text{PV Factor})$$

$$\text{Net Investment} \div \text{Annuity} = \text{PV Factor}$$

The solution yields a present value factor for the number of annuity periods corresponding to the project's life at an interest rate equal to the internal rate of return. Finding this factor in the PV of an annuity table and reading the interest rate at the top of the column in which the factor is found provides the internal rate of return.

To illustrate an IRR computation for a project with a simple annuity, information in Exhibit 18–6 pertaining to EastBay's potential investment in an alarm system is used. The alarm system would be installed in EastBay's corporate headquarters and would generate cost savings in property insurance costs over the 5-year life of the system. The system has no expected salvage value.

The NPV equation is solved for the present value factor.

$$\text{NPV} = -\text{Net Investment} + (\text{Annuity} \times \text{PV Factor})$$

$$0 = -\$35,471 + (\$9,000 \times \text{PV Factor})$$

$$+\$35,471 = (\$9,000 \times \text{PV Factor})$$

$$+\$35,471 \div \$9,000 = \text{PV Factor}$$

$$3.9412 = \text{PV Factor}$$

Note that the present value factor needed to approximate the internal rate of return is equal to the payback period for a project returning only an annuity.

The PV of an ordinary annuity table (Table 2, Appendix A) is examined to find the internal rate of return. A present value factor is a function of time and the discount rate. In the table, find the row representing the project's life (in this case, five periods). Look across the table in that row for the PV factor found upon solving the equation. In row 5, a factor of 3.9927 appears under the column headed 8 percent and a 3.8897 factor appears under 9 percent. Thus, the internal rate of return for this machine is between these two rates. Using interpolation, a computer program, or a programmable calculator shows the IRR for this project to be 8.5 percent.[7]

[7] Interpolation is the process of finding a term between two other terms in a series. The interpolation process using the actual PV factor and the table factors gives the following computation:

$$\text{Actual rate} = 8\% + [(.0515 \div .103)(1.0)]$$

$$= 8\% + (.50)(1.0)$$

$$= 8.5\%$$

EXHIBIT 18-7

Graph of NPVs and Rates of Return for Alarm Project

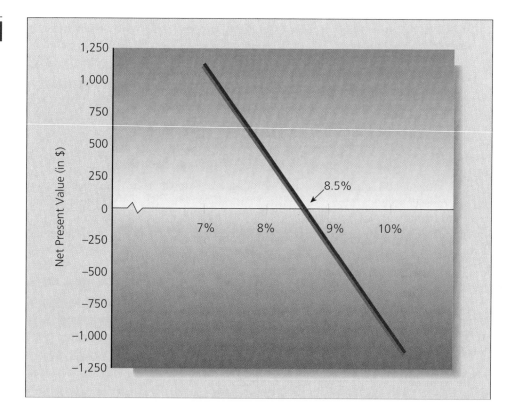

Exhibit 18–7 plots the net present values that result from discounting the alarm project cash flows at various rates of return. For example, the NPV at 4 percent is $4,595 and the NPV at 15 percent is −$5,301. (These computations are not provided here, but can be performed by discounting the $9,000 annual cash flows and subtracting $35,471 of investment cost.)

The internal rate of return is located on the graph's horizontal axis at the point where the NPV equals zero (8.5 percent). Note that the graph reflects an inverse relationship between rates of return and NPVs. Higher rates yield lower present values because, at the higher rates, fewer dollars need to be currently invested to obtain the same future value.

Manually finding the IRR of a project that produces unequal annual cash flows is more complex and requires an iterative trial-and-error process. An initial estimate is made of a rate believed to be close to the IRR and the NPV is computed. If the resulting NPV is negative, a lower rate is estimated (because of the inverse relationship mentioned above) and the NPV is computed again. If the NPV is positive, a higher rate is tried. This process is continued until the net present value equals zero, at which time the internal rate of return has been found. For example, Exhibit 18–5 indicates that the IRR for EastBay's skin growth hormone product is very close to 11 percent.

hurdle rate

The project's internal rate of return is then compared with management's preestablished **hurdle rate,** which is the rate of return specified as the lowest acceptable return on investment. Like the discount rate mentioned earlier, this rate should generally be at least equal to the cost of capital. In fact, the hurdle rate is commonly the discount rate used in computing net present value amounts. If a project's IRR is equal to or greater than the hurdle rate, the project is considered viable from a financial perspective. As indicated in the following passage, hurdle rates are no longer simply an American concept.

> Faced with higher capital costs, Japanese managers are beginning to embrace such previously little-known Western concepts as "hurdle rates" and "required rates of return." That's a big switch for executives who once concerned themselves only with market share.

Says Tsunehiko Ishibashi, general manager of finance for Mitsubishi Kasei, a major petrochemical company: "As a result of the higher cost of capital, the profitability standards for new investments must be raised."[8]

The higher the internal rate of return, the more financially attractive is the investment proposal. In choosing among alternative investments, however, managers cannot look solely at the internal rates of return on projects. The rates do not reflect the dollars involved. An investor would normally rather have a 10 percent return on $1,000 than a 100 percent return on $10!

Using the internal rate of return has three drawbacks. First, when uneven cash flows exist, the iterative process is inconvenient. Second, unless present value tables are available that provide factors for fractional interest rates, finding the precise IRR on a project is difficult. These two problems can be eliminated with the use of a computer or a programmable calculator. The last problem is that it is possible to find several rates of return that will make the net present value of the cash flows equal to zero. This phenomenon usually occurs when there are net cash inflows in some years and net cash outflows in other years of the investment project's life (other than time 0).

In performing discounted cash flow analyses, accrual-based accounting information sometimes needs to be converted to cash flow data. One accrual that deserves special attention is depreciation. Although depreciation is not a cash flow item, it has cash flow implications because of its deductibility for income tax purposes.

THE EFFECT OF DEPRECIATION ON AFTER-TAX CASH FLOWS

Income taxes are an integral part of the business environment and decision-making process in our society. Tax planning is a central part of management planning and has a large impact on overall business profitability. Managers typically make decisions only after examining how company taxes will be affected by those decisions. In evaluating capital projects, managers should use after-tax cash flows to determine project acceptability.

Note that depreciation expense is not a cash flow item. Although no funds are paid or received for it, depreciation on capital assets, similar to interest on debt, affects cash flows by reducing a company's tax obligation. Thus, depreciation provides a **tax shield** against the payment of taxes. The tax shield produces a **tax benefit** equal to the amount of taxes saved (the depreciation amount multiplied by the tax rate). The concepts of tax shield and tax benefit are shown on the income statements below. The tax rate is assumed to be 40 percent.

tax shield

tax benefit

NO DEPRECIATION DEDUCTION INCOME STATEMENT		DEPRECIATION DEDUCTION INCOME STATEMENT	
Sales	$500,000	Sales	$500,000
Cost of goods sold	(350,000)	Cost of goods sold	(350,000)
Gross margin	$150,000	Gross margin	$150,000
Expenses other than depreciation	(75,000)	Expenses other than depreciation	(75,000)
Depreciation expense	0	→Depreciation expense	(75,000)
Income before taxes	$ 75,000	Income before tax	$ 0
Tax expense (40%)	(30,000)←	→Tax expense (40%)	0
Net income	$ 45,000	Net income	$ 0

The tax shield is the depreciation expense amount of $75,000. The tax benefit is the $30,000 difference between $30,000 of tax expense on the first income statement and $0 of tax expense on the second income statement. The tax benefit is also equal to the 40 percent tax rate multiplied by the tax shield of $75,000, or $30,000. Because taxes are reduced by $30,000, the pattern of cash flows is improved.

It is the *depreciation for purposes of computing income taxes rather than the amount used for financial accounting purposes* that is relevant in discounted cash flow analysis. Income

---

[8] John J. Curran, "Japan Tries to Cool Money Mania," *Fortune* (January 28, 1991), p. 66.

tax laws regarding depreciation deductions are subject to revision. In making their analyses of capital investments, managers should use the most current tax regulations for depreciation. Different depreciation methods may have significant impacts on after-tax cash flows. For a continuously profitable business, an accelerated method of depreciation, such as the modified accelerated cost recovery system (MACRS), will produce higher tax benefits in the early years of asset life than will the straight-line method. These higher tax benefits will translate into a higher net present value over the life of the investment project.

Changes in the availability of depreciation methods or in the length of an asset's depreciable life may dramatically affect projected after-tax cash flows and also affect the net present value, profitability index, and internal rate of return expected from the capital investment. Because capital projects are analyzed and evaluated before investments are made, managers should be aware of the inherent risk of tax law changes. Original assumptions made about the depreciation method or asset life may not be valid by the time an investment is actually made and an asset is placed into service. However, once purchased and placed into service, an asset can generally be depreciated using the method and tax life allowed when the asset was placed into service regardless of the tax law changes occurring after that time.

Changes may also occur in the tax rate structure. Rate changes may be relatively unpredictable. For example, the maximum federal corporate tax rate for many years was 46 percent; the Tax Reform Act of 1986 lowered this rate to 34 percent, and the present top marginal U.S. tax rate is 35 percent.[9] A tax rate reduction lowers the tax benefit provided by depreciation because the impact on cash flow is lessened. Tax law changes (such as asset tax-life changes) can cause the expected outcomes of the capital investment analysis to vary from the project's actual outcomes.[10]

To illustrate such variations, assume that EastBay is considering investing $400,000 in a warehouse facility. The facility has a 40-year economic life and would produce expected annual cash operating savings of $50,000. Assume the company's after-tax cost of capital is 10 percent. Further assume that corporate assets are depreciated on a straight-line basis for tax purposes.[11]

In late 1996, prior to the warehouse investment, EastBay's cost accountant, Jennifer Marlowe, calculated the project's net present value. The results of her calculations are shown in Exhibit 18–8 under Situation A. Note that depreciation is added to income after tax to obtain the amount of after-tax cash flow. *Even though depreciation is deductible for tax purposes, it is still a noncash expense.* The present value amounts are obtained by multiplying the after-tax cash flows by the appropriate PV of an annuity factor from Table 2 in Appendix A at the end of the text. The NPV evaluation technique indicated the acceptability of the capital investment. At the time of Ms. Marlowe's analysis, EastBay's tax rate was 30 percent and the tax laws allowed a 15-year depreciable life on this property.

Because Ms. Marlowe was concerned about proposed changes in the U.S. tax rate, she also analyzed the project assuming tax rates changed. Exhibit 18–8 shows the different after-tax cash flows and net present values that result if the same project is subjected to either a 25 percent (Situation B) or 40 percent (Situation C) tax rate.

This example demonstrates the expected NPV change when a different tax rate is used. If the tax rate changes to either 25 or 40 percent, the NPV changes. An increase in the tax rate makes the warehouse a less acceptable purchase, based on its net present value, and a decrease in the tax rate has the opposite effect.

---

[9] Surtaxes that apply to corporations may drive the top marginal rate above 35 percent for certain income brackets.

[10] Additionally, managers should be careful to consider effects of both applicable foreign and state tax laws.

[11] To simplify the presentation, the authors have elected to ignore a tax rule requirement called the half-year (or mid-quarter) convention that applies to personal assets and a mid-month convention that applies to most real estate improvements. Under tax law, only a partial year's depreciation may be taken in the year an asset is placed into service. The slight difference that such a tax limitation would make on the amounts presented is immaterial for purposes of illustrating these capital budgeting concepts.

EXHIBIT 18–8

Warehouse Analyses

FACTS:

Initial investment	$400,000
Expected annual before-tax cash flows	50,000
Straight-line depreciation (15 years)	26,667
Expected economic life	40 years

Situation (A): Tax rate of 30% (actual rate in effect)
Situation (B): Tax rate of 25%
Situation (C): Tax rate of 40%

	SITUATIONS		
	A	*B*	*C*
YEARS 1–15:			
Before-tax cash flow	$50,000	$50,000	$50,000
Depreciation	(26,667)	(26,667)	(26,667)
Income before tax	$23,333	$23,333	$23,333
Tax	(7,000)	(5,833)	(9,333)
Net income	$16,333	$17,500	$14,000
Depreciation	26,667	26,667	26,667
Cash flow after tax	$43,000	$44,167	$40,667
YEARS 16–40:			
Before-tax cash flow	$50,000	$50,000	$50,000
Depreciation	0	0	0
Income before tax	$50,000	$50,000	$50,000
Tax	(15,000)	(12,500)	(20,000)
Net income (after-tax cash flow)	$35,000	$37,500	$30,000

SITUATION A—NPV CALCULATIONS ASSUMING A 10% DISCOUNT RATE:

PV @ 10% of $43,000 for years 1–15 (factor = 7.6061)	$327,062
PV @ 10% of $35,000 for years 16–40 (factor = 2.1730)	76,055
	$403,117
Cost	(400,000)
NPV	$ 3,117

SITUATION B—NPV CALCULATIONS ASSUMING A 10% DISCOUNT RATE:

PV @ 10% of $44,167 for years 1–15 (factor = 7.6061)	$335,939
PV @ 10% of $37,500 for years 16–40 (factor = 2.1730)	81,488
	$417,427
Cost	(400,000)
NPV	$ 17,427

SITUATION C—NPV CALCULATIONS ASSUMING A 10% DISCOUNT RATE:

PV @ 10% of $40,667 for years 1–15 (factor = 7.6061)	$309,317
PV @ 10% of $30,000 for years 16–40 (factor = 2.1730)	65,190
	$374,507
Cost	(400,000)
NPV	$(25,493)

Understanding how depreciation and taxes affect the various capital budgeting techniques will allow managers to make the most informed decisions about capital investments.[12] Well-informed managers are more likely to have confidence in capital investments made by the company if they can justify the substantial resource commitment required. That justification is partially achieved by considering whether a capital project fits into strategic plans. To be confident of their conclusions, managers must also comprehend the assumptions and limitations of each capital budgeting method.

ASSUMPTIONS AND LIMITATIONS OF METHODS

As summarized in Exhibit 18–9, each financial capital budget evaluation method has its own underlying assumptions and limitations. To maximize benefits of the capital budgeting process, managers should understand the similarities and differences of the various methods and use several techniques to evaluate a project.

All the methods have two similar limitations. First, except to the extent that payback indicates the promptness of the investment recovery, none of the methods provides a mechanism to include management preferences in regard to the timing of cash flows. This limitation can be partially overcome by discounting cash flows further in the future at higher rates than those in earlier years, assuming that early cash flows are preferred. Second, all the methods use single, deterministic measures of cash flow amounts rather than probabilities. This limitation can be minimized through the use of probability estimates of cash flows. Such estimates can be input into a computer program to determine a distribution of answers for each method under various conditions of uncertainty.

THE INVESTMENT DECISION

Management must identify the best asset(s) for the firm to acquire to fulfill the company's goals and objectives. Making such an identification requires answers to the following four subhead questions.

Is the Activity Worthy of an Investment?

A company acquires assets when they have value in relation to specific activities in which the company is engaged. For example, Genentech invests heavily in research and development because it is the primary path to new product development (the activity). Before making decisions to acquire assets, company management must be certain that the activity for which the assets will be needed is worthy of an investment.

An activity's worth is measured by cost-benefit analysis. For most capital budgeting decisions, costs and benefits can be measured in monetary terms. If the dollars of benefits exceed the dollars of costs, then the activity is potentially worthwhile. In some cases, though, benefits provided by capital projects are difficult to quantify. However, difficulty in quantification is no reason to exclude benefits from capital budgeting analyses. In most instances, surrogate quantifiable measures can be obtained for qualitative benefits. For example, benefits from investments in day care centers for employees' children may be estimable based on the reduction in employee time off and turnover. At a minimum, managers should attempt to subjectively include such benefits in the analytical process.

In other circumstances, management may know in advance that the monetary benefits of the capital project will not exceed the costs, but the project is essential for other reasons. For example, a company may consider renovating the employee workplace with new carpet, furniture, paint, and artwork. The renovation would not make employee work any easier or safer, but would make it more comfortable. Such a

---

[12] These examples have all considered the investment project as a purchase. If a leasing option exists, the classification of the lease as operating or capital will affect the amounts deductible for tax purposes. A good illustration of this is provided in "The Lease vs. Purchase Decision," by Ralph L. Benke, Jr., and Charles P. Baril in *Management Accounting* (March 1990), pp. 42–46.

ASSUMPTIONS

LIMITATIONS

PAYBACK

- Speed of investment recovery is the key consideration
- Timing and size of cash flows are accurately predicted
- Risk (uncertainty) is lower for a shorter payback project

- Cash flows after payback are ignored
- Cash flows and project life in basic method are treated as deterministic without explicit consideration of probabilities
- Time value of money is ignored
- Cash flow pattern preferences are not explicitly recognized

NET PRESENT VALUE

- Discount rate used is valid
- Timing and size of cash flows are accurately predicted
- Life of project is accurately predicted
- If the shorter-lived of two projects is selected, the proceeds of that project will continue to earn the discount rate of return through the theoretical completion of the longer-lived project

- Cash flows and project life in basic method are treated as deterministic without explicit consideration of probabilities
- Alternative project rates of return are not known
- Cash flow pattern preferences are not explicitly recognized
- IRR on project is not reflected

PROFITABILITY INDEX

- Same as NPV
- Size of PV of net inflows relative to size of present value of investment measures efficient use of capital

- Same as NPV
- A relative answer is given but dollars of NPV are not reflected

INTERNAL RATE OF RETURN

- Hurdle rate used is valid
- Timing and size of cash flows are accurately predicted
- Life of project is accurately predicted
- If the shorter-lived of two projects is selected, the proceeds of that project will continue to earn the IRR through the theoretical completion of the longer-lived project

- The IRR rather than dollar size is used to rank projects for funding
- Dollars of NPV are not reflected
- Cash flows and project life in basic method are treated as deterministic without explicit consideration of probabilities
- Cash flow pattern preferences are not explicitly recognized
- Multiple rates of return can be calculated on the same project

ACCOUNTING RATE OF RETURN
(Presented in Appendix 2 of this chapter)

- Effect on company accounting earnings relative to average investment is key consideration
- Size and timing of increase in company earnings, investment cost, project life, and salvage value can be accurately predicted

- Cash flows are not considered
- Time value of money is not considered
- Earnings, investment, and project life are treated as deterministic without explicit consideration of probabilities

EXHIBIT 18–9

Selected Assumptions and Limitations of Capital Budgeting Methods

EXHIBIT 18–10

Capital Investment
Information

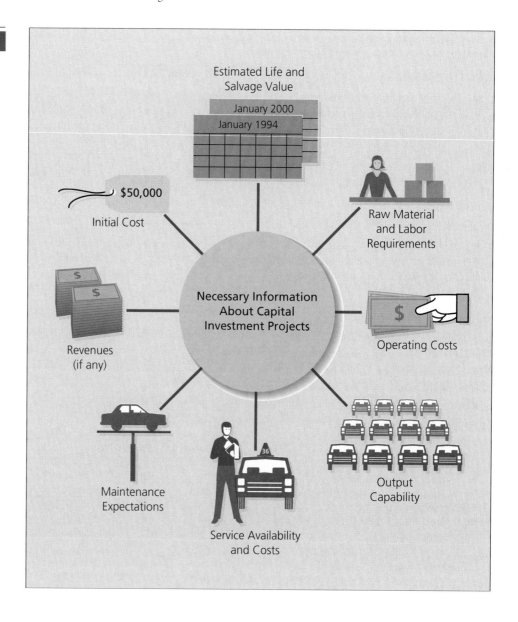

project may be deemed "worthy" regardless of cost-benefit analysis. Companies may also invest in unprofitable products to maintain market share of a product group, and, therefore, protect the market position of profitable products.

Which Assets Can Be Used for the Activity?

The determination of available and suitable assets to conduct the intended activity is closely related to the evaluation of the activity's worth. Management must have an idea of how much the needed assets will cost to determine whether the activity should be pursued. As shown in Exhibit 18–10, management should gather the following specific monetary and nonmonetary information for each asset to make this determination: initial cost, estimated life and salvage value, raw material and labor requirements, operating costs (both fixed and variable), output capability, service availability and costs, maintenance expectations, and revenues to be generated (if any). As mentioned in the previous section, information used in a capital project analysis may include surrogate, indirect measures. Management must have both quantitative and qualitative information on each asset and recognize that some projects are simply

The Big Gamble

NEWS
NOTE

Back in 1991, Intel was already the world's largest manufacturer of microprocessors, the brains of personal computers. Its latest chip, the 486, was beginning to take off. The successor, later dubbed Pentium, was barely on the drawing board. But just before a board meeting that year, Intel's chief, Andrew S. Grove, received a startling estimate of the capital spending needed to make the Pentium: $5 billion, or five times the amount for the 486 and a stunning 50 times that of the preceding 386 chip.

Until 1991, Intel and other semiconductor makers were slow to build new factories, traumatized by a mid-1980s capacity glut that ravaged chip prices and profits. But a controversial analysis by Senior Vice President Gerhard H. Parker concluded that the company had significantly underestimated potential demand for PCs and the more-costly Pentium.

If wrong, Intel could wind up with deadly overcapacity. "You had to have faith," says Arthur Rock, a celebrated venture capitalist and Intel director.

The board decided to gamble, with lasting repercussions for the $100 billion semiconductor industry. Sharply falling prices for PCs opened up a vast new consumer market and set off a chip boom that refuses to die. Last month, the Semiconductor Industry Association, a U.S. trade group, increased its estimate of 1995 world-wide unit growth for all types of chips to 39%, nearly three times its previous forecast of 15%.

Only Intel can meet the feverish demand. . . . Though rivals such as Motorola Inc. or International Business Machines Corp. are adding capacity, too, none can match the cash generated by Intel's 75% share of the microprocessor business. Intel has turned the spiraling cost of competition into a weapon.

Many analysts now believe that demand will propel the company to $8 billion to $11 billion in annual earnings in the year 2000. In contrast, the earnings last year of the most profitable companies—namely Exxon Corp., General Motors Corp., Ford Motor Co., AT&T and General Electric Co.—were clustered at slightly above or below $5 billion.

SOURCE: Don Clark, "A Big Bet Made Intel What It is Today; Now, It Wagers Again," *Wall Street Journal* (June 7, 1995), pp. A1, A5. Reprited by permission of *The Wall Street Journal*, © 1995 Dow Jones & Company, Inc. All Rights Reserved Worldwide.

more crucial to the firm's future than others. This point is illustrated in the News Note above.

Of the Available Assets for Each Activity, Which Is the Best Investment?

Using all available information, management should select the best asset from the candidates and exclude all others from consideration. In most instances, a company has a standing committee to discuss, evaluate, and approve capital projects. In judging capital project acceptability, this committee should recognize that two types of capital budgeting decisions need to be made: screening and preference decisions. A **screening decision** determines whether a capital project is desirable based on some previously established minimum criterion or criteria. If the project does not meet the minimum standard(s), it is excluded from further consideration. The second decision is a **preference decision** in which projects are ranked according to their impact on the achievement of company objectives.

Deciding which asset is the best investment requires the use of one or several of the evaluation techniques discussed previously. Some techniques may be used to screen the projects as to acceptability; other techniques may be used to rank the projects in order of preferability. Although different companies use different techniques for screening and ranking purposes, payback period is commonly used only

screening decision

preference decision

If an activity is judged worthy of a capital investment, then the best asset(s) in which to invest must be decided. In many situations, the variety of possible choices may be extremely wide.

for screening decisions. The reasons for this choice are that payback focuses only on the short run and does not consider the time value of money. The remaining techniques may be used to screen or rank capital projects.

Of the "Best Investments" for All Worthwhile Activities, in Which Ones Should the Company Invest?

Although many worthwhile investment activities exist, each company has limited resources available and must allocate them in the most profitable manner. Therefore, after choosing the best asset for each activity, management must decide which activities and assets to fund. Investment activities may be classified as mutually exclusive, independent, or mutually inclusive.

mutually exclusive projects

Mutually exclusive projects fulfill the same function. One project will be chosen from such a group, causing all others to be excluded from further consideration because they would provide unneeded or redundant capability. A proposal under consideration may be to replace a current asset with one that provides the same basic capabilities. If the company keeps the old asset, it will not buy the new one; if the new one is purchased, the old asset will be sold. Thus, the two assets are mutually exclusive. For example, if a bakery decided to buy a new delivery truck, it would no longer need its existing truck. The existing truck would be sold to help finance the new truck.

independent projects

Other investments may be **independent projects** because they have no specific bearing on one another. For example, the acquisition of an office microcomputer system is not related to the purchase of a factory machine. These project decisions are analyzed and accepted or rejected independently of one another. Although limited resources may preclude the acquisition of all acceptable projects, the projects themselves are not mutually exclusive.

mutually inclusive projects

Management may be considering certain investments that are all related to a primary project, or **mutually inclusive projects.** In a mutually inclusive situation, if the primary project is chosen, all related projects are also selected. Alternatively, rejection of the primary project will dictate rejection of the others. For example,

EXHIBIT 18–11

Typical Investment
Decision Process

Activity—Provide transportation for a sales force of ten people.

1. Is the activity worthy of an investment?
   Yes; this decision is based on an analysis of the cost of providing transportation in relationship to the dollars of gross margin to be generated by the sales force.
2. Which assets can be used for the activity?
   Available: Bus passes, bicycles, motorcycles, automobiles (purchased), automobiles (leased), automobiles (currently owned), small airplanes.
   Infeasible: Bus passes, bicycles and motorcycles are rejected as infeasible because of inconvenience and inability to carry a reasonable quantity of merchandise; airplanes are rejected as infeasible because of inconvenience and lack of proximity of landing sites to customers.
   Feasible: Various types of automobiles to be purchased (assume asset options A through G); various types of leasing arrangements (assume availability of leases 1 through 5); current fleet.
   Gather all relevant quantitative and qualitative information on all feasible assets (assets A-G; leases 1–5; current fleet).
3. Which asset is the best investment?
   Compare all relevant information and choose the best asset candidate from the purchase group (assume Asset D) and the lease group (assume Lease 2).
4. Which investment should the company make?
   Compare the best asset candidate from the purchase group (Asset D) and the lease group (Lease 2); this represents a mutually exclusive, multiple candidate project decision. The best candidate is found to be type D assets.
   Compare the type D assets to current fleet; this is a mutually exclusive, replacement project. The best investment is to sell the old fleet and purchase a new fleet of ten type D automobiles.

when the accounting firm of KPMG Peat Marwick selected Macintosh computers for its personnel, that selection dictated the acquisition of compatible brands of software and peripheral equipment.

Exhibit 18–11 shows a typical investment decision process in which a company is determining the best way to provide transportation for its sales force. Answers to the four questions asked in the subheadings to this section are provided for the transportation decision.

To ensure that capital funds are invested in the best projects available, managers must carefully evaluate all projects and decide which ones represent the most effective and efficient use of resources—a difficult determination. The evaluation process should consider activity priorities, cash flows, and risk of all projects. Projects should then be ranked in order of their acceptability. Ranking may be required for both independent projects and mutually exclusive projects. Ranking mutually exclusive projects is required to select the best project from the set of alternatives. Ranking independent projects is required to efficiently allocate scarce capital to competing uses.

RANKING MULTIPLE CAPITAL PROJECTS

When managers are faced with an accept/reject decision for a single asset, all time-value-of-money evaluation techniques will normally point to the same decision alternative. A project is acceptable under the NPV method when it has a nonnegative net present value. In a most-profit situation, acceptability of a capital asset is also indicated by a profitability index (PI) of 1.00 or more. Because the PI is an adaptation of the NPV method, these two evaluation techniques will always provide the same accept/reject decision.

To be acceptable using the IRR model, a capital acquisition must have an internal rate of return equal to or greater than the specified hurdle rate. The IRR method gives the same accept/reject decision as the NPV and PI methods if the hurdle rate and the discount rate used are the same.

More often, however, managers are faced with choosing from multiple projects. Multiple project decisions require that a selection ranking be made. This section of the chapter considers the use of the net present value, profitability index, and internal rate of return techniques in ranking mutually exclusive projects. Payback period also may be used to rank multiple projects. However, it does not provide as much useful information as NVP, PI, and IRR, because cash flows beyond the payback period are ignored.

Managers can use results from the evaluation techniques to rank projects in descending order of acceptability. For the NPV and PI methods, rankings are based, respectively, on magnitude of net present value and PI index. Although based on the same figures, the NPV and PI methods will not always provide the same order of ranking because the former is a dollar measure and the latter is a percentage. When the internal rate of return is used, rankings of multiple projects are based on expected rate of return. Rankings provided by the IRR method will not always be in the same order as those given by the NPV or PI methods.

reinvestment assumption

Conflicting results arise because of differing underlying **reinvestment assumptions** of the three methods. The reinvestment assumption presumes cash flows released during a project's life are reinvested until the end of the project's life. The NPV and PI techniques assume that released cash flows are reinvested at the discount rate which, at minimum, should be the weighted average cost of capital. The IRR method assumes reinvestment of released cash flows can be made at the expected internal rate of return, which may be substantially higher than the weighted average COC. If it is, the IRR method may provide a misleading indication of project success because additional projects may not be found that have such a high return.

Three situations are discussed in the following subsections to illustrate conflicting rankings of multiple projects. In each situation the weighted average cost of capital is the discount rate used to compute NPV as well as the hurdle rate against which to measure IRR.

Multiple Projects—Equal Lives, Constant Cash Flows, Unequal Investments

EastBay has gathered the following information pertaining to two potential projects. One project under consideration is the purchase of software that would improve the efficiency of certain lab analyses. The other investment being contemplated is a new air conditioner for corporate headquarters. The existing air conditioner is inefficient relative to current technology. Data on these projects are as follows:

	SOFTWARE	AIR CONDITIONER
Investment	$200,000	$40,000
Annual after-tax cash flows	$ 32,000	$ 7,000
Asset life	10 years	10 years
COC	8%	8%

Note that in this example the COC of 8 percent is to be used as the discount rate. The timelines, NPV, and PI computations appear in Exhibit 18–12 for both projects. The amounts on the timelines are shown in thousands of dollars. The IRR is approximated from the present value of an annuity table (Table 2, Appendix A), and the actual rate can be found using a computer or programmable calculator.

The net present value model indicates that the better investment for EastBay is the software with a NPV of $14,723. However, in applying the profitability index or internal rate of return models, the air conditioner would be selected because it has a higher PI and a higher IRR. Because these projects do not serve the same purpose, company management would most likely evaluate the selection based on priority needs rather than results of specific capital project evaluations. In the absence of a need to ration capital, EastBay may invest in both projects.

EXHIBIT 18-12

Multiple Projects;
Conflicting Rankings

SOFTWARE (IN THOUSANDS)

End of period	0	1	2	3	4	5	6	7	8	9	10
Inflows		+32	+32	+32	+32	+32	+32	+32	+32	+32	+32
Outflows	(200)										

PV of ordinary annuity of $32,000 discounted at 8% for 10 periods ($32,000 × 6.7101)	$214,723
Less cost (initial investment)	200,000
NPV	$ 14,723

PI = $214,723 ÷ $200,000 = 1.07

IRR factor = $200,000 ÷ $32,000 = 6.2500 (annuity for 10 periods)

The IRR is approximately 9.61%; calculator computations verify this finding.

AIR CONDITIONER (IN THOUSANDS)

End of period	0	1	2	3	4	5	6	7	8	9	10
Inflows		+7	+7	+7	+7	+7	+7	+7	+7	+7	+7
Outflows	(40)										

PV of ordinary annuity of $7,000 discounted at 8% for 10 periods ($7,000 × 6.7101)	$46,971
Less cost (initial investment)	40,000
NPV	$ 6,971

PI = $46,971 ÷ $40,000 = 1.17

IRR factor = $40,000 ÷ $7,000 = 5.7143 (annuity for 10 periods)

The IRR is approximately 11.73%; calculator computations verify this finding.

Multiple Projects—Unequal Lives, Constant But Unequal Cash Flows, Unequal Investments

The second illustration of conflicting rankings uses data on two other investment opportunities for EastBay. The weighted average cost of capital is assumed to be 8 percent.

	PACKAGING MACHINERY	OFFICE PHONE SYSTEM
Investment	$800,000	$593,000
Annual after-tax cash flows	210,000	110,000
Asset life	5 years	8 years

The timelines (in thousands of dollars) for the two investments are as follows:

PACKAGING MACHINERY (IN THOUSANDS)

End of period	0	1	2	3	4	5
Inflows		+210	+210	+210	+210	+210
Outflow	(800)					

OFFICE PHONE SYSTEM (IN THOUSANDS)

End of period	0	1	2	3	4	5	6	7	8
Inflows		+110	+110	+110	+110	+110	+110	+110	+110
Outflow	(593)								

EXHIBIT 18–13

Multiple Projects;
Conflicting Rankings

PACKAGING MACHINERY

PV of ordinary annuity of $210,000 discounted at 8% for 5 periods ($210,000 × 3.9927)	$838,467
Less cost (initial investment)	(800,000)
NPV	$ 38,467

$$PI = \$838,467 \div \$800,000 = 1.05$$
$$IRR\ factor = \$800,000 \div \$210,000 = 3.8095$$

By calculator, IRR = 9.81%

OFFICE PHONE SYSTEM

PV of ordinary annuity of $110,000 discounted at 8% for 8 periods ($110,000 × 5.7466)	$632,126
Less cost (initial investment)	(593,000)
NPV	$ 39,126

$$PI = \$632,126 \div \$593,000 = 1.07$$
$$IRR\ factor = \$593,000 \div \$110,000 = 5.3909$$

By calculator, IRR = 9.71%

The net present value, profitability index, and internal rate of return are calculated for each investment, and the calculated results are shown in Exhibit 18–13. If the net present value or profitability index method is used, the office phone system investment would be selected by EastBay. If the internal rate of return method is used to choose between the two projects, the packaging machinery appears to be the better investment.

Rankings using the internal rate of return are misleading because of the reinvestment assumption. The IRR method assumes that the cash inflows of $210,000 each year from the packaging machinery will be reinvested at a rate of 9.81 percent; the $110,000 of cash flows from the office phone system are assumed to be reinvested at 9.71 percent. The NPV method, however, assumes reinvestment of the cash flows at the weighted average cost of capital of 8 percent, which is a more reasonable rate of return. The NPV computations show the office phone system as the better investment.

There is a formal method of choosing the better investment. For EastBay's management to select the better investment, the difference in the annual cash flows between the packaging machinery and the office phone system investments must first be determined. The cash flow differences are then evaluated as if they resulted from a separate investment opportunity. Because the packaging machinery requires a higher investment than the office phone system, the packaging machinery is used as the comparison base. The investment opportunity resulting from the cash flow differences is referred to here as *project difference*. If project difference provides a positive net present value, the packaging machinery investment is ranked higher than the office phone system. This higher ranking is assigned because the additional investment required for the packaging machinery is more than compensated for by the additional cash flows. If project difference shows a negative net present value, the office phone equipment is the better investment. The NPV of project difference is negative as shown in Exhibit 18–14 using present value factors from Table 2, Appendix A.

EXHIBIT 18-14

Net Present Value of
Project Difference

End of Period	NET CASH FLOWS		
	Packaging Machinery	Office Phone System	Project Difference
0	− $800,000	− $593,000	− $207,000
1	210,000	110,000	+ 100,000
2	210,000	110,000	+ 100,000
3	210,000	110,000	+ 100,000
4	210,000	110,000	+ 100,000
5	210,000	110,000	+ 100,000
6	0	110,000	− 110,000
7	0	110,000	− 110,000
8	0	110,000	− 110,000

NPV of project difference:

PV of net positive flows of $100,000 discounted at 8% for years 1–5 ($100,000 × 3.9927)	$399,270
PV of net negative flows of $110,000 discounted at 8% for years 6–8 [$110,000 × (5.7466 − 3.9927)]	(192,929)
Total present value of net inflows	$206,341
Less difference in original investment	(207,000)
NPV of project difference	$ (659)

Multiple Projects—Equal Lives, Equal Investments, Unequal Cash Flows

EastBay's management is interested in two additional projects: automated quality control equipment and a research project for a governmental agency. The research and development project is somewhat unique in that no payment would be received from the governmental agency until the completion of the project. The company's cost of capital and discount rate are 8 percent. This set of projects illustrates another conflicting ranking situation; the relevant project data follow:

	AUTOMATED QUALITY CONTROL EQUIPMENT	RESEARCH PROJECT
Investment	$1,000,000	$1,000,000
Life	5 years	5 years
Net cash inflows		
Year 1	$ 360,000	$ 0
Year 2	360,000	0
Year 3	360,000	0
Year 4	360,000	0
Year 5	360,000	2,400,000

Using the same approach as presented in Exhibit 18–14, the following schedule computes a net present value for a project difference between the projects.

END OF PERIOD	AUTOMATED QUALITY CONTROL EQUIPMENT	RESEARCH PROJECT	PROJECT DIFFERENCE
0	$(1,000,000)	$(1,000,000)	$ 0
1	360,000	0	+ 360,000
2	360,000	0	+ 360,000
3	360,000	0	+ 360,000
4	360,000	0	+ 360,000
5	360,000	2,400,000	− 2,040,000

EXHIBIT 18–15

Comparison of Investment
Projects

AUTOMATED QUALITY CONTROL EQUIPMENT

PV of ordinary annuity of $360,000 discounted at 8% for 5 periods ($360,000 × 3.9927)	$1,437,372
Less cost (initial investment)	(1,000,000)
NPV	$ 437,372

$$PI = \$1,437,372 \div \$1,000,000 = 1.44$$
$$IRR\ factor = \$1,000,000 \div \$360,000 = 2.7778$$

The IRR is 23.4%

RESEARCH PROJECT

PV of an amount of $2,400,000 discounted at 8% at the end of year 5 ($2,400,000 × .6806)	$1,633,440
Less cost (initial investment)	(1,000,000)
NPV	$ 633,440

$$PI = \$1,633,440 \div \$1,000,000 = 1.63$$
$$IRR\ factor = \$1,000,000 \div \$2,400,000 = .4167$$

The IRR is 19.14%

PV of positive cash flows, discounted at 8% for years 1–4 ($360,000 × 3.3121)	$1,192,356
PV of negative cash flow, discounted at 8% for year 5 (−$2,040,000 × .6806)	(1,388,424)
NPV of project difference	$ (196,068)

Because the NPV of project difference is negative, the research project is the preferred investment.

Exhibit 18–15 presents the net present value, profitability index, and internal rate
of return computations for these projects. The investment in the automated quality
control equipment has the higher IRR, but the research project has a higher NPV
and PI. The best selection depends on assumptions made about the future reinvestment rate applied to each of the $360,000 cash flows from the automated quality
inspection equipment.

Fisher rate

The point of indifference between the two projects occurs when the $360,000
annuity can be discounted at a certain rate (the **Fisher rate**) and will equal $2,400,000
discounted for 5 years at that same rate. That rate is 14.43 percent and is calculated
by solving for a discount rate that causes the net present values of the two projects
to be equal. If worked manually, repeated trials are used; however, a computer or
programmable calculator can be used to find this rate quickly.

For reinvestment rates above 14.43 percent, the automated quality control equipment generates a higher net present value. For reinvestment rates below 14.43 percent, the research project is the superior investment.

The preceding situations demonstrate that different capital budgeting evaluation
methods often provide different rankings of projects. Because of this possibility, managers should select one primary evaluation method for capital projects. The critical
question is whether higher cash flows or a higher rate of return is preferable. The
answer is that higher present cash flows are *always* preferable to higher rates of return.

The net present value method is considered theoretically superior to the internal
rate of return in evaluating capital projects for two reasons. First, the reinvestment
assumption of the IRR method is less likely to occur than that of the NPV method.
Second, when a project has both positive and negative net annual cash flows during
its life, there is the arithmetic possibility that projects will have multiple internal rates
of return.

In addition, the net present value technique measures project results in dollars rather than rates, and dollar results are the objective of investment. To illustrate the problem that could occur by relying solely on the internal rate of return method, consider the following question: Would a manager rather receive a 100 percent return on a $1 investment or a 10 percent return on a $100 investment? The answer indicates the fallacy of focusing only on rates of return.

Although useful as a measure of evaluation under some circumstances, the profitability index is subject to the same concern as presented in the previous paragraph. Because monetary results *are* the objective of investments and the PI is expressed as a *rate* rather than as dollars, it can, if used by itself, lead to incorrect decisions. Taken together with other tools, however, the profitability index is a measure of capital efficiency and can assist decision makers in their financial investment analyses.

Managers rank capital projects to select those projects providing the greatest return on company investment. A company often finds that it has the opportunity to invest in more acceptable projects than it has money. In fact, most companies operate under some measure of **capital rationing,** which means that there is an upper dollar constraint on the amount of capital available to commit to capital asset acquisition.[13] When capital rationing exists, the selection of investment projects must fall within the capital budget limit. In these circumstances, the NPV model may not produce rankings that maximize the value added to the firm, because it does not consider differences in investment size.

Capital rationing is illustrated by the following situation. Assume that EastBay has a capital budget of $7,500,000 and is considering the various investment projects listed in Exhibit 18–16.

By all quantitative measures except NPV, Project 1 should be eliminated if the firm has only $7,500,000 available in the capital budget. Its NPV is larger than only Project 2, but deletion of Project 2 will not permit inclusion of any other project. The firm would need $8.1 million to complete all six projects and only $7.5 million is available. Because it does not help to eliminate Project 2, the project that would otherwise produce the smallest company NPV and return based on either the PI or IRR technique (Project 1) should be eliminated. Relatively speaking, Project 2 is of much less interest than Projects 3, 4, 5, and 6. Project 2 does meet minimum quantitative standards though.

Based on PIs, the attractiveness of the projects, in descending order, are 6, 4, 2, 5, and 3. Based on IRRs, the preferences would be 5, 3, 6, 4, and 2. Based on NPVs, the ranking would be 6, 5, 4, 3, and 2.

RANKING PROJECTS UNDER CAPITAL RATIONING

capital rationing

PROJECT	INITIAL PROJECT COST	PI	IRR	NPV
1. Product research	$1,000,000	1.15	12%	$ 145,712
2. Computer upgrade	100,000	1.43	17	43,214
3. Employee training	1,200,000	1.41	24	495,888
4. Safety enhancements	1,800,000	1.45	20	801,365
5. Manufacturing automation	2,000,000	1.42	24	839,481
6. Purchase patents	2,000,000	1.62	20	1,233,902
Total cost of projects	$8,100,000			

EXHIBIT 18–16

Potential Investment Projects

[13] Many publicly traded companies have the luxury of being able to obtain additional capital through new issuances of debt or stock. This possibility may limit the degree to which they are subject to capital rationing but does not eliminate it. Nonpublicly traded companies operate under much more strict rationing of capital resources.

EXHIBIT 18–17

Ranking Categories for
Capital Projects

CATEGORY 1—REQUIRED BY LEGISLATION

This category would include such items as pollution control equipment that has been mandated by law. Most companies can ill afford the fines or penalties that can be assessed for lack of installation; however, these capital acquisitions may not meet the company's minimum established economic criteria.

CATEGORY 2—ESSENTIAL TO OPERATIONS

This category would include capital assets without which the primary functions of the organization could not continue. This category could include new purchases of capital assets or replacements of broken or no longer usable assets. For example, the purchase of a kiln for a ceramics manufacturer would fall into this category.

CATEGORY 3—NONESSENTIAL BUT INCOME GENERATING

This category would include capital assets that would improve operations of the organization by providing cost savings or supplements to revenue. Robots in an automobile manufacturer would be included in this group.

CATEGORY 4—OPTIONAL IMPROVEMENTS

Items in this category would be those that do not provide any cost savings or revenue increases but would make operations run more smoothly or improve working conditions. The purchase of computer hardware or software that is faster than that currently being used and the installation of a microwave oven in the employees' lounge would be included here.

CATEGORY 5—MISCELLANEOUS

This category exists for "pet projects" that might be requested. Such acquisitions may be more for the benefit of a single individual and not the organization as a whole. Such projects may not even be related to organizational objectives. The installation of new carpeting in a manager's office could be an example of this group of investments. Items in this category will normally be chosen only when the organization has substantial, unencumbered resources at its disposal.

Although managers should select one *primary* evaluation technique, the EastBay example shows that capital project evaluation should not be performed using only one method. Each evaluation tool should be used in conjunction with others, not to the exclusion of others. Each method provides valuable information. Even the non-discounting technique of payback period can be helpful to management by indicating the quickness of return of investment.

In making their preference decisions, many company managers set ranking categories for projects such as those shown in Exhibit 18–17. Projects are first screened and placed into an appropriate category. Monetary resources are allocated to projects in a top-to-bottom fashion. Within each category, projects are usually ranked using net present value and profitability index techniques. Management's goal should be to select those projects that, within budget constraints, will maximize net present value to the firm. Selecting projects based solely on their internal rate of return rankings without consideration of the net present values may be incorrect.[14]

Regardless of the capital budgeting evaluation techniques used, managers must remember that the results provided are based on estimates of future events. The fact that estimates are involved indicates that a risk is associated with the decision. All project estimates should be carefully understood and analyzed using sound judgment. Capital project proposals are being "sold" by their sponsors using different reasons under different conditions.

[14] If the set of projects is very large, the selection of projects may require the use of integer programming techniques, which are outside the scope of this text.

When choosing among multiple projects, managers must consider the **risk** or uncertainty associated with each project. In accounting, risk reflects the possibility of differences between the expected and actual future returns from an investment. For example, the purchase of a $100,000, 10 percent treasury note would provide a virtually risk-free return of $10,000 annually because treasury notes are backed by the full faith and credit of the U.S. government. If the same $100,000 were used to purchase stock, the returns could range from −100 percent (losing the entire investment) to an abnormally high return. The potential for extreme variability makes the stock purchase a much more risky investment than the treasury note.

Managers considering a capital investment should understand and compensate for the degree of risk involved in that investment.[15] A manager may use three approaches to compensate for risk: the judgmental method, the risk-adjusted discount rate method, and sensitivity analysis. These methods do not *eliminate* risk, but they do help managers understand and evaluate risk in the decision-making process.

Judgmental Method

The **judgmental method** of risk adjustment allows the decision makers to use logic and reasoning to decide whether a project provides an acceptable rate of return in relation to its risk. The decision maker is presented with all available information for each project, including the payback period, NPV, PI, and IRR. After reviewing the information, the decision maker chooses from among acceptable projects based on personal judgment of the risk-to-return relationship. The judgmental approach provides no *formal* process for adjusting data for the risk element.

Risk-Adjusted Discount Rate Method

A more formal method of taking risk into account requires making adjustments to the discount or hurdle rate. Under the **risk-adjusted discount rate method,** the decision maker increases (decreases) the rate used for discounting future cash inflows (outflows) to compensate for increased risk. As the discount rate is increased (decreased), the present values of the cash flows are reduced (increased). Therefore, larger cash inflows are required to "cover" the investment and provide an acceptable rate of return. Changes in the discount rate should be reflective of the degree of cash flow variability and timing, other investment opportunities, and corporate objectives. If the internal rate of return is being used for project evaluation, the risk-adjusted discount rate method would increase the hurdle rate against which the IRR is compared for higher-risk projects.

Assume that the management of EastBay Company is considering developing a product that would be licensed to another pharmaceutical company for 10 years. The rights to the product would then be sold to the highest bidder. Estimates of the cost and annual cash flows for the product are as follows:

Initial development cost	$150,000,000
After-tax net cash flows	
Years 1–5	20,000,000
Years 6–10	30,000,000
Year 10 (sale)	60,000,000

EastBay management uses its 8 percent weighted average cost of capital as the discount rate in evaluating capital projects under the NPV method. However, Donna Greene, a board member, feels that above-normal risk is created in this endeavor by two factors. First, revenues realized through licensing fees may differ from those planned. Second, the market value of the product rights in 10 years may vary substantially from the estimate of $60 million.

COMPENSATING FOR RISK IN CAPITAL PROJECT EVALUATION

risk

judgmental method

risk-adjusted discount rate method

---

[15] Information about the degree of risk is indicated by variability measures such as the standard deviation and the coefficient of variation. These measures and their use in capital project evaluations are discussed in Appendix 3 to this chapter.

EXHIBIT 18–18

Product Development
Evaluation

NPV using 8% discount rate	
Cash flows, years 1–5 ($20,000,000 × 3.9927)	$ 79,854,000
Cash flows, years 6–10 [$30,000,000 × (6.7101−3.9927)]	81,522,000
Cash flow, year 10 ($60,000,000 × .4632)	27,792,000
PV of total cash flows	$189,168,000
Initial investment	(150,000,000)
Net present value of cash flows	$ 39,168,000
NPV using 15% discount rate	
Cash flows, years 1–5 ($20,000,000 × 3.3522)	$ 67,044,000
Cash flows, years 6–10 [$30,000,000 × (5.0188 − 3.3522)]	49,998,000
Cash flow, year 10 ($60,000,000 × .2472)	14,832,000
PV of total cash flows	$131,874,000
Initial investment	(150,000,000)
Net present value of cash flows	$(18,126,000)

Ms. Greene wants to compensate for these risk factors by using a 15 percent discount rate rather than the 8 percent cost of capital rate. Determination of the amount of adjustment to make to the discount rate (from 8 to 15 percent, for example) is most commonly an arbitrary one. Thus, even though a formal process is used to compensate for risk, the process still involves a degree of judgment on the part of the project evaluators. Exhibit 18–18 presents the NPV computations using both discount rates. When the discount rate is adjusted upward, the NPV of the project is lowered and, in this case, shows the project to be unacceptable.

The same type of risk adjustment may be used for payback period or accounting rate of return (Appendix 2). If the payback period method is being used, managers may choose to shorten the maximum allowable payback period to compensate for increased risk. This adjustment assumes that cash flows occurring in the more distant future are more risky than those occurring in the near future. If the accounting rate of return (ARR) method is used, managers may increase the preestablished acceptable rate against which the ARR is compared to compensate for risk. Another way in which risk can be included in the decision process is through the use of sensitivity analysis.

Sensitivity Analysis

sensitivity analysis

Sensitivity analysis is a process of determining the amount of change that must occur in a variable before a different decision would be made. In a capital budgeting situation, the variable under consideration could be the discount rate, annual net cash flows, or project life. Sensitivity analysis looks at the question, What if a variable is different than originally expected?

Except the initial purchase price, all information used in capital budgeting is estimated. Use of estimates allows for introduction of errors, and sensitivity analysis identifies an "error range" for the various estimated values over which the project will still be acceptable. The following considers how sensitivity analysis relates to the discount rate, cash flows, and life of the asset.

RANGE OF THE DISCOUNT RATE   A capital project providing a rate of return equal to or greater than the discount or hurdle rate is considered an acceptable investment. But returns from a project are not certain because, for instance, the cost of capital may increase due to increases in interest rates on new issues of debt.

Sensitivity analysis allows a company to determine what increases may occur in the estimated cost of capital before a project becomes unacceptable. The upper limit

The cost of installing a ski lift can be up to $12 million. Managers of ski resorts will generally use sensitivity analysis in justifying investments because of the variability surrounding the cash flows that might be generated.

of increase in the discount rate is the project's internal rate of return. At the IRR, a project's net present value is zero; therefore, the present value of the cash inflows equals the present value of cash outflows. As long as the IRR for a project is equal to or above the cost of capital, the project will be acceptable.

To illustrate use of sensitivity analysis, EastBay's air conditioner project that was analyzed in Exhibit 18–12 using an 8 percent discount rate is reconsidered:

After-tax cash flows for 10 years
   discounted at 8% (7,000 × 6.7101) $46,971
Initial investment   (40,000)
NPV $ 6,971

The project provides a positive net present value and is considered an acceptable investment candidate.

EastBay management wants to know how high the discount rate can rise before the project would become unacceptable. To find the upper limit of the discount rate, the present value factor for an annuity of 10 periods at the unknown interest is computed as follows:

$$\text{Cash flow (PV factor)} = \text{Investment}$$

$$\$7,000 \text{ (PV factor)} = \$40,000$$

$$\text{PV factor} = 5.7143$$

As indicated in Exhibit 18–12, the IRR for this project is approximately 11.75 percent. Using a computer or programmable calculator, the actual IRR is found to be 11.73 percent. As long as EastBay's cost of capital is less than or equal to 11.73 percent, this project will be acceptable. As the discount or weighted average cost of capital rate is increased toward the project's IRR, the project becomes less desirable. These calculations assume that the cash flows and project life have been properly estimated.

RANGE OF THE CASH FLOWS   Another factor sensitive to changes in estimation is the investment's projected cash flows. EastBay's data for the air conditioner project from Exhibit 18–12 is also used to illustrate how to determine the range of acceptable cash flows. Company management wants to know how small the net cash inflows can be and still have the project remain desirable. This determination requires that the present value of the cash flows for 10 periods, discounted at 8 percent, be equal to or greater than the investment cost. The PV factor for 10 periods at 8 percent is 6.7101. The equation from the preceding section can be used to find the lowest acceptable annuity:

$$\text{Cash flow (PV factor)} = \text{Investment}$$
$$\text{Cash flow (6.7101)} = \$40{,}000$$
$$\text{Cash flow} = \$40{,}000 \div 6.7101$$
$$\text{Cash flow} = \$5{,}961$$

As long as the net annual cash flow equals or exceeds $5,961, the air conditioner project will be financially acceptable.

RANGE OF THE LIFE OF THE ASSET   Asset life is related to many factors, some of which, like the quantity and timing of maintenance on equipment, are controllable. Other factors, such as technological advances and actions of competitors, are non-controllable. An error in the estimated life will change the number of periods from which cash flows are to be derived. These changes could affect the accept/reject decision for a project.

The EastBay air conditioner example is used to demonstrate how to find the minimum length of time the cash flows must be received from the project for it to be acceptable. The solution requires setting the present value of the cash flows discounted at 8 percent equal to the investment. This computation yields the PV factor for an unknown number of periods:

$$\text{Cash flow (PV factor)} = \text{Investment}$$
$$\$7{,}000 \text{ (PV factor)} = \$40{,}000$$
$$\text{PV factor} = 5.7143$$

Review the present value of an annuity table in Appendix A under the 8 percent interest column to find the 5.7143 factor. The project life is almost 8 years (7 years and 11 + months). If the project cash flows were to stop at any point before 7 years and 11 months, the project would be unacceptable.

Sensitivity analysis does not reduce the uncertainty surrounding the estimate of each variable. It does, however, provide management with a sense of the tolerance for estimation errors by providing upper and lower ranges for selected variables. The above presentation simplistically focuses on single changes in each of the variables. If all factors change simultaneously, the above type of sensitivity analysis is useless. More advanced treatments of sensitivity analysis, which allow for simultaneous ranging of all variables, can be found under the topic of simulation in an advanced mathematical modeling text. The concept of simulation is demonstrated in the accompanying News Note.

POSTINVESTMENT AUDIT

postinvestment audit

In a **postinvestment audit** of a capital project, information on actual project results is gathered and compared to expected results. This process provides a feedback or control feature to both the persons who submitted and those who approved the original project information. Comparisons should be made using the same technique or techniques as were originally used to determine project acceptance. Actual data should be extrapolated to future periods where such information would be appropriate. In cases where significant learning or training is necessary, start-up costs of the first year may not be appropriate indicators of future costs. Such projects should be given a chance to stabilize before making the project audit.

Fuzzy Logic

Capital budgeting analysis requires several important assumptions to be made. For example, assumptions are made about disposal values, annual cash flows, reinvestment interest rates, and project life. In conducting sensitivity analysis, traditional methods allow only one variable at a time to change. However, it is realistic to assume that two or more variables may vary from assumptions that were made in evaluating an investment project. One approach to allowing several assumptions to vary simultaneously involves fuzzy logic.

Fuzzy logic allows managers to specify a "belief distribution" for one or several variables. The fuzzy distribution is merely a likely range of values that could be assumed by a variable. Using the fuzzy distribution, a project NPV (or other project evaluation measure) can be computed. Rather than getting a single, deterministic NPV number, a probability distribution of net present values is generated. This distribution is a reflection of the likely values or distributions of all important variables in the NPV analysis.

The advantage of the fuzzy logic approach is that it allows for the use of more information in making capital budgeting decisions. Rather than being required to insert a single value for, say, disposal value, managers can insert the distribution of possible values. The outcome is more information about the project's NPV.

SOURCE: Adapted from Peter C. Brewer, Amy W. Gatian and James M. Reeve, "Managing Uncertainty," *Management Accounting* (October 1993), pp. 39–45. Reprinted from *Management Accounting*. Copyright by Institute of Management Accountants, Montvale, NJ.

As the size of the capital expenditure increases, a postinvestment audit becomes more crucial. Although an audit cannot change a past investment decision, it can pinpoint areas of project operations that are out of line with expectations so that problems can be corrected before they get out of hand. Secondarily, an audit can provide feedback on the accuracy of the original estimates for project cash flows. Sometimes, project sponsors may be biased in favor of their own projects and provide overly optimistic forecasts of future revenues or cost savings. Individuals providing unrealistic estimates should be required to explain all major variances. Knowing that post investment audits will be made may cause project sponsors to provide realistic cash flow forecasts in their capital requests.

Performing a postinvestment audit is not an easy task. The actual information may not be in the same form as were the original estimates, and some project benefits may be difficult to quantify. Project returns fluctuate considerably over time, so results gathered at a single point may not be representative of the project. But, regardless of the difficulties involved, postinvestment audits provide management with information that can help to make better capital investment decisions in the future.

REVISITING

Genentech, Inc.

Genentech, Inc., competes in an industry that is growing very rapidly. Genentech's present and future success depends critically on the firm's ability to bring new products to market before its competitors do. Research and development (R & D) activities provide the main avenue to innovation and product development. Consequently, Genentech must carefully manage its investment in R & D to be successful. The capital budget is the primary tool available to Genentech to carefully monitor and manage the R & D investment.

In a more mature industry, R & D would be relatively less important to firms, and in their capital budgets managers would be more concerned with projects to control quality and product and distribution costs. Thus, the life cycle of the firm and its industry will change the focus in capital budgeting over time.

Genentech's investments also reflect the importance of investing in its community and in human resources. In addition to its huge commitment to R & D, in 1995 Genentech

- donated more than $3 million for scientific research through medical and academic research organizations.
- identified, trained, and equipped outstanding high school educators to improve the teaching of science and biology in U.S. high schools.
- provided research materials to academic researchers worldwide.

SOURCE: 1995 Annual Report of Genentech, Inc.

CHAPTER SUMMARY

Capital budgeting is concerned with evaluating long-range projects involving the acquisition, operation, and disposition of one or more capital assets. A variety of criteria is employed to evaluate potential projects. Among the financial criteria used are payback period, net present value (NPV), profitability index (PI), and internal rate of return (IRR).

The payback period is the length of time needed for a firm to recoup its investment from the cash inflows of a project. If a project's payback period is less than a preestablished maximum, the project is acceptable. This method ignores the time value of money and all cash flows beyond the payback period.

Net present value, profitability index, and internal rate of return are discounted cash flow methods. As such, these methods require management to discount a project's cash inflows and outflows using a desired rate of return. The minimum rate at which the discount rate should be set is the cost of capital. Managers may compensate for a project's above-normal risk by using a discount rate that is higher than the cost of capital.

Under the NPV method, the total present value of future cash flows is reduced by the current investment to derive the net present value. If the NPV is equal to or greater than zero, the project provides a rate of return equal to or greater than the discount rate. A positive NPV makes the project acceptable for investment.

The profitability index equals the present value of the net cash flows divided by the investment cost. The profitability index is considered an indicator of the company's efficiency in its use of capital. Revenue-producing projects should have a PI of 1.00 or more.

The internal rate of return method computes the rate of return expected on the investment project. The IRR is equal to the discount rate at which the net present value of all cash flows equals zero. If the internal rate of return of a project exceeds management's desired hurdle rate, the project is acceptable.

Each capital project evaluation technique is based on certain assumptions and, therefore, has certain limitations. To compensate for these limitations, managers subject capital projects to more than one evaluation technique.

Depreciation expense and changes in tax rates affect after-tax cash flows. The tax rates and allowable depreciation methods estimated when the investment is analyzed may not be the same as when the project is implemented. Such changes can cause a significant difference in the actual net present value and internal rate of return amounts from those originally estimated on the project.

Management should select investment projects that will help to achieve the organization's objectives and provide the maximum return on capital resources utilized. The company must determine whether the activities in which it wishes to engage are worthy of an investment and which assets can be used for those activities. Then, decisions must be made about the best investment to accept from all available. These decisions require that investment projects be ranked as to their desirability in relationship to one another.

Often the NPV, PI, and IRR computations will produce the same rankings of multiple investment projects. In some situations, however, the NPV, PI, and IRR methods produce different project rankings. The primary reason for differences is the underlying assumption of each method regarding the reinvestment rate of cash flows released during the life of the project. The NPV and PI methods assume reinvestment at the discount rate, whereas the IRR method assumes reinvestment at the internal rate of return provided by the project. The assumption of the NPV and PI methods is more likely to be realized than that of the IRR method.

Capital rationing indicates that management has imposed a spending limit in the capital budget. When capital rationing exists, the NPV model may provide the best first-cut ranking of projects in which the returns to the firm will be maximized. Projects can be listed also in descending order of their PI and IRR rates of return. Only projects having an IRR in excess of the weighted average cost of capital should be considered and then only to the extent of the budget. In addition, managers need to consider legal requirements as well as the goals and objectives of the firm when ranking projects. Categorization of projects (such as is shown in Exhibit 18–17) is a useful way to rank investments.

Different risks can be associated with each capital project. Risk is defined as uncertainty about the expected returns from an asset. Project risk can be assessed and included in decision making judgmentally, or more formally, by calculating a risk-adjusted discount/hurdle rate. Sensitivity analysis can also be employed to compensate for risk by calculating a range for each of the variables (discount rate, cash flows, and life of project) in a capital budgeting problem. Sensitivity analysis assists management in determining the effect on project outcome of a change in the estimate of one or more of the critical variables in deriving the accept/reject conclusion about the project.

After a capital project is accepted and implemented, a postinvestment audit should be undertaken to compare actual results with expected results. The audit will help managers identify and correct any problems that may exist, evaluate the accuracy of estimates used for the original investment decision, and help improve the forecasts of future investment projects.

APPENDIX 1

Time Value of Money

The time value of money can be discussed in relationship to either its future or its present value. **Future value** (FV) refers to the amount to which a sum of money invested at a specified interest rate will grow over a specified number of time periods. Present value (PV) is the amount that future cash flows are worth currently, given a specified rate of interest.[16] Thus, future and present values depend on three things: (1) amount of the cash flow, (2) rate of interest, and 3) timing of the cash flow. Only present values are discussed in this appendix because they are most relevant to the types of management decisions discussed in this text.

future value

---

[16] Interest can be earned or owed, received or paid. To simplify the discussion for definitional purposes, the topic of interest is viewed only from the inflow standpoint.

Future and present values are related. A present value is a future value discounted back the same number of periods at the same rate of interest. The rate of return used in present value computations is called the discount rate.

In computing future and present values, simple or compound interest may be used. **Simple interest** means that interest is earned only on the original investment or principal amount. **Compound interest** means that interest earned in prior periods is added to the original investment so that, in each successive period, interest is earned on both principal and interest. The time between each interest computation is called the **compounding period.** The more often interest is compounded, the higher is the actual rate of interest being received relative to the stated rate. The following discussion is based on use of compound interest, because most transactions use this method.

simple interest

compound interest

compounding period

Interest rates are typically stated in annual terms. To compensate for more frequent compounding periods, the number of years is multiplied by the number of compounding periods per year and the annual interest rate is divided by the number of compounding periods per year.

Present Value of a Single Cash Flow

Assume that Tanya Jenning's bank pays interest at 10 percent per year compounded semiannually. Tanya wants to accumulate $26,802 in 3 years and wants to know what amount to invest now to achieve that goal. The formula to solve for the present value is

$$PV = \frac{FV}{(1 + i)^n}$$

where
$$PV = \text{present value of a future amount}$$
$$FV = \text{future value of a current investment}$$
$$i = \text{interest rate per compounding period}$$
$$n = \text{number of compounding periods}$$

Substituting known values into the formula gives the following:

$$PV = \$26,802 \left[\frac{1}{(1 + .05)^6} \right]$$

$$PV = \$26,802 \left[\frac{1}{1.3401} \right]$$

$$PV = \$20,000$$

Note that the interest rate used in this example is 5 percent. This is half of the annual rate of 10 percent and corresponds to the rate of interest earned during one compounding period.

In capital budgeting analyses, many future value amounts need to be converted to present values. Rather than using the formula $[1 \div (1 + i)^n]$ to find PVs, a table of factors for the present value of $1 (Table 1) for a variety of "i" and "n" values is provided in Appendix A at the end of the text for ease of computation. Such factors are also available in programmable calculators, making the use of tables unnecessary.

Present Value of an Annuity

An annuity is a cash flow (either positive or negative) that is repeated over consecutive periods. For an **ordinary annuity,** the first cash flow occurs at the end of each period. In contrast, the cash flows for an **annuity due** occur at the beginning of each period.

ordinary annuity

annuity due

To illustrate the computation of the present value of an annuity, consider the following situation. Mary and Mike Smith are planning for their daughter's college education. Their daughter, Keri, will need $15,000 per year for the next four years.

The Smith's want to know how much to invest currently at 8 percent so that Keri can withdraw $15,000 per year. The following diagram presents the situation:

Time period	t0	t1	t2	t3	t4
Future value		$15,000	$15,000	$15,000	$15,000
Present value	?				

The present value of each single cash flow can be found using 8 percent factors in Table 1 as follows:

PV of first receipt:	$15,000 (.9259)	$13,888
PV of second receipt:	$15,000 (.8573)	12,860
PV of third receipt:	$15,000 (.7938)	11,907
PV of fourth receipt:	$15,000 (.7350)	11,025
		$49,680

The present value factor for an ordinary annuity can be determined also by adding the present value factors for all periods having a future cash flow. Table 2 in Appendix A provides present value of ordinary annuity factors for various interest rates and time periods. From this table, the factor of 3.3121 can be obtained and multiplied by $15,000 to yield approximately the same result as above. (The difference is caused by decimal-fraction rounding.)

Nested Annuities

Situations often exist in which an annuity is "nested" or surrounded by unequal flows. The present value of each cash flow of the annuity could be found separately using the factors for the present value of $1 (Table 1). The alternative is to use Table 2 (PV of a $1 annuity), which is more direct but does require a slight modification.

Lester Delivery Service has provided the following information that illustrates a nested annuity. The project under consideration requires a $40,000 investment and will return the amounts shown below for a 10-year period. The company's discount rate is 12 percent.

1/1/97 current investment	($40,000)
Returns at year-end:	
12/31/97	+$8,000
12/31/98	+10,000
12/31/99	+11,000
12/31/00	+12,000
12/31/01	+12,000
12/31/02	+12,000
12/31/03	+12,000
12/31/04	+12,000
12/31/05	+8,000
12/31/06	+18,000

A $12,000 annuity starts at the end of 2000 and terminates in 2004. The present value of each annual cash flow, including the five annuity installments, could be computed separately by multiplying the cash flow amount by the present value factor for that period. Annual computations for the present value of the $12,000 annuity are as follows:

YEAR	CASH FLOW	PRESENT VALUE FACTOR	PRESENT VALUE
4	+$12,000	.6355	$ 7,626
5	+ 12,000	.5674	6,809
6	+ 12,000	.5066	6,079
7	+ 12,000	.4524	5,429
8	+ 12,000	.4039	4,847
Totals		2.5658	$30,790

The above approach requires that five factors be extracted from the PV table and five multiplications be made. Alternatively, the five factors could be summed (2.5658) and multiplied by $12,000 to provide the same result.

However, because the situation involves an annuity, there is another method of making this computation. Table 2 (PV of an ordinary annuity of $1) can be used to find the present value at a 12 percent rate. Because the $12,000 annuity stops at the end of year eight, start with the PV factor for eight periods (4.9676). Because the annuity did not begin until after the end of the third period, subtract the PV factor for three periods (2.4018). This subtraction gives a factor of 2.5658, representing the PV of an ordinary annuity lasting for five periods between and including periods four through eight.

APPENDIX 2

Accounting Rate of Return

accounting rate of return

The **accounting rate of return** (ARR) measures the rate of earnings obtained on the average capital investment over a project's life. This evaluation method is consistent with the accounting model and uses profits shown on accrual-based financial statements. It is the one evaluation technique that is *not* based on cash flows. The formula to compute the accounting rate of return is

$$ARR = \frac{\text{Average Annual Profits from Project}}{\text{Average Investment in Project}}$$

Investment includes project cost as well as any other costs needed for working capital items (such as inventory) for project support. Investment cost, salvage value, and working capital released at the end of the project's life are summed and divided by two to obtain the average investment.[17]

Information below pertains to a new product line being considered by an electronics retailer. The information is used to illustrate after-tax calculation of the ARR.

Beginning investment:
Initial cost of equipment and fixtures	$40,000
Additional working capital needed for the product line	20,000

Return over life of project:
Average increase in retailing profits after tax	10,000

Return at end of project:
Salvage value of equipment and fixtures in 10 years (end of life of product)	4,000
Working capital released at the end of 10 years	20,000

Solving the formula for the accounting rate of return gives

$$ARR = \$10,000 \div [(\$60,000 + \$24,000) \div 2]$$
$$= \$10,000 \div \$42,000$$
$$= 23.81\%$$

[17] Sometimes ARR is computed using initial cost rather than average investment as the denominator. Such a computation ignores the return of funds at the end of the project life and is less appropriate than the computation shown.

The 23.81 percent ARR on this project can be compared with a preestablished hurdle rate set by management. This hurdle rate may not be the same as the desired discount rate because the data used in calculating the accounting rate of return is not cash flow information. The ARR hurdle rate may be set higher than the discount rate because the discount rate automatically compensates for the time value of money. In addition, the 23.81 percent ARR for this project should be compared with ARRs on other projects under investment consideration by the electronics retailer to see which projects have the higher accounting rates of return.

APPENDIX 3

Measurement of Risk

Risk is inherent in capital budgeting because most factors used in the decision process involve estimates of future occurrences. Capital budgeting risks include variations in estimated asset life, cash flow amounts, timing of cash flows, and expected salvage value of the property at the end of its life. In addition, changes in tax laws or in general economic conditions can render the original estimates obsolete. It is highly unlikely that predictions made before the capital asset's acquisition will occur precisely as forecasted. The best that can be hoped for is that the variability of any or all of the estimates will be minimal.

The life of a capital asset is treated in capital budgeting decisions as an exact number. It would be more realistic to assume that the asset's life is a function of its specific application, level of maintenance performed, and changes in technology. Use of a variety of factors would provide a range of years for asset life rather than a specific period of time. Information about the range of life is useful to managers for planning purposes, but such information is difficult to integrate into the capital budgeting model. Thus, the naive but practical single point (deterministic) estimate of expected years is used.

Cash flows can be seriously affected by changes in depreciation methods or in tax rates. Capital budgeting analysis is most often performed using single point dollar estimates for annual cash flows and for salvage values. This practice disregards the inherent variability in the cash flows, and thus, the risk associated with a project. It would be more useful to prepare a probability distribution of the expected cash flows. A **probability distribution** is a range of possible values for which each value is assigned a likelihood of occurrence.

probability distribution

To illustrate probability distributions, assume that two alternative projects exist for EastBay. Each project requires a $200,000 initial investment. Both projects are expected to produce annual after-tax cash flows of $40,000 for 10 years, assuming continued current economic conditions. The projects appear to be equally desirable; discounting the cash flows at EastBay's 8 percent cost of capital yields a net present value of $68,404 for each project.

Bill Larson, EastBay's chief financial officer, has estimated that the projects will have different annual cash flows if there is a change in economic conditions. Larson's cash flow projections under three economic conditions (rapid expansion, continued conditions, and recession) appear in Exhibit 18–19 with their related probabilities of occurrence.[18] The exhibit also presents each project's total expected value of annual cash flows.

The **total expected value** of annual cash flows for a project is equal to the sum of individual cash flow amounts in a probability distribution multiplied by their re-

total expected value

---

[18] In evaluating the investment, analysis can focus on annual cash flows because all other factors are alike. In more complex project comparisons, analyses of additional factors (such as project life) and, ultimately, the NPV variability need to be considered.

EXHIBIT 18-19

EastBay's Investment
Alternatives—Probability
Distribution

			CASH FLOWS	
Economic Conditions	Percent Probability of Occurrence		Project A	Project B
Rapid expansion	20		$48,000	$60,000
Continued current	70		40,000	40,000
Recession	10		24,000	0

EXPECTED VALUE OF PROJECT A

(1) Cash Flows	(2) Probability of Occurrence	(3) Expected Values (1) × (2)
$48,000	.20	$ 9,600
40,000	.70	28,000
24,000	.10	2,400
Total		$40,000

EXPECTED VALUE OF PROJECT B

(1) Cash Flows	(2) Probability of Occurrence	(3) Expected Values (1) × (2)
$60,000	.20	$12,000
40,000	.70	28,000
0	.10	0
Total		$40,000

lated probabilities. The variability of the annual cash flows for Project A ranges from $24,000 to $48,000, whereas the variability of Project B cash flows extends from $0 to $60,000. This wider range of possible cash flows makes Project B a more risky investment than Project A.

Standard Deviation

standard deviation

One measure used to determined the variability of a probability distribution is the **standard deviation,** the measure of variability of data around the average (or mean) value of a set of data. It has been mathematically determined that any population average plus or minus 1 standard deviation contains approximately 68 percent of the outcomes in a normal distribution. If ± 2 standard deviations are considered, approximately 95 percent of all measurements are encompassed, and if ± 3 standard deviations are used, 99 percent of all measurements are included.

The standard deviation calculation uses expected values and the probabilities assigned to the expectations. The formula for the standard deviation (σ) is

$$\sigma = \sqrt{\sum_{i=1}^{n} [(R_i - \overline{R})^2 P_i]}.$$

where n = number of levels of possible cash flows in the probability distribution; number of economic conditions
    i = indication of the particular condition
    R_i = expected cash flow of condition i
    $\overline{R}$ = average for the cash flows
    P_i = probability for the expected cash flow of condition i

Project A

	R_i	$(\overline{R})$	$(R_i - \overline{R})$	$(R_i - \overline{R})^2$	P_i	$(R_i - \overline{R})^2(P_i)$
Rapid expansion	$48,000	$40,000	$ 8,000	$ 64,000,000	20%	$12,800,000
Continued current	40,000	40,000	0	0	70%	0
Recession	24,000	40,000	-16,000	256,000,000	10%	25,600,000
					$\sigma^2 =$	$38,400,000
					$\sigma =$	$ 6,197

Project B

	R_i	$(\overline{R})$	$(R_i - \overline{R})$	$(R_i - \overline{R})^2$	P_i	$(R_i - \overline{R})^2(P_i)$
Rapid expansion	$60,000	$40,000	$20,000	$ 400,000,000	20%	$ 80,000,000
Continued current	40,000	40,000	0	0	70%	0
Recession	0	40,000	-40,000	1,600,000,000	10%	160,000,000
					$\sigma^2 =$	$240,000,000
					$\sigma =$	$ 15,492

EXHIBIT 18–20

Standard Deviation
Calculations for Projects

Data regarding EastBay's evaluation of Projects A and B are used in Exhibit 18–20 to illustrate the calculation of the standard deviations for the projects. Using information from the columns, the standard deviations for each project are calculated. Project B has a much larger standard deviation than Project A. Because the standard deviation measures variability, the following statements are true: The higher the standard deviation, the higher the variability; the higher the variability of a project, the greater the risk. Thus, calculation of the standard deviation demonstrates that Project B is the more risky of the two projects being considered by EastBay.

Situations may arise where one project has a substantially higher total expected value but the same standard deviation as another project. In these cases, it is reasonable to assume that the project with the lower expected value has the greater risk. The **coefficient of variation** is a useful measure of risk when the standard deviations are approximately the same size on two or more projects but the expected values are significantly different. The coefficient of variation (V) is calculated as

coefficient of variation

$$V = \frac{\sigma}{\overline{R}}$$

where
σ = expected standard deviation
$\overline{R}$ = expected cash flow

The smaller the value of the coefficient of variation, the lower is the project's risk relative to its expected value.

The projects under consideration by EastBay do not need to be analyzed for risk using the coefficient of variation because they have different standard deviations. However, using the data for those projects yields coefficients of variation as follows:

PROJECT A	PROJECT B
$\sigma = \$6,197$	$\sigma = \$15,492$
$\overline{R} = \$40,000$	$\overline{R} = \$40,000$
$V = \sigma \div \overline{R}$	$V = \sigma \div \overline{R}$
$V = \$6,197 \div \$40,000$	$V = \$15,492 \div \$40,000$
$V = .15$	$V = .39$

Project B, which has the higher coefficient of variation, is also the project with the greater risk.

Using standard deviations and coefficients of variation in analyzing capital budgeting projects can help managers assess the risk of a project. This assessment is useful to managers in making judgments about processes such as adjusting the discount rate used in making net present value and profitability index computations or developing a hurdle rate against which to measure the internal rate of return.

KEY TERMS

accounting rate of return (p. 844)
annuity (p. 812)
annuity due (p. 842)
capital asset (p. 807)
capital rationing (p. 833)
cash flow (p. 809)
coefficient of variation (p. 847)
compound interest (p. 842)
compounding period (p. 842)
cost of capital (p. 812)
discount rate (p. 812)
discounting (p. 812)
financing decision (p. 809)
Fisher rate (p. 832)
future value (p. 841)
hurdle rate (p. 818)
independent projects (p. 826)
internal rate of return (p. 816)
investment decision (p. 809)
judgmental method (of risk adjustment) (p. 835)
mutually exclusive projects (p. 826)
mutually inclusive projects (p. 826)
net present value (p. 814)
net present value method (p. 814)

opportunity cost of capital (p. 813)
ordinary annuity (p. 842)
payback period (p. 811)
postinvestment audit (p. 838)
preference decision (p. 825)
present value (p. 812)
probability distribution (p. 845)
profitability index (p. 815)
project (p. 807)
return of capital (p. 813)
return on capital (p. 813)
reinvestment assumption (p. 828)
risk (p. 835)
risk-adjusted discount rate method (p. 835)
screening decision (p. 825)
sensitivity analysis (p. 836)
simple interest (p. 842)
standard deviation (p. 846)
tax benefit (of depreciation) (p. 819)
tax shield (of depreciation) (p. 819)
timeline (p. 811)
total expected value (for a project) (p. 845)

SOLUTION STRATEGIES

Prepare a timeline to illustrate all moments in time when cash flows are expected to occur. The discount rate used to determine PVs should be the cost of capital.

PAYBACK PERIOD

1. For projects with an equal annual cash flow:

$$\text{Payback Period} = \text{Investment} \div \text{Annuity Amount}$$

2. For projects with unequal annual cash flows:
   Sum the annual cash flows until investment is reached to find payback period.

If payback period is equal to or less than a preestablished maximum number of years, the project is acceptable.

NET PRESENT VALUE

– Investment made currently (always valued at a factor of 1.000)
+ PV of future cash inflows or cost savings
– PV of future cash outflows
= NPV

If NPV is equal to or greater than zero, the project is returning a rate equal to or greater than the discount rate and the project is acceptable.

PROFITABILITY INDEX

$+$ PV of future cash inflows or cost savings
$-$ PV of future cash outflows
$=$ PV of net cash flows

$$PI = \frac{PV \text{ of Net Cash Flows}}{PV \text{ of Net Investment}}$$

If PI is 1.00 or greater, the project is returning a rate equal to or greater than the discount rate and it is acceptable.

INTERNAL RATE OF RETURN

1. For projects with equal annual cash flows:

$$PV \text{ Factor} = \frac{Net \text{ Investment}}{Cash \text{ Flow Annuity}}$$

Find the PV factor (or the one closest to it) in the table on the row for the number of periods of the cash flows. The percentage at the top of the column where this factor is found will approximate the IRR. (Note: For projects with equal annual cash flows, this factor is also equal to the payback period.)

2. For projects with unequal annual cash flows:
Make an estimate of rate provided by project; compute NPV. If NPV is positive (negative), try a higher (lower) rate until the NPV is zero.

Compare IRR to the discount or preestablished hurdle rate. If the IRR equals or is greater than the hurdle rate, the project is acceptable.

TAX BENEFIT OF DEPRECIATION = DEPRECIATION AMOUNT × TAX RATE

ACCOUNTING RATE OF RETURN

$$ARR = \frac{Average \text{ Annual Profits from Project}}{Average \text{ Investment in Project}}$$

Average Investment = (Beginning Investment + Recovery of Investment at End of Project Life) ÷ 2

Compare calculated ARR to hurdle ARR. If the calculated ARR is equal to or greater than the hurdle ARR, the project is acceptable.

BASIC CONCEPTS OF CAPITAL BUDGETING TECHNIQUES

	PAYBACK	NPV	PI	IRR	ARR
Uses time value of money?	No	Yes	Yes	Yes	No
Provides a rate of return?	No	No	No	Yes	Yes
Uses cash flows?	Yes	Yes	Yes	Yes	No
Considers returns during life of project?	No	Yes	Yes	Yes	Yes
Discount rate used in calculation?	No	Yes	Yes	No*	No*

*Discount rate is not used in the calculation, but it may be used as the hurdle rate.

MEASURING RISK OF CAPITAL INVESTMENT

STANDARD DEVIATION (σ)

$$\sigma = \sqrt{\sum_{i=1}^{n} [(R_i - \overline{R})^2 P_i]} \, .$$

where   n = number of levels of possible cash flows in the
            probability distribution, or number of conditions
       i = indication of the particular condition
    R_i = expected cash flow of condition i
    $\overline{R}$ = average for the cash flows
    P_i = probability for the expected cash flow of condition i

COEFFICIENT OF VARIATION

$$V = \frac{\sigma}{\overline{R}}$$

where σ = expected standard deviation
         $\overline{R}$ = expected cash flow

DEMONSTRATION PROBLEM

Seiford Wholesaling is considering the purchase of a computerized system to track its delivery trucks and vans. The new system would lower operating costs by coordinating delivery vehicles and drivers to reduce total miles traveled per dollar of revenue. The technology would cost $600,000 and have an expected life of 6 years with an expected salvage value of $50,000 at the end of its life. Near the end of the fourth year, it is anticipated that the communication equipment in the new system would require maintenance by the manufacturer costing $75,000. This amount is fully deductible for tax purposes in the year incurred. Management requires that investments of this type be paid back in 5 years or less. Cost savings are anticipated to be $145,000 in each of the first 4 years, and $100,000 in each of the next 2 years. The company's discount rate is 10 percent; its tax rate is 35 percent; and the equipment would be depreciated for tax purposes using the straight-line method with no consideration of salvage value over a period of 5 years.

Required:

a. Prepare a timeline for displaying cash flows. Be certain to consider the effects of taxes.
b. Calculate the after-tax payback period.
c. Calculate the after-tax net present value on the project.
d. Discuss the appropriateness of making such an investment.

Solution to Demonstration Problem

a.

End of period	0	1	2	3	4	5	6
Investment	− $600,000						
Operating inflows[1]		+ $94,250	+ $94,250	+ $94,250	+ $94,250	+ $65,000	+ $65,000
Depreciation[2]		+ $42,000	+ $42,000	+ $42,000	+ $42,000	+ $42,000	
Operating outflows[3]					− $48,750		
Salvage value[4]							+ $32,500

[1]$145,000 \times (1 - .35) = \$94,250$
$100,000 \times (1 - .35) = \$65,000$
[2]$(\$600,000 \div 5) \times .35 = \$42,000$
[3]$75,000 \times (1 - .35) = \$48,750$
[4]$50,000 \times (1 - .35) = \$32,500$

Note that all proceeds received from the sale of the equipment are taxable because the entire cost of the equipment was depreciated. Expected salvage value is ignored in computing depreciation deductions.

b.

YEAR	ANNUAL FLOW	CUMULATIVE FLOW
0	− $600,000	− $600,000
1	+ 136,250	− 463,750
2	+ 136,250	− 327,500
3	+ 136,250	− 191,250
4	+ 87,500	− 103,750
5	+ 107,000	+ 3,250

The payback is complete in 4.97 years or in the last month of the fifth year. The portion of the fifth year (.97) required to complete the payback is equal to $\$103,750 \div \$107,000$.

c.

YEAR	CASH FLOW	10% PV FACTOR	PV
0	− $600,000	1.0000	− $600,000
1–3	+ 136,250	2.4869	+ 338,840
4	+ 87,500	.6830	+ 59,763
5	+ 107,000	.6209	+ 66,436
6	+ 97,500	.5645	+ 55,039
NPV			− $ 79,922

d. The project is acceptable based on the payback period but fails to qualify based on the NPV criterion. Accordingly, from strictly a financial perspective, the project is not acceptable. However, nonquantitative factors must be considered. These factors may include effects on quality, competitive position, and ability to adopt future technological advances.

QUESTIONS

1. What is a capital asset? How is it distinguished from other assets?
2. Why do firms use multiple criteria in evaluating potential capital investments?
3. Why do capital budgeting evaluation methods use cash flows rather than accounting income?
4. Why are cash flows related to financing not included in evaluating a capital project?
5. Why are timelines helpful in evaluating capital projects?
6. What does the payback method measure? What are its major weaknesses?
7. Why is the time value of money important in capital budgeting? Which evaluation methods use this concept? Which do not?
8. Differentiate between a return of capital and a return on capital.
9. What is the net present value of a potential project? If the net present value of a project equals zero, is it an acceptable project? Explain.
10. Will the NPV amount determined in the capital budgeting process be the same amount as that which actually occurs after a project is undertaken? Why or why not?
11. How is the profitability index related to the NPV method? What does the PI measure?

12. Under what circumstance will the PI exceed 1? Discuss the rationale for your answer.

13. What is measured by the internal rate of return? Under what circumstance is a project considered acceptable using this method?

14. What is the relationship between NPV and internal rate of return? Why does this relationship hold true?

15. Depreciation does not represent a cash flow. Why, then, is it important in capital budgeting evaluation techniques that use discounted cash flows?

16. What is the difference between the tax shield of depreciation and the tax benefit of depreciation?

17. What are four questions that managers should ask in choosing the investment proposals to be funded?

18. How would managers rank projects using each of the following methods: net present value, profitability index, internal rate of return, payback period, and accounting rate of return?

19. Why should managers use several techniques to rank capital projects? Which technique should be used as the primary evaluator?

20. Why does capital rationing exist, and how do managers deal with it in ranking capital projects?

21. How is risk defined in capital budgeting analysis? List several aspects of a project in which risk is involved and how risk can affect the net present value of a project.

22. How is sensitivity analysis used in capital budgeting?

23. Why are postinvestment audits performed? When should they be performed?

24. *(Appendix 1)* What is meant by the term *time value of money?* Why is a present value always less than the future value to which it relates?

25. *(Appendix 1)* How does an annuity differ from a single cash flow?

26. *(Appendix 2)* How is the accounting rate of return computed? How does this rate differ from the discount rate and the internal rate of return?

27. *(Appendix 3)* What is the difference between the standard deviation and the coefficient of variation in measuring risk?

EXERCISES

28. *(Payback period)* Lautenburg Ceramics is considering the purchase of an energy-efficient natural gas kiln. The new kiln would require an initial investment of $250,000 and have an expected life of 10 years. At the end of its life, the kiln would have no value. By installing the new kiln, the firm's annual energy costs would decline by $50,000.
    a. Compute the payback period for this investment (ignore tax).
    b. Assume, now, that the annual cost savings would vary according to the following schedule:

	ANNUAL COST SAVINGS
Years 1–5	$25,000
Years 6–10	50,000

    Compute the payback period under the revised circumstances (ignore tax).

29. *(Payback)* H & H Variety Store is considering a new product line, a flower shop. The new product line would require an investment of $30,000 in equipment and fixtures and $20,000 in working capital. H & H managers expect the following pattern of net cash inflows from the new flower shop over the life of the investment.

YEAR	AMOUNT
1	$11,000
2	14,000
3	16,000
4	18,000
5	15,000
6	14,000
7	12,000

a. Compute the payback period for the proposed flower shop. If H & H requires a 4-year pretax payback on its investments, should it invest in the new product line? Explain.

b. Should H & H use any other capital project evaluation methods before making an investment decision? Explain.

30. *(NPV)* Miami Fish Processing Company is considering the installation of an automated product handling system. The initial cost of such a system would be $200,000. This system would generate labor cost savings over its 10-year life as follows:

YEARS	ANNUAL LABOR COST SAVINGS
1–2	$35,000
3–5	42,500
6–8	43,200
9–10	31,000

The system will have no salvage at the end of its 10-year life, and the company uses a discount rate of 12 percent. What is the pretax net present value of this potential investment?

31. *(NPV)* Georgia Mechanical has been approached by one of its customers about producing 400,000 special-purpose parts for a new farm implement product. The parts would be required at a rate of 50,000 per year for 8 years. To provide these parts, Georgia Mechanical would need to acquire several new production machines. These machines would cost $500,000 in total. The customer has offered to pay Georgia Mechanical $50 per unit for the parts. Managers at Georgia Mechanical have estimated that, in addition to the new machines, the company would incur the following costs to produce each part.

Direct labor	$ 8
Direct materials	10
Variable overhead	4
Total	$22

In addition, annual fixed (out-of-pocket) costs would be $40,000. The new machinery would have no salvage value at the end of its 8-year life. The company uses a discount rate of 8 percent to evaluate capital projects.

a. Compute the net present value of the machine investment (ignore tax).

b. Based on the NPV computed in part a, is the machine a worthwhile investment? Explain.

c. Aside from the NPV, what other factors should Georgia Mechanical's managers consider in making the investment decision?

32. *(PI)* Callihan Carpets is interested in purchasing a computer and software that would allow its salespeople to demonstrate to customers how a finished carpet installation would appear. Managers have estimated the cost of the computer, software, and peripheral equipment to be $12,000. Based on this cost, the managers have determined that the net present value of the investment is $3,000. Compute the profitability index of the investment (ignore tax).

33. *(PI)* The Potomac Transit Authority (PTA) is considering adding a new bus route. To add the route, PTA would be required to purchase a new bus, which would have a life of 10 years and cost $180,000. If the new bus is purchased, PTA managers expect that net cash inflows from bus ridership would rise by $31,000 per year for the life of the bus. The PTA uses a 9 percent required rate of return for evaluating capital projects. No salvage value is expected from the bus at the end of its life.

  a. Compute the profitability index of the bus investment (ignore tax).

  b. Should the PTA buy the new bus?

  c. What is the minimum acceptable value for the profitability index for an investment to be acceptable?

34. *(Multiple methods)* Bubba's Meat Market is considering buying a delivery truck at a cost of $38,000. Presently, Bubba relies on a delivery service to deliver his products to area grocers and restaurants. The truck is expected to last 6 years and have a $5,000 salvage value. Annual operating savings (in delivery costs) are expected to be $10,000 for each of the first 2 years, $8,000 for each of the next 2 years, and $7,000 for the last 2 years. The company's cost of capital is 11 percent and this rate was set as the discount rate.

  a. Calculate the payback period (ignore tax).

  b. Calculate the net present value (ignore tax).

  c. Calculate the profitability index (ignore tax).

35. *(IRR)* Sweetwater Marina is considering adding facilities to provide more services to its marina occupants. The facilities would cost $320,000 and would generate $41,442 annually in new cash inflows. The expected life of the facilities would be 10 years, and there would be no expected salvage value. The firm's cost of capital and discount rate is 11 percent.

  a. Calculate the internal rate of return for the proposed machine (round to the nearest whole percent, ignore tax).

  b. Based on your answer to part a, should the company purchase the machine?

  c. How much annual cash inflow would be required for the project to be minimally acceptable?

36. *(Multiple methods)* Toys for Thoughts is considering purchasing a robot to assemble its simple toys. The robot will cost $1,400,000 and will produce annual labor and quality cost savings of $180,000. The robot is expected to last 12 years and have no salvage value.

  a. What is the payback period (ignore tax)?

  b. If Toys for Thoughts' discount rate is 10 percent, what is the net present value (ignore tax)?

  c. Using a 10 percent discount rate, what is the profitability index (ignore tax)?

  d. What is the internal rate of return (to the nearest .5 percent) (ignore tax)?

37. *(Depreciation)* Texas System Solutions operates consulting offices in three locations in Dallas. The firm is presently considering an investment in a new main frame computer and communication software. The computer would cost $1,000,000 and have an expected life of 8 years. For tax purposes, the computer can be depreciated using the straight-line method over 5 years. No salvage value is recognized in computing depreciation expense and no salvage is expected at the end of the life of the equipment. The company's cost of capital is 10 percent and its tax rate is 35 percent.

  a. Compute the present value of the depreciation tax benefit if the company uses the straight-line depreciation method.

  b. Compute the present value of the depreciation tax benefit assuming the company uses the double declining balance method of depreciation with a five year life.

  c. Why is the depreciation tax benefit computed in part b larger than that computed in part a?

38. *(Alternative depreciation methods; NPV)* New England Papermill Company is considering an investment in a revolutionary new paper-making mill. The mill will cost $20,000,000, have a life of 8 years, and generate annual net before-tax cash flows from operations of $4,200,000. The paper mill will have no value at the end of its 8-year estimated life. New England Papermill's tax rate is 30 percent, and its cost of capital is 8 percent.
   a. If New England Papermill uses straight-line depreciation for tax purposes, is the project acceptable using the net present value method?
   b. Assume the tax law allows the company to take accelerated annual depreciation on this asset in the following manner:

   Years 1–2:   23 percent of cost
   Years 3–8:   9 percent of cost

   What is the net present value of the project? Is it acceptable?
   c. Recompute parts a and b, assuming the tax rate is increased to 50 percent.

39. *(Tax effects of asset sale)* Southwest Industrial purchased a material conveyor system 3 years ago. Now, the company is going to sell the system and acquire more advanced technology. Data relating to this equipment follow:

Market value now	$15,000
Original cost	24,000
Book value now, for tax purposes	8,000
Book value now, for financial accounting purposes	15,000
Corporate tax rate	40%

   a. How much depreciation has been claimed on the conveyor system for tax purposes? For financial accounting purposes?
   b. What will be the after-tax cash flow from the sale of this asset?

40. *(Project ranking)* Two independent potential capital projects are under evaluation by Burdett Company. Project 1 costs $800,000, will last 10 years, and will provide an annual annuity of after-tax cash flows of $170,000. Project 2 will cost $1,200,000, last 10 years, and provide an annual annuity of $220,000 in annual after-tax cash flows.
   a. At what discount rate would management be indifferent between these two projects?
   b. What is this indifference rate called?
   c. If the firm's cost of capital is 10 percent, which project would be ranked higher?

41. *(Uncertain annual cash flow)* Conch and Associates, CPAs, is considering the installation of a voice mail system. The initial cost of the system would be $50,000. The expected life of the technology is 5 years.
   a. Given that the company's cost of capital is 10 percent, how much annual after-tax labor savings are necessary to minimally justify the investment.
   b. Given your answer in part a and the fact that the company's tax rate is 40 percent, how much pretax labor savings are necessary to justify the investment (ignore tax)?

42. *(Uncertain project life)* Caldwell Hydraulic is evaluating a potential investment project that would have an initial cost of $200,000 and will return $75,000 annually for 6 years. The company's cost of capital is 10 percent. Assume that the company is fairly certain regarding the initial cost and the annual return of $75,000, but uncertain as to how many years the $75,000 cash flows will be realized. How many years must the project generate cash flows of $75,000 to be minimally acceptable (ignore tax)?

43. *(Uncertain cash flow; uncertain discount rate)* Quixote Wind Systems manufactures wind-powered electricity generators. The company is considering investing in new technology to allow storage of wind-generated power in batteries. Initial

cost of the technology is expected to be $400,000. The investment is expected to increase after-tax cash flows by $68,000 for 11 years. The company uses its 8 percent cost of capital rate to discount cash flows for purposes of capital budgeting.

a. What is the lowest acceptable annual cash flow that would allow this project to be considered acceptable (ignore tax)?

b. Assume the company is uncertain as to its actual cost of capital. What is the maximum the company's cost of capital could be (rounded to the nearest whole percent) and still allow this project to be considered acceptable (ignore tax)?

44. *(Appendix 1)* You have just invested $10,000 in a bank account that guarantees to pay you 8 percent interest, compounded semiannually. At the end of 5 years, how much money will have accumulated in your investment account (ignore tax)?

45. *(Appendix 1)* You have just purchased a new car. Assume you made a down payment of $5,000 and financed the balance of the purchase cost on an installment credit plan. According to the credit agreement, you agreed to pay $450 per month for a period of 48 months. If the credit agreement was based on a monthly interest rate of 1 percent, what was the cost of the car?

46. *(Appendix 1)* Use the tables in Appendix A to determine the answers to the following questions.

a. Edith Roundtree wishes to have $25,000 in 8 years. She can make an investment today which will earn 7 percent each year, compounded annually. What amount of investment should she make to achieve her goal (ignore tax)?

b. Lillith Frazier is going to receive $100,000 on her fiftieth birthday, 20 years from today. Lillith has the opportunity to invest money today in a government-backed security paying 6 percent, compounded semiannually. How much would she be willing to receive today instead of the $100,000 in 10 years (ignore tax)?

c. Demi Ward has $45,000 today that she intends to use as a down payment on a house. How much money did Demi invest 8 years ago in order to have $45,000 now, if her investment earned 9 percent compounded annually (ignore tax)?

d. Pat Sawhack is the host of a television game show that gives away thousands of dollars each day. One prize on the show is an annuity, paid to the winner, in equal installments of $10,000 at the end of each year for the next 5 years. If the winner has an investment opportunity to earn 5 percent, semiannually, what present amount would the winner take in exchange for the annuity (ignore tax)?

e. Rebecka Howe is going to be paid modeling fees for the next 10 years as follows: year 1, $15,000; year 2, $25,000; year 3, $28,000; years 4–8, $50,000; year 9, $30,000, and year 10, $21,000. Rebecka can invest her money at 6 percent, compounded semiannually. What is the present value of her future modeling fees (ignore tax)?

f. Your friend has just won the lottery. The lottery will pay her $100,000 per year for the next 10 years. If this is the only asset owned by your friend, is she a millionaire (one who has a net worth of $1,000,000 or more)? Explain (ignore tax).

47. *(Appendix 2)* Allison Aftercare operates a rehabilitation center for physically disabled individuals. The company is considering the purchase of a new piece of equipment that costs $750,000, has a life of 5 years, and has no salvage value. The company depreciates its assets on a straight-line basis. The expected annual cash flow on a before-tax basis for this piece of equipment is $250,000. Allison requires that an investment be recouped in less than 5 years and have an accounting rate of return (pretax) of at least 18 percent.

a. Compute the payback period and the accounting rate of return for this piece of equipment (ignore taxes).

b. Is the equipment an acceptable investment for Allison? Explain.

48. *(Appendix 2; comprehensive)* Corner Publishing is evaluating the purchase of a state-of-the-art desktop publishing system that costs $100,000. The company's controller has estimated that the system will generate $32,000 of annual cash receipts for 6 years. At the end of that time, the system will have zero salvage value. The controller also has estimated that cash operating costs will be $4,000 annually. The company's tax rate is expected to be 34 percent during the life of the asset, and the company uses straight-line depreciation.

a. Determine the annual after-tax cash flows from the project.

b. Determine the after-tax payback period for the project.

c. Determine the after-tax accounting rate of return for the project. (Assume tax and financial accounting depreciation are equal.)

49. *(Comprehensive)* Star-O-Rama operates a video arcade in the Hamilton Mall. The owner of Star-O-Rama, Jennifer Shaw, is considering acquiring a new "center-piece" video machine. The cost of the new equipment would be $120,000. The equipment would have an expected life of 4 years and no salvage value. Straight-line depreciation would be used for both financial and tax purposes.

Ms. Shaw expects the new machine to generate an additional $50,000 per year in net, pretax cash flows. The cost of capital and tax rate for Ms. Shaw are 10 percent and 28 percent, respectively.

a. Determine the after-tax cash flows from the new machine.

b. Determine the net present value of the machine.

c. Determine the accounting income of the machine.

d. Determine the accounting rate of return and the payback period on an after-tax basis.

50. *(Appendix 3)* Assume that the following represent probabilities of the range of cash flows for potential Projects 1 and 2:

		CASH FLOWS	
ECONOMIC CONDITION	**PROBABILITY**	**PROJECT 1**	**PROJECT 2**
Strong	.20	$90,000	$95,000
Moderate	.50	70,000	70,000
Weak	.30	40,000	32,500

For each project, calculate

a. the expected value.

b. the standard deviation.

c. the coefficient of variation.

51. *(Technology acquisition)* General Motors recently announced that it was preparing to invest $850 million to update its metal-stamping operations. The new metal-stamping operations will be more flexible and less labor intense. GM's Metal Fabricating Division is expecting to reduce employment of hourly workers by 30,000 and salaried workers by 4,000.

Much of the new investment will be spent on modern transfer presses. Unlike some of GM's older presses, such units can accept different dies, or forms for shaping sheet metal. As Japanese auto makers have proved, such flexible machinery is much more efficient, because it allows an auto maker to alter its production mix to match what's selling and to compensate for breakdowns.

[SOURCE: Rebecca Blumenstein, "GM to Spend $850 Million to Update Its Sheet-Metal Stamping Operations," *Wall Street Journal* (May 21, 1996), p. A12. Reprinted by permission of *The Wall Street Journal*, © 1996 Dow Jones & Company, Inc. All Rights Reserved Worldwide.]

COMMUNICATION ACTIVITIES

a. Assume that the only justification for upgrading the metal-stamping machinery is the labor costs to be saved; also, assume the average pay of the 34,000 workers to be displaced by the upgraded machinery is $25,000. Compute the payback period for the upgrade project (ignore tax).

b. The two major financial dimensions of the upgrade project that are mentioned in the news article are the initial cost of $850 million and the labor cost savings. Prepare a brief oral report in which you identify other cost savings and other costs of the upgrade project.

52. *(Change in investment assumption)* Five Star Linen Supply Company provides laundered items to various commercial and service establishments in a large metropolitan city. Five Star is scheduled to acquire some new cleaning equipment in mid-1997 that should provide some operating efficiencies. The new equipment would enable Five Star to increase the volume of laundry it handles without any increase in labor costs. In addition, the estimated maintenance costs in terms of pounds of laundry would be reduced slightly with the new equipment.

The new equipment was justified on the basis not only of reduced cost but also of expected increase in demand starting in late 1997. However, since the original forecast was prepared, several potential new customers have either delayed or discontinued their own expansion plans in the market area that is serviced by Five Star. The most recent forecast indicates that no great increase in demand can be expected until late 1998 or early 1999.

Identify and explain the factors that Five Star Linen Supply Company should consider in deciding whether to delay the investment in the new cleaning equipment. In the presentation of your response, distinguish between those factors that tend to indicate that the investment should be made as scheduled versus those that tend to indicate that the investment should be delayed.

(CMA)

53. *(Links between short- and long-term operations)* As is the case of Genentech, Inc., drug companies rely on their research activities as the primary source of future revenues and profits. The capital budget is the principal tool used to allocate resources to research activities.

Merck & Co., a giant in the drug industry, recently unveiled a list of its products in early development stages. The products included drugs to treat major maladies such as arthritis and cancer. Analysts who were present at the unveiling were unimpressed. Some of the analysts commented that it is not Merck's long-term prospects that are in question; rather, "its short-term pipeline contains no clear breakthroughs. That poses potential problems for the bottom line, because the company's core products—cardiovascular drugs—face increasing competition, and several new drugs have fallen short of expectations."

[SOURCE: Robert Langreth, "Drug Pipeline at Merck Gets Weak Review," *Wall Street Journal* (May 22, 1996), p. B6. Reprinted by permission of *The Wall Street Journal*, © 1996 Dow Jones & Company, Inc. All Rights Reserved Worldwide.]

Prepare a written report in which you explain how short-term operations and plans are linked to long-term operations and plans. This report should be directed at an audience that is expected to have little knowledge of formal business planning systems. The major point to be explained in your report is why stock analysts would meet Merck's announcement of an aggressive R&D program with apathy because success of current operations is marginal.

PROBLEMS

54. *(Timeline; payback; NPV)* Lola of Lola's General Store is considering leasing an adjoining building to stock additional merchandise for travelers and tourists. The owner of the building has offered Lola an 8-year lease. Lola anticipates that upfront repairs and improvements costing $60,000 would be necessary to make the building suitable for her purposes. Although Lola would need to invest in

additional inventory, her suppliers are willing to provide inventory on a consignment basis. Annual incremental fixed cash costs (including the cost of the lease) of the facility are expected to be as follows:

YEAR	AMOUNT
1	$3,700
2	4,800
3	4,800
4	4,800
5	5,300
6	6,300
7	6,500
8	7,500

Lola estimates that annual cash inflows could be increased by $80,000 from the additional merchandise sales. The firm's contribution margin is typically 20 percent of sales. At the end of the lease, Lola would not be entitled to any payment for improvements she makes to the building. The firm uses a 9 percent discount rate.
a. Construct a timeline for the building lease.
b. Determine the payback period (ignore tax).
c. Calculate the net present value of the project (ignore tax).

55. *(Timeline; payback; NPV)* Dudley's Delivery Service is considering the purchase of a new van to replace an existing truck. The van would cost $25,000 and would have a life of 8 years with no salvage value at that time. The truck could be sold currently for $3,000; alternatively, if it is kept, it will have a remaining life of 8 years with no salvage value. By purchasing the van, Dudley's would anticipate operating cost savings as follows.

YEAR	AMOUNT
1	$3,700
2	3,800
3	4,000
4	5,000
5	5,000
6	5,100
7	5,200
8	5,500

Dudley's cost of capital and capital project evaluation rate is 11 percent.
a. Construct a timeline for the purchase of the van.
b. Determine the payback period (ignore tax).
c. Calculate the net present value of the van (ignore tax).

56. *(Payback; IRR)* Excel Tax Service prepares tax returns for individuals and small businesses. The firm employs four professional people in the tax practice. Currently, all tax returns are prepared on a manual basis. The firm's owner, Joseph Harraba, is considering purchasing a computer system that would allow the firm to service all its existing clients with the use of only three employees. To evaluate the feasibility of the computerized system, Joseph has gathered the following information:

Initial cost of the hardware and software	$45,000
Expected salvage value in 4 years	0
Annual depreciation	10,000
Annual operating costs	6,500
Annual labor savings	23,000
Expected life of the computer system	4 years

Joseph has determined that he will invest in the computer system if its pretax payback is less than 3.5 years and its pretax IRR exceeds 12 percent.

   a. Compute the payback period for this investment. Does the payback meet Joseph's criterion? Explain.

   b. Compute the IRR for this project to the nearest .5 percent. Based on the computed IRR, is this project acceptable to Joseph?

57. *(NPV; PI)* Dallas Warehousing provides storage services for industrial firms. Usual items stored include records, inventory, and waste items. The company is evaluating more efficient methods of moving inventory items into and out of storage areas. One vendor has proposed to sell Dallas Warehousing a conveyor system that would offer high-speed routing of inventory items. The required equipment would have an initial cost of $2,500,000 including installation. The vendor has indicated that the machinery would have an expected life of 7 years, with an estimated salvage value of $200,000. Below are estimates of the annual labor savings as well as the additional costs associated with the operation of the new equipment:

Annual labor cost savings (14 workers)	$465,000
Annual maintenance costs	20,000
Annual property taxes	14,000
Annual insurance costs	22,000

   a. Assuming the company's cost of capital is 9 percent, compute the NPV of the investment in the conveyor equipment (ignore tax).

   b. Based on the NPV, should the company invest in the new machinery?

   c. Compute the profitability index for this potential investment (ignore tax).

   d. What other factors should the company consider in evaluating this investment?

58. *(NPV; PI; payback; IRR)* Bill Ward Construction Company provides custom paving of sidewalks and driveways for residential and commercial customers. One of the most labor-intensive aspects of the paving operation is the preparation and mixing of materials. Paul Wilson, corporate engineer, has learned of a new computerized technology to mix (and monitor mixing of) materials. According to information received by Mr. Wilson, the cost of the required equipment would be $840,000, and the equipment would have an expected life of 7 years. If purchased, the new equipment would replace manually operated equipment. Data relating to the old and new mixing equipment follow.

OLD TECHNOLOGY:

Original cost new	$ 75,000
Present book value	32,000
Annual cash operating costs	220,000
Current market value	12,000
Market value in 7 years	0
Remaining useful life	7 years

NEW TECHNOLOGY:

Cost	$840,000
Annual cash operating costs	40,000
Market value in 7 years	0
Useful life	7 years

   a. Assume that the cost of capital in this company is 12 percent, which is the rate to be used in a discounted cash flow analysis. Compute the net present value and profitability index of investing in the new machine. Ignore taxes. Should the machine be purchased? Why or why not?

   b. Compute the payback period for the investment in the new machine. Ignore taxes.

   c. Rounding to the nearest whole percentage, compute the internal rate of return for the new technology investment.

59. *(NPV; taxes)* The manager of Bayou Cold Storage is considering the installation of a new refrigerated storage room. She has learned that the installation would require an initial cash outlay of $520,000. The installation would have an expected life of 20 years with no salvage value. The installation would increase annual labor and maintenance costs by $37,000. The firm's cost of capital is estimated to be 9 percent, and its tax rate is 30 percent. The storage room is expected to generate net annual cash revenues (before tax, labor, and maintenance costs) of $85,000.

    a. Using straight-line depreciation, calculate the after-tax net present value of the storage room.

    b. Based on your answer to part a, is this investment financially acceptable? Explain?

60. *(After-tax cash flows; payback; NPV; PI; IRR)* Ludwig Fashions is considering the purchase of computerized clothes designing software. The software is expected to cost $125,000, have a useful life of 5 years, and have a zero salvage value at the end of its useful life. Assume tax regulations permit the following depreciation patterns for this asset

YEAR	PERCENT DEDUCTIBLE
1	20
2	32
3	19
4	15
5	14

    The company's tax rate is 30 percent, and its cost of capital is 8 percent. The software is expected to generate the following cash savings and cash expenses:

YEAR	CASH SAVINGS	CASH EXPENSES
1	$40,000	$ 5,000
2	55,000	5,000
3	60,000	10,000
4	50,000	5,000
5	40,000	3,000

    a. Prepare a timeline presenting the after-tax operating cash flows.

    b. Determine the following on an after-tax basis: payback period, net present value, profitability index, and internal rate of return.

61. *(NPV; project ranking; risk)* Arkansas Financial Consultants is expanding operations, and the firm's president, Ms. Hillary Rose, is trying to make a decision about new office space. The following are Ms. Rose's options:

Maple Commercial Plaza:	5,000 square feet; cost, $800,000; useful life, 10 years; salvage, $400,000
High Tower:	20,000 square feet; cost, $3,400,000; useful life, 10 years; salvage, $1,500,000

    If the Maple Commercial Plaza is purchased, the company will occupy all of the space. If High Tower is purchased, the extra space will be rented for $620,000 per year. If purchased, either building will be depreciated on a straight-line basis. For tax purposes, the buildings would be depreciated assuming a 25-year life. By purchasing either building, the company will save $210,000 annually in rental payments. All other costs of the two purchases (such as land cost) are expected to be the same. The firm's tax rate is 40 percent.

    a. Determine the before-tax net cash flows from each project for each year.

    b. Determine the after-tax cash flows from each project for each year.

c. Determine the net present value for each project if the cost of capital for Arkansas Financial Consultants is 11 percent. Which purchase is the better investment based on the NPV method?

d. Ms. Rose is concerned about the ability to rent the excess space in High Tower for the 10-year period. To compute the NPV for that portion of the project's cash flows, she has decided to use a discount rate of 20 percent to compensate for risk. Compute the NPV and determine which investment is more acceptable.

 62. *(NPV; PI; IRR; Fisher rate)* Howard Marley Investments, which has a weighted average cost of capital of 12 percent, is evaluating two mutually exclusive projects (A and B), which have the following projections:

	PROJECT A	PROJECT B
Investment	$48,000	$80,000
After-tax cash flows	$12,800	$15,200
Asset life	6 years	10 years

a. Determine the net present value, profitability index, and internal rate of return for Projects A and B.

b. Using the answers to part a, which is the more acceptable project? Why?

c. What is the Fisher rate for the two projects?

63. *(Capital rationing)* Following are the capital projects being considered by the management of Hollywood Productions:

PROJECT	COST	ANNUAL AFTER-TAX CASH FLOWS	NUMBER OF YEARS
Film studios	$36,000,000	$5,600,000	15
Cameras and equipment	6,400,000	1,600,000	8
Land investment	10,000,000	2,360,000	10
Motion picture #1	35,600,000	9,940,000	5
Motion picture #2	22,800,000	7,840,000	4
Motion picture #3	15,600,000	4,200,000	7
Corporate aircraft	4,800,000	1,540,000	5

Assume that all projects have no salvage value and that the firm uses a discount rate of 10 percent. Company management has decided that only $50,000,000 can be spent in the current year for capital projects.

a. Determine the net present value, profitability index, and internal rate of return for each of the seven projects.

b. Rank the seven projects according to each method used in part a.

c. Indicate how you would suggest to the management of Hollywood Productions that the money be spent. What would be the total net present value of your selected investments?

64. *(Sensitivity analysis)* A 50-room motel is for sale in Houston and is being considered by the Lone Star Motel Chain as an investment. The current owners indicate that the occupancy of the motel averages 80 percent each day of the year that the motel is open. The motel is open 300 days per year. Each room rents for $75 per day, and variable cash operating costs are $10 per day that the room is occupied. Fixed annual cash operating costs are $100,000.

An acquisition price of $2,000,000 is being offered by Lone Star. The chain plans on keeping the motel for 14 years and then disposing of it. Because the market for motels is so difficult to predict, Lone Star estimates the salvage value to be zero at the time of disposal. Depreciation will be taken on a straight-line basis for tax purposes. In making the following computations, assume that there will be no tax consequences of the sale in 14 years. The chain's tax rate is estimated at 35 percent for all years.

a. Determine the after-tax net present value of the motel to Lone Star, assuming a cost of capital rate of 13 percent.

b. What is the highest level that the discount rate can be and still allow this project to be considered acceptable by Lone Star? If this discount rate exceeds the highest rate shown in the table (20 percent), simply state this fact and provide supporting computations and reasons.

c. How small can the net after-tax cash flows be and still allow the project to be considered acceptable by Lone Star, assuming a cost of capital rate of 13 percent?

d. What is the shortest number of years for which the net after-tax cash flows can be received and still have the project be considered acceptable?

e. Assume that the answer to part c is $217,425. If all costs remain as they are currently stated and the motel continues to stay open 300 days per year, approximately how many rooms would have to be rented each night to achieve this level of cash flows?

65. (*Postinvestment audit*) Ten years ago, based on a before-tax NPV analysis, Midwestern Industrial decided to add a new product line. The data used in the analysis were as follows:

Discount rate	12%
Life of product line	10 years
Annual sales increase:	
Years 1–4	$250,000
Years 5–8	350,000
Years 9–10	200,000
Annual fixed cash costs	$ 40,000
Contribution margin ratio	40%
Cost of production equipment	$250,000
Investment in working capital	20,000
Salvage value	0

As the product line was discontinued this year, corporate managers decided to conduct a postinvestment audit to assess the accuracy of their planning process. Accordingly, the actual cash flows generated from the product line were estimated to be as follows:

Actual investment:	
Production equipment	$240,000
Working capital	35,000
Total	$275,000
Actual:	
Years 1–4	$220,000
Years 5–8	400,000
Years 9–10	210,000
Actual fixed cash costs:	
Years 1–4	$ 30,000
Years 5–8	35,000
Years 9–10	50,000
Actual contribution margin ratio	35%
Actual salvage value	$ 10,000
Actual cost of capital	12%

a. Determine the projected NPV on the product line investment.

b. Determine the NPV of the project based on the postinvestment audit.

c. Identify the factors that are most responsible for the differences between the projected NPV and the postinvestment audit NPV.

66. *(Appendix 2; payback; NPV)* Fullerton Department Stores is a growing business that is presently considering adding a new product line. The firm would be required by the manufacturer to incur setup costs of $800,000 to handle the new product line. Fullerton has estimated that the product line would have an expected life of 8 years. Following is a schedule of revenues and annual fixed operating expenses (including $100,000 of annual depreciation on the investment) associated with the new product line. Variable costs are estimated to average 65 percent of revenues. All revenues are collected as earned. All expenses shown, except for the included amount of straight-line depreciation, are paid in cash when incurred.

YEAR	REVENUES	EXPENSES
1	$360,000	$180,000
2	400,000	160,000
3	480,000	160,000
4	640,000	180,000
5	800,000	160,000
6	800,000	160,000
7	560,000	160,000
8	340,000	140,000

The company has a cost of capital of 12 percent. Management uses this rate in discounting cash flows for evaluating capital projects.
a. Calculate the accounting rate of return (ignore tax).
b. Calculate the payback period (ignore tax).
c. Calculate the net present value (ignore tax).

67. *(Comprehensive; Appendix 2)* The management of Westlake Manufacturing Company is evaluating a proposal to purchase a new turning lathe as a replacement for a less efficient piece of similar equipment that would then be sold. The cost of the new lathe including delivery and installation is $175,000. If the equipment is purchased, Westlake will incur $5,000 of costs in removing the present equipment and revamping service facilities. The present equipment has a book value of $100,000 and a remaining useful life of 10 years. Due to new technical improvements that have made the equipment outmoded, it presently has a resale value of only $40,000.

Management has provided you with the following comparative manufacturing cost tabulation:

	PRESENT EQUIPMENT	NEW EQUIPMENT
Annual production in units	400,000	500,000
Cash revenue from each unit	$.30	$.30
Annual costs:		
Labor	$30,000	$25,000
Depreciation (10% of asset		
book value or cost)	10,000	17,500
Other cash operating costs	48,000	20,000

Management believes that if the equipment is not replaced now, the company must wait 7 years before replacement is justified. The company uses a 15 percent discount or hurdle rate in evaluating capital projects and expects all capital project investments to recoup their costs within 5 years.

Both pieces of equipment are expected to have a negligible salvage value at the end of 10 years.
a. Determine the net present value of the new equipment (ignore tax).
b. Determine the internal rate of return on the new equipment (ignore tax).
c. Determine the payback period for the new equipment (ignore tax).
d. Determine the accounting rate of return for the new equipment (ignore tax).
e. Using an incremental approach, determine whether the company should keep the present equipment or purchase the new.

68. *(Appendix 3)* Manhattan Office Systems is comparing two projects (X and Y), each of which requires investments of $80,000, produces expected after-tax annual cash flows of $18,000, and will last 9 years. Discounting the expected cash flows at 9 percent, the company's cost of capital yields the same net present value for each project.

Corporate president, Bill Henson, believes, however, that the levels of annual cash inflows each year will differ between the two projects depending on economic conditions. He constructed the following schedule to reflect his assessment of cash flows under various conditions:

	PERCENT	CASH FLOWS FROM	
	PROBABILITY		
ECONOMIC CONDITION	OF OCCURRENCE	PROJECT M	PROJECT N
Rapid expansion	15	$40,000	$32,000
Continued current	60	20,000	24,000
Recession	25	8,000	3,200
Expected value		20,000	20,000

a. Calculate the standard deviation of the range of cash flows for each project.
b. Calculate the coefficient of variation for each project.
c. Discuss which project is more desirable and provide reasons for your choice.

69. *(Probabilities; Appendix 3)* Gulf Coast Marine Company is comparing the investment profiles of two projects. The first project is a shrimp boat that costs $500,000 and provides net annual after-tax cash flows of $80,000. The life of the boat is 10 years. The second project is an $850,000 yacht that can be rented to corporate executives for meetings and parties. The yacht has a useful life of 8 years and is expected to produce annual after-tax cash flows of $165,000. Gulf Coast Marine Company uses a cost of capital rate of 11 percent to determine net present values.

a. Using an incremental approach, determine which of the two investments is the better choice for Gulf Coast Marine.
b. If the returns from the yacht are expected to be only $150,000 each year for 8 years, which is the better project?
c. The returns of each project are probabilistic. The probabilities are related to how well or how poorly the oil business does. If the oil business "booms," people will have more money, the selling price of shrimp will rise, and the yacht will be rented more often. Below are probabilities associated with changes in the oil business and how those changes will affect the returns from the projects:

	PERCENT	CASH	CASH
CONDITION	PROBABILITY	FLOWS—BOAT	FLOWS—YACHT
"Boom"	10	$95,000	$185,000
Continued as is	80	80,000	165,000
"Depressed"	10	70,000	120,000

What is the total expected value for each project?
d. Using the expected value from part c, compute the standard deviation and the coefficient of variation for the two projects.

70. *(NPV)* Michigan Motor Company is considering a proposal to acquire new manufacturing equipment. The new equipment has the same capacity as the current equipment but will provide operating efficiencies in direct and indirect labor, direct material usage, indirect supplies, and power. Consequently, the savings in operating costs are estimated to be $150,000 annually.

CASES

The new equipment will cost $300,000 and will be purchased at the beginning of the year when the project is started. The equipment dealer is certain that the equipment will be operational during the second quarter of the year it is installed. Therefore, 60 percent of the estimated annual savings can be obtained in the first year. Michigan Motor will incur a one-time expense of $30,000 to transfer the production activities from the old equipment to the new equipment. No loss of sales will occur, however, because the plant is large enough to install the new equipment without disrupting operations of the current equipment. The equipment dealer states that most companies use a 5-year life when depreciating this equipment.

The current equipment has been fully depreciated and is carried in the accounts at zero book value. Management has reviewed the condition of the current equipment and has concluded that it can be used an additional 5 years. Michigan Motor would receive $5,000 net of removal costs if it elected to buy the new equipment and dispose of its current equipment at this time.

Michigan Motor currently leases its manufacturing plant. The annual lease payments are $60,000. The lease, which will have 4 years remaining when the equipment installation would begin, is not renewable. Michigan Motor would be required to remove any equipment in the plant at the end of the lease. The cost of equipment removal is expected to equal the salvage value of either the old or the new equipment at the time of removal.

The company uses the sum-of-the-years' digits depreciation method for tax purposes. A full-year's depreciation is taken in the first year an asset is put into use.

The company is subject to a 40 percent income tax rate and requires an after-tax return of at least 12 percent on an investment.

a. Calculate the annual incremental after-tax cash flows for Michigan Motor Company's proposal to acquire the new manufacturing equipment.

b. Calculate the net present value of Michigan Motor's proposal to acquire the new manufacturing equipment using the cash flows calculated in part a and indicate what action Michigan Motor's management should take. Assume all recurring cash flows occur at the end of the year.

(CMA)

71. *(Postinvestment audit)* Smyth Brothers Inc. has formal policies and procedures to screen and approve capital projects. Proposed capital projects are classified as one of the following types:

1. Expansion requiring new plant and equipment
2. Expansion by replacement of present equipment with more productive equipment
3. Replacement of old equipment with new equipment of similar quality

All expansion projects and replacement projects that will cost more than $50,000 must be submitted to the top management capital investment committee for approval. The investment committee evaluates proposed projects considering the costs and benefits outlined in the supporting proposal and the long-range effects on the company.

The projected revenue and/or expense effects of the projects, once operational, are included in the proposal. Once a project is accepted, the committee approves an expenditure budget for the project from its inception until it becomes operational. The expenditures required each year for the expansions or replacements are also incorporated into Smyth Brothers's annual budget procedure. The budgeted revenue and/or cost effects of the projects, for the periods in which they become operational, are incorporated into the 5-year forecast.

Smyth Brothers Inc. does not have a procedure for evaluating projects once they have been implemented and become operational. The vice-president of finance has recommended that Smyth Brothers establish a postcompletion audit program to evaluate its capital expenditure projects.

a. Discuss the benefits a company could derive from a postcompletion audit program for capital expenditure projects.

b. Discuss the practical difficulties in collecting and accumulating information that would be used to evaluate a capital project once it becomes operational.

(CMA)

72. *(Multiple methods)* Southwest Products Inc. is considering the various benefits that may result from shortening the development stage of its products' life cycles by changing from the company's present manual system to a computer-aided manufacturing (CAD/CAM) system. The proposed system can provide productive time equivalent to the 20,000 hours currently available with the manual system. The incremental, annual out-of-pocket costs of maintaining the manual system are $20 per hour.

The incremental, annual out-of-pocket costs of maintaining the CAD/CAM system are estimated to be $200,000 with an initial investment of $580,000 in the proposed system. The estimated useful life of this system is 6 years. Southwest Products requires a minimum rate of return of 20 percent on projects of this type. Full capacity will be utilized.

a. Compute the relevant annual after-tax cash flows related to the CAD/CAM project.

b. Based on the computation in part a, compute the payback period, internal rate of return (round to the nearest .5 percent), net present value, and profitability index.

c. Based on the company's investment evaluation criterion, is the project acceptable? Explain.

(CMA)

---

73. In February 1996, the German firm, Jos. L. Meyer GmbH was negotiating for the right to build ships in the United States.

ETHICS AND QUALITY DISCUSSION

The family-owned German shipbuilder, which specializes in cruise ships, gas tankers and other complex, labor-intensive vessels would employ as many as 2,000 workers at the U.S. shipyard where wages and benefit rates would be significantly lower than in Germany.

Under the plan being negotiated, Meyer Werft (as the company is known) would invest $60 million in the Philadelphia yard and seek additional private and public funding of about $300 million. The money would be used to enclose one of the yard's huge drydocks, and to fund worker retraining and facility improvements.

[SOURCE: Daniel Machalaba, "Germany's Meyer Werft Seeks to Build Ships at Philadelphia's Naval Yard," *Wall Street Journal* (February 16, 1996), p. A4. Reprinted by permission of *The Wall Street Journal*, © 1996 Dow Jones & Company, Inc. All Rights Reserved Worldwide.]

a. For labor-intensive operations, such as shipbuilding, how would labor quality considerations affect capital budgeting (and location) decisions of firms with global operations?

b. In addition to labor rates, what other factors might be considered in global firms' location decisions for new capital investment?

74. In the United States, companies generally respond to economic downturns by reducing spending on capital projects. A frequently observed strategy is to delay investment in new capital projects and products and to cut spending on research and development activities, advertising, and customer-service activities.

a. In economic downturns how can companies cut costs and activities without affecting quality or service?

b. What are the likely effects of short-term cost cutting strategies such as those outlined above on long-term profitability and quality control?

75. *Dial Corp., a onetime bus company that now sells everything from soap to nuts, said it will separate into consumer products and services concerns, splitting a company with about $3 billion in current stock market value.*

The Phoenix-based company's consumer businesses, with revenue last year of about $1.3 billion, will continue to operate under the Dial name. Its diverse airline-catering, convention, travel and money-order businesses, among others, will operate as a separate, as-yet-unnamed unit that last year had revenue of about $2.2 billion.

Dial joins a host of U.S. companies that have decided that the sum of the parts is worth more than the whole. Companies that have announced or completed spinoffs include AT&T Corp., ITT Corp., Minnesota Mining & Manufacturing Co., Dun & Bradstreet Corp., and Melville Corp. The stocks of companies that announce spinoffs outperform the overall stock market, according to a J.P. Morgan & Co. study.

[SOURCE: Steven Lipin, "Dial to Split Into Two Companies," *Wall Street Journal* (February 16, 1996), p. A3. Reprinted by permission of *The Wall Street Journal*, © 1996 Dow Jones & Company, Inc. All Rights Reserved Worldwide.]

a. The conglomerate form of business is perhaps the most difficult to manage in terms of directing new capital investments. Spin-offs can be likened to "undoing" a prior capital investment in a business. What ethical obligation do managers of conglomerates have to stockholders in the event that a higher stock price could be obtained if a business was spun-off rather than held?

b. What obligation do managers have to employees who are affected by spin-offs?

76. The Fore Corporation has operations in over two dozen countries. Fore's headquarters is in Chicago, and company executives frequently travel to visit Fore's foreign and domestic operations.

Fore owns two business jets with international range and six smaller aircraft for shorter flights. Company policy is to assign aircraft to trips based on cost minimization, but its practice is to assign aircraft based on organizational rank of the traveler. Fore offers its aircraft for short-term lease or for charter by other organizations whenever Fore employees do not plan to use the aircraft. Fore surveys the market often to keep its lease and charter rates competitive.

William Earle, Fore's vice-president of finance, claims that a third business jet can be justified financially. However, some people in the Controller's office think the real reason Earle wants a third business jet is that people outranking Earle keep the two business jets busy. Thus, Earle usually must travel in the smaller aircraft.

The third business jet would cost $11 million. A capital expenditure of this magnitude requires a formal proposal with projected cash flows and net present value computations using Fore's minimum required rate of return. If Fore's president and finance committee approve the proposal, it will be submitted to the full board. The board has final approval on capital expenditures exceeding $5 million and has established a policy of rejecting any discretionary proposal that has a negative net present value.

Earle asked Rachel Arnett, assistant corporate controller, to prepare a proposal on a third business jet. Arnett gathered the following information:
- Acquisition cost of the jet, including instrumentation and interior furnishings.
- Operating cost of the jet for company use.
- Projected avoidable commercial airfare and other avoidable costs from company use of the plane.
- Projected value of executive time saved by using the third business jet.
- Projected contribution margin from incremental lease and charter activity.
- Estimated resale value of the jet.
- Estimated income tax effects of the proposal.

When Earle reviewed Arnett's completed proposal and saw the large negative net present value figure, he returned the proposal to Arnett and insisted she had made an error in her calculations.

Feeling some pressure, Arnett checked her computations and found no errors. However, Earle's message was clear. Arnett discarded her projections and estimates and replaced them with figures that had a remote chance of actually occurring but were more favorable to the proposal. For example, she used first-class airfares to refigure the avoidable commercial airfare costs, even though the company policy is to fly coach. She found revising the proposal to be distressing.

The revised proposal still had a negative net present value. Earle's anger was evident as he told Arnett to revise the proposal again and to start with a $100,000 positive net present value and work backward to compute supporting estimates and projections.

a. Explain whether Rachel Arnett's revision of the proposal was in violation of the Standards of Ethical Conduct for Management Accountants. (Refer back to Chapter 1.)

b. Was William Earle in violation of the Standards of Ethical Conduct for Management Accountants by telling Arnett specifically to revise the proposal? Explain your answer.

c. What elements of the projection and estimation process would be compromised in preparing an analysis for which a preconceived result is sought?

d. Identify specific controls over the capital budgeting process that Fore Corporation could implement to prevent unethical behavior on the part of the vice-president of finance.

(CMA)

INTERNET ACTIVITIES

77. Find the home page of the Institute of Management Accountants (IMA). From the home page, locate articles addressing the processes of budgeting. Among these materials is a discussion of the master budget and its component budgets including the capital budget. Read these materials and write a summary of how the capital budget affects, and is affected by, the other budgets that comprise the master budget.

78. Exhibit 18–2 presents a summary of the products that Genentech, Inc. has under development. Find the Internet home page of Genentech. From the home page find the most recent annual financial report of the company. Review the annual report and find the discussion of products under development. Prepare an oral report in which you discuss what has happened to the products appearing in Exhibit 18–2. Be sure to address the amount of sales currently derived from these products. Also, identify any products that are now under development that were not presented in Exhibit 18–2.

79. Several of the capital budgeting techniques presented in this chapter depend on discounted cash flow concepts. These concepts are applied in business in a variety of settings. Charter Mortgage Investment Corporation is a firm that has developed services that rely directly on discounted cash flow analysis. Find this company's home page and prepare an oral presentation in which you discuss the services offered by this firm and how the services utilize concepts of discounted cash flow analysis.

CHAPTER

19

Responsibility Accounting and Transfer Pricing in Decentralized Organizations

LEARNING OBJECTIVES

After completing this chapter, you should be able to answer these questions:

1. Why is decentralization appropriate for some companies but not for others?

2. How are responsibility accounting and decentralization related?

3. What are the differences among the four types of responsibility centers?

4. Why are transfer prices for products used in organizations?

5. What are the advantages and disadvantages of each type of transfer price?

6. How can multinational companies use transfer prices?

Entergy Corporation

In the early 1990s, Entergy Corporation stepped out on its way to becoming a major force in the evolving electric energy industry. It is one of the larger investor-owned public utility holding companies in the United States and is the leading electricity supplier in the Middle South Region through its operating companies in Arkansas, Louisiana, and Mississippi.

Entergy Corporation's nonregulated businesses fall into two broad categories: power development and new technology related to the utility business. The company has investments in Argentina's and Pakistan's electric energy infrastructures and is also pursuing additional projects in Central America, South America, Europe, and Asia.

Entergy's core retail utility business is organized along functional lines. A fossil group manages all aspects of generation at the company's 88 fossil-fueled units. A nuclear group manages Entergy's five nuclear units. An operations group manages the transmission and distribution of electricity, as well as customer service. By organizing along functional rather than geographical lines, Entergy has been able to perform as a single, efficient company.

In the area of energy services, the company has a subsidiary, Entergy Systems and Services, Inc., focused on providing energy-efficient lighting, heating, ventilation, air-conditioning, and refrigeration systems. Entergy also has a pilot project with First Pacific Networks, Inc., for the development of a "smart" telecommunications switching technology that would enable customers to program appliances for cost-efficient energy uses, and ultimately, to control all kinds of telecommunications coming into their homes or businesses.

Entergy management is working to create shareholder value by expanding into regulated and nonregulated-but-related businesses and improving operating and financial activities by decreasing costs, increasing revenues, redeploying cash, and reducing the cost of capital. Such ambitious diversification requires considerable decentralization and use of responsibility accounting so that corporate headquarters can be assured that Entergy is providing high quality and continuous improvement for its customers and its shareholders.

SOURCES: Entergy Corporation, *1992 Annual Report*, pp. Cover, 3, and 5; and Entergy Corporation, *1994 Annual Report*, pp. 14 and 28.

A n organization's structure evolves as its goals, technology, and employees change, and the progression is typically from highly centralized to highly decentralized. When the majority of authority is retained by top management, centralization exists. Decentralization refers to top management's downward delegation of decision-making authority to subunit managers. Entergy recognizes the need for decentralization in its corporate structure because the company's global operations demand that local managers be able to most effectively use corporate resources.

This chapter describes the degree to which top managers delegate authority to subordinate managers and the accounting methods (responsibility accounting and transfer pricing) that are appropriate in decentralized organizations.

Hewlett-Packard operates in a very decentralized manner. Such a structure allows individual business units and teams considerable autonomy to define and pursue business opportunities more creatively than would be possible under centralization.

DECENTRALIZATION

The degree of centralization reflects a chain of command, authority and responsibility relationships, and decision-making capabilities, and can be viewed as a continuum. In a completely centralized firm, a single individual (usually the company owner or president) performs all major decision making and retains full authority and responsibility for that organization's activities.

Alternatively, a purely decentralized organization would have virtually no central authority, and each subunit would act as a totally independent entity. Either end of the continuum represents a clearly undesirable arrangement. In the totally centralized company, the single individual may have neither the expertise nor sufficient and timely information to make effective decisions in all areas. In the totally decentralized firm, subunits may act in ways that are inconsistent with the organization's goals. Each of these possibilities was recognized by Johnson & Johnson in the management of its 160 almost wholly autonomous businesses operating in 50 countries. Although decentralization gives managers a sense of ownership and control and the ability to act on information more quickly, in the words of Johnson & Johnson's chairman, Ralph Larsen, "The glue that binds this company together" is an ethical code of conduct—which Johnson & Johnson dubs its "credo"—that is literally set in stone at the company's headquarters.[1]

Each organization tends to structure itself in light of pure centralization versus pure decentralization factors presented in Exhibit 19–1. Most businesses are, to some extent, somewhere in the middle part of the continuum because of practical necessity. The combination of managers' personal characteristics, the nature of decisions required for organizational growth, and the nature of organizational activities lead a

[1] "Dusting the Opposition," *The Economist* (April 29, 1995), p. 71.

EXHIBIT 19-1

Degree of Decentralization
in an Organizational
Structure

FACTOR	CONTINUUM	
	Pure Centralization ⟶	Pure Decentralization
Age of firm	Young ⟶	Mature
Size of firm	Small ⟶	Large
Stage of product development	Stable ⟶	Growth
Growth rate of firm	Slow ⟶	Rapid
Expected impact on profits of incorrect decisions	High ⟶	Low
Top management's confidence in subordinates	Low ⟶	High
Historical degree of control in firm	Tight ⟶	Moderate or loose

company to find the appropriate degree of decentralization. To be more responsive to market needs, Hewlett-Packard recently decentralized, as reflected in the News Note "Giant Goes from Stodgy to Nimble."

Decentralization does not necessarily mean that a unit manager has the authority to make all decisions concerning that unit. Top management selectively determines the types of authority to delegate and the types to withhold. For example, after Alcoa implemented a major reorganization program to decentralize in 1991, Chairman Paul H. O'Neill still viewed safety, environmental matters, quality, insurance, and infor-

VIDEO
VIGNETTE

Nissan Motor Corporation

Giant Goes from Stodgy to Nimble

Hewlett-Packard has turned into an ultra-flexible technology company. It's huge and powerful, yet it's made up of more pieces than an Erector Set. Pull one piece off, bolt a couple others together and—*voila!*—the company can quickly change and attack any emerging market.

"Inflexible people simply don't survive in the current environment," says H-P's Lew Platt, CEO since November 1992. "Inflexible companies don't, either."

The formula is working any way you measure it. At a time when big computer companies such as IBM and Digital Equipment are struggling, H-P is soaring. . . .

Platt started running the company like a conglomerate of little ventures, each responsible for its own success. He changed the focus of H-P from technology to people. In other words, the company isn't creating technology and then seeing if customers buy it. Instead, it's asking customers what problems they have, then saying H-P has the talent to create technology to solve those problems.

Reacting to customers keeps H-P growing and changing, grafting different pieces of itself together, spitting out new products. "It's more like a biological system than a company," says Jim Collins of Stanford University's business school.

NEWS NOTE

EXHIBIT 19–2

Advantages and
Disadvantages of
Decentralization

ADVANTAGES

- Helps top management recognize and develop managerial talent
- Allows managerial performance to be comparatively evaluated
- Can often lead to greater job satisfaction
- Makes the accomplishment of organizational goals and objectives easier
- Allows the use of management by exception

DISADVANTAGES

- May result in a lack of goal congruence or suboptimization
- Requires more effective communication abilities
- May create personnel difficulties upon introduction
- Can be extremely expensive

VIDEO
VIGNETTE

MED Center, Inc. and/or The
Delstar Group (Blue Chip
Enterprises)

mation strategy to be "central resource" issues. He thinks that centralization is the most sensible and cost-effective method of handling those specific functions.[2]

As with any management technique, decentralization has advantages and disadvantages. These pros and cons are discussed in the following sections and are summarized in Exhibit 19–2.

Advantages of Decentralization

Decentralization has many personnel advantages. Decentralized units provide excellent settings for training personnel and for screening aspiring managers for promotion. Managers in decentralized units have the need and occasion to develop their leadership qualities, creative problem-solving abilities, and decision-making skills. Managers can be comparatively judged on their job performance and on the results of their units relative to those headed by other managers; such comparisons can encourage a healthy level of organizational competition. Decentralization also often leads to greater job satisfaction for managers because it provides for job enrichment and gives a feeling of increased importance to the organization.[3] Employees are given more challenging and responsible work, providing greater opportunities for advancement.

In addition to the personnel benefits, decentralization is generally more effective than centralization in accomplishing organizational goals and objectives. The decentralized unit manager has more knowledge of the local operating environment, which means (1) a reduction of decision-making time; (2) a minimization of difficulties that may result from attempting to communicate problems and instructions through an organizational chain of command; and (3) quicker perceptions of environmental changes than is possible for top management. Thus, the manager of a decentralized unit is both in closest contact with daily operations and charged with making decisions about those operations.

A decentralized structure also allows the management by exception principle to be implemented. Top management, when reviewing divisional reports, can address issues that are out of the ordinary rather than dealing with operations that are proceeding according to plans.

Disadvantages of Decentralization

All aspects of decentralization are not positive. For instance, the authority and responsibility for making decisions may be divided among too many individuals. This division of authority and responsibility may result in a lack of goal congruence among the organizational units. **Goal congruence** exists when personal goals of the decision

goal congruence

[2] Paul H. O'Neill, *Remarks at Alcoa Organizational Meeting* (Pittsburgh Hilton Hotel, August 9, 1991), p. 5.
[3] Job enrichment refers to expanding a job to provide for personal achievement and recognition.

Why Some Functions Should Be
Home Office Functions

If decentralized management is increasingly popular among corporations, it also has its dark side. Consider this cautionary tale: KFC . . . kicked off a quality-improvement drive for its 2,000 company-owned restaurants [in 1990]. Instead, it got a bureaucratic mess [because] the chain's autonomous regional divisions failed to coordinate their efforts. "There was so much redundancy [that] the process became dysfunctional," says Edward A. Meager III, a vice president of the PepsiCo Inc. unit.

Facing the same problem, a growing number of U.S. companies are now reasserting central authority over a range of corporate activities. Bill Eaton, a senior vice president of Levi Strauss & Co., is replacing six separate order-processing computer systems with one system under centralized control. [M]any retailers complained that they had to deal with a plethora of different divisions—each with its own procedures—to buy the company's goods, Mr. Eaton says.

Companies still want to decentralize operations closest to customers because they "realize they must be more nimble in the marketplace," says Jim Down, who directs the Boston office of Mercer Management Consulting Inc. But at the same time, companies are consolidating less-visible internal functions such as personnel, "where there can be massive economies of scale," says John J. Parkington [of] consultants Wyatt Co. in New York.

Indeed, saving money is a major motive for recentralizing, particularly in tough times. McDonnell Douglas Corp. cites reduced defense spending as the main reason for its recent consolidation of college-recruiting efforts. As many as five different recruiting teams, each from different units, used to visit the same schools. "We saw there was a great duplication of effort," says David Hutchins, a McDonnell Douglas employment manager.

Besides cost-cutting, another motive for centralization is the need for a company-wide focal point. Avery Dennison Corp., an office supplies maker in Pasadena, Calif., has about 60 largely independent divisions. The company recently created a central office to spearhead a corporate drive to improve customer service [because] "each sector had a different slant on what was important" to customers.

SOURCE: Gilbert Fuchsberg, "Decentralized Management Can Have Its Drawbacks," *Wall Street Journal* (December 9, 1992), pp. B1, B8. Reprinted by permission of *The Wall Street Journal*, © 1992 Dow Jones & Company, Inc. All Rights Reserved Worldwide.

maker, goals of the decision maker's unit, and goals of the broader organization are mutually supportive and consistent. In a decentralized company, unit managers are essentially competing with each other because results of unit activities are compared. Because of this competition, unit managers may make decisions that positively affect their own units, but are detrimental to other organizational units or to the company. (This process results in suboptimization, which is discussed later in the chapter.) These difficulties may cause management to keep certain organizational functions at "headquarters" or recentralize some functions if they have been delegated to unit managers. The News Note regarding "Home Office Functions" discusses some companies' decisions to retain (or regain) central authority for certain organizational functions.

A decentralized organization requires that more effective methods of communicating plans, activities, and achievements be established because decision making is removed from the central office. Top management has delegated the authority to make decisions to unit managers, but the responsibility for the ultimate effects of those decisions is retained by top management. Thus, to determine whether those operations are progressing toward established goals, top management must maintain an awareness of operations at lower levels—something that may go unrecognized, as indicated in the following example about Daewoo, a Korean company.

At Daewoo, day-to-day control was ceded by Chairman Kim Woo-Choong to the presidents of individual Daewoo companies. It didn't work.

At Daewoo Shipbuilding, labor costs had risen tenfold over a decade and no attempt had been made to trim other expenses. Workers received free haircuts in the shipyard at a cost of $60 each a month, including lost hours. Kim personally took over Daewoo Shipbuilding for 18 months. Removing the barber shops saved $8 million a year. For bigger savings, Kim eliminated thousands of positions. From near-bankruptcy, the unit projected a $144 million profit for 1991.[4]

In attempts to introduce decentralization policies, some top managers may have difficulty relinquishing the control they previously held over the segments or may be unwilling or unable to delegate effectively. Reasons for this unwillingness or inability include the belief of managers that they can do the job better than anyone else, a lack of confidence in the lower-level managers' abilities, and a lack of ability to communicate directions and assignments to subordinates.

A final disadvantage of decentralization is that it may be extremely costly. In a large company, all subordinate managers are unlikely to have equally good decision-making skills. Thus, companies must often incur a cost to train lower-level managers to make better decisions. Another potential cost is that of poor decisions, because decentralization requires managerial tolerance if and when subordinates make mistakes. The potentially adverse consequences of poor decisions by subordinates cause some top managers to resist a high degree of decentralization.

Decentralization also requires that a company develop and maintain a sophisticated planning and reporting system. With more organizations like Entergy having decentralized units worldwide, integrated ways to transfer information are extremely important. A manager at an Entergy office in Australia may need to work with an Entergy manager in Argentina on a report for the home office in New Orleans, Louisiana. For companies having operations spanning the globe, modems, fax machines, interactive computer networks, management information systems, and videoconferencing are no longer on capital budgeting "wish lists;" they become capital investment necessities. Frito Lay, for example, has installed a network that links all the senior staff and field managers at all levels nationwide and allows decisions to be made quickly from a well-informed perspective. The company refers to its system (shown in Exhibit 19–3) as "directed decentralization."

In a decentralized organization, top management delegates decision-making authority but retains ultimate responsibility for decision outcomes. Thus, a reporting system must be implemented to provide top management with information about, as well as the ability to measure, the overall accountability of the subunits. This accounting and information reporting system is known as a responsibility accounting system.

RESPONSIBILITY ACCOUNTING SYSTEMS

A responsibility accounting system is an important tool in making decentralization work effectively by providing information to top management about the performance of organizational subunits. As companies became more decentralized, responsibility accounting systems evolved from the increased need to communicate operating results through the managerial hierarchy. Responsibility accounting implies subordinate managers' acceptance of *communicated* authority from top management.

Responsibility accounting is consistent with standard costing and activity-based costing because each is implemented for a common purpose—that of control. Responsibility accounting focuses attention on organizational subunit performance and the effectiveness and efficiency of that unit's manager. Standard costing traces variances to the person (or machine) having responsibility for a particular variance (such as tracing the material purchase price variance to the purchasing agent). Activity-

---

[4] Laxmi Nakarmi, "At Daewoo, a 'Revolution' at the Top," *Business Week* (February 18, 1991), pp. 68–69.

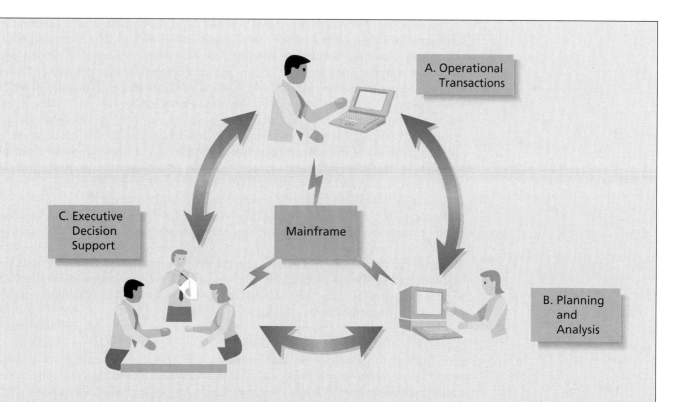

Frito Lay's system is built on a relational database. Any information entered into the system is immediately accessible to all users.

A.   A salesperson processes an order on his or her [laptop] computer. The purchasing, manufacturing, and logistics facilities are notified immediately and begin processing the order. Each successive transaction is entered as it occurs; that is, the company can track where the order is in manufacturing, when it left the plant, and when it will be delivered.

B.   At the same time, this information is available to the planning and analysis system. This allows the brand manager, the channel manager, and the area manager to spot trends in consumption. Competitive information from supermarket scanners is also fed into the mix, enabling managers to see their markets in wider perspective and to develop appropriate strategies to respond to market needs.

C.   This information, broader and more general in scope, becomes instantly available to top management. This allows managers to understand what is going on throughout the company, where the firm is losing market share, and why. This in turn allows the executive process to enter the picture sooner and with greater impact.

SOURCE: Charles S. Field, "Directed Decentralization: The Frito Lay story," *Financial Executive* (November/December 1990), p. 25. Reprinted with permission from *Financial Executive* November/December 1990, copyright 1990 by Financial Executives Institute, 10 Madison Avenue, P.O. Box 1938, Morristown, N.J. 07962-1938., (201)898-4600.

---

based costing traces as many costs as possible to the activities causing the costs to be incurred rather than using highly aggregated allocation techniques. Thus, each technique reflects cause-and-effect relationships.

A responsibility accounting system produces **responsibility reports** that assist each successively higher level of management in evaluating the performances of its subordinate managers and their respective organizational units. Much of the information communicated in these reports is of a monetary nature, although some nonmonetary data may be included. The reports about unit performance should be tailored to fit the planning, controlling, and decision-making needs of subordinate managers. Top managers review these reports to evaluate the performance of each unit and each unit manager.

EXHIBIT 19–3

Frito Lay's Directed Decentralization System

responsibility report

The number of responsibility reports issued for a decentralized unit depends on the degree of influence that unit's manager has on day-to-day operations and costs. If a manager strongly influences all operations and costs of a unit, one report will suffice for both the manager and the unit because responsibility reports should reflect only the revenues and/or costs *under the control* of the manager. Normally, though, some costs of an organizational unit are not controlled (or are only partially or indirectly controlled) by the unit manager. In such instances, the responsibility accounting report takes one of two forms. First, a single report can be issued showing all costs incurred in the unit, separately classified as either controllable or noncontrollable by the manager. Alternatively, separate reports can be prepared for the organizational unit and the unit manager. The unit's report would include all costs; the manager's would include only costs under his or her control.

Responsibility accounting systems help to establish control procedures at the point of cost incurrence rather than allocating such costs in a potentially arbitrary manner to all units, managers, and/or products. Control procedures are implemented by managers for three reasons. First, managers attempt to cause actual operating results to conform to planned results; this conformity is known as effectiveness. Second, managers attempt to cause the standard output to be achieved at minimum possible input costs; this conformity is known as efficiency.

Third, managers need to ensure reasonable plant and equipment utilization, which is primarily affected by product or service demand. At higher volumes of activity or utilization, fixed capacity costs can be spread over more units, resulting in a lower unit cost. Reasonable utilization must be tied to demand, and thus does not mean producing simply for the sake of lowering fixed cost per unit if sales demand cannot support production. To illustrate this concept, consider that bank credit cards require huge front-end technology and marketing costs. Robert H. Burke, general manager of the Bank of New York's credit card operation, says, "In effect, you're running a factory, and the more volume you can push through your fixed costs, the better the profits are."[5] BNY, though, selectively targets potential customers and does not send credit card applications to every adult in the United States.

A responsibility accounting system helps organizational unit managers in conducting the five basic control functions shown in Exhibit 19–4. First, a budget is prepared and used to officially communicate output expectations (sales, production, and so forth) and delegate authority to spend. Ideally, subunit managers negotiate budgets and standards for their units with top management for the coming year. The responsibility accounting system should be designed so that actual data are captured in conformity with budgetary accounts. Thus, during the year, the system can be used to record and summarize data for each organizational unit.

Operating reports comparing actual account balances with budgeted or standard amounts are prepared periodically and issued to unit and top managers for their review. However, because of day-to-day contact with operations, unit managers should have been aware of any significant variances *before* they were reported, identified the variance causes, and attempted to correct the causes of the problems. Top management, on the other hand, may not know about operational variances until responsibility reports are received. By the time top management receives the reports, the problems causing the variances should have been corrected, or subordinate managers should have explanations as to why the problems were not or could not have been resolved.

Responsibility reports for subordinate managers and their immediate supervisors normally compare actual results with flexible budget figures. These comparisons are more useful for control purposes because both operating results and flexible budget figures are based on achieved levels of activity. In contrast, top management may receive responsibility reports comparing actual performance to the master budget. Such a budget-to-actual comparison yields an overall performance evaluation, be-

[5] Douglas R. Sease and Robert Guenther, "Big Banks Are Plagued by a Gradual Erosion of Key Profit Centers," *Wall Street Journal* (August 1, 1990), p. A14.

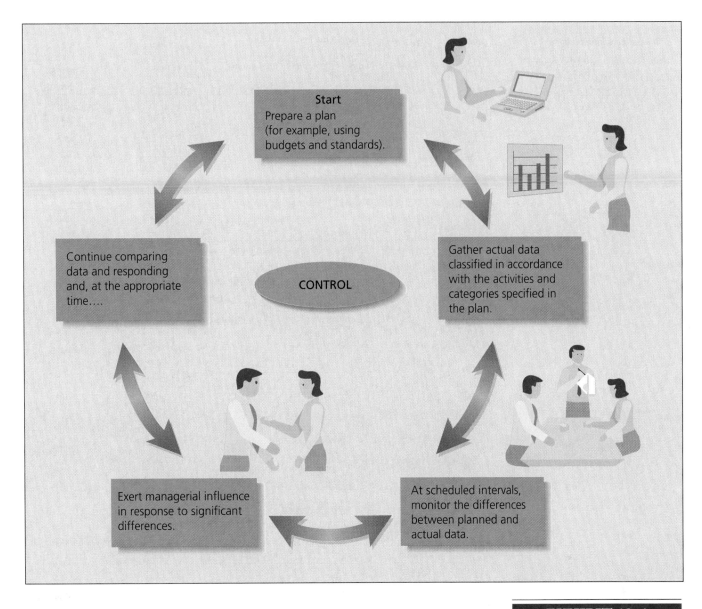

Start
Prepare a plan
(for example, using
budgets and standards).

CONTROL

Continue comparing
data and responding
and, at the appropriate
time....

Gather actual data
classified in accordance
with the activities and
categories specified in
the plan.

Exert managerial influence
in response to significant
differences.

At scheduled intervals,
monitor the differences
between planned and
actual data.

EXHIBIT 19–4

Basic Steps in
a Control Process

cause the master budget reflects management's expectations about volume, mix, costs, and prices. This type of comparison is especially useful when accompanied by a supporting detailed variance analysis identifying the effect of sales volume differences on segment performance.

Regardless of the type of comparison provided, responsibility reports reflect the upward flow of information from operational units to company top management and illustrate the broadening scope of responsibility. Managers receive detailed information on the performance of their immediate areas of control and summary information on all organizational units for which they are responsible. Summarizing results causes a pyramiding of information. Like the information received by the executives in the Frito-Lay exhibit, reports at the lowest level units are highly detailed, whereas more general information is reported at the top of the organization. Upper-level managers desiring more detail than provided in summary reports can obtain it by reviewing the responsibility reports prepared for their subordinates.

Exhibit 19–5 illustrates a set of performance reports for the Bingo Bongo Island Power Company. The division's flexible budget is presented for comparative purposes. Data for the generating department are aggregated with data of the other

EXHIBIT 19–5

Bingo Bongo Island Power Company Performance Reports for Costs Incurred

PRESIDENT'S PERFORMANCE REPORT
MAY 1997

	BUDGET	ACTUAL	VARIANCE FAV. (UNFAV.)
Administrative office—president	$ 298,000	$ 299,200	$(1,200)
Financial vice president	236,000	234,100	1,900
Production vice president	737,996	744,400	(6,404)
Sales vice president	275,000	276,400	(1,400)
Totals	$1,546,996	$1,554,100	$(7,104)

PRODUCTION VICE PRESIDENT'S
PERFORMANCE REPORT MAY 1997

	BUDGET	ACTUAL	VARIANCE FAV. (UNFAV.)
Administrative office—VP	$180,000	$182,200	$(2,200)
Distribution and storage	124,700	126,000	(1,300)
Generating	433,296	436,200	(2,904)
Totals	$737,996	$744,400	$(6,404)

DISTRIBUTION AND STORAGE MANAGER'S PERFORMANCE
REPORT MAY 1997

	BUDGET	ACTUAL	VARIANCE FAV. (UNFAV.)
Direct materials	$ 36,000	$ 35,400	$ 600
Direct labor	54,500	55,300	(800)
Supplies	4,700	5,300	(600)
Indirect labor	12,400	12,900	(500)
Power	11,200	10,900	300
Repairs and maintenance	3,500	3,700	(200)
Other	2,400	2,500	(100)
Totals	$124,700	$126,000	$(1,300)

GENERATING MANAGER'S PERFORMANCE
REPORT MAY 1997

	BUDGET	ACTUAL	VARIANCE FAV. (UNFAV.)
Fuel consumption	$119,300	$122,500	$(3,200)
Direct labor	190,880	188,027	2,853
Supplies	17,656	18,500	(844)
Indirect labor	46,288	47,020	(732)
Depreciation	38,653	38,653	0
Repairs and maintenance	12,407	12,900	(493)
Other	8,112	8,600	(488)
Totals	$433,296	$436,200	$(2,904)

departments under the production vice president's control. (These combined data are shown in the middle section of Exhibit 19–5.) In a like manner, the total costs of the production vice president's area of responsibility are combined with other costs for which the company president is responsible and are shown in the top section of Exhibit 19–5.

Variances are the responsibility of the manager under whose direct supervision they occur. Variances are individually itemized in performance reports at the lower levels so that the appropriate manager has the necessary details to take any required corrective action related to significant variances.[6] Under the management by exception principle, major deviations from expectations are highlighted under the subor-

[6] In practice, the variances presented in Exhibit 19–5 would be further separated into the portions representing price and quantity effects as is shown in Chapter 11 on standard costing.

- Departmental/divisional throughput
- Number of defects (by product, product line, supplier)
- Number of orders backlogged (by date, quantity, cost, and selling price)
- Number of customer complaints (by type and product); method of complaint resolution
- Percentage of orders delivered on time
- Manufacturing (or service) cycle efficiency
- Percentage of reduction of non-value-added time from previous reporting period (broken down by idle time, storage time, move time, and quality control time)
- Number of employee suggestions considered significant and practical
- Number of employee suggestions implemented
- Number of unplanned production interruptions
- Number of schedule changes
- Number of engineering change orders; percentage change from previous period
- Number of safety violations; percentage change from previous period
- Number of days of employee absences; percentage change from previous period

EXHIBIT 19–6

Nonmonetary Information for Responsibility Reports

dinate manager's reporting section to assist upper-level managers in making decisions about when to become involved in subordinates' operations. If no significant deviations exist, top management is free to devote its attention to other matters. In addition, such detailed variance analysis alerts operating managers to items that may need to be explained to superiors. For example, the items of fuel consumption and direct labor in Exhibit 19–5 on the generating manager's section of the report would probably be considered significant and require explanations to the production vice president.

In addition to the monetary information shown in Exhibit 19–5, many responsibility accounting systems are now providing information on critical nonmonetary measures of the period's activity. Some examples of these types of information are shown in Exhibit 19–6. Many of these measures are equally useful for manufacturing and service organizations and can be used to judge performance in addition to basic financial measurements.

The performance reports of each management layer are reviewed and evaluated by each successively higher management layer. Managers are likely to be more careful and alert in controlling operations, knowing that the reports generated by the responsibility accounting system will reveal financial accomplishments and problems. Thus, in addition to providing a means for control, responsibility reports can motivate managers to influence operations in ways that will reflect positive performance.

The focus of responsibility accounting is on the managers who are responsible for a particular cost object. In a decentralized company, the cost object is an organizational unit such as a division, department, or geographical region. The cost object under the control of a manager is called a **responsibility center**.

responsibility center

Responsibility accounting systems identify, measure, and report on the performance of people controlling the activities of responsibility centers. Responsibility centers are classified according to their manager's scope of authority and type of financial responsibility. Companies may define their organizational units in various ways based on management accountability for one or more income-producing factors—costs, revenues, profits, and/or asset base. The four types of responsibility centers are illustrated in Exhibit 19–7 (on p. 882) and discussed in the following sections.

TYPES OF RESPONSIBILITY CENTERS

Cost Centers

In a **cost center,** the manager has the authority only to incur costs and is specifically evaluated on the basis of how well costs are controlled. Theoretically, revenues cannot exist in a cost center because the unit does not engage in revenue-producing

cost center

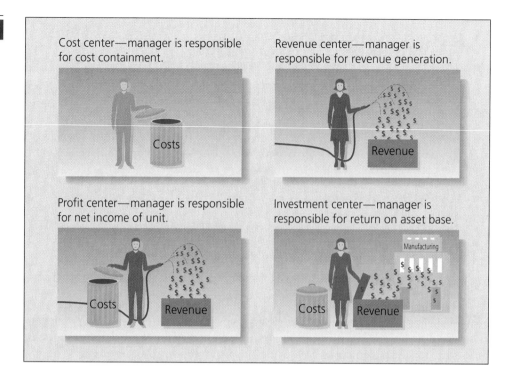

activity. Cost centers commonly include the service and administrative departments discussed in Chapter 5. For example, the placement center in a university may be a cost center because it does not charge for its services, but it does incur costs.

In other instances, revenues do exist for a cost center, but they are either not under the manager's control or are not effectively measurable. The first type of situation exists in a governmental agency that is provided a specific proration of sales tax dollars, but has no authority to levy or collect the related taxes. The second situation could exist in engineered and discretionary cost centers in which the outputs (revenues or benefits generated from the cost inputs) are not easily measured.[7] In these two types of situations, the revenues should not be included in the manager's responsibility accounting report.

In the traditional manufacturing environment, a standard costing system is generally used and variances are reported and analyzed. In such an environment, the highest priority in a cost center is often the minimization of unfavorable cost variances. Top management may often concentrate only on the unfavorable variances occurring in a cost center and ignore the efficient performance indicated by favorable variances. To illustrate this possibility, the May 1997 operating results for the Generating Department are shown in Exhibit 19–8.

Dawn Ho is the manager of the Generating Department. During the month, the department produced 477,200 units of electricity at a unit cost of $.914. The standard production cost for these units is $.908. Top management's analysis of the responsibility report issued for the Generating Department for May might focus on the large unfavorable fuel consumption variance rather than on the large favorable variance for the direct labor. Ms. Ho's job is to control costs and she did so relatively well when both favorable and unfavorable variances are reviewed.

Significant favorable variances should not be disregarded if the management by exception principle is applied appropriately. Using this principle, top management should investigate all variances (both favorable and unfavorable) that fall outside the range of acceptable deviations. The unfavorable fuel consumption variance in the Generating Department should be investigated further to find its cause. For example, a substandard grade of fuel may have been purchased and caused excessive usage. If this is the case, the purchasing agent, not Ms. Ho, should be assigned the respon-

---

[7] Engineered and discretionary costs are discussed in Chapter 16.

A university's placement office is a cost center. Many costs are incurred for salaries, equipment, supplies, and facilities, but no revenues are generated because neither students nor potential employers are charged for the services.

EXHIBIT 19–8

Generating Department's May 1997 Production Costs

Units of electricity produced: 477,200

Standard cost per unit of production:

Fuel consumption		$.250
Direct labor		.400
Overhead		
Supplies	$.037	
Indirect labor	.097	
Depreciation (units of production method)	.081	
Repairs and maintenance	.026	
Other	.017	.258
Total		$.908

	STANDARD COST	ACTUAL COST	VARIANCE FAV. (UNFAV.)
Fuel consumption	$119,300	$122,500	$(3,200)
Direct labor	190,880	188,027	2,853
Supplies	17,656	18,500	(844)
Indirect labor	46,288	47,020	(732)
Depreciation	38,653	38,653	0
Repairs and maintenance	12,407	12,900	(493)
Other	8,112	8,600	(488)
Total	$433,296	$436,200	$(2,904)

sibility for the variance. Other possible causes for the unfavorable fuel consumption variance include increased fuel prices, excess waste, or some combination of all causes. Only additional inquiry will determine whether the variance could have been controlled by Ms. Ho.

The favorable direct labor variance should also be analyzed for causes. Ms. Ho may have used inexperienced personnel who were being paid lower rates. This might explain the favorable direct labor variance and, to some extent, the unfavorable fuel consumption variance (because of a lack of employee skill and possible overuse of fuel). Alternatively, the people working in the Generating Department could have been very efficient this period.

Revenue Centers

A **revenue center** is strictly defined as an organizational unit for which a manager is accountable only for the generation of revenues and has no control over setting selling prices or budgeting costs. In many retail stores, the individual sales departments are considered independent units, and managers are evaluated based on the total revenues generated by their departments. Departmental managers, however, may not be given the authority to change selling prices to affect volume, and often they do not participate in the budgeting process. Thus, the departmental managers may have no impact on costs. In most instances, however, *pure revenue* centers do not exist. Managers of revenue centers are typically not only responsible for revenues, but also are involved in the planning and control over some (but not necessarily all) costs incurred in the center. A more appropriate term for this organizational unit is a *revenue and limited cost center.*

For example, Jerry Smith is the district sales manager for the Commercial Sales Division of Bingo Bongo Island Power Company and is responsible for the sales revenues generated in his territory. In addition, he is accountable for controlling the mileage and other travel-related expenses of his sales staff. Jerry is not, however, able to influence the types of cars his sales staff obtain because cars are acquired on a fleetwide basis by top management.

Salaries, if directly traceable to the center, are often a cost responsibility of the "revenue center" manager. This situation reflects the traditional retail environment in which sales clerks are assigned to a specific department and are only allowed to check out customers wanting to purchase that department's merchandise. Most stores, however, have found such a checkout situation to be detrimental to business because customers are forced to wait for the appropriate clerk. Clerks in many stores are now allowed to assist all customers with all types of merchandise. Such a change in policy converts what was a traceable departmental cost into an indirect cost. Those stores carrying high-cost, high-selling-price merchandise normally retain the traditional system. Managers of such departments are thus able to trace sales salaries as a direct departmental cost.

The effects of price, sales mix, and volume variances from budget are illustrated in the following revenue variance model:

The following revenue statistics are presented for the Consumer Products Division of Bingo Bongo Island Power Company for May 1998:

BUDGET	UNITS	UNIT PRICE	REVENUE	STANDARD MIX		
Fuses [F]	1,000	$1.80	$1,800	1,000 ÷ 2,700 =	37.0%
Socket caps [S]	500	.80	400	500 ÷ 2,700 =	18.5%
Wattsavers [W]	1,200	1.00	1,200	1,200 ÷ 2,700 =	44.5%
Totals	2,700		$3,400		100.0%

ACTUAL				
Fuses	1,100	$2.00	$2,200
Socket caps	540	.70	378
Wattsavers	1,180	1.10	1,298
Totals	2,820		$3,876

Using the revenue variance model and the information presented for the Consumer Products Division of Bingo Bongo, variances can be determined as follows:

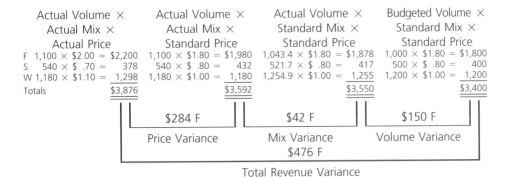

Actual Volume × Actual Mix × Actual Price	Actual Volume × Actual Mix × Standard Price	Actual Volume × Standard Mix × Standard Price	Budgeted Volume × Standard Mix × Standard Price
F 1,100 × $2.00 = $2,200	1,100 × $1.80 = $1,980	1,043.4 × $1.80 = $1,878	1,000 × $1.80 = $1,800
S 540 × $ .70 = 378	540 × $ .80 = 432	521.7 × $ .80 = 417	500 × $ .80 = 400
W 1,180 × $1.10 = 1,298	1,180 × $1.00 = 1,180	1,254.9 × $1.00 = 1,255	1,200 × $1.00 = 1,200
Totals $3,876	$3,592	$3,550	$3,400

$284 F — Price Variance

$42 F — Mix Variance

$150 F — Volume Variance

$476 F

Total Revenue Variance

Inspection of the results reveals that (1) prices increased (except for socket caps), causing an overall favorable price variance; (2) the actual mix included more of the high-priced products (fuses and wattsavers) than the standard mix, causing an overall favorable mix variance; and (3) the total actual units (2,820) was greater than the budgeted total units (2,700), causing a favorable volume variance. The Consumer Products Division's manager should be commended for a good performance.

Profit Centers

In a **profit center,** the manager is responsible for generating revenues and planning and controlling expenses related to current activity. (Expenses not under a profit center manager's control are those related to long-term investments in plant assets; such a situation creates a definitive need for separate evaluations of the subunit and the subunit's manager.) A profit center manager's goal is to maximize the center's net income. Profit centers should be independent organizational units whose managers have the ability to obtain resources at the most economical prices and to sell products at prices that will maximize revenue. If managers do not have complete authority to buy and sell at objectively determined costs and prices, a meaningful evaluation of the profit center is difficult to make. In fact, it's also sometimes a difficult change for the people involved when their organization becomes a profit center. To illustrate, consider the News Note about "Renaissance Faires" on the following page.

Profit centers are not always manufacturing divisions or branches of retail stores. Banks may view each department (checking and savings accounts, loans, and credit cards) as a profit center; trucking companies may view each 18-wheeler as a profit center; and a university may view certain educational divisions as profit centers (undergraduate education, non-degree-seeking night school, and the law school).

To illustrate the computations for a profit center, assume that Atlantic Electric Company uses 18-wheelers to deliver products in the United States and each truck is considered a profit center. The segment margin income statement budgeted and actual results of the "Red Dog," a truck for which Dick Lucas is responsible, are shown in Exhibit 19–9. These comparisons can be used to explain to top management why the budgeted income was not reached. The profit center should be judged on the $34,400 of profit center income, but Dick Lucas should be judged on the controllable margin of $63,900. Because actual volume was greater than budgeted, the comparison in Exhibit 19–9 shows unfavorable variances for all of the variable costs. A comparison of actual results to a flexible budget at the actual activity level would provide better information for assessing cost control in the profit center.

profit center

VIDEO VIGNETTE

Riverwood Enterprises and/or Steiner/Bressler Advertising (Blue Chip Enterprises)

Investment Centers

An **investment center** is an organizational unit in which the manager is responsible for generating revenues and planning and controlling expenses. In addition, the center's manager has the authority to acquire, use, and dispose of plant assets in a manner that seeks to earn the highest feasible rate of return on the center's asset base. Many

investment center

NEWS NOTE

Ye Olde Bottom Line Is a New Attraction at Renaissance Faires

William Watters, squire to the court of Elizabeth I, is steamed. "There's some resentment out here," whispers the bearded, velvet-clad computer programmer. "We're being run by corporate suits."

There definitely is trouble afoot at Mr. Watters place of part-time employment, the Renaissance Pleasure Faire. The oldest and biggest of the free-form celebrations of Elizabethan fun and games, held at sites in southern and northern California, was acquired last spring by publicly traded Renaissance Entertainment Corp., of Boulder, Colo.

Now, the past isn't what it used to be.

It's time for Renaissance re-engineering, layoffs and more attention to ye olde bottom line, sometimes at the expense of authenticity and merriment. Renaissance Entertainment has downsized the faire's back-office staff to 30, from 50. It has booted the town criers in the faire's Southern California edition and has plans to trim the hundreds of part-time actors by 10%.

Anachronistic paraphernalia, such as baseball caps and key chains, now permeate the late-summer encampment. "They're selling teriyaki!" exclaims Jessica Cohen, a 17-year faire veteran equipped with low-cut dress, dagger and tankard of beer. "I feel like the golden age for faires is over."

Miles Silverman, Renaissance Entertainment's chief executive officer, thinks the profit-making era has just begun. . . .

His company, which already owned a faire in Kenosha, Wis., and a jousting outfit called Heroes & Villains Inc., acquired the California faires for about $1.5 million in the stock of a nonprofit company headed by the faire's 63-year old creator, Phillis Patterson. She had been on the verge of closing the faires despite robust attendance.

"She was losing $1 million a year," Mr. Silverman says. "It's hard for me to imagine a faire grossing $8 million and losing money. In Kenosha, we gross $2.5 million and make $700,000."

SOURCE: Quentin Hardy, "Ye Olde Bottom Line Is a New Attraction at Renaissance Faires," *Wall Street Journal* (September 28, 1995), pp. A1, A8. Reprinted with permission of *The Wall Street Journal*, © 1995 Dow Jones & Company, Inc. All Rights Reserved Worldwide.

EXHIBIT 19–9

Profit Center Comparisons for "Red Dog" for Month Ended May 31, 1997

	BUDGET	ACTUAL	VARIANCE
Fees	$120,000	$124,000	$4,000 F
Cost of services rendered			
Direct labor	$ 3,000	$ 3,200	$ 200 U
Gas and oil	25,200	26,300	1,100 U
Variable overhead	5,200	5,800	600 U
Total	$ 33,400	$ 35,300	$1,900 U
Contribution margin	$ 86,600	$ 88,700	$2,100 F
Fixed overhead—controllable	(24,600)	(24,800)	200 U
Controllable segment margin	$ 62,000	$ 63,900	$1,900 F
Fixed overhead—not controllable by profit center manager	(28,000)	(29,500)	1,500 U
Profit center income	$ 34,000	$ 34,400	$ 400 F

investment centers are independent, free-standing divisions or subsidiaries of a firm. This independence allows investment center managers the opportunity to make decisions about all matters affecting their organizational units and to be judged on the outcomes of those decisions.

Assume that the Light Bulb Division of Atlantic Electric Company is an investment center headed by Tammy Jones. The 1997 income statement for the plant is as follows:

Sales	$1,720,000
Variable expenses	(900,000)
Contribution margin	$ 820,000
Fixed expenses	(690,000)
Income before tax	$ 130,000

Ms. Jones has the authority to set selling prices, incur costs, and acquire and dispose of plant assets. The plant has an asset base of $1,480,000 and thus the rate of return on assets for the year was approximately 8.8 percent ($130,000 ÷ $1,480,000). This rate of return would be compared with the rates desired by Atlantic Electric management and would also be compared with other investment centers in the company. Rate of return and other performance measures for responsibility centers are treated in greater depth in Chapters 20 and 21.

Because of their closeness to daily divisional activities, responsibility center managers should have more current and detailed knowledge about sales prices, costs, and other market information than top management does. If responsibility centers are designated as profit or investment centers, managers are encouraged, to the extent possible, to operate those subunits as separate economic entities that exist for the same organizational goals.

Regardless of the size, type of ownership, or product or service being sold, one goal for any business is to generate profits. For other organizations, such as a charity or governmental entity, the ultimate financial goal may be to break even. The ultimate goal will be achieved through the satisfaction of organizational critical success factors—those items that are so important that, without them, the organization would cease to exist. Five critical success factors organizations frequently embrace are quality, customer service, efficiency, cost control, and responsiveness to change. If all these factors are managed properly, the organization should be financially successful; if they are not, sooner or later the organization will fail. All members of the organization—especially those in management—should work toward the same basic objectives if the critical success factors are to be satisfied. Losing sight of the organizational goal while working to achieve an independent responsibility center's conflicting goal results in suboptimization.

Suboptimization is a situation in which individual managers pursue goals and objectives that are in their own and/or their segments' particular interests rather than in the company's best interests. Because of their greater degree of flexibility in financial decisions, profit and investment center managers must remember that their operations are integral parts of the entire corporate structure. Therefore, all actions taken should be in the best long-run interest of both the responsibility center and the organization. Unit managers should be aware of and accept the need for goal congruence throughout the entity.

For suboptimization to be limited or minimized, top management must be aware that it can occur and should develop ways to avoid it. A primary way managers can try to limit suboptimization is by communicating corporate goals to all organizational units, regardless of the types of responsibility centers. Exhibit 19–10 depicts other ways of limiting suboptimization as stairsteps to the achievement of corporate goals. These steps are not in a hierarchical order. If any steps are missing, the climb toward achieving corporate goals and objectives becomes more difficult for divisional managers.

With the exception of the use of internal and operational audit functions, these steps are discussed throughout the text. Internal and operational auditing are briefly introduced at this point and should be covered in more depth in an auditing course.

SUBOPTIMIZATION

suboptimization

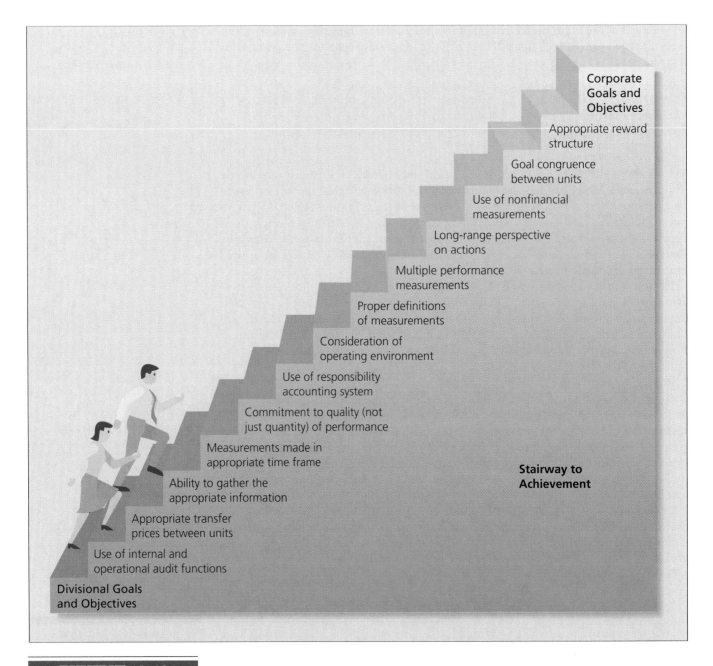

Stairway to Achievement

Corporate Goals and Objectives

Appropriate reward structure

Goal congruence between units

Use of nonfinancial measurements

Long-range perspective on actions

Multiple performance measurements

Proper definitions of measurements

Consideration of operating environment

Use of responsibility accounting system

Commitment to quality (not just quantity) of performance

Measurements made in appropriate time frame

Ability to gather the appropriate information

Appropriate transfer prices between units

Use of internal and operational audit functions

Divisional Goals and Objectives

EXHIBIT 19–10

Performance Measures to Limit Suboptimization

An internal or operational audit function is used to monitor and evaluate the effectiveness and efficiency of the various organizational units and programs. Part of the evaluation includes an assessment of subordinate managers' knowledge of company goals and objectives and of whether the managers are striving for and achieving those goals. Operational auditors are expected to act as a kind of management consultant team. Their expertise and abilities should be focused on recognizing suboptimal behavior. Rigorous and systematic monitoring by such a team can be highly advantageous to companies, especially large, decentralized ones.

To properly evaluate segments and their managers, useful information about performance must be available. When the various segments of a firm exchange goods or services among themselves, a "price" for those goods or services must be set so that the "selling" segment can measure its revenue and the "buying" segment can measure its costs. Such an internal price is known as a transfer price.

Responsibility centers often provide goods or services to other company segments. Such transfers require that a price be established to account for the flow of these goods or services within the company. **Transfer prices** (or prices in a chargeback system) are *internal* charges established for the exchange of goods or services between organizational units of the same company. Although a variety of transfer prices may be used for internal reporting purposes, intercompany inventory transfers should be presented on an external balance sheet at the producing segment's actual cost. Internal transfers would be eliminated for external income statement purposes altogether. Thus, if transfers are "sold" at an amount other than cost, any intersegment profit in inventory, expense, and/or revenue accounts must be eliminated.

Transfer prices may be established to promote goal congruence, make performance evaluation among segments more comparable, and/or "transform" a cost center into a profit center. The appropriate transfer price should ensure optimal resource allocation and promote operating efficiency. A number of different approaches are used to establish a transfer price for goods or services. The basic caveat is that intracompany transfers should be made only if they are in the best interest of the total organization. Within this context, the general rules[8] for choosing a transfer price are as follows:

- The maximum price should be no greater than the lowest market price at which the buying segment can acquire the goods or services externally.
- The minimum price should be no less than the sum of the selling segment's incremental costs associated with the goods or services plus the opportunity cost of the facilities used.

From the company's perspective, any transfer price set between these two limits is generally considered appropriate. To illustrate the use of these rules, assume that a product is available from external suppliers at a price below the lower limit (selling division's incremental costs plus opportunity cost). The immediate short-run decision might be that the selling division is to stop production and allow the purchasing division to buy the product from the external suppliers. This decision may be reasonable because compared with the external suppliers, the selling division does not appear to be cost efficient in its production activities. Stopping production would release the facilities for other, more profitable purposes. A longer-run solution may be to have the selling division improve its efficiency and reduce the internal cost of making the product. This solution could be implemented without stopping internal production, but possibly reducing it by making some external purchases until costs were under control.

After the transfer price range limits have been established, one criterion used to select a particular price in the range is the ease by which that price can be determined. Managers should be able to understand the computation of a transfer price and to evaluate the impact of that transfer price on their responsibility centers' profits. The more complex the method used to set a transfer price, the less comfortable managers will be with both the method and the resulting price. In addition, from a cost standpoint, it takes more time and effort to administer and account for a complicated transfer pricing system than a simple one.

The difference between the upper and lower transfer price limits is the corporate "profit" (or savings) generated by producing internally rather than buying externally. The transfer price chosen acts to "divide the corporate profit" between the buying and selling segments. For external statements, it is irrelevant which segment shows the profits from transfers because such internal profit allocations are eliminated in

TRANSFER PRICING

transfer price

---

[8] These rules are more difficult to implement when the selling division is in a "captive" relationship, in that it is not able to transfer its products to customers outside the corporate entity. Captive relationships often exist when the selling division was acquired or established in a company's move toward vertical integration. In such situations, opportunity cost must be estimated to provide the selling division an incentive to transfer products.

EXHIBIT 19–11

Foster Company Spool
Division

Standard unit production cost:		
Direct materials	A$.20	
Direct labor	.06	
Variable overhead	.10	
Variable selling and administrative	.04	
Total variable costs		A$.40
Fixed overhead*	A$.09	
Fixed selling and administrative*	.03	
Total fixed cost		.12
Total cost		A$.52
Normal markup on variable cost (50%)		.20
List selling price		A$.72

Estimated annual production: 700,000 spools
Estimated sales to outside entities: 400,000 spools
Estimated intracompany transfers: 300,000 spools
*Fixed costs are allocated to all units produced based on estimated annual production.

preparing these statements. For internal reporting, though, this division of profits may be extremely important. Use of transfer prices affects the responsibility reports that are prepared, and top management may have established a subunit performance measurement system that is affected by such "profit" allocations.

Segment managers in a decentralized company often have competing vested interests if managerial performance is evaluated on a competitive basis. Such internal competition could lead to suboptimization because both buying and selling segment managers want to maximize their financial results in the responsibility accounting reports. The supplier-segment manager attempts to obtain the highest transfer (selling) price, whereas the buying-segment manager attempts to acquire the goods or services at the lowest transfer (purchase) price. Thus, transfer prices should be agreed on by the company's selling and buying segments.

Many top managers believe in giving subunit managers a considerable amount of autonomy to negotiate divisional transfer prices. Division managers are expected to make choices that will maximize the effectiveness and efficiency of their divisions as well as contribute to overall company performance.

Three traditional methods are used for determining transfer prices: cost-based prices, market-based prices, and negotiated prices. Following is a discussion of each method and its advantages and disadvantages. This discussion will use information on the Foster Company, an Australian subsidiary of Atlantic Electric Company. Foster Company is composed of two investment centers: an electric wire producing division (managed by Pam Davies) and a spool-making plant (managed by Larry Thomas). The managers are attempting to establish a reasonable transfer price for a particular size of spool on which to wind the wire. The Spool Division data (shown in Exhibit 19–11 in Australian dollars) are used to illustrate various transfer pricing approaches. Note that the Spool Division is capable of supplying all external and internal production needs.

Cost-Based Transfer Prices

A cost-based transfer price is, on the surface, an easily understood concept until one realizes the variations that can exist in the definition of the term *cost*. Different companies use different definitions of cost in conjunction with transfer pricing. These definitions range from variable production cost to absorption cost plus additional amounts for selling and administrative costs (and, possibly, opportunity costs) of the selling unit. Another consideration in a cost-based transfer price is whether actual or standard cost is used. Actual costs may vary according to the season, production volume, and other factors, whereas standard costs can be specified in advance and are stable measures of efficient production cost. For these two reasons, standard costs provide a superior basis for transfer pricing. When standard costs are used, any variances from standard are borne by the selling segment because otherwise the selling division's efficiencies or inefficiencies are passed on to the buying division.

COST ALTERNATIVE-VARIABLE COST   Using the data provided in Exhibit 19–11, a variable cost transfer price for spools can be either A$.36 (production variable costs only) or A$.40 (total variable costs). The difference depends on whether *variable cost* is defined as variable production cost or total variable cost. Even using A$.40 as the transfer price provides little incentive to Mr. Thomas to sell to the Wire division. Fixed costs of the Spool Division are not reduced by selling internally, and no contribution margin is being generated by the transfers to help cover fixed costs. The low transfer prices could result in a poor financial showing for the Spool Division that, in turn, could detrimentally affect Mr. Thomas' performance evaluation.

Considering the total standard cost per unit of A$.52, a loss of A$.12 will result for Mr. Thomas's division on each spool sold internally at a transfer price of A$.40. If all sales and transfers occur as expected and there are no variances from standard costs, Mr. Thomas's responsibility report will appear as follows:

Sales
External (400,000 × A$.72)	A$288,000	
Internal (300,000 × A$.40)	120,000	A$408,000

Costs:
Total variable and fixed costs (700,000 × A$.52)		(364,000)
Income before tax		A$ 44,000

Had the Spool Division been able to sell all its production externally, it would have shown a net income for the period of A$140,000:

Sales (700,000 × A$.72)	A$504,000
Costs (shown previously)	(364,000)
Income before tax	A$140,000

This A$96,000 difference can be reconciled as the 300,000 units multiplied by the A$.32 per unit (A$.72 − A$.40) "lost" revenue from making internal sales.

Assume, on the other hand, that the 400,000 units represented the total number of units that could be sold externally and the Spool Division has no other opportunity to use the facilities. In this instance, the opportunity cost of the facilities used is zero and the division is no worse off by transferring the 300,000 spools internally than by sitting with idle capacity. Relating this situation to the general transfer pricing rules, the transfer price of A$.40 is at its lower limit.

COST ALTERNATIVE—ABSORPTION COST   Transfer prices based on absorption cost (direct materials, direct labor, and variable and fixed overhead) at least provide a contribution toward covering the selling division's fixed production overhead. Such a transfer price does not produce the same amount of income that would be generated if the transferring division sold the goods externally, but it does provide for coverage of all production costs. Absorption cost for a spool is A$.45 (A$.20 DM + A$.06 DL + A$.10 VOH + A$.09 FOH). The Spool Division's income statement would appear as follows using absorption cost as the transfer price:

Sales:
External (400,000 × A$.72)	A$288,000	
Internal (300,000 × A$.45)	135,000	A$423,000
Costs (shown previously)		364,000
Income before tax		A$ 59,000

Although the absorption cost transfer price provides a reasonable coverage of costs to the selling segment, that same cost could create a suboptimization problem because of the effects on the buying segment.

Suppose the Wire Division of Foster Company can purchase spools externally from United Spools for A$.44 and that the externally purchased spools are of the same quality and specifications as those produced internally. If the transfer price is set at the absorption cost of A$.45, the Wire Division may decide to purchase the spools from United Spools for A$.44. Purchasing at the lower price would give the buying unit's manager more favorable financial results than would making the acquisition internally. In such an instance, Foster Company is paying A$.44 for a product its Spool Division can make for a variable cost of A$.40. Thus, although the buying segment manager *appears* to "save" A$.01 per spool, the *company* would be better off by A$12,000 if the spools were purchased internally rather than externally:

Unit cost to Electric Wire Division to purchase externally	A$.44
Unit cost to produce and deliver in Spool Division (out-of-pocket costs)	.40
Net advantage of company to produce per unit	A$.04
Multiplied by number of units transferred	× 300,000
Total savings to produce internally	A$ 12,000

These facts assume that the Spool Division does not have an opportunity cost of more than A$.04 per spool for the use of the facilities devoted to the 300,000 units. If, however, the Spool Division can sell all the units it produces at list price, the division should do so. The Wire Division could then purchase its spools from United Spools, and Foster Company would be optimizing its resources. Computations to arrive at this conclusion are

Spool Division's additional contribution margin from outside sales (300,000 × A$.32)	A$96,000
Additional cost caused by Wire Division's purchase from outside source (300,000 × A$.04)	(12,000)
Net incremental income to company before tax	A$84,000

The company is better off by A$84,000 because the A$.32 contribution margin (A$.72 − A$.40) realized on each additional unit sale to outsiders is greater than the A$.04 difference between the A$.44 external purchase price paid by the Wire Division and the A$.40 incremental cost of the Spool Division to produce the units.

Under the above circumstances, the general transfer pricing rules also would have yielded the decision not to make the internal transfer. The sum of the A$.40 incremental cost to produce and the A$.32 opportunity cost of additional contribution on external sales is A$.72, which exceeds the upper limit of the A$.44 market price. Foster Company should not make the transfer as long as the Wire Division can purchase the units externally for a price less than A$.72.

COST ALTERNATIVE—MODIFICATIONS TO VARIABLE AND/OR ABSORPTION COST Modifications can be made to minimize the definitional and motivational problems associated with cost-based transfer prices. When variable cost is used as a base, an additional amount can be added to cover some fixed costs and provide a measure of profit to the selling division. This adjustment is an example of a "cost-plus" arrangement. Some company managers think cost-plus arrangements are acceptable substitutes for market-based transfer prices, especially when market prices for comparable substitute products are unavailable.

Absorption cost can be modified by adding an amount equal to an average of the nonproduction costs associated with the product and/or an amount for profit to the selling division. In contrast, a transfer price could be set at less than absorption cost on the theory that there might be no other use for the idle capacity, and the selling division should receive some benefit from partial coverage of its fixed factory overhead. Alternatively, absorption cost can be reduced by the estimated savings in production costs on internally transferred goods. For example, packaging may not be necessary or as expensive if the inventory is sold intracompany rather than externally.

Market-Based Transfer Prices

To eliminate the problems of defining "cost," some companies simply use a market price approach to setting transfer prices. Market price is believed to be an objective, arm's-length measure of value that simulates the selling price that would be offered and paid if the subunits were independent, autonomous companies. If a selling division is operating efficiently relative to its competition, it should be able to show a profit when transferring products or services at market prices. Similarly, an efficiently operating buying division should not be troubled by a market-based transfer price because that is what it would have to pay for the goods or services if the alternative of buying internally did not exist. Using such a system, the Spool Division would transfer all spools to the Wire Division at the A$.72 price charged to external purchasers.

Although this approach appears logical, several problems may exist with the use of market prices for intracompany transfers. First, transfers may involve products having no exact counterpart in the external market. Second, market price may not be entirely appropriate because of cost savings on internal sales arising from reductions in bad debts and/or in packaging, advertising, or delivery expenditures. Third, difficulties can arise in setting a transfer price when the external market is depressed because of a temporary reduction in demand for the product. Should the current depressed price be used as the transfer price or should the expected long-run market price be used? Fourth, different prices are quoted and different discounts and credit terms are allowed to different buyers. Which market price is the "right" one to use?

Negotiated Transfer Prices

Because of the problems associated with both cost- and market-based prices, **negotiated transfer prices** are often set through a process of bargaining between the selling and purchasing unit managers. Such prices are typically below the normal market purchase price of the buying unit, but above the sum of the selling unit's incremental and opportunity costs. A negotiated price meeting these specifications falls within the range limits of the transfer pricing rules.

negotiated transfer price

A negotiated transfer price for the Foster Company would be bounded on the top side by the Wire Division's external buying price and on the bottom side by the A$.40 incremental variable costs of the Spool Division. If some of the variable selling costs could be eliminated, the incremental cost would be less. If the Spool Division could not sell any additional spools externally or downsize its facilities, no opportunity cost would be involved. Otherwise, the amount of the opportunity cost would need to be determined, and it could be as much as the A$.32 contribution margin (if all units could be sold externally).

Ability to negotiate a transfer price implies that segment managers have the autonomy to sell or buy products externally if internal negotiations fail. Because such extensive autonomy may lead to dysfunctional behavior and suboptimization, top management may provide a means of arbitrating a price in the event that the units cannot agree. This arbitration arrangement must be specified and agreed on in advance and be skillfully handled or the segment managers may perceive that their autonomy is being usurped by upper-level management.

To encourage cooperation between the transferring divisions, top management may consider joint divisional profits as one performance measurement for both the selling and buying unit managers. Another way to reduce difficulties in establishing a transfer price is simply to use a dual pricing approach.

Dual Pricing

dual price arrangement

Because a transfer price is used to satisfy internal managerial objectives, a **dual pricing arrangement** can be used to provide for different transfer prices for the selling and buying segments. Such an arrangement lets the selling division record the transfer of goods or services at a market or negotiated market price and the buying division to record the transfer at a cost-based amount.[9] Use of dual prices would provide a profit margin on the goods transferred and thus reflect a "profit" for the selling division. The arrangement would also provide a minimal cost to the buying division. Dual pricing eliminates the problem of having to divide the profits artificially between the selling and buying segments and allows managers to have the most relevant information for both decision making and performance evaluation.

When dual pricing is used, the sum of the individual segment performances will not equal the companywide performance. The selling segment's recorded sales price is not equal to the buying segment's recorded purchase price for the same transaction. The difference is assigned to an internal reconciliation account used to adjust revenues and costs when company financial statements are prepared. Such a reconciliation is the same as would exist in preparing consolidated statements when sales are made between the consolidated entities at an amount other than cost.

Three distinct benefits can result from the use of dual transfer pricing. First, it "provides the selling department with an incentive to maximize profits while at the same time it provides the buying department with the relevant cost information for making short-run decisions."[10] Second, goal congruence may be enhanced because each manager is motivated to engage in intracompany transfers. In the selling division, internal transfers are reflected in an equitable manner to external sales; in the buying division, internal purchases would be at a cost lower than that for external purchases. Third, dual transfer prices should reduce potential managerial conflict arising through attempts to negotiate "equitable" transfer prices. (On the other hand, although reducing conflict, dual pricing could also eliminate some of the benefits of managerial competition, such as the understanding and cooperation resulting from negotiation and the opportunity for creative solutions to mutual problems.)

Using the information for the Spool and Wire Divisions of Foster Company, journal entries to record transfers under various transfer pricing systems are shown in Exhibit 19–12.

Selecting a Transfer Pricing System

Setting a reasonable transfer price is not an easy task. Everyone involved in the process must be aware of the positive and negative aspects of each type of transfer price and be responsive to suggestions of change if the need is indicated. The determination of the type of transfer pricing system to use should reflect the organizational units' characteristics as well as corporate goals. No one method of setting a transfer price is best in all instances. Also, transfer prices are not permanent; they are frequently revised in relation to changes in costs, supply, demand, competitive forces, and other factors. Such cost adjustments allow a department "to stimulate consumption during its slack times and ration consumption during peak demand times, thus encouraging efficient use of resources."[11]

Regardless of what method is used, a thoughtfully set transfer price will provide

- an appropriate basis for the calculation and evaluation of segment performance;
- the rational acquisition or use of goods and services between corporate divisions;

---

[9] Typically, the cost-based amount used by the buying division reflects only the variable costs of the selling division.

[10] Herbert S. Cassel, "The Transfer Pricing Dilemma—And a Dual Pricing Solution," *Journal of Accountancy* (September 1987), p. 172.

[11] Leon B. Hoshower and Robert P. Crum, "Controlling Service Center Costs," *Management Accounting* (November 1987), p. 45.

Assume that 1,000 spools are transferred from the Spool Division to the Wire Division:
  Variable production cost (1,000 × A$.36) = A$360
  Full production cost (1,000 × A$.45) = A$450
  External selling price (1,000 × A$.72) = A$720

SITUATION	SPOOL DIVISION (S)			WIRE DIVISION (W)		
Transfer at variable production cost	A/R—Division W	360		Inventory	360	
	Intracompany Sales		360	A/P—Division S		360
	Intracompany CGS	450				
	Finished Goods		450			
Transfer at full production cost	A/R—Division W	450		Inventory	450	
	Intracompany Sales		450	A/P—Division S		450
	Intracompany CGS	450				
	Finished Goods		450			
Transfer at external selling price	A/R—Division W	720		Inventory	720	
	Intracompany Sales		720	A/P—Division S		720
	Intracompany CGS	450				
	Finished Goods		450			
Transfer at dual price of external selling price for selling division and full production cost for buying division	A/R—Division W	450		Inventory	450	
	Intracompany Sales in Excess of Assigned Costs	270		A/P—Division S		450
	Intracompany Sales		720			
	Intracompany CGS	450				
	Finished Goods		450			

NOTE: Entries for negotiated transfer prices would be similar to those at full production cost, except that the negotiated transfer price would be shown for the first entry for the selling division and the purchase entry for the buying division.

- the flexibility to respond to changes in demand or market conditions; and
- a means of motivation to encourage and reward goal congruence by managers in decentralized operations.

EXHIBIT 19–12

Journal Entries for
Transfer Prices

**TRANSFER PRICES
FOR SERVICE
DEPARTMENTS**

The practice of setting prices for products transferred between one organizational segment and another is well established. Instituting transfer prices for services is a less common but effective technique for some types of service departments.

Setting Service Transfer Prices

Setting transfer prices for services requires that practical internal guidelines be developed to provide meaningful information for both the user and provider departments. For an organization to be profitable, service department costs must be covered by revenue-producing areas. These costs can be allocated internally to user departments based on the methods shown in Chapter 5 or services can be "sold" to user departments using transfer prices. In either case, service department costs are included in the costs of revenue-producing departments so that those departments' sales can cover the service departments' costs. The decision as to the most useful information is at the discretion of top management.

Transfer prices for services can take the same forms as those for products: cost-based, market-based, negotiated, or dual. A Price Waterhouse survey on service transfer prices indicated that "[m]ost companies (72 percent) reported that transfer prices are negotiated between buyer and seller. This is especially true for services because value is often added by means that cannot be measured effectively—such as expertise, reliability, convenience and responsiveness."[12] The type of transfer price

---

[12] Daniel P. Keegan and Patrick D. Howard, "Transfer Pricing for Services: A Price Waterhouse Survey," *Journal of Accountancy* (March 1988), p. 98.

EXHIBIT 19–13

Types of Service
Department Transfer Costs

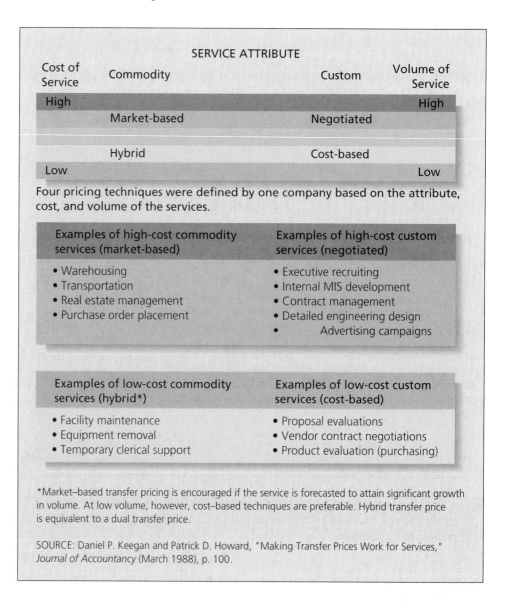

SERVICE ATTRIBUTE

Cost of Service	Commodity		Custom	Volume of Service
High				High
	Market-based		Negotiated	
	Hybrid		Cost-based	
Low				Low

Four pricing techniques were defined by one company based on the attribute, cost, and volume of the services.

Examples of high-cost commodity services (market-based)	Examples of high-cost custom services (negotiated)
• Warehousing • Transportation • Real estate management • Purchase order placement	• Executive recruiting • Internal MIS development • Contract management • Detailed engineering design • Advertising campaigns

Examples of low-cost commodity services (hybrid*)	Examples of low-cost custom services (cost-based)
• Facility maintenance • Equipment removal • Temporary clerical support	• Proposal evaluations • Vendor contract negotiations • Product evaluation (purchasing)

*Market–based transfer pricing is encouraged if the service is forecasted to attain significant growth in volume. At low volume, however, cost–based techniques are preferable. Hybrid transfer price is equivalent to a dual transfer price.

SOURCE: Daniel P. Keegan and Patrick D. Howard, "Making Transfer Prices Work for Services," *Journal of Accountancy* (March 1988), p. 100.

to use should depend on the cost and volume level of the service as well as whether comparable substitutes are available. Exhibit 19–13 presents an example of a model that can help determine the suitable transfer price for different types of services.

Advantages of Service Transfer Prices

A company should weigh the advantages and disadvantages of service transfer prices before instituting such a transfer policy. Transfer prices are useful when service departments provide distinct, measurable benefits to other areas or provide services having a specific cause-and-effect relationship. Transfer prices in these circumstances can provide certain organizational advantages in both the revenue-producing and service departments. These advantages (listed in Exhibit 19–14) are as follows. First, transfer prices can encourage more involvement between service departments and their users. Service departments are more likely to interact with users to determine the specific services that are needed and to eliminate or reduce services that are not cost-beneficial. If charged a transfer price, users may be more likely to suggest ways the service department could reduce costs and improve its performance, and thereby lower the transfer prices charged.

EXHIBIT 19–14

Advantages of Transfer
Prices for Services

	Revenue Departments	Service Departments
User Involvement	Suggestions of ways to improve services to benefit users	Promotes development of services more beneficial to users
Cost Consciousness	Relates to services used; restrict usage to those necessary and cost beneficial	Relates to cost of services provided; must justify transfer price established
Performance Evaluations	If control over amount of services used exists, costs can be included in making performance evaluations	Can make a service department a profit center rather than a cost center and this provides more performance evaluation measures

Data processing departments are excellent candidates for utilizing transfer prices. These centers perform substantial services for other organizational areas and management may decide to "charge" other units for DP activities.

Second, using transfer prices for services should cause service department and user department managers to be more cost conscious and eliminate wasteful usage. If service departments incur excessive costs, a reasonable transfer price may not cover those costs or a high transfer price may not be justifiable to users. If user departments are charged for all services they receive, they may decide their service demands have been excessive. For example, if the Management Information Department charged other departments for the number of reports received, managers would be less likely to request reports simply to be "on the receiving list," as sometimes occurs.

Last, transfer prices result in useful information for performance evaluations. Responsibility reports show a controllable service department cost relative to the actual services used by individual managers instead of noncontrollable allocated expense amounts. The use of transfer prices would also allow service departments to be established as profit rather than cost centers. However, although transfer prices are effective responsibility accounting tools, there are disadvantages to their use.

DISADVANTAGES OF TRANSFER PRICES

Transfer prices (whether for services or products) do have certain disadvantages. First, there can be (and most often is) disagreement among organizational unit managers as to how the transfer price should be set. Second, implementing transfer prices in the accounting system requires additional organizational costs and employee time. Third, transfer prices do not work equally well for all departments or divisions. For example, service departments that do not provide measurable benefits or cannot show a distinct cause-and-effect relationship between cost behavior and service use by other departments should not attempt to use transfer prices. Fourth, the transfer price may cause dysfunctional behavior among organizational units or may induce certain services to be under- or overutilized. Last, U.S. tax regulations regarding transfer prices in multinational companies are quite complicated.

TRANSFER PRICES IN MULTINATIONAL SETTINGS

Because of the differences in tax systems, customs duties, freight and insurance costs, import/export regulations, and foreign-exchange controls, setting transfer prices for products and services becomes extremely difficult when the company is engaged in multinational operations. In addition, as shown in Exhibit 19–15, the internal and external objectives of transfer pricing policies differ in multinational enterprises (MNEs).

Because of these differences, the determination of transfer prices in MNEs has no simple resolution. Multinational companies may use one transfer price when a product is sent to or received from one country and a totally different transfer price for the same product when it is sent to or received from another. However, some guidelines on transfer pricing policies should be set by the company and be followed on a consistent basis. For example, a company should not price certain parent company services to foreign subsidiaries in a manner that would send the majority of those costs to the subsidiary in the country with the highest tax rate *unless that method of pricing were reasonable and equitable to all subsidiaries.* The general test of reasonableness is that transfer prices should reflect an arm's-length transaction. Multinational transfer prices are now being carefully scrutinized by tax authorities in both the home and host countries because such prices determine which country taxes the income from the transfer. The U.S. Congress is concerned about both U.S. multinationals

EXHIBIT 19–15

Multinational Company Transfer Pricing Objectives

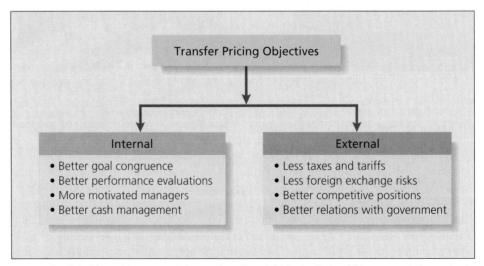

SOURCE: Reprinted from *Management Accounting.* Copyright by Institute of Management Accountants, Montvale, NJ.

United States Allows More Flexible Transfer Pricing

The U.S. Treasury yesterday unveiled tax rules to allow companies greater flexibility in determining the transfer prices of cross-border transactions with foreign subsidiaries or parents.

Transfer pricing, in which companies assign prices to internal transactions for taxation purposes, has become a highly contentious part of the international tax arena.

Foreign companies operating in the U.S. have often been accused of manipulating transfer prices in order to reduce their tax liability. In the 1992 U.S. election campaign, Mr. Bill Clinton hit at foreign companies for paying too little tax.

The new rules, which formalize and extend temporary regulations introduced last year, give companies more leeway over the methods they use to determine their transfer prices.

However, the Internal Revenue Service will be able to impose penalties of 20 to 40 percent where it has determined that tax has been underpaid due to transfer price adjustments.

The final regulations are "intended to maximize the extent to which relevant information may be taken into account in evaluating a taxpayer's results under the arm's-length standard," the Treasury says.

SOURCE: Ken Warn, "U.S. Allows More Flexible Transfer Pricing," *(London) Financial Times,* (July 6, 1994), p. 6.

operating in low-tax-rate countries and foreign companies operating in the United States. In both situations, Congress believes that companies could avoid paying U.S. corporate income taxes because of misleading or inaccurate transfer pricing. Thus, the Internal Revenue Service (IRS) may be quick to investigate U.S. subsidiaries that operate in low-tax areas (such as Ireland, Singapore, and Puerto Rico) and suddenly have unusually high profits. If foreign companies charge their U.S. subsidiaries higher prices than what they would charge subsidiaries in their home country, U.S. taxable income and thus the tax base will decline—which may also provoke an IRS review. The accompanying News Note discusses taxation concerns and the current approach of the U.S. Treasury regarding cross-border transactions of foreign subsidiaries or parents.

Final IRS regulations regarding transfer pricing became effective on February 9, 1996 and include the following highlights:

- Taxpayers are required to update their transfer pricing analyses of data through the end of the tax year.
- Additional guidance is provided on the required scope of the search for data (defined in the regulations as a "reasonably thorough search") which may be determined based on the relative "cost/benefit" of obtaining the data.
- It is not necessary to exhaustively evaluate all of the applicable transfer pricing methods, but taxpayers still must make a comparison with other methods and consider all the available data in choosing the best method.[13]

As discussed earlier in the text, transfers among nations are becoming easier through the institution of trade integration arrangements such as the European Union and the North American Free Trade Agreement. These arrangements should help reduce the significance of transfer price manipulations through (among other features) the harmonization of tax structures and the reduction in import/export fees, tariffs, and capital movement restrictions.

[13] "IRS Issues Final Transfer Pricing Penalty Regulations," *Deloitte & Touche Review* (February 19, 1996), pp. 5–6.

To determine the effectiveness of their transfer pricing policies, multinational company managers should consider the following two questions:

(a) does the system achieve economic decisions that positively affect MNE performance, including international capital investment decisions, output level decisions for both intermediate and final products, and product pricing decisions for external customers? and (b) do subsidiary managers feel that they are being fairly evaluated and rewarded for their divisional contributions to the MNE as a whole?[14]

If the answers to both of these questions are yes, then the company appears to have a transfer pricing system that appropriately coordinates the underlying considerations, minimizes the internal and external goal conflicts, and balances the short- and long-range perspectives of the multinational company.

REVISITING

Entergy Corporation

Entergy Corporation would like to invest about $150 million annually in business expansion activities. By 1998, the firm would like to have about $1 billion invested in noncore electric power ventures. It had invested almost half of that amount at the end of 1994. [Whenever Entergy's component organizations internally transfer goods or services between divisions or other subunits, management must assure itself that such transfers are economically beneficial and that the transfer prices used enhance organizational effectiveness and efficiency and are set in such a way as to avoid the risk of tax, tariff, or other regulatory penalties.]

Management recognizes that risk is higher overseas, which is why it expects higher returns on these investments. The firm manages the risk by working with partners knowledgeable about the countries in which it invests [that is, by using decentralization], by assessing each project individually [that is, using responsibility accounting], and by limiting excessive exposure in any one country. Also, the firm is structured so that its core business is insulated from its nonregulated ventures, which are managed by separate legal entities and personnel.

Company management is preparing for the competitive near future with the following key initiatives:

- To have Best-in-Class programs to become low-cost producers in our Fossil and Nuclear generation organizations.
- To aggressively reduce costs and improve efficiencies in our other business units.
- To reduce our prices to be competitive with alternative sources of electricity.
- To check every aspect of the regulatory environment for ways to improve and streamline it.
- To make significant investments in electric energy businesses that should produce growth and returns superior to our core electric utility business.

SOURCE: Entergy Corporation, *Annual Report*, 1994, pp. 11 and 12.

---

[14] Wagdy M. Abdallah, "Guidelines for CEOs in Transfer Pricing Policies," *Management Accounting* (September 1988), p. 61. Reprinted from *Management Accounting*. Copyright by Institute of Management Accountants, Montvale, NJ.

CHAPTER SUMMARY

A decentralized organization is composed of operational units led by managers who have some degree of decision-making autonomy. The degree to which a company is decentralized depends on top management philosophy and on the ability of unit managers to perform independently. Decentralization provides managers the opportunity to develop leadership qualities, creative problem-solving abilities, and decision-making skills. It also lets the individual closest to the operational unit make decisions for that unit, thereby reducing the time spent in communicating and making decisions.

One disadvantage of decentralization is that responsibility may be spread too thinly throughout the organization. Competition can also result among the managers of decentralized units, which could lessen the organizational goal congruence. Some disruption may occur during a transition to decentralization because top managers resist delegating a portion of their authority to subordinates. Last, the costs of incorrect decisions made by the decentralized unit managers could be high.

Responsibility accounting systems are used to provide information on the revenues and/or costs under the control of unit managers. Responsibility reports reflect the upward flow of information from each decentralized unit to top management. Managers receive information regarding the activities under their immediate control as well as the control of their direct subordinates. The information is successively aggregated, and the reports allow the application of the management by exception principle.

Responsibility centers are classified as cost, revenue, profit, or investment centers. Cost center and revenue center managers have control primarily over, respectively, costs and revenues. Profit center managers are responsible for maximizing their segments' incomes. Investment center managers must generate revenues and control costs to produce a satisfactory return on the asset base under their influence. All responsibility center managers should perform their functions within the framework of organizational goal congruence, although there is a possibility of suboptimization of resources.

A transfer price is an intracompany charge for goods or services bought and sold between segments of a decentralized company. A transfer price for products is typically cost-based, market-based, or negotiated. The upper limit of a transfer price is the lowest market price at which the product can be acquired externally. The lower limit is the incremental cost of production plus the opportunity cost of the facilities used. A dual pricing system may also be used that assigns different transfer prices to the selling and buying units. Top management should promote a transfer pricing system that enhances goal congruence, provides segment autonomy, motivates managers to strive for segment effectiveness and efficiency, is practical, and is credible in measuring segment performance.

Setting transfer prices in multinational enterprises is a complex process because of the differences existing in tax structures, import/export regulations, customs duties, and other factors of the international subsidiaries and divisions. A valid transfer price for a multinational company achieves economic benefit for the entire company and support from the domestic and international managers using the system.

KEY TERMS

cost center (p. 881)
dual pricing arrangement (p. 894)
goal congruence (p. 874)
investment center (p. 885)
negotiated transfer price (p. 893)
profit center (p. 885)

responsibility center (p. 881)
responsibility report (p. 877)
revenue center (p. 884)
suboptimization (p. 887)
transfer price (p. 889)

SOLUTION STRATEGIES

Transfer Prices (Cost-Based, Market-Based, Negotiated, Dual)

Upper Limit: Lowest price available from external suppliers

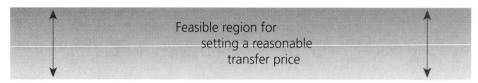

Feasible region for
setting a reasonable
transfer price

Lower Limit: Incremental costs of producing and selling the transfer goods
or services plus the opportunity cost for the facilities used

DEMONSTRATION PROBLEM

Patrick Guffey Enterprises is a diversified company of which one segment makes high-quality fishing rods and another produces fishing reels. Costs for a reel produced by the Reel Division are

Direct materials	$12	
Direct labor	5	
Variable overhead	3	
Variable S&A (both for external and internal sales)	1	
Total variable cost		$21
Fixed overhead*	$ 3	
Fixed S&A	2	
Total fixed cost		5
Total cost per reel		$26
Markup on total variable cost (33 1/3%)		7
List price to external customers		$33

*Fixed costs are allocated to all units produced based on estimated annual production.

- Estimated annual production: 400,000 reels
- Estimated sales to outside entities: 300,000 reels
- Estimated sales by the Reel Division to the Rod Division: 100,000 reels

The managers of the two divisions are currently negotiating a transfer price.

Required:

a. Determine a transfer price based on variable product cost.
b. Determine a transfer price based on total variable cost plus markup.
c. Determine a transfer price based on full production cost.
d. Determine a transfer price based on total cost per reel.
e. Assume that the Reel Division has no alternative use for the facilities that make the reels for internal transfer. Also assume that the Rod Division can buy equivalent reels externally for $25. Calculate the upper and lower limits for which the transfer price should be set.
f. Compute a transfer price that divides the "profit" between the two divisions equally.
g. In contrast to the assumption in part e, assume that the Reel Division can rent the facilities in which the 100,000 reels are produced for $100,000. Determine the lower limit of the transfer price.

Solution to Demonstration Problem

a.
Direct materials	$12
Direct labor	5
Variable overhead	3
Transfer price	$20

b.
Total variable cost	$21
Markup	7
Transfer price	$28

c.
Variable production cost	$20
Fixed production cost	3
Transfer price	$23

d.
Total variable cost	$21
Total fixed cost	5
Transfer price	$26

e. Upper limit: Rod Division's external purchase price = $25
   Lower limit: Total variable cost of Reel Division = $21

f. (Lower limit + Upper limit) ÷ 2 = ($21 + $25) ÷ 2 = $23

g. $100,000 ÷ 100,000 reels = $1 opportunity cost per reel
   Lower limit: Incremental cost of Reel Division + Opportunity cost = $21 + $1 = $22

---

1. What is the distinction between a centralized organizational structure and a decentralized organizational structure? In what types of companies is decentralization appropriate and why?

2. "A company's operations are either centralized or decentralized." Discuss this statement.

3. Tim Roy is the president and chief operating officer of Reagan Enterprises. Tim founded the company and has led it to its prominent place in the electronics field. Reagan has manufacturing plants and outlets in 25 states, including Alaska and Hawaii. Tim, however, is finding that he cannot "keep track" of things the way he did in the past. Discuss the advantages and disadvantages of decentralizing the firm's decision-making activities among the various local and regional managers.

4. Even in a decentralized company, some functions may be best performed centrally. List several of these functions and the reasons you have for suggesting them.

5. Why is it suggested that decentralization has many costs associated with it? Describe some of the significant costs associated with decentralization.

6. How does decentralization affect accounting?

7. Why are responsibility reports prepared?

8. Is it appropriate for a single responsibility report to be prepared for a division of a major company? Why or why not?

9. Discuss the way in which a performance report consolidates information at each successively higher level of management.

10. Why might firms use both monetary and nonmonetary measures to evaluate the performance of subunit managers?

11. Discuss the differences among the various types of responsibility centers.

12. Why might salaries be included in the responsibility report of a revenue center manager?

13. What is suboptimization and what factors contribute to suboptimization in a decentralized firm?

14. What are transfer prices and why are they used by companies?

15. How or would transfer prices be used in each of the following types of responsibility centers: cost, revenue, profit, and investment?

16. How could the use of transfer prices improve goal congruence? Impair goal congruence?

17. What are the high and low limits of transfer prices and why do these limits exist?

18. A company is considering the use of a cost-based transfer price. What arguments favor the use of standard rather than actual cost?

19. What problems may be encountered in attempting to implement a cost-based transfer pricing system?

20. What practical problems may impede the use of a market-based transfer price?

21. Why would the element of negotiation be "potentially both the most positive and the most negative aspect of negotiated transfer prices?"

22. What is dual pricing? What is the intended effect of dual pricing on the performance of each division affected by the dual price?

23. How can service departments use transfer prices and what advantages do transfer prices have over cost allocation methods?

24. "Activity-based costing for service departments is essentially the same as using transfer pricing for service departments." Is this statement true or false? Why?

25. What are some of the major disadvantages of using transfer pricing?

26. Explain why the determination of transfer prices may be more complex in a multinational setting than in a domestic setting.

EXERCISES

27. *(Terminology)* Match the following lettered terms on the left with the appropriate numbered description on the right.

a. Cost center
b. Investment center
c. Profit center
d. Revenue center
e. Centralized organization
f. Decentralized organization
g. Dual pricing arrangement
h. Goal congruence
i. Suboptimization
j. Transfer price

1. Situation in which buying division is charged a price that differs from that credited to the selling division
2. Structure in which most decisions are made by segment managers
3. Situation in which decisions are made that are sometimes not in the best interest of whole firm
4. Segment whose manager is responsible primarily for costs
5. Segment whose manager is primarily responsible for revenues, expenses, and assets
6. Segment whose manager is responsible for both revenues and expenses
7. Segment whose manager is primarily responsible for revenues
8. Structure in which most decisions are made by top management
9. An internal exchange price
10. Situation in which mutual support exists among goals of individual managers and the organization

28. *(Decentralization advantages and disadvantages)* Indicate which of the following is a potential advantage (A), disadvantage (D), or neither (N) of decentralization.
   a. Promotion of goal congruence
   b. Support of training in decision making
   c. Development of leadership qualities
   d. Complication of communication process
   e. Cost of developing the planning and reporting system
   f. Placement of decision maker closer to time and place of problem
   g. Speed of decisions
   h. Use of management by exception principle by top management
   i. Provision of greater job satisfaction
   j. Delegation of ultimate responsibility

29. *(Centralization versus decentralization)* For each situation below, indicate whether the firm would tend to be more centralized (C) or more decentralized (D), or the tendency is indefinite (I).
   a. The firm's growth rate is rapid.
   b. The firm is small.
   c. The firm is in a growth stage of product development.
   d. Top management expects that incorrect subordinate management decisions could have a disastrous impact on company profits.
   e. The company was founded two years ago.
   f. Top management has a high level of confidence in subordinates' judgment and skills.
   g. Top management is proud of its record of tight control.
   h. Both d and f.
   i. Both c and g.
   j. Both a and b.

30. *(Revenue variances)* The Sales Department of Elegant Glazes is responsible for sales of two porcelain figurines. One is called "Peaceful Child" and the other is called "Barefoot Beau." For April 1997, the Sales Department's actual and budgeted sales were as follows:

	PEACEFUL CHILD		BAREFOOT BEAU	
	DOLLARS	**UNITS**	**DOLLARS**	**UNITS**
Budgeted sales	$10,000	1,000	$15,000	3,000
Actual sales	9,000	750	15,750	3,500

For April 1997, compute each of the following for the Sales Department of Elegant Glazes:
   a. Price variance
   b. Mix variance
   c. Volume variance

31. *(Revenue variances)* Good Life Products Inc. manufactures two products: purses and fur-lined, elbow-length gloves. For 1998, the firm budgeted the following:

	PURSES	GLOVES
Sales	$400,000	$600,000
Unit sales price	40	30

At the end of 1998, managers were informed that total actual sales amounted to 35,000 units and totaled $1,225,000. Glove sales for the year amounted to 20,000 units at an average price of $35.
   a. Compute the total revenue variance for 1998.
   b. Compute the price variance for 1998.
   c. Compute the mix variance for 1998.
   d. Compute the volume variance for 1998.

32. *(Transfer pricing)* Autochip Division, a decentralized plant of Spaceage Motor Company, is considering what transfer price to charge the Engine Division for transfers of computer chips to that division. The following data on production cost per computer chip have been gathered:

Direct materials	$1.50
Direct labor	4.00
Variable overhead	1.70
Fixed overhead	2.40
Total	$9.60

The Autochip Division sells the computer chips to external buyers for $21.75. Managers of the Engine Division have received external offers to provide the division comparable chips, ranging from $15 at one company to $23 at another.

a. Determine the upper and lower limits for the transfer price between the Autochip Division and the Engine Division.

b. If the Autochip Division is presently selling all the chips it can produce to external buyers, what is the minimum price it should set for transfers to the Engine Division?

33. *(Transfer pricing)* Allied Products Company is decentrally organized. One of its divisions, Surestop Division, manufactures truck and trailer brake pads for sale to other company divisions as well as to outside entities. Corporate management treats Surestop Division as a profit center. The normal selling price for a pair of Surestop's brake pads is $12; costs for each pair are:

Direct materials	$2.00
Direct labor	1.40
Variable overhead	.80
Fixed overhead (based on production of 700,000 pairs)	2.75
Variable selling expense	.50

Another division of Allied Products, the Trailer Division, wants to purchase 25,000 pairs of brake pads from Surestop Division during next year. No selling costs are incurred on internal sales.

a. If Surestop's manager can sell all the brake pads it produces externally, what should the minimum transfer price be? Explain.

b. Assume that Surestop Division is experiencing a slight slowdown in external demand and will be able to sell only 600,000 pairs of brake pads to outsiders next year at the $12 selling price. What should be the minimum selling price to the Trailer Division under these conditions? Explain.

c. Assume that Mr. Conan, the manager of Trailer Division, offers to pay Surestop Division's production costs plus 25 percent for each pair of brake pads. He receives an invoice for $217,187.50, and he was planning on a cost of $131,250. How were these amounts determined? What created the confusion? Explain.

34. *(Transfer pricing)* Two investment centers of Seattle Technology Company are the Fire Safety Division and the Kitchen Equipment Division. The Fire Safety Division manufactures an electronic heat sensor that can be sold externally and is also used by the Kitchen Equipment Division in making motors for its kitchen equipment. The following information is available about the heat sensor:

Total production annually—200,000 units; internal requirements are 150,000 units; all others are sold externally
List selling price—$25.60
Variable production costs—$12
Fixed overhead—$300,000; allocated on the basis of units of production
Variable selling costs—$3; includes $1 per unit in advertising cost
Fixed selling costs—$400,000

Determine the transfer price under each of the following methods:
a. Total variable cost
b. Full production cost
c. Total variable production cost plus necessary selling costs
d. Market price

35. *(Transfer pricing and management motivation)* Hunter Food Stores operates 12 large supermarkets in Knoxville, Tennessee. Each store is evaluated as a profit center, and store managers have complete control over purchases and their inventory policy. The policy is that if a store runs short of an item and a sister store has a sufficient supply, a transfer will be made between stores. Company policy requires that all such transfers be made at cost.

   During a recent period of rapid increases in food prices, company management officials have noted that transfers between stores have decreased sharply. Store managers have indicated that if they ran short of a particular item, they could not locate a sister store with sufficient inventory to make the transfer.

   Company management officials have observed several recent cases in which a store manager inquired about the availability of a particular item and was told that the sister store did not have sufficient inventory to make a transfer. Further checking indicated that the sister store had more than sufficient inventory to make the transfer.
   a. Why were the store managers reluctant to make the transfers?
   b. How could the transfer pricing policy be changed to avoid this situation?

36. *(Transfer pricing in service departments)* Indicate whether each of the following statements constitutes a potential advantage (A), disadvantage (D), or neither (N) of using transfer prices for service department costs.
   a. Can make a service department into a profit center.
   b. May reduce goal congruence.
   c. Can make users and providers more cost conscious.
   d. May increase resource waste.
   e. Can increase disagreements among departments.
   f. Can put all service departments on an equal footing.
   g. Can cause certain services to be under- or overutilized.
   h. Can improve ability to evaluate performance.
   i. Can increase communication about what additional services are needed and which may be reduced or eliminated.
   j. May require additional organizational data and employee time.

37. *(Transfer pricing for services)* The data processing operation of Bank of Atlanta is developing a transfer price for its services. Capacity is defined as minutes of computer time. Expected capacity for next year (1998) is 350,000 minutes and full capacity is 450,000 minutes. Costs of the computer area for 1998 are expected to total $280,000.
   a. What is the transfer price based on expected capacity?
   b. What is the transfer price based on full capacity?
   c. Assume the actual cost of operating the computer area in 1998 is $297,500. What is the total variance from budget of that department? What are some possible causes of that variance?

38. *(Essay)* Briefly indicate why you do or do not agree with each of the following statements.
   a. Decentralization is always superior to centralization in an organization.
   b. Noncontrollable costs should be reported on responsibility reports.

COMMUNICATION ACTIVITIES

39. *(Selection of type of transfer pricing)* A multiple-division company is considering the effectiveness of its transfer pricing policies. One of the items under consideration is whether the transfer price should be based on variable production cost, absorption production cost, or external market price. Describe the circumstances in which each of these transfer prices would be most appropriate.

40. *(Cost center performance)* Melissa Furgeson is the production supervisor at the Pittsburgh plant of Midwest Metalworks. As plant production supervisor, Ms. Furgeson is evaluated based on her ability to meet standard production costs. At the Pittsburgh plant, the firm manufactures steel cattle panels (fence sections). The standard costs to produce a single cattle panel are given below:

Metal pipe	($.20 per foot)	$12.00
Paint	($10 per gallon)	2.00
Direct labor	($15 per hour)	3.00
Overhead		
Welding supplies	$ .90	
Utilities	1.10	
Indirect labor	.80	
Machine maintenance/repairs	.40	
Equipment depreciation	2.20	
Miscellaneous	.80	6.20
Total		$23.20

In May 1997, the Pittsburgh plant produced 35,000 cattle panels and incurred the following costs:

Metal pipe	($.25 per foot)	$507,500
Paint	($ 9.40 per gallon)	65,800
Direct labor	($14.90 per hour)	104,300
Overhead		
Welding supplies	$34,900	
Utilities	38,300	
Indirect labor	25,500	
Machine maintenance/repairs	21,200	
Equipment depreciation	77,000	
Miscellaneous	29,500	226,400
Total		$904,000

a. For May 1997, compute the variance for each production cost category in the Pittsburgh plant.

b. Based on the variances computed in part a, evaluate the performance of Melissa Furgeson. Which variances might deserve closer scrutiny by top management? Explain.

41. *(Revenue center performance)* Mark Schwartz manages the sales department at the Boston Lighting Company. Mark is evaluated based on his ability to meet budgeted revenues. For June 1998, Mark's revenue budget was as follows:

	PRICE PER UNIT	UNIT SALES
Floor lamps	$120	1,600
Hanging lamps	65	2,150
Ceiling fixtures	80	4,200

The actual sales generated by Mr. Schwartz's sales department in June were as follows:

	PRICE PER UNIT	TOTAL SALES IN DOLLARS
Floor lamps	$115	$195,500
Hanging lamps	70	141,400
Ceiling fixtures	75	311,250

a. Compute the revenue price variance.

b. Compute the revenue mix variance.

c. Compute the revenue volume variance.

d. Based on your answers to parts a through c, evaluate the performance of Mr. Schwartz.

e. If Mr. Schwartz is to be held accountable for meeting the revenue budget, why might it be advisable to also give him the authority to set the salesperson salary and commission structure?

42. *(Transfer pricing and performance measurement)* Sloan Industries consists of eight divisions that are evaluated as profit centers. All transfers between divisions are made at market price. Quality Bearing is a division of Sloan that sells approximately 20 percent of its output externally. The remaining 80 percent of the output from Quality Bearing is transferred to other divisions within Sloan. No other division of Sloan Industries transfers internally more than 10 percent of its output.

Based on any profit-based measure of performance, Quality Bearing is the leading division within Sloan Industries. Other divisional managers within Sloan always find that their performance is compared to that of Quality Bearing. These managers argue that the transfer pricing situation gives Quality Bearing a competitive advantage.

a. What factors may contribute to any advantage that the Quality Bearing division might have over the other divisions?

b. What alternative transfer price or performance measure might be more appropriate in this situation?

43. *(Responsibility accounting reports)* Gold Finch Inc. manufactures small industrial tools and has an annual sales volume of approximately $3.5 million. Sales growth has been steady during the year and there is no evidence of cyclical demand. The company's market has expanded only in response to product innovation; therefore, R&D is very important to the company.

Cynthia Tatum, controller, has designed and implemented a new budget system. An annual budget has been prepared and divided into 12 equal segments to use for monthly performance evaluations. The vice president of operations was upset upon receiving the following responsibility report for the Machining Department for October 1997:

MACHINING DEPARTMENT—RESPONSIBILITY REPORT
FOR THE MONTH ENDED OCTOBER 31, 1997

	BUDGET	ACTUAL	VARIANCE
Volume in units	3,000	3,185	185F
Variable manufacturing costs:			
Direct material	$24,000	$ 24,843	$ 843U
Direct labor	27,750	29,302	1,552U
Variable factory overhead	33,300	35,035	1,735U
Total	$85,050	$ 89,180	$4,130U
Fixed manufacturing costs:			
Indirect labor	$ 3,300	$ 3,334	$ 34U
Depreciation	1,500	1,500	0
Tax	300	300	0
Insurance	240	240	0
Other	930	1,027	97U
Total	$ 6,270	$ 6,401	$ 131U
Corporate costs:			
Research and development	$ 2,400	$ 3,728	$1,328U
Selling and administration	3,600	4,075	475U
Total	$ 6,000	$ 7,803	$1,803U
Total costs	$97,320	$103,384	$6,064U

Handwritten annotations: next to Direct material "8/units", next to Direct labor "9.25", next to Variable factory overhead "11.10".

a. Identify the weaknesses in the responsibility report for the Machining Department.

b. Prepare a revised responsibility report for the Machining Department that reduces or eliminates the weaknesses indicated in part a.

c. Deviations in excess of 5 percent of budget are considered material and worthy of investigation. Should any of the variances of the Machining Department be investigated? Regardless of materiality, is there any area that the vice president of operations might wish to discuss with the manager of the Machining Department?

(CMA adapted)

44. *(Multinational company transfers)* The South Carolina Instruments Company (SCIC) is considering establishing a division in Ireland to manufacture integrated circuits. Some of the circuits will be shipped to the United States and incorporated into the firm's line of computers. The remaining output from the Ireland division will be sold in the European Union. SCIC plans to operate the Ireland division as a profit center. Compose a report describing some of the problems related to transfer pricing that SCIC must consider in establishing the Ireland division.

PROBLEMS

45. *(Profit center performance)* Frona Greene, the head of the accounting department at Mammoth State University has felt increasing pressure to raise external monies to compensate for dwindling state financial support. Accordingly, in early January 1998, she conceived the idea of offering a three-day accounting workshop on income taxation for local CPAs. She asked Mel Price, a tenured tax professor, to supervise the planning process for the seminar, which was to be held in late March 1998. In early February, Professor Price presented Ms. Greene with the following budget plan:

Revenues ($400 per participant)		$40,000
Expenses		
Speakers ($500 each)	$ 5,000	
Rent on facilities	3,600	
Advertising	2,100	
Meals and lodging	18,000	
Departmental overhead allocation	3,500	(32,200)
Profit		$ 7,800

Explanations of budget items: The facilities rent of $3,600 is a fixed rental, which is to be paid to a local hotel for use of its meeting rooms. The advertising is also a fixed budgeted cost. Meal expense is budgeted at $5 per person per meal (a total of 9 meals are to be provided for each participant); lodging is budgeted at the rate of $45 per participant per night. The departmental overhead includes a specific charge for supplies costing $10 for each participant as well as a general allocation of $2,500 for use of departmental secretarial resources. After reviewing the budget, Ms. Greene gave Professor Price approval to proceed with the seminar.

a. Recast the above income statement in a segment margin income statement format.

b. Assume the actual financial results of the seminar were as follows:

Revenues (120 participants)		$38,500
Expenses		
Speakers ($750 each)	$ 7,500	
Rent on facilities	4,200	
Advertising	2,900	
Meals and lodging	21,600	
Departmental overhead allocation	3,700	(39,900)
Loss		$(1,400)

Explanation of actual results: Because signups were running below expectations, the seminar fee was reduced from $400 to $300 for late enrollees and advertising expense was increased. In budgeting for the speakers, Professor Price neglected to include airfare, which averaged $250 per speaker. After the fees were reduced and advertising increased, the number of participants grew and was larger than expected; therefore, a larger meeting room had to be rented from the local hotel. Recast the actual results in a segment margin income format.

c. Compute variances between the budgeted segment margin income statement and the actual segment income statement. Identify and discuss the factors that are primarily responsible for the difference between the budgeted profit and the actual loss on the tax seminar.

46. *(Transfer prices)* In each of the following cases, the Electronic Division can sell all its production of audio speakers to outside customers or it can sell some of them to the Hi Fi Division and the remainder to outside customers. Electronic Division's capacity for production of these speakers is 200,000 units annually. The data related to each independent case are:

	ELECTRONIC DIVISION	
	CASE #1	CASE #2
Production costs per unit:		
Direct materials	$30	$20
Direct labor	10	8
Variable overhead	3	2
Fixed overhead (based on capacity)	1	1
Other variable selling and delivery costs per unit*	6	4
Selling price to outside customers	75	60

*In either case, $1 of the selling expenses will not be incurred on intracompany transfers.

	HI FI DIVISION	
Number of speakers needed annually	40,000	40,000
Current unit price being paid to outside supplier	$65	$52

a. For each case, determine the upper and lower limits for a transfer price for speakers.

b. For each case, determine a transfer price for the Electronic Division that will provide a $10 contribution margin per unit.

c. Using the information developed for part b, determine a dual transfer price for Case #1 assuming that Hi Fi is to be able to acquire the speakers from Electronic at $10 below Hi Fi's purchase price from outside suppliers.

47. *(Transfer price)* Two of the divisions of Heavy-Duty Equipment Company are the Motor Division and the Implement Division. The Motor Division produces motors used by both the Implement Division and a variety of external industrial customers.

For external sales, sales orders are generally produced in 50-unit lots. Using this typical lot size, the cost per motor is as follows:

Variable production costs	$1,050
Fixed manufacturing overhead	450
Variable selling expenses	150
Fixed selling expense	210
Fixed general and administrative expense	320
Total unit cost	$2,180

The Motor Division normally earns a profit margin of 20 percent by setting the external selling price at $2,616. Because a significant number of sales are being made internally, Motor Division managers have decided that $2,616 is the appropriate price to use for all transfers to the Implement Division.

When the managers in the Implement Division heard of this change in the transfer price, they became very upset because the change would have a major negative impact on Implement's net income figures. Because of competition, Implement has asked the Motor Division to lower its transfer price; by reducing the transfer price, Motor's profit margin will be 15 percent. Implement managers have asked Heavy-Duty whether the Division can buy motors externally. Bud Dawkins, Heavy-Duty's president, has gathered the following price information to help the two divisional managers negotiate an equitable transfer price:

Current external sales price	$2,616
Total variable production cost plus a 20% profit margin ($1,050 × 1.2)	1,260
Total production cost plus a 20% profit margin ($1,500 × 1.2)	1,800
Bid price from external supplier (if motors are purchased in 50-unit lots)	2,320

a. Discuss advantages and disadvantages of each of the above transfer prices to both the selling and buying divisions and to Heavy-Duty Equipment.

b. If the Motor Division could sell all its production externally at $2,616, what is the appropriate transfer price and why?

48. *(Intracompany transfers)* The Clutch Division of James Industries makes a variable-speed clutch that it sells commercially at $500 per unit. Standard unit costs for the variable-speed clutch are

Direct material	$ 75
Direct labor	150
Overhead	150
Total unit cost	$375

The standard direct labor rate is $10 per hour, and overhead is assigned at 100 percent of the direct labor rate. Expected capacity direct labor hours are 75,000, and the overhead rate is $4 variable and $6 fixed. The Clutch Division is operating at 80 percent of capacity.

A coal-hauling system is being rebuilt by the Materials Handling Division of James Industries. This job requires 50 variable-speed clutches. A clutch that meets the job specifications can be purchased for $450 a unit from an outside supplier. The clutch made by the Clutch Division exceeds the specifications for the coal-handling system job. Interdivisional transfers in James Industries are made at market price when available, and all divisions are evaluated as profit centers.

a. From the perspective of James corporate officials, is James Industries better off if the Materials Handling Division purchases the clutches from the outside supplier at $450 a unit or from the Clutch Division at $500 a unit? Would your answer change if the Clutch Division agreed to transfer the clutches at $450 a unit? Explain.

b. From the perspective of the Materials Handling Division manager, should the division purchase the clutches externally at $450 a unit or internally at $500 a unit? Would your answer change if the Clutch Division agreed to transfer the clutches at $450 a unit? Explain.

c. If the Clutch Division is operating at 80 percent of capacity, what is the lowest price at which it would consider transferring the clutches to the Materials Handling Division? Would your answer change if the Clutch Division was operating at 100 percent of capacity? Explain.

d. Because both divisions are evaluated as profit centers, what is the most useful transfer price if the Clutch Division is operating at 80 percent capacity? Explain. Would your answer change if the Clutch Division were operating at 100 percent of capacity? Explain.

49. *(Calculation of income using transfer pricing)* Enchanting Scents Ltd. manufactures a line of perfume in a series of mixing operations with the addition of certain aromatic and coloring ingredients. The finished products are packaged in a company-produced glass bottle and packed in cases containing six bottles.

Management believes that product sales are heavily influenced by the appearance of the bottle and has therefore devoted considerable effort to the bottle production process. This attention has resulted in the development of certain unique bottle production processes in which management takes considerable pride.

The two areas (perfume production and bottle manufacturing) have evolved over the years in an almost independent manner; in fact, rivalry has developed between management personnel about which division is more important to Enchanting Scents. This attitude is probably intensified because the bottle manufacturing plant was purchased intact 10 years ago and no real interchange of management personnel or ideas (except at the top corporate level) has taken place.

Since the Bottle Division was acquired, its entire production has been absorbed by the Perfume Division. Each area is considered a separate profit center and evaluated as such. As the new corporate controller, you are responsible for the definition of a proper transfer price to use in crediting the bottle production profit center and in debiting the perfume production profit center. At your request, the general manager of the Bottle Division has asked certain other bottle manufacturers to quote a price for the quantity and sizes demanded by the Perfume Division. These competitive prices for cases of six bottles each are as follows:

VOLUME	TOTAL PRICE	PRICE PER CASE
2,000,000 cases	$ 4,000,000	$2.00
4,000,000 cases	7,000,000	1.75
6,000,000 cases	10,020,000	1.67

A cost analysis of the internal bottle plant indicates that it can produce bottles at these costs:

VOLUME	TOTAL PRICE	PRICE PER CASE
2,000,000 cases	$ 3,200,000	$1.60
4,000,000 cases	5,200,000	1.30
6,000,000 cases	7,200,000	1.20

The above analysis represents fixed costs of $1,200,000 and variable costs of $1 per case.

These figures have given rise to considerable corporate discussion about the proper value to use in the transfer of bottles to the Perfume Division. This interest is heightened because a significant portion of a division manager's income is an incentive bonus based on profit center results.

The Perfume Division has the following costs in addition to the bottle costs:

VOLUME	TOTAL COST	COST PER CASE
2,000,000 cases	$16,400,000	$8.20
4,000,000 cases	32,400,000	8.10
6,000,000 cases	48,420,000	8.07

Market research has furnished you with the following price-demand relationships for the finished product:

SALES VOLUME	TOTAL SALES REVENUE	SALES PRICE PER CASE
2,000,000 cases	$25,000,000	$12.50
4,000,000 cases	45,600,000	11.40
6,000,000 cases	63,900,000	10.65

a. Enchanting Scents Ltd. has used market-based transfer prices in the past. Using the current market prices and costs, and assuming a volume of 6,000,000 cases, calculate the income for the Bottle Division, the Perfume Division, and Enchanting Scents Ltd.

b. The production and sales level of 6,000,000 cases is the most profitable volume for which of the following: the Bottle Division, the Perfume Division, or Enchanting Scents? Explain your answer.

(IMA adapted)

50. *(Transfer pricing policy)* Tennessee Corporation operates with 25 profit centers. Company policy requires all transfers between corporate units to be at market price. Memphis Division was requested to produce 10,000 standard parts for Knoxville Division. This order represents 10 percent of the division's capacity, stated in terms of machine hours. Memphis Division quoted a $35 price per unit, but Knoxville Division found an external company that would sell the parts for $28. Because corporate policy states that external market prices must be used, Memphis was required to sell the units at $28. Memphis' total variable cost for the parts is $22.

a. What amount of contribution margin will Memphis Division earn at the originally quoted price? At the externally quoted price?

b. What effect does the use of the externally quoted price have on Tennessee Corporation's income before tax?

c. Some of the time required by Knoxville Division's order could be used to produce a special order for an outside company. Only 10,000 hours of machine time are available in Memphis Division. Discuss how Memphis management should make the choice between producing the order for Knoxville versus the outside company. What factors should be considered?

d. Should market price always be used to set a transfer price between organizational units? If so, discuss why. If not, discuss why not and when it is appropriate.

51. *(Transfer pricing and decision making)* The Controls Division of Johnson Electric Motors manufactures a starter with the following standard costs:

Direct material	$ 5
Direct labor	30
Overhead	15
Total unit cost	$50

The standard direct labor rate is $15 per hour, and overhead is assigned at 50 percent of the direct labor rate. Normal capacity direct labor hours are 20,000, and the overhead rate is $2.50 variable and $5.00 fixed per direct labor hour based on normal capacity.

The starters sell for $75, and the Controls Division is currently operating at a level of 16,000 direct labor hours for the year. All transfers in Johnson are made at market price. If mutually agreed upon, the divisional managers are permitted to negotiate a transfer price.

The Motor Division currently purchases 2,000 starters from the Controls Division at market price. The divisional manager of the Motor Division indicates that she can purchase the starters from a foreign supplier for $65. Because she is free to select a supplier, she has indicated that she would like to negotiate a new transfer price with the Controls Division. The managers of the Controls Division indicate that they believe the foreign supplier is attempting to "buy in" by selling the starters at what they consider to be an excessively low price.

a. From the perspective of the firm, should the Motors division purchase the starters internally or externally? How much will the firm's pretax income change if the starters are purchased from the foreign supplier?

b. From the view of the Motor Division, should the starters be purchased from the Controls Division or the foreign supplier? How much will the pretax income of the division change if the starters are purchased from the foreign supplier?

c. From the perspective of the Controls Division, how much will its net income change if the starters are purchased from the foreign supplier? What is the minimum price at which the Controls Division would transfer the starters? What is the change in the pretax income of the Controls Division if the transfers are made at $65 a unit?

d. If the Controls Division were operating at 100 percent of capacity and the Motor Division wanted to purchase the starters externally, from the point of view of the firm, the Motor Division, and the Controls Division, what should be done if

   (1) The Controls Division could not sell the additional starters externally to continue operating at full capacity?

   (2) The Controls Division could sell the additional starters externally to continue at full capacity?

52. *(Journal entries)* Sports Bag Division makes top-of-the-line travel bags that are sold to external buyers and are also being used by the Wholesale Sporting Goods Division as part of a complete tennis racket set. During the month just ended, Wholesale Sporting Goods acquired 2,000 bags from Sports Bag Division. Sports Bag's standard unit costs are

Direct materials	$10
Direct labor	3
Variable factory overhead	4
Fixed factory overhead	6
Variable selling	2
Fixed selling and administrative	3

Wholesale Sporting Goods can acquire comparable bags externally for $40 each. Give the entries for each division for the past month if the transfer is to be recorded

a. at Wholesale Sporting Goods' external purchase price.

b. at a negotiated price of variable cost plus 15 percent of production cost.

c. by Sports Bag at Wholesale Sporting Goods' external price and by Wholesale Sporting Goods at Sports Bag's variable production cost.

d. at Sports Bag's absorption cost.

53. *(Internal versus external sale)* Providence Products Inc. consists of three decentralized divisions: Park Division, Quayside Division, and Ridgetop Division. The president of Providence Products has given the managers of the three divisions the authority to decide whether to sell internally at a transfer price determined by the division managers, or externally. Market conditions are such that sales made internally or externally will not affect market or transfer prices. Intermediate markets will always be available for Park, Quayside, and Ridgetop to purchase their manufacturing needs or sell their product. Division managers attempt to maximize their contribution margin at the current level of operating assets for the division.

The Quayside Division manager is considering the following two alternative orders.

The Ridgetop Division needs 3,000 units of a motor that can be supplied by the Quayside Division. To manufacture these motors, Quayside would purchase components from the Park Division at a transfer price of $600 per unit; Park's variable cost for these components is $300 per unit. Quayside Division would further process these components at a variable cost of $500 per unit.

If the Ridgetop Division cannot obtain the motors from the Quayside Division, the motors will be purchased from Essex Company for $1,500 per unit.

Essex Company would also purchase 3,000 components from Park at a price of $400 for each of these motors; Park's variable cost for these components is $200 per unit.

The Saxon Company wants to buy 3,500 similar motors from the Quayside Division for $1,250 per unit. Quayside would again purchase components from the Park Division at a transfer price of $500 per unit; Park's variable cost for these components is $250 per unit. Quayside Division would further process these components at a variable cost of $400 per unit.

The Quayside Division's plant capacity is limited and, as such, the company can accept either the Saxon contract or the Ridgetop order, but not both. The president of Providence Products and the manager of Quayside Division agree that it would not be beneficial in the short or long run to increase capacity.

a. If the Quayside Division manager wants to maximize short-run contribution margin, determine whether the Quayside Division should (1) sell motors to the Ridgetop Division at the prevailing market price or (2) accept the Saxon Company contract. Support your answer with appropriate calculations.

b. Without prejudice to your answer to part a, assume that the Quayside Division decides to accept the Saxon Company contract. Determine whether this decision is in the best interest of Providence Products Inc. Support your answer with appropriate calculations.

(CMA adapted)

54. *(Transfer prices; regular use of direct method of allocation from Chapter 5)* Williams & Associates, CPAs, has three revenue departments: Auditing and Accounting (A&A), Tax (T), and Consulting (C). In addition, the company has two support departments: Administration and EDP. Administration costs are allocated to the three revenue departments on the basis of number of employees. The EDP department's fixed costs are allocated to revenue departments on the basis of peak hours of monthly service expected to be used by each revenue department. EDP's variable costs are assigned to the revenue departments at a transfer price of $40 per hour of actual service. Following are the direct costs and the allocation bases associated with each of the departments:

	DIRECT COSTS (BEFORE TRANSFER COSTS)	NUMBER OF EMPLOYEES	ALLOCATION BASES PEAK HOURS	EDP HOURS USED
Administration	$450,000	4	30	290
EDP—Fixed	300,000	2	N/A	N/A
EDP—Variable	90,000	2	N/A	N/A
A&A	200,000	10	80	1,220
T	255,000	5	240	650
C	340,000	3	25	190

a. Was the variable EDP transfer price of $40 adequate? Explain.

b. Allocate the other service department costs to A&A, T, and C using the direct method. (See Chapter 5 for the direct method of allocation.)

c. What are the total costs of the revenue-producing departments after allocation?

55. *(Justification of cost allocations)* Wales Company recently reorganized its computer and data processing activities. The small installations located within the accounting departments at its plants and subsidiaries have been replaced with a single data processing department at corporate headquarters responsible for the operations of a newly acquired large-scale computer system. The new department has been in operation for 2 years and has been producing reliable and timely data for the past 12 months.

Because the department has focused its activities on converting applications to the new system and producing reports for the plant and subsidiaries managements, little attention has been devoted to the costs of the department. Now that the department's activities are operating relatively smoothly, company management has requested that the department manager recommend a cost accumulation system to facilitate cost control and the development of suitable rates to charge users for service.

For the past 2 years, the departmental costs have been recorded in one account. The costs have then been allocated to user departments on the basis of computer time used. The schedule below reports the costs and charging rate for calendar year 1997:

(1) Salaries and benefits	$ 622,600
(2) Supplies	40,000
(3) Equipment maintenance contract	15,000
(4) Insurance	25,000
(5) Heat and air-conditioning	36,000
(6) Electricity	50,000
(7) Equipment and furniture depreciation	285,400
(8) Building improvements depreciation	10,000
(9) Building occupancy and security	39,300
(10) Corporate administrative charges	52,700
Total costs	$1,176,000
Computer hours for user processing*	2,750
Hourly rate ($1,176,000 ÷ 2,750)	$428

*Use of available computer hours:

Testing and debugging programs	250
Setup of jobs	500
Processing jobs	2,750
Downtime for maintenance	750
Idle time	742
Total hours of usage	4,992

The department manager recommends that the department costs be accumulated by five activity centers within the department: Systems Analysis, Programming, Data Preparation, Computer Operations (Processing), and Administration. She also suggests that the costs of the Administration activity be allocated to the other four activity centers before a separate rate for charging users is developed for each of the first four activities. The manager made the following observations regarding the charges to the several subsidiary accounts within the department after reviewing details of the accounts:

1. Salaries and benefits—records the salary and benefit costs of all employees in the department.
2. Supplies—records paper costs for printers, and a small amount for miscellaneous other costs.
3. Equipment maintenance contracts—records charges for maintenance contracts; all equipment is covered by maintenance contracts.
4. Insurance—records costs of insurance covering the equipment and furniture.
5. Heat and air-conditioning—records a charge from the corporate heating and air-conditioning department; estimated to be the incremental cost to meet the special needs of the computer department.
6. Electricity—records the charge for electricity based on a separate meter in the department.
7. Equipment and furniture depreciation—records the depreciation charges for all owned equipment and furniture in the department.
8. Building improvements—records the amortization charges for the building changes required to provide proper environmental control and electrical service for the computer equipment.
9. Building occupancy and security—records the computer department's share of the depreciation, maintenance, heat, and security costs of the building; allocated to the department on the basis of square feet occupied.

10. Corporate administrative charges—records the computer department's share of the corporate administrative costs; allocated to the department on the basis of number of employees in the department.

   a. For each of the ten cost items, state whether it should be distributed to the five activity centers. For each cost item that should be distributed, recommend the basis on which it should be distributed. Justify your conclusion in each case.

   b. Assume the costs of the Computer Operations (processing) activity will be charged to the user departments on the basis of computer hours. Using the analysis of computer utilization shown, determine the total number of hours that should be employed to determine the charging rate for Computer Operations (processing). Justify your answer.

(CMA adapted)

CASES

56. *(Interdivisional transfers; deciding on alternatives)* Alice Appleby, a management accountant, has recently been employed as controller in the Designer Division of Global Traveler, Inc. The company is organized on a divisional basis with considerable vertical integration.

Designer Division makes several luggage products, including a slim leather portfolio. Sales of the portfolio have been steady, and the marketing department expects continued strong demand. Alice is looking for ways the Designer Division can contain its costs and thus boost its earnings from future sales. She discovered that the Designer Division has always purchased its supply of high-quality tanned leather from another division of Global Traveler, the Guissepi Division. Guissepi Division has been providing the three square feet of tanned leather needed for each portfolio for $9 per square foot.

Alice wondered whether it might be possible to purchase Designer's leather needs from a supplier other than Guissepi at a lower price for comparable quality. Top management at Global Traveler reluctantly agreed to allow the Designer Division to consider purchasing outside the company.

The Designer Division will need leather for 100,000 portfolios during the coming year. Designer management has requested bids from several leather suppliers. The two best bids are $8 and $7 per square foot from Keonig and Thompson, respectively. Alice has been informed that another subsidiary of Global Traveler, Ridley Chemical, supplies Thompson with chemicals that have been an essential ingredient of the tanning process for Thompson. Ridley Chemical charges Thompson $2 for enough chemicals to prepare three square feet of leather. Ridley's profit margin is 30 percent.

The Guissepi Division wants to continue supplying Designer's leather needs at the same price per square foot as in the past. Jim Scott, Guissepi's controller, has made it clear that he believes Designer should continue to purchase all its needs from Guissepi to preserve Guissepi's healthy profit margin of 40 percent of sales.

You, as Global Traveler's vice president of finance, have called a meeting of the controllers of Designer and Guissepi. Alice is eager to accept Thompson's bid of $7. She points out that Designer's earnings will show a significant increase if the division can buy from Thompson.

Jim Scott, however, wants Global to keep the business within the company and suggests that you require Designer to purchase its needs from Guissepi. He emphasizes that Guissepi's profit margin should not be lost to the company.

From whom should the Designer Division buy the leather? Consider both Designer's desire to minimize its costs and Global's corporate goal of maximizing profit on a companywide basis.

(IMA adapted)

57. *(Transfer prices; discussion)* Better Products Inc. is a decentralized company. Each division has its own sales force and production facilities and is operated as an investment center. Top management uses return on investment (ROI) for performance evaluation. The Hazlett Division has just been awarded a contract for a product that uses a component manufactured by the Andalusia Division as well as by outside suppliers. Hazlett used a cost figure of $3.80 for the component when the bid was prepared for the new product. This cost figure was supplied by Andalusia in response to Hazlett's request for the average variable cost of the component.

Andalusia has an active sales force that is continually soliciting new customers. Andalusia's regular selling price for the component Hazlett needs for the new product is $6.50. Sales of the component are expected to increase. Andalusia management has the following costs associated with the component:

Standard variable manufacturing cost	$3.20
Standard variable selling and distribution expenses	.60
Standard fixed manufacturing cost	1.20
Total	$5.00

The two divisions have been unable to agree on a transfer price for the component. Corporate management has never established a transfer price because interdivisional transactions have never occurred. The following suggestions have been made for the transfer price:

- Regular selling price
- Regular selling price less variable selling and distribution expenses
- Standard manufacturing cost plus 15 percent
- Standard variable manufacturing cost plus 20 percent

a. Compute each of the suggested transfer prices.
b. Discuss the effect each of the transfer prices might have on the Andalusia Division management's attitude toward intracompany business.
c. Is the negotiation of a price between the Hazlett and Andalusia Divisions a satisfactory method to solve the transfer price problem? Explain your answer.
d. Should the corporate management of Better Products Inc. become involved in this transfer controversy? Explain your answer.

(CMA adapted)

58. *(Effect of service department allocations on reporting and evaluation)* Janson Corporation is a diversified manufacturing company with corporate headquarters in Jacksonville, Florida. The three operating divisions are the Canaveral Division, the Plastic Products Division, and the Metalic Products Division. Much of the manufacturing activity of the Canaveral Division is related to work performed for the government space program under negotiated contracts.

Janson Corporation headquarters provides general administrative support and computer services to each of the three operating divisions. The computer services are provided through a computer time-sharing arrangement. The central processing unit (CPU) is located in Jacksonville, and the divisions have remote terminals that are connected to the CPU by telephone lines. One standard from the Cost Accounting Standards Board provides that the cost of general administration may be allocated to negotiated defense contracts. Further, the standards provide that, in situations in which computer services are provided by corporate headquarters, the actual costs (fixed and variable) of operating the computer department may be allocated to the defense division based on a reasonable measure of computer usage.

The general managers of the three divisions are evaluated based on the before-tax performance of each division. The November 1997 performance evaluation reports (in millions of dollars) for each division are presented below.

	CANAVERAL DIVISION	PLASTICS PRODUCTS DIVISION	METALIC PRODUCTS DIVISION
Sales	$23	$15	$55
Cost of goods sold	(13)	(7)	(38)
Gross profit	$10	$ 8	$17
Selling and administrative:			
Division selling and administration costs	$ 5	$ 5	$ 8
Corporate general administration costs	1	—	—
Corporate computing	1	—	—
Total	$ 7	$ 5	$ 8
Profit before taxes	$ 3	$ 3	$ 9

Without a charge for computing services, the operating divisions may not make the most cost-effective use of the Computer Systems Department's resources. Outline and discuss a method for charging the operating divisions for use of computer services that would promote cost consciousness by the operating divisions and operating efficiency by the Computer Systems Department.

(CMA adapted)

ETHICS AND QUALITY DISCUSSION

59. Schneider Corporation has decided to open a subsidiary in Holland. Hans Post has been asked to go overseas and help in the startup of the subsidiary. Hans is still going to be responsible for his division in Concord during the startup phase of the Holland plant. The Concord Division manufactures the same products that the Holland Division will, although planned production costs for the Holland products are less. Hans's performance will be judged on the continued success of the Concord plant as well as his abilities in getting the Holland plant on line. Hans was chosen for the assignment in part because of his knowledge of the language; Hans's wife is from Holland and her family still lives there. When the Holland plant is on line, Hans and his family will return to Concord.

   a. What impact will the fully operational Holland plant have on the performance of the Concord plant?

   b. What conflicts will Hans face in getting the Holland plant on-line? Do these conflicts relate to ethical or performance measurement problems? How can they be resolved?

   c. Was it reasonable of the company to ask Hans to take on the new position under these conditions?

60. A large American corporation participates in a highly competitive industry. To meet the competition and achieve profit goals the company has chosen the decentralized form of organization. Each manager of a decentralized center is measured on the basis of profit contribution, market penetration, and return on investment. Failure to meet the objectives established by corporate management for these measures is not accepted and usually results in demotion or dismissal of a center manager.

   An anonymous survey of managers in the company revealed that the managers felt pressure to compromise their personal ethical standards to achieve the corporate objectives. For example, certain plant locations felt pressure to reduce quality control to a level that could not ensure that all unsafe products would be rejected. Also, sales personnel were encouraged to use questionable sales tactics to obtain orders, including offering gifts and other incentives to purchasing agents.

The chief executive officer is disturbed by the survey findings. In her opinion, such behavior cannot be condoned by the company. She concludes that the company should do something about this problem.

a. Discuss what might be the causes for the ethical problems described.

b. Outline a program that could be instituted by the company to help reduce the pressures on managers to compromise personal ethical standards in their work.

(CMA)

61. The Moreno Company has several plants, one of which produces military equipment for the federal government. Many of the contracts are negotiated on a cost-plus basis. Some of the other plants have been only marginally profitable. The home office has engaged a consultant, Mr. Ladron, to meet with top management. Ladron observes that the company isn't using some of the more "creative" accounting techniques to shift costs toward the plant serving the federal government and away from the marginally profitable plants. He notes that "transfer pricing and service department allocations involve a lot of subjectivity and there is plenty of room to stack the deck and let the taxpayer foot the bill. Taxpayers will never know and even if the government suspects, it can't prove motive if we document the procedures with contrived business jargon." One of the staff stated that "this would be a way to get back some of those exorbitant income taxes we have had to pay all these years." The company president ended the meeting and asked for some time to consider the matter.

a. What is the purpose of setting transfer prices and making service department allocations?

b. Can or should transfer prices and service department allocations be used to shift income from one plant to another? If so, under what conditions?

c. Do you think that what the consultant is suggesting is legal? Ethical? Has it ever been done? Discuss your reasoning for each answer.

INTERNET ACTIVITIES

62. Entergy Corporation, featured in the opening vignette to this chapter, recently began operations in Australia. Find the home page of Entergy Corporation and read materials there discussing the new Australian operations. In applying concepts of decentralization and responsibility accounting to its operations, write a report discussing whether the Australian operations should be evaluated differently than U.S. operations.

63. Find the home page of Coopers & Lybrand LLP. From there, locate web pages discussing governmental consulting services offered by the firm. How is Coopers & Lybrand applying the concepts of decentralization and responsibility accounting to the public sector? What services does Coopers & Lybrand offer governmental units?

64. Recently, International Thomson Publishing acquired the publisher of this textbook, West Educational Publishing, in a transaction valued at $3.4 billion. Find the Thomson Corporation home page and read materials provided there discussing the merger. What was the apparent motivation for the merger? As a member of the top management team at Thomson, what recommendations would you make for the design of the responsibility accounting system to be used to evaluate West's management?

PERFORMANCE EVALUATION

CHAPTER

20

Measuring Short-Run Organizational Performance

LEARNING OBJECTIVES

After completing this chapter, you should be able to answer these questions:

1. How are performance measures tied to organizational missions and strategies?

2. What roles does performance measurement serve in organizations?

3. What guidelines or criteria apply to the design of performance measures?

4. What are traditional short-term financial performance measures of profit and investment centers?

5. How may the Statement of Cash Flows be useful for performance measurement?

6. How are return on investment and residual income similar? How do they differ?

7. Why may the use of ROI create suboptimization in investment decisions?

Unity Telephone Company

[In the late 1980s tiny Unity Telephone Company was considering entering the emerging cellular phone market. The firm applied to the Federal Communications Commission for a cellular license and it was awarded the rights to serve Penobscot County, Maine. However, before the company could actually begin cellular phone service, it had to obtain the financing for needed equipment. In turn, to obtain financing, the company needed to develop a plan to demonstrate to potential lenders that the venture would be profitable.

[With the aid of a Big Six accounting firm, a five-year plan was established. The plan indicated that the cellular phone service would achieve profitability by the fourth year of operation. The plan called for the construction of five cellular towers with three of the towers being constructed in the first year and the other two prior to the end of the fifth year. Even with the plan in hand, no Maine bank was willing to provide financing for the venture. Eventually, Unity was able to obtain 100 percent debt financing from a manufacturer of cellular phones in exchange for a mortgage on the cellular phone system. A new company, Unicel, was created to launch the venture.

[The next challenge faced by Unity was to establish a system to track the success of the new cellular phone company. Again with the aid of the accounting firm, an operating budget was established that tied to the five-year plan developed previously.] Statistics were available [for the industry] regarding the amount of the average subscriber bill, which was reported to be approximately $97 per month, and the cost of activating a cellular subscriber, which was reported to be around $600 per subscriber. These statistics provided a couple of financial targets to be included in the operating budget, but the remaining expenses and other items of income and expense had to be budgeted based on best guess.

During the second half of 1989 [only the second year of the five-year plan] the five-year business plan became obsolete when Unicel constructed the remaining two cells to complete the system. Why was the construction schedule accelerated?

SOURCE: Kathryn Stewart, "On the Fast Track to Profits," *Management Accounting* (February 1995), pp. 44–50. Reprinted from *Management Accounting.* Copyright by Institute of Management Accountants, Montvale, NJ.

O rganizational strategy and subunit missions were introduced in Chapter 2. The three generic missions for an organizational subunit are build, hold, and harvest. Unicel's mission is build; that is, it is expected to be a growth-oriented subunit of Unity Telephone Company. Once the company was created, managers of Unity and Unicel understood that they needed to establish a measurement system to determine whether Unicel was pursuing its mission successfully. Accordingly, they created a system of accounting-based measurements that compared Unicel's performance with industry norms and with performance accomplishments in its own short history. Managers used these measurements as the basis for making changes to improve the effectiveness and efficiency of operations.

This chapter and the next two cover general concepts of performance measurement. The focus of this chapter is *traditional*, shorter-term performance measures; Chapter 21 covers performance measurement over the longer term and nonfinancial performance measures. Chapter 22 discusses how and why managerial rewards are linked to organizational performance measures. Discussion in the following section explains how performance measures are used in organizations.

ORGANIZATIONAL ROLES OF PERFORMANCE MEASURES

Organizations have reasons or missions for which they exist. In fulfilling organizational missions, managers design and implement strategies that apply organizational resources to activities. The activities are intended to execute management's strategies. Management talent and time are dedicated to planning, decision making, controlling, and *evaluating performance* with respect to these activities. The intent in these managerial processes is for management to take actions that maximize the efficiency and effectiveness of resources used. For an organization to be successful in its missions, managers must devise appropriate information systems to track resource applications.

Gauging effective and efficient management of resources is possible only if (1) the terms *effective* and *efficient* can be defined, and (2) measures that are consistent with the definitions can be formulated. Definitions of effective and efficient could be relative to historical performance, competitors, or expectations. Once defined, effectiveness and efficiency of performance can be assessed by comparing measures of actual performance with defined performance goals.

Performance measurement has been identified as a weakness of American businesses in several national surveys. For example, a 1987 survey found that 60 percent of U.S. executives were dissatisfied with their systems of performance measurement.[1] A more recent survey study (1994) co-sponsored by the Institute of Management Accountants identified control and performance measurement as one of the key areas in which a gap exists between the knowledge accounting graduates should have and do have.[2] The only areas perceived to have greater gaps between knowledge needed and knowledge possessed by accounting graduates were budgeting, product costing, and strategic cost management. The studies demonstrate the relative importance of performance measurement in businesses today.

Performance measurement provides a foundation for[3]

■ judging organizational performance,
■ relating organizational missions and goals to managerial performance,
■ fostering the growth of subordinate managers,
■ stimulating managerial motivation,
■ enhancing organizational communication,
■ making judgments about promotion, and
■ implementing organizational control.

As mentioned in prior chapters, and as discussed in detail in Chapter 22, by linking performance measures to managerial rewards, managers can provide incentives to concentrate on improving specific performance areas. As the measured dimensions of performance are improved, managerial rewards are increased. The linkage of management rewards to organizational performance measures creates the incentive that drives managers to take desired actions.

Performance measures should be devised for all critical resources consumed by operations. Additionally, the performance measurements should lead to insights about how to improve resource use and how to achieve organizational changes that allow firms to remain competitive. The following subsections provide details of performance measurement information in areas that are critical to survival in the global market.

Information for Evaluating Capital Market Performance

A traditional area of performance measurements relates to the effective and efficient use of capital resources. This area is the domain of financial accounting. Generally accepted accounting principles (GAAP) are formulated for providing information to

---

[1] Robert A. Howell, James D. Brown, Stephen R. Soucy, and Allen H. Seed, *Management Accounting in the New Manufacturing Age* (Montvale, NJ: National Association of Accountants, 1987).
[2] "What America Wants in Entry-Level Accountants," IMA Internet homepage, URL: http://www.rutgers.edu/Accounting/raw/ima/entry/entry3.htm#summary.
[3] Adapted from Harry Levinson, "Management by Whose Objectives?" *Harvard Business Review* (July/August 1970), pp. 125–134.

capital markets and other external users that provide data that are comparable across firms. This comparability facilitates investor/creditor judgments about which firms are worthy of capital investments. On the other side of the capital equation, to obtain needed capital at competitive rates, managers must demonstrate to investors that the managers' firms offer excellent returns relative to the risks assumed. Absent an ability to acquire capital at reasonable rates, a firm will stagnate for want of funds to capitalize on growth opportunities.

Another consideration that makes managers focus on capital management is stockholders. Stockholders, acting through their boards of directors, have the right to determine who will manage their businesses. Naturally, stockholders are interested in hiring a management team that will maximize the return on the stockholders' investment in the firm. So, managers must compete with other managers to obtain and maintain their positions. Only if managers satisfy the demands of shareholders will these managers be allowed to maintain their positions, be promoted, and enhance their personal human capital.

Stockholders achieve returns on their investments through dividends and appreciation in stock prices. Both types of returns depend on the ability of the firm to generate future earnings. Accordingly, stockholders and other capital providers are most intensely interested in measures of performance that indicate the ability of the firm to generate profits. To do this, firms must be able to establish a position in a market and successfully serve the customers of that market. Additional performance measures are established to gauge the success of the firm in this critical performance dimension.

Information for Evaluating Organizational Learning and Change

The emerging global market has created a pronounced trend in designing performance measures. The quality and quantity of firms competing in markets has placed the consumer at the center of attention, and success in a market depends on the ability of a firm to satisfy some segment of the market better than can any rival firm. In recent years, managers have focused more attention on assessment of their firms' performance in serving customers.

Although the level of profit achieved may be the arbiter's ultimate measure of success in serving customers, profit is a very aggregated measure. Other measures

NEWS NOTE

U.S. Firms Lag in Measurement of Critical Performance Areas

In 1991, Ernst & Young, in conjunction with the American Quality Foundation, conducted an international survey in an attempt to understand the "best practices" of total quality management. Although the research focused primarily on quality management initiatives, the survey summary provides some striking insights into U.S. firms' use of performance measures. Three major findings were as follows:

- More than 50% of businesses in all countries evaluate quality performance at least monthly. However, almost 20% of U.S. firms review quality indicators less than annually or not at all.
- While German and Japanese firms regularly translate customer expectations into the design of new products or services, almost one-third of American firms never or only occasionally use customer satisfaction measures in their design.
- Only one-third of U.S. firms place primary emphasis on competitors' performance data when developing strategic plans.

SOURCE: Michael R. Vitale and Sarah C. Mavrinac, "How Effective Is Your Performance Measurement System?" *Management Accounting* (August 1995), pp. 43–47. Reprinted from *Management Accounting*. Copyright by Institute of Management Accountants, Montvale, NJ.

can be developed that give indications of relative success in specific areas of market performance.

For example, under the forces of global competition, markets are always evolving as firms constantly search for ways to be innovative in providing customers with more value at less cost. To compete in this environment, a firm must develop an organizational culture that fosters learning and innovation. Measures can be used to track a firm's performance against customer expectations. Other measures can be designed to identify waste and assess relative efficiency in resource consumption.

With appropriate measures in place, the focus of managers and workers is on the success of the firm in serving its customers. As the organization strives to improve its performance, a climate embracing change and organizational evolution is created. Such a culture is necessary for a firm to be opportunistic and aggressive as it confronts world-class competition. The measures may also provide the incentive that is necessary to foster cooperation across functional specialties in an organization.

Managers develop products and organizational structures to support strategies that have been devised to serve a firm's customers. Once these strategies are deployed, measures must be developed to assess the performance of the products and organizational structure.

Information for Evaluating Product/Subunit Performance

A company may place its products in a market to compete on the dimensions of price, quality, and/or functionality (or product features).[4] Superior performance in any of these three performance areas can provide the competitive advantage needed for a firm to be successful. By developing specific performance measures for each competitive dimension, alternative ways can be identified to leverage the firm's competencies. As the above News Note indicates, American firms have substantial opportunity to improve their systems of quality and functionality measurements.

The organizational structure reflects the manner in which a firm assigns and coordinates its people in deploying strategies. By subdividing the overall firm, subunits can be created and charged with making specific contributions to the business. Man-

---

[4] For more details, see Robin Cooper, *When Lean Enterprises Collide* (Boston: Harvard Business School Press, 1995).

agers of each subunit can then concentrate on developing the skills and competencies necessary to satisfy their organizational roles.

The extent to which each subunit succeeds in its mission can be assessed using carefully designed performance measures. Such measures must be tailored to capture the important performance dimensions of each subunit.

Through the linkage of performance measures to a reward structure, managers are given an incentive to improve measured performance. Once this incentive has been created, it will work to advance the organization toward its established missions, or it will cause managers to act in manners contrary to the missions. The outcome depends largely on how well performance measures have been designed to capture the performance dimensions that are critical to accomplishing the organization's missions. Exhibit 20–1 identifies warning signs of performance measures that are flawed.

Each manager in a firm is expected to make a particular contribution to the organization. This concept was introduced in Chapter 19 in discussing responsibility centers and responsibility accounting. The performance measurements selected need to be appropriate for the type of responsibility assigned and the type of behavior desired. The point *that performance measures are created to cause managers to act* cannot be overemphasized. The critical question to address in evaluating a performance evaluation measure is: What managerial actions will this performance measure encourage? This section discusses important issues to be considered in designing a system of performance measurement.

DESIGNING A SYSTEM OF PERFORMANCE MEASUREMENT

Selecting Performance Measures

As discussed previously, benchmarks must be established against which accomplishments can be measured to evaluate performance. A benchmark can be a monetary one (such as a standard cost or a budget appropriation) or a nonmonetary one (such as zero defects or the market share of another organization). Regardless of the specific measures that are used (whether monetary or nonmonetary), four general criteria should be considered in designing a performance measurement system.

- The measures should be established to assess progress toward organizational goals and objectives.
- The persons being evaluated should be aware of the measurements to be used and have had some input in developing them.
- The persons being evaluated should have the appropriate skills, equipment, information, and authority to be successful under the measurement system.
- Feedback of accomplishment should be provided in a timely and useful manner.

One key to designing an effective system of performance measurement is to recognize that no single performance measure is capable of capturing all the important dimensions of performance.

- Performance is acceptable in all dimensions except profit.
- Customers don't buy even when prices are competitive.
- No one notices when performance measurement reports aren't produced.
- Managers spend significant time debating the meaning of the measures.
- Share price is lethargic despite solid financial performance.
- You haven't changed your measures in a long time.
- You've recently changed your corporate strategy.

EXHIBIT 20–1

Seven Warning Signs of Problems with Performance Measures

SOURCE: Michael R. Vitale and Sarah C. Mavrinac, "How Effective Is Your Performance Measurement System?" *Management Accounting* (August 1995), pp. 43–47. Reprinted from *Management Accounting.* Copyright by Institute of Management Accountants, Montvale, NJ.

NEWS NOTE

Performance Measurement and Organizational Performance

[In 1994, Kodak's CEO, George Fisher received performance incentives valued at about $1.7 million. This compensation was in addition to his base salary of $2 million.] The incentives were paid even as Kodak's earnings "were below target," according to the proxy [statement], as the company took charges for restructuring that included some 4,000 new layoffs. But the photography and imaging company did see stronger revenues as well as higher cash flow resulting from Kodak's lucrative sales of its health businesses for a total of $7.9 billion.

Those factors contributed to fattened executive bonuses, which were calculated on the basis of a 40% weighting for cash-flow levels and 20% on the basis of revenue according to the proxy statement. The remaining 40% weighting factor for determining bonuses was tied to earnings.

For 1995, however, Mr. Fisher has proposed substantial changes to the formula for determining management incentives as well as increases in base salaries for top executives. The proposed plan says 50% of bonuses will be based on shareholder satisfaction, including earnings and revenue growth as well as improved return on net assets and cash flow. Another 30% of bonuses will be linked to market-share growth, reduction in product defects, improved customer satisfaction and speed of bringing products to market.

The remaining 20% would reward managers for increasing the number of women and minorities in their division, ensuring at least 20 hours of training for employees and decreasing health, safety and environment violations.

SOURCE: Wendy Bounds, "Kodak's CEO Got $1.7 Million Bonus in 1994 Despite Below-Target Profit," *Wall Street Journal* (March 13, 1995), p. B9. Reprinted by permission of *The Wall Street Journal*, © 1995 Dow Jones & Company, Inc. All Rights Reserved Worldwide.

Multiple Performance Measures

The first criterion establishes the reason for using multiple performance measures rather than a single measure or measures of only a single type. Organizations have a variety of operational objectives. A primary objective is to be financially viable. If the organization is a profit-oriented one, this objective is satisfied by generating a net income amount considered by the owners to be satisfactory relative to the assets invested. That level of "satisfactory" earnings may change over time or differ based on the type of business or subunit mission. Therefore, financial performance measures must be relevant for the type of company or organizational subunit being evaluated. Also, any financial measures chosen must reflect an understanding of accounting information and its potential for manipulation. The above News Note discusses changes the CEO of Kodak proposed to measure his performance to include a broader range of performance dimensions.

In addition to financial success, many companies are now establishing operational targets of total customer satisfaction, zero defects, minimal lead time to market, and social responsibility for the environment. These goals cannot be defined directly using traditional, financial terms. Even though poor or excellent performance in these areas will eventually be reflected in financial measures, alternative short-term performance measures are needed to capture the nonfinancial dimensions of performance. Nonfinancial performance measures can be developed that indicate progress, or lack thereof, toward the achievement of these important critical success factors of a world-class company.

Exhibit 20–2 illustrates a "balanced scorecard" that considers all aspects of performance. The various company objectives and suggested measures of performance are provided for an illustrative company in the semiconductor business.

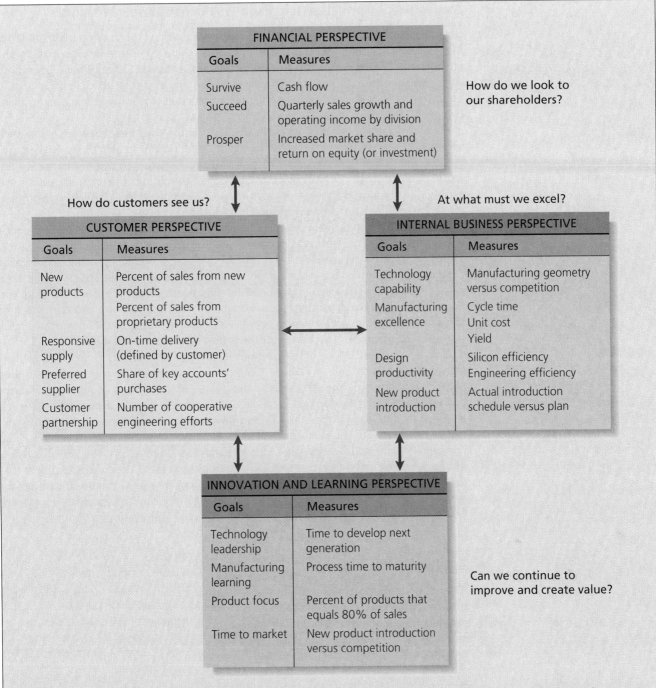

FINANCIAL PERSPECTIVE

Goals	Measures
Survive	Cash flow
Succeed	Quarterly sales growth and operating income by division
Prosper	Increased market share and return on equity (or investment)

How do we look to our shareholders?

How do customers see us?

At what must we excel?

CUSTOMER PERSPECTIVE

Goals	Measures
New products	Percent of sales from new products
	Percent of sales from proprietary products
Responsive supply	On-time delivery (defined by customer)
Preferred supplier	Share of key accounts' purchases
Customer partnership	Number of cooperative engineering efforts

INTERNAL BUSINESS PERSPECTIVE

Goals	Measures
Technology capability	Manufacturing geometry versus competition
Manufacturing excellence	Cycle time
	Unit cost
	Yield
Design productivity	Silicon efficiency
	Engineering efficiency
New product introduction	Actual introduction schedule versus plan

INNOVATION AND LEARNING PERSPECTIVE

Goals	Measures
Technology leadership	Time to develop next generation
Manufacturing learning	Process time to maturity
Product focus	Percent of products that equals 80% of sales
Time to market	New product introduction versus competition

Can we continue to improve and create value?

SOURCE: Reprinted by permission of *Harvard Business Review*. An excerpt from "The Balanced Scorecard–Measures that Drive Performance," by Robert S. Kaplan and David P. Norton (January–February 1992), pp. 72, 76. Copyright © 1992 by the President and Fellows of Harvard College; all rights reserved.

EXHIBIT 20–2

Illustrative "Balanced Scorecard"

Awareness of and Participation in Performance Measures

Regardless of the number or types of measures chosen, top management must set high performance standards and communicate them to lower-level managers and employees. Additionally, the measures should promote harmonious operations among organizational units. This factor is important to minimize the effects of sub-optimization (as discussed in the previous chapter) that might occur in a decentralized company.

People will normally act specifically in accordance with how they are to be measured. Thus, the individuals must know of and understand the performance measures used, so that managers can make decisions in light of the effects of alternative decision choices on the performance measures. Withholding information about measures will not allow employees to perform at their highest level, which is frustrating for them and does not foster feelings of mutual respect and cooperation.

To illustrate, assume your teacher said, "Turn in the answer to Problem 7 and it will be graded." You work the problem and turn in *only* the answer, as requested. Your homework is returned and you receive two points out of a possible ten because the teacher's grading key assigned points to supporting computations of the final answer. Do you believe your performance has been properly measured? Had you known that supporting computations were to be counted, and you chose not to turn them in, would your performance have been properly measured? Thus, proper measurement is influenced by proper information about what is expected.

If actual-to-standard or actual-to-budget comparisons are to be used as performance measures, people are more likely to be committed to the process if they participated in setting the standards or the budget. Participation captures the interest and attention of those persons involved and results in a "social contract" between participants and evaluators. This allows individuals to demonstrate a mutual respect for each other's ability to contribute effectively to the development process. The participants who will be evaluated clearly understand and accept the reasonableness of the standards or budget and generally attempt to achieve the results to affirm that the plans were well-founded. Employee involvement in a performance measurement system is so important that "management attempts to bolster productivity will plateau without employee support, which is the key to achieving maximum productivity."[5]

Appropriate Tools for Performance

Anyone who has accepted a job understands that there will be a performance measurement and evaluation process. For performance measures to be fair, placement personnel must first put the right individuals in the available jobs. If candidates placed in jobs do not have the appropriate skills, they are usually destined to fail. Thus, the organization is responsible for making certain that either job skills exist or can be obtained through available training. Given job competence, people must then be given the necessary tools (equipment, information, and authority) to perform their jobs in a manner consistent with the measurement process. No matter where an employee is in the organizational hierarchy, each job has certain requirements. A carpenter must have a saw and a drawing or idea of the product to be made; an accountant must have transaction information and/or source documents and a manual or electronic means by which to capture monetary changes; the company president must have the authority to obtain the needed resources to accomplish organizational objectives. Competent individuals having the necessary job "tools" can be held re-

[5] Dan J. Seidner and Glenn Kieckhaefer, "Using Performance Measurement Systems to Create Gain-sharing Programs," *(Grant Thornton) Manufacturing Issues* (Summer 1990), p. 8. Reprinted by permission, © 1990.

It is essential that workers have the appropriate tools to perform their jobs. Employees at Mazda's Flat Rock, Michigan, plant gain the tool of knowledge as they assemble flashlights in timed tests as part of training activities.

sponsible for their performance. If the appropriate tools are unavailable, people cannot be presumed to be able to accomplish their tasks.

In decentralized firms, upper-level managers have little opportunity to observe the actions of subordinates. These managers are able only to observe the outcomes as captured by performance measures. This fact makes it imperative that the performance measures selected be those that are (1) highly correlated with the subunit mission, (2) fair and complete reflections of the subunit manager performance, and (3) reflect performance that is under the subunit manager's control.

Need for Feedback

Managerial performance should be *monitored* (though not *evaluated*) on a continuous basis, and feedback should be provided to the appropriate individuals. Thus, performance monitoring and feedback should be ongoing activities, whereas performance evaluation should be scheduled for specified points in time. Positive feedback serves to motivate employees to future success by encouraging continuation of favorable behaviors. Employees receiving negative feedback are made aware of problems and can attempt to change behaviors. Waiting to provide feedback on performance until some "measurement date" is reached allows employees no opportunity for early adjustment. As indicated by the survey data presented in Exhibit 20–3 on the next page, some employees do not believe that the feedback they are receiving is of the highest quality.

Performance measurement has typically relied on information generated from the cost management system during the management control process. Exhibit 20–4 provides a diagram of the basic management control process and indicates the point at which performance has traditionally been evaluated. Although this type of measurement system was easy to implement, it often focused on performance traits that were not the most conducive to sound, competitive positions. Because of this, traditional performance measures are being supplemented with additional ones.

Feedback and Performance
Measurement

Regular feedback is the ultimate tool for shaping workers' performance, yet few employees feel their managers give it. Nor do workers really believe that performance leads to promotion, according to a survey of more than 1,000 employees in 15 small, midwestern companies. None of the following statements managed to earn a full "agree" rating–a dismal comment on the quality of employee feedback. (The shaded area represents the average response.)

Strongly disagree	Disagree	Agree	Strongly agree
I receive adequate	feedback on my performance.		
Promotions are based	on employee performance.		
Performance is	evaluated regularly.		
Managers communicate	openly and honestly.		
Performance reviews	are fair.		
My supervisor provides feedback	on performance.		
The feedback I receive is balanced —	negative and positive.		
Negative feedback expressed in our the problem, not the person.	organization addresses		

SOURCE: Ross Culbert Lavery and Russman Inc. (New York), compiled from company organizational audits, Perz Inc., Maumee, Ohio, 1992; presented in *Inc.* (September 1992), p. 32. Reprinted with permission of *Inc.* magazine. © 1992 by Goldhirsh Group, Inc.

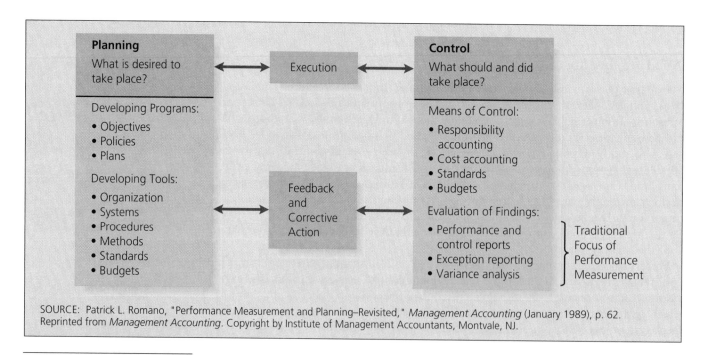

Planning What is desired to take place?	Execution	**Control** What should and did take place?
Developing Programs: • Objectives • Policies • Plans		Means of Control: • Responsibility accounting • Cost accounting • Standards • Budgets
Developing Tools: • Organization • Systems • Procedures • Methods • Standards • Budgets	Feedback and Corrective Action	Evaluation of Findings: • Performance and control reports • Exception reporting • Variance analysis } Traditional Focus of Performance Measurement

SOURCE: Patrick L. Romano, "Performance Measurement and Planning–Revisited," *Management Accounting* (January 1989), p. 62. Reprinted from *Management Accounting*. Copyright by Institute of Management Accountants, Montvale, NJ.

Diagram of Management
Control

A traditional focus of performance evaluation at the managerial level is on the financial aspects of operations and concentrates on monetary measures such as divisional profits, achievement of budget objectives, individual and total variances from budget or standard, and cash flow. Each of these measures provides different information that can be used to analyze the effectiveness and efficiency of managerial performances.

The type of responsibility center being evaluated affects the performance measure(s) used because managers should only be evaluated using performance measures relating to their authority and responsibility. In a cost center, the primary financial performance measure is the materiality of the variances from budgeted costs. Performance in a pure revenue center can be primarily judged by comparing budgeted with actual revenues. These two responsibility centers are accountable for only one type of monetary object—costs and revenues, respectively. When a manager is responsible for only one monetary item, the financial measurements appropriate for performance evaluations are limited to those relevant to that single monetary item. However, nonmonetary performance measures are now being coupled with monetary measures to provide multidimensional views of responsibility center performance.

Profit and investment center managers are responsible for both the revenues and expenses of those centers. Given this greater accountability, more financial performance measures can be used for these responsibility centers than the rather simplistic ones used by cost and revenue centers.

Divisional Profits

The segment margin of a profit or investment center is a frequently used measure of divisional performance.[6] This amount is compared with the center's budgeted income objective, and variances are computed to determine where objectives were exceeded or were not achieved.

One problem with the use of segment margin for measuring performance is that the individual components used to derive it (like any other accounting income-based amount) are subject to manipulation. Segment margin manipulation can take many forms, for example:

- If the center is using a cost flow method other than FIFO, inventory purchases can be accelerated or deferred at the end of the period to change the Cost of Goods Sold amount for the period.
- Replacement of workers who have resigned or been terminated can be deferred to minimize salary expense for the period.
- Routine maintenance can be delayed or eliminated to reduce expenses.
- If actual overhead is being allocated to inventory, production can be increased so that cost per unit declines.
- Sales recognition can be shifted between periods.
- Advertising expenses or other discretionary costs can be delayed or accelerated.
- Depreciation methods may be changed.

All the above tactics can be used to "cause" reported segment margin to conform to budget expectations, but such manipulations are normally not in the center's long-run best interest.

Divisional segment margin (or profit) represents a short-term, rather than a long-term, objective. Most reward systems (promotions, pay raises, bonuses) are based on short-term performance. Although short-run efficiency is important, companies should not use the quarterly or annual segment margin as the only performance measure of a profit or investment center's manager. A year is often too short a time over which to judge managerial performance. The performance measurement period should coincide with the time it takes to evaluate the quality of the center manager's

TRADITIONAL SHORT-TERM FINANCIAL PERFORMANCE MEASURES

---

[6] The term *segment margin* is defined in Chapter 13 as segment sales minus (direct variable expenses and avoidable fixed expenses). Thus, the margin would not include allocated common costs.

decisions.[7] Similarly, the performance measures should be matched to the subunit's mission. Short-term measures are more appropriate for hold and harvest missions and less appropriate for build missions.

Cash Flow

Managers who have authority over operating, investing, and financing activities know that for their entities to succeed, two requirements must be met: (1) long-run profitability and (2) continuous liquidity. Because external financial statements use accrual-based figures, management's attention can become diverted from the size and direction of cash inflows and outflows. The Statement of Cash Flows (SCF) helps to correct this situation by providing information about the cash impacts of the three major categories of business activities (operating, investing, and financing). The SCF explains the change in the cash balance by reflecting the entity's sources and uses of cash. Such knowledge can assist in judging the entity's ability to meet current fixed cash outflow commitments, to adapt to adverse changes in business conditions, and to undertake new commitments. Further, because the cash flow statement identifies the relationships between segment margin (or net income) and net cash flow from operations, the SCF assists managers in judging the quality of the entity's earnings.

Although the cash budget presented in Chapter 14 is essential to current cash management, the budgeted SCF gives managers a more global view of cash flows by arranging them by major activity. Such an arrangement permits management to judge whether the anticipated flows are consistent with the entity's strategic plans and, thus, provides an opportunity to evaluate performance. In addition, the cash budget disregards significant noncash transactions that are incorporated into a schedule or narrative on a Statement of Cash Flows. Because most noncash transactions will ultimately result in cash flows, disclosure of noncash transactions provides a more complete picture of future operations and their potential affect on cash availability. Analysis of the SCF in conjunction with budgets and other financial reports provides information on cost reductions, collection policies, dividend payout, impact of capital projects on total cash flows, and liquidity position.

Like segment margins and income, cash flow can be manipulated and relates to the short run rather than the long run. As a measure of performance, cash flow suffers from some of the same problems as divisional profits because managers can defer purchases of inventory and equipment or misassign collections to a period to enhance the appearance of cash flow. But adequate cash flow is a *necessity* for conducting business activities. Inadequate cash flow may reflect poor judgment and decision making on the part of the profit or investment center manager. There are many useful financial ratios (such as the current ratio, quick ratio, and number of days' collections in accounts receivable) that involve cash flow available to assist managers in the effective conduct of their functions. Three other financial measures often used to evaluate divisional performance in an investment center are return on investment, residual income, and economic value added.

Return on Investment

The difference between a profit center and an investment center is that the investment center manager also has responsibility for assets under the center's control. Giving the manager responsibility for acquisition, use, and disposal of assets increases the number of financial performance measures available because another dimension of accountability is added. **Return on investment** (ROI) is a ratio relating income

return on investment

---

[7] Quality and financial benefits to the organization should be measured concurrently. The accounting system should be designed to capture both types of information (qualitative and quantitative) that can be used as valid predictors of long-term profitability. See Sue Y. Whitt and Jerry D. Whitt, "What Professional Services Firms Can Learn From Manufacturing," *Management Accounting* (November 1988), pp. 39–42.

QUESTION	PREFERABLE ANSWER
Is income defined as segment or operating income?	Segment income
Is income on a before- or after-tax basis?	Before-tax
Should assets be defined as	
■ total assets utilized; ■ total assets available for use; or ■ net assets (equity)?	Total assets available for use
Should plant assets be included at	
■ original cost; ■ depreciated book value; or ■ current value?	Current values
Should beginning, ending, or average assets be used?	Average assets

EXHIBIT 20–5

ROI Definitional Questions and Answers

generated by the investment center to the resources (or the asset base) used to produce that income. The return on investment formula is

$$\text{ROI} = \frac{\text{Income}}{\text{Assets Invested}}$$

Before ROI can be used effectively, both terms in the formula must be specifically defined. To do this, Exhibit 20–5 asks and answers several definitional questions about this ratio. Once definitions have been assigned to the terms, ROI can be used to evaluate individual investment centers as well as to make intracompany, intercompany, and multinational comparisons. However, managers making these comparisons must consider differences in the entities' characteristics and accounting methods.

Using segment margin rather than operating income is preferred in the ROI calculation because the investment center manager does not have control in the short run over unavoidable fixed expenses and allocated corporate costs. Therefore, unavoidable fixed expenses and allocated corporate costs should not be a part of the performance evaluation criteria.[8] The same logic applies to the exclusion of taxes (or corporate interest) from investment center income. Company tax rates are determined based on total company income. Investment centers might pay higher or lower rates if they were separate taxable entities.

Investment center managers may have a substantial number of assets that are not being used. Eliminating these assets from the ROI denominator provides no encouragement for the manager to dispose of duplicate or unnecessary assets. Thus, total assets available for use is preferable to total assets utilized. Disposition of idle assets will provide the manager with additional cash flow that could be used for alternative projects. In contrast, if the objective is to measure how well the segment is performing, given the funds stockholders have provided for that segment, then net assets should be used to measure return on equity funds.

Use of the original cost of plant assets is more appropriate than net book value in determining the amount of assets invested. As assets age and net book value declines, an investment center earning the same income each year would show a continuously

---

[8] When assets and costs cannot be directly traced and must be allocated to an investment center, ROI calculations may not carry the same credibility as when allocations are not necessary. ROI calculations for an entire company or its autonomous, free-standing divisions are easier to make and are more meaningful than are ROI calculations for units requiring such allocations. Criticism of ROI comparisons may also arise when such comparisons are made among divisions of very unequal sizes or at different stages of growth and product development.

EXHIBIT 20-6

Data for Spydell National Cellular Service

	GAINESVILLE	OMAHA	SEATTLE	TOTAL
Revenues	$3,200,000	$675,000	$430,000	$4,305,000
Direct costs:				
Variable	(1,120,000)	(310,500)	(172,000)	(1,602,500)
Fixed (avoidable)	(550,000)	(117,500)	(60,000)	(727,500)
Segment margin	$1,530,000	$247,000	$198,000	$1,975,000
Unavoidable fixed and allocated costs	(372,000)	(78,000)	(50,000)	(500,000)
Operating income	$1,158,000	$169,000	$148,000	$1,475,000
Taxes (35%)	(405,300)	(59,150)	(51,800)	(516,250)
Net income	$ 752,700	$109,850	$ 96,200	$ 958,750
Current assets	$ 48,500	$ 33,125	$ 20,000	
Plant assets	6,179,000	4,610,000	900,000	
Total asset cost	$6,227,500	$4,643,125	$920,000	
Accumulated depreciation	(1,232,500)	(1,270,000)	(62,500)	
Asset book value	$4,995,000	$3,373,125	$857,500	
Liabilities	(2,130,000)	(600,000)	(162,500)	
Net assets	$2,865,000	$2,773,125	$695,000	
Proportion of total assets utilized	100%	88%	80%	
Current value of plant assets	$4,975,000	$2,180,000	$875,000	

NOTE: A summarized corporate balance sheet would not balance with the investment center balance sheets because of the existence of general corporate assets and liabilities.

increasing return on investment solely because of the diminishing asset base. Such apparent increasing returns could cause erroneous assessments of a manager's performance. The use of current plant asset values is, however, preferable to original costs. Current values measure the opportunity cost of using the assets. Such values, though, are more difficult to obtain and may be determined only by very subjective methods.

Regardless of which plant asset base is chosen for the ROI denominator, that value should be a periodic average. Because income is earned over a period rather than at a specific point in time, the averaging period for the denominator should be the same as that used to determine the ROI numerator.

Data for Spydell National Cellular Service (Exhibit 20–6) are used to illustrate return on investment computations. The company has divisions located in Gainesville, Omaha, and Seattle, which are all operated as separate investment centers. All three divisions operate in the same industry and offer the same types of services to their subscribers. Also, each division is charged with a hold mission. The similarity in mission and business line allows comparisons to be made among the three investment centers.

Return on investment computations (using a variety of bases) for Spydell National Cellular Service's investment centers are shown in Exhibit 20–7. This exhibit illustrates that ROI figures differ dramatically depending on the definitions used for the formula terms. Therefore, how the numerator and denominator in the ROI computation are to be determined must be precisely specified before making computations or comparisons.

The ROI formula can be restated to provide useful information about individual factors that compose the rate of return. This restatement indicates that ROI is affected by both profit margin and asset turnover. **Profit margin** is the ratio of income

profit margin

EXHIBIT 20–7

ROI Computations

	GAINESVILLE	OMAHA	SEATTLE
Operating Income	$1,158,000	$ 169,000	$148,000
Assets Utilized	$4,995,000	$2,968,350	$686,000
ROI	23.2%	5.7%	21.6%
Operating Income	$1,158,000	$ 169,000	$148,000
Asset Current Value	$4,975,000	$2,180,000	$875,000
ROI	23.3%	7.8%	16.9%
Segment Margin	$1,530,000	$ 247,000	$198,000
Total Asset Cost	$6,227,500	$4,643,125	$920,000
ROI	24.6%	5.3%	21.5%
Segment Margin	$1,530,000	$ 247,000	$198,000
Asset Book Value	$4,995,000	$3,373,125	$857,500
ROI	30.6%	7.3%	23.1%
Segment Margin	$1,530,000	$ 247,000	$198,000
Asset Current Value	$4,975,000	$2,180,000	$875,000
ROI	30.8%	11.3%	22.6%
Segment Margin	$1,530,000	$ 247,000	$198,000
Net Assets	$2,865,000	$2,773,125	$695,000
ROI	53.4%	8.9%	28.5%

to sales and indicates what proportion of each sales dollar is *not* used for expenses and, thus, becomes profit. **Asset turnover** measures asset productivity and shows the number of sales dollars generated by each dollar of assets. The restatement of the ROI formula is referred to as the **Du Pont model** and is

asset turnover

Du Pont model

$$ROI = \text{Profit Margin} \times \text{Asset Turnover}$$

$$= \frac{\text{Income}}{\text{Sales}} \times \frac{\text{Sales}}{\text{Assets}}$$

As with the original ROI formula, terms in the restated formula must be specifically defined before the formula is usable for comparative or evaluative purposes. The Du Pont model provides refined information about an investment center's opportunities for improvement. Profit margin can be used to judge the center's operating leverage by indicating management's efficiency in regard to the relationship between sales and expenses. Asset turnover can be used to judge marketing leverage in regard to the effectiveness of asset use relative to revenue production.

Calculations showing the ROI components using the Spydell National Cellular Service information are given in Exhibit 20–8 and use segment margin and total historical cost asset valuation as the income and asset base definitions. Thus, these computations provide the same answers as those given in the third calculation of Exhibit 20–7.

The calculations indicate that the Omaha investment center is performing very poorly relative to the other two divisions. Its performance trails for both profit margin and asset turnover measures. Based on the amount of accumulated depreciation, the Omaha investment center appears to be the oldest, which may be related to its poor performance. For age-related reasons or others that cannot be identified from the data shown, the Omaha investment center is generating too little revenue relative to both the expenses it is incurring and the assets it is employing. Omaha's manager might consider purchasing more modern facilities to generate more sales dollars and

EXHIBIT 20–8	Gainesville Investment Center:
ROI Components	ROI = (Income ÷ Sales) × (Sales ÷ Assets)

EXHIBIT 20–8

ROI Components

Gainesville Investment Center:
ROI = (Income ÷ Sales) × (Sales ÷ Assets)

$$= (\$1,530,000 \div \$3,200,000) \times (\$3,200,000 \div \$6,227,500)$$

$$= .478 \times .514 = 24.6\%$$

Omaha Investment Center:
ROI = (Income ÷ Sales) × (Sales ÷ Assets)

$$= (\$247,000 \div \$675,000) \times (\$675,000 \div \$4,643,125)$$

$$= .366 \times .145 = 5.3\%$$

Seattle Investment Center:
ROI = (Income ÷ Sales) × (Sales ÷ Assets)

$$= (\$198,000 \div \$430,000) \times (\$430,000 \div \$920,000)$$

$$= .460 \times .467 = 21.5\%$$

NOTE: for purposes of these computations, income is defined as segment margin and assets are defined as total asset cost.

greater profits. Such an acquisition could, however, cause ROI to decline, because the asset base would be increased. Rate of return computations can encourage managers to retain and use old plant assets (especially when accumulated depreciation is excluded from the asset base) to keep ROIs high as long as those assets are effective in keeping revenues up and expenses down.

Gainesville enjoys both the highest profit margin and the highest turnover. It appears that Gainesville may be benefiting from economies of scale relative to the other divisions which may partially account for its superior performance. Additionally, Gainesville is better leveraging its assets because they are 100 percent utilized. The Seattle investment center appears to be the youngest of the three. It has a lower level of accumulated depreciation relative to its investment, and it has a lower level of asset utilization. Even so, it is generating an ROI that is close to that generated by Gainesville. With greater utilization of its assets, the Seattle investment center should be able to generate a higher asset turnover and raise its ROI.

ROI is affected by decisions involving sales prices, volume and mix of products sold, expenses, and capital asset acquisitions and dispositions. Return on investment can be increased through various management actions including (1) improving profit margins by raising sales prices if doing so will not impair demand, (2) decreasing expenses, and (3) decreasing dollars invested in assets, especially if those assets are no longer productive. Action should be taken only after considering all the interrelationships that determine ROI. A change in one of the component elements can affect others. For instance, an increase in price could reduce sales volume if demand is elastic with respect to price.

Assessments about whether profit margin, asset turnover, and return on investment are favorable or unfavorable can be made only by comparing actual results for each component with some valid benchmark. Bases of comparison include expected results, prior results, or results of other similar entities. Many companies establish target rates of return either for the company, or alternatively, for the division based on the industry or market in which that division operates. Favorable results should generate rewards for investment center managers.

Unfavorable rates of return should be viewed as managerial opportunities for improvement. Factors used in the computation should be analyzed for more detailed information. For example, if asset turnover is low, additional calculations can be made for inventory turnover, accounts receivable turnover, machine capacity level experi-

Profitability Performance
  Profit margin
  Return on assets (ROI)
Asset Utilization Performance
  Average collection period
  Inventory turnover
  Fixed asset turnover
Performance in Generating Revenues
  Percentage increase in retail revenues
  Percentage increase in subscribers
  Percentage increase in roaming revenues
  Percentage increase in total revenues
Financial Strength—short term
  Current ratio
  Quick ratio
Financial Strength—long term
  Times interest earned
  Debt ratio
  Debt/Equity ratio

SOURCE: Kathryn Stewart, "On the Fast Track to Profits," *Management Accounting* (February 1995), pp. 44–50. Reprinted from *Management Accounting.* Copyright by Institute of Management Accounting, Montvale, NJ.

EXHIBIT 20–9

Unicel's Internal
Performance Measures

enced, and other rate-of-utilization measures. This investigation should help to indicate to the manager the direction of any problem(s) involved, so that causes may be determined and adjustments made. Exhibit 20–9 displays the measures utilized by Unicel to diagnose inefficiency in its operations.

Residual Income

An investment center's **residual income** (RI) is the profit earned that exceeds an amount "charged" for funds committed to the center. The amount charged for funds is equal to a specified rate of return multiplied by the asset base. Top management establishes a target minimum rate of return against which the investment center's ROI can be judged.[9] This target rate is comparable to an imputed rate of interest on the assets used by the division. The rate can be changed from period to period consistent with market rate fluctuations or to compensate for risk. The residual income computation is as follows:

residual income

$$\text{Residual Income} = \text{Income} - (\text{Target Rate} \times \text{Asset Base})$$

The advantage of residual income over return on investment is that residual income is concerned with a dollar figure rather than a percentage. It would always be to a company's advantage to obtain new assets if they would earn a dollar amount of return greater than the dollar amount required by the rate charged for the additional investment. Expansion (or additional investments in assets) could occur in an investment center as long as positive residual income is expected on the additional investment.

Continuing the Spydell National Cellular Service example, residual income is calculated for each investment center. Spydell has established 14 percent as the target rate of return on total assets and has defined income as segment margin. The cal-

[9] The target rate established for measuring residual income is similar to the discount rate used in capital budgeting (discussed in Chapter 18). For management to invest in a capital project, that project must earn at least a specified rate of return. In the same manner, ROI of an investment center must be equal to or higher than the target rate used to compute residual income.

EXHIBIT 20–10

Spydell National Cellular
Service Residual Income

Residual Income = Income − (Target Rate × Asset Base)

Gainesville:
$1,530,000 − (.14 × $6,227,500) = $1,530,000 − $871,850 = $ 658,150

Omaha:
$ 247,000 − (.14 × $4,643,125) = $ 247,000 − $650,038 = $(403,038)

Seattle:
$ 198,000 − (.14 × $ 920,000) = $ 198,000 − $128,800 = $ 69,200

NOTE: for purposes of these computations, income is defined as segment margin and assets are defined as total asset cost.

culations are shown in Exhibit 20–10. The Gainesville and Seattle investment centers show positive residual income, which means that these responsibility centers are earning above what top management considers a reasonable charge for funds. The residual income computation for the Omaha investment center indicates that income is being significantly underproduced relative to the asset investment. The division manager should be apprised of the situation so that he or she can take steps to discover the cause of and correct this unsatisfactory result.

Top management must interpret the performance measures in the light of the organizational mission of each investment center. In the case of Spydell, all divisions have the same organizational mission. However, this is not always the case as is demonstrated in the following News Note.

economic value added

Closely related to residual income is a recently developed measure called economic value added. **Economic value added** (EVA) is a measure of the extent to which income exceeds the dollar cost of capital. Its computation is as follows:

$$\text{Economic Value Added} = \text{Income} - (\text{Invested Capital} \times \text{Cost of Capital \%})$$

This measure captures market performance of a business or segment in terms of whether the income generated exceeds the costs incurred for use of the capital re-

NEWS NOTE

Saturn, The Money-Losing Winner of General Motors

[After investing $5 billion in its Saturn Division, General Motors is yet to realize any profit from its investment. Despite this fact, General Motors is preparing to expand Saturn's product line beyond the original compact sedan first sold in 1990.

[One analyst likes the decision]: it's time for GM to expand the Saturn beyond the single sedan and coupe line. "It's a fine small car, but it's not exceptional, compared to all those good Japanese cars out there," he says. "But with Saturn, you've got world-class customer satisfaction at the dealer level, and no one can copy you without creating a brand new dealer network."

[Another consultant to the auto industry also likes GM's decision:] "One of GM's toughest challenges is to win over young people—a new generation of buyers. It's really tough to reposition Buick or Oldsmobile. But Saturn's already doing it— They're already getting young import buyers."

SOURCE: Gabriella Stern, "Saturn Experiment Is Deemed Successful Enough to Expand," *Wall Street Journal* (April 18, 1995), pp. B1, B2. Reprinted by permission of *The Wall Street Journal*, © 1995 Dow Jones & Company, Inc. All Rights Reserved Worldwide.

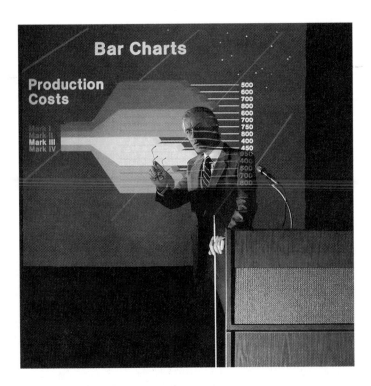

A typical short-term performance measure is profitability. Managers need to be aware of fluctuations in costs that will, in turn, be reflected in increased or decreased income amounts.

quired for operations. This information is useful to top managers in determining which business or segments are adding to, or deducting from, stockholder value. The measure of income used in calculating EVA is normally an after-tax amount. This is appropriate because EVA is a market-based performance measure and only the income remaining after payment of taxes is available for distribution to equity investors.

When used to measure investment center performance, each of the financial measures of performance discussed has certain limitations. For example, the limitations of divisional profit and cash flow are their potential for income and cash flow manipulation.

Limitations of Return on Investment and Residual Income

ROI and residual income have three primary limitations. The first limitation is a triple dimension problem related to income. Income can be manipulated on a short-run basis. This possibility was explained earlier in the chapter on the use of divisional segment margin as a performance measure. Income also depends on the accounting methods selected, for items such as inventory cost flow or depreciation. Secondarily, for perfectly valid ROI and RI comparisons to be made among investment centers, all centers must use the same accounting methods. Finally, income is based on accrual accounting, which does not consider the pattern of cash flows or the time value of money, and therefore, may not always provide the best basis for evaluating investment center performance.

The second limitation is also a triple dimension problem related to the asset investment base on which both of these measures rely. Asset investment is difficult to properly measure and assign to center managers. Some expenditures have residual values beyond the accounting period, but are not capitalized (for example, research and development costs), and therefore, create an understated asset base.[10] Also, assets included in the asset base might be the result of decisions made by previous investment center managers. Thus, current managers can potentially be judged on investment decisions over which they had no control. Third, "[w]hen fixed assets and inventory are not restated for [rising] price level changes after acquisition, net income

---

[10] Life-cycle accounting (discussed in Chapter 6) can help to eliminate this problem.

is overstated and investment is understated. Thus managers who retain older, mostly depreciated assets [often] report much higher ROIs than managers who invest in new assets."[11]

The third limitation of these measures is a single, possibly critical problem. ROI and RI both focus attention on how well an investment center performs in isolation, rather than how well that center performs relative to companywide objectives. Such a focus can result in suboptimization of resources, meaning that the firm is not maximizing its operational effectiveness and efficiency.

The Seattle Division of Spydell is used to illustrate the effects of suboptimization. As indicated in Exhibit 20–6, the Seattle Division has revenues of \$430,000, direct costs of \$232,000, and an asset base of \$920,000. ROI for the division is 21.5 percent (\$198,000 ÷ \$920,000). Assume that the Seattle Division has an opportunity to increase income by \$60,000 from installation of a new cellular tower. This venture requires an additional capital investment of \$300,000. Considered separately, this venture would result in a return on investment of 20 percent (\$60,000 ÷ \$300,000). If Seattle Division accepts this opportunity, divisional return on investment will fall:

$$ROI = (Original\ income + New\ income) \div (Original\ assets + New\ assets)$$
$$= (\$198,000 + \$60,000) \div (\$920,000 + \$300,000)$$
$$= \$258,000 \div \$1,220,000$$
$$= 21.1\%$$

If top management evaluates investment center managers on the ROIs of their divisions, the Seattle Division manager will not accept this investment opportunity because it would cause the division's ROI to drop.

Assume, however, that Spydell National Cellular Service has established a target rate of return of 16 percent on investment dollars. The decision by the Seattle manager to reject the new opportunity suboptimizes the companywide returns. This venture should be accepted because it provides a return higher than the firm's target rate. Top management should be informed of such opportunities, made aware of the effects acceptance will have on divisional performance measurements, and be willing to reward such acceptance based on the impact on company performance.

REVISITING

Unity Telephone Company

[Why did Unity Telephone Company have to build the two cellular towers so much earlier than planned? The simple answer is that competition forced the company to do so.] Subscribers are attracted to a company by the amount of cellular coverage within the serving area as well as quality of service. Cellular coverage is determined by the number of cells [towers] in each company's cellular system. Unicel had put up its three-cell system approximately four months ahead of United States Cellular [a very large competitor] in order to gain the edge of the market share of customers . . . [Their decision to add the two additional towers early was similarly motivated.

[The decision to install the towers early had substantial financial implications. The cost of a tower is in the \$250,000 to \$500,000 range depending on its height. After borrowing funds to construct the towers, the interest and principal payments became an added burden on profits and cash flows. However, the company understood the strategic consequences of failing to accelerate the investment.

[11] Robert S. Kaplan, "Yesterday's Accounting Undermines Production," *Harvard Business Review* (July/August 1984), p. 99.

Aiding in the decision to accelerate the investment were the performance criteria selected by top management. The performance criteria were appropriate for the strategic objectives of Unicel, which stressed both improving financial results and growth in market share.

[Unicel managers had developed performance measurement criteria that allowed the managers to evaluate Unicel's performance relative to the industry and to Unicel's historical performance. Managers understood that they had to interpret the performance criteria in light of the unique characteristics of Unicel such as the 100 percent debt financing and the small scale of operations. By carefully tracking the selected performance criteria, Unicel managers were able to identify the company's weak spots and improve the efficiency of operations. Even as industry performance was deteriorating, Unicel was able to make year-to-year gains in virtually all of its performance measures.

[Unicel has continued its growth trend and has improved its financial performance. In 1994, the firm merged with InterCel, Inc., a cellular company located in Alabama.]

SOURCE: Kathryn Stewart, "On the Fast Track to Profits," *Management Accounting* (February 1995), pp. 44–50. Reprinted from *Management Accounting.* Copyright by Institute of Management Accountants, Montvale, NJ.

CHAPTER SUMMARY

Organizations exist to achieve specific missions. In fulfilling organizational missions, managers design and implement strategies that apply organizational resources to activities. If the organization is to be successful, managers must apply resources with the objective of maximizing effectiveness and efficiency. Only if a properly designed performance measurement system exists can managers gauge their success. Performance measures should be designed for all critical resources consumed by operations. Also, the measurement system should lead to insights about how resource usage can be improved and create a climate for desired organizational changes to be implemented. By linking performance measures to rewards, managers are provided incentives to concentrate on improving specific performance areas. Some of the most critical performance areas for businesses today include capital market performance, organizational learning, and product and subunit evaluation.

There are standard design considerations in developing performance measurement systems. Performance measures must be appropriate for the type of responsibility center under review and can be either financial or nonfinancial. The measures selected should be sensitive to the strategies and missions of the organizations and their subunits. These measures should assess progress toward goals and objectives and should be accepted by persons being evaluated. Persons to be evaluated should have the appropriate skills, equipment, information, and authority for meeting their organizational responsibilities. Moreover, feedback on accomplishment should be provided in a timely and useful manner. Using multiple measures regarding the firm's critical success factors is more effective than using single measures. Those persons to be evaluated should participate in the development of the measures by which their performance will be evaluated. The performance measurements should lead to insights about how to improve resource use and how to achieve organizational changes that allow firms to remain competitive.

Of the short-term financial performance measures, divisional profits and cash flow are frequently used performance measures. Care must be taken that these measures are not manipulated. Two additional major financial measures of performance for investment centers are return on investment and residual income. Return on investment is income divided by assets. Residual income is the amount of income in excess of income calculated by using an imputed interest charge on the asset base. Although both measures provide important information about the efficiency and effectiveness of managers, neither should be used alone nor without recognizing the limitations inherent in the measure. Financial measures should be coupled with nonfinancial measures to provide a more complete and useful picture of performance, and long-term measures should be coupled with short-term measures.

KEY TERMS

asset turnover (p. 939)
Du Pont model (p. 939)
economic value added (p. 942)

profit margin (p. 938)
residual income (p. 941)
return on investment (p. 936)

SOLUTION STRATEGIES

PERFORMANCE MEASURES FOR RESPONSIBILITY CENTERS

- Cost Center
  Budgeted costs
  − Actual costs
  Variances (consider materiality)

- Revenue Center
  Budgeted revenues
  − Actual revenues
  Variances (consider materiality)

- Profit Center
  Budgeted profits
  − Actual divisional profits
  Variances (consider materiality)

  Cash inflows
  − Cash outflows
  Net cash flow (adequate to operations?)

- Investment Center
  Budgeted profits
  − Actual profits
  Variances (consider materiality)

  Cash inflows
  − Cash outflows
  Net cash flow (adequate to operations?)

Return on Investment = Income ÷ Assets (high enough rate?)

Du Pont Model = Profit Margin × Asset Turnover
= (Income ÷ Sales) × (Sales ÷ Assets)(high enough rate?)
Residual Income = Income − (Target Rate × Asset Base)(positive or negative? amount?)
Economic Value Added = Income − (Invested Capital × Cost of Capital %) (positive or negative? amount?)

Lancaster Industries is one of the larger divisions of McCallister Corporation. Lancaster produces numerous products used in construction of large, commercial buildings. For 1997, McCallister and Lancaster executives negotiated performance targets for Lancaster as follows:

PERFORMANCE MEASURE	TARGET LEVEL
Profit margin	7%
Asset turnover	2 times
Return on investment	14%
Residual income (target return rate is 10%)	$520,000

Actual results and other data for 1997 are summarized below:

Total assets at beginning of year	$12,200,000
Total assets at end of year	14,600,000
Sales	24,560,000
Operating expenses	22,720,000

Required:

a. Calculate the profit margin for Lancaster.
b. Determine asset turnover for Lancaster.
c. Compute the return on investment for Lancaster.
d. Prove your answer to part c using ratios computed in parts a and b.
e. Calculate residual income.
f. Evaluate Lancaster's performance for 1997.

Solution to Demonstration Problem

a. Profit margin = Operating income ÷ Sales

= ($24,560,000 − $22,720,000) ÷ $24,560,000

= $1,840,000 ÷ $24,560,000

= 7.49%

b. Asset turnover = Sales ÷ Average total assets

= $24,560,000 ÷ [($12,200,000 + $14,600,000) ÷ 2]

= $24,560,000 ÷ $13,400,000

= 1.83

c. ROI = Operating income ÷ Average total assets

= $1,840,000 ÷ $13,400,000

= 13.73%

d. ROI = Profit margin × Asset turnover

= 7.49% × 1.83

= 13.71% (answer differs from that in part c due to rounding)

e. RI = Operating income − (Target rate × Average total assets)

= $1,840,000 − (.10 × $13,400,000)

= $1,840,000 − $1,340,000

= $500,000

f. Lancaster achieved performance very close to target levels. Favorable performance was recorded for the profit margin on sales. However, the division experienced unfavorable results in asset turnover. Rather than turning assets over twice, turnover was only 1.83 times. The negative turnover effect dominated the positive profit margin effect to produce an ROI slightly below the target level. Residual income was $20,000 below the target level of $520,000. This is less than a 4 percent deviation from the target.

QUESTIONS

1. Why is performance measurement important to the success of businesses today?

2. How are organizational missions and strategies related to performance measures?

3. Why is it necessary to establish benchmarks for performance measurements to be meaningful?

4. What roles does performance management serve in the management of an organization?

5. Why do firms need to track measures regarding capital market performance?

6. In today's environment of world-class competition, why do organizations need to develop a culture that is accepting of change?

7. How do managers use information regarding performance of specific product groups and specific subunits?

8. In designing a performance measurement system, why should managerial rewards be linked to the performance measures?

9. How should one decide on a basis for measuring the performance of a responsibility center?

10. Should performance measures be qualitative, quantitative, or both? Justify your answer.

11. Can the same quantitative measures of performance be used for all types of responsibility centers? If so, why; if not, why not?

12. How can feedback, both positive and negative, be used to improve managerial performance?

13. What is the traditional financial performance measure for a cost center? A revenue center?

14. Why is managerial manipulation of reported results an important concern in designing performance evaluation measures? Are internal or external measures more susceptible to manipulation? Explain.

15. How can cash flow be used as a performance measure? In what ways is cash flow a relatively stronger or weaker performance measure than accrual measures such as segment income?

16. Do the Statement of Cash Flows and the Cash Budget provide identical information on performance? Explain.

17. The president of Toys for Boys evaluates the performance of Annie and Andy, the divisional managers, on the basis of a variety of net income measures. Drew, the controller, informs the president that such measures could be misleading. What are the major concerns in defining the "income" measure?

18. What is the major difference between a profit center and an investment center? How does this difference create the need for a different financial performance measure in an investment center relative to a profit center?

19. What is the Du Pont model? What are its component ratios?

20. The senior managers of Jambino's Bakery Inc. were gathering for their monthly breakfast meeting when Mr. Jambino came in. Norm Henry, the cost accountant, was overhead to say, ". . . turnover looks good." Mr. Jambino, in a rather unpleasant mood that morning, turned to Norm and hollered, "Of course, the turnovers are good, but what does that have to do with the return this company should be making on its investment?" Norm calmly explained that he was discussing ROI. What kind of turnover was Norm discussing and how does it relate to ROI?

21. What is residual income and how is it used to measure divisional performance? How is it similar to, and different from, the return on investment measure? How is residual income similar to, and different from, economic value added?

22. Identify and discuss the major weaknesses associated with use of ROI and RI as performance measures.

23. Describe the circumstances in which use of ROI would be likely to create a suboptimization problem. Under what circumstances would use of this measure be less likely to create a suboptimization problem?

---

24. *(ROI)* Lansing Industries has three autonomous divisions. Data for each division for the year 1997 follow:

EXERCISES

	DIVISION 1	DIVISION 2	DIVISION 3
Segment income	$ 50,000	$ 150,000	$ 400,000
Asset investment	200,000	1,000,000	4,000,000

Compute the return on investment for each division.

25. *(ROI)* Carolina Classics has asked you to help its managers determine the ROI for the year just ended. You gather the following information: average assets invested, $1,200,000; revenues, $4,400,000; and expenses, $4,100,000.
  a. Calculate return on investment.
  b. Calculate profit margin.
  c. Calculate asset turnover.
  d. Using parts b and c, prove your answer to part a.

26. *(ROI)* Your cost accounting class has been assigned a case, but the teacher only provides partial information. You have been told that a division of Texas Mills has an ROI of 12.5 percent, average total assets of $3,400,000, and total direct expenses of $1,275,000. You have been asked to
  a. determine segment income.
  b. determine revenues.
  c. determine asset turnover.
  d. determine profit margin.
  e. prove that ROI is 12.5 percent from the amounts calculated in parts a to d.

27. *(ROI)* James Clowe, a division manager of Northfield Oil, provides you with the following information regarding his division:

Beginning of the year assets, $150,000
End of the year assets, $194,000
Revenues for year, $150,500
Expenses for year, $122,500
Variable expenses, 30 percent of total revenues; remaining expenses, fixed.

  a. Compute the profit margin for the year.
  b. Compute average assets for the year.
  c. Compute asset turnover for the year.
  d. Compute return on investment for the year.

e. If Mr. Clowe could increase revenues next year by 25 percent with an increase in advertising of $15,000 and no changes in asset investment, what would be his new rate of return?

28. *(ROI)* For the most recent fiscal year, the Washington Division of Cotter Wholesaling generated an asset turnover ratio of 5 and a profit margin (as measured by the segment margin) ratio of 4 percent on sales of $400,000.
  a. Compute the average assets employed.
  b. Compute the segment margin.
  c. Compute the ROI.

29. *(RI)* The European Division of Global Department Stores accepted a 12 percent target ROI for 1997. The following data have been gathered for the division's operations for 1997: average total assets, $5,600,000; revenues, $15,000,000; and expenses, $14,280,000. What is the division's residual income? Did the division successfully meet the target ROI?

30. *(RI)* Northwest Real Estate Management has two divisions that are operated as investment centers. Information about these divisions is shown below.

	DIVISION 1	DIVISION 2
Sales	$1,200,000	$2,100,000
Total variable costs	300,000	1,435,000
Total fixed costs	700,000	250,000
Average assets invested	1,100,000	3,050,000

  a. What is the residual income of each division if the "charge" on invested assets is 10 percent? Which division is doing a better job?
  b. If the only change expected for next year is a sales increase of 15 percent, what will be the residual income of each division? Which division will be doing a better job financially?
  c. Why did the answers to the second questions in parts a and b differ?

31. *(ROI, RI)* East L.A. Law, Inc. has a target rate of return of 14 percent for its Criminal Law Division. For 1998, the Criminal Law Division generated gross fees of $10,000,000 on average assets of $5,000,000. The Criminal Law Division's variable costs were 35 percent of sales, and fixed costs were $3,750,000. For 1998, compute the following for the Criminal Law Division:
  a. ROI
  b. Residual income
  c. Profit margin
  d. Asset turnover

32. *(Missing data)* Fill in the missing numbers in the following three independent cases.

	CASE	CASE 2	CASE 3
Revenue	a	$225,000	k
Expenses	$200,000	f	l
Segment income	b	g	$80,000
Average total assets	$600,000	h	m
Asset turnover	c	4	2.5
Profit margin	d	8%	n
Achieved ROI	e	i	12%
Residual income	$ 30,000	$ 2,500	o
Target ROI	12%	j	14%

33. *(Missing data)* Tamara Billings is doing a case for her cost accounting class for which she has only partial information. She knows that a company has an ROI of 14 percent, average total assets of $7,080,000, and total expenses of $6,375,000. She needs to know the income, revenues, asset turnover, and profit margin.

a. Find each of the amounts needed by Tamara.

b. Prove that ROI is 14 percent from the amounts computed in part a.

34. *(Missing data)* Powder Valley Manufacturing relies on a residual income measure to evaluate the performance of certain segment managers. The target rate of return for all segments is 14 percent. One segment, Lawn Furniture, generated net income of $800,000 for the year just ended. For the same period, the segment's residual income was $240,000.

a. Compute the amount of average assets employed by the Lawn Furniture segment.

b. Compute the ROI for the Lawn Furniture segment.

35. *(Investment acquisition)* ABC Corporation has a target rate of return of 12 percent. C Division is analyzing a new investment that promises to generate an ROI of 20 percent, and a residual income of $40,000.

a. What is the acquisition cost of the investment C Division is considering?

b. What is the estimated net income from the new project?

36. *(Performance measures and suboptimization)* Myron Stiles is a division manager of Birmingham Rubber Products. He is presently evaluating a potential revenue-generating investment that has the following characteristics:

Initial cost $4,000,000

Net annual increase in divisional income before consideration of depreciation:

Year 1	$ 400,000
Year 2	600,000
Year 3	760,000
Year 4	3,200,000
Year 5	3,200,000

The project would have a 5-year life with no salvage value. All assets are depreciated according to the straight-line method. Myron is evaluated and compensated based on the amount of pretax profit his division generates. More precisely, he receives an annual salary of $150,000 plus a bonus equal to 8 percent of divisional segment income. Before consideration of the above project, Myron anticipates that his division will generate $4,600,000 in pretax profit.

a. Compute the effect of the new investment on the level of divisional pretax profits for years 1 through 5.

b. Determine the effect of the new project on Myron's compensation for each of the five years.

c. Based on your computations in part b, will Myron be hesitant to invest in the new project? Explain.

d. Would upper management likely view the new investment favorably? Explain.

37. *(Selecting performance measures)* Conway Property Management provides management services for a variety of commercial real estate development projects. The firm has recently created a new division to market video game services to the company's existing clients. The new division will purchase and maintain the video equipment that is placed in client buildings. Clients will be paid 20 percent of gross video equipment revenues.

Assume that you have been hired as a management consultant by Conway Property Management. You have been charged with the task of preparing a written report recommending performance measures to be used to monitor and evaluate the success of the new division and its manager. Begin your report with a discussion of your perception of the strategic mission of the new division.

COMMUNICATION ACTIVITIES

38. *(Choosing performance standards)* Caldwell Oil Field Services Company is a division of Langston Petroleum. Prior to the current year, the manager of Caldwell and corporate managers agreed to a target ROI for Caldwell of 13 percent. Subsequently, an incentive pay contract was executed between Jeannie Green, the manager of Caldwell, and corporate management. The contract stipulated that in the event Caldwell achieved an ROI of 13 percent, certain bonus payments would be made to Ms. Green. Any achieved ROI below 13 percent would result in no bonus payments. At year end, the measured ROI of Caldwell Oil Field Services Company was 5 percent.

Ms. Green has approached corporate management with the following information as the basis of arguing that she deserves a bonus payment for the year, despite the fact that her division failed to meet the stipulated 13 percent ROI.

ROI of top competitor for the year	2.7 percent
Average ROI in the industry for the year	−2.9 percent

You have been selected to be an arbitrator between Ms. Green and Langston Petroleum's top managers. Prepare a brief oral report in which you interpret the meaning of the additional information provided by Ms. Green.

39. *(Comparing performance of divisions)* Training Services Ltd. has two divisions operating in the management training field. One division, Domestic, operates strictly in the United States; the other division, Foreign, operates exclusively in the Pacific Rim countries. Both divisions are evaluated, in part, based on a measure of ROI. For the most recent year, Domestic's ROI was 14 percent and Foreign's ROI was 8 percent. One of the tasks of upper management is to evaluate the relative performance of the divisions so that an appropriate performance pay bonus can be determined for each manager. In evaluating relative performance, provide arguments as to why the determination of relative performance should

a. include a comparison of the ROI measures in the two divisions.
b. not include a comparison of ROI measures in the two divisions.

40. *(Performance measurement manipulation)* Below are a number of transactions affecting a specific division within a multiple-division company. For each described transaction, indicate whether the transaction would increase (IN), decrease (D), have no effect (N), or have an indeterminate (I) effect on the following measures: asset turnover, profit margin, ROI, and RI for the present fiscal year. Each transaction is independent.

a. The division writes down an inventory of obsolete finished goods. The journal entry is

Cost of Goods Sold	$80,000
Finished Goods Inventory	$80,000

b. A special overseas order is accepted. The sales price for this order is well below the sales price on normal business but is sufficient to cover all costs traceable to this order.
c. A piece of equipment is sold for $150,000. The equipment's original cost was $900,000. At the time of sale, the book value of the equipment is $180,000. The sale of the equipment has no effect on product sales.
d. The division fires its R&D manager. The manager will not be replaced during the current fiscal year.
e. The company raises its target rate of return for this division from 10 percent to 12 percent.
f. At mid-year, the divisional manager decides to increase scheduled annual production by 1,000 units. This decision has no effect on scheduled sales.
g. During the year, the division manager spends an additional $250,000 on advertising. Sales immediately increase thereafter.

h. The divisional manager replaces a labor-intense operation with machine technology. This action has no effect on sales, but total annual expenses of the operation are expected to decline by 10 percent.

41. (*Selecting performance criteria*) The Chicago Trading and Production Company is a large, divisionalized manufacturing company. Each division is viewed as an investment center and has virtually complete autonomy for product development, marketing, and production.

   Performance of division managers is evaluated periodically by senior management. Divisional return on investment (ROI) is the sole criterion used in performance evaluation under current corporate policy. Corporate management believes ROI is an adequate measure because it incorporates quantitative information from the divisional income statement and balance sheet in the analysis.

   Some division managers complained that a single criterion for performance evaluation is insufficient and ineffective. These managers have compiled a list of criteria that they believe should be used in evaluating a division manager's performance. The criteria include profitability, market position, productivity, product leadership, personnel development, employee attitudes, public responsibility, and balance between short-range and long-range goals.

   a. Discuss the shortcomings or possible inconsistencies of using return on investment as the sole criterion to evaluate divisional management performance.
   b. Discuss the advantages of using multiple criteria versus a single criterion to evaluate divisional management performance.
   c. Discuss some ways in which each of the multiple criteria listed by the managers could be evaluated.
   d. Describe the problems or disadvantages that can be associated with the implementation of the multiple performance criteria measurement system suggested to the Chicago Trading and Production Company by its division managers.

   (*CMA*)

42. (*Divisional profit*) Conroe Division of the Southwest Fabrics Company produces and markets floor covering products to wholesalers in Texas, New Mexico, Arizona, and California. The manager of Conroe is Michael Wilson. Southwest Fabrics evaluates all its division managers on the basis of a comparison of budgeted profit to actual profit achieved. The profit measure used is pretax income. For 1998, the budgeted income for Conroe was as follows:

PROBLEMS

Sales	$12,000,000
Variable costs	(8,400,000)
Contribution margin	$ 3,600,000
Fixed costs	(2,400,000)
Pretax income	$ 1,200,000

   At the end of 1998, the actual results for Conroe Division were determined. Those results follow.

Sales	$13,000,000
Variable costs	(9,750,000)
Contribution margin	$ 3,250,000
Fixed costs	(2,410,000)
Pretax income	$ 840,000

   a. Based on the preceding information, evaluate the performance of the Conroe Division. What was the principal reason for the poor profit performance?
   b. Why do complete income statements provide a more complete basis to evaluate the profit performance of a manager than mere comparisons of the bottom lines of the budgeted and actual income statements?

43. *(Cash flow)* Jeri Jackson, the controller of Nevada Gaming Systems Inc., has become increasingly disillusioned with the company's system of evaluating the performance of profit centers and their managers. The present system focuses on a comparison of budgeted to actual income from operations. Ms. Jackson's major concern with the current system is the ease with which the measure "income from operations" can be manipulated by profit center managers. The "basic business" of Nevada Gaming Systems is the design and production of slot machines and other gaming devices. Most sales are made on credit and most purchases are made on account. The profit centers are organized according to product line. Below is a typical quarterly income statement for a profit center, Slot Machines, that appears in the responsibility report for the profit center:

Sales	$5,500,000
Cost of goods sold	(4,500,000)
Gross profit	1,000,000
Selling and administrative expenses	(750,000)
Income from operations	$ 250,000

Ms. Jackson has suggested to top management that the company replace the accrual income evaluation measure, "income from operations," with a measure called "cash flow from operations." Ms. Jackson suggests that this measure will be less susceptible to manipulation by profit center managers. To defend her position, she compiles a cash flow income statement for the same profit center:

Cash receipts from customers	$4,400,000
Cash payments for production labor, materials, and overhead	(3,600,000)
Cash payments for selling and administrative activities	(700,000)
Cash flow from operations	$ 100,000

a. If Ms. Jackson is correct about profit center managers manipulating the income measure, where are manipulations likely taking place?

b. Is the proposed cash flow measure less subject to manipulation than the income measure?

c. Could manipulation be reduced if both the cash flow and income measures were utilized? Explain.

d. Do the cash and income measures reveal different information about profit center performance?

e. Could the existing income statement be used more effectively in evaluating performance? Explain.

44. *(Statement of Cash Flows)* The Wichita Grain Corporation's controller prepared the following Statements of Cash Flows (in thousands of dollars) for the past 3 years and the budget for next year (1998):

	BUDGET 1995	1996	1997	1998
NET CASH FLOWS FROM OPERATING ACTIVITIES				
Net income	$ 41,700	$ 39,200	$ 43,700	$ 45,100
Add net reconciling items	2,200	4,300	3,000	4,000
Total	$ 43,900	$ 43,500	$ 46,700	$ 49,100
NET CASH FLOWS FROM INVESTING ACTIVITIES				
Purchase of plant and equipment	$(18,700)		$(12,200)	$(4,600)
Sale (purchase) of investments	8,700	$ (3,600)	(12,600)	(15,800)
Other investing inflows	1,200	800	600	2,400
Total	$ (8,800)	$ (2,800)	$(24,200)	$(18,000)

NET CASH FLOWS FROM FINANCING ACTIVITIES

Payment of notes payable	$(12,000)	$(24,000)	$(15,000)	$(7,000)
Payment of dividends	(20,000)	(7,000)	(13,300)	(20,000)
Total	$(32,000)	$(31,000)	$(28,300)	$(27,000)
Net change in cash	$ 3,100	$ 9,700	$ (5,800)	$ 4,100

After preparation of the above budgeted SCF for 1998, Monique Jones, the company president, asked you to recompile it based on a separate set of facts. She is evaluating a proposal to purchase a local area network (LAN) computer system for the company at a total cost of $50,000. The proposal has been deemed to provide a satisfactory rate of return. However, she does not want to issue additional stock and she would prefer not to borrow any more money to finance the project.

Projecting the market value of the accumulated investments for the previous 3 years ($3,600 and $12,600) reveals an estimate that these investments could be liquidated for $18,400. Ms. Jones said the investments scheduled for 1998 did not need to be purchased and that dividends could be reduced to 40 percent of the budgeted amount. These are the only changes that can be made to the original forecast.

a. Evaluate the cash trends for the company over the past 3 years.

b. Giving effect to the changes above, prepare a revised 1998 budgeted Statement of Cash Flows and present the original and revised in a comparative format.

c. Based on the revised budgeted SCF, can the LAN computer system be purchased if Ms. Jones desires an increase in cash of at least $1,000?

d. Comment on the usefulness of the report prepared in part b to Monique Jones.

45. *(ROI)* Larson Lumber operates a chain of lumber and hardware stores. For 1998, corporate management examined industry-level data and determined the following performance targets for lumber retail stores:

Asset turnover	2.4
Profit margin	6%

The actual 1998 results for the lumber retail stores are summarized below:

Total assets at beginning of year	$19,200,000
Total assets at end of year	25,600,000
Sales	53,760,000
Operating expenses	50,420,000

a. For 1998, how did the lumber retail stores perform relative to their industry norms?

b. Where, as indicated by the performance measures, are the most likely areas to improve performance in the retail lumber stores?

c. What are the advantages and disadvantages of setting a performance target at the start of the year compared with one that is determined at the end of the year based on actual industry performance?

46. *(Adjusting income for ROI purposes)* Sheila White manages a division of Gulf Chemical. She is evaluated on the basis of return on investment and residual income. Near the end of November 1998, Ms. White was at home reviewing the division's financial information as well as some activities projected for the remainder of the year. The information she was reviewing is shown below.

1. Sales for the year are projected at 100,000 units. Each unit has a selling price of $30. Ms. White has received a purchase order from a new customer for 5,000 units. The purchase order states that the units should be shipped on January 3, 1999, for arrival on January 5.

2. The division had a beginning inventory for the year of 500 units, each costing $10. Purchases of 99,500 units have been made steadily throughout the year, and the cost per unit has been constant at $10. Ms. White intends to make a purchase of 5,200 units before year-end. This purchase will leave her with a 200-unit balance in inventory after she makes the shipment to the new customer. Carrying costs for the units are quite high, but ordering costs are extremely low. The division uses a LIFO cost flow assumption for inventory.

3. Ms. White has just received a notice from her primary supplier that he is going out of business and is selling his remaining stock of 15,000 units for $9.00 each. Ms. White makes a note to herself to place her final order for the year from this supplier.

4. Shipping expenses are $.50 per unit sold.

5. Advertising is $5,000 per month. The advertising for the division is in newspapers and television spots. No advertising has been discussed for December; Ms. White intends to have the sales manager call the paper and TV station early next week.

6. Salaries are projected through the end of the year at $700,000. This assumes that the position to be vacated by Ms. White's personnel manager is filled on December 1. The personnel manager's job pays $66,000 per year. Ms. White has an interview on Monday with an individual who appears to be a good candidate for the position.

7. Other general and administrative costs for the full year are estimated to total $590,000.

8. As Ms. White is preparing her pro forma income statement for the year, she receives a telephone call from the maintenance supervisor at the office. He informs Ms. White that electrical repairs to the office heating system are necessary, which will cost $10,000. She asks if the repairs are essential, to which the supervisor replies, "No, the office won't burn down if you don't make them, but they are advisable for energy efficiency and long-term operation of the system." Ms. White tells the supervisor to see her on Monday at 8:00 A.M.

   Ms. White was fairly pleased with her pro forma results. Although the results did provide the 13 percent rate of return on investment desired by corporate management, the results did not reach the 16 percent rate needed for Ms. White to receive a bonus. Ms. White has an asset investment base of $4,500,000.

   a. Prepare a pro forma income statement for Ms. White's division. Determine the amount of residual income for the division.

   b. Ms. White's less-than-scrupulous friend, Ms. Green, walked into the house at this time. When she heard that Ms. White was not going to receive a bonus, Ms. Green said, "Here, let me take care of this for you." She proceeded to recompute the pro forma income statement and showed Ms. White that, based on her computation of $723,000 in income she would be receiving her bonus. Prepare Ms. Green's pro forma income statement.

   c. What future difficulties might arise if Ms. White acts in a manner that will make Ms. Green's pro forma income statement figures a reality?

47. (ROI, RI) ABC Wholesaling sells a broad line of clothing goods to specialty retail and department stores. For 1998, the company's Mexican Division had the following performance targets:

Asset turnover	1.8
Profit margin	8%

Actual information concerning the performance of the Mexican Division in 1998 follows:

Total assets at beginning of year	$2,400,000
Total assets at end of year	3,600,000
Sales	6,000,000
Operating expenses	5,640,000

a. For 1998, did the Mexican Division achieve its target objectives for ROI, asset turnover, and profit margin?

b. Where, as indicated by the performance measures, are the most likely areas to improve performance?

c. If the company has an overall target return of 13 percent, what was the Mexican Division's residual income for 1998?

48. *(Decisions based on ROI, RI)* Seattle Aviation evaluates the performance of its two division managers using an ROI formula. For the forthcoming period, divisional estimates of relevant measures are

	PLEASURE	COMMERCIAL	TOTAL COMPANY
Sales	$24,000,000	$96,000,000	$120,000,000
Expenses	21,600,000	84,000,000	105,600,000
Divisional assets	20,000,000	60,000,000	80,000,000

The managers of both operating divisions have the autonomy to make decisions regarding new investments. The manager of Pleasure Crafts is contemplating an investment in an additional asset that would generate an ROI of 14 percent, and the manager of Commercial Crafts is considering an investment in an additional asset that would generate an ROI of 18 percent.

a. Compute the projected ROI for each division disregarding the contemplated new investments.

b. Based on your answer in part a, which of the managers is likely to actually invest in the additional assets under consideration?

c. Are the outcomes of the investment decisions in part b likely to be consistent with overall corporate goals? Explain.

d. If the company evaluated the division managers' performances using a residual income measure with a target return of 17 percent, would the outcomes of the investment decisions be different from those described in part b? Explain.

CASES

49. *(ROI, RI)* Raddington Industries produces tool and die machinery for manufacturers. The company expanded vertically in 1993 by acquiring one of its suppliers of alloy steel plates, Reigis Steel Company. To manage the two separate businesses, the operations of Reigis are reported separately as an investment center.

Raddington monitors its divisions on the basis of both unit contribution and return on average investment (ROI), with investment defined as average operating assets employed. Management bonuses are determined based on ROI. All investments in operating assets are expected to earn a minimum return of 11 percent before income taxes.

Reigis's cost of goods sold is considered to be entirely variable, whereas the division's administrative expenses are not dependent on volume. Selling expenses are a mixed cost with 40 percent attributed to sales volume. Reigis's ROI has ranged from 11.8 percent to 14.7 percent since 1993. During the fiscal year ended November 30, 1997, Reigis contemplated a capital acquisition with an estimated ROI of 11.5 percent; however, division management decided that the investment would decrease Reigis's overall ROI.

The 1997 income statement for Reigis follows. The division's operating assets employed were $15,750,000 at November 30, 1997, a 5 percent increase over the 1996 year-end balance.

REIGIS STEEL DIVISION
INCOME STATEMENT
FOR THE YEAR ENDED NOVEMBER 30, 1997
($000 OMITTED)

Sales revenue		$25,000
Less expenses		
Cost of goods sold	$16,500	
Administrative expenses	3,955	
Selling expenses	2,700	(23,155)
Income from operations before income taxes		$ 1,845

a. Calculate the unit contribution for Reigis Steel Division if 1,484,000 units were produced and sold during the year ended November 30, 1997.

b. Calculate the following performance measures for 1997 for the Reigis Steel Division:
   (1) Pretax return on average investment on operating assets employed (ROI)
   (2) Residual income calculated on the basis of average operating assets employed

c. Explain why the management of the Reigis Steel Division would have been more likely to accept the contemplated capital acquisition if residual income rather than ROI were used as a performance measure.

d. The Reigis Steel Division is a separate investment center within Raddington Industries. Identify several items that Reigis should control if it is to be evaluated fairly by either the ROI or residual income performance measures.

(CMA)

50. *(ROI and management incentives)* The Notewon Corporation is a highly diversified company that grants its divisional executives a significant amount of authority in operating the divisions. Each division is responsible for its own sales, pricing, production, costs of operations, and the management of accounts receivable, inventories, accounts payable, and use of existing facilities. Cash is managed by corporate headquarters; all cash in excess of normal operating needs of the divisions is transferred periodically to corporate headquarters for redistribution or investment.

The divisional executives are responsible for presenting requests to corporate management for investment projects. The proposals are analyzed and documented at corporate headquarters. The final decision to commit funds to acquire equipment, to expand existing facilities, or for other investment purposes rests with corporate management.

The corporation evaluates the performance of division executives by the return on investment (ROI) measure. The asset base is composed of fixed assets employed plus working capital exclusive of cash.

The ROI performance of a divisional executive is the most important appraisal factor for salary changes. In addition, the annual performance bonus is based on the ROI results with increases in ROI having a significant impact on the amount of the bonus.

The Notewon Corporation adopted the ROI performance measure and related compensation structure about 10 years ago. The corporation did so to increase the awareness of divisional management of the importance of the profit/asset relationship and to provide additional incentive to the divisional executives to seek investment opportunities.

The corporation seems to have benefited from the program. The ROI for the corporation as a whole increased during the first years of the program. Although ROI has continued to grow in each division, the corporate ROI has declined in recent years. The corporation has accumulated a large amount of cash and short-term marketable securities in the past 3 years.

The corporate management is concerned about the increase in the short-term marketable securities. A recent article in a financial publication suggested that the use of ROI was overemphasized by some companies with results similar to those experienced by Notewon.

a. Describe the specific actions division managers might have taken to cause the ROI to grow in each division but decline for the corporation. Illustrate your explanations with appropriate examples.

b. Explain, using the concepts of goal congruence and motivation of divisional executives, how Notewon Corporation's overemphasis on the ROI measure might result in the recent decline in the corporation's return on investment and the increase in cash and short-term marketable securities.

c. Discuss how divisional statements of cash flows might provide some additional useful information to divisional executives and corporate management.

d. What changes could be made in Notewon Corporation's compensation policy to avoid the current problems? Explain your answer.

(CMA adapted)

51. *(Providing feedback on performance)* Terry Travers is the manufacturing supervisor of the Aurora Manufacturing Company, which produces a variety of plastic products. Some of these products are standard items that are listed in the company's catalog, whereas others are made to customer specifications. Each month, Travers receives a performance report displaying the budget for the month, the actual activity for the period, and the variance between budget and actual. Part of Travers' annual performance evaluation is based on his department's performance against budget. Aurora's purchasing manager, Bob Christensen, also receives monthly performance reports and is evaluated in part on the basis of these reports.

The most recent monthly reports had just been distributed, on the 21st of the month, when Travers met Christensen in the hallway outside their offices. Scowling, Travers began the conversation, "I see we have another set of monthly performance reports hand-delivered by that not very nice junior employee in the budget office. He seemed pleased to tell me that I was in trouble with my performance again."

Christensen: "I got the same treatment. All I ever hear about are the things I haven't done right. Now, I'll have to spend a lot of time reviewing the report and preparing explanations. The worst part is that the information is almost a month old, and we spend all this time on history."

Travers: "My biggest gripe is that our production activity varies a lot from month to month, but we're given an annual budget that's written in stone. Last month, we were shut down for three days when a strike delayed delivery of the basic ingredient used in our plastic formulation, and we had already exhausted our inventory. You know that, of course, since we had asked you to call all over the country to find an alternate source of supply. When we got what we needed on a rush basis, we had to pay more than we normally do."

Christensen: "I expect problems like that to pop up from time to time—that's part of my job—but now we'll both have to take a careful look at the report to see where charges are reflected for that rush order. Every month, I spend more time making sure I should be charged for each item reported than I do making plans for my department's daily work. It's really frustrating to see charges for things I have no control over."

Travers: "The way we get information doesn't help, either. I don't get copies of the reports you get, yet a lot of what I do is affected by your department, and by most of the other departments we have. Why do the budget and accounting people assume that I should be told only about my operations even though the president regularly gives us pep talks about how we all need to work together as a team?"

Christensen: "I seem to get more reports than I need, and I am never getting asked to comment until top management calls me on the carpet about my department's shortcomings. Do you ever hear comments when your department shines?"

Travers: "I guess they don't have time to review the good news. One of my problems is that all the reports are in dollars and cents. I work with people, machines, and materials. I need information to help me solve this month's problems—not another report of the dollars expended last month or the month before."

a. Based on the conversation between Terry Travers and Bob Christensen, describe the likely motivation and behavior of these two employees resulting from the Aurora Manufacturing Company's performance reporting system.

b. When properly implemented, both employees and companies should benefit from performance reporting systems.

   (1) Describe the benefits that can be realized from using a performance reporting system.

   (2) Based on the situation presented above, recommend ways for Aurora Manufacturing Company to improve its performance system so as to increase employee motivation.

(CMA adapted)

52. *(ROI and suboptimization)* Northstar Offroad Company (NOC), a subsidiary of Allston Automotive, manufactures go-carts and other recreational vehicles. Family recreational centers that feature go-cart tracks, miniature golf, batting cages, and arcade games have increased in popularity. As a result, NOC has been receiving some pressure from Allston Automotive top management to diversify into some of these other recreational areas. Recreational Leasing Inc. (RLI), one of the largest firms that leases arcade games to family recreation centers, is looking for a friendly buyer. Allston Automotive management believes that RLI's assets could be acquired for an investment of $3.2 million and has strongly urged Bill Grieco, division manager of NOC, to consider acquiring RLI.

Grieco has reviewed RLI's financial statements with his controller, Marie Donnelly, and they believe that the acquisition may not be in the best interest of NOC. "If we decide not to do this, the Allston Automotive people are not going to be happy," said Grieco. "If we could convince them to base our bonuses on something other than return on investment, maybe this acquisition would look more attractive. How would we do if the bonuses were based on residual income using the company's 15 percent cost of capital?"

Allston Automotive has traditionally evaluated all its divisions on the basis of return on investment, which is defined as the ratio of operating income to total assets; the desired rate of return for each division is 20 percent. The management team of any division reporting an annual increase in the return on investment is automatically eligible for a bonus. The management of divisions reporting a decline in the return on investment must provide convincing explanations for the decline to be eligible for a bonus, and this bonus is limited to 50 percent of the bonus paid to divisions reporting an increase.

Following are condensed financial statements for both NOC and RLI for the fiscal year ended May 31, 1997.

	NOC	RLI
Sales revenue	$10,500,000	
Leasing revenue		$2,800,000
Variable expenses	(7,000,000)	(1,000,000)
Fixed expenses	(1,500,000)	(1,200,000)
Operating income	$ 2,000,000	$ 600,000
Current assets	$ 2,300,000	$1,900,000
Long-term assets	5,700,000	1,100,000
Total assets	$ 8,000,000	$3,000,000
Current liabilities	$ 1,400,000	$ 850,000
Long-term liabilities	3,800,000	1,200,000
Shareholders' equity	2,800,000	950,000
Total liabilities and shareholders' equity	$ 8,000,000	$3,000,000

a. Under the present bonus system, how would the acquisition of RLI affect Mr. Grieco's bonus expectations?

b. If Mr. Grieco's suggestion to use residual income as the evaluation criterion is accepted, how would acquisition of RLI affect Mr. Grieco's bonus expectations?

c. Given the present bonus arrangement, is it fair for Allston Automotive management to expect Mr. Grieco to acquire RLI? Explain.

d. Is the present bonus system consistent with Allston Automotive's goal of expansion of NOC into new recreational products? Why or why not?

(CMA)

ETHICS AND QUALITY DISCUSSION

53. *We often think that a performance system can be devised for a given position within a firm that will be appropriate for any individual who might be selected to fill that position. However, a recent survey has indicated that there are substantial differences among the U.S. population in terms of factors that motivate them. Further, many people in the current workforce have been through traumas, such as downsizing, that has caused them to be less loyal than their predecessors to (and less trusting of) their employers.*

   Another alarming result of the study is that the American workforce is experiencing significant problems in dealing with the issue of diversity. For example, the study found:

   - *Employees under age 25 are no more likely than older employees to indicate a preference for working with employees of other races or ethnicities*
   - *Half of all respondents indicated a preference to work with other employees of the same race, sex, gender, and level of education*
   - *Employees of all types indicated the likelihood of minorities advancing in the organization was less than for other worker groups*
   - *One-fifth of minority workers indicated they had been discriminated against in the workplace*
   - *Women were more than twice as likely as men to rate their job advancement opportunities as "poor" or only "fair"*
   - *Nonfinancial employee benefits were more likely to be highly correlated with job satisfaction than pay*

   [SOURCE: Sue Shellenbarger, "Work-Force Study Finds Loyalty Is Weak, Divisions of Race and Gender Are Deep," *Wall Street Journal* (September 3, 1993), pp. B1, B2. Reprinted by permission of *The Wall Street Journal*, © 1993 Dow Jones & Company, Inc. All Rights Reserved Worldwide.]

   a. Does the lack of progress in achieving widespread acceptance of worker diversity have implications for the quality of work in American businesses? Discuss.

   b. What actions might managers take to encourage greater acceptance of diversity?

54. *Could any philosophy or cast-of-mind be seen as more vile these days than that of being "anti-business"? It is like being "soft-on-communism" back when there were communists to be soft on.*

And according to prominent corporate executives, an antibusiness view, disgraceful and opprobrious though it may be, has permeated an unlikely home—the Financial Accounting Standards Board. This seemingly banal organization, which sets the rules governing corporate accounting, reflects "an implicit antibusiness bias." It fails to recognize "business reality" and is unresponsive to business's "valid concerns."

This broadside has been leveled by the Financial Executives Institute, a 14,000-member corporate executives group, and it is only the latest in a series of attacks on FASB from business. . . . But what gives rise to the "antibusiness" rhetoric and the overall virulence of the FEI attack? P. Norman Roy, its president, said his members think FASB has become an accounting "policeman" (a role he would prefer to see played by individual auditors). FASB's thick encyclicals, he added, are too "prescriptive." Naturally, executives want flexibility over how they report earnings.

[SOURCE: Robert Lowenstein, "Can FASB Be Considered Antibusiness?" *Wall Street Journal* (March 21, 1996), p. C1. Reprinted by permission of *The Wall Street Journal*, © 1996 Dow Jones & Company, Inc. All Rights Reserved Worldwide.]

  a. Why would corporate executives desire more flexibility in how they report earnings?

  b. How would more managerial flexibility in the reporting of accounting data affect the quality of accounting information?

  c. What are the ethical obligations of the FASB in setting rules for reporting financial information?

55. Bailey Manufacturing has just initiated a formula bonus plan whereby plant managers are rewarded for various achievements. One of the current criteria for bonuses is the improvement of asset turnover. The plant manager of the Carson City Plant told Horace Appleby, his young assistant, to meet him Saturday when the plant is closed. Without explanation, the plant manager specified certain raw materials to be loaded on one of the plant's dump trucks. When the truck was loaded, the plant manager and Horace drove to a secluded mountain road where, to Horace's astonishment, the plant manager flipped a switch and the truck dumped the raw materials down a steep ravine. The plant manager grinned and said that these were obsolete raw materials and the company would run more smoothly without them. For the next several weekends, Horace observed the plant manager do the same thing. The following month, the plant manager was officially congratulated for improving asset turnover.

  a. How did the dumping improve asset turnover?

  b. What are the ethical problems in this case?

  c. What are Horace's options? Which should he choose and why?

56. Manhattan Electronics Corporation produces a variety of computer products. Recently the firm has revealed plans to expand into new office automation products. To realize the expansion plans, the firm will need to go to the stock market for additional capital in October of this year. Present plans call for raising $200,000,000 in new common equity. Historically, the firm's small notebook computer has been a significant contributor to corporate profits. However, a competitor has recently introduced a notebook model that has rendered Manhattan Electronic's notebook computer obsolete. At some point, the controller has informed the president, the inventory of notebooks needs to be "written down" to realizable value. Because Manhattan Electronics has a large inventory of the notebooks on hand, the write-down will have a very detrimental affect on both the balance sheet and income statement.

The president, whose compensation is determined in part by corporate profits and in part by stock price, has suggested that the write-downs be deferred until the next fiscal year (next January). He argues that, by deferring the write-down, existing shareholders will realize more value from the shares to be sold in October because the stock market will not be informed of the pending write-downs.

a. What effects are the performance evaluation measures of the president likely to have on his decision to defer the write-down of the obsolete inventory?

b. Is the president's decision to defer the write-down of the inventory an ethical treatment of existing shareholders? Of potential new shareholders?

c. If you were the controller of Manhattan Electronics, how would you respond to the president's decision to defer the write-down until after issuance of the new stock?

57. *A typical executive is in his mid-40's, frequently travels on business, says he values "self-respect," and is very likely to commit financial fraud.*

That, anyway, is the conclusion of four business school professors, whose study on fraud was published in the February issue of the Journal of Business Ethics.

After getting nearly 400 people (more than 85% of them men) over the past seven years to play the role of a fictional exec named Todd Folger, the professors found that 47% of the top executives, 41% of the controllers and 76% of the graduate-level business students they surveyed were willing to commit fraud by understating write-offs that cut into their companies' profits.

[SOURCE: Dawn Blalock, "Study Shows Many Execs Are Quick to Write Off Ethics," *Wall Street Journal* (March 16, 1996), pp. C1, C13. Reprinted by permission of *The Wall Street Journal*, © 1996 Dow Jones & Company, Inc. All Rights Reserved Worldwide.]

a. What creates the incentive for managers to understate write-offs?

b. How does the use of accounting as a performance measurement system of managers affect the objectivity of accounting information?

c. What are the ethical obligations of accountants in dealing with managers who desire to manipulate accounting information for their personal benefit?

INTERNET ACTIVITIES

58. Computer Consulting Services Corporation provides services related to software development. The company's Internet home page provides a description of the services offered. One unique characteristic of the company is that it employs both short-term and long-term employees. Discuss how the measurement of employee performance would be complicated by the use of both short-term and long-term employees, and outline a plan by which you would provide appropriate performance measures for both groups of employees.

59. Search the Internet using the term *economic value added*. Read articles you find that discuss how firms, such as Quaker Oats Company, are using the economic value added concept to measure performance. Write a summary of your findings.

60. Many governmental units, such as the City of Grand Prairie, Alberta, are revising the methods they use to evaluate the performance of employees and managers. Search the Internet for discussions of performance evaluation in government and read articles discussing recent revisions made to systems of performance evaluation. Then, write an article that discusses the changes that have been made and the change in operational results that are expected because of the changes.

Measuring Long-Run Organizational Performance

LEARNING OBJECTIVES

After completing this chapter, you should be able to answer these questions:

1. Why should company management focus on long-run performance?

2. Why is a vision statement so important to a firm?

3. How do long-run objectives differ from short-run objectives?

4. Of what value are nonfinancial performance measures to managers?

5. What should managers consider in selecting nonfinancial performance measures?

6. Why is it important for managers to develop bases for comparison for performance measures?

7. What difficulties are encountered in trying to measure performance for multinational firms?

8. How can activity-based costing be used in long-run performance evaluation?

9. *(Appendix 2)* What are some major areas of a manufacturing company for which performance measures and their cost drivers have been delineated?

10. *(Appendix 2)* What effects do learning curves have on the setting of labor standards?

Dell Computer Corporation

At age 19, Michael Dell was selling customized computers out of the trunk of his car at 15% below the going retail price. He was a freshman at the University of Texas at Austin when he confessed to his parents that he wanted to quit school to start his own computer company to "Compete with IBM." Talk about vision!

For fiscal 1995, the company's income grew to $149.2 million, while revenues increased to $3.5 billion. At age 30, Michael Dell is a long way from his days as a high-tech *enfant terrible*. Several years back, the company was growing so fast that it couldn't handle all the problems.

Dell made some big changes. He imported seasoned talent from companies like Motorola, Hewlett-Packard, Sun Microsystems, and Apple Computer to help him run his company like the big business it had become. He also refocused emphasis on profitability and liquidity while slowing the company's growth. This reflected his realization that it is important to balance short-run and long-run objectives in managing his business.

Dell selected the strategy of forgoing the retail market for the direct sales market, focusing on the high-margin customers rather than fighting the price wars for the retail home computer market. Dell says that the reason his firm has grown so fast is simple: "Its focus." He has reoriented his company from a strategy of *growth, growth, growth* to *liquidity, profit, and growth*.

SOURCE: Judy Ward, "Runaway Horse," *Financial World* (October 24, 1995), pp. 36–37, and Rahul Jacob, "The Resurrection of Michael Dell," *FORTUNE* (September 18, 1995), pp. 118–134. Excerpted from *Financial World* 1328 Broadway, New York, NY 10001. © Copyrighted 1995 by Financial World Partners. All rights reserved.

Historically, managers focused on short-run performance measures almost exclusively while ignoring long-run performance. Such tunnel vision was caused, in part, because managers and managerial accountants did not have a body of knowledge about the availability or usage of long-run performance measures. Then global competition emerged and world-class companies began to use and to tout the virtues of using long-run performance measures.

Professional literature in recent years has appropriately extolled the benefits of long-run performance measurements and given less coverage to the somewhat already replete set of paradigms concerning short-term performance measures. However, enlightened managers such as Michael Dell are well aware that a balanced scorecard for measuring long-run and short-run performance is necessary for a company to thrive in today's global economy.

Management must conduct company affairs in such a way that both the short-term and long-term needs of the firm are being met. Short-term needs are associated with the management functions of operating, financing, and investing during the current period. These short-term needs tend to be primarily financial and are discussed in Chapter 20. This chapter addresses meeting the measurement needs of the long-range performance of a firm. Additionally, Appendix 2 discusses an important reason that short-run measures should not be used to reflect long-run expectations. Company personnel gain knowledge and skill as they move down the learning curve. What seems efficient in the short run is often not considered adequate in the long run.

VISION AND MISSION STATEMENTS

vision

vision statement

Vision is a conceptualization of a future state for the organization that is better than the current state. Developing a company vision statement is a necessary step in the chain of management endeavors to perform well in the future.

A well-articulated **vision statement** provides a unifying focus on which all company personnel can base their decisions and behaviors so that everyone is working for the same long-run results. Employees at all organizational levels can know with confidence that their efforts fit together with the efforts of their colleagues and thus, will feel more empowered and energized. A model vision statement was created by Collis P. Huntington, founder of the Newport News Shipbuilding and Dry Dock Company in 1886. It reads:

> We shall build good ships here.
> At a profit—if we can.
> At a loss—if we must.
> But always good ships.[1]

Notice that customer satisfaction with the quality of the ships is given a more important place than profits in this vision statement. The long-run consideration has prevailed all of these years and empowered managers and workers with a unifying theme.

A similar objective of customer satisfaction is expressed by Hewlett-Packard, in a 1989 statement of overriding values, along with a number of other elements of corporate strategy including integrity, teamwork, and innovation:

> To provide products and services of the highest quality and greatest possible value to our customers, thereby gaining and holding their respect and loyalty.[2]

mission statement

Within the firm's vision statement, managers should construct a **mission statement** that expresses how the company uniquely meets its targeted customers' needs with its products or services. The vision and mission statements provide the basis for setting goals (abstract targets to be achieved) and objectives. (In contrast with goals, objectives are more concrete targets for which quantifiable performance measures and expected completion dates of achievement are established.)

DIFFERENCES IN OBJECTIVES

Traditionally, managing for the long run has been viewed as managing a series of short runs. Theory held that if a firm performed well in each of its short runs, then its future was secure. Although this approach has some appeal, it fails when the firm has not kept pace with long-term technical and competitive improvement trends. Lead time is frequently required for an organization to improve its technology, human resources, and modes of operations. If managers think in terms of short-run performance measures and ignore the required lead times to make long-term improvements, the firm may be doomed in the global competitive environment.

In a sense, the long run never arrives because future periods become the short run as soon as they become current and other periods replace them as the future. Even so, managers must focus on continuous improvements for the long run so that when the future becomes "now," the company will be strategically able to survive and prosper. For example, much of Japanese industry has worked to improve quality over recent decades so that, over the longer run, these industries have gained market share. Their strategy has been based on the belief that profitability and liquidity, both short-run measures, will result as the long run becomes the present.

One can also assert that the Japanese had no other option than to use a patient, long-run strategy. Consider that in the 1950s, Japan's automobile manufacturing companies were poorly financed and struggling to survive. Managers in these firms were motivated to adopt approaches such as kaizen, total quality management, and

---

[1] Richard C. Whiteley, *The Customer Driven Company* (Reading, Mass.: Addison-Wesley, 1991), p. 21.
[2] Hewlett-Packard, *The Organizational Framework for Our Objectives* (Palo Alto, Calif.: Hewlett-Packard Company, 1989), p. 5.

How to Implement Performance Measurement in Your Organization

With today's focus on competing aggressively for marketshare, satisfying customers, ensuring quality, and maintaining healthy relationships with employees, regulators and suppliers, managing performance requires a lot of information. Furthermore, that information must be designed and distributed to people in a way that will influence the best possible behavior. Managing performance is, therefore, highly dependent on the availability of a well-designed performance measurement system which provides clear linkage between strategy and human behavior.

Most organizations have conducted business with managers located in functional structures where layers of people concern themselves with measurements of functional performance. Over the past 10 years, most organizations have removed those layers of management and have placed more emphasis on individual performance. In an environment with fewer managers, functional organizational structures exist to co-ordinate individuals with a shared-activity orientation (skill base) to supply resources and activities to cross-functional processes. Processes are the sequence of cross-functional activities performed by people and machines which combine valuable resources to convert inputs into outputs. It is the processes which provide the linkage between organizational level goals and the work performed by people.

SOURCE: Reprinted from an article appearing in *CMA Magazine* by Paul Sharman, "How to Implement Performance Measurement in Your Organization," (May 1995), p. 33, with permission of The Society of Management Accountants of Canada.

just-in-time processes to efficiently deliver quality and incur low costs. These methods normally require years of dedication and commitment before implementation is truly effective and substantial benefits can be realized. Managing the long run requires building long-term relationships, proactively making investments in people and technology, and exerting effort according to a plan confidently believed to yield beneficial results in the future.

Short-run objectives generally reflect a focus on the effective and efficient management of current operating, financing, and investing activities. These objectives are predominantly financial, although they may also be concerned with immediate customer satisfaction issues such as quality, delivery, cost, and service. In contrast, a firm's long-term objectives involve resource investments and proactive efforts conceived to enhance the firm's competitive position. Although the firm is always striving toward achieving these objectives, the results will not be known until the future has become the present. By that time, the long-term objectives have normally been revised in a continuous round of planning and replanning for desired improvements.

The company's competitive position results from a multiplicity of performance factors, most of which only tend to indirectly yield the desired objectives. For example, companies may expend significant resources in training employees to better serve customers so that a greater share of the market may be gained. However, market share is also affected by the quality of products and services, speed of delivery, price, changing reputation, and other factors relative to the corresponding factors of competitors. The above News Note discusses the rationale behind a well-designed performance measurement system.

Long-term measures tend to be more indirect to long-term objectives than are short-term measures to short-term objectives. Long-term objectives require lead time for their achievement.

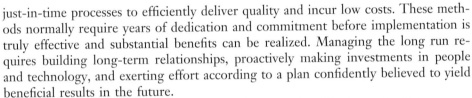

Managerial performance can be evaluated using both qualitative and quantitative measures. Qualitative measures are often subjective; for example, a manager may be evaluated using simple low-to-high rankings on job skills, such as knowledge, quality of work, and need for supervision. The rankings can be given for an individual on a

**NONFINANCIAL
PERFORMANCE
MEASURES**

Combining the ideas of innovation with customer satisfaction produced the concept of custom-sized "Perfect Pair" jeans by Levi Strauss. One nonfinancial measure of the success of this new product line is the number of repeat orders.

stand-alone basis, in relationship to other managers, or on a group or team basis. Although such measures provide useful information, at some point and in some way, performance should also be compared to a quantifiable—but not necessarily financial—standard.

Selection of Nonfinancial Measures

Managers are generally more comfortable with and respond better to quantitative measures of performance because such measures provide a defined target at which to aim. Quantifiable performance measures are of two types: nonfinancial and financial. Nonfinancial measures "rely on data outside of a conventional financial or cost system, such as on-time delivery, manufacturing cycle time, set-up time, productivity for the total work force and various measures of quality."[3] According to the IMA's *Statement on Management Accounting 4D*, nonfinancial performance measures have two distinct advantages over financial performance measures:

1. Nonfinancial indicators directly measure an entity's performance in the activities that create shareholder wealth, such as manufacturing and delivering quality goods and services and providing service for the customer.
2. Because they measure productive activity directly, nonfinancial measures may better predict the direction of future cash flows. For example, the long-term financial viability of some industries rests largely on their ability to keep promises of improved product quality at a competitive price.[4]

The advantages provided by nonfinancial measures should be considered when establishing a performance measurement system. The accompanying News Note discusses the growing use of these performance measures. Choosing appropriate performance measures can significantly help a company focus on the activities that cause its costs to be incurred and, thereby, attempt to control those costs and improve processes. These measures may be activity cost drivers as discussed in Chapter 6 on

[3] Peter R. Santori, "Manufacturing Performance in the 1990s: Measuring for Excellence," *Journal of Accountancy* (November 1987), p. 146.
[4] Institute of Management Accountants (formerly National Association of Accountants), *Statements on Management Accounting Number 4D: Measuring Entity Performance* (Montvale, N.J.: NAA, January 3, 1986), p. 12.

Measure What You Want to Manage

Faced with global competition, the reengineering fallout of the 1980s merger wave, and increasingly active institutional investors, corporations are focusing more than ever on new performance measures. Historical and purely financial performance measures, developed to meet regulatory and financial reporting requirements, were seen by [a Conference Board's study group] as better suited to report on the stewardship of assets entrusted to management's care than to chart the strategic direction of a business. Traditional accounting-based measures were found to (1) be too historical, (2) lack predictive behavior, (3) reward the wrong behavior, (4) focus on inputs, not outputs, (5) reflect functions, not cross-functional processes, and (6) give inadequate consideration to hard-to-quantify resources such as intellectual capital.

A small but growing number of major companies are developing performance measures characterized as "non-traditional" or "non-financial." The study group concluded that these measures should be labeled "key"—to be converted through a company's process of strategic achievement into more recognizable financial outputs such as sales, profits, and rate of return on investment. Typical key measures, which are meant to capture not only the value of existing assets, but also the potential for future performance, include:

- Quality of output
- Customer satisfaction/retention
- Employee training
- Research and development investment and productivity
- New product development
- Market growth/success
- Environmental competitiveness

Key measures are intended not to replace, but to augment, more traditional historical and financial performance measures. Only those activities that are actionable and will lead to enhanced performance should be measured. By tying key measures to the strategic vision of the company, there is assurance that as the vision changes so do the measures.

SOURCE: Deloitte & Touche LLP, "Challenging Traditional Measures of Performance," *Deloitte & Touche Review* (August 7, 1995), pp. 1–2.

activity-based management (ABM), or are frequently related to them. Control the activity and the cost resulting from that activity is controlled.

Traditionally, managers have conducted performance evaluations based almost solely on financial results. But concentrating on financial results alone is analogous to a baseball player, in hopes of playing well, focusing solely on the scoreboard. Both the game score and financial measures reflect the *results of past decisions.* Success in playing baseball and in managing a business require that considerable attention be placed on actionable steps for effectively competing in the stadium, whether it is the baseball stadium or the global marketplace. The baseball player must focus on hitting, fielding, and pitching; the company must focus on performing well in activities such as customer service, product development, manufacturing, marketing, and delivery. Performance measurement for improving the conduct of these activities requires tracking statistical data about the actionable steps that the activities involve.[5] Nevertheless, companies have historically disregarded nonfinancial measures. Consider the observations about the problem of disregarding nonfinancial measures in the News Note on the following page.

The nonfinancial performance measures (NFPM) that could be used are limited only by the imagination. Notwithstanding this, using a very large number of NFPMs

[5] Joseph Fisher, "Use of Nonfinancial Performance Measures," *Journal of Cost Management* (Spring 1992), p. 31.

Problems with Existing Manufacturing Performance Measures

Many performance measurement systems use financial measurements that are too abstract because they are too hard to relate to activities taking place on the shop floor. Financial measurements often fail to provide information that is useful for decision making.

For example, managers may want to know how often a machine breaks down because of a certain critical part, but that information is usually unavailable because the company's information system collects only financial data. Unless the maintenance department collects data about repairs and develops an appropriate database, this information is simply unavailable. Although most companies develop and maintain financial databases well, few keep nonfinancial information with the same degree of accuracy and detail. As a result, financial performance measures are developed even when they are inappropriate simply because the information is available.

SOURCE: Dileep G. Dhavale, "Problems with Existing Manufacturing Performance Measures," *Journal of Cost Management* (Winter 1996), p. 50. Reprinted with permission from *The Journal of Cost Management for the Manufacturing Industry* (Winter 1996), © 1996, Warren Gorham & Lamont, 31 St. James Avenue, Boston, MA 02116. All rights reserved.

is counterproductive and wasteful. Management should strive to identify the firm's critical success factors and to choose a few qualitative attributes of each NFPM to monitor for continuous long-run improvement. Critical success factors are those believed to be the direct causes of achievement or nonachievement of organizational goals and objectives.

Nonfinancial critical success factors could include quality, customer satisfaction, manufacturing efficiency and effectiveness, technical excellence, and rapid response to market demands. For each success factor chosen, management should select some short-run and long-run attribute measures to properly steer the company's activities toward both immediate and long-range success. For example, a short-range success measure for quality is the number of customer complaints in the current period and a long-range success measure for quality is the number of patents obtained for quality improvements of the company's products.

Establishment of Comparison Bases

Once the NFPMs are selected, managers should establish acceptable performance levels to provide bases of comparison against which actual statistical data can be compared. These benchmark comparison bases can be developed internally (such as from another established world-class division) or determined from external sources (such as competitors, regardless of whether they are in the company's industry). Unless a manager analyzing data has a basis for comparison, usually little meaning can be assigned to actual results. An appropriate basis for comparison allows the manager to breathe life and meaning into the actual data.

Managers need to agree to assign specific responsibility for performance and to be evaluated in each area in which a performance measurement is to be made. In this regard, a system of monitoring and reporting comparative performance levels should be established at appropriate intervals, as presented in Exhibit 21–1. This exhibit reflects a responsibility hierarchy of performance standards, with the broader issues addressed by higher levels of management and the more immediately actionable issues addressed by the lower management levels. It represents a good blend of short-run and long-run performance measurements. Note also that the lower-level activities are monitored more frequently (continuously, daily, or weekly), whereas the upper-level measures are investigated less frequently (monthly, quarterly, and annually). Those measures used by middle management (in Exhibit 21–1, the Plant

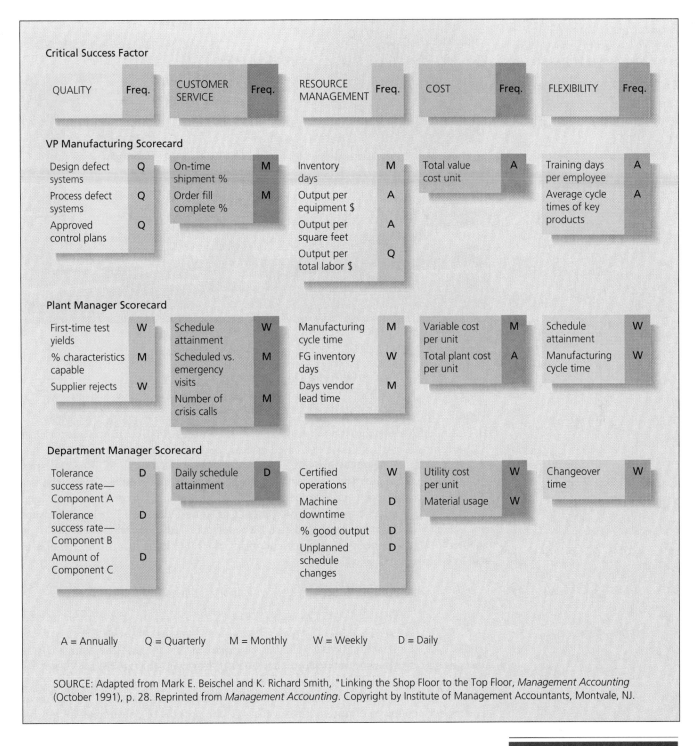

Critical Success Factor

QUALITY	Freq.	CUSTOMER SERVICE	Freq.	RESOURCE MANAGEMENT	Freq.	COST	Freq.	FLEXIBILITY	Freq.

VP Manufacturing Scorecard

Design defect systems	Q	On-time shipment %	M	Inventory days	M	Total value cost unit	A	Training days per employee	A
Process defect systems	Q	Order fill complete %	M	Output per equipment $	A			Average cycle times of key products	A
Approved control plans	Q			Output per square feet	A				
				Output per total labor $	Q				

Plant Manager Scorecard

First-time test yields	W	Schedule attainment	W	Manufacturing cycle time	M	Variable cost per unit	M	Schedule attainment	W
% characteristics capable	M	Scheduled vs. emergency visits	M	FG inventory days	W	Total plant cost per unit	A	Manufacturing cycle time	W
Supplier rejects	W	Number of crisis calls	M	Days vendor lead time	M				

Department Manager Scorecard

Tolerance success rate— Component A	D	Daily schedule attainment	D	Certified operations	W	Utility cost per unit	W	Changeover time	W
Tolerance success rate— Component B	D			Machine downtime	D	Material usage	W		
Amount of Component C	D			% good output	D				
				Unplanned schedule changes	D				

A = Annually   Q = Quarterly   M = Monthly   W = Weekly   D = Daily

SOURCE: Adapted from Mark E. Beischel and K. Richard Smith, "Linking the Shop Floor to the Top Floor, *Management Accounting* (October 1991), p. 28. Reprinted from *Management Accounting*. Copyright by Institute of Management Accountants, Montvale, NJ.

EXHIBIT 21–1

Performance Measurement Factors and Timetables

Manager) are intermediate linkages between the lower- and upper-level performance measures and require monitoring at intermediate points (weekly, monthly, and annually). The annual measurements can be plotted to reveal long-run trends and progress toward long-run objectives.

A general model for measuring the relative success of an activity compares a numerator representing number of successes with a logical and valid denominator representing total activity volume. For example, delivery success could be measured (with statistics given within the example) for the period as follows:

Federal Express is known for its effective delivery system. The company's benchmark of performance is 100% on-time deliveries. Deviations from this measure are carefully analyzed so that the same problems will not occur again.

$$\text{Number of On-time Deliveries} \div \text{Total Deliveries Made} =$$
$$822 \div 1{,}000 = 82.2\%$$

If a competitive benchmark for on-time delivery success had been previously set at 85 percent, success would be evaluated at close to but slightly below the mark.

In contrast, management may prefer that a failure rate be measured. If near-perfect to perfect performance were the expectation, the failure rate would indicate the degree to which perfect performance did not occur. If success were defined as total quality, the benchmark would be 100 percent on-time deliveries. For example, suppose that a world-class firm expected zero defects. The general model could be adapted to measure nonperformance and, using the same basic information as above, would be calculated as follows:

$$\text{Number of Late Deliveries} \div \text{Total Deliveries Made} =$$
$$178 \div 1{,}000 = 17.8\%$$

In this case, the benchmark is implied as zero percent errors, and the company was unsuccessful at achieving its performance goal. If, however, this failure rate were less than the prior period's, the conclusion can be drawn that improvement is occurring. Analysis of the types and causes of the 178 late deliveries should allow management to consider actions to eliminate these causes in the process of continuous long-term improvement. The accompanying News Note presents a technique to determine whether long-term quality improvement programs are on schedule.

Appendix 1 to this chapter presents a variety of nonfinancial performance measures that can also be viewed as the cost drivers of an activity-based costing system. Care must be taken, though, to evaluate all selected measures relative to one another and make certain that any competing or inhibiting measures are eliminated. Additionally, the number of performance measurements used for any given area must be limited. Top management should choose several measures on which to concentrate during a period; those measures should be the ones most reflective of the company's objectives for that time frame.

Performance Measures for Cell Manufacturing and Focused Factory Systems

Under continuous improvement programs, all aspects of the operations of manufacturing cells and focused factories improve over time. These improvements can be measured by various performance measures. For example, an improvement in quality may be measured by defective parts per million (ppm), a rate that should decrease over time as quality improves. A *half-life* measure can estimate how soon and by how much the ppm will decrease, which helps managers determine whether quality improvement programs are on track or not.

In nuclear physics, the half-life of a radioactive substance is the time it takes for half of the material to disintegrate. The half-life of any given element is constant. The concept of half-lives has also been successfully applied to improvements made under continuous improvement programs. The half-life, or time required for a 50 percent change, is approximately constant for a given type of improvement.

In quality control, for example, if it takes eight months to reduce ppm from 20,000 to 10,000, then it should take another eight months to reduce the ppm from 10,000 to 5,000. A further reduction to 2,500 will take another eight months, and so on. Half-lives, in this example, indicate the progress of a quality improvement program. If it takes longer than eight months for the ppm rate to drop from, say, 2,500 to 1,250, a company might start reviewing its quality improvement program to determine if it is encountering any problems.

It is important, however, to remember that half-lives are not a mathematical constant in manufacturing as they are in physics. Some deviations should be expected. In the example just given, the half-life might range from six to ten months, or even longer.

SOURCE: Dileep G. Dhavale, "Performance Measures for Cell Manufacturing and Focused Factory Systems," *Journal of Cost Management* (Spring 1996), pp. 59–60. Reprinted with permission from *The Journal of Cost Management* (Spring 1996), Warren Gorham & Lamont, 31 St. James Avenue, Boston, MA 02116. All rights reserved.

Use of Multiple Measures

A progressively designed performance measurement system should encompass various types of measures, especially those that track factors considered necessary for world-class status. The "performance pyramid" depicted in Exhibit 21–2 summarizes the types of measures needed at different organizational levels and for different purposes. Within the pyramid are measures that consider both long- and short-term organizational objectives. These measures can be financial and nonfinancial.

Nonfinancial measures are becoming more important because performance can no longer be evaluated solely on internal measurements, and external measures are often of the nonfinancial type. Performance is now primarily judged externally by a company's customers. Good performance is typically defined by customers as having a product or service that equals or exceeds their quality, cost, and delivery expectations. Companies that cannot measure up will find themselves without customers and without a need for financial measures of performance.

Knowing that performance is to be judged using some external criteria of success should cause companies to begin implementing concepts such as just-in-time inventory management, total quality management, and continuous improvement. The common themes of these concepts are to make the organization, its products, and its processes (production and customer responsiveness) better and to lower costs to provide better value.

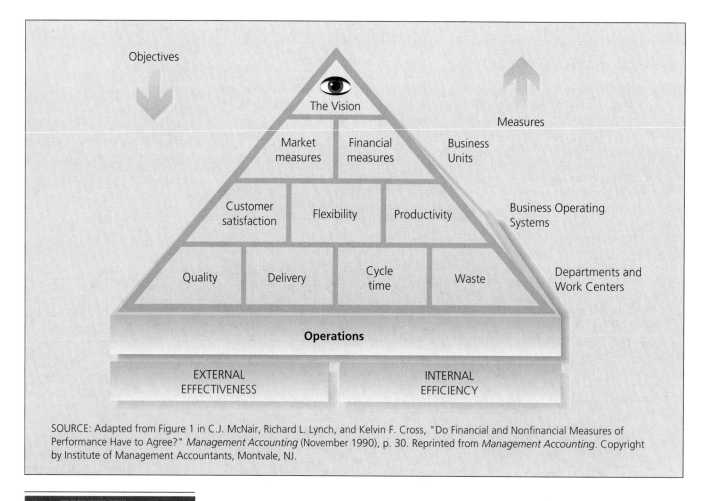

Objectives

Measures

The Vision

Market measures | Financial measures | Business Units

Customer satisfaction | Flexibility | Productivity | Business Operating Systems

Quality | Delivery | Cycle time | Waste | Departments and Work Centers

Operations

EXTERNAL EFFECTIVENESS | INTERNAL EFFICIENCY

SOURCE: Adapted from Figure 1 in C.J. McNair, Richard L. Lynch, and Kelvin F. Cross, "Do Financial and Nonfinancial Measures of Performance Have to Agree?" *Management Accounting* (November 1990), p. 30. Reprinted from *Management Accounting*. Copyright by Institute of Management Accountants, Montvale, NJ.

EXHIBIT 21–2

The Performance Pyramid

Exhibit 21–3 provides some ideas for judging the performance of managers in four areas of operations. Some measures suggested in this exhibit should be monitored for both short-run and long-run evaluations. For example, a short-run measure of market improvement is the rate of growth of the number of sales transactions. A long-run measure is the rate of growth of the pool of repeat customers who constitute the customer base. Forming employee groups to "brainstorm" about the identification of both short-run and long-run measures can be an effective approach to identifying what measures to use. As Robert W. Hall's observations about performance measures indicate in the following passages from his book, *Attaining Manufacturing Excellence*, a particular set of performance measures reflects a company management's expectations and philosophies. If management's philosophy changes, many of the performance measures will also change.

Performance measurements are the emblems of a management philosophy because people measure what they consider important. When the philosophy of management changes, the measurement systems change—or should change. However, changing measurement systems is more difficult than reworking a machine. Performance measurement is the basis of every system in a company: cost systems, planning systems, capital budgeting systems, personnel assignments, promotions, reorganizations, budget allocations—the mechanisms, built up over years, by which everything *runs*.

Major overhauls bring out the same emotions as if the perpetrators were to hold a rock concert in a cemetery. Performance measurement changes are only possible with strong leadership at the top of the company—and those leaders have to be careful if their performance is judged by a horde of impatient investors.[6]

[6] Robert W. Hall, *Attaining Manufacturing Excellence* (Homewood, Ill.: Dow Jones-Irwin, 1987), pp. 43–44.

	QUALITATIVE	QUANTITATIVE	
		Nonfinancial	*Financial*
PERSONNEL	Acceptance of additional responsibility Increased job skills Need for supervision Interaction with upper- and lower-level employees	Proportion of direct to indirect labor (low or high depending on degree of automation) Diversity of ethnic background in hiring and promotion Hours of continuing professional education Scores on standardized examinations	Comparability of personnel pay levels with those of competitors Savings from using part-time personnel
MARKET	Addition of new product features Increased product durability Improved efficiency of product Improved effectiveness of product	Number of sales transactions Number of repeat customers Generation of new ideas Number of customer complaints Number of days to deliver an order Proportion of repeat business Number of new patents obtained Number of new (lost) customers	Increase in revenue from previous period Percent of total market revenue Revenue generated per advertising dollar
COSTS	Better traceability of costs Increased cost consciousness Better employee suggestions for cost reductions Increased usage of automated equipment for routine tasks	Time to design new products Number of engineering change orders issued for new products Proportion of product defects Number of different product parts Number of days of inventory in stock Length of process time Proportion of material generated as scrap/waste Reduction in setup time since prior period	Reduction in production cost since prior period—individually for material, labor, and overhead, and collectively Reduction in distribution and scrap/waste cost since prior period Cost of engineering changes Variances from standard
RETURNS (PROFITABILITY)	Customer satisfaction Product brand loyalty	Proportion of on-time deliveries Degree of accuracy in sales forecasts of demand Frequency of customer willingness to accept an exchange rather than a refund	Increase in market price per share Return on investment Increase in net income Increase in cash flow

EXHIBIT 21–3

Examples of Performance Measurements

THROUGHPUT AS A NONFINANCIAL PERFORMANCE MEASURE

synchronous management

process productivity

process quality yield

One innovative, nonfinancial indicator of performance gaining wide acceptability is throughput. This term refers to the number of good units or quantity of services produced *and sold* by an organization within a time period. An important aspect of this definition is that the company must sell the units and not simply produce them for inventory stockpiles. Because a primary goal of a profit-oriented organization is to make money, inventory must be sold for that goal to be achieved. All endeavors helping an organization achieve its goal(s) are considered to be **synchronous management** techniques. "Synchronous management's strategic objective is to simultaneously increase throughput, while reducing inventory and operating expenses."[7]

One way to measure performance is to determine the extent to which the company is meeting its goal of making money by having rapid and high-quality throughput. Some of the benefits of improving throughput are increasing the ability to be more responsive to customer needs and demands, reducing costs of production, and reducing inventory levels.

Throughput, as mentioned, simply reflects how many good units are produced and sold for each available processing hour. Throughput can be analyzed as a set of component elements (in a manner similar to which the Du Pont model, presented in the previous chapter, includes components of return on investment). Components of throughput include manufacturing cycle efficiency, process productivity, and process quality yield.[8] Throughput can be measured as follows:

$$\text{Manufacturing Cycle Efficiency} \times \text{Process Productivity} \times \text{Process Quality Yield} = \text{Throughput}$$

$$\frac{\text{Value-Added Processing Time}}{\text{Total Time}} \times \frac{\text{Total Units}}{\text{Value-Added Processing Time}} \times \frac{\text{Good Units}}{\text{Total Units}} = \frac{\text{Good Units}}{\text{Total Time}}$$

The manufacturing cycle efficiency (as defined in Chapter 6) is the proportion of total processing that is value-added time from beginning to completion of production or service performance. This time relates to activities that increase the product's worth to the customer. For example, assume that Small Computer Company worked a total of 20,000 hours in May 1998 producing microcomputers. Of these hours, only 3,000 were considered value added; thus, the company had a manufacturing cycle efficiency of 15 percent.

Total units started during the period are divided by the value-added processing time to determine **process productivity.** Small Computer Company produced 30,000 units in May's 3,000 hours of value-added processing time and all units were sold. Thus, the company had a productivity rate of 10 (meaning that 10 units could be produced in each value-added processing hour).

Production activities serve to produce both good and defective units. The proportion of good units resulting from activities is the **process quality yield.** This measure reflects the quality of the production process. If only 27,000 of the 30,000 units produced by Small Computer Company in May were good units, the company had a 90 percent process quality yield for the period.

The total product throughput of Small Computer Company in May was 1.35 (.15 × 10 × .90); that is, the company produced and sold only 1.35 good units for every hour of total actual processing time. This is significantly different from the 10 units indicated as process productivity. The company can increase throughput by

---

[7] Victor Lippa, "Measuring Performance with Synchronous Management," *Management Accounting* (February 1990), p. 54.

[8] These terms and formulas are based on the following article: Carole Cheatham, "Measuring and Improving Throughput," *Journal of Accountancy* (March 1990), pp. 89–91. One assumption that must be made in regard to this model is that the quantity labeled "throughput" is sold. Another assumption is that the units started are always completed before the end of the measurement period.

Back to the Past

NEWS
NOTE

To build a factory of the future, Sony Corp. is taking a page from the workshops of the past.

At a plant here, men are dismantling conveyor belts on which as many as 50 people assembled camcorders. Nearby, Sony has set up tables to form a snail-shaped shop for four people. Walking through this "spiral line," workers assemble an entire camera themselves, doing everything from soldering to testing.

This is progress, Sony says. Output per worker on the experimental line is 10% higher than on a conventional one. The spiral performs better, Sony says, because it frees efficient assemblers to churn out more product instead of limiting them to a conveyor belt's speed. It reduces handling time, the seconds consumed as goods under production are passed from worker to worker. And if something goes wrong, only a small section of the plant is affected. . . .

Sony is one of a growing number of companies that are reorganizing assembly operations by updating an old idea: craft work. In industries where it is suitable, a new kind of factory is being created.

SOURCE: Michael Williams, "Back to the Past," *Wall Street Journal* (October 24, 1994), p. A1. Reprinted by permission of *The Wall Street Journal*, © 1994 Dow Jones & Company, Inc. All Rights Reserved Worldwide.

decreasing non-value-added activities, increasing total production and sales of the computers, decreasing the per-unit processing time, or increasing the process quality yield.

Manufacturing firms have increased throughput significantly using flexible manufacturing systems. Using technologies associated with computers such as bar coding, CIM, and electronic data interchange has enhanced throughput at many firms. Merely reorganizing the assembly operations can sometimes yield greater throughput. The News Note "Back to the Past" indicates that some world-class companies are finding productivity gains from rearranging assembly operations.

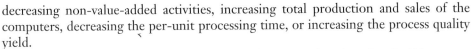

Traditional performance measurements in accounting are ladened with factors that contribute to non-value-added activities. Materials standards are developed that include factors for waste, and labor standards are developed that include estimates of idle time. Predetermined overhead rates are set using estimates of expected annual capacity usage rather than full capacity usage. Inventories are produced to meet budget expectations rather than sales demand. Detailed treatments of how to account for spoiled and defective units are used. Exhibit 21–4 (p. 978) provides some traditional performance indicators and potential suboptimizing results they may create.

ACTIVITY-BASED MANAGEMENT AND PERFORMANCE EVALUATION

Activity-based management (ABM) is concerned with reducing non-value-added activities as one way to increase throughput. Activity-based costing (ABC) measures cost from a longer-run perspective than does traditional costing. Fixed costs are viewed in ABC as long-run variable costs. ABC can be used to determine the impact on overhead of reengineering company processes to streamline activities and minimize nonquality work. As quality improves, management's thresholds of acceptable performance become more demanding and performance is evaluated against progressively more rigorous benchmarks.

If companies are to move toward world-class operations, acceptance of ABM must become sufficiently pervasive to remove the implied acceptance of non-value-added (NVA) activities from performance and to substitute an efficient level of value-added (VA) activities. The adages "you get what you measure" and "measure what you want to get" are appropriate. Activity-based management encourages and rewards workers for developing new skills, accepting greater responsibilities, and making suggestions for improvements in plant layout, product design, and worker utilization. Each of these improvements reduces non-value-added time and cost. In addition, by

EXHIBIT 21–4

Traditional Performance
Measurements and Results

MEASUREMENT	ACTION	RESULT
Purchase price variance	Purchasing agent increases order quantity to get lower price and ignores quality and speed of delivery	Excess inventory; increased carrying cost; suppliers with the best quality and delivery are overlooked
Machine utilization percentage	Supervisor produces in excess of daily unit requirements to maximize machine utilization percentage	Excess inventory; wrong inventory
Scrap built into standard cost	Supervisor takes no action if there is no variance (from the lax standard)	Inflated standard; scrap threshold built in
Overhead rate based on expected capacity	Supervisor overproduces WIP or FG to have a favorable fixed overhead volume variance	Excess inventory; wrong inventory
Cost center reporting	Managers focus on cost centers instead of activities	Cost reduction opportunities are missed because common activities among cost centers are overlooked

SOURCE: Charles Porter, *Cost Management in the New Manufacturing Environment* (Coopers & Lybrand LLP presentation, Directory XAT8803A).

focusing on activities and costs, ABM is better able to provide more appropriate measures of performance than are found in more traditional systems.

Performance measurements should concentrate on that which is of value to the customer. Focusing on the idea of value-added activities underlies activity-based management. Measures can be quantitative or qualitative, nonfinancial or financial. Selection of the measurement should definitely be related to the performance that management wishes to either encourage or discourage. Probably the two most important performance measures of U.S. businesses at this time are quality and service.

Because companies are extremely concerned about the cost of quality (COQ) (and the non-value-added activities associated with lack of quality), measurements related to COQ such as those presented in Exhibit 21–5 should be developed. For example, if a performance measurement is the cost of defective units produced during a period, the original assumption is that management is expecting defects to occur and will accept some stated or understood defect cost. Instead, if the performance objective is zero defects, the assumption is that no defects are to occur. Managers would strive harder to eliminate defects under the second measurement than under the first. Thus, "performance measurements must be externally focused. They . . . must be linked to and support the business goals. They must measure what is of value to the customer."[9]

A commitment to quality requires that companies make major adjustments in the way they design products, train and develop their work force, make decisions on acquisition and utilization of plants and equipment, and interact with suppliers and customers. Products should be designed to provide the maximum quality possible for

[9] Thomas O'Brien, "Measurements in the New Era of Manufacturing," proceedings from *Cost Accounting for the '90s: Responding to Technological Change* (Montvale, N.J.: National Association of Accountants, 1988), p. 72.

EXHIBIT 21–5

Cost of Quality
Measurements

ELEMENT OF COQ	OPERATIONAL COST DRIVERS	MEASURE	VA OR NVA
Prevention	Investment in reducing overall COQ operations	$\dfrac{\text{Prevention Cost*}}{\text{Total COQ}}$	VA
Appraisal	Setup frequency Tight tolerance operations Complex design	Number of inspections	NVA
Internal failure	Machine reliability Tooling age or condition Design error Operator error	Number of pieces rejected	NVA
External failure	Order entry errors Incorrect assembly instructions Product failure Operator error	Number of customer complaints	NVA

*Ideally, the formula should equal 1. Prevention costs are, by definition, all value-added costs. As non-value-added costs included in the denominator are eliminated, total COQ is composed of only value-added costs. Therefore, the formula ideally ends up equaling 1 (value-added costs ÷ value-added costs), which is the target measurement.

SOURCE: Michael R. Ostrenga, "Return on Investment Through the Cost of Quality," *Journal of Cost Management* (Summer 1991), p. 43. Reprinted with permission from *The Journal of Cost Management for the Manufacturing Industry* (Summer 1991), © 1991, Warren Gorham & Lamont, 31 St. James Avenue, Boston, MA 02116. All rights reserved.

the forecasted selling price. Spoilage and defects should not be built into product or service costs. ABM, with its focus on value-added and non-value-added activities, helps to eliminate building such costs into a product. According to Philip B. Crosby, quality itself is free. Unfortunately, the cost of nonquality work is very expensive.

One measure of service is how quickly the customer receives the goods needed or requested. The appropriate performance measure is a nonfinancial one: lead time. If lead time is measured, products should be available to customers more rapidly. In addition, a manufacturer would tend to make products that would have fewer parts, parts that are more interchangeable, and parts that require few or no engineering changes after the production process is begun. Lead time measurement should also force rearrangement of building layout, increase work force productivity, and reduce defects and reworks, because these changes would minimize lead time. Lastly, lead time measurement should cause managers to observe and correct any phenomena that are creating production, performance, or processing delays. These phenomena are caused by non-value-added activities or by constraints in the system.

Some performance measurements, such as zero defects, are the same regardless of divisional locale. However, because multinational settings are more complex than domestic settings, they require some additional considerations in performance measurement and evaluation.

PERFORMANCE EVALUATION IN MULTINATIONAL SETTINGS

Many large, decentralized companies are heavily involved in overseas operations. In an attempt to measure and evaluate such operations, upper-level management often uses income as the overriding criterion in the evaluation of all subunits, regardless of their locales. Such a singular focus is generally not appropriate for domestic responsibility centers; it is even less appropriate for multinational segments. This conclusion is valid regardless of whether the organization is Dell Computer Corporation headquarters in Austin, Texas with manufacturing operations in Limerick, Ireland

Attempting to compare financial performance results between Wal-Marts in Mexico and in other locations would be extremely difficult, especially given recent Mexican currency devaluations. It would be reasonable, however, to use a nonfinancial measure such as number of customer complaints to evaluate the various store locations.

VIDEO
VIGNETTE

New Skills for Global Managers

and Penang, Malaysia, or ABB (Asea Brown Boveri) domiciled in Zurich with operations in the United States, Finland, Thailand, and Brazil.

Differences among cultures and economies are as important as differences in accounting standards and reporting practices when attempting comparisons of multinational organizational units. In Japan, for instance, a company president views shareholders as basically inconsequential. When the head of a large Japanese conglomerate was asked "whether stock-market movements would ever affect his business decisions, he answered in a single word: 'Never!'"[10] This type of attitude allows Japanese companies to focus on both long-run and short-run business decisions. Such a concept is relatively unheard of in the United States where top management is often removed by stockholders for making decisions that appear not to maximize current shareholder value.

The dollar amount of investments in different countries necessary to create the same type of organizational unit may differ substantially. For example, because of the exchange rate and legal costs, it is significantly more expensive for a U.S. company to open a Japanese subsidiary than an Indonesian one. If performance is measured using a concept such as residual income, the Japanese unit would be placed at a distinct disadvantage because of its large investment base. On the other hand, the company may have believed that the possibility of future joint ventures with the Japanese was a primary corporate goal that justified the larger investment. One method of handling such a discrepancy in investment bases is to assign a lower target rate to compute residual income for the Japanese subsidiary than for the Indonesian one. This type of a differential would also be appropriate because of the lower political, financial, and economic risks.

Income comparisons between multinational units may be invalid because of important differences in trade tariffs, income tax rates, currency fluctuations, and the possibility of restrictions on the transfer of goods or currency from a country. Income earned by a multinational unit may also be affected by conditions totally outside its control, such as protectionism of local companies, government aid in some countries, and varying wage rates caused by differing standards of living, level of industrial development, and/or quantity of socialized services. If the multinational subunit adopts the local country's accounting practices, differences in international standards can make income comparisons among units difficult and inconvenient even after the statements are translated to a single currency basis.

[10] Alan S. Blinder, "Doing It Their Way," *Business Edge* (October 1992), p. 27.

The diverse economic, legal/political, and tax structures of countries have affected the development and practice of accounting. The International Accounting Standards Committee is working to achieve harmonization of accounting standards. However, many of the standards issued to date by this organization reflect compromise positions, allow for a significant number of alternatives, and are accepted only through voluntary compliance. In addition, within the constraints of moral and social responsibility, managers may be able to transfer goods between segments at prices that minimize profits or tariffs in locations where taxes are high by shifting profits or cost values to more advantageous climates.

U.S. firms having multinational profit or investment centers (or subsidiaries) need to establish flexible systems of measuring profit performance for those units. Such systems should recognize that differences in sales volumes, accounting standards, economic conditions, and risk may be outside the control of an international subunit's manager. In such cases, qualitative factors may become significantly more useful. Performance evaluations can include measures such as market share increases, quality improvements (defect reductions), improvement of inventory management with the related reduction in working capital, and new product development. Use of measures that limit suboptimization of resources is vital to the proper management of both domestic and multinational responsibility centers.

In conclusion, companies need to make a variety of decisions regarding performance measurements. This package of decisions can be labeled a performance management system and is depicted in Exhibit 21–6. No one system is appropriate for all companies or, possibly, even all responsibility centers within the same company. The measurement of performance is the measurement of people. Because people are unique and have multiple facets, the performance management system must reflect those characteristics.

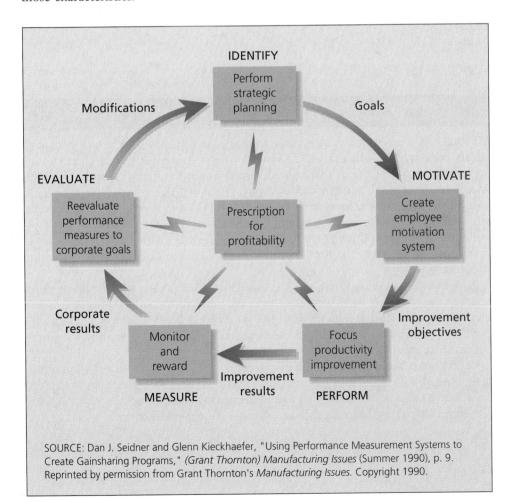

EXHIBIT 21–6

Performance
Management System

SOURCE: Dan J. Seidner and Glenn Kieckhaefer, "Using Performance Measurement Systems to Create Gainsharing Programs," *(Grant Thornton) Manufacturing Issues* (Summer 1990), p. 9. Reprinted by permission from Grant Thornton's *Manufacturing Issues.* Copyright 1990.

REVISITING

![gray bar]

Dell Computer Corporation

The big issue for the company now isn't so much growth *per se* as the *right* growth. "In a lot of ways we have too many opportunities," Dell says. "That's a fortunate situation, but it requires that we be very diligent in our evaluation of those opportunities." He goes on about "sequencing" those options and "prioritizing them."

The company's growth depends in part on the widening circle of consumers willing to buy computers they can't see and touch ahead of time. Dell speculates that while only representing 20% of the total market today, direct sales could grow to 30% by 2000. [Examples of performance measurements concerned with growth and other strategic factors are presented in Exhibit 21–3.]

What's the lure? Rather than producing massive numbers of standardized PCs based on forecasts of overall demand, Dell custom-builds each computer to the customer's specifications when ordered. [Tracking the numbers of new and repeat customers is a relevant performance measurement for this marketing and manufacturing strategy.]

"Their fingers are more on the pulse of what their customers are buying, so they are able to fairly accurately time technology transitions," maintains Scott Miller, an industry analyst at Dataquest, a San Jose, California–based market research company. "They know how the market is changing as it changes. Very few other companies can say that."

SOURCE: Judy Ward, "Runaway Horse," *Financial World* (October 24, 1995), p. 37. Excerpted from *Financial World*, 1328 Broadway, New York, NY 10001. © Copyrighted by Financial World Partners. All rights reserved.

CHAPTER SUMMARY

A firm's long-term objectives are always associated with investments and proactive efforts conceived to enhance the company's long-run competitive position. Long-term performance measures should be designed within the firm's vision and mission statements and should assess progress toward goals and objectives. Managers should assure themselves that persons to be evaluated have the appropriate skills, equipment, information, and authority for accomplishment. Moreover, feedback on progress toward accomplishment should be provided in a timely and useful manner. Using multiple measures regarding the firm's critical success factors is more effective than using single measures.

An innovative, nonfinancial measure of performance is throughput. Throughput refers to the goods or services started, finished, and sold by an organization. When throughput is increased, the company goal of making money is enhanced. Activity-based management also provides an excellent base from which to identify long-term performance measurements.

Performance measures of multinational units may be more difficult to establish than those of domestic units because of differences in taxes, tariffs, currency exchange rates, and transfer restrictions. Top management may wish to consider extending the use of qualitative performance measures because of such differences.

APPENDIX 1

Performance Measurement Areas and Cost Drivers

Exhibit 21–7 is from a joint study by the Institute of Management Accountants (formerly the National Association of Accountants) and the international public accounting firm of Coopers & Lybrand LLP. The exhibit indicates some activity cost drivers that need to be measured to determine performance in the six specified areas.

EXHIBIT 21–7

Performance Measures

Performance Measurement Area: Design for Manufacturability

KEY CHARACTERISTICS	COST DRIVERS/MEASURES
Quantity and quality of engineering changes	Number of engineering changes
	Severity of engineering changes
Test results	First pass reject rate
	Materials used versus design specification
	Manufacturing skills required
Part standardization	Number of products
	Percent common parts per product
Engineering cycle time	Lead time to engineer (design) a finished product
	Startup time from design to production
Product complexity	Number of components per finished product
	Number of manufacturing operations per finished product
	Number of tools required per finished product

Performance Measurement Area: Zero Defects

KEY CHARACTERISTICS	COST DRIVERS/MEASURES
Product specification	Tolerances of critical components
	Historical capability of process versus current performance
Parts quality	First pass reject rate versus test results
	Units scrapped by cell
	Cell downtime due to quality problems
	Yield of finished product per raw material batch
	Units reworked by cell
Quality control checkpoints	Sampling requirements for incoming materials
	Time required for sample/test procedures
	Production time loss due to quality control procedures/queues
	Number of checkpoints
	Effectiveness—number of returned units

Performance Measurement Area:
Minimize Raw and In Process Inventory

KEY CHARACTERISTICS	COST DRIVERS/MEASURES
Supplier performance	Number and location of vendors
	Number/frequency of deliveries
	Lead time from order initiation to delivery
	Flexibility in order quantity, delivery and variety
Component standardization	Complexity of components
	Number of components to support total production
Market characteristics	Demand variation
	Forecast accuracy
	Availability/accuracy of information

Performance Measurement Area: Zero Lead Time

KEY CHARACTERISTICS	COST DRIVERS/MEASURES
Velocity of units through cell	Actual production time
	Queue time between operations
	Move, setup, and inspection times
	Manufacturing cycle efficiency = value-added time ÷ total time
Quality of components	Scrap percent
	Rework percent
	Yield percent
Customer service levels	Late deliveries
	On-time deliveries
	Back orders
	Cancelled orders
Complexity of flow	Mix of products
	New product introductions
	Routing required per product

Performance Measurement Area: Minimize Process Time

KEY CHARACTERISTICS	COST DRIVERS/MEASURES
Product design ■ Complexity ■ Tolerance ■ Materials ■ Producibility	Number of components
	Number of manufacturing procedures/steps
	Required tolerance versus matching optimum
	Maximum tolerance range per component
	Packaging of component versus use configuration
	Quality of components
	Availability/ease of use
	Skills necessary to meet engineering requirements
Process capabilities and limitations	Information system capabilities
	Plant layout: optimum versus current
	Work rules: percent changed

Performance Measurement Area: Optimize Production	
KEY CHARACTERISTICS	COST DRIVERS/MEASURES
Resource limitations	Bottleneck capacity level
	Setup time
	Lot size constraints
	Labor availability, qualifications, flexibility
	Material resources (e.g., availability, lead time, quality, proximity)
	Number of distribution centers
	Number of storerooms
Demand fluctuation	Volume variations (total units produced)
	Mix changes (number and magnitude)
	Schedule changes (number and magnitude)
Configuration of plant	Plant layout (e.g., move time, move distance, number of total moves)
Information processing constraints	Information accuracy and availability
	Data accuracy in planning execution (routing, bills, standards)

SOURCE: C. J. McNair, William Mosconi and Thomas Norris, *Meeting the Technology Challenge: Cost Accounting in a JIT Environment* (Montvale, N.J.: National Association of Accountants, now Institute of Management Accountants, 1988), pp. 199–210. Copyright by Institute of Management Accountants (formerly National Association of Accountants), Montvale, NJ.

APPENDIX 2

Learning Curves

Performance measurements are influenced by the standards against which those measurements are to be compared for evaluation. However, standards set for short-run comparisons are based on current expectations of good performance. Some current standards are not a proper basis for evaluating long-run performance because of intervening changes occurring beyond the short run. Labor standards for repetitive tasks that require some degree of skill are an example of this phenomena. With practice, personnel gain from experience and become more proficient. This gain in efficiency by personnel is known as the learning curve. The company's performance measurement team should recognize the existence of learning curves in devising long-run performance measurements.

A **learning curve** is a model that helps predict how labor time will decrease as people become more experienced at performing a task and are able to eliminate the inefficiencies associated with unfamiliarity. The learning curve model can be used for manufacturing, assembly, or office personnel, although the degree of learning differs dramatically among occupations and tasks. For example, the learning curve for a person attempting to use a new computer program is much higher and lasts much longer than one for a person learning to assemble boxes in a warehouse.

In a learning curve situation, labor time is reduced in a distinct pattern as production is increased. Statistical studies show that the pattern is related to the doubling of the output level. The learning curve pattern indicates that, *as total production quantities double, the level of work time required per unit declines by a specified percentage.* The size of the learning curve percentage depends on the skills necessary to perform the task.

learning curve

EXHIBIT 21-8

85% Learning Curve

TOTAL PACKING QUANTITY	PREDICTED AVERAGE PACKING MINUTES PER UNIT (PREVIOUS TIME × 85%)	PREDICTED TOTAL PRODUCTION MINUTES (TIME PER UNIT × PACKING QUANTITY)
1	3.0000 (given)	3.0000
2	2.5500	5.1000
4	2.1675	8.6700
8	1.8424	14.7392
16	1.5660	25.0560

Assume that Dell Computer hires Rajev Mehta to box computers. It took Rajev 3 minutes to pack his first box. Dell has noticed an 85 percent learning curve applies to its other packers. Using this information, the company can predict the time necessary for future packing activities using the number of minutes spent the first time. The predictions are shown in Exhibit 21–8. Note that predictions are computed only for doubled production quantity levels.

The time shown in the Predicted Average column is an *average* for all the boxes that have been packed at that point. It does not provide information on the actual time per box for any box except the first one. The second box is expected to take Rajev 2.10 minutes: the 5.10 total minutes for the first two boxes minus the 3.00 minutes for the first box. The next two boxes are expected to take 3.57 minutes (8.67 − 5.10) or an average of 1.785 minutes for each box.

An important workplace application of learning curves relates to the installation of new computer applications. The time it takes for an employee to become proficient at various applications on alternative computer software programs must be considered when deciding which programs to purchase. Computer programs that can show users have a lower-percentage learning curve are more cost efficient than those having higher-percentage learning curves assuming that each program has virtually the same level of rigor to start.

Learning curves are applicable in developing labor time standards for efficiency and piecework. However, reductions in labor time are most noticeable when employees first begin performing a task. At some point, after some degree of learning has occurred, the learning curve becomes almost flat and only minimal improvements are achieved. This point is referred to as the **steady state phase** and depends on the complexity of the work and the original level of the learning curve.

steady state phase

The most effective labor time standards are based on a time (per unit or per task) achieved at some point *after* start-up activities have begun and *before* the steady state occurs. If standards are set at the beginning of the learning process, they will rapidly become too easy to achieve and ineffectual for cost control. Cost estimates based on such standards would be significantly overstated for future jobs. Standards based on the steady state phase will be too tight and will result in unrealistic ideas about production time. Such a planning error would occur for two reasons: (1) all workers do not reach the steady state phase at the same time and (2) the labor force changes over time with new workers being added who are at the beginning of the learning curve. Standards set based on the steady state phase may also be poor motivators because they could be perceived by new employees as being unattainable.

Additionally, the learning process can affect raw material usage because waste and spoilage may be higher than normal early in the learning phase. The cost accountant should be aware of all the implications of learning curves when establishing both short- and long-run performance standards for material usage and labor time and estimating time and costs for new types of production or new operations involving repetitive actions. Management should also be aware of the influence of learning curves in measuring short- and long-term employee performance at tasks requiring some skill proficiency.

KEY TERMS

MEASURING THROUGHPUT

$$\frac{\text{Manufacturing}}{\text{Cycle Efficiency}} \times \frac{\text{Process}}{\text{Productivity}} \times \frac{\text{Process}}{\text{Quality Yield}} = \text{Throughput}$$

$$\frac{\text{Value-Added Processing Time}}{\text{Total Time}} \times \frac{\text{Total Units}}{\text{Value-Added Processing Time}} \times \frac{\text{Good Units}}{\text{Total Units}} = \frac{\text{Good Units}}{\text{Total Time}}$$

SOLUTION STRATEGIES

LEARNING CURVES

For doublings of production quantities:

1. Determine time to produce first unit.
2. Double production quantity.
3. Multiply previous time by learning curve percentage to estimate average production time per unit produced.
4. Multiply average production time per unit times production quantity to estimate total production time.
5. Repeat steps 2 through 4.

Andrew Brown Company makes computer chips. During November 1997, managers compiled the following data:

DEMONSTRATION PROBLEM

Total chips processed	370,500
Good chips	345,800
Total hours	3,800
Value-added processing hours	2,850

Required:

a. Calculate the manufacturing cycle efficiency.
b. Calculate the process productivity.
c. Calculate the process quality yield.
d. Calculate the throughput using one ratio.
e. Confirm your answer to part d using the results of parts a, b, and c.

Solution to Demonstration Problem

a. $\dfrac{\text{Value-Added Processing Time}}{\text{Total Time}} = \dfrac{2,850}{3,800} = .750$

b. $\dfrac{\text{Total Chips Produced}}{\text{Value-Added Processing Time}} = \dfrac{370,500}{2,850} = 130$

c. $\dfrac{\text{Good Chips}}{\text{Total Chips Produced}} = \dfrac{345{,}800}{370{,}500} = .933$

d. $\dfrac{\text{Good Chips}}{\text{Total Time}} = \dfrac{345{,}800}{3{,}800} = 91$

e. $(.750 \times 130 \times .933) = 91$ chips per hour
(rounded)

QUESTIONS

1. What are the possible adverse consequences of ignoring the long-term requirements of the firm?

2. What are the benefits of a vision statement to the firm?

3. How do long-run objectives differ from short-run objectives?

4. Why should management focus on long-run performance?

5. Of what value are nonfinancial performance measures to managers?

6. What criteria should managers consider in selecting nonfinancial performance measures?

7. How does development of bases for comparison for performance measures assist managers?

8. What difficulties are encountered in trying to measure performance for multinational firms?

9. According to the NAA's (now IMA's) Statement 4D, what are the two distinct advantages of using nonfinancial performance measures?

10. What is a benchmark and what is its role in the use of nonfinancial performance measures?

11. Why is throughput defined on the basis of goods sold rather than goods produced?

12. How can activity-based costing concepts be used to design performance measures?

13. *(Appendix 1)* Birmingham Metalworks manufactures iron railings for ornamental fences. Recently, the company has become much more concerned about reducing the number of flaws in its completed products. Identify some performance measures that the company could use to monitor the effectiveness of its efforts to improve product quality.

EXERCISES

14. *(Terminology)* Match the following lettered terms on the left with the appropriate numbered descriptions on the right.

a. Learning curve	1. Point after which little learning occurs
b. Process productivity	2. Predicts labor decrease as workers gain experience
c. Synchronous management	3. Concept of future state that is better than present
d. Process quality yield	4. Way in which a firm's products meets customers' needs
e. Throughput	5. Relation between total units and value-added time
f. Steady state phase	6. Reflections of the quality of production process
g. Vision	
h. Mission	
i. None of the above	

7. Cost that changes proportionately with activity
8. All endeavors helping firm achieve its goals
9. Good units produced and sold by firm during a period

15. *(Throughput)* Lucky Duck Bottling Company is interested in examining its throughput. Analysis of May production revealed the following:

Good units produced and sold	6,000
Total units produced	8,000
Total processing time	144,000
Value-added time	48,000

a. Determine the manufacturing cycle efficiency.
b. Determine the process productivity.
c. Determine the process quality yield.
d. Determine the throughput.

16. *(Throughput)* Barbarossa Cannery packs dates for shipment all over the world. Abdul Barbarossa has asked you to analyze the cannery's throughput. You find that in June, the cannery generated the following:

Cans packed and shipped	10,000
Total cans (some defective)	12,500
Value-added processing time	25,000
Total processing time	75,000

a. Calculate the manufacturing cycle efficiency.
b. Calculate the process productivity.
c. Calculate the process quality yield.
d. Calculate the throughput using only good units and total time.
e. Verify your answer to part d by using your answers to parts a, b, and c.

17. *(Appendix 2)* Tom's Bicycle Shop hires college students at Christmas to assemble bikes for customers. Tom heard about learning curves and asked you to help him estimate improvement. The literature in the sporting goods industry indicates that bicycle assembly has an 80 percent learning curve. The college student Tom just hired took 5 hours to assemble the first bike, and Tom was visibly upset. Tom would like to know what he can expect will be the average time required for this worker to assemble 32 bicycles.

18. *(Appendix 2)* Pat Jones inherited a patio furniture shop from her deceased Uncle Fred. Pat decided she would start learning the business and began by making her first wrought iron table. It took her three days and she figured that unless she could make tables at a rate of more than one per day, she'd make more money at her old job as a short-order cook at the local diner. She was about to close the business when someone told her about the learning curve. Industry literature reveals a 60 percent learning curve for making this type of table. How many tables will Pat have to make before she has become proficient enough to produce an average of more than one table per day?

19. *(Vision statement)* The board of directors of your company has asked you to explain what a vision statement is and to devise several criteria that might be used in preparing a good vision statement. Write a brief report complying with the board's request. In your report, also explain how a well-prepared vision statement will benefit the firm.

COMMUNICATIONS ACTIVITIES

20. *(Nonfinancial performance measures)* One of the "old time" accountants in your company says that nonfinancial performance measures are not accounting and should be left for others to accumulate and evaluate. How would you respond?

21. *(Long-run performance)* As the new controller of your company, you have been asked by the company president to comment on any deficiencies of the firm. After saying you believe that the firm needs long-run performance measurement, the president says that the long run is really just a series of short runs. He says that if you do a good job of evaluating these short-run performances, that the long run will take care of itself. He sees that you are unconvinced and agrees to keep an open mind if you can make a good case for measuring and evaluating long-run performance. He suggests that you prepare a report stating your case.

22. *(ABC and long-run performance measurement)* A consultant has just recommended to top management that activity-based management would help the company generate much of the information necessary for long-run performance measurements. The company CEO has asked you to suggest how ABM could be used for this purpose. Prepare a brief report explaining some of the ways ABM would help in long-run measurement.

23. *(Nonfinancial measures)* In 1995, CDB Research & Consulting developed an eight-point "Hidden Value Index" of nonfinancial performance measures. Information on this index was reported in the July 4 and September 12, 1995, issues of *Financial World*. Work in a team of three or four to do the following:
    a. Prepare a report about why your team believes each of the eight items were selected for the index and how success in each of these items would help predict long-run financial success for an organization.
    b. Use the most recently-available Hidden Value Index of companies to choose two organizations (one with an index score of above 7.7 and one with a score of below 6.0). Gather information (including annual reports and news stories) to compare and contrast the two organizations and assess why your team believes the index scores were or were not reasonable.

24. *(Appendix 2)* Julia Cox is developing labor standards for the staff at the Chalmette Diagnostic Clinic. The staff will be performing six tests on each lab specimen received. She has asked you to explain learning curves and how they may assist her in setting her labor standards. How would you respond?

PROBLEMS

25. *(Throughput)* The Chocolate Bar Company has historically evaluated divisional performance exclusively on financial measures. Top managers have become increasingly concerned with this approach and are now actively seeking alternative measures that more accurately assess success in the activities that generate value for customers. One promising measure is throughput. To experiment with an annual throughput measure, management has gathered the following historical information on one of its larger operating divisions:

Units started into production	200,000
Total good units completed	130,000
Total value-added hours of processing time	80,000
Total hours of divisional time	120,000

    a. What is the manufacturing cycle efficiency of the division?
    b. What is the process productivity of the division?
    c. What is the process quality yield of the division?
    d. What is the total throughput per hour?

26. *(Throughput)* Fernando Sanchez is concerned about the quantity of goods being produced by the Mexican Division of the Auto Products Company. The following production data are available for April 1997:

Total units completed	30,000
Total good units completed	26,400
Total value-added hours of processing time	12,000
Total hours of division time	19,000

Determine each of the following for this division for April.

a. What is the manufacturing cycle efficiency?

b. What is the process productivity?

c. What is the process quality yield?

d. What is the total throughput per hour?

e. If Fernando can eliminate 20 percent of the non-value-added time, how would throughput per hour for these data differ?

f. If Fernando can increase quality output to a yield of 94 percent and eliminate 20 percent of the non-value-added time, how would throughput per hour for these data differ?

g. How would Fernando determine how the non-value-added time was being spent in the division? What suggestions do you have for Fernando to decrease non-value-added time and increase yield?

h. If only 22,500 of the units produced in April had been sold, would your answers to any of the above questions differ? If so, how? If not, why not?

27. *(Appendix 2)* Nadja Corporation is considering the purchase of one of two software packages that perform the same function. The application requires 5 hours of employee time when an employee first uses either package. The cost per employee hour is $35. Package #1 has a 70 percent learning curve; package #2 has a 90 percent learning curve.

a. What is the employee cost if the package is used 16 times?

b. Which package should Nadja Corporation purchase?

28. *(Appendix 2)* Home Medical Services is a firm that has been experiencing financial difficulties. Its founder, Dr. Stephen Ross, has been studying the possibility of instituting a standard cost system. The firm's product is a basic physical examination that is administered in the client's home. Dr. Ross is aware that more experienced examiners (all employees are registered nurses) can conduct the basic exam in significantly less time than the firm's new hires. New hires typically require 60 minutes to complete their first exam. Dr. Ross is also aware of the learning curve concept, but has no idea of how it affects his business or its profitability. He has recently experienced significant employee turnover. Most of the employees who have quit have been with Dr. Ross for more than 2 years. He pays all employees a basic hourly wage of $25 plus fringe benefits.

a. Assume that the administration of the health care examination is characterized by a 70 percent learning curve. Determine the average time required per exam to conduct 32 exams.

b. Alternatively, assume that the administration of a health care examination is characterized by a 90 percent learning curve. Determine the average time required per exam to conduct 32 exams.

c. Is it possible that Dr. Ross's employee turnover is related to the learning curve? Explain. Would the 70 percent or the 90 percent learning curve better explain the pattern in employee turnover? Why?

29. *(Appendix 2)* Dan's Manufacturing is trying to decide how much to offer as a bid (selling) price for the manufacture of 1,400 mechanical log splitters that are needed by a large retail sports chain. Because Dan has never made a log splitter before, he wants to first estimate a standard cost for the product. He has already estimated direct material to be $25 per unit. His cost accountant has suggested that an 85 percent learning curve be used and that the standard cost for labor be based on estimated time for 128 log splitters on the learning curve. Dan will be paying production workers $14 per direct labor hour. Assume that variable overhead has previously been estimated at $8 per direct labor hour. The first log splitter took 3 hours to build.

a. Calculate the amount of time on the 85 percent learning curve required to build 128 log splitters.

b. What is the standard direct labor cost per log splitter?

c. What is the total standard variable production cost per log splitter?

d. Suppose Dan wants to make 40 percent above standard variable unit production cost on the manufacture of the log splitter. How much should he bid to deliver the 1,400 log splitters?

30. *(Appendix 2)* Spacetech Corporation has been a supplier to the Orion Project since the program's inception. Two years ago, Spacetech received a contract to produce 960 telecommunications devices to be used in space exploration. Funding for the project has been curtailed, and Spacetech has received a contract modification decreasing the quantity of devices to be delivered to 240 units.

Direct material cost for each telecommunications device is $80,000 per unit. The direct labor is subject to a 95 percent learning curve. The average direct labor cost was estimated to be $50,000 per unit for the first lot of 30 units. This average direct labor cost figure and the 95 percent learning curve were used to develop the original bid for the contract. Variable manufacturing overhead was estimated to be 70 percent of direct labor cost. In calculating the original bid price, Spacetech added its regular markup of 35 percent on all variable manufacturing costs.

The learning curve of 95 percent has proven to be accurate over the first 60 units. Maximum efficiency is expected to be achieved with the production of 240 units.

a. Describe the theory underlying the use of learning curves.

b. Determine Spacetech's cumulative average cost of labor for producing 240 units.

c. If Spacetech Corporation should be asked to produce additional telecommunication devices beyond the 240 covered by the amended contract, calculate the unit price Spacetech should bid, employing the same markup that was used in the original bid. (Hint: Determine the average cost of labor of the last 120 units.)

(CMA adapted)

ETHICS AND QUALITY DISCUSSION

31. *A few New Orleans hoteliers have reneged on promises to set aside hotel rooms for the National Football League's Super Bowl XXXI, a senior NFL executive and New Orleans tourism executives said.*

And tourism officials said they feared the conflict is creating ill will with the football league, which could make future Super Bowls more difficult to land.

. . . According to Jim Steeg, director of special events for the NFL, several hoteliers have decided to ignore the promise and sell about 400 [of approximately 15,000] rooms reserved for the NFL.

[SOURCE: Stewart Yerton, "Some Hotels Stiff NFL for Rooms," *(New Orleans) Times-Picayune* (September 4, 1996), p. C-1. Reprinted by permission of The Times-Picayune Publishing Corp.]

a. Discuss the strategy of the hotels reneging on their promise to the NFL. Do you think that these hotels are considering the long-run implications of their actions?

b. Is it possible for a few hotels to hurt the larger community in which they operate? How or why?

c. Suggest an alternative strategy to the managers of these hotels.

32. A News Note entitled "Price Isn't Everything," presented in Chapter 16 tells of a company that relied heavily on the support of a technologically-capable supplier to help develop a new product. However, the contract for the raw materials to make the product was awarded to a lower bidder than the supplier who

provided all the assistance. The company lost a valuable ally by exploiting this supplier in such a way. Other examples are reported in the literature in which companies *take advantage* of customers and/or suppliers.

a. Form a team to discuss other examples of exploitation of external providers of assistance.

b. Discuss the motivation of a company to engage in exploitative behavior and whether such behavior is really within the best long-run interests of the company.

c. Formulate a strategic policy for a company for the future use of non-contractual external assistance.

---

33. Find the Ernst & Young home page. From there, go to the discussion of financial reporting developments. Read the discussion provided. Prepare a summary of the discussion which represents some of the key proposals for change in reporting of financial results. How do these proposals compare to internal reporting trends regarding performance measurement?

34. Find the home page of the Texas Agricultural Extension Service. Four goals of the extension service are presented on this page. On linked pages are the objective measures that have been established to determine whether the service is successfully achieving these four goals. Review the goals, the performance measures for each goal, and the budgeted and actual performance measurements for each performance measure. Write a report discussing whether the performance measures selected are appropriate for measuring achievement of the goals, and by comparing the budgeted and actual performance measurements whether the service is achieving its goals.

35. Find the home page of Rockford Consulting Group. This organization consults with businesses regarding reengineering to improve their performance levels. Review the integrated change model presented on the home page for change management and prepare an oral discussion in which you present the elements of the model and highlight the role that performance measurement plays in the model.

INTERNET ACTIVITIES

CHAPTER 22

Rewarding Performance

LEARNING OBJECTIVES

After completing this chapter, you should be able to answer these questions:

1. How are employee compensation and maximization of stockholder wealth related?

2. What are the alternative means of rewarding performance?

3. Why is there a movement toward rewarding group, as well as individual, performance?

4. What are the potential positive and negative consequences of incentive pay programs?

5. Why do many financial incentive programs involve shares of, or options for, common stock?

6. Of what importance are nonmonetary rewards in motivating managers?

7. How do taxes affect the design of compensation plans?

8. Why should ethics be considered in designing a compensation package?

9. What concerns need to be addressed in developing compensation packages for expatriates?

ABB Vetco Gray Inc.

[ABB Vetco Gray manufactures equipment and provides other services for the oil and gas industries. Its worldwide headquarters is in Houston, Texas. Prior to 1991, the firm used a typical pay-for-performance plan: merit pay coupled with a system to periodically review performance. James L. Wilkerson, vice president of Human Resources for the company, describes why the company changed its pay-for-performance plan in 1991]:

Force one. We began a reengineering project in the United States to change the way we did our business fundamentally, that is, to focus more on our customers. It wasn't long before we discovered that the cultural values associated with salary level and performance measurement—based on past performance—emphasized control, enshrined hierarchy, and were inconsistent with the reengineered environment of a customer-focused organization. There was virtually no relationship between how we paid people and profitability.

Force two. The second reason we started to look seriously at our pay and performance system was the results of an employee survey. It was clear that our current merit-pay system was viewed as unfair, had no relationship to performance, and was considered an entitlement.

Force three. The last impetus that we needed to make some adjustments in our pay system was our year-end financial analysis. The year-end results showed that even though our organization was going through a difficult market downturn, which reduced revenues and put pressure on profits, our labor costs continued to rise at a compounding rate. It was time for change.

SOURCE: James L. Wilkerson, "They Just Don't Work," *Management Accounting* (June 1995), pp. 40–45. Reprinted from *Management Accounting.* Copyright by Institute of Management Accountants, Montvale, NJ.

After revision of ABB Vetco Gray's strategies and other management systems, James Wilkerson became aware that the company's performance evaluation and reward systems were no longer effective. Wilkerson recognized that in the modern competitive environment, the firm was afflicted with one of the deadly diseases identified by management guru, Dr. W. Edwards Deming: Evaluation of performance using merit rating or annual review.[1] Wilkerson described the problem:

> Deming's analysis of classic performance appraisal systems tells us they are deadly because they focus on individuals, not systems; they have too much variability; and they presume stable systems and processes exist. As a consequence, performance appraisals are not objective, consistent, dependable or fair.[2]

The performance evaluation and reward systems in an organization are the key tools to align the incentives of workers, managers, and owners. When workers help to control costs and the bottom line increases, stockholders benefit through increased dividends and/or stock market prices. Throughout American business management literature, the expressed primary function of managers is to maximize stockholder value or stockholder wealth.

[1] W. E. Deming, *Out of the Crisis*, (Cambridge, Mass.; Massachusetts Institute of Technology, Center for Advanced Engineering Study, 1986), pp. 97–98.
[2] James L. Wilkerson, "They Just Don't Work," *Management Accounting* (June 1995), pp. 40–45. Reprinted from *Management Accounting.* Copyright by Institute of Management Accountants, Montvale, NJ.

Stockholders are granted this special attention because they (acting through the board of directors) have the unique power to hire, fire, and set compensation for top managers who, in turn, can hire, fire, and set compensation for workers.[3] On the other hand, workers and managers are naturally selfish to some degree and would prefer to maximize their own wealth rather than that of the stockholders. Consequently, the burden of motivating employees to maximize stockholder wealth is clearly borne by the stockholders through their specifications of managerial pay and other performance rewards and of the performance measurement system.

Accounting frequently plays a primary role in defining expected performance, monitoring and measuring actual performance, and determining the quantity and quality of appropriate employee rewards. In the two prior chapters, a variety of techniques to measure employee performance are discussed. This chapter explores the relationship of organizational plans, strategies, and performance to employee rewards as well as the tax and ethical implications of various compensation systems.

COMPENSATION STRATEGY

As noted in prior chapters, many changes (technological advances, globalization, customer and quality orientation) have occurred in business in the recent past. These changes have created problems and opportunities in establishing responsibility and rewarding individuals for organizational performance. Each organization has a unique compensation plan. A rational compensation plan will tie its component elements (organizational goals and strategies, performance measurements, and employee rewards) together into a cohesive package. The relations and interactions among these elements are shown in Exhibit 22–1. In this model, the organizational strategic goals are determined by the board of directors (the governing body representing stockholder interests) and top management. From these strategic goals, the organization's critical success factors are identified and operational performance targets are defined. Operational targets, for example, could include specified annual net income, unit sales of a specific product, quality measures, customer service measures, or costs.

compensation strategy

The board of directors and top management must also decide on a **compensation strategy** for the organization. This strategy provides a foundation for the compensation plan by addressing the role compensation should play in the organization. This strategy should be made known to everyone, from the board of directors to the lowest-level worker.

financial incentive

The traditional American compensation strategy differentiates among three employee groups that are compensated differently. Top managers' compensation contains a salary element and significant **financial incentives** that are provided for performance above targeted objectives. Usually these targeted objectives are specified in some financial accounting measure such as companywide net income or earnings per share. Middle managers are given salaries with the opportunity for future raises based on some—again, usually accounting-related—measure of performance such as segment income or divisional return on investment. Workers are paid wages (usually specified by union contract or tied to the minimum wage law) for the number of hours worked or production level achieved; current or year-end bonuses may arise when performance is above some specified quantitative measure. If provided, worker performance bonuses are usually fairly small relative to the level of wages. Significant incentive pay is generally limited to top management (and possibly the sales force)—regardless of the levels of employees who may have contributed to increased profits.

This type of traditional compensation system provides little motivation for lower-level managers to improve organizational performance.

Compensation systems that reward sales growth or near-term accounting profits and personnel systems that reward managers for increasing the size of their organizations are a problem. Top executives should be rewarded in a way comparable with how shareholders

---

[3] The authors use the term *employees* to refer to all of the personnel of an organization. The terms *workers* and *managers* are used to identify mutually exclusive groups of employees.

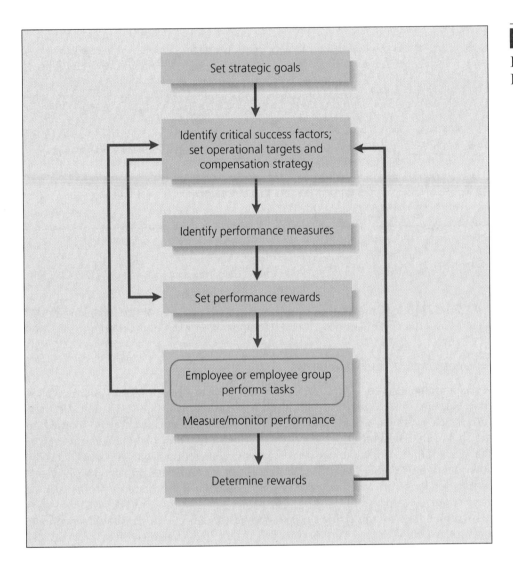

EXHIBIT 22–1

Plan-Performance-
Reward Model

are rewarded; line managers should be rewarded for managing the value drivers under their control. Incentive compensation should be a large part of any manager's compensation.[4]

The trend in pay scheme innovation is to tie compensation strategy to performance by providing incentive-based compensation systems (such as that now in place at ABB Vetco Gray Inc.) to all employees, regardless of organizational level or function.

Compensation plans should encourage higher levels of employee performance and loyalty, while concurrently lowering overall costs and raising profits. Such plans must encourage behavior essential to achieving organizational goals and maximizing stockholder value.

**PAY-FOR-
PERFORMANCE PLANS**

Correlation with Organizational Goals

In a pay-for-performance plan, the defined performance measures must be highly correlated with the organization's operational targets. Otherwise, suboptimization may occur and workers could earn incentive pay even though the broader organizational objectives are not achieved.

[4] David L. Wenner and Richard W. LeBer, "Managing for Shareholder Value—From Top to Bottom," *Harvard Business Review* (November-December 1989), pp. 64–65.

EXHIBIT 22–2

Components of Pay-for-
Performance Plan at
ABB Vetco Gray

■ A market-driven base pay for each job in the organization. The market midpoint becomes our point of departure, and employees have the opportunity to move to two higher levels within that particular job by demonstrating organizational capabilities and/or acquiring or demonstrating skills that will enable them to create additional value to the company in the future. As long as Sally and John are senior accountants, they will be paid exactly the same rate—unless they make improvements.

■ "Fun" time to celebrate great and small successes through the President's Awards and the supervisor's discretionary rewards budget.

■ A profit-sharing plan for all employees based on budgeted targets for our operations, with department targets to assist employees to see how they can affect our bottom line.

SOURCE: James L. Wilkerson, "They Just Don't Work," *Management Accounting* (June 1995), pp. 40–45. Reprinted from *Management Accounting.* Copyright by Institute of Management Accountants, Montvale, NJ.

Exhibit 22–2 lists the major components of the new employee pay plan at ABB Vetco Gray Inc. The plan has a notable emphasis on creating goal congruence.

Appropriate Time Horizon

A second important consideration in designing a performance-based system involves time horizon. One recent criticism leveled at American businesses is that the measures (such as annual net income) used to monitor performance are too focused on the short run. Alternatively, the espoused primary function of American business is the maximization of shareholder wealth, which is inherently a long-run consideration. The message of this criticism is that short-run measures are not necessarily viable proxies for long-run wealth maximization. In particular, short-term profits may be garnered at the expense of long-term growth.

In responding to this criticism, pay-for-performance criteria should encourage workers to adopt a long-run perspective. Many financial incentives now involve shares of corporate common stock. When employees become stockholders in their employer company, they tend to develop the same perspective as other stockholders: long-run wealth maximization.

Subunit Mission

Each organizational subunit has a unique organizational mission and must possess unique competencies. Both the performance measurement system and the reward structure should be crafted with the mission of the subunit in mind. What is measured and rewarded affects the focus of the subunit employees, and the focus of the employees should be specific to factors that determine the success of each subunit's operations.

Consideration of Employee Age

Employee age is another important factor in designing employee incentive plans. Younger employees, for natural reasons, may have a longer-term perspective than older employees who expect to retire from the firm within a few years. In designing employee incentives, this difference in perspective between younger and older employees should be given due regard.

To illustrate how age can affect decision processes, consider the case of James Ellis, a division manager evaluating two new projects. Each project would require an initial investment of $500,000. The projects promise to generate the following annual net returns:

YEAR	PROJECT 1	PROJECT 2
1	$ (250,000)	$300,000
2	(150,000)	200,000
3	0	0
4	300,000	(100,000)
5	600,000	(300,000)
6	500,000	(40,000
Total	$1,000,000	$ 60,000

Assume that, based on the net present value criterion, Project 1 is acceptable and Project 2 is unacceptable. Consequently, Project 1 increases shareholder value and Project 2 decreases shareholder value. Further, assume that James is evaluated, in part, based on the return on investment (ROI) generated by his division. If James is 2 years from retirement, he would be reluctant to invest in Project 1 because he would never realize the positive ROI effects of this project. The positive benefits from Project 1 (as well as the negative effects of Project 2) would be realized by his successor. James would be more enthusiastic about investing in Project 2, because in the 2 years prior to his retirement, his division's ROI would be enhanced. A younger manager with a longer-term time perspective would likely find Project 1 acceptable and Project 2 unacceptable.

Balance Group and Individual Benefits

Another consideration in designing worker incentives is to balance the incentives provided for both groups (or teams) and individuals. In automated production systems, workers function more by indirectly monitoring and controlling machinery and are, therefore, less directly involved in hands-on production. Additionally, evolving organizational and managerial philosophies, such as total quality management and quality circles, have stressed group performance and the performance of work in teams.

Incentives for small groups and individuals are often virtual substitutes. As the group grows larger, incentives must be in place for both the group and the individual. Group incentives are necessary to encourage cooperation among workers. On the other hand, if *only* group incentives are offered, the incentive compensation system may be ineffective because the reward for individual effort goes to the group. The larger the group size, the smaller the individual's share of the group reward becomes. Eventually, individual workers will be encouraged to shirk or "free-ride" on the group. **Shirking** occurs when individuals perceive their proportional shares of the group reward as insufficient to compensate for their efforts. Managing the balance between individual and group rewards requires skill and a careful consideration of incentives. These issues are demonstrated in the News Note on the next page.

shirking

Management Ownership

A final consideration in designing a performance reward system for upper management rewards is the degree of management ownership. Unlike at many small firms, managers of large firms are often not owners. When the managers and owners are different groups, a new set of organizational performance issues emerges. The two groups do not automatically have compatible interests with respect to using organizational resources. Consequently, incentive systems must be designed to align the interests of the two groups.

NEWS
NOTE

Managing the Individual by Managing the Team

Rewarding teamwork effectively is increasingly crucial. Today, two-thirds of big U.S. companies assign some workers to self-managed teams, up from 28% in 1987. . . . Now, many of these employers are revamping their pay systems, especially for their self-managed teams, because hierarchical pay plans centered on individuals no longer make sense for them.

Textron Inc.'s Defense Systems subsidiary . . . introduced both teams and team-pay incentives for 900 of its 1,000 employees in March 1993. Each member, after a review by management, can earn an equal share of a team's annual performance bonus. But the Wilmington, Mass., unit soon realized that "even in a team environment, there often are key players," says Chester Labetz, the subsidiary's human resources vice president.

As a result, the unit recently sweetened individual recognition awards. Along with their team-pay incentives, employees can earn an additional 3% to 10% of their base salaries for special achievements, such as devising an important patent or taking what is considered an intelligent though unsuccessful risk. More than 100 people got such awards in January [1995].

SOURCE: Joann S. Lublin, "My Colleague, My Boss," *Wall Street Journal* (April 12, 1995), pp. R4, R12. Reprinted by permission of *The Wall Street Journal*, © 1995 Dow Jones & Company, Inc. All Rights Reserved Worldwide.

EXHIBIT 22–3

Profit Benefits When
Executives Own Stock

Companies in which chief executives own a relatively large amount of company stock typically have greater stock-price performance, according to Wyatt Co.

INDUSTRY	ANNUALIZED TOTAL RETURN TO SHAREHOLDERS (1988–1993)
RETAIL	
High-ownership companies	13.1%
Low-ownership companies	10.3
CHEMICAL	
High-ownership companies	11.1%
Low-ownership companies	5.8
CONSUMER PRODUCTS	
High-ownership companies	14.7%
Low-ownership companies	7.3
BANKING	
High-ownership companies	14.5%
Low-ownership companies	13.9
MANUFACTURING	
High-ownership companies	9.1%
Low-ownership companies	8.0

SOURCE: Lauren Young, "The Owner Mentality," *Wall Street Journal* (April 12, 1995), p. R12. Reprinted by permission of *The Wall Street Journal*, © 1995 Dow Jones & Company, Inc. All Rights Reserved Worldwide.

Many companies (including Eastman Kodak, Xerox, Union Carbide, and Hershey Foods) are beginning to either mandate or encourage top management stock ownership. As indicated in Exhibit 22–3, a recent survey found that chief executive stock ownership seems to enhance corporate profits.

Once the target objectives and compensation strategy are known, performance measures for individual employees or employee groups can be determined based on their required contribution to the operational plan. Performance measures should, directly or indirectly, link the basic business strategies with individual actions. As discussed in the previous two chapters, employee performance is typically measured relative to some designated set of financial and nonfinancial performance standards.

CONSIDERATIONS IN SETTING PERFORMANCE MEASURES

Degree of Control over Performance Output

As companies shift from evaluating workers through observing their inputs to evaluating them based on their outputs, new problems for the pay and performance relationship are created. Earlier chapters stressed the importance of evaluating managers and workers only on the basis of controllable factors. Most performance measures tend to capture results that are a function of both controllable and noncontrollable factors.

Actual performance is a function of worker effort, worker skill, and random effects. The random effects include performance measurement error, problems or inefficiencies created by coworkers or adjacent work stations, illness, and weather-related production problems. After the actual performance is measured, determining the contributions of the controllable and noncontrollable factors to the achieved performance is impossible in many instances. Consequently, the worker bears the risk of the outcome effects of both types of factors. Thus, using performance-based pay systems causes workers to bear more risk than when fairly strict input-output measurements are used to determine compensation. Efforts should be made to identify performance measures that minimize the risk borne by the workers.

At the worker level, performance measures should be specific and typically have a short-run focus—usually on cost and/or quality control. Each higher level in the organizational hierarchy should include increasingly more elements related to the critical success factors under an individual's control and responsibility. Performance measures should, by necessity, become less specific, focus on a longer time horizon, and be more concerned with organizational longevity rather than short-run cost control or income.

Once the operational targets, compensation strategy, and performance measurements are determined, appropriate target rewards can be specified. These rewards should motivate individual employees to contribute in a manner congruent with the operational objectives, and employees must be able to relate their performance to the reward structure.

Incentives Relative to Organizational Level

As with performance measures, an employee's organizational level and current compensation should affect the types of rewards chosen. Individuals at different levels of employment typically view monetary rewards differently because of the relationship of pay to standard of living. Relative pay scales are essential to recognizing the value of monetary rewards to different employees. At lower employee levels, more incentives should be monetary and short term; at higher levels, more incentives should be nonmonetary and long term. The system should, though, include some nonmonetary and long-term incentives for lower-level employees and some monetary and short-term incentives for top management. Such a two-facet compensation system provides lower-paid people with tangible rewards (more money) that directly enhance their lifestyles, but also provides rewards (such as stock options) that cause them to take a long-run "ownership" view of the organization. In turn, top managers, who are well paid by most standards, should receive more rewards (such as stock and stock options) that cause them to be more concerned about the organization's long-term well-being rather than short-term personal gains. The following News Note describes the benefits of stock-based pay.

Stock-Based Performance Pay Plans Align Incentives

At Great Western Financial Corp. in Chatsworth, California, chief executive James Montgomery saw his 1993 bonus plummet by two-thirds to $142,500, because the company's earnings fell. For the first time, Great Western paid half of his bonus in stock options. He got no other options last year. The nation's second-biggest thrift believed that this approach "would more closely align the interests of the executive officers with those of the company's shareholders," its proxy statement says.

A no-cash, all stock package may represent the ultimate in politically correct CEO pay, compensation critics suggest. The unusual concept is starting to attract interest. Dennis Hendrix, the chief executive of Panhandle Eastern Corp. in Houston, has been paid entirely in stock since taking the helm of the natural-gas company in November 1990. Mr. Hendrix, who now owns 427,000 shares, has said he mainly lives on Panhandle's quarterly dividend of 21 cents a share.

Ted Newall, president and CEO of Nova Corp. of Alberta, recently decided to take stock instead of any salary or bonus for at least the next two years. In 1993, his salary totaled 609,000 Canadian dollars. The 58-year-old chief of the Canadian natural-gas pipeline company says he will support himself and his wife by selling some shares in other concerns.

The arrangement truly "puts me at risk with shareholders," Mr. Newall notes. "That's what corporate governance is all about."

SOURCE: Joann S. Lublin, "Looking Good: For CEOs, the Pay Gains Haven't Stopped; It's Just the Packaging that Has Changed," *Wall Street Journal* (April 13, 1994), p. R1. Reprinted by permission of *The Wall Street Journal,* © 1994 Dow Jones & Company, Inc. All Rights Reserved Worldwide.

Performance Plans and Feedback

As employees perform their required tasks, performance related to the measurement standards is monitored. The two feedback loops in the model shown in Exhibit 22–1 exist so that any problems identified in one period can be corrected in future periods. The first feedback loop relates to the monitoring and measurement of performance, which must be considered in setting targets for the following periods. The second feedback loop relates to the rewards given and the compensation strategy's effectiveness. Both loops are essential in the managerial planning process.

Just as there are numerous ways to tie organizational performance to employee rewards, there is also a wide variety of reward plans available to organizations. The major types of compensatory arrangements in use for workers and managers are discussed next.

WORKER COMPENSATION

In addition to the recent changes in competitive focus, organizational culture, local laws, union affiliation, and political considerations will affect the choice of pay plan. For example, although the piece rate pay plan may work effectively for some U.S. businesses, such a compensation plan may not work at all in a Japanese plant. The Japanese workforce is more attuned to the group and organization than to the individual. A plan that determines worker compensation based on individual performance would clash with the Japanese culture. And, installing a performance-based pay plan in any firm can be difficult if the plan's objectives are not clearly specified and/or if the organizational culture is not suited to such a plan. Even the differences in labor laws across countries can affect the design of pay plans. Exhibit 22–4 indicates how stock-based plans would be received in various regions of the world.

periodic compensation   The most basic of all reward plans consists of hourly, weekly, monthly, or other **periodic compensation,** which is based on time spent at work rather than on tasks accomplished. Different workers may command different periodic pay rates/amounts because of seniority, skill, or education level. However, this type of compensation

EXHIBIT 22–4

Thinking About a Stock-Based Compensation Plan in that Foreign Sub?

[Below are predicted reactions to the installation of a stock-based compensation plan in various parts of the world]:

Belgium Problematic. Some stock plans conflict with a government-imposed wage freeze.

Brazil Impossible. Foreign-exchange controls prohibit out-of-country stock investment; phantom stock plans are a headache.

Britain Easy. But sometimes labor unions can get in the way.

Eastern Europe Forget it. Even if you get government permission, chances are you've talked to the wrong bureaucrat.

Germany Can I get that in deutsche marks? U.S. plans suffer when the dollar is weak.

Israel Difficult. Exchange controls forced National Semiconductor to a third-party system, but plan has only scant participation.

Luxembourg Tax haven. Great place to set up a trust to administer stock plans.

Mexico May regret it. Labor laws can force a one-time stock grant into an annual event.

Netherlands No thanks. Employees may like the stock options, but they won't appreciate a hefty tax bill upfront.

Philippines Time-consuming. Requires government approval and lots of worker education.

SOURCE: Tara Parker-Pope, "Culture Clash: Do U.S.-Style Stock Compensation Plans Make Sense in Other Countries?" *Wall Street Journal* (April 13, 1995), p. R7. Reprinted by permission of *The Wall Street Journal*, © 1995 Dow Jones & Company, Inc. All Rights Reserved Worldwide.

provides no immediate link between performance and reward. The only motivational aspects of periodic compensation are the prospects for advancement to a higher periodic pay rate/amount, demotion to a lower pay rate/amount, or dismissal. Because this pay plan provides little incentive to achieve, worker performance is monitored by superiors rather than tracked by financial records. Organizational performance is ensured through monitoring and instruction instead of the motivation of the performance/reward relationship.

Worker Pay and Performance Links

The competitive environment in many industries, such as that of ABB Vetco Gray, has undergone substantial changes that have, among other effects, led to companies using greater automation and fewer labor-intensive technologies. Also, evolving management philosophies are now emphasizing the need for workers to perform in teams and groups. An interesting paradox has been created by these changes. Workers are more detached from the production function and more involved with higher-technology tasks, so it is more difficult to control workers through direct oversight and supervision. These changes require firms to rely more on results-based evaluations even though identifying appropriate performance evaluation criteria is now more difficult because of the more indirect worker/production relationship. Nevertheless, the trend is to rely more on performance-based evaluation and less on direct supervision to control worker behavior. This trend is consistent with the movement to empower workers and decrease levels of supervision and layers of management.

merit pay

One common performance-based pay plan is **merit pay,** in which a pay increment is earned after achieving a specific performance level. Although merit pay typically represents a raise in the base pay that continues throughout the worker's tenure with the firm, some merit pay plans may expire at a future date or be made contingent on a continuing high level of performance.

contingent pay

A variety of other performance-based pay plans exists. For some workers, the basic wage may be partly replaced with a contingent pay plan. **Contingent pay** is not guaranteed like the basic wage, but is dependent on the achievement of some performance objective. The contingent pay plan adds a pay-for-performance dimension to the compensation package. The contingent pay can be a fixed amount or may vary with, for example, the level of achieved sales or profit. It can be paid in cash, stock, or another form. Also, the plan can be structured to apply to group or individual performance.

piece rate

At the extreme end of the performance-based pay incentive plans are **piece rate** payment arrangements wherein workers are paid a flat rate for each unit of work accomplished. Some alternatives may combine the piece rate with a basic hourly rate to guarantee workers a minimal return on their time and effort. Such combination-type piece rate plans serve to protect workers from poor judgments or errors in setting piece rates.

Promoting Overall Success

A significant problem with piece rate payment plans is their failure to provide incentives for workers to consider overall organizational success. Alternative performance-based plans exist for this purpose, many of which have the expressed goal of getting common stock into the hands of employees. One popular arrangement is profit sharing, which provides incentive payments to employees. These current and/or deferred incentive payments are contingent on organizational performance and may be in the form of cash or stock. Allocation of the total profit-sharing payment among individual employees is made on the basis of personal performance measurements, seniority, team performance, managerial judgment, or specified formulas.

VIDEO
VIGNETTE

Holt, Hughes & Stamell (Blue Chip Enterprises)

stock option

In addition to profit-sharing arrangements, some firms pay employees a portion of their compensation in stock options or stock appreciation rights. **Stock options** allow the holder to purchase shares of company common stock at specified terms. These terms usually relate to price and designate the future time frame during which the stock may be purchased. **Stock appreciation rights** allow employees to receive cash, stock, or a combination of cash and stock based on the difference between a specified amount per share of stock and the quoted market price per share at some future date. In each situation, the amount of compensation is not determinable with certainty at the date the incentive reward is received, but rather the options or rights will become more valuable if the price of the common stock rises.

stock appreciation rights

Employee Stock Ownership Plan

Another popular profit-sharing compensation program is the **Employee Stock Ownership Plan** (ESOP), in which investments are made in the securities of the employer. An ESOP must conform to rules in the Internal Revenue Code, but offers both tax and incentive advantages. Under an ESOP arrangement, the employer makes tax-deductible payments of cash or stock to a trust fund. If cash is contributed, it is used by the trust to purchase shares of the employing company's stock. The trust beneficiaries are the employees, and their wealth grows with both the employer contributions and advances in the per-share price of the stock.

Nonfinancial Incentives

Besides various forms of monetary compensation, workers may also be motivated by nonfinancial factors. Although all employees value and require money to satisfy basic human needs, other human needs cannot necessarily be fulfilled with monetary wealth. Employees desire some compensation that satisfies the higher-order social

Money is not the only reward for performance. At Sun Microsystems, the company picnic is a benefit that allows employees to relax and enjoy their accomplishments individually and in teams.

needs of humans. For example, workers and managers will typically be more productive in environments in which they think their efforts are appreciated. Simple gestures such as compliments and small awards can be used by superiors to formally recognize contributions of subordinates. Allowing subordinates to participate in decisions affecting their own welfare and the welfare of the firm also contributes to making employment socially fulfilling. Such efforts provide assurance to employees that they are serving productive roles in the firm and that superiors are attentive to, and appreciative of, employee contributions. One of the three components of ABB Vetco Gray's performance pay plan (second component in Exhibit 22–2) was created, in part, to exploit benefits of nonfinancial rewards.

Lastly, the concept of job security, which is so prevalent in Japanese companies, is a powerful incentive to offer. For example, although A. T. Cross & Company (makers of Cross pens and mechanical pencils) does offer a modest profit-sharing plan and comparable wages, CEO Brad Boss believes the company's high quality standards partially result from employee loyalty. "The company has never had a layoff. When new, more efficient production technology is introduced, workers are retrained and generally promoted."[5]

Managers are primary decision makers in organizations and are subject to less direct supervision than workers. They are more likely than workers to be evaluated and compensated based on the results they achieve and the contributions they make to achieving the organization's strategic objectives. Frequently, top-level managerial compensation is directly linked to company stock price or to corporate earnings performance. As indicated in the News Note on p. 1006, bonuses based on organizational performance comprise a significant portion of the income of chief executive officers in most United States industries.

Prior chapters discuss various incentive-compatible ways to evaluate managerial performance. For example, Chapter 20 indicates that residual income, economic value added, and return on investment are three useful financial performance measures for managers of decentralized operations. Other chapters discuss the roles of standard costing, variance analysis, and budget-to-actual comparisons in performance evaluation. Chapter 21 discusses a variety of nonfinancial indicators used as bases to assess the efficiency and effectiveness of managerial efforts. Managers will find improving these performance measures to be much more important when the reward

MANAGERIAL COMPENSATION

[5] Louis S. Richman, "What America Makes Best," *Fortune* (Spring–Summer, 1991), p. 81.

NEWS NOTE

CEO Compensation Survey Results

A study conducted by Deloitte-Touche evaluated 1994 CEO compensation in a variety of industries. Results of the study indicate that CEOs receive a substantial portion of their compensation as bonuses, and that total compensation varies significantly across industries. Following is a summary of findings indicating, by industry, total compensation and compensation in salary. Total compensation is the sum of bonuses and salary.

INDUSTRY	MEDIAN TOTAL COMPENSATION	MEDIAN SALARY
Financial Services/ Investment	$1,469,000	$500,000
Telecommunications	1,235,000	650,000
Communications	929,000	600,000
Insurance	893,000	526,000
Commercial Banking	826,000	550,000
Construction	695,000	533,000
Manufacturing	675,000	425,000
Energy/Natural Resources	582,000	383,000
Transportation	575,000	387,000
Retail Trade	567,000	410,000
Diversified Service	523,000	368,000
Utilities	507,000	401,000
Wholesale Trade	459,000	309,000

SOURCE: Deloitte & Touche LLP, "Compensation of Top Executives," *Deloitte & Touche Review* (February 5, 1996) p. 1.

EXHIBIT 22–5

Different Strategic Missions: Implications for Incentive Compensation

	BUILD	HOLD	HARVEST
Percent of compensation as bonus	Relatively high	⟶	Relatively low
Bonus criteria	Emphasis on nonfinancial criteria	⟶	Emphasis on financial criteria
Bonus determination approach	More subjective	⟶	More formula-based
Frequency of bonus payment	Less frequent	⟶	More frequent

SOURCE: Vijay Govindarajan and John K. Shank, "Strategic Cost Management: Tailoring Controls to Strategies," *Journal of Cost Management* (Fall 1992), pp. 14–24. Reprinted with permission from *The Journal of Cost Management for the Manufacturing Industry* (Fall 1992), © 1992, Warren Gorham & Lamont, 31 St. James Avenue, Boston, MA 02116. All rights reserved.

---

structure is directly linked to them. "When many things are measured but only financial results are rewarded, it is obvious which measures will be regarded as most important."[6] Thus, the rewards to be provided in a performance-based compensation plan should be based on both monetary and nonmonetary, short-term and long-term measures. The mixture of long-term/short-term and financial/nonfinancial measures is related to the mission of the organizational subunit, as is shown in Exhibit 22–5.

[6] Robert G. Eccles and Philip J. Pyburn, "Creating a Comprehensive System to Measure Performance," *Management Accounting* (October 1992), p. 44.

PERQUISITE OFFERED	COMPANY SALES OF LESS THAN $1M	COMPANY SALES OF $1–$50M
Company car allowance	40.3%	63.4%
Key-person insurance	30.3%	47.0%
Special parking	16.0%	21.6%
Luncheon clubs	14.3%	14.9%
Financial counseling/tax services	14.3%	17.2%
Employment contracts	13.4%	20.1%
Severance pay for executives	12.6%	17.2%
Country clubs	12.6%	19.4%
Deferred compensation	7.6%	5.2%

EXHIBIT 22–6

Popular Perks

SOURCE: Ernst & Young, 1992 Executive Compensation Middle Market Survey of 669 Companies with Annual Sales of $50 Million or Less (New York City); shown in *Inc.* (August 1992), p. 82. Reprinted with permission, *Inc. Magazine,* August 1992. Copyright 1992 by Goldhirsh Group, Inc., 38 Commercial Wharf, Boston, MA 02110.

In addition to the monetary benefits, managers frequently are offered a variety of perquisites, or **perks,** for short. Perks are fringe benefits provided by the employer and include items such as vacations, free child care, free parking, personal assistants or private secretaries, health care, recreational club memberships, an office with a view, or flexible work hours. Perks can be offered as an incidental benefit of the position or they can be offered as compensation for specific performance. Exhibit 22–6 indicates some popular perks and the proportion of a sample group of companies that offer them to managers.

perk

Because economic value added (EVA) has become a frequently-used organizational performance measure, more firms are examining how their compensation structures align with the objective of maximizing EVA. The News Note on p. 1008 discusses how a variety of forms of compensation can be used to balance incentives of executives consistent with maximizing value creation.

The pay and performance relationships discussed earlier are not equally applicable to all types of organizations. The discussion that follows addresses the unique aspects of not-for-profit and governmental organizations.

The prior discussion assumed that employee performance and rewards would be determined under the oversight of a self-interested group of stockholders who are concerned about the effectiveness and efficiency of operations. The stockholders assume this oversight role because they are the residual claimants who are entitled to be paid only after all other involved parties have received their compensation—be it wages, salaries, perks, or interest payments.

NOT-FOR-PROFIT AND GOVERNMENTAL COMPENSATION

Not-for-profit and governmental organizations have no direct counterpart to stockholders. No single self-interest group has the financial incentive to seek assurances that employees and managers perform their work effectively and efficiently. This one distinct factor may partially account for the horror stories, detailing out-of-control purchasing practices in the Pentagon or other governmental units, that occasionally appear in the press. Although some link exists between pay and performance in not-for-profit and governmental agencies, this relationship is typically not as direct or strong as that existing in private companies.

The historical norm for public and not-for-profit organizations is time-based pay plans. The use of such plans has several nonperformance advantages, including the ease of predicting and budgeting costs and the avoidance of pay disputes. But as far back as 1988, employees were expressing substantial dissatisfaction with the performance evaluation and reward system in the federal government. "A poll of some 4,000 federal workers indicated that 70% of the workers regarded the pay as unfair, 74% felt that the bonus and merit pay systems were unfair, and a whopping 90% supported

Pay Strategies to Balance Long-Term and Short-Term Incentives of Executives Use a Portfolio of Pay Elements

Even within executive compensation, executives generally receive a portfolio of devices adding to the overall package. These are designed to attract, retain, provide incentive and reward for performance over various time frames. It generally takes more than one or two vehicles to do all that. It's the rare executive who, like Lee Iacocca, has been compensated entirely with stock or stock options plus, say, a $1 salary. In fact, recipients discount the value of packages that are highly skewed toward risky elements. Typical packages include:

- Base salary, rising by level of responsibility and subject to periodic merit increases on after-the-fact perceptions of performance. This can attract and reward; it may not provide as much incentive, and it only retains until someone tops it.
- Annual bonuses, the design drivers of which differ sharply among various companies. These are typically after-the-fact judgmental rewards for short-term performance, but some are far more complex and contain objective incentive elements that may or may not reinforce EVA.
- Long-term incentives, whether stock-related or formula-related. Payouts tend to be calculated by a predetermined formula, with only the judgment of the compensation committee available as a last "sanity check." These arrangements are designed to motivate and retain in the meantime, and reward later.
- Participation in benefit plans available applicable to most employees. Supplemental executive benefits programs such as deferred compensation plans, and perquisites such as executive financial counseling. (The latter is quite helpful to the executive in sorting out the personal implications of the rest of the package!). It is possible to do a fairly good job of normalizing these diverse vehicles so as to compare their overall value against competitive marketplaces for executive services.

SOURCE: Jim Fisher, "How Effective Executive Compensation Plans Work," *CMA Magazine* (June 1995), pp. 36–39.

innovation in pay plans that would more closely link pay and performance."[7] Such complaints are not unusual in many governmental and not-for-profit entities. The trend in these organizations has been to try and tighten the linkage between pay and performance so that the best and brightest employees do not leave the public sector.

Several experiments are ongoing, particularly in federal government, to attract and retain the most qualified employees. The financial and nonfinancial incentives for producing quality products and services that are becoming an essential part of private industry compensation plans are also being considered for adoption in public-sector and not-for-profit agencies. However, according to a survey by Coopers & Lybrand, LLP, only 20 percent of not-for-profit entities currently provide bonus plans for their top executives.[8]

Whether employees work in the private sector, not-for-profits, or the government, the effects of income taxation should be considered when the compensation system is designed. The following section indicates that fringe benefits and certain other forms of compensation may be preferred to cash compensation because of the relative tax benefits.

[7] Albert C. Hyde, "The New Environment for Compensation and Performance Evaluation in the Public Sector," *Public Personnel Management* (Winter 1988), pp. 351–358.
[8] Internet, Coopers & Lybrand Home Page: http://www.colybrand.com/.

In recent years, individual tax rates have been as high as 50 percent and corporate tax rates have been as high as 46 percent of taxable income. Currently, tax rates for individuals and corporations are well below these levels. But, because current tax rates are still significant, one important consideration is the tax consequences of the alternative rewards provided by compensation packages. Differences in tax treatments are important because they affect the amount of after-tax income received by the employee and the after-tax cost of the pay plan to the employer. There are three different tax treatments for employee compensation: full and immediate taxation, deferral of taxation, and exemption from taxation.[9] **Tax deferral** indicates taxation occurs at a future, rather than current, date. **Tax exemption** is the most desirable form of tax treatment because the amount is never subject to income taxation.

Most forms of compensation are fully and currently taxable to the employee and fully and currently deductible by the employer. For instance, wages represent income that is taxable to the employee when earned and tax deductible to the employer when incurred. The special, favorable tax treatments of deferral and exemption are provided under the tax code to encourage certain socially desirable behavior on the part of employers and employees.

For two reasons, the discussion of the tax aspects of compensation must center on the federal income tax and its effect on the employer and employee. First, although other taxes (such as payroll taxes, state income taxes, and unemployment taxes) may be affected differently by choices in reward structures, the impact of such taxes is rather minimal relative to the corporate and individual federal income taxes. Second, the impact of state income tax will vary from state to state, and thus, is beyond the scope of this text.

Fringe Benefits

When analyzing the compensation plan, employers and employees must consider the entire package—not simply one element of the package. For the employer, compensation other than wages and salaries will create additional costs; for employees, such compensation creates additional benefits. Fringe benefits may include employee health insurance, child care, physical fitness facilities, and pension plans. However, different types of fringe benefits have different tax consequences.

Certain employee fringe benefits are not treated as taxable income to the employee, but are fully and currently deductible by the employer.[10] One important type of these fringe benefits is employer-provided accident and health insurance plans. Premiums on such plans can be deducted for tax purposes when paid by the employer, but the premium is not treated as taxable income to the employee. If each employee purchased the insurance individually, there might also be certain tax benefits. However, the tax treatment available when employees spend after-tax earnings for the services is not as preferable as the full exemption from taxation that occurs in an employer-provided plan.

The importance of various fringe benefits is directly related to an individual employee's needs and wants, which is why some companies have instituted flexible fringe benefit programs called **cafeteria plans**. These plans contain a "menu" of fringe benefit options including cash compensation and nontaxable benefits alternatives. If the employee elects to receive cash in lieu of nontaxable fringe benefits, the cash is fully taxable. However, employees who elect fringe benefits such as health care, group term life insurance, or child care, receive these benefits free of tax. Flexibility is the greatest benefit of cafeteria plans because employees, based on their perceptions of the benefits' value, choose which benefits to receive.

TAX IMPLICATIONS OF COMPENSATION ELEMENTS

tax deferral

tax exemption

cafeteria plan

---

[9] Myron S. Scholes and Mark A. Wolfson, *Taxes and Business Strategy: A Planning Approach* (Englewood Cliffs, N.J.: Prentice-Hall, 1992), p. 33.

[10] For more information on the taxation of fringe benefits, see the current edition of *West's Federal Taxation: Individual Income Taxes* by William H. Hoffman, James E. Smith, and Eugene Willis (St. Paul, Minn.).

Deferred Compensation

Various forms of deferred compensation were identified earlier in this discussion. **Deferred compensation** represents pay related to current performance that will be received at a later point in time, typically after retirement. Among the diverse types of deferred compensation plans are profit-sharing arrangements, pensions, and various stock-based plans (including the ESOP). Many of these plans receive substantially identical treatment under the tax rules. The employer is allowed a current deduction for payments made to the plan, but the employee is not taxed until distributions are received from the plan. This treatment creates two significant tax benefits. First, no immediate taxable income is created for the employee by the employer's contribution. Second, no taxation of earnings on the plan occurs between the year of contribution and the year of distribution. In short, the employer's contributions and the earnings on the contributions are accorded tax-deferred treatment. When the employee reaches retirement and receives payments from the plan, all receipts are wholly taxable. However, the employee is frequently in a lower tax bracket at that time and will have enjoyed tax-free growth in the contributions over his or her working career.

Although the tax treatment to the employee of the various types of deferred compensation may not be significantly different, substantial differences exist in incentive effects. For example, the growth in the value of a pension plan may be largely unrelated to the employing corporation's stock performance. However, reward plans involving the employing company's stock have both a compensatory and an incentive element. Growth in the value of the deferred compensation depends on both the current contribution amounts and the change in the stock's value. Hence, employees are motivated to be concerned with stock performance—which is partly determined by corporate earnings. Exhibit 22–7 provides a summary of the pay elements and their relationships to the various concepts discussed in the chapter.

Because the self-serving motives of managers, workers, and stockholders frequently diverge, a proper reward structure needs to balance the interests of the three groups. Each group is entitled to an adequate return for the risks they bear and contributions they make to the organization's success. Inevitably, ethical dilemmas will be encountered when opportunities arise for one of the three groups to gain advantage over one or both of the other groups.

ETHICAL CONSIDERATIONS OF COMPENSATION

A phenomenon that has accompanied corporate growth is the emergence of professional managers and the dispersion of organizational ownership. In the largest corporations, no individual or group may own a large enough portion of common stock to directly influence the efforts and decisions of professional managers. This circumstance gives top managers greater discretion in operating the business and may also allow them to feel insulated from stockholders and their desires. Some observers argue that this atmosphere of discretion and insulation may be used to the managers' benefit rather than to the stockholders'. A number of ethical issues need to be resolved in the 1990s and beyond with regard to organizational governance and compensation of workers and managers.

Organizational Governance

Some argue that laws protecting the rights of stockholders failed to evolve with the dispersion of corporate ownership in the United States. Further, stockholder interests have become more diverse as institutional traders (such as pension funds) have moved into the capital markets along with individuals and industrial firms. Institutions have historically been passive investors and have not been diligent in voting their shares or monitoring managerial performance. Thus, professional managers have become less sensitive to stockholder concerns and have occasionally forgotten their primary duty is to act in good faith for the organization.

	LINK TO PERFORMANCE	TIED TO COMPANY OBJECTIVES	PROMOTES QUALITY	LEVEL OF MOTIVATION	TIME FOCUS	TAXABLE TO EMPLOYEE*	DEDUCTIBLE BY EMPLOYER*
HOURLY WAGES/ MONTHLY SALARY	Little	No	No	Low	Short term	Currently	Currently
MERIT PAY	Some	Possibly	Possibly	Medium	Short term	Currently	Currently
CONTINGENT PAY	High	Possibly	Possibly	Medium	Short term	Currently	Currently
PIECE RATE	High	Possibly	No	High	Short term	Currently	Currently
PROFIT SHARING	Some	Yes	Yes	Medium	Depends	Depends	Currently
STOCK OPTIONS/ APPRECIATION RIGHTS	High	Yes	Yes	Medium	Long term	Deferred	Depends
ESOPS	High	Yes	Yes	Medium	Long term	Deferred	Currently
PERKS	Some	Possibly	Possibly	Medium	Short term	Exempt	Currently
HEALTH INSURANCE	Little	No	No	Low	Short term	Exempt	Currently
CAFETERIA PLAN	Little	Possibly	Possibly	Medium	Depends	Depends	Currently
PENSIONS	Some	Possibly	Possibly	Medium	Depends	Deferred	Currently

*Subject to proper compliance and to potential regulatory changes.

EXHIBIT 22–7

Summary of Pay Plans

Role of Capital Markets

Under these circumstances, the capital markets have assumed an important role in ensuring that management teams are disciplined in their use of corporate resources. For example, partly as a response to ineffective, entrenched management groups, the 1970s and 1980s were witness to many attempted and successful hostile takeovers. In a **takeover,** an outside or inside investor acquires managerial control of a corporation by acquiring enough common stock and stockholder votes to control the board of directors, and thereby control management. The adjective *hostile* (as opposed to *friendly*) indicates that the takeover is not welcomed by management and frequently indicates that one objective of the takeover is to replace the management.

takeover

Raiders is a pejorative term used to describe firms or individuals who specialize in hostile takeovers. Raiders commonly identify firms as takeover targets when those firms are believed to be undervalued because managers are not acting in the stockholders' best interests. For example, managers of some conglomerates could increase stockholder value by selling pieces of the conglomerate that are not synergistic with other pieces.

raider

Managers may have golden parachutes written into their compensation packages. These benefits provide payments in the event management is displaced in an organizational merger or takeover.

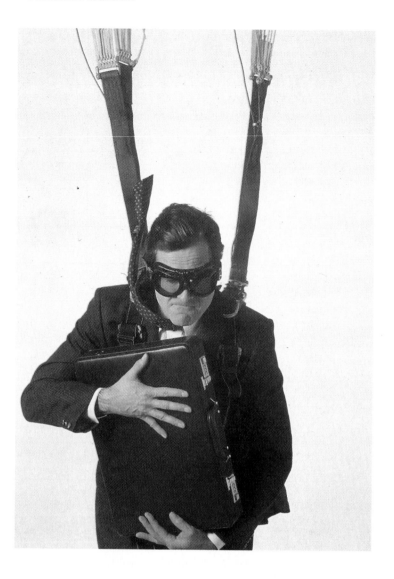

golden parachute

Takeovers can have either positive or negative effects on existing shareholders and employees, depending on the acquiring firm's objectives and the actions taken by the management of the target firm. A takeover can represent an attempt to steal value from the existing managers and workers; alternatively, it can represent an effective mechanism to revitalize an organization plagued by ineffective management. In either case, managers have often been permitted to include certain elements in their compensation packages that allow a retention of power in the face of a hostile takeover.

One compensation device that has helped discourage takeover attempts and protect managers is the **golden parachute,** which is a benefits package payable to incumbent managers if those managers are terminated following a successful hostile takeover (or in some cases a friendly merger). Both the ethical and incentive effects of golden parachutes are difficult to assess. Some proponents argue that golden parachutes serve stockholder interests because "top managers are free to devote their attention to serving the interests of existing stockholders in the face of a takeover threat."[11] The parachute is viewed as providing managers with financial protection that will keep them unbiased in their actions, regardless of the outcome.

However, critics view the golden parachute as a means for entrenched managers to protect themselves in the event they are ousted. Proponents of this perspective

[11] Bob L. Sellers, "Bankers Discover the Golden Parachute," *Bankers Monthly* (June 1988), p. 54.

are offended by the notion that managers who mismanage and create the conditions that originally attracted a takeover effort should profit by a takeover removing them for inept performance.

Golden parachutes also have some taxation issues. When these devices were first introduced, corporations were allowed to deduct the payments as normal business expenses. Such deductibility was affected significantly by the 1984 Deficit Reduction Act, which added a 20 percent excise tax on amounts received by an executive that are in excess of three times a 5-year average salary. Although many companies have agreed to pay this tax as part of a manager's severance package, a corporate deduction is disallowed for the excess payment.

Compensation Differentials

A major issue of discussion and contention involves perceptions of disparity between the pay of ordinary workers and top managers. Plato argued that no one should earn more than 5 times income earned by the lowest-paid worker. In the early 1900s, however, J. P. Morgan stated that the differential should be no more than 20 times. Exhibit 22–8 provides average total compensation (including cash pay, stock options, benefits, and perquisites) for four categories of employees in several countries. The exhibit indicates that, in general, neither Plato's nor Morgan's compensation relationships are currently true in the United States. All other countries surveyed, however, are well within at least Morgan's guidelines.

A new, major conflict between workers and managers has surfaced in the 1990s. As more bonus plans of upper managers have been revised to make them more

EXHIBIT 22–8

Average Compensation Levels for Employees

Manufacturing Employee	White-Collar Employee	Manager	CEO
Germany $36,857	Britain $74,761	Italy $219,573	United States $717,237
Canada $34,935	France $62,279	France $190,354	France $479,772
Japan $34,263	Germany $59,916	Japan $185,437	Italy $463,009
Italy $31,537	Italy $58,263	Britain $162,190	Britain $439,441
France $30,019	United States $57,675	United States $159,575	Canada $416,066
United States $27,606	Canada $47,231	Germany $145,627	Germany $390,933
Britain $26,084	Japan $40,990	Canada $132,877	Japan $390,723

SOURCE: Amanda Bennett, "Managers' Incomes Aren't Worlds Apart," *Wall Street Journal* (October 12, 1992), B1. Reprinted by permission of *The Wall Street Journal*, © 1992 Dow Jones & Company, Inc. All Rights Reserved Worldwide.

EXHIBIT 22–9

CEOs Receive Increased
Bonus Pay as They
Fire Workers

COMPANY	JOB CUTS 3/91 TO 4/94	CEO'S 1993 COMPENSATION	CHANGE IN CEO PAY FROM 1992 TO 1993
Sears Roebuck	50,000	$3,095,000	+198%
United Technologies	10,697	1,479,000	+115%
Citicorp	13,000	4,150,000	+ 90%
General Motors	74,000	1,375,000	+ 84%
McDonnell Douglas	10,200	1,055,000	+ 54%
Martin Marietta	15,000	1,651,000	+ 18%
Pacific Telesis	10,000	1,630,000	+ 18%
General Electric	10,250	4,013,000	+ 15%
AT&T	83,500	2,517,000	+ 11%
Boeing	30,000	1,421,000	+ 3%
TRW	10,000	1,558,000	− 1%
GTE	32,150	1,746,000	− 6%
Unisys	10,000	1,573,000	− 15%
Xerox	12,500	1,316,000	− 30%

SOURCE: Molly Baker, "I Feel Your Pain?" *Wall Street Journal* (April 12, 1995), p. R6. Reprinted by permission of *The Wall Street Journal*, © 1995 Dow Jones & Company, Inc. All Rights Reserved Worldwide.

sensitive to stockholder issues, top managers have become more aggressive in controlling costs to generate profits. Simultaneously, technological advantages have allowed firms to increase their productivity, that is, generate more output using fewer workers. These two forces have combined to create an historically rare circumstance: firms reporting record levels of profits while they concurrently are firing hundreds or thousands of workers. Thus, as top executives are receiving record levels of pay, many average workers are losing their jobs. The combined effects are reported in Exhibit 22–9.

Salary differentials between workers and CEOs are often created by a type of self-fulfilling prophecy caused by the board of directors. Although it is the job of the board of directors to protect the interests of stockholders, the composition of boards are usually split between outsiders and insiders. Insiders may be officers of the corporation and naturally identify more with the management group than the owners. Accordingly, they are sympathetic with the manager's position in stockholder/manager conflicts.

Oftentimes, a company's board of directors will survey a group of similar organizations to determine the "average" compensation for an executive. If the company's executive appears to be underpaid, the board will increase his or her compensation. Therefore, the next time the survey is performed, the average will be increased—regardless of managerial performance. Such indiscreet consumption of organizational resources can cause common stock prices to decline and undermines the stockholder value maximization goal.

Thus, the greatest ethical dilemmas involve circumstances that pit the welfare of employees against those of stockholders or the welfare of managers against the welfare of workers. Only if there is a perception of equity across the contributions and entitlements of labor, management, and capital will the organization be capable of achieving the efficiency to compete in global markets.

GLOBAL COMPENSATION

As more companies engage in multinational operations, compensation systems must be developed that compensate **expatriate** employees and managers on a fair and equitable basis. Expatriates are parent-company company and third-country nationals assigned to a foreign subsidiary or foreign nationals assigned to the parent company. Relocating individuals in foreign countries requires consideration of compensation. A fair and reasonable compensation package in one locale may not be fair and rea-

expatriate

The opportunity to live in a foreign locale is often part of the performance reward system. Although expatriates must become accustomed to new surroundings and customs, compensation should be determined so that these individuals have the same basic standard of living as they did previously—adjusted for cost of living factors, such as housing, clothing, and meals.

sonable in another. A recent survey of 45 multinationals indicated that every respondent considered differing pay levels, benefits, and perks as one of the biggest problems in developing an international workforce.[12]

The compensation package paid to expatriates must reflect labor market factors, cost-of-living considerations, and currency fluctuations as well as give consideration to tax consequences. Typically, an expatriate's base salary and fringe benefits should reflect what he or she would have been paid domestically. This base should then be adjusted for reasonable cost-of-living factors. These factors could be quite apparent (such as obtaining housing, education, and security needs similar to those that would have been obtained in the home country or compensating for a spouse's loss of employment) or they could be less obvious (such as a need to hire someone in the home country to care for an elderly relative or to handle real estate investments).

Because expatriates have a variety of monetary needs, these individuals may be paid in the currency of the country in which they reside or in their home currency or a combination of both. Frequently, price-level adjustment clauses will be built into the compensation system to counteract any local currency inflation or deflation. But, regardless of the currency makeup of the pay package, the fringe benefit related to retirement must be related to the home country and should be paid in that currency.

Income taxes are important in the compensation package of expatriates because they may pay taxes in the local country, home country, or both. Some countries (such as the United States and Great Britain) exempt expatriates from taxation on a specified amount of income earned in a foreign country. If a tax treaty exists and local taxes are paid on the balance of the nonexempt income of expatriates, such taxes may be credited against the expatriate's home nation income taxes. Regardless of how the package is ultimately determined, an ethical company will make certain that the system is as fair as possible to all employees involved and that it is cost beneficial and not an administrative nightmare.

[12] Organizational Resources Counselors Inc., "Global Headaches," cited in *Wall Street Journal* (April 21, 1993), p. R5.

Tying compensation to performance is essential because everyone in business recognizes that what gets measured and rewarded is what gets accomplished. Businesses must focus their reward structures to motivate employees to succeed at all activities that will create shareholder and personal value. In this highly competitive age, the new paradigm of success is to provide quality products and services at a reasonable price while generating a reasonable profit margin. Top management compensation has traditionally been tied to financial measures of performance; more and more companies are beginning to tie compensation to nonfinancial performance measures.

REVISITING

ABB Vetco Gray Inc.

[Top managers at ABB Vetco Gray decided to radically change their system of evaluating and rewarding employees. James Wilkerson, vice president of Human Resources describes the process for achieving change]:

Our "new" organization had to focus on customers through partnerships, quality service, and quick responses; partner with suppliers; control costs; manage change; be strong globally while focusing on the local operation; and be innovative. Our challenge was to develop a system that communicated expected employee performance correlated with salary level. This system also would reinforce our organization's capabilities and competitive advantage. We know that before designing the system we had to translate our organization's business strategy into the pay system's objectives. It is impossible to design a reward system that adds value to the organization without delineating the kind of people to be attracted and retained, the behaviors that are rewarded, and the desired organizational structure.

We realized that to shift to the desired culture, management and employees must be provided with new processes to modify existing habits, perceptions, and knowledge that were barriers to change. We knew that one way to drive this desired change was to give employees the opportunity to link their pay to their value to the organization.

We settled on four objectives to align our employees' total pay and performance communication package:

- Shift employee focus to the organization's business results.
- Tie total pay to the cyclical nature of the business.
- Move to a "Career Management Process" that stimulated productivity instead of continuing an ineffective and negative performance appraisal system.
- Create an environment for high-performance employees where desired behaviors and qualities can grow.

SOURCE: James L. Wilkerson, "They Just Don't Work," *Management Accounting* (June 1995), pp. 40–45. Reprinted from *Management Accounting*. Copyright by Institute of Management Accountants, Montvale, NJ.

CHAPTER SUMMARY

In American industry, corporate stockholders play a unique role. Stockholders do not receive benefit from their investments until all other parties have been paid for their contributions. For bearing this risk, stockholders have the right to establish the contributions to be made and rewards to be received by the corporation's employees.

Although maximizing stockholder value is the maintained objective of profit-oriented corporations, employees are not naturally concerned with stockholder welfare. Thus, employees must be provided incentives to motivate them to maximize their own wealth while concurrently maximizing that of the stockholders.

In the past, compensation was often based solely on individual performance and short-run, financial results. Because of operational changes and shifts in managerial philosophies, performance measurements and their related rewards now encompass group success, nonfinancial performance attributes, and long-run considerations. Some of the rewards provide short-run satisfaction (merit pay and bonuses), whereas others provide long-run satisfaction (common stock ownership).

Pay plans are available that involve current compensation, deferred compensation, and perks. Three important dimensions of pay plans are incentive effects, tax effects, and ethical considerations. Incentive effects vary from plan to plan. The periodic pay plan is the least effective in directly motivating employees to perform and provides the weakest link between performance and reward. At the other extreme, the piece rate pay plan provides a direct link between the work accomplished and the employee reward, as long as it promotes quality and group cooperation.

Not-for-profit and governmental entity employees have historically been dissatisfied with their compensation plans. Some of these organizations are now attempting to strengthen the association between compensation and performance to encourage retention of high-quality employees in public-sector careers.

Tax benefits vary among reward structure types. For the employee, rewards may be fully and currently taxable, tax deferred, or tax exempt. Although regular pay is generally fully and currently taxable, certain employer-provided fringe benefits are tax exempt to employees while providing current deductions for employers. Additionally, some elements of incentive compensation plans can be structured to defer taxation.

In designing reward structures, consideration should be given to ethical questions. Three changes that have influenced the power structure in the corporate world are the rise of professional managers, dispersion of stock ownership, and extensive involvement of institutional investors in capital markets. Additionally, some top managers' compensation grossly exceeds pay to ordinary workers. Such excesses can be counterproductive, causing a demoralizing effect within the firm, and ultimately, the failure to succeed in maximizing long-term stockholder wealth. Additional stress between management and workers is being created by employee layoffs that are driven by management's pursuit of higher profits. These situations create ethical issues that should be considered when establishing a compensation strategy that will ensure fairness, effectiveness, and efficiency in an organization.

KEY TERMS

cafeteria plan (p. 1009)
compensation strategy (p. 996)
contingent pay (p. 1004)
deferred compensation (p. 1010)
Employee Stock Ownership Plan
   (ESOP) (p. 1004)
expatriate (p. 1014)
financial incentive (p. 996)
golden parachute (p. 1012)
merit pay (p. 1004)

periodic compensation (p. 1002)
perk (p. 1007)
piece rate (p. 1004)
raider (p. 1011)
shirking (p. 999)
stock appreciation rights (p. 1004)
stock option (p. 1004)
takeover (p. 1011)
tax deferral (p. 1009)
tax exemption (p. 1009)

SOLUTION STRATEGIES

The design of an effective reward structure heavily depends on each organization's unique characteristics. It is impossible to design a generic incentive model that would be effective in a variety of firms. However, affirmative answers to the following questions provide guidance as to the applicability of a proposed incentive and reward plan for a particular organization.

1. Will the organizational objectives be achieved if the proposed compensation structure is implemented?
2. Is the proposed structure consistent with the organizational design, culture, and management philosophy?
3. Are there reasonable and objective performance measures that are good surrogates for the organizational objectives and subunit missions?
4. Are factors beyond employee/group control minimized under the performance measures of the proposed compensation structure?
5. Is there minimal ability of employees to manipulate the performance measurements tied to the proposed compensation structure?
6. In the light of the interests of managers, workers, and stockholders, is the proposed reward structure fair and does it encourage and promote ethical behavior?
7. Is proposed reward structure arranged to take advantage of potential employee/ employer tax benefits?
8. Does the proposed reward structure promote harmony among employee groups?
9. Is there an adequate balance between group and individual incentives?

QUESTIONS

1. How are organizational strategies linked to managerial reward structures?
2. Why would an effective compensation strategy treat top managers, middle managers, and other workers differently?
3. The trend in American business is away from automatic pay increases and toward more use of incentive compensation plans. Why has this trend developed?
4. If worker performance measures used in a pay-for-performance plan are not highly correlated with corporate goals, what is the likely result for the organization? For the workers?
5. How does the time perspective of a performance-based plan affect the selection of performance measures?
6. Why should different missions for two subunits result in different performance reward structures for the managers of the two subunits?
7. Why should worker age be taken into account in designing performance-based pay systems?
8. If a firm offers substantial group-level performance incentives, but no individual performance incentives, how might workers respond?
9. Why are performance-based worker evaluations more risky for workers than evaluations based on direct observation by superiors?
10. Why are additional performance measurement and reward issues created by the circumstance of managers not being shareholders?
11. How do performance-based rewards create risk for the managers and employees who are so evaluated?
12. How is feedback used in a performance-based reward system?
13. Identify the more important differences between periodic compensation and contingent compensation. Why do you believe these to be important?
14. Why is piece-rate pay the extreme form of a performance-based pay system?

15. Many pay structures involve both cash compensation and stock-based compensation. Why do managers want employees to be holders of the firm's common stock?

16. How is the mix of financial and nonfinancial, and short-term and long-term, rewards affected by the mission of an organizational subunit?

17. What are perks? What are the advantages associated with the use of perks in rewarding performance?

18. Why must reward structures in not-for-profit and governmental organizations be structured differently than those for profit-oriented firms?

19. Why must income taxation be taken into account in designing a reward system? What are the alternative tax treatments of the various compensation alternatives?

20. Why is flexibility the distinguishing characteristic of cafeteria plans? Why is flexibility important?

21. What are raiders? What positive and negative roles is served by raiders in capital markets?

22. What is a golden parachute? What are the alternative explanations for the existence of such plans?

23. What are some of the important equity issues in designing reward structures? Why is the achievement of equity in the reward structure important? Globally, where does the United States rank in the pay differential between the average worker and the CEO?

24. For global enterprises, what are the additional concerns in designing a reward system, relative to single-country operations?

25. *(Terminoloy)* Match the following lettered terms on the left with the appropriate numbered description on the right.

EXERCISES

a. Stock option
b. Merit pay
c. Cafeteria plan
d. Deferred compensation
e. Tax-exempt income
f. Expatriate
g. Profit sharing
h. Contingent pay
i. Perk
j. Shirking

1. A right for the holder to purchase common shares
2. A menu of fringe benefit options
3. An employer-provided fringe benefit
4. An increase in pay earned through performance
5. Free-riding
6. Income that is not subject to tax
7. Pay that is dependent on performance
8. Pay for current performance to be received in the future
9. A specific type of contingent pay plan
10. A foreign national assigned to the parent company

26. *(Characteristics of alternative pay plans)* For each of the following pay plan alternatives, indicate whether it provides a high (H) or low (L) level of motivation; whether the time focus is short term (S) or long term (LT); and whether there is a strong (ST), weak (W), or moderate (M) link with employee performance.

a. Periodic pay plan
b. Cafeteria plan
c. Pension
d. ESOP
e. Profit sharing
f. Merit pay
g. Contingent pay
h. Piece rates
i. Stock option
j. Perks

27. *(Pay plan and suboptimization)* Susan Smyth is a division manager of Midwest Manufacturing Inc. She is presently evaluating a potential revenue-generating investment that has the following characteristics:

Initial cost	$2,000,000

Net annual increase in divisional income before consideration of depreciation:

Year 1	$ 200,000
Year 2	300,000
Year 3	380,000
Year 4	1,600,000
Year 5	1,600,000

The project would have a 5-year life with no salvage value. All assets are depreciated according to the straight-line method. Susan is evaluated and compensated based on the amount of pretax profit her division generates. More precisely, she receives an annual salary of $200,000 plus a bonus equal to 2 percent of divisional pretax profit. Before consideration of the above project, Susan anticipates that her division will generate $2,000,000 in pretax profit.

   a. Compute the effect of the new investment on the level of divisional pretax profits for years 1 through 5.
   b. Determine the effect of the new project on Susan's compensation for each of the 5 years.
   c. Based on your computations in part b, will Susan be hesitant to invest in the new project? Explain.
   d. Would upper management likely view the new investment favorably? Explain.

28. *(Pay plan, age, and suboptimization)* Bama Beans Inc. has operations in 13 states. Bama Beans is in the business of growing soybeans and processing the beans into two products: soybean oil and soybean meal. These products are then sold for various commercial uses. Operations in each state are under the control of an autonomous state manager whose performance is evaluated (in large part) based on the magnitude of annual profit. State managers typically receive an annual bonus equal to .5 percent of net state profits. The manager of North Carolina operations is Beano DuMars. Beano has just turned 63 years old and has been with Bama Beans for 39 years. He would like to sell his existing bean crusher and purchase a new, technologically superior one. To evaluate the feasibility of such a move, Beano's controller prepared the information presented below. This information has created a tremendous dilemma for Beano.

Incremental cost of the new crusher:	$2,000,000
Expected remaining life of the old crusher:	5 years
Expected life of the new crusher:	5 years
Expected effect of the new crusher on net profit for the next 5 years:	
Year 1: Decrease in operating costs:	$ 600,000
Loss on disposal of old crusher	1,500,000
Net change in profit	$ (900,000)
Year 2: Net increase in profit	400,000
Year 3: Net increase in profit	400,000
Year 4: Net increase in profit	510,000
Year 5: Net increase in profit	600,000

   a. Assume Beano expects to retire when he reaches age 65. Compute the effect of purchasing the new crusher on Beano's divisional profit and his compensation over his remaining career with Bama Beans.
   b. If Beano had just turned 60 rather than 63, what would be the effect of purchasing the new crusher on Beano's compensation over his remaining career?

c. Is Beano's age likely to be an important factor in his decision regarding the purchase of the new crusher?

d. Would Beano's superiors prefer that he purchase the new crusher? Explain.

---

29. *(Performance measurement)* You have just reviewed a proposal issued by the College of Business at your university. The proposal is about the methods to be used for evaluating the performance of, and rewarding of, professors. The principal provision of the proposal is to change the measures for evaluating performance of professors to emphasize achievements in research and professional service and to deemphasize teaching achievements. Another important provision is to more tightly link merit pay raises and promotion to the performance measurements.

Assume you have been nominated to provide the student perspective in responding to this proposal. Prepare a written report that will be presented to the college dean that summarizes your response.

30. *(Suboptimization)* Compensation consultant, Craig Schneier, describes an experience by one of his clients who decided to pay the purchasing department employees bonuses if they kept the cost of purchases down:

"The problem was, to make that happen they were relying on second-tier sources and accepting poor-quality materials. The company was in the middle of a very big order, and the fasteners were lousy and ended up costing millions of dollars, while the [purchasing] department walked away with big bonuses."

[SOURCE: Adapted from Amanda Bennett, "Paying Workers to Meet Goals Spreads, But Gauging Performance Proves Tough," *Wall Street Journal* (September 10, 1991), pp. B1, B4. Reprinted by permission of *The Wall Street Journal*, © 1991 Dow Jones & Company, Inc. All Rights Reserved Worldwide.]

a. Using the plan-performance-reward model in Exhibit 22–1, identify where the company described above went awry in structuring the performance-based pay plan.

b. How can the company use the feedback received regarding the purchasing department's performance to improve the design of the pay plan?

c. How could the purchasing department's behavior be changed by combining the purchasing department with the production department for group-level performance evaluation purposes?

31. *(Pay and incentives)* Peach Chemical Corporation is a multinational firm that markets a variety of chemicals for industrial uses. One of the many autonomous divisions is the North America Petro-Chemical Division (NAPCD). The manager of NAPCD, Karyn Kravitz, was recently overheard discussing a vexing problem with her controller, William Michaels. The topic of discussion was whether the division should replace its existing chemical-handling equipment with newer technology that is safer, more efficient, and cheaper to operate.

According to an analysis by Mr. Michaels, the cost savings over the life of the new technology would pay for the initial cost of the technology several times over. However, Ms. Kravitz remained reluctant to invest. Her most fundamental concern involved the disposition of the old processing equipment. Because the existing equipment has been in use for only 2 years, it has a very high book value relative to its current market value. To illustrate, Ms. Kravitz noted that if the new technology is not purchased, the division will earn a net income of $4,000,000 for the year. However, if the new technology is purchased, the old equipment will have to be sold, and Ms. Kravitz noted that the division can probably sell the equipment for $1.2 million. This equipment has an original cost of $8 million and $1.5 million in depreciation has been recorded. Thus a book loss of $5.3 million ($6.5m − $1.2m) would be recorded on the sale.

COMMUNICATION ACTIVITIES

Ms. Kravitz' boss, Jim Heitz, is the president of the Western Chemical Group, and his compensation is based almost exclusively on the amount of ROI generated by his group, which includes NAPCD.

After thoroughly analyzing the facts, Ms. Kravitz concluded, "The people in the Western Chemical Group will swallow their dentures if we book a $5.3 million loss."

a. Why is Ms. Kravitz concerned about the book loss on disposal of the old technology in her division?

b. What are the weaknesses in the performance pay plan in place for Western Chemical Group that are apparently causing Ms. Kravitz to avoid an investment that meets all of the normal criteria to be an acceptable investment (ignoring the ROI effect)?

32. *(Incentive compensation) General Motors Corp. earned record profit in 1995—but because results fell short of aggressive targets set by the board, bonus payouts to top GM executives were cut.*

For John F. Smith Jr., GM's chairman and chief executive officer, that meant a 9.2% reduction in salary and bonus to $5.6 million from his 1994 total of $6.1 million. The cut in compensation continues efforts by the GM board to hold management accountable for meeting financial-performance goals. Corporate governance experts observe that much of corporate America has been criticized for not tying executive compensation directly to company performance.

Unlike GM, Ford Motor Co. and Chrysler Corp. both reported earnings declines for 1995. They both cut executive bonuses accordingly.

[SOURCE: Rebecca Blumenstein, "GM Cuts Bonuses of Top Executives, Citing Unmet Goals Despite '95 Profit," *Wall Street Journal* (April 10, 1996), p. A3. Reprinted by permission of *The Wall Street Journal*, © 1996 Dow Jones & Company, Inc. All Rights Reserved Worldwide.]

Assume you are an advocate of John Smith Jr. Prepare a brief oral argument suggesting a reason or reasons why Mr. Smith should have been awarded a larger bonus.

33. *(Performance measurement) Boston Scientific is giving Baxter International Inc. a run for its money.*

Boston Scientific, a small but growing maker of medical devices, doesn't compete directly with health-care giant Baxter. But Baxter's top executives are keenly watching the performance of their new rival. Their compensation, in part, is based on it.

Baxter's payout of stock to its senior managers is linked to how the company's shares perform compared with the Standard & Poor's Medical Products and Supplies Index, which includes the two companies plus seven others.

It's the latest twist in executive pay: awarding stock benefits according to how well a corporation stacks up against its rivals. Many comparisons, like Baxter's, are based on total shareholder return, though some use other measures such as return on assets. Whatever they use, the purpose is the same: to ensure that managers keep a gimlet eye on other companies competing for the same customer and investor dollars.

[SOURCE: Lauren Young, "Compare and Contrast: More Pay Plans are Linked to How Well a Corporation Fares Against Its Rivals. The Problem: Finding an Appropriate Rival," *Wall Street Journal* (April 11, 1996), p. R8. Reprinted by permission of *The Wall Street Journal*, © 1996 Dow Jones & Company, Inc. All Rights Reserved Worldwide.]

Write a report in which you discuss the benefits and risks of evaluating and rewarding performance based on comparisons with competitors.

CASES

34. *(Pay plans and goal congruence)* In 1997, the lead story in your college newspaper reports the details of the hiring of your new football coach. Your old football coach was fired for failing to win games and attract fans. In his last season his record was 1 win and 11 losses. The news story states the new coach's contract provides for a base salary of $100,000 per year plus an annual bonus computed as follows:

Win less than 5 games	$ 0.00
Win 5 to 7 games	$ 25,000
Win 8 games or more	$ 75,000
Win 8 games and conference championship	$ 95,000
Win 8 games, win conference, get a bowl bid	$150,000

The coach's contract has essentially no other features or clauses.

The first year after the new coach is hired, the football team wins 3 games and loses 8. The second year the team wins 6 games and loses 5. The third year the team wins 9 games, wins the conference championship, and is invited to a prestigious bowl. Shortly after the bowl game, articles appear on the front page of several national sports publications announcing your college football program has been cited by the National Collegiate Athletic Association (NCAA) for nine major rule violations including cash payoffs to players, playing academically ineligible players, illegal recruiting tactics, illegal involvement of alumni in recruiting, etc. All the national news publications agree that your football program will be disbanded by the NCAA. One article also mentioned that over the past 3 years only 13 percent of senior football players managed to graduate on time. Additional speculation suggests the responsible parties including the coaching staff, athletic director, and college president will be dismissed by the board of trustees.

a. Compute the amount of compensation paid to the new coach in each of his first 3 years.

b. Did the performance measures in the coach's contract foster goal congruence? Explain.

c. Would the coach's actions have been different if other performance measures were added to the compensation contract? Explain.

d. What performance measures should be considered for the next coach's contract, assuming the football program will be kept alive?

35. *(Incentive compensation)* According to a news article, the chairman of HCA-Hospital Corporation of America, Thomas Frist, received $127 million in compensation for 1992. Of that amount, $125.9 million came from exercising stock options that had been received in 1989. According to the same article, many of the other HCA top managers also exercised substantial amounts of stock options in 1992. The stock options gave the officers the right to purchase the stock from the corporation for a price that was substantially below the market value.

One of the reasons cited by the managers for exercising the stock options in 1992 was an expectation that tax laws were going to change. Specifically, the managers expected two tax law changes to be enacted in 1993 or later years:

1. An increase in the tax rate on personal income.

2. A limit of $1,000,000 on the annual amount of compensation paid to top executives that would be deductible for tax purposes by corporations.

[SOURCE: Helene Cooper, "HCA Chairman's 1992 Compensation Hit $127 Million Due to Stock Options," *Wall Street Journal* (March 24, 1993), p. B7. Reprinted by permission of *The Wall Street Journal*, © 1993 Dow Jones & Company, Inc. All Rights Reserved Worldwide.]

a. Were the stock options exercised in 1992 compensation for job performance in 1992 or compensation for other years? Explain.

b. If the tax law changes expected by the managers were passed as anticipated, was exercising the stock options a wise move for the managers? For HCA? Explain.

c. For 1992, HCA's net income was $28.1 million. Given the level of compensation received by Mr. Frist for 1992, does Mr. Frist's pay appear to be equitable? Explain.

d. If Mr. Frist and the other top managers had not only exercised their stock options, but also sold their stock in 1992, how would this have potentially affected their incentives?

ETHICS AND QUALITY DISCUSSION

36. In a survey published in 1990, 649 managers responded to a questionnaire and provided their opinions from an ethical perspective as to the acceptability of manipulating accounting earnings to achieve higher managerial compensation. One of the questions dealt with the acceptability of changing a sales practice to pull some of next year's sales into the current year so that reported current earnings could be pushed up. The results of the survey indicated that about 43 percent of the respondents felt this practice was ethically acceptable, 44 percent felt the practice was ethically questionable, and 13 percent felt the practice was ethically unacceptable.

Other results of the survey indicate the managers felt large manipulations were more unethical than small manipulations, and income-increasing manipulations were more ethically unacceptable than income-decreasing manipulations.

[SOURCE: Adapted from William J. Bruns and Kenneth A. Merchant, "The Dangerous Morality of Managing Earnings," *Management Accounting* (August 1990), pp. 22–25. Reprinted from *Management Accounting*. Copyright by Institute of Management Accountants, Montvale, NJ.]

a. If managers are able to manipulate earnings to effect a change in their pay, is this a signal of a weakness in the pay-for-performance plan? Explain.

b. In your view, does the materiality of a manipulation partly determine the extent to which the manipulation is ethically acceptable?

c. Describe any circumstances in which you believe manipulations would be ethically acceptable.

37. General Dynamics is one of the many firms that has instituted bonus plans. Below is an excerpt from a description of the implementation:

[O]ne element of the plan is a gain-sharing provision that gives senior executives annual bonuses equal to their base salaries, under one condition: that General Dynamics stock trades for 10 consecutive days at a price at least $10 a share above where it stood when the plan was adopted. . . . At least half of each bonus paid as a direct result of increasing shareholder value must remain in a General Dynamics account, the value of which we intend to link directly to the company's long-term performance until the individual participant reaches age 65. . . . Consequently, every manager who is part of gain-sharing has a continuing, tangible incentive to work to increase shareholder value over the long term.

The plan was adopted in February of 1991. On May 6, 1991, the stock price met the conditions specified above and managers split a pool of $5.1 million.

[SOURCE: William A. Anders, "Hefty Bonuses for Hefty Gains," *Wall Street Journal* (May 20, 1991), p. A18. Reprinted by permission of *The Wall Street Journal*, © 1991 Dow Jones & Company, Inc. All Rights Reserved Worldwide.]

a. Do you think that General Dynamics' managers could take actions between February 1991 and May 1991 that were so significant that share price would rise by $10? Explain.

b. As a shareholder, would you have been suspicious of the timing of the implementation of this plan? Explain.

c. In your view, is there any ethical problem with the implementation of the General Dynamics plan?

d. What factors, other than managerial actions, could have caused the stock price to rise?

38. During the recessionary times of the late 1980s and early 1990s, many companies turned to their workers for pay concessions in response to sagging profits. In other words, as profits declined, managers asked ordinary workers to make sacrifices in their compensation levels. However, the managers were not willing to participate in the worker's pain. For example:

- While profits plunged 97 percent in 1989 for Commodore International Ltd., Chief Executive Irving Gould received a 40 percent pay hike. His salary was larger than the company's net income for the year.
- According to a survey of 325 large corporations in 1989, corporate profits fell 4.2 percent and executive cash compensation rose by 8 percent.

- In 1989 at General Motors, Chairman Roger Smith's annual bonus fell by 7 percent to $1.4 million, profits fell by 13 percent, and worker bonuses dropped by 81 percent.

[SOURCE: Adapted from Carol Hymowitz, "More Employees, Shareholders Demand that Sacrifices in Pay Begin at the Top," *Wall Street Journal* (November 8, 1990), pp. B1, B5. Reprinted by permission of *The Wall Street Journal*, © 1990 Dow Jones & Company, Inc. All Rights Reserved Worldwide.]

   a. Based on the examples above and the data in Exhibit 22–8, do you perceive any equity problem or ethical problem in the relative pay treatments of ordinary workers and top managers?

   b. Why do you think the pay gap between top managers and workers appears to be more pronounced in the United States than in other countries?

   c. In the two examples above involving Commodore and General Motors, did the top managers act ethically in accepting the high level of pay, given the circumstances?

39. Recall from your academic career the various ways that your academic performance has been measured and rewarded. Have the ways that your class grades been determined always provided the best indications of performance? Provide at least two positive and two negative examples. What would you have done to change the measurement system in the negative examples?

40. When David P. Gardner, president of the University of California, announced his retirement unexpectedly in April 1992, he received a severance package worth $1 million—in a year in which the university's budget was cut by $255 million. The university also announced that student fees would rise for the third straight year—for a 3-year total increase of 85 percent.

   Mr. Gardner, who retired early at age 58, earned an official salary of $243,500—double that of California's governor. But his actual compensation was more than $400,000. And although his official pension will be $126,000 a year, he received an additional $933,000 when he departed.

   In addition to Mr. Gardner's base salary, the regents found ways to pay him an additional $160,000 annually. Deferred income, severance pay, and a special supplemental retirement program made the difference. In fact, a secret deferred-income plan was established by the regents in 1988 for about a dozen top UC executives, after a private study concluded that their compensation lagged behind that of top administrators in a nationwide comparison group of universities. (The conclusions of the study have since been challenged by the California Postsecondary Education Commission, an independent state agency.)

[SOURCE: Adapted from Jon Wiener, "Lavish Compensation Is Not Appropriate for Top Executives at Public Universities," *Chronicle of Higher Education* (November 25, 1992), p. B3.]

   a. Assume you were one of the students in the UC system. Discuss your perceptions about Mr. Gardner's compensation package.

   b. How ethical do you think it was for Mr. Gardner to accept such a compensation package. Consider both the information in the comparative study and the budget problems that California has experienced.

   c. Could this simply be a case of trying to retain the "best and the brightest" in a not-for-profit institution? Discuss the rationale for your answer.

41. *At least five Bush Cabinet secretaries authorized tens of thousands of dollars in bonuses for senior employees, both political appointees and career civil servants, in the closing minutes of their tenures.*

   Five minutes before Bill Clinton took the oath of office [in January 1993], outgoing Interior Secretary Manuel Lujan proposed $170,000 in bonuses for 12 senior career officials at the Interior Department.

   Former Labor Secretary Lynn Martin awarded eight bonuses totaling $22,000 for departing political appointees between November 1 and Inauguration Day, and the Agriculture Department gave year-end bonuses of up to $12,500 to more than 50 senior employees, spokesmen said. Several senior employees at the Department of Housing and Urban Development also received bonuses, according to a department source who spoke on condition of anonymity.

In his last weeks in office, former Attorney General William Barr awarded more than $108,000 in bonuses to 37 Justice Department employees, including members of his security detail, his secretary and two of his closest aides.

The practice of giving cash bonuses to government employees is legal, and Bush administration officials say it occurred under earlier presidents.

[SOURCE: Marcy Gordon, "Bush Officials Awarded Bonuses at Last Minute," [*New Orleans*] *Times-Picayune* (February 11, 1993) p. A17.]

a. The proposed bonuses were to be reviewed as to merit, but the deadline for such bonuses was January 22, so they were within the appropriate time frame. Regardless of merit, what is your opinion about the timing of the bonus nominations? Provide some valid reasons why bonus nominations might need to wait until after the end of the calendar year.

b. Because many of the individuals to receive bonuses will not be retained by the new administration, the bonus pay could not have a retention basis. What are the ethical issues of paying bonuses to government employees in the current environment of a skyrocketing federal government deficit?

c. Do you see an ethical problem in outgoing government employees receiving bonuses at the "last hour?" Would your answer differ if the organization under consideration were a business being taken over by new management rather than the government? Discuss the rationale for your answers.

42. *Donald Hudgens thinks ConAgra Inc.'s chairman and chief executive officer, Philip B. Fletcher, has it too easy.*

"Maybe I'm naive," says Mr. Hudgens, a retired railroad chemist. "I've never had a high-powered job." Still, he contends that ConAgra's CEO should be working harder for his millions.

As a consequence, ConAgra shareholders will vote later this month on Mr. Hudgens' proposal that the company revise a special long-term incentive plan directors approved for Mr. Fletcher last year. Under that plan, the chairman would receive 50,000 ConAgra common shares for every percentage point over 10% the company's per-share earnings rise during the next four fiscal years.

For example, if earnings grow at a compound annual rate of 14%, as they did last year, Mr. Fletcher would get 200,000 shares of stock—that is, four percentage points times 50,000 shares. The payout would occur in July 1998. At ConAgra's current price, every 50,000 shares would be valued at $1.6 million.

"They'll do it [exceed 10%] in spite of any incentive award," Mr. Hudgens says. He has some statistical support. . . . ConAgra's per-share earnings have grown at a 15.4% compounded annual rate; ConAgra's longtime internal goal is for per-share earnings [growth] to exceed 14% a year, on average.

Thus, Mr. Hudgens wants ConAgra to compare its performance with that of other food companies [instead of its own growth targets] and he has drawn up a list of 13 [competitors]. . . . Moreover, per-share growth must come from continuing operations, the 54-year-old shareholder says.

ConAgra, the nation's largest independent food company, opposes Mr. Hudgens' suggestion. Initially, the company said it wouldn't allow shareholders to consider it at all, only to have the Securities and Exchange Commission disagree.

[SOURCE: Richard Gibson, "ConAgra Holder Is Seeking Changes in Incentive Plan," *Wall Street Journal* (September 6, 1994), p. B5. Reprinted by permission of *The Wall Street Journal*, © 1994 Dow Jones & Company, Inc. All Rights Reserved Worldwide.]

a. Why would managers of ConAgra oppose Mr. Hudgens' proposal?

b. What is your opinion regarding the payment of bonuses for performance that is merely average?

c. What are the ethical responsibilities of top management and the board of directors in setting the performance criteria that determine bonus payments?

43. Executive Alliance is a firm that specializes in designing executive compensation services. Find the home page of this company and review the services it offers. Assume that you are on the board of directors of a mid-size manufacturing company. Discuss how you might use the services of a firm like Executive Alliance to develop a compensation strategy for your firm.

44. National Center for Employee Ownership is a nonprofit organization that distributes information regarding employee ownership of businesses. Review the materials provided on the home page of this organization. Assume that you work for a company that is about to introduce an incentive stock option plan for its employees. Prepare an oral report in which you present to your company's top executives a strategy as to how materials from this organization could be used to introduce the idea of stock ownership to your employees.

45. Find the home page of Columbia/HCA Healthcare Corporation. This company is the United States' largest healthcare provider. Review the information provided by the company on its home page. Assume that you are a top executive of Columbia and that you have been charged with designing a compensation system for the doctors and nurses employed by the firm. Describe the major concerns that you would have in designing the compensation system and the major features you would incorporate in the compensation system.

Present Value Tables

Table 1 Present Value of $1

Period	1.00%	2.00%	3.00%	4.00%	5.00%	6.00%	7.00%	8.00%	9.00%	9.50%	10.00%	10.50%	11.00%
1	0.9901	0.9804	0.9709	0.9615	0.9524	0.9434	0.9346	0.9259	0.9174	0.9132	0.9091	0.9050	0.9009
2	0.9803	0.9612	0.9426	0.9246	0.9070	0.8900	0.8734	0.8573	0.8417	0.8340	0.8265	0.8190	0.8116
3	0.9706	0.9423	0.9151	0.8890	0.8638	0.8396	0.8163	0.7938	0.7722	0.7617	0.7513	0.7412	0.7312
4	0.9610	0.9239	0.8885	0.8548	0.8227	0.7921	0.7629	0.7350	0.7084	0.6956	0.6830	0.6707	0.6587
5	0.9515	0.9057	0.8626	0.8219	0.7835	0.7473	0.7130	0.6806	0.6499	0.6352	0.6209	0.6070	0.5935
6	0.9421	0.8880	0.8375	0.7903	0.7462	0.7050	0.6663	0.6302	0.5963	0.5801	0.5645	0.5493	0.5346
7	0.9327	0.8706	0.8131	0.7599	0.7107	0.6651	0.6228	0.5835	0.5470	0.5298	0.5132	0.4971	0.4817
8	0.9235	0.8535	0.7894	0.7307	0.6768	0.6274	0.5820	0.5403	0.5019	0.4838	0.4665	0.4499	0.4339
9	0.9143	0.8368	0.7664	0.7026	0.6446	0.5919	0.5439	0.5003	0.4604	0.4419	0.4241	0.4071	0.3909
10	0.9053	0.8204	0.7441	0.6756	0.6139	0.5584	0.5084	0.4632	0.4224	0.4035	0.3855	0.3685	0.3522
11	0.8963	0.8043	0.7224	0.6496	0.5847	0.5268	0.4751	0.4289	0.3875	0.3685	0.3505	0.3334	0.3173
12	0.8875	0.7885	0.7014	0.6246	0.5568	0.4970	0.4440	0.3971	0.3555	0.3365	0.3186	0.3018	0.2858
13	0.8787	0.7730	0.6810	0.6006	0.5303	0.4688	0.4150	0.3677	0.3262	0.3073	0.2897	0.2731	0.2575
14	0.8700	0.7579	0.6611	0.5775	0.5051	0.4423	0.3878	0.3405	0.2993	0.2807	0.2633	0.2471	0.2320
15	0.8614	0.7430	0.6419	0.5553	0.4810	0.4173	0.3625	0.3152	0.2745	0.2563	0.2394	0.2237	0.2090
16	0.8528	0.7285	0.6232	0.5339	0.4581	0.3937	0.3387	0.2919	0.2519	0.2341	0.2176	0.2024	0.1883
17	0.8444	0.7142	0.6050	0.5134	0.4363	0.3714	0.3166	0.2703	0.2311	0.2138	0.1978	0.1832	0.1696
18	0.8360	0.7002	0.5874	0.4936	0.4155	0.3503	0.2959	0.2503	0.2120	0.1952	0.1799	0.1658	0.1528
19	0.8277	0.6864	0.5703	0.4746	0.3957	0.3305	0.2765	0.2317	0.1945	0.1783	0.1635	0.1500	0.1377
20	0.8195	0.6730	0.5537	0.4564	0.3769	0.3118	0.2584	0.2146	0.1784	0.1628	0.1486	0.1358	0.1240
21	0.8114	0.6598	0.5376	0.4388	0.3589	0.2942	0.2415	0.1987	0.1637	0.1487	0.1351	0.1229	0.1117
22	0.8034	0.6468	0.5219	0.4220	0.3419	0.2775	0.2257	0.1839	0.1502	0.1358	0.1229	0.1112	0.1007
23	0.7954	0.6342	0.5067	0.4057	0.3256	0.2618	0.2110	0.1703	0.1378	0.1240	0.1117	0.1006	0.0907
24	0.7876	0.6217	0.4919	0.3901	0.3101	0.2470	0.1972	0.1577	0.1264	0.1133	0.1015	0.0911	0.0817
25	0.7798	0.6095	0.4776	0.3751	0.2953	0.2330	0.1843	0.1460	0.1160	0.1034	0.0923	0.0824	0.0736
26	0.7721	0.5976	0.4637	0.3607	0.2812	0.2198	0.1722	0.1352	0.1064	0.0945	0.0839	0.0746	0.0663
27	0.7644	0.5859	0.4502	0.3468	0.2679	0.2074	0.1609	0.1252	0.0976	0.0863	0.0763	0.0675	0.0597
28	0.7568	0.5744	0.4371	0.3335	0.2551	0.1956	0.1504	0.1159	0.0896	0.0788	0.0693	0.0611	0.0538
29	0.7493	0.5631	0.4244	0.3207	0.2430	0.1846	0.1406	0.1073	0.0822	0.0719	0.0630	0.0553	0.0485
30	0.7419	0.5521	0.4120	0.3083	0.2314	0.1741	0.1314	0.0994	0.0754	0.0657	0.0573	0.0500	0.0437
31	0.7346	0.5413	0.4000	0.2965	0.2204	0.1643	0.1228	0.0920	0.0692	0.0600	0.0521	0.0453	0.0394
32	0.7273	0.5306	0.3883	0.2851	0.2099	0.1550	0.1147	0.0852	0.0634	0.0058	0.0474	0.0410	0.0355
33	0.7201	0.5202	0.3770	0.2741	0.1999	0.1462	0.1072	0.0789	0.0582	0.0500	0.0431	0.0371	0.0319
34	0.7130	0.5100	0.3660	0.2636	0.1904	0.1379	0.1002	0.0731	0.0534	0.0457	0.0391	0.0336	0.0288
35	0.7059	0.5000	0.3554	0.2534	0.1813	0.1301	0.0937	0.0676	0.0490	0.0417	0.0356	0.0304	0.0259
36	0.6989	0.4902	0.3450	0.2437	0.1727	0.1227	0.0875	0.0626	0.0449	0.0381	0.0324	0.0275	0.0234
37	0.6920	0.4806	0.3350	0.2343	0.1644	0.1158	0.0818	0.0580	0.0412	0.0348	0.0294	0.0249	0.0210
38	0.6852	0.4712	0.3252	0.2253	0.1566	0.1092	0.0765	0.0537	0.0378	0.0318	0.0267	0.0225	0.0190
39	0.6784	0.4620	0.3158	0.2166	0.1492	0.1031	0.0715	0.0497	0.0347	0.0290	0.0243	0.0204	0.0171
40	0.6717	0.4529	0.3066	0.2083	0.1421	0.0972	0.0668	0.0460	0.0318	0.0265	0.0221	0.0184	0.0154
41	0.6650	0.4440	0.2976	0.2003	0.1353	0.0917	0.0624	0.0426	0.0292	0.0242	0.0201	0.0167	0.0139
42	0.6584	0.4353	0.2890	0.1926	0.1288	0.0865	0.0583	0.0395	0.0268	0.0221	0.0183	0.0151	0.0125
43	0.6519	0.4268	0.2805	0.1852	0.1227	0.0816	0.0545	0.0365	0.0246	0.0202	0.0166	0.0137	0.0113
44	0.6455	0.4184	0.2724	0.1781	0.1169	0.0770	0.0510	0.0338	0.0226	0.0184	0.0151	0.0124	0.0101
45	0.6391	0.4102	0.2644	0.1712	0.1113	0.0727	0.0476	0.0313	0.0207	0.0168	0.0137	0.0112	0.0091
46	0.6327	0.4022	0.2567	0.1646	0.1060	0.0685	0.0445	0.0290	0.0190	0.0154	0.0125	0.0101	0.0082
47	0.6265	0.3943	0.2493	0.1583	0.1010	0.0647	0.0416	0.0269	0.0174	0.0141	0.0113	0.0092	0.0074
48	0.6203	0.3865	0.2420	0.1522	0.0961	0.0610	0.0389	0.0249	0.0160	0.0128	0.0103	0.0083	0.0067
49	0.6141	0.3790	0.2350	0.1463	0.0916	0.0576	0.0363	0.0230	0.0147	0.0117	0.0094	0.0075	0.0060
50	0.6080	0.3715	0.2281	0.1407	0.0872	0.0543	0.0340	0.0213	0.0135	0.0107	0.0085	0.0068	0.0054

11.50%	12.00%	12.50%	13.00%	13.50%	14.00%	14.50%	15.00%	15.50%	16.00%	17.00%	18.00%	19.00%	20.00%
0.8969	0.8929	0.8889	0.8850	0.8811	0.8772	0.8734	0.8696	0.8658	0.8621	0.8547	0.8475	0.8403	0.8333
0.8044	0.7972	0.7901	0.7832	0.7763	0.7695	0.7628	0.7561	0.7496	0.7432	0.7305	0.7182	0.7062	0.6944
0.7214	0.7118	0.7023	0.6931	0.6839	0.6750	0.6662	0.6575	0.6490	0.6407	0.6244	0.6086	0.5934	0.5787
0.6470	0.6355	0.6243	0.6133	0.6026	0.5921	0.5818	0.5718	0.5619	0.5523	0.5337	0.5158	0.4987	0.4823
0.5803	0.5674	0.5549	0.5428	0.5309	0.5194	0.5081	0.4972	0.4865	0.4761	0.4561	0.4371	0.4191	0.4019
0.5204	0.5066	0.4933	0.4803	0.4678	0.4556	0.4438	0.4323	0.4212	0.4104	0.3898	0.3704	0.3521	0.3349
0.4667	0.4524	0.4385	0.4251	0.4121	0.3996	0.3876	0.3759	0.3647	0.3538	0.3332	0.3139	0.2959	0.2791
0.4186	0.4039	0.3897	0.3762	0.3631	0.3506	0.3385	0.3269	0.3158	0.3050	0.2848	0.2660	0.2487	0.2326
0.3754	0.3606	0.3464	0.3329	0.3199	0.3075	0.2956	0.2843	0.2734	0.2630	0.2434	0.2255	0.2090	0.1938
0.3367	0.3220	0.3080	0.2946	0.2819	0.2697	0.2582	0.2472	0.2367	0.2267	0.2080	0.1911	0.1756	0.1615
0.3020	0.2875	0.2737	0.2607	0.2483	0.2366	0.2255	0.2149	0.2049	0.1954	0.1778	0.1619	0.1476	0.1346
0.2708	0.2567	0.2433	0.2307	0.2188	0.2076	0.1969	0.1869	0.1774	0.1685	0.1520	0.1372	0.1240	0.1122
0.2429	0.2292	0.2163	0.2042	0.1928	0.1821	0.1720	0.1625	0.1536	0.1452	0.1299	0.1163	0.1042	0.0935
0.2179	0.2046	0.1923	0.1807	0.1699	0.1597	0.1502	0.1413	0.1330	0.1252	0.1110	0.0986	0.0876	0.0779
0.1954	0.1827	0.1709	0.1599	0.1496	0.1401	0.1312	0.1229	0.1152	0.1079	0.0949	0.0835	0.0736	0.0649
0.1752	0.1631	0.1519	0.1415	0.1319	0.1229	0.1146	0.1069	0.0997	0.0930	0.0811	0.0708	0.0618	0.0541
0.1572	0.1456	0.1350	0.1252	0.1162	0.1078	0.1001	0.0929	0.0863	0.0802	0.0693	0.0600	0.0520	0.0451
0.1410	0.1300	0.1200	0.1108	0.1024	0.0946	0.0874	0.0808	0.0747	0.0691	0.0593	0.0508	0.0437	0.0376
0.1264	0.1161	0.1067	0.0981	0.0902	0.0830	0.0763	0.0703	0.0647	0.0596	0.0506	0.0431	0.0367	0.0313
0.1134	0.1037	0.0948	0.0868	0.0795	0.0728	0.0667	0.0611	0.0560	0.0514	0.0433	0.0365	0.0308	0.0261
0.1017	0.0926	0.0843	0.0768	0.0700	0.0638	0.0582	0.0531	0.0485	0.0443	0.0370	0.0309	0.0259	0.0217
0.0912	0.0826	0.0749	0.0680	0.0617	0.0560	0.0509	0.0462	0.0420	0.0382	0.0316	0.0262	0.0218	0.0181
0.0818	0.0738	0.0666	0.0601	0.0543	0.0491	0.0444	0.0402	0.0364	0.0329	0.0270	0.0222	0.0183	0.0151
0.0734	0.0659	0.0592	0.0532	0.0479	0.0431	0.0388	0.0349	0.0315	0.0284	0.0231	0.0188	0.0154	0.0126
0.0658	0.0588	0.0526	0.0471	0.0422	0.0378	0.0339	0.0304	0.0273	0.0245	0.0197	0.0160	0.0129	0.0105
0.0590	0.0525	0.0468	0.0417	0.0372	0.0332	0.0296	0.0264	0.0236	0.0211	0.0169	0.0135	0.0109	0.0087
0.0529	0.0469	0.0416	0.0369	0.0327	0.0291	0.0258	0.0230	0.0204	0.0182	0.0144	0.0115	0.0091	0.0073
0.0475	0.0419	0.0370	0.0326	0.0289	0.0255	0.0226	0.0200	0.0177	0.0157	0.0123	0.0097	0.0077	0.0061
0.0426	0.0374	0.0329	0.0289	0.0254	0.0224	0.0197	0.0174	0.0153	0.0135	0.0105	0.0082	0.0064	0.0051
0.0382	0.0334	0.0292	0.0256	0.0224	0.0196	0.0172	0.0151	0.0133	0.0117	0.0090	0.0070	0.0054	0.0042
0.0342	0.0298	0.0260	0.0226	0.0197	0.0172	0.0150	0.0131	0.0115	0.0100	0.0077	0.0059	0.0046	0.0035
0.0307	0.0266	0.0231	0.0200	0.0174	0.0151	0.0131	0.0114	0.0099	0.0087	0.0066	0.0050	0.0038	0.0029
0.0275	0.0238	0.0205	0.0177	0.0153	0.0133	0.0115	0.0099	0.0086	0.0075	0.0056	0.0043	0.0032	0.0024
0.0247	0.0212	0.0182	0.0157	0.0135	0.0116	0.0100	0.0088	0.0075	0.0064	0.0048	0.0036	0.0027	0.0020
0.0222	0.0189	0.0162	0.0139	0.0119	0.0102	0.0088	0.0075	0.0065	0.0056	0.0041	0.0031	0.0023	0.0017
0.0199	0.0169	0.0144	0.0123	0.0105	0.0089	0.0076	0.0065	0.0056	0.0048	0.0035	0.0026	0.0019	0.0014
0.0178	0.0151	0.0128	0.0109	0.0092	0.0078	0.0067	0.0057	0.0048	0.0041	0.0030	0.0022	0.0016	0.0012
0.0160	0.0135	0.0114	0.0096	0.0081	0.0069	0.0058	0.0049	0.0042	0.0036	0.0026	0.0019	0.0014	0.0010
0.0143	0.0120	0.0101	0.0085	0.0072	0.0060	0.0051	0.0043	0.0036	0.0031	0.0022	0.0016	0.0011	0.0008
0.0129	0.0108	0.0090	0.0075	0.0063	0.0053	0.0044	0.0037	0.0031	0.0026	0.0019	0.0013	0.0010	0.0007
0.0115	0.0096	0.0080	0.0067	0.0056	0.0046	0.0039	0.0033	0.0027	0.0023	0.0016	0.0011	0.0008	0.0006
0.0103	0.0086	0.0077	0.0059	0.0049	0.0041	0.0034	0.0028	0.0024	0.0020	0.0014	0.0010	0.0007	0.0005
0.0093	0.0077	0.0063	0.0052	0.0043	0.0036	0.0030	0.0025	0.0020	0.0017	0.0012	0.0008	0.0006	0.0004
0.0083	0.0068	0.0056	0.0046	0.0038	0.0031	0.0026	0.0021	0.0018	0.0015	0.0010	0.0007	0.0005	0.0003
0.0075	0.0061	0.0050	0.0041	0.0034	0.0028	0.0023	0.0019	0.0015	0.0013	0.0009	0.0006	0.0004	0.0003
0.0067	0.0054	0.0044	0.0036	0.0030	0.0024	0.0020	0.0016	0.0013	0.0011	0.0007	0.0005	0.0003	0.0002
0.0060	0.0049	0.0039	0.0032	0.0026	0.0021	0.0017	0.0014	0.0011	0.0009	0.0006	0.0004	0.0003	0.0002
0.0054	0.0043	0.0035	0.0028	0.0023	0.0019	0.0015	0.0012	0.0010	0.0008	0.0005	0.0004	0.0002	0.0002
0.0048	0.0039	0.0031	0.0025	0.0020	0.0016	0.0013	0.0011	0.0009	0.0007	0.0005	0.0003	0.0002	0.0001
0.0043	0.0035	0.0028	0.0022	0.0018	0.0014	0.0012	0.0009	0.0007	0.0006	0.0004	0.0003	0.0002	0.0001

Table 2 Present Value of an Ordinary Annuity of $1

Period	1.00%	2.00%	3.00%	4.00%	5.00%	6.00%	7.00%	8.00%	9.00%	9.50%	10.00%	10.50%	11.00%
1	0.9901	0.9804	0.9709	0.9615	0.0524	0.9434	0.9346	0.9259	0.9174	0.9132	0.9091	0.9050	0.9009
2	1.9704	1.9416	1.9135	1.8861	1.8594	1.8334	1.8080	1.7833	1.7591	1.7473	1.7355	1.7240	1.7125
3	2.9410	2.8839	2.8286	2.7751	2.7233	2.6730	2.6243	2.5771	2.5313	2.5089	2.4869	2.4651	2.4437
4	3.9020	3.8077	3.7171	3.6299	3.5460	3.4651	3.3872	3.3121	3.2397	3.2045	3.1699	3.1359	3.1025
5	4.8534	4.7135	4.5797	4.4518	4.3295	4.2124	4.1002	3.9927	3.8897	3.8397	3.7908	3.7429	3.6959
6	5.7955	5.6014	5.4172	5.2421	5.0757	4.9173	4.7665	4.6229	4.4859	4.4198	4.3553	4.2922	4.2305
7	6.7282	6.4720	6.2303	6.0021	5.7864	5.5824	5.3893	5.2064	5.0330	4.9496	4.8684	4.7893	4.7122
8	7.6517	7.3255	7.0197	6.7327	6.4632	6.2098	5.9713	5.7466	5.5348	5.4334	5.3349	5.2392	5.1461
9	8.5660	8.1622	7.7861	7.4353	7.1078	6.8017	6.5152	6.2469	5.9953	5.8753	5.7590	5.6463	5.5371
10	9.4713	8.9826	8.5302	8.1109	7.7217	7.3601	7.0236	6.7101	6.4177	6.2788	6.1446	6.0148	5.8892
11	10.3676	9.7869	9.2526	8.7605	8.3064	7.8869	7.4987	7.1390	6.8052	6.6473	6.4951	6.3482	6.2065
12	11.2551	10.5753	9.9540	9.3851	8.8633	8.3838	7.9427	7.5361	7.1607	6.9838	6.8137	6.6500	6.4924
13	12.1337	11.3484	10.6350	9.9857	9.3936	8.8527	8.3577	7.9038	7.4869	7.2912	7.1034	6.9230	6.7499
14	13.0037	12.1063	11.2961	10.5631	9.8986	9.2950	8.7455	8.2442	7.7862	7.5719	7.3667	7.1702	6.9819
15	13.8651	12.8493	11.9379	11.1184	10.3797	9.7123	9.1079	8.5595	8.0607	7.8282	7.6061	7.3938	7.1909
16	14.7179	13.5777	12.5611	11.6523	10.8378	10.1059	9.4467	8.8514	8.3126	8.0623	7.8237	7.5962	7.3792
17	15.5623	14.2919	13.1661	12.1657	11.2741	10.4773	9.7632	9.1216	8.5436	8.2760	8.0216	7.7794	7.5488
18	16.3983	14.9920	13.7535	12.6593	11.6896	10.8276	10.0591	9.3719	8.7556	8.4713	8.2014	7.9452	7.7016
19	17.2260	15.6785	14.3238	13.1339	12.0853	11.1581	10.3356	9.6036	8.9501	8.6496	8.3649	8.0952	7.8393
20	18.0456	16.3514	14.8775	13.5903	12.4622	11.4699	10.5940	9.8182	9.1286	8.8124	8.5136	8.2309	7.9633
21	18.8570	17.0112	15.4150	14.0292	12.8212	11.7641	10.8355	10.0168	9.2922	8.9611	8.6487	8.3538	8.0751
22	19.6604	17.6581	15.9369	14.4511	13.1630	12.0416	11.0612	10.2007	9.4424	9.0969	8.7715	8.4649	8.1757
23	20.4558	18.2922	16.4436	14.8568	13.4886	12.3034	11.2722	10.3711	9.5802	9.2209	8.8832	8.5656	8.2664
24	21.2434	18.9139	16.9355	15.2470	13.7986	12.5504	11.4693	10.5288	9.7066	9.3342	8.9847	8.6566	8.3481
25	22.0232	19.5235	17.4132	15.6221	14.0939	12.7834	11.6536	10.6748	9.8226	9.4376	9.0770	8.7390	8.4217
26	22.7952	20.1210	17.8768	15.9828	14.3752	13.0032	11.8258	10.8100	9.9290	9.5320	9.1610	8.8136	8.4881
27	23.5596	20.7069	18.3270	16.3296	14.6430	13.2105	11.9867	10.9352	10.0266	9.6183	9.2372	8.8811	8.5478
28	24.3164	21.2813	18.7641	16.6631	14.8981	13.4062	12.1371	11.0511	10.1161	9.6971	9.3066	8.9422	8.6016
29	25.0658	21.8444	19.1885	16.9837	15.1411	13.5907	12.2777	11.1584	10.1983	9.7690	9.3696	8.9974	8.6501
30	25.8077	22.3965	19.6004	17.2920	15.3725	13.7648	12.4090	11.2578	10.2737	9.8347	9.4269	9.0474	8.6938
31	26.5423	22.9377	20.0004	17.5885	15.5928	13.9291	12.5318	11.3498	10.3428	9.8947	9.4790	9.0927	8.7332
32	27.2696	23.4683	20.3888	17.8736	15.8027	14.0840	12.6466	11.4350	10.4062	9.9495	9.5264	9.1337	8.7686
33	27.9897	23.9886	20.7658	18.1477	16.0026	14.2302	12.7538	11.5139	10.4664	9.9996	9.5694	9.1707	8.8005
34	28.7027	24.4986	21.1318	18.4112	16.1929	14.3681	12.8540	11.5869	10.5178	10.0453	9.6086	9.2043	8.8293
35	29.4086	24.9986	21.4872	18.6646	16.3742	14.4983	12.9477	11.6546	10.5668	10.0870	9.6442	9.2347	8.8552
36	30.1075	25.4888	21.8323	18.9083	16.5469	14.6210	13.0352	11.7172	10.6118	10.1251	9.6765	9.2621	8.8786
37	30.7995	25.9695	22.1672	19.1426	16.7113	14.7368	13.1170	11.7752	10.6530	10.1599	9.7059	9.2870	8.8996
38	31.4847	26.4406	22.4925	19.3679	16.8679	14.8460	13.1935	11.8289	10.6908	10.1917	9.7327	9.3095	8.9186
39	32.1630	26.9026	22.8082	19.5845	17.0170	14.9491	13.2649	11.8786	10.7255	10.2207	9.7570	9.3299	8.9357
40	32.8347	27.3555	23.1148	19.7928	17.1591	15.0463	13.3317	11.9246	10.7574	10.2473	9.7791	9.3483	8.9511
41	33.4997	27.7995	23.4124	19.9931	17.2944	15.1380	13.3941	11.9672	10.7866	10.2715	9.7991	9.3650	8.9649
42	34.1581	28.2348	23.7014	20.1856	17.4232	15.2245	13.4525	12.0067	10.8134	10.2936	9.8174	9.3801	8.9774
43	34.8100	28.6616	23.9819	20.3708	17.5459	15.3062	13.5070	12.0432	10.8380	10.3138	9.8340	9.3937	8.9887
44	35.4555	29.0800	24.2543	20.5488	17.6628	15.3832	13.5579	12.0771	10.8605	10.3322	9.8491	9.4061	8.9988
45	36.0945	29.4902	24.5187	20.7200	17.7741	15.4558	13.6055	12.1084	10.8812	10.3490	9.8628	9.4163	9.0079
46	36.7272	29.8923	24.7755	20.8847	17.8801	15.5244	13.6500	12.1374	10.9002	10.3644	9.8753	9.4274	9.0161
47	37.3537	30.2866	25.0247	21.0429	17.9810	15.5890	13.6916	12.1643	10.9176	10.3785	9.8866	9.4366	9.0236
48	37.9740	30.6731	25.2667	21.1951	18.0772	15.6500	13.7305	12.1891	10.9336	10.3913	9.8969	9.4449	9.0302
49	38.5881	31.0521	25.5017	21.3415	18.1687	15.7076	13.7668	12.2122	10.9482	10.4030	9.9063	9.4524	9.0362
50	39.1961	31.4236	25.7298	21.4822	18.2559	15.7619	13.8008	12.2335	10.9617	10.4137	9.9148	9.4591	9.0417

11.50%	12.00%	12.50%	13.00%	13.50%	14.00%	14.50%	15.00%	15.50%	16.00%	17.00%	18.00%	19.00%	20.00%
0.8969	0.8929	0.8889	0.8850	0.8811	0.8772	0.8734	0.8696	0.8658	0.8621	0.8547	0.8475	0.8403	0.8333
1.7012	1.6901	1.6790	1.6681	1.6573	1.6467	1.6361	1.6257	1.6154	1.6052	1.5852	1.5656	1.5465	1.5278
2.4226	2.4018	2.3813	2.3612	2.3413	2.3216	2.3023	2.2832	2.2644	2.2459	2.2096	2.1743	2.1399	2.1065
3.0696	3.0374	3.0056	2.9745	2.9438	2.9137	2.8841	2.8850	2.8263	2.7982	2.7432	2.6901	2.6386	2.5887
3.6499	3.6048	3.5606	3.5172	3.4747	3.4331	3.3922	3.3522	3.3129	3.2743	3.1994	3.1272	3.0576	2.9906
4.1703	4.1114	4.0538	3.9976	3.9425	3.8887	3.8360	3.7845	3.7341	3.6847	3.5892	3.4976	3.4098	3.3255
4.6370	4.5638	4.4923	4.4226	4.3546	4.2883	4.2236	4.1604	4.0988	4.0386	3.9224	3.8115	3.7057	3.6046
5.0556	4.9676	4.8821	4.7988	4.7177	4.6389	4.5621	4.4873	4.4145	4.3436	4.2072	4.0776	3.9544	3.8372
5.4311	5.3283	5.2285	5.1317	5.0377	4.9464	4.8577	4.7716	4.6879	4.6065	4.4506	4.3030	4.1633	4.0310
5.7678	5.6502	5.5364	5.4262	5.3195	5.2161	5.1159	5.0188	4.9246	4.8332	4.6586	4.4941	4.3389	4.1925
6.0698	5.9377	5.8102	5.6869	5.5679	5.4527	5.3414	5.2337	5.1295	5.0286	4.8364	4.6560	4.4865	4.3271
6.3406	6.1944	6.0535	5.9177	5.7867	5.6603	5.5383	5.4206	5.3069	5.1971	4.9884	4.7932	4.6105	4.4392
6.5835	6.4236	6.2698	6.1218	5.9794	5.8424	5.7103	5.5832	5.4606	5.3423	5.1183	4.9095	4.7147	4.5327
6.8013	6.6282	6.4620	6.3025	6.1493	6.0021	5.8606	5.7245	5.5936	5.4675	5.2293	5.0081	4.8023	4.6106
6.9967	6.8109	6.6329	6.4624	6.2989	6.1422	5.9918	5.8474	5.7087	5.5755	5.3242	5.0916	4.8759	4.6755
7.1719	6.9740	6.7848	6.6039	6.4308	6.2651	6.1063	5.9542	5.8084	5.6685	5.4053	5.1624	4.9377	4.7296
7.3291	7.1196	6.9198	6.7291	6.5469	6.3729	6.2064	6.0472	5.8947	5.7487	5.4746	5.2223	4.9897	4.7746
7.4700	7.2497	7.0398	6.8399	6.6493	6.4674	6.2938	6.1280	5.9695	5.8179	5.5339	5.2732	5.0333	4.8122
7.5964	7.3658	7.1465	6.9380	6.7395	6.5504	6.3701	6.1982	6.0342	5.8775	5.5845	5.3162	5.0700	4.8435
7.7098	7.4694	7.2414	7.0248	6.8189	6.6231	6.4368	6.2593	6.0902	5.9288	5.6278	5.3528	5.1009	4.8696
7.8115	7.5620	7.3257	7.1016	6.8889	6.6870	6.4950	6.3125	6.1387	5.9731	5.6648	5.3837	5.1268	4.8913
7.9027	7.6447	7.4006	7.1695	6.9506	6.7429	6.5459	6.3587	6.1807	6.0113	5.6964	5.4099	5.1486	4.9094
7.9845	7.7184	7.4672	7.2297	7.0049	6.7921	6.5903	6.3988	6.2170	6.0443	5.7234	5.4321	5.1669	4.9245
8.0578	7.7843	7.5264	7.2829	7.0528	6.8351	6.6291	6.4338	6.2485	6.0726	5.7465	5.4510	5.1822	4.9371
8.1236	7.8431	7.5790	7.3300	7.0950	6.8729	6.6629	6.4642	6.2758	6.0971	5.7662	5.4669	5.1952	4.9476
8.1826	7.8957	7.6258	7.3717	7.1321	6.9061	6.6925	6.4906	6.2994	6.1182	5.7831	5.4804	5.2060	4.9563
8.2355	7.9426	7.6674	7.4086	7.1649	6.9352	6.7184	6.5135	6.3198	6.1364	5.7975	5.4919	5.2151	4.9636
8.2830	7.9844	7.7043	7.4412	7.1937	6.9607	6.7409	6.5335	6.3375	6.1520	5.8099	5.5016	5.2228	4.9697
8.3255	8.0218	7.7372	7.4701	7.2191	6.9830	6.7606	6.5509	6.3528	6.1656	5.8204	5.5098	5.2292	4.9747
8.3637	8.0552	7.7664	7.4957	7.2415	7.0027	6.7779	6.5660	6.3661	6.1772	5.8294	5.5168	5.2347	4.9789
8.3980	8.0850	7.7923	7.5183	7.2613	7.0199	6.7929	6.5791	6.3776	6.1872	5.8371	5.5227	5.2392	4.9825
8.4287	8.1116	7.8154	7.5383	7.2786	7.0350	6.8060	6.5905	6.3875	6.1959	5.8437	5.5277	5.2430	4.9854
8.4562	8.1354	7.8359	7.5560	7.2940	7.0482	6.8175	6.6005	6.3961	6.2034	5.8493	5.5320	5.2463	4.9878
8.4809	8.1566	7.8542	7.5717	7.3075	7.0599	6.8275	6.6091	6.4035	6.2098	5.8541	5.5356	5.2490	4.9898
8.5030	8.1755	7.8704	7.5856	7.3193	7.0701	6.8362	6.6166	6.4100	6.2153	5.8582	5.5386	5.2512	4.9930
8.5229	8.1924	7.8848	7.5979	7.3298	7.0790	6.8439	6.6231	6.4156	6.2201	5.8617	5.5412	5.2531	4.9930
8.5407	8.2075	7.8976	7.6087	7.3390	7.0868	6.8505	6.6288	6.4204	6.2242	5.8647	5.5434	5.2547	4.9941
8.5567	8.2210	7.9090	7.6183	7.3472	7.0937	6.8564	6.6338	6.4246	6.2278	5.8673	5.5453	5.2561	4.9951
8.5710	8.2330	7.9191	7.6268	7.3543	7.0998	6.8615	6.6381	6.4282	6.2309	5.8695	5.5468	5.2572	4.9959
8.5839	8.2438	7.9281	7.6344	7.3607	7.1050	6.8659	6.6418	6.4314	6.2335	5.8713	5.5482	5.2582	4.9966
8.5954	8.2534	7.9361	7.6410	7.3662	7.1097	6.8698	6.6450	6.4341	6.2358	5.8729	5.5493	5.2590	4.9972
8.6058	8.2619	7.9432	7.6469	7.3711	7.1138	6.8732	6.6479	6.4364	6.2377	5.8743	5.5502	5.2596	4.9976
8.6150	8.2696	7.9495	7.6522	7.3754	7.1173	6.8761	6.6503	6.4385	6.2394	5.8755	5.5511	5.2602	4.9980
8.6233	8.2764	7.9551	7.6568	7.3792	7.1205	6.8787	6.6524	6.4402	6.2409	5.8765	5.5517	5.2607	4.9984
8.6308	8.2825	7.9601	7.6609	7.3826	7.1232	6.8810	6.6543	6.4418	6.2421	5.8773	5.5523	5.2611	4.9986
8.6375	8.2880	7.9645	7.6645	7.3855	7.1256	6.8830	6.6559	6.4431	6.2432	5.8781	5.5528	5.2614	4.9989
8.6435	8.2928	7.9685	7.6677	7.3881	7.1277	6.8847	6.6573	6.4442	6.2442	5.8787	5.5532	5.2617	4.9991
8.6489	8.2972	7.9720	7.6705	7.3904	7.1296	6.8862	6.6585	6.4452	6.2450	5.8792	5.5536	5.2619	4.9992
8.6537	8.3010	7.9751	7.6730	7.3925	7.1312	6.8875	6.6596	6.4461	6.2457	5.8797	5.5539	5.2621	4.9993
8.6580	8.3045	7.9779	7.6752	7.3942	7.1327	6.8886	6.6605	6.4468	6.2463	5.8801	5.5541	5.2623	4.9995

Using the Ethics Discussion Questions

B

There are few more difficult issues facing business graduates or people in the business world today than those pertaining to ethical dilemmas. Some of these situations are specifically covered by professional codes of conduct; others reflect the differences among what is ethical, what is legal, and what is professionally accepted. Most traditional coverage of ethics in accounting courses focuses on the teachings of the various professional codes of ethics. While teaching about codes of ethics is important, it can be greatly enhanced by presenting cases involving questionable breaches of proper conduct in the myriad of everyday business transactions. By covering such situations, college faculty have an opportunity to make a significant contribution to their students' success and well-being in the area of day-to-day ethics.

The text provides a series of end of chapter situations that can be used to give the student practice in recognizing ethical issues and an opportunity to develop appropriate responses. Some of the questions address what appear to be fairly innocuous issues (price setting for a price bid); others address mainstream environmental and ethical matters (the handling of environmentally destructive waste materials). Both types of situations, however, have important underlying ethical conflicts and require a logical thought process to arrive at the most ethical solution rather than simply *rationalizing* any solution chosen. Students need to recognize that it may be easy to make an unethical decision when the stakes are not very high; however, when the stakes increase, the pattern of unethical decision making may already be in place. If the minor ethical decisions can be analyzed and resolved ethically, the major decisions are more likely to be addressed in a thoughtful and ethical manner.

It is important that students be prepared, while they are in school, for ethical conflicts with which they may be confronted in the workplace. An essential part of such preparation is obtaining the *ability* to recognize ethical problems before they become realities and learning how, when, and to whom to respond to such problems. The purpose of cost accounting is not to provide a philosophy lecture, but students should be made aware of at least some of the major existing ethical theories and problem-solving models before being asked to analyze and resolve ethical conflict situations. Thus, the following information may be useful to both the faculty member teaching this course as well as the students taking it.

Ethics can be viewed and taught at two levels: (1) as a set of general theories and (2) as a set of specific principles.

Ethical Theories

Viewing ethics as a set of general theories allows people to learn the background used in developing specific principles and, therefore, be able to develop their own principles or guidelines when confronted with unique situations in which the existing principles seem to have no relevance. This type of teaching is usually performed in philosophy courses, but some of the basic theories can be briefly defined and illustrated at this point.

UTILITARIANISM   This theory holds that the primary method of determining what is right or ethical is the usefulness of an action or a policy in producing other actions or experiences that people value. It emphasizes the consequences that an action has on all the people directly and/or indirectly affected by that action. Utilitarianism reflects a societal viewpoint of the "greatest good for the greatest number." While this theory may provide extremely valid ethical decisions, it is highly unworkable in its theoretical state in practice. This model would require determining *all* possible solutions to a dilemma, determining *all* possible stakeholders for each solution, determining *all* the costs and benefits of *each* solution to *each* stakeholder, summing such costs and benefits, and choosing the decision that maximized the benefits of the most stakeholders. Thus, when utilitarianism is applied as a model of ethical decision making, certain shortcuts are normally taken, such as considering only certain types of stakeholders or solutions within a certain type of framework. When such shortcuts are taken, however, the decision maker should occasionally review them to make sure that such simplifications have not automatically ignored important constituencies, reference points, interests, or values. (Utilitarianism is a type of cost-benefit analysis.)

CATEGORICAL IMPERATIVES   This set of rules requires that a person act on the premise that whatever he or she does would become a universal law. Categorical imperatives form the basis of duties that are considered inherently right. Because actions are determined to be inherently right or wrong (regardless of the positive or negative consequences), the decision maker is responsible for behavior, not for consequences. Thus, the model emphasizes treating all persons equally and as the person acting would like to be treated. Additionally, the model emphasizes respect for individuals and their freedoms. (Categorical imperatives reflect a basic "Do unto others as you would have them do unto you" concept.)

The theory of rights asserts that people have some fundamental rights that must be respected in all types of decisions and is a variation of the duty-based analysis. Rights advocates suggest that there are liberty rights and welfare rights for all persons. Liberty rights basically have been embedded in the U.S. Constitution and include:

- the right of free consent (people should be treated only as they knowingly and willingly consent to be treated)
- the right to privacy (outside the work environment)
- the right to freedom of conscience
- the right to free speech
- the right to due process

Welfare rights reflect the rights of all people to some minimum standard of living; these rights typically have fallen into the realm of governmental or corporate social responsibilities.

The theory of justice requires that people make decisions based on equity, fairness, and impartiality. While the theory of justice requires that people who are similar must be treated in a similar manner, it allows people who are different in a *relevant* way to be treated differently. The relevant ways affecting when people can be treated differently cannot relate to arbitrary characteristics; the differences must be related to the task that is to be performed or differences in people's needs. In using the theory of justice, a decision maker must be careful to make certain that the characteristic(s) on which he or she is making the distinction is(are) relevant and not discriminatory.

(While these are not the only ethical theories that exist, they do provide a foundation from which to begin ethical discussions.)

Ethics as a Set of Principles

Teaching ethics as a set of specific principles provides individuals with a means to answer concrete, problem-oriented situations. This method is typically how ethics are treated in an auditing course or in discussions of codes of ethics.

It is important to point out to students the difference between ethics and legality. Ethics can be viewed as a nonjurisdictional system of moral rights. It represents the moral rights that people have regardless of where or when they live, whether these rights are recognized or not. Legality merely refers to what is permissible under the law in a particular society. Sometimes society may condone an act as legal because of the surrounding circumstances even though the act itself may be viewed as unethical. (For example, it is unethical to kill another human being, but society may make it legal to do so under certain situations.) Legitimizing a "wrong" act because of circumstances does not make that act any more moral.

In making ethical decisions, a person must first have the sensitivity to recognize that an ethical dilemma exists and exert the self-control to attempt to resolve it. This conflict may be at the personal, organizational, or societal level. All feasible alternatives should be considered along with their influencing factors such as values, laws, resource constraints, pressures, and cultural mores. *Once all ramifications are considered and the decision maker selects an alternative using whatever theories or processes he or she chooses, the decision maker must also be willing to accept the outcomes from and responsibility for that choice.* An individual acts as an autonomous agent when he or she acts on the basis of principles that have been consciously evaluated and accepted by the individual as the correct principles to direct behavior; individuals cannot be considered autonomous when they act based on principles that have been imposed from the outside (through peer pressure or by some authority) or that have been internalized as a matter of mere habit.

The making of ethical choices is not a science; it is subjective and cannot be resolved from a societal point of view. Different individuals will always have different viewpoints as to what is ethical and what is the proper decision for an ethical dilemma. The challenge is to create a means for students to foresee potential problems, recognize they have an obligation to derive internal and personal criteria by which to resolve such dilemmas, and accept personal, organizational, societal, and legal determinations as to the ethical or unethical nature of solutions chosen when (or if) those solutions are made public.

Glossary

ABC   see activity-based costing

ABC analysis   a process of separating inventory items into three groups (A, B, and C) based on annual cost-to-volume usage

ABM   see activity-based management

abnormal loss   a decline in units in excess of normal expectations during a production process

absorption costing   a cost accumulation and reporting method that treats the costs of all manufacturing components (direct materials, direct labor, variable overhead, and fixed overhead) as inventoriable or product costs; is the traditional approach to product costing; must be used for external financial statements and tax returns

accounting rate of return (ARR)   the rate of earnings obtained on the average capital investment over the life of a capital project; computed as average annual profits divided by average investment; not based on cash flow

accretion   an increase in units or volume caused by the addition of materials or by factors inherent in the production process

activity   a repetitive action performed in fulfillment of business functions

activity analysis   the process of detailing the various repetitive actions that are performed in making a product or providing a service, classifying them as value-added and non-value-added, and devising ways of minimizing or eliminating non-value-added activities

activity-based costing (ABC)   a process using multiple cost drivers to predict and allocate costs to products and services; an accounting system collecting financial and operational data on the basis of the underlying nature and extent of business activities; an accounting information and costing system that identifies the various activities performed in an organization, collects costs on the basis of the underlying nature and extent of those activities, and assigns costs to products and services based on consumption of those activities by the products and services

activity-based management (ABM)   a discipline that focuses on the activities incurred during the production/performance process as the way to improve the value received by a customer and the resulting profit achieved by providing this value

activity center   a segment of the production or service process for which management wants to separately report the costs of the activities performed

activity driver   a measure of the demands on activities and, thus, the resources consumed by products and services; often indicates an activity's output

actual cost system   a valuation method that uses actual direct materials, direct labor, and overhead charges in determining the cost of Work in Process Inventory

ad hoc discount   a price concession made under competitive pressure (real or imagined) that does not relate to quantity purchased

administrative department   an organizational unit that performs management activities benefiting the entire organization; includes top management personnel and organization headquarters

algebraic method   a process of service department cost allocation that considers all interrelationships of the departments and reflects these relationships in simultaneous equations

algorithm   a logical step-by-step problem-solving technique (generally requiring the use of a computer) that continuously searches for an improved solution from the one previously computed until the best answer is determined

allocate   assign based on the use of a cost driver, a cost predictor, or an arbitrary method

allocation   the systematic assignment of an amount to a recipient set of categories

annuity   a series of equal cash flows (either positive or negative) per period

annuity due   a series of equal cash flows being received or paid at the beginning of a period

applied overhead   the amount of overhead that has been assigned to Work in Process Inventory as a result of productive activity; credits for this amount are to an overhead account

appraisal cost   a quality control cost incurred for monitoring or inspection; compensates for mistakes not eliminated through prevention activities

appropriation   a budgeted maximum allowable expenditure

approximated net realizable value at split-off allocation   a method of allocating joint cost to joint products using a simulated net realizable value at the split-off point; approximated value is computed as final sales price minus incremental separate costs

asset turnover   a ratio measuring asset productivity and showing the number of sales dollars generated by each dollar of assets

attribute-based costing (ABC II)   an extension of activity-based costing using cost-benefit analysis (based on increased customer utility) to choose the product attribute enhancements that the company wants to integrate into a product

authority   the right (usually by virtue of position or rank) to use resources to accomplish a task or achieve an objective

autonomation   the use of equipment that has been programmed to sense certain conditions

backflush costing   a streamlined cost accounting method that speeds up, simplifies, and minimizes accounting effort in an environment that minimizes inventory balances, requires few allocations, uses standard costs, and has minimal variances from standard

batch-level cost   a cost that is caused by a group of things being made, handled, or processed at a single time

benchmarking   the process of investigating how others do something better so that the investigating company can imitate, and possibly improve upon, their techniques

benefits-provided ranking   a listing of service departments in an order that begins with the one providing the most service to all other corporate areas; the ranking ends with the service department providing service primarily to revenue-producing areas

bill of materials   a document that contains information about the product materials components and their specifications (including quality and quantities needed)

bottleneck   any object or facility whose processing speed is sufficiently slow to cause the other processing mechanisms in its network to experience idle time

break-even chart   a graph that depicts the relationships among revenues, variable costs, fixed costs, and profits (or losses)

break-even point   the level of activity, in units or dollars, at which total revenues equal total costs

budget   a financial plan for the future based on a single level of activity; the quantitative expression of a company's commitment to planned activities and resource acquisition and use

budgeted cost   a planned expenditure

budgeting   the process of formalizing plans and committing them to written, financial terms

budget manual   a detailed set of documents that provides information and guidelines about the budgetary process

budget slack   an intentional underestimation of revenues and/or overestimation of expenses in a budgeting process for the purpose of including deviations that are likely to occur so that results will occur within budget limits

budget variance   the difference between total actual overhead and budgeted overhead based on standard hours allowed for the production achieved during the period; computed as part of two-variance overhead analysis; also referred to as the controllable variance

build mission   a mission of increasing market share, even at the expense of short-term profits and cash flow; typically pursued by a business unit that has a small market share in a high-growth industry; appropriate for products that are in the early stages of the product life cycle

business intelligence (BI) system   a formal process for gathering and analyzing information and producing intelligence to meet decision making needs; requires information about internal processes as well as knowledge, technologies, and competitors

business process reengineering (BPR)   the process of combining information technology to create new and more effective business processes with a continuous improvement movement to lower costs, eliminate unnecessary work, upgrade customer service, and increase speed to market

business-value-added activity   an activity that is necessary for the operation of the business but for which a customer would not want to pay

by-product   an incidental output of a joint process; is salable, but the sales value of by-products is not substantial

enough for management to justify undertaking the joint process; viewed as having a higher sales value than scrap

cafeteria plan   a "menu" of fringe benefit options that include cash or nontaxable benefits

capacity   a measure of production volume or some other activity base

capital asset   an asset used to generate revenues or cost savings by providing production, distribution, or service capabilities for more than one year

capital budget   management's plan for investments in long-term property, plant, and equipment

capital budgeting   a process of evaluating an economic entity's proposed long-range projects or courses of future activity for the purpose of allocating limited resources to desirable projects

capital rationing   a condition that exists when there is an upper-dollar constraint on the amount of capital available to commit to capital asset acquisition

carrying cost   the variable costs of carrying one unit of inventory in stock for one year; includes the opportunity cost of the capital invested in inventory

CASB   see Cost Accounting Standards Board

cash flow   the receipt or disbursement of cash; when related to capital budgeting, cash flows arise from the purchase, operation, and disposition of a capital asset

centralization   a management style that exists when top management makes most decisions and controls most activities of the organizational units from the company's central headquarters

Certified Management Accountant (CMA)   a professional designation in the area of management accounting that recognizes the successful completion of an examination, acceptable work experience, and continuing education requirements

charge-back system   a system using transfer prices; see transfer price

coefficient of correlation   a measure of dispersion that indicates the degree of relative association existing between two variables

coefficient of determination   a measure of dispersion that indicates the "goodness of fit" of the actual observations to the least squares regression line; indicates what proportion of the total variation in y is explained by the regression model

coefficient of variation   a measure of risk used when the standard deviations for multiple projects are approximately the same but the expected values are significantly different

committed cost   a cost related either to the long-term investment in plant and equipment of a business or to the organizational personnel whom top management deem permanent; a cost that cannot be changed without long-run detriment to the organization

common body of knowledge (CBK)   the minimum set of knowledge needed by a person to function effectively in a particular field

compensation strategy   a foundation for the compensation plan that addresses the role compensation should play in the organization

compound interest   a method of determining interest in which interest that was earned in prior periods is added to the original investment so that, in each successive period, interest is earned on both principal and interest

compounding period the time between each interest computation

computer-aided design (CAD) a system using computer graphics for product designs

computer-aided manufacturing (CAM) the use of computers to control production processes through numerically controlled (NC) machines, robots, and automated assembly systems

computer integrated manufacturing (CIM) the integration of two or more flexible manufacturing systems through the use of a host computer and an information networking system

concurrent engineering see simultaneous engineering

confrontation strategy an organizational strategy in which company management decides to confront, rather than avoid, competition; an organizational strategy in which company management still attempts to differentiate company products through new features or to develop a price leadership position by dropping prices even though management recognizes that competitors will rapidly bring out similar products and match price changes; an organizational strategy in which company management identifies and exploits current opportunities for competitive advantage in recognition of the fact that those opportunities will soon be eliminated

constraint a restriction inhibiting the achievement of an objective

contingent pay compensation pay that is dependent on the achievement of some performance objective

continuous budgeting a process in which there is an ongoing twelve-month budget at all points in time during a budget period because a new budget month (twelve months into the future) is added as each current month expires

continuous improvement an ongoing process of enhancing employee task performance, level of product quality, and level of company service through eliminating non-value-added activities to reduce lead time, making products (performing services) with zero defects, reducing product costs on an ongoing basis, and simplifying products and processes

continuous loss any reduction in units that occurs uniformly throughout a production process

contract manufacturer an external party that has been granted an outsourcing contract to produce a part or component for an entity

contract vendor an external party that has been granted an outsourcing contract to provide a service activity for an entity

contribution margin the difference between selling price and variable cost per unit, or in total for the level of activity; indicates the amount of each revenue dollar remaining after variable costs have been covered and going toward the coverage of fixed costs and the generation of profits

contribution margin ratio the proportion of each revenue dollar remaining after variable costs have been covered; computed as contribution margin divided by sales

control chart a graphical presentation of the results of a specified activity; indicates the upper and lower control limits and those results that are out of control

controllable cost a cost over which a manager has the ability to authorize incurrence or directly influence magnitude

controllable variance the budget variance of the two-variance approach to analyzing overhead variances

controller the chief accountant (in a corporation) who is responsible for maintaining and reporting on both the cost and financial sets of accounts but does not handle or negotiate changes in actual resources

controlling the process of exerting managerial influence on operations so that they conform to previously prepared plans

conversion the process of transformation or change

conversion cost the total of direct labor and overhead cost; the cost necessary to transform direct materials into a finished good or service

core competency a higher proficiency relative to competitors in a critical function or activity; a root of competitiveness and competitive advantage; anything that is not a core competency is a viable candidate for outsourcing

correlation analysis an analytical technique that uses statistical measures of dispersion to reveal the strength of the relationship between variables

cost the cash or cash equivalent value necessary to attain an objective such as acquiring goods and services used, complying with a contract, performing a function, or producing and distributing a product

cost accounting a technique or method for determining the cost of a project, process, or thing through direct measurement, arbitrary assignment, or systematic and rational allocation

Cost Accounting Standards Board (CASB) a body established by Congress in 1970 to promulgate cost accounting standards for defense contractors and federal agencies; disbanded in 1980 and reestablished in 1988; previously issued pronouncements still carry the weight of law for those organizations within its jurisdiction

cost accumulation the approach to product costing that determines which manufacturing costs are recorded as part of product cost

cost allocation the assignment, using some reasonable basis, of any indirect cost to one or more cost objects

cost avoidance the practice of finding acceptable alternatives to high-cost items and/or not spending money for unnecessary goods or services

cost-benefit analysis the analytical process of comparing the relative costs and benefits that result from a specific course of action (such as providing information or investing in a project)

cost center a responsibility center in which the manager has the authority to incur costs and is evaluated on the basis of how well costs are controlled

cost consciousness a company-wide attitude about the topics of cost understanding, cost containment, cost avoidance, and cost reduction

cost containment the practice of minimizing, to the extent possible, period-by-period increases in per-unit variable and total fixed costs

cost control system a logical structure of formal and/or informal activities designed to analyze and evaluate how well expenditures are managed during a period

cost driver a factor that has a direct cause-effect relationship to a cost; an activity creating a cost

cost driver analysis the process of investigating, quantifying, and explaining the relationships of cost drivers and their related costs

cost leadership the position in a competitive environment of being the low cost producer of a product or provider of a service; provides one method of avoiding competition

cost management system (CMS) a set of formal methods developed for planning and controlling an organization's cost-generating activities relative to its goals and objectives

cost object anything to which costs attach or are related

cost of goods manufactured the total cost of the goods completed and transferred to Finished Goods Inventory during the period

cost of production report a process costing document that details all operating and cost information, shows the computation of cost per equivalent unit, and indicates cost assignment to goods produced during the period

cost-plus contract a contract in which the customer agrees to reimburse the producer for the cost of the job plus a specified profit margin over cost

cost pool a collection of monetary amounts incurred either for the same purpose, at the same organizational level, or as a result of the occurrence of the same cost driver

cost presentation the approach to product costing that determines how costs are shown on external financial statements or internal management reports

cost reduction the practice of lowering current costs, especially those that may be in excess of what is necessary

cost structure the relative composition of an organization's fixed and variable costs

cost tables databases providing information about the impact on product costs of using different input resources, manufacturing processes, and design specifications

cost-volume-profit (CVP) analysis a procedure that examines changes in costs and volume levels and the resulting effects on net income (profits)

critical success factors those items (such as quality, customer service, efficiency, cost control, and responsiveness to change) so important that, without them, the organization would cease to exist

CVP see cost-volume-profit analysis

cycle time the time between the placement of an order to the time the goods arrive for usage or are produced by the company; is equal to value-added time plus non-value-added time

data bits of knowledge or facts that have not been summarized or categorized in a manner useful to a decision maker

decentralization a management style that exists when top management grants subordinate managers a significant degree of autonomy and independence in operating and making decisions for their organizational units

decision making the process of choosing among the alternative solutions available to a course of action or a problem situation

decision variable an unknown item for which a linear programming problem is being solved

defective unit a unit that has been rejected at a control inspection point for failure to meet appropriate standards of quality or designated product specifications; can be economically reworked and sold through normal distribution channels

deferred compensation pay related to current performance that will be received at a later time, typically after retirement

degree of operating leverage a factor that indicates how a percentage change in sales, from the existing or current level, will affect company profits; calculated as contribution margin divided by net income; is equal to $(1 \div \text{margin of safety percentage})$

dependent variable an unknown variable that is to be predicted using one or more independent variables

differential cost a cost that differs in amount among the alternatives being considered

differentiation a technique for avoiding competition by distinguishing a product or service from that of competitors through adding sufficient value (including quality and/or features) that customers are willing to pay a higher price than that charged by competitors

direct cost a cost that is distinctly traceable to a particular cost object

direct costing see variable costing

direct labor the time spent by individuals who work specifically on manufacturing a product or performing a service; the cost of such time

direct material a readily identifiable part of a product; the cost of such a part

direct method a process of service department cost allocation that assigns service department costs directly to revenue-producing areas with only one set of intermediate cost pools or allocations

discounting the process of reducing future cash flows to present value amounts

discount rate the rate of return used to discount future cash flows to their present value amounts; should equal or exceed an organization's weighted average cost of capital

discrete loss a reduction in units that occurs at a specific point in a production process

discretionary cost a cost that is periodically reviewed by a decision maker in a process of determining whether it continues to be in accord with ongoing policies; a cost that arises from a management decision to fund an activity at a specified cost amount for a specified period of time, generally one year; a cost that can be reduced to zero in the short run if necessity so dictates

dispersion the degree of variability or difference; is measured as the vertical distance of an actual point from the estimated regression line in least squares regression analysis

distribution cost a cost incurred to warehouse, transport, or deliver a product or service

dividend growth method a method of computing the cost of common stock equity that indicates the rate of return that common shareholders expect to earn in the form of dividends on a company's common stock

dollar days (of inventory) a measurement of the value of inventory for the time that inventory stays in an area

dual pricing arrangement a transfer pricing system that allows a selling division to record the transfer of goods or services at one price (e.g., a market or negotiated market price) and a buying division to record the transfer at another price (e.g., a cost-based amount)

dumping selling products abroad at lower prices than those charged in the home country or in other national markets

Du Pont model a model that indicates the return on investment as it is affected by profit margin and asset turnover

economic order quantity (EOQ) an estimate of the number of units per order that will be the least costly and provide the optimal balance between the costs of ordering and the costs of carrying inventory

economic production run (EPR) an estimate of the number of units to produce at one time that minimizes the total costs of setting up production runs and carrying inventory

economically reworked when the incremental revenue from the sale of reworked defective units is greater than the incremental cost of the rework

economic value added (EVA) a measure of the extent to which income exceeds the dollar cost of capital; calculated as income minus (invested capital times the cost of capital percentage)

effectiveness a measure of how well an organization's goals and objectives are achieved; compares actual output results to desired results; determination of the successful accomplishment of an objective

efficiency a measure of the degree to which tasks were performed to produce the best yield at the lowest cost from the resources available; the degree to which a satisfactory relationship occurs when comparing outputs to inputs

electronic data interchange (EDI) the computer-to-computer transfer of information in virtual real time using standardized formats developed by the American National Standards Institute

Employee Stock Ownership Plan (ESOP) a profit-sharing compensation program in which investments are made in the securities of the employer

employee time sheet a source document that indicates, for each employee, what jobs were worked on during the day and for what amount of time

empowerment the process of giving workers the training and authority they need to manage their own jobs

engineered cost a cost that has been found to bear an observable and known relationship to a quantifiable activity base

engineering change order (ECO) a business mandate that changes the way in which a product is manufactured or a service is performed by modifying the design, parts, process, or even quality of the product or service

environmental constraint any limitation on strategy options caused by external cultural, fiscal, legal/regulatory, or political situations; limiting factors that are not under the direct control of an organization's management; tend to be fairly long-run in nature

equivalent units of production an approximation of the number of whole units of output that could have been produced during a period from the actual effort expended during that period; used in process costing systems to assign costs to production

European Union (EU) an economic alliance originally created in 1957 as the European Economic Community by France, Germany, Italy, Belgium, the Netherlands, and Luxembourg and later joined by the United Kingdom, Ireland, Denmark, Spain, Portugal, and Greece; prior to the Maastricht Treaty of 1993 was called the European Community; has eliminated virtually all barriers to the flow of capital, labor, goods, and services among member nations

expatriate a parent company or third-country national assigned to a foreign subsidiary or a foreign national assigned to the parent company

expected annual capacity a short-run concept that represents the anticipated level of capacity to be used by a firm in the upcoming year

expected standard a standard set at a level that reflects what is actually expected to occur in the future period; anticipates future waste and inefficiencies and allows for them; is of limited value for control and performance evaluation purposes

expired cost an expense or a loss

failure cost a quality control cost associated with goods or services that have been found not to conform or perform to the required standards as well as all related costs (such as that of the complaint department); may be internal or external

feasible region the graphical space contained within and on all of the constraint lines in the graphical solution to a linear programming problem

feasible solution a solution to a linear programming problem that does not violate any problem constraints

FIFO method (of process costing) the method of cost assignment that computes an average cost per equivalent unit of production for the current period; keeps beginning inventory units and costs separate from current period production and costs

financial accounting a discipline in which historical, monetary transactions are analyzed and recorded for use in the preparation of the financial statements (balance sheet, income statement, statement of owners/stockholders' equity, and statement of cash flows); focuses primarily on the needs of external users (stockholders, creditors, and regulatory agencies)

financial budget a budget that aggregates monetary details from the operating budgets; includes the cash and capital budgets of a company as well as the pro forma financial statements

financial incentive a monetary reward provided for performance above targeted objectives

financing decision a judgment made regarding the method of raising funds that will be used to make acquisitions; is based on an entity's ability to issue and service debt and equity securities

Fisher rate the rate of return that equates the present values of the cash flows of all the multiple projects being considered; the rate of indifference

fixed cost a cost that remains constant in total within a specified range of activity

fixed overhead spending variance the difference between the total actual fixed overhead and budgeted fixed overhead; computed as part of the four-variance overhead analysis

fixed overhead volume variance see volume variance

flexible budget a series of individual budgets that present costs according to their behavior at different levels of activity

flexible manufacturing system (FMS) a production system in which a single factory manufactures numerous variations of products through the use of computer-controlled robots

focused factory arrangement an arrangement in which a vendor (which may be an external party or an internal corporate division) agrees to provide a limited number of products according to specifications or to perform a limited number of unique services to a company that is typically operating on a just-in-time system

Foreign Corrupt Practices Act (FCPA) a law passed by Congress in 1977 that makes it illegal for a company to engage in various "questionable" foreign payments and makes it mandatory for a company to maintain accurate accounting records and a reasonable system of internal control

full costing see absorption costing

functional classification a separation of costs into groups based on the similar reason for their incurrence; includes cost of goods sold and detailed selling and administrative expenses

future value the amount to which one or more sums of money invested at a specified interest rate will grow over a specified number of time periods

General Agreement on Tariffs and Trade (GATT) a treaty among many nations setting standards for tariffs and trade for signees

global economy an economy characterized by the international trade of goods and services, the international movement of labor, and the international flows of capital and information

globalization a changeover in market focus from competition among national or local suppliers to competition among international suppliers

goal a desired abstract achievement

goal congruence a circumstance in which the personal and organizational goals of decision makers throughout a firm are consistent and mutually supportive

golden parachute a benefits package that is triggered by the termination of a manager's employment

grade (of product or service) the addition or removal of product or service characteristics to satisfy additional needs, especially price

grapevine the informal relationships and channels of communication that exist in an organization

growth rate an estimate of the increase expected in dividends (or in market value) per share of stock

harvest mission a mission that attempts to maximize short-term profits and cash flow, even at the expense of market share; typically pursued by a business unit that has a large market share in a low-growth industry; appropriate for products in the final stages of the product life cycle

high-low method a technique used to determine the fixed and variable portions of a mixed cost; uses only the highest and lowest levels of activity and related costs within the relevant range

historical cost a cost incurred in the past; the recorded purchase price of an asset; a sunk cost

hold mission a mission that attempts to protect the business unit's market share and competitive position; typically pursued by a business unit with a large market share in a high-growth industry

horizontal price fixing a practice by which competitors attempt to regulate prices through an agreement or conspiracy

hurdle rate a preestablished rate of return against which other rates of return are measured; is usually the cost of capital rate when used in evaluating capital projects

hybrid costing system a costing system combining characteristics of both job order and process costing systems

ideal capacity see theoretical capacity

ideal standard a standard that provides for no inefficiencies of any type; impossible to attain on a continuous basis

idle time the amount of time spent in storing inventory or waiting at a production operation for processing

imposed budget a budget developed by top management with little or no input from operating personnel; operating personnel are then informed of the budget objectives and constraints

incremental analysis a process of evaluating changes that focuses only on the factors that differ from one course of action or decision to another

incremental cost the cost of producing or selling an additional contemplated quantity of output

incremental revenue the revenue resulting from an additional contemplated sale

incremental separate cost the cost that is incurred for each joint product between the split-off point and the point of sale

independent project an investment project that has no specific bearing on any other investment project

independent variable a variable that, when changed, will cause consistent, observable changes in another variable; a variable used as the basis of predicting the value of a dependent variable

indirect cost a cost that cannot be traced explicitly to a particular cost object; a common cost

information bits of knowledge or fact that have been carefully chosen from a body of data and arranged in a meaningful way

input-output coefficients numbers (prefaced as multipliers to unknown variables) that indicate the rate at which each decision variable uses up (or depletes) the scarce resource

inspection time the time taken to perform quality control activities

Institute of Management Accountants (IMA) an organization composed of individuals interested in the field of management accounting; was previously the National Association of Accountants; coordinates the Certified Management Accountant program through its affiliate organization (the Institute of Certified Management Accountants)

integer programming a mathematical programming technique in which all solutions for variables must be restricted to whole numbers

intellectual capital   the intangible assets of skill, knowledge, and information that exist in an organization; encompasses human and structural capital

internal control   any measure used by management to protect assets, promote the accuracy of records, ensure adherence to company policies, or promote operational efficiency; the totality of all internal controls represents the internal control system

internal rate of return (IRR)   the expected or actual rate of return from a project based on, respectively, the assumed or actual cash flows; the discount rate at which the net present value of the cash flows equals zero

interpolation   the process of finding a term between two other terms in a series

inventoriable cost   see product cost

investment center   a responsibility center in which the manager is responsible for generating revenues and planning and controlling expenses and has the authority to acquire, dispose of, and use plant assets to earn the highest rate of return feasible on those assets within the confines and to the support of the organization's goals

investment decision   a judgment about which assets will be acquired by an entity to achieve its stated objectives

ISO 9000   a comprehensive series of international quality standards that define the various design, material procurement, production, quality-control, and delivery requirements and procedures necessary to produce quality products and services

JIT   see just-in-time

job   a single unit or group of units identifiable as being produced to distinct customer specifications

job cost record   see job order cost sheet

job order cost sheet   a source document that provides virtually all the financial information about a particular job; the set of all job order cost sheets for uncompleted jobs composes the Work in Process Inventory subsidiary ledger

job order costing system   a system of product costing used by an entity that provides limited quantities of products or services unique to a customer's needs; focus of record-keeping is on individual jobs

joint cost   the total of all costs (direct materials, direct labor, and overhead) incurred in a joint process up to the split-off point

joint process   a manufacturing process that simultaneously produces more than one product line

joint products   the primary outputs of a joint process; each joint product individually has substantial revenue-generating ability

judgmental method (of risk adjustment)   an informal method of adjusting for risk that allows the decision maker to use logic and reason to decide whether a project provides an acceptable rate of return

just-in-time (JIT)   a philosophy about when to do something; the when is "as needed" and the something is a production, purchasing, or delivery activity

just-in-time manufacturing system   a production system that attempts to acquire components and produce inventory only as needed, to minimize product defects, and to reduce lead/setup times for acquisition and production

kaizen   the Japanese word for continuous improvement

kaizen costing   a costing technique to reflect continuous efforts to reduce product costs, improve product quality, and/or improve the production process after manufacturing activities have begun

kanban   the Japanese word for card; the original name for a JIT system because of the use of cards that indicated a work center's need for additional components during a manufacturing process

key variable   a critical factor that management believes will be a direct cause of the achievement or nonachievement of the organizational goals and objectives

labor efficiency variance   the number of hours actually worked minus the standard hours allowed for the production achieved multiplied by the standard rate to establish a value for efficiency (favorable) or inefficiency (unfavorable) of the work force

labor mix variance   (actual mix × actual hours × standard rate) minus (standard mix × actual hours × standard rate); presents the financial effect associated with changing the proportionate amount of higher or lower paid workers in production

labor rate variance   the actual rate (or actual weighted average rate) paid to labor for the period minus the standard rate multiplied by all hours actually worked during the period; actual labor cost minus (actual hours × standard rate)

labor yield variance   (standard mix × actual hours × standard rate) minus (standard mix × standard hours × standard rate); shows the monetary impact of using more or fewer total hours than the standard allowed

lead time   see cycle time

learning curve   a model that helps predict how labor time will decrease as people become more experienced at performing a task and eliminate the inefficiencies associated with unfamiliarity

least squares regression analysis   a statistical technique that investigates the association between dependent and independent variables; determines the line of "best fit" for a set of observations by minimizing the sum of the squares of the vertical deviations between actual points and the regression line; can be used to determine the fixed and variable portions of a mixed cost

life cycle costing   the accumulation of costs for activities that occur over the entire life cycle of a product from inception to abandonment by the manufacturer and consumer

limited liability company   an organizational form that is a hybrid of the corporate and partnership organizational forms and used to limit the personal liability of the owners; typically used by small professional (such as accounting) firms

limited liability partnership   an organizational form that is a hybrid of the corporate and partnership organizational forms and used to limit the personal liability of the owners; typically used by large professional (such as accounting) firms

line employee   an employee who is directly responsible for achieving the organization's goals and objectives

linear programming   a method of mathematical programming used to solve a problem that involves an objective function and multiple limiting factors or constraints

long-term variable cost a cost that was traditionally viewed as a fixed cost

loss an expired cost that was unintentionally incurred; a cost that does not relate to the generation of revenues

make-or-buy decision a decision that compares the cost of internally manufacturing a component of a final product (or providing a service function) with the cost of purchasing it from outside suppliers or from another division of the company at a specified transfer price

management accounting a discipline that includes almost all manipulations of financial information for use by management in performing their organizational functions and in assuring the proper use and handling of an entity's resources; includes the discipline of cost accounting

Management Accounting Guidelines (MAGs) pronouncements of the Society of Management Accountants of Canada that advocate appropriate practices for specific management accounting situations

management control system (MCS) an information system that helps managers gather information about actual organizational occurrences, make comparisons against plans, effect changes when they are necessary, and communicate among appropriate parties; should serve to guide organizations in designing and implementing strategies so that organizational goals and objectives are achieved

management information system (MIS) a structure of interrelated elements that collects, organizes, and communicates data to managers so they may plan, control, evaluate performance, and make decisions; the emphasis of the MIS is on internal demands for information rather than external demands; some or all of the MIS may be computerized for ease of access to information, reliability of input and processing, and ability to simulate outcomes of alternative situations

management style the preference of a manager in how he/she interacts with other stakeholders in the organization; influences the way the firm engages in transactions and is manifested in managerial decisions, interpersonal and interorganizational relationships, and resource allocations

manufacturer a company engaged in a high degree of conversion that results in a tangible output

manufacturing cell a linear or U-shaped production grouping of workers or machines

manufacturing cycle efficiency (MCE) a ratio resulting from dividing the actual production time by total lead time; reflects the proportion of lead time that is value-added

manufacturing resource planning (MRP II) a fully integrated materials requirement planning system that involves top management and provides a basis for both strategic and tactical planning

maquiladora a business (typically U.S.-owned on the Mexican side of the United States-Mexico border) that exists under a special trade agreement in which foreign companies import materials into Mexico duty-free for assembly, then export the goods back out of Mexico, and only pay duty on the value added to inventory in the process

margin of safety the excess of the budgeted or actual sales of a company over its breakeven point; can be calculated in units or dollars or as a percentage; is equal to (1 ÷ degree of operating leverage)

mass customization personalized production generally accomplished through the use of flexible manufacturing systems; reflects an organization's increase in product variety from the same basic component elements

master budget the comprehensive set of all budgetary schedules and the pro forma financial statements of an organization

material price variance total actual cost of materials purchased minus (actual quantity of materials × standard price); the amount of money spent below (favorable) or in excess (unfavorable) of the standard price for the quantity of materials purchased; can be calculated based on the actual quantity of materials purchased or the actual quantity used

material quantity variance (actual quantity × standard price) minus (standard quantity allowed × standard price); the standard cost saved (favorable) or expended (unfavorable) due to the difference between the actual quantity of materials used and the standard quantity of materials allowed for the goods produced during the period

material requisition form a source document that indicates the types and quantities of materials to be placed into production or used in performing a service; causes materials and their costs to be released from the Raw Materials Inventory warehouse and sent to Work in Process Inventory

materials mix variance (actual mix × actual quantity × standard price) minus (standard mix × actual quantity × standard price); computes the monetary effect of substituting a nonstandard mix of materials

materials requirements planning (MRP) a computer-based information system that simulates the ordering and scheduling of demand-dependent inventories; a simulation of the parts fabrication and subassembly activities that are required, in an appropriate time sequence, to meet a production master schedule

materials yield variance (standard mix × actual quantity × standard price) minus (standard mix × standard quantity × standard price); computes the difference between the actual total quantity of input and the standard total quantity allowed based on output and uses standard mix and standard prices to determine variance

mathematical programming a variety of techniques used to allocate limited resources among activities to achieve a specific objective

matrix structure an organizational structure in which functional departments and project teams exist simultaneously so that the resulting lines of authority resemble a grid

merit pay a pay increment earned by achieving a specific level of performance

method of least squares see least squares regression analysis

method of neglect a method of treating spoiled units in the equivalent units schedule as if they did not occur; used for continuous normal spoilage

mission statement a written expression of organizational purpose that describes how the organization uniquely meets its targeted customers' needs with its products or services

mix any possible combination of materials or labor inputs

mixed cost   a cost that has both a variable and a fixed component; changes with changes in activity, but not proportionately

modified FIFO method (of process costing)   the method of cost assignment that uses FIFO to compute a cost per equivalent unit but, in transferring units from a department, the costs of the beginning inventory units and the units started and completed are combined and averaged

MRP   see materials requirements planning

MRP II   see manufacturing resource planning

multiple regression   a statistical technique that uses two or more independent variables to predict a dependent variable

multiprocess handling   the ability of a worker to monitor and operate several (or all) machines in a manufacturing cell or perform all steps of a specific task

mutually exclusive projects   a set of proposed capital projects from which one is chosen, causing all the others to be rejected

mutually inclusive projects   a set of capital projects that are all related and that must all be chosen if the primary project is chosen

National Association of Accountants (NAA)   the previous name of the Institute of Management Accountants

negotiated transfer price   an intracompany charge for goods or services set through a process of negotiation between the selling and purchasing unit managers

net cost of normal spoilage   the cost of spoiled work less the estimated disposal value of that work

net present value (NPV)   the difference between the present values of all cash inflows and outflows for an investment project

net present value method   a process that uses the discounted cash flows of a project to determine whether the rate of return on that project is equal to, higher than, or lower than the desired rate of return

net realizable value approach   a method of accounting for by-products or scrap that requires that the net realizable value of these products be treated as a reduction in the cost of the primary products; primary product cost may be reduced by decreasing either (1) cost of goods sold when the joint products are sold or (2) the joint process cost allocated to the joint products

net realizable value at split-off allocation   a method of allocating joint cost to joint products that uses, as the proration base, sales value at split-off minus all costs necessary to prepare and dispose of the products; requires that all joint products be salable at split-off point

network organization   a flexible organization structure that establishes a working relationship among multiple entities, usually to pursue a single function

noncontrollable variance   the fixed overhead volume variance; computed as part of the two-variance approach to overhead analysis

non-negativity constraint   a restriction in a linear programming problem stating that negative values for physical quantities cannot exist in a solution

non-value-added activity   an activity that increases the time spent on a product or service but that does not increase its worth or value to the customer

normal capacity   the long-run (5–10 years) average production or service volume of a firm; takes into consideration cyclical and seasonal fluctuations

normal cost system   a valuation method that uses actual costs of direct materials and direct labor in conjunction with a predetermined overhead rate or rates in determining the cost of Work in Process Inventory

normal loss   an expected decline in units during the production process

normal spoilage   spoilage that has been planned or foreseen; is a product cost

North American Free Trade Agreement (NAFTA)   an agreement among Canada, Mexico, and the United States establishing the North American Free Trade Zone, with a resulting reduction in trade barriers

objective   a desired quantifiable achievement for a period of time

objective function   the linear mathematical equation that states the purpose of a linear programming problem

operating budget   a budget expressed in both units and dollars

operating leverage   the proportionate relationship between a company's variable and fixed costs

operational plan   a formulation of the details of implementing and maintaining an organization's strategic plan; typically formalized in the master budget

operations flow document   a document listing all operations necessary to produce one unit of product (or perform a specific service) and the corresponding time allowed for each operation

opportunity cost   a potential benefit that is foregone because one course of action is chosen over another

opportunity cost of capital   the highest rate of return that could be earned by using capital for the most attractive alternative project(s) available

optimal mix of capital   the combination of capital sources at which the lowest weighted average cost of capital is achieved

optimal solution   the solution to a linear programming problem that provides the best answer to the objective function

ordering cost   the variable cost associated with preparing, receiving, and paying for an order

order point   the level of inventory that triggers the placement of an order for additional units; is determined based on usage, lead time, and safety stock

ordinary annuity   a series of equal cash flows being received or paid at the end of a period

organizational culture   the set of basic assumptions about the organization and its goals and ways of doing business; a system of shared values about what is important and beliefs about how things get accomplished; provides a framework that organizes and directs employee behavior at work; describes an organization's norms in internal and external, as well as formal and informal, transactions

organizational-level cost   a cost incurred to support the ongoing facility or operations

organizational structure   the manner in which authority and responsibility for decision making is distributed in an entity

organization chart a depiction of the functions, divisions, and positions of the people/jobs in a company and how they are related; also indicates the lines of authority and responsibility

organization form an entity's legal nature (for example, sole proprietorship, partnership, corporation)

outlier an abnormal or nonrepresentative point within a data set

out-of-pocket cost a cost that is a current or near-current cash expenditure

outsourcing the use, by one company, of an external provider of a service or manufacturer of a component

overapplied overhead the amount of overhead that remains at the end of the period when the applied overhead amount is greater than the actual overhead that was incurred

overhead any factory or production cost that is indirect to the product or service; does not include direct materials or direct labor; any production cost that cannot be directly traced to the product

overhead application rate see predetermined overhead rate

overhead efficiency variance the difference between total budgeted overhead at actual hours and total budgeted overhead at standard hours allowed for the production achieved; computed as part of a three-variance analysis; same as variable overhead efficiency variance

overhead spending variance the difference between total actual overhead and total budgeted overhead at actual hours; computed as part of three-variance analysis; equal to the sum of the variable and fixed overhead spending variances

Pareto analysis a method of ranking the causes of variation in a process according to the impact on an objective

Pareto principle a rule which states that the greatest effects in human endeavors are traceable to a small number of causes (the *vital few*), while the majority of causes (the *trivial many*) collectively yield only a small impact; this relationship is often referred to as the 20:80 rule

participatory budget a budget that has been developed through a process of joint decision making by top management and operating personnel

payback period the time it takes an investor to recoup an original investment through cash flows from a project

perfection standard see ideal standard

performance evaluation the process of determining the degree of success in accomplishing a task; equates to both effectiveness and efficiency

period cost a cost other than one associated with making or acquiring inventory

periodic compensation a pay plan based on the time spent on the task rather than the work accomplished

perk a fringe benefit provided by the employer

phantom profit a temporary absorption-costing profit caused by producing more inventory than is sold

physical measurement allocation a method of allocating a joint cost to products that uses a common physical characteristic as the proration base

piece rate a pay plan in which workers are paid a flat rate for each unit of work accomplished

planning the process of creating the goals and objectives for an organization and developing a strategy for achieving them in a systematic manner

postinvestment audit the process of gathering information on the actual results of a capital project and comparing them to the expected results

practical capacity the physical production or service volume that a firm could achieve during normal working hours with consideration given to ongoing-expected operating interruptions

practical standard a standard that can be reached or slightly exceeded with reasonable effort by workers; allows for normal, unavoidable time problems or delays and for worker breaks; often believed to be most effective in inducing the best performance from workers, since such a standard represents an attainable challenge

predetermined overhead rate an estimated constant charge per unit of activity used to assign overhead cost to production or services of the period; calculated by dividing total budgeted annual overhead at a selected level of volume or activity by that selected measure of volume or activity; is also the standard overhead application rate

predictor an activity measure that, when changed, is accompanied by consistent, observable changes in another item

preference decision the second decision made in capital project evaluation in which projects are ranked according to their impact on the achievement of company objectives (see also screening decision)

present value (PV) the amount that one or more future cash flows is worth currently, given a specified rate of interest

present value index see profitability index

prevention cost a cost incurred to improve quality by preventing defects from occurring

price fixing a practice by which firms conspire to set a products price at a specified level

prime cost the total cost of direct materials and direct labor for a product

probability distribution a range of possible values for which each value has an assigned likelihood of occurrence

process benchmarking benchmarking that focuses on practices and how the best-in-class companies achieved their results

process costing system a method of accumulating and assigning costs to units of production in companies producing large quantities of homogeneous products; accumulates costs by cost component in each production department and assigns costs to units using equivalent units of production

processing time the actual time consumed performing the functions necessary to manufacture a product

process map a flowchart or diagram indicating every step that goes into making a product or providing a service

process productivity the total units produced during a period using value-added processing time

process quality yield the proportion of good units that resulted from the activities expended

product complexity an assessment about the number of components in a product or the number of processes or operations through which a product flows

product contribution margin the difference between selling price and variable cost of goods sold

product cost a cost associated with making or acquiring inventory

productive capacity the number of total units that could be produced during a period based on available equipment time

productive processing time the proportion of total time that is value-added time; also known as manufacturing cycle efficiency

product- (or process-) level cost a cost that is caused by the development, production, or acquisition of specific products or services

product life cycle a model depicting the stages through which a product class (not necessarily each product) passes

product line margin see segment margin

product variety the number of different types of products produced (or services rendered) by a firm

profit center a responsibility center in which managers are responsible for generating revenues and planning and controlling all expenses

profit margin the ratio of income to sales

profit sharing an incentive payment to employees that is contingent on organizational or individual performance

profit-volume graph a visual representation of the amount of profit or loss associated with each level of sales

profitability index (PI) a ratio that compares the present value of net cash flows to the present value of the net investment

program budgeting an approach to budgeting that relates resource inputs to service outputs

project the purchase, installation, and operation of a capital asset

pull system a production system dictated by product sales and demand; a system in which parts are delivered or produced only as they are needed by the work center for which they are intended; requires only minimal storage facilities

purchasing cost the quoted price of inventory, minus any discounts allowed, plus shipping charges

push system the traditional production system in which work centers may produce inventory that is not currently needed because of lead time or economic production/order requirements; requires that excess inventory be stored until needed

quality all the characteristics of a product or service that make it able to meet the stated or implied needs of the person acquiring it; relates to both performance and value; the pride of workmanship; conformance to requirements

quality assurance the process of determining that product or service quality conforms to designated specifications usually through an inspection process

quality audit a review of product design activities (although not for individual products), manufacturing processes and controls, quality documentation and records, and management philosophy

quality control the implementation of all practices and policies designed to eliminate poor quality and variability in the production or service process; places the primary responsibility for quality at the source of the product or service

raider a firm or individual that specializes in taking over other firms

realized value approach a method of accounting for by-products or scrap that does not recognize any value for these products until they are sold; the value recognized upon sale can be treated as other revenue or other income

red-line system an inventory ordering system in which a red line is painted on the inventory container at a point deemed to be the reorder point

regression line any line that goes through the means (or averages) of the set of observations for an independent variable and its dependent variables; mathematically, there is a line of "best fit," which is the least squares regression line

reinvestment assumption an assumption made about the rates of return that will be earned by intermediate cash flows from a capital project; NPV and PI assume reinvestment at the discount rate; IRR assumes reinvestment at the IRR

relevant cost a cost that is logically associated with a specific problem or decision

relevant costing a process that compares, to the extent possible and practical, the incremental revenues and incremental costs of alternative decisions

relevant range the specified range of activity over which a variable cost per unit remains constant or a fixed cost remains fixed in total; is generally assumed to be the normal operating range of the organization

replacement cost an amount that a firm would pay to replace an asset or buy a new one that performs the same functions as an asset currently held

residual income the profit earned by a responsibility center that exceeds an amount "charged" for funds committed to it

responsibility the obligation to accomplish a task or achieve an objective

responsibility accounting system an accounting information system for successively higher-level managers about the performance of segments or subunits under the control of each specific manager

responsibility center a cost object under the control of a manager

responsibility report a report that reflects the revenues and/or costs under the control of a particular unit manager

results benchmarking benchmarking in which an end product or service is examined; the focus is on product/service specifications and performance results

return of capital the recovery of the original investment (or principal) in a project

return on capital income; is equal to the rate of return multiplied by the amount of the investment

return on investment a ratio that relates income generated by the investment center to the resources (or asset base) used to produce that income

revenue center a responsibility center for which a manager is accountable only for the generation of revenues and has no control over setting selling prices, or budgeting or incurring costs

risk uncertainty; reflects the possibility of differences between the expected and actual future returns from an investment

risk-adjusted discount rate method a formal method of adjusting for risk in which the decision maker increases the rate used for discounting the future cash flows to compensate for increased risk

Robinson-Patman Act a law that prohibits companies from pricing the same products at different amounts when those amounts do not reflect related cost differences

rolling budget see continuous budgeting

routing document see operations flow document

safety stock a buffer level of inventory kept on hand by a company in the event of fluctuating usage or unusual delays in lead time

sales mix the relative combination of quantities of sales of the various products that make up the total sales of a company

sales value at split-off allocation a method of assigning joint cost to joint products that uses the relative sales values of the products at the split-off point as the proration basis; use of this method requires that all joint products are salable at split-off

scarce resource a resource that is essential to production activity, but is available only in some limited quantity

scattergraph a graph that plots all known activity observations and the associated costs; is used to separate mixed costs into their variable and fixed components and to examine patterns reflected by the plotted observations

scrap an incidental output of a joint process; is salable but the sales value from scrap is not enough for management to justify undertaking the joint process; is viewed as having a lower sales value than a by-product; leftover materials that have a minimal but distinguishable disposal value

screening decision the first decision made in evaluating capital projects that indicates whether a project is desirable based on some previously established minimum criterion or criteria (see also preference decision)

segment margin the excess of revenues over direct variable expenses and avoidable fixed expenses for a particular segment

sensitivity analysis a process of determining the amount of change that must occur in a variable before a different decision would be made

service company an individual or firm engaged in a high or moderate degree of conversion that results in service output

service department an organizational unit that provides one or more specific functional tasks for other internal units

service time the actual time consumed performing the functions necessary to provide a service

setup cost the direct or indirect cost of getting equipment ready for each new production run

shirking the process of an individual free-riding on a group effort because the individual's share of the group reward is insufficient to compensate for his or her separate effort

shrinkage a decrease in units arising from an inherent characteristic of the production process; includes decreases caused by evaporation, leakage, and oxidation

simple interest a method of determining interest in which interest is earned on only the original investment (or principal) amount

simple regression a statistical technique that uses only one independent variable to predict a dependent variable

simplex method an iterative (sequential) algorithm used to solve multivariable, multiconstraint linear programming problems

simultaneous engineering an integrated approach in which all primary functions and personnel contributing to a product's origination and production are involved continuously from the beginning of a product

slack variable a variable used in a linear programming problem that represents the unused amount of a resource at any level of operation; associated with less-than-or-equal-to constraints

Society of Management Accountants of Canada the professional body representing an influential and diverse group of over 26,000 Certified Management Accountants; this body produces numerous publications that address business management issues

special order decision a situation in which management must determine a sales price to charge for manufacturing or service jobs outside the company's normal production/service realm

split-off point the point at which the outputs of a joint process are first identifiable or can be separated as individual products

spoilage an occurrence in the production process that causes unacceptable units to be produced

spoiled unit a unit that is rejected at a control inspection point for failure to meet appropriate standards of quality or designated product specifications; cannot be economically reworked to be brought up to standard

staff employee an employee responsible for providing advice, guidance, and service to line personnel

standard a model or budget against which actual results are compared and evaluated; a benchmark or norm used for planning and control purposes

standard cost a budgeted or estimated cost to manufacture a single unit of product or perform a single service

standard cost card a document that summarizes the direct materials, direct labor, and overhead standard quantities and prices needed to complete one unit of product

standard cost system a valuation method that uses predetermined norms for direct materials, direct labor, and overhead to assign costs to the various inventory accounts and cost of goods sold

standard deviation the measure of variability of data around the average (or mean) value of a set of data

standard error of the estimate a measure of dispersion that reflects the average difference between actual observations and expected results provided by a regression line

standard overhead application rate a predetermined overhead rate used in a standard cost system; can be a separate variable or fixed rate or a combined overhead rate

standard quantity allowed the quantity of input (in hours or some other cost driver measurement) required at standard for the output actually achieved for the period

Statements on Management Accounting (SMAs) pronouncements developed and issued by the Management Accounting Practices Committee of the Institute of Management Accountants; application of these statements is through voluntary, not legal, compliance

statistical process control (SPC) the use of control techniques that are based on the theory that a process has natural variations in it over time, but uncommon variations are typically the points at which the process produces "errors," which can be defective goods or poor service

steady-state phase that point at which the learning curve becomes flat and only minimal improvements in performance are achieved

step cost a cost that increases in distinct amounts because of increased activity

step method a process of service department cost allocation that assigns service department costs to cost objects after considering the interrelationships of the service departments and revenue-producing departments

stock appreciation rights the right to receive cash, stock, or a combination of cash and stock based on the difference between a specified dollar amount per share of stock and the quoted market price per share at some future date

stock option a right allowing the holder to purchase shares of common stock during some future time frame and at a specified price

stockout the condition of not having inventory available upon need or request

strategic planning the process of developing a statement of long-range (5–10 years) goals for the organization and defining the strategies and policies that will help the organization achieve those goals

strategic resource management the organizational planning for the deployment of resources to create value for customers and shareholders; key variables in the process include the management of information and the management of change in response to threats and opportunities

strategic staffing an approach to personnel management that requires a department to analyze its staffing needs by considering its long-term objectives and those of the overall company and determining a specific combination of permanent and temporary employees with the best skills to meet those needs

strategy the link between an organization's goals and objectives and the activities actually conducted by the organization

strict FIFO method (of process costing) the method of cost assignment that uses FIFO to compute a cost per equivalent unit and, in transferring units from a department, keeps the cost of the beginning units separate from the cost of the units started and completed during the current period

suboptimization a situation in which an individual manager pursues goals and objectives that are in his/her own and his/her segment's particular interests rather than in the company's best interests

substitute good an item that can replace another item to satisfy the same wants or needs

sunk cost a cost incurred in the past and not relevant to any future courses of action; the historical or past cost associated with the acquisition of an asset or a resource

surplus variable a variable used in a linear programming problem that represents overachievement of a minimum requirement; associated with greater-than-or-equal-to constraints

synchronous management the use of all techniques that help an organization achieve its goals

tactical planning the process of determining the specific means or objectives by which the strategic plans of the organization will be achieved; are short-range in nature (usually 1–18 months)

takeover the acquisition of managerial control of the corporation by an outside or inside investor; control is achieved by acquiring enough stock and stockholder votes to control the board of directors and management

target costing a method of determining what the cost of a product should be based on the product's estimated selling price less the desired profit

tax benefit (of depreciation) the amount of depreciation deductible for tax purposes multiplied by the tax rate; the reduction in taxes caused by the deductibility of depreciation

tax-deferred income current compensation that is taxed at a future date

tax-exempt income current compensation that is never taxed

tax shield (of depreciation) the amount of depreciation deductible for tax purposes; the amount of revenue shielded from taxes because of the depreciation deduction

theoretical capacity the estimated maximum production or service volume that a firm could achieve during a period

theory of constraints a method of analyzing the bottlenecks (constraints) that keep a system from achieving higher performance; states that production cannot take place at a rate faster than the slowest machine or person in the process

throughput the total completed and sold output of plant during a period

timeline a tool that visually illustrates the amounts and timing of all cash inflows and outflows; is used in analyzing cash flow from a capital project

total contribution margin see contribution margin

total cost to account for the sum of the costs in beginning inventory and the costs of the current period

total expected value (for a project) the sum of the individual cash flows in a probability distribution multiplied by their related probabilities

total overhead variance the difference between total actual overhead and total applied overhead; the amount of underapplied or overapplied overhead

total quality management (TQM) a structural system for creating organization-wide participation in planning and implementing a continuous improvement process that exceeds the expectations of the customer/client; the application of quality principles to all company endeavors; also known as total quality control

total units to account for the sum of the beginning inventory units and units started during the current period

total variance the difference between total actual cost incurred and total standard cost for the output produced during the period

transfer price an internal charge established for the exchange of goods or services between organizational units of the same company

transfer time the time consumed by moving products or components from one place to another

treasurer an individual in a corporation who handles the actual resources of the organization but who does not have access to the accounting records

two-bin system an inventory ordering system in which two containers (or stacks) of raw materials or parts are available for use; when one container is depleted, the removal of materials from the second container begins and a purchase order is placed to refill the first container

underapplied overhead the amount of overhead that remains at the end of the period when the applied overhead amount is less than the actual overhead that was incurred

unexpired cost an asset

unit-level cost a cost caused by the production or acquisition of a single unit of product or the delivery of a single unit of service

units started and completed the difference between the number of units completed for the period and the units in beginning inventory; can also be computed as the number of units started during the period minus the units in ending inventory

usage the quantity of inventory used or sold each time interval

value the characteristic of meeting the highest number of customer needs at the lowest possible price

value-added activity an activity that increases the worth of the product or service to the customer

value chain the set of processes that convert inputs into products and services for the firm's customers; includes the processes of suppliers as well as internal processes

value chart a visual representation indicating the value-added and non-value-added activities and time spent in those activities from the beginning to the end of a process

variable cost a cost that varies in total in direct proportion to changes in activity; is constant on a per unit basis

variable costing a cost accumulation and reporting method that includes only variable production costs (direct materials, direct labor, and variable overhead) as inventoriable or product costs; treats fixed overhead as a period cost; is not acceptable for external reporting and tax returns

variable cost ratio the proportion of each revenue dollar represented by variable costs; computed as variable costs divided by sales or as (1 − contribution margin ratio)

variable overhead efficiency variance the difference between budgeted variable overhead based on actual hours and variable overhead applied to production

variable overhead spending variance the difference between total actual variable overhead and the budgeted amount of variable overhead based on actual hours

variance a difference between an actual and a standard or budgeted cost; is favorable if actual is less than standard and is unfavorable if actual is greater than standard

variance analysis the process of categorizing the nature (favorable or unfavorable) of the differences between standard and actual costs and determining the reasons for those differences

vertex a corner produced by the intersection of lines on a graph

vertical price fixing a practice of collusion between a producing business and its distributors to control the prices at which the business's products may be sold to consumers

vision a conceptualization of a future state for the organization that is better than the current state

vision statement a written expression about the organization's future upon which all company personnel can base their decisions and behavior so that everyone is working toward the same long-run results

volume variance a fixed overhead variance that represents the difference between budgeted fixed overhead and fixed overhead applied to production of the period; is also referred to as the noncontrollable variance

waste a residual output of a production process that has no sales value and must be disposed of

weighted average cost of capital a composite of the cost of the various sources of funds that comprise a firm's capital structure; the minimum rate of return that must be earned on new investments so as not to dilute shareholder interests

weighted average method (of process costing) the method of cost assignment that computes an average cost per equivalent unit of production for all units completed during the current period; combines beginning inventory units and costs with current production and costs, respectively, to compute the average

World Trade Organization (WTO) the arbiter of global trade that was created in 1995 under the General Agreement on Tariffs and Trade; each signatory country has one vote in trade disputes

yield the quantity of output that results from a specified input

yield ratio the expected or actual relationship between input and output

zero-base budgeting a comprehensive budgeting process that systematically considers the priorities and alternatives for current and proposed activities in relation to organization objectives; requires the rejustification of ongoing activities

Author Index

Organization Index

Subject Index

Photography Credits